CASES AND MATERIALS ON ADMINISTRATIVE LAW

By

S. H. BAILEY, M.A., LL.B. (Cantab)
Professor of Public Law
University of Nottingham

B. L. JONES, M.A., LL.B. (Cantab)
Professor of Environmental Liability
De Montford University, Leicester

A. R. MOWBRAY, LL.B. (Warw), Ph.D. (Edin)
Senior Lecturer in Law
University of Nottingham

THIRD EDITION

R.T.C. LIBRARY

D1347059

LONDON
SWEET & MAXWELL LTD
1997

First Edition.............................1977
Second Edition 1992
Third Edition...........................1997

Published in 1997 by
Sweet & Maxwell Ltd, 100 Avenue Road,
Swiss Cottage, London NW3 3PF

(http://www.smlawpub.co.uk)

Computerset by
MFK Information Services Ltd, Hitchin
Printed in England by
Clays Ltd., St Ives plc

No natural forests were destroyed to make this product:
only farmed timber was used and replanted

A CIP catalogue record for this book is available from the
British Library

ISBN 0 421 59770 4

All rights reserved. U.K. statutory material in this
publication is acknowledged as Crown copyright.
No part of this publication may be reproduced or transmitted,
in any form or by any means, or stored in a retrieval system
of any nature, without prior written permission, except for
permitted fair dealing under the Copyright, Designs
and Patents Act 1988, or in accordance with the terms
of a licence issued by the Copyright Licensing Agency
in respect of photocopying and/or reprographic reproduction.
Application for permission to reproduce extracts in
other published works shall be made to the publishers.
Full acknowledgment of author, publisher and source must be given.

©
S.H. Bailey, B.L. Jones & A.R. Mowbray
1997

PREFACE

The first edition of this book appeared in 1977 and the second in 1992. We are pleased that the third has appeared after a more appropriate interval. There have, nevertheless, been important changes. These include the decisions of the House of Lords in *ex p. Page*, confirming the breadth and general applicability of the *Anisminic* principle, and *R. v. Wicks*, casting doubt on attempts to narrow the scope of collateral challenge to byelaws and other decisions while emphasising that all ultimately turns on the particular statutory context. The decision of the Court of Appeal in *R. v. Ministry of Defence, ex p. Smith* contains some interesting observations on the scope of judicial review for irrationality. The chapter on contract, tort and restitution has been very substantially revised to take account of important (and not wholly consistent) new case law, the section on tort now being based on the House of Lords decisions in *X v. Bedfordshire County Council* and *Stovin v. Wise*. The material on jurisdictional control has been reorganised to highlight what are the key issues today. The rule against bias has been redefined by the House of Lords in *R. v. Gough* and its ambit significantly widened in *ex p. Kirkstall Valley Campaign Ltd.* Many other developments in both administrative practice and the case law have been dealt with in the notes and questions.

At the time of writing this preface (July 1997), we stand on the brink of significant constitutional changes which are likely to have profound implications for the ground covered in the book. The next five years or so promises to be even more interesting than the last for administrative lawyers.

S.H.B.
B.L.J.
A.R.M.

ACKNOWLEDGMENTS

Grateful acknowledgment is made to the following authors and publishers for permission to quote from their works:

ACAS: Extracts from Annual Report 1995.

Baldwin, R.: *Rules and Government: Non-Statutory Rules and Administrative Law* (1985). Reproduced with permission of Oxford University Press.

Baldwin and Houghton: Extract from "Circular Arguments: The Status and Legitimacy of Administrative Rules" [1986] P.L. 239.

Beloff, M.: Extract from "Pitch, Pool, Rink ... Court? Judicial Review in the Sporting World" [1989] P.L. 95.

Bradley, A.: Extract from "The Role of the Ombudsman in Relation to the Protection of Citizens' Rights" (1980) C.L.J. 304.

Bridges, Meszaros and Sunkin: *Judicial Review in Perspective* (1995). Reproduced with permission of Cavendish Publishing Ltd.

Butterworths Law Publishers Ltd: Extracts from the All England Law Reports.

Charles Knight & Co. Ltd: Extract from the judgment of *Re Hurle-Hobbs, ex p. Riley* taken from *The Law Relating to District Audit* (2nd ed., 1955).

Commission for Local Administration in England: Extracts from the Annual Reports of the Local Ombudsmen.

Daintith, T.: "The Executive Power Today: Bargaining and Economic Control" in Jowell and Oliver, *The Changing Constitution* (2nd ed., 1989). Reproduced by permission of Oxford University Press.

Daintith, T.: "Techniques of Government" in Jowell and Oliver, *The Changing Constitution* (3rd ed., 1994). Reproduced with permission of Oxford University Press.

Daintith, T.: Extract from "The Regulation of Contract: The New Prerogative" (1979) C.L.P. 41, Oxford University Press.

Fredman, S. & Morris, G.: Extract from "Public or Private? State Employees and Judicial Review" (1991) 107 L.Q.R. 298.

Ganz, G.: Extract from *Quasi Legislation: Recent Developments in Secondary Legislation* (1987) Sweet & Maxwell.

Genn, H.: "Tribunal Review of Administrative Decision-Making" in Richardson and Genn, *Administrative Law and Government Action* (1994). Reproduced with permission of Oxford University Press.

Harden, I.: An extract from "A Constitution for Quangos" [1987] P.L. 27.

HMSO: Controller of HMSO for extracts from Crown and Parliamentary copyright material.

The Incorporated Council of Law Reporting for England and Wales: Extracts from the Law Reports.

Jackson, P.: Extract from "Fairness and Natural Justice" (1980) 96 L.Q.R. 497.

McAuslan, P.: Extract from "Administrative Law—Collective Consumption and Judicial Policy" (1983) 46 M.L.R. 1. Reproduced with permission of Blackwell Publishing.

Marsh, N.S.: Extract from *Public Access to Government Held Information* (1987) Sweet & Maxwell.

Wade, W.: Extract from *Administrative Law* (5th ed.). Reproduced with permission of Oxford University Press.

Wade, W.: Extract from *Administrative Law* (6th ed.). Reproduced with permission of Oxford University Press.

While every care has been taken to establish and acknowledge copyright, and contact copyright owners, the publishers tender their apologies for any accidental infringement. They would be pleased to come to a suitable arrangement with the rightful owners in each case.

CONTENTS

Part I
Administrative Authorities, Procedures and Non-judicial Mechanisms of Redress

Part II
Judicial Review

TABLE OF CASES

TABLE OF STATUTES

TABLE OF STATUTORY INSTRUMENTS

TABLE OF REPORTS

ABBREVIATIONS

Allen: Sir Carleton Kemp Allen, *Law and Orders* (3rd ed., 1965, Stevens)

Cane: P. Cane, *An Introduction to Administrative Law* (3rd ed., 1996, Clarendon Press, Oxford)

Craig: P.P. Craig, *Administrative Law* (3rd ed., 1994, Sweet & Maxwell)

Cross: S.H. Bailey, *Cross on Local Government Law* (9th ed., 1996, Sweet & Maxwell)

de Smith, Woolf and Jowell: Lord Woolf and J. Jowell, *de Smith, Woolf and Jowell, Judicial Review of Administrative Action* (5th ed., 1995, Sweet & Maxwell)

de Smith CA: S.A. de Smith and R. Brazier, *Constitutional and Administrative Law* (7th ed., 1994, Penguin)

Emery and Smythe: C.T. Emery and B. Smythe, *Judicial Review: Legal Limits of Official Power* (1986, Sweet & Maxwell)

Garner: B.L. Jones and K. Thompson, *Garner's Administrative Law* (8th ed., 1996, Butterworths)

Harlow and Rawlings: C. Harlow and R. Rawlings, *Law and Administration* (1984, Weidenfeld & Nicolson)

Lewis: C. Lewis, *Judicial Remedies in Public Law* (1992, Sweet & Maxwell)

Wade and Forsyth: Sir William Wade and C.F. Forsyth, *Administrative Law* (7th ed., 1994, Clarendon Press, Oxford)

Zamir and Woolf: Lord Woolf and J. Woolf, *Zamir, The Declaratory Judgment* (2nd ed., 1993, Sweet & Maxwell)

Part I

ADMINISTRATIVE AUTHORITIES, PROCEDURES AND NON-JUDICIAL MECHANISMS OF REDRESS

INTRODUCTORY NOTE TO PART I

THE purpose of this collection of materials is, first, to provide a selective overview of the institutional framework within which modern public administration operates, in order to facilitate an understanding of the nature of the major bodies governed by administrative law. Many fundamental changes are occurring in the existing system. For example, the appointments processes and membership of Non-Departmental Public Bodies, often termed QUANGOs, have been a matter of serious political controversy (as part of the "sleaze" in government debate), which has been partially resolved by the work of the Nolan Committee on Standards in Public Life. Secondly, we examine selected features of some of the most important procedures adopted by public authorities so that we can gain an insight into the ways in which these organisations actually perform their duties. These materials reveal a number of tensions existing in the use of various procedures; *e.g.* over the fairest method of conducting inquiries—a topic hotly debated by Sir Richard Scott V.-C. (as he now is) and some prominent witnesses at his inquiry into the export of defence equipment to Iraq (often referred to as "Iraqgate" by the media) and in the increasing powers being given to the regulators of public utilities whilst the Government is committed to a crusade of deregulation. Thirdly, we include a consideration of the important, but low profile, work of the Council on Tribunals, which supervises over 50 different tribunal systems determining many hundreds of thousands of individual cases per year. Fourthly, we consider the increasing workload of the proliferating statutory ombudsmen, together with the adoption of this model of grievance-resolution by many private sector trade associations (*e.g.* the creation of a Funerals Ombudsman). Finally, we note some of the effects of the Citizen's Charter on public administration.

Within the diverse collection of materials contained in Part I it is possible to discern at least four recurring themes in contemporary Government policy. First, there is the increasing pace of the restructuring of public organisations. Today, nearly 70 per cent of civil servants are working in Next Steps Agencies, rather than in traditional central government departments. Similarly, local government is being reshaped in the form of unitary authorities, which are replacing the established two-tier system throughout many parts of England and the whole of Wales. Secondly, the subjection of the provision of public services to greater competition. Hence, local authorities are today obliged to offer for tender the supply of professional services as well as manual ones. Likewise, an expanding range of central government administration is being subjected to "market testing" with competition from private sector companies (*e.g.* computer services). Legislation even provides for competition in the supply of schools inspectors. Consequently, the new structures of public administration are becoming purchasers, rather than direct providers, of many public services. Thirdly, the privatisation of all the major public utilities, together with many other former public corporations, has resulted in the need for the creation of new regulatory offices with extensive statutory powers to control the pricing and competition policies of the resulting private sector monopolies. Therefore, regulation has assumed a central role as a method of contemporary public administration. Finally, aspects of all the above policies intersect in the programme of charterism initiated with the Citizen's Charter. This policy views citizens as consumers of public services being guided by a plethora of "league tables" measuring the services provided by individual organisations. Symbolically, charterism has also refocused attention on the provision of redress for aggrieved individuals by internal and other non-judicial mechanisms.

Chapter 1

ADMINISTRATIVE INSTITUTIONS

(A) Central Government

The central government exercises its many functions nominally by way of advice to the Crown, although statute in some instances confers powers on Ministers personally.[1] These functions so exercised by Ministers of the Crown may take the form of initiating delegated legislation (by Orders in Council or by Regulations, orders, directions, etc., made by ministers), of exercising discretionary powers,[2] of determining appeals from the decisions of other government bodies, such as local authorities, and by carrying on the every day activities of administration. These and other administrative procedures are exercised over a wide field of activity, especially in the fields of social security, town and country planning and the environment generally, immigration and foreign relations, home affairs and the regulation of the economy and industrial relations, etc.

In the exercise of their functions, the decisions of Ministers are as subject to judicial review as are the decisions of other public bodies, subject always of course to the terms of any relevant enabling statutes.

For further reading see *Garner*, Chap. 2; *Wade and Forsyth*, Chap. 3; *Craig*, Chap. 3; J.F. McEldowney, *Public Law* (1994), Chap. 10.

(i) Departments

Until the late 1980s almost all of the administrative tasks allocated to ministers had been performed by government departments. These are "branches of the central administration which are staffed by civil servants, paid for out of Exchequer funds and headed by a Minister responsible to Parliament".[3] In 1988 the following report to the Prime Minister, from a group in the Cabinet Office concerned with efficiency inside the government machine, was published. The report derived from interviews with 150 Ministers and officials, together with the evidence collected by earlier investigations into the civil service.

EFFICIENCY UNIT; IMPROVING MANAGEMENT IN GOVERNMENT: THE NEXT STEPS

(HMSO) 1988

10. Seventh, the Civil Service is too big and too diverse to manage as a single entity. With 600,000 employees it is an enormous organisation compared

---

[1] In such instances the minister may be sued in the courts: see, *e.g. Padfield v. Minister of Agriculture, Fisheries and Food* below, p. 303. A decision by a subordinate in the name of the minister will normally be accepted by the courts without proof of express delegation: *Carltona Ltd v. Commissioners of Works* below, p. 249.
[2] *e.g.* as in *British Oxygen Co. Ltd v. Minister of Technology* below, p. 263.
[3] Wade and Bradley, *Constitutional and Administrative Law* (11th ed., 1993), p. 289.

with any private sector company and most public sector organisations. A single organisation of this size which attempts to provide a detailed structure within which to carry out functions as diverse as driver licensing, fisheries protection, the catching of drug smugglers and the processing of Parliamentary Questions is bound to develop in a way which fits no single operation effectively.

11. At present the freedom of an individual manager to manage effectively and responsibly in the Civil Service is severely circumscribed. There are controls not only on resources and objectives, as there should be in any effective system, but also on the way in which resources can be managed. Recruitment, dismissal, choice of staff, promotion, pay, hours of work, accommodation, grading, organisation of work, the use of IT equipment, are all outside the control of most Civil Service managers at any level....

12. In our discussions it was clear that the advantages which a unified Civil Service are intended to bring are seen as outweighed by the practical disadvantages, particularly beyond Whitehall itself. We were told that the advantages of an all-embracing pay structure are breaking down, that the uniformity of grading frequently inhibits effective management and that the concept of a career in a unified Civil Service has little relevance for most civil servants, whose horizons are bounded by their local office or, at most, by their department.

19. **We recommend that "agencies" should be established to carry out the executive functions of government within a policy and resources framework set by a department.** An "agency" of this kind may be part of government and the public service, or it may be more effective outside government. We use the term "agency" not in its technical sense but to describe any executive unit that delivers a service for government. The choice and definition of suitable agencies is primarily for Ministers and senior management in departments to decide. In some instances very large blocks of work comprising virtually a whole department will be suitable to be managed in this way. In other instances, where the scale of activity is too small for an entirely separate organisation, it may be better to have one or even several smaller agencies within departments.

20. These units, large or small, need to be given a well defined framework in which to operate, which sets out the policy, the budget, specific targets and the results to be achieved. It must also specify how politically sensitive issues are to be dealt with and the extent of the delegated authority of management. The management of the agency must be held rigorously to account by their department for the results they achieve.

21. The framework will need to be set and updated as part of a formal annual review with the responsible Minister, based on a long-term plan and an annual report. The main strategic control must lie with the Minister and Permanent Secretary. But once the policy objectives and budgets within the framework are set, the management of the agency should then have as much independence as possible in deciding how those objectives are met....

To strengthen operational effectiveness, there must be freedom to recruit, pay, grade and structure in the most effective way as the framework becomes sufficiently robust and there is confidence in the capacity of management to handle the task.

23. Placing responsibility for performance squarely on the shoulders of the manager of an agency also has implications for the way in which Ministers answer to Parliament on operational issues. Clearly Ministers have to be wholly responsible for policy, but it is unrealistic to suppose that they can actually have knowledge in depth about every operational question. The convention that they do is in part the cause of the overload we observed. We believe it is possible for Parliament, through Ministers, to regard managers as directly responsible for operational matters and that there are precedents for this and precisely defined ways in which it can be handled.

24. The detailed nature of the relationship between a department and an agency will vary with the job to be done or the service to be delivered. The agency structure could be used to cover a substantial proportion of the activities of the Civil Service. It is clear from our discussions with Permanent Secretaries that some departments are already moving towards this concept. What is needed is a substantial acceleration and broadening of this trend through a major initiative. Ultimately some agencies could be in a position where they are no longer inside the Civil Service in the sense they are today. Any decision of this kind should be taken pragmatically—the test must always be adopting the structure which best fits the job to be done.

44. The aim should be to establish a quite different way of conducting the business of government. The central Civil Service should consist of a relatively small core engaged in the function of servicing Ministers and managing departments, who will be the "sponsors" of particular government policies and services. Responding to these departments will be a range of agencies employing their own staff, who may or may not have the status of Crown servants, and concentrating on the delivery of their particular service, with clearly defined responsibilities between the Secretary of State and the Permanent Secretary on the one hand and the Chairmen or Chief Executives of the agencies on the other. Both departments and their agencies should have a more open and simplified structure.

Notes

1. In February 1988, Mrs Thatcher gave her general endorsement to the report. She expressed the view that the new agencies would "generally be within the Civil Service, and their staff will continue to be civil servants".[4]

2. By July 1988, the Minister for the Civil Service stated that 29 activities, involving 170,000 persons in central government, had been identified as potential agency functions. These included Her Majesty's Stationery Office, the Meteorological Office and the Companies Registration Office.[5]

3. The House of Commons Select Committee on the Treasury expressed concern about the vagueness of the Report, particularly in relation to the accountability of the new agencies to Parliament, and noted that 20 years earlier the Fulton Committee on the Civil Service had recommended the "hiving off" of discrete responsibilities to autonomous agencies (Cmnd. 3638).[6]

4. The Cabinet Office produces an annual review of the Next Steps Agencies. By 1994 there were 102 separate agencies employing 268,000 civil servants (plus 85,000

[4] H.C.Deb., Vol. 127, cols. 1149–1156.
[5] Annexe, *Treasury & Civil Service Select Committee 8th Report 1987–88*, H.C. 494 (1987–1988).
[6] *Ibid.*

civil servants working in 59 executive units, operating on Next Steps principles, for the two revenue departments). 62 per cent of the civil service were working for these agencies. Before an agency is created and thereafter at regular five-yearly intervals a series of questions (called "prior options") will be asked by government. These include: whether an activity needs to continue, whether government has to be responsible for it (or can it be left to the market), does government have to undertake the activity itself (or can it buy those services from outside providers—see further the programme of "Market Testing" discussed in the Contracting section below, p. 93) and is the agency properly structured and focused? Common features of established agencies encompass: (1) clearly defined tasks established in published framework documents, (2) annual performance targets announced to Parliament by Ministers (*e.g.* financial targets), (3) each agency is headed by a chief executive (the majority have been appointed through open competition and over half of these have come from outside the civil service) and (4) staff in agencies remain civil servants and are bound by the same rules of conduct as those employed in departmental headquarters.[7] By the end of 1995, 69 per cent of the Home Civil Service was working in agencies (or in organisations operating according to similar principles). A further 8 per cent of the civil service is working in departmental organisations which have been identified as definite or possible agency candidates.[8]

5. M. Freedland has questioned whether the *Carltona* principle (see below, p. 249) can be applied to the exercise of discretionary powers by agencies' staff in the light of the separate financial accountability of each agency from its parent department: see "The rule against delegation and the *Carltona* doctrine in an agency context" [1996] P.L. 19.

6. During 1994 the Government published a White Paper articulating its policies for the future of the civil service. Whilst being committed to sustaining the key principles governing the service, namely "integrity, political impartiality, objectivity, selection and promotion on merit and accountability through Ministers to Parliament", the Government believed that "there is considerable potential for further improvement in both quality of service, within what can be afforded, and in efficiency". To achieve these goals the overall size of the service should be reduced to "significantly below 500,000". Senior posts in departments and agencies will always be considered for open competition when vacancies arise. Members of the new Senior Civil Service would have written contracts of employment (some would be appointed on fixed or rolling contracts) and more flexibility would be introduced in their pay structure (*e.g.* performance-related pay).[9] The Parliamentary Commissioner for Administration has expressed concern that the planned reductions in the size of the civil service will result in more cases of maladministration. "There is a risk that fewer staff will lead both to slower service to the public and to more mistakes because civil servants will have less time for thought to enable them to pursue considered and prudent action. I doubt whether automation and technology will compensate fully for cuts in human resources. I foresee more, not less, maladministration, despite the references to efficiency savings."[10]

7. For an examination of the Next Steps programme see G. Drewry, "Revolution in Whitehall: The Next Steps and Beyond" in J. Jowell and D. Oliver (eds.), *The Changing Constitution* (3rd ed., 1994). A critical evaluation of the competitive environment in which the Forensic Science Service must now operate is provided by P. Roberts in "What Price a Free Market in Forensic Science Services" (1996) 36 Brit.J.Criminol. 37. P. Giddings (ed.), *Parliamentary Accountability: A Study of Parliament and Executive Agencies* (1995). An extensive list of official publications concerning the programme can be found in Cm. 3164 at 355.

---

[7] *Next Steps Agencies in Government Review 1994*, Cm. 2775 (1994).
[8] *Next Steps Agencies in Government Review 1995*, Cm. 3164 (1996).
[9] *The Civil Service Continuity and Change*, Cm. 2627 (1994).
[10] Annual Report 1995, H.C. 296 (1995–96).

(ii) Non-Departmental Public Bodies

During the eighteenth and nineteenth centuries, the Board system was a commonly used form of administrative organisation. The key feature of these organisations (ranging from the Poor Law Commission to the General Board of Health) was that they were not directly accountable to Parliament. However, they were gradually replaced by departments as the dominant form of central government administration. Nevertheless, there remain a number of bodies which perform public functions at the national government level that are not part of the ordinary departmental/Next Steps agencies structure. Administrative lawyers are particularly interested in the legal personality of such Non-Departmental Public Bodies (hereafter NDPBs) and the judicial remedies available to control them. But, first it is necessary to consider the general issues of the modern functions performed by NDPBs, together with their accountability to Parliament, Ministers and the public generally.

For further reading see *Craig*, pp. 85–90, I. Harden, N. Lewis and P. Birkinshaw, *Government by Moonlight* (1989).

REPORT ON NON-DEPARTMENTAL PUBLIC BODIES (PLIATZKY REPORT)

Cmnd. 7797 (1979)

[Soon after the election of the Conservative government in 1979, this report was prepared with the objectives of, *inter alia*, surveying the existing NDPBs and commenting upon the arrangements for their control and accountability. This report divided NDPBs into three categories, "executive bodies" that carried out a wide range of operational or regulatory functions, various scientific and cultural activities, and some commercial work; "advisory bodies" which provided external advice to ministers; and "tribunals". In this section we shall concentrate upon the first two categories and tribunals will be examined in the next chapter.]

3. Organisations in the executive etc. group generally employ staff and spend money, in some cases large amounts, on their own account. Advisory bodies and tribunals are not normally employers of staff or spenders of money themselves, but their expenses and the cost of staff working on their behalf are met by their sponsor Departments, that is, the Government Departments concerned with their affairs. In addition, Departments incur staff costs, in some cases substantial, through their own Departmental functions arising from their sponsorship role in relation to all three types of body.

4. Some non-Departmental organisations cover the whole of Great Britain, and a few cover the whole of the United Kingdom, *i.e.* including Northern Ireland. But in many cases Scotland, Wales and Northern Ireland have separate institutions.

5. At the start of this review there were 489 bodies in the executive group. Between them last year they were the channel for expenditure on capital and current account approaching £5,800 million and had around 217,000 staff. In addition Departments spent about £24 million in their sponsoring capacity for these bodies.

7. At the same date there were 1,561 advisory bodies, involving expenditure of about £13 million by their sponsor Departments. Two-thirds of this total is accounted for by as few as 22 networks of advisory bodies, each of which includes eight or more separate bodies, in some cases as many as 100 or 200, so as to cover all areas.

11. Executive-type bodies are mostly set up under a specific Act of Parliament, though some are set up by administrative action—in some cases by forming a company under the Companies Acts; a Department does not need specific legislation in order to form a company, though it needs Parliamentary approval for any money provided to the company. With advisory bodies the reverse is the case; that is to say, most of them are set up by purely administrative action, but some of them have a statutory basis. Tribunals and other judicial bodies are set up to meet a specific statutory requirement. The feature common to all these cases is that they are in some sense part of the apparatus of government, without being Government Departments or divisions or branches or directorates of Departments, so that they do not come under the day to day direction of Ministers and Permanent Secretaries in charge of Departments; nor are they part of a local authority Department.

12. The case in principle for having an advisory committee with representation from outside the Department (as distinct from the justification in detail for all the committees which exist) is that the Department's own staff cannot provide the necessary advice by themselves, or that it may be desirable to enlist the participation of outside interests in order to formulate publicly acceptable proposals.

14. The case for having bodies of the executive type is more complex. It is that Parliament, or the Government with Parliamentary approval for the money involved, have decided that a certain function should be carried out for reasons of public policy, but that it is best carried out at arm's length from central government. There can be a number of reasons for this—because the work is of an executive character which does not require Ministers to take responsibility for its day to day management; because the work is more effectively carried out by a single-purpose organisation rather than by a Government Department with a wide range of functions; in order to involve people from outside government in the direction of the organisation; or, as a self-denying ordinance on the part of Government and Parliament, in order to place the performance of particular functions outside the party political arena.

15. Some fringe bodies go back a long way. The Development Commission, for instance, was set up in 1909, and the Horserace Totalisator Board—the Tote—goes back in one form or another to 1928. Organisations handling large sums of money, such as the New Town Development Corporations, have been set up by successive Governments since the second world war. A further fillip was given to this trend by the Fulton Committee's Report on the Civil Service in 1968 (Cmnd. 3638) which recommended the creation of accountable units of management within Departments and examination of the possibility of a considerable extension of "hiving off" of autonomous bodies from Departments. Subsequent developments included the hiving off of a large part of the functions of the Department of Employment to the Manpower Services Commission, the Health and Safety Commission and the Advisory, Conciliation and Arbitration Service.

34. What is involved in being on a non-Departmental body differs a great deal from one kind of body to another. Generally speaking it is in the executive group that salaried posts are to be found, and even there a typical board will consist of a full-time or less than full-time chairman with a number of part-time members, though there are full-time members in some cases; a

board of this kind tends to have a full-time chief executive or equivalent officer whom it appoints.

35. The arrangements for advisory committees vary a great deal from case to case, as does the amount of work involved. Any remuneration paid usually takes the form of an honorarium or daily fee, but a high proportion of these appointments are unpaid.

38. The feature common to non-Departmental bodies generally is that Ministers appoint the chairman and members (though not the staff of bodies which have their own employees) and are accountable to Parliament for these appointments. In the case of some public appointments, not confined to those covered by this report, the relevant legislation provides for certain bodies, such as local authorities or representative organisations of employers or employees, to be consulted about appointments or to make nominations, or requires that the people appointed must have certain qualifications or experience. Otherwise, and subject to the special arrangements for tribunals, Ministers are free to seek the names of possible candidates from any source.

39. There is a Public Appointments Unit in the Civil Service Department which keeps a central list of potential members of public bodies, and some Departments keep a list of people with special qualifications for appointment to the bodies with which they are concerned. Departmental Ministers can obtain names from these sources but are free to seek suggestions from other sources within and outside government circles.

41... On various major appointments, such as the chairmanship of an executive board, Departmental Ministers naturally seek the Prime Minister's concurrence.

74. Legislation under which fringe bodies are set up, whether they are financed by grants or by other methods, generally gives the Minister concerned powers to give directions of at least a general character. Suitable powers of direction are an appropriate safeguard, though they are no substitute for an effective financial regime and a sensible working relationship.

75. Annual reports and accounts of fringe bodies, whether financed by grant in aid or from other sources, should be as informative as possible, not simply in giving news about their activities but also, in all cases where the nature of the operation lends itself to this approach, in providing material designed to help in forming a judgment on the cost-effectiveness of the organisation's activities or on the costs and benefits involved, where this is a more relevant concept.

76. Reports and accounts should include enough information about the remuneration and expenses of the chairman and members of the governing body and its employees to obviate any reasonable grounds for concern on this score. The material published about remuneration should go at least as far as that required of companies by the Companies Act....

77. When a new fringe body is set up with a fairly finite mission, the legislation should contain provisions for its winding up when the mission is complete. But in general it would not make for good management and morale and successful recruitment to go beyond this and give it only a short initial lease of life, subject to periodical renewal. On the other hand, fringe bodies should not be allowed to continue indefinitely in set ways without a fresh look being taken from time to time both at the need for their continued existence and at the success or otherwise of their form of organisation and method of operations.

79. As a general rule advisory committees should be set up either with a finite remit, which will automatically lead to the dissolution of the committee when the remit is discharged, or with a finite lease of life, after which the Committee would be disbanded unless a positive decision is taken to give it a new lease of life.

81. Between them these suggestions contain most of the ingredients indicated by experience for making up an alternative to a competitive market régime for those public bodies to which in their nature such a régime cannot apply. Within a framework of this kind the function of securing efficiency and economy must rest with the organisation's own management, while the main responsibility for oversight of its performance lies with its sponsoring Minister and Department.

82. There remains one further important ingredient in a régime of this kind, that is, monitoring by an external body. An important part of this function is discharged by the audit-based scrutinies carried out by the Public Accounts Committee of those bodies whose accounts are audited by the Comptroller and Auditor General, or his audits of Departmental expenditure involving non-Departmental bodies to whose books he has access. For the future, a further important contribution will be made by the 14 new Select Committees of the House of Commons set up in response to recommendations from the Select Committee on Procedure to examine the expenditure, administration and policy of the principal Government Departments and associated public bodies, and similar matters within the responsibilities of the Secretary of State for Northern Ireland.

Notes

1. Following the publication of the Pliatzky Report (above), the Civil Service Department issued a document in 1981 entitled *Non-Departmental Public Bodies: A Guide for Departments*, a second edition of this guide was promulgated during 1985 and a third edition in 1992. The Guide has been described as the informal constitution for NDPBs because, whilst primarily addressed to officials, it details both current government policy towards these bodies and the basic legal/administrative processes for their creation and dissolution. The Guide begins by stating that, "new NDPBs should be set up only if the functions they are to carry out are essential and need to be in the public sector, and it is clear that an NDPB is the most suitable and cost-effective machinery".[11] Subsequent chapters identify the legal means by which NDPBs may be created (*e.g.* through being granted a Royal Charter or incorporation under the Companies Act); advice on the appointment and conditions of service of members; the forms of public disclosure of information relating to NDPBs (*e.g.* through annual reports and accounts); and the procedures for dissolving such bodies (*e.g.* how to wind-up a Royal Commission).

Harden has made a number of criticisms of the Guide. He believes that it fails to provide an accurate demarcation between Government and non-government bodies, and is opaque about the appointments process. Furthermore:

"the constitutional danger is that the publicly visible 'NDPB regime' embodied in the guide, and the limited form of public accountability through Parliament which it endorses, will be outflanked in a number of ways. First, 'ministerial responsibility' may become almost as much of a shield for the real activities of quasi-government as

[11] p. 4.

it is for those of government itself. Whilst, secondly, bargaining over public policy with powerful interest groups will be structured through quasi-non-government processes and institutions which remain unacknowledged even as 'public'."

I. Harden, "A Constitution for Quangos?" [1987] P.L. 27 at 35.

2. The Cabinet Office publishes an annual statistical guide to NDPBs. In 1995 there were 320 executive NDPBs (compared with 492 in 1979), their total staff amounted to 109,200 persons (compared with 217,000 persons in 1979) and their collective expenditure was approximately £21 billion (compared with £6 billion in 1979). The number of advisory NDPBs had been reduced from 1,485 in 1979 to 699 in 1995.[12]

3. Over recent years there has been growing public concern over the powers of patronage exercised by Ministers regarding NDPBs (*e.g.* over appointments of members of the governing boards of such bodies) and the ethical principles governing the behaviour of board members and staff of these organisations. Hence, the terms of reference of the Nolan Committee on Standards in Public Life made express reference to members and senior staff of NDPBs. After elaborating the seven principles of public life which should govern the behaviour of all holders of public office (selflessness, integrity, objectivity, accountability, openness, honesty and leadership: see further First Report, p. 14), the Committee made a number of recommendations concerning appointments to and the conduct of members/staff of an NDPB. The committee proposed, *inter alia*, that: (1) appointments of board members should always be on the basis of merit; (2) Ministers should continue to make these appointments; however, a new independent Public Appointments Commissioner should be created to regulate, monitor and report on the public appointments process; (3) the Commissioner should take over the Cabinet Office's role in promoting best practice in the appointments process; (4) all appointments processes should involve candidates being approved by an advisory panel with an independent element in its membership; (5) all NDPBs should have codes of conduct governing the behaviour of members and staff and (6) internal and external audit procedures should encompass matters of propriety as well as finance.[13]

The Government accepted the above recommendations. It was anticipated that all appointments to executive NDPBs would involve Advisory Panels containing an independent element (*i.e.* person(s) not having an "operational role within the bodies or Government departments concerned") by July 1996. However, advisory NDPBs are not subject to this regime and they will also, initially, be outside the formal jurisdiction of the Public Appointments Commissioner.[14] In his first annual report the Commissioner, Sir Len Peach, criticised three chairpersons of NDPBs for selecting members through the "old boy network" rather than through open advertisements. He also expressed the wish that more women and members of ethnic minority groups would apply for the 89,000 positions on NDPBs.[15]

In January 1997, the Public Services Minister, Roger Freeman, announced that at least one-third of all departmental appointees to public bodies should be women. This was a minimum "benchmark". Some departments (*e.g.* the Scottish Office and the Home Office) had already appointed women to over 40 per cent of such positions; however, the Ministry of Defence only appointed women to 5 per cent of its public bodies.

In a second report, published during May 1996, the Nolan Committee reviewed the

[12] *Public Bodies: 1995* (HMSO, 1995).
[13] Standards in Public Life, Cm. 2850 (1995).
[14] The Government's Response to the First Report from the Committee on Standards in Public Life, Cm. 2931 (1995).
[15] *The Times*, October 17, 1996.

practices of 4,500 public bodies spending over £16 billion a year providing services at a local level (*e.g.* training and enterprise councils, and housing associations). The Committee concluded that, "nothing in this report points to any fundamental malaise in any of the sectors which we have examined". But it was recommended that the principles of public life should be applied to these bodies (*e.g.* through fair and open appointments systems, public access to the board meetings of these organisations and members terms of office being limited to four years).

4. H.M. Treasury has produced a "Code of Best Practice for Board Members of Public Bodies" which is designed to provide guidance for executive NDPBs and related organisations, analogous to that provided by the Cadbury Report on Corporate Governance for private sector companies. Although the Code has no legal force, it elaborates the relationship of bodies to their sponsoring Departments and the roles of Board Chairpersons, Board members (*e.g.* "The Chairman and other Board members should declare any personal or business interests which may conflict with their responsibilities as Board members": paragraph 17) and accounting officers.

Questions

1. In what ways does the legal form of a NDPB affect its accountability to Parliament, Ministers and the Courts?

2. Are there similarities between NDPBs and voluntary self-regulatory agencies (such as the Takeover Panel or the Jockey Club) and, if so, should they be subject to a common administrative law framework?

3. Are the Nolan Committee proposals adequate to eliminate public concerns about partisan appointments and "sleaze" in the activities of some NDPBs?

(iii) Public Corporations

Public corporations are a particular sub-species of NDPBs with the distinguishing feature that they always have a separate corporate personality. Their constituent statutes normally provide them with such sweeping powers that the courts are virtually powerless to exercise any substantial supervision over the actions of public corporations. The major issue that has been litigated concerned the question whether a particular corporation was entitled to Crown immunity from suit or from the application of specific legislation; see *Nottingham No. 1 Area Hospital Management Committee v. Owen* [1958] 1 Q.B. 50 (National Health Service hospital immune from criminal proceedings for an alleged statutory nuisance caused by smoke emitted from one of its chimneys) and *British Medical Association v. Greater Glasgow Health Board* [1989] A.C. 1211 (Scottish health authority not immune from interdict proceedings by virtue of the Crown Proceedings Act 1947).

Public corporations have been closely associated with the post-Second World War nationalisation of major industries (*e.g.* steel, coal and the railways). However, a major element in the post-1979 Conservative Government's economic and industrial strategy has been to subject these public corporations to various forms of privatisation. This development has resulted in relatively little direct litigation. An exception concerned the flotation of the trustee savings banks on the stock market in 1986. Under the Trustee Savings Banks Act 1985, the existing statutory trustee savings banks were abolished and replaced by successor limited liability companies. Depositors in the statutory banks brought actions in which they claimed that they were entitled to the surplus assets of the statutory banks when they were abolished. The House of Lords determined that the depositors' rights were limited to receiving their principal sums invested together with the interest due on those investments. Consequently, the surplus assets of the banks would pass to the successor companies and their new private shareholders: *Ross v. Lord Advocate* [1986] 1 W.L.R. 1078. In a later case several local authorities had their claim that the privatisation of public water authorities, by the Water Act 1989, infringed valuable property rights possessed by the council struckout. Sir Nicolas Browne-Wilkinson V.-C. (as he then was) concluded that the councils had no legal or equitable interests in the assets of the water authorities which were privatised: *Sheffield City Council v. Yorkshire Water Services Ltd and related actions* [1991] 2 All E.R. 280.

The privatisation of many former public corporations has placed much more emphasis on the regulation of the pricing, ownership and competition policies of the now private sector public utility companies: see below, the section on Regulation at p. 81.

For readings on public corporations see: *Garner*, Chap. 2, *Craig*, pp. 99–101, *Wade and Forsyth*, Chap. 6, T. Prosser, *Nationalised Industries and Public Control* (1988). Readings on privatisation include: D. March, "Privatisation under Mrs. Thatcher: A Review of the Literature" (1991) 61 *Public Administration* 459; Graham and Prosser, *Privatising Public Enterprises, Constitutions, the State and Regulation in Comparative Perspective* (1991); Foster, *Privatisation, Public Ownership and the Regulation of Natural Monopoly* (1992) and Daintith and Sah, "Privatisation and the Economic Neutrality of the Constitution" [1993] P.L. 465.

Question
Should the actions of public corporations be subject to greater judicial scrutiny?

(B) LOCAL GOVERNMENT

In this section we will deal with the special position of local authorities, the relationship between members and officers *inter se* and in relation to other persons. Many of the problems that arise in connection with local authorities, in particular in relation to judicial control over their discretionary powers, are similar to those that arise in connection with agencies of central government and public corporations, and are considered elsewhere in this book. For general reading see *Garner*, Chaps. 13–17; *Wade and Forsyth*, Chap. 4; *Craig*, Chap. 3; M. Loughlin, *Local Government in the Modern State* (1987) and *Legality and Locality* (1996), and J.F. McEldowney, *Public Law*, Chap. 12. Detailed consideration of the law relating to local government can be found in the *Encyclopedia of Local Government Law*, and *Cross*.

Particular aspects of local government law illustrated elsewhere in this book include: the application of the *ultra vires* principle to local authorities (below pp. 182 *et seq.*); delegation (pp. 253 *et seq.*); assurances given by officers to members of the public (pp. 286 *et seq.*), the fiduciary duty owed by local authorities to their rate/ council tax-payers (pp. 321 *et seq.*); appeals against local authority decisions (pp. 543 *et seq.*); and the liability of local authorities in tort and contract (Chap. 11).

(i) The Characteristics and Value of Local Government

THE CONDUCT OF LOCAL AUTHORITY BUSINESS

Cmnd. 9797 (1986)

Committee of Inquiry chaired by D. Widdicombe Q.C.

The constitutional position of local government
3.3 In Great Britain Parliament is sovereign. Although local government has origins pre-dating the sovereignty of Parliament, all current local authorities are the statutory creations of Parliament and have no independent status or right to exist. The whole system of local government could lawfully be

abolished by Act of Parliament. Central government is not itself sovereign, and indeed its powers are—or may be—circumscribed by Parliament just as much as those of local government. In practice, however, central government is drawn from the political party with a majority in Parliament and its de facto political strength is accordingly much greater than that of local government.

The legislative form of local government
3.7 The principal characteristics of modern local authorities in Great Britain can be traced to the origins of elected local government in the 19th century. There have however been important changes, particularly in the functions they undertake and in their size. The system has never been a static one. Major re-organisations took place in 1974 and, in Scotland 1975, following the reports of the Redcliffe-Maud[16] and Wheatley[17] Commissions. Although a further re-organisation took place in London and the metropolitan counties on April 1, 1986 the characteristics of the great majority of local authorities were determined by those re-organisations, and can be summarised as follows:

(a) they are directly elected by popular franchise;
(b) they are multi-purpose: in most areas responsibilities are divided between two tiers of multi-purpose authorities;
(c) they cover large areas as measured in population (about 120,000 people on average for lower tier authorities);
(d) they have substantial responsibilities for the delivery of services. Indeed this is one of the reasons why it has been felt necessary to create such large authorities. The extent of autonomy from central government in the delivery of services varies between services;
(e) they may only act within the specific powers set by Parliament. It would be possible for Parliament to grant local government a "general competence" to act for the good of its area. Instead they rely primarily on specific powers granted service by service;
(f) they may raise their own revenue. About 60 per cent of national local government expenditure is currently financed from locally determined and collected rates* and rents, from other charges for services and from borrowing. The balance is financed from central government grant;
(g) they are corporate bodies. The powers of local authorities are vested corporately in their councillors as a whole. They are not vested in the majority party, nor in individual councillors, nor in officers. They rely on full-time professional officers, however, for the day-to-day discharge of their functions.

THE VALUE OF LOCAL GOVERNMENT

3.11 The value of local government stems from its three attributes of:

---

[16] Report of the Royal Commission on Local Government in England, 1969. Cmnd. 4040.
[17] Report of the Royal Commission on Local Government in Scotland, 1969. Cmnd. 4150.
 * (Editor's note) Subsequently replaced by the Community Charge (Poll Tax) in relation to domestic dwellings in England and Wales (Local Government Finance Act 1988) and now by the Council Tax (Local Government Finance Act 1992).

(a) pluralism, through which it contributes to the national political system;
(b) participation, through which it contributes to local democracy;
(c) responsiveness, through which it contributes to the provision of local needs through the delivery of services.

Pluralism

3.13 The case for pluralism is that power should not be concentrated in one organ of state but should be dispersed, thereby providing political checks and balances, and a restraint on arbitrary government and absolutism. This is not an argument for fragmentation of the state, nor for divided sovereignty, but rather for increasing the cohesiveness and stability of the state by making it less brittle and allowing within it some safety valve for the expression of contrary views.

Participation

3.18 Arguments about participation are less concerned with local government's position in the wider political system and more concerned with the quality of democracy within local government. As such they are relatively modern arguments, originating with the introduction of a popular franchise and remain in a continuing state of development as the nature of democracy itself continues to develop.

3.20 Local government offers two kinds of participation; participation in the expression of community views and participation in the actual delivery of services. It does so both through the process of electing representatives as councillors and through the opportunity to influence local government more directly through consultation, co-option, and local lobbying. These factors have led to much recent debate as to the quality of local democracy and how it might best be promoted.

Responsiveness

3.26 Proponents of local government argue that it is an **effective** means of delivering services because it has the ability, unlike a non-elected system of local administration, to be responsive to local needs. There is an important distinction between efficiency and effectiveness. Efficiency is concerned solely with output, effectiveness is concerned also with the meeting of needs. It is a distinction which applies in industry as much as it does in government. Efficiency in the production of manufactured goods is of little value if there is no market for those goods. A successful private industry needs to be responsive to its customers. Similarly those delivering local services need to be responsive to the local community, and it is argued that local government alone possesses that ability.

Notes

1. For an analysis of this report in its political context see P. McAuslan, "The Widdicombe Report: Local Government Business or Politics?" [1987] P.L. 154. Professor McAuslan described central-local government relations thus, "the government's overriding aim which it has pursued with a fair degree of consistency since 1979 is to reduce the role, status, powers, financial independence, functions and, in some cases, the very existence of local government" (p. 162).

2. The views of councillors and other academics on the Widdicombe Report can be found in a special edition of the journal *Local Government Studies*, Vol. 12, No. 6 (1986).

3. Part II of the Local Government Act 1992 establishes a Local Government Commission for England (replacing the Local Government Boundary Commission for England), whose remit includes the task of examining the structure of local government in England outside London with a view to moving, where appropriate, to single-tier authorities. Central government favours the creation of single-tier unitary authorities and in 1993 the Secretary of State for the Environment issued statutory policy guidance to the Local Government Commission stating, *inter alia*, that: "Unitary authorities can reduce bureaucracy and costs and improve the coordination and quality of services. ... In some areas the Commission may wish to recommend a continuation of the existing two-tiered structure. But the Government expects that to be the exception, and that the result will be a substantial increase in the number of unitary authorities in both urban and rural areas." Two local authorities brought judicial review actions against the Secretary to challenge this guidance. The High Court held that the final sentence of the guidance quoted above was unlawful as it undermined the statutory criteria, laid down in section 13 of the 1992 Act, which Parliament had elaborated to govern the working of the Commission (see *R. v. Secretary of State for the Environment, ex p. Lancashire County Council/Derbyshire County Council* [1994] 4 All E.R. 165).

4. The Local Government (Wales) Act 1994, has created a new structure for local government in the principality. 21 new unitary authorities ("principal councils") have been created. Elections for the new authorities took place in May 1995 and they formally assumed responsibility for the provision of local services in April 1996.

(ii) The Control by District Audit

PICKWELL v. CAMDEN LONDON BOROUGH COUNCIL

[1983] 1 Q.B. 962; [1983] 1 All E.R. 602; 80 L.G.R. 798, D.C. (Q.B.D.)

In February 1979 members of the National Union of Public Employees (NUPE) began indefinite strike action in the London Borough of Camden with a serious effect upon council services. The controlling group of Labour councillors agreed to negotiate with the local branch of NUPE, despite the existence of contemporaneous national negotiations over local authority wage rates. A local settlement between NUPE and Camden resulted in an agreement that the relevant employees would receive at least £60 for a 35-hour week, which was approved by the Council on March 7, 1979. The next day the national negotiations resulted in a nationwide settlement which was less favourable to employees. However, the Camden employees continued to receive their extra pay. The District Auditor considered that the Camden pay settlement resulted in a £950,000 excess payment by the Council between 1978–1981. He accordingly applied to the High Court for a declaration under s.161(1) of the Local Government Act 1972, that these items of account were contrary to law. In addition he sought an order under s.161(2) of the Act, in terms the court thought fit to make. The respondents were the Council and the 31 Labour councillors who had voted for the local settlement.

FORBES J. . . . I should now look at the provisions of the Local Government Act 1972 which govern these proceedings before this court, but before doing so I propose to glance briefly at the statutory provisions which preceded them. In doing this I am not seeking to derive assistance in the interpretation of the Act of 1972 but to contrast the past and present position of the court and the district auditor and to indicate the statutory background against which some of the authorities were decided.

The first situation to look at is that obtaining before 1933 under the Public Health Act 1875 (38 & 39 Vict. c. 55). I do not propose to read the statute in extenso. It is sufficient to say that it provided for the annual audit of local accounts by district auditors and contained these provisions:

"247 . . . (6) Any ratepayer or owner of property in the district may be present at the audit, and may make any objection to such accounts before the auditor; and such ratepayers and owners shall have the same right of appeal against allowances by an auditor as they have by law against disallowances: (7) Any auditor acting in pursuance of this section shall disallow every item of account contrary to law, and surcharge the same on the person making or authorising the making of the illegal payment, and shall charge against any person accounting the amount of any deficiency or loss incurred by the negligence or misconduct of that person, or of any sum which ought to have been but is not brought into account by that person, and shall in every such case certify the amount due from such person, and on application by any party aggrieved shall state in writing the reasons for his decision . . ."

The section also provides so far as is relevant that any person so surcharged, or any ratepayer or owner aggrieved by a refusal to disallow, may apply to the Divisional Court for certiorari or alternatively appeal to the Local Government Board. The duties of that board were subsequently taken over by the Minister of Health.

The features of this procedure were thus that the district auditor himself made the surcharge, and he was under a mandatory duty to do so, wherever the item of account was contrary to law. The challenge to that decision before the courts was by certiorari. This inevitably meant that the court was exercising a supervisory and not an appellate jurisdiction. It also meant that the onus was on the applicant to show that the district auditor was wrong. Where the court is exercising a supervisory jurisdiction its approach to the matter in hand is necessarily different from its approach when acting as a Court of Appeal. The approach is often referred to as the *Wednesbury* doctrine because the elements are conveniently summarised in the judgment of Lord Greene M.R. in *Associated Provincial Picture Houses Ltd v. Wednesbury Corporation* [1948] 1 K.B. 223. . . .

The principles of *Wednesbury* can therefore be seen as the corollary of the assertion of a supervisory rather than an appellate jurisdiction and involve, so far as is material here, the three brief propositions: (1) an authority must not be affected by immaterial nor ignore material considerations: (2) an authority must not act in such a way that it can be said of it that no reasonable authority, properly directing itself to what was material, could have concluded that it was entitled so to act: and (3) in reviewing the acts of an authority the court will not substitute its own view of how a discretion should be exercised for that of the authority entrusted by Parliament with the discretion....

The Local Government Act 1933 repealed the provisions of the Public Health Act 1875. The provisions relating to district auditors are to be found in Part X. There is again a provision for a right of objection to the accounts which the district auditor is engaged in auditing. The right was given, not to a ratepayer or property owner, as in the Act of 1875, but, curiously, to any local government elector for the local authority area. The duties of the district auditor, however, remained the same, and in the same mandatory form. The arrangements for challenging the district auditor's decisions were markedly different. Any person aggrieved by any decision of the district auditor, whether to disallow or to refuse to do so, could appeal either to the High Court or Minister. The powers of the court or Minister are given in section 229(2) which, so far as is relevant, is in these terms:

> "The court or Minister on such an appeal shall have power to confirm, vary or quash the decision of the auditor, and to remit the case to the auditor with such directions as the court or Minister thinks fit for giving effect to the decision on appeal . . ."

I think that it has never been doubted that these words effectively mean that the court's jurisdiction was still intended to be a supervisory one and that therefore the principles which, merely as a convenient shorthand, one refers to as the *Wednesbury* principles apply. Subject to that explanation the position remained precisely as it was under the Act of 1875: the mandatory duty lay on the district auditor, the onus lay on the party aggrieved to show that he had been wrong, and the question still remained: Was the item of account contrary to law?

The modern position is to be found in section 161 of the Local Government Act 1972. I need not look at the provisions governing the audit itself. A local government elector for the area still has his right of objection to the accounts. I should read section 161(1) to (3):

> "(1) Where the audit of any accounts under this Part of this Act is carried out by a district auditor and it appears to him that any item of account is contrary to law he may apply to the court for a declaration that the item is contrary to law except where it is sanctioned by the Secretary of State. (2) On an application under subsection (1) above the court may make or refuse to make the declaration asked for, and where the court makes that declaration then, subject to subsection (3) below, it may also—(a) order that any person responsible for incurring or authorising any expenditure declared unlawful shall repay it in whole or in part to the body in question and, where two or more persons are found to be responsible, that they shall be jointly and severally liable to repay it as aforesaid; and (b) if any such expenditure exceeds £2,000 and the person responsible for incurring or authorising it is a member of a local authority, order him to be disqualified from being a member of a local authority for a specified period; and (c) order rectification of the accounts. (3) The court shall not make an order under

R.T.C. LIBRARY, LETTERKENNY

subsection (2)(a) or (b) above if the court is satisfied that the person responsible for incurring or authorising any such expenditure acted reasonably or in the belief that the expenditure was authorised by law, and in any other case shall have regard to all the circumstances, including that person's means and ability to repay that expenditure or any part of it."

It is clear that there has been a fundamental change in the position of the district auditor in relation to items in the account which may be contrary to law. The district auditor is no longer under a duty to disallow such items nor to surcharge the amounts on the persons responsible. He has a discretionary power to make an application to the court for a declaration. The court, too, is in a fundamentally different situation. It is not to embark on the process of seeing whether the district auditor was right. It must itself decide all questions which arise, both of fact and law. The onus is also altered: the onus of satisfying the court that the item of account is contrary to law is now on the district auditor....

[After citing *Roberts v. Hopwood* [1925] A.C. 578: see below, p. 321]

The case seems to me to decide no more than this, that where the inevitable inference which must be drawn is that an obviously excessive wage payment was agreed to be paid without any regard to any commercial consideration and solely on some extraneous principle, as, for instance, philanthropy, such a payment can only be regarded as a gift and is not covered by a statutory power to pay reasonable wages. Looking back, as we do, over 60 years of progress in the field of social reform and industrial relations some of their Lordships' observations may, with the benefit of this hindsight, appear unsympathetic. But what has changed over those years is our attitudes to what should be regarded as pure philanthropy; the basic legal principle, that a payment is illegal which cannot be justified by reference to the objects for which a statutory power is granted, still remains....

Of course it is plain that a local authority owes a fiduciary duty to its ratepayers: it also owes a duty, laid on it specifically by Parliament, to provide a wide range of services for its inhabitants, be they ratepayers, electors or neither. It is entitled as an employer to have regard to the interests and welfare of its workforce, as any good employer should. It must therefore often be involved in balancing fairly these interests which may frequently conflict....

But I think despite this the district auditor in considering the accounts, and certainly the court in considering any application for a declaration under section 161, must have due regard to the other duties which the local authority has to discharge. If it can be shown, and the onus is now on the district auditor to show it, that a local authority has deliberately topped the balance in favour of one interest over others then, whether this be put as taking into account irrelevant material or as the brand of unreasonableness to which *Wednesbury* refers, it is plainly something beyond the power which was entrusted to it....

The position is thus that on February 13, 1979, the Labour group's decision to agree to a £60 minimum earnings level and a 35-hour week was not taken freely and voluntarily and without pressure. The council was faced with a position where vital services had been so disrupted that real hardship was being caused, not only to the elderly and handicapped, but to the commercial concerns who pay rates but have no elective voice, and where the whole administrative machine of the borough was in imminent danger of having to close down. To this should be added a belief, not unreasonable in the circumstances, that negotiations at national level were not being pursued as effectively or speedily as was required. It seems to me that in this climate we are worlds away from Poplar in the 1920s where a calm and deliberate decision to indulge in what then passed for philanthropy was being taken. Nor do I regard it as the inevitable inference to be drawn from the payment in those circumstances of what might in others be regarded as excessive wages that the group ignored the interests of the ratepayers or any other relevant consideration or in any way can be regarded as unreasonable as that term is understood in *Associated Provincial Picture Houses Ltd v. Wednesbury Corporation* [1948] 1 K.B. 223. I remain wholly unsatisfied that the district auditor has made out a case for declaring the decision to concede the £60 minimum and the 35-hour week unlawful....

The district auditor was of course right to make this application. The power to do so falls just as much within his discretion as did the power to pay the wages he seeks to challenge, and, although different factors affect the two discretions. I do not wish to give any impression that the district auditor exercised his discretion wrongly in this matter. Much publicity, and much of it hostile, was attracted to the Camden decision. It is clear that the district auditor thought that Camden had given in too easily, and without a fight, to the strikers' demands. But there is nothing here to suggest that there was any collusion or collaboration between councillors and the strikers. If there had been this would of course have been wholly improper and would have struck directly at the good faith of the council's decision to pay these wages. But as it is I can reiterate that in my view it is not possible in the circumstances of this case to draw the inference that the council here ignored relevant material, were guided by improper motives, or acted in such a way as no reasonable council could properly act. I would refuse the declaration asked.

ORMROD L.J. gave a separate judgment in which he upheld the lawfulness of the expenditure.

Notes

1. Crawford believed that the case clarified the role of the auditor and the courts in relation to the burden of proof under s.161 of the 1972 Act; he also reported that some local authorities had greeted the decision with euphoria as an important defence against the value-judgments of the auditor: C. Crawford, "Auditors, Local Government and the Fiduciary Duty" [1983] P.L. 248.

2. The system of local government audit was subject to further reforms by the Local Government Finance Act 1982. The Act, *inter alia*, created a new body called the Audit Commission. The Commission was given the functions of: (a) appointing auditors for local authorities in England and Wales; (b) preparing a code of audit practice to govern local authority; and (c) undertaking studies to promote economy, efficiency and effectiveness in the provision of local government services. The code of practice has subsequently been regularly updated by the Commission and approved by Parliament. In 1994 the Commission created a separate agency, called District Audit, to provide auditing services to local authorities and other public bodies. Parliament increased the remit of the Commission to include giving directions to local authorities regarding the

production of performance indicators in the Local Government Act 1992. The Commission has identified value for money improvements of £620 million in local authority expenditure between 1988–1994.

3. The House of Lords has held that in the performance of certain district functions (notably the issuing of a certificate under the Local Government Finance Act 1982, s.20(1), that a member of a local authority has been guilty of wilful misconduct which has caused the authority to incur a financial loss) the District Auditor is required to act fairly: see *Lloyd v. McMahon* [1987] A.C. 625, below, p. 487.

4. The longest investigation of alleged wilful misconduct by councillors took the district auditor of Westminster City Council, John Magill, seven years to complete. In his May 1996 report he found that three councillors, including Dame Shirley Porter (the former leader of the council) and three officers were liable to repay £31.6 million expended on an unlawful policy of designated housing sales. He considered that this policy amounted to "disgraceful and improper gerrymandering" by means of the selective selling of council housing, encouraging home ownership and expelling the homeless from eight marginal wards with the purpose of converting them into Conservative areas.

(iii) Disclosure of Interest by Members

RANDS v. OLDROYD

[1959] 1 Q.B. 204; [1958] 3 W.L.R. 583; 128 J.P. 1; 102 S.J. 811;
[1958] 3 All E.R. 344; 56 L.G.R. 429, D.C. (Q.B.D.)

The defendant was managing director of and held a controlling interest in a building company and was also a member of the local council. The company had taken part in various building contracts for the council, but had not tendered for any such contracts since 1954. In 1956, in view of his position on the council, the defendant decided that the company would not tender in future for any building contracts for the council. In 1957, at a meeting of the council, a motion was proposed that, where it was required that tenders should be obtained, the borough engineer should submit a tender on behalf of his department, and where necessary, the direct labour force should be increased to implement that policy. The motion was subsequently amended by deleting that part referring to the increase of the direct labour force, and the defendant voted in favour of the motion as amended. An information was preferred against the defendant under section 76 of the Local Government Act 1933 (now section 94 of the Local Government Act 1972).

LORD PARKER C.J. .... It is clear that the member of the council concerned, namely, the defendant, can only have an indirect pecuniary interest in this case if the company itself has a direct pecuniary interest. Therefore one can limit the matter to simply this: Did Henry Rands & Son Ltd in the circumstances of this case have a direct pecuniary interest in any contract or proposed contract or other matter which was the subject of discussion at the meeting? There is no question here of any contract or proposed contract. If the company had a direct pecuniary interest it was because they had a direct pecuniary interest in an "other matter", and what is said quite shortly is this, that the matter under discussion was a matter which, to put it generally, seriously affected the company in a pecuniary way in that, if the original motion was carried, the company of the borough engineer might well be such as to prevent the company, if they tendered, from ever getting a contract. It is said that, accordingly, they had a financial interest and a direct financial interest in the matter to be discussed, and which was discussed at that meeting.

The all-important matter is to consider the mischief aimed at by section 76. One can say it is obvious, and indeed it is. It was put by Lord Esher M.R. in *Nutton v. Wilson* ((1889) 22 Q.B.D. 744 at 747) a case considering a rather similar provision in the Public Health Act, 1875 in these words: "I adhere to what I have before said with regard to provisions of this kind. They are intended to prevent the members of local boards, which may have occasion to enter into contracts, from being exposed to temptation, or even to the semblance of temptation." Lindley L.J. in the same case said (at 748): "To interpret words of this kind, which have no very definite meaning, and which perhaps were purposely employed for that very reason, we must look at the object to be attained. The object obviously was to prevent the conflict between interest and duty that might otherwise inevitably arise."

That is clearly the object of section 76 of the Local Government Act, 1933, and whereas, of course, a consideration of the mischief aimed at does not enable the court to construe the words in a wider sense than they appear, it at least means that the court would not be acute to cut down words otherwise wide merely because this was a penal statute. Mr Wilson in his very able argument has contended that, nevertheless, the words "having a direct pecuniary interest in any contract or proposed contract or other matter", are not as wide, properly construed, as one would otherwise think. He relies in particular on the words "or other matter", and he says that whether one looks at the matter as a case of *ejusdem generis* or of *noscitur a sociis*, at any rate "other matter" must be something confined to what he would say was a specific transaction, and not a matter of what might be said to be general policy. Apart from relying on that principle he also points out that in the Municipal Corporations Act 1882, which was repealed by the Local Government Act 1933, the corresponding section, section 22(3), was in these terms: "A member of the council shall not vote or take part in the discussion of any matter before the council, or a committee, in which he has, directly or indirectly, by himself or by his partner, any pecuniary interest." He points out that that is quite general; there is no reference there to a specific contract or proposed contract, and he invites the court to say that section 76 was intended to be a limitation on what heretofore had been a very general provision. I find it impossible to give any satisfactory narrower meaning, even if I were so minded, to those words "any contract or proposed contract or other matter". I do not propose to go through the number of illustrations which have been canvassed in this court, but the more one does consider the matter the more difficult and impossible it is to cut down those words "or other matter" to something which was definable and which was a limitation on what appear to be general words. Bearing in mind the mischief aimed at by this Act, I do not think those words are to be read in other than a very general way, and I see no ground for introducing a limitation which, as I said, is one which cannot satisfactorily be defined.

Mr Wilson pointed out that if you construe section 76 in a very wide way you may make business at council meetings impossible, it may stultify the whole proceedings, and that he invokes as another ground for cutting down the general meaning of those words. I quite appreciate the force of that argument, but I think the limitation to be found in section 76 is not in regard to the words "in any contract or proposed contract or other matter", but in the consideration of whether the person under consideration—the company here—had a direct pecuniary interest. I think the limitation is to be found in that word "direct" as opposed to a pecuniary interest which is too remote. In the present case I am satisfied that the company did have a direct pecuniary interest, and that that interest was not too remote to bring them within the words of the section. All these cases, of course, must be determined ultimately on their particular facts, but I think that some help is to be gained by a consideration of one of the only two cases which have come before this court on this question, namely, *Brown v. Director of Public Prosecutions* ([1956] 2 Q.B. 369; [1956] 2 W.L.R. 1087; [1956] 2 All E.R. 189). The question there to be debated was as to lodgers' allowances to be paid by tenants of council houses, and three of the councillors who were on the council considering this matter were in fact tenants of council houses, albeit they had not any lodgers. The court were clearly of opinion that those councillors who were already tenants, albeit they did not have lodgers as yet and might never have lodgers, did have a pecuniary interest in the contract or proposed contract of tenancy. The court went on to contrast the position of those councillors who might become tenants of a council house in the future but who as yet had not become tenants. It is enough, I think, to refer to two passages, first, in the judgment of Lord Goddard C.J., where he said ([1956] 2 Q.B. 369 at 376): "I think that Parliament has laid down that on any matter in which a member of a local authority has a pecuniary interest—and he undoubtedly has a pecuniary interest if he is paying rent for a house owned by the council—he should not vote at all. . . ." A little further on he refers to what might be thought to be anomalies; he said (at 377): "It is true that anomalies may occur—if they are really anomalies, though I do not think they are—for instance, councillors might vote on those matters knowing, perhaps, that in a few months' time they might themselves be the occupiers of council houses and pay rent to the council. One cannot deal with every point which arises, but if a person occupies a council house, I think that he is debarred by the terms of section 76 from voting. Again, Donovan J. in his judgment ([1956] 2 Q.B. 369 at 378) after stating: "The object of section 76(1) is clearly to prevent councillors from voting on a matter which may affect their own pockets and which may therefore affect their judgment," goes on to say: "I am referring to the three who had not taken any lodgers or sublet at the time, but who each had a council house which was a potential income-producing asset. Their case is different from a councillor who merely had a hope of obtaining such a house in the future." The facts there were quite different. What was being considered was a contract of tenancy, but I think the relevance of it is that in laying down the limitation in the case of councillors who had not yet got tenancies, the court were making the very point I am trying to make, namely, that one has to consider whether the pecuniary interest was direct or remote, and they were really saying that the interest of councillors who had not a council house was too remote, whereas those that did have a council house came within the words of the section. In the present case the company clearly had a direct pecuniary interest in the matter under discussion.

Finally, I should say this: The justices found that not only since 1954 had the company not tendered, but that the defendant himself had decided that in view of his position as vice-chairman of the housing and town planning committee of the council, his company would not tender in the future for any building contracts of the council. Further, the justices say: "We were of opinion that the [defendant] was sincere in his statement to us that his company did not intend to tender for any further council work." I cannot think that that can affect the question whether there has been an offence committed or not. It goes very clearly to mitigation but not, I think, to defence because at any time the defendant and the company could have changed their minds and could have tendered. It is a matter which the justices very properly took into consideration in mitigation and they gave what I think is a very appropriate sentence namely an absolute discharge. In my view, the justices, who dealt very ably with a difficult case, came to a correct decision, and I would dismiss this appeal.

CASSELS and STREATFEILD JJ. delivered concurring judgments.

Appeal dismissed.

Notes

1. In 1975 the Government and local authorities agreed a voluntary National Code of Local Government Conduct. Paragraph 3 of the Code required councillors to withdraw from meetings where they had relevant non-pecuniary interests (*e.g.* friendship with a person affected by the local authority's decision). The Widdicombe Report disclosed that the Code had been formally adopted by 82 per cent of local authorities,[18] while the Local Government Ombudsmen normally regarded breaches of the Code as maladministration in so far as the Code related to matters within their jurisdiction.

2. Now, the Local Government and Housing Act 1989, s.31, empowers the Secretary of State, after consultation with local authorities, to issue a statutory code, which must be approved by both Houses of Parliament. The code was issued in 1990. Where the Local Ombudsmen find a councillor has acted in breach of the statutory code they must generally name the councillor in their report (s.32). See DoE Circular No. 8/90.

3. The Widdicombe Report also noted that 50 per cent of local authorities had introduced non-statutory registers of members' interests.[19] They favoured this development and recommended that all councils should be obliged to produce a public register of their members' pecuniary and non-pecuniary interests. Section 19 of the Local Government and Housing Act 1989 enables the Secretary of State to promulgate regulations obliging councillors to notify their authority of the councillors' prescribed direct and indirect pecuniary interests. Failure to supply the prescribed information or supplying false/misleading information is made a criminal offence. The regulations may require the registers to be kept open for public inspection. See the Local Authorities (Members' Interests) Regulations 1992 (S.I. 1992 No. 618 as amended by S.I. 1995 No. 789). See *Garner*, pp. 484–487.

Questions

1. The defendant in *Rands v. Oldroyd* contended that the *ejusdem generis* rule or the *noscitur a sociis* rule should be applied to the words "other matter" in the phrase "having a direct pecuniary interest in any contract or proposed contract or other matter". What, in your view, would have been the consequence in practical terms if the court had accepted this contention?

[18] Report, para. 6:17.
[19] Report, para. 6:44.

2. If a member having an interest votes on a matter in contravention of these provisions, is the decision of the authority (or committee) void in law?

3. Compare the cases on the rules against interest and bias (the *nemo judex* rule of natural justice) below, pp. 516 *et seq.*

(iv) Rights of the Public to Attend Meetings

R. v. LIVERPOOL CITY COUNCIL, ex p. LIVERPOOL TAXI FLEET OPERATORS' ASSOCIATION

[1975] 1 All E.R. 379; [1975] 1 W.L.R. 701; 119 S.J. 166; (1974) 73 L.G.R. 143, D.C. (Q.B.D.)

[The relevant facts appear in the judgment.]

LORD WIDGERY C.J.: In these proceedings counsel moves on behalf of the Liverpool Taxi Fleet Operators' Association for a variety of forms of relief under the prerogative orders. More especially, and in my judgment central to his motion, is an application for an order of certiorari to remove into this court with a view to its being quashed a resolution of the Liverpool City Council ("the corporation") dated October 9, 1974, the effect of which was to authorise the grant of an increased number of hackney carriage licences to operate within the city boundaries.

The substantial ground for the relief sought is that the committee meeting leading up to the decision of the corporation on October 9, 1974 was itself held in breach of the provisions of the Public Bodies (Admission to Meetings) Act 1960 in that it is alleged the public were not admitted to the relevant committee meeting as required by that Act.

There is a certain history to this application. I mention it very briefly because it seems to me to have no real bearing on the issue which is before the court. A very similar matter was before this court, and subsequently the Court of Appeal, in *Re Liverpool Taxi Owners' Association* ([1972] 2 All E.R. 589; [1972] 2 Q.B. 299, below, p. 448). That was a case which again had raised the vexed issue of whether there should be additional hackney carriage licences in Liverpool, this being a matter of very considerable interest to those whose livelihood depends on obtaining and retaining licences to operate such cabs, and indeed to those who already operate such cabs and who wish to be protected against unfair competition by an undue increase in the number. In the matter which was before the court in 1972 it was laid down that the corporation in exercising their undoubted jurisdiction to grant or withhold the grant of licences were required to act fairly, and in particular were required to give interested parties an opportunity of making representations before any decision in regard to the grant of new licences was taken.

Further intervention by this court occurred as recently as July 1974 because the corporation, being minded to alter the number of hackney carriage licences, and mindful of the directions of this court and the Court of Appeal in 1972, had invited representations before embarking on their decision but unhappily had not made that invitation sufficiently all embracing to bring in all those who were interested, and accordingly an application for prohibition in this court on 19th July to prohibit the corporation from acting on the then current resolution was successful because the corporation conceded that it was in the wrong and the resolution then made by the corporation was duly set aside.

It is in the autumn of 1974 that the corporation make their third attempt to deal with this problem and they began by publishing a public notice dealing with their plans. The notice went out on or about 14th August and it says in the plainest terms, it being a notice in the public press, that the corporation are proposing to review the present issue of licences for taxi cabs. It recognises in terms that the corporation are under a duty to hear representations before reaching a conclusion and invites all those who wish to make representations to attend at a meeting of the Highways and Environment Committee to be held on September 18, 1974.

If I may pause there, so far so good. The corporation appear to be following to the letter the lessons which they have learnt, if I may say so without giving offence, in the two previous proceedings before us here. The notice of course came to the attention of the applicants, who are a representation of a very large number of taxi drivers in Liverpool. In the first instance the applicants seem to have been minded to appear at the committee meeting fixed for 18th September and to make representations. But in the end they decided that they would not make representations, but they informed the corporation that they wished to attend the meeting in order to listen to the representations which were made by other people.

So one comes to the meeting of 18th September. It is at this meeting that the resolution was passed, which on adoption by the corporation on 9th October becomes the resolution under attack in the present case. On 18th September the room set aside for the meeting of the committee had 55 seats. When those concerned began to assemble it became apparent that there were 22 members of the corporation who wished to sit on the committee on that day, or at least to be present on that day. That in itself was some indication of how keen is the interest in this matter in Liverpool. In addition to the 22 members of the corporation who wanted seats there were 17 officials. One feels bound to say that seems rather a large number of officials, but it is not for us in this court to decide what was or was not necessary in that respect. There were also two police officers. So of the original 55 seats, 41 were absorbed in that way, leaving only 14 vacant. Those 14 had to serve for the claims of the press, the public and those individuals who were making representations to the committee.

It is not difficult to understand that the number of seats was clearly inadequate for that purpose: all the more so, because when the meeting was about to start there were something like 40 people outside waiting to come in being either members of the public or interested persons minded to make representations or otherwise concerned to be present. There were 40 of them there, coming to deal with a subject on which, as I have said, feelings ran high.

The decision as to what to do in that event fell on Mrs Jones, who was the chairman of the committee, and she tells us in her affidavit what the position was. She said that having regard to the numbers to which I have already referred it was clear that it was not possible to throw the meeting open to members of the public in the ordinary sense of the word. There just was not room for that purpose. Again there was no very obvious way in which individual members of the public could be selected to occupy such seats as there were. This was not a case where there was a public gallery set aside and marked out for use as such, and it was not a case where there was an orderly queue of people from whom the first six or eight, or whatever number it was, could be taken. If there had been an indication to the assembled 40 outside that there were 14 seats, the possibility of an ugly rush was clear enough.

But not only that, in Mrs Jones's mind there were strong reasons for saying in this case that each person coming forward to make his representations about the issue should be entitled to make those representations to the committee not in the presence of others making conflicting representations. Whether that was a sensible point of view or not is not for us to comment on, but I am bound to say that I see no reason at all why that should be regarded as other than a tenable conclusion in the rather unusual facts and circumstances of this case.

Having regard to all those matters, Mrs Jones put it to the committee and the committee agreed that the public should be excluded from the meeting but the press should be allowed to attend. No doubt Mrs Jones thought there would probably be room for the press, and this on the face of it, it may be, was a perfectly sensible compromise. But be that as it may, the committee adopted Mrs Jones's suggestion on those lines and the resolution makes reference to that fact. It is resolution 101 of the relevant committee on the 18th September, and it says:

> "Exclusion of Public. Resolved that members of the public, with the exception of the Press, be excluded from the meeting during consideration of the following item in view of the limitations of available space and in order that the business of the Committee may be carried out satisfactorily."

That is the reason recorded in the minutes for the exclusion of the public. The contention that these proceedings were irregular, and irregular to the point that the resolution should be set aside, is entirely based on the provisions of the 1960 Act to which I have already referred. Section 1(1) provides:

> "Subject to subsection (2) below, any licence of a local authority or other body exercising public functions, being an authority or other body to which this Act applies, shall be open to the public."

The expression "body" there does include, as counsel have been kind enough to agree, this committee by virtue of the extension of the 1960 Act produced by s.100 of the Local Government Act 1972. So the committee was a body within the meaning of that subsection and thus required to open its proceedings to the public subject to s.1(2) of the 1960 Act, which s.1(2) says:

> "A body may, by resolution, exclude the public from a meeting (whether during the whole or part of the proceedings) whenever publicity would be prejudicial to the public interest by reason of the confidential nature of the business to be transacted or for other special reasons stated in the resolution and arising from the nature of that business or of the proceedings; and where such a resolution is passed, this Act shall not require the meeting to be open to the public during proceedings to which the resolution applies."

So under s.1(2) it is permissible for the committee to resolve to exclude the public for special reasons stated in the resolution and arising from the nature of that business, that is to say the business of the body or of the proceedings.

The first question I think we have to decide here is whether the public really were excluded or not in this particular case. It is, I think, important to stress that authorities arranging committee meetings and other meetings to which the 1960 Act applies must have regard to their duty to the public. That means they must have regard when making the arrangements for the committee meeting to the provision of reasonable accommodation for the public. If a committee was minded to choose to meet in a very small room and turned round and said "We cannot have the public in because there is no room", it would be acting in bad faith and it would not be beyond the long arm of this court. The committee must in the first instance so organise its affairs as to recognise its obligation to the public. But of course if the interest in the matter is unexpectedly great, if the estimates of persons attending are proved to be too low, and if the accommodation reasonably allotted to the public is filled up, then other members of the public will be excluded but not excluded by order of the committee; they will be excluded for the simple reason that no more can get in the space provided.

If that situation is reached, it is wrong to speak of the exclusion of the public at all in the context in which we use the phrase in this case, but in my judgment that was not this case, and I am moved to that conclusion most by the fact that the committee themselves did not regard this as a case in which the public were only turned back because the last seat had gone. The last seat indeed had not gone. The committee quite deliberately decided to exclude the public, and their conduct must be justified, if at all, under the terms of s.1(2) of the 1960 Act.

Next I turn to consider what was the reason which prompted the exclusion order and we cannot do better than take the account given by Mrs Jones. Indeed I think that is the only source to which one can go. As I read her affidavit, extracts from which I have already given, there were really two reasons in her mind somewhat overlapping and perhaps slightly confusing each other because they do overlap.

I think she was mindful of the fact that with only a minimum number of seats available there was no practical way in which the public could be selected to come and occupy those seats. In so far as that was her reason, and later the reason of the committee which adopted her suggestion, I would have thought that was a perfectly good reason under s.1(2). It would not be a case of a body declining to face up to its responsibility and provide accommodation for the public. It would be a case of a body which found that its arrangements, apparently sensibly made, had been swamped by the number of people who sought to attend. If in those circumstances the committee said "The only way out of this is to keep all the members of the public out", and if they took that view fairly and honestly, then I think that that would be a reason arising from the nature of the business or the proceedings within the meaning of s.1(2).

But, equally, as it seems to me, the second reason which Mrs Jones put forward is a valid one as well. The second reason, it will be remembered, was that it was desirable that individual applicants should be heard in the absence of competing applicants. That seems to me to be a conclusion which could properly be reached by this committee if so minded, and indeed there is a hint of something rather like that in s.1(3), a subsection to which I need not refer in detail.

Accordingly, if the committee had said either separately or in addition to their first reason that they wanted to exclude the public in order that individual applicants could be individually heard, I would have thought that could be regarded as a special reason arising from the nature of the business or the proceedings within the terms of s. 1(2).

So it seems to me that the acceptable reasons were there and that they were the reasons which caused Mrs Jones to give the committee the advice she did and caused the committee to adopt the resolution which it adopted.

The only remaining stumbling block is whether those reasons have been correctly stated in the minute as required by the section. I have read the minute and in so far as the reason was based on lack of available space that reason is mentioned in the minute. But in so far as the refusal of admission to the public was based on the desire to hear applicants individually, then in my judgment that reason cannot be discovered from the terms of the minute itself. It seems to me that the expression "that the business of the committee may be carried out satisfactorily", is too vague to meet the requirement of the statute where it insists that reasons for this kind of decision be given. Therefore I would be bound to say that looked at by themselves those words did not adequately show as a reason why the committee thought that individual applicants should be individually heard.

Accordingly, the final question which has to be decided is whether, given adequate reasons, the decision of the committee becomes irregular, whether as a nullity or otherwise by reason of the failure properly to state the reasons in the resolution.

At this point I think that one must distinguish between statutory provisions which are clearly imperative or mandatory and those which are merely directory. In my opinion the requirement that the reasons shall be stated in the resolution is a purely directory requirement. The effect of that is that the resolution does not automatically become a nullity by reason of the failure to state the reasons within its terms. It stands unless and until set aside by this court, and it would not be set aside by this court unless there were good reasons for setting it aside on the footing that someone had suffered a significant injury as a consequence of the irregularity. No such injury is suggested in this case, and it seems to me therefore that the corporation has perhaps at long last produced a resolution on this subject which is not subject to attack in this court. For the reasons I have given I would refuse the application.

MELFORD STEVENSON and WATKINS JJ. agreed.

Application refused.

Notes

1. In *R. v. Brent Health Authority, ex p. Francis* [1985] 1 Q.B. 869, the district health authority had convened three meetings to approve reductions in expenditure and each session had been disrupted by members of the public present at the meetings. Therefore, the chairman resolved to hold a fourth meeting with the press in attendance, but other members of the public being excluded. That meeting was held and approved the chairman's decision to exclude the public. On an application for certiorari to quash the chairman's decision brought by a member of the public, the High

Court held that section 1(8) of the 1960 Act preserved the common law power of exclusion from meetings of disorderly citizens. Furthermore, the court interpreted the power of exclusion to include the prevention of persons coming to a meeting and the expulsion of those already present at a meeting. In the context of the previous disruptions to their meetings the health authority's resolution to exclude the public was, therefore, lawful.

2. Whilst the 1960 Act continues to apply to meetings of certain public bodies (*e.g.* parish councils), it has been supplemented by the Local Government (Access to Information) Act 1985, inserting a new Part VA in the Local Government Act 1972, which governs the major local authorities (*i.e.* county and district councils). The latter Act extends the public's right of access to the meetings of committees and sub-committees of these authorities. However, the public must be excluded when confidential information is discussed and they may be excluded in a range of designated circumstances (*e.g.* when personal information about council employees is being considered). The High Court has upheld the decision of a planning committee to go into closed session (thereby excluding the developer and objectors) in order to hear the advice of a legal officer regarding the likelihood of a successful appeal against their decision being brought by the developer: see *R. v. Kensington and Chelsea London Borough Council, ex p. Stoop, The Times*, September 10, 1991. There are also rights of access to agenda and connected reports, minutes and other documents after meetings and background papers.

Questions
1. Towards the end of his judgment Lord Widgery C.J. said: "I think one must distinguish between statutory provisions which are clearly imperative or mandatory and those which are merely directory. In my opinion the requirement that the reasons shall be stated in the resolution is a purely directory requirement." On what grounds did the Lord Chief Justice come to this conclusion? What was the effect of his reaching this conclusion?

2. From the principles emerging in this case can you visualise a circumstance where a person who considered himself improperly excluded from a local authority committee meeting could apply for an order of certiorari to remove a resolution of the committee into the court with a view to its being quashed?

(v) The Duties of Officers

Re HURLE-HOBBS, ex p. RILEY AND ANOTHER

(Unreported) Divisional Court (Q.B.D.)

[This case is not reported, but a full note of the judgment appears in the appendix to C.R.H. Hurle-Hobbs, *The Law Relating to District Audit* (2nd ed., 1955, Charles Knight & Co. Ltd).]

At the beginning of 1939 the Council of the Borough of Finsbury were greatly concerned about the provision of shelters for the people of Finsbury. The second appellant, the Town Clerk of Finsbury, was closely associated with the first appellant Alderman Riley in this project. The respondent in the case was the District Auditor. He had caused a surcharge to be made against each of the appellants in respect of certain expenditure incurred in an abortive deep shelter project. He had taken the view after a long inquiry, that a contract in respect of this shelter, and which was the cause of the surcharge, was one which was open to grave criticism, that it called for the exercise by the council, as trustees of public funds, of the highest degree of care in their examination of it and of the scheme for which it provided; that the council entirely failed to exercise that care, and that such failure was due to the fact that they were kept by the appellants in complete ignorance of almost everything material to be considered. The District Auditor was satisfied that in order to get the agreements sealed, the council were deliberately kept in the dark by the appellants as to the material parts of the agreement, as to the adverse criticism of the London County Council and as to the condemnation of the scheme by an independent consulting engineer, whose opinion had been sought on the advice of Counsel, and that the appellants so acted in flagrant disregard of the liabilities and risks involved. In the District Auditor's view the council might well have rejected the scheme if they had known the truth, and it was for that reason that the appellants hid the truth from them.

The Town Clerk's answer to the Auditor's criticism was that while he knew that there ought to have been a fuller and better disclosure of information, especially the consultant's report, to the council, he was under the domination of Alderman Riley, who threatened him at least once with dismissal from his post, and that if he had taken steps to let the council have all the proper information, he would have lost his position.

LORD CALDECOTE C.J.: ... I can deal more shortly with the case as it concerns the Town Clerk. Mr Turner did not dispute that the Town Clerk had a duty to disclose information which was in fact kept back, but he submitted that being subordinate to Alderman Riley, he was not guilty of misconduct. Imprudence there may have been, but imprudence is not misconduct. Notwithstanding the strenuous contention of Counsel on his behalf, the Town Clerk seems to me wholly to misconceive his duty when he says that although he thought that the matters I have discussed ought to have been disclosed to the Council, he was entitled to stand by without taking such steps as were open to him merely because he would otherwise have been liable to dismissal from his office without notice. It was a little surprising to me that such an argument should be advanced on his behalf. It seems to me to be tantamount to an admission of misconduct. It suggests that the Town Clerk put his private interests above his duty in his office. The office of Town Clerk is an important part of the machinery of local government. He may be said to stand between the Borough Council and the ratepayers. He is there to assist by his advice and action the conduct of public affairs in the Borough, and if there is a disposition on the part of the Council, still more on the part of any member of the Council, to ride roughshod over his opinions, the question must at once arise as to whether it is not his duty forthwith to resign his office or, at any rate, to do what he thinks right and await the consequences. This is not so dangerous or heroic a course as it may seem. The integrity of the administration of public affairs is such that publicity may be safely relied upon to secure protection for anyone in the position in which the Town Clerk was said to have been placed.

I think the Respondent was right in holding that the Town Clerk was a party to Alderman Riley's scheme and that without the Town Clerk's assistance Alderman Riley could not have carried it through the Council.

On the whole case, therefore, I am of opinion that the Respondent rightly found that the sums which he has surcharged on these two Appellants represent losses incurred by their negligence and misconduct.

Appeal dismissed.

THE BOGNOR REGIS INQUIRY

[The Report of the Bognor Regis Inquiry presented by the Minister of Housing and
Local Government and the Chairman and Members of the Bognor Regis Urban Dis-
trict Council by Mr J. Ramsay Willis Q.C. (HMSO, 1965) contains, at p. 64, the fol-
lowing comments on the observations of the Lord Chief Justice quoted above. The
Inquiry was appointed to examine the circumstances leading to the dismissal of Mr
Paul Smith as Clerk of the Council.]

231. Mr Smith considers that the Clerk of a Council, if he is a lawyer,
should act as the Council's legal adviser; in so doing he is advising the Council
in his speciality just as the Engineer advises on engineering matters, and all
other Chief Officers provide the Council with the benefit of their professional
and technical knowledge. But the Clerk is also the Chief Administrative Officer of the Council, unless it is specifically stated to the contrary, and as such
the Clerk is "first among equals" in his relationship with the Council's other
Chief Officers.

232. With this view of the office of Clerk, the Bognor Regis Council, the
Society of Clerks of Urban District Councils and nearly everyone in the world
of local government would, I think, agree with Mr Smith.

233. Mr Smith, however, goes further, and believes that the Clerk of a
Council bears a unique responsibility among Chief Officers in that he enjoys a
very special relationship with the ratepayers. He finds support for this view, as
he has said on a number of occasions, in the judgment given by Lord Chief
Justice Caldecote in the case of *Hurle-Hobbs ex. p. Riley*, 1944, known as the
"Finsbury Case", which is concerned with district audit. The section of the
judgment which Mr Smith considers to be relevant appears in his letter of 25th
May to all Councillors (see Chapter 28(b)) and is as follows. [Mr Ramsay
Willis then quoted the passage printed above beginning with the words "The
office of Town Clerk is an important part of the machinery of local
government."]

234. The observations of the Lord Chief Justice were made in the context of
the facts of the Finsbury Case and seem to me not to have been necessary to his
decision on that case. Whether I am right or not, I think it is clear that Lord
Caldecote was not intending to lay down a principle of local government
practice of universal application and irrespective of the circumstances.

235. The acceptance of the passage quoted above as definitive of the Clerk's
duties in all circumstances and at all times would place him in a unique position indeed. It would seem to follow from the acceptance of that view that in
any situation in which a Clerk found himself in conflict with his Council over
an important issue of policy, he would have a duty, if it was his opinion that
the wishes of the Council were opposed to the best interests of the ratepayers,
"to do what he thinks right"; indeed, the Clerk might conceive it to be his duty
to make every effort to frustrate the will of his Council and to appeal, over
their heads, for the support of the ratepayers. If a Clerk were to interpret the
words of Lord Caldecote in the way suggested above, it is clear that he would
consider that his first duty was to the ratepayers and that he was virtually
independent of his council.

236. But if a Clerk is not answerable to his Council he is answerable to no
one. In my view he is the employee of his Council and it is to them that his

primary loyalty and duty lie and it is to them that he is answerable for his actions. In the course of advising his Council there is clearly no objection to a Clerk telling them that he considers their proposals to be wrong and, if he thinks fit, submitting his views to them in writing. I consider, however, that he should express his opinion in a manner that will not embarrass his Council and that once his view is known to them he should leave them to come to their own decision. It is the duty of Councillors to formulate the policy for the local authority and they are directly answerable for their actions to the ratepayers at the polls. This was the view of their own and their Clerk's function that was held by the Bognor Regis Council, as I think, correctly.

237. In exceptional circumstances, such as those in the Finsbury Case, there could well be a justification for a Clerk departing from what I have suggested should be his normal behaviour *vis-à-vis* Councillors. If he believes that a member of the Council has either consciously or unconsciously committed, or is putting himself in a position in which he might commit, an offence then I think he should first broach the matter with the Councillor himself; if that fails he should inform the Chairman of the Council of his concern and, perhaps, consult the Leader on the Council of the Party to which the Councillor in question belongs. If after all these efforts the Clerk finds that no notice has been taken of his warning, naturally, he finds himself in a difficult situation. If he is satisfied that there is a prima facie case of, for example, an offence under section 76 of the Local Government Act, 1933 [now section 94 of the Local Government Act 1972], after making efforts to alert the Chairman and Councillor concerned, I think he would be justified in confiding his suspicions to the Director of Public Prosecutions.

238. However, it seems to me that it would be quite improper if the Clerk were to do anything which might create the impression in the minds of the public or the Press that he was suspicious of his Council or any member of it. It is perhaps otiose to add that a man is innocent until the Courts have found him guilty, but the public seems all too ready to believe that the mere suggestion of impropriety is sufficient proof of guilt.

239. I have heard evidence from the Society of Clerks of Urban District Councils and from people who have served for many years in local government either as Councillors or Officers. I am satisfied that none of them share the view—quoted by Mr Smith on several occasions—that the Clerk "may be said to stand between the Borough Council and the ratepayers."

Note

The Widdicombe Report considered that "the chief executive should be head of the authority's paid staff with clear authority over other officers, and should have ultimate managerial responsibility for the way in which officers discharge the functions of the council".[20] In addition the Committee of Inquiry recommended that all councils should be statutorily required to appoint a chief executive. By section 4 of the Local Government and Housing Act 1989, local authorities (primarily county councils, district councils and London borough councils) must designate one of their officers as "head of paid service". This officer must be provided with sufficient staff and other resources to perform his duties laid down under the section. The major obligations of such an officer are to report to the authority on the way in which the discharge of its functions are co-ordinated, and the organisation of its staff. Section 5 of the 1989 Act

[20] Report, para. 6:151.

requires these authorities to appoint a "monitoring officer", who must report to the authority if it appears that any proposal, decision or omission by the authority (or one of its committee or officers) may be contrary to law or a statutory code of practice, or maladministration. The report must be considered within 21 days and implementation is postponed until then. The report is not binding on the authority, but members who decline to follow its recommendations may open themselves to action by the auditor. The authority's chief financial officer has similar responsibilities in respect of unlawful expenditure (Local Government Finance Act 1988, s.114). The monitoring officer may be the head of paid service but may not be the chief finance officer.

Questions

Until the coming into force of the Local Government Act 1972 certain officers of local authorities (including the clerk of a county council) could not be dismissed except with the consent of a minister. This change in the law was in line with government policy to reduce the degree of central control over the exercise of local authority discretion. Is there, in your view, a case for the reintroduction of ministerial control over the dismissal of officers? If you see a case for such control to which officer or officers should it be extended? If you see no case for ministerial control what safeguards, if any, already exist for the protection of officers who may be placed in the situation of the town clerk in the *Finsbury* case? If there are such safeguards, are they, in your view, adequate? Could and should they be strengthened, and in what way?

(vi) The Powers of Members

R. v. BIRMINGHAM CITY DISTRICT COUNCIL, ex p. O

[1983] A.C. 578; [1983] 1 All E.R. 497; 81 L.G.R. 259 (House of Lords)

The council acted as an adoption agency (under the Adoption Act 1958 and the Local Authority Social Services Act 1970) and had delegated its powers and duties under those Acts to a social services committee. During 1976 the social services department of the council "fostered out" a child with the applicants (a married couple with four children). Later, the applicants fell into arrears with their council tenancy and appeared before the council's housing committee. A member of that committee, Mrs Willetts, became alarmed at the suitability of the applicants to foster or adopt the child. After communication with the social services department and the chairperson of the social services committee, Councillor Willetts sought access to the social services' files concerning the applicants. The council's solicitor advised that it was reasonably necessary for Councillor Willetts to see the files in order to properly carry out her duties as a councillor. However, before Councillor Willetts was given access to the files, the applicants sought an order of prohibition to prevent the council disclosing the files to her on the grounds that she was not a member of the social services committee and, therefore, had no duties which required her to be acquainted with social services' files. The Divisional Court refused the application. On appeal by the applicants, the Court of Appeal (by a majority) allowed the appeal. The council appealed to the House of Lords.

LORD BRIGHTMAN [with whom all the other Law Lords agreed]:
My Lords, I entertain no doubt as to the correctness of the decision of the Divisional Court and of Donaldson L.J. The general principle must be, that a councillor is entitled by virtue of his office to have access to all written material in the possession of the local authority of which he is a member, provided that he has good reason for such access. I apprehend that there can

be no challenge to that general principle, which was undisputed half a century ago: see *R. v. Barnes Borough Council, ex p. Conlan* [1938] 3 All E.R. 226. At the risk of being repetitive, I would like to read an extract from the judgment of the Divisional Court in that case, at 230, which was quoted by Donaldson L.J. in his written judgment:

> "As to the right of a councillor to inspect all documents in possession of the council, there was no dispute at the bar that such a right exists, so far as his access to the documents is reasonably necessary to enable the councillor properly to perform his duties as a member of the council. The common law right of a councillor to inspect documents in the possession of the council arises from his common law duty to keep himself informed of all matters necessary to enable him properly to discharge his duty as a councillor. There must be some limit to this duty. To hold that each councillor of such a body as, for instance, the London County Council, is charged with the duty of making himself familiar with every document in the possession of that body would be to impose an impossible burden upon individual councillors. The duties are therefore divided amongst various committees and sub-committees. In our judgment, it is plain that, as was decided in *R. v. Southwold Corporation, ex p. Wrightson* (1908) 97 L.T. 431: 'a councillor has no right to a roving commission to go and examine books or documents of a corporation because he is a councillor. Mere curiosity or desire to see and inspect documents is not sufficient.' "

In the case of a committee of which he is a member, a councillor as a general rule will ex hypothesi have good reason for access to all written material of such committee. So I do not doubt that each member of the social services committee is entitled by virtue of his office to see all the papers which have come into the possession of a social worker in the course of his duties as an employee of the council. There is no room for any secrecy as between a social worker and a member of the social services committee.

In the case of a committee of which the councillor is not a member, different considerations must apply. The outside councillor, as I will call him, has no automatic right of access to documentary material. Of him, it cannot be said that he necessarily has good reason, and is necessarily entitled, to inspect all written material in the possession of the council and every committee and the officers thereof. What Donaldson L.J. described as a "need to know" must be demonstrated. As he put it, [1982] 1 W.L.R. 690:

> "No official has any right to acquire any part of the authority's stock of information, whether or not confidential, save in so far as it is needed by him in order that he should be able to do his job. In a word, he has to have a 'need to know'."

The "need to know" test involves the application of a screening process, and this in turn raises the question of the nature of the screen and who is to apply it. To my mind, in the case of an area as delicate and confidential as that of child care and adoption, the screening process should be administered with great strictness. The utmost care must be taken to prevent the unnecessary dissemination within the council of details relating to the child, to its natural parents, to any foster or adoptive parents, and of sources of information. More than that need not be said, because the subject matter sufficiently speaks for itself.

The decision whether the outside councillor has a good reason for access to the information is ultimately one to be taken by the councillors themselves sitting in council. But the council may expressly, or by implication, delegate to others the right to decide whether an application for access to material is to be acceded to, subject to resort to a meeting of the council if the decision of the delegate is challenged. . . .

The decision of the council is the final word, subject only to an application for judical review under section 31 of the Supreme Court Act 1981 on *Wednesbury* principles: see *Associated Provincial Picture Houses Ltd v. Wednesbury Corporation* [1948] 1 K.B. 223. . . .

This leads to the final question arising on this appeal, namely, whether the decision to permit access to relevant files was one which could have been taken by a reasonable local authority. Unless this question is decided in the negative, this appeal must inevitably succeed. . . .

I would urge your Lordships to hesitate before deciding that access to information is being unreasonably allowed, particularly when such access is approved by the immediate possessor of the information, namely, the social services committee, as well as by the council's solicitor, the council's general purposes committee, and the council itself. Viewing the matter broadly, I do not think that there is anything unreasonable in the council's forming the view that the interests of Emma and the legitimate interests of the applicants will in no way be prejudiced by the fact that Mrs Willetts is permitted to have access in confidence to files about her and about those who desire to adopt her.

Appeal allowed.

Notes

1. One commentator fears that this decision may encourage a more cautious attitude to note-making by social workers, a less candid flow of information from clients and external bodies, together with the increased danger of politically motivated intervention in social work decision-making. See H. Carty (1983) *Journal of Social Welfare Law* 179.

2. The principle endorsed in the *Birmingham* case has now been extended to encompass a councillor's right to attend appropriate committee and sub-committee meetings. In *R. v. Hackney London Borough Council, ex p. Gamper* [1985] 1 W.L.R. 1229, the applicant councillor was a member of the authority's Public Services Committee, but he had been prevented from attending the meetings of the Direct Labour Organisation sub-committee. After citing the *Birmingham* decision, Lloyd L.J. stated (at 1240):

"there is no logical distinction between access to documents and attendance at meetings. As in the case of access to documents, the answer must depend on whether the councillor needs to attend the meeting in order to perform his duties properly as a member of the council."

The court declared that the council had acted unlawfully in denying councillor Gamper access to the sub-committee meetings.

3. Parliament has supplemented the above common law powers of councillors by enacting the Local Government (Access to Information) Act 1985, which amended the Local Government Act 1972. Section 100F of the 1972 Act provides councillors with a general right of access to documents in the possession of their council, but this right is subject to the numerous exempted categories of information listed in Schedule 12A (*e.g.* action taken in connection with the prevention of crime).

Question
What remedy is available to a member who believes that he is improperly prevented from seeing a document held by the authority? Against whom will the remedy lie?

CHAPTER 2

ADMINISTRATIVE PROCEDURES

Decision-making in Government may take many forms and different processes are used to arrive at various types of decisions. In the course of these processes the law has a variety of roles to play (*e.g.* in establishing minimum standards of procedural fairness).

A full study of decision-making is not here possible[1]; suffice it for us to examine a selection of the materials dealing with the following important administrative procedures.

(A) Conciliation

Conciliation is a well-developed process which is frequently used in the resolution of industrial disputes. Since 1974 such conciliation has been one major function of an independent public body, the Advisory, Conciliation and Advisory Service (commonly called ACAS): see the Trade Union and Labour Relations Act 1992. ACAS seeks to achieve agreed solutions to both collective disputes (those between a union and an employer) and individual disputes (those involving a specific worker and an employer).

ADVISORY, CONCILIATION AND ARBITRATION SERVICE ANNUAL REPORT 1995

Preventing and resolving industrial disputes

ACAS adopts a flexible approach to helping employers, employees and their representatives prevent and resolve industrial relations problems. The key to success is the acceptability and credibility of ACAS as an independent, impartial third party, professionally competent and able to facilitate problem-solving through the direct involvement of the parties themselves.

When specific disputes occur, often arising when employer and trade union representatives fail to agree on substantive issues affecting terms and conditions of employment, *collective conciliation* by ACAS is usually appropriate. In less adversarial situations or where problems are more deep-rooted and affecting relationships at work, ACAS may propose *advisory mediation*, seeking to develop a co-operative approach to joint problem-solving. In practice, these techniques frequently interlink and overlap to ensure that the most effective approach is adopted in response to any particular situation.

Collective conciliation

Conciliation is normally appropriate in circumstances where existing

---

[1] For a valuable snapshot of organisation theory, see *Craig*, pp. 445–456.

Completed collective conciliation cases
by cause of dispute

pay and terms & conditions of employment — 48%

redundancy — 17%

dismissal and discipline — 12%

trade union recognition — 9%

other trade union matters — 7%

changes in working practices — 3%

others — 4%

procedures have been exhausted. The Service can offer conciliation at the request of either or both parties but is clearly unable, in a purely voluntary process, to conciliate in disputes where one party is opposed to ACAS involvement. ACAS will often run alongside a dispute in its early stages, using professional judgement about timing and the attitudes of the parties to decide if and when to intervene and propose conciliation.

ACAS has continued to provide a valued and effective conciliation service during the year. In 88 per cent of cases industrial action was avoided and mutually acceptable solutions were found. Even when settlements were not reached under ACAS auspices, the conciliation process often contributed to a better understanding or clarification of issues, which ultimately assisted the parties to resolve their differences.

Trends in casework

We dealt with 1,321 requests for conciliation in 1995, marginally higher than the previous year (1,313) and completed action in 1,229 cases. ACAS also maintained private and informal contact with the parties in a further 366 disputes, without becoming involved in formal talks. Most casework is carried out by ACAS's regional offices. Head Office generally deals with disputes which have a national dimension.

The largest proportion of our collective conciliation cases continued to occur in the private sector. The food and drink industry accounted for 12 per cent of completed cases; transport 12 per cent; mechanical and electrical engineering 8 per cent; and the textile industry 4 per cent. Work in the education and health sectors held steady in 1995. These areas accounted for 13 per cent of casework in the year compared with 12 per cent last year and only 5 per cent some five years ago.

In our last Annual Report we noted that cases involving pay were the highest since 1990. This trend continued in 1995, with 593 requests being received—nearly 50 per cent of the total caseload. This compares with 590 requests in 1994. Some pay issues, however, reflect wider concerns arising from the pressures of change, for example in working practices or hours worked in the week. At 203 cases, redundancy related conciliations remained at proportionately the same level as a year ago.

. . .

Conciliating in actual and potential claims to industrial tribunals

ACAS conciliation officers have a statutory duty to seek to promote settlements of complaints which have been or could be made to an industrial tribunal under a wide variety of enactments providing individual employment rights and protection. In 1995 we received 91,568 cases, an increase of about 15 per cent on the 1994 total, which had previously been the highest number of cases ever received. The greatest increase was centred on our North West region, which saw a 31 per cent increase in cases, while the next highest were in Scotland and Northern region, with increases of 20 and 18 per cent respectively. Formal complaints to industrial tribunals (IT1 cases) accounted for 98 per cent of cases; in the remainder (non-IT1 cases) there was a claim to ACAS that action had been taken in respect of which a complaint could be made to a tribunal.

Notes

1. Individual conciliation was used for disputes over alleged: unfair dismissal (45 per cent of cases), unlawful deduction of pay under the Wages Act 1986 (24 per cent of cases), breach of contract claims (17 per cent of cases) and also smaller numbers of sex and race discrimination claims. *Annual Report 1995*. For a discussion of the work of ACAS, see I.T. Smith and G. Thomas, *Industrial Law* (6th ed., 1996), p. 30.

2. Conciliation is also used by other public agencies, including the Equal Opportunities Commission in the field of gender discrimination and local rent officers in disagreement between landlords and tenants.

(B) Adjudication

A proportion of the disputes generated in the field of administrative law can be resolved by the application of pre-existing rules. These rules vary in precision and in origin (see Administrative Rule-making, below). The application of reasonably precise rules of law in the resolution of a dispute is a function typically performed by a court of law, although there are many examples of such processes being entrusted to other institutions, and courts of law do fulfil other kinds of function. The task of adjudication in a particular area may be divided among several persons or bodies. For example, Part II of the Social Security Administration Act 1992, "Adjudication", includes examples of adjudication (1) by the Secretary of State, on such matters as whether a person is an earner (s.17(1)(a)); (2) by an Adjudication Officer, on "any claim for benefit" (s.20(1)(a)); (3) by a local Social Security Appeal Tribunal, on an appeal from the decision of an Adjudication Officer (s.22); and (4) by a Social Security Commissioner, on appeal on a point of law from any decision of a local tribunal (s.23).

Adjudication by tribunals was considered over four decades ago by the Franks Committee (below). Part II of their Report concerned "Tribunals in General" (below). Many, although not all, of its recommendations were accepted, the main ones being included in the Tribunals and Inquiries Act 1958 (consolidated in the Act of 1992, below), and see Chapter 3 regarding the Council on Tribunals.

There have been a number of research studies on tribunals in general and on particular tribunals. Official and semi-official studies include the Francis Committee on the Rent Acts (Cmnd. 4609 (1971)) and the work of Professor Kathleen Bell, "National Insurance Local Tribunals: A Research Study", 3 *Journal of Social Policy* 289; and "Research Study on Supplementary Benefit Appeal Tribunals" (HMSO, 1975). Also, H. Genn and Y. Genn, *Representation at Tribunals* (1989), concerning mental health review tribunals, social security appeal tribunals and immigration adjudicators. More recent research on social security adjudication is contained in J. Baldwin, N. Wikeley and R. Young, *Judging Social Security* (1992).

Generally see *Garner*, Chap. 11; *Wade*, Chap. 23; *Craig*, Chap. 4; J. Peay, *Tribunals on Trial* (1989); P. Birkinshaw, *Grievances, Remedies and the State* (2nd ed., 1994); H.W.R. Wade, "Administrative Tribunals and Administrative Justice" (1981) 55 *Australian Law Journal* 374; N.V. Lowe and H.F. Rawlings, "Tribunals and the Laws Protecting the Administration of Justice" [1982] P.L. 418; A.R. Mowbray, "Customs and Excise Public Notices: The Tribunal Response" (1987) 11 *British Tax Review* 381; R. Sainsbury, "Social Security Appeals: in Need of Review?" in W. Finnie *et al.*, *Edinburgh Essays in Public Law* (1991); N. Wikeley and R. Young, "The Administration of Benefits in Britain" [1992] P.L. 238; H. Genn, "Tribunals and Informal Justice" (1993) 56 M.L.R. 393.

REPORT OF THE COMMITTEE ON ADMINISTRATIVE TRIBUNALS AND ENQUIRIES

(HMSO, Cmnd. 218, July 1957)

CHAIRMAN: Sir Oliver Franks.
[The Committee's terms of reference were:

"To consider and make recommendations on:
  (a) The constitution and working of tribunals other than the ordinary courts of law, constituted under any Act of Parliament by a Minister of the Crown or for the purposes of a Minister's functions.
  (b) The working of such administrative procedures as include the holding of an enquiry or hearing by or on behalf of a Minister on an appeal or as the result of objections or representations, and in particular the procedure for the compulsory purchase of land."]

PART I: *INTRODUCTION*

CHAPTER 2: THE SCOPE AND NATURE OF OUR ENQUIRY

5. Our terms of reference involve the consideration of an important part of

the relationship between the individual and authority. At different times in the history of this country it has been necessary to adjust this relationship and to seek a new balance between private right and public advantage, between fair play for the individual and efficiency of administration. The balance found has varied with different governmental systems and different social patterns. Since the war the British electorate has chosen governments which accepted general responsibilities for the provision of extended social services and for the broad management of the economy. It has consequently become desirable to consider afresh the procedures by which the rights of individual citizens can be harmonised with wider public interests.

6. The problem is not confined to this country. In recent years most other Western governments have been called upon to govern more extensively and more intensively, and finding a right relationship between authority and the individual has consequently become a matter of concern on both sides of the Atlantic.

Disputes between the individual and authority

7. How do disputes between the individual and authority arise in this country at the present time? In general the starting point is the enactment of legislation by Parliament. Many statutes apply detailed schemes to the whole or to large classes of the community (for example national insurance) or lay on a Minister and other authorities a general duty to provide a service (for example education or health). Such legislation is rarely sufficient in itself to achieve all its objects, and a series of decisions by administrative bodies, such as government departments and local authorities is often required. For example, in a national insurance scheme decisions have to be given on claims to benefit, and in providing an educational service decisions have to be taken on the siting of new schools. Many of these decisions affect the rights of individual citizens, who may then object.

8. Once objection has been raised, a further decision becomes inevitable. This further decision is of a different kind: whether to confirm, cancel or vary the original decision. In reaching it account must be taken not only of the original decision but also of the objection.

The resolution of these disputes

9. These further decisions are made in various ways. Some are made in courts of law and therefore by the procedure of a court of law. For example, an order made by a local authority for the demolition of an insanitary house may be appealed against to the county court. Frequently the statutes lay down that these further decisions are to be made by a special tribunal or a Minister. For example, a contested claim to national insurance benefit has to be determined by a special tribunal, and the decision whether or not to confirm an opposed scheme for the compulsory acquisition of land by a local authority must be made by the Minister concerned. In these cases the procedure to be followed in dealing with objections to the first decision and in arriving at the further decision is laid down in the statute or in regulations made thereunder.

10. But over most of the field of public administration no formal procedure

is provided for objecting or deciding on objections. For example, when foreign currency or a scarce commodity such as petrol or coal is rationed or allocated, there is no other body to which an individual applicant can appeal if the responsible administrative authority decides to allow him less than he has requested. Of course the aggrieved individual can always complain to the appropriate administrative authority, to his Member of Parliament, to a representative organisation or to the Press. But there is no formal procedure on which he can insist.

11. There are therefore two broad distinctions to be made among these further decisions which we have been discussing. The first is between those decisions which follow a statutory procedure and those which do not. The second distinction is within the group of decisions subject to a statutory procedure. Some of these decisions are taken in the ordinary courts and some are taken by tribunals or by Ministers after a special procedure.

12. These two distinctions are essential for understanding our terms of reference. We are not instructed to consider those many cases in which no formal procedure has been prescribed. Nor are we instructed to consider decisions made in the ordinary courts. What we are instructed to consider are the cases in which the decision on objections, the further decision as we have called it, is taken by a tribunal or by a Minister after a special procedure has been followed.

13. At this stage two comments may be added. First, although the foregoing broad analysis holds good over nearly all the field covered by our terms of reference, there are a few tribunals (for example Rent Tribunals) which determine disputes not between the individual and authority but between citizen and citizen. Secondly, we have said that we are not required to consider decisions made in the ordinary courts. This is adequate as a general statement, but it should be qualified by adding that our terms of reference clearly permit us to consider appeals to the courts from decisions of tribunals or of Ministers after a special procedure.

14. We have already said that our terms of reference do not instruct us to consider the vast majority of what we have termed further decisions—because they do not result from a formal procedure involving a tribunal or inquiry. It may be thought that in these cases the individual is less protected against unfair or wrong decision. But we are not asked to go into questions of maladministration which may arise in such cases.

15. It follows therefore that the celebrated case of Crichel Down, which is widely regarded as a principal reason for our appointment, itself in fact falls outside the subjects with which we have been asked to deal. It is true that an inquiry was held in this case, but it was an ad hoc inquiry for which there was no statutory requirement. It resulted from the exercise of those informal methods of raising objection to which we have referred in paragraph 10, and was therefore unlike the inquiries with which we are concerned.

Developments since the Donoughmore Report

16. Our subject corresponds broadly to that defined by the second part of the terms of reference of the Committee on Ministers' Powers, which reported in 1932 (Cmd. 4060). The first part of its terms of reference related to delegated legislation, which we were not asked to consider. That Committee is

generally referred to as the Donoughmore Committee, and for convenience we use this short title in the rest of this Report.

17. At the time when the Donoughmore Committee was appointed there already existed a number of tribunals, almost entirely in the field of unemployment insurance and contributory and war pensions; and local authorities already possessed considerable powers to acquire or restrict the use of private land. Since then the expansion of governmental activities and responsibilities has led to corresponding developments and innovations in our field on a large scale. Old tribunals have been adapted to wider purposes, and new tribunals have been established. More extensive powers exist, and more extensive use is made of powers, to acquire land and control its use.

18. The general impact of decisions by tribunals and Ministers on the public today is illustrated by the fact that Rent Tribunals have in some recent years dealt with as many as 15,000 cases and that the annual number of planning appeals is about 6,000. Although the number of cases heard by National Insurance and Industrial Injuries Local Tribunals (50,000 to 60,000 annually) is smaller than the number of unemployment insurance cases heard in the years just before the war, the scheme is now on a wider basis and potentially affects nearly everyone.

19. The subject of our inquiry, though only part of the relationship between authority and the individual, is thus large and important. The sketch which we have given of its increasingly widespread impact upon the individual illustrates the living background to the abstract formulations of our terms of reference.

CHAPTER 3: THE TWO PARTS OF THE TERMS OF REFERENCE

20. It is noteworthy that Parliament, having decided that the decisions with which we are concerned should not be remitted to the ordinary courts, should also have decided that they should not be left to be reached in the normal course of administration. Parliament has considered it essential to lay down special procedures for them.

Good administration

21. This must have been to promote good administration. Administration must not only be efficient in the sense that the objectives of policy are securely attained without delay. It must also satisfy the general body of citizens that it is proceeding with reasonable regard to the balance between the public interest which it promotes and the private interest which it disturbs. Parliament has, we infer, intended in relation to the subject-matter of our terms of reference that the further decisions or, as they may rightly be termed in this context, adjudications must be acceptable as having been properly made.

22. It is natural that Parliament should have taken this view of what constitutes good administration. In this country government rests fundamentally upon the consent of the governed. The general acceptability of these adjudications is one of the vital elements in sustaining that consent.

Openness, fairness and impartiality

23. When we regard our subject in this light, it is clear that there are certain

general and closely linked characteristics which should mark these special procedures. We call these characteristics openness, fairness and impartiality.

24. Here we need only give brief examples of their application. Take openness. If these procedures were wholly secret, the basis of confidence and acceptability would be lacking. Next take fairness. If the objector were not allowed to state his case, there would be nothing to stop oppression. Thirdly, there is impartiality. How can the citizen be satisfied unless he feels that those who decide his case come to their decision with open minds?

25. To assert that openness, fairness and impartiality are essential characteristics of our subject-matter is not to say that they must be present in the same way and to the same extent in all its parts. Difference in the nature of the issue for adjudication may give good reason for difference in the degree to which the three general characteristics should be developed and applied. Again, the method by which a Minister arrives at a decision after a hearing or inquiry cannot be the same as that by which a tribunal arrives at a decision. This difference is brought out later in the Report. For the moment it is sufficient to point out that when Parliament sets up a tribunal to decide cases, the adjudication is placed outside the department concerned. The members of the tribunal are neutral and impartial in relation to the policy of the Minister, except in so far as that policy is contained in the rules which the tribunal has been set up to apply. But the Minister, deciding in the cases under the second part of our terms of reference, is committed to a policy which he has been charged by Parliament to carry out. In this sense he is not, and cannot be, impartial.

The allocation of decisions to tribunals and Ministers

26. At this stage another question naturally arises. On what principle has it been decided that some adjudications should be made by tribunals and some by Ministers? If from a study of the history of the subject we could discover such a principle, we should have a criterion which would be a guide for any future allocation of these decisions between tribunals and Ministers.

27. The search for this principle has usually involved the application of one or both of two notions, each with its antithesis. Both notions are famous and have long histories. They are the notion of what is judicial, its antithesis being what is administrative, and the notion of what is according to the rule of law, its antithesis being what is arbitrary.

28. What is judicial has been worked out and given expression by generations of judges. Its distinction from what is administrative recalls great constitutional victories and marks the essential difference in the nature of the decisions of the judiciary and of the executive.

29. The rule of law stands for the view that decisions should be made by the application of known principles or laws. In general such decisions will be predictable, and the citizen will know where he is. On the other hand there is what is arbitrary. A decision may be made without principle, without any rules. It is therefore unpredictable, the antithesis of a decision taken in accordance with the rule of law.

30. Nothing that we say diminishes the importance of these pairs of antitheses. But it must be confessed that neither pair yields a valid principle on which one can decide whether the duty of making a certain decision should be laid upon a tribunal or upon a Minister or whether the existing allocation of

decisions between tribunals and Ministers is appropriate. But even if there is no such principle and we cannot explain the facts, we can at least start with them. An empirical approach may be the most useful.

31. Starting with the facts, we observe that the methods of adjudication by tribunals are in general not the same as those of adjudication by Ministers. All or nearly all tribunals apply rules. No ministerial decisions of the kind denoted by the second part of our terms of reference is reached in this way. Many matters remitted to tribunals and Ministers appear to have, as it were, a natural affinity with one or other method of adjudication. Sometimes the policy of the legislation can be embodied in a system of detailed regulations. Particular decisions cannot, single case by single case, alter the Minister's policy. Where this is so, it is natural to entrust the decisions to a tribunal, if not to the courts. On the other hand it is sometimes desirable to preserve flexibility of decision in the pursuance of public policy. Then a wise expediency is the proper basis of right adjudication, and the decision must be left with a Minister.

32. But in other instances there seems to be no such natural affinity. For example, there seems to be no natural affinity which makes it clearly appropriate for appeals in goods vehicle licence cases to be decided by the Transport Tribunal when appeals in a number of road passenger cases are decided by the Minister.

33. We shall therefore respect this factual difference between tribunals and Ministers and deal separately with the two parts of the subject. When considering tribunals we shall see how far the three characteristics of openness, fairness and impartiality can be developed and applied in general and how far their development and application must be adapted to the circumstances of particular tribunals. We shall then proceed to the decisions of Ministers after a hearing or inquiry and consider how far the difference in method of adjudication requires a different development and application of the three characteristics.

Policy is not our concern

34. Before concluding this Introduction we wish to emphasise that our terms of reference relate to the "constitution and working" of tribunals and to the "working" of certain administrative procedures. We have no concern with the policies which have given rise to the various tribunals or administrative procedures, and are not to be understood as approving or disapproving of these policies.

PART II: TRIBUNALS IN GENERAL

CHAPTER 4: INTRODUCTORY

The choice between tribunals and courts of law

38. We agree with the Donoughmore Committee that tribunals have certain characteristics which often give them advantages over the courts. These are cheapness, accessibility, freedom from technicality, expedition and expert knowledge of their particular subject. It is no doubt because of these advan-

tages that Parliament, once it has decided that certain decisions ought not to be made by normal executive or departmental processes, often entrusts them to tribunals rather than to the ordinary courts. But as a matter of general principle we are firmly of the opinion that a decision should be entrusted to a court rather than to a tribunal in the absence of special considerations which make a tribunal more suitable.

39. Moreover, if all decisions arising from new legislation were automatically vested in the ordinary courts the judiciary would by now have been grossly overburdened. The Permanent Secretary to the Lord Chancellor said in his written evidence (Days 6–7, pp. 191–192):—"It is plain, I think, that if all the disputes now determined by administrative tribunals had to be transferred to the ordinary courts, such a transfer would necessarily involve the creation of a large number of additional judges, particularly in the county court. ... many of the disputes in question do not warrant, at least in my judgment, the services of a highly remunerated judge. ... I believe that it is essential for the administration of justice as a whole that, because the Bench should be of the highest possible quality, any proposals for dilution should be jealously regarded. ... These are some of the reasons why I believe, with others, that the system of administrative tribunals as it has grown up in this country has positively contributed to the preservation of our ordinary judicial system." We agree with the Permanent Secretary to the Lord Chancellor that any wholesale transfer to the courts of the work of tribunals would be undesirable. We have not excluded from consideration whether the jurisdiction of any existing tribunal should be transferred to the ordinary courts, though we make no such recommendation. We therefore proceed to consider what improvements and safeguards, including appeals to the courts, should be introduced into the present structure.

Tribunals as machinery for adjudication

40. Tribunals are not ordinary courts, but neither are they appendages of government departments. Much of the official evidence, including that of the Joint Permanent Secretary to the Treasury, appeared to reflect the view that tribunals should properly be regarded as part of the machinery of administration, for which the Government must retain a close and continuing responsibility. Thus, for example, tribunals in the social service field would be regarded as adjuncts to the administration of the services themselves. We do not accept this view. We consider that tribunals should properly be regarded as machinery provided by Parliament for adjudication rather than as part of the machinery of administration. The essential point is that in all these cases Parliament has deliberately provided for a decision outside and independent of the department concerned, either at first instance (for example in the case of Rent Tribunals and the Licensing Authorities for Public Service and Goods Vehicles) or on appeal from a decision of a Minister or of an official in a special statutory position (for example a valuation officer or an insurance officer). Although the relevant statutes do not in all cases expressly enact that tribunals are to consist entirely of persons outside the government service, the use of the term "tribunal" in legislation undoubtedly bears this connotation, and the intention of Parliament to provide for the independence of tribunals is clear and unmistakable.

The application of the principles of openness, fairness and impartiality

41. We have already expressed our belief, in Part I, that Parliament in deciding that certain decisions should be reached only after a special procedure must have intended that they should manifest three basic characteristics: openness, fairness and impartiality. The choice of a tribunal rather than a Minister as the deciding authority is itself a considerable step towards the realisation of these objectives, particularly the third. But in some cases the statutory provisions and the regulations thereunder fall short of what is required to secure these objectives. Our main task in this Part and in Part III will be to assess the extent to which the three objectives are capable of attainment in the field of tribunals and to suggest appropriate measures.

42. In the field of tribunals openness appears to us to require the publicity of proceedings and knowledge of the essential reasoning underlying the decisions; fairness to require the adoption of a clear procedure which enables parties to know their rights, to present their case fully and to know the case which they have to meet; and impartiality to require the freedom of tribunals from the influence, real or apparent, of departments concerned with the subject-matter of their decisions.

Notes

1. J.A. Farmer, *Tribunals and Government* (1974) should be read as a corrective to the assumption that tribunals can and do operate solely as part of the judicial system. He points out that "some tribunals really constitute alternatives to departmental or ministerial decision-making rather than court substitutes" (*ibid.*, p. 3), that "the judicial system itself cannot necessarily be regarded as falling outside the business of the State" (*ibid.*, p. 4), and that the allocation of new jurisdiction to courts or tribunals has not always been done "as a rational exercise in decision-making" (*ibid.*, p. 4). In his concluding chapter on "The Role of Administrative Tribunals", Farmer shows that there is a fundamental distinction between "policy-oriented tribunals" (such as the Transport Tribunal, the transport licensing authorities, and the Civil Aviation Authority) and courts and "court-substitute tribunals" (such as the majority of those subject to the supervision of the Council on Tribunals), in that the former remain subject to ministerial control over important matters of policy. He suggests that there is "enormous potential ... for the growth and greater use of policy-oriented tribunals" (*ibid.*, p. 191) in the administration and application of general policies laid down by Ministers. Another important point made is that the differences between courts and court-substitute tribunals have been greatly exaggerated (*ibid.*, p. 192) in that various tribunals have established informal systems of precedents while denying that precedents are formally binding (*ibid.*, Chap. 7).

2. It must not be thought that the quality of decision-making by tribunals is always ideal. Farmer (*op. cit.*, pp. 167–169) lists 10 illustrations of "the fragile nature of the procedures by which tribunals obtain the material upon which their decisions as to the facts of cases must be based", and which might be said to constitute procedural unfairness. The former Supplementary Benefit Appeal Tribunals (now superseded by Social Security Appeal Tribunals) were subject to particular criticism. H. Hodge considered that they could not distinguish policy from law, they allowed presenting officers (from the DHSS) to introduce entirely irrelevant prejudicial matter, and they had little concept of how to weigh up evidence (*L.A.G. Bulletin*, February 1973). Furthermore, N. Lewis believed that the decision-making of these tribunals did not fulfil the basic standards required by law, for example the rules against fettering or abuse of discretion ([1973] P.L. 257). Even in more recent times Professor Genn, drawing upon

her extensive empirical research into the workings of tribunals, believes that their decision-making and procedures can be daunting for unrepresented individuals.

"In practice, however, from the perspective of tribunal applicants, the conditions that operate in many tribunals are far from perfect. Despite their conventional characterization as informal, accessible, and non-technical, frequently tribunals are not particularly quick, there is considerable variation in the degree of informality, and the issues dealt with are highly complex in terms of both the regulations to be applied and the factual situations of applicants. This study of tribunal processes and decision-making has highlighted the complexity of many areas of law with which tribunals must deal and the impact of this complexity on decision-making. Although tribunal procedures are generally more flexible and straightforward than court hearings, the nature of tribunal adjudication means that those who appear before tribunals without representation are often at a disadvantage. The short-comings of tribunals as effective checks on administrative decisions are the result of misdescription of procedures as informal and misconceptions about simple decision-making and the scope for unrepresented applicants to prepare, present and advocate convincing cases."

H. Genn, "Tribunal Review of Administrative Decision-Making", Chap. 11 at p. 285 in G. Richardson and H. Genn (eds.), *Administrative Law and Government Action* (1994).
3. The Franks Report is discussed in the following articles apart from the textbooks already cited: J.A.G. Griffith (1956) III J.S.P.T.L.(N.S.) 207–219; G.W. Keeton (1958) 11 C.L.P. 88–103; W.A. Robson [1958] P.L. 12–31; E.C.S. Wade (1957) 73 L.Q.R. 470–491.

TRIBUNALS AND INQUIRIES ACT 1992

(An Act to consolidate the Tribunals and Inquiries Act 1971 and certain other enactments relating to tribunals and inquiries.)

[Sections 1 to 4 prescribe the constitution and functions of the Council on Tribunals established by the 1958 Act. These provisions are summarised in the Council's Annual Report for 1994–95, Appendix D (below, Chap. 3 pp. 103–104.]

Composition and procedure of tribunals and inquiries

Recommendations of Council as to appointment of members of tribunals

5.—(1) Subject to section 6 but without prejudice to the generality of section 1(1)(a), the Council may make to the appropriate Minister general recommendations as to the making of appointments to membership of any tribunals mentioned in Schedule 1 or of panels constituted for the purposes of any such tribunals; and (without prejudice to any statutory provisions having effect with respect to such appointments) the appropriate Minister shall have regard to recommendations under this section.
(2) In this section "the appropriate Minister", in relation to appointments of any description, means the Minister making the appointments or, if they are not made by a Minister, the Minister in charge of the government department concerned with the tribunals in question. ...

Appointment of chairmen of certain tribunals

6.—(1) The chairman, or any person appointed to act as chairman, of any of the tribunals to which this subsection applies shall (without prejudice to any statutory provisions as to qualifications) be selected by the appropriate authority from a panel of persons appointed by the Lord Chancellor.

(2) Members of panels constituted under this section shall hold and vacate office under the terms of the instruments under which they are appointed, but may resign office by notice in writing to the Lord Chancellor; and any such member who ceases to hold office shall be eligible for re-appointment.

(3) Subsection (1) applies to any tribunal specified in paragraph 7, 38(a), 41(a), (b), (c) or (e) or 43 of Schedule 1.

(4) In relation to the tribunals specified in paragraph 41(a), (b) and (c) of Schedule 1, this section has effect subject to sections 41 (social security appeal tribunals), 43 (disability appeal tribunals) and 50 (medical appeal tribunals) of the Social Security Administration Act 1992.

(5) The person or persons constituting any tribunal specified in paragraph 31 of Schedule 1 shall be appointed by the Lord Chancellor, and where such a tribunal consists of more than one person the Lord Chancellor shall designate which of them is to be the chairman.

(6) In this section, "the appropriate authority" means the Minister who apart from this Act would be empowered to appoint or select the chairman, person to act as chairman, members or member of the tribunal in question.

(7) A panel may be constituted under this section for the purposes either of a single tribunal or of two or more tribunals, whether or not of the same description. . . .

Concurrence required for removal of members of certain tribunals

7.—(1) Subject to subsection (2), the power of a Minister, other than the Lord Chancellor, to terminate a person's membership of any tribunal specified in Schedule 1, or of a panel constituted for the purposes of any such tribunal, shall be exercisable only with the consent of—

- (a) the Lord Chancellor, the Lord President of the Court of Session and the Lord Chief Justice of Northern Ireland, if the tribunal sits in all parts of the United Kingdom;
- (b) the Lord Chancellor and the Lord President of the Court of Session, if the tribunal sits in all parts of the Great Britain;
- (c) the Lord Chancellor and the Lord Chief Justice of Northern Ireland, if the tribunal sits both in England and Wales and in Northern Ireland;
- (d) the Lord Chancellor, if the tribunal does not sit outside England and Wales;
- (e) the Lord President of the Court of Session, if the tribunal sits only in Scotland;
- (f) the Lord Chief Justice of Northern Ireland, if the tribunal sits only in Northern Ireland.

(2) This section does not apply to any tribunal specified in paragraph 3, 4, 12, 14, 17, 18, 21A, 26, 33(a), 33A, 34, 35(d) or (e), (g) or (h), 36(a), 36A, 39(b), 40, 43, 48, 56(a) or 57A of Schedule 1.

(3) For the purposes of this section in its application to any tribunal specified in paragraph 22(a) of Schedule 1, an adjudicator who has sat only in England and Wales, who has sat only in Scotland or who has sat only in Northern Ireland shall be deemed to constitute a tribunal which does not sit outside England and Wales, which sits only in Scotland or which sits only in Northern Ireland, as the case may be.

Procedural rules for tribunals

8.—(1) The power of a Minister, the Lord President of the Court of Session, the Commissioners of Inland Revenue or the Foreign Compensation Commission to make, approve, confirm or concur in procedural rules for any tribunal specified in Schedule 1 shall be exercisable only after consultation with the Council.

(2) The power of the Treasury to make—

(a) regulations under section 48(3) of the Building Societies Act 1986 (regulations with respect to appeals to the tribunal established under section 47 of that Act), or
(b) regulations under section 30 of the Banking Act 1987 (regulations with respect to appeals under Part I of that Act), or
(c) regulations under section 60 of the Friendly Societies Act 1992 (regulations with respect to appeals under section 58 of that Act),

shall be exercisable only after consultation with the Council. ...

(4) In this section "procedural rules" includes any statutory provision relating to the procedure of the tribunal in question.

Procedure in connection with statutory inquiries

9.—(1) Subject to section 14, the Lord Chancellor, after consultation with the Council, may make rules regulating the procedure to be followed in connection with statutory inquiries held by or on behalf of Ministers; and different provision may be made by any such rules in relation to different classes of such inquiries.

(2) Any rules made by the Lord Chancellor under this section shall have effect, in relation to any statutory inquiry, subject to the provisions of the enactment under which the inquiry is held, and of any rules or regulations made under that enactment.

(3) Subject to subsection (2), rules made under this section may regulate procedure in connection with matters preparatory to such statutory inquiries as are mentioned in subsection (1), and in connection with matters subsequent to such inquiries, as well as in connection with the conduct of proceedings at such inquiries. ...

Judicial control of tribunals etc.

Reasons to be given for decisions of tribunals and Ministers

10.—(1) Subject to the provisions of this section and of section 14, where—

    (a) any tribunal specified in Schedule 1 gives any decision, or
    (b) any Minister notifies any decision taken by him—
          (i) after a statutory inquiry has been held by him or on his behalf, or
          (ii) in a case in which a person concerned could (whether by object-
              ing or otherwise) have required a statutory inquiry to be so held,

it shall be the duty of the tribunal or Minister to furnish a statement, either written or oral, of the reasons for the decision if requested, on or before the giving or notification of the decision, to state the reasons.

(2) The statement referred to in subsection (1) may be refused, or the specification of the reasons restricted, on grounds of national security.

(3) A tribunal or Minister may refuse to furnish a statement under subsection (1) to a person not primarily concerned with the decision if of the opinion that to furnish it would be contrary to the interests of any person primarily concerned.

(4) Subsection (1) does not apply to any decision taken by a Minister after the holding by him or on his behalf of an inquiry or hearing which is a statutory inquiry by virtue only of an order made under section 16(2) unless the order contains a direction that this section is to apply in relation to any inquiry or hearing to which the order applies.

(5) Subsection (1) does not apply—

    (a) to decisions in respect of which any statutory provision has effect, apart from this section, as to the giving of reasons,
    (b) to decisions of a Minister in connection with the preparation, making, approval, confirmation, or concurrence in regulations, rules or byelaws, or orders or schemes of a legislative and not executive character,
  (ba) to decisions of the Pensions Compensation Board referred to in paragraph 35(h) of Schedule 1, or
    (c) to decisions of the Occupational Pensions Board referred to in paragraph 35(d) of Schedule 1.

(6) Any statement of the reasons for a decision referred to in paragraph (a) or (b) of subsection (1), whether given in pursuance of that subsection or of any other statutory provision, shall be taken to form part of the decision and accordingly to be incorporated in the record.

(7) If, after consultation with the Council, it appears to the Lord Chancellor and the Lord Advocate that it is expedient that—

    '(a) decisions of any particular tribunal or any description of such decisions, or
    (b) any description of decisions of a Minister,

should be excluded from the operation of subsection (1) on the ground that the subject-matter of such decisions, or the circumstances in which they are made, make the giving of reasons unnecessary or impracticable, the Lord Chancellor and the Lord Advocate may by order direct that subsection (1) shall not apply to such decisions.

(8) Where an order relating to any decisions has been made under subsection (7), the Lord Chancellor and the Lord Advocate may, by a subsequent order made after consultation with the Council, revoke or vary the earlier order so that subsection (1) applies to any of those decisions.

Appeals from certain tribunals

11.—(1) Subject to subsection (2), if any party to proceedings before any tribunal specified in paragraph 8, 15(a), (d) or (e), 16, 18, 24, 26, 31, 33(b), 37, 40A, 44 or 45 of Schedule 1 is dissatisfied in point of law with a decision of the tribunal.he may, according as rules of court may provide, either appeal from the tribunal to the High Court or require the tribunal to state and sign a case for the opinion of the High Court.

(2) Subsection (1) shall not apply in relation to proceedings before industrial tribunals which arise under or by virtue of any of the enactments mentioned in section 136(1) of the Employment Protection (Consolidation) Act 1978.

(3) Rules of court made with respect to all or any of the tribunals referred to in subsection (1) may provide for authorising or requiring a tribunal, in the course of proceedings before it, to state, in the form of a special case for the decision of the High Court, any question of law arising in the proceedings; and a decision of the High Court on a case stated by virtue of this subsection shall be deemed to be a judgment of the Court within the meaning of section 16 of the Supreme Court Act 1981 (jurisdiction of Court of Appeal to hear and determine appeals from judgments of the High Court).

(4) In relation to proceedings in the High Court or the Court of Appeal brought by virtue of this section, the power to make rules of court shall include power to make rules prescribing the powers of the High Court or the Court of Appeal with respect to—

(a) the giving of any decision which might have been given by the tribunal;
(b) the remitting of the matter with the opinion or direction of the court for re-hearing and determination by the tribunal;
(c) the giving of directions to the tribunal;

and different provisions may be made for different tribunals.

(5) An appeal to the Court of Appeal shall not be brought by virtue of this section except with the leave of the High Court or the Court of Appeal.

(6) Subsection (1) shall apply to a decision of the Secretary of State on an appeal under section 41 of the Consumer Credit Act 1974 from a determination of the Director General of Fair Trading as it applies to a decision of any

of the tribunals mentioned in that subsection, but with the substitution for the reference to a party to proceedings of a reference to any person who had a right to appeal to the Secretary of State (whether or not he has exercised that right); and accordingly references in subsections (1) and (4) to a tribunal shall be construed, in relation to such an appeal, as references to the Secretary of State. ...

(10) In this section "decision" includes any direction or order, and references to the giving of a decision shall be construed accordingly.

Supervisory functions of superior courts not excluded by Acts passed before August 1, 1958

12.—(1) As respects England and Wales—

(a) any provision in an Act passed before August 1, 1958 that any order or determination shall not be called into question in any court, or
(b) any provision in such an Act which by similar words excludes any of the powers of the High Court,

shall not have effect so as to prevent the removal of the proceedings into the High Court by order of certiorari or to prejudice the powers of the High Court to make orders of mandamus. ...

(3) Nothing in this section shall apply—

(a) to any order or determination of a court of law, or
(b) where an Act makes special provision for application to the High Court or the Court of Session within a time limited by the Act.

Power to apply Act to additional tribunals and to repeal or amend certain provisions

13.—(1) The Lord Chancellor and the Lord Advocate may by order amend Part I or Part II of Schedule 1 by adding to that Part any such tribunals, other than any of the ordinary courts of law, as may be provided by the order.

(2) The Lord Chancellor and the Lord Advocate may by order make provision, as respects any tribunal for the time being specified in Schedule 1, not being a tribunal mentioned in section 6, for amending that section so as to apply any of the provisions of that section to the tribunal or for providing for the appointment by the Lord Chancellor, the Lord President of the Court of Session or the Lord Chief Justice of Northern Ireland of the chairman of the tribunal and of any person to be appointed to act as chairman.

(3) The Lord Chancellor and the Lord Advocate may by order amend section 11 so as to apply that section to any tribunal for the time being specified in Schedule 1.

(4) Any order under subsection (1), (2) or (3) may make any such adaptations of the provisions of this Act as may be necessary or expedient in consequence of the order.

(5) The Lord Chancellor and the Lord Advocate may by order—

    (a) repeal or amend section 7(3) of this Act or any of paragraphs 5, 6, 9, 13, 16, 20, 22, 23, 24, 29, 30, 32, 35(a) and (d), 37, 39(c), 43, 44, 47, 49, 51, 54, 55, 56(d), 57(a), 58, 59 and 63 of Schedule 1;

    (b) repeal the reference in section 6 to paragraph 43 of Schedule 1;

    (c) repeal the reference in section 8(1) to the Foreign Compensation Commission and the reference in section 14(1) to paragraph 20 of Schedule 1;

    (d) repeal the references in section 11 to any of paragraphs 16, 24, 37, 44, 51, 59 and 63 of Schedule 1; and

    (e) repeal the references in paragraphs 21 and 53 of Schedule 1 to sections 16, 17B and 25 of the Forestry Act 1967....

Restricted application of Act in relation to certain tribunals

14.—(1) References in this Act to the working or a decision of, or procedural rules, for,—

    (a) any tribunals specified in paragraph 14(a), 20, 33, 34, 39(a) or (b), 40, 48, 56 or 60 of Schedule 1,

    (b) the Director General of Fair Trading referred to in paragraph 17 of Schedule 1, or

    (c) the Controller of Plant Variety Rights referred to in paragraph 36(a) of Schedule 1,

do not include references to their working, decisions or procedure in the exercise of executive functions.

(1A) In this Act—

    (a) references to the working of the Occupational Pensions Regulatory Authority referred to in paragraph 35(g) of Schedule 1 are references to their working so far as relating to matters dealt with by them by means of a formal hearing or on review, and

    (b) references to procedural rules for the Authority are references to regulations under—

        (i) section 96(5) of the Pensions Act 1995 (procedure to be adopted with respect to reviews), or

        (ii) paragraph 13 of Schedule 1 to that Act (procedure of the Authority), so far as the regulations relate to procedure on any formal hearing by the Authority.

(3) For the purposes of this Act, the functions of the Civil Aviation Authority referred to in paragraph 3 of Schedule 1 are to be taken to be confined to those prescribed for the purposes of section 7(2) of the Civil Aviation Act 1982.

Rules and orders

15. Any power of the Lord Chancellor and the Lord Advocate or either of them to make rules or orders under this Act shall be exercisable by statutory instrument subject to annulment in pursuance of a resolution of either House of Parliament.

Interpretation

16.—(1) In this Act, except where the context otherwise requires—

"decision", "procedural rules" and "working", in relation to a tribunal, shall be construed subject to section 14,
"Council" means the Council on Tribunals,
"Minister" includes any Board presided over by a Minister,
"Scottish Committee" means the Scottish Committee of the Council on Tribunals,
"statutory inquiry" means—
    (a) an inquiry or hearing held or to be held in pursuance of a duty imposed by any statutory provision, or
    (b) an inquiry or hearing, or an inquiry or hearing of a class, designated for the purposes of this section by an order under subsection (2), and
"statutory provision" means a provision contained in, or having effect under, any enactment.

(2) The Lord Chancellor and the Lord Advocate may by order designate for the purposes of this section any inquiry or hearing held or to be held in pursuance of a power conferred by any statutory provision specified or described in the order, or any class of such inquiries or hearings.

(3) References in this Act to members of tribunals include references to the person constituting a tribunal consisting of one person....

TRIBUNALS AND INQUIRIES ACT 1992

SCHEDULE 1

TRIBUNALS UNDER GENERAL SUPERVISION OF COUNCIL

PART I

TRIBUNALS UNDER DIRECT SUPERVISION OF COUNCIL

Matters with which tribunal concerned	*Tribunal and statutory authority*
Agriculture	1. (a) The Agricultural Land Tribunals established under section 73 of the Agriculture Act 1947 (c. 48); (b) arbitrators appointed (otherwise than by agreement) under Schedule 11 to the Agricultural Holdings Act 1986 (c. 5).

Matters with which tribunal concerned	*Tribunal and statutory authority*
Aircraft and shipbuilding industries	2. The Aircraft and Shipbuilding Industries Arbitration Tribunal established under section 42 of the Aircraft and Shipbuilding Industries Act 1977 (c. 3).
Antarctica	2A. The Tribunal established under Regulation 11 of the Antarctic Regulations 1995.
Aviation	3. The Civil Aviation Authority established under section 2 of the Civil Aviation Act 1982 (c. 16).
Banking	4. An appeal tribunal constituted under section 28 of the Banking Act 1987 (c. 22).
Betting levy	5. An appeal tribunal for England and Wales established under section 29 of the Betting, Gaming and Lotteries Act 1963 (c. 2).
Building societies	6. The tribunal constituted in accordance with section 47 of the Building Societies Act 1986 (c. 53).
Child support maintenance	7. (a) The child support appeal tribunals established under section 21 of the Child Support Act 1991 (c. 48); (b) a Child Support Commissioner appointed under section 22 of that Act and any tribunal presided over by such a Commissioner.
Children's homes, voluntary homes, nursing homes, mental nursing homes and residential care homes	8. Registered Homes Tribunals constituted under Part III of the Registered Homes Act 1984 (c. 23).
Commons	9. The Commons Commissioners and assessors appointed under section 17(2) and (3) of the Commons Registration Act 1965 (c. 64).
Conveyancing	10. A Conveyancing Appeals Tribunal constituted under section 39 of the Courts and Legal Services Act 1990 (c. 41).
Copyright	11. The Copyright Tribunal constituted under section 145 of the Copyright, Designs and Patents Act 1988 (c. 48).
Criminal injuries compensation	12. The Criminal Injuries Compensation Board constituted under Part VII of the Criminal Justice Act 1988 (c. 33).
	12. The adjudicators appointed under section 5 of the Criminal Injuries Compensation Act 1995 (c. 53).

Matters with which tribunal concerned	*Tribunal and statutory authority*
Dairy produce quotas	13. The Dairy Produce Quota Tribunal for England and Wales constituted under regulation 35(1) of the Dairy Produce Quotas Regulations 1991 (S.I. 1991 No. 2232).
Data protection	14. (a) The Data Protection Registrar appointed under section 3 of the Data Protection Act 1984 (c. 35); (b) the Data Protection Tribunal constituted under that section.
Education	15. (a) Independent Schools Tribunals constituted under section 72 of, and Schedule 6 to, the Education Act 1944 (c. 31); (b) appeal committees constituted in accordance with Part I of Schedule 2 to the Education Act 1980 (c. 20); (c) appeal committees constituted for the purposes of [paragraph 5(1) of Schedule 6 to the Education Act 1993]; (d) a tribunal constituted in accordance with Schedule 3 to the Education (Schools) Act 1992 (c. 38); (e) the Special Educational Needs Tribunal constituted under section 177 of the Education Act 1993.
Employment	16. The industrial tribunals for England and Wales established under section 128 of the Employment Protection (Consolidation) Act 1978 (c. 44).
Fair trading	17. The Director General of Fair Trading in respect of his functions under the Consumer Credit Act 1974 (c. 39) and the Estate Agents Act 1979 (c. 38), and any member of the Director's staff authorised to exercise those functions under paragraph 7 of Schedule 1 to the Fair Trading Act 1973 (c. 41).
Financial services	18. The Financial Services Tribunal established by section 96 of the Financial Services Act 1986 (c. 60).
Food	19. Tribunals constituted in accordance with regulations under Part II of the Food Safety Act 1990 (c. 16).
Foreign compensation	20. The Foreign Compensation Commission constituted under section 1 of the Foreign Compensation Act 1950 (c. 12).

Matters with which tribunal concerned	*Tribunal and statutory authority*
Forestry	21. Committees appointed for the purposes of section 16, 17B, 20, 21 or 25 of the Forestry Act 1967 (c. 10), being committees the members of which are appointed by the Minister having functions under those sections as respects England or Wales.
Friendly Societies	21A. An appeal tribunal constituted under section 59 of the Friendly Societies Act 1992.
Immigration appeals	22. (a) The adjudicators established under section 12 of the Immigration Act 1971 (c. 77); (b) the Immigration Appeal Tribunal established under that section.
Indemnification of justices and clerks	23. Any person appointed under section 53(3) of the Justices of the Peace Act 1979 (c. 55).
Industrial training levy exemption	24. Referees established by the Industrial Training (Levy Exemption References) Regulations 1974 (S.I. 1974 No. 1335).
Industry	25. An arbitration tribunal established under Schedule 3 to the Industry Act 1975 (c. 68).
Insolvency practitioners	26. The Insolvency Practitioners Tribunal referred to in section 396 of the Insolvency Act 1986 (c. 45).
Land	27. The Lands Tribunal constituted under section 1(1)(b) of the Lands Tribunal Act 1949 (c. 42).
Local taxation	28. Valuation tribunals established by regulations under Schedule 11 to the Local Government Finance Act 1988 (c. 41).
London Building Acts	29. The tribunals of appeal constituted in accordance with section 109 of the London Building Acts (Amendment) Act 1939 (c. 97).
Mental health	30. The Mental Health Review Tribunals constituted or having effect as if constituted under section 65 of the Mental Health Act 1983 (c. 20).
Mines and quarries	31. Tribunals for the purposes of section 150 of the Mines and Quarries Act 1954 (c. 70).

Matters with which tribunal concerned	*Tribunal and statutory authority*
Misuse of drugs	32. The Misuse of Drugs Tribunal in England and Wales constituted under Part I of Schedule 3 to the Misuse of Drugs Act 1971 (c. 38).
National Health Service	33. (a) Family Health Services Authorities established in pursuance of section 10 of the National Health Service Act 1977 (c. 49); (b) the tribunal constituted under section 46 of that Act; (c) service committees of Family Health Services Authorities, being committees constituted in accordance with regulations made under that Act.
National Health Service	33. (a) Health Authorities established under section 8 of the National Health Service Act 1977 (c. 49) in respect of their functions under the National Health Service (Service Committees and Tribunal) Regulations 1992 or any regulations amending or replacing those Regulations; (b) the tribunal constituted under section 46 of that Act; (c) committees of Health Authorities established under regulation 3 of those Regulations or any provision amending or replacing that regulation.
National Lottery	33A. The Director General of the National Lottery in respect of his functions under section 10 of and Schedule 3 to the National Lottery, etc., Act 1993 (c. 39), and any member of the Director General's staff authorised under paragraph 4 of Schedule 2 to that Act to exercise any of those functions.
National Savings Bank and National Savings Stock Register	33B. An adjudicator appointed under section 84 of the Friendly Societies Act 1992.
Patents, designs and trade marks	34. The comptroller-general of patents, designs, and trade marks, and any officer authorised to exercise the functions of the comptroller under section 62(3) of the Patents and Designs Act 1907 (c. 29).
Pensions	35. (a) Pensions Appeal Tribunals for England and Wales established under section 8 of the War Pensions (Administrative Provisions) Act 1919 (c. 53);

Matters with which tribunal concerned	*Tribunal and statutory authority*
	(b) Pensions Appeal Tribunals constituted under the Pensions Appeal Tribunals Act 1943 (c. 39), being tribunals appointed for England and Wales; (c) appeal tribunals constituted in accordance with a scheme in force under section 26 of the Fire Services Act 1947 (c. 41); (d) the Occupational Pensions Board constituted under section 2 of the Pension Schemes Act 1993; (e) the Pensions Ombudsman established under Part X of the Pension Schemes Act 1993 in respect of his functions under or by virtue of section 146(2) section 146(1) (c) and (d) of that Act; (f) tribunals appointed under regulations under section 1 of the Police Pensions Act 1976 (c. 35) to hear such appeals as by virtue of the regulations lie to tribunals so appointed; (g) the Occupational Pensions Regulatory Authority established by section 1 of the Pensions Act 1995; (h) the Pensions Compensation Board established by section 78 of that Act.
Plant varieties	36. (a) The Controller of Plant Variety Rights and any officer authorised to exercise the functions of the Controller under section 11(5) of the Plant Varieties and Seeds Act 1964 (c. 14); (b) the Plant Varieties and Seeds Tribunal established by section 10 of that Act.
Police	36A. An appeals tribunal constituted in accordance with Schedule 5 to the Police Act 1964 (c. 48).
Rents	37. Rent assessment committees constituted in accordance with Schedule 10 to the Rent Act 1977 (c. 42).
Reserve forces	38. (a) The Reinstatement Committees appointed under paragraph 1 of Schedule 2 to the Reserve Forces (Safeguard of Employment) Act 1985 (c. 17); (b) the umpire and any deputy umpire appointed under paragraph 5 of Schedule 2 to that Act.

Matters with which tribunal concerned	*Tribunal and statutory authority*
Revenue	39. (a) The Commissioners for the general purposes of the income tax acting under section 2 of the Taxes Management Act 1970 (c. 9) for any division in England and Wales; (b) the Commissioners for the special purposes of the Income Tax Acts appointed under section 4 of that Act; (c) the tribunal constituted for the purposes of Chapter I of Part XVII of the Income and Corporation Taxes Act 1988 (c. 1).
Road traffic	40. (a) The traffic commissioner for any area constituted for the purposes of the Public Passenger Vehicles Act 1981 (c. 14); (b) a parking adjudicator appointed under section 73(3)(a) of the Road Traffic Act 1991 (c. 40).
Sea fish (conservation)	40A. The Sea Fish Licence Tribunal established under section 4AA of the Sea Fish (Conservation) Act 1967 (c. 84).
Social security	41. (a) Social security appeal tribunals constituted under section 41 of the Social Security Administration Act 1992 (c. 5); (b) disability appeal tribunals constituted under section 43 of that Act; (c) medical appeal tribunals constituted under section 50 of that Act; (d) a Commissioner appointed under section 52 of that Act and any tribunal presided over by a Commissioner so appointed; (e) a tribunal constituted under regulations made under section 58 of that Act.
Transport	42. The Transport Tribunal constituted as provided in Schedule 4 to the Transport Act 1985 (c. 67).
Vaccine damage	43. The tribunals constituted under section 4 of the Vaccine Damage Payments Act 1979 (c. 17).
VAT and duties	44. VAT and duties tribunals for England and Wales and for Northern Ireland, constituted in accordance with Schedule [12 to the Value Added Tax Act 1994].
Wireless telegraphy	45. The tribunal established under section 9 of the Wireless Telegraphy Act 1949 (c. 54).

Note
For a criticism of the Tribunals and Inquiries Act 1958, see J.A.G. Griffith (1959) 22 M.L.R. 145.

(C) INQUIRIES

Public inquiries are held for many different purposes. The most formal ones are those constituted under the Tribunals of Inquiry (Evidence) Act 1921, to inquire into matters of "urgent public importance". However, only 21 such bodies have been created (*e.g.* to examine the Aberfan landslide disaster: H.C. 33 (1967–1968)), with the result that one commentator has criticised successive governments for their reluctance to invoke this power of investigation (see Z. Segal, "Tribunals of Inquiry: A British Invention Ignored in Britain" [1984] P.L. 207). According to R.E. Wraith and G.B. Lamb, *Public Inquiries as an Instrument of Government* (1971), other functions performed by inquiries include (1) "post-mortems" into public scandals or major disasters (*e.g.* the inquiry chaired by Desmond Fennell Q.C. into the King's Cross Underground Fire: H.C. 499 (1987–1988)); (2) considering objections to administrative decisions (*e.g.* the public local inquiry held to investigate objections to the draft M40 motorway extension which featured in *Bushell v. Secretary of State for the Environment* [1981] A.C. 75, below, p. 496); and (3), most frequently, hearing appeals against administrative decisions (particularly in the field of town and country planning applications).

For further reading see *Garner*, Chap. 11; *Wade*, Chap. 24; *Craig*, Chap. 4; JUSTICE—All Souls Review of Administrative Law, *Administrative Justice: Some Necessary Reforms*, Chap. 11; D.G.T. Williams, "Public Local Inquiries—Formal Administrative Adjudication" (1980) 29 I.C.L.Q. 701; W. Le-Las, *Playing the Public Inquiry Game* (1987).

For a detailed study of the longest public inquiry held in the United Kingdom (the Sizewell B pressurised water nuclear power station inquiry chaired by Sir Frank Layfield Q.C., which opened in January 1983, closed in March 1985, with the report being presented to the Secretary of State for Energy in December 1986) see T. O'Riordan, R. Kemp and M. Purdue, *Sizewell B: An Anatomy of the Inquiry* (1988).

A well-known recent example of an inquiry falling into Wraith and Lamb's "post-mortems" category is the inquiry conducted by Sir Richard Scott V.-C. (*Report of the Inquiry into the Export of Defence Equipment and Dual-Use Goods to Iraq and Related Prosecutions*, H.C. 115 (1995–1996). Several witnesses at the inquiry, including Lord Howe and Douglas Hurd (both former Foreign Secretaries) were critical of the procedure followed by Sir Richard. Lord Howe was especially critical of the inability of witnesses to have lawyers represent their views before the inquiry and conduct cross-examination of other persons giving evidence: "When I first complained that this was to be an inquiry at which—as never before in modern times—'defence lawyers may be seen but not heard', I had scarcely believed myself. But Sir Richard had indeed explicitly discarded almost every one of the established principles." He concluded, "The risk is that [the Scott Inquiry] may, in Dennis Healy's phrase, have done for public or judicial inquiries what the Boston Strangler did for door-step selling. And that would be—for me and for many others—a serious loss from the British constitutional armoury." Lord Howe of Aberavon, "Procedure at the Scott Inquiry" [1996] P.L. at 446–447 and 460. However, Sir Richard sought to distinguish the appropriate procedures for inquiries from those used in ordinary court proceedings. "There is, however, a significant and fundamental difference between litigation and Inquiries that makes procedural comparisons unsafe. Litigation in this country, whether civil or criminal, is adversarial in character. The nature of an Inquiry on the other hand is, with very rare exceptions, investigative or inquisitorial." He then went on to examine whether the six principles articulated in Lord Justice Salmon's report (Report of the Royal Commission on Tribunals of Inquiry, Cmnd. 3121 (1966) were truly applicable to inquiries such as his. Sir Richard concluded: "The overall problem, in my view, with the six Salmon 'cardinal principles' is that they are too heavily based on procedural requirements of fairness in an adversarial system. ... Fairness does not, in my opinion, require that adversarial procedures such as the right to cross-examine other witnesses, the right to have an examination-in-chief or a re-examination conducted orally by a party's lawyer ... should always be incorporated into the procedure at inquisitorial Inquiries. The golden rule ... is that there should be procedural flexibility, with procedures to achieve fairness tailored to suit the circumstances of each Inquiry." Sir Richard Scott, "Procedures at Inquiries—The Duty to be Fair" (1995) 111 L.Q.R. 596 at pp. 597, 610 and 616. For criticism of the procedure adopted by General Sir John Learmount in his inquiry into "The Review of Prison Service Security in England and Wales and the Escape from Parkhurst Prison on Tuesday January 3, 1995" (Cm. 3020), see Sir L. Blom-Cooper, "Witnesses before Public Inquiries: An Example of Unfairness", [1996] P.L. 11. The Autumn 1996 edition of *Public Law* is devoted to a series of articles on the Scott Inquiry. The Council on Tribunals has provided the Lord Chancellor with its advice on procedural issues arising from the establishing of ad hoc inquiries. The Council concluded that it is not possible to prescribe a uniform procedure, because of the diversity of such inquiries. However, the procedures adopted must ensure effectiveness, fairness, speed and economy: (1996) 146 N.L.J. 1714.

THE TOWN AND COUNTRY PLANNING (INQUIRIES PROCEDURE) RULES 1992

(S.I. 1992 No. 2038)

Citation and commencement

1. These Rules may be cited as the Town and Country Planning (Inquiries Procedure) Rules 1992 and shall come into force on September 30, 1992.

Interpretation

2. In these Rules, unless the context otherwise requires—

"applicant", in the case of an appeal, means the appellant;
"assessor" means a person appointed by the Secretary of State to sit with an inspector at an inquiry or re-opened inquiry to advise the inspector on such matters arising as the Secretary of State may specify;
"the Commission" means the Historic Buildings and Monuments Commission for England;
"conservation area consent" has the meaning given in section 74(1) of the Listed Buildings Act;
"development order" has the meaning given in section 59 of the Planning Act;
"document" includes a photograph, map or plan;
"inquiry" means a local inquiry in relation to which these Rules apply;
"inspector" means a person appointed by the Secretary of State to hold an inquiry or a re-opened inquiry;
"land" means the land, tree or building to which an inquiry relates;
"the Listed Buildings Act" means the Planning (Listed Buildings and Conservation Areas) Act 1990;
"listed building consent" has the meaning given in section 8(7) of the Listed Buildings Act;
"local planning authority" means—
        (i) in relation to a referred application, the body who would otherwise have dealt with the application;

(ii) in relation to an appeal, the body who were responsible for dealing with the application occasioning the appeal;

"outline statement" means a written statement of the principal submissions which a person proposes to put forward at an inquiry;

"the Planning Act" means the Town and Country Planning Act 1990;

"pre-inquiry meeting" means a meeting held before an inquiry to consider what may be done with a view to securing that the inquiry is conducted efficiently and expeditiously, and where two or more such meetings are held references to the conclusion of a pre-inquiry meeting are references to the conclusion of the final meeting;

"referred application" means an application of any description mentioned in rule 3(1) which is referred to the Secretary of State for determination;

"relevant date" means the date of the Secretary of State's written notice to the applicant and the local planning authority of his intention to cause an inquiry to be held, and "relevant notice" means that notice;

"the 1988 Rules" means the Town and Country Planning (Inquiries Procedure) Rules 1988;

"statement of case" means, and is comprised of, a written statement which contains full particulars of the case which a person proposes to put forward at an inquiry, and a list of any documents which that person intends to refer to or put in evidence;

"statutory party" means—

(a) a person mentioned in paragraph (1)(b)(i) of article 22A of the Town and Country Planning General Development Order 1988 whose representations the Secretary of State is required by paragraph (3) of that article to take into account in determining the referred application or appeal to which an inquiry relates; and, in the case of an appeal, such a person whose representations the local planning authority were required by paragraph (1) of that article to take into account in determining the application occasioning the appeal; and

(b) a person whose representations the Secretary of State is required by paragraphs (3)(b) and (5) of regulation 6 of the Planning (Listed Buildings and Conservation Areas) Regulations 1990 to take into account in determining the referred application or appeal to which an inquiry relates; and, in the case of an appeal, a person whose representations the local planning authority were required by paragraph (3)(b) of that regulation to take into account in determining the application occasioning the appeal.

"tree preservation order" has the meaning given in section 198 of the Planning Act.

Application of rules

3.—(1) These Rules apply in relation to any local inquiry caused by the Secretary of State to be held in England or Wales before he determines—

(a) an application in relation to planning permission referred to him under section 77, or an appeal to him under section 78, of the Planning Act;

(b) an application for consent referred to him under a tree preservation order or an appeal to him under such an order, with the exceptions that rule 4(1) shall not apply and the references to a statutory party shall be omitted;

(c) an application for listed building consent referred to him under section 12, or for variation or discharge of conditions referred to him under that section as applied by section 19, or an appeal to him under section 20, of the Listed Buildings Act;

(d) an application for conservation area consent referred to him under section 12 (including an application to which that section is applied by section 19), or an appeal to him under section 20, of the Listed Buildings Act as those sections are applied by virtue of section 74(3) of that Act,

but do not apply to any local inquiry by reason of the application of any provision mentioned in this paragraph by any other enactment.

(2) Where these Rules apply in relation to an appeal which at some time fell to be disposed of in accordance with the Town and Country Planning Appeals (Determination by Inspectors) (Inquiries Procedure) Rules 1992 or Rules superseded by those Rules, any step taken or thing done under those Rules which could have been done under any corresponding provision of these Rules shall have effect as if it had been taken or done under that corresponding provision.

Preliminary information to be supplied by local planning authority

4.—(1) The local planning authority shall, on receipt of a notice from the Secretary of State of his intention to cause an inquiry to be held ("the relevant notice"), forthwith inform him and the applicant in writing of the name and address of any statutory party who has made representations to them; and the Secretary of State shall as soon as practicable thereafter inform the applicant and the local planning authority in writing of the name and address of any statutory party who has made representations to him.

(2) This paragraph applies where—

(a) the Secretary of State has given to the local planning authority a direction restricting the grant of planning permission for which application was made; or

(b) in a case relating to listed building consent, the Commission has given a direction to the local planning authority pursuant to section 14(2) of the Listed Buildings Act as to how the application is to be determined; or

(c) the Secretary of State or any other Minister of the Crown or any government department, or any body falling within rule 11(1)(c), has expressed in writing to the local planning authority the view that the application should not be granted either wholly or in part, or should be granted only subject to conditions, or, in the case of an application for consent under a tree preservation order, should be granted together with a direction requiring replanting; or

(d) any authority or person consulted in pursuance of a development order has made representations to the local planning authority about the application.

(3) Where paragraph (2) applies, the local planning authority shall forthwith after the date of the relevant notice ("the relevant date") inform the person or body concerned of the inquiry and, unless they have already done so, that person or body shall thereupon give the local planning authority a written statement of the reasons for making the direction, expressing the view or making the representations, as the case may be.

Procedure where Secretary of State causes pre-inquiry meeting to be held

5.—(1) The Secretary of State may cause a pre-inquiry meeting to be held if it appears to him desirable and where he does so the following paragraphs apply.

(2) The Secretary of State shall serve with the relevant notice a notification of his intention to cause a meeting to be held and a statement of the matters about which he particularly wishes to be informed for the purposes of his consideration of the application or appeal in question; and where another Minister of the Crown or a government department has expressed in writing to the Secretary of State a view which is mentioned in rule 4(2)(c), the Secretary of State shall set this out in his statement and shall supply a copy of the statement to the Minister or government department concerned.

(3) The local planning authority shall cause to be published in a newspaper circulating in the locality in which the land is situated a notice of the Secretary of State's intention to cause a meeting to be held and of the statement served in accordance with paragraph (2).

(4) The applicant and the local planning authority shall, not later than 8 weeks after the relevant date, each serve an outline statement on the other and on the Secretary of State.

(5) Where rule 4(2) applies, the local planning authority shall—

(a) include in their outline statement the terms of—
   (i) any direction given together with a statement of the reasons therefor; and
   (ii) any view expressed or representation made on which they intend to rely in their submissions at the inquiry; and
(b) within the period mentioned in paragraph (4), supply a copy of their statement to the person or body concerned.

(6) The Secretary of State may in writing require any other person who has notified him of an intention or a wish to appear at the inquiry to serve, within 4 weeks of being so required, an outline statement on him, the applicant and the local planning authority.

(7) The meeting (or, where there is more than one, the first meeting) shall be held not later than 16 weeks after the relevant date.

(8) The Secretary of State shall give not less than 3 weeks written notice of

the meeting to the applicant, the local planning authority, any person known at the date of the notice to be entitled to appear at the inquiry and any other person whose presence at the meeting seems to him to be desirable; and he may require the local planning authority to take, in relation to notification of the meeting, one or more of the steps which he may under rule 10(6) require them to take in relation to notification of the inquiry.

(9) The inspector shall preside at the meeting and shall determine the matters to be discussed and the procedure to be followed, and he may require any person present at the meeting who, in his opinion, is behaving in a disruptive manner to leave and may refuse to permit that person to return or to attend any further meeting, or may permit him to return or attend only on such conditions as he may specify.

(10) Where a pre-inquiry meeting has been held pursuant to paragraph (1), the inspector may hold a further meeting. He shall arrange for such notice to be given of a further meeting as appears to him necessary; and paragraph (9) shall apply to such a meeting.

Service of statements of case, etc.

6.—(1) Subject to paragraph (4), the local planning authority shall, not later than—

    (a) 6 weeks after the relevant date, or
    (b) where a pre-inquiry meeting is held pursuant to rule 5, 4 weeks after the conclusion of that meeting,

serve a statement of case on the Secretary of State, the applicant and any statutory party.

(2) Where rule 4(2) applies, the local planning authority shall, unless they have already done so in an outline statement, include in their statement of case the matters mentioned in rule 5(5)(a) and shall supply a copy of the statement to the person or body concerned.

(3) Subject to paragraph (4), the applicant shall, not later than—

    (a) in the case of a referred applicant where no pre-inquiry meeting is held pursuant to rule 5, 6 weeks after the relevant date, or
    (b) in the case of an appeal where no such meeting is held, 9 weeks after the relevant date, or
    (c) in any case where a pre-inquiry meeting is held pursuant to rule 5, 4 weeks after the conclusion of that meeting,

serve a statement of case on the Secretary of State, the local planning authority and any statutory party.

(4) The statement of case mentioned in paragraph (1) or, as the case may be, paragraph (3) shall be served no later than the day which is 4 weeks before the date fixed for the holding of the inquiry, where that day falls within whichever of the periods mentioned in either of those paragraphs is applicable to the case.

(5) The applicant and the local planning authority may each require the

other to send to them a copy of any document, or of the relevant part of any document, referred to in the list of documents comprised in that party's statement of case; and any such document, or relevant part, shall be sent as soon as practicable to the party who required it.

(6) The Secretary of State may in writing require any other person who has notified him of an intention or a wish to appear at an inquiry to serve a statement of case, within 4 weeks of being so required, on the applicant, the local planning authority, the Secretary of State and any (or any other) statutory party.

(7) The Secretary of State shall supply any person from whom he requires a statement of case in accordance with paragraph (6) with a copy of the applicant's and the local planning authority's statement of case and shall inform that person of the name and address of every person on whom his statement of case is required to be served.

(8) The Secretary of State or an inspector may require any person who has served a statement of case in accordance with this rule to provide such further information about the matters contained in the statement as he may specify; and a person so required shall provide the Secretary of State, or as the case may be, the inspector, with that information in writing and shall, at the same time, send a copy to any other person on whom the statement of case has been served.

(9) Any person other than the applicant who serves a statement of case on the local planning authority shall serve with it a copy of any document, or of the relevant part of any document, referred to in the list comprised in that statement, unless a copy of the document or part of the document in question is already available for inspection pursuant to paragraph (11).

(10) Unless he has already done so, the Secretary of State shall in the case of a referred application, and may in the case of an appeal, not later than 12 weeks from the relevant date serve a written statement of the matters referred to in rule 5(2) on the applicant, the local planning authority, any statutory party and any person from whom he has required a statement of case.

(11) The local planning authority shall afford to any person who so requests a reasonable opportunity to inspect and, where practicable, take copies of any statement of case or other document which, or a copy of which, has been served on them in accordance with this rule, and of their statement of case together with a copy of any document, or of the relevant part of any document, referred to in the list comprised in that statement or otherwise served by them pursuant to this rule; and shall specify in their statement of case the time and place at which the opportunity will be afforded.

Further power of inspector to hold pre-inquiry meetings

7.—(1) Where no pre-inquiry meeting is held pursuant to rule 5, an inspector may hold one if he thinks it desirable.

(2) An inspector shall arrange for not less than 2 weeks written notice of a meeting he proposes to hold under paragraph (1) to be given to the applicant, the local planning authority, any person known at the date of the notice to be entitled to appear at the inquiry and any other person whose presence at the meeting appears to him to be desirable.

(3) Rule 5(9) shall apply to a meeting held under this rule.

Inquiry timetable

8.—(1) Where a pre-inquiry meeting is held pursuant to rule 5 an inspector shall, and in any other case may, arrange a timetable for the proceedings at, or at part of, an inquiry and may at any time vary the timetable.

(2) An inspector may specify in a timetable arranged pursuant to this rule a date by which any proof of evidence and summary required by rule 13(1) to be sent to him shall be so sent.

Notification of appointment of assessor

9. Where the Secretary of State appoints an assessor, he shall notify every person entitled to appear at the inquiry of the name of the assessor and of the matters on which he is to advise the inspector.

Date and notification of inquiry

10.—(1) The date fixed by the Secretary of State for the holding of an inquiry shall be, unless he considers such a date impracticable, not later than—

(a) 22 weeks after the relevant date; or
(b) in a case where a pre-inquiry meeting is held pursuant to rule 5, 8 weeks after the conclusion of that meeting.

(2) Where the Secretary of State considers it impracticable to fix a date in accordance with paragraph (1), the date fixed shall be the earliest date after the end of the relevant period mentioned in that paragraph which he considers to be practicable.

(3) Unless the Secretary of State agrees a lesser period of notice with the applicant and the local planning authority, he shall give not less than 4 weeks written notice of the date, time and place fixed by him for the holding of an inquiry to every person entitled to appear at the inquiry.

(4) The Secretary of State may vary the date fixed for the holding of an inquiry, whether or not the date as varied is within the relevant period mentioned in paragraph (1); and paragraph (3) shall apply to a variation of a date as it applied to the date originally fixed.

(5) The Secretary of State may vary the time or place for the holding of an inquiry and shall give such notice of any such variation as appears to him to be reasonable.

(6) The Secretary of State may require the local planning authority to take one or more of the following steps—

(a) not less than 2 weeks before the date fixed for the holding of an inquiry, to publish a notice of the inquiry in one or more newspapers circulating in the locality in which the land is situated;

(b) to serve a notice of the inquiry on such persons or classes of persons as he may specify, within such period as he may specify;

(c) to post a notice of the inquiry in a conspicuous place near to the land, within such period as he may specify.

(7) Where the land is under the control of the applicant he shall, if so required by the Secretary of State, affix a notice of the inquiry firmly to the land or to some object on or near the land, in such manner as to be readily visible to and legible by members of the public; and he shall not remove the notice, or cause or permit it to be removed, for such period before the inquiry as the Secretary of State may specify.

(8) Every notice of inquiry published, served or posted pursuant to paragraph (6), or affixed pursuant to paragraph (7), shall contain—

(a) a clear statement of the date, time and place of the inquiry and of the powers enabling the Secretary of State to determine the application or appeal in question;

(b) a written description of the land sufficient to identify approximately its location; and

(c) a brief description of the subject matter of the application or appeal.

Appearances at inquiry

11.—(1) The persons entitled to appear at an inquiry are—

(a) the applicant;

(b) the local planning authority;

(c) any of the following bodies if the land is situated in their area and they are not the local planning authority—

    (i) a country or district council;

    (ii) a National Park Committee within the meaning of paragraph 5 of Schedule 17 to the Local Government Act 1972;

    (iii) a joint planning board constituted under section 2(1) of the Planning Act or a joint planning board or special planning board reconstituted under Part I of Schedule 17 to the Local Government Act 1972;

    (iv) an urban development corporation established under section 135 of the Local Government, Planning and Land Act 1980;

    (v) an enterprise zone authority designated under Schedule 32 to the Local Government, Planning and Land Act 1980;

    (vi) the Broads Authority, within the meaning of the Norfolk and Suffolk Broads Act 1988;

    (vii) a housing action trust specified in an order made under section 67(1) of the Housing Act 1988;

(d) where the land is in an area designated as a new town, the development corporation for the new town or the Commission for the New Towns as its successor;

(e) a statutory party;

(f) the council of the parish or community in which the land is situated, if that council made representations to the local planning authority in respect of the application in pursuance of a provision of a development order;

(g) where the application was required to be notified to the Commission under section 14 of the Listed Buildings Act, the Commission;

(h) any other person who has served a statement of case in accordance with rule 6(6) or who has served an outline statement in accordance with rule 5(6).

(2) Nothing in paragraph (1) shall prevent the inspector from permitting any other person to appear at an inquiry, and such permission shall not be unreasonably withheld.

(3) Any person entitled or permitted to appear may do so on his own behalf or be represented by counsel, solicitor or any other person.

Representatives of government departments and other authorities at inquiry

12.—(1) Where—

(a) the Secretary of State or the Commission has given a direction such as is described in rule 4(2)(a) or (b); or

(b) the Secretary of State or any other Minister of the Crown or any government department, or any body falling within rule 11(1)(c), has expressed a view such as is described in rule 4(2)(c) and the local planning authority have included the terms of the expression of view in a statement served in accordance with rule 5(4) or 6(1); or

(c) another Minister of the Crown or any government department has expressed a view such as is described in rule 4(2)(c) and the Secretary of State has included its terms in a statement served in accordance with rule 5(2) or 6(10),

the applicant may, not later than 2 weeks before the date of an inquiry, apply in writing to the Secretary of State for a representative of the Secretary of State or of the other Minister, department or body concerned to be made available at the inquiry.

(2) Where an application is made in accordance with paragraph (1), the Secretary of State shall make a representative available to attend the inquiry or, as the case may be, transmit the application to the other Minister, department or body concerned, who shall make a representative available to attend the inquiry.

(3) A person attending an inquiry as a representative in pursuance of this rule shall state the reasons for the direction or expressed view and shall give evidence and be subject to cross-examination to the same extent as any other witness.

(4) Nothing in paragraph (3) shall require a representative of a Minister or a government department to anwer any question which in the opinion of the inspector is directed to the merits of government policy.

Proofs of evidence

13.—(1) A person entitled to appear at an inquiry who proposes to give, or to call another person to give, evidence at the inquiry by reading a proof of evidence shall send a copy of the proof to the inspector together with, subject to paragraph (2), a written summary.

(2) No written summary shall be required where the proof of evidence proposed to be read contains no more than 1500 words.

(3) The proof and any summary shall be sent to the inspector not later than—

(a) 3 weeks before the date fixed for the holding of the inquiry, or
(b) where a timetable has been arranged pursuant to rule 8 which specifies a date by which the proof and any summary shall be sent to the inspector, that date.

(4) Where the applicant or the local planning authority send a copy of a proof to an inspector in accordance with paragraph (1), with or without a summary, they shall at the same time send a copy of that proof and any summary to the other party, and to any statutory party; and where any other party so sends a copy of such documents he shall at the same time send a copy to the applicant, the local planning authority and any (or any other) statutory party.

(5) Where a written summary is provided in accordance with paragraph (1), only that summary shall be read at the inquiry, unless the inspector permits or requires otherwise.

(6) Any person required by this rule to send a copy of a proof to any other person shall send with it a copy of the whole, or the relevant part, of any document referred to in it, unless a copy of the document or part of the document in question is already available for inspection pursuant to rule 6(11).

(7) The local planning authority shall afford to any person who so requests a reasonable opportunity to inspect and, where practicable, take copies of any document sent to or by them in accordance with this rule.

Procedure at inquiry

14.—(1) Except as otherwise provided in these Rules, the inspector shall determine the procedure at an inquiry.

(2) Unless in any particular case the inspector with the consent of the applicant otherwise determines, the applicant shall begin and shall have the right of final reply; and the other persons entitled or permitted to appear shall be heard in such order as the inspector may determine.

(3) A person entitled to appear at an inquiry shall be entitled to call evidence and the applicant, the local planning authority and a statutory party shall be entitled to cross-examine persons giving evidence, but, subject to the foregoing and paragraphs (4) and (5), the calling of evidence and the cross-examination of persons giving evidence shall otherwise be at the inspector's discretion.

(4) The inspector may refuse to permit—

(a) the giving or production of evidence,
(b) the cross-examination of persons giving evidence, or
(c) the presentation of any other matter,

which he considers to be irrelevant or repetitious; but where he refuses to permit the giving of oral evidence, the person wishing to give the evidence may submit to him any evidence or other matter in writing before the close of the inquiry.

(5) Where a person gives evidence at an inquiry by reading a summary of his evidence in accordance with rule 13(5), the proof of evidence referred to in rule 13(1) shall, unless the person required to provide the summary notifies the inspector that he now wishes to rely on the contents of that summary only, be treated as tendered in evidence, and the person whose evidence the proof contains shall then be subject to cross-examination on it to the same extent as if it were evidence he had given orally.

(6) The inspector may direct that facilities shall be afforded to any person appearing at an inquiry to take or obtain copies of documentary evidence open to public inspection.

(7) The inspector may require any person appearing or present at an inquiry who, in his opinion, is behaving in a disruptive manner to leave and may refuse to permit that person to return, or may permit him to return only on such conditions as he may specify; but any such person may submit to him any evidence or other matter in writing before the close of the inquiry.

(8) The inspector may allow any person to alter or add to a statement of case served under rule 6 so far as may be necessary for the purposes of the inquiry; but he shall (if necessary by adjourning the inquiry) give every other person entitled to appear who is appearing at the inquiry an adequate opportunity of considering any fresh matter or document.

(9) The inspector may proceed with an inquiry in the absence of any person entitled to appear at it.

(10) The inspector may take into account any written representation or evidence or any other document received by him from any person before an inquiry opens or during the inquiry provided that he discloses it at the inquiry.

(11) The inspector may from time to time adjourn an inquiry and, if the date, time and place of the adjourned inquiry are announced at the inquiry before the adjournment, no further notice shall be required.

Site inspections

15.—(1) The inspector may make an unaccompanied inspection of the land before or during an inquiry without giving notice of his intention to the persons entitled to appear at the inquiry.

(2) The inspector may, during an inquiry or after its close, inspect the land in the company of the applicant, the local planning authority and any statutory party; and he shall make such an inspection if so requested by the applicant or the local planning authority before or during an inquiry.

(3) In all cases where the inspector intends to make an inspection of the kind referred to in paragraph (2) he shall announce during the inquiry the date and time at which he proposes to make it.

(4) The inspector shall not be bound to defer an inspection of the kind referred to in paragraph (2) where any person mentioned in that paragraph is not present at the time appointed.

Procedure after inquiry

16.—(1) After the close of an inquiry, the inspector shall make a report in writing to the Secretary of State which shall include his conclusions and his recommendations or his reasons for not making any recommendations.

(2) Where an assessor has been appointed, he may, after the close of the inquiry, make a report in writing to the inspector in respect of the matters on which he was appointed to advise.

(3) Where an assessor makes a report in accordance with paragraph (2), the inspector shall append it to his own report and shall state in his own report how far he agrees or disagrees with the assessor's report and, where he disagrees with the assessor, his reasons for that disagreement.

(4) If, after the close of an inquiry, the Secretary of State—

(a) differs from the inspector on any matter of fact mentioned in, or appearing to him to be material to, a conclusion reached by the inspector, or

(b) takes into consideration any new evidence or new matter of fact (not being a matter of government policy),

and is for that reason disposed to disagree with a recommendation made by the inspector, he shall not come to a decision which is at variance with that recommendation without first notifying the persons entitled to appear at the inquiry who appeared at it of his disagreement and the reasons for it; and affording to them an opportunity of making written representations to him within 3 weeks of the date of the notification, or (if the Secretary of State has taken into consideration any new evidence or new matter of fact, not being a matter of government policy) of asking within that period for the re-opening of the inquiry.

(5) The Secretary of State may, as he thinks fit, cause an inquiry to be re-opened, and he shall do so if asked by the applicant or the local planning authority in the circumstances and within the period mentioned in paragraph (4); and where an inquiry is re-opened (whether by the same or a different inspector)—

(a) the Secretary of State shall send to the persons entitled to appear at the inquiry who appeared at it a written statement of the matters with respect to which further evidence is invited; and

(b) paragraphs (3) to (8) of rule 10 shall apply as if the references to an inquiry were references to a re-opened inquiry.

Notification of decision

17.—(1) The Secretary of State shall notify his decision on an application or appeal, and his reasons for it, in writing to all persons entitled to appear at the inquiry who did appear, and to any other person who, having appeared at the inquiry, has asked to be notified of the decision.

(2) Where a copy of the inspector's report is not sent with the notification of

the decision, the notification shall be accompanied by a statement of his conclusions and of any recommendations made by him; and if a person entitled to be notified of the decision has not received a copy of that report, he shall be supplied with a copy of it on written application made to the Secretary of State within 4 weeks of the date of the decision.

(3) In this rule "report" includes any assessor's report appended to the inspector's report but does not include any other documents so appended; but any person who has received a copy of the report may apply to the Secretary of State in writing, within 6 weeks of the date of the Secretary of State's decision, for an opportunity of inspecting any such documents and the Secretary of State shall afford him that opportunity.

Procedure following quashing of decision

18. Where a decision of the Secretary of State on an application or appeal in respect of which an inquiry has been held is quashed in proceedings before any court, the Secretary of State—

    (a) shall send to the persons entitled to appear at the inquiry who appeared at it a written statement of the matters with respect to which further representations are invited for the purposes of his further consideration of the application or appeal; and

    (b) shall afford to those persons the opportunity of making, within 3 weeks of the date of the written statement, written representations to him in respect of those matters or of asking for the re-opening of the inquiry; and

    (c) may, as he thinks fit, cause the inquiry to be reopened (whether by the same or a different inspector) and if he does so paragraphs (3) to (8) of rule 10 shall apply as if the references to an inquiry were references to a re-opened inquiry.

Allowing further time

19. The Secretary of State may at any time in any particular case allow further time for the taking of any step which is required or enabled to be taken by virtue of these Rules, and references in these Rules to a day by which, or a period within which, any step is required or enabled to be taken shall be construed accordingly.

Service of notices by post

20. Notices or documents required or authorised to be served or sent under these Rules may be sent by post.

Notes

1. These Rules are a refinement of The Town and Country Planning (Inquiries Procedure) Rules 1988 (S.I. 1988 No. 944). The 1988 Rules had as their main objective "to make the inquiry process at all stages as efficient and effective as possible, whilst

impairing neither the fairness and impartiality of the proceedings, nor the ability of participants to make representations which are relevant to the decision" (Joint Dept of the Environment/Welsh Office Circular 10/88 (DoE), para. 6). The major changes introduced by the 1988 Rules were: (1) the enhancement of information exchanges between the parties prior to the commencement of the inquiry; (2) the specific power of the Secretary of State to appoint assessors to advise inspectors; and (3) the explicit power of inspectors to regulate conduct at inquiries.

2. Whilst the DoE believed that: "it is generally acknowledged that the 1988 Rules have largely achieved their principal objective. The benefits to be gained from the increased exchanges of information during the pre-inquiry period are now widely recognised, the disciplines imposed by the timetabling provisions have helped to improve the efficiency of the inquiry process . . . it is considered that further procedural improvements can be achieved, in the interests of efficiency and clarity, whilst maintaining the principles of natural justice" (Joint DoE/Welsh Office Circular 24/92 (DoE), para. 7). Therefore, the 1992 Rules sought to expedite inquiry proceedings by, *inter alia*, requiring proofs of evidence to be accompanied by summaries and, where appropriate, for the summaries to be read out at inquiries, rather than the whole proofs.

3. The role of the Council on Tribunals in the evolution of the 1992 Rules is considered in Chapter 3 at p. 114.

4. Despite the procedural reforms introduced by the 1988 and 1992 Rules, some experienced practitioners still feel that "the inquiry process is failing to deliver the level of efficiency and effectiveness achievable. The chief problem lies in the failure to use pre-inquiry time productively, often resulting in the inquiry being longer and more costly than necessary." They have proposed that a statement of agreed facts (*e.g.* concerning the description and planning history of the site) should be produced by the parties; that inspectors should routinely hold a pre-inquiry review to ensure that all preparatory procedures have been complied with; and that parties should be empowered to serve a "notice of cost penalty" on other parties who have failed to comply with time limits laid down in the Rules (if the breach was not rectified within seven days of service of a notice the defaulter would be deemed to have acted "unreasonably" and thereby exposed himself to a costs award). They conclude, "these improvements will not only benefit the principal parties but also the public, who should find that issues are better defined and their factual basis established at an early stage, facilitating public understanding and participation in what is the public inquiry process." G. Graves, R. Max and T. Kitson, "Inquiry Procedure—Another Dose of Reform?" [1996] J.P.L. 99 at 105–106. See also Sir Frank Layfield, "The Planning Inquiry: An Inspector's Perspective" [1996] J.P.L. 370. The Department of the Environment has issued a consolidating circular regarding planning inquiries: DoE 15/96.

5. The Secretary of State's obligation to give reasons for his decision under rule 17(1) has been considered by the House of Lords in *Save Britain's Heritage v. No. 1 Poultry Ltd* [1991] 1 W.L.R. 153. The case concerned extremely valuable land in the City of London (the Mappin & Webb site). The property developers who owned the land sought permission from the local authority to demolish the existing listed buildings on the site and replace them with a prestigious new development. Permission was refused and the developers appealed to the Secretary of State who appointed an inspector to hold an inquiry into the matter. The Inspector recommended allowing the development to take place, and the Secretary of State accepted that advice by incorporating the Inspector's major reasoning in his formal decision letter. A preservation group, which had objected to the development, applied to the court challenging the Secretary's decision on the ground that he had failed to give adequate reasons for the decision as required by rule 17(1). Lord Bridge held that: "Whatever may be the position in any other legislative context, under the planning legislation, when it comes to deciding in any particular case whether the reasons given are deficient, the question is not to be

answered *in vacuo*. The alleged deficiency will only afford a ground for quashing the decision if the court is satisfied that the interests of the applicant have been substantially prejudiced by it" (at 166–167). In this case his Lordship concluded that the Secretary's reasons were adequate and that the granting of planning permission was therefore lawful. Other cases on the Rules include: *Portsmouth Water v. Secretary of State for the Environment* (1993) 66 P. & C.R. 410 and *Coal Contractors v. Secretary of State for the Environment* (1994) 68 P. & C.R. 285. See further, below, p. 577.

6. Other important sets of inquiry rules include the Town and Country Planning Appeals (Determination by Inspectors) (Inquiries Procedure) Rules 1992, S.I. 1992 No. 2039 and the Highways (Inquiries Procedure) Rules 1994, S.I. 1994 No. 3263. Highways inquiries were particularly controversial in the 1970s, when a number were disrupted by objectors (see J. Tyme, *Motorways versus Democracy* (1978): Mr Tyme was one of the best-known objectors; F. Sharman [1977] J.P.L. 293; D.G.T. Williams (1980) 29 I.C.L.Q. 701, 708–709). Steps were taken to improve the amount of information made available to objectors (see the *Report on the Review of Highway Inquiry Procedures*, Cmnd. 7133 (1978). Note, however, P. McAuslan's view that, notwithstanding these developments, and, more generally, the changes brought about by the Franks Report, "the overriding purpose of the public local inquiry ... was and is to advance the administration's version of the public interest" (*The Ideologies of Planning Law* (1980), p. 73; road inquiries are considered at pp. 55–73).

7. Where an application for development under the Planning Acts in England and Wales is of major public interest because of its national or regional implications, or the extent or complexity of the environmental, safety, technical or scientific issues involved, the relevant department may decide to apply a non-statutory Code of Practice to the procedures leading up to the public inquiry into the application. The Code is contained in Annex 1 to the above Joint Circular 10/88. Its purpose is "to enable the Inspector to structure the inquiry in such a way as to ensure that the proceedings run smoothly, speedily and efficiently, and to help participants to concentrate on the real issues that have to be resolved" (para. 1). This is achieved by, *inter alia*, the establishment of an inquiry secretariat which will register interested participants and the holding of a pre-inquiry "programme meeting" at which the administrative arrangements for the inquiry will be determined.

8. A significant development in the 1970s and 1980s was the desire of certain pressure groups (particularly environmental groups) to question matters of national government policy before specific inquiries. The judiciary sought to limit the legal obligations on inspectors to hear such challenges (*Bushell v. Secretary of State for the Environment*, below, p. 496) and reach conclusions on them (*R. v. Secretary of State for Transport, ex p. Gwent County Council* [1988] Q.B. 429 and see A.R. Mowbray, "Public Inquiries and Government Policy" (1987) 137 N.L.J. 418). Furthermore, studies have demonstrated the weaknesses in this use of inquiries. "Where Government policy is fundamental to the issues which are the subject-matter of an inquiry, a Government witness provides a useful function in explaining and elaborating this policy. .... However, if Government policies are unclear or in a state of flux, the witness will be put in a difficult position. In the case of the Sizewell B Inquiry this tendency has been increased by the length of the inquiry. As a result, we would argue that it would be unwise to look to public inquiries as a formal mechanism for any definitive assessment of Government policy, especially in those areas which are either unclear or prone to substantial policy flux" M. Purdue *et al.*, "The Government at the Sizewell B Inquiry" [1985] P.L. 475 at 488–489.

9. The European Court of Human Rights has considered the planning appeals system in *Bryan v. The United Kingdom* (1996) 21 E.H.R.R. 342. The Court determined that proceedings before Inspectors were "fair", but the power of the Secretary of State to revoke an Inspector's jurisdiction deprived the Inspector of the appearance of independence required by Article 6(1) of the European Convention on Human Rights. However, the appellant's right of appeal on a point of law to the High Court meant

that the combined remedies of an appeal to an Inspector coupled with the possibility of a further appeal to the High Court satisfied the demands of Article 6. From a planning perspective, see S. Crow, "Lessons from Bryan" [1996] J.P.L. 359.

(D) INSPECTION

Inspection involves the direct examination of an activity or object by an officially appointed person. "Inspectors" have historically often been employed by central or local government and in turn the subject of their inspection may be private citizens (*e.g.* television licence inspectors), an institution (*e.g.* factory inspections), or a public authority (*e.g.* inspection of local police forces). Some inspectors in central government are dignified by a Crown appointment (*e.g.* Her Majesty's Chief Inspector of Prisons). Other so-called "inspectors" do not in fact inspect anything, except incidentally in the performance of their main functions. The main example of these are Department of the Environment planning inspectors who conduct inquiries on behalf of the Secretary of State (see above, Inquiries at p. 63). As with many aspects of modern public administration, in recent years the Government has sought to introduce competition into the provision of inspection services. For example, the Education (Schools) Act 1992, required the new Chief Inspector of Schools in England to encourage competition in the provision of services by registered inspectors (s.2(3)(e)).[2] Consequently, many such inspections are now carried out by registered inspectors, together with their chosen teams, drawn from persons outside the ranks of Her Majesty's Inspectors of Schools. The purposes of inspection include the enforcement of law, the enforcement of efficiency, improving performance, the provision of advice on "best practices" and the obtaining of information.

REPORT OF HER MAJESTY'S CHIEF INSPECTOR OF PRISONS 1994–95

H.C. 760 (1994–1995)

Preface

By His Honour Judge Stephen Tumim

"The Government will ensure that the Prisons Inspectorate remains strong and independent in the future."

—Extract from the Citizen's Charter

In 1995 it may be useful to consider precisely what was meant by these words. This is an Inspectorate where no Chief Inspector has been a former member of the Prison Service. He is an outsider and must rely, particularly at the start, on the professional knowledge of his team. An outsider may have some advantages. In Dr Robert Stevens' book, *The Independence of the Judiciary*, he considers the basis for the appointment of a Judge to chair a non-judicial Commission. In 1951 the Lord Chancellor had asked a Judge to do such a job. The Judge accepted noting that "as I know nothing whatever about the matter, at any rate I come to it with an open mind". The Lord Chancellor repeated this to the Minister: he knows "nothing whatsoever about the subject in dispute which is, I think, a decided advantage". Dr Stevens commented: "Such

---

[2] Note, the consolidating Schools Inspection Act 1996.

statements sound odd in the light of modern studies of the psychology of decision-making; the statements, however, clearly represented the basic view of the English judicial establishment. Ignorance, impartiality and independence were seen largely as synonymous."

The experience of the Inspectorate over the 15 years of its existence does tend to show the advantage of an outsider, although perhaps not entirely for the reasons proposed by Dr Stevens. An outsider is not tempted to put forward unfairly the interests of former colleagues and friends. He is impartial. He looks with a fresh eye so as to make what is genuinely a "lay" inspection. He needs, and he gets, the support and advice of long-term leaders and professionals in every aspect of prison life. He can be selected himself from many different groups of experienced people: he will need to be able to write and speak quickly and accurately, and to remain calm in testing circumstances. He will not, I hope, always be selected from the ranks of the judiciary, particularly at a stage of radical changes by Government of policy towards prisoners, when the stresses on a Chief Inspector are likely to be wholly different to those on a Judge, and he may feel his independence at risk.*

But of whom or what is the Inspectorate to be independent? Clearly it must be independent of the Prison Service, and free to inspect or visit wherever appropriate without obstruction from the Service. There has never been any suggestion of such obstruction, and the nearest we have got to it is failure from time to time by the Service to prepare Inspectorate reports for publication with reasonable speed. I believe this to be due to administrative failures and not to anything more sinister, and there has indeed been much improvement in speed.

Independence in relation to Ministers is a more complicated issue, where it is the first duty of the Chief Inspector to report to and advise Ministers on prison questions. It would be of no use to Ministers to receive a report prepared to soothe rather than to instruct. From time to time in history Ministers have resented such an independent approach. "Those wretched colonies", wrote Disraeli, "will all be independent, too, in a few years, and are a millstone round our necks." I do not believe that Ministers currently perceive the Inspectorate reports as a millstone, but it is not easy always to receive with grace a very critical report about an institution for which the Minister is responsible. It is sometimes difficult for the public to appreciate that the media selects the bad reports and largely ignores the reports which praise, and this also can be embarrassing to Ministers. I have no complaints to make of unfair reception of advice by Ministers, or unreasonable refusal to act upon recommendations. The need for independence has to be borne in mind as much by Ministers as by Inspectors, if the system is to work.

There is an important and not wholly resolved issue of how far Inspectors should go in commending policy solutions to Ministers, but without such freedom to comment it is difficult to see how Inspectors could properly perform their duties.

There are matters of policy where it is essential for the Chief Inspector to comment, if he is to perform any useful function. ...

The Charter statement is not limited to the word "independent". It also undertakes that the Government will ensure that the Inspectorate remains "strong". In the period since 1980, the number of prisons has gone up by

---

* (Editor's note) Judge Tumim's successor is a retired army General (Sir David Ramsbotham).

about a third. It is clearly likely to increase again, and there will be more prisoners and more staff. The Inspectorate remains almost precisely the same in
size as it was fifteen years ago. We have made no attempt to acquire a larger
budget to increase our numbers, but we have greatly increased our production. We attempt to make a full report on each prison every five years, and
a short report about halfway through that period. All these reports have to be
prepared for publication, and should be delivered to Ministers, if they are to
be useful rather than historic, in about three months from inspection. One or
two absentees, through illness or courses or whatever, makes performance of
this task very hard. In the year from April 1994 to March 1995 we made 22
full inspections with a team of Inspectors and specialists for about a week
each; and 18 short inspections, normally unexpected, for 2 or 3 days, with a
smaller team. The pace is intense. We have inevitably from time to time lost an
Inspector temporarily or permanently. There is a considerable pressure on the
teams and others if we are to preserve the high quality of our reports, and the
time will soon come for a need to increase the staff.

I report that at present we do remain strong and independent and, I hope,
constructive in our recommendations. But I must warn that we need sympath-
etic monitoring and a supportive approach if we are going to keep it up.

Notes

1. Regular summaries of the Prison Inspectorate's work can be found in the "Penal
Policies File" section of the *Howard Journal of Criminal Justice*.

2. For the role of the judiciary in reviewing the actions of the prison authorities, see
R. v. Hull Prison Board of Visitors, ex p. St Germain [1979] 1 All E.R. 701; *Leech v.
Parkhurst Prison Deputy Governor* [1988] 1 All E.R. 485; *R. v. Deputy Governor of
Parkhurst Prison, ex p. Hague* [1992] 1 A.C. 58 and *Doody v. Secretary of State for the
Home Department* [1993] 3 All E.R. 92 (below, p. 509): see Mowbray [1992] 3 *Jour-
nal of Forensic Psychiatry* 536. More generally on prisoners' rights see: S. Livingstone
and T. Owen, *Prison Law: Text and Materials* (1993) and Creighton and King, *Prisoners and the Law* (1996).

3. On inspection generally see: *Garner*, p. 41, O.W. Hartley, "Inspectorates in British Central Government" [1972] *Public Administration* 447, P. Wusteman, *Her Majesty's Inspectors of Factories 1833–1983* (1983), K. Hawkins, *Environment and
Enforcement* (1984), B. Hutter, "An Inspector Calls: The Importance of Proactive
Enforcement in the Regulatory Context" (1986) 26 *British Journal of Criminology*
114, R. Baldwin, *Rules and Government* (1995) and W. Upton and R. Harwood, "The
Stunning Powers of Environmental Inspectors" [1996] J.P.L. 623.

Question

Will the implementation of inspectors' reports be dependent upon the legal sanctions
available to them?

(E) REGULATION

Governmental control over an activity by means of regulation is a very well-established administrative procedure, Professor Ogus traces its origins back to the times of
the Tudors and Stuarts. "Almost all areas of industry and trade were at that time subject to very detailed legislative controls, although some were governed by what we
would now call 'self-regulation', since guilds were given monopoly rights of supply
with powers to regulate the methods of production."[2a] A common form of regulation is

[2a] A.I. Ogus, *Regulation: Legal Form and Economic Theory* (1994), p. 6.

by means of licensing, the best-known example being the sale by retail of intoxicating liquor, which is regulated by a complex body of law. This was considered at length in the Report of the Departmental Committee on Liquor Licensing.[3] The regulation of development under the Town and Country Planning Acts can also be regarded as a licensing process.

Other examples of licensing, illustrated by cases cited elsewhere in this book, include hackney carriage licenses (*R. v. Liverpool Corporation*, p. 448), gaming licences (*R. v. Gaming Board*, p. 472), sex shops (*R. v. Chester Borough Council*, p. 248) and airlines (*R. v. Secretary of State for Transport*, p. 476). One point of difficulty has been whether an authority in deciding to grant, renew or revoke a licence is required to observe any form of procedural fairness: see *McInnes v. Onslow-Fane*, p. 454.

REPORT OF THE DIRECTOR GENERAL OF TELECOMMUNICATIONS 1995

H.C. 295 (1995–1996)

1.1 1995 was a year when we began to put into action many of the concepts we have been working on over the last few years. The different strands of OFTEL's work came together to create a regime more appropriate for the multi-operator liberalised market of the 1990s and beyond, of which telecoms will be but a part.

1.2 An important part of this regime is to move away from the era of OFTEL "instructing" through detailed prescriptive licence conditions. This might have been acceptable for the weaker phase of competition we saw before the 1991 changes took effect. But now real competition in the market-place is starting. We need simple over-arching principles backed up where necessary by guidelines framed in the familiar language of U.K. and E.U. competition law. In other words, OFTEL will be more the industry specific competition authority.

1.3 We are not there yet and effective competition is still some way off in significant parts of the market. ...

1.4 It has been suggested that the regulatory regime is causing economic uncertainty for companies in the telecommunications market. There will be uncertainty but as the market develops it will be competition which causes it—not regulation. That's what effective markets are about. Customers with real choice will rule, and predicting—and investing to meet—their demands will be a difficult business.

1.9 I have recently heard even BT express the view that the future of telecommunications is a mosaic of interconnecting networks—a view of OFTEL has been putting forward for a considerable time. Network competition is central to our policy. This makes it essential that we get the interconnection rules right. ...

1.12 ... We put more resources into investigating alleged anti-competitive behaviour and as a result used our current regulatory powers more effectively to deal with proven cases. We are fully committed to pursuing these cases. ...

1.14 Many of our recent consultations have reinforced the view that OFTEL needs more effective powers under the Telecommunications Act to deal with anti-competitive behaviour, particularly by dominant operators. ...

[3] Cmnd. 5154.

1.17 This is the crucial angle as far as OFTEL is concerned. So how is the customer doing?

1.18 All customers continued to benefit from the RPI–7.5% constraint on BT's prices. In 1995 this brought the change from unit pricing to per second pricing. Not only did the new system make call charges and bills much easier to understand but substantial price reductions were introduced at the same time.

1.20 The broadband networks of the cable operators are in a phase of rapid growth. Their millionth telephone subscriber had been signed up by June. These networks offer real choice to both residential and business customers. They also offer lots of potential for access to advanced services.

1.21 The mobile operators too are competing fiercely for customers. During the eight years of mobile duopoly there was little marketing from the two network operators. But with four operators the marketing effort is alive and vibrant—a sign of real competition.

1.22 Perhaps the customer is beginning to feel overwhelmed by choice. Life is straightforward with only one option. ... But we believe customers will adapt to a proliferation of choice very quickly and the next generation will expect nothing less.

1.23 ... In a world of real competition the telecommunications company must respond to survive. When the barriers to competition are gone, changing your telecoms supplier tomorrow could be as easy as changing your telephone today. Remember how difficult that was 20 years ago.

1.25 ... We are therefore moving ahead to ensure that people with disabilities have an equal opportunity to share the benefits available from modern telecommunications through the mechanism of the universal service fund. These arrangements will focus on people with profound hearing loss or serious speech impairment as they have particular difficulty—and extra expense—in communicating by telephone at a basic level.

1.26 Second, we have been looking at deploying the concept of universal service to help schools link up to the advanced services of the "information superhighway". ...

1.28 In 1995 OFTEL began a review of future price controls, as the current arrangements in BT's licence run out in July 1997. This is an aspect of regulation that has a direct impact on customers, competitors and the national economy. ... Our approach is essentially deregulatory. It recognises that real competition is reaching parts of the market and may become truly effective in restraining prices within the timespan of a conventional price control period.

1.37 Recently we published the first set of comparable performance indicators from telecommunications operators. These compare "like with like" for the first time and give customers valuable information about different companies' strengths on which to base their choice. This project will continue and expand to include more indicators and more companies.

Notes

1. There has naturally been a close relationship between the Government's privatisation programme concerning the major public utilities and the creation of new national regulatory offices. The formal powers of the telecommunications, gas, electricity and water industries regulators were considerably enhanced by the Competition and Service (Utilities) Act 1992. This legislation empowered all these offices to, *inter alia*, establish performance standards for licensed undertakers, approve mandatory

complaints handling procedures and authorise regulators to resolve disputes involving undertakers. However, public concerns have grown in relation to some licensed undertakers, *e.g.* over domestic servicing by the former British Gas plc and the installation of equipment by various cable television companies.

2. Judicial scrutiny of the major national regulatory offices has been limited. Successful actions based upon natural justice (*R. v. Director General of Gas Supply, ex p. Smith* (1989)) and jurisdiction (*R. v. Director General of Electricity Supply, ex p. Redrow Homes* (1995)) have been brought, but have not been widely reported. Also, proceedings for a declaration in a private law action before the Commercial Court concerning the proper interpretation of BT's Public Telecommunication Operator's licence have been allowed by the House of Lords (*Mercury Communications Ltd v. Director General of Telecommunications and another* [1996] 1 All E.R. 575. See A. McHarg, "Regulation as a private law function?" [1995] P.L. 539.

3. Whilst the above utility regulatory systems have expanded, another strand of Government policy has been to reduce the amount of public regulation of business activities. Throughout the 1980s a major element of economic policy was to promote enterprise by reducing the burdens imposed via administrative and legislative regulation. In a White Paper entitled "Lifting the Burden"[4] the view was expressed that "too many people in central and local government spend too much of their time regulating the activities of others".[5] Subsequently a central body, the Enterprise and Deregulation Unit, was established to promote deregulation throughout Whitehall.[6] All departments were obliged to develop a rolling annual programme of reviewing existing regulation.[7] This programme was relaunched as the Deregulation Initiative under the terms of the Citizen's Charter in 1992. Lord Sainsbury chaired eight task forces which examined the existing regulatory provisions and systems operating in different sectors of the economy (*e.g.* engineering and tourism). The task forces made several hundred detailed proposals for reducing existing regulatory schemes.[8] However, to effect such changes would require a mass of primary legislation repealing or amending the earlier regulatory provisions. Therefore, the Government sought the enactment of the Deregulation and Contracting Out Act 1994. Chapter 1 of the Act empowers Ministers to introduce delegated legislation to repeal burdensome regulatory provisions. Parliamentary opposition to such wide powers being conferred on Ministers led to an elaborate legislative procedure being established for the enactment of deregulation orders. Ministers must lay a draft of the proposed order before each House, accompanied by an explanatory report giving details of the order and the consultations with affected persons which have preceded the drafting of the order. The draft order will then be examined by a new House of Commons' Deregulation Committee and by the House of Lords' Delegated Powers Scrutiny Committee. This procedure has subsequently been used on many occasions. One example is The Deregulation (Greyhound) Racing Order 1995 (S.I. 1995 No. 3231), which amends and repeals portions of the Betting, Gaming and Lotteries Act 1963. The deregulation alterations provide, *inter alia*, for operators of dog racecourses to be able to make permanent structures available to bookmakers on the track and allows the taking of bets on dog races by means of a totalisator in advance of the day of the races.

4. For further readings see: R. Baldwin and C. McCrudden (eds.), *Regulation and Public Law* (1987); A.I. Ogus, *op. cit.*; T. Prosser, "Regulation" in J. Jowell and D. Oliver (eds.), *The Changing Constitution* (3rd ed., 1994); D. Miers, "Regulation and the Public Interest: Commercial Gambling and the National Lottery" (1996) 56 M.L.R. 489.

---

[4] Cmnd. 9571 (1985).
[5] *ibid.*, para. 1.7.
[6] *Building Businesses ... Not Barriers*, Cmnd. 9794 (1986), Chap. 3.
[7] *Releasing Enterprise*, Cm. 512 (1988).
[8] *Deregulation. Task Forces Proposals for Reform* (1994).

(F) Prosecution

Under this heading may be included offences such as the following:

(1) failure to obtain a licence before commencing or continuing an activity, or acting in breach of licence conditions (*e.g.* breaches of planning control: Planning and Compensation Act 1991);

(2) failing to observe prescribed standards (*e.g.* in relation to food hygiene, trading standards or pollution levels);

(3) false claims for rights and privileges, such as social security benefits (in December 1996, the Comptroller and Auditor General reported that fraudulent income support claims cost £1.4 billion per year);

(4) obstruction of public officials when exercising statutory functions (*e.g. Stroud v. Bradbury* [1952] 2 All E.R. 76).

Notes

1. A major official study concluded that prosecutions by central and local government bodies, excluding the police (and now, of course, the Crown Prosecution Service), amounted to almost one-fifth of non-traffic criminal cases. These agencies included the following in descending order of their use of the courts: the Post Office (television licence prosecutions), the British Transport Police (rail fare "dodgers"), the Department of the Environment (vehicle excise tax cases), local authorities (numerous types of criminal behaviour) and the revenue departments (tax fraud, etc.). See K.W. Lidstone *et al., Royal Commission on Criminal Procedure: Prosecutions by Private Individuals and Non-Police Agencies*, Research Study No. 10 (HMSO, 1980).

2. Against the background of an expanding "black economy" (see the *National Federation* case below, p. 663) and growing sophistication in tax avoidance schemes, the prosecution practices of the Inland Revenue, together with the Customs and Excise, were subject to detailed scrutiny by the Committee on Enforcement Powers of the Revenue Departments (chaired by Lord Keith), Cmnd. 8822 and see the commentary by D.W. Williams [1984] P.L. 28.

3. Research indicates that administrative bodies may for a variety of reasons prefer to use other enforcement strategies, rather than prosecution. For example, the Commissioners of Customs and Excise use their statutory power to compound proceedings (*i.e.* refrain from prosecuting an alleged offender in return for a monetary penalty being paid) in thousands of petty smuggling cases per year. Such alternatives to prosecution raise important legal questions concerning the basic rights of individuals, including the procedure by which such offers are made, the legal status of these agreements and the forms of redress available to aggrieved individuals. For a detailed study see A.R. Mowbray, "The Compounding of Proceedings by the Customs and Excise: Calculating the Legal Implications" (1988) *British Tax Review* 290.

4. Sir Richard Scott examined the role of the Customs and Excise department as a prosecuting authority in his Report on defence exports to Iraq (see above, Inquiries at p. 63). He stated that:

"it is an important constitutional principle that a prosecuting authority should be independent, free from political interference and free from direction by Government. Both the Crown Prosecution Service under the Director of Public Prosecutions and the Serious Fraud Office are independent prosecuting authorities in the sense I have mentioned. Both are subject to the superintendence of the Attorney General but it is recognised that, in that capacity, the Attorney General exercises a quasi-judicial role and does not act as a Cabinet Minister. ... Many Government Departments have statutory prosecution functions [*e.g.* the Department of Trade and Industry, Department of Transport and the Post Office]. ... Departments cannot, in my opinion, when exercising their statutory prosecution functions be regarded as independent of the executive in quite the sense that the CPS and the SFO are independent. They are, no doubt, independent in the sense of being free from political interference; but their prosecuting function will usually involve the enforcement of laws in respect of which there will be some departmental policy and prosecutions can often legitimately be regarded as a means of enforcing departmental policy in the area in question. Customs, in relation to offences in connection with its revenue functions, has more in common with a departmental prosecuting authority than with the CPS or the SFO. .... Customs is entitled, in deciding what prosecutions to bring, to take some account of departmental policy relating to the collection of the revenue in question. In relation to export control offences, however, Customs has no departmental responsibility save that of enforcer of the law. In its investigation of these offences, it has a similar function to that of the police in respect of ordinary crime; in prosecuting these offences Customs' role is analogous to that of the CPS or the SFO. Customs should, in my opinion, in takings its decisions on whether to investigate or prosecute export control offences, be as independent as are the police when investigating crime and as are the CPS and the SFO when taking prosecution decisions. These decisions should not be based on what is believed by Customs to be Government policy on export controls. It is, in my opinion, fundamentally unsatisfactory for Customs to regard its function in enforcing export control law as being the enforcement of Government policy." H.C. 115 (1995–1996) paras. K4.6–4.9.

Sir Richard recommended, *inter alia*, that the Attorney General should supervise the bringing of export control prosecutions by the Commissioners of Customs and Excise. This would involve regular reporting by Customs officials to the Law Officers and the Attorney General becoming answerable to Parliament for the conduct of such prosecutions (*ibid.*, para. K4.11). More generally on Sir Richard's Report, see R. Austin (ed.), *Iraqgate: The Constitutional Implications of the Matrix-Churchill Affair* (1996).

Question

Should all agencies bringing prosecutions on behalf of the public observe the same evidential and public interest criteria in deciding whether to prosecute in particular cases? Note the Director of Public Prosecutions' Code of Practice to Crown Prosecutors, which governs their discretion to prosecute: see J.R. Spencer, *Jackson's Machinery of Justice* (1989), pp. 237–240 and S.H. Bailey and M.J. Gunn, *Smith and Bailey on the Modern English Legal System* (3rd ed., 1996), pp. 712–718.

(G) DEFAULT POWERS

A number of statutes give powers to Ministers to act in default of proper action taken by local authorities (*e.g.* the Public Health Act 1936 and the Education Act 1944 as amended by the Education Reform Act 1988). See, for example, *Wade*, pp. 756–760 and *Craig*, pp. 547–548. Whilst these powers are not formally invoked frequently, their use may be threatened against recalcitrant authorities and Ministers have had resort to them in periods of intense central-local government conflict (see, *e.g. Asher (and Others) v. Secretary of State for the Environment* [1974] 1 Ch. 208). Local authorities also have default powers to take action where individuals fail to comply with statutory notices (*e.g.* to repair unfit houses under the Housing Act 1985). Another respect in which the existence of a default power may be significant is where a person aggrieved by administrative action is refused a remedy in the courts as a result. A request to the authority with power to act in default, or to give instructions to the recalcitrant authority is regarded as the proper course of action; see *Watt v. Kesteven County Council* [1955] 1 Q.B. 408.

R. v. SECRETARY OF STATE FOR THE ENVIRONMENT, ex p. NORWICH CITY COUNCIL

[1982] 1 Q.B. 808; [1982] 1 All E.R. 737; 80 L.G.R. 498
(Court of Appeal)

The Housing Act 1980 provided local authority tenants with the right to buy their homes. Under section 10(1) the landlord council had "as soon as practicable" to serve on a tenant, with an established right to buy, a notice stating what, in the council's opinion, was to be the price for the conveyance and what provisions should be contained therein. Section 11 enabled the tenant to have the value determined by the district valuer. By section 23(1),

"where it appears to the Secretary of State that tenants of a particular landlord ... have or may have difficulty in exercising the right to buy effectively and expeditiously, he may, after giving the landlord ... notice in writing of his intention to do so ... use his powers under the ... section."

Subsection (3) empowers the Secretary of State to "do all such things as appear to him necessary or expedient" to enable the tenant to exercise the right to buy.

Within the first month Norwich Council had received 452 applications to buy, but after seven months no sales had been completed. Tenants began to complain about the time taken by the council to complete sales and meetings were held between officials of both the department and the council. These were followed by meetings between Ministers and councillors.

In December 1981, the Secretary of State made an order under section 23 of the Act and wrote to the leader of Norwich Council in the following terms:

"in my view the conduct of your council with respect to the notices required to be served on your council's secure tenants under section 10 of the Housing Act 1980 could well amount to non-compliance with the statutory requirements of Chapter 1 of Part 1 of that Act. But whether or not this is the case I would still conclude that secure tenants of your council have or may have difficulty in exercising the right to buy effectively and expeditiously ... I cannot however ignore the further delays and difficulties referred to above."

On the same day the council applied to the High Court for an order of certiorari to quash the decision of the Secretary of State. The Divisional Court dismissed the application and the council appealed to the Court of Appeal.

LORD DENNING M.R....

"Default power"

... Our present statute, the Housing Act 1980, in section 23 goes as far as anything that I have seen hitherto. It enables the Minister to take over the function himself—to do it all himself by his own civil servants—and to charge the cost to the local authority....

This "default power" enables the central government to interfere with a high hand over local authorities. Local self-government is such an important part of our constitution that, to my mind, the courts should be vigilant to see that this power of the central government is not exceeded or misused. Wherever the wording of the statute permits, the courts should read into it a provision that the "default power" should not be exercised except in accordance with the rules of natural justice. That follows from such cases as *Board of Education v. Rice* [1911] A.C. 179 and *Ridge v. Baldwin* [1964] A.C. 40. After all, the Minister is dismissing the local authority for default in carrying out their duty. He is replacing them by his own civil servants. He is making them pay all the costs and depriving them of the interest they would have received. Simple fairness requires that this should not be done unless they are told what is alleged against them and they have had an opportunity of answering it.

Apart from this, the very decision of the Minister himself is open to judicial review. If the Minister does not act in good faith, or if he acts on extraneous considerations which ought not to influence him, or if he misdirects himself in fact or in law, the court will in a proper case intervene and set his order aside. That follows from such cases as *Padfield v. Minister of Agriculture, Fisheries and Food* [1968] A.C. 997 and *Secretary of State for Employment v. ASLEF (No. 2)* [1972] 2 Q.B. 455, 493, approved by Lord Wilberforce in *Secretary of State for Education and Science v. Tameside Metropolitan Borough Council* [1977] A.C. 1014, 1047. Also if the Minister assumes to interfere with a decision of the local authority to which they came quite reasonably and sensibly, the court may intervene to stop the Minister....

The district valuer

It is quite clear that many local councils, in order to state the price under section 10(1) at which they were ready to sell, consulted the district valuer at the outset. He made the initial valuation on which that price was fixed. That saved the council time and money. Instead of their own staff making the initial valuation in the council's time—and instead of putting out the work to private valuers—the council got the district valuer to do it at no expense to the council at all. This speeded up valuations greatly in many of the other councils. ...

Pointing to section 11, the Norwich City Council said that the district valuer was like an appeal body. He should not be employed to make the initial valuation where he would sit on appeal from it to make the final valuation. That point impressed me much for some time. It seemed contrary to the accepted principle that "justice should not only be done, but should manifestly and undoubtedly be seen to be done": see *per* Lord Hewart C.J. in *R. v. Sussex Justices, ex p. McCarthy* [1924] 1 K.B. 256, 259 and *F.G.C. Metropolitan Properties Co. Ltd v. Lannon* [1969] 1 Q.B. 577, 599. But this principle—like that of natural justice—must not be carried too far. It is flexible and must be adapted as the case may require. ...

[After detailing the method of calculation of rateable values.] A similar system is applied in these valuations under the Housing Act 1980. The initial valuation under section 10(1) (on which the local council fixes the price) is made by one of the clerks in the office. If the tenant takes objection and refers the matter to the district valuer under section 11, then the decision is made by the valuation officer himself or his deputy. This system works perfectly well. That is shown by the fact that in 50 per cent of the cases the valuation is reduced: and also by the even more striking fact that no tenant has ever taken any objection to the system. The only person to take objection has been the Norwich City Council.

So justice is *in fact* done by reason of the final valuation being done by a senior officer quite distinct from the one who made the initial valuation. It is *seen* to be done by reason of the fact that no tenant has ever complained of it.

Application to this case

... the concern of this court, as always, is to protect the individual from the misuse or abuse of power by those in authority. The individual here is the tenant. He has been given by Parliament the right to buy the house in which he lives. Yet in the exercise of that right he has met with intolerable delay. The responsibility for that delay is, beyond doubt, the responsibility of the Norwich City Council. They acted—or failed to act—in complete good faith. But they were misguided. And they must answer for it. They were badly advised on many matters; such as to insist on scale 1:500 when scale 1:1250 would do. They were badly advised to refuse to employ the district valuer, when it would have speeded things up greatly. No one can excuse himself for his own mistakes by saying that he did it on bad advice: see *Federal Commerce & Navigation Co. Ltd v. Molena Alpha Inc.* [1978] Q.B. 927, 979. The council here showed too little concern for the rights of the tenants. They should have given them higher priority. They were unreasonable not to do so.

What is the remedy? What recourse have the tenants for redress? None by coming to the courts. Nothing could be done effectively by mandamus. The statute has provided a remedy. It has enabled the Secretary of State to make a "default order". It is a very great power to be used only after careful consideration. The Secretary of State here did give it careful consideration. He gave the council every opportunity to mend their ways. He gave them ample notice of what was alleged against them. He heard all that they had to say before he made his order. He gave them clear warning of the consequences. His order, strong as it was, was within his statutory powers. It cannot be upset in this court.

We were told that, pending these proceedings, the Secretary of State had allowed the Norwich City Council to carry on with the selling of the houses, and had not taken them out of their hands. This holds out hope for a solution. Surely the City Council will agree now to use the district valuer to make the initial valuations. Surely they will speed up the procedure so as to avoid any further complaints. If they do this, there may be no need for the Secretary of State to act upon his order. But that his order was good, I have no doubt. I would dismiss this appeal.

KERR and MAY L.JJ. gave separate judgments dismissing the appeal.

Note

Following the Court of Appeal's decision, Norwich Council co-operated with the Secretary of State by providing an office for his representatives, taking on more staff to process tenants' applications and using the district valuer for first valuations of properties. The Secretary of State withdrew his section 23 notice after three-and-a-half years in May 1985. Two academic commentators assessed the outcome of the Environment Secretary's actions in the following terms:

"in the aftermath of the service of notice of intervention Norwich had held on to administration and co-operated in the best interests of tenants and ratepayers. Although defeat in the courts was unfortunate and the notice had remained in operation longer than had been hoped Norwich can reasonably be regarded to have coped satisfactorily with the circumstances. For central government the outcome was more favourable. Success in the courts had strengthened their hand in relations with other authorities, closeness to detailed day-to-day administration had informed them of problems and issues and again strengthened their position through increasing knowledge."

R. Forrest and A. Murie, *An Unreasonable Act? Central-Local Government Conflict and the Housing Act 1980*, pp. 129–130 (1985). See also the case commentary by S.H. Bailey [1983] P.L. 8.

Question
Is Parliament too willing to grant coercive default powers to Ministers?

(H) CONTRACTING

This section will examine the use of contractual powers by central and local government for the purpose of securing policy goals. The liability of such bodies is considered later at p. 709.

For general reading see *Garner*, pp. 330–340 and 263–265; *Craig*, pp. 685–699; *Wade and Forsyth*, pp. 801–804; S. Arrowsmith, *Government Procurement and Judicial Review* (1988) [for a Commonwealth perspective]; C. Turpin, *Government Procurement and Contracts* (1989); I. Harden, *The Contracting State* (1992).

REGULATION BY CONTRACT: THE NEW PREROGATIVE*

Terence Daintith (1979) *Current Legal Problems* 41

The anti-inflation policy pursued by the last Labour Government from 1975 to 1979[9] had many striking features, but for lawyers, that which surely still demands discussion and analysis is the reinforcement of this "voluntary" policy, until December 1978, by a programme of sanctions upon employers operated almost entirely without statutory support. During this period, an undertaking to comply with the policy was a prerequisite for the award of almost all government contracts and of some government industrial assistance; a known breach of the policy disqualified from consideration for such contracts and assistance; compliance with the policy was secured for the future as a legally enforceable term thereof.[10] The purpose of this paper is not

---

* Note: some footnotes have been omitted.
[9] See references in the White Papers: *The Attack on Inflation*, Cmnd. 6151 (1975), paras. 22–23; *The Attack on Inflation, the Second Year*, Cmnd. 6507 (1976), para. 21; *The Attack on Inflation after July 31, 1977*, Cmnd. 6882 (1977), para. 16; *Winning the Battle against Inflation*, Cmnd. 7293 (1978), para. 25. Sanctions were withdrawn by the Government following an adverse vote in the House of Commons in December 1978: see 960 H.C. Deb., col. 920 (December 14, 1978).
[10] See, *e.g.* Department of Environment, PSA General Conditions GC/Works/1, Supplementary Condition No. 186 (Counter-inflation—Incomes Policy) (February 1978), and for an earlier, less draconian example, Supplementary Condition No. 163, Disallowance in Prices of Increases in Remuneration (November 1975).

to discuss the details of the incomes policy, but to attempt to place the tools for its enforcement in an appropriate legal context, as an example—the most egregious to date—of the use by the Government of its contractual forms and procedures as an instrument of regulation of the behaviour of the subject.[11]

Obviously, any government contract constrains, by law, the behaviour of both contracting parties, for the purpose of achieving their joint objective— the erection of an office building, say, or the provision of 10,000 pairs of wellington boots. In the traditional conception of contract, the legal obligations imposed are individualised by reference to this particular objective. With the widespread adoption, in ordinary commerce, of the standard form contract, the distinction between the consensual, individualised contract and the imposed, general regulation is already blurred. Government contracting shares fully in this movement but also, in the examples I wish to discuss, goes far beyond it; for it incorporates, into standard terms and allocation procedures, clauses and requirements reflecting public interests which by their breadth and importance pass far beyond the mutual objectives of the contracting parties and which, therefore, might normally be promoted by statutory regulation. This is why the paper's title refers to prerogative: government has discovered means of using its increasing economic strength *vis-à-vis* private industry so as to promote certain policies in a style, and with results, which for a long time we have assumed must be the hallmark of parliamentary legislation: that is to say, officially promulgated rules backed by effective general compulsion. This means the power to rule without parliamentary consent, which is the hallmark of prerogative....

Such an inquiry falls naturally into two parts, corresponding to the two types of power related to government contracts: first, the power of Government to decide who will be its contractors, and on what terms; secondly, its power to control contractors' (and indeed subcontractors') behaviour in terms of the contract itself. These powers will be referred to respectively as *Precontractual* and *Contractual*.

Precontractual powers

In discussing the precontractual phase, it is necessary to distinguish the position of the Crown—that is to say, the legal personification of central government—from that of most other public authorities. The reason is that the Crown enjoys a common law capacity to make contracts, while most other public authorities, being created by statute, only enjoy such contractual capacity as their constitutive statute allots them....

To sum up, therefore, on the precontractual phase, in which the public authority is taking its unilateral decision as to who shall be its contractor and

---

[11] A comprehensive and perceptive discussion of the legality of sanctions is provided by Ferguson and Page, "Pay Restraint: The Legal Constraints" (1978) 128 N.L.J. 515. See also, on this topic, Harden and Scott, "Sound Administration Must Rest on a Sound Legal Basis" (1978) 128 N.L.J. 4; M. Elliott, "Government Contracts and Counter-Inflation Policy," (1978) 7 Ind.L.J. 120. There is little writing on the general issue of the regulatory use of government contracts in the U.K. See in general Turpin, *Government Contracts* (1972), Chap. 9, and on the Fair Wages clause Kahn-Freund, "Legislation through Adjudication: the Legal Aspect of Fair Wages Clauses and Recognised Conditions" (1948) 11 M.L.R. 269, 429; B. Bercusson, *Fair Wages Resolutions* (1978).

on what terms, the situation of the public authority, reflecting the common law respect for freedom of contract in general, is in domestic law one of almost complete discretion. This is so whether the power to contract is based in common law or in statute. The discretion is large enough to permit the pursuit of a wide range of regulatory policies through the contractual process—a very convenient discovery in a period of minority government. Such real legal constraints as exist are external, the product of the system of EEC law, operating on some central and local government contracts through the medium of co-ordination of contractual procedures, and on some of the contractual activity of public enterprises through the rules of competition policy.

Contractual powers

. . .

Let us, then, look back over the different phases of the exercise of contractual powers by Government, to see what is the effect, in law, of using these powers, rather than statutory powers, as an instrument of public regulation. We have just noted that, with minor exceptions, the courts have applied, to the exercise of purely contractual powers, techniques of review of a type and intensity broadly similar to those which fill the pages of de Smith's *Judicial Review of Administrative Action*. At this stage, therefore, there is little to be gained, in terms of administrative freedom of manoeuvre, from the use of contractual techniques. But in the precontractual phase, in selecting contractual partners and deciding the terms it will offer them, the Government enjoys almost unfettered freedom and total immunity from judicial review by reason of the absence of general rules of domestic law to control this process. There are important constraints on this process stemming from the activity of the European Community in the fields of public procurement and of competition law, but their full potential, and the possibility of their operation in the domestic legal arena have not yet been adequately appreciated. In consequence Government enjoys far greater freedom and discretion in the elaboration of contractual schemes of regulation than it could reasonably hope to possess as the operator of a statutory scheme under powers conferred by Parliament. Moreover, even if Parliament might itself on occasion be prepared to grant Government such wide and ill-defined powers by statute, the availability to Government of the contractual option denies to Parliament the very possibility of discussing and deciding the issue. In a recent report, the parliamentary select committee on the ombudsman showed its sensitivity to the problem of contractual regulation in recommending that the ombudsman's powers be extended to enable him to look at the process of awarding government contracts.[12] Consideration of this sensible proposal must not distract Parliament from the far more fundamental question of whether it is prepared to see a reduction of its formal supremacy by allowing Government to develop and ramify a technique of regulation in which legislative authorisation plays no effective part. It would be sad, but not surprising, if Parliament, at the time of

[12] Fourth Report from the Select Committee on the Parliamentary Commissioner for Administration (1977–1978) H.C. 444.

its greatest real authority over Government in recent years, were to sit quietly by while Government fashioned for itself a new prerogative.

Notes

1. Subsequently, Professor Daintith has classified the power of government contracting as an element of "dominium" (*i.e.* the ability of Government to secure its policy objectives through the use of public wealth). He argued:

> "a case might also be made for subjecting the use by central government of a dominant economic position to the same kinds of constraints as are imposed on private firms and some public-sector bodies by competition legislation, in particular the Fair Trading Act 1973. Useful as such improvements might be, we should not expect them to hold government back on the occasions when it feels that major political or economic gains can result from sweeping or unorthodox use of its dominium powers."

"The Executive Power Today: Bargaining and Economic Control" in J. Jowell and D. Oliver, *The Changing Constitution* (2nd ed., 1989), Chap. 8 at p. 217.

An increasingly important form of control over Government's use of the power to award contracts is the European Community. Professor Daintith has observed that:

> "While in its early years the Commission, as the Community's executive arm, naturally concentrated its attention on the removal of the most obvious regulatory and fiscal barriers, such as quotas and tariffs, it has more recently been able to focus on the less visible distortions of competition flowing from the use of State *dominium*, particularly through the granting of State aids, the favourable treatment of public enterprises (as by making capital available on advantageous terms) and discriminatory public procurement. All these feature strongly in the 1992 programme for the completion of the single market, embarked on in 1985. In consequence, decisions which once would have represented a highly discretionary exercise of *dominium* now need to be cleared with the Commission, and failure to do this may result in their reversal."

"The Techniques of Government" in J. Jowell and D. Oliver, *The Changing Constitution* (3rd ed., 1994), Chap. 8 at p. 232.

2. Another major theme in central government's approach to the exercise of contractual powers by public bodies has been the desire to subject the provision of public services to competition from the private sector. Part I of the Local Government Act 1988, empowered the Secretary of State for the Environment to require local authorities to offer private contractors the opportunity to compete for contracts to provide basic services on behalf of the authorities. Initially the services subject to competitive tendering requirements were manual operations (*e.g.* refuse collection and the cleaning of public buildings); however, now professional services (*e.g.* the provision of legal work) are also subject to these requirements (see, *e.g.* the Local Government Act 1988 (Competition) (Legal and Construction Services) (Police Authorities) Regulations (S.I. 1995 No. 3302)). Central government departments and their associated agencies began to experience similar competitive pressures through the Government's introduction of a "market-testing" programme in 1991 (see *Competing for Quality*, Cm. 730 (1991)). This initiative sought to subject discrete government activities to competition from the private sector by requiring the existing public sector providers to bid against private contractors for the right to undertake these activities in the future. Contracts have been won by companies to undertake a wide range of activities from servicing R.A.F. aeroplanes to providing building management services. One of the

largest contracts, valued at over £1 billion, was awarded to an American company (Electronic Data Services) to provide computer facilities for the Inland Revenue over a 10-year period. Part II of the Deregulation and Contracting Out Act 1994, allows Ministers to make orders enabling themselves or "office-holders" (*i.e.* persons holding an office created by a public general Act: section 79) to authorise any person (*e.g.* commercial organisations) to undertake specified statutory or common law functions on behalf of the Minister/office-holder. These powers are designed to widen the range of central government activities that can be subjected to market testing. See further: M. Freedland, "Government by Contract and Public Law" [1994] P.L. 86 and "Privatising *Carltona*: Part II of the Deregulation and Contracting Out Act 1994" [1995] P.L. 21.

LOCAL GOVERNMENT ACT 1988

Local and other public authority contracts: exclusion of non-commercial considerations

17.—(1) It is the duty of every public authority to which this section applies, in exercising, in relation to its public supply or works contracts, any proposed or any subsisting such contract, as the case may be, any function regulated by this section to exercise that function without reference to matters which are non-commercial matters for the purposes of this section.

(2) The public authorities to which this section applies are those specified in Schedule 2 to this Act.

(3) The contracts which are public supply or works contracts for the purposes of this section are contracts for the supply of goods or materials, for the supply of services or for the execution of works; but this section does not apply in relation to contracts entered into before the commencement of this section.

(4) The functions regulated by this section are—

    (a) the inclusion of persons in or the exclusion of persons from—
        (i) any list of persons approved for the purposes of public supply or works contracts with the authority, or
        (ii) any list of persons from whom tenders for such contracts may be invited;
    (b) in relation to a proposed public supply or works contract with the authority—
        (i) the inclusion of persons in or the exclusion of persons from the group of persons from whom tenders are invited,
        (ii) the accepting or not accepting the submission of tenders for the contract,
        (iii) the selecting the person with whom to enter into the contract, or
        (iv) the giving or withholding approval for, or the selecting or nominating, persons to be sub-contractors for the purposes of the contract; and
    (c) in relation to a subsisting public supply or works contract with the authority—
        (i) the giving or withholding approval for, or the selecting or nominating, persons to be sub-contractors for the purposes of the contract, or
        (ii) the termination of the contract.

(5) The following matters are non-commercial matters as regards the public supply or works contracts of a public authority, any proposed or any subsisting such contract, as the case may be, that is to say—

(a) the terms and conditions of employment by contractors of their workers or the composition of, the arrangements for the promotion, transfer or training of or the other opportunities afforded to, their workforces;
(b) whether the terms on which contractors contract with their subcontractors constitute, in the case of contracts with individuals, contracts for the provision by them as self-employed persons of their services only;
(c) any involvement of the business activities or interests of contractors with irrelevant fields of Government policy;
(d) the conduct of contractors or workers in industrial disputes between them or any involvement of the business activities of contractors in industrial disputes between other persons;
(e) the country or territory of origin of supplies to, or the location in any country or territory of the business activities or interests of, contractors;
(f) any political, industrial or sectarian affiliations or interests of contractors or their directors, partners or employees;
(g) financial support or lack of financial support by contractors for any institution to or from which the authority gives or withholds support;
(h) use or non-use by contractors of technical or professional services provided by the authority under the Building Act 1984 or the Building (Scotland) Act 1959.

(6) The matters specified in subsection (5) above include matters which have occurred in the past as well as matters which subsist when the function in question falls to be exercised.

(7) Where any matter referable to a contractor would, as a matter specified in subsection (5) above, be a non-commercial matter in relation to him, the corresponding matter referable to—

(a) a supplier or customer of the contractor;
(b) a sub-contractor of the contractor or his supplier or customer;
(c) an associated body of the contractor or his supplier or customer; or
(d) a sub-contractor of an associated body of the contractor or his supplier or customer;

is also, in relation to the contractor, a non-commercial matter for the purposes of this section.

(8) In this section—

"approved list" means such a list as is mentioned in subsection (4)(a) above;
"associated body", in relation to a contractor, means any company which (within the meaning of the Companies Act 1985) is the contractor's hold-

ing company or subsidiary or is a subsidiary of the contractor's holding company;

"business" includes any trade or profession;

"business activities" and "business interests", in relation to a contractor or other person, mean respectively any activities comprised in, or any investments employed in or attributable to, the carrying on of his business and "activity" includes receiving the benefit of the performance of any contract;

"contractor", except in relation to a subsisting contract, means a "potential contractor," that is to say—

(a) in relation to functions as respects an approved list, any person who is or seeks to be included in the list; and

(b) in relation to functions as respects a proposed public supply or works contract, any person who is or seeks to be included in the group of persons from whom tenders are invited or who seeks to submit a tender for or enter into the proposed contract, as the case may be;

"exclusion" includes removal;

"Government policy" falls within "irrelevant fields" for the purposes of this section if it concerns matters of defence or foreign or Commonwealth policy and "involve", as regards business activities and any such field or policy, includes the supply of goods or materials or services to, or the execution of works for, any authority or person having functions or carrying on business in that field and, as regards business interests and any such field of policy, includes investments in any authority or person whose business activities are so involved;

"industrial dispute" has, as regards a dispute in Great Britain, the same meaning as trade dispute in the Trade Union and Labour Relations (Consolidation) Act 1992 and "involve", as regards business activities and an industrial dispute, includes the supply of goods, materials or services to or by, or the execution of works for or by, any party to the dispute, any other person affected by the dispute, or any authority concerned with the enforcement of law and order in relation to the dispute;

"political, industrial or sectarian affiliations or interests" means actual or potential membership of, or actual or potential support for, respectively, any political party, any employers' association or trade union or any society, fraternity or other association;

"suppliers or customers" and "sub-contractors" includes prospective suppliers or customers and sub-contractors; and "supplier", in relation to a contractor, includes any person who, in the course of business, supplies him with services or facilities of any description for purposes of his business.

and "employers' association" and "trade union" have, as regards bodies constituted under the law of England and Wales or Scotland, the same meaning as in the Trade Union and Labour Relations (Consolidation) Act 1992.

(9) This section is subject to section 18 below.

Notes

1. Schedule 2 to the Act subjects many public bodies to the above restrictions, including local authorities, police authorities and national parks planning boards.

2. Breach of section 17 does not amount to a criminal offence, but is actionable by any person who in consequence suffers loss or damage. Furthermore, potential or former potential contractors are given *locus standi* for the purposes of bringing judicial review proceedings (s.19(7)).

3. As to the scope of section 17, a departmental circular has expressed the view that the section prohibits relevant local authorities from banning contracts with contractors who have worked on nuclear missile sites, but enables authorities to make reasonable inquiries about contractors' health and safety records: Department of the Environment Circular 8/88.

4. Section 18 of the 1988 Act entitles local authorities to ask questions about contractors'/potential contractors' behaviour under race relations legislation, provided that the Secretary of State has approved the questions asked. The Environment Secretary has, after consultation with the Commission for Racial Equality, approved six questions under section 18; *e.g.* "in the last three years has any finding of unlawful racial discrimination been made against your organisation by any court or industrial tribunal?" All the authorised questions are listed in Annex B to Circular 8/88.

Question

Should the same legal principles apply to the processes of government contracting at the central and local authority levels?

(I) Administrative Rule-making

Following the pioneering writings of the American commentator Professor K.C. Davis (particularly in his book *Discretionary Justice: A Preliminary Inquiry* (1969)), recent years have witnessed a growing interest by British academics in the important process of administrative rule-making. Despite the lack of publicity surrounding many of these provisions it is now generally recognised that the creation of non-statutory rules by central government departments, together with other public bodies, has significant influence on the actual operation of numerous administrative programmes and, consequently, raises many fundamental legal questions about the creation, status and enforcement of such norms. Craig suggests that there are at least four explanations for the creation of administrative rules:

(1) the organisational needs of bureaucratic agencies when faced with the obligation to exercise discretionary powers;
(2) the ability to use non-technical language in such provisions (*e.g.* in the Highway Code);
(3) the flexibility of these provisions compared with formal delegated legislation;
(4) the assertion that such provisions are not legally binding (but see below).

The Citizen's Charter programme (see below, p. 167) combined with the Government's Code of Practice on Access to Government Information, which entered into effect in April 1994, has begun to encourage central government departments and agencies to publish their more important internal administrative guidance. The Inland Revenue has now published all its major internal guidance manuals (explaining its interpretations and policies towards the collection of relevant taxes) and the Benefits Agency has published over 50 of its internal codes and manuals (which perform similar functions in relation to the administration of benefits).

General readings:
Craig, pp. 271–277; *Wade,* pp. 869–873; G. Ganz, *Quasi-Legislation: Recent Developments in Secondary Legislation* (1987) and R. Baldwin, *Rules and Government* (1995).

THE PARLIAMENTARY COMMISSIONER AND ADMINISTRATIVE GUIDANCE

Alastair R. Mowbray, [1987] P.L. 570*

Study of the P.C.A.'s reports soon discloses that there is a myriad of individual pieces of administrative guidance being used by departments, not necessarily under this name.[13] Consequently it is necessary to devise a method of classifying these provisions which allows the aggregation of similar forms of guidance into distinct classes. For the purpose of the present study, a threefold functional classification, which in part was derived from United States law,[14] has been adopted. This classification distinguishes between forms of administrative guidance which relate to (a) policy, (b) procedure and (c) interpretation. The first class, *policy* guidance, specifies the formal objectives of a departmental programme, such as the designation of approved company auditors, and provides the detailed criteria by which officials are to determine the cases of individuals affected by the programme. The source of this guidance is to be found in the political value judgments espoused by Ministers.[15] Secondly, *procedural* guidance informs subordinate officials and/or persons outside the department of the form to be followed in the relevant decision-making process.[16] This guidance is derived from the organisational expertise possessed by departments, supplemented occasionally by legal norms. Finally, *interpretative* guidance seeks to explain the departmental view of what Parliament or any other legislator (in the case of delegated legislation) meant by enacting a particular provision.[17] Inevitably this class of guidance relies upon legal knowledge derived from lawyers. . . .

(a) *Policy guidance*

Provisions falling within this class of guidance are utilised by virtually all the departments subject to the scrutiny of the P.C.A. Examples extend from

---

* Note: some footnotes have been omitted.

[13] Thus the Scottish Office terms these provisions "guidelines" C126/77, H.C. 126 (1977–1978) p. 268; the Inland Revenue calls them "departmental instructions" C87/82, H.C. 8 (1982–1983), p. 92; and the Home Office refers to them as "standing orders" C264/G, H.C. 290 (1972–1973) p. 119.

[14] See Administrative Procedure Act, s.553 and more generally the discussion of American rule-making in K.C. Davis, *Discretionary Justice: A Preliminary Inquiry;* R. Baldwin and K. Hawkins, "Discretionary Justice: Davis Reconsidered" [1984] P.L. 570; M. Asimow, "Delegated Legislation: U.S. and U.K." (1983) 3 O.J.L.S. 253.

[15] See the P.C.A.'s explanation of why the rules governing the sale of surplus government land were changed in 1980, C384/81 H.C. 132 (1981–1982), p. 8.

[16] *e.g.* the procedure to be observed by war pension medical boards, C260/77, H.C. 126 (1977–1978), p. 108. Also see A.D. Jergesen, "The Enforcement of Administrative Procedures in G.B. and the U.S." (1982) 30 Am.J.Comp.L. 267 and P. Birkinshaw, "Departments of State, Citizens and the Internal Resolution of Grievances" (1985) C.J.Q. 15.

[17] *e.g.* the Public Notices issued by the Customs and Excise on the scope of the legislation administered by their department, C316/68, H.C. 129 (1968–1969), p. 20.

the Ministry of Overseas Development's rules stating eligibility for foreign income supplements to the DHSS's criteria entitling disabled persons to financial help towards the costs of running a private car. The bulk of policy guidance encountered was concerned with the departments' aims towards the public at large who came within their responsibilities. These aims encompassed all the major functions of the modern state, including regulating conduct, providing benefits (in kind or in cash), and taxing. Such guidance regulated all types of discretionary powers, with 21 instances governing statutory and prerogative powers, 10 applying to extra-statutory discretions (mainly in the field of taxation), and the remaining two sets of provisions having no direct link with any statutory scheme. . . .

(b) *Procedural guidance*

The overwhelming majority of pieces of procedural guidance discovered by the P.C.A. regulated civil servants' conduct towards members of the public, with the remainder governing the form of relations between departments and other public authorities. The largest number of cases dealing with procedural guidance affecting the public elaborated the practices to be followed for the allocation of public largesse (such as the process of determining eligibility for war pensions), although a significant minority of cases concerned procedural guidance controlling the actions of officials in the revenue departments.

(c) *Interpretative guidance*

Unsurprisingly, six of the eight cases revealing interpretative guidance contained interpretations of primary legislation, which ranged in subject-matter from the Purchase Tax Act 1963 to the Countryside Act 1968. However, this category of guidance differed from the two previous categories in that almost all the individual pieces of interpretative guidance had been published. One explanation for this distinction may have been the departments' desire to persuade affected citizens of the accuracy and legitimacy of their interpretations, which could be achieved only via a public promulgation of the interpretations. . . .

CONCLUSIONS

From the reports of the P.C.A. that were surveyed for the purposes of the present article, valuable insight may be gained into the significant role played by administrative guidance in decision-making across the whole spectrum of central government departments. The reports have disclosed, *inter alia*, policy guidance detailing when the former Ministry of Transport would refuse to appoint garages as approved vehicle testing stations; procedural guidance specifying the method by which capital grants for farmers could be obtained from the Ministry of Agriculture, Fisheries and Food; and interpretative guidance issued by the Department of the Environment elaborating the duties of councils as highway authorities. Hence there is a pressing need for a deeper consideration of the status of such provisions in contemporary public law.

Definitive answers have yet to be established regarding the circumstances in which departments should be able to create and use these provisions, the situations in which departments ought to be bound by the terms of their guidance, and the grounds upon which affected individuals can challenge the content and application of guidance. The broader constitutional issues include the extent to which departments should be under a legal duty to consult the public about the creation of individual pieces of administrative guidance (particularly policy guidance), and to publish (or at least make available to the public) the final version of their internally promulgated guidance.[18]

From the perspective of the P.C.A., the adaptable concept of maladministration has been used to examine the departmental application of all three classes of guidance. Successive Commissioners have scrutinised officials' decision-making to ensure that relevant guidance has been applied with regard to all the material facts of the case. Furthermore, the P.C.A. now demands that officials should not deviate from the requirements of their procedural guidance without good reason. Departments have also had the substance of their procedural, and in exceptional circumstances their interpretative, guidance subjected to critical evaluation by the P.C.A. In developing these responses towards administrative guidance, the P.C.A. has demonstrated a marked tendency towards consistency in assessing whether departmental utilisation of guidance violates the concept of maladministration. Yet this consistency has been obtained without the explicit reference to previous cases that one expects in a formal system of precedential decision-making.

By undertaking the above investigations, the P.C.A. has helped to protect the vital rights, interests and duties of citizens[19] from some of the adverse effects of the creation and application of administrative guidance by departments. His role has been particularly valuable in cases where the relevant guidance had not been published and consequently it would have been virtually impossible for the citizen to seek a judicial remedy. Furthermore, the P.C.A.'s responses towards administrative guidance are in many ways more advanced than the newly emerging judicial cognisance of these provisions. For example, since the earliest post-Sachsenhausen days, the P.C.A. has operated on the basis of the presumption that departments should apply their policy guidance to determine all individual cases coming within its scope, unless there are exceptional circumstances; whereas the courts have only recognised a similar legal presumption since 1984. Nevertheless, there is a great potential for the cross-fertilisation of ideas between the P.C.A. and the courts, in their respective assessments of the limits placed upon the departmental creation and utilisation of guidance by the standards of maladministration and illegality (*e.g.* the acceptability of particular pieces of procedural guidance when assessed against the criteria of "good administrative practice" and procedural fairness/impropriety). It may be concluded that the Parliamentary Commissioner deserves a central place in lawyers' understanding of the mech-

---

[18] On the issue of publication see Donald C. Rowat (ed.), *Administrative Secrecy in Developed Countries* (1979).
[19] Including, their right to legal advice in quasi-criminal proceedings (C486/81, n. 66, above); their interest in securing lawful consideration of their parole applications (C264/G, n. 20, above); their duty to pay the correct amount of tax (C316/68, n. 46, above).

anisms that currently provide a check on the administration's use of administrative guidance in its decision-making.

Notes

1. A landmark decision in the judicial scrutiny of the way in which public authorities utilise administrative rules was delivered by the House of Lords in *British Oxygen Co. Ltd v. Minister of Technology* [1971] A.C. 610 (see below, p. 263). In *R. v. Secretary of State for the Home Department, ex p. Khan* [1984] 1 W.L.R. 1337, the Court of Appeal reached an equally significant decision by upholding a claim that the Home Secretary was legally obliged to observe the requirements of his own administrative rules which he had published. Hence, English law was beginning to accord legal weight to the contents of such provisions (see A.R. Mowbray, "Administrative Guidance and Judicial Review" [1985] P.L. 558). After a wide-ranging study of the use and legal characteristics of administrative rules R. Baldwin and J. Houghton concluded:

> "the seeds of a more rational approach do exist, but a disinclination to deal with the effects of informal rules has rendered rule-makers unaccountable and exposed a useful device to exploitation. Questionable decisions have been taken to use informal rules in areas where fundamental liberties and issues of central political contention have been involved (*e.g.* picketing, policing, immigration, prisons). More than anything, such executive activity should prompt the courts to take action."

"Circular Arguments: The Status and Legitimacy of Administrative Rules" [1986] P.L. 239.

2. Professor Ganz has produced an alternative agenda to regulate the creation and use of administrative rules. She proposes the development of a Code of Practice to control the procedures followed by administrative bodies when making such rules (and see below, note 4). In addition she advocates the establishment of a permanent agency:

> "to advise on the creation of quasi-legal or voluntary rules instead of legal rules and evolve criteria for their use. At present they seem to come into existence largely on an ad hoc basis, often as an afterthought, in response to conflicting pressures to do nothing or to legislate. If the rules are to be observed, rather than be political window dressing, they must be adopted for better reasons than political expediency."

(*Quasi-Legislation: Recent Developments in Secondary Legislation*, p. 108)

3. Administrative rules may also come within the purview of particular administrative tribunals. In a study of Value Added Tax Tribunals, it was discovered that the tribunals' response to such rules depended on (a) the breadth of the jurisdiction granted to the tribunals by Parliament and (b) the legal form of the specific administrative rule at issue. Generally, VAT tribunals asserted their independence from the executive by proclaiming their unwillingness to be bound by the Customs and Excise's interpretations of legislative provisions contained in administrative rules. See A.R. Mowbray, "Customs and Excise Public Notices: The Tribunal Response" (1987) *British Tax Review* 381.

4. There are also many hybrid forms of guidance created by public authorities which have a statutory basis, but are not subordinate legislation.[20] One particular form of

[20] See S.H. Bailey and M.J. Gunn, *Smith and Bailey on The Modern English Legal System* (3rd ed., 1996), pp. 302–308.

such guidance is the statutory code of practice. There are now over 40 different statutory provisions relating to codes of practice, most of which have been enacted since 1974. Because of the increasing practical importance of these codes, Parliament expressed its concern that not all the codes were subject to parliamentary proceedings.[21] The Government responded by producing a document entitled "Guidance on Codes of Practice and Legislation",[22] directed at officials and parliamentary draftsmen contemplating the proposing of new statutory provisions empowering the issuing of codes of practice. The document states that "a code of practice is an authoritative statement of practice to be followed in some field" (para. 2:1). Codes differ from legislation because, (1) they offer guidance rather than imposing obligations; (2) their provisions are not directly enforceable in legal proceedings and (3) they often contain explanatory materials and argument. The document asserts that codes should not be used to impose specific legal obligations (para. 4:1); their contents should clearly distinguish between prescriptive and explanatory text (para. 9:3); and where their contents have indirect legal effects (either civil or criminal) they ought to be subject to parliamentary proceedings (*e.g.* affirmative or negative resolutions) (para. 10:1).

See further: Lord Campbell, "Codes of Practice as an Alternative to Legislation" [1985] Stat.L.R. 127; A. Samuels, "Codes of Practice and Legislation" [1986] Stat.L.R. 29; C. McCrudden, "Codes in a Cold Climate: Administrative Rule-Making by the Commission for Racial Equality" (1988) 51 M.L.R. 409.

5. In a theoretical and empirical study (involving the work of the Factory Inspectorate) Baldwin has divided the rules made by Government into secondary legislation and "tertiary rules" (*e.g.* administrative guidance and codes of practice). He argues that the use of such provisions should be evaluated according to five "legitimacy claims": (1) the achieving of legislative objectives, (2) accountability to representative bodies, (3) respect for due process values in the operation of governmental programmes, (4) the facilitation of expert judgments in the administration of such programmes and (5) efficiency in the provision of public services. He concludes that:

"In applying such rationales to the body of secondary and tertiary rules encountered in British government it is remarkable how weak many potential claims to legitimacy are. Secondary legislation, for example, often lacks clear authorization, it is subject to weak systems of accountability and control, and the participatory rights of affected parties are often ill protected. These problems are all the more severe in relation to tertiary rules and where secondary or tertiary rules are employed to implement European Community Directives, or in pursuance of policies emanating from the European Union, or within the contractual frameworks of government, special problems of legitimation are encountered. On the positive side, however, secondary and tertiary rules have an important role to play in defining and clarifying statutory mandates and in producing expertise and efficiency gains. The conclusion to be drawn is that, if such rules are to be used, all possible steps should be taken to improve the legitimacy claims to be made on behalf of them—notably by increasing obligations to disclose rules: by linking tertiary and secondary rules more clearly to statutory provisions, and by making the status and force of such rules more clear."
Rules and Government (1995) at pp. 300–301.

---

[21] Debate in the House of Lords, January 15, 1986: *Hansard*, Vol. 469, cols. 1075–1104.
[22] Produced in December 1987 by H.M. Government: the full text of the document is reproduced in 10 Stat.L.R. 214 (1989).

CHAPTER 3

THE COUNCIL ON TRIBUNALS

THE Franks Committee[1] recommended the creation of two standing councils, one for England/Wales and one for Scotland, to keep the constitution and working of tribunals under constant review. Although the Committee perceived the councils as primarily having an advisory role it also recommended the allocation of certain executive functions to the councils (*e.g.* the power to appoint members of tribunals).[2] Parliament, however, created a single council with limited advisory powers by the Tribunals and Inquiries Act 1958. This Act was broadened by the Tribunals and Inquiries Act 1966, and by numerous statutory instruments and was continued in existence by the (consolidating) Tribunals and Inquiries Acts 1971 and 1992.

In an early assessment of the Council's work, Professor Garner concluded that its scrutiny of draft rules governing the procedure of individual tribunals was "extremely valuable" and that the Council acted as a useful interface between senior civil servants and informed outsiders.[3] But the Council was generally unable to provide redress for specific complainants and the Council needed a clear mandate for departments to consult it about primary legislation involving tribunals. Subsequently, Professor Sir David Williams, a former member of the Council, noted that despite its restricted formal powers the Council had built up a strong relationship with departments. Consequently, they regularly consulted the Council about new legislation affecting tribunals and allowed members of the Council to participate in departmental working parties considering such matters.[4]

Further discussion of the Council's activities can be found in *Garner*, Chap. 11; *Wade and Forsyth*, Chap. 23; *Harlow and Rawlings*, Chap. 6; *Craig*, Chap. 4; H.W.R. Wade, "Administrative Tribunals and Administrative Justice" (1981) 55 *Australian Law Journal* 374.

(A) CONSTITUTION AND POWERS

ANNUAL REPORT OF THE COUNCIL ON TRIBUNALS
1994/1995

Appendix D: A note on the constitution and functions of the Council

H.C. 64 (1995–1996)

1. The Council were set up by the Tribunals and Inquiries Act 1958 and now operate under the Tribunals and Inquiries Act 1992.

---

[1] *Report of the Committee on Administrative Tribunals and Enquiries*, Cmnd. 218 (1957).
[2] *ibid.*, Chap. 11.
[3] J.F. Garner, "The Council on Tribunals" [1965] P.L. 321.
[4] D.G.T. Williams, "The Council on Tribunals: The First 25 Years" [1984] P.L. 73.

2. The Council are to consist of not more than 15 or less than 10 members appointed by the Lord Chancellor and the Lord Advocate. In addition, the Parliamentary Commissioner for Administration (the Parliamentary Ombudsman) is a member by virtue of his office. In appointing members, regard is to be had to the need for representation of the interests of persons in Wales.

3. The Scottish Committee of the Council is to consist of two or three members of the Council designated by the Lord Advocate, and three or four non-members of the Council appointed by him. The Parliamentary Ombudsman is also an ex-officio member of the Committee.

4. The Council have 15 members, of whom one is appointed primarily to represent the interests of people in Wales. The Scottish Committee has seven members of whom three are members of the Council.

5. The principal functions of the Council as laid down in the Tribunals and Inquiries Act 1992 are:

(a) to keep under review the constitution and working of the tribunals specified in Schedule 1 to the Act, and, from time to time, to report on their constitution and working;

(b) to consider and report on matters referred to the Council under the Act with respect to tribunals other than the ordinary courts of law, whether or not specified in Schedule 1 to the Act; and

(c) to consider and report on these matters, or matters the Council may consider to be of special importance, with respect to administrative procedures which involve or may involve the holding of a statutory inquiry by or on behalf of a Minister.

6. The term "statutory inquiry" means (i) an inquiry or hearing held in pursuance of a statutory duty, or (ii) a discretionary inquiry or hearing designated by an order under section 16(2) of the Act. The relevant order now in force is the Tribunals and Inquiries (Discretionary Inquiries) Order 1975 (S.I. 1975 No. 1379) as amended (S.I. 1976 No. 293, S.I. 1983 No. 1287, S.I. 1990 No. 526 and S.I. 1992 No. 2171).

7. The Council must be consulted before procedural rules are made for any tribunal specified in Schedule 1 to the 1992 Act, and on procedural rules made by the Lord Chancellor or the Lord Advocate in connection with statutory inquiries. They must also be consulted before any exemption is granted from the requirement in section 10 of the Act to give reasons for decisions. They may make general recommendations to Ministers about appointments to membership of the scheduled tribunals.

Appendix C: The committees of the Council

1. There are at present six committees of the Council, apart from the Scottish Committee.

2. Much committee business is transacted by correspondence, but meetings are held as and when required, generally on the day of the monthly Council meeting. In practice, committees (or, in cases of great urgency, their chairmen) deal with straightforward business within their sphere of interest, reporting to the Council as necessary.

3. The committees, with an indication of their respective areas of activity, are (in alphabetical order):

Education Tribunals Committee	The procedures of Education Appeal Committees (both local authority and grant-maintained).
Health and Social Security Committee	Most matters concerning social security, health and related subjects, including tribunals and inquiries dealing with social security, medical and disability issues.
Legal Committee	Matters having a strong legal content, including the drafting of primary and subordinate legislation.
Planning Procedures Committee	Town and country planning, highways, and other related subjects which may involve public inquiries or related procedures, including the drafting of primary and subordinate legislation.
Representation and Assistance Committee	Matters concerning the provision of professional or other representation or assistance in tribunal and inquiry proceedings.
Visits Committee	The Council's visits policy and the planning and organisation of visits by members of the Council to tribunals, inquiries, training seminars and conferences.

THE FUNCTIONS OF THE COUNCIL ON TRIBUNALS: SPECIAL REPORT

Cmnd. 7805 (1980)

5.1 The Functions of the Council Committee examined a number of weaknesses in our statutory powers and material resources.

5.2 These weaknesses are particularly striking when the scope of our statutory task is taken into account. The number of different types of tribunal within our jurisdiction has greatly increased since the Tribunals and Inquiries Act 1958 was passed, and now exceeds 50. Tribunals placed under our supervision since that time include the Local Valuation Courts, Immigration Adjudicators and the Immigration Appeal Tribunal, the Director General of Fair Trading (in respect of certain of his functions), Mental Health Review Tribunals, Rent Assessment Committees, Value Added Tax Tribunals, Children's Hearings (in Scotland) and Industrial Tribunals.

5.4 Under the heading of matters requiring statutory attention, our committee considered the lack of clarity as to the extent of our general jurisdiction in relation to tribunals; our lack of a specific power to investigate complaints;

and the absence of any requirement that we be consulted on proposed primary legislation affecting tribunals or inquiries, and of any power to require our views (expressed in response to statutorily prescribed consultation) to be made public.

5.6 Other matters governed by statute are the difference between the statutory expression of our powers in relation to inquiries and that in relation to tribunals; the absence of any obligation on the part of Ministers (other than the Lord Chancellor) to consult us on draft rules in connection with statutory inquiries; and the need to clarify the right of our members to attend private hearings and to remain at the deliberation stage of tribunals' proceedings ... we consider that all of them require suitable attention from Parliament, so that we can act with greater confidence and authority under a clear, logical and somewhat broadened remit.

5.7 Under the heading of resources, we refer to our constitution. ... We believe that the Council should not be larger than now, and should continue to rely on the standing and the distinctive contribution of each member; but there is an obvious connection between our resources and the strength of our secretariat. A part-time body requires a great deal of professional and technical support if it is to do its job effectively. A staff as small as ours must be occupied almost exclusively by day-to-day business, and find hardly any opportunity for undertaking the wider studies and preparation of background material which are so important in our specialist field of work. We therefore recommend a modest increase in our staff.

8.6 Lord Franks made it clear, in discussion with our Functions of the Council Committee, that after a period of more than 20 years he still attached significance to the phrase "supervision of tribunals" which appears in his report as the heading to the chapter dealing with the creation of the Council of Tribunals. He felt that we should not lose sight of this rôle, because for him it still embodied the Council's essential function. Other witnesses, with practical experience as tribunal chairmen, voiced their concern about the lack of supervision of the kind envisaged by the Franks Committee—notably the absence of detailed knowledge about how tribunals are actually working, the appropriateness of their jurisdictions, the quality of decision-making in different classes of tribunals and, in general, what in fact happens at ground level. Sporadic visiting, although valuable in other respects, cannot provide this kind of systematic knowledge. It can come only from studies in depth.

8.10 We envisage that some of the research to which we have just referred would be carried out directly by our own staff. Particularly sensitive subjects would certainly have to be dealt with in this way. On other matters we would commission studies from outside researchers, or advise on research mounted on their own initiative by academic investigators. We see particular scope for directly commissioning research by academic consultants. The Administrative Conference of the United States succeeds in engaging consultants at a very modest cost to prepare reports on specific subjects in collaboration with committees of the Conference.

9.9 Looking ahead, therefore, we see an increasingly important constitutional rôle for the Council on Tribunals. In the changing constitutional climate our organisation has potentialities as yet unrealised—a point of view we share with all those with whom we had discussions. At present, movement generally is towards greater openness in public administration; there is growing demand for opening up procedures which have hitherto been closed, for explanations of how official decisions have been reached and for adjudication external to the agency in cases of unresolved disputes. Emphasis is on the legal aspects of citizens' rights and on effective procedures for their protection. In fact, the reconciliation of the requirements of efficient government with the rule of law has assumed greater significance within recent years. Indeed, some authorities are thinking in terms of a new constitutional settlement starting from a reaffirmation of the fundamental importance of the rule of law.

SPECIFIC RECOMMENDATIONS

10.1 We divide our proposals into those which would require legislation and those which could be given effect by administrative action, either with or without accompanying legislation.

Proposals requiring legislation

(i) The Council should be given a clear general power (in addition to the supervision of the tribunals named in Schedule 1 to the Act of 1971) to act as an advisory body over the whole area of administrative adjudication and the general pattern and organisation of tribunal structure.

(ii) The Council should be given a clear right to be consulted, and empowered to offer views, in relation to matters arising on draft primary legislation affecting our area of jurisdiction.

(iii) The entitlement of the Council to be consulted about procedural rules should be restated in clearer and more general terms.

(iv) When primary or secondary legislation on which the Council have been consulted is brought before Parliament, the Minister concerned should be obliged to disclose the substance of the Council's final advice.

(v) The differences between the wording of the Council's jurisdiction in connection with tribunals and that in connection with inquiries should be removed. In relation to both tribunals and inquiries, the Council should have a wide power to offer advice on general or particular matters, whether or not on request and without a matter having to be regarded as one of "special importance".

(vi) The Council should have a statutory power to investigate and issue findings upon certain complaints raising matters of principle in relation to the proceedings of tribunals and inquiries. In this connection the Council should be empowered to call for relevant papers from tribunals and government departments.

(vii) Members of the Council should be specifically empowered to visit private hearings of tribunals under the Council's supervision and to attend the deliberation stage of the proceedings of those tribunals.

(viii) At an appropriate time, further consideration should be given to the supervision of administrative tribunals and public inquiries in Northern Ireland.

Proposals not requiring legislation

(ix) A code for consultation with the Council should be agreed by the Lord Chancellor and government departments.

(x) The financial and staff resources of the Council should be strengthened.

10.2 We appreciate that the developments advocated in this report will need to be spread over a period of time. We are also mindful of economic restraints. The intention, therefore, is to indicate the way forward by setting out a programme which can be initiated in the near future and thereafter progressively implemented.

Notes

1. Lord Tweedsmuir delivered the Government's formal response to the Special Report on April 27, 1981. The Government considered that the case for substantially widening the Council's powers had not been made out. It was also concerned about the public expenditure implications of the Council's recommendations. However, the Government accepted that it would be desirable for the Council's right to be consulted about procedural rules to be restated in clearer terms. Furthermore, it was often appropriate for departments to consult the Council about draft primary legislation affecting matters within the latter's jurisdiction. In reply the Council regretted that its major recommendations had not been accepted (Annual Report [hereafter A.R.] 1980–1981, H.C. 89 (1981–1982), p. 7).

2. The above extracts demonstrate that the procedure of departments consulting the Council is central to the latter's working. Therefore in 1981 the Council formulated a Code of Practice on Consultation with the Council, which was accepted by the Lord Chancellor (and the Lord Advocate for Scotland). It then sent it to Ministers in relevant departments asking them to bring it to the attention of their officials working on appropriate draft legislation. The Code states that departments should always allow the Council as much time as possible to prepare and submit their comments on proposed legislation. The minimum periods for consideration by the Council should be four weeks for routine proposals which do not raise major questions of principle, and six weeks where major issues of principle are involved. The Code also emphasises that where the Council has expressed views on an important question of principle and a Minister intends to make public the fact of consultation he ought to state the general tenor of the Council's advice. In 1983 the Government refused to provide a statutory endorsement of the latter requirement. (A.R. 1983–1984), H.C. 42 (1984–1985), para. 2.6.) Next year the Council reported that there had been a general improvement in the way in which departments consulted the Council. However, it was still not always given adequate time for consultation (*e.g.* by the DHSS (as it was then called) who sent them draft Regulations on July 26 and then laid them before Parliament on August 2—A.R. 1984–1985, H.C. 54 (1985–1986), para. 2.3). In an attempt to encourage wider adherence to the code, the Council reissued it to departments during 1986. The full text of the Code can be found in Appendix C to the 1986–1987 Annual Report, H.C. 234 (1987–1988).

3. Professor Sir David Williams has predicted that the Council will continue in its present form for some time to come ([1984] P.L. 87). The *JUSTICE/All Souls Review* (1988) recommended that the Council should continue in existence with a widened jurisdiction covering all tribunals and with greater financial resources (Chap. 9). Furthermore, the Review proposed the creation of a permanent and independent Administrative Review Commission to exercise general oversight across the whole administrative system. Close collaboration, possibly including overlapping membership, between the Council and the Commission was advocated (Chap. 4). Whilst welcoming the creation of such a new institution, Professor Williams believes that it is unlikely to command governmental support for some years and, therefore, the Council will remain the dominant standing body in administrative law ("The Tribunal System—Its Future Control and Supervision," (1990) 9 C.J.Q. 27).

4. The Council has frequently renewed the plea for new legislation to enable its functions to be clarified and widened. The Council believes that reference to the 1980 Special Report "as a touchstone of our aims is subject inevitably to the law of diminishing returns". Nevertheless, legislation ought to empower the Council to advise departments on proposals to establish new tribunals, and those affecting the constitution and working of scheduled tribunals. Secondly, the Council wishes to be entitled to advise on proposals which would affect the administrative procedures involving a statutory inquiry. Thirdly, the Council wants the removal of inconsistencies in its current powers (*e.g.* its differential powers of scrutiny over tribunals and inquiries contained in Tribunals and Inquiries Act 1992, s.1). The Council has discussed these changes with the Lord Chancellor and his officials, but Government approval and the finding of legislative time is still awaited. (A.R. 1988–1989, H.C. 114 (1989–1990) pp. 14–18.) Subsequently, the Council has had further discussions with the Lord Chancellor's department and there is "general agreement in principle that there is considerable merit in our proposals"; but no legislative measures have yet been laid before Parliament (A.R. 1989–1990, H.C. 64 (1990–1991), p. 30; A.R. 1990–1991, H.C. 97 (1991–1992), pp. 37–38.) These matters were not addressed by the consolidation of the Tribunals and Inquiries Act in 1992. The Council has continued to press for these changes to its primary legislation, but Parliamentary time has not been made available (A.R. 1993–1994, H.C. 22 (1994–1995), p. 9.). The Council has also noted that "a small group of tribunals" within its existing jurisdiction have routinely refused to allow members of the Council to attend the deliberative stage of the tribunals' decision-making (*ibid.*, p. 9).

(B) THE WORK OF THE COUNCIL ON TRIBUNALS

(i) The Scrutiny of Tribunal Procedures

ANNUAL REPORT OF THE COUNCIL ON TRIBUNALS 1985–1986

H.C. 42 (1986–1987)

2.5. In all our work we have been persistent in pursuing certain basic aims, as illustrated below. A good general guide to the Council's approach is embodied in the phrase "openness, fairness and impartiality". This was a constant theme of the Franks Report. However, over the years other standards have been significant. For example, efficiency, expedition and economy have also been prominent. Openness has to be expressed in practical steps to ensure accountability, so that it is clear where the responsibilities for different tribunals lie. The needs of users of the system have, rightly, received more emphasis.

2.6. We recommend that tribunals be clearly independent of the bodies over whose decisions they adjudicate: this has recently been implemented in connection with Social Security Appeal Tribunals: their members are no longer appointed by the Secretary of State in the department which was seen to be a party to appeals; they are now appointed and administered by the President of SSATs. It has been implemented in other ways in connection with Social Security Commissioners and specialist tax appeals (VAT Tribunals and Special Commissioners of Income Tax): the administrative responsibility for these tribunals has been transferred to the Lord Chancellor's Department.

2.8. We have been vigilant in seeking to ensure that people are granted a hearing in connection with proposals which affect their interests; that rights of appeal against administrative decisions are given wherever appropriate and are not eroded where they already exist, *e.g.* concerning the Social Fund, immigration appeals, expulsion and suspension from school, the Social Security Commissioners, the Transport Tribunal, and patents; that parties to tribunal proceedings are treated equitably and neither side is given an unfair advantage; that clerks to tribunals play a defined and appropriate part in the proceedings; that reasons are normally given in writing for all decisions and that they are adequate and comprehensible; that proceedings should be simple and clear, and should normally be in public: the proceedings must be "not done in a corner"; and that resources should not be wasted—for example in Local Valuation Panels where many appeals are lodged but few are heard.

2.9. In short the procedure should make the tribunal easily accessible to the public; it should be cheap, swift and free from technicality. The whole proceedings should be, and be seen to be, independent and impartial, and fair to the powerful and the professional, but also to the vulnerable.

2.11. We have long stood out for the right of representation for parties before tribunals and inquiries. We believe that non-legal aid would sometimes be more suitable for parties before tribunals than professional assistance from a lawyer. We also believe that legal aid or assistance by way of representation should be extended to virtually all kinds of tribunal but subject to a "sieve" to ensure that it would not be granted in cases which did not really merit it. At present legal aid is only available in the Lands Tribunals and the Commons Commissioners, and free legal representation before Mental Health Review Tribunals.

Notes

1. This is the most important function performed by the Council. A very dramatic example of this process in operation occurred in relation to appeals under the Social Fund. During 1985 the Government announced that it intended to replace single payments under the supplementary benefits system (for items such as replacement furniture) with loans and grants payable out of a new Social Fund.[5] Under these proposals, claimants would lose their right of appeal to a Social Security Appeal Tribunal against an adjudication officer's decision regarding their claim for a single payment. The Council felt so strongly about this alteration in appellate rights that it issued a special report.[6] The report stated that annually around 36,000 appeals regarding single payments were heard by SSATs and that 25 per cent of them were successful. The Council concluded:

> "the people most affected by this proposal are amongst the most vulnerable in our society. Very good reasons are needed before the abolition of the right to an independent appeal in such circumstances, an appeal which has existed for over 50 years. It would probably be the most substantial abolition of a right of appeal to an independent tribunal since the Council on Tribunals were set up by Parliament in 1958, following the Franks Report. It is for these reasons that we are so critical of the proposal."[7]

[5] *Reform of Social Security*, Vol. 1, Cmnd. 9517 (1985).
[6] *Social Security—Abolition of Independent Appeals Under the Proposed Social Fund*, Cmnd. 9722 (1986).
[7] Above, pp. 6–7.

Despite the Council's offer to advise the Government on a modified right of appeal for Social Fund disputes, the Government made no formal response to the Council until after the enactment of the Social Security Act 1986, which created the Fund.[8] However, during the report stage of the Bill the Government responded to parliamentary pressure and introduced a scheme for reviewing most challenged Social Fund decisions by a new group of Social Fund Inspectors appointed by a Social Fund Commissioner. Drabble and Lynes found that the Social Fund Inspectors were "approaching their task with a commendable degree of objectivity".[9] But "it is too early to say how well a cadre of some 40 legally unqualified inspectors under the part-time supervision of a solicitor will perform the essentially legal task that has been assigned to them".[10] The Council has maintained its view that Social Fund appeals should be determined by an independent tribunal.[11] For a detailed account of the Social Fund see A.I. Ogus and N.J. Wikeley, *The Law of Social Security* (4th ed., 1994), Chap. 14; also D. Feldman, "The Constitution and the Social Fund: A Novel Form of Legislation" (1991) 41 L.Q.R. 39.

2. In its Annual Report for 1989–1990[12] the Council expressed the fear that financial considerations may be establishing a trend of compromising the standards expected of adjudicative bodies under their supervision.

The Council was particularly critical of the Government for creating one-person tribunals, an example being the Pensions Ombudsman established by the Social Security Act 1990.

"The more usual tripartite constitution of the majority of tribunals possesses distinct advantages where the jurisdiction of the tribunal comprehends subject-matters of substantial complexity affecting the status, livelihood or financial well-being of individual appellants, permitting as it does the combination of an independent, adjudicative approach with the availability of expertise in, or experience of the subject-matter in question."[13]

Generally, the Council concluded,

"we believe that where a decision affects a citizen's liberty, livelihood, status or other basic rights, particularly where a grievance concerns a decision of a public authority, nothing less is apt for the purpose than a properly equipped independent body able to bring an adjudicative approach to bear on the matter at issue. ... we shall be vigilant in assessing appeals procedures on the general criteria indicated and in warning the Government and the public in cases where new appeal or review procedures are in our view inadequate for the purposes for which they are proposed."[14]

3. The Council "deplored" the removal of appellate rights from foreign visitors and certain categories of students, because of administrative expediency, by the Asylum and Immigration Appeals Act 1993 (A.R. 1992–1993, H.C. 78 (1993–1994), p. 2.).

4. The Council has also noted situations where failings by public agencies outside of its jurisdiction have created problems for tribunals operating under the Council's supervision. For example, delays have been caused in the decision-making of Child Support Appeal Tribunals due to the late submission of case documents by officers of the Child Support Agency. Furthermore, "it is clear from reports on monitoring that the quality of the work carried out at the initial decision-making stage, on review and in the preparation of the appeal submissions leaves much to be desired".

---

[8] *Annual Report 1985–86*, H.C. 42 (1986–1987) para. 3.85.
[9] R. Drabble and T. Lynes, "The Social Fund—Discretion or Control?" [1989] P.L. 297 at 315.
[10] *ibid.*, at 318.
[11] A.R. 1987–1988, H.C. 102 (1988–1989), para. 3.36.
[12] H.C. 64 (1990–1991).
[13] *ibid.*, para. 1.11.
[14] *ibid.*, para. 1.14.

(A.R. 1994–1995, H.C. 64 (1995–1996), p. 11.). However, the Council thanked the Department of Social Security for consulting it at any early period in the pre-legislative stages of what became the Child Support Act 1995.

(ii) Visits to Tribunals and Inquiries

ANNUAL REPORT OF THE COUNCIL ON TRIBUNALS 1994–1995

H.C. 64 (1995–1996)

Our visits policy

3.21 Our visits to tribunals are the most effective means by which we can discharge our statutory duty to "keep under review the constitution and working" of the tribunals we supervise. The duty we have in relation to inquiries is assisted in the same way. We never visit unannounced but make an appointment in advance. The visit is always preceded by a letter which refers to our independence, to the fact that our purpose is solely to observe, and which emphasises that we will take no part in the proceedings or be involved in the decisions taken. It is accompanied by a leaflet summarising our role and explaining how we operate. We are anxious that those whom we are likely to visit should know something about us and about our work, and we have asked the heads of tribunals this year to make the leaflet available in future to all new members soon after their appointment.

3.22 It is important to our advisory function for members to develop through their visits a practical knowledge of the tribunals that we supervise. That is one of their main purposes. We particularly value the opportunity which visits give us to see how the procedures we have helped to create or on which we have advised are operating; and we welcome the opportunity to talk to those who are closely involved in the day-to-day operation of the tribunal, and to listen to what they have to say about its working and any procedural or other problems they may be experiencing. We are also glad to accept invitations to visit training seminars and conferences. These more informal occasions provide us with a further opportunity to meet people working in tribunals and to develop our knowledge and understanding of their problems, as well as to tell them something about the Council and our work.

3.23 Members provide a written report to the Council following each visit. The purpose is to inform other members about the visit and to draw attention to any points raised during the course of it. The Council as a whole are then able to consider any procedural or other issues which come to light either from what was seen or from the member's discussion with the tribunal. We amass considerable information about the workings of a particular tribunal over a period of time. Occasionally this provides evidence of a need for change, requiring action to be taken by the tribunal or the Department. If, after substantial experience of the practical workings of a tribunal, we see features in it which fall short of the standards we expect, we will pass our concerns to the appropriate tribunal authority or the Department and suggest action to remedy the defect.

3.24 We visit approximately 100 hearings conducted by a variety of tribunals and inquiries in England and Wales each year. We take care in ing our annual programme to ensure that it covers a representative sample of tribunals in various parts of the country so that we have a good picture of how a particular tribunal and its procedures are operating. High in the programme are those tribunals which we have decided should be subject to a detailed review (we usually select one tribunal for close scrutiny each year) and those which, from our earlier visits, suggest there is cause for concern. Subsequent visits enable us to test the validity of earlier observations or to establish how widespread the features are which cause us concern. But our visits are not confined to the major tribunals. We also look for the opportunity each year to visit hearings conducted by the smaller tribunals under our supervision, many of which sit only rarely. The number of visits we are able to make to any particular major tribunal system each year covers only a small segment of its total activity. But significant patterns do emerge from our visits over a period of time. We have occasionally used this evidence, in anonymised form, to support the case for change which we put to the relevant Department. We have found this practice useful: the cumulative effect of comments taken from our visit reports over time has a telling impact, bringing home through description of events observed the need for change.

Feedback to tribunals

3.25 We know that many tribunals would welcome something more by way of formal feedback from us following a visit. Our members welcome any opportunity afforded by the tribunal when they visit to discuss matters of mutual interest and concern, either before or after the proceedings. We always find these discussions helpful and we are not averse to sharing our experiences with a tribunal during our visit. However, it is important to the effective discharge of our functions that we should do nothing which suggests that our role is something more than it is. We attend hearings as observers and not inspectors, and we are observing tribunal procedures rather than tribunal personnel. Nevertheless, towards the end of 1995 we hope to be producing feedback reports summarising our visits to certain Child Support Appeal Tribunal and Immigration Adjudicator hearings during the past year. The reports, which will be sent to the tribunals concerned and to the relevant Departments, will draw attention both to issues of good practice and to any perceived shortcomings in the procedures or working of the tribunals we have observed.

Notes
1. The late Professor Street expressed the view, in his Hamlyn lectures, that the underfunding of the Council meant "... that its supervision of tribunals is so slight as to be ineffective. It is unlikely to discover the existence of incompetent tribunal members."[15]

2. During 1994–1995 members of the Council (together with its Scottish Committee and members of the Council's secretariat) made a total of 154 visits to tribunals and inquiries. Of this total, 10 visits were to inquiries and the remainder to tribunals (A.R. 1994–1995, H.C. 64 (1995–1996), p. 60 and Appendix B). In the same period, Industrial Tribunals in England and Wales decided 21,003 cases (*ibid.*, Appendix E).

3. Professor D. Foulkes, a former member of the Council, has noted that major tribunals are always visited and special attention is given to new tribunals together with those tribunals which previous visits have revealed to be experiencing problems.

[15] H. Street, *Justice in the Welfare State* (2nd ed., 1975), p. 63.

He concludes that: "visits are essential to enable Council members to acquire a practical understanding of the work of tribunals. There is in them an element of inspection: of premises, of procedure, and of the chairman's performance. Visits do not constitute a system of inspection of tribunals as a whole, but visits are undertaken on a rational and systematic basis. When a full programme of monitoring a tribunal system is set up the Council can provide useful additional information. The body of knowledge built up from a series of visits is particularly valuable. The Council is able to influence official action significantly. It is sometimes referred to as a 'watchdog'. In choosing which tribunals to visit, and how often, in seeking out tribunals that may be in difficulties and otherwise following up various leads, the Council may perhaps be seen as a 'bloodhound', as it was suggested [by R.A. Butler] it might be": "The Council on Tribunals: Visits Policy and Practice" [1994] P.L. 564 at 571–572.

Question

Who should have the primary responsibility for monitoring the administrative performance of tribunals—Presidents of Tribunals, the Parliamentary Commissioner for Administration, the courts or some other institution?

(iii) The Scrutiny of Inquiry Procedures

ANNUAL REPORT OF THE COUNCIL ON TRIBUNALS 1991–1992

H.C. 316 (1992–1993)

Planning Inquiries Procedural Rules—Proposals for Change

2.66 In our Annual Report for 1987/1988 we discussed the important changes introduced in that year by the new Planning Inquiries Procedure Rules. This year we report on the consideration which has subsequently been given to ways in which the 1988 Rules could be further improved.

2.67 In his Report following the Hinkley Point inquiry, the inspector, Mr Michael Barnes Q.C., included a chapter on procedure, in which he made a number of suggestions (not amounting to recommendations) for improvements in the inquiry process. He requested that the chapter be sent to us, noting that members of the Council had attended the proceedings at the Hinkley Point inquiry on several occasions. We invited Mr Barnes to one of our meetings to discuss his suggestions.

2.68 Hinkley Point was an example of the very biggest type of inquiry, lasting for some fourteen months. The procedure was governed by the Electricity Generating Stations and Overhead Lines (Inquiries Procedure) Rules 1987 (now replaced by the 1990 Rules). This was the first set of Rules to be made following the major review which also led to the Planning Inquiries Procedure Rules of 1988, and both incorporated the same improvements in procedure.

2.69 Some of the suggestions put forward by Mr Barnes would not have entailed changes to the Rules. They related to such matters as the preparation of an informal written account of procedures in advance of the inquiry, the setting aside of time at pre-inquiry meetings to deal informally with procedural queries from members of the public, the control of cross-examination, the holding of "informal" sessions of the inquiry where strict compliance with the Rules was not insisted upon, and the need to limit the number of documents admitted as evidence. Taken as a whole, we regarded these suggestions as providing helpful guidance in relation to inquiries on the scale of Hinkley Point, though we would be cautious about extending them to the ordinary or even moderately big inquiry.

2.70 Two of Mr Barnes's suggestions would have required changes to the procedural rules. In the light of his experience at Hinkley Point, Mr Barnes suggested removing from the Rules the concept of "section 34 parties" (now "qualifying objectors"), that is, people who, by making objections in accordance with the statutory provisions, thereby acquire the right to receive copy documents and to appear at the inquiry. Mr Barnes also suggested that, save with the permission of the inspector, all evidence in chief should be in writing, submitted at least three weeks in advance, and taken wholly as read.

2.71 As regards qualifying objectors, there were nearly 10,000 of them at Hinkley, and strict compliance with the rules about copying documents would have entailed huge expense. However, the Rules were subsequently changed to give the Secretary of State a discretion to modify the right of such objectors to be provided with copies of statements of case. Mr Barnes's suggestion would have entailed taking away the right to appear at the inquiry. Mr Barnes considered that nobody would be disadvantaged by this, since objectors could still appear at the inspector's discretion, and a serious objector would undoubtedly always be allowed to do so. Nonetheless, we were not persuaded that it would be right to curtail existing rights in this way. The Department of Energy shared our view.

2.72 We also could not support the suggestion that all evidence in chief should be in writing, submitted in advance, and taken wholly as read. In the case of an inquiry of the size of Hinkley Point, there are obvious advantages in encouraging those entitled to appear to put their evidence in writing beforehand, but we do not consider that this is necessary or desirable in the case of ordinary or moderately big inquiries. We also do not favour evidence in chief being taken wholly as read. While it is in nobody's interest for time to be wasted at the inquiry by the reading of evidence, it is often helpful if parties are given the opportunity to explain and expand on difficult aspects of technical evidence and to draw out principal points.

2.73 Our consideration of these matters fell at the same time as the initiation of the review of the Planning Inquiries Procedure Rules being carried out by the Department of the Environment and in due course we were consulted about their proposals for change. Most of the proposals represented useful improvements, some of which have already been incorporated into sets of rules made since 1988, such as the Compulsory Purchase Inquiries Procedure Rules of 1990. Our concerns centred on the proposals for the extended use of summaries of proofs of evidence.

2.74 The 1988 Rules introduced provisions enabling an inspector to require a summary of a proof of evidence to be prepared. Only the summary would be read at the inquiry, unless the inspector permitted otherwise. We welcomed this innovation at the time, since it enabled much valuable time to be saved, while ensuring that third parties were able to understand the broad outline of the matters under consideration.

2.75 The Department of the Environment proposed to extend these provisions so as to require summaries of proofs of evidence in all cases. Summaries were to be provided at the same time as the proof, and normally only the summary would be read at the inquiry. We had misgivings about these proposals. We thought that some well-drafted proofs would already be so short as not to lend themselves to being summarised. We considered that the requirement for the summary to be provided at the same time as the proof was unnecessary and burdensome; we were not convinced by the Department's argument that such a requirement would assist in avoiding disputes as to whether the summary contained additional material. We were also very doubtful whether it would be right, where summaries were provided as of course, to insist that normally only the summary should be read at the inquiry. It was in our view important that parties be given the opportunity to explain technical evidence and to draw out salient points. Finally, we doubted the benefit or practicability of requiring summaries of supplementary proofs, in cases where time was very short. We considered that, at the very least, the Rules giving effect to the new proposals would need to give the inspector, as a matter of law, a discretion to dispense with the requirements, and that the Circular accompanying the Rules should emphasise the Department's expectation that inspectors would adopt a reasonably flexible approach.

2.76 The Department met our concerns to the extent of dispensing with the requirement for summaries in the case of proofs of not more than 1,500 words. They adhered to their view that summaries should be provided at the same time as the proofs, and that normally only the summary should be read at the inquiry. They did not favour making an exception in the case of supplementary proofs. However, they took account of some of our misgivings in drafting the Circular to accompany the new Rules, and undertook to monitor closely how the new proposals work out in practice. We propose to do likewise.

Notes

1. The Council's involvement in the formulation of the 1988 Rules can be found in the second edition of this book at pp. 138–141.
2. The 1992 Rules are reproduced and commented upon above at pp. 64 *et seq.*

(iv) Examining Complaints from Individuals

ANNUAL REPORT OF THE COUNCIL ON TRIBUNALS 1994–1995

H.C. 64 (1995–1996)

Complaints

3.20 Most of the complaints we receive are handled by our Secretariat. But our governing Act does not give us the authority to adjudicate on complaints, and we have to make it clear to many of those who complain that we have no power to change a tribunal decision or to interfere with the conduct of a case. Since most complainants seek that form of remedy from us we are unable to offer them any effective redress. To suggest that we can, for example by pursuing the complaint with the tribunal concerned, raises false expectations in the minds of complainants who then feel let down. It is also a source of annoyance to tribunal members. Accordingly, when our Secretariat acknowledge a complaint the letter is accompanied by a leaflet which explains what our functions are, why we cannot take action and where to turn for advice. Sometimes the information adds to our understanding of the difficulties arising at a particular tribunal and we are able to acknowledge this in the reply which is sent, even though we cannot take action on the complaint itself. On a few occasions the allegation may suggest that proper procedures are not being followed. Our Secretariat will then forward the correspondence to the head of the tribunal who has a direct interest in remedying shortcomings of this kind. But we look more closely at complaints which reveal evidence of unreasonable delay in holding a hearing, or indicate that the procedures of a particular tribunal or inquiry may be defective or inadequate. These may point to administrative or procedural shortcomings on which the tribunal or Department need to take action and, in some cases, we may ask our Secretariat to make further inquiries about the nature and extent of the problem. But this takes time and, regrettably, any recommendations we may make at the end of the day are unlikely to benefit the person who made the original complaint.

Chapter 4

OMBUDSMEN AND OTHER
COMPLAINTS MECHANISMS

(A) Introduction

THE idea of an "Ombudsman", or inquirer into the complaints of grievances suffered by citizens at the hands of some organ of the administration, is of Scandinavian origin, where it was conceived as a check on corrupt officials. Imported from Sweden into Denmark in 1954 where he is almost an inspector of the administration, the Ombudsman acts on his own motion, and relies on publicity and public opinion to achieve the redress of grievances. The idea was familiarised in this country chiefly by the activities of JUSTICE. A Parliamentary Commissioner was established by the Act of 1967, and he was followed by the Health Service Commissioners for Scotland (National Health Service Reorganisation Act 1972), and for England and Wales (National Health Service Reorganisation Act 1973), and by the Commissions for Local Administration (Local Government Act 1974). Meanwhile, the Parliamentary Commissioner (Northern Ireland) Act was passed in 1969, and also that jurisdiction established a separate local government commissioner, by the Commissioner for Complaints (Northern Ireland) Act 1969.

In the United Kingdom, the Parliamentary Commissioner for Administration (hereafter the P.C.A.) was initially limited to investigating complaints (referred by Members of Parliament) of "maladministration" causing injustice created by central government departments. However, in 1987 his jurisdiction was extended to encompass over 50 Non-Departmental Public Bodies (*e.g.* the Sports Council), and subsequently many "Next Steps" agencies have been subjected to his jurisdiction.

During the 1960s and the 1970s the Ombudsman idea spread across many legal systems (*e.g.* the New Zealand Ombudsman was created in 1962 and the French Mediateur in 1973). Whilst the 1980s witnessed the emergence of private sector Ombudsmen in the United Kingdom (initially to deal with consumer complaints in the financial services industries—see below, p. 165). And the current decade opened with Parliament establishing the Legal Services Ombudsman under the Courts and Legal Services Act 1990 followed by the Pensions Ombudsman (Pensions Schemes Act 1993, s.145). The creation of these various Ombudsmen has enabled many grievances to be resolved by the distinct techniques adopted by such officers. Indeed, the Treaty on European Union (Maastricht Treaty) created a European Ombudsman who can receive complaints from, *inter alios*, citizens of the Union alleging that they suffered maladministration at the hands of a Community institution (excluding the Court of Justice and the Court of First Instance acting in their judicial roles) as a means of providing such redress at an international level of administration (E.C. Treaty Article 138e, as amended). See further: E.A. Marias (ed.), *The European Ombudsman*, (1994); details of his work and annual reports can be obtained via the World Wide Web (internet) from http://www.europa.eu.int. During his first year of office in 1995–1996 the E.U. Ombudsman, Mr Jacob Soderman (formerly the Finnish Ombudsman), received 537 complaints; the largest numbers of complaints came from Britons, Germans and the Spanish.

Today, 75 countries have created ombudsmen, with a number of "emerging democracies" in Central and Eastern Europe, Latin America and Africa utilising these offices to try and safeguard human rights. Consequently, Professor Gregory has observed: "looking back over the history of the Ombudsman around the world, what I notice is a combination of three inter-related developments, summed up by the ugly words: *proliferation*—as regards numbers; *diversification*—as regards categories and types; and *mutation and variation*—as regards functions and purpose."[1]

Selected general readings include: *Garner*, pp. 126–150; *Craig*, pp. 127–138; *Wade and Forsyth*, pp. 79–107; F. Stacey, *Ombudsmen Compared* (1978); *JUSTICE/All Souls Report*, Chap. 5; P. Birkinshaw, *Grievances, Remedies and the State* (2nd ed., 1994), Chap. 5; M. Seneviratne, *Ombudsmen in the Public Sector* (1994).

(B) THE PARLIAMENTARY COMMISSIONER FOR ADMINISTRATION

(i) Constitutional and Jurisdictional Matters

PARLIAMENTARY COMMISSIONER ACT 1967

Appointment and tenure of office

1.—(1) For the purpose of conducting investigations in accordance with the following provisions of this Act there shall be appointed a Commissioner, to be known as the Parliamentary Commissioner for Administration.

(2) Her Majesty may by Letters Patent from time to time appoint a person to be the Commissioner, and any person so appointed shall (subject to [subsections (3) and (3A)] of this section) hold office during good behaviour.

(3) A person appointed to be the Commissioner may be relieved of office by Her Majesty at his own request, or may be removed from office by Her Majesty in consequence of Addresses from both Houses of Parliament, and shall in any case vacate office on completing the year of service in which he attains the age of sixty-five years.

[(3A) Her Majesty may declare the office of Commissioner to have been vacated if satisfied that the person appointed to be the Commissioner is incapable for medical reasons—

    (a) of performing duties of his office; and
    (b) of requesting to be relieved of it.] ...[2]

Salary and pension

2.—(1) There shall be paid to the holder of the office of Commissioner a salary at the rate (subject to subsection (2) of this section) of £8,600 a year.

(2) The House of Commons may from time to time by resolution increase the rate of the salary payable under this section, and any such resolution may

---

[1] R. Gregory, Address to the British and Irish Ombudsman Association: AGM May 16, 1996, para. 7.
[2] Subsection (3A) added by the Parliamentary and Health Service Commissioners Act 1987, s.2(1).

take effect from the date on which it is passed or such other date as may be specified therein. ...

(5) Any salary, pension or other benefit payable by virtue of this section shall be charged on and issued out of the Consolidated Fund.

Administrative provisions

3.—(1) The Commissioner may appoint such officers as he may determine with the approval of the Treasury as to numbers and conditions of service.

(2) Any function of the Commissioner under this Act may be performed by any officer of the Commissioner authorised for that purpose by the Commissioner [or may be performed by any officer so authorised—

(a) of the Health Service Commissioner for England;
(b) of the Health Service Commissioner for Scotland; or
(c) of the Health Service Commissioner for Wales].[3]

(3) The expenses of the Commissioner under this Act, to such amount as may be sanctioned by the Treasury, shall be defrayed out of moneys provided by Parliament.

Appointment of acting Commissioners

[3A.—(1) Where the Office of Commissioner becomes vacant, Her Majesty may, pending the appointment of a new Commissioner, appoint a person under this section to act as the Commissioner at any time during the period of twelve months beginning with the date on which the vacancy arose.

(2) A person appointed under this section shall hold office during Her Majesty's pleasure and, subject to that, shall hold office—

(a) until the appointment of a new Commissioner or the expiry of the period of twelve months beginning with the date on which the vacancy arose, whichever occurs first; and
(b) in other respects, in accordance with the terms and conditions of his appointment which shall be such as the Treasury may determine.

(3) A person appointed under this section shall, while he holds office, be treated for all purposes, except those of section 2 of this Act, as the Commissioner.

(4) Any salary, pension or other benefit payable by virtue of this section shall be charged on and issued out of the Consolidated Fund.][4]

Departments, etc., subject to investigation

[4.—(1) Subject to the provisions of this section and to the notes contained in Schedule 2 to this Act, this Act applies to the government departments, corporations and unincorporated bodies listed in that Schedule; and references in this Act to an authority to which this Act applies are references to any such corporation or body.

---

[3] Amended by the Parliamentary and Health Service Commissioners Act 1987, s.3.
[4] Added by the Parliamentary and Health Service Commissioners Act 1987, s.6(1).

(2) Her Majesty may by Order in Council amend Schedule 2 to this Act by the alteration of any entry or note, the removal of any entry or note or the insertion of any additional entry or note.

(3) An Order in Council may only insert an entry if—

(a) it relates—
   (i) to a government department; or
   (ii) to a corporation or body whose functions are exercised on behalf of the Crown; or
(b) it relates to a corporation or body—
   (i) which is established by virtue of Her Majesty's prerogative or by an Act of Parliament or on Order in Council or order made under an Act of Parliament or which is established in any other way by a Minister of the Crown in his capacity as a Minister or by a government department;
   (ii) at least half of whose revenues derive directly from money provided by Parliament, a levy authorised by an enactment, a fee or charge of any other description so authorised or more than one of those sources; and
   (iii) which is wholly or partly constituted by appointment made by Her Majesty or a Minister of the Crown or government department.

(4) No entry shall be made in respect of a corporation or body whose sole activity is, or whose main activities are, included among the activities specified in subsection (5) below.

(5) The activities mentioned in subsection (4) above are—

(a) the provision of education, or the provision of training otherwise than under the Industrial Training Act 1982;
(b) the development of curricula, the conduct of examinations or the validation of educational courses;
(c) the control of entry to any profession or the regulation of the conduct of members of any profession;
(d) the investigation of complaints by members of the public regarding the actions of any person or body, or the supervision or review of such investigations or of steps taken following them.

(6) No entry shall be made in respect of a corporation or body operating in an exclusively or predominantly commercial manner or a corporation carrying on under national ownership an industry or undertaking or part of an industry or undertaking.

(7) Any statutory instrument made by virtue of this section shall be subject to annulment in pursuance of a resolution of either House of Parliament.

(8) In this Act—

(a) any reference to a government department to which this Act applies includes a reference to any of the Ministers or officers of such a department; and
(b) any reference to an authority to which this Act applies includes a reference to any members or officers of such an authority.][5]

[5] Substituted by the Parliamentary and Health Services Commissioners Act 1987, s.1(1).

Matters subject to investigation

5.—(1) Subject to the provisions of this section, the Commissioner may investigate an action taken by or on behalf of a government department or other authority to which this Act applies, being action taken in the exercise of administrative functions of that department or authority, in any case where—

(a) a written complaint is duly made to a member of the House of Commons by a member of the public who claims to have sustained injustice in consequence of maladministration in connection with the action so taken; and

(b) the complaint is referred to the Commissioner, with the consent of the person who made it, by a member of that House with a request to conduct an investigation thereon.

(2) Except as hereinafter provided, the Commissioner shall not conduct an investigation under this Act in respect of any of the following matters, that is to say—

(a) any action in respect of which the person aggrieved has or had a right of appeal, reference or review to or before a tribunal constituted by or under any enactment or by virtue of Her Majesty's prerogative;

(b) any action in respect of which the person aggrieved has or had a remedy by way of proceedings in any court of law;

Provided that the Commissioner may conduct an investigation notwithstanding that the person aggrieved has or had such a right or remedy if satisfied that in the particular circumstances it is not reasonable to expect him to resort or have resorted to it.

(3) Without prejudice to subsection (2) of this section, the Commissioner shall not conduct an investigation under this Act in respect of any such action or matter as is described in Schedule 3 to this Act.

(4) Her Majesty may by Order in Council amend the said Schedule 3 so as to exclude from the provisions of that Schedule such actions or matters as may be described in the Order; and any statutory instrument made by virtue of this subsection shall be subject to annulment in pursuance of a resolution of either House of Parliament.

(5) In determining whether to initiate, continue or discontinue an investigation under this Act, the Commissioner shall, subject to the foregoing provisions of this section, act in accordance with his own discretion; and any question whether a complaint is duly made under this Act shall be determined by the Commissioner.

[(6) For the purposes of this section, administrative functions exercisable by any person appointed by the Lord Chancellor as a member of the administrative staff of any court or tribunal shall be taken to be administrative functions of the Lord Chancellor's Department or, in Northern Ireland, of the Northern Ireland Court Service.][6];

6 Added by the Courts and Legal Services Act 1990, s.110(1).

[(7) For the purposes of this section, administrative functions exercisable by any person appointed as a member of the administrative staff of a relevant tribunal—

(a) by a government department or authority to which this Act applies; or
(b) with the consent (whether as to remuneration and other terms and conditions of service or otherwise) of such a department or authority,

shall be taken to be administrative functions of that department or authority.

(8) In subsection (7) of this section, "relevant tribunal" means a tribunal listed in Schedule 4 to this Act.

(9) Her Majesty may by Order in Council amend the said Schedule 4 by the alteration or removal of any entry or the insertion of any additional entry; and any statutory instrument made by virtue of this subsection shall be subject to annulment in pursuance of a resolution of either House of Parliament.][7]

Provisions relating to complaints

6.—(1) A complaint under this Act may be made by any individual, or by any body of persons whether incorporated or not, not being—

(a) a local authority or other authority or body constituted for purposes of the public service or of local government or for the purposes of carrying on under national ownership any industry or undertaking or part of an industry or undertaking;
(b) any other authority or body whose members are appointed by Her Majesty or any Minister of the Crown or government department, or whose revenues consist wholly or mainly of moneys provided by Parliament.

(2) Where the person by whom a complaint might have been made under the foregoing provisions of this Act has died or is for any reason unable to act for himself, the complaint may be made by his personal representative or by a member of his family or other individual suitable to represent him; but except as aforesaid a complaint shall not be entertained under this Act unless made by the person aggrieved himself.

(3) A complaint shall not be entertained under this Act unless it is made to a member of the House of Commons not later than twelve months from the day on which the person aggrieved first had notice of the matters alleged in the complaint; but the Commissioner may conduct an investigation pursuant to a complaint not made within that period if he considers that there are special circumstances which make it proper to do so.

(4) [Except as provided in subsection (5) below] a complaint shall not be entertained under this Act unless the person aggrieved is resident in the United

---

[7] Added by the Parliamentary Commissioner Act 1994, s.1(1).

Kingdom (or, if he is dead, was so resident at the time of his death) or the complaint relates to action taken in relation to him while he was present in the United Kingdom or on an installation in a designated area within the meaning of the Continental Shelf Act 1964 or on a ship registered in the United Kingdom or an aircraft so registered, or in relation to rights or obligations which accrued or arose in the United Kingdom or on such an installation, a ship or aircraft.

[(5) A complaint may be entertained under this Act in circumstances not falling within subsection (4) above where—

    (a) the complaint relates to action taken in any country or territory outside the United Kingdom by an officer (not being an honorary consular officer) in the exercise of a consular function on behalf of the Government of the United Kingdom; and

    (b) the person aggrieved is a citizen of the United Kingdom and Colonies who, under section 2 of the Immigration Act 1971, has the right of abode in the United Kingdom.][8]

Procedures in respect of investigations

7.—(1) Where the Commissioner proposes to conduct an investigation pursuant to a complaint under this Act, he shall afford to the principal officer of the department of authority concerned, and to any person who is alleged in the complaint to have taken or authorised the action complained of, an opportunity to comment on any allegations contained in the complaint.

(2) Every such investigation shall be conducted in private, but except as aforesaid the procedure for conducting an investigation shall be such as the Commissioner considers appropriate in the circumstances of the case; and without prejudice to the generality of the foregoing provision the Commissioner may obtain information from such persons and in such manner, and make such inquiries, as he thinks fit, and may determine whether any person may be represented, by counsel or solicitor or otherwise, in the investigation.

(3) The Commissioner may, if he thinks fit, pay to the person by whom the complaint was made and to any other person who attends or furnishes information for the purposes of an investigation under this Act—

    (a) sums in respect of expenses properly incurred by them;

    (b) allowances by way of compensation for the loss of their time,

in accordance with such scales and subject to such conditions as may be determined by the Treasury.

(4) The conduct of an investigation under this Act shall not affect any action taken by the department or authority concerned, or any power or duty of that department or authority to take further action with respect to any matters subject to the investigation; but where the person aggrieved has been removed

---

[8] Added by the Parliamentary Commissioner (Consular Complaints) Act 1981, s.1.

from the United Kingdom under any Order in force under the Aliens Restriction Acts 1914 and 1919 or under the Commonwealth Immigrants Act 1962, he shall, if the Commissioner so directs, be permitted to re-enter and remain in the United Kingdom, subject to such conditions as the Secretary of State may direct, for the purposes of the investigation.

Evidence

8.—(1) For the purposes of an investigation under this Act the Commissioner may require any Minister, officer or member of the department or authority concerned or any other person who in his opinion is able to furnish information or produce documents relevant to the investigation to furnish any such information or produce any such document.

(2) For the purposes of any such investigation the Commissioner shall have the same powers as the Court in respect of the attendance and examination of witnesses (including the administration of oaths or affirmations and the examination of witnesses abroad) and in respect of the production of documents.

(3) No obligation to maintain secrecy or other restriction upon the disclosure of information obtained by or furnished to persons in Her Majesty's service, whether imposed by any enactment or by any rule of law, shall apply to the disclosure of information for the purposes of an investigation under this Act; and the Crown shall not be entitled in relation to any such investigation to any such privilege in respect of the production of documents or the giving of evidence as is allowed by law in legal proceedings.

(4) No person shall be required or authorised by virtue of this Act to furnish any information or answer any question relating to proceedings of the Cabinet or of any committee of the Cabinet or to produce so much of any document as relates to such proceedings; and for the purposes of this subsection a certificate issued by the Secretary of the Cabinet with the approval of the Prime Minister and certifying that any information, question, document or part of a document so relates shall be conclusive.

(5) Subject to subsection (3) of this section, no person shall be compelled for the purposes of an investigation under this Act to give any evidence or produce any document which he could not be compelled to give or produce in [civil][9] proceedings before the Court.

Obstruction and contempt

9.—(1) If any person without lawful excuse obstructs the Commissioner or any officer of the Commissioner in the performance of his functions under this Act, or is guilty of any act or omission in relation to any investigation under this Act which, if that investigation were a proceeding in the Court, would constitute contempt of court, the Commissioner may certify the offence to the Court.

---

[9] Added by the Civil Evidence Act 1968, s.17(1)(b).

(2) Where an offence is certified under this section, the Court may inquire into the matter and, after hearing any witnesses who may be produced against or on behalf of the person charged with the offence, and after hearing any statement that may be offered in defence, deal with him in any manner in which the Court could deal with him if he had committed the like offence in relation to the Court.

(3) Nothing in this section shall be construed as applying to the taking of any such action as is mentioned in subsection (4) of section 7 of this Act.

Reports by Commissioner

10.—(1) In any case where the Commissioner conducts an investigation under this Act or decides not to conduct such an investigation, he shall send to the member of the House of Commons by whom the request for investigation was made (or if he is no longer a member of that House, to such member of that House as the Commissioner thinks appropriate) a report of the results of the investigation or, as the case may be, a statement of his reasons for not conducting an investigation.

(2) In any case where the Commissioner conducts an investigation under this Act, he shall also send a report of the results of the investigation to the principal officer of the department or authority concerned and to any other person who is alleged in the relevant complaint to have taken or authorised the action complained of.

(3) If, after conducting an investigation under this Act, it appears to the Commissioner that injustice has been caused to the person aggrieved in consequence of maladministration and that the injustice has not been, or will not be, remedied, he may, if he thinks fit, lay before each House of Parliament a special report upon the case.

(4) The Commissioner shall annually lay before each House of Parliament a general report on the performance of his functions under this Act and may from time to time lay before each House of Parliament such other reports with respect to those functions as he thinks fit.

(5) For the purposes of the law of defamation, any such publication as is hereinafter mentioned shall be absolutely privileged, that is to say—

   (a) the publication of any matter by the Commissioner in making a report to either House of Parliament for the purposes of this Act;
   (b) the publication of any matter by a member of the House of Commons in communicating with the Commissioner or his officers for those purposes or by the Commissioner or his officers in communicating with such a member for those purposes;
   (c) the publication by such a member to the person by whom a complaint was made under this Act of a report or statement sent to the member in respect of the complaint in pursuance of section (1) of this section;
   (d) the publication by the Commissioner to such a person as is mentioned in subsection (2) of this section of a report to that person in pursuance of that subsection.

Provision for secrecy of information

11.—(1) ...[10]

(2) Information obtained by the Commissioner or his officers in the course of or for the purposes of an investigation under this Act shall not be disclosed except—

(a) for the purposes of the investigation and of any report to be made thereon under this Act;

(b) for the purposes of any proceedings for an offence under [the Official Secrets Act 1911 to 1989][11] alleged to have been committed in respect of information obtained by the Commissioner or any of his officers by virtue of this Act or for an offence of perjury alleged to have been committed in the course of an investigation under this Act or for the purposes of an inquiry with a view to the taking of such proceedings; or

(c) for the purposes of any proceedings under section 9 of this Act;

and the Commissioner and his officers shall not be called upon to give evidence in any proceedings (other than such proceedings as aforesaid) of matters coming to his or their knowledge in the course of an investigation under this Act.

[(2A) Where the Commissioner also holds office as a Health Service Commissioner and a person initiates a complaint to him in his capacity as such a Commissioner which relates partly to a matter with respect to which that person has previously initiated a complaint under this Act, or subsequently initiates such a complaint, information obtained by the Commissioner or his officers in the course of or for the purposes of investigating the complaint under this Act may be disclosed for the purposes of his carrying out his functions in relation to the other complaint.][12]

(3) A Minister of the Crown may give notice in writing to the Commissioner, with respect to any document or information specified in the notice, or any class of documents or information so specified, that in the opinion of the Minister the disclosure of that document or information, or of documents or information of that class, would be prejudicial to the safety of the State or otherwise contrary to the public interest; and where such a notice is given nothing in this Act shall be construed as authorising or requiring the Commissioner or any officer of the Commissioner to communicate to any person or for any purpose any document or information specified in the notice, or any document or information of a class so specified.

(4) The references in this section to a Minister of the Crown include references to the Commissioners of Customs and Excise and the Commissioners of Inland Revenue.

[10] Repealed by the Official Secrets Act 1989, s.16(4), Sched. 2.
[11] Substituted by the Official Secrets Act 1989, s.16(3), Sched. 1, para. 1.
[12] Added by the Parliamentary and Health Service Commissioners Act 1987, s.4(1).

Consultations between Parliamentary Commissioner and Health Service Commissioners

[11.A.—(1) Where, at any stage in the course of conducting an investigation under this Act, the Commissioner forms the opinions that the complaint relates partly to a matter within the jurisdiction of the Health Service Commissioner for England, Wales or Scotland, he shall—

    (a) unless he also holds office as that Commissioner, consult about the complaint with him; and

    (b) if he considers it necessary, inform the person initiating the complaint under this Act of the steps necessary to initiate a complaint under [the Health Service Commissioners Act 1993].[13]

(2) Where by virtue of subsection (1) above the Commissioner consults with the Health Service Commissioner in relation to a complaint under this Act, he may consult him about any matter relating to the complaint, including—

    (a) the conduct of any investigation into the complaint; and

    (b) the form, content and publication of any report of the results of such an investigation.

(3) Nothing in section 11(2) of this Act shall apply in relation to the disclosure of information by the Commissioner or any of his officers in the course of consultations held in accordance with this section.][14]

Investigation by the Commissioner

[11.B—(1) For the purposes of this Act, administrative functions exercisable by an administrator of the Criminal Injuries Compensation Scheme ("Scheme functions") shall be taken to be administrative functions of a government department to which this Act applies.

(2) For the purposes of this section, the following are administrators of the Scheme—

    (a) a claims officer appointed under section 3(4)(b) of the Criminal Injuries Compensation Act 1995;

    (b) a person appointed under section 5(3)(c) of that Act;

    (c) the Scheme manager, as defined by section 1(4) of that Act, and any person assigned by him to exercise functions in relation to the Scheme.

(3) The principal officer in relation to any complaint made in respect of any action taken in respect of Scheme functions is—

[13] Substituted by the Health Service Commissioners Act 1993, Sched. 2
[14] Added by the Parliamentary and Health Service Commissioners Act 1987, s.4(2).

(a) in the case of action taken by a claims officer, such person as may from time to time be designated by the Secretary of State for the purposes of this paragraph;

(b) in the case of action taken by a person appointed under section 5(3)(c) of the Act of 1995, the chairman appointed by the Secretary of State under section 5(3)(b) of that Act; or

(c) in the case of action taken by the Scheme manager or by any other person mentioned in subsection (2)(c) of this section, the Scheme manager.

(4) The conduct of an investigation under this Act in respect of any action taken in respect of Scheme functions shall not affect—

(a) any action so taken; or

(b) any power or duty of any person to take further action with respect to any matters subject to investigation.][15]

Interpretation

12.—(1) In this Act the following expressions have the meanings hereby respectively assigned to them, that is to say—

"action" includes failure to act, and other expressions connoting action shall be construed accordingly;

"the Commissioner" means the Parliamentary Commissioner for Administration;

"the Court" means, in relation to England and Wales the High Court, in relation to Scotland the Court of Session, and in relation to Northern Ireland the High Court of Northern Ireland;

"enactment" includes an enactment of the Parliament of Northern Ireland and any instrument made by virtue of an enactment;

"officer" includes employee;

"person aggrieved" means the person who claims or is alleged to have sustained such injustice as is mentioned in section 5(1)(a) of this Act;

"tribunal" includes the person constituting a tribunal consisting of one person.

(2) References to this Act to any enactment are references to that enactment as amended or extended by or under any other enactment.

(3) It is hereby declared that nothing in this Act authorises or requires the Commissioner to question the merits of a decision taken without maladministration by a government department or other authority in the exercise of a discretion vested in that department or authority....

---

[15] Added by the Criminal Injuries Compensation Act 1995, s.10(1).

SCHEDULE 2

DEPARTMENTS, ETC., SUBJECT TO INVESTIGATION

Advisory, Conciliation and Arbitration Service.
Agricultural Wages Committees.
Ministry of Agriculture, Fisheries and Food.
Arts Council of England.
Arts Council of Great Britain.
Arts Council of Wales (Cyngor Celfyddydau Cymru).
Scottish Arts Council.
British Council.
British Library Board.
Building Societies Commission.
Bwrdd yr Iaith Gymraeg (Welsh Language Board).
Certification Officer.
Charity Commission.
Civil Service Commission.
Coal Authority.
Co-operative Development Agency.
Countryside Commission.
Countryside Council for Wales.
Crafts Council.
Crofters Commission.
Crown Estate Office.
Customs and Excise.
Data Protection Registrar.
Ministry of Defence.
Development Commission.
Education Assets Board.
Central Bureau for Educational Visits and Exchanges.
Office of the Director General of Electricity Supply.
The Department for Education and Employment.
Environment Agency.
Equal Opportunities Commission.
Export Credits Guarantee Department.
Office of the Director General of Fair Trading.
British Film Institute.
Foreign and Commonwealth Office.
Forestry Commission.
Friendly Societies Commission.
Registry of Friendly Societies.
Office of the Director General of Gas Supply.
Health and Safety Commission.
Health and Safety Executive.
Department of Health.
Historic Buildings and Monuments Commission for England.
Home Office.
Horserace Betting Levy Board.
Housing Corporation.
Housing for Wales.
Human Fertilisation and Embryology Authority.
Central Office of Information.
Inland Revenue.

The International Rail Regulator.
Intervention Board for Agricultural Produce.
Land Registry.
Legal Aid Board.
The following general lighthouse authorities—
    (a) the Corporation of the Trinity House of Deptford Strond;
    (b) the Commissioners of Northern Lighthouses.
Local Government Commission for England.
Lord Chancellor's Department.
Lord President of the Council's Office.
Medical Practices Committee.
Scottish Medical Practices Committee.
Museums and Galleries Commission.
National Debt Office.
Department of National Heritage.
Trustees of the National Heritage Memorial Fund.
Office of the Director General of the National Lottery.
National Rivers Authority.
Department for National Savings.
Office for National Statistics.
Nature Conservancy Council for England.
Commission for the New Towns.
Development corporations for new towns.
Northern Ireland Court Service.
Northern Ireland Office.
Occupational Pensions Board.
Occupational Pensions Regulatory Authority.
Ordnance Survey.
Director of Passenger Rail Franchising.
Pensions Compensation Board.
Office of Population Censuses and Surveys.
Office of the Commissioner for Protection Against Unlawful Industrial Action.
Registrar of Public Lending Right.
Public Record Office.
Office of Public Service ...
Commission for Racial Equality.
Rail Regulator.
Red Deer Commission.
Department of the Registers of Scotland.
General Register Office, Scotland.
Biotechnology and Biological Sciences Research Council.
Economic and Social Research Council.
Engineering and Physical Sciences Research Council.
Medical Research Council.
Natural Environment Research Council.
Particle Physics and Astronomy Research Council.
Council for the Central Laboratory of the Research Councils.
Residuary Bodies.
Office of the Commissioners for the Rights of Trade Union Members.
Royal Mint.
Office of Her Majesty's Chief Inspector of Schools in England.
Office of Her Majesty's Chief Inspector of Schools in Wales.
Scottish Courts Administration.
Scottish Environment Protection Agency.
Scottish Homes.

Scottish Legal Aid Board.
Scottish Natural Heritage.
Scottish Office.
Scottish Record Office.
Council for Small Industries in Rural Areas.
Department of Social Security.
Central Council for Education and Training in Social Work.
Sports Council.
Scottish Sports Council.
Sports Council for Wales.
Staff Commission for Wales (Comisiwn Staff Cymru).
Stationery Office.
Office of the Director General of Telecommunication.
English Tourist Board.
Scottish Tourist Board.
Wales Tourist Board.
Board of Trade.
Department of Trade and Industry.
Traffic Director for London.
Agricultural Training Board.
Clothing and Allied Products Industry Training Board.
Construction Industry Training Board.
Engineering Industry Training Board.
Hotel and Catering Industry Training Board.
Plastics Processing Industry Training Board.
Road Transport Industry Training Board.
Department of Transport.
Treasury.
Treasury Solicitor.
United Kingdom Ecolabelling Board.
Urban development corporations.
Urban Regeneration Agency.
Development Board for Rural Wales.
Office of the Director General of Water Services.
Welsh Office.[16]

SCHEDULE 3

MATTERS NOT SUBJECT TO INVESTIGATION

1. Action taken in matters certified by a Secretary of State or other Minister of the Crown to affect relations or dealings between the Government of the United Kingdom and any other Government or any international organisation of States or Governments.

---

[16] For reasons of space it is not possible to include the Notes which detailed the specific functions of the above bodies that may be investigated by the Parliamentary Commissioner. Nor is it possible to specify the precise legislative basis for the many additions and deletions to the above Schedule.

2. Action taken, in any country or territory outside the United Kingdom, by or on behalf of any officer representing or acting under the authority of Her Majesty in respect of the United Kingdom, or any other officer of the Government of the United Kingdom other than action which is taken by an officer (not being an honorary consular officer) in the exercise of a consular function on behalf of the Government of the United Kingdom. ....

3. Action taken in connection with the administration of the government of any country or territory outside the United Kingdom which forms part of Her Majesty's dominions or in which Her Majesty has jurisdiction.

4. Action taken by the Secretary of State under the Extradition Act 1870 or the Fugitive Offenders Act 1881, the Fugitive Offenders Act 1967 or the Extradition Act 1989.

5. Action taken by or with the authority of the Secretary of State for the purposes of investigating crime or of protecting the security of the State, including action so taken with respect to passports.

6. The commencement or conduct of civil or criminal proceedings before any court of law in the United Kingdom, of proceedings at any place under the Naval Discipline Act 1957, the Army Act 1955 or the Air Force Act 1955, or of proceedings before any international court or tribunal.

6A. Action taken by any person appointed by the Lord Chancellor as a member of the administrative staff of any court or tribunal, so far as that action is taken at the direction, or on the authority (whether express or implied), of any person acting in a judicial capacity or in his capacity as a member of the tribunal.

6B.—(1) Action taken by any member of the administrative staff of a relevant tribunal, so far as that action is taken at the direction, or on the authority (whether express or implied), of any person acting in his capacity as a member of the tribunal.

(2) In this paragraph, "relevant tribunal" has the meaning given by section 5(8) of this Act.

6C. Action taken by any person appointed under section 5(3)(c) of the Criminal Injuries Compensation Act 1995, so far as that action is taken at the direction, or on the authority (whether express or implied), of any person acting in his capacity as an adjudicator appointed under section 5 of that Act to determine appeals.

7. Any exercise of the prerogative of mercy or of the power of a Secretary of State to make a reference in respect of any person to the Court of Appeal, the High Court of Justiciary or the Courts-Martial Appeal Court.

8. Action taken on behalf of the Minister of Health or the Secretary of State by a Regional Health Authority, an Area Health Authority, a District Health Authority, a special health authority, except the Rampton Hospital Review Board . . . the Rampton Hospital Board, the Broadmoor Hospital Board or the Moss Side and Park Lane Hospitals Board, a Family Practitioner Committee, a Health Board or the Common Services Agency for the Scottish Health Service, by the Dental Practice Board or the Scottish Dental Practice Board, or by the Public Health Laboratory Service Board.

9. Action taken in matters relating to contractual or other commercial transactions, whether within the United Kingdom or elsewhere, being transactions of a government department or authority to which this Act applies or of any such authority or body as is mentioned in paragraph (a) or (b) of subsection (1) of section 6 of this Act and not being transactions for or relating to—

(a) the acquisition of land compulsorily or in circumstances in which it could be acquired compulsorily;

(b) the disposal as surplus of land acquired compulsorily or in such circumstances as aforesaid.

10.—(1) Action taken in respect of appointments or removals, pay, discipline, superannuation or other personnel matters, in relation to—

(a) service in any of the armed forces of the Crown, including reserve and auxiliary and cadet forces;

(b) service in any office or employment under the Crown or under any authority to which this Act applies; or

(c) service in any office or employment, or under any contract for services, in respect of which power to take action, or to determine or approve the action to be taken, in such matters is vested in Her Majesty, any Minister of the Crown or any such authority as aforesaid.

(2) Sub-paragraph (1)(c) above shall not apply to any action (not otherwise excluded from investigation by this Schedule) which is taken by the Secretary of State in connection with:

(a) the provision of information relating to the terms and conditions of any employment covered by an agreement entered into by him under section 12(1) of the Overseas Development and Cooperation Act 1980 or

(b) the provision of any allowance, grant or supplement or any benefit (other than those relating to superannuation) arising from the designation of any person in accordance with such an agreement.

11. The grant of honours, awards or privileges within the gift of the Crown, including the grant of Royal Charters.[17]

Notes

1. The key concept in delimiting the jurisdictional powers of the P.C.A. is that of "maladministration." This concept had its origins in the JUSTICE report of 1961,[18] as they believed that this norm of administrative behaviour would prevent the Parliamentary Commissioner from unduly encroaching upon the exercise of discretionary powers by examining if the particular decisions reached were "wrong or unwelcome". During the enactment of the 1967 Act, the Leader of the House of Commons (Richard Crossman) acknowledged that the government had not been able to define comprehensively the concept of maladministration. Instead, he proposed a non-statutory list containing some of the characteristics of this concept including, "bias, neglect, inattention, delay, incompetence, inaptitude, perversity, turpitude, arbitrariness and so on".[19] Subsequently, this description of maladministration has become known as the "Crossman catalogue".

After several years the P.C.A.'s use of maladministration was analysed by Dr G. Marshall. He concluded, "the view (that certainly follows from the Crossman catalogue approach) that maladministration may be inferred from, and can consist in, a complete lack of merits implies that the distinction between merits and maladministration drawn in the 1967 Act is incoherent ...".[20] Consequently, he favoured the abandonment of the concept of maladministration with all its ambiguities as the foundation of the P.C.A.'s jurisdiction.

In 1977 another report from JUSTICE[21] suggested the replacement of "maladministration", with the P.C.A. being empowered to investigate "unreasonable, unjust, or oppressive action" by government departments. However, this idea was rejected by the Select Committee on the P.C.A. as they did not believe that the new jurisdiction would enable the Parliamentary Commissioner to investigate or criticise anything that did not already come within his authority.[22]

The JUSTICE/All Souls report accepted the view of Sir Cecil Clothier (who was P.C.A. during the early 1980s) that "maladministration" was "a wholly adequate basis for his investigations." Therefore, they did not propose any alterations to this concept.[23]

In 1994 the P.C.A. expressed the view that: "to define maladministration is to limit it. Such a limitation could work to the disadvantage of individual complainants with justified grievances which did not fit within a given definition." However, he supplemented the Crossman catalogue with other examples of maladministration including: unwillingness to treat the complainant as a person with rights; refusal to answer reasonable questions; knowingly giving advice which is misleading or inadequate; and

---

[17] The legislative origins of the amendments to this Schedule are not included for reasons of space.
[18] *The Citizen and the Administration* (1961).
[19] H.C.Deb. Vol. 754, col. 51 (1966).
[20] G. Marshall, "Maladministration" [1973] P.L. 32.
[21] *Our Fettered Ombudsman.*
[22] *Review of Access and Jurisdiction* (1977–1978) H.C. 615.
[23] Report, Chap. 5.

showing bias whether because of colour, sex or any other grounds. (Annual Report for 1993–1994, para. 7; H.C. 290 (1993–1994)).

A practical appreciation of the way in which the concept of maladministration has been invoked by various Parliamentary Commissioners can be ascertained from the extracts below at p. 138, examining the casework of the Ombudsman.

2. In 1993 the Select Committee on the P.C.A. (see below, p. 150), published a major report on *The Powers, Work and Jurisdiction of the Ombudsman* (H.C. 33 (1993–1994)). The Committee recommended, *inter alia*, that complainants should continue to be referred by M.P.s (the so-called M.P. filter) because a majority of M.P.s favoured the existing system (all M.P.s were sent a questionnaire, 333 replied with 58 per cent supporting the filter and 38 per cent favouring direct access to the Ombudsman). Furthermore, constitutional issues underpinned the filter: "we continue to believe that the Member of Parliament has an irreplaceable role in pursuing complaints of the public against the Executive, notwithstanding the development within public bodies of an array of direct access complaint and redress mechanisms for the citizen" (paragraph 75). But it was proposed that legislation should be enacted to enable the Ombudsman to launch an investigation where a matter was raised with him by the Committee, even where no individual had complained to an M.P. Also, the Committee felt that the "current system of jurisdiction is both bureaucratic and confusing" (paragraph 50). Therefore, the report advocated amending the 1967 Act to provide that the P.C.A. would have jurisdiction over all central government bodies unless his jurisdiction was specifically excluded. The Government was unwilling to accept the proposal to allow the Select Committee to initiate investigations by the Ombudsman. "While a power to initiate investigations without having received a complaint from a member of the public would allow the Ombudsman to be more proactive, it would also, as he has noted, represent a fundamental change from the concept that his basic role is to investigate and suggest redress for people's grievances" (H.C. 619 (1993–1994): paragraph 18). As to the proposal to alter the legislative structure of the Ombudsman's jurisdiction, the Government replied that it would "look carefully" at whether the 1967 Act could be amended in that way, but priority should be given to publicising the existing jurisdiction of the Ombudsman.

3. In recent years a number of Departments have appointed their own complaints officers to deal with grievances raised by citizens. These officers have differing powers and titles; *e.g.* the Inland Revenue and the Customs and Excise have an "adjudicator", Companies House has appointed a "complaints adjudicator" and the prison service in England and Wales has appointed an "ombudsman". The Select Committee on the P.C.A. has criticised such persons being termed ombudsmen when the Department/agency is within the jurisdiction of the P.C.A. (H.C. 33 (1993–1994) paragraph 28). The Government agreed that it was important to avoid public confusion about the status of different "ombudsmen", but it would be difficult to change the formal titles of existing complaints officers (H.C. 619 (1993–1994)). The P.C.A. has continued to receive complaints against departments where such officers operate. For a discussion of the background to one complaints officer see: D. Oliver, "The Revenue Adjudicator: A New Breed of Ombudsperson" [1993] P.L. 407 and P.E. Morris, "The Revenue Adjudicator—The First Two Years" [1996] P.L. 309. The latter has concluded that: "the Adjudicator scheme earns high marks for openness (the remit of the Adjudicator and key principles are clearly articulated, and the Adjudicator herself is accessible to the media and outside researchers), fairness (both sides to the dispute can clearly put their case during the process of complaint investigation) and effectiveness (her recommendations are always followed and changes in administrative practices have been achieved). However, the scheme is clearly flawed in terms of perceived independence and accountability. Some form of institutional re-structuring is obviously needed to satisfy these criteria" (at 321).

(ii) The Work of the Parliamentary Commissioner

(a) *Workload*

P.C.A. ANNUAL REPORT FOR 1995

H.C. 296 (1995–1996)

Cases Received, Screened and Investigated

Note
546 M.P.s referred a total of 1,706 complaints to the P.C.A. during 1995. This was an increase of nearly 28 per cent over the number of complaints received during 1994.

Outcome of Investigations

Justified:
153 cases

62%

34%

Partly justified:
83 cases

Not justified:
9 cases

4%

Notes

1. Of the 1,229 cases rejected or discontinued by the P.C.A., 43 per cent were not concerned with administrative matters, 25 per cent involved cases where the complainant had a right of appeal to a tribunal, 8 per cent were directed against a body outside the P.C.A.'s jurisdiction and 4 per cent involved public service personnel matters.

2. In 154 of the cases where the P.C.A. found for the complainant he was able to secure a remedy going beyond an apology.

3. The Department of Social Security and its related agencies accounted for 49 per cent of the complaints referred to the P.C.A., followed by the Inland Revenue with 9 per cent. The Child Support Agency was the subject of 25 per cent of the complaints reaching the P.C.A. (thereby significantly contributing to the total for the D.S.S.). The P.C.A. produced two special reports on his investigations into the Agency in 1995 and decided that thereafter he would only investigate further complaints if they involved, *inter alia*, novel matters or actual financial loss.

(b) *Casework*

R. v. PARLIAMENTARY COMMISSIONER FOR ADMINISTRATION, ex p. DYER

[1994] 1 W.L.R. 621, [1994] 1 All E.R. 375 (High Court)

Miss Dyer had complained to her M.P. (Rt Hon. Roy Hattersley) about a number of matters concerning her claims for various benefits administered by the Department of Social Security. Mr Hattersley had referred her complaints to the P.C.A. who had decided to investigate some of them. In his report the P.C.A. found that Miss Dyer had suffered maladministration and he criticised the local office of the Department for various mistakes in its handling of her claims. The Department apologised and made an *ex gratia* payment of £500. The P.C.A. considered these remedies to be a satisfactory outcome to his investigation. However, Miss Dyer was not satisfied and sought judicial review of the P.C.A.'s decision not to reopen his investigation into her complaints. She alleged that the P.C.A. had acted unlawfully by: (1) deciding to investigate some of her original complaints (rather than investigating all of them), (2) giving the Department an opportunity to comment on the factual accuracy of his draft report (whilst denying her such an opportunity) and (3) regarding himself as being precluded from reopening an investigation once he had issued a report.

SIMON BROWN L.J.: ... This is the first substantive application for judicial review of the P.C.A. to come before the courts (an application for leave in an earlier case having been refused). The first question raised for decision upon it concerns the proper ambit of this court's supervisory jurisdiction over the P.C.A. Mr Stephen Richards on his behalf submits to us that, certainly so far as the P.C.A.'s discretionary powers are concerned, this court has no review jurisdiction whatever over their exercise. In the alternative he submits that the court should intervene only in the most exceptional cases of abuse of discretion, essentially on the same limited basis held by the House of Lords in *Nottinghamshire C.C. v. Secretary of State for the Environment* [1986] 1 All E.R. 199; [1986] A.C. 240 and *Hammersmith and Fulham London B.C. v. Secretary of State for the Environment* [1990] 3 All E.R. 589; [1991] 1 A.C. 521 to be appropriate in the particular area of decision-making there in question.

The resolution of this initial jurisdictional issue clearly depends essentially on the legislation which created the P.C.A.'s office and governs the discharge of his functions. ...

As to his wider proposition—that this court has literally no right to review the P.C.A.'s exercise of his discretion under the 1967 Act (not even, to give the classic illustration, if he refused to investigate complaints by red-headed complainants)—Mr Richards submits that the legislation is enacted in such terms as to indicate an intention that the P.C.A. should be answerable to Parliament alone for the way he performs his functions. The P.C.A. is, he suggests, an officer of the House of Commons, and, the argument runs, the parliamentary control provided for by the statute displaces any supervisory control by the courts. Mr Richards relies in particular on these considerations: first, the stipulation under s.5 that a complaint must be referred to the P.C.A. by a member of Parliament before even his powers of investigation are engaged; second, the requirement under s.10(1) to report back to the member of Parliament (and, in certain circumstances, to each House of Parliament—see s.10(3)); third, the requirement under s.10(4) annually to lay a general report before Parliament; fourth, the provision under s.1(3) of the Act for the P.C.A.'s removal from office only in the event of addresses from both Houses of Parliament. Mr Richards points also to the P.C.A. being always answerable to the select committee.

Despite these considerations I, for my part, would unhesitatingly reject this argument. Many in government are answerable to Parliament and yet answerable also to the supervisory jurisdiction of this court. I see nothing about the P.C.A.'s role or the statutory framework within which he operates so singular as to take him wholly outside the purview of judicial review.

I turn next, therefore, to Mr Richards's alternative and narrower submission that, by analogy with the two House of Lords cases already mentioned, the courts should regard their powers as restricted with regard to reviewing the P.C.A.'s exercise of the discretions conferred upon him by this legislation.

I need cite one passage only from the speeches in those two cases, this from Lord Bridge's speech in *Hammersmith and Fulham London B.C. v. Secretary of State for the Environment* [1990] 3 All E.R. 589 at 637; [1991] 1 A.C. 521 at 597:

> "The restriction which the *Nottinghamshire* case [1986] 1 All E.R. 199; [1986] A.C. 240 imposes on the scope of judicial review operates only when the court has first determined that the ministerial action in question does not contravene the requirements of the statute, whether express or implied, and only then declares that, since the statute has conferred a power on the Secretary of State which involves the formulation and the implementation of national economic policy and which can only take effect with the approval of the House of Commons, it is not open to challenge on the grounds of irrationality short of the extremes of bad faith, improper motive or manifest absurdity. Both the constitutional propriety and the good sense of this restriction seem to me to be clear enough. The formulation and the implementation of national economic policy are matters depending essentially on political judgment. The decisions which shape them are for politicians to take and it is in the political forum of the House of Commons that they are properly to be debated and approved or disapproved on their merits. If the decisions have been taken in good faith within the four corners of the Act, the merits of the policy underlying the decisions are not susceptible to review by the courts and the courts would be exceeding their proper function if they presumed to condemn the policy as unreasonable."

Mr Richards concedes that the analogy between the position considered there and that arising here is not a very close one. He submits, however, that the underlying rationale for restricting the scope of judicial review in those cases applies also here. Although, as counsel recognises, the P.C.A.'s functions are manifestly not political, nevertheless, he submits, the provisions here for parliamentary control afford this case a comparable dimension.

This submission too I would reject. There seems to me no parallel whatever between, on the one hand, decisions regarding the formulation and implementation of national economic policy—decisions "depending essentially on political judgment ... for politicians to take ... in the political forum of the House of Commons"—and, on the other hand, decisions of the P.C.A. regarding the matters appropriate for investigation and the proper manner of their investigation.

All that said, however, and despite my rejection of both Mr Richards's submissions on the question of jurisdiction, it does not follow that this court will readily be persuaded to interfere with the exercise of the P.C.A.'s discretion. Quite the contrary. The intended width of these discretions is made strikingly clear by the legislature: under s.5(5), when determining whether to initiate, continue or discontinue an investigation, the commissioner shall "act in accordance with his own discretion"; under s.7(2), "the procedure for conducting an investigation shall be such as the commissioner considers appropriate in the circumstances of the case". Bearing in mind too that the exercise of these particular discretions inevitably involves a high degree of subjective judgment, it follows that it will always be difficult to mount an effective challenge on what may be called the conventional ground of *Wednesbury* unreasonableness (see *Associated Provincial Picture Houses Ltd v. Wednesbury Corp.* [1947] 2 All E.R. 680; [1948] 1 K.B. 223).

Recognising this, indeed, one may pause to wonder whether in reality the end result is much different from that arrived at by the House of Lords in the two cases referred to, where the decisions in question were held "not open to challenge on the grounds of irrationality short of the extremes of bad faith, improper motive or manifest absurdity". True, in the present case "manifest absurdity" does not have to be shown; but inevitably it will be almost as difficult to demonstrate that the P.C.A. has exercised one or other of his discretions unreasonably in the public law sense. ...

Recognising the full width of our jurisdiction but with those considerations in mind I turn to Miss Dyer's grounds of challenge.

As to her contention that the P.C.A. investigated some only of her original grounds of complaint, that is undoubtedly the case. But is she entitled to criticise the P.C.A. for taking that course? More particularly, was the P.C.A. acting outside the proper ambit of his discretion under s.5(5) of the 1967 Act in doing so? ...

In my judgment, the P.C.A. was entitled in the exercise of his discretion to limit the scope of his investigation, to be selective as to just which of Miss Dyer's many detailed complaints he addressed, to identify certain broad categories of complaint (the six main aspects as he called them) and investigate only those. Inevitably such an approach carried the risk that some of the problems which Miss Dyer complained of having experienced with the local office would continue, and that indeed is what Miss Dyer says has occurred. But no investigation should be expected to solve all problems for all time and it cannot in my judgment be said that the approach adopted here by the P.C.A. was not one properly open to him.

Turning to Miss Dyer's complaint that the draft report was sent to the department for comment on the facts but not to her, the respondent's evidence indicates that this is a practice which has existed for 25 years, and is known to and acquiesced in by the select committee. The reasons for it are explained as follows. First, that it is the department rather than the complainant who may subsequently be called upon to justify its actions before the select committee and, if it is shown the draft report and does not point out any inaccuracy, it will then be unable to dispute the facts stated in it. Second, the practice affords the department an opportunity to give notice in writing to the P.C.A., as expressly provided for by s.11(3) of the 1967 Act, of any document or information the disclosure of which, in the opinion of the relevant minister, would be prejudicial to the safety of the state or otherwise contrary to the public interest. Third, sight of the draft report gives the department the opportunity to propose the remedy it is prepared to offer in the light of any findings of maladministration and injustice contained in it. The commissioner can then include in his final report what that proposed remedy is and indicate whether he finds that it satisfactorily meets the need.

Miss Dyer recognises, I think, that the same reasons do not exist for sending the draft report to her. Indeed, having regard to s.11(3), it could not be sent to her unless and until it had already been cleared by the department. Therefore, to graft on to the existing practice a need to show the draft report to complainants too would introduce a further stage into the process. Does natural justice require this? I do not think so. As Lord Bridge said in *Lloyd v. McMahon* [1987] 1 All E.R. 1118 at 1161; [1987] A.C. 625 at 702:

"My Lords, the so-called rules of natural justice are not engraved on tablets of stone. To use the phrase which better expresses the underlying concept, what the requirements of fairness demand when any body, domestic, administrative or judicial, has to make a decision which will affect the rights of individuals depends on the character of the decision-making body, the kind of decision it has to make and the statutory or other framework in which it operates."

Assuming, as I do, and indeed as Mr Richards concedes, that the P.C.A. makes "a decision which will affect the rights of" Miss Dyer, it should nevertheless be borne in mind that it is the department and not her who is being investigated and who is liable to face public criticism for its acts. I cannot conclude that fairness here demanded that she too be shown the draft report. Rather it seems to me that the P.C.A., in determining the procedure for conducting his investigation as provided for by s.7(2), was amply entitled to consider it appropriate to follow his long-established practice.

I come finally to Miss Dyer's complaint about the P.C.A.'s refusal to reopen this investigation. This I can deal with altogether more shortly. It seems to me that the P.C.A. is clearly correct in his view that, once his report had been sent to Mr Hattersley and the DSS (as required by s.10(1) and (2)), he was *functus officio* and unable to reopen the investigation without a further referral under s.5(1). Section 5(5), as already indicated, confers a wide discretion indeed; it does not, however, purport to empower the P.C.A. to reopen an investigation once his report is submitted. It would seem to me unfair to the department and outside the scheme of this legislation to suppose that the P.C.A. could do as Miss Dyer wished. ...

It follows that, in my judgment, none of Miss Dyer's grounds of challenge can be made good and this application accordingly fails. ...

Application refused.

Notes

1. Norman S. Marsh, the Chairman of the Committee which proposed the creation of the P.C.A., has criticised Simon Brown L.J.'s reasoning concerning Miss Dyer's allegation that it was unlawful for the P.C.A. to allow departments to comment upon the factual accuracy of his draft reports. Marsh believes there may be factual inaccuracies which relate to complainants' cases and they should be given an opportunity to explain them to the P.C.A. "The impression given by this part of Simon Brown L.J.'s judgment is almost that the underlying purpose of the Parliamentary Commissioner Act is to give government departments a better opportunity to refute accusations of maladministration made against them" (at 349). N.S. Marsh, "The Extent and Depth of Judicial Review of the Decisions of the Parliamentary Commissioner for Administration" [1994] P.L. 347.

2. The first successful action for judicial review of a report issued by the P.C.A. occurred in 1996: *R. v. Parliamentary Commissioner for Administration, ex p. Balchin* (25/10/1996 Lexis). The applicants' former home had been seriously affected by planning blight, caused by a proposed nearby road scheme. The Balchins had complained to the P.C.A. about the actions of the Department of Transport in confirming the scheme. In his report the P.C.A. rejected the applicants' complaints. However, Sedley J. held that the P.C.A. had unlawfully failed to have regard to a relevant consideration (whether if the Department had brought a new statutory power to pay compensation to property owners to the attention of the local highway authority the applicants might have received compensation) in reaching his conclusions.

THE BARLOW CLOWES AFFAIR

P.C.A. Annual Report for 1989: H.C. 353 (1989–1990)

64. [This investigation report] was by far the longest and most detailed produced by the Office. It also resulted in the provision of the most substantial financial remedy ever to result from an investigation. I refer to my investigation into the Barlow Clowes affair—which I had decided to conduct following the publication, in October 1988, of the report[24] on the fact-finding investigation carried out by Sir Godfray Le Quesne Q.C. at the request of the then Secretary of State for Trade and Industry. My own investigation was the subject of a special report[25] which I made to Parliament (under the provisions of section 10(4) of the Parliamentary Commissioner Act) on December 19, 1989. The investigation involved my enquiring into the exercise of licensing duties under the Prevention of Fraud (Investments) Act 1958 by the Department of Trade and Industry over a period of some 14 years. I found that there had been significant maladministration by the Department, in their dealings with Barlow Clowes' partnerships and their successor companies, in five main areas. The businesses concerned had been engaged in the management of client monies running into millions of pounds. They had led the investors to believe that their monies were being put into British Government stocks. Much of the marketing of the businesses' services had been directed to those in retirement and others seeking a risk-free but tax-efficient form of investment, and a substantial part of the attraction to investors had been the use—until it was severely curtailed in 1985—of the tax-avoidance device known as "bond-washing". The volume of the business thus transacted had already grown considerably when, in 1984, the Department sought to bring the operation within the licensing framework having, in 1976 and in the intervening years, allowed it—as described in my report—to continue unlicensed. Partnerships, with identical names but with differing members, had been operating in both the United Kingdom and in Jersey, but the Department had failed to realise that a separate Jersey partnership existed, or to appreciate the need to extend to the Jersey partnership the enquiries they proposed to make into the suitability of the United Kingdom partnership for a licence. I concluded that an examination of the Jersey partnership's affairs would have disclosed that its role was more than that of an investment vehicle for expatriates (as had been represented to DTI), that there had been intermingling between the funds it managed and those of the mainland partnership, and that—at the audit date selected for the examination of the mainland partnership's funds—securities held by the Jersey partnership on behalf of clients fell short of the amount needed to discharge obligations to investors by at least £3.65 million. Had these facts been discovered, the firm's operations would in my view almost certainly have been brought to an end early in 1985. As it was, licences were issued to the United Kingdom business in 1985, 1986 and 1987 (that in 1987 being closely followed by the appointment of Inspectors by the Secretary of State to investigate the company's affairs in the light of serious concerns about

[24] Barlow Clowes Report of Sir Godfray Le Quesne Q.C. to the Secretary of State for Trade and Industry H.C. 671.
[25] First Report—Session 1989–1990 H.C. 76.

its viability and integrity); and, in 1988, the United Kingdom and offshore branches of the business were put into liquidation owing investors many millions of pounds. The final total of the losses had not emerged when my report was issued, but seemed likely to exceed £100 million. Apart from the centrally important errors in relation to the Jersey partnership, I also found that the viability of the schemes offered by Barlow Clowes had not been adequately considered, and that the decision to renew the licence for a third time, in 1987, had involved both excessive delay in responding to worrying information about the company and errors in correctly identifying the options available to the Department.

65. When I put my findings to the Department they told me, to my disappointment, that the Government disagreed with them and proposed to set out its own views in a separate document to be published at the same time as my report. The Department also said that my report raised a number of important issues about the responsibilities of regulators (on which the document to be published by the Government would also set out the Government's views). They went on to say, however, that the Government recognised that the case had created very great hardship and involved a unique combination of unusual features. In the light of that the Government was, in the exceptional circumstances and without admission of fault or liability, prepared to make a substantial payment to investors who had suffered loss. This payment (the proposed detailed calculation of which the Department explained to me) would be made to investors in both Barlow Clowes Gilt Managers Limited and Barlow Clowes International Limited in return for their assigning to the Secretary of State their rights in the liquidation and against third parties, and giving an undertaking to provide reasonable assistance in the pursuit of those rights. The payments would not distinguish between early and late investors.

66. I concluded that this outcome of the investigation—providing as it would for more than 99 per cent of the investors to receive at least 85 per cent of their capital (and 90 per cent in the case of those with investments of £50,000 or less) and, in addition, payments in lieu of interest lost on that amount since the collapse—was not unsatisfactory. The Government published its observations[26] on my Findings on December 19. However, I saw ground for satisfaction in that the Government—with whatever reservations—was prepared to act as it proposed in providing a fair remedy for what, as I had seen things, had been an injustice suffered by investors as a result of maladministration.

Notes

1. For an analysis of this major investigation, see R. Gregory and G. Drewry, "Barlow Clowes and the Ombudsman" [1991] P.L. 192 and 408.

2. Another major investigation has been the P.C.A.'s combined inquiries into a number of complaints about alleged planning blight (*i.e.* the loss of value caused to property near a proposed development) caused by the protracted deliberations over the route for a new high speed rail link from London to the Channel tunnel. The Ombudsman found maladministration in the way in which the Department of Transport dealt with several claims for compensation for alleged planning blight. However, the Department refused to accept the P.C.A.'s findings of maladministration. Therefore, the P.C.A. took the unusual step, for only the second time in the history of the office, of

[26] Observations by the Government on the Report of the Parliamentary Commissioner for Administration on Barlow Clowes H.C. 99.

submitting a special report on the matter to Parliament (under s.10(3) of the 1967 Act): *The Channel, Tunnel Rail Link and Blight,* H.C. 193 (1994–1995). The Select Committee on the P.C.A. subsequently took evidence from the Permanent Secretary of the Department and the Secretary of State (Dr B. Mawhinney). Later the Committee issued a report recommending that the Department accept the P.C.A.'s findings: H.C. 270 (1994–1995). In response the new Transport Secretary (Sir George Young) repeated the Department's position that they were not guilty of maladministration, but "out of respect for the Select Committee and the office of the P.C.A." he agreed to consider whether compensation should be paid to those suffering extreme and exceptional hardship. For a discussion of these events see, R. James and D. Longley [1996] P.L. 38.

Right to Advice: A Case Study

A RIGHT TO OFFICIAL ADVICE: THE PARLIAMENTARY COMMISSIONER'S PERSPECTIVE*

Alastair R. Mowbray [1990] P.L. 68

In the context of our contemporary society, it is inevitable that a great deal of sought after information is located within government departments, particularly where they are responsible for generating the detailed provisions that govern today's numerous administrative programmes. Therefore, a vital element in the relationship between citizens and the state concerns the nature of the obligation on the latter to provide advice to citizens regarding matters falling within the competence and expertise of those departments.

Of all the administrative grievance-handling agencies, it is the Parliamentary Commissioner for Administration (hereafter the P.C.A. or the Commissioner) who has contributed the most towards the development of a citizen's right to advice from the government in our modern public law....

Today, the importance of the right to advice is reflected in the fact that during recent years advice cases have represented approximately 20 per cent of all the investigations published by the P.C.A. in his selected case reports (see table below).

Year	Number of Reported Cases	Number of Advice Cases
1985	59	12
1986	63	13
1987	51	9
Totals	173	34

THE SCOPE OF THE RIGHT TO ADVICE

A study of the Commissioner's published cases during 1985–1987 enables us to delimit the boundaries of the right as currently enforced by the P.C.A. A clear example of the principle that individuals have a right to advice is given by a complaint against the DHSS.[27] The complainant asked an officer at the local

* *Note—not all the footnotes have been reproduced.*

[27] C573/84 (1984–1985) H.C. 150.

office whether he would be entitled to an increase in his supplementary benefit payments if he was to take out a mortgage on a new house. Because of a confusion over case papers the office failed to provide the complainant with a reply to his request and subsequently the building society refused to grant the complainant a mortgage. The P.C.A. concluded that the department's failure to provide the requested information meant that the complainant's criticisms were fully justified. Moreover, the P.C.A. has adopted a wide usage of the concept of "advice". He treats both the provision of essentially factual information to individuals (*e.g.* the extent of a complainant's pension contributions[28]) and the expression of officers' opinions as amounting to statements of advice. Officers' opinions can be about matters of current departmental policy (*e.g.* whether a company's short-time working schedule complied with existing departmental rules governing the payment of unemployment benefit[29]) or future situations involving the department (*e.g.* the level of benefits an individual would receive if she began reclaiming social security allowances in several months' time[30]).

(a) *The subject-matter of official advice*

Of the 34 advice cases published during 1985–1987, the overwhelming majority concerned what may be termed personal queries, where individuals sought advice from departments about their eligibility for public benefit (21 cases) or liability to make a payment to the state (four cases)....

(b) *The form of official advice*

... In half the cases studied (17), the relevant advice took the form of a personal letter sent to the complainant. A typical example of advice being presented in such a form arose in a case involving the overseas branch of the DHSS.[31] The complainant was a United Kingdom citizen who had taken up employment in France and he sought advice from the department about his future entitlement to retirement pensions in Britain and France. The department wrote expressing their views on the levels of pensions he could expect from both countries under European Community regulations. Later the complainant received a much lower French pension than the DHSS had predicted and he complained to the P.C.A. The Commissioner found that the department had inadvertently misinterpreted the E.C. regulations.

The second most common form of advice was that of oral statements (14 cases). This type of advice was normally given in two distinct circumstances. First, in response to a personal visit by a citizen to departmental premises. An example occurred where a managing director went to his local VAT office to discover if a proposed purchase of manufacturing assets would be liable to tax.[32] He was informed by the officer at the counter that VAT would be payable; but the District Surveyor later determined that tax was not due. The

[28] C223/85 (1984–1985) H.C. 590.
[29] C466/84 (1984–1985) H.C. 324.
[30] C665/84 (1984–1985) H.C. 590.
[31] C494/83 (1984–1985) H.C. 150.
[32] C567/84 (1984–1985) H.C. 590.

other context in which oral advice was obviously present was where an individual telephoned the department for advice. For example, a complainant telephoned his local DHSS office to seek advice on social security benefits he could claim whilst undergoing a M.S.C. training course.[33] In reply the officer expressed a view as to what types of benefits would be payable. When it subsequently transpired that not all these benefits were available the P.C.A. was asked to investigate.

Lastly, in three of the cases studied, advice took the form of leaflets and booklets published by the department. In a case against the Department of Employment,[34] a woman complained that she satisfied the conditions required for employment under the Job Release Scheme, administered by the department, as explained in an official leaflet. But the department refused to allow her to take up such a post, because they asserted that she did not meet all the requirements laid down for the scheme. The P.C.A. upheld her complaint, noting that,

"there was nothing in the leaflet then current to suggest that eligibility was also governed by other rules ... the leaflet was clearly misleading in this respect and the Principal Officer of D.E. has acknowledged that it should have provided a clearer definition of the term 'unemployed'."

In such a case the offending advice was directed towards sections of the community at large....

THE QUALITY OF OFFICIAL ADVICE

As members of the public have a prima facie right to advice concerning their personal queries about programmes being administered by departments, what is the quality of the advice they can expect from officials? The P.C.A. has invoked the adaptable concept of maladministration to condemn advice which he considers to be defective. Incorrect and misleading statements were the most common forms of defects found in the cases studied, 10 cases involving incorrect advice and eight misleading advice. Although the Commissioner has not provided specific definitions of these terms, we can gain an understanding of his usage by examining the substance of his criticisms in individual cases.

The P.C.A. equates the notion of "wholly wrong" with the term "incorrect" as a characteristic of defective advice. For example, after a complainant received a reduction in his social security benefits he queried the level of his new payments with the department. The local office replied that the change was caused by the fact that the department would now be paying his rent and rates directly to the local authority. Subsequently, it emerged that this was not the true position and his benefits had been reduced because his wife had become entitled to a pension in her own right. The P.C.A. noted, "it is clear from my investigation that ... the local office did inform the complainant quite specifically and *quite wrongly*, that from November 22 he would no longer have to pay rent and rates."[35]

[33] C712/86 (1987–1988) H.C. 103.
[34] C313/84 (1984–1985) H.C. 150.
[35] C701/84 (1985–1986) H.C. 536.

In contrast, the Commissioner uses the term "misleading" advice in relation to statements which are partially wrong, with the consequence that the citizen is unable to comprehend his true position. An example involved a case where a woman was receiving benefits from the DHSS including a higher long-term scale rate of supplementary benefit. The claimant asked the local office what her entitlements would be if she were to register for a training course and then later reclaim social security benefits. The office replied that her attendance on the course would have no effect on her future eligibility for supplementary benefit. Some months later, after completing the course, the woman reapplied for supplementary benefit, but was awarded only a lower rate payment, because the rules provided that where a person receiving a higher rate benefit stopped claiming the benefit for more than eight weeks they were subsequently entitled only to the lower rate. The P.C.A. considered that the office had given the complainant misleading advice and criticised them "for their failure to provide the complainant with a *full and correct* explanation of the consequences of her planned attendance on the TOPS course".[36]

"Inadequate" advice also results in citizens being incompletely informed of their true position. The P.C.A. found that the DHSS had provided a widow with inadequate advice about her eligibility for invalidity benefit by failing to warn her of the need to submit medical evidence regularly to the local office.[37] The difference between misleading and inadequate advice, therefore, appears to be that the former category contains statements which are partially erroneous whereas in the latter case the advice is correct but incomplete. ...

THE INJUSTICE SUFFERED THROUGH RELIANCE ON DEFECTIVE OFFICIAL ADVICE

According to section 5(1)(a) of the Parliamentary Commissioner Act 1967, the P.C.A. can investigate complaints only where, *inter alia*, the complainant claims to have "sustained injustice in consequence of maladministration". So if the P.C.A. is to uphold a citizen's complaint in regard to defective advice he must also find that he or she has sustained an injustice through relying or acting upon the advice. In contrast to the Local Ombudsman, the P.C.A. tends not to make an express finding of both maladministration and injustice, but instead concludes that he upholds the citizen's complaint. However, according to the substance of his reports in this context, the P.C.A. has generally equated injustice with a tangible and direct financial disadvantage experienced by the citizen relying upon the defective advice.

The most common form of financial disadvantage experienced by complainants was a loss of state benefits, which occurred in eight of the 34 cases. One example involved a woman who suffered from agoraphobia with the result that she could not use public transport.[38] The complainant asked the DHSS mobility allowance unit if she was entitled to any form of benefit to help pay the cost of taxi fares to work. The unit informed her that she was not entitled to mobility allowance and failed to provide her with a leaflet listing other available benefits as their internal procedures required. Eight months

---

[36] C665/84 (1984–1985) H.C. 590.
[37] C277/86 (1986–1987) H.C. 312.
[38] C141/86 (1987–1988) H.C. 41.

later the complainant was awarded one of these other benefits, the existence of which she had discovered from a magazine. The P.C.A. criticised the unit's failure and approved the payment of an *ex gratia* sum equivalent to the lost eight months' benefit. . . .

R.T.C. LIBRARY, LETTERKENNY

CONCLUSIONS

What then are the contours of the right to advice from departments of state as currently enforced by the P.C.A.? Provided citizens have complied with a series of preliminary obligations, including the full disclosure of relevant information and the seeking of advice at the earliest opportunity, they can legitimately expect answers to the overwhelming majority of queries concerning the application of departmental programmes to their personal circumstances. If the answers are incorrect, misleading or inadequate, the P.C.A. will characterise the department's conduct as amounting to maladministration. He will then determine whether the citizen has suffered a direct financial loss through acting or relying upon the defective advice. Where such a loss is established the P.C.A. will then treat the citizen as having sustained an injustice in consequence of maladministration. A suitable remedy will then be recommended by the P.C.A., in most cases involving the department in making a quantified *ex gratia* payment to the citizen to compensate for his or her loss.

The only significant weakness discovered in the P.C.A.'s response to advice complaints was the lack of clarity in his reports regarding the calculation of the level of financial loss suffered by citizens and the corresponding compensation required to alleviate the injustice. The inclusion of a more precise assessment of the extent of the pecuniary loss flowing from the defective advice would end any lingering suspicion that the P.C.A.'s calculations are based more on subjective inclination than objective evaluation. . . .

Despite persistent criticisms of the notion of "maladministration", the reports disclose that the indefinite nature of the concept has enabled the P.C.A. to develop and refine its application to cover virtually all forms of departmental advice concerning personal queries about collective consumption programmes. Furthermore, the success of the P.C.A. in securing redress for justified complaints (financial compensation was paid in 20 cases), means that despite his lack of formal coercive powers the P.C.A.'s findings in advice cases satisfy the minimum jurisprudential requirements of a right. As Stoljar explains, "you cannot have a right unless it can be claimed or demanded or insisted upon, indeed claimed effectively or enforceably".[39] The achievements of the Commissioner in relation to advice complaints certainly enable individuals effectively to insist upon the provision of accurate advice within the limits elucidated in this article.

Finally, we can assess the value of this right in the context of the continuing debate over freedom of information in the United Kingdom. Marsh observes that one justification put forward by proponents of a statutory right of access to government information is that the current position reflects:

"disequilibrium between the state with its command over a wide field of information and the private organisation or individual, from whom infor-

---

[39] S. Stoljar, *An Analysis of Rights* (1984), pp. 3–4.

mation of all kinds is demanded by the state, from which, however, information can only be obtained with difficulty, or not at all."[40]

Against this backdrop, the right to official advice has the potential to help redress that imbalance on the level of dealings between individuals and departments, because it can assist a citizen in discovering his or her position in relation to the administrative norms governing specific programmes. However, the right only extends to those activities which fall within the P.C.A.'s jurisdiction and it fails to provide a general right of access to governmental information for interested citizens (qua campaigners, journalists or academics) where they are not directly affected by a particular administrative scheme. Therefore, whilst the right is clearly not a substitute for a balanced Freedom of Information Act, it offers a modest ray of sunshine in an otherwise gloomy landscape of increasing official secrecy.

Notes

1. The right to advice is merely one of many administrative norms developed by the P.C.A. in his casework (*cf.* his principles governing the use of administrative guidance noted previously in Chap. 2 at p. 98). Professor Bradley has analysed this aspect of the P.C.A.'s work in the following terms:

"it was to be expected that 'arbitrary discretion' of the kind which the 1967 Act vested in the British Ombudsman should evolve into a more or less settled body of ascertainable principles which might even harden into rules.... Thus, inevitably, the British Ombudsman has developed principles, standards and rules of what he believes to constitute good administration, since otherwise no notion of maladministration could have emerged. As the process of investigation and report continues in every fresh case, so the individual complainant receives the benefit of the Ombudsman's enforcement of the rules and principles which have emerged from the previous case-work. And it may not be pressing this analysis too far to conclude that the individual citizen thus acquires what may properly be called new rights to the maintenance of a certain quality of administration."

"The Role of the Ombudsman in Relation to the Protection of Citizens' Rights" [1980] C.L.J. 304 at 310–311.

2. Because of the M.P. filter, the relationship between Members of the House of Commons and the Parliamentary Commissioner is crucial to the operation of the scheme. A major survey of M.P.s' attitudes towards the P.C.A., conducted in 1993, revealed that 16 per cent of respondents considered his work to be "very satisfactory" and 64 per cent described it as "quite successful". Furthermore, 52 per cent of respondents referred complaints to the P.C.A. "sometimes"; but, rather worryingly, 40 per cent of respondents "seldom" passed on such complaints. See "The Powers, Work and Jurisdiction of the Ombudsman", H.C. 33 (1993–1994).

3. A positive aspect of the P.C.A.'s relationship with the House of Commons has been the support given to him by the Select Committee on the P.C.A., created in 1967 to monitor his work. Professor Gregory, in a study of the early work of the Committee, discovered that it concentrated upon three tasks. First, seeking to ensure that remedies were provided for complainants where the P.C.A. upheld their claims against departments. If a department was unwilling to provide the redress suggested by the P.C.A., then the Select Committee would call the Permanent Secretary of the department to

[40] N.S. Marsh (ed.), *Public Access to Government Held Information* (1987), p. 4.

give evidence before the Committee explaining his department's actions. Secondly, to examine defects in administrative procedures discovered by the P.C.A. in the course of his investigations. And, thirdly, to keep under review the adequacy of the P.C.A.'s powers. Gregory concluded that the Committee had been most successful in performing the first function, because of parliamentary and media concerns with personal "human interest" matters: see R. Gregory, "The Select Committee on the P.C.A. 1967–80" [1982] P.L. 49. In recent times the Committee has continued to support the P.C.A. in the, rare, cases where executive bodies have refused to provide redress (*e.g.* the Channel tunnel rail-link cases noted above, p. 144). We have also seen how the Committee has continued to periodically review the powers and jurisdiction of the P.C.A. (above, p. 136). A new development in the work of the Committee has been its decision to undertake "thematic inquiries" into the matters raised during the course of the P.C.A.'s casework. The first such report was published on "Maladministration and Redress", H.C. 112 (1994–1995), and recommended, *inter alia*, criteria for the assessment of redress offered by executive bodies (*e.g.* the person who has suffered injustice as a consequence of maladministration should be put back in the same position as he/she would have been had things gone right in the first place).

(C) THE LOCAL GOVERNMENT OMBUDSMEN

(i) Constitutional and Jurisdictional Matters

Once again it was a report by JUSTICE[41] that advocated the creation of ombudsmen for local government. Because of the large number of local authorities and their responsibility for the provision of many direct services to the public, thereby increasing the likelihood of consumer complaints, it was not considered possible to appoint a single local ombudsman. Instead, the idea of several local commissioners was proposed. When local authorities in England and Wales were restructured during 1974, Parliament took the opportunity to create separate local ombudsman systems for these two parts of the United Kingdom. Northern Ireland's Parliament had already established a local ombudsman (the Commissioner for Complaints) and separate legislation[42] has instituted a Local Commissioner for Scotland.

Part III of the Local Government Act 1974 creates the Commission for Local Administration in England which currently has three full time Commissioners (commonly called the Local Government Ombudsmen). The Commissioners are appointed by the Queen on the advice of the Environment Secretary. Each Commissioner deals with complaints originating from different regions of England. Originally there was a "councillor filter" requirement for complainants, but since 1988[43] the Local Government Ombudsmen can receive complaints directly from members of the public. They may investigate complaints against a number of specified local bodies including, county councils, district councils and urban development corporations.[44] Much of their jurisdiction is modelled on the language of the Parliamentary Commissioner Act 1967. Hence, the Local Government Ombudsmen can investigate complaints that members of the public have "sustained injustice in consequence of maladministration" in connection with the performance of administrative functions by local authorities.[45] However, certain functions are excluded from the Local Government Ombudsmen's remit, *e.g.* contractual/commercial transactions and personnel matters.[46] Their

---

[41] *The Citizen and his Council* (1969).
[42] Local Government (Scotland) Act 1975, as amended by the Scottish Legal Services Ombudsman and Commissioner for Local Administration in Scotland Act 1997.
[43] Local Government Act 1988.
[44] 1974 Act, s.25.
[45] *ibid.*, s.26(1).
[46] *ibid.*, Sched. 5.

investigations are to be conducted in private and have the backing of the High Court's powers of contempt.[47] When a Local Government Ombudsman has conducted an investigation he or she must send copies of his or her report to, *inter alios*, the complainant and the local authority. As with the Parliamentary Commissioner, the Local Government Ombudsmen have no power to compel the provision of redress by local authorities where they uphold a complaint.

Notes

1. On several occasions, notably in 1978, 1980 and 1984, the English Local Government Ombudsmen formally reviewed their existing jurisdiction. After each review they sought to have their remit extended, but with little support from local authorities or the Environment Secretary. Before the Widdicombe Committee examining "The Conduct of Local Government Business", the Local Government Ombudsmen renewed their jurisdictional pleas—in particular for:

(1) direct access by complainants;
(2) contractual/commercial transactions and personnel matters to be open to investigation;
(3) the Local Ombudsmen to be given the power to investigate on their own motion without receiving a specific complaint from a member of the public.

The Committee favoured direct access to the Local Government Ombudsmen because:

"... we believe it is wrong in principle that complainants should be expected to direct their complaints against a council through a member of the executive decision making body for that council".[48]

The Local Government Ombudsmen's desire to investigate commercial transactions was also endorsed:

"we have not been convinced that cases involving commercial and contractual transactions with members of the public are different in kind from cases involving other local authority dealings with the public and that they should therefore as a matter of general principle be excluded from the ombudsman's remit."[49]

But the Committee was only willing to recommend that complaints about appointment procedures used by councils should be within the Ombudsmen's jurisdiction, not general personnel matters. This was due to the Committee's belief that "... the primary function of the ombudsmen is in our view to provide support for the consumers of local government services rather than for those who are employed to provide them".[50] The Committee approved a modified power for the Local Government Ombudsmen to initiate investigations, provided they were based upon "good grounds for concern" and directed towards individual injustice.[51]

As indicated above, the Government accepted the desirability of direct public access to the Local Government Ombudsmen and this was enacted in 1988. However, the other proposed changes to the Ombudsmen's jurisdiction were not so well received. Regarding commercial transactions the Government felt:

[47] *ibid.*, ss.28–29.
[48] *The Conduct of Local Government Business*, Cmnd. 9797 (1986), para. 9.64.
[49] *ibid.*, para. 9.73.
[50] *ibid.*, para. 9.72.
[51] *ibid.*, para. 9.76.

"Ombudsmen—central and local—are concerned with the inter-action between the executive arm of government and the general public. Actions taken by public bodies in buying and selling goods and services are fundamentally different. The law already provides various safeguards and remedies for the parties involved in such commercial transactions, and there is no case for providing further protection through the local Ombudsman...."[52]

For the same underlying reason the Government did not accept that personnel complaints were appropriate for Local Government Ombudsmen. The idea of self-initiated action by the Ombudsmen was rejected, because the Government felt that it could result in the Ombudsmen losing goodwill if they were perceived as general purpose watchdogs. Instead the Government proposed that the Ombudsmen be given a new power to publish general guidance to local authorities on good administrative practice. This has now been enacted in section 23 of the Local Government and Housing Act 1989.

2. In June 1995, the Environment Secretary announced that a comprehensive review of the work of the Local Ombudsmen would be undertaken by Sir Geoffrey Chipperfield. The first stage of the review would consider, *inter alia*, whether the functions of the Local Ombudsmen were necessary. The full terms of reference of the review can be found in Appendix 6 of the *Local Government Ombudsman: Annual Report 1994/95*.

Sir Geoffrey concluded that the Local Ombudsmen would not be able to handle effectively the increasing number of complaints that he foresaw citizens making. Therefore, he recommended that each local authority should be under a statutory duty to operate its own complaints system (involving both internal and external adjudicators). The role of the Local Ombudsmen would be to monitor these local complaints procedures, but not to investigate individual complaints.

The Local Ombudsmen were concerned that, under Sir Geoffrey's recommendations, the persons investigating citizens' complaints against local government would not be independent of those authorities and that complainants challenging local government would be treated differently from those having access to the Parliamentary Commissioner and Health Service Commissioner. The local authority associations and the National Association of Citizens' Advice Bureaux were also opposed to Sir Geoffrey's proposals.

After considering the Chipperfield report and associated representations, the Government concluded that:

"We recognise the importance of all local authorities having their own effective local complaints systems, although we are not persuaded of the need to seek legislation imposing a new statutory duty on local authorities to establish and maintain such systems. Nor do we believe that the case has been made that there is at present no continued need for the [Local Ombudsmen's] role as a wholly independent body to investigate complaints of maladministration" (*per* Mr David Curry: Minister of State at the Department of the Environment, H.C.Deb., Vol. 271, col. 402 (February 12, 1996)).

Therefore, the Department initiated the second stage of the review, to be undertaken by a senior official (Andrew Whetnall), which involved examining the efficiency and effectiveness of the Local Ombudsmen's procedures. That review was concluded in August 1996 and subsequently published (*Report of the Financial Management and Policy Review of the Commission for Local Administration in England: DoE, November 1996*). It recommended, *inter alia*, that the Local Ombudsmen be brought within

---

[52] *The Government's Response to the Report of the Widdicombe Committee of Inquiry*, Cm. 433 (1988), para. 6.27.

the jurisdiction of the Select Committee on the Parliamentary Commissioner for Administration (so that the Committee could consider matters of policy, administration and resources concerning the Local Ombudsmen, but not the investigation of individual complaints), and that the relationship between the Local Ombudsmen and the courts should develop in the light of Lord Woolf's report (*Access to Justice: Final Report to the Lord Chancellor on the Civil Justice System in England and Wales: July 1996*). The Government's response was given on November 28, 1996, by Mr Curry:

> "On the issues raised by the Review's First Stage, we have concluded that there needs to be a wholly independent body—an Ombudsman—to which citizens who are aggrieved in their dealings with public bodies can turn, if there is to be a guarantee that complaints of maladministration will be fully and equitably investigated. Accordingly, we confirm our earlier provisional view ... that the [Local Ombudsmen's] principal role should continue to be as a wholly independent, investigatory body for complaints of maladministration relating to local government in England. ... The Review's Second Stage concludes that the cost of the [Local Ombudsmen] is a fraction of the cost of resolving a similar number of complaints through legal processes, and makes a range of recommendations for performance improvements covering issues of accountability, jurisdiction, powers, management systems and financial accountability, and quality of service. We believe that overall these recommendations provide a package of measures for significantly modernising and improving the Local Government Ombudsman service in England, and we intend to take them forward. ...."

The Government does not have any current plans to extend the jurisdiction of the Select Committee on the P.C.A. to encompass the Local Ombudsmen. However, it will seek to obtain legislation allowing the appointment of Advisory Commissioners (representing the interests of local authorities and complainants, etc.) who will be able to "introduce a more independent contribution to the [Local Ombudsmen's] thinking". Also, the Government intends to postpone consideration of the relationship between the Local Ombudsmen and the courts for the time being, because other aspects of Lord Woolf's report have been given priority (*e.g.* the creation of unified Rules of Court): *Government Response to the Financial Management and Policy Review of the Commission for Local Administration in England: DoE, November 1996*).

(ii) The Courts and the Local Government Ombudsmen

R. v. LOCAL COMMISSIONER FOR ADMINISTRATION FOR THE SOUTH, ex p. EASTLEIGH B.C.

[1988] 1 Q.B. 855; [1988] 3 All E.R. 151 (Court of Appeal)

A householder complained to the Local Government Ombudsman, for his area of England, that Eastleigh B.C. had failed properly to inspect the construction of a defective sewer connected to his house as required by the Building Regulations 1976. The Local Ombudsman produced a report (extracts of which appear in the judgment below) in which he stated that the Council had not inspected the sewer at all the relevant stages of its construction and consequently the sewer had not been thoroughly inspected. He went on to find that the householder had sustained injustice as a consequence of the Council's maladministration, but that even if the final inspection of the sewer had been carried out properly he could not be certain that the defect would have been discovered. Therefore, the Ombudsman recommended that Eastleigh B.C. pay only a part of the costs of remedial work.

The Council sought judicial review of the Local Ombudsman's report on the grounds that (1) it was contrary to section 34(3) of the Local Government Act 1974, in that the Ombudsman had questioned a discretionary decision taken without maladministration by the council and (2) it was also contrary to section 26(1) of the 1974 Act, in that the Ombudsman had made a report when it was not certain that the householder had suffered injustice in consequence of an act of maladministration by Eastleigh B.C. In the High Court Nolan J. upheld the Council's submissions, but refused to grant them a declaration. The Council appealed against the refusal of a remedy and the Local Government Ombudsman cross-appealed against the findings of *ultra vires*.

LORD DONALDSON OF LYMINGTON M.R.: ... The ombudsman's conclusions are stated in paragraphs 30 and 31 of his report:

"30. In my view good administration dictates that the council should carry out an inspection under the Building Regulations in respect of all stage inspections for which they have received notice from the owner or builder as the case may be. Where inspections have not been made at a particular stage I consider that special attention should be given on the final inspection to remedy the omission. In the case of drains it is a relatively easy matter to carry out a full test, such as a ball test or its equivalent, at the final inspection stage and I consider that a council have a duty to ensure that this is done because a final inspection should mean that, so far as the council are concerned, they have with reasonable diligence and expenditure of officer time found no defect under the Building Regulations. I am satisfied that in this case the private foul sewer in question was not fully or thoroughly inspected. The defects in piping discovered as a result of the soil and vent pipe test should have alerted officers to the possibility of other defects in the pipe work.

31. I find, therefore, that the complainant has sustained injustice as a result of the council's maladministration. However, I cannot say, categorically, whether had the council carried out the final inspection in accordance with the dictates of good administration, the trouble at the centre of this complaint would not have arisen. Equally, I have taken account of the argument that with synthetic piping of the sort employed in this case soil compaction can cause undulation at a later date. I have also considered the fact that the original fault was the builder's and that that (and the council's fault) occurred some years ago. On the other hand the final inspection was, in my view, incomplete and the council could have become aware of the problem at an early stage because of the difficulties experienced by the owner of house 3. Having considered these factors I feel on balance it would be inequitable to ask the council to defray the whole cost of the necessary remedial work. Accordingly, upon the residents' agreement to pay a proportion of the reasonable cost, I consider that the council themselves should take the action which the Assistant Director of Technical Services commended to the residents (see paragraph 29, above)."

The action referred to in paragraph 29 consisted of exposing that part of the sewer which lay between two manholes and adjusting the pipe work to eliminate the undulation.

The ombudsman's cross-appeal

Section 34(3)

This subsection is in the following terms:

"It is hereby declared that nothing in this Part of this Act authorises or requires a Local Commissioner to question the merits of a decision taken without maladministration by an authority in the exercise of a discretion vested in that authority."

"Maladministration" is not defined in the Act, but its meaning was considered in *R. v. Local Commissioner for Administration for the North and East Area of England, ex p. Bradford Metropolitan City Council* [1979] Q.B. 287. All three judges (Lord Denning M.R., at 311, Eveleigh L.J., at 314, and Sir David Cairns, at 319) expressed themselves differently, but in substance each was saying the same thing, namely, that administration and maladministration in the context of the work of a local authority is concerned with the *manner* in which decisions by the authority are reached and the *manner* in which they are or are not implemented. Administration and maladministration have nothing to do with the nature, quality or reasonableness of the decision itself.

The key to this part of the cross-appeal lies in identifying the policy decision of the council in relation to the inspection of drains. This was, as I have stated, to inspect at four of the more important of nine stages in construction. It did not condescend to the nature of the inspections. . . .

Nolan J. read paragraph 30 of the ombudsman's report, which I have set out in full, as questioning the merits of that policy. I do not so read it. I can best illustrate my understanding of that paragraph by adding words which render explicit what, in my judgment, is implicit:

"In my view good administration dictates that the council should carry out an inspection under the Building Regulations in respect of all stage inspections for which they have received notice from the owner or builder as the case may be. [However I recognise that, on the authority of *Anns'* case [1978] A.C. 728 to which I have referred at length earlier in this report, it was open to the council in the exercise of their discretion and taking account of the competing claims of efficiency and thrift to decide to inspect on fewer occasions. This the council has done and I accept its decisions. That said] Where inspections have not been made at a particular stage I consider that special attention should be given on the final inspection to remedying the omission. [In saying this I am not calling for an expenditure of time and effort which would nullify the council's discretionary decision on the resources to be devoted to building regulation inspections.] In the case of drains it is a relatively easy matter to carry out a full test, such as a ball test or its equivalent, at the final inspection stage. . . . [The choice of test must be a matter for the council's officers and I would not criticise them for not using the ball test, if they had used some equivalent test. However an air pressure test, such as the council's officers used, is not such an equivalent, because it only reveals whether or not the sewer is watertight. It tells the inspector nothing about its gradient or its ability to self-clear and efficiently carry away matter discharged into it as required by regulation N10.] I consider that [this is of considerable importance and that] a council have a duty to ensure that this is done because a final inspection [if the council decide to make one, as this council did] should mean that, so far as the council are concerned, they have with reasonable diligence and expenditure of officer time found no defect under the Building Regulations. I am satisfied that in this case the private foul sewer in question was not fully or thoroughly inspected [in terms of the council's own 1977 policy. Even if in other circumstances a lesser inspection might have been justified in terms of that policy] the defects in piping discovered as a result of the soil and vent pipe tests should have alerted officers to the possibility of other defects in the pipe work."

So read, and I do so read it, paragraph 30 loyally accepts the council's discretionary decision on the inspection of drains. It simply criticises the way in which that decision was implemented. I do not, therefore, think that this complaint by the council is made out.

Section 26(1)

This subsection is in the following terms:

"Subject to the provisions of this Part of this Act where a written complaint is made by or on behalf of a member of the public who claims to have sustained injustice in consequence of maladministration in connection with action taken by or on behalf of an authority to which this Part of this Act applies, being action taken in the exercise of administrative functions of that authority, a Local Commissioner may investigate that complaint."

... [I]t does mean that he cannot report adversely upon an authority unless his investigation reveals not only maladministration, but injustice to the complainant sustained as a consequence of that maladministration.

The mischief at which this subsection is directed is not difficult to detect. Every local authority has living within its boundaries a small cadre of citizens who would like nothing better than to spend their spare time complaining of maladministration. The subsection limits the extent to which they can involve the ombudsman by requiring, as a condition precedent to his involvement, that the complainant shall personally have been adversely affected by the alleged maladministration. If he was not so affected, he did not himself suffer injustice. If he was, he did. ...

Like Nolan J., I am loath to criticise a busy Local Commissioner on merely semantic grounds, but I think that he laid himself open to criticism by finding maladministration in paragraph 30 and then proceeding, without any explanation, to his conclusion of consequential injustice. ...

... [I]n the end I have come to the conclusion that the ombudsman was intending to say that, whilst there could be no absolute certainty that a proper inspection would have revealed the defects and it was a possibility that the undulation occurred after the date of the inspection, on the balance of probabilities he was satisfied that the defects were present at the time of the inspection, that a proper inspection would have revealed them and that he was therefore satisfied that the complainant had suffered injustice in consequence of the maladministration.

An ombudsman's report is neither a statute nor a judgment. It is a report to the council and to the ratepayers of the area. It has to be written in everyday language and convey a message. This report has been subjected to a microscopic and somewhat legalistic analysis which it was not intended to undergo. Valid criticisms have been made, particularly of paragraph 31, but in my judgment they go to form rather than substance and, notwithstanding occasional dicta to the contrary, judicial review is concerned with substance. I would therefore allow the ombudsman's cross-appeal.

The council's appeal

As Parker and Taylor L.JJ. are minded to dismiss the ombudsman's appeal, it is necessary to consider the council's appeal. I would allow it.

Nolan J. considered that there was no need for any declaration that the ombudsman had exceeded his remit by contravening the limits upon his jurisdiction set by section 34(3). He said that this was a free country and that there was nothing to prevent the council responding to the report with equal publicity. He concluded by saying that, since Parliament had not thought it necessary to create a right of appeal against the findings in the Local Commissioner's report, and in the absence of impropriety, it seemed to him that the courts ought not to provide the equivalent of such a right by judicial review.

I have to say that I profoundly disagree with this approach. Let me start with the fact that Parliament has not created a right of appeal against the findings in a Local Commissioner's report. It is this very fact, coupled with the public law character of the ombudsman's office and powers, which is the foundation of the right to relief by way of judicial review.

Next there is the suggestion that the council should issue a statement disputing the right of the ombudsman to make his findings and that this would provide the council with an adequate remedy. Such an action would wholly undermine the system of ombudsman's reports and would, in effect, provide for an appeal to the media against his findings. The Parliamentary intention was that reports by ombudsmen should be loyally accepted by the local authorities concerned. This is clear from section 30(4) and (5), which require the local authority to make the report available for inspection by the public and to advertise this fact, from section 31(1), which requires the local authority to notify the ombudsman of the action which it has taken and proposes to take in the light of his report and from section 31(2), which entitles the ombudsman to make a further report if the local authority's response is not satisfactory.

Whilst I am very far from encouraging councils to seek judicial review of an ombudsman's report, which, bearing in mind the nature of his office and duties and the qualifications of those who hold that office, is inherently unlikely to succeed, in the absence of a successful application for judicial review and the giving of relief by the court, local authorities should not dispute an ombudsman's report and should carry out their statutory duties in relation to it.

If Nolan J. thought that the publication of his judgment in favour of the council was itself an adequate remedy, he did not say so, and, in any event, I think that he would have been mistaken, because this by itself does not relieve the council of its obligations to respond to the report in accordance with section 31(1) and, assuming that the report should never have been made, it is wrong that the council should be expected to respond.

I would grant a declaration in terms which reflect the decision of this court on the ombudsman's appeal against the decision of Nolan J.

PARKER L.J.: ... On a fair reading of the whole of paragraph 30 it appears to me that the ombudsman is not concluding that there was maladministration because there was no inspection at all nine stages, but merely that the inspections of the sewer which were called for by the policy of inspecting at the four most important stages were not fully or thoroughly carried out. This conclusion was not dependent upon the view expressed in the opening sentence and indeed it could not have been because the policy did call for drain inspections, indeed two drain inspections....

I conclude therefore that the ombudsman's conclusion in paragraph 30 was valid, but if the council felt it necessary to seek some declaratory relief with regard to the opening words of the paragraph I would be prepared to consider granting it.

I turn to the second question raised on the cross-appeal, namely, whether the conclusion that the complainant had suffered injustice as a result of the maladministration can be sustained. This depends upon paragraph 31 of the report. Had the ombudsman stopped at the first sentence, I should have had no doubt that the decision was sustainable. It seems to me abundantly clear that the complainant had suffered injustice if the failure to inspect properly led to the subsequent expenditure and the ombudsman could in my view easily have determined that it had. It is submitted however that, having stated his conclusion in the opening sentence, he proceeds to negate it and that the paragraph read as a whole really amounts to this: "I cannot say whether the failure to inspect led to the expenditure, but as the council were at fault it would be fair that they should contribute to the cost of remedial measures." For the ombudsman it is submitted that this is not so and that on a fair reading the paragraph says no more than: "I cannot be absolutely sure, but on the balance of probabilities I conclude...."

I regret to say that, unlike Lord Donaldson M.R. I cannot accept this construction. It appears to me that to do so involves applying legal concepts of differing standards of proof in order to uphold a paragraph which, like its predecessor, must be broadly considered. I have, despite its opening words, been able, by a broad reading and the correctness of the ombudsman's directions to himself on the law, to uphold the conclusion in paragraph 30. In the case of paragraph 31 I am unable to do so.

I would therefore dismiss the cross-appeal and allow the appeal.

TAYLOR L.J.: ... The crucial issue therefore is whether the ombudsman's findings in both paragraphs 30 and 31 of his report can be upheld and his cross-appeal thus allowed. I agree with Nolan J. that both paragraphs contain findings which cannot be justified.

[Regarding paragraph 30.] In my judgment its tenor shows the ombudsman to be trespassing into the field of discretion by laying down what policy as to inspections the dictates of good administration require, and what tests the council ought to ensure are carried out. That is quite different from finding that a test specifically required by the council's policy has not been carried out or has been carried out inefficiently. I therefore agree with Nolan J. that the ombudsman was in breach of section 34(3) of the Local Government Act 1974 in his conclusion that maladministration was established.

As to paragraph 31, I agree with Parker L.J. Only by straining the language used by the ombudsman and attributing to him speculatively considerations as to the burden of proof, could one render his finding on causation sound. I do not think such straining and speculation is justified.

Accordingly I conclude that in respect of both paragraphs 30 and 31 of the report, Nolan J. reached the correct conclusions. I would therefore dismiss the cross-appeal and allow the council's appeal.

Notes

1. M. Jones comments: "in *Eastleigh*, the court's interpretation of s.34(3) affirms the orthodox view, and the legislature's intent, that the Commissioners ought not to usurp the policy-making discretions of democratically elected local authorities; ... [nevertheless] the local ombudsmen may continue to find maladministration in the processes by which discretionary decisions are made upon grounds which closely resemble the *Wednesbury* principles of review employed by the courts—relevancy, proper purposes and so on. And there may still be room for a finding of maladministration where a Commissioner considers that the terms of an authority's policy transcend to the bounds of reasonableness, and step into perversity, capriciousness, or what the courts now term 'irrationality' " ("The Local Ombudsman and Judicial Review" [1988] P.L. 608 at 615–616.)

Whilst, on the issue of whether the Local Government Ombudsman had found that the complainant's injustice was caused by the Council's maladministration, Mowbray observed:

> "the division of opinion on this question by the Court of Appeal again clearly reflected the differing judicial attitudes towards the margin of appreciation to be accorded to the Local Ombudsman in performing his functions. Lord Donaldson was willing to allow the Ombudsman a wide latitude of freedom because, in his opinion, the Ombudsman was not required to produce the kind of reasoned decision expected of a superior court of law. But the majority were unwilling to make similar allowances when scrutinising the Ombudsman's logic. Therefore, if the Local Ombudsman is to avoid such criticisms in the future his reports will have to adopt a more precise and definitive form of reasoning." ("Maladministration and the Local Ombudsmen" (1988) S.J. 1442 at 1444.)

2. Despite the above opinion of Lord Donaldson that an action for judicial review of a Local Government Ombudsman's report "is inherently unlikely to succeed", the High Court found that a report made in 1986 by the Chairman of the English Commission for Local Administration was *ultra vires*. In *R. v. Commissioner for Local Administration, ex p. Croydon L.B.C.* [1989] 1 All E.R. 1033, the Local Government Ombudsman had investigated a complaint by parents about the way in which an education appeal committee, established by the council, had rejected their appeal regarding which school their daughter should attend. The Ombudsman concluded that the committee had been guilty of maladministration by giving undue weight to council policy concerning school admissions. In response, the council sought judicial review of the report arguing, *inter alia*, that the Ombudsman should not have investigated this

complaint as the parents had a remedy before a court of law (section 26(6) of the Local Government Act 1974 provides: "A Local Commissioner shall not conduct an investigation ... in respect of the following matters, ... (c) any action in respect of which the person aggrieved has or had a remedy by way of proceedings in any court of law: Provided that a Local Commissioner may conduct an investigation notwithstanding the existence of such a right or remedy if satisfied that in the particular circumstances it is not reasonable to expect the person aggrieved to resort or have resorted to it...").

In the judgment of Woolf L.J., the Ombudsman must consider whether the complainant comes within section 26(6) both before and during the course of an investigation. Furthermore, the High Court stressed its predominant role in the scrutiny of tribunals:

"the Commissioner should also have well in mind, even when the holder of the office is a distinguished lawyer as in the case here, that his expertise is not the same as that of a court of law. Issues whether an administrative tribunal has properly understood the relevant law and the legal obligations which it is under when conducting an inquiry are more appropriate for resolution by the High Court than by a Commissioner, however eminent" (at 1045).

The Court went on to conclude that there was no foundation for the Ombudsman's finding of maladministration.

Writing extra-judicially, Sir Harry Woolf (now Lord Woolf M.R.) has suggested that the Ombudsman (whether central or local) should have an express power to refer an issue to the court, whether before, during or after an investigation, "either because there is a point of law of significance involved or because the courts are in a better situation to provide a remedy than he is" (*Protection of the Public—A New Challenge* (1990), pp. 90–91). This would "make the best of both systems available to the public" (*ibid.*).

3. The willingness of some local authorities to seek judicial review of the Local Commissioners' reports (which can be contrasted with the absence of such litigation by central government bodies against the Parliamentary Commissioner) indicates that the relationship between councils and Local Government Ombudsmen is not always harmonious. A continuing example of this discord is the fact that in about 6 per cent of cases (by 1995–1996) where the Ombudsmen find a local authority guilty of maladministration causing injustice the authority fails to provide a remedy that is acceptable to the Ombudsmen. Consequently, the Local Government Ombudsmen argued before the Widdicombe Committee that, as in Northern Ireland, where a local authority failed to provide a suitable remedy the complainant should have the right to go to the County/Sheriff Court for a binding judicial order of compensation or remedial action. The Committee endorsed this method of strengthening the remedial powers of the Local Government Ombudsmen (Report, para. 9.69).

At about the same time, the Select Committee on the P.C.A. proposed an alternative system for dealing with recalcitrant local authorities, that involved the Select Committee extending its remit to encompass such bodies. The Select Committee suggested that where a council failed to provide a suitable remedy then the leaders of the council could be called to give evidence before the Committee which, as we have already noted, is how reluctant Departments are dealt with. (*Local Government Cases: Enforcement of Remedies*, H.C. 448 (1985–1986)).

The Government accepted that non-compliance was a problem, "although a rate of compliance of 95 per cent might in other circumstances be considered good for a voluntary system, it is the other 5 per cent of 'failures' which not unnaturally attract attention. There is no doubt that these cases serve to produce a particularly marked sense of grievance on the part of the complainants, as well as undermining the credibility of the Local Ombudsman system as a whole."[53] However, the Government rejected the solution of judicial enforcement because "... local authorities might be less willing to co-operate, and investigations would become increasingly formalised, lengthy, legalistic and costly. Complainants might find the process more intimidating and flexibility would be lost."[54] Moreover, the Select Committee's idea was also dismissed:

> "although this has its attractions in that it builds on the existing voluntary principle, it is unlikely to be readily acceptable to local government who do not see themselves as accountable to Parliament—though recognising that they operate within a statutory framework laid down by Parliament."[55]

Instead it was decided to increase the local pressure on councils to comply with Ombudsmen's reports. This approach has now been enacted in Part II of the Local Government and Housing Act 1989. Where a report finding injustice in consequence of maladministration has been made the relevant local authority must consider the report and notify the Local Government Ombudsman of the action they have taken within three months. If the authority does not notify the Ombudsman, or he is not satisfied with the action taken, he may issue a second report. Again, the authority must consider and notify the Ombudsman of its action regarding the second report. If the Ombudsman is still not satisfied with the authority's conduct he may publish an account of his recommendations in two editions of a local newspaper. This lengthy process is clearly less forceful than the Local Government Ombudsmen's desire for judicial enforcement of their reports.

By 1996 the Local Ombudsmen had required the publication of 69 statements in local newspapers where a satisfactory remedy had not been provided. The futility of this process has been noted by the Local Ombudsmen when they commented that the newspaper statements "... often costs the council considerably more than the sum the Ombudsman had recommended should be paid in compensation to the complainant in the first place" (Annual Report 1992/1993, p. 8.).

During 1995–1996 the Local Ombudsmen undertook research into the reasons why local authorities failed to provide the recommended remedies. The major explanation was that the local authority concerned disagreed with the Local Ombudsman's finding of maladministration. The second reason was that authorities disputed the Ombudsmen's findings that complainants had suffered injustice. Consequently, the Ombudsmen have introduced a number of measures to encourage greater compliance with their recommendations. These include: (1) explaining the nature of maladministration and the reasoning behind individual findings of its existence; (2) giving authorities advance notice of potential criticisms which may be included in a final report and (3) publishing guidance on how the Ombudsmen assess remedies (Annual Report 1995–1996, p. 4). Time will show if this strategy is successful in reducing the rate of non-compliance.

---

[53] *The Government's Response to the Report of the Widdicombe Committee of Inquiry*, para. 6.21.
[54] *ibid.*, para. 6.22.
[55] *ibid.*, para. 6.23.

(iii) The Work of the Local Ombudsmen

THE LOCAL OMBUDSMEN: ANNUAL REPORT 1995–1996

Chapter 7

Complaints Received by Category 1995/1996

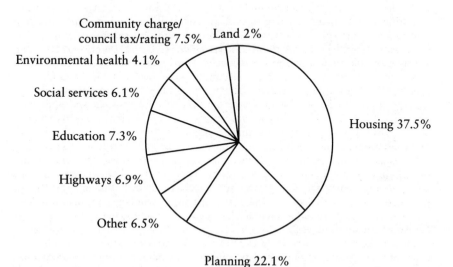

Community charge/council tax/rating 7.5%

Land 2%

Environmental health 4.1%

Social services 6.1%

Education 7.3%

Highways 6.9%

Other 6.5%

Housing 37.5%

Planning 22.1%

Analysis of Outcome of Complaints 1995/1996

	Number of complaints	Percentage of total (excluding premature complaints and those outside jurisdiction)
Local settlements	2,552	22.1%
Maladministration causing injustice	410	3.5%
Maladministration, no injustice	76	0.7%
No maladministration, or no or insufficient injustice	8,534	73.7%
Premature complaints	2,759	
Outside jurisdiction	2,013	
Total	16,344	

Notes

1. In 1995–1996 it took the Local Ombudsmen on average 71.6 weeks to reach a decision on a complaint that was fully investigated (as opposed to being settled via a local agreement or being rejected for being outside the Ombudsmen's jurisdiction). In the same year the average cost, for the Local Ombudsmen, per complaint was £395.

2. A survey undertaken for the Local Ombudsmen in 1995–1996 revealed that 59 per cent of social groups A, B and C1 were aware of this complaints service. However, only 32 per cent of "non-white" ethnic minority groups had such an awareness. The Ombudsmen are concerned that awareness is not higher, but recognise that action to redress this problem would create more complaints and therefore necessitate more resources. Consequently, this is another matter for consideration during the current review of the future of the Local Ombudsmen service (*Annual Report 1995–96*, p. 7).

3. After a major empirical study, Professor N. Lewis and his colleagues reported that, "the impact of the Local Ombudsman upon local government has been impressive, both in relation to securing redress for complainants and in improving procedures" (Report, p. 59) They were impressed with the general quality of the investigations conducted by the Ombudsmen. However, despite the efforts of the Ombudsmen, public awareness about the Local Commissioners was low (a survey indicated that only 38 per cent of the electorate were aware of the Ombudsmen's existence). The researchers were critical of the concept of "maladministration"; "the interpretation afforded to maladministration has been inconsistent and unpredictable" (Report, p. 228) They, consequently, suggested empowering the Local Ombudsmen to investigate "a matter relating to administration" with the objective of discovering if it complied with statutory codes of good administrative practice. Also these commentators recommended the abolition of the Representative Body (comprised wholly of local authority nominees) to whom the Local Ombudsmen historically reported. They felt that it was too executive-minded. Instead, the Report proposed a new body with a wider membership, including consumer interests (N. Lewis, M. Seneviratne, S. Cracknell, *Complaints Procedures in Local Government* (University of Sheffield, 1987)).

4. In another study, C. Crawford and B. Thompson concluded that it was difficult to determine the specific reasoning and principles behind many reports of the Local Ombudsmen: *Decisions of Local Ombudsmen* (Dept of the Environment/Scottish and Welsh Offices, 1987, unpublished). Does this finding support the stance taken by the local authority in the *Eastleigh* case, above?

5. Crawford has advocated the creation of a new institution ("the Commission for Local Administration") to whom the Local Ombudsmen would be responsible. The Commission would have a broad composition, including local authorities' representatives (but not a dominant number), private sector groups, legal and other professional associations, and lay bodies. Amongst the proposed functions of the Commission would be:

(1) enforcement of the Ombudsmen's reports by means of second opinions;
(2) administrative audit through the issuing of codes of guidance on administrative behaviour;
(3) keeping under review the jurisdiction and casework of the Local Ombudsmen.

He believes that the creation of such an institution would help to secure the provision of an integrated complaints system for local government (C. Crawford, "Complaints, Codes, and Ombudsmen in Local Government" [1988] P.L. 246).

6. Parliament has now abolished the Representative Bodies for England and Wales (Local Government and Housing Act 1989, s.25). From 1989 onwards the English and Welsh Local Government Ombudsmen must submit their annual reports to persons who represent local authorities (*e.g.* organisations such as the Association of District Councils). The funding of the Local Government Ombudsmen has been transferred to central government (1989 Act, s.24). Also they may have advisers appointed as fellow members of their respective Commissions (1989 Act, s.22).

(D) PRIVATE SECTOR OMBUDSMEN

The financial services industry has taken the lead in the creation of ombudsmen to resolve disputes between consumers and commercial organisations. In 1980 three insurance companies agreed to create a voluntary ombudsman scheme for this industry and their innovative arrangements were later developed by the banking and building society industries. The insurance scheme has no statutory basis and, therefore, utilises the legal concept of a private unlimited company. A Board of Directors (dominated by representatives of the insurance industry) is responsible for the financing of the scheme, whilst a lay-dominated Council appoints the Insurance Ombudsman and receives his annual report. The Insurance Ombudsman is an independent person who can investigate specified consumer complaints against member companies. Where he upholds the complaint he can make a binding award of up to £100,000 against the member company. Five years later the major high street banks decided to follow the example of the insurance industry. The Banking Ombudsman scheme is broadly similar, though banks can remove individual complaints from the Ombudsman's remit where novel points of law are involved. Subsequently, Parliament passed the Building Societies Act 1986, which provided the impetus for the establishment of a Building Societies Ombudsman whose jurisdiction is based upon the requirements laid down in this Act.

The above ombudsmen have maintained close links and adopted a common conception of their role as impartial decision-makers. They tend to use similar techniques of investigation (notably the reliance on documentary evidence and the utilisation of experts to resolve questions of fact). Complainants were successful in 20–30 per cent of the cases which were subject to formal reports by the various ombudsmen. Although these figures may appear low when compared with the public sector ombudsmen, they can be explained by the need for complainants to have exhausted internal redress before raising the matter with the private sector ombudsmen and the latter's attempts to achieve conciliated settlements.

Criticisms of the banking scheme have been made by the Jack Committee on Banking Services.[56] The Committee were particularly concerned about the apparent influence of the Board of Directors over the terms of reference of the Banking Ombudsman and the failure of some smaller banks to join the scheme. One structural reform might be the integration of the Banking and Building Societies Ombudsmen into one combined Commission (analogous to the Commission for Local Administration in England) dealing with complaints against both of these industries now that many of their services are similar.

Overall, the above financial services ombudsmen have evolved without many express references to the heritage of the public sector ombudsmen. But their original methods of investigation may be of relevance to the public sector ombudsmen (especially the P.C.A.) in developing a range of efficient techniques adapted to different types of complaints. See further, A.R. Mowbray, "Ombudsmen: The Private Sector Dimension" in Finnie, Himsworth and Walker (eds.), *Edinburgh Essays in Public Law* (1991); R. James, "The Building Societies Ombudsman Scheme" (1992) 11 C.J.Q. 157; R.W. Hodges, "Ombudsman and other Complaints Procedures in the Financial Services Sector in the U.K." (1992) 21 Anglo-Am.L.R. 1; A. McGee, *The Financial Services Ombudsmen* (1992); P. Rawlings and C. Willett, Ombudsmen Schemes in the United Kingdom's Financial Sector" (1994) 17 *Journal of Consumer Policy* 307; and P.E. Morris, "The Investment Ombudsman—A Critical Review" [1996] J.B.L. 1.

In 1993 a voluntary organisation, the United Kingdom Ombudsman Association, was created to enable public and private sector ombudsmen (together with other interested persons, *e.g.* academics) to share their experiences, to promote best practices, to

---

[56] *Banking Services: Law and Practice*, Cm. 622 (1989).

define the criteria for using the term "ombudsman" and to accord public recognition to those ombudsmen schemes which met the defined criteria ((1) independence of the ombudsmen from the organisations over which they have jurisdiction, (2) effectiveness, (3) fairness and (4) public accountability). Subsequently, the Association was broadened to cover ombudsmen working in Ireland and renamed the British and Irish Ombudsman Association. The Association has, *inter alia*, held conferences to discuss matters affecting ombudsmen, made representations to Government and the European Union, and drafted recommendations for best practice on topics such as the consistency of ombudsmen's decisions and conflicts of interest affecting ombudsmen. By 1995 there were 22 different ombudsmen schemes recognised by the Association. Private sector ombudsmen were still primarily operating in the area of financial services but new members included the Corporate Estate Agents Ombudsman (dealing with complaints against the large chains of estate agents from private individuals as actual or potential buyers or sellers of residential property in the United Kingdom) and the Funeral Ombudsman (investigating complaints against funeral directors belonging to the major trade associations).

Not all private sector ombudsmen have been successful in providing independent and effective redress for aggrieved individuals. Many of the so called "ombudsmen" created by national newspapers to deal with readers' complaints have been relatively powerless and lacking in credible independence: see A.R. Mowbray, "Newspaper Ombudsmen: The British Experience" (1991) 12 *Journal of Media Law and Practice* 91.

Lord Woolf M.R. has advocated that private sector ombudsmen "should be extended to new fields; that they should remain separate from the courts, but there should be a relationship between them and the courts which enable them to support one another" (The Tom Sargant Memorial Lecture 1996 (1996) 146 N.L.J. 1701 at 1702). This relationship would involve the ombudsmen being able to refer questions of law to the courts and the civil courts having the power to refer disputed issues of fact for investigation by ombudsmen.

(E) OTHER COMPLAINTS MECHANISMS

The various Ombudsmen's offices discussed in this chapter must be seen in the wider context of the formal and informal complaint mechanisms that exist in respect of the multifarious activities of the state, and which have come under increasing scrutiny in recent years. On the role of M.P.s in handling complaints, see R. Rawlings, "Parliamentary Redress of Grievance" in C. Harlow (ed.), *Public Law and Politics* (1986) and "The MP's Complaints Service" (1990) 53 M.L.R. 22 and 149. On the handling of complaints in local government, see N. Lewis and P. Birkinshaw, "Taking Complaints Seriously: A Study in Local Government Practice" in M. Partington and J. Jowell (eds.), *Welfare Law and Social Policy* (1979); N. Lewis, M. Seneviratne and S. Cracknell, *Complaints Procedures in Local Government* (1987), summarised by the latter two authors at (1988) 66 *Public Administration* 181; P. McCarthy *et al.*, *Grievances, Complaints and Local Government* (1992). In 1978, the Local Authorities Association published a Code of Practice, *Complaints Procedures: A Code of Practice for Local Government and Waters Authorities for dealing with queries and complaints* which has been supplemented by a Code of Practice issued by the Local Government Ombudsmen entitled "Devising a Complaints System". More generally, see P. Birkinshaw, *Grievances, Remedies and the State* (2nd ed., 1994), Chap. 2.

Birkinshaw (*op. cit.*) has noted the historically "pervasive" practice among government departments of adopting informal or formal but unpublished mechanisms for dealing with complaints, as an aid to discretion or as a means of avoiding "a more rigorous and formal statutory process of hearing grievances or complaints" (Birkinshaw, in P. McAuslan and John F. McEldowney (eds.), *Law, Legitimacy and the Con-*

stitution (1985), pp. 164–165). Even today, "... in spite of many statutory appeal or complaints procedures, departments make widespread resort to informal methods for the resolution of grievances" (Birkinshaw, *Grievances* (op. cit.), p. 39). The Council on Tribunals has protested against the introduction of internal review procedures as a substitute for a right of appeal to an independent body: see Annual Reports for 1989–1990 (1990–1991 H.C. 64), paras. 1.6–1.10, and 1990–1991 (1991–1992 H.C. 97), paras. 3.25–3.28.

The importance of complaints procedures has received a new emphasis in the Government's *Citizen's Charter*, Cm. 1599 (1991). The Charter applies to all public services, including government departments and agencies, local authorities, the NHS, the courts, police and emergency services, and to the key utilities in the private sector. The following extract sets out what the citizen is entitled to expect.

THE CITIZEN'S CHARTER: RAISING THE STANDARD

Cm. 1599 (1991)

The Principles of Public Service

Every citizen is entitled to expect:

● **Standards**
Explicit standards, published and prominently displayed at the point of delivery. These standards should invariably include courtesy and helpfulness from staff, accuracy in accordance with statutory entitlements, and a commitment to prompt action, which might be expressed in terms of a target response or waiting time. If targets are to be stretched, it may not be possible to guarantee them in every case; minimum, as well as average, standards may be necessary. There should be a clear presumption that standards will be progressively improved as services become more efficient.

● **Openness**
There should be no secrecy about how public services are run, how much they cost, who is in charge, and whether or not they are meeting their standards. Public servants should not be anonymous. Save only where there is a real threat to their safety, all those who deal directly with the public should wear name badges and give their name on the telephone and in letters.

● **Information**
Full, accurate information should be readily available, in plain language, about what services are being provided. Targets should be published, together with full and audited information about the results achieved. Wherever possible, information should be in comparable form, so that there is a pressure to emulate the best.

● **Choice**
The public sector should provide choice wherever practicable. The people affected by services should be consulted. Their views about the services they use should be sought regularly and systematically to inform decisions about what services should be provided.

● **Non-discrimination**

Services should be available regardless of race or sex. Leaflets are being printed in minority languages where there is a need. In Wales public bodies are aware of the needs of Welsh speakers.

● **Accessibility**

Services should be run to suit the convenience of customers, not staff. This means flexible opening hours, and telephone inquiry points that direct callers quickly to someone who can help them.

● **And if things go wrong?**

At the very least, the citizen is entitled to a good explanation, or an apology. He or she should be told **why** the train is late, or **why** the doctor could not keep the appointment. There should be a well-publicised and readily available complaints procedure. If there is a serious problem, it should be put right. And lessons must be learnt so that mistakes are not repeated. Nobody wants to see money diverted from service improvement into large-scale compensation for indifferent services. But the Government intends to introduce new forms of redress where these can be made to stimulate rather than distract from efficiency.

Notes

1. The Government published a special report in 1995 to mark four years of the Charter programme. The report noted that there were now 40 main charters covering key public services at a national level (*e.g.* the Taxpayer's Charter issued by the Inland Revenue) and several thousand covering local service providers (*e.g.* Nottingham City Council's charter regarding the collection of household refuse). In addition, the Charter Mark award scheme, which recognises excellence and innovation in public service, had resulted in 227 awards being made to particular public sector organisations and privatised utilities. Achievements in promoting the principles articulated in the original Citizen's Charter were detailed, these included: (1) targets and performance information are published for almost all public services (*i.e.* what are commonly known as "league tables"); (2) 50 telephone helplines now exist to offer advice on public services (*e.g.* on the existence of tax rebates); (3) remedies are provided where "things go wrong" in the provision of public services (*e.g.* in 1994–1995 British Rail paid £3.5 million in compensation to customers under the terms of the Passenger's Charter). The link between the Charter programme and the Government's underlying ideology towards public services was made clear in the statement that: "privatisation of public sector industries and organisations has also achieved a major improvement in the efficiency and value of services to businesses and households. Privatisation has meant real pressure on costs; it has meant major improvements in service standards; and it has secured a major increase in infrastructure investment" (at p. 42): *The Citizen's Charter: The Facts and Figures*, Cm 2970 (1995).

2. Not all aspects of the Charter programme have been successful. The most notorious failure was the "Cones Hotline" which provided a telephone number which road users could call to report road cones which appeared to be obstructing roads unnecessarily. Over three years the scheme received 27,000 calls, but only five sets of cones were removed as a result of these calls! The Government ended the scheme in 1995.

3. Professor G. Drewry considers: "One's view of the merits of the Citizen's Charter depends on one's views about the political philosophy to which it relates. Disciples of Public Choice will presumably welcome it as a desirable move to redress an imbalance of power between the providers and the consumers of public services; those who do not

subscribe to such a philosophy may nevertheless be willing to recognise the Charter as a logical extension of recent policy tendencies—though those who are hostile to those tendencies may see it as a cynical way of squeezing extra productivity out of a rapidly shrinking and over-stretched public sector": "Mr Major's Charter: Empowering the Consumer" [1993] P.L. 248 at 256.

4. Professor P. Birkinshaw's assessment of charterism is that "the image is of a government maximising its discretion in government while creating a market for self-interested individuals to complain about other's shortcoming while successfully cocooning themselves from effective censure": *Grievances, Remedies and the State, op. cit.*, at p. 18. For different views see: W. Waldegrave, *The Reality of Reform and Accountability in Today's Public Service* (1993); A. Barron and C. Scott, "The Citizen's Charter Programme" (1992) M.L.R. 526, and R. Bellamy and J. Greenway, "The New Right Conception of Citizenship and the Citizen's Charter", (1995) 30 *Government and Opposition* 469.

5. The Labour Party has stated that it would not end the Charter programme if elected to government. The possibility of allowing citizens to complain of alleged violations of Charter standards by means of the Internet would be explored: *The Guardian*, July 31, 1996. Now we shall have to wait and see what they achieve in office.

Part II

JUDICIAL REVIEW

INTRODUCTORY NOTE TO PART II

THE remainder of this book is concerned with the role of the *courts* in relation to the administration of government. A person affected by an act or omission of a public authority may be able to bring the matter before a court in any of the following circumstances:

(i) where the act is *ultra vires* (*i.e.* beyond the powers of the authority); or where the authority has omitted to perform a legal duty of a public nature;

Here the normal procedure will be to seek an *application for judicial review* in the High Court under Ord. 53 R.S.C. The various *grounds of challenge* for judicial review will be considered in detail in Chapters 6–10: matters of *procedure and remedy* in applications for judicial review will be dealt with in Chapter 12.

In addition to proceedings for judicial review a matter may be taken to a court:

(ii) where statute provides for a right of *appeal* to a court against a decision taken or a proposed course of action. Such appeal will be to the *kind* of court specified in the statutory provision, and the *grounds of appeal* will be as wide or as narrow as there defined. In this context we shall have occasion to note certain contexts—"statutory applications to quash"—in which although in form the procedure resembles an appeal, in terms of the grounds of challenge the *substance* is more akin to judicial review. These various matters will form the subject-matter of Chapter 11;

(iii) where the act or omission constitutes the commission of a tort or a breach of contract or where a proprietary or restitutionary claim may lie. The liability of public authorities in contract and tort is considered in Chapter 13. Such claims may either be brought by the ordinary procedures of civil litigation, or may form a part of the remedies sought in an application for judicial review.

Although, understandably, the matter of recourse to the courts is of particular concern to lawyers, it will be apparent from the materials in Part I of this book that this is but one way of seeking redress of a grievance. We have already considered, and stressed the importance of, other non-judicial procedures—for example, appeals to specially created tribunals, opportunities to raise objections at public inquiries, complaints to and investigations by Ombudsmen, intervention of M.P.s or local councillors to seek to secure resolution of the matter. The collective significance of these matters should be remembered in assessing the subject-matter which follows.

Appreciation that judicial review is but one of a number of means of seeking redress should not, however, lead to its significance being underestimated. The last three decades have witnessed notable developments in the substance, and in the improvement and simplification of the procedures, of judicial review. A period of "judicial activism" dating from the early 1960s has developed and refined the various grounds of challenge; and the "new" R.S.C. Ord. 53 introduced, in 1977, rationalised procedures for judicial review challenges. At the same time there has been a very considerable increase in the number of judicial review applications being brought before the courts, a specialist Bar has emerged, and the procedural reforms have led to these cases (the Crown Office List) being handled by a nucleus of designated judges with substantial expertise in this area.

Moreover, the significance of judicial review should not be measured simply by the quantity of case-law generated, substantial as this now is. At its heart is the notion of the "rule of law"—that government possesses only those powers which have been bestowed upon it, and must exercise those powers in accordance with certain principles of presumed Parliamentary intention. The substance of judicial review is an examination of how the judges have operated this "police" jurisdiction over the administration. The principles of judicial review should, in outline at least, be known to administrators and should influence the exercise of their functions. Concern that this was not sufficiently the case led the Treasury to issue to administrators, in 1987, a brief guide to the grounds of judicial review (*The Judge Over Your Shoulder*—Treasury Solicitor's Department). The purpose of the guide was stated to be to give administrators some basic grounding in the principles of review so that they would be less likely to act in ways which would give rise to a successful challenge. It is significant that on the first page of the document it is stated that "scarcely a day passes without the *Times Law Report* containing one or more cases where someone is challenging the decisions, or actions, of central or local government or a public body".

The next five chapters will comprise a detailed examination of the various grounds of challenge by way of judicial review. Most of the various grounds of challenge are, at root, aspects of the notion of *ultra vires*. It may be helpful if this notion, and the essence of each of the potential grounds of challenge, is outlined in this Introduction before they are discussed in detail.

THE *ULTRA VIRES* PRINCIPLE—GROUNDS OF CHALLENGE BY WAY OF JUDICIAL REVIEW

The supervisory, judicial review, jurisdiction inherent in the High Court is intended to ensure that persons or bodies exercising functions under statute (or, exceptionally, the royal prerogative) do not exceed or abuse their *powers*; and also to ensure that such persons or bodies perform such *duties* as have been so imposed upon them. An act or decision which is beyond the powers of the actor/decision-maker is said to be *ultra vires*, and, subject to the matters to be discussed below in Chapters 14 and 15, may be regarded as having no legal validity.

There are a variety of ways in which a body may exceed or abuse its powers. This is reflected in the emergence, in judicial opinions and in the writings of commentators, of a "catalogue" of grounds of challenge.

Each of these grounds is, however, no more than a sub-species of the broader governing notion of *ultra vires*. Some of the grounds "overlap", so that it may sometimes be successfully argued that a decision is tainted on more than one ground—and some decisions of courts expressly taken on the basis of one ground of challenge might equally well have been based on one of the other grounds. Moreover, the various grounds may not, as we shall see, cover the entire field of *ultra vires*—the door remains open for further grounds of challenge to develop.

Nevertheless, the various so-called "grounds of challenge" are of considerable value as a check-list by which to assess the *vires* of an act or decision. The "catalogue" is also of importance for its explanatory power—helping in the demonstration of, and providing constant reminder of, the subtlety and sophistication of the judicial elaboration of the *ultra vires* doctrine. For these reasons we have in this book preferred the traditional categorisation of the grounds of review to that suggested by Lord Diplock in the *CCSU* case (see below). His Lordship's simple division of challenges into those alleging "illegality", those alleging "irrationality", and those alleging "procedural impropriety" is valuable in drawing important distinctions between the intellectual bases of the various traditional grounds of review. We do not, however, consider that this trilogy of labels should be substituted for the more traditional "catalogue".

The traditional catalogue—in outline

(i) "Simple" *Ultra Vires* and "Jurisdictional Control"

By "simple" *ultra vires* we mean the situation where a body which has power to do X and Y, in fact does Z. The purported act or decision Z will be *ultra vires*. See below, pp. 182–191.

By "jurisdictional control" we mean the situation where a body's power to do X is not conferred "at large", but has been conferred to be exercisable only in certain circumstances defined in the legislation: *i.e.* power to do X where conditions A and/or B prevail. In this situation if the body purports to do X in circumstances where A and/or B do *not* prevail its act or decision will be *ultra vires*.

In each of these situations the task for the reviewing court is to determine the meaning in law of the jurisdictional parameters to the conferment of power, and then to determine whether on the facts the body challenged has acted within or beyond its powers.

For many years the approach of the courts was to consider that a body which had exceeded its powers might have done so either because of an erroneous understanding as regards the circumstances in which its powers were exercisable (error of jurisdictional law) or because of an erroneous appreciation of a prevailing factual precondition to the existence of power (error of jurisdictional fact).

As will be seen below (pp. 191–193), the present approach of the courts is to maintain a distinction between errors of fact which "go to jurisdiction" and non-jurisdictional factual errors (see pp. 193–209 for cases illustrating this doctrine of "precedent fact"); but they no longer seek to draw a distinction, always an elusive one, between errors of law which should be regarded as going to jurisdiction and other errors of law which would not have such effect. The modern approach, involving a broad power of review simply for "error of law" is evident from the speeches of their Lordships in *Page*. It acknowledges the practical effect of the decision of the House of Lords, two decades earlier, in *Anisminic*: if not the more circumspect statements of principle to be found in the speeches delivered in that earlier decision. In this respect it may be observed that some potential for intellectual confusion would seem to flow from the practice of judges and lawyers of referring to the new-found broad jurisdiction to review for "error of law" as the "*Anisminic* principle".

The abandonment by the courts of their attempt to distinguish between jurisdictional and non-jurisdictional errors of law has rendered redundant a former ground of review in respect of which this distinction had for long not been of significance. Where a decision of a reviewable body displayed what the courts regarded as "error of law on the face of the record" it had since early modern times been accepted that certiorari would lie. With the extension in recent times, by judicial decisions and by legislation, of the concept of "the record" this seemingly slightly archaic ground of challenge for error of law (and not founded upon any notions of *ultra vires*) became a valuable, if unsung, ground of challenge. The recent extension of the scope of review, as confirmed by the speeches in *Page*, extends review to error of law generally, and not just to error of law manifest from review of the "record" of a decision impugned. In the light of these developments the doctrine of error of law on the face of the record no longer seems to warrant detailed treatment. Any who are curious may like to look at Chapter 10 of the previous edition of this book. Although detailed treatment no longer seems apposite, it seems appropriate to have alerted readers to its previous existence and significance in order that they may not overestimate the magnitude of the steps taken culminating in *Page*. It might even be thought that that step was scarcely resistible: a matter of "when" rather than "whether".

(ii) Failure to "Retain Discretion" as to Exercise of Discretionary Power

Here the challenger does not dispute that a particular power is, in the circumstances, possessed by the body challenged. The challenge is based, rather, on failure to have complied with an obligation, which the courts imply from the legislative grant of power, to retain and to exercise a free and unfettered discretion as to the exercise or non-exercise of that power. Such fettering of discretion may occur in various ways, and gives rise to sub-divisions of this ground of challenge. See below, pp. 236–239 (acting under dictation), pp. 255–266 (over-rigid adherence to self-created policy), pp. 266–282 (fettering discretion by contractual or other undertakings affecting exercise of power), pp. 299–300 (fettering discretion by unduly narrow construction of scope of discretionary power).

In this section it will be appropriate also to consider the "rule against delegation" of powers. This can be regarded as a want of power in the delegate, or a failure personally to exercise the power by the delegator. See below, pp. 239–255. It will be an appropriate place also to consider the issue of estoppel in public law—to what extent may a body's past assertions/assurances as to the scope of its powers, or as to how it will exercise those powers, prevent it from subsequently denying such power, or prevent it from exercising powers so as to defeat expectations which its assurances may have engendered—see below, pp. 282–299 and 379–397.

(iii) Challenge for "Abuse of Discretion"

Such challenges are based on the contention that a power has been exercised by the body in question for a purpose other than one for which the power was conferred— below, pp. 301–321; or that in determining how to exercise the power the body took into account considerations which were irrelevant to the proper exercise of the power; or that there was a failure to have taken into account all the considerations which were relevant—below, pp. 321–348; or on the ground that the manner of exercise of the power was patently unreasonable—not such as any reasonable body could have determined—below, pp. 349–379.

(iv) Challenges on Grounds of Procedural Irregularity

This covers:

(a) failure to have complied with a procedural requirement expressly provided in the legislative grant of power. The task for the reviewing court is to determine whether or not in all the circumstances the failure to comply should make the decision or act invalid. See below, pp. 407–418.

(b) failure to comply with natural justice requirements which are implied by the judges, in some contexts, into statutory conferments of power. The rules of natural justice are two:
   —that a decision-maker should not decide a matter in respect of which he has a financial interest or in respect of which there may be reason to suspect he may be biased—see below, pp. 520–537;
   —that no person should be seriously affected by the exercise of power without having first been informed of the intention to exercise the power and having been given an appropriate opportunity to make representations before a final decision is taken—see below, pp. 418–519.

THE ROLE OF THE JUDGES

Judicial decision-making in any branch of law is not simply a mechanical process of logical reasoning, with the judges finding the facts and applying precisely formulated legal rules to those facts. In all areas of law it is now well appreciated that the judges possess some degree of freedom as regards the view they may take of the evidence presented, and also as regards their understanding of the relevant legal rules. The way in which individual judges hearing individual cases may behave, within this limited area of freedom of decision-making, will depend upon, and reflect, certain values of a legal, moral and political nature held by individual judges and possessed collectively by judges as a group. This latter aspect is significant. Simply because we may recognise the non-mechanical nature of the task of judging cases, and acknowledge that judges must make choices which will reflect values, we need not subscribe to any extreme view of the significance, case by case, of the presiding judge's personal political, moral or ethical views. An interpretation is possible which recognises that judges may have, in addition to their own personal scheme of values, a view as to what values they should, in their role as judges, allow to have some limited influence on the exercise of their judicial functions. This is perhaps particularly true of decision-making in public law, where many of the "substantive rules" (the grounds for judicial review) are in fact broadly drawn principles, and where the trend is, if anything, for the grounds of review to become less rather than more specific (see for example, the case law on procedural *ultra vires*, on the duty to act fairly and on standing (below, pp. 407–519, 663–679). Moreover, remedies in administrative law are almost invariably discretionary (pp. 679–690). Thus, in practice, the judges possess considerable leeways of choice, and it becomes important to attempt to discern the values that may influence their decision-making. One difficulty here is that it is unusual for these values to be expressly articulated. Another is that such non-articulated values may change from one period of time to another.

Commentators have identified a variety of themes. J.A.G. Griffith (*The Politics of the Judiciary* (4th ed., 1991)), for example, has noted the homogeneity of the background of the judiciary (almost all male, predominantly public school and Oxbridge) and argues that:

> "These judges have by their education and training and the pursuit of their profession as barristers, acquired a strikingly homogenous collection of attitudes, beliefs and principles, which to them represent the public interest.... The judicial conception of the public interest, seen in the cases discussed in this book, is threefold. It concerns, first, the interest of the state (including its moral welfare); secondly, the preservation of law and order, broadly interpreted; and, thirdly, the promotion of certain political views normally associated with the Conservative Party" (pp. 275, 278).

In his book Griffith seeks to demonstrate his thesis in relation to a variety of areas of judicial decision-making. One of his chapters (Chapter 4) examines and discusses cases on the control of discretionary powers. Griffith's views are strong. Not all would agree that his selection of cases to discuss is representative; nor agree with his analysis of those cases and conclusions. Nevertheless, his discussion is thought-provoking and will repay study. For published critiques of Griffith's views see, *e.g.* Lord Devlin (1978) 41 M.L.R. 501 and S. Lee, *Judging Judges* (1988), Chapter 4. Lee comments (p. 35):

> "Yet Griffith is merely saying that he disagrees with the decisions. One would get the impression that he would almost always decide the opposite way against property, stability, the Conservative Party, etc. But would this be preferable? Would it be more democratic? ... Does the evidence really show that judges act in this way? Is law really explicable in terms of class interests?"

Quite apart from whether Griffith's views truly reflect the position when originally formulated (the mid-1970s), how true are his contentions as regards the present day? Note, for example, the disquiet which seems to have existed in Conservative Party circles at the readiness of the judges to have condemned acts and decisions of Ministers.

A second, much discussed critique, was that of P. McAuslan ("Administrative Law, Collective Consumption and Judicial Policy" (1983) 46 M.L.R. 1). He detected from case-law in the 1970s and early 1980s (such as the *Bromley* case (below, pp. 330–339)) that the "only coherent jurisprudence of administrative law" that had emerged was "basically antipathetic" to the processes of "collective consumption". This term refers to the services (such as education, health care, social welfare, environmental and cultural facilities, highways, public transport, public housing, land use regulation and urban planning) that are organised, planned and managed on a collective public basis by central or local government or quangos, and are consumed collectively ((1983) 46 M.L.R. at 2). McAuslan also detected a "most significant division of judicial opinions":

"This is between the Divisional Court, staffed for the most part by judges whose whole working life and success has coincided with, and indeed has been in large part formed by, the growth of the processes of collective consumption and the judges in the Court of Appeal and House of Lords, who for the most part either passed their formative and working years in different political milieu, or are generally not over-sympathetic to or understanding of the processes of collective consumption. The former judges with their greater understanding of modern administration and politics, and their more recent involvement as lawyers in those processes, are clearly much more reluctant to get drawn into the maelstrom of political and ideological conflicts which masquerade as legal issues justiciable in courts. They appear to be more sensibly aware of the long-term dangers of judges appearing to adopt a partisan political role through their judgments in the courts. In the higher reaches of the judiciary, it seems to be believed that if your judgment is long and full of extracts of statutes and previous decisions, no one will notice that it is a political statement and if anybody does and says so, they can be dismissed as "prejudiced" and in some obscure way "failing to uphold the rule of law" (footnotes omitted; *ibid.*, 19).

If McAuslan's views about the influence of age and generation are correct what should we expect to find now, a decade or more later? All our judges have spent their adult lives in post-war Britain. They must understand and be familiar with the "processes of collective consumption". Has this produced the consequences McAuslan foresaw? Can it be contended that the new generation of judges were themselves too old to review "neutrally" the acts and decisions of the Conservative administrations between 1979 and 1997?

A third commentator, D. Feldman ("Public Law Values in the House of Lords" (1990) 106 L.Q.R. 246) suggested that the dominant political theory among law lords in the 1980s was "democratic elitism", which:

"restricts public participation to a periodic take-it-or-leave-it choice between competing political élites, freeing the elected group to do much as it will between elections".

(*ibid.*, at p. 247). In his discussion Feldman notes the limited applicability of review for irrationality where action has been approved by Parliament (below, pp. 354–357) or where the decision-maker is responsible to Parliament (*e.g. R. v. Secretary of State for Trade and Industry, ex p. Lonrho plc*, below, pp. 311–315); the marked deference to the political judgment of Ministers where national security is in issue; and a lack of enthusiasm for a more participatory model of democracy (*cf.* the *Bushell* case, below,

p. 496). Other values identified include deference to the professional expertise of administrators (*cf.* the *Puhlhofer* case, below, p. 208) and the limited recognition of individual rights.

"Where rights are recognised they are important: schemes which interfere with rights will be zealously scrutinised; but those dependent on public benefits are not generally seen as having rights, so administrators of schemes conferring benefits are given a freer rein" (*ibid.* at p. 259).

Moreover, the European Convention on Human Rights has not been seen as conferring on individuals rights to be protected by English law (*cf.* the *Brind* case, decided more recently than Feldman's article). Finally, Feldman notes that "principled consistency" has tended to give way to pragmatism, usually in the interests of government (*e.g.* the comparison between *Manchester City Council v. Greater Manchester County Council* and *Re Westminster City Council* (below, p. 191)). In developing this analysis Feldman pointed out that the general picture does conceal heterogeneous approaches, with certain judges giving greater weight (usually in dissent) to rights or to principled consistency.

Feldman's discussion was based on his interpretation of decisions of (only) the House of Lords during an earlier decade. Readers should consider whether his statements are applicable to decision-making in public law cases in the courts generally today.

A matter which should not simply be assumed to be constant is the extent to which public authorities have been willing to take action known or suspected to be unlawful. There are well-known cases where Labour local councils have taken steps fairly clearly in defiance of the law (*e.g.* some aspects of "Poplarism" in the 1920s: see below, p. 328; the Clay Cross affair: above, p. 86; the proceedings arising out of the wilful misconduct of Liverpool City councillors in delaying making a rate: below, pp. 487–490). On the other hand, it has been said that the (Conservative):

"governments since 1979 have become increasingly careless of their obligations to comply with the law in the implementation of their policies. Indeed so general has become this abuse and excess of power, and the taking of actions of doubtful legality that observers would be forgiven for thinking that there was a studied practice of such behaviour."

(P. McAuslan and J.F. McEldowney, "Legitimacy and the Constitution: The Dissonance between Theory and Practice" in McAuslan and McEldowney (eds.), *Law, Legitimacy and the Constitution* (1985), Chapter 1, p. 28, giving (at pp. 28–31) 12 of the "more noteworthy examples of this casual approach to the use of governmental power" between 1979 and 1985). A decade later some observers who may have been sceptical about this analysis might more nearly have become convinced.

THE "GROWTH" OF JUDICIAL REVIEW

1. Research on the statistics of judicial review has been conducted by Maurice Sunkin (see "What has been Happening to Applications for Judicial Review" (1987) 50 M.L.R. 432 (covering 1981–1986); "The Judicial Review Case-Load 1987–1989" [1991] P.L. 490; and by Lee Bridges, George Meszaros and Maurice Sunkin, *Judicial*

Review in Perspective (1995)). The research shows that while the overall figures show a substantial growth in applications for judicial review in civil matters (533 applications for leave in 1981; 1,580 in 1989; over 3,200 in 1994), the figures are dominated by applications in particular subject areas, especially immigration and housing. Note the conclusions drawn by Bridges, Meszaros and Sunkin in 1995:

"In other fields the problem with judicial review is certainly not one of over-use. Growth in the number of applications other than in immigration, homelessness and crime has been relatively modest during the past decade. The limited use of judicial review is demonstrated not only by the relatively small overall number of applications outside of these 'core' areas. It is also shown in the limited extent to which judicial review has penetrated into the practices of solicitors in private practice and into law centres, and in the infrequent appearance of pressure groups directly as applicants. It is further indicated by the surprisingly low rates of use of judicial review to challenge the actions of most central government departments. Outside the fields of immigration and housing, it is used far more readily against local authorities than central government. Although these are early days, our data reveal little evidence that the drive toward privatisation and contracting out of public services has resulted in any significant increase in the use of judicial review against either the new executive agencies or private organisations performing public functions" (Judicial Review in Perspective, p. 193).

It may, however, be wrong to judge the efficacy of judicial review solely by reference to the case load. Harlow and Rawlings (Law and Administration (1984), p. 258) acknowledge that "the number of cases is infinitesimal compared with the millions of decisions taken daily by public authorities" but emphasise that one court decision may affect "perhaps thousands of similar cases" and that "the mere existence of judicial review and the creation of precedent may influence administrative behaviour" (ibid., p. 261).

Research conducted by M. Sunkin and A.P. Le Sueur ("Can Government Control Judicial Review?" (1991) C.L.P. 161) noted the establishment of an official group of high level civil servants to examine the growth in the number of successful applications against government Departments, and the consequent steps taken within the civil service. Civil servants were encouraged to reduce the risks of legal challenge by anticipating and planning for challenge throughout their decision-making. Legislation should be expressed in the clearest possible terms; steps should be taken to improve and broaden the quality of legal awareness (note the earlier mentioned circulation of the pamphlet The Judge Over Your Shoulder), and there should be developed closer relationships between policy-makers and departmental lawyers. Moreover, the aims seems not to have been entirely negative and defensive. Interviewees told the researchers that, for example, legal awareness training was "aimed at inculcating habits of good administrative conduct" (p. 172). The overall impression was:

"that if the new ethos [was] having an effect it [was] to encourage officials to become more cautious in their work and more aware of the need to explain and justify action" (p. 175).

Judicial review was, moreover, only one of many external constraints, which included the P.C.A., M.P.s, Select Committees, the media, pressure and interest groups and, increasingly, the European Community and the ECHR. These had all to be set alongside the "internal organisational, policy, financial and other constraints which encroach upon operational practice".

"When decision-makers are constantly forced to balance competing and possibly conflicting constraints, risks of challenge are incurred as an inevitable part of administrative life. The new ethos can do little to change this, save that by obliging decision-takers consciously to address the legal implications of their action, risk-taking may become a more informed, deliberate and explicit process" (*ibid.*).

The point is also made that:

"despite the perceptions of the senior officials that we interviewed, ignorance of the most elementary legal principles (let alone understanding of how they will be applied by the courts) is still likely to be endemic particularly amongst those charged with routine decision-making".

2. The vast majority of the cases on judicial review concern powers based on statute. However, exercises of power by reference to the royal prerogative are also subject to judicial review. The courts have for centuries asserted the power to ensure that a prerogative power which is relied upon does in truth exist (*Case of Proclamations* (1611) 12 Co.Rep. 74; *Burmah Oil Co. v. Lord Advocate* [1965] A.C. 75) and has not been superseded by statute (*Att.-Gen. v. De Keyser's Royal Hotel Ltd* [1920] A.C. 508; *R. v. Secretary of State for the Home Department, ex p. Northumbria Police Authority* [1989] Q.B. 26).

The House of Lords in *Council of Civil Service Unions v. Minister for the Civil Service* [1985] A.C. 374 held that at least delegated powers referable to the prerogative were in principle subject to judicial review for abuse of discretion or procedural impropriety. However, not all the prerogative powers were justiciable; *per* Lord Roskill at 418:

"Prerogative powers such as those relating to the making of treaties, the defence of the realm, the prerogative of mercy, the grant of honours, the dissolution of Parliament and the appointment of ministers as well as others are not, I think, susceptible to judicial review because their nature and subject matter is such as not to be amenable to the judicial process."

Powers that have been held to be justiciable include the administration of the civil service, other than where action was necessitated by the requirements of national security (the *CCSU* case); the issue or denial of passports (*R. v. Secretary of State for Foreign and Commonwealth Affairs, ex p. Everett* [1989] Q.B. 811); the case of a warrant authorising telephone tapping (*R. v. Secretary of State for the Home Department, ex p. Ruddock* [1987] 1 W.L.R. 1482, and see now the Interception of Communications Act 1985); and, notwithstanding Lord Roskill's general reference to "the prerogative of mercy" in his list of aspects of the prerogative likely not to be susceptible to review, it was held in *R. v. Secretary of State for the Home Department, ex p. Bentley* [1994] Q.B. 349 that a decision of the Home Secretary which evidenced a misappreciation of the scope of prerogatival discretion as regards forms of pardon which might be granted, could be reviewed.

Other challenges to prerogatival actions have, however, raised issues which the courts have regarded as falling in the area of non-justiciability. For example, in *ex p. Molyneux* [1986] 1 W.L.R. 331 a challenge was made to the validity of an agreement entered into between the Governments of the United Kingdom and the Republic of Ireland. Taylor J. dismissed the action on various grounds, including that "the agreement ... is in the field of international relations. It is akin to a treaty. It concerns relations between the United Kingdom and another foreign State and it is not the function of the court to inquire into the exercise of the prerogative in entering into such an agreement" (at 336). Note also *R. v. Secretary of State for Home Affairs, ex p. Rees Mogg* [1994] 2 W.L.R. 115. In *Solicitor-General, ex p. Taylor* (CO 2117–94, July 31,

1993) the conventional unreviewability of discretionary decisions taken by the law officers of the Crown was confirmed: Solicitor-General's decision not to bring contempt proceedings in respect of adverse newspaper publicity in a criminal case. Held, law officer "answerable to Parliament alone for his decision".

The exercise of contractual powers by public authorities has also been held to be subject to judicial review in some contexts. See below, pp. 633–634; and S. Arrowsmith, "Judicial Review and the Contractual Powers of Public Authorities" (1990) 106 L.Q.R. 277.

On the *CCSU* case, see H.W.R. Wade (1985) 101 L.Q.R. 153; G.S. Morris [1985] P.L. 177; S. Lee [1985] P.L. 186; K. Ewing [1985] C.L.J. 1; C.F. Forsyth (1985) 36 N.I.L.Q. 25; I.S. Dickinson (1985) 30 J.L.S. 112.

On judicial review and the prerogative, see C. Walker, "Review of the Prerogative: The Remaining Issues" [1987] P.L. 62; B. Hough, "Judicial Review where the Attorney-General Refuses to Act: Time for a Change" (1988) 8 L.S. 189; B.V. Harris, "Judicial Review of the Prerogative of Mercy?" [1991] P.L. 386.

3. For general speculations about the underlying principles which do, or should, found the modern scope of review, see D. Oliver, "Is the *Ultra Vires* Doctrine the Basis for Judicial Review?" [1987] P.L. 343. Note also the following discursive treatments by eminent judges and practitioners in the field of judicial review: Sir John Laws, in M. Supperstone and Goudie (eds.), *Judicial Review* (1992) Chapter 4; at [1993] P.L. 59 ("Is the High Court the Guardian of Fundamental Constitutional Rights"); at (1994) 57 M.L.R. 213 ("Judicial Remedies and the Constitution"); and at [1995] P.L. 72 ("Law and Democracy"); Lord Irvine of Lairg [1996] P.L. 59 ("Judges and Decision-makers: The Theory and Practice of *Wednesbury* Review"); and Sir R. Carnwath [1996] P.L. 244 ("The Reasonable Limits of Local Authority Powers").

CHAPTER 5

JURISDICTIONAL CONTROL

(A) "SIMPLE" ULTRA VIRES—THE BASIC PRINCIPLES

ATTORNEY-GENERAL v. FULHAM CORPORATION

[1921] 1 Ch. 440; 90 L.J. Ch. 281; 125 L.T. 14; 85 J.P. 213;
37 T.L.R. 156 (Chancery Division, Sargant J.)

THE defendant, a statutory authority, had power under the Baths and Wash-houses Acts 1846 to 1878 to establish baths, wash-houses and open bathing places. In the exercise of these powers it had for many years operated a wash-house at which persons coming to the wash-house had an opportunity of washing their clothes. The only assistance given, beyond the provision of the facilities, was that an attendant operated the "hydro-extractor" (wringer), and another attendant controlled the "box mangle". In due course, the corporation resolved to "confer a lasting benefit on all classes of the community" by "establishing a system of mechanical washing" in the borough. A public notice was issued, headed—"Household problem solved! A boon to house-wives!!!." The notice continued: "the Council has established a department at the baths and wash-house, for the purpose of relieving Housewives to a great extent of this most laborious work". The new scheme involved the purchase of a bag. This the customer would fill with washing and leave at the wash-house. The laundered washing would later be delivered to the customer, or the customer could collect.

SARGANT J.: This is an action by the Attorney-General, at the relation of the ratepayers of Fulham, against the municipal borough of Fulham, to restrain it, to use a short phrase, from carrying on a laundry, or something in the nature of a laundry.

In considering what the corporation may do, and what it may not do, I have to take as my guiding authority the words of Lord Selborne L.C. in *Attorney-General v. Great Eastern Ry Co.* (1880) 5 App.Cas. 473, 478. He says: "I assume that your Lordships will not now recede from anything that was determined in *Ashbury Ry Co. v. Riche* (1875) L.R. 7 H.L. 653. It appears to me to be important that the doctrine of *ultra vires*, as it was explained in that case, should be maintained. But I agree with James L.J. that this doctrine ought to be reasonably, and not unreasonably, understood and applied, and that whatever may fairly be regarded as incidental to, or consequential upon, those things which the Legislature has authorized, ought not (unless expressly prohibited) to be held, by judicial construction, to be *ultra vires*." That recognizes that in every case it is for a corporation of this kind to show that it has affirmatively an authority to do particular acts; but that in applying that principle, the rule is not to be applied too narrowly, and the corporation is entitled to do not only that which is expressly authorized but that which is reasonably incidental to or consequential upon that which is in terms authorized. And it is, of

182

course, for the defendant corporation to point out the authority under which it has acted in what it has done. [His Lordship stated the facts, as set out above, including the new laundry scheme, and continued:] Now that is the new scheme and the method of carrying it out, and the question I have to consider is this, whether that scheme is authorized by the Baths and Wash-houses Act 1846, and the Baths and Wash-houses Act, 1847.

It is quite clear that the new scheme of the corporation is not directly authorized by those Acts, but I have also to see, whether, although it is not authorized in terms by the Acts, it is something which in the language I have cited, "may fairly be regarded as incidental to or consequent upon those things which the Legislature has authorized". For that purpose I have to look at the two Acts. [His Lordship summarised the principal provisions of the Acts, and continued:]

Now what is the effect of that legislation? It appears to me to be quite clear that the whole scheme is to afford facilities for persons who have not such facilities themselves and cannot pay for them, so that they may, so far as the wash-houses are concerned, do their own washing. Throughout there is no sort of suggestion, as far as I can see, that anything is to be provided for those persons except facilities for their doing the work themselves. ...

Under the new system which has been inaugurated what has been provided for the persons who become customers is, in my judgment, not facilities for doing their own washing, but the washing itself. It seems to me that, in view of the fact that the control of the articles in question is entirely parted with, that the articles are washed up to a certain point absolutely and entirely irrespective of the labours or attention or care of the customers, and that the articles when that process has been gone through are redelivered in their semi-finished state to the customers, it is impossible to say that the council have been doing anything else except the washing of the clothes down to a certain point for the particular customers. Now is that something which may fairly be regarded as incidental to or consequential upon the provision of facilities for washing? In my judgment, it is not. ...

There will therefore be a declaration that the defendant corporation is not entitled to carry on any enterprise which involves the total or partial washing of clothes for others by the defendant corporation, as distinguished from facilities for enabling others to come to the wash-house to wash their clothes; and there will be an injunction to restrain the defendant corporation, its officers, servants and agents, acting in contravention of this declaration. ...

Notes

1. A feature of the case which seems to have weighed with Sargant J. in reaching his decision that the municipal enterprise of operating the laundry was *ultra vires* was that, notwithstanding the opinion of the council sub-committee which had recommended the scheme, it appeared that the laundry was to be a substantial loss-making activity. Sargant J. discussed, in this connection, the economics of an aspect of this scheme which involved the establishment of a horse and van delivery service, and concluded:

"the service is being performed at about half ... of the cost to the Council. That is an instance I think ... of the light way in which operations are conducted by persons who have not their own pockets to consider, but who have behind them what they regard as the unlimited or nearly unlimited purse of the ratepayers."

2. This is an example of a relator action: see further below, p. 695.

3. Other, modern, examples of successful challenges of this sort include the following. In *R. v. Manchester City Council, ex p. Fulford* (1982) 81 L.G.R. 292, the schools sub-committee of the education committee resolved that corporal punishment should be abolished in all the city's schools. This resolution was confirmed by the education committee and the council, but was quashed by certiorari on the ground that it concerned the general direction of the conduct of the school rather than its general educational character and was thus for the school governors to determine and not the council, in accordance with the Articles of Government for County Secondary Schools.

In *Re Westminster City Council* [1986] A.C. 668, the House of Lords held that a proposed grant of £40 million to the Inner London Education Authority by the Greater London Council, approved shortly before the latter's abolition under the Local Government Act 1985, was *ultra vires*. The 1985 Act made complete and comprehensive provision for the financing of the new ILEA, and only a clear express provision in the Act enabling the GLC to make such a grant could have given it power to do so. Moreover, grants to certain "umbrella bodies" for distribution to named voluntary associations after abolition should they not otherwise be funded, and to the revenue reserve for the funding of an arts centre, were also *ultra vires*. These grants offended the principle that local government finance is conducted on an annual basis. (*cf. R. v. Greater London Council, ex p. London Residuary Body* (1986) 19 H.L.R. 175.)

See also *R. v. Greater London Council, ex p. Bromley LBC, The Times*, March 27, 1984 (*cf. R. v. Bromley LBC, ex p. Lambeth LBC, The Times*, June 16, 1984); *R. v. Director of Passenger Services, ex p. Save Our Railways, The Times*, December 12, 1985; *Credit Suisse v. Allerdale B.C.* [1996] 4 All E.R. 129; *Credit Suisse v. Waltham Forest LBC* [1996] 4 All E.R. 176); *R. v. Kensington and Chelsea Royal B.C., ex p. Brandt, The Times*, December 21, 1995.

4. The principle applies also the vires of delegated or subordinate legislation. See below, pp. 833–838; and note the recent broad application of the principle in *R. v. Secretary of State for Social Security, ex p. Joint Council for the Welfare of Immigrants* [1996] 4 All E.R. 385, C.A. (in order to be valid subordinate legislation must not only be within the powers of the enabling (social security) statute, it must also not conflict with, or render nugatory, statutory rights conferred by other primary legislation (asylum claims)).

ATTORNEY-GENERAL v. CRAYFORD URBAN DISTRICT COUNCIL

[1962] 1 Ch. 575; [1962] 2 W.L.R. 998; 126 J.P. 308; 106 S.J. 175; [1962] 2 All E.R. 147; 60 L.G.R. 261 (Court of Appeal)

The defendant council as housing authority entered into an arrangement with the Municipal Mutual Insurance Ltd whereby they agreed to recommend to their tenants that they should insure their household furniture and effects with that insurance company. The council acted as agents for the company, the insurance premiums (5d. per week) being collected by council rent-collectors with the rent and rates. The council retained 15 per cent of the premiums as commission, and made a profit out of the transaction; 893 out of 3,100 tenants took advantage of the scheme.

The Attorney-General, at and by the relation of the Prudential Staff Union, a trade union established with the object, *inter alia*, of maintaining, protecting and advancing the interests of its members, sought a declaration that the council was not empowered to effect the insurance of the personal and household goods belonging to persons occupying housing accommodation provided by it or to collect premiums in respect of such insurance and that the effecting of the insurance and the collection of the premiums were *ultra vires* the council, and an injunction to restrain the council by itself, its servants or agents or otherwise from so acting.

It was established in evidence that since 1945 similar collective insurances had been made by the company with 53 local authorities. The scheme was started as it was felt that the tenants were, as a rule, weekly wage earners or elderly people, who, when faced with the financial strain of burglary, fire or other disaster, would either be unable to pay their rent or would have to be supported by the council. There had been flooding in the area in 1958. The council relied on their powers of "general management" under the Housing Act 1957. No evidence was tendered on behalf of the plaintiffs.

Pennycuick J. held, dismissing the action, that the power of a local authority under section 111 (1) of the Housing Act 1957 to manage its houses was limited to such acts as might fairly be regarded as acts of general management by a prudent landlord of property in the ordinary sense of that term, and that the facilitation of insurance of household goods and personal effects by way of a collective policy in the particular circumstances was such an act of management notwithstanding that it was incidentally concerned with the private possessions of the tenants.

The Attorney-General appealed.

LORD EVERSHED M.R.: ... The real complaint ... is that the council is acting as agent for a particular insurance company in effecting insurances of the private effects of the tenants. The interest of the relators is because they represent, as their name implies, persons interested in a rival insurance business. The union as such is not a ratepayer, and, in any event, it is clear that the effect of what the council is doing does not impose any burden on the ratepayers. It is perhaps to be noted that the challenge was first contained in a letter in which the protest, vigorously made, was stated to be on the grounds: "(a) The district council are restricting insurance to one specific office. (b) They are instructing rent collectors to become part-time insurance men in the ratepayers' time. (c) They are depriving full-time agents, who are ratepayers, of remuneration. (d) The insurance office concerned has a very bad record regarding recognition of a bona fide trade union."

When the case was opened, we expressed some curiosity in regard to the action, brought as it is by the Attorney-General at the relation of the union. It seems, however, quite clear that once the Attorney-General has initiated such proceedings, no question can be raised in regard to the nature of the action by reason of the interest or the lack of interest of the relator as a ratepayer or otherwise. ...

[His Lordship stated further facts and continued:] Section 111 (1) of the Housing Act 1957 reads as follows: "The general management, regulation and control of houses provided by a local authority under this Part of this Act shall be vested in and exercised by the authority, and the authority may make such reasonable charges for the tenancy or occupation of the houses as they may determine." The question involved may, then, be simply stated thus: Are the activities, above described and challenged by the plaintiff, acts of "general management", within the terms of the subsection? ...

The principle of law to be applied I take from the speech of Lord Selborne L.C. in *Attorney-General v. Great Eastern Railway* Co. The noble Lord there states (1880) 5 App.Cas. 473, 478, H.L., after reference to *Ashbury Railway Carriage and Iron Co. v. Riche* (1875) L.R. 7 H.L. 653: "I agree with James L.J. that this doctrine ought to be reasonably and not unreasonably, understood and applied, and that whatever may fairly be regarded as incidental to, or consequential upon, those things which the legislature has authorised, ought not (unless expressly prohibited) to be held, by judicial construction, to be *ultra vires.*" ... The evidence also showed quite clearly ... that the class comprehended in the term "Council house tenants" consists generally of persons of small means who are, in the ordinary course, unable to find substantial sums, whether for the purpose of replacing losses or damage through such calamities as fire, flood, burglary and the like, and equally unable to find substantial sums at intervals in the way of insurance premiums, payment of electricity and other like charges. It was also proved that in the event of losses of their effects through calamities of the kind mentioned, the tenants were frequently inclined to default in their rent payments and, indeed, to come to the council for assistance in replacing their lost effects. In the light of these circumstances, the evidence also showed that it was the fairly general practice of councils, and had been for some time, to make arrangements for insuring the tenants, as well as themselves, against liabilities arising from that common phenomenon of the day and age, namely, the erection of television aerials, and also for the payment of electricity charges by way in each case of collecting small sums weekly from the tenants with the rent, the councils themselves paying the premiums or charges on their respective due dates. In my view it is legitimate, in considering the question before us, to take these facts into account, to have regard to the well-known and established facts as to the resources of council house tenants and also to the consequences as regards rent payment of such losses as these policies covered. In other words, we are, as it seems to me, concerned with the standard of management appropriate not to a private land owner concerned to turn to account to his best advantage his own estate but with the standard of management appropriate to a local authority providing dwellings for a particular class of the community under a statutory duty so to do, such class of the community having the limitations to which I have referred.

It must be the concern, if not the duty, of a local authority to maintain the general quality and standard of its housing estate which it is its duty to provide and to take such steps as may fairly be regarded as prudent to that end, and also so as to ensure, so far as may be, that the rents due to it will be paid and that the council will not be unduly involved in the consequences that would follow from a tenant's failure to pay his rent and observe the ordinary obligations of his tenancy. [Counsel for the Att.-Gen.] said that these objectives could be achieved if the council were to enter itself into a policy covering failure to recover rent from its tenants. But apart from the fact that such a course would be much more expensive to the council than the present activities, the objectives would not be achieved of maintaining the standards of the dwellings in the way I have indicated or the avoidance of the consequences of defaults by the tenants.

I refer to certain other sections of the Part of the Act, Part V, in which section 111 occurs. The Part begins at section 91 and is headed in the statute: "Provision of housing accommodation. General powers and duties of local authorities." The first example I take is from section 93, the first subsection of which states: "The powers of a local authority under this Part of this Act to provide housing accommodation shall include a power (either by themselves or jointly with any other person) to provide and maintain with the consent of the Minister in connection with any such housing accommodation any building adapted for use as a shop, any recreation grounds, or other buildings or land which in the opinion of the Minister will serve a beneficial purpose in connection with the requirements of the persons for whom the housing accommodation is provided." Section 94 contains a power to "... fit out, furnish and supply any house erected, converted or acquired by them under section 92 of this Act with all requisite furniture, fittings and conveniences", and goes on to provide that they may let and sell furniture under hire-purchase contracts. Section 95 contains a power to provide, among other things, laundry facilities for the council house tenants. I pass over a number of sections and will content myself finally with a reference to section 113 which, in the statement of the arrangement of sections at the beginning of the Act, is described as "Conditions to be observed in management of local authority's houses". Subsection (2) states: "The local authority shall secure that in the selection of their tenants a reasonable preference is given to persons who are occupying insanitary or overcrowded houses, have large families or are living under unsatisfactory housing conditions." It is true, as [Counsel for the Att.-Gen.] observed, that certain things are specifically mentioned and specific power in regard to them is given to local authorities, and so, as he submitted, according to ordinary principles, these express references should be taken to exclude other activities of a comparable nature not expressly mentioned. I see the force of the argument, but I still think that it is shown by the references I have made that a council housing estate is, from the point of view of management, *sui generis*. If the plaintiffs are right, it would appear inevitably to follow that the arrangements such as those relating to insurance of television aerials and arrangements in regard to Electricity Board charges and the like would be equally open to challenge—a challenge that has never hitherto been suggested.

[Counsel for the council] went further and said that the true inference from the circumstances and from Part V of the Act was that the management of council housing estates comprehended what could be fairly described as welfare considerations of all kinds and he referred to a statement of Romer J. in *Belcher v. Reading Corporation* [1950] Ch. 380, 391. Pennycuick J. rejected this broad argument and in the circumstances it is unnecessary for me to express a view upon it, though I am for my part disposed to think that the obligations of the council do, as Romer J. thought, at least comprehend a welfare element. At least, such considerations would justify the view taken by my predecessor, Lord Greene M.R., in *Shelley v. London County Council* [1948] 1 K.B. 274, 286 affd [1949] A.C. 56 that the widest significance should be given to the word "management" in this connection ... I think this appeal fails and should be dismissed.

HARMAN and DONOVAN L.JJ. delivered concurring judgments.

Notes
1. The notion of implied incidental/consequential powers was first worked out in the nineteenth century in relation to the powers of statutory undertakers such as the railway companies. Hence the cases referred to in *Fulham*. Note also, *Baroness Wenlock v. River Dee Company* (1884–1885) 10 App.Cas. 354. The respondent company was empowered by an Act of 1851 to borrow up to £25,000 on mortgage. The company subsequently borrowed on mortgage over £150,000. The House of Lords held that the lender's executors could only recover £25,000. In the course of his speech Lord Watson said (at 362): "I am of opinion not only that the objects which the corporation may

legitimately pursue must be ascertained from the Act itself, but that the powers which the corporation may lawfully use in furtherance of those objects must be expressly conferred or derived by reasonable implication from its provisions. That appears to me to be the principle recognised by this House in *Ashbury Company v. Riche* ..., and in *Attorney-General v. Great Eastern Railway Company....*"

2. The doctrine of implied or incidental powers gives some flexibility to the courts in their operation of the doctrine of *ultra vires*. See also, *Att.-Gen. v. Manchester Corp.* [1906] 1 Ch. 643—extent to which a parcels service could be regarded as ancillary to express powers to operate a tramway service; and *Att.-Gen. v. Smethwick Corp.* [1932] 1 Ch. 562—establishment of printing, bookbinding and stationery works *intra vires* as being incidental to performance by local authority of its express functions.

This beneficial principle must not, however, be pressed too far. In *London County Council v. Attorney-General* [1902] A.C. 165, the House of Lords held *ultra vires* the operation of an omnibus service by a local authority authorised to operate tramways. In the words of Lord Macnaghten: "It is quite true that the two businesses can be worked conveniently together; but the one is not incidental to the other. The business of an omnibus proprietor is no more incidental to the business of a tramway company than the business of steamship owners is incidental to the undertaking of a railway company which has its terminus at a seaport."

Likewise in a decision denying that legislation of 1871 conferred on trade unions power to collect and administer funds for political purposes, Lord Macnaghten insisted that the incidental powers idea should not be used to *enlarge* upon the powers conferred by Parliament, as distinct from simply sanctioning matters which by reasonable implication Parliament must have intended to authorise: see *Amalgamated Society of Railway Servants v. Osborne* [1910] A.C. 87.

3. Note the terms of section 111 of the Local Government Act 1972:

"Subsidiary powers of local authorities

111.—(1) Without prejudice to any powers exercisable apart from this section but subject to the provisions of this Act and any other enactment passed before or after this Act, a local authority shall have power to do any thing (whether or not involving the expenditure, borrowing or lending of money or the acquisition or disposal of any property or rights) which is calculated to facilitate, or is conducive or incidental to, the discharge of any of their functions. ...

(3) A local authority shall not by virtue of this section raise money, whether by means of rates, precepts or borrowing, or lend money except in accordance with the enactments relating to those matters respectively. ...."

This gives statutory force in the context of local government to the common law doctrine of incidental powers.

Section 111 has been held to authorise the release of a member of staff to a joint committee of trade unions in the interests of good industrial relations (but not the release of staff in support of a campaign against government policy) (*R. v. Greater London Council and Another, ex p. Westminster City Council, The Times,* December 27, 1984); and the establishment of a council working party comprising staff and officers to consider ways of improving the council's structure and efficiency (*R. v. Eden District Council, ex p. Moffatt, The Times,* November 24, 1988).

Several modern decisions display what might be considered to be a carefully cautious attitude to claims that conduct is justified by this section. In *Hazell v. Hammersmith and Fulham London Borough Council* [1990] 2 Q.B. 722–723 the House of Lords held that interest rate swap transactions entered into on behalf of the council (and also many other local authorities) were *ultra vires*. These were speculative transactions on the money markets, entered into in order to make a profit. Profits were dependent on interest rates falling, but in fact they increased. The council's auditor obtained a declaration under section 19 of the Local Government Finance Act 1982 that these transactions were contrary to law; otherwise, the council stood to lose in excess of £100m. The transactions were not authorised by Schedule 13 to the Local Government Act 1972, which covered borrowing by local authorities, nor by the, more generally worded, section 111 of that Act. At first instance Woolf L.J. said:

> "What is a function for the purposes of the subsection is not expressly defined but in our view there can be little doubt that in this context 'functions' refers to the multiplicity of specific statutory activities the council is expressly or impliedly under a duty to perform or has power to perform under the other provisions of the Act of 1972 or other relevant legislation. The subsection does not of itself, independently of any other provision, authorise the performance of any activity. It only confers, as the sidenote to the section indicates, a subsidiary power. A subsidiary power which authorises an activity where some other statutory provision has vested a specific function or functions in the council and the performance of the activity will assist in some way in the discharge of that function or those functions."

This was approved by the Court of Appeal [1990] 2 Q.B. 697, 785, and the House of Lords [1991] 2 W.L.R. 372, 383. In the House of Lords, Lord Templeman accepted that "borrowing" was a "function" for these purposes, but that interest rate swap transactions neither "facilitated" nor were "conducive" or "incidental to" borrowing. A power was not incidental merely because it was convenient or desirable or profitable. See further on *Hazell*: M. Loughlin, "Innovative Financing in Local Government Law: The Limits of Legal Instrumentalism" [1990] P.L. 372 and [1991] P.L. 568.

In *R. v. Wirral Metropolitan Borough Council, ex p. Milstead* (1989) 87 L.G.R. 611, the Divisional Court held that a "factoring" agreement to sell, for a current payment, the right to receive the proceeds of future sales of land was not lawful under section 111. Entering the agreement was not incidental to the sale of the land, but was concerned with the sale of sums of money cleaved from the proceeds of sale of the land.

In *R. v. Richmond upon Thames London Borough Council, ex p. McCarthy & Stone (Developments) Ltd* [1991] 3 W.L.R. 941, the House of Lords, reversing the Court of Appeal, held that section 111 did not authorise the levy of a charge on developers in respect of pre-planning application meetings and discussions. The consideration and determining of planning applications *was* a function of the council; the giving of pre-application advice facilitated and was conducive and incidental to that function, but was not *itself* a "function". Charging was thus "incidental to the incidental", which was too remote a relationship (*cf.* Farwell J. in *Att.-Gen. v. Manchester Corporation* [1906] 1 Ch. 643, 656). Lord Lowry rejected the Court of Appeal's argument that while no charge could be made without express authority in respect of the performance of a *duty*, a charge could be made in respect of a function which it had *power* to provide.

In *Allsop v. North Tyneside Metropolitan Borough Council* (1992) L.G.R. 462, the Court of Appeal held that section 111 did not authorise payments under a voluntary redundancy scheme in excess of the limits permitted under statutory regulations authorising redundancy payments. These regulations took effect by virtue of the Superannuation Act 1972, which was an "other enactment" for the purposes of section 111.

4. A further general power is conferred by the following section (set out as amended).

"Power of local authorities to incur expenditure for certain purposes not otherwise authorised

137.—(1) A local authority may, subject to the provisions of this section, incur expenditure which in their opinion is in the interests of [, and will bring direct benefit to,] their area or any part of it or all or some of its inhabitants, but a local authority shall not, by virtue of this subsection, incur any expenditure—

[(a)] for a purpose for which they are, either unconditionally or subject to any limitation or to the satisfaction of any condition, authorised or required to make any payment by or by virtue of any other enactment [; nor
(b) unless the direct benefit accruing to their area or any part of it or to all or some of the inhabitants of their area will be commensurate with the expenditure to be incurred].

[(1A) In any case where—

(a) by virtue of paragraph (a) of subsection (1) above, a local authority are prohibited from incurring expenditure for a particular purpose, and
(b) the power or duty of the authority to incur expenditure for that purpose is in any respect limited or conditional (whether by being restricted to a particular group of persons or in any other way),

the prohibition in that paragraph shall extend to all expenditure to which that power or duty would apply if it were not subject to any limitation or condition.]

(2) It is hereby declared that the power of a local authority to incur expenditure under subsection (1) above includes power to do so by contributing towards the defraying of expenditure by another local authority in or in connection with the exercise of that other authority's functions. . . .

[(2C) A local authority may incur expenditure under subsection (1) above on publicity only—

(a) [...]
(b) by way of assistance to a public body or voluntary organisation where the publicity is incidental to the main purpose for which the assistance is given;

but the following provisions of this section apply to expenditure incurred by the local authority under section 142 below on information as to the services provided by them under this section, or otherwise relating to their functions under this section, as they apply to expenditure incurred under this section.

(2D) In subsection (2C) above—

"publicity" means any communication, in whatever form, addressed to the public at large or to a section of the public; and
"voluntary organisation" means a body which is not a public body but whose activities are carried on otherwise than for profit.]

(3) A local authority may, subject [to the following provisions of this section], incur expenditure on contributions to any of the following funds, that is to say—

(a) the funds of any charitable body in furtherance of its work in the United Kingdom; or
(b) the funds of any body which provides any public service [(whether to the public at large or to any section of it)] in the United Kingdom otherwise than for the purposes of gain; or
(c) any fund which is raised in connection with a particular event directly affecting persons resident in the United Kingdom on behalf of whom a public appeal for contributions has been made by the Lord Mayor of London or the chairman of a principal council or by a committee of which the Lord Mayor of London or the chairman of a principal council is a member. . . ."

The amount that can be spent was formerly the product of a 2p rate. Following the abolition of domestic rating, it is now calculated by multiplying the local authority's "relevant population" by a sum prescribed in regulations: different sums being prescribed in relation to different kinds of authority—namely counties, metropolitan districts, non-metropolitan districts. A separate account must be kept of expenditure under s.137.

Section 137 was substantially amended by the Local Government and Housing Act 1989. Part III of this Act now makes express provision in respect of the promotion of economic development by local authorities, which now falls outside section 137.

The use of section 137 in practice was considered by C. Crawford and V. Moore, *The Free Two Pence* (CIPFA, 1983). In *Manchester City Council v. Greater Manchester Metropolitan County Council* (1980) 78 L.G.R. 560, the House of Lords upheld the validity of payments under section 137 by the county council to a trust established by that council for the provision of free or assisted places at independent schools for children of parents in the area. (Education was not one of the county council's functions.) The payment was held not to infringe the principle that local government expenditure be conducted on an annual basis; although most of the money would be held by the trustees for expenditure in future years, the expenditure was properly incurred within the county council's budget in one year. (*cf. Re Westminster City Council* [1986] A.C. 668 above, p. 188.)

5. From time to time concern has been expressed that the *ultra vires* doctrine may unduly cramp municipal enterprise and initiative. The Committee on the Management of Local Government (Chairman: Sir John Maud (later Lord Redcliffe-Maud)) (HMSO, 1967) considered that the *ultra vires* doctrine had "a deleterious effect on local government because of the narrowness of the legislation governing local authorities' activities. The specific nature of legislation discourages enterprise, handicaps development, robs the community of services which the local authority might render, and encourages too rigorous oversight by the central government. It contributes to the excessive concern over legalities and fosters the idea that the clerk should be a lawyer" (para. 283). It recommended the enactment of a "general competence" clause, of the kind now incorporated in section 137 of the Local Government Act 1972 (above) although it did *not* recommend financial limits to spending under the recommended general power.

Similarly, the Royal Commission on Local Government in England 1966–69 (Chairman: Lord Redcliffe-Maud, Cmnd. 4040) suggested that the only limit on a "general power to spend money for the benefit of their areas or inhabitants" should be "the wishes of the electors and such restrictions as have to be placed on local government expenditure in the interests of national economic and financial policy" (para. 323). This suggestion also was not accepted.

(B) Jurisdictional Review

Overview: Development of Current Scope of Review

In the cases considered above (pp. 182–191) the principal question for the courts has been relatively straightforward: whether the actions of a public body were, or were not, authorised (expressly or impliedly) by the terms of legislation.

What is essentially the same question may arise, however, in a different and slightly more complex way. It may be that there is no dispute between the parties that in certain circumstances the body in question may do what it has done. The contention of the applicant is not that what has been done is, in the simple sense considered above, beyond the powers of the public body in question. Rather, the challenge will be founded on the contention that power to do what has been done has not been conferred by the legislation to be exercised "at large"—whenever the body in question so pleases—but has been conferred subject to limitations as to the circumstances which must prevail before the power may validly be exercised. To put the matter another way: it is the difference between legislative grant of power to do "X"; and the grant of power to do "X" in (and, implicitly, *only* in) defined circumstances.

What should be the scope of review where power has been conferred in this latter way? It is clear that if it is the role of the High Court to keep grantees of powers within the bounds of the powers conferred, the judges must be willing to review the jurisdictional parameters set by the legislation in question. The notion that such a grantee of power might be given power conclusively to determine the existence or non-existence of the circumstances upon which the validity of such power might depend was acknowledged as a legislative possibility (Parliament being sovereign) in the *Income Tax Commissioners* case (below, p. 202): but this idea has not been applied in any subsequent decision.

The courts will, in the exercise of the jurisdictional control described above, be confronted with arguments of two principal kinds. On the one hand it may be argued that a public body has come to an incorrect conclusion as regards the circumstances which must exist in order for it to possess the power in question. This will involve a question of disputed interpretation of the legislative text. Alternatively, it might be that there is simply a dispute about the existence or non-existence of the circumstances which it is agreed must prevail if there is to be a valid exercise of the statutory power. In other words the critical issues may be ones of law, or may be ones of fact.

The first cases in the section which follows this overview involve the issue of the willingness of the High Court to review issues of fact upon which, it is argued, the existence of statutory power may depend. It will be seen that there are cases (*White and Collins*; *Khawaja*) where the courts have demonstrated a preparedness to review the existence of facts which are, therefore, said to be "precedent to jurisdiction". In other cases—and the legislative and factual context may here be critical—the courts may be less willing to intervene (*Dowty*; *Puhlhofer*), leaving a measure of judgment here to the executive body.

Issues of jurisdictional *law* have tended to arise in the context of the functioning of adjudicatory (as distinct from purely administrative) bodies; giving rise to more complex issues for the courts as regards the kinds of errors which should, and which should not, found judicial review. It may be helpful to an understanding of the cases which follow (*Anisminic* and its progeny) to explain this point a little more fully.

The law which is relevant to an adjudicatory body in the exercise of its functions will cover a variety of matters. In respect of each matter it will be necessary for the body to come to determinations. The issue to be considered is: in relation to what kinds of such questions will a wrong decision by an adjudicatory body result in its proceedings or decision being *ultra vires*?

It may help, first, to consider the kinds of legal questions which such a body may have to determine. These may relate to any, or all, of the following matters:

—the *proper composition* of the tribunal,
—the *types of case* which the tribunal has power to hear,
—the *procedural rules* to be followed in hearing and determining cases,
—the *substantive rules* to be applied to the facts in reaching decisions,
—the *order or orders* to be made consequent upon the decision reached.

The question with which we are concerned may be restated: given that tribunals may make errors in respect of each and any of these matters, which errors will give rise to successful judicial review proceedings and which not?

It is not difficult to see how errors in respect of the first, second, third and fifth of the kinds of legal question listed above are likely to qualify for jurisdictional review. Functions are given to tribunals on an assumption that the statutorily designated membership presides over cases; that the body hears, and only hears, the kinds of dispute within its jurisdictional remit; and also restricts itself to making the kinds of orders which statute has authorised.

But what of the "correctness" of the tribunal's actual substantive decisions? This would seem to represent a situation where, unless review and appeal are to become one and the same, it may be necessary for the reviewing court to draw back and consider that a properly constituted tribunal hearing a case within its jurisdiction *has jurisdiction* to make errors of law (and of fact) in coming to its actual decision in that case. Such errors would be remediable only if an appropriately widely defined right to *appeal* exists.

Although this may well be a logical application of the basic principles of jurisdictional review to the actions of adjudicatory bodies, it has not in recent times, as will shortly be seen, found favour with the judges.

That this is so can perhaps be explained on a number of grounds. In the first place the notion of "jurisdiction to err" is perhaps not an easy one to explain to disappointed judicial review applicants. The temptation for a judge to intervene if an error of law appears to have been made by a tribunal in reaching a decision is inevitably great. More so, given the power (referred to above, p. 174) to intervene for *error on the face of the record* (in cases where the error so appears) whether or not that error is in respect of a jurisdictional matter. It is not, therefore, surprising that the courts have held that their power to review decisions of tribunals extends not just to their proper composition and the nature of the cases they hear, but also to their decisions on points of substantive law.

The difficulty for the courts for a number of years, exemplified by the speeches in *Anisminic* (below, p. 210), was how to devise a formula so that some errors in the course of coming to decisions would qualify for review, whilst others would not. In this context the courts sometimes stated a distinction between "errors which go to jurisdiction" and "errors which go to the merits" of the particular case. But this, of course, was simply to ask the basic question in a different guise, rather than the provision of any guiding test. The search by the courts for a suitable guiding test proved an elusive one; and also one in respect of which, over the passage of time a number of differing approaches prevailed.

Happily, the modern approach, exemplified in the speeches in the House of Lords in *Page* (below, p. 225) appears to have made otiose much of the "old learning" to be found in *Anisminic* and its successor cases. Nevertheless, *Anisminic* remains an important case and is extracted below. Its name seems now indelibly associated with the new broad doctrine of "review for error of law" (see comment above at p. 174); and an appreciation of the decision is important to a comprehension of the speeches in *Page*. Moreover, it contains important statements on the matter of the judicial interpretation of statutory provisions purporting to exclude judicial review (on which, see below, pp. 796–810).

In the light of the discussion above, the materials which follow are organised in the following sequence: (a) Precedent fact review; (b) Review for error of law.

(a) *Precedent fact review*

Re RIPON (HIGHFIELD) CONFIRMATION ORDER 1938, WHITE & COLLINS v. MINISTER OF HEALTH

[1939] 2 K.B. 838; 180 L.J.K.B. 768; 161 L.T. 109; 55 T.L.R. 956; 83 S.J. 622; [1939] 3 All E.R. 548; 103 J.P. 331 (Court of Appeal)

Under Part V of the Housing Act 1936, a local authority had power to acquire land compulsorily for the provision of houses for the working classes. By section 75 nothing in the Act was to authorise the compulsory acquisition of land "which at the date of the

compulsory purchase forms part of any park, garden or pleasure ground or is otherwise required for the amenity or convenience of any house". Ripon Borough Council
made an order for the compulsory purchase of about 23 acres of land, forming part of
the grounds of a house at Ripon called "Highfield", which comprised in all about 35
acres. The 23 acres were at the time let for grazing purposes. The owners (the present
appellants) objected that the land was part of a park and required for the amenity or
convenience of the house, and that the order was therefore contrary to section 75. The
Minister, after causing a public inquiry to be held, confirmed the order. The owners
applied to the High Court for the order to be quashed. Further evidence was given by
affidavit. Charles J. dismissed the motion on the ground that the question was one of
fact, and that it was not open to the court to interfere by rehearing the case and evidence. The owners appealed to the Court of Appeal.

MacKinnon L.J.: ... The only evidence filed on this motion was three affidavits by Mr Rennoldson, and Mr Denman, for the applicants, and by Mr
Wrigley for the respondents. The only material evidence on the question
whether this land is part of a park is that of Mr Denman, who says: [*inter alia*]
"... The house itself is an imposing stone-built residence. It is a house of the
type and size to which it is invariably expected to find paddock and park land
attached. Without them the house and grounds are not such as to attract a
purchaser or tenant. To the west and north-west of the dwelling house and
gardens lies an expanse of open grass land studded with trees of an approximate acreage of 23.46. This land is undoubtedly the park land attaching to the
house of 'Highfield'. It is obvious on inspection of the site that the architect in
designing 'Highfield' so placed the house as to benefit by the amenity of the
open stretch of land on its west side.... Often the land can be utilized for
running horses, etc., but usually it is let off to neighbouring farmers or owners
for grazing purposes, and the fact that this land is so let does not render it the
less properly described in the market as park land...."
   ... Upon the evidence before us I am satisfied that this land was part of a
park within the meaning of section 75 of the Act of 1936, that its compulsory
purchase was therefore not within the powers of the Act, and that therefore
the order of the Minister ought to be quashed. I say "upon the evidence before
us". I have said that we do not know what materials were before the Minister,
though para. 3 of Mr Wrigley's affidavit refers to but does not specify those
materials. But I would add that, if Mr Hall [the inspector] and the Minister in
his turn accepted the contention of Mr Peaker at the inquiry—that this land
had ceased to be a park when, and because, it was let for grazing—that was
manifestly an erroneous view. It is notorious that hundreds of undoubted
"parks" throughout the country are so let for grazing. I should not be surprised to hear that this obtains at Chatsworth or Badminton, or even in Windsor Great Park....
   Mr Valentine Holmes impressed upon us the importance of the duties of
local authorities as to rehousing under this Act, and deprecated interference
with them. I appreciate that importance, but it must be subject to observance
of the clear words of section 75 of the Act, and I might point out that that
section only refers to land "which forms *part* of any park", etc. There would
be nothing to prevent the Ripon Council acquiring compulsorily the whole of
the Highfield property, including the house, or the whole of the Holmfield
property, as to part of which they made a previous unsuccessful attempt. The
owners would have no power to interfere with them. Perhaps they would have

the consolation that, however much they suffered sentimentally, they did not suffer financially.

In the result, I think Charles J. was wrong in dismissing this application, that the appeal should be allowed, and the Minister's order be quashed.

LUXMOORE L.J.: ... The evidence before the inspector was not given on oath, and the proceedings were necessarily far less formal than in a court of law. I have carefully considered the transcript and can find but little evidence directed to prove that the land in question is part of the park of Highfield and none to justify a finding that it is not part thereof: but there is some evidence to support the view that the land is not required for the amenities or convenience of the house. The evidence in the affidavits in support of the application is uncontradicted, and leads only to the conclusion that the land is part of the park. This evidence was not before the Minister, and, although it was before Charles J. when he heard the motion, he does not appear to have considered it, for, in refusing to quash the order of the borough council and its confirmation by the Minister, he based that refusal on the ground that the Minister had decided that the land in question was not part of the park or required for the amenity or convenience of the house, and that, as these were questions of fact, he would not interfere with the findings, as he had no power to retry or to rehear the case.

In my judgment Charles J. was in error in deciding as he did. As I have already pointed out, the proceeding before Charles J. was not by way of appeal from any order made by the borough council or its confirmation by the Minister of Health, but was a new and independent proceeding and not a rehearing or a retrial.

The first and most important matter to bear in mind is that the jurisdiction to make the order is dependent on a finding of fact; for, unless the land can be held not to be part of a park or not to be required for amenity or convenience, there is no jurisdiction in the borough council to make, or in the Minister to confirm, the order. In such a case it seems almost self-evident that the court which has to consider whether there is jurisdiction to make or confirm the order must be entitled to review the vital finding on which the existence of the jurisdiction relied upon depends. If this were not so, the right to apply to the court would be illusory.

There is however ample authority that the court is entitled so to act, for the point has been considered in a number of cases. It is sufficient to refer to the case of *Bunbury v. Fuller* (9 Ex. 111, 140). In that case Coleridge J. delivering the judgment of the Court of Exchequer Chamber said: "it is a general rule, that no court of limited jurisdiction can give itself jurisdiction by a wrong decision on a point collateral to the merits of the case upon which the limit to its jurisdiction depends; and however its decision may be final on all particulars, making up together that subject-matter which, if true, is within its jurisdiction, and however necessary in many cases it may be for it to make a preliminary inquiry, whether some collateral matter be or be not within the limits, yet, upon this preliminary question, its decision must always be open to inquiry in the superior court. Then to take the simplest case—suppose a judge with jurisdiction limited to a particular hundred, and a matter is brought before him as having arisen within it, but the party charged contends that it arose in another hundred, this is clearly a collateral matter independent of the merits; on its being presented, the judge must not immediately forbear to proceed, but must inquire into its truth or falsehood and for the time decide it, and either proceed or not with the principal subject-matter according as he finds on that point; but this decision must be open to question, and if he has improperly either forborne or proceeded on the main matter in consequence of an error, on this the Court of Queen's Bench will issue its mandamus or prohibition to correct his mistake."

As in *Bunbury v. Fuller* and also in *R. v. Bradford* [1908] 1 K.B. 365, so also in the present case, the decision on the question whether the particular land is part of a park or not is preliminary to the exercise of the jurisdiction to make and confirm the order conferred by the Housing Act 1936, s.75, and is therefore open to review in this court. Charles J. in arriving at his decision stated that he agreed with the decision of du Parcq J. in *Re Newhill Compulsory Purchase Order*, 1937, *Payne's Application* [1938] 2 All E.R. 163, and of Swift J. in *Bowman's* case [1932] 2 K.B. 621, 627, 634 in support of the view that he had no power to review the decision of the Minister of Health, because the question to be determined was one of fact.

... Reliance in this Court was placed on the statement of Swift J. that an aggrieved person "is not entitled to come here and complain that the local authority have made a mistake of fact in making the order. He is not entitled to say that his house is not insanitary or unfit for human habitation and therefore the order should not have been made." If this statement was intended by the learned judge to be of universal application to all cases under section 11(3) of the 1930 Act, and therefore also to all cases under the second clause of the Second Schedule to the 1936 Act, I should have no hesitation in saying that it went too far, for it ignores the rule laid down in *Bunbury v. Fuller* to which reference has already been made: a decision which Swift J. had no power to overrule; indeed no reference appears to have been made to it during the argument of *Bowman's* case. I think the remarks of Swift J. must be read in the light of the facts of the case before him, and especially with regard to the provisions of the Act of 1930, s.1, which appear in express terms to make the local authority the judge whether the houses in question are fit for habitation or not; for the material words of that section are: "Where a local authority upon consideration of an official representation or other information in their possession are satisfied" that the houses in the area are unfit, then an order may be made.

This provision differs materially from the present case; section 75 of the Act of 1936 does not refer in terms to the local authority being satisfied that the land is not part of a park. The making of the order for compulsory purchase is prohibited if the land is part of a park, a matter which can only be proved or disproved by evidence....

The true position with regard to applications under cl. 2 of the Second Schedule to the 1936 Act appears to me to be that the judge to whom the application is made is bound to consider the available evidence, whether given at the local inquiry or by the affidavits in support of or in opposition to the motion, and, if there is a conflict with regard to the facts raised, or if the evidence is insufficient to enable him to come to a conclusion, he is free to direct that oral evidence be given, whether by way of cross-examination or of additional evidence....

In the present case, as I have already stated, I am satisfied that there was no evidence before the inspector sufficient to entitle the local authority or the

Minister to come to a conclusion that the land in question was not part of the park of Highfield; I am further satisfied that on the affidavit evidence ... the only conclusion open to the court is that the land was part of the park of Highfield.... In my judgment the appeal must be allowed.

HUMPHREYS J. agreed.

Order quashed.

Notes

1. These proceedings were in the form of a "statutory application to quash"—proceedings which are something of a hybrid between appeal and review. See further on this procedure below, p. 552. The statements in the case about the basis and scope of review for error of jurisdictional fact remain authoritative as to the substance of this ground of judicial review, although in the particular context of statutory applications to quash the modern approach may now be as stated by Lord Denning M.R. in *Ashbridge Investments Ltd v. Minister of Housing and Local Government*—see further below, p. 555.

2. The reasons given in the case for distinguishing *Re Bowman* may not reflect the more recent approach of the courts to powers conferred in "subjective" form—*i.e.* power to do "X" where *in the opinion* of the body in question "Y" exists. See further below, p. 369.

R. v. SECRETARY OF STATE FOR THE HOME DEPARTMENT, ex p. KHAWAJA

[1984] A.C. 74; [1983] 1 All E.R. 765; [1983] 2 W.L.R. 32 (House of Lords)

In this case two separate appeals to the House of Lords raising the same legal issues were heard together. The appellants, Khera and Khawaja, were both persons who, having been admitted to the United Kingdom as immigrants, had later been detained and ordered for removal as "illegal entrants" under the Immigration Act 1971. Argument centred on two questions—(i) the meaning of the term "illegal entrant" and (ii) the scope of review of the exercise of power to remove such persons from the United Kingdom.

These two questions had earlier been considered by the House of Lords in *Zamir v. Secretary of State for the Home Department* [1980] A.C. 930. In that case it had been held that the term "illegal entrant" included one who had obtained permission to enter after having failed positively to disclose some matter which would have led to the refusal of permission to enter had that information been known at the time. This was so even though no request for such information may have been made by any official—in other words, *Zamir* imposed a positive duty to disclose relevant information to immigration officers, even beyond answering truthfully the various questions which might specifically have been asked by the officers. In *Khawaja* the House of Lords overruled *Zamir* on this point, holding that a person who had been admitted entry was only an "illegal entrant" where some positive deception had been practised.

Our concern, however, is with the second of the two questions: in proceedings for judicial review is it sufficient for the Secretary of State to satisfy the court that when he exercised his power to order removal he had reasonable grounds to believe the appellant to be an illegal entrant? Or is not the critical issue whether the appellant does, or does not, in fact fall within that statutory category? *Zamir* had decided that the scope of review was of the former extent. The appellants called upon the House of Lords to reconsider the matter.

LORD FRASER: ... The second general issue relates to the function of the courts and of this House in its judicial capacity when dealing with applications for judicial review in cases of this sort: is their function limited to deciding whether there was evidence on which the immigration officer or other appropriate official in the Home Office could reasonably come to his decision (provided he acted fairly and not in breach of the rules of natural justice), or does it extend to deciding whether the decision was justified and in accordance with the evidence? On this question I agree with my noble and learned friends Lord Scarman and Lord Bridge that an immigration officer is only entitled to order the detention and removal of a person who has entered the country by virtue of an *ex facie* valid permission if the person *is* an illegal entrant. That is a "precedent fact" which has to be established. It is not enough that the immigration officer reasonably believes him to be an illegal entrant if the evidence does not justify his belief. Accordingly, the duty of the court must be beyond inquiring only whether he had reasonable grounds for his belief. In both the present cases the immigration officers stated, in what appears to be a standard formula, that there were "reasonable grounds to conclude, etc.". That formula indicates, in my opinion, that they applied the wrong test....

LORD SCARMAN: ... [In *Zamir*] ... [t]he House approved a line of authority (beginning with *R. v. Secretary of State for the Home Department, ex p. Hussain* [1978] 1 W.L.R. 700) which put a gloss on the words of the critical provision in the 1971 Act, *i.e.* Sched. 2, para. 9 to the Act. The paragraph declares an illegal entrant to be liable to removal. It provides that where an illegal entrant is not given leave to enter or remain in the United Kingdom an immigration officer may give directions for his removal. Unless he (or the Secretary of State, para. 10) gives such directions, no power to detain him arises; for para. 16(2) provides a power to detain only in respect of a person who may be so removed....

The gloss which the House in *Zamir's* case put on the words of para. 9 was to read them as meaning not "where a person *is* an illegal entrant" but "where the immigration officer *has reasonable grounds for believing a person to be* an illegal entrant" he may be removed if not given leave to enter. If it be sought to justify the gloss as a proper construction of the statutory language, there is a difficulty. The gloss requires the introduction into the paragraph of words that are not there. Must they, then, be implied? This question lies at the heart of the problem.

In *Zamir's* case the House was impressed with the difficulties arising if the implication were not to be made. The House attached importance to three considerations: (1) the line of cases beginning with *Hussain,* in which the Court of Appeal had held it necessary to make the implication; (2) the scheme of the Immigration Act; and, especially, (3) the nature and process of the power of decision conferred by the Act on immigration officers.

These considerations, in the view of the House, made it necessary to reject the appellant's argument based on the well-established principle that, where the exercise of an executive power depends on the precedent establishment of an objective fact, it is for the court, if there be a challenge by way of judicial review, to decide whether the precedent requirement has been satisfied. In *R. v. Governor of Pentonville Prison, ex p. Azam* [1974] A.C. 18, 34 Lord

Denning M.R. (in the Court of Appeal) considered the principle applicable in the case of removal of an illegal entrant. The House recognised the existence of the principle, but, following and approving *Hussain's* case, opted for a construction of the legislation which would oust it.

In rejecting the appellant's argument based on the "precedent fact" principle of review Lord Wilberforce said [in *Zamir*] [1980] A.C. 930, 948:

> "My Lords, for the reasons I have given I am of opinion that the whole scheme of the Act is against this argument. It is true that it does not, in relation to the decisions in question, use such words as 'in the opinion of the Secretary of State' or 'the Secretary of State must be satisfied', but it is not necessary for such a formula to be used in order to take the case out of the 'precedent fact' category. The nature and process of decision conferred on immigration officers by existing legislation is incompatible with any requirement for the establishment of precedent objective facts whose existence the court may verify."

He therefore implied into para. 9 the words needed to bring it outside the "precedent fact" category of provision. My Lords, in most cases I would defer to a recent decision of your Lordships' House on a question of construction, even if I thought it wrong. I do not do so in this context because for reasons which I shall develop I am convinced that the *Zamir* reasoning gave insufficient weight to the important (I would say fundamental) consideration that we are here concerned with, the scope of judicial review of a power which inevitably infringes the liberty of those subjected to it. This consideration, if it be good, outweighs, in my judgment, any difficulties in the administration of immigration control to which the application of the principle might give rise. The *Zamir* construction of para. 9 deprives those subjected to the power of that degree of judicial protection which I think can be shown to have been the policy of our law to afford to persons with whose liberty the executive is seeking to interfere. It does therefore, in my view, tend to obstruct the proper development and application of the safeguards our law provides for the liberty of those within its jurisdiction. . . .

Accordingly, faced with the jealous care our law traditionally devotes to the protection of the liberty of those who are subject to its jurisdiction, I find it impossible to imply into the statute words the effect of which would be to take the provision, para. 9 of Sched. 2 to the 1971 Act, "out of the 'precedent fact' category" (see *Zamir* [1980] A.C. 930 at 948, *per* Lord Wilberforce). If Parliament intends to exclude effective judicial review of the exercise of a power in restraint of liberty, it must make its meaning crystal clear.

LORD BRIDGE: . . . [T]he authorities from R. *v. Secretary of State for the Home Department, ex p. Hussain* to *Zamir* have consistently affirmed the principle that the decision of an immigration officer to detain and remove a person as an illegal entrant under these provisions can only be attacked successfully on the ground that there was no evidence on which the immigration officer could reasonably conclude that he was an illegal entrant.

It will be seen at once that this principle gives to an executive officer, subject, no doubt, in reaching his conclusions of fact to a duty to act fairly, a draconian power of arrest and expulsion based on his own decision of fact. . . . It will be further observed that to justify the principle important words have to be read into para. 9 of Sched. 2 by implication. That paragraph, on the face of the language used, authorises the removal of a person who is an illegal entrant. The courts have applied it as if it authorised the removal of a person whom an immigration officer on reasonable grounds believes to be an illegal entrant. The all-important question is whether such an implication can be justified.

The presently prevailing doctrine was first enunciated in *R. v. Secretary of State for the Home Department, ex p. Hussain* by Geoffrey Lane L.J. He explained the suggested basis of the doctrine rather more fully in *R. v. Secretary of State for the Home Department, ex p. Choudhary* [1978] 1 W.L.R. 1177, 1183, where he said:

"The whole object of this part of the Immigration Act 1971, read as a whole, is to ensure that there is a procedure, and a readily available and easy procedure, whereby the Secretary of State can detain pending removal any person such as the appellant in this case. The Secretary of State obviously, from the nature of things, has no desire to detain a man longer than is necessary to get him out of this country and back to Pakistan, or wherever it was he came from. It is conceded by [counsel for Mr Choudhary], and, if I may say so, rightly conceded, that a reasonable belief held by the Secretary of State is sufficient to justify the initial detention of the man; but it is said that, once the Secretary of State's inquiries are at an end, then one has to examine the basis of fact and, if that shows that the Secretary of State had got the factual basis wrong, then the whole of the detention from the moment the inquiries have come to an end and onwards is unlawful. With that submission I cannot agree. It seems to me that the detention in circumstances such as these is throughout a matter for the discretion of the Secretary of State; and, if he was acting on reasonable grounds and acting *bona fide* on those reasonable grounds, then he is protected."

In *Zamir* [1980] A.C. 930, 948–949 Lord Wilberforce said:

"The nature and process of decision conferred on immigration officers by existing legislation is incompatible with any requirement for the establishment of precedent objective facts whose existence the court may verify.

The immigration officer, whether at the stage of entry or at that of removal, has to consider a complex of statutory rules and non-statutory guidelines. He has to act on documentary evidence and such other evidence as inquiries may provide. Often there will be documents whose genuineness is doubtful, statements which cannot be verified, misunderstandings as to what was said, practices and attitudes in a foreign state which have to be estimated. There is room for appreciation, even for discretion."

He proceeds to contrast the disadvantageous position of the Divisional Court as a fact-finding tribunal in the relevant field. . . .

My Lords, we should, I submit, regard with extreme jealousy any claim by the executive to imprison a citizen without trial and allow it only if it is clearly justified by the statutory language relied on. The fact that, in the case we are considering, detention is preliminary and incidental to expulsion from the country in my view strengthens rather than weakens the case for a robust exercise of the judicial function in safeguarding the citizen's rights.

So far as I know, no case before the decisions under the Act which we are presently considering has held imprisonment without trial by executive order to be justified by anything less than the plainest statutory language, with the sole exception of the majority decision of your Lordships' House in *Liversidge v. Anderson* [1942] A.C. 206. No one needs to be reminded of the now celebrated dissenting speech of Lord Atkin in that case, or of his withering condemnation of the process of writing into the statutory language there under consideration the words which were necessary to sustain the decision of the majority. Lord Atkin's dissent now has the approval of your Lordships' House in *R. v. Inland Revenue Commissioners, ex p. Rossminster Ltd* [1980] A.C. 952.

A person who has entered the United Kingdom with leave and who is detained under Sched. 2, para. 16(2) pending removal as an illegal entrant on the ground that he obtained leave to enter by fraud is entitled to challenge the action taken and proposed to be taken against him both by application for habeas corpus and by application for judicial review. On the view I take, para. 9 of Sched. 2 must be construed as meaning no more and no less than it says. There is no room for any implication qualifying the words "illegal entrant". From this it would follow that, while, prima facie, the order for detention under para. 16(2) would be a sufficient return to the writ of habeas corpus, proof by the applicant that he had been granted leave to enter would shift the onus back to the immigration officer to prove that the leave had been obtained in contravention of s.26(1)(c) of the Act, in other words by fraud....

LORDS WILBERFORCE and TEMPLEMAN delivered concurring speeches.

Notes

1. See N.P. Gravells (1983) 99 L.Q.R. 363; I.A. Macdonald, and N.J. Blake, *Macdonald's Immigration Law and Practice* (4th ed., 1995), Chaps. 16, 18; G.L. Peiris, "Judicial Review and Immigration Policy: Emerging Trends" (1988) 8 L.S. 201.

2. In *R. v. Secretary of State for the Environment, ex p. Davies* (1990) 61 P. & C.R. 487, the Court of Appeal held that the question whether a person had an "interest in land" to which an enforcement notice related, and so was entitled to appeal to the Secretary of State under the Town and Country Planning Act 1971, s.88 (now the 1990 Act, s.174), was a matter that went to the jurisdiction of the Secretary of State. Neill L.J. said (at 492) that:

"it is now clear that it is common ground that where the decision-maker had to determine a preliminary question as to his own jurisdiction and this determination involved the inferences to be drawn from correspondence and other documents, the test to be applied by the court on judicial review is not that of perversity or unreasonableness. It is accepted that the court is entitled to look at the matter afresh and make up its own mind.

The only remaining question between the parties on this first issue is as to the weight, if any, to be attached to the decision of the Secretary of State....

As will become clear, we are concerned in this case with a claim by the appellant that at the material time she was in adverse possession of land and thus, it is said, had an interest in the land for the purposes of section 88(1) of the 1971 Act. It is necessary for her to establish an interest in land in order that she can appeal to the Secretary of State. It seems to me that in such circumstances, where the decision impugned involves a question as to the jurisdiction of the decision-maker and where the primary facts are contained in documents and do not involve any questions of credibility or policy, the court should look at the matter afresh and make up its own mind. That means, however, that the court must look at the matter on the basis of the evidence which was before the Secretary of State at the time when he reached his decision, because it is his decision against which judicial review is sought."

The court concluded on the facts, in agreement with the Secretary of State, that the applicant did not have an interest in the land.

For further illustrations of this ground of challenge, in a variety of contexts, see, *e.g. Re Butler, Camberwell (Wingfield Mews) (No. 2) Clearance Order 1936* [1939] 1 K.B. 570 (whether clearance order buildings were "houses"); *Relton and Sons (Contracts) Ltd v. Whitstable UDC* (1967) 201 *Estates Gazette* 955 (whether street a "new street"); *R. v. Agricultural Land Tribunal for Wales and Monmouth Area, ex p. Davies* [1953] 1 W.L.R. 722 (whether conditions existed upon which depended ministerial power to consent to eviction); *R. v. Greenwich LBC, ex p. Williams, The Times,* December 29, 1995 (whether vehicle exhaust pollution justified exercise of traffic restriction powers dependent upon danger to "road users").

3. The notion that a body which has powers exercisable in certain defined situations or circumstances cannot by its *own* decision determine conclusively that such conditions exist needs qualification. Parliament under our constitution is sovereign and therefore there is no reason in principle why a statute should not confer powers on a body, make them exercisable in defined circumstances only, yet also make that body the conclusive judge as to whether those circumstances exist.

This possibility, much limiting the review powers of the courts, was adverted to by Lord Esher M.R. in *R. v. Income Tax Special Purposes Comrs* (1888) 21 Q.B.D. 313, C.A. His Lordship adverted to two types of case. In the first type the jurisdictional facts are fully subject to review. In the second type:

"the legislation may entrust the ... body with a jurisdiction which includes the jurisdiction to determine whether the preliminary state of facts exists as well as the jurisdiction, on finding that it does exist, to proceed further or do something more".

The problem for the courts is to decide in each case whether the legislative grant of power is of the former or the latter kind. In deciding this question the particular wording of the legislation will, of course, be of critical importance (and here we should note the reticence of the judges to interpret legislation as excluding a jurisdiction they might wish to exercise—see *Anisminic*, below, p. 210). However, of equal significance are likely to be factors such as the *formulation* of the jurisdictional yardsticks (*e.g.* are they precise factual matters upon which a court can confidently rule, or less clear-cut matters upon the existence of which reasonable persons might differ), and the *nature* of the decision-making body (*e.g.* is it accountable for its actions in other ways, such as by being an elected body; is it a body whose membership makes it specially qualified to make judgments on these matters?).

R. v. CITY OF LONDON, ETC., RENT TRIBUNAL, ex p. HONIG

[1951] 1 K.B. 641; [1951] 1 T.L.R. 41; [1951] 1 All E.R. 195; 115 J.P. 42; 49 L.G.R. 252, D.C. (King's Bench Division)

In 1949, the applicant, Emanuel Honig, let two furnished rooms in a house to one Albert Shomade, on a weekly tenancy. In 1950, S was given a week's notice to quit, to expire on a Monday. A month later, having remained in possession, he referred his contract of tenancy to the rent tribunal under the Furnished Houses (Rent Control) Act 1946, in order to secure a reduction of rent. At the rent tribunal hearing, H argued that the notice to quit was valid and that therefore there was no "contract of tenancy" subsisting which could be referred to the tribunal. The tribunal held, however, that as the notice to quit was invalid, the tenancy being from Saturday to Saturday, they had jurisdiction to reduce the rent. H applied for certiorari to quash this reduction, on the ground that the tribunal had no jurisdiction to inquire whether the notice to quit was good or bad.

LORD GODDARD C.J.: The question in the present case is whether the tribunal can, first of all, decide the question of the existence of a tenancy. Unless they can do so, they can only proceed in a case in which both parties agree that a contract is in existence. If they did not so agree, it would, of course, always be open to a landlord to dispute the existence of the tenancy, in which case the parties would first of all be relegated to the county court to have that preliminary matter determined.... I cannot think that it was intended that anything of that kind should take place in connection with proceedings under this Act.

It is not necessary, however, to embark upon any inquiry of that kind because the principles upon which these tribunals can act appear to me to be well established by decided cases. The first thing to consider is whether the tribunal, in order to obtain jurisdiction, must find that a certain state of affairs exists which is collateral to the main question. The question whether there is a contract or not seems to me to be collateral, and clearly collateral, to the main question which the tribunal have jurisdiction to decide, namely, what is the fair rent under a contract of tenancy. If there is no contract, they cannot, of course, determine that question. If there is a contract, they can determine it, and therefore they must decide for themselves in the first instance whether or not the contract exists....

[His Lordship cited *R. v. Commissioners for Special Purposes of the Income Tax* (1881) 21 Q.B.D. 313, 319, *per* Lord Esher M.R. (see above, p. 202) and *R. v. Lincolnshire JJ., ex p. Brett* [1926] 2 K.B. 192, 201.]

I am of opinion that the tribunal in the present case had power to inquire into the collateral fact, namely, whether there was a contract, because it was only if there was a contract that they could exercise the jurisdiction which the Act of Parliament has given them. When they have decided that, it is open to the person who complains of that decision to ask this court to inquire into it by means of certiorari. In many cases—at any rate in some cases—this court has been able to inquire into the matter by means of documents and other information put before it and has come to the conclusion in some cases that the tribunal decided erroneously, and in others that it acted rightly.

In a case like the present, depending as it did on oral statement against oral statement, although it is not impossible for this court to inquire into the matter it appears to me to be quite impossible for us to hold that the tribunal below were wrong. At any rate, the onus of showing that they were wrong is upon the person who applies for certiorari. The matter here depended entirely on oral statements, and the tribunal saw the witnesses and heard them. It is true that they were not cross-examined on oath, because the proceedings before the tribunals are not conducted on oath. That, again, is a matter for the legislature and not for the courts. These tribunals act on all kinds of evidence which no court of law would look at for a minute. That is one of the difficulties which frequently arise in these cases, and very often arguments are addressed to the court on that ground. But this court has nothing to do with that. If Parliament chooses to set up a tribunal to decide disputed questions of fact not on oath, that is a matter for Parliament and not for this court. Where, as in the present instance, the matter depends on oral statements with flat contradictions on one side or the other, the only people who can come to a decision are those who see and hear the witnesses—I use that word in the colloquial sense of people called before a tribunal to depose to certain facts. The tribunal here heard both parties and came to a decision on the question of fact, and there is nothing before us which can satisfy us that they came to a wrong conclusion. Therefore, certiorari cannot issue and the application must be refused.

HILBERY J. and PARKER J. concurred.

Application refused.

DOWTY BOULTON PAUL LTD v. WOLVERHAMPTON CORPORATION (No. 2)

[1976] Ch. 13 [1973] 2 W.L.R. 618; [1973] 2 All E.R. 491;
71 L.G.R. 323; 25 P. & C.R. 282 (Court of Appeal)

On August 27, 1935, the plaintiffs entered into an agreement with the defendants. The agreement stated that the Corporation would apply to the Air Council, under the Air Navigation Act 1920, for permission to establish and maintain an aerodrome on land to be acquired by them; that they would lease a site on the western side of the aerodrome to the plaintiffs for the purpose of a factory and that they would allow the plaintiffs to use the aerodrome in connection with their business of manufacturing aircraft.

In 1936 the Corporation conveyed the fee simple of the factory site to the plaintiffs instead of leasing it. By clause 2 of the conveyance, the plaintiffs covenanted to erect a factory and use it for the purpose of manufacturing, etc., aircraft and aeronautical equipment or parts thereof and for the purpose of carrying on a school for the training and teaching of flying. By clause 3 the Corporation covenanted to allow the plaintiffs to use the airport for the purpose of test, delivery and other flights in connection with their business, and for the purpose of flying in connection with the flying school, for 99 years from December 1, 1935, or as long as the corporation maintained the airport as a municipal aerodrome whichever was longer. The conveyance further provided that, without prejudice to the Corporation's powers to deal with the aerodrome, they should not, in exercise of their powers, unreasonably affect the plaintiff's rights. At the time the Corporation welcomed the establishment of a factory which would be a substantial employer of labour in the area.

By 1957, the plaintiffs were no longer manufacturing aircraft, and thereafter used the factory for making airframes and equipment. They no longer used the aerodrome for test flying, but only for executive flights. They had never operated a flying school. There were only 26 flights by the plaintiffs to or from the aerodrome in 1967, 56 in 1968, 16 in 1969 and none in 1970. The need in the area for land for housing purposes had substantially increased, and in 1971 the Corporation resolved to reappropriate the land forming the aerodrome for planning purposes, namely a comprehensive development for housing, shops and schools, acting under section 163 (1) of the Local Government Act 1933. This provided that: "Any land belonging to a local authority and not required for the purposes for which it was acquired or has since been appropriated may be appropriated for any other purpose approved by the Minister for which the local authority are authorised to acquire land. ..."

Once planning permission for the redevelopment was granted, the Corporation would have power under section 127 of the Town and Country Planning Act 1971 (formerly section 81 of the 1962 Act and now section 237 of the 1990 Act) to carry out works which in effect would destroy the plaintiffs' airfield rights, on payment of compensation. By writ dated September 22, 1970, the plaintiffs sought, *inter alia*, declarations that, so long as the plaintiffs used the land in accordance with the conveyance and required the aerodrome for their purposes, the Corporation were under an obligation to maintain it; the plaintiffs were entitled to use it; and, in the event of the Corporation, in breach of contract, failing to maintain it, the plaintiffs were entitled to maintain it. By originating summons taken out in 1971, the plaintiffs sought declarations that on the true construction of (1) sections 81 and 87 of the Town and Country Planning Act 1962 and section 163 of the Local Government Act 1933, (2) the conveyance and (3) the agreement, the Corporation were not entitled to vary the appropriation of the land in breach of convenant so that the aerodrome could be used for a purpose other than that of an aerodrome.

The case came before Pennycuick V.-C. in November, 1970 on a motion for interlocutory relief, in anticipation of the Corporation's resolution, which was refused: see [1971] 1 W.L.R. 204, below, p. 275. Plowman J. heard the action and summons together, and dismissed them both ([1973] Ch. 94). The plaintiffs appealed. They contended that there had not been a valid appropriation for planning purposes on the ground that it could not be said that the airfield site was not required for use as an airfield, having regard to the existence of the rights of the plaintiffs under the 1936 conveyance. They contended that it was for the court to decide whether the factual precondition of a non-requirement existed; that it was not necessary to show that the Corporation had acted *mala fide*, nor that no local authority on the facts could reasonably form the view that land was not required for airfield purposes; that the airfield purpose of the original appropriation or acquisition included flight use by the plaintiffs who still required so to use it, and accordingly the airfield purpose was not spent; that on the evidence the land was required for use as such by the plaintiffs both now and potentially to a greater extent in the future should they revert to manufacture of aircraft requiring flight testing.

The Corporation relied on the decision of Maugham J. in *Att.-Gen v. Manchester Corp.* [1931] 1 Ch. 254 that the question whether the land was not relevantly required was for the decision of the local authority acting bona fide and not for the court.

RUSSELL L.J.: ... The question whether land is not required for the purpose for which it was acquired has long been posed in statutory enactments relating to corporations and authorities with the ability compulsorily to acquire land. In general the situation was that land not so required had to be disposed of: it was regarded as basically wrong that it should be retained for some other purpose when the authority no longer needed it for the purpose for which is was compulsorily acquired. Subsequently, the statutory system has been to allow a local authority in such a case to appropriate the land to some other purpose for which it has powers of compulsory acquisition, I suppose to avoid the double step of (a) sale and (b) further compulsory acquisition. Section 163 of the Local Government Act 1933 is one example: as originally enacted, the exercise of the power of appropriation required the approval of the Minister, but that requirement was later dropped by amendment. It is a curious fact that no decision directly on this point is to be found, save in that of Maugham J. in *Attorney-General v. Manchester Corporation* [1931] 1 Ch. 254: the question

there arose under section 175 of the Public Health Act 1875, as amended by
section 95 of the Public Health Acts (Amendment) Act 1907: thereunder land
not required for the purpose for which it had been acquired might be appropriated for any other purpose, etc. The terms of the statutory provision were
not relevantly different from that now under consideration. The land in question had been acquired for street improvements, and the corporation purported to appropriate it for the purpose of a tuberculosis dispensary with the
approval (then required) of the Minister of Health. One argument was
whether inconsistent public rights had been acquired over the site; but the
question was also raised whether the site could be said to be not required for
the purpose for which it had been acquired. Maugham J. said, at 269:

"I have already said that in my view prima facie the defendant corporation,
having acquired lands for a particular purpose, and having applied the
lands with an intention that that application should be permanent, are not
entitled to alter the purpose in question and to apply the land for a different
one except under proper statutory authority or except under, it may be, the
provisions of a general Act enabling them to do so. This leads me to what I
consider to be the real point of this case—namely, the true construction of
section 95 of the Public Health Acts (Amendment) Act 1907, which I have
already mentioned. That section was no doubt passed, or partly passed, to
prevent the evil which it was thought arose from the decision of the Court of
Appeal in the case of *Attorney-General v. Hanwell Urban District Council*
[1900] 2 Ch. 377. The headnote says (inter alia): 'A local authority have no
power to apply permanently land which they have acquired for one purpose
to another purpose inconsistent with the original purpose, even though the
land cannot possibly be required for that original purpose, and they will be
restrained from so doing at the suit of the Attorney-General.' Section 95
provides that [His Lordship read the section, and continued:] Two questions arise under that section which are, I think, of considerable importance
and of some difficulty. In the first place the question arises, What is the
meaning of the phrase 'not required for the purposes for which those lands
have been acquired'? Who is to be the judge of that? Is it a question of fact
on which the court may express an opinion, or is it a question on which the
determination of the local authority is to prevail? In answering that question, I think that I have to compare section 175 of the Public Health Act
1875. That section, after providing power to purchase, goes on to say: [His
Lordship read the section, and continued:] I think that in such a case, either
under section 175 of the earlier Act or under section 95 of the amending
Act, the local authority, acting in good faith, must be the sole judges of
whether the land is no longer required, or is not required for the purpose for
which the land was acquired. Of course they must act honestly. I need
hardly say that the contrary is not suggested here. But I do not see any
ground for thinking that the court can substitute its judgment upon such a
question for the local authority who are given by these Acts wide powers of
local government. Accordingly, I must take it that, in the circumstances of
this case, it has been determined in good faith by the corporation that the
land in question is not required for the purpose for which it was acquired in
1875.…"

Now that decision, on an indistinguishable section, has we are told been ever since noticed in relevant textbooks without adverse comment. Counsel were unable to find any criticism in any learned articles, over a period in which there has been intensive study and analysis of the powers of the court to disagree with and substitute its own view of the validity of administrative acts for that of, for example, a local authority. Moreover, it is by no means without significance, and is indeed persuasive—though not, of course, conclusive— that the legislature has enacted the same formula in statutes subsequent to that clear decision. Further, for my part, I consider the decision to be correct. It is a function of a local authority to study and keep under review the needs of the inhabitants of the locality and to exercise to the best of its ability its powers with those needs in mind. This must involve the authority in consideration of the relative importance of different needs, not least in connection with the use to which lands of the authority are to be put for the public benefit. I would construe "not required" in the section as meaning "not needed in the public interest of the locality" for the original purpose: and it appears that Maugham J. so construed them. Now that question, it is plain to me, involves matters both of degree and of comparative needs, as to which there can be no question but that the local authority is better qualified than the court to judge, assuming it to be acting bona fide and not upon a view that no reasonable local authority could possibly take. In the present case lack of bona fides is no longer pursued, the abandonment of the site as a municipal airport is in no way criticised, and I can see no ground for holding that the decision of Maugham J., with which I agree, is not directly applicable. Moreover, in so far as the degree of *private* need for use of the airfield as such is said to be relevant, the evidence of likely need to use it for purposes of the plaintiffs' business (other than flight testing of aircraft manufactured at the plaintiffs' factory) is extremely small in extent, and related to convenience rather than need: and the evidence directed to the possibility of future manufacture of aircraft, for which it might fairly be said that there would be a need for the airfield, is purely speculative and on balance of probability unlikely.... It was argued for the plaintiffs that authority showed that the court will always inquire into and decide upon the existence of a factual pre-condition of an administrative step; that non-requirement here was such; and that the views of Maugham J. were erroneous. It seems to me that this depends on what is meant by a factual pre-condition, or rather what sort of factual pre-condition is in question. We were referred to *Eleko v. Officer Administering the Government of Nigeria* [1931] A.C. 662, where the administrative or executive step that was challenged could only be taken if the appellant was a native chief in the particular area. That, of course, was a simple factual pre-condition which the court was as competent to decide as anyone else. In *Re Ripon (Highfield) Housing Confirmation Order 1938; White and Collins v. Minister of Health* [1939] 2 K.B. 838 a compulsory order was quashed on the ground that the land formed part of a park, and such land was excluded from the power of compulsory purchase: a similar type of case....

Accordingly, in my judgment, the contention that the appropriate resolution was invalid on the ground that the land was still required for the purpose for which it was originally acquired or appropriated is unsound and the appeal should be dismissed.

Buckley L.J. (*dubitante*) and Lawton L.J. delivered concurring judgments.

Appeal dismissed.

Notes

1. Section 163 was re-enacted, with modifications, as section 122 of the Local Government Act 1972.

2. A similar approach was adopted a little more recently in *Puhlhofer v. Hillingdon London Borough Council* [1986] A.C. 484. Under the Housing (Homeless Persons) Act 1977 (see now, Housing Act 1985) local authorities had certain duties to secure accommodation for homeless persons. Homeless persons were defined as persons with no "accommodation", and the notion of "no accommodation" was further elaborated by the legislation. In *Puhlhofer* the applicants were a couple with two young children, who were all living in one room in a guest house. The local authority had determined that they therefore were not persons without accommodation and so the duties imposed by the legislation on local authorities did not apply. The issue for the House of Lords was whether the condition of homelessness was fully reviewable by the courts in judicial review proceedings alleging that a determination by a local authority on that issue was wrong either in fact or in law; or, alternatively, whether the legislation should be regarded as conferring on *local authorities* power to determine the ambit of their housing duties by making *them* the proper judges of the meaning and application of the statutory jurisdictional tests. Was this a situation like the *White and Collins* case or was it more like the *Dowty* case? Their Lordships preferred the latter approach and the words of Lord Brightman are instructive: He said:

> "I am troubled at the prolific use of judicial review for the purpose of challenging the performance by local authorities of their functions under the 1977 Act. Parliament intended the local authority to be the judge of fact ... Where the existence or non-existence of a fact is left to the judgment and discretion of a public body and that fact involves a broad spectrum ranging from the obvious to the debatable to the just conceivable, it is the duty of the court to leave the decision of that fact to the public body to whom Parliament has entrusted the decision-making power save in a case where it is obvious that the public body, consciously or unconsciously; is acting perversely."

In other words, provided the authority makes its determination without disclosing expressly or implicitly a misunderstanding of the legislative words applicable, and provided it does not act for an improper purpose or on the basis of irrelevant considerations, and provided there is no procedural irregularity tainting its decision, then its decision as to homelessness will be unchallengeable even though that decision is not the same decision as the reviewing court might have come to had it regarded itself as qualified to make its own determination of that matter. Note, however, the legislative response to this decision: Housing and Planning Act 1986, amending Housing Act 1985, ss.58 and 69 (persons only to be regarded as "accommodated" if accommodation "reasonable for him to continue to occupy").

3. For more recent examples of the approach exemplified by *Puhlhofer* and *Dowty*, see *R. v. Westminster City Council, ex p. Tansey* (1988) 20 H.L.R. 520 (issue whether accommodation "suitable"); *R. v. Monopolies and Mergers Commission, ex p. South Yorkshire Transport Ltd* [1992] 1 W.L.R. 291 (whether a "substantial part" of the United Kingdom); *R. v. Brent London Borough Council, ex p. Grossett* (1994) 28 H.L.R. 9 (issue whether applicant could have "afforded rent payments" a matter for local authority, not an issue of precedent jurisdictional fact for the court); *R. v. South*

Hams District Council, ex p. Gibbs [1995] Q.B. 158 (applicants status as "gypsies" not a matter of precedent jurisdictional fact: rather a question for the local authority, whose decision unassailable so long as correct legal test applied and decision arrived at not unreasonable); *R. v. Secretary of State for the Environment, ex p. Gosforth Allotments and Gardens Association* (1995) 70 P. & C.R. 480 (whether "adequate provision" made under alternative allotment rules); *R. v. Radio Authority, ex p. Guardian Media Group* [1995] 1 W.L.R. 334; *R. v. Brent LBC, ex p. S* [1994] 1 F.L.R. 203, C.A.

Note also the decision of the Court of Appeal in *R. v. Secretary of State for the Home Department, ex p. Onibiyo* [1996] 2 All E.R. 901, where Sir Thomas Bingham M.R. stated (at 911, 912):

"The applicant argued that whether or not a fresh 'claim for asylum' had been made was a matter of precedent fact to be decided, in case of dispute, by the court. The Secretary of State argued that the question was one for him and his decision, while not immune from challenge, could be challenged only on grounds of irrationality. The cases already referred to contain tentative expressions of opinion both ways.

The judge did not rule on this question, and it is not clear to what extent it was argued before him. It was not raised in the notice of appeal, and not explored in the applicant's skeleton argument in this court. No authority was cited to us. For reasons given below, I do not regard the answer to the question as determinative of this appeal. Since the issue is one of importance, and also in my opinion of considerable difficulty, I accordingly proffer a tentative answer only.

The role of the court in the immigration field varies, depending on the legislative and administrative context. Where an exercise of administrative power is dependent on the establishment of an objective precedent fact the court will, if called upon to do so in case of dispute, itself rule whether such fact is established to the requisite standard. Thus, for example, where power to detain and remove is dependent on a finding that the detainee is an illegal entrant, one who has entered clandestinely or by fraud and deceit, the court will itself rule whether the evidence is such as to justify that finding (see *Khawaja v. Secretary of State for the Home Dept* [1983] 1 All E.R. 765; [1984] A.C. 74). By contrast, the decision whether an asylum-seeker is a refugee is a question to be determined by the Secretary of State and the immigration appellate authorities, whose determinations are susceptible to challenge only on *Wednesbury* principles (see *Bugdaycay v. Secretary of State for the Home Dept* [1987] 1 All E.R. 940; [1987] A.C. 514). I am of opinion, although with some misgivings, that the judgment whether a fresh 'claim for asylum' has been made should be assimilated with the latter, and not the former, class of judgment. If the test propounded in (1) above is correct, the answer to the question whether or not a fresh 'claim for asylum' has been made, will depend not on the finding of any objective fact, nor even on a literal comparison of the earlier and the later claim, but on an exercise of judgment, and this is a field in which the initial judgments are very clearly entrusted to the Secretary of State."

4. It is not uncommon for statutory conferments of power to be couched in terms which limit power or jurisdiction not to the *existence* of defined facts or circumstances, but either (a) to the donee of the power's *belief* in the existence of the statutory requirement; or (b) the donee's *reasonable belief* in that matter. For the scope of review in such circumstances see below, pp. 367–369 and 369–379. Compare the power asserted by the courts to review subjectively worded conferments of power with the statements in the *Income Tax Commissioners* case (referred to above, at p. 202); and the limited scope of review exerted in the *Dowty* and *Puhlhofer* cases (see above, pp. 204–208).

(b) *Review for error of law*

ANISMINIC LTD v. THE FOREIGN COMPENSATION COMMISSION AND ANOTHER

[1969] 2 A.C. 147; [1969] 2 W.L.R. 163; 113 S.J. 55; [1969] 1 All E.R. 208 (House of Lords)

Anisminic Ltd was a British company which in 1956 owned a mining property in Egypt, which they claimed was worth over £4 million. On the outbreak of hostilities between Israel and Egypt the property was occupied by Israeli forces and damaged to the extent of some £500,000. On November 1, 1956, property in Egypt belonging to British subjects had been sequestrated by the Egyptian Government. On April 29, 1957, after the Israeli forces had withdrawn, the Egyptian Government authorised a sale of the appellants' property, and it was sold to an Egyptian organisation, TEDO. The appellants' property had included a large quantity of manganese ore, and they took steps to dissuade their customers from buying ore from TEDO. This apparently embarrassed the Egyptian authorities, and on November 23, 1957, an agreement was made between the appellants, TEDO and the Sequestrator General whereby the appellants purported to sell to TEDO, for £500,000, their whole business in Egypt. This was not, however, to include any claim which the appellants might "be entitled to assert against any governmental authority other than the Egyptian Government, as a result of loss suffered by, or of damage to or reduction in the value of" their business or assets during the events of October and November 1956.

In 1959 a treaty was concluded between the British and Egyptian Governments under which compensation was paid to the British Government in respect of certain properties, including the appellants', listed in Annex E to the treaty. It was accepted that at that stage the disposal of the sum was in the discretion of the British Government. The distribution of the compensation was entrusted to the Foreign Compensation Commission by the Foreign Compensation (Egypt) (Determination and Registration of Claims) Order 1959 (subsequently amended), made under the Foreign Compensation Act 1950. Article 4 of the 1962 Order provided that:

"(1). The Commission shall treat a claim under this Part of the Order as established if the applicant satisfies them of the following matters:—(a) that his application relates to property in Egypt which is referred to in Annex E; (b) if the property is referred to in paragraph (1)(a) or paragraph (2) of Annex E—(i) that the applicant is the person referred to in paragraph (1)(a) or in paragraph (2), as the case may be, as the owner of the property or is the successor in title of such person; and (ii) that the person referred to as aforesaid and any person who became successor in title of such person on or before February 28, 1959, were British nationals on October 31, 1956, and February 28, 1959;...

(2)...

(3) For the purposes of sub-paragraphs (b)(ii) and (c)(ii) of paragraph (1) of this article, a British national who died, or in the case of a corporation or association ceased to exist, between October 31, 1956, and February 28, 1959, shall be deemed to have been a British national on the latter date and a person who had not been born, or in the case of a corporation or association had not been constituted, on October 31, 1956, shall be deemed to have been a British national on that date if such person became a British national at birth or when constituted, as the case may be; provided that a converted company shall for the purposes of sub-paragraphs (b)(ii) and (c)(ii) of paragraph (1) of this article be deemed not to have been a British national...."

The appellants submitted a claim for compensation to the Commission. After various proceedings, the Commission made a provisional determination to the effect that Anisminic Ltd had failed to establish entitlement to a claim under the Order, in respect of the sequestrated property, on the ground that TEDO, which had become the successor in title to the appellants, was not at any time a British national. Section 4(4) of the 1950 Act provided that "The determination by the Commission of any application made to them under this Act shall not be called in question in any court of law." Browne J. ([1969] 2 A.C. 223; [1969] C.L.J. 230) made a declaration that the Commission's provisional determination was a nullity, and that the Commission were under a statutory duty to treat the appellants' claim as established. The Court of Appeal ([1968] 2 Q.B. 852) set aside his judgment. Anisminic Ltd appealed to the House of Lords.

The main questions were as follows:

(1) Was the nationality of a "successor-in-title" relevant where the claimant was the original owner of property mentioned in Annex E of the Treaty? Lords Reid, Pearce and Wilberforce held that it was not. In their view, Article 4(1) was defectively drafted. It was meant to convey (1) that if a person claimed as the original owner, he had to show he was a British national on the dates specified, and (2) that if he claimed as the universal successor, for example after the death of an original owner or the liquidation of an original owning company, he had to show that both he and the original owner were British nationals. (See Lord Reid [1969] 2 A.C. 173–175; Lord Pearce, 201–205; Lord Wilberforce, 212–214.) Lord Morris of Borth-y-Gest did not express a final opinion on this point. Lord Pearson (219–223) thought the Commission correct in holding that "successor-in-title" meant "successor-in-title" to the claim of the owners against the Egyptian Government, and that this claim had been sold to TEDO as part of the business assets in Egypt.

(2) Did the error cause the Commission to exceed their jurisdiction, or was it an error within jurisdiction? Lords Reid, Pearce and Wilberforce held that there was an excess of jurisdiction. Lord Pearson (215) accepted that had they made such an error it would have taken them outside their jurisdiction. Lord Morris was of the opinion that it was a matter within their jurisdiction.

(3) If the determination was made in excess of jurisdiction, was it nevertheless protected by section 4(4)? All five members of the House of Lords were agreed that it was not. (Exclusion of judicial review is considered further in Chap. 13.)

[The extracts given here are mainly concerned with the second and third questions.]

LORD REID: ... The next argument was that, by reason of the provisions of section 4(4) of the 1950 Act, the courts are precluded from considering whether the respondent's determination was a nullity, and therefore it must be treated as valid whether or not inquiry would disclose that it was a nullity. Section 4(4) is in these terms:

"The determination by the commission of any application made to them under this Act shall not be called in question in any court of law."

The respondent maintains that these are plain words only capable of having one meaning. Here is a determination which is apparently valid: there is nothing on the face of the document to cast any doubt on its validity. If it is a nullity, that could only be established by raising some kind of proceedings in court. But that would be calling the determination in question, and that is expressly prohibited by the statute. The appellants maintain that that is not the meaning of the words of this provision. They say that "determination" means a real determination and does not include an apparent or purported determination which in the eyes of the law has no existence because it is a nullity. Or, putting it in another way, if you seek to show that a determination is a nullity you are not questioning the purported determination—you are maintaining that it does not exist as a determination. It is one thing to question a determination which does exist: it is quite another thing to say that there is nothing to be questioned.

Let me illustrate the matter by supposing a simple case. A statute provides that a certain order may be made by a person who holds a specified qualification or appointment, and it contains a provision, similar to section 4(4), that such an order made by such a person shall not be called in question in any court of law. A person aggrieved by an order alleges that it is a forgery or that the person who made the order did not hold that qualification or appointment. Does such a provision require the court to treat that order as a valid order? It is a well established principle that a provision ousting the ordinary jurisdiction of the court must be construed strictly—meaning, I think, that, if such a provision is reasonably capable of having two meanings, that meaning shall be taken which preserves the ordinary jurisdiction of the court.

Statutory provisions which seek to limit the ordinary jurisdiction of the court have a long history. No case has been cited in which any other form of words limiting the jurisdiction of the court has been held to protect a nullity. If the draftsman or Parliament had intended to introduce a new kind of ouster clause so as to prevent any inquiry even as to whether the document relied on was a forgery, I would have expected to find something much more specific than the bald statement that a determination shall not be called in question in any court of law. Undoubtedly such a provision protects every determination which is not a nullity. But I do not think that it is necessary or even reasonable to construe the word "determination" as including everything which purports to be a determination but which is in fact no determination at all. And there are no degrees of nullity. There are a number of reasons why the law will hold a purported decision to be a nullity. I do not see how it could be said that such a provision protects some kinds of nullity but not others: if that were intended it would be easy to say so.

The case which gives most difficulty is *Smith v. East Elloe Rural District Council* [1956] A.C. 736 where the form of ouster clause was similar to that in the present case. But I cannot regard it as a very satisfactory case. The plaintiff was aggrieved by a compulsory purchase order. After two unsuccessful actions she tried again after six years. As this case never reached the stage of a statement of claim we do not know whether her case was that the clerk of the council had fraudulently misled the council and the Ministry, or whether it was that the council and the Ministry were parties to the fraud. The result would be quite different, in my view, for it is only if the authority which made the order had itself acted in mala fide that the order would be a nullity. I think that the case which it was intended to present must have been that the fraud was only the fraud of the clerk because almost the whole of the argument was on the question whether a time limit in the Act applied where fraud was alleged; there was no citation of the authorities on the question whether a clause ousting the jurisdiction of the court applied when nullity was in question, and there was little about this matter in the speeches. I do not therefore regard this case as a binding authority on this question. The other authorities are dealt with in the speeches of my noble and learned friends, and it is unnecessary for me to deal with them in detail. I have come without hesitation to the conclusion that in this case we are not prevented from inquiring whether the order of the commission was a nullity.

It has sometimes been said that it is only where a tribunal acts without jurisdiction that its decision is a nullity. But in such cases the word "jurisdiction" has been used in a very wide sense, and I have come to the conclusion that it is better not to use the term except in the narrow and original sense of the tribunal being entitled to enter on the inquiry in question. But there are many cases where, although the tribunal had jurisdiction to enter on the inquiry, it has done or failed to do something in the course of the inquiry which is of such a nature that its decision is a nullity. It may have given its decision in bad faith. It may have made a decision which it had no power to make. It may have failed in the course of the inquiry to comply with the requirements of natural justice. It may in perfect good faith have misconstrued the provisions giving it power to act so that it failed to deal with the question remitted to it and decided some question which was not remitted to it. It may have refused to take into account something which it was required to take into account. Or it may have based its decision on some matter which, under the provisions setting it up, it had no right to take into account. I do not intend this list to be exhaustive. But if it decides a question remitted to it for decision without committing any of these errors it is as much entitled to decide that question wrongly as it is to decide it rightly. I understand that some confusion has been caused by my having said in *R. v. Governor of Brixton Prison, ex p. Armah* [1968] A.C. 192, 234 that if a tribunal has jurisdiction to go right it has jurisdiction to go wrong. So it has, if one uses "jurisdiction" in the narrow original sense. If it is entitled to enter on the inquiry and does not do any of those things which I have mentioned in the course of the proceedings, then its decision is equally valid whether it is right or wrong subject only to the power of the court in certain circumstances to correct an error of law. I think that, if these views are correct, the only case cited which was plainly wrongly decided is *Davies v. Price* [1958] 1 W.L.R. 434. But in a number of other cases some of the grounds of judgment are questionable.

I can now turn to the provisions of the Order under which the commission acted, and to the way in which the commission reached their decision. It was said in the Court of Appeal that publication of their reasons was unnecessary and perhaps undesirable. Whether or not they could have been required to publish their reasons, I dissent emphatically from the view that publication may have been undesirable. In my view, the commission acted with complete propriety, as one would expect looking to its membership.

The meaning of the important parts of this Order is extremely difficult to discover, and, in my view, a main cause of this is the deplorable modern drafting practice of compressing to the point of obscurity provisions which would not be difficult to understand if written out at rather greater length.

The effect of the Order was to confer legal rights on persons who might previously have hoped or expected that in allocating any sums available discretion would be exercised in their favour. We are concerned in this case with article 4 of the Order and more particularly with para. (1)(b)(ii) of the article. Article 4 is as follows:

[His Lordship read Article 4.]

The task of the commission was to receive claims and to determine the rights of each applicant. It is enacted that they shall treat a claim as established if the applicant satisfies them of certain matters....

The main difficulty in this case springs from the fact that the draftsman did not state separately what conditions have to be satisfied (1) where the applicant is the original owner and (2) where the applicant claims as the successor in title of the original owner. It is clear that where the applicant is the original owner he must prove that he was a British national on the dates stated. And it is equally clear that where the applicant claims as being the original owner's successor in title he must prove that both he and the original owner were British nationals on those dates, subject to later provisions in the article about persons who had died or had been born within the relevant period. What is left in obscurity is whether the provisions with regard to successors in title have any application at all in cases where the applicant is himself the original owner. If this provision had been split up as it should have been, and the conditions, to be satisfied where the original owner is the applicant had been set out, there could have been no such obscurity.

This is the crucial question in this case. It appears from the commission's reasons that they construed this provision as requiring them to inquire, when the applicant is himself the original owner, whether he had a successor in title. So they made that inquiry in this case and held that TEDO was the applicant's successor in title. As TEDO was not a British national they rejected the appellants' claim. But if, on a true construction of the Order, a claimant who is an original owner does not have to prove anything about successors in title, then the commission made an inquiry which the Order did not empower them to make, and they based their decision on a matter which they had no right to take into account. If one uses the word "jurisdiction" in its wider sense, they went beyond their jurisdiction in considering this matter. It was argued that the whole matter of construing the Order was something remitted to the commission for their decision. I cannot accept that argument. I find nothing in the Order to support it. The Order requires the commission to consider whether they are satisfied with regard to the prescribed matters. That is all they have to do. It cannot be for the commission to determine the limits of its powers. Of course if one party submits to a tribunal that its powers are wider than in fact they are, then the tribunal must deal with that submission. But if they reach a wrong conclusion as to the width of their powers, the court must be able to correct that—not because the tribunal has made an error of law, but because as a result of making an error of law they have dealt with and based their decision on a matter with which, on a true construction of their powers, they had no right to deal. If they base their decision on some matter which is not prescribed for their adjudication, they are doing something which they have no right to do and, if the view which I expressed earlier is right, their decision is a nullity. So the question is whether on a true construction of the Order the applicants did or did not have to prove anything with regard to successors in title. If the commission were entitled to enter on the inquiry whether the applicants had a successor in title, then their decision as to whether TEDO was their successor in title would I think be unassailable whether it was right or wrong: it would be a decision on a matter remitted to them for their decision. The question I have to consider is not whether they made a wrong decision but whether they inquired into and decided a matter which they had no right to consider.

... In themselves the words "successor in title" are, in my opinion, inappropriate in the circumstances of this Order to denote any person while the original owner is still in existence, and I think it most improbable that they were ever intended to denote any such person. There is no necessity to stretch them to cover any such person. I would therefore hold that the words "and any person who became successor in title to such person" in Article 4(1)(b)(ii) have no application to a case where the applicant is the original owner. It follows that the commission rejected the appellants' claim on a ground which they had no right to take into account and that their decision was a nullity. I would allow this appeal.

LORD MORRIS OF BORTH-Y-GEST: [dissenting: stated the facts and continued:] This is not a case in which there has been any sort of suggestion of irregularity either of conduct or procedure on the part of the commission. It has not been said that anything took place which disqualified the commission from making a determination. No occasion arises, therefore, to refer to decisions which have pointed to the consequences of failing to obey or of defying the rules of natural justice: nor to decisions relating to bias in a tribunal: nor to decisions in cases where bad faith has been alleged: nor to decisions in cases where a tribunal has not been properly constituted. If a case arose where bad faith was alleged the difficult case of *Smith v. East Elloe Rural District Council* [1956] A.C. 736 would need consideration: but the present case can, in my view, be approached without any examination of or reliance upon that case.

The provisions of section 4(4) of the Act do not, in my view, operate to debar any inquiry that may be necessary to decide whether the commission has acted within its authority or jurisdiction. The provisions do operate to debar contentions that the commission while acting within its jurisdiction has come to wrong or erroneous conclusions. There would be no difficulty in pursuing, and in adducing evidence in support of, an allegation such as an allegation that those who heard a claim had never been appointed or that those who had been appointed had by some irregular conduct disqualified themselves from adjudicating or continuing to adjudicate. There would be no difficulty in raising any matter that goes to the right or power of the commission to adjudicate (see *R. v. Bolton* (1841) 1 Q.B. 66). What is forbidden is to question the correctness of a decision or determination which it was within the area of their jurisdiction to make.

It is, of course, clear that no appeal is given from a determination of the commission. When Parliament sets up a tribunal and refers matters to it, it becomes a question of policy as to whether to provide for an appeal. Sometimes that is thought to be appropriate. Thus, where (by the Indemnity Act 1920), provision was made for the assessment by the War Compensation Court of certain claims for compensation for acts done in pursuance of prerogative powers it was enacted that though the decision of the tribunal (presided over by a judge) was to be final there could be an appeal by a party aggrieved by a direction or determination of the tribunal on any point of law. Sometimes, on the other hand, it is not thought appropriate to provide for an appeal. In reference to the Foreign Compensation Tribunal it was presumably thought that the advantages of securing finality of decision outweighed any disadvantages that might possibly result from having no appeal procedure. It was presumably thought that there was every prospect that right determinations would be reached if those appointed to reach them were persons in whom there could be every confidence.

I return, then, to the question as to how the appellants can justify the calling in question by them of the determination of the commission. The answer is that they boldly say that what looks like a determination was in fact no determination but was a mere nullity. That which, they say, should be disregarded as being null and void, is a determination explained in a carefully reasoned document nearly 10 pages in length which is signed by the chairman of the commission. There is no question here of a sham or spurious or merely purported determination. Why, then, is it said to be null and void? The answer given is that it contains errors in law which have caused the commission to exceed their jurisdiction. When analysed this really means that it is contended that when the commission considered the meaning of certain words in Article 4 of the Order in Council they gave them a wrong construction with the consequence that they had no jurisdiction to disallow the claim of the applicants.

It is not suggested that the commission were not acting within their jurisdiction when they entertained the application of the appellants and gave it their consideration nor when they heard argument and submissions for four days in regard to it. The moment when it is said that they strayed outside their allotted jurisdiction must, therefore, have been at the moment when they gave their "determination".

The control which is exercised by the High Court over inferior tribunals (a categorising but not a derogatory description) is of a supervisory but not of an appellate nature. It enables the High Court to correct errors of law if they are revealed on the face of the record. The control cannot, however, be exercised if there is some provision (such as a "no certiorari" clause) which prohibits removal to the High Court. But it is well settled that even such a clause is of no avail if the inferior tribunal acts without jurisdiction or exceeds the limit of its jurisdiction.

In all cases similar to the present one it becomes necessary, therefore, to ascertain what was the question submitted for the determination of a tribunal. What were its terms of reference? What was its remit? What were the questions left to it or sent to it for its decision? What were the limits of its duties and powers? Were there any conditions precedent which had to be satisfied before its functions began? If there were, was it or was it not left to the tribunal itself to decide whether or not the conditions precedent were satisfied? If Parliament has enacted that provided a certain situation exists then a tribunal may have certain powers, it is clear that the tribunal will not have those powers unless the situation exists. The decided cases illustrate the infinite variety of the situations which may exist and the variations of statutory wording which have called for consideration. Most of the cases depend, therefore, upon an examination of their own particular facts and of particular sets of words. It is, however, abundantly clear that questions of law as well as of fact can be remitted for the determination of a tribunal.

If a tribunal while acting within its jurisdiction makes an error of law which it reveals on the face of its recorded determination, then the court, in the exercise of its supervisory function, may correct the error unless there is some provision preventing a review by a court of law. If a particular issue is left to a tribunal to decide, then even where it is shown (in cases where it is possible to show) that in deciding the issue left to it the tribunal has come to a wrong conclusion, that does not involve that the tribunal has gone outside its jurisdiction. It follows that if any errors of law are made in deciding matters which are left to a tribunal for its decision such errors will be errors within jurisdiction. If issues of law as well as of fact are referred to a tribunal for its determination, then its determination cannot be asserted to be wrong if Parliament has enacted that the determination is not to be called in question in any court of law.

[His Lordship cited passages from the judgments in *R. v. Governor of Brixton Prison, ex p. Armah* [1968] A.C. 192, 234 (Lord Reid); *R. v. Northumberland C.A.T., ex p. Shaw* [1952] 1 K.B. 338, 346 (Denning L.J.); *R. v. Nat Bell Liquors Ltd* [1922] 2 A.C. 128, 156 (Lord Sumner).]

If, therefore, a tribunal while within the area of its jurisdiction committed some error of law and if such error was made apparent in the determination itself (or, as it is often expressed, on the face of the record) then the superior court could correct that error unless it was forbidden to do so. It would be so forbidden if the determination was "not to be called in question in any court of law". If so forbidden it could not then even hear argument which suggested that error of law had been made. It could, however, still consider whether the determination was within "the area of the inferior jurisdiction".

So the question is raised whether in the present case the commission went out of bounds. Did it wander outside its designated area? Did it outstep the confines of the territory of its inquiry? Did it digress away from its allotted task? Was there some preliminary inquiry upon the correct determination of which its later jurisdiction was dependent?

For the reasons which I will endeavour to explain it seems to me that at no time did the commission stray from the direct path which it was required to tread. Under Article 4 of the Order in Council the commission was under a positive duty to treat a claim under Part III as established if the applicant satisfied them of certain matters. If they had stated that they were satisfied of those matters but had then declined to treat a claim as established, there would have been a situation very different from that now under consideration and one in which the court could clearly act. So also if they had stated that they were not satisfied of the matters but had nevertheless treated the claim as established. They would have had no right to treat the claim as established unless they were satisfied of the matters. The present is a case in which, faithfully following the wording of Article 4, they stated that they were not satisfied of the matters and, therefore, did not treat the claim as established. In stating why they were not satisfied of the matters they have set out the processes of their reasoning. The more that reasoning is examined the more apparent does it, in my view, become that the members of the commission applied their minds very carefully to a consideration of the matters about which the applicant had to satisfy "them". To no one else were the matters remitted but to "them". It was for them to be satisfied and not for anyone else. The words of Article 4 state their terms of reference. In those terms were certain words and certain phrases. The commission could not possibly discharge their duty without considering those words and phrases and without reaching a decision as to their meaning. The commission could not burke that task. It seems to me that the words which stated that it was for the commission to be satisfied of certain matters, and defined those matters, inevitably involved that any necessary interpretation of words within the compass of those matters was for the commission. They could not come to a conclusion as to whether they were satisfied as to the specified matters unless and until they gave meaning to the words which they had to follow. Unless such a phrase as "successor in title" was defined in the Order—and it was not—it was an inescapable duty of the commission to consider and to decide what the phrase signified. Doubtless they heard ample argument before forming a view. The same applies in regard to many other words and sequences of words in Article 4. But the forming of views as to these matters lay in the direct path of the commission's duties. They were duties that could not be shirked. They were central to the exercise of their jurisdiction. When their fully reasoned statement of their conclusions (which in this case can be regarded as a part of their "determination") is studied it becomes possible for someone to contend that an alternative construction of Article 4 should be preferred to that which was thought correct by the commission. But this calling in question cannot, in my view, take place in any court of law. Parliament has forbidden it. . . .

In this case there has been much concentration on the question whether the commission correctly decided that the phrase "successor in title" included an assignee. But this was but one of very many matters which might receive determination by the commission. A perusal of the Orders in Council shows that they bristle with words and phrases needing construction. For my part I cannot accept that if, in regard to any one of the many points in respect of which interpretation and construction became necessary a view can be formed that the commission made an error, the consequence follows that their determination became a nullity as being made in excess of jurisdiction. . . .

The claim of the applicants had to be determined by the commission and the applicants were under the obligation of satisfying the commission as to certain stated matters. They could not decide whether or not they were satisfied until they had construed the relevant parts of the Order in Council. When they were hearing argument as to the meaning of those relevant parts they were not acting without jurisdiction. They were at the very heart of their duty, their task and their jurisdiction. It cannot be that their necessary duty of deciding as to the meaning would be or could be followed by the result that if they took one view they would be within jurisdiction and if they took another view that they would be without. If at the moment of decision they were inevitably within their jurisdiction because they were doing what they had to do, I cannot think that a later view of someone else, if it differed from theirs, could involve that they trespassed from within their jurisdiction at the moment of decision.

It is sometimes the case that the jurisdiction of a tribunal is made dependent upon or subject to some condition. Parliament may enact that if a certain state of affairs exists then there will be jurisdiction. If in such case it appears that the state of affairs did not exist, then it follows that there would be no jurisdiction. Sometimes, however, a tribunal might undertake the task of considering whether the state of affairs existed. If it made error in that task such error would be in regard to a matter preliminary to the existence of jurisdiction. It would not be an error within the limited jurisdiction intended to be conferred. An illustration of this appeared in 1853 in *Bunbury v. Fuller* (1853) 9 Ex. 111. . . . [T]here is here no room for any suggestion that the commission failed to satisfy any condition precedent or failed to state the existence of any matter essential to their jurisdiction. . . .

In the submissions on behalf of the appellants a phrase much used was that the commission had asked themselves wrong questions. The phrase can be employed when consideration is being given to a question whether a tribunal has correctly decided some point of construction. If, however, the point of construction is fairly and squarely within the jurisdiction of the tribunal for them to decide, then a suggestion that a wrong question has been posed is no more than a means of deploying an argument: and if construction has been left to the tribunal the argument is unavailing. The phrase is, however, valuable and relevent in cases where it can be suggested that some condition precedent has not been satisfied or where jurisdiction is related to the existence of some state of affairs.... So in some cases a tribunal may reveal that by asking some wrong question it fails to bring itself within the area of the demarcation of its jurisdiction. In *Maradana Mosque Trustees v. Mahmud* [1967] 1 A.C. 13, P.C., one part of the decision was that the rules of natural justice had been violated. The other part of the decision, relevant for present purposes, was that where statutory authority was given to a Minister to act if he was satisfied that a school *is* being administered in a certain way he was not given authority to act because he was satisfied that the school *had been* administered in that way. It could be said that the Minister had asked himself the wrong question: so he had, but the relevant result was that he never brought himself within the area of his jurisdiction....

I would dismiss the appeal.

LORD PEARCE: My Lords, the courts have a general jurisdiction over the administration of justice in this country. From time to time Parliament sets up special tribunals to deal with special matters and gives them jurisdiction to decide these matters without any appeal to the courts. When this happens the courts cannot hear appeals from such a tribunal or substitute their own views on any matters which have been specifically committed by Parliament to the tribunal.

Such tribunals must, however, confine themselves within the powers specially committed to them on a true construction of the relevant Acts of Parliament. It would lead to an absurd situation if a tribunal, having been given a circumscribed area of inquiry, carved out from the general jurisdiction of the courts, were entitled of its own motion to extend that area by misconstruing the limits of its mandate to inquire and decide as set out in the Act of Parliament.

If, for instance, Parliament were to carve out an area of inquiry within which an inferior domestic tribunal could give certain relief to wives against their husbands, it would not lie within the power of that tribunal to extend the area of inquiry and decision, that is, jurisdiction, thus committed to it by construing "wives" as including all women who have, without marriage, cohabitated with a man for a substantial period, or by misconstruing the limits of that into which they were to inquire. It would equally not be within the power of that tribunal to reduce the area committed to it by construing "wives" as excluding all those who, though married, have not been recently co-habiting with their husbands. Again, if it is instructed to give relief wherever on inquiry it finds that two stated conditions are satisfied, it cannot alter or restrict its jurisdiction by adding a third condition which has to be satisfied before it will give relief. It is, therefore, for the courts to decide the true construction of the statute which defines the area of a tribunal's jurisdiction. This is the only logical way of dealing with the situation and it is the way in which the courts have acted in a supervisory capacity.

Lack of jurisdiction may arise in various ways. There may be an absence of those formalities or things which are conditions precedent to the tribunal having any jurisdiction to embark on an inquiry. Or the tribunal may at the end make an order that it has no jurisdiction to make. Or in the intervening stage, while engaged on a proper inquiry, the tribunal may depart from the rules of natural justice; or it may ask itself the wrong questions; or it may take into account matters which it was not directed to take into account. Thereby it would step outside its jurisdiction. It would turn its inquiry into something not directed by Parliament and fail to make the inquiry which Parliament did direct. Any of these things would cause its purported decision to be a nullity.

Further, it is assumed, unless special provisions provide otherwise, that the tribunal will make its inquiry and decision according to the law of the land. For that reason the courts will intervene when it is manifest from the record that the tribunal, though keeping within its mandated area of jurisdiction, comes to an erroneous decision through an error of law. In such a case the courts have intervened to correct the error.

The courts have, however, always been careful to distinguish their intervention whether on excess of jurisdiction or error of law from an appellate function. Their jurisdiction over inferior tribunals is supervision, not review:

> "That supervision goes to two points: one is the area of the inferior jurisdiction and the qualifications and conditions of its exercise; the other is the observance of the law in the course of its exercise" (*R. v. Nat Bell Liquors Ltd* [1922] 2 A.C. 128, 156).

It is simply an enforcement of Parliament's mandate to the tribunal. If the tribunal is intended on a true construction of the Act to inquire into and finally decide questions within a certain area, the courts' supervisory duty is to see that it makes the authorised inquiry according to natural justice and arrives at a decision whether right or wrong. They will intervene if the tribunal asks itself the wrong questions (that is, questions other than those which Parliament directed it to ask itself). But if it directs itself to the right inquiry, asking the right questions, they will not intervene merely because it has or may have come to the wrong answer, provided that this is an answer that lies within its jurisdiction.

It is convenient to set out the matter in broad outline because there has been evolution over the centuries and there have been many technicalities. There have also been many border-line cases. And the courts have at times taken a more robust line to see that the law is carried out and justice administered by inferior tribunals, and at times taken a more cautious and reluctant line in their anxiety not to seem to encroach or to assume an appellate function which they have not got....

[His Lordship held that section 4(4) did not protect a purported determination made without jurisdiction.]

In my opinion, the subsequent case of *Smith v. East Elloe Rural District Council* [1956] A.C. 736 does not compel your Lordships to decide otherwise. If it seemed to do so, I would think it necessary to reconsider the case in the light of the powerful dissenting opinions of my noble and learned friends, Lord Reid and Lord Somervell. It might possibly be said that it related to an administrative or executive decision, not a judicial decision, and somewhat different considerations might have applied; certainly none of the authorities relating to absence or excess of jurisdiction were cited to the House. I agree with Browne J. that it is not a compelling authority in the present case. Again, the fact that this commission was expressly exempted from the provisions of section 11 of the Tribunals and Inquiries Act passed in 1958, though no doubt a tribute to the high standard of the commission and the fact that its chairman was a lawyer of distinction, cannot have any bearing on the construction of the Foreign Compensation Act, 1950.

If, therefore, the commission by misconstruing the Order in Council which gave them their jurisdiction and laid down the precise limit of their duty to inquire and determine, exceeded or departed from their mandate, their determination was without jurisdiction and Brown J. was right in making the order appealed from.

Pursuant to the Foreign Compensation Act 1950 the Order in Council which deals with the present claim gave a wide power to determine the amount of compensation. But with regard to the establishment of the claims under Article 4 it gave narrow powers. It gave no general discretion at all. If the applicant satisfies them of certain listed matters, the commission shall treat the claim as established. The only listed matters so far as relevant to the present claim were, the appellants argue, (1) the fact that the property referred to in Annex E was in Egypt; (2) the identity of the claimant as referred to in Annex E; and (3) the nationality of the claimant on certain dates. There is no dispute that on these matters they satisfied the commission. Therefore, on the appellants' argument, the commission had a mandatory duty to treat their claim as established. If their construction of Article 4 is correct, the appellants are right in this contention. There was no discretion in the commission, no jurisdiction to put further hurdles, other than those listed, in the path of the appellants' claim or to embark on inquiries other than those which the Order in Council directed. The commission, on the other hand, construed the Order as giving them jurisdiction to inquire and be satisfied on two further points; since they were not satisfied on these they rejected the claim. If *their* construction is correct, they were entitled to do so and have not exceeded their jurisdiction.

[His Lordship held that the commission's construction was erroneous.]

LORD WILBERFORCE: ... In every case, whatever the character of a tribunal, however wide the range of questions remitted to it, however great the permissible margin of mistake, the essential point remains that the tribunal has a derived authority, derived, that is, from statute: at some point, and to be found from a consideration of the legislation, the field within which it operates is marked out and limited. There is always an area, narrow or wide, which is the tribunal's area; a residual area, wide or narrow, in which the legislature has previously expressed its will and into which the tribunal may not enter. Equally, though this is not something that arises in the present case, there are certain fundamental assumptions, which without explicit restatement in every case, necessarily underlie the remission of power to decide such as (I do not attempt more than a general reference, since the strength and shade of these matters will depend upon the nature of the tribunal and the kind of question it has to decide) the requirement that a decision must be made in accordance with principles of natural justice and good faith. The principle that failure to fulfil these assumptions may be equivalent to a departure from the remitted area must be taken to follow from the decision of this House in *Ridge v. Baldwin* [1964] A.C. 40. Although, in theory perhaps, it may be possible for Parliament to set up a tribunal which has full and autonomous powers to fix its own area of operation, that has, so far, not been done in this country. The question, what is the tribunal's proper area, is one which it has always been permissible to ask and to answer, and it must follow that examination of its extent is not precluded by a clause conferring conclusiveness, finality, or unquestionability upon its decisions. These clauses in their nature can only relate to decisions given within the field of operation entrusted to the tribunal. They may, according to the width and emphasis of their formulation, help to ascertain the extent of that field, to narrow it or to enlarge it, but unless one is to deny the statutory origin of the tribunal and of its powers, they cannot preclude examination of that extent....

The courts, when they decide that a "decision" is a "nullity", are not disregarding the preclusive clause. For, just as it is their duty to attribute autonomy of decision of action to the tribunal within the designated area, so, as the counterpart of this autonomy, they must ensure that the limits of that area which have been laid down are observed (see the formulation of Lord Sumner in *R. v. Nat Bell Liquors Ltd* [1922] 2 A.C. 128, 156). In each task they are carrying out the intention of the legislature, and it would be misdescription to state it in terms of a struggle between the courts and the executive. What would be the purpose of defining by statute the limit of a tribunal's powers if, by means of a clause inserted in the instrument of definition, those limits could safely be passed?...

[His Lordship cited *R. v. Commissioners for Special Purposes of the Income Tax* (1888) 21 Q.B.D. 313, 319 (Lord Esher M.R.); *R. v. Shoreditch Assessment Committee, ex p. Morgan* [1910] 2 K.B. 859, 880 (Farwell L.J.); and *R. v. Northumberland C.A.T., ex p. Shaw* [1952] 1 K.B. 338, 346 (Denning L.J.).]

These passages at least answer one of the respondents' main arguments, to some extent accepted by the members of the Court of Appeal, which is that *because* the commission has (admittedly) been given power, indeed required, to decide some questions of law, arising out of the construction of the relevant Order in Council, it must necessarily have power to decide those questions which relate to the delimitation of its powers; or conversely that if the court has power to review the latter, it must also have power to review the former. But the one does not follow from the other: there is no reason why the Order in Council should not (as a matter of construction to be decided by the court) limit the tribunal's powers and at the same time (by the same process of construction) confer upon the tribunal power, in the exercise of its permitted task, to decide other questions of law, including questions of construction of the Order. I shall endeavour to show that this is what the Order has done.

The extent of the interpretatory power conferred upon the tribunal may sometimes be difficult to ascertain and argument may be possible whether this or that question of construction has been left to the tribunal, that is, is within the tribunal's field, or whether, because it pertains to the delimitation of the tribunal's area by the legislature, it is reserved for decision by the courts. Sometimes it will be possible to form a conclusion from the form and subject-matter of the legislation. In one case it may be seen that the legislature, while stating general objectives, is prepared to concede a wide area to the authority it establishes: this will often be the case where the decision involves a degree of policy-making rather than fact-finding, especially if the authority is a department of government or the Minister at its head. I think that we have reached a stage in our administrative law when we can view this question quite objectively, without any necessary predisposition towards one that questions of law, or questions of construction, are necessarily for the courts. In the kind of case I have mentioned there is no need to make this assumption. In another type of case it may be apparent that Parliament is itself directly and closely concerned with the definition and delimitation of certain matters of comparative detail and has marked by its language the intention that these shall accurately be observed. If *R. v. Minister of Health* [1939] 1 K.B. 232 was rightly decided, it must be because it was a case of the former type. The dispute related to a superannuation allowance and the statute provided that "any dispute" should be determined by the Minister. The basis of the decision is not very clearly expressed but can, I think, be taken to be that, as the context and subject-matter showed, the Minister had a field of decision extending to the construction of the superannuation provisions of the Act. The present case, by contrast, as examination of the relevant Order in Council will show, is clearly of the latter category.

I do not think it desirable to discuss further in detail the many decisions in the reports in this field. But two points may perhaps be made. First, the cases in which a tribunal has been held to have passed outside its proper limits are not limited to those in which it had no power to enter upon its inquiry or its jurisdiction, or has not satisfied a condition precedent. Certainly such cases exist (for example *ex p. Bradlaugh* (1878) 3 Q.B.D. 509) but they do not exhaust the principle. A tribunal may quite properly validly enter upon its task and in the course of carrying it out may make a decision which is invalid—not merely erroneous. This may be described as "asking the wrong question" or "applying the wrong test"—expressions not wholly satisfactory since they do not, in themselves, distinguish between doing something which is not in the tribunal's area and doing something wrong within that area—a crucial distinction which the court has to make. Cases held to be of the former kind (whether, on their facts, correctly or not does not affect the principle) are *Estate and Trust Agencies (1927) Ltd v. Singapore Improvement Trust* [1937] A.C. 898, 915–917; *Seereelall Jhuggroo v. Central Arbitration and Control Board* [1953] A.C. 151, 161 ("whether [the board] took into consideration matters outside the ambit of its jurisdiction and beyond the matters which it was entitled to consider"); *R. v. Fulham, Hammersmith and Kensington Rent Tribunal, ex p. Hierowski* [1953] 2 Q.B. 147. The present case, in my opinion, and it is at this point that I respectfully differ from the Court of Appeal, is of this kind. Secondly, I find myself obliged to state that I cannot regard *Smith v. East Elloe Rural District Council* [1956] A.C. 736 as a reliable solvent of this appeal, or of any case where similar questions arise. The preclusive clause was indeed very similar to the present but, however inevitable the particular decision may have been, it was given on too narrow a basis to assist us here. I agree with my noble and learned friends, Lord Reid and Lord Pearce, on this matter.

LORD PEARSON dissented.

Appeal allowed.

Notes

1. This was for several years the most significant modern case on jurisdictional control, and it generated a series of important articles; see H.W.R. Wade (1969) 85 L.Q.R. 198; S.A. de Smith [1969] C.L.J. 161; B.C. Gould [1970] P.L. 358; J.A. Smillie (1969) 47 Can. Bar Rev. 623; D. Gordon (1971) 34 M.L.R. 1. See also D.G.T. Williams [1969] A.S.C.L. 125–126, 129–130; Cooke J. [1975] N.Z.L.J. 529; Sykes and Maher (1970) 7 Melbourne U.L.R. 385; J.K. Bentil (1976) U. of W.A.L.R. 543.

2. The judgments of Browne J. (at first instance) and of Diplock L.J. (in the Court of Appeal) contain valuable analyses of the issues and of the case law.

3. The sequel to *Anisminic* was summarised by S.A. de Smith [1969] C.L.J. at 164–166. See the Foreign Compensation Act 1969, s.3. Points of interest in section 3 include the express power of the Commission "to determine any question as to the construction or interpretation of any provision of an Order in Council under section 3 of the 1950 Act with respect to claims failing to be determined by them" (1969 Act, s.3(1)); the provision of an appeal by way of case stated on a point of law to the Court of Appeal (s.3(4)–(7)); and the provision that a "determination" (which includes a "provisional determination" and "anything which purports to be a determination" (s.3(3))) is not to be called in question in any court of law (s.3(9)) except on the ground of breach of natural justice (s.3(10)).

4. The question whether *all* errors of law (or just some: and if so, which) should be regarded as going to jurisdiction was considered in a somewhat troublesome line of decisions in the years following *Anisminic*. In 1979 Lord Denning M.R. in *Pearlman v. Keepers and Governors of Harrow School* [1979] Q.B. 56 expressed the view that the search for a test by which to distinguish errors of law which were jurisdictional from those which were not should be abandoned: and that thenceforth all errors of law upon which a decision-maker's decision depended should be regarded as jurisdictional. The other judges of the Court of Appeal expressed more limited opinions. Both Eveleigh L.J. and Lane L.J. approached the matter on the basis that the distinction remained significant. The former regarded the error in question as going to jurisdiction; the latter viewed the error as non-jurisdictional.

Then in *Re Racal* [1981] A.C. 374 Lord Diplock offered influential thoughts as regards the scope of review for error of law. His Lordship drew a distinction for purposes of the scope of such review between different kinds of body subject to review. In his opinion the decision on a point of law of a county court judge (as in *Pearlman*) was reviewable only where the error was such as to go to jurisdiction in the traditional (albeit somewhat unclear sense). *Pearlman* should therefore be regarded as wrongly decided, and the approach of Lane L.J. (regarding the alleged error of law as non-jurisdictional) was supported. Lord Diplock drew a distinction, however, between such cases and the more usual situation where the body under challenge was an "administrative tribunal" or "administrative authority". In such cases the distinction between jurisdictional and non-jurisdictional errors of law should be regarded as redundant. The decision in *Anisminic* should, it was argued, be regarded as an instance of the application of this wider power of review for error of law *simpliciter*: the Foreign Compensation Commission being a statutory tribunal. Having so explained this leading case, His Lordship proceeded, in language which has found much favour since, to describe this undifferentiated power of review as the "*Anisminic* principle".

Lord Diplock returned to this matter in his opinion in *O'Reilly v. Mackman* [1983] 2 A.C. 237. In order to clarify the position as regards the scope of review of certain inferior courts of law (but not disturbing the approach towards the county court) his Lordship revised his formulation of the bodies subject to the "*Anisminic* principle" so as now to comprise "inferior courts, administrative and statutory tribunals and administrative authorities".

R. v. LORD PRESIDENT OF THE PRIVY COUNCIL, ex p. PAGE

[1993] A.C. 682; [1993] 1 All E.R. 97 (House of Lords)

In 1988 Mr Page, who had held a lectureship at the University of Hull since 1966, was given three months' written notice terminating his employment on the ground of redundancy. His appointment was subject to the terms of his letter of appointment and also the statutes of the university.

Mr Page commenced an action in the High Court for wrongful dismissal. This was struck out on the grounds that Mr Page's complaint lay within the exclusive jurisdiction of the visitor of the university, Her Majesty the Queen. Mr Page petitioned the visitor for a declaration that his purported dismissal was contrary to the statutes of the university, was *ultra vires* and of no effect.

The Lord President of the Council took advice from Lord Jauncey of Tullichettle (a Lord of Appeal in Ordinary) as regards the proper construction of the statutes. The advice tendered was that on the true construction of the statutes the dismissal was valid and *intra vires*. The visitor therefore dismissed the petition.

Mr Page then commenced proceedings by way judicial review to seek to quash the visitor's decision. Two issues were raised: (i) did the High Court have jurisdiction to review decisions of the university visitor; and (ii) if it did, had the visitor rejected the petition on the basis of a misconstruction of the statutes?

The Divisional Court answered both questions in the affirmative. The Court of Appeal recognised jurisdiction in the High Court to review abuse of power by visitors (including misconstruction of statutes), but held that there had been no such misconstruction in this case. Mr Page appealed to the House of Lords on the point of construction: the visitor and the university appealed on the issue of the power of judicial review in respect of visitors.

Their Lordships were unanimous that the visitor had made no error in the interpretation of the statutes. On the issue of the power to review decisions of visitors a majority of their Lordships (Lords Browne-Wilkinson, Griffiths and Keith) held that visitors were not subject to review for misconstruction of the statutes laying down the domestic law of their charitable foundation. A visitor would be subject to review, however, should he or she act outside jurisdiction in the sense of embarking upon a dispute where this was beyond the visitor's functions laid down in the governing statutes. Equally, a visitor was subject to review for breach of natural justice. The minority (Lords Mustill and Slynn) considered that visitors' decisions should be reviewable also for error of law.

Their Lordships' speeches contain important general statements of principle as regards the scope of review for error of law. It is on this broad question, rather than the specific construction issue or the issue of the partial immunity of visitors from review, that the extracts below focus.

LORD GRIFFITHS: ... It is in my opinion important to keep the purpose of judicial review clearly in mind. The purpose is to ensure that those bodies that are susceptible to judicial review have carried out their public duties in the way it was intended they should. In the case of bodies other than courts, in so far as they are required to apply the law, they are required to apply the law correctly. If they apply the law incorrectly they have not performed their duty correctly and judicial review is available to correct their error of law so that they may make their decision upon a proper understanding of the law.

In the case of inferior courts, that is courts of a lower status than the High Court, such as the justices of the peace, it was recognised that their learning and understanding of the law might sometimes be imperfect and require correction by the High Court and so the rule evolved that certiorari was available to correct an error of law of an inferior court. At first it was confined to an error on the face of the record but it is now available to correct any error of law made by an inferior court. But despite this general rule Parliament can if it wishes confine a decision on a question of law to a particular inferior court and provide that the decision shall be final so that it is not to be challenged either by appeal or by judicial review. Such a case was *Pearlman v. Keepers and Governors of Harrow School* [1979] 1 All E.R. 365; [1979] Q.B. 56, in which the dissenting judgment of Geoffrey Lane L.J. was approved by the majority of the House of Lords in *Re Racal Communications Ltd* [1980] 2 All E.R. 634; [1981] A.C. 374.

The common law has ever since the decision in *Philips v. Bury* (1694) Holt K.B. 715; 90 E.R. 1294 recognised that the visitor acting as a judge has exclusive jurisdiction and that his decision is final in all matters within his jurisdiction. The common law courts have through three centuries consistently resisted all attempts to appeal decisions of the visitor. The courts have, however, been prepared to confine the visitor to his proper role as a judge of the internal affairs of the foundation by the use of the writs of prohibition and mandamus.

When I said in *Thomas*'s case [1987] 1 All E.R. 834 at 850; [1987] A.C. 795 at 825:

> "... I have myself no doubt that in the light of the modern development of administrative law, the High Court would have power, upon an application for judicial review, to quash a decision of the visitor which amounted to an abuse of his powers"

I used the words "an abuse of his powers" advisedly. I do not regard a judge who makes what an appellate court later regards as a mistake of law as abusing his powers. In such a case the judge is not abusing his powers: he is exercising them to the best of his ability albeit some other court thinks he was mistaken. I used the phrase "abuse of his powers" to connote some form of misbehaviour that was wholly incompatible with the judicial role that the judge was expected to perform. I did not intend it to include a mere error of law.

The decision in the *Racal* case shows that Parliament can by the use of appropriate language provide that a decision on a question of law whether taken by a judge or by some other form of tribunal shall be considered as final and not be subject to challenge either by way of appeal or judicial review. ...

LORD BROWNE-WILKINSON: ... Under the modern law, certiorari normally lies to quash a decision for error of law. Therefore, the narrow issue in this case is whether, as Mr Page contends and the courts below have held, certiorari lies against the visitor to quash his decision as being erroneous in point of law notwithstanding that the question of law arises under the domestic law of the university which the visitor has "exclusive" jurisdiction to decide. ...

The decision of Holt C.J. in *Philips v. Bury* is the locus classicus of the law of visitors. It has been repeatedly applied for the last 300 years, most recently in *Thomas v. University of Bradford*. For present purposes it is important for three reasons. (1) It shows that the court can and will inquire whether the visitor has jurisdiction to determine the question, *i.e.* to enter into the matter. (2) If the visitor has such jurisdiction, the court has no power to ignore it or review it by way of mandamus or in any other way. (3) The reason for such lack of jurisdiction to review in the court is that an eleemosynary corporation is governed by a system of private law which is not of "the common known laws of the kingdom" but the particular laws and constitutions assigned by the founder. ...

In my judgment this review of the authorities demonstrates that for over 300 years the law has been clearly established that the visitor of an eleemosynary charity has an exclusive jurisdiction to determine what are the internal laws of the charity and the proper application of those laws to those within his jurisdiction. The court's inability to determine those matters is not limited to the period pending the visitor's determination but extends so as to prohibit any subsequent review by the court of the correctness of a decision made by the visitor acting within his jurisdiction and in accordance with the rules of natural justice. This inability of the court to intervene is founded on the fact that the applicable law is not the common law of England but a peculiar or domestic law of which the visitor is the sole judge. This special status of a visitor springs from the common law recognising the right of the founder to lay down such a special law subject to adjudication only by a special judge, the visitor.

How then is it contended that the courts have power to review the visitor's decision as to the effect of the domestic law of the university in this case? The Divisional Court and the Court of Appeal did not consider in any detail the old authorities to which I have referred. They started from the position, in my judgment incorrectly, that the references in *Thomas*'s case to the visitor's jurisdiction being exclusive meant simply that the court did not have concurrent jurisdiction with him. Then, since this House in *Thomas*'s case had accepted that judicial review by way of certiorari did lie to the visitor at least to restrain an abusive process, they held that there was jurisdiction to correct errors of law since "illegality" is one of the accepted heads of judicial review.

Before your Lordships, Mr Burke Q.C. refined this argument. He relied upon the great development that has recently taken place in the law of judicial review whereby the courts have asserted a general jurisdiction to review the decisions of tribunals and inferior courts. He points to the way in which the law has developed from a maze of individual sets of circumstances in which one or other of the prerogative writs would lie to a general principle under which courts will review decisions on the three grounds of illegality, irrationality and procedural impropriety: see *Council of Civil Service Unions v. Minister for the Civil Service* [1984] 3 All E.R. 935 at 950; [1985] A.C. 374 at 410 *per* Lord Diplock. Mr Burke submits that, if judicial review lies at all, then it is not possible to pick and choose between Lord Diplock's three categories: it must lie on all three grounds or not at all. As to illegalilty, recent developments in the law have shown that any relevant error of law made by the decision-maker, whether as to his powers or as to the law he is to apply, may lead to his decision being quashed. In the present case, since the decision in *Thomas*'s case shows that judicial review does lie against the visitor, so his decision is capable of being reviewed on any one of Lord Diplock's three grounds, including illegality. If, therefore, the visitor has made an error in construing the statutes of the university, his decision can be quashed on judicial review.

I accept much of Mr Burke's submissions. Over the last 40 years the courts have developed general principles of judicial review. The fundamental principle is that the courts will intervene to ensure that the powers of public decision-making bodies are exercised lawfully. In all cases, save possibly one, this intervention by way of prohibition or certiorari is based on the proposition that such powers have been conferred on the decision-maker on the underlying assumption that the powers are to be exercised only within the jurisdiction conferred, in accordance with fair procedures and, in a *Wednesbury* sense (see *Associated Provincial Picture Houses Ltd v. Wednesbury Corp* [1947] 2 All E.R. 680; [1948] 1 K.B. 223), reasonably. If the decision-maker exercises his powers outside the jurisdiction conferred, in a manner which is procedurally irregular or is *Wednesbury* unreasonable, he is acting *ultra vires* his powers and therefore unlawfully: see Wade, *Administrative Law* (6th ed., 1988), pp. 39 *et seq*. The one possible exception to this general rule used to be the jurisdiction of the court to quash a decision taken within the jurisdiction of the decision-taker where an error of law appeared on the face of the record: *R. v. Northumberland Compensation Appeal Tribunal, ex p. Shaw* [1952] 1 All E.R. 122; [1952] 1 K.B. 338.

In my judgment the decision in *Anisminic Ltd v. Foreign Compensation Commission* [1969] 1 All E.R. 208; [1969] 2 A.C. 147 rendered obsolete the distinction between errors of law on the face of the record and other errors of law by extending the doctrine of *ultra vires*. Thenceforward it was to be taken that Parliament had only conferred the decision-making power on the basis that it was to be exercised on the correct legal basis: a misdirection in law in making the decision therefore rendered the decision *ultra vires*. Professor Wade considers that the true effect of the *Anisminic* case is still in doubt: see Wade, pp. 299 *et seq*. But in my judgment the decision of this House in *O'Reilly v. Mackman* [1982] 3 All E.R. 1124; [1983] 2 A.C. 237 establishes the law in the sense that I have stated. Lord Diplock, with whose speech all the other members of the committee agreed, said that the decision in the *Anisminic* case—

"has liberated English public law from the fetters that the courts had theretofore imposed upon themselves so far as determinations of inferior courts and statutory tribunals were concerned, by drawing esoteric distinctions between errors of law committed by such tribunals that went to their jurisdiction, and errors of law committed by them within their jurisdiction. The breakthrough that *Anisminic* made was the recognition by the majority of this House that if a tribunal whose jurisdiction was limited by statute or subordinate legislation mistook the law applicable to the facts as it had found them, it must have asked itself the wrong question, *i.e.* one into which it was not empowered to inquire and so had no jurisdiction to determine. Its purported 'determination', not being 'a determination' within the meaning of the empowering legislation, was accordingly a nullity." (See [1982] 3 All E.R. 1124 at 1129; [1983] 2 A.C. 237 at 278.)

Therefore, I agree with Mr Burke that in general any error of law made by an administrative tribunal or inferior court in reaching its decision can be quashed for error of law.

At this point I must notice an argument raised by Mr Beloff Q.C. for the university. He suggests that the recent decision of this House in *R. v. Independent Television Commission, ex p. TSW Broadcasting Ltd*, *The Independent*, March 27, 1992, has thrown doubt on the proposition that all errors of law vitiate the decision. In my judgment this is a misreading of that authority. This House was asserting that the mere existence of a mistake of law made at some earlier stage does not vitiate the actual decision made: what must be shown is a relevant error of law, *i.e.* an error in the actual making of the decision which affected the decision itself. This is demonstrated by Lord Templeman's quotation from the well-known judgment of Lord Greene M.R. in the *Wednesbury* case [1947] 2 All E.R. 680 at 682–683: [1948] 1 K.B. 223 at 229 (including the passage "a person entrusted with a discretion must, so to speak, direct himself properly in law") and the manner in which thereafter he applied those principles to the facts of the case before the House.

Although the general rule is that decisions affected by errors of law made by tribunals or inferior courts can be quashed, in my judgment there are two reasons why that rule does not apply in the case of visitors. First, as I have sought to explain, the constitutional basis of the courts' power to quash is that the decision of the inferior tribunal is unlawful on the grounds that it is *ultra vires*. In the ordinary case, the law applicable to a decision made by such a body is the general law of the land. Therefore, a tribunal or inferior court acts *ultra vires* if it reaches its conclusion on a basis erroneous under the general law. But the position of decisions made by a visitor is different. As the authorities which I have cited demonstrate, the visitor is applying not the general law of the land but a peculiar, domestic law of which he is the sole arbiter and of which the courts have no cognisance. If the visitor has power under the regulating documents to enter into the adjudication of the dispute (*i.e.* is acting within his jurisdiction in the narrow sense) he cannot err in law in reaching this decision since the general law is not the applicable law. Therefore he cannot be acting *ultra vires* and unlawfully by applying his view of the domestic law in reaching his decision. The court has no jurisdiction either to say that he erred in his application of the general law (since the general law is not applicable to the decision) or to reach a contrary view as to the effect of the domestic law (since the visitor is the sole judge of such domestic law).

The second reason is closely allied to the first. In *Pearlman v. Keepers and Governors of Harrow School* [1979] 1 All E.R. 365; [1979] Q.B. 56 a statute provided that the decision of the county court as to whether works constituted an "improvement" within the meaning of the Act should be "final and conclusive". A tenant claimed that the installation of a central heating system constituted an "improvement". The county court judge ruled that it did not. The tenant then applied to the Divisional Court by way of judicial review to quash the judge's decision. The majority of the Court of Appeal held that it had jurisdiction to quash the judge's order. However, Geoffrey Lane L.J. dissented. He held that the judge had done nothing which went outside the proper area of his inquiry. The question was not whether the judge had made a wrong decision but whether he had inquired into and decided a matter which he had no right to consider. Therefore he held that the court had no jurisdiction to review the decision of the county court judge for error of law.

This dissenting judgment of Geoffrey Lane L.J. has been approved by the Privy Council in *South East Asia Fire Bricks Sdn Bhd v. Non-Metallic Mineral Products Manufacturing Employees Union* [1980] 2 All E.R. 689 at 692; [1981] A.C. 363 at 370 and by a majority in this House in *Re Racal Communications Ltd* [1980] 2 All E.R. 634 at 639, 644–645; [1981] A.C. 374 at 384, 390–391. In the latter case, Lord Diplock pointed out that the decision in *Anisminic* applied to decisions of administrative tribunals or other administrative bodies made under statutory powers: in those cases there was a presumption that the statute conferring the power did not intend the administrative body to be the final arbiter of questions of law. He then contrasted that position with the case where a decision-making power had been conferred on a court of law. In that case no such presumption could exist; on the contrary where Parliament had provided that the decision of an inferior court was final and conclusive the High Court should not be astute to find that the inferior court's decision on a question of law had not been made final and conclusive, thereby excluding the jurisdiction to review it.

In my judgment, therefore, if there were a statutory provision that the decision of a visitor on the law applicable to internal disputes of a charity was to be "final and conclusive", courts would have no jurisdiction to review the visitor's decision on the grounds of error of law made by the visitor within his jurisdiction (in the narrow sense). For myself, I can see no relevant distinction between a case where a statute has conferred such final and conclusive jurisdiction and the case where the common law has for 300 years recognised that the visitor's decision on questions of fact and law are final and conclusive and are not to be reviewed by the courts. Accordingly, unless this House is prepared to sweep away long-established law, there is no jurisdiction in the court to review a visitor's decision for error of law committed within his jurisdiction.

Mr Burke urged that the position of a visitor would be anomalous if he were immune from review on the grounds of error of law. He submitted that the concept of a peculiar domestic law differing from the general law of the land was artificial since in practice the charter and statutes of a university are expressed in ordinary legal language and applied in accordance with the same principles as those applicable under the general law. He pointed to the important public role occupied by universities and submitted that it was wrong that they should be immune from the general law of the land: "There must be no Alsatia in England where the King's writ does not run": see *Czarnikow v. Roth Schmidt & Co.* [1922] 2 K.B. 478 at 488; [1922] All E.R. Rep. 45 at 50 *per* Scrutton L.J. He further suggested that to permit review of a visitor's decision for error of law would not impair the effectiveness of the visitor's domestic jurisdiction.

I accept that the position of the visitor is anomalous, indeed unique. I further accept that where the visitor is, or is advised by, a lawyer the distinction between the peculiar domestic law he applies and the general law is artificial. But I do not regard these factors as justifying sweeping away the law which for so long has regulated the conduct of charitable corporations. There are internal disputes which are resolved by a visitor who is not a lawyer himself and has not taken legal advice. It is not only modern universities which have visitors: there are a substantial number of other long-established educational, ecclesiastical and eleemosynary bodies which have visitors. The advantages of having an informal system which produces a speedy, cheap and final answer to internal disputes has been repeatedly emphasised in the authorities, most recently by this House in the *Thomas v. University of Bradford* [1987] 1 All E.R. 834 at 850; [1987] A.C. 795 at 825 *per* Lord Griffiths; see also *Patel v. University of Bradford Senate* [1978] 3 All E.R. 841 at 852; [1978] 1 W.L.R. 1488 at 1499–1500. If it were to be held that judicial review for error of law lay against the visitor I fear that, as in the present case, finality would be lost not only in cases raising pure questions of law but also in cases where it would be urged in accordance with the *Wednesbury* principle that the visitor had failed to take into account relevant matters or taken into account irrelevant matters or had reached an irrational conclusion. Although the visitor's position is anomalous, it provides a valuable machinery for resolving internal disputes which should not be lost.

I have therefore reached the conclusion that judicial review does not lie to impeach the decisions of a visitor taken within his jurisdiction (in the narrow sense) on questions of either fact or law. Judicial review does lie to the visitor in cases where he has acted outside his jurisdiction (in the narrow sense) or abused his powers or acted in breach of the rules of natural justice. Accordingly, in my judgment the Divisional Court had no jurisdiction to entertain the application for judicial review of the visitor's decision in this case. ...

LORD SLYNN OF HADLEY: ... On this appeal questions as to the court's jurisdiction and as to the proper construction of the university's statutes have been raised.

The jurisdiction issue seems to me to divide into two parts. First, does judicial review by way of certiorari ever lie to review error of law where there is no issue as to excess of jurisdiction or breach of natural justice? If it does not, it cannot in any event lie against a visitor on that basis. If it does, the second question is whether certiorari can lie in respect of the decision of a visitor.

As to the first question it is clear that views as to the availability and scope of certiorari together with its actual use have varied from time to time. In particular distinctions were drawn between errors of law going to jurisdiction and errors of law within jurisdiction and between errors of law on the face of the record and other errors on law which in neither case went to jurisdiction.

For my part and despite the advice of the Privy Council in *South East Asia Fire Bricks Sdn Bhd v. Non-Metallic Mineral Products Manufacturing Employees Union* [1980] 2 All E.R. 689; [1981] A.C. 363. I would now follow the opinion of Lord Diplock in *Re Racal Communications Ltd* [1980] 2 All E.R. 634; [1981] A.C. 374 (with which Lord Keith of Kinkel agreed) and in *O'Reilly v. Mackman* [1982] 3 All E.R. 1124; [1983] 2 A.C. 237 (with which the other members of the Appellate Committee agreed). In the former case Lord Diplock said ([1980] 2 All E.R. 634 at 638–639; [1981] A.C. 374 at 382–383):

"The breakthrough made by *Anisminic* was that, as respects administrative tribunals and authorities, the old distinction between errors of law that went to jurisdiction and errors of law that did not was for practical purposes abolished."

In the latter case Lord Diplock said that the decision in *Anisminic Ltd v. Foreign Compensation Commission* [1969] 1 All E.R. 208; [1969] 2 A.C. 147—

"has liberated English public law from the fetters that the courts had theretofore imposed upon themselves so far as determinations of inferior courts and statutory tribunals were concerned, by drawing esoteric distinctions between errors of law committed by such tribunals that went to their jurisdiction, and errors of law committed by them within their jurisdiction. The breakthrough that the *Anisminic* case made was the recognition by the majority of this House that if a tribunal whose jurisdiction was limited by statute or subordinate legislation mistook the law applicable to the facts as it found them, it must have asked itself the wrong question, *i.e.* one into which it was not empowered to inquire and so had no jurisdiction to determine. Its purported 'determination', not being a 'determination' within the meaning of the empowering legislation, was accordingly a nullity." (See [1982] 3 All E.R. 1124 at 1129; [1983] 2 A.C. 237 at 278.)

I accordingly accept that certiorari is now available to quash errors of law in a decision albeit those errors do not go to the jurisdiction of the tribunal. ...

Notes

1. The question of the scope of review for error of law was considered by Lord Cooke of Thorndon in the House of Lords in *Williams v. Bedwellty Justices* [1996] 3 All E.R. 737 at 742, 743:

"In approaching the appeal I will avoid as far as reasonably practicable that which the certified question successfully avoids, namely the use of the term 'jurisdiction'. It is a term used in a number of different senses, and possibly its popularity and convenience are partly due to its very ambiguity. For instance one can say, without any distortion of ordinary language, (i) that a superior court of general jurisdiction, such as the High Court of Justice, has jurisdiction to determine, subject to any provisions for appeal, the limits of its own jurisdiction; (ii) that the authorities now establish that the Queen's Bench Division of the High Court has normally in judicial review proceedings jurisdiction to quash a decision of an inferior court, tribunal or other statutory body for error of law, even though the error is neither apparent on the face of the record nor so serious as to deprive the body of jurisdiction in the original and narrow sense of powers to enter on the inquiry and to make against persons subject to its jurisdiction the kind of decision in question; and (iii) that the second proposition may often be otherwise expressed by saying that the body acts outside its jurisdiction if it asks itself the wrong question. Such familiar propositions illustrate some (but not all) of the diverse shades of meaning which the term can bear.

Perhaps it is indeed the versatility rather than the precision of the term that has lent persuasiveness to some leading judgments of the past. A sufficient illustration is the judgment of Lord Sumner in the Privy Council case of *R. v. Nat Bell Liquors Ltd* [1922] 2 A.C. 128 at 151–152; [1922] All E.R. Rep. 335 at 348, with its statement:

'A justice who convicts without evidence is doing something that he ought not to do, but he is doing it as a judge, and if his jurisdiction to entertain the charge is not open to impeachment, his subsequent error, however grave, is a wrong exercise of a jurisdiction which he has, and not a usurpation of a jurisdiction which he has not. How a magistrate, who has acted within his jurisdiction up to the point at which the missing evidence should have been, but was not, given, can, thereafter, be said by a kind of relation back to have had no jurisdiction over the charge at all, it is hard to see.'

To convict or commit for trial without any admissible evidence of guilt is to fall into an error of law. As to the availability of certiorari to quash a committal for such an error, I understood at the end of the arguments that all your Lordships were satisfied that in principle the remedy is available and that the only issue presenting any difficulty relates to the exercise of the court's discretion. This conclusion about principle reflects the position now reached in the development of the modern law of judicial review in England through a sequence of cases beginning with *R. v. Northumberland Compensation Appeal Tribunal, ex p. Shaw* [1952] 1 All E.R. 122; [1952] 1 K.B. 338 and extending by way most notably of *Anisminic Ltd v. Foreign Compensation Commission* [1969] 1 All E.R. 208; [1969] 2 A.C. 147 to (at present) *Page v. Hull University Visitor* [1993] 1 All E.R. 97; [1993] A.C. 682. The path of the authorities is traced in such leading textbooks as Wade and Forsyth *Administrative Law* (7th ed., 1994), pp. 301–311 and de Smith, Woolf and Jowell *Judicial Review of Administrative Action* (5th ed., 1995), pp. 237–256. To attempt to repeat the exercise here would be surplusage. It is enough to take *Page*'s case as stating the developed law.

In *Page*'s case the five members of the Appellate Committee (Lord Keith of Kinkel, Lord Griffiths, Lord Browne-Wilkinson, Lord Mustill and Lord Slynn of Hadley) were unanimous that usually any error of law made by an administrative tribunal or inferior court in reaching its decision can be quashed by certiorari for error of law. There were, however, observations to the effect that as regards an inferior court of law a statutory provision that its decision is to be "final and conclusive" or the like will confine the remedy to cases of abuse of power, acting outside jurisdiction in the narrow sense, or breach of natural justice. Moreover, there was a division of opinion on whether the university visitor was applying a peculiar domestic law of which, historically and for reasons of policy, he was to be treated as the sole arbiter."

2. If all errors of law go to jurisdiction the scope of the concept "error of law" becomes critical, and may itself become the vehicle by which courts of review may extend or limit their scope of review. See further, below, pp. 564–574.

3. In *Page* reference is made to the notion of review for "lack of jurisdiction in the narrow sense". This ground of review will be applicable even as regards bodies not subject to review for error of law in the sense described in *Page* (*e.g.* those exercising visitorial jurisdictions, the county court as in *Pearlman*).

What is meant by "lack of jurisdiction in the narrow sense"? In addition to the illumination of the concept given in the extract above, the following points seem established by the case law. The proper composition of a tribunal is usually a jurisdictional matter. For example, in *Howard v. Borneman (No. 2)* [1976] A.C. 301, the House of Lords had to decide whether a provision (the Finance Act 1960, s.28(7)) that a tribunal shall consist of a chairman "and two or more persons appointed by the Lord Chancellor as having special knowledge of and experience in financial or commercial matters" meant that the tribunal was only validly constituted for a particular case if all the appointed members took part. The House decided that the tribunal was validly constituted provided that the chairman and not less than two of the appointed members took part. See also, *R. v. Merseyside Coroner, ex p. Carr* [1993] 4 All E.R. 65 (improperly summoned jury).

It is quite common for Parliament to provide that the acts of a tribunal or other body shall be valid notwithstanding a defect in the appointment of a person purporting to be a member. An example is paragraph 20(2) of Schedule IX to the Agriculture Act 1947, which was held by the Court of Appeal to cure the defective appointments of two members of an agricultural land tribunal in *Woollett v. Minister of Agriculture* [1955]

1 Q.B. 103. (The defects were that they were appointed neither by the Minister as specified by para. 15 of Sched. IX, nor by a properly authorised civil servant.) Denning L.J. said at 121:

> "I cannot help remarking that it would be most unfortunate if we came to any other conclusion. The members of the land tribunals in the eastern province have been appointed in this way for several years. They have made decisions in a great many disputes and people have acted on the faith of their decisions. Indeed, we have had cases in this court where these tribunals have given consent to notices to quit by landlords to tenants; and many landlords have recovered their lands on the basis that the decisions are valid: see *Martin-Smith v. Smale* [1954] 1 W.L.R. 247. If all the decisions were now invalidated by a technical defect, it would produce great confusion and injustice. It is just the thing which paragraph 20(2) was made to avoid."

Other similar statutory provisions include section 82 of the Local Government Act 1972 (members of local authorities) and section 193 of the Licensing Act 1964 (licensing justices (see *Paterson's Licensing Acts* (1991 ed.), pp. 510 *et seq.*)).

The question of the proper composition of a tribunal may be described as a preliminary jurisdictional requirement, or equally properly as a question of procedural *ultra vires*. Questions of composition are also raised by allegations of bias against a tribunal member, on which see pp. 516–537, below, and by the general rule that no person ought to participate in the deliberations of a judicial or quasi-judicial body unless he is a member of it (see *Ward v. Bradford Corporation* (1971) 70 L.G.R. 27). See further: P. Jackson (1974) 90 L.Q.R. 158 and (1975) 91 L.Q.R. 469.

The geographical competence of a tribunal is usually regarded as a jurisdictional question. For example, each panel of General Commissioners for Income Tax exercises jurisdiction in respect of a particular geographical area or "division". The allocation of the various kinds of proceedings which may come before the General Commissioners, to the appropriate panel, is governed by section 44 and Schedule 3 to the Taxes Management Act 1970. These rules may include the determination of such questions as where trade is "carried on", or where the appellant "ordinarily resides". See *Lack v. Doggett* (1970) 46 T.C. 497, C.A. and *R. v. Inland Revenue Commissioners, ex p. Knight* [1973] 3 All E.R. 721, C.A.

A tribunal may lack jurisdiction where proceedings before it are not properly instituted. *cf. Campbell v. Wallsend Slipway & Engineering Co. Ltd* [1978] I.C.R. 1015 where the Divisional Court held that justices did have jurisdiction to proceed with certain informations laid by an inspector of the Health and Safety Executive. The justices had dismissed the informations on the ground that the inspector was not competent to prosecute. The court held (1) that the presumption *omnia praesumuntur rite esse acta* applied in favour of the validity of the appointment of the Executive, and of the inspector, which presumption could only be rebutted by evidence; and (2) that provisions of the Health and Safety at Work Act, etc., 1974, requiring certain formalities on the appointment of the Executive, were directory only.

CHAPTER 6

REVIEW OF THE EXERCISE OF DISCRETION— RETENTION OF DISCRETION

IN this and the following chapter we shall be considering judicial review in relation to the exercise of discretionary powers. By "discretionary power" we mean the situation where a body has a power of choice, in the circumstances, to do "X" or not to do "X"; or to do "X" and/or "Y" or do neither. We shall be concerned to see what principles of review are applied by the courts in supervising such discretionary powers. We are not here concerned with the situation where a body has had a "duty" imposed upon it to act in a designated way in defined circumstances, involving no exercise of discretion on the part of that body.

In the cases which follow there is usually no argument as to whether the body challenged has, in the circumstances, the discretionary power in question. In this way the cases differ from those which have formed the subject-matter of Chapter 5. In the cases which follow the challenge is made on the ground that a body on which the statutory power in question has been conferred *either*:

(i) **has failed properly to retain that degree of free and unfettered power of judgment** as to whether, and, if so how, it should exercise its discretionary powers, which Parliament is assumed by the courts to have intended that donees of such powers should have retained. Such failure may arise in a number of ways, and we shall look at the decisions under the following sub-headings—"acting under dictation", "failure to retain discretion by unauthorised delegation of power", "over-rigid adherence to self-created rules of policy", "fettering discretion by contractual or similar undertakings", and "fettering discretion by estoppel". These matters are considered in this chapter.

or,

(ii) **has exercised its powers in a way which the reviewing court may categorise as an "abuse of power".** The courts have consistently stated that powers must be exercised for "proper purposes," must be exercised on the basis of consideration of "relevant" matters and the exclusion from consideration of "irrelevant" matters, and the manner of the exercise of power must not in substance be "unreasonable"— must not be a manner of exercising the power which no reasonable person/body could have chosen. These various grounds of challenge for "abuse of power" form the principal subject-matter of Chapter 7.

(A) ACTING UNDER DICTATION

R. v. THE MAYOR, ALDERMEN AND COUNCILLORS OF STEPNEY

[1902] 1 K.B. 317; 71 L.J.K.B. 238; 86 L.T. 21; 18 T.L.R. 98;
66 J.P. 183; 46 S.J. 106; 50 W.R. 412, D.C. (King's Bench Division)

Mr Jutsum was clerk to the vestry of Mile End Old Town from 1872 to 1901. In 1901 this parish was included in the new metropolitan borough of Stepney. The existing parish officers were transferred to the borough council. Under the London Government Act 1899, s.30(1), the council had power to abolish the office of any officer transferred to them, whose office they deemed unnecessary. They accordingly abolished J's office. He was now entitled to compensation calculated in accordance with the Local Government Act 1888, s.120. This stated that regard should be had, *inter alia*, to the conditions on which his appointment was made, to the nature of his office or employment, to the duration of his service "and to all the other circumstances of the case, and the compensation shall not exceed the amount which, under the Acts and Rules relating to Her Majesty's Civil Service, is paid to a person on abolition of office".

J held his post on a part-time basis, as he was also a solicitor in private practice. The town clerk of Stepney wrote to the Treasury asking what their rule was as to the amount of compensation paid to a person in the civil service on abolition of an office, held part time. The reply was that the Treasury's practice was to calculate the compensation allowance as if the office was full time, but to deduct a quarter of the amount so arrived at. The council acted on this letter and assessed the compensation accordingly.

J applied for mandamus to compel the council to deal with his claim properly. He could have appealed to the Treasury under section 120(4), who had power to determine what sum "ought to be granted".

CHANNELL J.: ... I think that the mandamus ought to go because the local authority have not in fact exercised their discretion upon this matter. They have, by a mistake, thought that they were bound by a practice of the Treasury as though it were a rule, and consequently they exercised no discretion in the matter. In my opinion, if they had said "We quite know that we are not bound by this absolutely, but we think it right to follow the Treasury practice", and had so followed it, they would have exercised their discretion and would have been right; but they thought that they were bound when they were not bound, and consequently it is a case for a mandamus calling upon them to exercise their discretion in the matter.... It is clearly settled that the Court does not grant a prerogative writ of mandamus when there is another remedy, if that other remedy is equally convenient and adequate.... I think he has another remedy; but I do not think on the whole, after some consideration, that it is equally convenient, because I think that the local tribunal is the one that is best to investigate in the first instance the particular facts about this gentleman's employment. They will know much more about it than the Treasury can know, and it is much better that they should investigate the facts in the first instance. I think, therefore, that although the applicant here could, in the present state of things, go to the Treasury and get them to decide finally the amount of the allowance which he ought to have—and very likely he will have to go there in the end, and the Treasury will ultimately have to decide the matter—yet I do not think that that is an equally convenient remedy where the local authority have not exercised their discretion, because if he goes to the Treasury now he will have to go without the preliminary investigation, which might or might not be useful to him in going there. . . .

LORD ALVERSTONE C.J. and DARLING J. delivered concurring judgments.

Notes

1. In *Roncarelli v. Duplessis* (1959) 16 D.L.R. (2d) 689, it was found that D, the Prime Minister and Attorney-General of Quebec, ordered the Quebec Licensing Commission to revoke R's liquor permit, in response to R's activities in acting in over 380 cases as surety for Jehovah's Witnesses charged with distributing literature (some of which was thought to be seditious) without a licence. The discretion to revoke was legally the Commission's, but there was "ample evidence to sustain the finding of the trial judge that the cancellation . . . was the result of instructions given by the respondent to the Managers of the Commission" (Martland J. at 737). D stated in a press interview: "It was I, as Attorney-General of the Province charged with the protection of good order, who gave the order to annul [R's] permit. By so doing not only have we exercised a right but we have fulfilled an imperious duty. The permit was cancelled not temporarily but definitely and for always." This was held to be unlawful on the ground that the Commission acted under dictation, and also because "it was a gross abuse of legal power expressly intended to punish [R] for an act wholly irrelevant to the statute . . ." (Rand J. at 706).

2. Below, p. 411 we draw attention to the common practice of Parliament, in conferring grants of power, of imposing an obligation to consult with specified or unspecified persons or bodies prior to exercising the power. As will be seen, also, when we consider review for failure to comply with procedural requirements, this obligation to consult is one which the courts have regarded as of being of a "mandatory" nature. See below, p. 407. Even beyond instances where an express statutory obligation to consult may exist, the process of consultation prior to coming to a decision may be regarded as part of the required process by which, as we shall see (below, p. 321), a decision-maker must seek to inform himself of *all relevant circumstances* in relation to the decision he is to take. More generally still, the process of consultation has been regarded as part and parcel of the process of "good administration"—as providing a mechanism, by which decision-makers may take account of, and benefit from, a broad range of expertise and opinion in coming to their eventual decisions.

This present ground of challenge shows that those exercising statutory powers must steer a proper course between the process, voluntary or mandatory, of consultation and the requirement that the ultimate power of decision must remain in their hands. A context in which consultation is, perhaps, most likely to drift into dictation is where there is consultation of one organ of government by another. See, *e.g. Lavender v. Minister of Housing and Local Government* (below, p. 258) where it could be said that the respondent Minister had acted under the dictation of the Minister of Agriculture.

3. In some instances legislation may expressly empower one body to issue "guidance" to another as to the exercise of the latter's powers. In *Laker Airways v. Department of Trade* [1977] Q.B. 643, the Court of Appeal considered the provisions of the Civil Aviation Act 1971 under which the Secretary of State was empowered to give "guidance" to the Civil Aviation Authority as to the exercise of its functions, and the CAA was, in turn, obliged to "perform those functions in such manner as it considers is in accordance with" such guidance (1971 Act, s.3(2)). Construing the scope of this power to issue guidance, the Court of Appeal held that it did not cover guidance which contradicted the general policy objectives which were expressly stated in the 1971 Act itself. The power to issue guidance was restricted to power to explain, amplify or supplement those objectives. As regards the CAA's duty to follow guidance given under the Act, Lord Denning M.R. explained (at 699):

"So long as the 'guidance' given by the Secretary of State keeps within the due bounds of guidance, the Authority is under a duty to follow his guidance. Even so, the Authority is allowed some degree of flexibility. It is to perform its functions 'in such manner as it considers is in accordance with the guidance'. So, whilst it is obliged to follow the guidance, the manner of doing so is for the Authority itself. . . ."

Note that a power, in the 1971 Act, under which the Secretary of State could give "directions" to the CAA was interpreted as denoting power to give orders which had to be obeyed by the CAA and which could, unlike the guidance, be contrary to the Act's general objectives.

In determining the extent to which a body is obliged to follow statutory guidance the particular terms of the legislation must be considered. For example, an Act may use a formula under which a body exercising powers is required simply to take guidance into account, without being obliged to follow the guidance. Such was the case in *R. v. Police Complaints Board, ex p. Madden* [1983] 1 W.L.R. 447. The Police Complaints Board was required by the Police Act 1976 to "have regard to" certain guidance given to it by the Secretary of State. The Board adopted a policy of following the guidance given. McNeill J. held that the Board had thereby failed properly to exercise its own discretion as to the exercise of its powers. It had erred in regarding its obligation to "have regard to" the guidance as an obligation to "comply with" the guidance. Rather the Board, "as an independent body, ought to [have been] asserting its independence" (at 470). Certainly it was obliged to take the guidance into account in reaching its own decisions. It fell into error in regarding the legislation as conferring a power of dictation on the Minister. See also *R. v. Secretary of State for the Environment, ex p. Lancashire County Council* [1994] 4 All E.R. 165.

4. A local education authority may not use its power to dismiss school governors as a means of imposing its views on educational matters on the governors; it is the policy of the Education Act 1944 that the governors and the authority should have different spheres of responsibility: *R. v. Inner London Education Authority, ex p. Brunyate* [1989] 1 W.L.R. 542, H.L.; *R. v. Trustee of the Roman Catholic Diocese of Westminster, ex p. Andrews, The Times*, August 18, 1989. On the other hand, a decision that all council-appointed governors should face reappointment and replacement in order to ensure that the number of governors appointed by each political party continued to be in proportion with party representation on the council was held to be lawful in *R. v. Warwickshire County Council, ex p. Dill-Russell* (1990) 89 L.G.R. 640, D.C. and C.A.; and a local council can change the membership of one of its committees, which is not an independent body, in order to ensure that council policy is followed in committee: *R. v. Greenwich London Borough Council, ex p. Lovelace* [1991] 1 W.L.R. 506. Note, however, that these cases might now be subject to the restrictions imposed on council appointments by the Local Government and Housing Act 1989, ss.15–17, which requires a political balance on committees and certain other bodies.

5. The extent to which a decision by a councillor to vote in accordance with the "party line" can fall foul of the rule against the fettering of discretion was considered in the following case. In *R. v. Waltham Forest London Borough Council, ex p. Baxter* [1988] Q.B. 419, members of the majority group on the council held a private, party meeting where they discussed what the policy of the group would be as to the setting of the rate at the forthcoming council meeting. After discussion, the group agreed to support a rate increase of 62 per cent for the domestic rate and 56.6 per cent for the non-domestic rate. The group's standing orders provided that members were required to refrain from voting in opposition to group decisions, the sanction being withdrawal of the party whip. A number of members who voted against this level of increase at the group meeting voted in favour at the council meeting, at which a resolution to increase the rate by the previously agreed amounts was passed by 31 votes to 26. A number of ratepayers sought judicial review on a variety of grounds. The Divisional Court rejected arguments to the effect (i) that the councillors had fettered their discretion by

regarding themselves as bound by the terms of their election manifesto to undertake expenditure which rendered such a rate inevitable: (ii) that the resolution was "irrational" or "*Wednesbury* unreasonable"; (iii) that there was no genuine or adequate consultation with representatives of commerce and industry; and (iv) that six or seven councillors had voted contrary to their personal views. The Court of Appeal dismissed an appeal confined to issue (iv). The court held that had the councillors in question voted for the resolution not because they were in favour of it but because their discretion had been fettered by the vote at the group meeting, then the councillors would have been in breach of their duty to make up their own minds as to what rate was appropriate. However, that was not established on the facts. The councillors were entitled to take account of party loyalty and party policy as relevant considerations provided that this did not dominate so as to exclude other considerations. The court noted that the sanction was only withdrawal of the party whip: there was nothing to prevent a councillor who voted against the party line continuing as an independent member. Furthermore, these procedures were widely adopted by political groups throughout the country and had not been regarded by the Widdicombe Committee on the Conduct of Local Authority Business, Cmnd. 9797 (1986), as a matter for concern.

(B) Unauthorised Delegation of Power

This ground of challenge reflects a presumption of statutory interpretation known as the principle *delegatus non potest delegare*—the principle that where a function has been entrusted by statute to body "X", the function should be performed by "X" and not delegated by "X" for performance by body "Y". The theory is that the legislature has delegated power to "X" and that a delegate does not itself have power further to delegate such power.

It is convenient to consider this ground of challenge here. Body "X" may be said in these circumstances to have failed properly to exercise its discretion by having delegated its power of decision to another body. Alternatively, we could have considered this topic in the context of "want of jurisdiction" (see above, pp. 182 *et seq.*). The purported exercise of power by the body to whom there has been an unlawful delegation is challengeable as an act beyond the powers of that body.

This principle, taken to an extreme, could operate as a severe restraint on administrative decision-making. The materials which follow demonstrate not only the operation of the principle, but also important legislative and case-law limits. Thus we shall note that:

(i) the principle does not prevent the exercise by civil servants of powers entrusted by legislation to the ministerial head of a Department or entrusted to the Department itself—the *Carltona* principle (below, p. 249);

(ii) Parliament may provide express authority to a body, on whom it has conferred powers, to delegate, and even for that delegate to subdelegate, those powers. The maxim *delegatus non potest delegare* is a presumption of interpretation which must give way to clear contrary legislative intention. Where a power of delegation does exist, the courts may still, of course, be called upon to consider whether the delegate has acted within or beyond the scope of the powers delegated. An important legislative provision of this kind, permitting wide powers of delegation in the context of the exercise of functions conferred on local authorities, is the Local Government Act 1972, s.101 (below, p. 253);

(iii) The rule against delegation has been interpreted as requiring that the ultimate power of decision as to the whether and how a discretionary power is to be exercised should be retained by the designated statutory body. It does not preclude that body from delegating to another body some preliminary tasks leading up to that final decision. In so doing the appointed body is adopting a procedure by which it seeks assistance in reaching what can still be regarded as its own decision on the matter. Thus a body may delegate certain fact-finding tasks to, and even seek recommendations from, another body (or its own sub-committee). It must, however, retain to itself the power of final decision—it must not allow itself to be dictated to by the delegate, not can it confer power to make any binding decision (as distinct from non-binding recommendation) on the delegate. In truth this is no exception to the principle stated above—it is simply a situation where a court may hold that no delegation of the power of decision has in fact occurred. As we shall see the courts have been more tolerant of such decision-making arrangements in relation to the exercise of administrative functions than in relation to the exercise of judicial powers. See, generally, below, pp. 244–249.

Note

On delegation, see generally J. Willis, "Delegatus Non Potest Delegare" (1943) 21 Can. Bar Rev. 257; *Allen*, pp. 177–195; P.H. Thorp (1972) 2 Auck.U.L.J. 85.

HUTH v. CLARKE

(1890) 25 Q.B.D. 391; 59 L.J.Q.B. 559; 63 L.T. 348; 6 T.L.R. 373; 55 J.P. 86; [1886–1890] All E.R. Rep. 542 (Queen's Bench Division)

By Schedule 6 to the Contagious Diseases (Animals) Act 1878 a county council had power to appoint an executive committee with all the council's powers under the Act. In turn, the executive committee could appoint a sub-committee and delegate all or any of the committee's powers to it. A delegation could be revoked or altered from time to time. In 1889, West Sussex County Council appointed an executive committee. On October 9, 1889, the executive committee appointed local sub-committees, and authorised them to exercise certain powers, including power under the Rabies Order 1887, to make regulations for the muzzling of dogs. No such regulations were in fact made by the local sub-committee, but on March 21, 1890, the executive committee made an order under the Rabies Order that no dog should be at large within the district of Chichester local sub-committee unless it was effectively muzzled or kept under proper control. The appellant was summonsed for a breach of this order. He argued in his defence that the order was *ultra vires*, on the ground that it could only be made by the Chichester sub-committee. The justices stated a case for the opinion of the High Court.

LORD COLERIDGE C.J.: ... [W]e ... have a regulation in force in the district made by the proper authority and dealing with a subject-matter with which they were competent to deal. It is suggested, however, that, because there was another authority which might (had it chosen) have violated good sense by making an inconsistent order, the executive committee had no power to make the regulation in question. But delegation does not imply a denudation of power and authority; the 6th schedule of the Act provides that the delegation may be revoked or altered and the powers resumed by the executive committee. The word "delegation" implies that powers are committed to another person or body which are as a rule always subject to resumption by the power delegating, and many examples of this might be given. Unless, therefore, it is controlled by statute, the delegating power can at any time resume its authority. Here the executive committee has exercised the power which the sub-committee might have exercised—but did not—and no question of conflict of jurisdiction arises. I think, therefore, that the justices came to a perfectly right conclusion, and the conviction must be upheld.

WILLS J. delivered a concurring judgment.

Notes

1. In holding that delegation does not mean parting with authority altogether, this case conflicts with *Blackpool Corporation v. Locker* [1948] 1 K.B. 349. It is suggested that *Huth v. Clarke* is correct on this point (see *de Smith*, pp. 362–363) and that *Blackpool Corporation v. Locker* must be read in the light of its special facts. (See generally on this case *Allen*, pp. 187 *et seq.*; C.K. Allen, *Law and Disorders*, p. 87; "Squaring the Circular", 11 M.L.R. 338; 12 M.L.R. 37; 64 L.Q.R. 306; 66 L.Q.R. 14.)

2. A principal may at any time revoke authority which it has given to a delegate. The revocation of authority will, however, be of prospective effect only—it will not affect the validity of any acts already done under delegated authority: see *Battelley v. Finsbury Borough Council* (1958) 56 L.G.R. 165. Note also, that acts of an *unauthorised* body may be ratified or adopted by a body which *has* authority in the matter. This adoption will, however, be of prospective effect only—it does not give retrospective validity to the acts of the unauthorised body: see *Firth v. Staines* [1897] 2 Q.B. 70; *Warwick RDC v. Miller-Mead* [1962] Ch. 441, [1962] 1 All E.R. 212; *Stoke-on-Trent City Council v. B&Q Retail Ltd* [1984] Ch. 1, discussed in *Cross*, paras. 4–75–4–84; *Webb v. Ipswich Borough Council* (1989) 21 H.L.R. 325; *R. v. Rochester upon Medway City Council, ex p. Hobday* (1989) 58 P. & C.R. 424. And see Lanham D. (1981) 5 Otago L.R. 35.

BARNARD AND OTHERS v. NATIONAL DOCK LABOUR BOARD AND OTHERS

[1953] 2 Q.B. 18; [1953] 2 W.L.R. 995; 97 S.J. 331; [1953] 1 All E.R. 1113; [1953] 1 Lloyd's Rep. 371 (Court of Appeal)

The Dock Workers (Regulation of Employment) Order 1947 set up a scheme to ensure greater regularity of employment for dock workers, and to secure an adequate number of dock workers available for the efficient performance of dock work. The National Dock Labour Board was established by the Order to administer the scheme. It was required by the Order to delegate to local boards all appropriate functions. These included the operation of a disciplinary code. Under Clause 16 the local board could suspend for seven days a registered dock worker who failed to comply with any of the provisions of the scheme. One of the local boards, the London Dock Labour Board, passed a resolution which had the effect of leaving the power of suspension to the London port manager, Mr Hogger. As the result of a dispute, Mr Hogger suspended the plaintiffs. They exercised their rights of appeal to an appeal tribunal set up under the Order, which only had power to revise penalties imposed by the local board. Their appeals were dismissed. Further industrial action followed. Eventually the plaintiffs applied to the High Court for declarations that their suspensions had been wrongful in the light of the facts of the dispute. At the discovery of documents stage, the plaintiffs learned for the first time that they had been suspended, not by the local board, but by the port manager. They amended their pleadings and claimed a further declaration that the original notices of suspension were *ultra vires* and invalid. Counsel for the Board argued that the disciplining of dock workers was an administrative function, which could be delegated.

McNair J. held that the local board had power to delegate its disciplinary functions to the port manager.

The Court of Appeal reversed McNair J. on this point.

DENNING L.J.: ... It was urged on us that the local board had power to delegate their functions to the port manager on the ground that the power of suspension was an administrative and not a judicial function. It was suggested that the action of the local board in suspending a man was similar in character to the action of an employer in dismissing him. I do not accept this view. Under the provisions of the scheme, so far from the board being in the position of an employer, the board are put in a judicial position between the men and the employers; they are to receive reports from the employers and investigate them; they have to inquire whether the man has been guilty of misconduct, such as failing to comply with a lawful order, or failing to comply with the provisions of the scheme; and if they find against him they can suspend him without pay, or can even dismiss him summarily. In those circumstances they are exercising a judicial function just as much as the tribunals which were considered by this court in the corn-porters' case, *Abbott v. Sullivan* [1952] 1 K.B. 189 and in *Lee v. Showmen's Guild of Great Britain* [1952] 2 Q.B. 329 the only difference being that those were domestic tribunals, and this is a statutory one. The board, by their procedure, recognize that before they suspend a man they must give him notice of the charge and an opportunity of making an explanation. That is entirely consonant with the view that they exercise a judicial function and not an administrative one, and we should, I think, so hold.

While an administrative function can often be delegated, a judicial function rarely can be. No judicial tribunal can delegate its functions unless it is enabled to do so expressly or by necessary implication. In *Local Government Board v. Arlidge* [1915] A.C. 120 the power to delegate was given by necessary implication; but there is nothing in this scheme authorizing the board to delegate this function, and it cannot be implied. It was suggested that it would be impracticable for the board to sit as a board to decide all these cases; but I see nothing impracticable at all; they have only to fix their quorum at two members and arrange for two members, one from each side, employers and workers, to be responsible for a week at a time: probably each pair would only have to sit on one day during their week.

Next, it was suggested that even if the board could not delegate their functions, at any rate they could ratify the actions of the port manager; but if the board have no power to delegate their functions to the port manager, they can have no power to ratify what he has done. The effect of ratification is to make it equal to a prior command; but just as a prior command, in the shape of a delegation, would be useless, so also is a ratification....

We have to consider here two decisions: first, the decision to suspend the men; second, the decision of the appeal tribunal. So far as the decision to suspend is concerned, as I see it, ... we are asked to interfere with the position of a usurper. The port manager (if he will forgive my saying so) is a usurper, or, at any rate, is in the position of a usurper. I do not mean this unkindly, because I know that he acted in good faith on the authority of the board; nevertheless, he has assumed a mantle which was not his, but that of another. This is not a case of a tribunal which has a lawful jurisdiction and exercises it; it is a case of a man acting as a tribunal when he has no right to do so. These courts have always had jurisdiction to deal with such a case.... We can declare that the suspension ordered by the port manager was unlawful and void. We can declare it to be the nullity which in law it was.

So far as the decision of the appeal tribunal is concerned, it seems to me that, once the port manager's order is found to be a nullity it follows that the order of the appeal tribunal is also a nullity. The appeal tribunal has no original jurisdiction of its own; it cannot itself make a suspension order; it can only affirm or disaffirm a suspension order which has already been made. If none has been made because it is a nullity, the tribunal can do nothing. It cannot make something out of nothing any more than anybody else can: see *Toronto Railway Co. v. Corporation of the City of Toronto* [1904] A.C. 809, 815....

SINGLETON and ROMER L.JJ. delivered concurring judgments.

Notes

1. See case notes at 69 L.Q.R. 451; 16 M.L.R. 506.
2. As regards the issue of the power to delegate administrative, as distinct from judicial, functions compare the statements of Denning L.J. in *Barnard* with the decision of the House of Lords in *Vine v. National Dock Labour Board* [1957] A.C. 488, where the facts were similar. The plaintiff, a registered dockworker, was dismissed by a disciplinary committee appointed by the South Coast Local Dock Labour Board. Ormerod J. awarded him £250 damages and granted a declaration that the purported dismissal was *ultra vires*. His judgment was upheld in the House of Lords. Their Lordships were agreed that delegation was not permissible in the circumstances—the matter was "too important to delegate" (Lord Kilmuir L.C. at 499), and "of a judicial character" (Lord Morton at 502). Lord Cohen (at 505) doubted "whether the mere fact that it was an administrative act would be conclusive of the matter", but did not explore the point as he was satisfied that the local board was acting "in a judicial capacity". Lord Somervell (at 512) said:

"In deciding whether a 'person' has power to delegate one has to consider the nature of the duty and the character of the person. Judicial authority normally cannot, of course, be delegated, though no one doubted in *Arlidge*'s case that the Local Government Board, which consisted of the President, the Lord President of the Council, the Secretaries of State, the Lord Privy Seal and the Chancellor of the Exchequer (Local Government Board Act 1871), could act by officials duly deputed for the purpose, whether or not the act to be done had judicial ingredients. There are, on the other hand, many administrative duties which cannot be delegated. Appointment to an office or position is plainly an administrative act. If under a statute a duty to appoint is placed on the holder of an office, whether under the Crown or not, he would, normally, have no authority to delegate. He could take advice, of course, but he could not by a minute authorize someone else to make the appointment without further reference to him. I do not, therefore, find it necessary to consider what judicial requirements might be held implicit in the local board's proceedings under clause 16. I am, however, clear that the disciplinary powers, whether 'judicial' or not, cannot be delegated. The non-entitlement to pay, the suspension, the notice or the dismissal must be a step taken by the board and not by a delegate. The penalties, in some cases, may be slight but, in some cases, very great. A man who has worked all his life in the docks may find himself precluded altogether from doing so. Today it may be easy for him to get other work, but that has not always been so. The constitution of the board also supports the conclusion. It is clearly constituted so as to inspire confidence and weigh fairly the interests of employers and employed. The purported delegation in the present case was to a representative of each side, but it is impossible to imply a limited right of delegation. *Osgood v. Nelson* (1872) L.R. 5 H.L. 636 [below, p. 244] decides that in somewhat similar circumstances the appointment of a committee to take evidence and report is not in itself a delegation of authority. If there are administrative difficulties, this may be an answer to them."

See note by E.C.S. Wade [1957] C.L.J. 6.

3. Denning L.J. held that the board's decision could not retrospectively validate the decision of the unauthorised port manager. Compare the approach of the courts to the "curative" effect of appeal proceedings where the decision appealed from is tainted by failure to have complied with the principles of natural justice. See below, p. 506.

OSGOOD v. NELSON

(1872) L.R. 5 H.L. 636; 41 L.J.Q.B. 329 (House of Lords)

From 1856 to 1867, Mr Osgood held the office of Registrar of the Sheriff's Court of the City of London. He was appointed by resolution of the Court of Common Council of the City. In August 1866 allegations of neglect in the performance of his duties were made against the plaintiff. These were referred by the Council to their "Officers and Clerks' Committee". Mr Osgood appeared before the committee and had access to the relevant documents. The committee took evidence, and reported that in their opinion irregularities had occurred, such as seriously interfered with the proper conduct of public business. The matter was considered by the Council on May 2, 1867. Mr Osgood was present, represented by counsel (Mr Serjeant Tindal Atkinson). The council had before them the committee's report and a transcript of the notes of evidence. The council resolved to dismiss Mr Osgood, and appoint Mr Nelson in his place. The plaintiff brought an action in the Court of Queen's Bench to recover the fees of his office, in order to challenge the validity of the dismissal. The Court of Queen's Bench gave judgment for the defendant, and this was upheld in the Court of Exchequer Chamber. The case was then taken to the House of Lords on Error.

One issue was whether there had been an unlawful delegation to the committee.

Mr Baron Martin [speaking in the name of the Judges present said:] . . . In our opinion there was no delegation at all. What was done was, that a complaint having been made to the body which had control in the matter, *viz.*, the Mayor, Aldermen, and Commons of the City of London, as to the conduct of Mr Osgood, it was referred by them to a committee, which seems to have been long used in the Corporation of London, known as the "Officer and Clerk's Committee"; and what they were directed to do was to make inquiry with reference to the alleged complaint, to take evidence, and to ascertain the truth of it, not for the purpose of that committee coming to any judgment or decision themselves, but for the purpose of their report being submitted to the Mayor, Aldermen, and Commons in order that they might come to a judgment upon it. The argument of the learned counsel is erroneous in point of fact. That has not taken place which they allege to have taken place, and therefore there was no delegation.

. . . [W]e are of opinion, that in the proceedings before the committee in the first place, every possible opportunity that could be given to any man was given to Mr Osgood in this matter. He was allowed to cross-examine witnesses, and he was permitted also to call as many witnesses as he pleased. He was repeatedly asked whether he had any farther evidence to produce, and he was permitted to address the Court himself, and to state his view of the matter, and to comment on the evidence. These proceedings having occupied four days, it was on March 21, that the committee came to a decision upon the matter. Therefore, as it seems to us, so far as the proceedings before this committee are concerned, it is impossible that any one can have had a fuller and fairer opportunity than Mr Osgood had of bringing forward his case, with any evidence he might have to support it.

It was on March 21, that the report of the committee was presented to the Court of Common Council. The Common Council permitted a period of more than six weeks to elapse before proceeding to discuss it. It was then discussed, and Mr Serjeant Tindal Atkinson, who was counsel on the part of Mr Osgood, then repeated what Mr Osgood had before said, and stated that he did not require any farther particularity in the charge. He was content to take the case as it then stood. He was requested by the Recorder to state whether or not he desired to offer any farther evidence than that which appeared on the shorthand writer's notes, and he stated that he did not, and then proceeded to address the Court at considerable length in regard to this matter. Throughout the whole of the proceedings Mr Osgood had the presence either of the Recorder or of the Common Serjeant for the purpose of assisting the Committee and the Common Council. Therefore, it does seem to us that it is impossible for any man to have had what I may call a fairer trial than Mr *Osgood* had with reference to this matter....

LORD COLONSAY: ... I quite agree with the observation made by the learned Baron, that there was no violation of the rule against delegation in this case. The mode adopted was the mode in which such inquiries are ordinarily conducted, and necessarily conducted, by such a tribunal. What was the course which [counsel for Mr Osgood] stated to have been requisite? It was that after this committee had made their report, if they did make such a report, there should have been an assembling of the Common Council, there should have been a prosecutor appointed, and there should have been a new trial, with all the formalities of a criminal trial, before they could have arrived at a conclusion. But the committee appointed to inquire into this matter having made the inquiry in the ordinary way, having collected the evidence in the ordinary way, and allowed the party, who had been present at the collecting of that evidence, to state his case by counsel, I cannot conceive a more fair mode of proceedings....

Notes

1. In *Jeffs and Others v. New Zealand Dairy Production and Marketing Board* [1967] 1 A.C. 551, the Board had power to define zones from which particular factories could get cream and milk. The Board set up a committee of three of its members to investigate the question of supply to two factory-owning dairy companies. The committee, acting on its own initiative, held a public hearing at which farmers and other interested parties gave evidence and made oral and written submissions. The farmers opposed zoning. The committee made a written report, and recommended certain zonings, which were accepted by the Board without alteration. The report did not record, even in a summary form, the evidence given at the hearing, but did state the submissions that had been made. The Board conceded that it was under a duty to act judicially in determining zoning questions affecting the rights of individuals. The Privy Council held that the Board acted in breach of natural justice in failing to hear the interested parties, but that they would have complied with natural justice had the

evidence and submissions been fully summarised. The appointment of a person or persons to hear evidence and submissions was appropriate where the credibility of witnesses was not involved. See K.J. Keith (1968) 31 M.L.R. 87.

2. In *R. v. Race Relations Board, ex p. Selvarajan* [1975] 1 W.L.R. 1686, C.A., S's complaint of unlawful discrimination was investigated by a conciliation committee appointed under section 15(2)(a) of the Race Relations Act 1968, and then reinvestigated by the Board under section 15(5). The Board had power under section 14(4) to act by a group of members selected by the chairman, and the reinvestigation was undertaken by the Board's employment committee of seven. Each committee member was given a copy of the conciliation committee's report of over 100 pages and some other notes. Further information was collected by one of the Board's conciliation officers. When the employment committee met to consider the matter only three of the members had seen the full papers. The other four only had the officer's summary of the results of her inquiries. The committee decided that there had been no unlawful discrimination. Lord Denning M.R. inferred that the four "were not in a position to form an opinion of their own. They must have gone by the opinion of the other three.... If this had been a judicial body, I do not think this would be right. Every member of a judicial body must have access to all the evidence and papers in the case, he must have heard all the arguments, and he must come to his own conclusion. The maxim *delegatus non potest delegare* applies strictly to judicial functions. But it is different with a body which is exercising administrative functions or which is making an investigation or conducting preliminary inquiries, especially when it is a numerous body" ([1975] 1 W.L.R. 1686 at 1695). Lord Denning distinguished *Jeffs v. New Zealand Dairy Board* on the ground that the Dairy Board, unlike the Race Relations Board, had no power to delegate its functions.

For contrasting decisions applying these principles see *R. v. Hertsmere Borough Council, ex p. Woolgar* (1995) 160 L.G.R. 261 and *R. v. West Dorset District Council, ex p. Gerrard* (1994) 27 H.L.R. 150.

3. For modern illustrations of judicial reticence as regards the delegation of judicial functions see, for example, *R. v. Gateshead Justices, ex p. Tesco Stores Ltd* [1981] Q.B. 470; [1981] 1 All E.R. 1027 (held to be an unlawful delegation of a judicial function for magistrates to have delegated to their clerks certain decision-making functions in respect of the issuance of summonses: note, however, the provision now so permitting contained in S.I. 1993 No. 1183, adding r.4 to Justices Clerks Rules 1970); *R. v. D.P.P., ex p. First Division Association* [1988] NJLR 158, *The Times*, May 24, 1988 (successful challenge to policy under which the initial screening of prosecutions had been delegated by the DPP not to legally qualified Crown Prosecutors, as expressly permitted by the legislation, but to non-legally qualified civil servants. The decisions delegated involved evaluation of evidence and the exercise of judgment as to whether the public interest required a prosecution to take place); *R. v. Manchester Stipendiary Magistrate, ex p. Hill* [1983] 1 A.C. 328; [1982] 2 All E.R. 963.

For decisions to remind us that recognition of a strict approach as regards judicial-type functions does not mean that the courts will not also apply the principle in relation to the exercise of administrative functions, see *Allingham v. Minister of Agriculture and Fisheries* [1948] 1 All E.R. 780; *R. v. Liverpool City Council, ex p. Professional Association of Teachers* (1984) 82 L.G.R. 648.

4. In *Attorney-General ex rel. McWhirter v. Independent Broadcasting Authority* [1973] 1 Q.B. 629 the Court of Appeal considered the duty imposed by statute on the IBA to "satisfy themselves that, so far as possible ... nothing is included in ... programmes which offends against good taste or decency or is likely ... to be offensive to public feeling ...". Discussing the extent to which the IBA could delegate this function, Lord Denning M.R. explained (at 650–652):

"Such being the statutory requirements, Parliament puts a duty on the Independent Broadcasting Authority to 'satisfy themselves' that they are complied with 'so far as possible'. This does not mean, of course, that the members of the authority are themselves to see every programme or go through it. They can and must leave a great deal to the staff. They are entitled in the ordinary way to accept the advice of their staff on the programmes in general, and on any programme in particular: see *Lewisham Metropolitan Borough and Town Clerk v. Roberts* [1949] 2 K.B. 608, 621, 629. It is only in a most exceptional case that they may be expected to see a programme for themselves in order to be 'satisfied'. But there are such exceptional cases, just as there are exceptional cases when a Minister must satisfy himself personally. It depends how serious is the case: see *Liversidge v. Anderson* [1942] A.C. 206, 223, 224.

Was this film a programme which they ought to have seen for themselves? Let me state the circumstances. (i) The programme was prepared by one of the programme companies called ATV Network Ltd. In its original form, the staff of the Independent Broadcasting Authority were so unhappy about it that they thought that the programme should be seen by the authority itself. (ii) ATV Network Ltd thereupon deleted some of the material and introduced the film with a warning that 'some people may find Warhol's views unusual and possibly offensive'. (iii) In the light of those modifications, the Director-General and staff of the Independent Broadcasting Authority felt able to recommend that the programme be transmitted as the usual network documentary on Tuesday, January 16, 1973, at 10.30 p.m. They made an intervention report to that effect. The Independent Broadcasting Authority accepted that recommendation but did not see the film themselves. (iv) On January 12 or 13, journalists were invited to a preview of the film. (v) On Sunday, January 14, and Monday, January 15, some of the journalists in their papers made severe criticisms of the film. If their accounts were correct, it included incidents which were indecent and likely to be offensive to public feeling. The *News of the World*, in particular, said that "Millions of viewers will find its frankness offensive." (vi) On reading those newspaper reports, the chairman and directors of one of the channels, Anglia Television, determined to have the film screened privately for them to see. They came to the unanimous conclusion that the programme, if broadcast, was likely to be offensive to public feeling. They announced that they were not going to supply it for broadcasting. (vii) The Independent Broadcasting Authority, however, did not see it. Some of them had an informal discussion with the senior staff, and, on their assurances, were prepared to let it be broadcast.

The question is: did the Independent Broadcasting Authority do what was sufficient or ought they not to have seen the film for themselves....

In the circumstances I think that the Independent Broadcasting Authority ought to have seen the film for themselves on the Monday or Tuesday before passing it. Since that time they have done so. So have the General Advisory Council. The members of the General Council are drawn from a broad cross-section of the people, and are as representative and responsible a body as you could find anywhere. The General Council, by a majority of 17 to one, passed this resolution: 'The Council felt that the staff were right to advise the Authority that the film which they had seen was suitable to be shown at the suggested time.' The members of the Independent Broadcasting Authority are likewise most representative and responsible. Ten out of the 11 saw the film and unanimously reaffirmed the decision:

> 'that the programme is suitable for transmission in the 10.30 p.m. documentary slot, and that it is satisfied that the programme complies with the requirements of Section 3(1)(a) of the Television Act 1964'.

If those decisions are to be accepted as valid, they are decisive. The Independent Broadcasting Authority are the people who matter. They are the censors. The courts have no right whatever—and I may add no desire whatever—to interfere with their decisions so long as they reach them in accordance with law...."

5. In *Mills v. London County Council* [1925] 1 K.B. 213, the L.C.C. had granted a

licence to Mills, a cinema proprietor, subject to the following condition: "That no film
... which has not been passed for universal exhibition by the British Board of Film
Censors shall be exhibited in the premises without the express consent of the Council
during the time that any child under ... the age of 16 is therein." Mills contended that
the condition was *ultra vires* because it involved delegation by the Council of that
body's functions under the Cinematograph Act 1909 to another body, the BBFC. The
Divisional Court upheld the condition. Lord Hewart C.J. said (at 220–221):

> "It is said, first of all, that this condition is bad, because it means that the London
> County Council have delegated, or transferred, to the British Board of Film Censors
> no small part of the duties of the London County Council under the Act, and refer-
> ence is made to *Ellis v. Dubowski* [1921] 3 K.B. 621. In that case the condition
> which was attached to the licence was in these terms: 'That no film be shewn ...
> which has not been certified for public exhibition by the British Board of Film Cen-
> sors.' It was held with some doubt that that condition was unreasonable and *ultra
> vires*. . . . But one thing was made very plain by that Court, both in the course of the
> argument and also in the judgment, that different considerations would have
> applied if the condition had been so framed as to make the certificate or the decision
> of the British Board of Film Censors not final, but subject to review. . . . In the present
> case that mischief is avoided. This condition with which we are now concerned pro-
> vides an exception where the express consent of the Council is given. In other words,
> there is an appeal in the matter from the decision of the British Board of Film Cen-
> sors to the Council itself. In my opinion, therefore, the first objection fails. . . ."

In *R. v. Greater London Council, ex p. Blackburn* [1976] 1 W.L.R. 550, the Court of
Appeal unanimously upheld the decision in *Mills.* Lord Denning M.R. explained (at
554–555):

> "I do not think the county councils can delegate the whole of their responsibilities to
> the board . . .; but they can treat the board as an advisory body whose views they can
> accept or reject, provided that the final decision—aye or nay—rests with the county
> council. If the exhibitor—or any member of the public—brings the film up before
> the county council, they ought themselves to review the decision of the British Board
> of Film Censors and exercise their own judgment on it. That is, I think, the right way
> to interpret *Mills v. London County Council.* When the board issues a certificate
> permitting the exhibition of a film—and the county council take no objection to
> it—that is equivalent to a permission by the county council themselves. When the
> board refuses a certificate, the exhibitor can appeal to the county council. The
> county council can then give their consent to the exhibition, and from their decision
> there is no appeal.
>   The upshot of it all is this. The county council are in law the body which has the
> power to censor films for exhibition in cinemas, but in practice it is the board which
> carries out the censorship, subject to review by the county council."

6. In *R. v. Chester Borough Council, ex p. Quietlynn Ltd* (1985) 83 L.G.R. 308, the
Court of Appeal considered the practice of the local authority in handling applications
for licences to operate sex shops, under the Local Government (Miscellaneous Provisions) Act 1982. The local authority had delegated its power to grant or refuse such
licences to its Environmental Services Committee. There was clear statutory authority
for this delegation (Local Government Act 1972, s.101, below, p. 253). That committee set up a licensing panel to consider applications and to make recommendations
to the committee. The panel consisted of five of the members of the committee. The
panel held a hearing at which the applicants appeared, and then made a recommendation to the Environmental Services Committee that the application be refused. Refusal
was on grounds relating to the character of the locality, the uses to which premises in

the vicinity were being put, and that it considered that the appropriate number of sex establishments in the area should be nil. This recommendation was put before a meeting of the committee, at which 13 members (including the five panel members) were present. At this meeting some detailed discussion first took place in connection with another application, that application eventually being granted. When the applicants' application came up for consideration there was no report made and no discussion—simply a vote taken, which refused the application. The applicants argued that there had been a failure to comply with the statutory obligation, under the 1982 Act, that the committee or sub-committee should afford a hearing to an applicant before refusing a licence; and that this obligation had not, in the circumstances, been satisfied by the hearing before the panel. The local authority argued that as the members of the panel had been present at the committee meeting and therefore were available to have given any information about the hearing had any such information been requested by the other members; and because the panel decision, based on "character of locality", was based on information within the knowledge of all the members, it was not necessary for there to have been anything by way of full report to the committee. The Court of Appeal upheld the applicants' contentions. Stephen Brown L.J. noted (at 316) that "no report of any kind was made to the decision-making committee. It may be that a report could have been a very short report indeed, but ... it is a requisite of the [legislation] that the applicants' representations should be considered by the committee making the decision." The decision of the authority was therefore quashed.

CARLTONA LTD v. COMMISSIONERS OF WORKS AND OTHERS

[1943] 2 All E.R. 560 (Court of Appeal)

The appellants were manufacturers of food products, and on November 4, 1942, their factory was requisitioned by the Commissioners of Works under regulation 51(1) of the Defence (General) Regulations, 1939:

> "A competent authority, if it appears to that authority to be necessary or expedient so to do in the interests of the public safety, the defence of the realm or the efficient prosecution of the war, or for maintaining supplies and services essential to the life of the community, may take possession of any land, and may give such directions as appear to the competent authority to be necessary or expedient in connection with the taking of possession of that land."

The notice of November 4 was signed by a Mr Morse for and on behalf of the Commissioners of Works. The letter said in part:

> "I have to inform you that the department have come to the conclusion that it is essential, in the national interest, to take possession of the above premises occupied by you."

The functions of the Commissioners of Works were made exercisable by the First Commissioner of Works, by the Crown Lands Act 1851 and 1852. Under the Minister of Works and Planning Act 1942 the functions of the First Commissioner were made exercisable by that minister. The appellants sought, *inter alia*, a declaration that the requisitioning notice was invalid, and an injunction restraining any action based on the notice. The action was dismissed by Hilbery J. Carltona Ltd appealed to the Court of Appeal.

LORD GREENE M.R. [stated the facts and continued]: ... The next point which was taken was that the requisition itself was bad quite apart from the notice because the persons constituting the requisitioning authority never brought their minds to bear on the question. That argument is based, as it seems to me—and I say this without the slightest disrespect to the argument—upon a complete misapprehension as to the facts. It appears to have been thought at the time of the trial that the proper persons to take into consideration the question of exercising the power under this regulation were the Commissioners of Works themselves, a body which, as I have said, never meets. If that idea ever was put forward, and I am not quite sure whether it was or not, a moment's consideration will show that the argument cannot be supported for the very simple reasons, first, that the person who has the statutory power to act for the Commissioners of Works is the First Commissioner, and, secondly, that the person acting for the First Commissioner in this matter was the assistant secretary. There is no point in the argument at all that the Commissioners of Works as such did not take the matter into consideration, nor is there, in my opinion, any substance in the argument that, at any rate, the First Commissioner did not personally direct his mind to the matter.

In the administration of government in this country the functions which are given to ministers (and constitutionally properly given to ministers because they are constitutionally responsible) are functions so multifarious that no minister could ever personally attend to them. To take the example of the present case no doubt there have been thousands of requisitions in this country by individual ministries. It cannot be supposed that this regulation meant that, in each case, the minister in person should direct his mind to the matter. The duties imposed upon ministers and the powers given to ministers are normally exercised under the authority of the ministers by responsible officials of the department. Public business could not be carried on if that were not the case. Constitutionally, the decision of such an official is, of course, the decision of the minister. The minister is responsible. It is he who must answer before Parliament for anything that his officials have done under his authority, and, if for an important matter he selected an official of such junior standing that he could not be expected competently to perform the work, the minister would have to answer for that in Parliament. The whole system of departmental organisation and administration is based on the view that ministers, being responsible to Parliament, will see that important duties are committed to experienced officials. If they do not do that, Parliament is the place where complaint must be made against them.

In the present case the assistant secretary, a high official of the Ministry, was the person entrusted with the work of looking after this particular matter ... The appeal must be dismissed. ...

GODDARD and DU PARCQ L.JJ. agreed.

Notes

1. In *Local Government Board v. Arlidge* [1915] A.C. 120, Arlidge sought certiorari to quash an order made by the Board. The Board's order had rejected A's appeal against his local authority's decision not to terminate a closure order it had made in respect of his house, which it considered to be unfit for human habitation. One of the grounds on which certiorari was sought was that neither the Board, nor anyone

lawfully authorised to act for them, had in fact determined the appeal. The matter had been investigated by one of the Board's housing inspectors, who had held an inquiry at which A had been represented. The inspector had submitted his report to the Board, together with a shorthand note of the speeches. The order of the Board did not indicate which officer of the Board had taken the final decision on the matter. In the House of Lords, Viscount Haldane L.C. said (at 133):

> "The Minister at the head of the Board is directly responsible to Parliament like other Ministers. He is responsible not only for what he himself does but for all that is done in his department. The volume of work entrusted to him is very great and he cannot do the great bulk of it himself. He is expected to obtain his materials vicariously through his officials, and he has discharged his duty if he sees that they obtain these materials for him properly. To try to extend his duty beyond this and to insist that he and other members of the Board should do everything personally would be to impair his efficiency. Unlike a judge in a court he is not only at liberty but is compelled to rely on the assistance of his staff. When, therefore, the Board is directed to dispose of an appeal that does not mean that any particular official of the Board is to dispose of it."

Lord Shaw of Dunfermline said (at 136):

> "... My Lords, how can the judiciary be blind to the well-known facts applicable not only to the constitution but to the working of such branches of the Executive? The department is represented in Parliament by its responsible head. On the one hand he manages its affairs with such assistance as the Treasury sanctions, and on the other he becomes answerable in Parliament for every departmental act. His Board—that is, all the members of it together—may never meet, or they may only be convened on some question of policy; but a determination, signed and sealed and issued in correct form, stands as the deliverance of the Board as such, for which determination the President becomes answerable to Parliament. This is the general rule, acknowledged and familiar, of departmental action and responsibility...."

2. The *Arlidge* and *Carltona* cases were each decided in wartime. They illustrate a degree of judicial self-restraint which is, perhaps, not surprising in such circumstances. Compare *Liversidge v. Sir John Anderson* [1942] A.C. 206, and below, p. 369, note 2. The English courts have not, however, in the years since the decision in *Carltona* seemed anxious to impose limits to the scope of that decision.

Thus, in *R. v. Skinner* [1968] 2 Q.B. 700, the Court of Appeal held that approval of the "Alcotest" breath-testing device by the Home Secretary required by section 7(1) of the Road Safety Act 1967 (which was a necessary precondition to a conviction for an offence under the breathalyser legislation), could be expressed by an assistant secretary in the police department of the Home Office, acting in the name of the Home Secretary. The court applied the *Carltona* case, and dicta in *Lewisham B.C. v. Roberts* [1949] 2 K.B. 608. The personal approval of the Home Secretary was not necessary even though this was an isolated matter unlike the thousands of requisitioning cases that arose during the war which no Minister could have considered personally. Widgery L.J. emphasised (at 707) that: "It is not strictly a matter of delegation; it is that the official acts as the Minister himself and the official's decision is the Minister's decision."

Then, in *Re Golden Chemical Products Ltd* [1976] Ch. 300, Brightman J. considered the exercise of powers contained in section 35 of the Companies Act 1967. This section empowered the Secretary of State to present a petition to the High Court for the winding-up of a company where "it appears [to the Secretary of State] ... that it is expedient in the public interest that the body be wound up ...". His Lordship held that the functions of the Secretary of State under section 35 need not be exercised by the

Secretary of State personally. His Lordship rejected the argument of counsel for the company, that unless a statute conferring a power on a Minister to do an act if it appears to him expedient provided otherwise, the initial decision-making process could be performed by someone other than the Minister only if it led to no serious invasion of the freedom or property rights of the subject. This argument ran counter to the *Carltona*, *Lewisham* and *Skinner* cases, and would result in a distinction which would be "impossibly vague" (*per* Brightman J. at 310). His Lordship accepted that the relationship between the Minister and his official was not one of delegation.

By way of contrast, some willingness by the courts to review the exercise by a Minister of his *Carltona* power to devolve decision-making has been indicated by the courts in the more recent case of *R. v. Secretary of State for the Home Department, ex p. Oladehinde* [1991] 1 A.C. 254; [1990] 3 All E.R. 393. This concerned the lawfulness of a practice by which the Home Secretary had "delegated" to immigration inspectors (officials in the civil service who are equivalent in grade to senior executive officers, and who have considerable experience in immigration matters) his powers under the Immigration Act 1971 to authorise service of notices of intention to deport persons from the United Kingdom. The inspectors reached their decisions in the light of reports compiled by immigration officers. Following the service of such notices a right of appeal in certain cases might lie to an independent immigration adjudicator or to the Immigration Appeal Tribunal. However, such appeals, by "overstayers" served with notices of intention to deport, were severely restricted by the Immigration Act 1988. Following an unsuccessful appeal, or in the absence of an appeal, the deportation department at the Home Office reviewed each case before a final decision as to the making of a deportation order was made by the Secretary of State, acting on the advice of his department and his Minister of State.

In the Divisional Court ([1991] 1 A.C. at 258) certiorari was granted to quash decisions of immigration inspectors. Woolf L.J. referred to the *Carltona* principle and stated that the principle should be "regarded as an implication which is read into a statute in the absence of any clear contrary indication by Parliament that the implication is not to apply" (at 264–265). Such implications might be express (see, *e.g.* 1971 Act, ss.13(5), 14(3), and 15(3) and (4)—requiring certain decisions to be taken by the Secretary of State personally) or implied. In determining whether the principle was impliedly excluded, a number of matters were of relevance. Woolf L.J. noted that the scheme of the legislation was, somewhat unusually, to divide responsibilities and to assign specific functions to the Secretary of State and to particular categories of official. In such circumstances an implication was appropriate that the Secretary of State could not, under the *Carltona* principle, devolve to those officials the powers which had been conferred on himself. In addition to the "structure" of the legislative allocation of power, Woolf L.J. paid regard to the nature of the power devolved, noting the serious consequences for the individuals affected which might follow from the making of a deportation order. Pill J. analysed the *Carltona* principle in similar terms and agreed that "Parliament did not intend the relevant powers given to the Secretary of State with respect to deportation to be exercised on his behalf by members of the immigration service" (at 270).

In the Court of Appeal ([1991] 1 A.C. at 278), Lord Donaldson M.R., giving the judgment of the court, stated (at 282) that the *Carltona* power to devolve decision-making was a "common law constitutional power, but one which is capable of being negatived or confined by ... clearly necessary implication". In this connection his Lordship said that such challenge would normally be on the basis that the decision to devolve was *Wednesbury* unreasonable—*i.e.* not an arrangement for the exercise of the function which any reasonable Minister could have chosen to adopt. The Court of Appeal differed, however, from the Divisional Court in its view as to whether in this case these limitations to the *Carltona* power to devolve applied. It stressed that in its view:

"there are clear advantages and no unfairness in the (provisional) decision to deport, which does not of itself affect the status of the immigrant ..., being taken by civil servants who are readily available and have considerable experience and expertise in immigration matters."

The House of Lords affirmed the decision of the Court of Appeal. On the issue of the ambit of the *Carltona* principle, Lord Griffiths noted that the 1971 Act contained three explicit limitations on the Secretary of State's power to devolve—see sections referred to above. In these circumstances a court should be "very slow to read into the statute a further implicit limitation". His Lordship continued (at 303):

"The immigration service is comprised of Home Office civil servants for whom the Home Secretary is responsible and I can see no reason why he should not authorise members of that service to take decisions under the *Carltona* principle *providing they do not conflict with or embarrass them in the discharge of their specific statutory duties under the Act and that the decisions are suitable to their grading and experience*" (emphasis added).

By way of example of a situation which would fall within the conflict/embarrassment limitation Lord Griffiths said (at 303): "it would not be right to authorise an inspector to take a decision ... in any case in which he had been engaged as an immigration officer, for to do so would be too much like asking a prosecutor to be judge in the same cause". Lords Keith, Templeman, Brandon and Ackner concurred with Lord Griffiths.

3. The *Carltona* principle applies to the devolution of functions to civil servants within a department of central government. Outside this context, it has been held not to be applicable simply because administrative convenience may be served by such a practice. Thus, in *Nelms v. Roe* [1969] 3 All E.R. 1379, a police inspector sought information from R under section 232(2)(a) of the Road Traffic Act 1960 as to the identity of the driver of R's car on an occasion when a traffic offence was allegedly committed. Under the section such information could be required "by or on behalf of a chief officer of police ..." but there was no written authority from the Metropolitan Police Commissioner either to the inspector or to the inspector's superior officer, the superintendent in charge of Croydon sub-division. The superintendent claimed that he had implied authority by virtue of his office, and stated that he had given the inspector verbal authority to act under section 232. The court held (1) that the *alter ego* doctrine applicable to Ministers and civil servants could not be applied to the superintendent *vis-à-vis* the commissioner (*per* Lord Parker C.J. at 1382: "It is not, I think, sufficient to say that it is a principle which is applicable whenever it is difficult or impracticable for a person to act himself ..."); but (2) that there was an implied delegation to the superintendent, which included power for the superintendent to sub-delegate to "a person in his unit in a responsible position".

4. See generally on the *Carltona* principle, D. Lanham, "Delegation and the *Alter Ego* Principle" (1984) 100 L.Q.R. 587.

LOCAL GOVERNMENT ACT 1972

Part VI

DISCHARGE OF FUNCTIONS

Arrangements for discharge of functions by local authorities

101.—(1) Subject to any express provision contained in this Act or any Act passed after this Act, a local authority may arrange for the discharge of any of their functions—

    (a) by a committee, a sub-committee or an officer of the authority; or
    (b) by any other local authority.

(2) Where by virtue of this section any functions of a local authority may be discharged by a committee of theirs, then, unless the local authority otherwise direct, the committee may arrange for the discharge of any of those functions by a sub-committee or an officer of the authority and where by virtue of this section any functions of a local authority may be discharged by a sub-committee of the authority, then, unless the local authority or the committee otherwise direct, the sub-committee may arrange for the discharge of any of those functions by an officer of the authority.

(3) Where arrangements are in force under this section for the discharge of any functions of a local authority by another local authority, then, subject to the terms of the arrangements, that other authority may arrange for the discharge of those functions by a committee, sub-committee or officer of theirs and subsection (2) above shall apply in relation to those functions as it applies in relation to the functions of that other authority.

(4) Any arrangements made by a local authority or committee under this section for the discharge of any functions by a committee, sub-committee, officer or local authority shall not prevent the authority or committee by whom the arrangements are made from exercising those functions.

(5) Two or more local authorities may discharge any of their functions jointly and, where arrangements are in force for them to do so,—

    (a) they may also arrange for the discharge of those functions by a joint committee of theirs or by an officer of one of them and subsection (2) above shall apply in relation to those functions as it applies in relation to the functions of the individual authorities; and
    (b) any enactment relating to those functions or the authorities by whom or the areas in respect of which they are to be discharged shall have effect subject to all necessary modifications in its application in relation to those functions and the authorities by whom and the areas in respect of which (whether in pursuance of the arrangements or otherwise) they are to be discharged.

(6) A local authority's functions with respect to levying, or issuing a precept for, a rate [...] shall be discharged only by the authority ...

Notes

1. This section gives very wide powers of delegation to local authorities. The general power of delegation to officers was new in the 1972 Act. Section 101(1) does not authorise the delegation of functions to a single member: *R. v. Secretary of State for Education and Science, ex p. Birmingham District Council* (1984) 83 L.G.R. 79, where it was held that a proposal by a local education authority to close a school had not been lawfully made where the date of closure had been fixed not by the authority but by its chairman. This view was confirmed by Woolf J. and the Court of Appeal in *R. v.*

Secretary of State for the Environment, ex p. Hillingdon London Borough Council [1986] 1 W.L.R. 192 and 867, in respect of the issue of enforcement notices. The word "committee" in the 1972 Act did not extend to a committee of one. Woolf J. recognised, however, that the difficulties could be circumvented by delegating a power to an officer acting *in consultation* with a member. This would enable urgent action to be taken between meetings of the relevant committee or sub-committee. Where it is arranged for decisions to be made by an officer in consultation with a councillor the ultimate decision must be the officer's: if the dominant role is taken by the councillor, the decision will be *ultra vires*: *R. v. Port Talbot Borough Council, ex p. Jones* [1988] 2 All E.R. 207. On the other hand, there is no objection to standing orders requiring the officer to obtain the approval of a member of the council, such as a committee chairman, before exercising the delegated power: *Fraser v. Secretary of State for the Environment* (1987) 56 P. & C.R. 386. The difference appears to be that, in the former case, the officer would not have made the positive decision in question had it not been for the intervention of the councillor. In the latter, the officer made a provisional decision independently, but was then required to obtain approval from a committee chairman before it could be made effective. The former situation was unlawful, the latter arrangement was lawful.

2. For indications that something analogous to the *Carltona* principle may have some limited operation in the context of *local* government decision-making, see *Provident Mutual Life Assurance Association v. Derby City Council* (1981) 79 L.G.R. 297, H.L. (enabling "administrative matters" in connection with rate collection to be dealt with by members of the treasurer's staff where power had been delegated to the treasurer), applied in *Cheshire County Council v. Secretary of State for the Environment* [1988] J.P.L. 30 and *Fitzpatrick v. Secretary of State for the Environment, The Times,* December 29, 1988. In *Fitzpatrick*, however, the member of the district secretary's staff was merely implementing an instruction by the council to the district secretary to issue an enforcement notice; as neither the member of staff nor the district secretary was exercising any independent discretion the problem of the delegation of power did not strictly arise. See also *R. v. Southwark London Borough Council, ex p. Bannerman* (1990) 22 H.L.R. 459.

(C) OVER-RIGID ADHERENCE TO SELF-CREATED RULES OF POLICY

The cases which follow demonstrate the balance which has been struck by the courts between:

(i) applying the presumption, often stated, that statutes conferring discretionary powers should be interpreted as intending that decisions as to whether and how that power is to be exercised should be taken in the light of individual consideration of the merits of each particular case; and,

(ii) appreciation that such individualised, case-by-case, decision-making may be less conducive to good and fair administration than an approach under which discretionary decisions are taken in the light of, though not unduly constrained by, previously determined (and perhaps promulgated) rules or principles of policy.

Individual justice is important. But decision-makers should also have regard to the "administrative justice" which is associated with consistency and predictability in decision-making. See further, below, pp. 379–397, on "inconsistency" as a ground of challenge.

In any case where a decision has been taken in accordance with a self-created rule of policy the following matters must be considered:

(i) is the policy intrinsically flawed? For example, does it require the decision-maker to take into account irrelevant considerations? Does it seek to utilise the powers for an improper purpose? Is the policy "unreasonable"? These grounds of challenge are considered in the next chapter;

(ii) assuming that there is nothing intrinsically objectionable about the policy, has the policy been applied over-rigidly and to the exclusion of the genuine exercise of discretion in the particular case? The tests applied by the courts in determining this question appear from the cases which follow.

Note

See generally H.L. Molot (1972) 18 McGill L.J. 310; D.J. Galligan [1976] P.L. 332.

R. v. PORT OF LONDON AUTHORITY, ex p. KYNOCH LTD

[1919] 1 K.B. 176; 88 L.J.K.B. 553; 120 L.T. 177; 35 T.L.R. 103; 83 J.P. 41; 16 L.G.R. 937 (Court of Appeal)

Kynoch Ltd owned land at Canvey Island on the north bank of the Thames. They applied to the Port of London Authority for a licence (under the Port of London Act 1908, s.7, and the Thames Conservancy Act 1894, s.109) to construct a deep-water wharf and other works. In November 1917 the Authority rejected the application "on the ground that the accommodation applied for, is of the character of that which Parliament has charged the Authority with the duty of providing in the port". Under the Port of London Act 1908, s.2(1), the Authority was under a duty "to take into consideration the state of the river and the accommodation and facilities afforded in the Port of London, and, subject to the provisions of this Act to take such steps as they may consider necessary for the improvement thereof". Under section 2(2) they had power (*inter alia*) to "construct, equip, maintain, or manage any docks, quays, wharves and other works in connection therewith ...". In April 1918 Kynoch Ltd gave notice of appeal to the Board of Trade under the 1908 Act. In September 1918 they withdrew this appeal and applied instead for mandamus to compel the Authority to exercise their discretion according to law. An affidavit from the Secretary to the Authority made it clear that the merits of the application had been fully considered by two committees and the Authority itself.

The Divisional Court refused to grant mandamus. Kynoch Ltd appealed to the Court of Appeal.

BANKES L.J.: ... The main ground [upon which the appellants sought mandamus] was that the Port authority had not heard and determined the application of June 8, 1917, for permission to carry out works of a very important character with a very extensive frontage to the river....

Every case must depend on its own particular circumstances; but decided cases furnish some rules which ought to govern the court in the exercise of its discretion to grant or refuse the prerogative writ of mandamus. There must be something in the nature of a refusal to exercise jurisdiction by the tribunal or authority to whom the writ is to be directed. A refusal may be conveyed in one of two ways: there may be an absolute refusal in terms, or there may be conduct amounting to a refusal. In the latter case it is often difficult to draw the line between those cases where the tribunal or authority has heard and determined erroneously upon grounds which it was entitled to take into consideration and those cases where it has heard and determined upon grounds outside and beyond its jurisdiction; but this conclusion may be drawn from decided cases, that there is no refusal to hear and determine unless the tribunal or authority has in substance shut its ears to the application which was made to it, and has determined upon an application which was not made to it. On this point I would refer to the words of Farwell L.J. in *R. v. Board of Education* [1910] 2 K.B. 165, 179: "If the tribunal has exercised the discretion entrusted to it *bona fide*, not influenced by extraneous or irrelevant considerations, and not arbitrally or illegally, the courts cannot interfere; they are not a Court of Appeal from the tribunal, but they have power to prevent the intentional usurpation or mistaken assumption of a jurisdiction beyond that given to the tribunal by law, and also the refusal of their true jurisdiction by the adoption of extraneous considerations in arriving at their conclusion or deciding a point other than that brought before them, in which cases the courts have regarded them as declining jurisdiction." Again, in *R. v. Bowman* [1898] 1 Q.B. 663, 667, where licensing justices had allowed their decision to be influenced by extraneous considerations, Wills J. said: "There has been no real hearing, and the mandamus must therefore go." Those two cases furnish a rough test for deciding when a tribunal, in considering matters outside its jurisdiction, has refused to exercise its true and proper jurisdiction.

In the present case there is another matter to be borne in mind. There are on the one hand cases where a tribunal in the honest exercise of its discretion has adopted a policy, and, without refusing to hear an applicant, intimates to him what its policy is, and that after hearing him it will in accordance with its policy decide against him, unless there is something exceptional in his case. I think counsel for the applicants would admit that, if the policy has been adopted for reasons which the tribunal may legitimately entertain, no objection could be taken to such a course. On the other hand there are cases where a tribunal has passed a rule, or come to a determination, not to hear any application of a particular character by whomsoever made. There is a wide distinction to be drawn between these two classes.... [His Lordship referred to *R. v. Sylvester* (1862) 31 L.J.M.C. 93, and *R. v. L.C.C., ex p. Corrie* [1918] 1 K.B. 68.]

Now to apply these principles to the facts of this case. There is the letter of November 2 written on behalf of the Port authority by their secretary ... and there is his affidavit. It negatives the suggestion that the only matter considered by the Port authority was that specified in the letter. We must decide this case upon the affidavit. Read carefully and fairly it amounts to a statement that the Port authority did nothing which could be properly described as a refusal to hear and determine. But I go a step further. Even assuming that the letter contains the only ground on which the application was refused, I think, considering the position of the Port authority, that the matters involved in that decision were rightly and properly considered by them, and warrant the adoption of a general policy in granting licences for works of this particular class. Therefore on the main point the rule must be discharged....

WARRINGTON L.J. agreed.

SCRUTTON L.J. delivered a concurring judgment.

Note

In *R. v. London County Council, ex p. Corrie* [1918] 1 K.B. 68, the local authority had made a byelaw prohibiting, without its written consent, the selling of any article in the parks, gardens and open spaces under its control. After having granted permissions in some cases to sell literature at meetings in certain parks the local authority changed its policy. It revoked existing permits and resolved that no further consents should be granted for such sales. The applicant then sought permission to sell a pamphlet, "The British Blind", at meetings to be held by the National League of the Blind. She was refused permission. The letter of refusal included the following statement: "the Council has decided that no permits for the sale of literature ... are to be issued. I regret that it is not possible to make an exception to this rule even in a most deserving case ...". The King's Bench Division granted mandamus to the applicant, requiring that the Council should hear her application on its merits. Avory J., agreeing with Darling and Sankey JJ., stated (at 74):

"I have come to the same conclusion, though somewhat reluctantly, because I doubt whether the [grant of mandamus] will be of any effective service to the [applicant], inasmuch as, when the application for permission is considered, the Council will probably refuse to give it.... I ... do not assent to the submission ... that the ... Council must give their consent unless they determine that the pamphlet is an improper one to be sold in parks.... No such duty is cast upon them by the by-laws. They may refuse their consent although, as an article, no exception can be taken to the pamphlet which it is proposed to sell."

LAVENDER (H.) & SON LTD v. MINISTER OF HOUSING AND LOCAL GOVERNMENT

[1970] 1 W.L.R. 1231; 114 S.J. 636; [1970] 3 All E.R. 871; (1969) 68 L.G.R. 408

The company applied for planning permission to extract sand, gravel and ballast from part of Rivernook Farm, Walton-on-Thames. Most of the site was within an area of high quality agricultural land reserved for that purpose in accordance with the Waters Report on Sand and Gravel, 1948–1953. The planning authority refused planning permission, and the company appealed to the Minister. The only substantial objection to the development came from the Ministry of Agriculture, which wished to see the land maintained as agricultural land. There was evidence that the company would be able to restore the land to a high standard of fertility after excavation. The inspector who conducted the public inquiry could find no reason to refuse planning permission apart from the objection of the Ministry of Agriculture. The Minister dismissed the appeal. His decision letter included the two sentences:

"It is the Minister's present policy that land in the reservations should not be released for mineral working unless the Minister of Agriculture, Fisheries and Food is not opposed to working. In the present case the agricultural objection has not been waived, and the Minister has therefore decided not to grant planning permission for the working of the appeal site."

The company applied to the High Court under section 179 of the Town and Country Planning Act 1962 (now section 288 of the 1990 Act) for the Minister's decision to be quashed.

WILLIS J.: ... It is those last two sentences in the decision letter which lie at the heart of the matter in issue; and it is submitted, first of all, by counsel for the applicants, that they show, in this case, that the Minister had so fettered his own discretion to decide the appeal by the policy which he had adopted that the decisive matter was not the exercise of his own discretion on a consideration of the report and other material considerations, but the sustained objection of the Minister of Agriculture. In effect, he says that the decision was not that of the Minister of Housing and Local Government, the tribunal entrusted with the duty to decide, but the Minister of Agriculture, who had no status save perhaps in a consultative capacity and certainly no status to make the effective decision....

... In general support of his main submission, counsel for the applicants has referred me to Professor de Smith's well-known work, *Judicial Review of Administrative Action* ((2nd ed., 1968), pp. 292–297) and to certain of the cases cited therein. He really puts his argument in two ways: (1) that the Minister has fettered his discretion by a self-created rule of policy; and (2) that the Minister, who has a duty to exercise his own discretion in determining an appeal, has in this case delegated that duty to the Minister of Agriculture, who has no such duty and is, statutorily, a stranger to any decision. It is, of course, common ground that the Minister is entitled to have a policy and to decide an appeal in the context of that policy. He can also differ from the inspector on any question of fact, and disagree with the inspector's conclusion and recommendations. He can, and no doubt should, reject any recommendation of an inspector which runs counter to his policy, since, as counsel for the Minister points out, it is of the very essence of the duties laid on the Minister by section 1 of the Minister of Town and Country Planning Act 1943 that he should secure consistency and continuity in the framing and execution of a national policy with respect to the use and development of land.

The courts have no authority to interfere with the way in which the Minister carries out his planning policy (see *per* Lord Denning M.R., *Lord Luke of Pavenham v. Minister of Housing and Local Government* [1968] 1 Q.B. 172 at 192). There is also no question but that the Minister, before making a decision whether or not to allow an appeal, may obtain the views of other government departments (see *Darlassis v. Minister of Education* (1954) 52 L.G.R. 304 at 318, *per* Barry J.). The duties of the Minister and their extent in relation to a matter such as the appeal in the present case, comprising in a hybrid form both administrative and quasi-judicial functions, were enunciated by Lord Greene M.R. in a well-known passage in *B. Johnson & Co. (Builders) Ltd v. Minister of Health* [1947] 2 All E.R. 395, at 397 and 399:

"The duty placed on the Minister with regard to objections is to consider them before confirming the order. He is also to consider the report of the person who held the inquiry. Having done that, his functions are laid down by the last words of the paragraph (*i.e.* para. 4 of Sched. 1 to the Housing Act 1936), *viz.*, 'and may then confirm the order either with or without modification'. Those words are important, because they make it clear that it is to the Minister that Parliament has committed the decision whether he will or will not confirm the order after he has done all that the statute requires him to do. There is nothing in that paragraph, or anywhere else in the Act, which imposes on the Minister any obligation with regard to the objections, save the obligation to consider them. He is not bound to base his decision on any conclusion that he comes to with regard to the objections, and that must be so when one gives a moment's thought to the situation. The decision whether to confirm or not must be made in relation to questions of policy, and the Minister, in deciding whether to confirm or not, will, like every Minister entrusted with administrative duties, weigh up the considerations which are to affect his mind, the preponderating factor in many, if not all, cases being that of public policy, having regard to all the facts of the case.... That decision must be an administrative decision, because it is not to be based purely on the view that he forms of the objections, *vis-à-vis* the desires of the local authority, but is to be guided by his view as to the policy which in the circumstances he ought to pursue."

Can there, nevertheless, come a point in this hybrid process when the court can interfere with a Ministerial decision which, *ex facie*, proceeds on a consideration of the inspector's report and concludes by applying Ministerial policy?

Counsel for the applicants submits that such a point can be reached and has been reached in this case. It is reached, he says, adopting the words of Professor de Smith (see p. 294), if a tribunal, entrusted with a discretion as the Minister was in the present case, disables itself from exercising that discretion in a particular case by the prior adoption of a general policy. In *R. v. Port of London Authority, ex p. Kynoch Ltd*, Bankes L.J. said: ... [His Lordship cited the passage "In the present case ... by whomsoever made" (above, p. 257)].

In another licensing case, *R. v. County Licensing (Stage Plays) Committee of Flint County Council, ex p. Barrett* [1957] 1 All E.R. 112 at 122, where the decision was given in the interests of consistency, Jenkins L.J. said:

"Then they went on ... to conclude ... that the Queen's Theatre licence must follow the fate of the Pavilion Theatre licence, because it was essential that the same rule should be applied in all cases or, in other words, that the committee should be consistent. I cannot think that that method of approach fulfils the requirement that the matter should be heard and determined according to law.... It seems to me that it wrongly pursues consistency at the expense of the merits of individual cases."

I have referred to these two cases since they were relied on by counsel for the applicants, but I am inclined to agree with counsel for the Minister that the considerations applicable to licensing cases are not of much assistance when considering the scope of a Minister's duties within a statutory framework....

It is, of course, clear that if the Minister has prejudged any genuine consideration of the matter before him, or has failed to give genuine consideration to (*inter alia*) the inspector's report, he has failed to carry out his statutory duties properly (see *Franklin v. Minister of Town and Country Planning* [1948] A.C. 87 [below, p. 526]).

In the present case counsel for the applicants does not shrink from submitting that the decision letter shows that no genuine consideration was given to the question whether planning permission could, in the circumstances, be granted. I have carefully considered the authorities cited by counsel, but I have not found any clear guide to what my decision should be in this case. I have said enough to make it clear that I recognise that in the field of policy, and in relation to Ministerial decisions coloured or dictated by policy, the courts will interfere only within a strictly circumscribed field (see *per* Lord Greene M.R. in *Associated Provincial Picture Houses Ltd v. Wednesbury Corp.* [see below, p. 349]). It is also clear, and is conceded by counsel for the Minister, that where a Minister is entrusted by Parliament with the decision of any particular case he must keep that actual decision in the last resort in his own hands (see *R. v. Minister of Transport, ex p. Grey Coaches* (1933) 77 S.J. 301). I return, therefore, to the words used by the Minister. It seems to me that he has said in language which admits of no doubt that his decision to refuse permission was solely in pursuance of a policy not to permit minerals in the Waters agricultural reserves to be worked unless the Minister of Agriculture was not opposed to their working. Counsel for the Minister submits that, read as a whole, the decision letter should be taken as implying some such words as "I have gone through the exercise of taking all material considerations into account, but you have not persuaded me that this is such an exceptional case as would justify me in relaxing my policy; therefore I stick to it and apply it." If that were the right construction perhaps counsel for the Minister would be justified in saying that there was no error in law. But in my judgment the language used is not open to any such such implication. There is no indication that this might be an exceptional case such as would or could induce the Minister to change his policy. It is common ground that the Minister must be open to persuasion that the land should not remain in the Waters reservation. How can his mind be open to persuasion, how can an applicant establish an "exceptional case" in the case of an inflexible attitude by the Minister of Agriculture? That attitude was well known before the inquiry, it was maintained during the inquiry, and presumably thereafter. The inquiry was no doubt, in a sense, into the Minister of Agriculture's objection, since, apart from that objection, it might well have been that no inquiry would have been necessary, but I do not think that the Minister, after the inquiry, can be said in any real sense to have given genuine consideration to whether, on planning (including agricultural) grounds, this land could be worked. It seems to me that by adopting and applying his stated policy he has in effect inhibited himself from exercising a proper discretion (which would of course be guided by policy considerations) in any case where the Minister of Agriculture has made and maintained an objection to mineral working in an agricultural reservation. Everything else might point to the desirability of granting permission, but by applying and acting on his stated policy I think that the Minister has fettered himself in such a way that in this case it was not he who made the decision for which Parliament made him responsible. It was the decision of the Minister of Agriculture not to waive his objection which was decisive in this case, and while that might properly prove to be the decisive factor for the Minister when taking into account all material considerations, it seems to me quite wrong for a policy to be applied which in reality eliminates all the material considerations save only the consideration, when that is the case, that the Minister of Agriculture objects. That means, as I think, that the Minister has by his stated policy delegated to the Minister of Agriculture the effective decision on any appeal within the agricultural reservations where the latter objects to the working...

If the Minister was intending to follow his stated policy, I think that it was very undesirable that it should not have been made known in advance. It is possible to imagine great hardship falling on appellants who, all unawares, embark on an expensive appeal foredoomed to failure by reason of a strict though unannounced policy. However, I agree with counsel for the Minister that the failure to publicise the policy is not a ground for questioning the decision...

On the main ground on which this case has been argued, however, I am satisfied that the applicants should succeed. I think that the Minister failed to exercise a proper or indeed any discretion by reason of the fetter which he imposed on his exercise in acting solely in accordance with his stated policy; and further that on the true construction of the Minister's letter the decision to dismiss the appeal, while purporting to be that of the Minister, was in fact, and improperly, that of the Minister of Agriculture.

Questions

1. Was *ex p. Kynoch* applied in this case, or was some different rule adopted? See Galligan, *op. cit.*, pp. 348–350.

2. When may it be desirable for a decision-maker to evaluate "the weight of at least some factors that may be relevant to an exercise of discretion *in the future*"? (our question mark) (Galligan, *op. cit.*, p. 350, emphasis added).

Notes

1. See case note by D.G.T. Williams [1971] C.L.J. 6. Other cases in which there has been successful challenge on this ground include: *R. v. Windsor Licensing Justices, ex p. Hodes* [1983] 1 W.L.R. 685 (justices failed to consider merits of particular application for liquor licence—applied their "store within store" supermarket policy over-rigidly); *R. v. Hampshire Education Authority, ex p. J* (1985) 84 L.G.R. 547 (over-rigid policy in respect of exercise of discretion to pay independent school fees); *R. v. Canterbury City Council, ex p. Gillespie* (1986) 19 H.L.R. 7 (over-rigid application of statutorily required general policy as to allocation of council accommodation); *R. v. Secretary of State for Transport, ex p. Sherriff and Sons Ltd, The Times,* December 18, 1986 (revocation of discretionary grant based on over-rigid wording of Ministry's Memorandum of Explanation as to the availability of grants; see A.W. Bradley [1987] P.L. 141 and [1989] P.L. 197); *R. v. Bexley LBC, ex p. Jones* [1994] C.O.D. J93 (local authority policy as regards award of dicretionary student grants held legitimate so long as authority prepared to consider exceptional cases: however, no reference in application form to the policy; nor, consequently, any opportunity to plead special circumstances).

2. *Stringer v. Minister of Housing and Local Government* [1970] 1 W.L.R. 1281 concerned (*inter alia*) the long-standing policy of the Ministry to discourage development which would interfere with the efficient operation of the Jodrell Bank radio telescope. Cooke J. held that the Minister was entitled to rely on this policy in refusing an appeal on application for planning permission, stating at 1298:

> "It seems to me that the general effect of the many relevant authorities is that a Minister charged with the duty of making individual administrative decisions in a fair and impartial manner may nevertheless have a general policy in regard to matters which are relevant to those decisions, provided that the existence of that general policy does not preclude him from fairly judging all the issues which are relevant to each individual case as it comes up for decision.
>
> I think that in this case the Minister was entitled to have a policy in regard to Jodrell Bank, and I think that his policy is not such as to preclude him from fairly considering a planning appeal on its merits. I do not think that it precluded him from fairly considering Mr Stringer's appeal. I do not think that the Minister has prejudged the case, or tied his own hands, or abdicated any of his functions."

Further aspects of *Stringer* are considered below, p. 274.

BRITISH OXYGEN CO. LTD v. MINISTER OF TECHNOLOGY

[1971] A.C. 610; [1970] 3 W.L.R. 488; [1970] T.R. 143; 114 S.J. 682; [1970] 3 All E.R. 165 (House of Lords)

The company manufactured, sold and delivered industrial and medical gases, which had to be kept in special containers of various kinds. One general class of container included individual cylinders of different sizes. The company bought a large number of these over three years, their total expenditure exceeding £4 million. They cost, on average, £20 each. The Board of Trade had a discretion to award investment grants under the Industrial Development Act 1966 in respect of new "plant". They had a rule of practice not to approve for grant, expenditure on items which cost individually less than £25, however great the number of such individual items purchased at any one time. The company applied for a declaration that the Board of Trade was not entitled to decline to make a grant on the sole ground that each cylinder cost less than £25. Buckley J. ([1969] 1 Ch. 57) granted the declaration, saying that this "would not be an exercise of the discretion but an abrogation of it ... every genuine and reasonable application ... must be considered on its merits. Refusals to consider an application merely on the ground of the low cost of the individual equipment provided involves ignoring whatever characteristics the application has meriting approval." The Court of Appeal allowed an appeal ([1969] 2 Ch. 174, *sub nom. British Oxygen Co. Ltd v. Board of Trade*). There was a further appeal to the House of Lords.

LORD REID: ... [I]t is necessary to consider what is the duty of the respondent in administering the Act and what rights, if any, the Act confers on those eligible for grants.

Section 1 of the Act provides that the Board of Trade "may" make grants.... But how were the Board intended to operate that discretion? Does the Act read as a whole indicate any policy which the Board is to follow or even give any guidance to the Board? If it does then the Board must exercise its discretion in accordance with such policy or guidance (*Padfield v. Minister of Agriculture, Fisheries and Food* [below, p. 303]). One generally expects to find that Parliament has given some indication as to how public money is to be distributed. In this Act Parliament has clearly laid down the conditions for eligibility for grants and it has clearly given to the Board a discretion so that the Board is not bound to pay to every person who is eligible to receive a grant. But I can find nothing to guide the Board as to the circumstances in which they should pay or the circumstances in which they should not pay grants to such persons.

[His Lordship referred to the long title, section 1(6) and sections 2 to 8 of the 1966 Act.]

Sections 11 and 12 are perhaps more relevant. Section 11 provides for the appointment of committees to advise the Board on the administration of the Act and it could be taken as an indication that otherwise the Board's discretion is unlimited. Section 12 provides for an annual report to Parliament so that Parliament can *ex post facto* consider the way in which this discretion has been exercised....

I cannot find that these provisions give any right to any person to get a grant. It was argued that the object of the Act is to promote the modernisation of machinery and plant and that the Board were bound to pay grants to all who are eligible unless, in their view, particular eligible expenditure would not promote that object. That might be good advice for an advisory committee to give but I find nothing in the Act to require the Board to act in that way. If the Minister who now administers the Act, acting on behalf of the Government, should decide not to give grants in respect of certain kinds of expenditure, I can find nothing to prevent him.... [I]f the Minister thinks that policy or good administration requires the operation of some limiting rule, I find nothing to stop him.

[His Lordship cited *R. v. Port of London Authority, ex p. Kynoch*, in particular the passage from the judgment of Bankes L.J. beginning—"There are on the one hand...", and ending—"between these two classes".]

I see nothing wrong with that. But the circumstances in which discretions are exercised vary enormously and that passage cannot be applied literally in every case. The general rule is that anyone who has to exercise a statutory discretion must not "shut his ears to an application" (to adapt from Bankes L.J.). I do not think there is any great difference between a policy and a rule. There may be cases where an officer or authority ought to listen to a substantial argument reasonably presented urging a change of policy. What the authority must not do is to refuse to listen at all. But a Ministry or large authority may have had to deal already with a multitude of similar applications and then they will almost certainly have evolved a policy so precise that it could well be called a rule. There can be no objection to that, provided the authority is always willing to listen to anyone with something new to say—of course I do not mean to say that there need be an oral hearing. In the present case the respondent's officers have carefully considered all that the appellants have had to say and I have no doubt that they will continue to do so....

VISCOUNT DILHORNE: ... [His Lordship read the passage from *ex p. Kynoch* quoted by Lord Reid above.]

Bankes L.J. clearly meant that in the latter case there is a refusal to exercise the discretion entrusted to the authority or tribunal but the distinction between a policy decision and a rule may not be easy to draw. In this case it was not challenged that it was within the power of the Board to adopt a policy not to make a grant in respect of such an item. That policy might equally well be described as a rule. It was both reasonable and right that the Board should make known to those interested the policy it was going to follow. By doing so fruitless applications involving expense and expenditure of time might be avoided. The Board says that it has not refused to consider any application. It considered the appellants'. In these circumstances it is not necessary to decide in this case whether, if it had refused to consider an application on the ground that it related to an item costing less than £25, it would have acted wrongly.

I must confess that I feel some doubt whether the words used by Bankes L.J. in the passage cited above are really applicable to a case of this kind. It seems somewhat pointless and a waste of time that the Board should have to consider applications which are bound as a result of its policy decision to fail. Representations could of course be made that the policy should be changed.

I cannot see any ground on which it could be said that it was *ultra vires* of the Board to decide not to make grants on items costing less that £25 ... In my opinion, this appeal should be dismissed.

Lord Morris of Borth-y-Gest, Lord Wilberforce and Lord Diplock concurred with Lord Reid.

Notes

1. Consider the views on the question of policy fetters expressed by the Court of Appeal in *Sagnata Investments Ltd v. Norwich Corporation* [1971] 2 Q.B. 614, below, pp. 543–550.

Sagnata raises the question whether a power to license an activity may, by the adoption of a policy of "no licences", be used by an authority to prohibit all such activity? To prevent authorities going beyond what Parliament may have intended the courts may hold either that the policy goes beyond what the legislation authorises as a legitimate exercise of power, or that the authority has been unwilling to consider the merits of individual applications and has operated the policy in an inflexible way.

Parliament has, on occasions, made clear by the wording of legislation that such "blanket" policies are permissible. See, *e.g.* Local Government (Miscellaneous Provisions) Act 1982—local authority may reject an application to operate a "sex establishment" on the ground, *inter alia*, that there are already an appropriate number of such establishments in the area; express provision that the local authority may take the view that the appropriate number is "nil".

It has been held that legislation authorising such "blanket" policy decisions should be construed narrowly—see *Walker v. Leeds City Council* [1976] 3 All E.R. 709, H.L.

2. In *R. v. Secretary of State for the Environment, ex p. Brent London Borough Council* [1982] Q.B. 593; [1983] 3 All E.R. 321, the Secretary of State had exercised powers to reduce the rate support grant payable to the applicant local authority. In so doing the Secretary of State had acted in accordance with a policy earlier formulated to deal with "overspending" authorities. He had refused to meet representatives of the local authority to discuss any alteration or amendment of the policy, regarding his policy on the matter as "settled". In the words of Ackner L.J. (at 644): "... the Secretary ... clearly decided to turn a deaf ear to any and all representations to change the policy ...". In so acting the Secretary of State was held by the Court of Appeal to have erred. Again in the words of Ackner L.J. (*ibid.*): "In our judgment [he] was obliged to listen to any objector who showed that he might have something new to say; putting it negatively, he was obliged not to declare his unwillingness to listen.... We accept that to be entitled to be heard it was for the objector to show that he had, or might have, something new to say...." The Secretary of State's decision was, accordingly, quashed. The court rejected the Secretary of State's argument that the "fettering" principle applied only to cases where a discretionary power conferred was of a general nature, to be exercised on more than one occasion and in relation to applications for the grant of some right which the person holding the power can confer, such as a permission or licence: see [1982] Q.B. at 640–642. See S.H. Bailey [1983] P.L. 8.

3. Note how this ground of challenge overlaps with others. To fail to give proper consideration to the merits of an individual matter may at one and the same time be to apply a policy over-rigidly and to fail to take into account a relevant consideration (see below, p. 321). Equally, to defend successfully a decision taken in accordance with a policy it may be necessary to show that one has "acted fairly" in the sense of having given notice of the policy which was to be followed, and having indicated that representations that an exception should be made or that the policy should be changed would be considered (see further on the "duty to act fairly," below, pp. 418 *et seq.*). The need to make the policy known to those who may be affected by it would seem to follow from the obligation to be receptive to representations. This obligation is only of substance if those affected are aware of the policy in respect of which they may raise arguments.

Note also that *failure* to have followed a published guideline or policy without good reason may give rise to successful challenge. See, for example, *R. v. Director of Public Prosecutions, ex p. C* (1994) 159 J.P. 227 (failure of Crown Prosecution Service to have followed its Code for Prosecutors); *Morbaine v. Secretary of State for the Environment* (1993) 68 P. & C.R. 525 (all facts pointed to one decision—following announced policy—different decision reached—court willing to infer absence of valid reason); *R. v. Leeds City Council, ex p. Hendy* (1994) 6 Admin. L.R. 439; *R. v. Secretary of State for the Environment, ex p. West Oxfordshire D.C.* (1993) 26 H.L.R. 417.

(D) FETTERING DISCRETION BY CONTRACTUAL OR SIMILAR UNDERTAKINGS

The cases which follow demonstrate the line which the courts have sought to draw between, on the one hand, contracts or other binding undertakings which they have upheld as having been entered into in the valid exercise of discretionary power (or valid performance of public duty), and, on the other hand, purported contractual or other commitments which the courts have held to be invalid as unduly infringing the requirement that bodies in whom discretionary powers have been vested should retain freedom as to the exercise of those discretionary powers.

The cases show how the courts have acknowledged the fact that public authorities will commonly need to enter into binding commitments with "outsiders" in order that they may perform their various statutory functions. Express provision to such effect may appear in legislation, or may appropriately be implied therefrom. At the same time, the courts have had regard to the principle that, notwithstanding an authority's possession of a power to enter into binding commitments, the authority's discretionary powers have been conferred on it to be exercised as the public interest may from time to time require. "Commitments" which seem unduly to restrict an authority from acting in the exercise of its powers as the public interest may in due course require will therefore be held invalid; and for a public body to regard itself as unable, because of "commitments" entered into, to exercise its powers as it may subsequently consider the public interest to require may involve that body in having failed to have retained sufficiently the broad scope of its discretionary power.

The following cases illustrate (i) the general principles applied by the courts as regards the performance/fettering of statutory powers; and (ii), the operation of the same, or at least a very similar, principle in respect of the capacity of the Crown to enter into binding commitments.

Note

See generally J.D.B. Mitchell, *The Contracts of Public Authorities* (1954), Chap. 2, esp. pp. 57–65; C. Turpin, *Government Contracts* (1972), pp. 19–25; P.W. Hogg (1970) 44 A.L.J. 154; E. Campbell (1971) 45 A.L.J. 338; P. Rogerson [1971] P.L. 288.

(i) The General Principles

BIRKDALE DISTRICT ELECTRIC SUPPLY CO. LTD v. SOUTHPORT CORPORATION

[1926] A.C. 355; 95 L.J.Ch. 587; 134 L.T. 673; 42 T.L.R. 303; 90 J.P. 77; 24 L.G.R. 157 (House of Lords)

In 1901 the appellants, an electricity company, took over, under an Electric Lighting Order (made under the Electric Lighting Acts), the local electricity supply undertaking from Birkdale UDC. Under a Supplemental Deed to the Main Deed of Transfer, it was agreed that the prices to be charged by the appellants to private consumers should not exceed those charged in the adjoining borough of Southport by Southport

Corporation, which also operated an electricity supply undertaking. In 1911 South-port Corporation "took over" Birkdale UDC. The appellants continued to supply the Birkdale area. In 1923, the Corporation applied for an injunction to restrain the appel-lants from charging prices in excess of the Southport prices (as had been done since 1921). The appellants argued that the 1901 agreement was an *ultra vires* fetter on their own power to fix the price (subject to statutory maxima) of electricity supplied by them. In the future they might be faced with a difficult situation, and need to raise their prices above those in Southport. The Corporation argued that the 1901 agreement was a business agreement which was not incompatible with the proper performance by the appellants of their statutory functions. The question of incompatibility had to be judged at the date of the agreement. The fact that the agreement might be improvident, and lead to lower profits, was a matter between the appellant company and their share-holders, but did not render the agreement *ultra vires*. Astbury J. dismissed the action ([1925] 1 Ch. 63), but was reversed by the Court of Appeal ([1925] 1 Ch. 794). The company appealed to the House of Lords.

LORD SUMNER: ... Are ... [the agreements] void at common law as being *ultra vires* the appellants, a trading company, incorporated to exercise statu-tory powers vested in them in the public interest under the authority of the Legislature? This is a doctrine, which it may be unwise to circumscribe within the limits of an inelastic definition. We have, however, a long series of decisions, extending over nearly a century, and at any rate illustrating the cases to which the rule has been understood to extend. With the exception of *York Corporation v. Henry Leetham & Sons* [1924] 1 Ch. 557 no case has been cited, in which a contract by a trading company to compound with a customer without limit of time for the price to be paid for services rendered to him, has been declared to be *ultra vires*, and we were told that the diligence of counsel had failed to find any other case. Certainly I have been able to go no further.

Hitherto the question has mainly arisen, where servitudes have been claimed over the property, which the alleged servient owner acquired under statutory authority and for the purposes of a public undertaking. In *R. v. Inhabitants of Leake* (1833) 5 B. & Ad. 469 a public right of way was alleged to exist over the bank of a drain constructed by statutory Commissioners and reparable as such by the inhabitants of Leake. In *Staffordshire and Worcester-shire Canal Navigation v. Birmingham Canal Navigations* (1866) L.R. 1 H.L. 254 a right was claimed to have water discharged from the respondents' canal into the canal of the appellants at the bottom of a flight of locks connecting the two navigations ... The right in these cases ... was rested on prescription and not on express grant, but the argument, which prevailed, was that the theory of dedication to the public use rests on an implied grant but none could be implied, since even an express grant would have been void as being *ultra vires*.

Parallel with these decisions there is a line of cases, in which the servitude claimed has been upheld on the ground that a dedication would not under the circumstances have been incompatible with full observance of the terms and full attainment of the purposes for which the statutory powers had been granted. This principle is stated as early as *R. v. Inhabitants of Leake*, in which the dedication was upheld, and was acted on in *Grand Junction Canal Co. v. Petty* (1888) 21 Q.B.D. 273, a case of a public right of walking on a towpath, and in *Greenwich Board of Works v. Maudslay* (1870) L.R. 5 Q.B. 397, a case of a footpath along a sea wall ... Parke J. says, in the *Leake* case, that, if the bank was vested in the Commissioners by statute, so that they were thereby bound to use it for some special purpose, incompatible with a public right of walking along it, they must be deemed to have been incapable in law of thus dedicating their property; otherwise they were in that regard in the same position as other landowners.... In the *Grand Junction* case Lindley L.J. says, that such incompatibility is a matter of evidence, and, in practice, evidence has regularly been given and considered for the purpose of testing the question.

My Lords, I do not think that these cases assist the appellants in any way, but in most respects are against them, for they show that, in default of proof of incompatibility in the present case, some other consideration of a cogent kind must be found. The incompetence of the company is only an incompetence *sub modo*, beyond which the powers necessary to its operation may be freely exercised.

Ayr Harbour Trustees v. Oswald (1883) 8 App.Cas. 323 introduces a new matter and is nearer to the present case. Harbour trustees, whose statutory power and duty were to acquire land, to be used as need might arise for the construction of works on the coast line of the harbour, sought to save money in respect of severance on the compulsory acquisition of a particular owner's land by offering him a perpetual covenant not to construct their works on the land acquired, so as to cut him off from access to the waters of the harbour, or otherwise to affect him injuriously in respect of land not taken but from which the acquired land was severed. It was held that such a covenant was *ultra vires*. Lord Blackburn's words should be quoted. "I think", he says, "that where the legislature confer powers on any body to take land compulsorily for a particular purpose, it is on the ground that the using of that land for that purpose will be for the public good. Whether that body be one which is seeking to make a profit for shareholders, or, as in the present case, a body of trustees acting solely for the public good ... a contract, purporting to bind them and their successors not to use those powers, is void."

Founding on this case, Russell J. held in *York Corporation v. Henry Leetham & Sons* [1924] 1 Ch. 557 that a contract, terminable only by the customer, to carry his traffic at a fixed annual sum was equally *ultra vires*. Just as the covenant in the *Ayr Harbour* case tied the hands of the successors to the then trustees, and prevented them from constructing works on the land acquired, however necessary they might have become for the proper management of the undertaking, so he held that the corresponding contracts with Leetham fettered the free management of the canal in perpetuity, no matter how urgent it might be to increase the revenues of the undertaking.

My Lords, I do not think that there is a true analogy between these cases. On examining the facts in the *Ayr Harbour* case it is plain that, in effect, the trustees did not merely propose to covenant in a manner that committed the business of the harbour to restricted lines in the future; they were to forbear, once and for all, to acquire all that the statute intended them to acquire, for, though technically they acquired the whole of the land, they were to sterilize part of their acquisition, so far as the statutory purpose of their undertaking was concerned. This is some distance from a mere contract entered into with regard to trading profits. The land itself was affected in favour of the former owner in the *Ayr* case just as a towpath is affected in favour of the owner of a dominant tenement, if he is given a personal right of walking along it. If the Ayr trustees had reduced the acquisition price by covenanting with the respondent for a perpetual right to moor his barges, free of tolls, at any wharf they might construct on the water front of the land acquired, the decision might, and I think would, have been different.

There is, however, another aspect of the *Ayr Harbour* case which ought to be loyally recognized. It is certainly some ground for saying that there may be cases where the question of competence to contract does not depend on a proved incompatibility between the statutory purposes and the user, which is granted or renounced, but is established by the very nature of the grants or the contract itself. It was not proved in the *Ayr* case that there was any actual incompatibility between the general purposes of the undertaking and the arrangement by which the particular proprietor was to be spared a particular interference with the amenities or the advantages of his back land. I think the case was supposed to speak for itself and that, in effect, the trustees were held to have renounced a part of their statutory birthright. The appellants, however, contend, and Russell J. appears to have thought, that your Lordships' House extended other principles, namely, those applicable to servitudes over land acquired, to mere contracts restricting the undertakers' future freedom of action in respect to the business management of their undertaking. This point of view ought therefore to be examined.

The appellants, as I understand them, say that the doctrine is not confined to the creation of servitudes or other derogations by grant from plenary ownership, but extends also to such covenants in perpetuity as may, in events not actually impossible, starve their undertaking and spell its ruin. Southport, they say, now standing in the shoes of the Birkdale Council as well as in its own (if I may somewhat distort their metaphor), has behind it the pockets of the ratepayers of both areas, and though these may be no more inexhaustible than their patience, at least they may prove deeper and more enduring than the paid-up or uncalled capital of the appellant company, or its shareholders' willingness to subscribe to new issues of debentures or of preference stock. The thing speaks for itself. The covenant is fraught with potential suicide for the covenantors, and so is *ultra vires*.

My Lords, this hypothesis is conceivable, though neither from the evidence nor the argument have I gathered why these machinations should be attributed to the respondents or be tolerated by their outraged ratepayers. Municipal finance is capable of much curious development, but I think that among ordinary ratepayers a passion to supply current below cost price to private consumers is purely academic. If it exists at Southport, I think it should be proved by testimony.

The argument must be either that it is one of the direct statutory objects of the Electric Lighting Order that the undertakers should make a profit or at least not suffer any loss, or else that this is an indirect statutory object, since, if the undertakers make no profit, they will either pursue the undertaking without zeal or will drop it, so soon as this imaginary rate-war exhausts their resources.

My Lords, I am afraid this is beyond me. It may be the policy of the Electric Lighting Acts to get trading companies to take up and work Electric Lighting Orders in hope of gain, but I cannot see that it is any part of the direct purposes of the Order, that money should be made or dividends distributed. The primary object of the Electric Lighting Order was to get a supply of electric energy for the area in question, a thing only feasible at the time by getting a trading company to undertake the business. It was not to secure that certain charges should be made or that certain results should be shown upon a profit and loss account. As for the indirect effect, which will follow if no money is made or enough money is lost, the Order itself imposes a maximum price for the current and conceivably, therefore, might itself lead to the exhaustion of the company's funds. How, then, can it be part of the legal objects of the grant of these powers, that they should never result in financial disaster? The Order is really as little concerned with the company's ultimate ability to continue the undertaking as with its earning of a profit. The latter is the company's own affair; the former will simply lead to the revocation of the Order and the grant of a more favourable one to someone else. If this is so, there is a wide and more than sufficient difference between the contract of the Ayr Harbour Trustees not to acquire all that they were intended to acquire, and that of the appellants to obtain the transfer of the Order by convenanting among other considerations for something, which obviously is not and may never be, incompatible with the fulfilment of all the purposes of the Order and most of the purposes of the company's trading as well.

In *York Corporation v. Henry Leetham & Sons* there were two navigations, both vested in the Corporation of York, which appear to have differed somewhat in their incidents, the Ouse Navigation and the Foss Navigation. The original Act of 1726, which authorized the former, empowered trustees to levy tolls on craft using the navigation when completed, and, for the purpose of constructing the navigation, authorized them to mortgage these prospective tolls and so to raise the necessary capital. The resources of the trustees were therefore of a character wholly different from those of a limited liability company. A later Act, that of 1732, fixed a schedule of rates and provided that all commodities carried "shall" bear them, and that it should be lawful for the trustees to take the rates "by this Act directed and no others", though, if the full revenue derived from these rates proved to be more than was required to maintain the undertaking, there was power to moderate them. The Act, which authorized the latter navigation, provided for the incorporation of a company having a capital of 25,400*l.* in 100*l.* shares and borrowing powers up to 10,000*l.* No distinction appears, from the judgment of Russell J., to have been drawn in argument between these two undertakings, but it is possible that the agreement in dispute, by which the undertakers compounded the rate with a particular customer, might be regarded as a direct breach of the mandatory charging clause of the Ouse Act of 1732, and consequently *ultra vires*. The same view could not arise on the Foss Act. The *ratio decidendi* of the judgment, however, proceeds entirely on the analogy of the *Ayr Harbour* case.

My Lords, with all respect to the learned judge, I am unable to adopt this reasoning. As I have said, it is no part of the intention of the Legislature that the appellants should make a profit or avoid a loss. If, again, the agreement is to be *ultra vires* at all, it must be *ultra vires* all through. In cases like the *Ayr Harbour* case the land acquired under statutory powers was fettered in the undertakers' hands from the time the agreement was made. In the present case the company's activities have not yet been and may never be impaired by the agreement at all. So far it may have been and probably has been safe and beneficial. How then, can it have been *ultra vires* hitherto? There is further, in my opinion, a wide distinction between the position of the appellants and of such undertakers as the Ayr Harbour Trustees. The scheme here is that a limited liability company, not deprived of its right, as such, to go into voluntary liquidation or otherwise to terminate its enterprise, obtained the Order with the Board of Trade's consent and with the like consent may part with it. In other words, the Board of Trade is here the constituted authority, by whose discretionary intervention the supply of electricity may be secured in the interest of the locality. This is a very different scheme from a constitution of undertakers, which under the same statute establishes their existence, confers their powers, and defines their purposes.

It appears to me that no line can be drawn between the agreement now in question and any ordinary trading contract, if the appellants are right in testing the validity of the contract by its ultimate and theoretic possibility of bringing upon them a crippling loss. I do not think that a speculation as to the possible effect of what they have done is a legitimate ground for relieving them from their bargain, and it seems to me that the appeal should be dismissed.

THE EARL OF BIRKENHEAD, LORD ATKINSON, LORD WRENBURY and LORD CARSON concurred.

Notes

1. The Earl of Birkenhead (at 364) formulated the basic principle as:

> "a well established principle of law, that if a person or public body is entrusted by the Legislature with certain powers and duties expressly or impliedly for public purposes, those persons or bodies cannot divest themselves of these powers and duties. They cannot enter into any contract or take any action incompatible with the due exercise of their powers or the discharge of their duties."

2. The leading modern case on the implied dedication of rights of way by statutory corporation is *British Transport Commission v. Westmorland C.C.* [1958] A.C. 126; [1957] 2 All E.R. 353. The House of Lords emphasised that the validity of express or implied dedications depends on the question of fact whether such dedication is incompatible with the corporation's statutory powers. Their Lordships rejected the Commission's argument that there could only be compatibility if it could be proved that in no conceivable circumstances could the proposed user at any future time and in any way possibly interfere with the statutory purpose for which the land was acquired. *Per* Viscount Simonds at 144:

> "to give to incompatibility such an extended meaning is in effect to reduce the principle to a nullity. For a jury, invited to say that in no conceivable circumstances and at no distance of time could an event possibly happen, could only fold their hands and reply that it was not for them to prophesy what an inscrutable Providence might in all the years to come disclose. I do not disguise from myself that it is difficult to formulate with precision what direction should be given to a jury. But, after all, we live in a world in which our actions are constantly guided by a consideration of reasonable probabilities of risks that can reasonably be foreseen and guarded against, and by a disregard of events of which, even if we think of them as possible, we can fairly say that they are not at all likely to happen. And it is, in my opinion, by such considerations as these, imprecise though they may be, that a tribunal of fact must be guided in determining whether a proposed user of land will interfere with the statutory purpose for which it was acquired."

Lord Radcliffe (at 155–156) referred to Lord Sumner's description of the *Ayr* case as an example of an attempt to renounce a part of the "statutory birthright" of the trustees:

> "Striking as the phrase is, it does not seem to me to offer much help in deciding which are the cases in which the principle of *Paterson's* case (1880–1881) 6 App.Cas. 833 and *Oswald's* case is to be applied, where, as he says, 'the very nature of the grants or the contract itself' provides the answer, and which are those many other cases in which the test to be applied is the humbler one of incompatibility proved by evidence. The birthright of a statutory corporation includes all those powers and rights with which it is thought proper to invest it at its creation: and I do not think it easy for a court of law to decide merely by the nature of the thing which of those powers are inalienably entailed and which can be disentailed and disposed of by ordinary grant.
>
> In my opinion, we are bound to recognize that the principle of these two cases cannot be applied in all circumstances and on all occasions to all statutory corporations and public bodies. That, indeed, has already been recognized by the decision of this House in the *Birkdale* case, in which the electric supply company had certainly made a contract which deprived themselves and their successors of power at any future time to raise the charges for their supply beyond a fixed limit, however much the needs of their undertaking might require it. It is of some importance to remember, when searching for a dividing line, that the two cases which 'spoke for themselves' were both concerned with defined areas of land of no great extent, and the possible consequence of renouncing powers over such areas could be stated as a matter of practical observation. But nothing like the same observation can be brought to bear when the factors of the problem are, on the one hand, all the general powers derived by a railway company from the Railway Clauses Consolidation Act, 1845, and, on the other hand, many miles of railway lines covering great varieties of setting. In such cases what I have called the pragmatic test is, I think, to be preferred...."

3. In *Stourcliffe Estates Co. Ltd v. Bournemouth Corporation* [1910] 2 Ch. 12, C.A., the defendant corporation purchased some land from the plaintiff to be used as a public park, and entered into a covenant not to erect any building except "such structures as summer houses a band stand or shelters." The corporation had power under the Bournemouth Improvement Act 1892 to build public conveniences on any of their public parks. The plaintiff was granted an injunction to restrain the corporation from erecting public conveniences on the land they had sold. The corporation's argument that the covenant was *ultra vires* was rejected. *Per* Cozens-Hardy M.R. at 18–19:

> "That ... is a proposition which seems to me to be startling. If the deed is wholly *ultra vires* I can understand it, but to suppose that the corporation could be allowed to retain the land and to repudiate the consideration or part of the consideration for it is a proposition to which certainly I could not give my adhesion."

His Lordship distinguished the *Ayr* case on the ground that in that case:

> "the Act of Parliament, for public purposes and in the public interest, declared that certain land should be purchased by the undertakers, who were given compulsory powers for the purpose. That land included Mr Oswald's land. Not only were they to make the harbour and a quay, but they had power—it was obviously part of the essence of the undertaking—to make over any part of the land so purchased, certain warehouses facing a certain road.... Here the corporation have general powers to purchase land for, *inter alia*, the purposes of a public park. They may go anywhere they like and may make a contract with anybody who is willing to enter into a

contract with them for these purposes, and to say that a vendor under those circumstances cannot rely upon a restrictive covenant entered into by the purchaser would really be to render it practically impossible for a municipal corporation ever to enter into a contract with a landowner for purposes of this kind."

Buckley L.J. pointed out (at 22) that the corporation "must acquire not for all and every purpose for which they can acquire land anywhere, but for some definite purpose, some one of the purposes in respect of which they are entitled to acquire land …". His Lordship saw no reason why the corporation should not take the land while binding themselves not to put a urinal there:

"It is said that that is divesting themselves of some power, because under s.85 of their Act of 1892 they could have put a urinal there. That section means that it is not an improper expenditure of money by the corporation to, amongst other things, erect urinals in proper places, but it is not necessary that the corporation should with every piece of land which they buy acquire also the right to put a urinal there."

4. In *William Cory & Son Ltd v. London Corporation* [1951] 2 K.B. 476; [1951] 2 All E.R. 85, C.A., the corporation as sanitary authority entered a contract with Cory's for the removal by Cory's barges of refuse from the City of London. Subsequently, the corporation as port health authority made new byelaws with requirements as to coamings and coverings that were more stringent than the terms of the contract. Compliance with the byelaws would have been onerous, requiring expenditure of over £400 per barge, and preventing the use of the barges for carrying coal on the return journey. The company purported to treat the making of the byelaws as repudiation by anticipatory breach, to accept the repudiation, and to claim rescission. They claimed that there was an implied term in the contract to the effect that the corporation should not use their powers to make byelaws to impose more onerous burdens than those provided by the contract. The Court of Appeal, affirming Lord Goddard C.J. ([1951] 1 K.B. 8) held that in general an implied term might be read into a contract that one party should not act so as to prevent the other from being able to perform its obligations. However, the court held that, given the statutory responsibilities of the sanitary authority, there was in this case no such implied term, and therefore no repudiation. In the words of Lord Asquith of Bishopstone at 484–485:

"I consider that such a term, whether implied or even express, could not be valid. The language of section 84(1)(a) of the Public Health (London) Act, 1936, is mandatory. The provision is as follows: '(1) Every sanitary authority shall make by-laws (a) for the prevention of nuisances arising from snow, ice, salt, dust, ashes, rubbish, offal, carrion, fish or filth or other matter or thing in any street.' If the suggested term were express, it would have to take some such form as this: 'True we are charged by Parliament with the duty of making such by-laws with reference to refuse as may be called for from time to time by considerations of public health. But even if these considerations call, and call peremptorily, for a provision not less stringent than that made by the 1948 by-laws, even if a second plague of London is likely to occur, unless such provision is made, we undertake in such an event to neglect or violate our statutory duty so far as the requirement of such a by-law may exceed the requirements imposed by cl. 1 of our contract with the claimants.' Such a contractual provision would seem to be plainly invalid. …"

His Lordship relied on the point that the corporation was not "a body trading for profit", unlike the body executing statutory duties in *Southport Corporation v. Birkdale District Electric Supply Co.*, and like the trustees in the *Ayr* case. Thus "the considerations which were thought relevant in the *Southport* case (so far as that decision threw doubt in [*sic*] the *York* case) have no application here".

It was accepted, however, that the contract had been frustrated from the date the byelaws came into effect.

5. In March 1967, Cheshire County Council and Congleton Rural District Council entered into an agreement with Manchester University, whereby the councils undertook to discourage development "within the limits of their powers" in a zone within the rural district. The aim was to protect the Jodrell Bank radio telescope, which was operated by a department of the University. The rural district council dealt with applications for planning permission as agents for the county council (the local planning authority).

In *Stringer v. Minister of Housing and Local Government* [1970] 1 W.L.R. 1281; [1971] 1 All E.R. 65, Cooke J. held that this agreement was *ultra vires* as inconsistent with the proper performance of the duties of a planning authority under the Town and Country Planning Act 1962, s.17(1). This required the authority to have regard to the provisions of the development plan, and to any other material considerations. It was admitted that after the agreement was signed the local planning authority did not override the Jodrell Bank objections to development, and the judge held that the intention of the agreement was to bind the authority to disregard considerations to which, under section 17(1), they were required to have regard. The judge held, further, that in refusing S's application for planning permission for 23 houses, the rural district council had intended to honour this agreement, it being immaterial whether or not it was legally binding, and so had failed to comply with section 17(1). The Rural District Council's determination was therefore void.

Nevertheless, Cooke J. ultimately decided against S. S had appealed to the Minister against the Rural District Council's determination. The Minister had dismissed the appeal on the ground that the development would give rise to a very serious danger to the continued operation of the telescope. S was now applying under s.179(1) of the 1962 Act for an order to quash the Minister's decision on the ground that it was not within the powers of the Act (see now s.288 of the 1990 Act and below, pp. 552–564). Cooke J. held that as the Minister had power to deal with appeals *de novo* (under s.23(4) of the 1962 Act; now, s.79(1) of the 1990 Act), he could entertain an appeal in this case even though the Rural District Council's determination was void. On the facts, the Minister had not been influenced by the 1967 agreement, and had not applied rigidly his policy to protect the telescope (see above, p. 262). S's application was dismissed.

Questions

1. Do public authorities need the protection of legal incapacity to enter "fettering" contracts? Should they be allowed to override express terms in contracts into which they enter freely without payment of compensation? Should they not be bound by the kinds of terms implied into contracts between private parties for their mutual protection? See P. Hogg, *Liability of the Crown* (2nd ed., 1989), pp. 134 *et seq.*

2. How satisfactorily is the *Ayr* case distinguished in the *Stourcliffe* case? Would the *Stourcliffe* case have been decided differently had the corporation been able to show that there was no other appropriate site for lavatories on the pleasure ground? Or in that part of Bournemouth?

3. How satisfactory is any distinction between a corporation acting solely for the public good and one trading for profit (*Cory*)? See Mitchell, *op. cit.*, p. 62.

DOWTY BOULTON PAUL LTD v. WOLVERHAMPTON CORPORATION

[1971] 1 W.L.R. 204; (1970) 115 S.J. 76; [1971] 2 All E.R. 277; 69 L.G.R. 192 (Chancery Division, Pennycuick V.-C.)

[The facts are stated above at pp. 204–205 in relation to the sequel to this application.]

By notice of motion dated September 23, 1970, the company sought an interlocutory injunction that the corporation should "... do nothing which would cause the Board of Trade [later the Department of Trade and Industry] to determine the existing licence enabling Pendeford Aerodrome, Wrottesley, Wolverhampton to be used as a licensed airfield and shall do nothing to prevent the company from using the airfield for their lawful purposes".

PENNYCUICK V.-C.: ... The first issue which has arisen upon the hearing of this motion is whether under the terms of the 1936 conveyance or under the general law the corporation is entitled to override the rights conferred upon the company under the 1936 conveyance. If it is so entitled that would be the end of the matter: the corporation will do no wrong to the company if it does nullify those rights by developing the airfield as a housing estate and the company will have no remedy whether by way of injunction or damages or otherwise.

Mr Bagnall for the company was content to rely on the plain terms of the 1936 conveyance. ...

Mr Newsom's [main] contention ... was that, under the general law regarding the exercise of statutory powers, the corporation is at any time entitled to override this licence, if it requires to use the airfield for any of its statutory purposes. These, of course, include its powers as a housing authority. Mr Newsom accepted that the grant of the licence under the 1936 conveyance was within the powers of the corporation. ...

Mr Newsom based his contention on the principle that a body entrusted with statutory powers cannot by contract fetter the exercise of those powers. He referred to a number of cases which establish beyond all doubt that principle. I refer shortly to three of those authorities.

[His Lordship referred to the *Ayr* case, *York Corporation v. H. Leetham* and *Southend-on-Sea Corporation v. Hodgson* [1962] 1 Q.B. 416 at 424.]

... That seems to me, however, a principle wholly inapplicable to the present case. What has happened here is that the corporation has made what is admittedly a valid disposition in respect of its land for a term of years. What is, in effect, contended by Mr Newsom is that such a disposition—and, indeed, any other possible disposition of property by a corporation for a term of years, for example, an ordinary lease—must be read as subject to an implied condition enabling the corporation to determine it should it see fit to put the property to some other use in the exercise of any of its statutory powers. Nothing in the cases cited supports this startling proposition. The cases are concerned with attempts to fetter in advance the future exercise of statutory powers otherwise than by the valid exercise of a statutory power. The cases are not concerned with the position which arises after a statutory power has been validly exercised. Obviously, where a power is exercised in such a manner as to create a right extending over a term of years, the existence of that right *pro tanto* excludes the exercise of other statutory powers in respect of the same subject-matter, but there is no authority and I can see no principle upon which that sort of exercise could be held to be invalid as a fetter upon the future exercise of powers....

[His Lordship referred to *Stourcliffe Ltd. v. Bournemouth Corporation* (above, p. 272) which had not been cited by counsel.]

I conclude for the purpose of this motion that the company has made out a *prima facie* case that it is entitled to this right and that the corporation is not entitled to override that right either under the terms of the 1936 conveyance or in exercise of its statutory power.

I turn now to consider the remedy available to the company should the corporation persevere in its intention to appropriate this land for housing. It seems to me that the remedy of the company must lie in damages only and that the company is not now entitled, and will not be entitled at the hearing of the action, if it is then otherwise successful, to any relief by way of injunction or mandatory order.

The right vested in the company necessarily involves the maintenance of the airfield as a going concern. That involves continuing acts of management, including the upkeep of runways and buildings, the employment of staff, compliance with the Civil Aviation Act 1949 and so forth, *i.e.* in effect the carrying on of a business. That is nonetheless so by reason that so far the corporation has elected to engage Don Everall Aviation Ltd to manage the airfield on its behalf. It is very well established that the court will not order specific performance of an obligation to carry on a business or, indeed, any comparable series of activities: see in this connection *Halsbury's Laws of England* (3rd ed., 1961), Vol. 36, pp. 267 to 269:

"The court does not enforce the performance of contracts which involve continuous acts and require the watching and supervision of the court."

... The principle is established, I should have thought, beyond argument. For this purpose there is no difference between an order for specific performance of the contract and a mandatory injunction to perform the party's obligation under the contract. In the present case the notice of motion is expressed as one for a negative injunction, but one has only to look at it to see that it does involve a mandatory order upon the corporation to maintain the airfield. In order that the corporation could continue to allow the company to use the airfield, it is essential that the corporation should maintain the airfield. It would be quite impossible for the company to use the airfield if the corporation did not maintain it. So an injunction in the terms asked would put upon the corporation a duty, to be observed for something over 60 years, to maintain the airfield.

I conclude therefore in the first place, always so far as this interlocutory motion is concerned, that the company has made out a *prima facie* case that it is entitled to the right conferred by the 1936 conveyance, and the corporation will do an actionable wrong if it prevents the company from exercising that right. I conclude further that the remedy and the only remedy of the company lies in damages, with the consequence that I must make no order on this motion.

Questions

1. Could the corporation's liability to pay damages for breach of covenant properly be regarded as a fetter on the exercise of their statutory housing powers? Are those powers among the primary powers of the local authority (*cf.* the *Stourcliffe* case, above, p. 272)?

2. If the corporation had covenanted not to build dwelling-houses on the airport site, and such a covenant would have been binding on a private covenantor, should an injunction have been granted?

Note

Given that any contract which a public authority has purported to make must be one which is itself within the scope of its legal powers, the issue for the courts may be regarded as one of determining the extent to which an authority's exercise of *one* of its powers may legitimately inhibit its freedom as regards its exercise of *other* powers. When looked at in this way it is, perhaps, understandable why a none too strict approach should be adopted by the courts.

The point was well illustrated in *R. v. Hammersmith and Fulham London Borough Council, ex p. Beddowes* [1987] Q.B. 1050. Here the Court of Appeal upheld a council resolution which purported to dispose of part of a run-down housing estate to a private developer and to accept a restrictive covenant over retained parts of the estate as to the types of lettings it would grant in those retained parts. The Court of Appeal acknowledged that:

"if a statutory power is lawfully exercised so as to create legal rights and obligations between the council and third parties, the result will be that the council will for the time being be bound, even though that hinders or prevents the exercise of other statutory powers" (*per* Fox L.J.).

In other words, the mere fact that the exercise of one power may fetter the exercise of another should not suffice to constitute a ground of challenge, provided that the decision so to exercise the former power was taken properly: that is, for proper purposes, on the basis of consideration of all relevant matters (including the extent to which it might fetter the exercise of other powers) and not unreasonably.

(ii) The Crown

REDERIAKTIEBOLAGET AMPHITRITE v. THE KING

[1921] 3 K.B. 500; 91 L.J.K.B. 75; 126 L.T. 63; 37 T.L.R. 985; [1921] All E.R.Rep. 542 (Rowlatt J.)

(Petition of Right)

ROWLATT J.: In this case the suppliants are a Swedish shipowning company who sue the Crown by petition of right for damages for breach of contract, the breach being that the ship *Amphitrite* was refused a clearance to enable her to leave this country, when she had entered a British port under an arrangement whereby she was promised that she should be given that clearance. Now undoubtedly the suppliants desired to get the clearest and most binding assurance that was possible. Their vessel was free; they might have employed her elsewhere; and they had experience of the difficulties encountered by foreign ships in getting away from this country when once they had come here. Accordingly they wrote on March 8, 1918, to the British Legation at Stockholm and asked whether, in the event of the vessel being put in trade between

Sweden and England, the Legation could give them a guarantee that she would be allowed free passage without being detained in Great Britain. The Legation replied that they were "instructed to say that the S.S. *Amphitrite* will earn her own release and be given a coal cargo if she proceed to the United Kingdom with a full cargo consisting of a least 60% approved goods". That reply was given by the British Legation after consulting the proper authorities, and I must take it that it was given with the highest authority with which it could be given on behalf of His Majesty's Government. And the British Government thereby undertook that if the ship traded to this country she should not be subjected to the delays which were sometimes imposed. The letters in which that undertaking was contained were written with reference to an earlier voyage which was allowed to go through, the undertaking being on that occasion observed. But the undertaking was renewed with respect to the voyage in connection with which the present complaint arises by a letter from the British Legation, in which it was stated that "the S.S. *Amphitrite* will be allowed to release herself in her next voyage to the United Kingdom"—that is to say, upon the same terms as before. Now under those circumstances what I have to consider is whether this was a contract at all. I have not to consider whether there was anything of which complaint might be made outside a Court, whether that is to say what the Government did was morally wrong or arbitrary; that would be altogether outside my province. All I have got to say is whether there was an enforceable contract, and I am of opinion that there was not. No doubt the Government can bind itself through its officers by a commercial contract, and if it does so it must perform it like anybody else or pay damages for the breach. But this was not a commercial contract; it was an arrangement whereby the Government purported to give an assurance as to what its executive action would be in the future in relation to a particular ship in the event of her coming to this country with a particular kind of cargo. And that is, to my mind, not a contract for the breach of which damages can be sued for in a Court of law. It was merely an expression of intention to act in a particular way in a certain event. My main reason for so thinking is that it is not competent for the Government to fetter its future executive action, which must necessarily be determined by the needs of the community when the question arises. It cannot by contract hamper its freedom of action in matters which concern the welfare of the State. Thus in the case of the employment of public servants, which is a less strong case than the present, it has been laid down that, except under an Act of Parliament, no one acting on behalf of the Crown has authority to employ any person except upon the terms that he is dismissible at the Crown's pleasure; the reason being that it is in the interests of the community that the ministers for the time being advising the Crown should be able to dispense with the services of its employees if they think it desirable. Again suppose that a man accepts an office which he is perfectly at liberty to refuse, and does so on the express terms that he is to have certain leave of absence, and that when the time arrives the leave is refused in circumstances of the greatest hardship to his family or business, as the case may be. Can it be conceived that a petition of right would lie for damages? I should think not. I am of opinion that this petition must fail and there must be judgment for the Crown.

Judgment for the Crown.

Note

This brief judgment is the source of the so-called "doctrine of executive necessity", under which the Crown may apparently plead executive necessity as a defence to an action for breach of contract. See P.W. Hogg, *Liability of the Crown* (2nd ed., 1989), pp. 169–172; J.D.B. Mitchell, *The Contracts of Public Authorities*, pp. 27–32, 52–57 and Chap. V; C. Turpin, *Government Contracts* (1972), pp. 19–25.

COMMISSIONERS OF CROWN LANDS v. PAGE

[1960] 2 Q.B. 274; [1960] 3 W.L.R. 446; 104 S.J. 642; [1960] 2 All E.R. 726 (Court of Appeal)

The Minister of Works, acting on behalf of the Crown, requisitioned in 1945 premises which had been demised in 1937 by the Commissioner of Crown Lands for a term of 25 years. There was no express covenant of quiet enjoyment. The premises were derequisitioned in 1955. The Commissioners claimed the arrears of rent. It was conceded that the Crown was one and indivisible as lessor and requisitioning authority. The lessee claimed that she had been "evicted", but the court held that there had been no "eviction", merely the requisitioning of the lessee's right of occupation (for which compensation was payable to the lessee). One point was whether the re-entry was "wrongful" as in breach of an *implied* covenant of quiet enjoyment. The Crown argued *inter alia* that the requisitioning was not done in the capacity of landlord, but as the Executive responsible for the government of the country.

DEVLIN L.J.: ... Has the Crown committed a fundamental breach of the covenant? To answer that question one must consider the true scope and object of the covenant in such a lease as this where the Crown is the grantor. On the face of it, and if the covenant is taken as read without any limitation, there has been a breach. The Crown has deprived the defendant of the enjoyment of the demised premises for a long and indefinite period, and has done so deliberately, and (if one ignores the compulsion of public duty) has done so of its own free will; its act was authorised, but was not required by the statute. But, it is said by the Crown, it is not an act done as landlord, and it lacks other necessary constituents of the act of eviction.

I think that it may well be that the covenant of quiet enjoyment is limited to acts that are done by the landlord in supposed assertion of his rights as landlord, and that other trespasses, however grave, are outside the covenant. But because the landlord in this case is also the Crown, I have found it on the whole simpler to answer the question in the case not by reference to any special limitation on the covenant of quiet enjoyment affecting all landlords, but by reference to the general limitation that affects all contracts or covenants entered into by the Crown, or for that matter by any other public authority.

When the Crown, or any other person, is entrusted, whether by virtue of the prerogative or by statute, with discretionary powers to be exercised for the public good, it does not, when making a private contract in general terms, undertake (and it may be that it could not even with the use of specific language validly undertake) to fetter itself in the use of those powers, and in the exercise of its discretion. This principle has been accepted in a number of authorities; it is sufficient to mention *Ayr Harbour Trustees v. Oswald* (1883) 8 App.Cas. 623; *Rederiaktiebolaget Amphitrite v. The King* [1921] 3 K.B.

500; *Board of Trade v. Temperley Steam Shipping Co. Ltd* (1926) 26 Ll.L.R. 76; affirmed (1927) 27 Ll.L.R. 230, C.A. and *William Cory & Sons Ltd v. City of London Corporation* [1951] 2 K.B. 476, C.A.

The covenant for quiet enjoyment in the present case is implied, and is not dissimilar to the contractual provision considered in the two cases last cited, which were both concerned with the implied obligation on one party to a contract not to interfere with the performance by the other party of his obligations under it. In *Board of Trade v. Temperley Steam Shipping Co. Ltd*, the Board were the charterers of the defendant's ship, and it was contended that they had prevented the defendants from making their ship efficient for her service under the charterparty because one of the Board's surveyors had refused a licence to do certain repairs.... [His Lordship summarised the *Cory* case, above, p. 273.]

I do not, however, rest my decision in the present case simply on the fact that the covenant for quiet enjoyment has to be implied. For reasons which I think will appear sufficient in the next paragraph, I should reach the same conclusion if the ordinary covenant was expressed.

In some of the cases in which public authorities have been defendants, the judgments have been put on the ground that it would be *ultra vires* for them to bind themselves not to exercise their powers; and it has also been said that a promise to do so would be contrary to public policy. It may perhaps be difficult to apply this reasoning to the Crown, but it seems to me to be unnecessary to delve into the constitutional position. When the Crown, in dealing with one of its subjects, is dealing as if it too were a private person, and is granting leases or buying and selling as ordinary persons do, it is absurd to suppose that it is making any promise about the way in which it will conduct the affairs of the nation. No one can imagine, for example, that when the Crown makes a contract which could not be fulfilled in time of war, it is pledging itself not to declare war for so long as the contract lasts. Even if, therefore, there was an express promise by the Crown that it would not do any act which might hinder the other party to the contract in the performance of his obligations, the covenant or promise must by necessary implication be read to exclude those measures affecting the nation as a whole which the Crown takes for the public good.

During the last war the Ministries of War Transport, Food and Supply were trading on a vast scale, and were also issuing orders under their statutory powers which quite frequently frustrated their own contracts, or those made by some other government department. The Minister of Supply, for example, might be found prohibiting all importation of a commodity of a sort which he had contracted to buy; or the Ministry of War Transport might fail to make cargo space available for another department's purchases. So far as I am aware, there is no case in which it has been contended that because of such action, the Crown was in breach of contract. That shows the general understanding under which such business was done. If at the time of making any such contract the "officious bystander" had asked whether it was clear that the Crown was not undertaking to limit the use of its general executive powers, I think that there could have been only one answer. That is the proper basis for a necessary implication. I need not examine the question whether, if the Crown sought to fetter its future action in express and specific terms, it could effectively do so. It is most unlikely that in a contract with the subject, it would ever make the attempt. For the purpose of this case it is unnecessary to go further than to say that in making a lease or other contract with its subjects, the Crown does not (at least in the absence of specific words) promise to refrain from exercising its general powers under a statute or under the prerogative, or to exercise them in any particular way. That does not mean that the Crown can escape from any contract which it finds disadvantageous by saying that it never promised to act otherwise than for the public good. The distinction was clearly put by Roche J. in *Board of Trade v. Temperley Steam Shipping Co. Ltd*, 26 Ll.L.R. 76 at 78, where he said: "I think and I hold that in this charterparty it is to be implied that the Crown should do nothing in connection with and in relation to and in the carrying out of the contract contained in the charterparty to prevent the shipowners from keeping the vessel seaworthy and to prevent them earning their hire. But I am utterly unable to imply in the charterparty a term or condition that the Crown should do nothing by virtue of some general legislation or by virtue of some executive action entirely remote from the charterparty and done by persons not connected with the performance of the contract directly or indirectly to bring about the results in question." That is a different thing from saying that the Crown can never bind itself in its dealings with the subject in case it might turn out that the fulfilment of the contract was not advantageous. The observations of Denning J. in *Robertson v. Minister of Pensions* [1949] 1 K.B. 227, 231, on the doctrine of "executive necessity" were, I think, directed to a case of that sort. Here we are dealing with an act done for a general executive purpose, and not an act done for the purpose of achieving a particular result under the contract in question.

I agree that the appeal should be dismissed.

[LORD EVERSHED M.R. and ORMEROD L.J. expressed no opinion on the effect of an express covenant, but agreed that an implied covenant of quiet enjoyment could not "extend to prevent the future exercise by the Crown of powers and duties imposed upon it in its executive capacity by statute" (*per* Lord Evershed M.R., at 287) or "be taken to go so far as to imply an undertaking by the Crown to refrain from exercising statutory powers in respect of the demised premises which the Crown may properly deem necessary" (*per* Ormerod L.J., at 289).]

Questions

1. Is the *Amphitrite* principle the same as that applied in *Ayr Harbour Trustees v. Oswald* and the other cases cited in the previous section (pp. 266–277)?

2. What limitations did Rowlatt J. place on the principle he applied? Are they sufficiently precise? Are they workable?

3. If the *Amphitrite* principle is not the *Ayr* principle in disguise, should any of the latter's limitations (*e.g.* the test of incompatibility) be applied to the Crown? See Turpin, *op. cit.*, p. 24.

4. Does the Crown need the protection of the *Amphitrite* principle? An injunction, or an order for specific performance cannot be awarded against the Crown (see s.21 of the Crown Proceedings Act 1947), and so the Crown in relying on this principle would merely be avoiding the payment of damages. See Hogg, *op. cit.*, p. 171, who suggests that the *Amphitrite* was wrongly decided, and Mitchell, *op. cit.* who accepts the statements of Rowlatt J. "as containing a sound general principle of law" (p. 222) but argues that compensation should be payable wherever contractual obligations are overridden in the public interest.

5. What would the position have been had the Crown covenanted expressly not to exercise any existing or future powers of entry under any legislation? Would that situation be strictly analogous with the *Amphitrite* case?

(E) FETTERING DISCRETION BY ESTOPPEL

The cases which follow raise the following questions:

(i) Whether a body which has held itself out as having greater powers than in fact it possesses will, in any subsequent legal proceedings, be prevented, "estopped", from relying on its lack of power in the matter in question? As we shall see (the *Rhyl* case, below p. 283), the courts have noted that to apply the doctrine of estoppel in such circumstances would be to allow an agency *by its own actions* to extend the ambit of the legal powers conferred on it by Parliament. The principle has therefore been clearly stated that no agency may extend its legal powers by the process of estoppel.

(ii) Whether a body may by process of estoppel disentitle itself from performance of a legal duty imposed on it? Again, it has been held (*Maritime Electric* case, below, p. 285), and for the same reason as in (i) above, that estoppel does not operate in public law to such effect.

(iii) Whether a body (the "principal") which possesses certain powers is bound by a *purported* exercise of those powers by an "agent"/"delegate" acting without strict legal authority to bind the "principal"? Here the courts have, over the years adopted a less clear and consistent approach. The judges have been torn between, on the one hand, sympathy for an applicant who may quite reasonably have relied on the apparent "authority" of an official employed by the body in question, or the apparent authority of one of its committees, as regards an (in fact) unauthorised assurance given or decision taken; and, on the other hand, their desire not to allow the notion of estoppel to undermine the fundamentals of the *ultra vires* doctrine. Critical questions which need to be asked in this context are:

(a) is the *substance* of the power in question *intra vires* the respondent body itself?;
(b) had that body chosen to have done so, would it have had *power to delegate the exercise of the power in question to the person/committee* which has purported to exercise that power?;
(c) was the assertion of authority of the "agent"/"delegate" assertion by the *respondent agency itself* as to the powers of its apparent "agent"/"delegate"; or was the assertion of authority that of the "agent"/"delegate" alone?

See on these issues, below, pp. 286–299.

We shall see that, after some equivocation, the courts have been reluctant to utilise the concept of estoppel for the benefit of applicants for review. Instead they have developed a doctrine under which bodies possessing discretionary powers may be held to have "abused" those powers if, having by their conduct engendered legitimate expectations as to how the powers will be exercised, they then exercise those powers, without good reason, in a way which defeats those expectations. We shall consider this developing doctrine when we look at the various grounds of review for abuse of discretion—see below, p. 379. For the moment we should just note that this emerging ground of challenge may involve some potential for inconsistency with the oft-stated obligation of bodies to retain an unfettered discretion as to the manner of exercise of their powers. The reconciliation may lie in limits to the new doctrine. The new doctrine says, in effect—"Don't defeat expectations you have created unless there are good reasons in the public interest for so doing"; the retention of discretion principle requires discretion to be retained *in order that* bodies may through the course of time exercise their powers as the public interest may be considered to require.

Note

See generally J.A. Andrews, "Estoppels against Statutes" (1966) 29 M.L.R. 1; G. Ganz [1965] P.L. 237; M.A. Fazal [1972] P.L. 43; P.P. Craig (1977) 93 L.Q.R. 398 and · *Craig*, Chap. 16; A.W. Bradley, "Administrative Justice and the Binding Effect of Official Acts" (1981) C.L.P. 1.

(i) No Enlargement of Powers by Estoppel

RHYL URBAN DISTRICT COUNCIL v. RHYL AMUSEMENTS LTD

[1959] 1 W.L.R. 465, [1959] 1 All E.R. 257, 57 L.G.R. 19 (Harman J.)

Rhyl UDC sought a declaration that a 31-year lease which they had in 1932 granted to the defendant company was void. The only power under which the lease might have been granted was contained in section 177 of the Public Health Act 1875. This required the consent of the Minister of Health to have been obtained. No such consent had been obtained.

HARMAN J.: It was ... argued by the defendants, and so pleaded, that the plaintiffs are now estopped from denying the validity of the lease. The plea is based on the fact that the relations of the parties have been regulated by it ever since 1932 and that in that year the defendants changed their position by surrendering their 1921 lease on a promise to grant the new one. The representation so acted on must have been that the plaintiffs had power to grant a valid new lease. If the plaintiffs were private people this would be a strong plea, but in my judgment a plea of estoppel cannot prevail as an answer to a claim that something done by a statutory body is *ultra vires*: see *Minister of Agriculture and Fisheries v. Hulkin* (1948), an unreported case alluded to by Cassels J. in *Minister of Agriculture and Fisheries v. Matthews* [1950] 1 K.B. 148, where he said (at 153):

"If, therefore, the Minister does something which is an *ultra vires* act, it is not the act of the Minister at all. In the unreported case of *Minister of Agriculture and Fisheries v. Hulkin* the present plaintiff was suing for the possèssion of a cottage and garden which was in the possession of the defendant. The action was brought in the county court and the county court judge took the view that under the relevant defence regulations it was competent for the County Agricultural Committee, acting under the authority of the Minister, and as the delegate of the Minister's own powers, to create a relationship of landlord and tenant between the Minister and the defendant.

The case went to the Court of Appeal and the appeal of the plaintiff was allowed. The first point which called for consideration was the finding of the county court judge that under the regulation the Minister had power to create a tenancy and that, by the document relied on in that case, he had in fact done so. In the Court of Appeal the defendant's counsel disclaimed any intention of attempting to support the county court judge's judgment on that point. He contended, however, that the Minister having done what he had done in that case was estopped from denying that the document, under which the defendant was in possession, created a tenancy.

In dealing with that contention, Lord Greene M.R. said: 'He (the defendant's counsel) suggested, first of all, that even assuming, as he conceded, that the regulations gave no power to the Minister to create a tenancy, nevertheless the Minister was estopped from denying that the document in question did create a tenancy and, accordingly, the relationship must be regarded as one of landlord and tenant. There is, I think, a very short answer to that. Accepting the view which Mr Bailleu (the defendant's counsel) accepts, that the Minister had no power under the regulations to grant a tenancy, it is perfectly manifest to my mind that he could not by estoppel give himself such power. The power given to an authority under a statute is limited to the four corners of the power given. It would entirely destroy the whole doctrine of *ultra vires* if it was possible for the donee of a statutory power to extend his power by creating an estoppel. That point, I think, can be shortly disposed of.' "

If I may say so with respect, this seems as good sense as it is good law.

It was ingeniously argued that the present was not a case of the plaintiff council having no power, but that they had a power if they obtained the necessary consent and that the doctrine does not apply except where no power exists, so that the plaintiffs might be estopped from denying that they obtained consent. If this be not, as I suspect, a quibble, a like answer could be made that it would destroy the necessity of ever obtaining consent if a statutory body omitting to obtain it could thereafter be held estopped. Such a body could by these means confer on itself a power which it had not got, and the *ultra vires* doctrine would be reduced to a nullity.

Declaration granted.

Notes

1. In *Vestry of the Parish of St Mary, Islington v. Hornsey UDC* [1900] 1 Ch. 695, C.A., the plaintiffs allowed certain Hornsey landowners to use the plaintiffs' sewer. These "rights" were acquired by the defendants, and the plaintiffs allowed the defendants to use the sewer for over 30 years. By 1900, heavy use of the sewer by the defendants caused a serious nuisance in Islington. The Court of Appeal held, first, that the

plaintiffs could not grant anything more than a revocable licence. A contract, or the grant of an easement, for the discharge of sewage through the plaintiffs' sewer would have been *ultra vires* as the Metropolis Management Acts only authorised persons within the metropolitan district to use metropolitan sewers. Islington was within, and Hornsey outside the metropolitan district. Secondly, the court held that the plaintiffs were not estopped or debarred by laches or acquiescence from revoking the licence. The only concession to the defendants' argument that disconnection would cause a public nuisance in Hornsey was that they were given 12 months to make alternative arrangements, with the plaintiffs given leave to apply for an injunction at the end of that time.

2. In *Yabbicom v. King* [1899] 1 Q.B. 444, D.C., Mr King deposited plans for a house with the urban district council which revealed that when built it would not comply with byelaws made by the Council under the Public Health Act 1875, s.157. The plans were nevertheless approved by the council. This approval was held to be no defence to a prosecution subsequently brought for breach of the byelaws by the council's successor, Bristol Corporation. *Per* Day J. at 488: "The district council could not control the law, and byelaws properly made have the effect of laws; a public body cannot any more than private persons dispense with laws ... they have no dispensing power whatever."

3. In *R. v. Lambeth Borough Council, ex p. Clayhope Properties Ltd* (1986) 18 H.L.R. 541 a local authority was held not to be estopped from asserting the invalidity of notices it had served under what is now the Housing Act 1985. As the notices were invalid the local authority was entitled to resist claims to, otherwise mandatory, repair grants.

(ii) No Release of Duty by Estoppel

MARITIME ELECTRIC CO. LTD v. GENERAL DAIRIES LTD

[1937] A.C. 610; 53 T.L.R. 391; [1937] 1 All E.R. 748
(Privy Council: Lords Atkin, Thankerton, Russell of Killowen, Alness and Maugham)

The plaintiffs, although a private electricity supply company, were under a statutory duty to furnish reasonably adequate service and facilities, and were strictly limited as to the charges they could make, which had to be in exact accordance with filed schedules open to public inspection. To determine the amount of electricity supplied it was necessary to multiply the meter dial reading by 10. Through the plaintiffs' error this was not done over 28 months in relation to the defendants, a dairy company, who as a result, were charged for only one-tenth of the electricity supplied in this period. The plaintiffs sought to recover the balance of nine-tenths. The defendants had relied on the accuracy of the sums actually charged them for electricity in fixing the amounts they paid to the farmers who supplied them, and in fixing the prices they charged their customers.

LORD MAUGHAM: . . . The sections of the Public Utilities Act which are here in question are sections enacted for the benefit of a section of the public, that is, on grounds of public policy in a general sense. In such a case—and their Lordships do not propose to express any opinion as to statutes which are not within this category—where, as here, the statute imposes a duty of a positive kind, not avoidable by the performance of any formality, for the doing of the very act which the plaintiff seeks to do, it is not open to the defendant to set up an estoppel to prevent it. This conclusion must follow from the circumstance that an estoppel is only a rule of evidence which under certain special circumstances can be invoked by a party to an action; it cannot therefore avail in such a case to release the plaintiff from an obligation to obey such a statute, nor can it enable the defendant to escape from a statutory obligation of such a kind on his part. It is immaterial whether the obligation is onerous or otherwise to the party suing. The duty of each part is to obey the law. . . .

A similar conclusion will be reached if the question put by the learned judge is looked at from a somewhat different angle. It cannot be doubted that if the appellants, with every possible formality, had purported to release their right to sue for the sums remaining due according to the schedules, such a release would be null and void. A contract to do a thing which cannot be done without a violation of the law is clearly void. It may be asked with force why, if a voluntary release will not put an end to the obligation of the respondents, an inadvertent mistake by the appellants acted upon by the respondents can have the result of absolving the appellants from their duty of collecting and receiving payment in accordance with the law. . . . Their Lordships are unable to see how the Court can admit an estoppel which would have the effect *pro tanto* and in the particular case of repealing the statute.

(iii) Estoppel, Agency and Delegation

WESTERN FISH PRODUCTS LTD v. PENWITH DISTRICT COUNCIL

[1981] 2 All E.R. 204; (1978) 38 P. & C.R. 7; (1978) 77 L.G.R. 185 (Court of Appeal)

In April 1976 W.F.P. bought an industrial site at Stable Hobba which included the buildings of a disused factory. The factory had previously been used for the production of fertiliser from fish and fishmeal. This use had ceased in 1975. W.F.P. wanted to use the site for the manufacture of fish oil and fishmeal, and for the preparation and packaging of fresh fish for human consumption. The company intended to spend considerable sums of money, demolishing some of the old buildings, repairing others, and building new buildings. On April 7, 1976, a meeting took place between the Chairman of W.P.F. (Mr de Savary) and an official (Mr Giddens) of the district council, deputy to and representing the council's chief planning officer. De S asserted that because of the previous factory use of the site there existed an "established user right" which entitled his company to carry on their intended processes without needing to obtain planning permission from the council. G said that W.F.P. should satisfy him of such entitlement in writing; and that if he was so satisfied, the council would do everything they could to assist the project.

W.F.P. then wrote two letters supplying G with information. G replied, on behalf of the chief planning officer. This letter included a statement which "confirmed that the limits of the various component parts of the commercial undertaking as now existing appear to be established". On the strength of this letter, which W.F.P. later stated they regarded as confirmation that planning permission for their proposed use of the land was not needed, the company began to demolish, renovate, repair, build, and install equipment. This work was carried out to the knowledge of the council's officials. Then, on July 6, G contacted W.F.P. and asked that it submit applications for planning permission in respect of the building operations, and for an "established use certificate" under section 94 of the Town and Country Planning Act 1971. G explained that the application for this certificate was purely a formality.

W.F.P. submitted applications for planning permission and for the certificate. On August 26 a full meeting of the council refused all the applications, and authorised the service of enforcement and stop notices in respect of the work in progress. In September the enforcement notices were issued and all work at the site stopped.

W.F.P. brought an action seeking declarations that they were entitled to existing use rights entitling them to use the factory for their intended purpose, or that they were entitled to be treated as having planning permission for that purpose. W.F.P. also claimed injunctions to prevent the enforcement of the notices, and damages. Walton J. dismissed the claims. The company appealed to the Court of Appeal.

MEGAW L.J. delivered the judgment of the Court (MEGAW, LAWTON and BROWNE L.JJ):

Outline of issues

This appeal raises points which may, very broadly, be stated as follows.

(A) Did the defendant council make representations to the plaintiffs as to what the plaintiffs were permitted to do on the Stable Hobba site in such circumstances that the defendant council became estopped from making decisions contrary to the representations, and so that, the defendant council having made or purported to make such decisions, the plaintiffs are entitled to damages and other relief?

(B) Did the defendant council make any determination under s.53 [see below, p. 293] or s.94 of the Town and Country Planning Act 1971, and, if so, what is the effect?

(C) Did the defendant council act in abuse of their statutory powers, or act negligently, so as to give the plaintiffs the right by action in a court of law to claim damages or any other remedy?

[His Lordship considered whether the company had existing use rights in respect of its proposed processes, and, concluding that it did not, held that planning permission was therefore required for such development. His Lordship then addressed the question whether by process of estoppel the company should be treated as having been given such permission:]

... Here arise various issues which we shall consider later, such as whether any oral statements which were made could be treated as giving rise to an estoppel, and if so, an estoppel as to what, whether the letter of April 26, 1976, from Mr Giddens constitutes a relevant representation of anything, and if so, what, and whether the plaintiffs did rely on any representation which may be contained, or which they thought was contained, in that letter....

Was the letter of April 26, a representation and, if so, of what?

... We are unable to accept that a person familiar with the relevant facts known to both the writer and the recipient of the letter, reading the letter with reasonable care, could reasonably have read it as giving the plaintiffs confirmation that there was an existing use right which would cover the uses contemplated by the plaintiffs' scheme without the necessity for planning permission in respect of use. Whether Mr de Savary's belief that the letter contained that confirmation was because he was so firmly convinced of the "incontrovertible right" that he did not read the letter with due care, or whether it was for some other reason, we are unable to see how, taking full account of the relevant circumstances and of the context of the letter itself and of the letters and conversations which had led up to it, the words "Accordingly it is confirmed that the limits of the component parts of the commercial undertaking as now existing appear to be established" could reasonably be understood to be a confirmation of that which the plaintiffs allege it did confirm.

At the most the letter means that Mr Giddens on behalf of the defendant council was satisfied that the buildings on the site had been used previously for the purposes written on the plan and that the dimensions of the respective buildings used for those various purposes were correctly shown. If and in so far as it could be interpreted as confirming any use right, it was no more than a use right for the purposes for which the site had previously been used.

It follows that no relevant estoppel, "proprietary" or otherwise, can be founded on any representation contained in that letter.

Did the plaintiffs rely on such representation as they allege?

Even if it were to be construed as having the meaning which the plaintiffs placed on it, it would still, in our judgment, not avail the plaintiffs as an estoppel. They did not act on it to their detriment.

The judge, as we understand his judgment, has held that the plaintiffs, through Mr de Savary, did rely on what he understood to be the representation. "I think", says the judge, "he acted on that assurance, by going ahead with his projects as a whole"; and again, "He regarded it as all important, and considered that, having obtained that confirmation, all his troubles were over...."

We regard the evidence provided by the contemporary documents and by Mr de Savary himself in the witness box as being overwhelmingly in support of the conclusion that, if the plaintiffs had not received the letter of April 26, or had not construed it as they did, they would have gone ahead with their planned project as they did go ahead with it, both in timing and other respects. Mr de Savary's absolute conviction of the incontrovertible status of his user rights in respect of his planned operations was such that he would not have been deterred by the absence of a confirmation from Mr Giddens....

Even if we had been satisfied that the defendant council through their officers had represented to the plaintiffs that all they wanted to do on the Stable Hobba site could be done because of the existing uses, planning permission being required only for new buildings and structures, and that they had acted to their detriment to the knowledge of the defendant council because of their representations, their claim would still have failed. There are two reasons for this: first, because they did not have the equitable right which has come to be called proprietary estoppel; and, second, because in law the defendant council could not be estopped from performing their statutory duties under the 1971 Act.

[His Lordship considered the doctrine of *proprietary estoppel*: "when A to the knowledge of B acts to his detriment in relation to his own land in the expectation, encouraged by B, of acquiring a right over B's land, such expectation arising from what B has said or done, the court will order B to grant A that right on such terms as may be just." His Lordship noted that "there was no question of [W.F.P.] acquiring any rights in relation to any other person's land, which is what proprietary estoppel is concerned with", and so held this argument inapplicable. His Lordship then proceeded to explain why the argument that the council could be estopped from the performance of its statutory duties failed:]

... The defendant council's officers, even when acting within the apparent scope of their authority, could not do what the 1971 Act required the defendant council to do; and if their officers did or said anything which purported to determine in advance what the defendant council themselves would have to determine in pursuance of their statutory duties, they would not be inhibited from doing what they had to do. An estoppel cannot be raised to prevent the exercise of a statutory discretion or to prevent or excuse the performance of a statutory duty (see *Spencer Bower and Turner on Estoppel by Representation* (3rd ed., 1977, p. 141) and the cases there cited). The application of this principle can be illustrated on the facts of this case: under section 29 of the 1971 Act the defendant council as the planning authority had to determine applications for planning permission, and when doing so had to have regard to the provision of the development plan and "to any other material considerations". The plaintiffs made an application for planning permission to erect a tall chimney on the site. When considering this application the defendant council had to "take into account any representations relating to that application" which were received by them following the publishing and posting of notices: see sections 26 and 29(2). This requirement was in the interests of the public generally. If any representations made by the defendant council's officers before the publication or posting of notices bound the council to act in a particular way, the statutory provision which gave the public opportunities of making representations would have been thwarted and the defendant council would have been dispensed from their statutory obligation of taking into account any representation made to them. The officers were appointed by the defendant council but the council's members were elected by the inhabitants of their area. Parliament by the 1971 Act entrusted the defendant council, acting through their elected members, not their officers, to perform various statutory duties. If their officers were allowed to determine that which Parliament had enacted the defendant council should determine there would be no need for elected members to consider planning applications. This cannot be. Under section 101(1) of the Local Government Act 1972 (which repealed section 4 of the 1971 Act, which re-enacted in an amended form section 64 of the Town and Country Planning Act 1968), a local authority may arrange for the discharge of any of their functions by an officer of the authority. This has to be done formally by the authority acting as such. In this case the defendant council issued standing orders authorising designated officers to perform specified functions including those arising under sections 53 and 94 of the 1971 Act. Their officers had no authority to make any other determinations under the 1971 Act. We can see no reason why Mr de Savary, acting on behalf of the plaintiffs, and having available the advice of lawyers and architects, should have assumed, if he ever did, that Mr Giddens could bind the defendant council generally by anything he wrote or said.

Counsel for the plaintiffs submitted that, notwithstanding the general principle that a statutory body could not be estopped from performing its statutory duties, there are exceptions recognised by this court. This case, he asserted, came within the exceptions.

There seem to be two kinds of exceptions. If a planning authority, acting as such, delegates to its officers powers to determine specific questions, such as applications under sections 53 and 94 of the 1971 Act, any decisions they make cannot be revoked. This kind of estoppel, if it be estoppel at all, is akin to *res judicata.* Counsel for the Department of the Environment accepted that there was this exception, as did counsel for the defendant council in his final submissions. *Lever (Finance) Ltd v. Westminster Corp.* [1970] 3 All E.R. 496; [1971] 1 Q.B. 222 can, we think, be considered as an application of this exception. The trial judge had found that it was a common practice amongst planning authorities, including the defendants, for planning officers to sanction immaterial modifications to plans sent with successful applications for planning permission. This is what one of the defendants' planning officers thought he was doing when he agreed with the plaintiffs' architect that they could make a modification to the plans of some houses which were being erected; but Lord Denning M.R. thought that what he had agreed to was not an immaterial modification: it was a material one. He should have told the plaintiffs that they required planning permission to make it. When the defendants found out what had happened as a result of complaints made by members of the public who were likely to be affected by the modification, they suggested to the plaintiffs that they should apply for planning permission. They did; and their application was refused. This court affirmed the declaration made by the trial judge that there was a valid planning permission for the modification. The members of this court gave different reasons for finding as they did. Sachs L.J. stated that the combined effect of the past practice, taken with the powers of delegation under section 64 of the 1968 Act, was that the oral agreement made between the plaintiffs' architect and the defendants' planning officer operated as if all the formalities of section 43 of the Town and Country Planning Act 1962 (now section 53 of the 1971 Act) had been complied with. The other members of the court (Lord Denning M.R. and Megaw L.J.) made no mention of this reasoning. It follows that it was not the *ratio decidendi* of the judgment. We do not agree with it, as appears later in this judgment. Lord Denning M.R. rested his judgment on estoppel and delegation. After referring to the authorities setting out the general rule that planning authorities cannot be estopped from doing their public duty, he went on as follows ([1970] 3 All E.R. 496 at 500, [1971] 1 Q.B. 222 at 230):

> "But those statements must now be taken with considerable reserve. There are many matters which public authorities can now delegate to their officers. If an officer, acting within the scope of his ostensible authority, makes a representation on which another acts, then a public authority may be bound by it, just as much as a private concern would be."

He went on to refer by way of illustration to *Wells v. Minister of Housing and Local Government* [1967] 2 All E.R. 1041; [1967] 1 W.L.R. 1000, which was concerned with what this court adjudged to be an informal application made under section 43 of the 1962 Act. It is pertinent to note too that Lord Denning M.R. used the words "may be bound". Megaw L.J. said that he agreed with the reasons for judgment given by Lord Denning M.R. This case, of course, binds us unless there is in the reasoning an element which can be said to be *"per incuriam"*. In our judgment it is not an authority for the proposition that every representation made by a planning officer within his ostensible authority binds the planning authority which employs him. For an estoppel to arise there must be some evidence justifying the person dealing with the planning officer for thinking that what the officer said would bind the planning authority. Holding an office, however senior, cannot, in our judgment, be enough by itself. In the *Lever (Finance) Ltd* case there was evidence of a widespread practice amongst planning authorities of allowing their planning officers to make immaterial modifications to the plans produced when planning permission was given. Lever (Finance) Ltd's architect presumably knew of this practice and was entitled to assume that the practice had been authorised by the planning authorities in whose areas it was followed. The need for some evidence of delegation of authority can be illustrated in this way. Had Lever (Finance) Ltd's architect produced plans showing material and substantial modifications to the planning permission for a large development in Piccadilly Circus already granted, he could not sensibly have assumed that the planning officer with whom he was dealing had authority to approve the proposed modifications without putting them before the planning authority. Whether anyone dealing with a planning officer can safely assume that the officer can bind his authority by anything he says must depend on all the circumstances. In the *Lever (Finance) Ltd* case [1970] 3 All E.R. 496 at 501, [1971] 1 Q.B. 222 at 231 Lord Denning M.R. said: "Any person dealing with them [*i.e.* officers of a planning authority] is entitled to assume that all necessary resolutions have been passed." This statement was not necessary for the conclusion he had reached and purported to be an addendum. We consider it to be *obiter*; with all respect, it stated the law too widely.

In this case there was no evidence of any relevant delegations of authority save in relation to applications under sections 53 and 94. We deal later in this judgment with the plaintiffs' submissions about the operation of those sections.

We can deal with the second exception shortly. If a planning authority waives a procedural requirement relating to any application made to it for the exercise of its statutory powers, it may be estopped from relying on lack of formality. Much, however, will turn on the construction of any statutory provisions setting out what the procedure is to be. *Wells v. Minister of Housing and Local Government* is an example of the exception. Both counsel for the Department of the Environment and counsel for the defendant council submitted that this case was wrongly decided. Counsel for the Department of the Environment said that the dissenting judgment of Russell L.J. was to be preferred and both he and counsel for the defendant council reserved the right to argue this point elsewhere. Save in relation to the plaintiffs' submissions as to the operation of sections 53 and 94 on the facts of this case, this exception cannot have any application to this case.

The extension of the concept of estoppel beyond these two exceptions, in our judgment, would not be justified. A further extension would erode the general principle as set out in a long line of cases of which the decision of the Privy Council in *Maritime Electric Co. Ltd v. General Dairies Ltd* [1937] 1 All E.R. 748; [1937] A.C. 610 and the judgment of the Divisional Court in

Southend-on-Sea Corp. v. Hodgson (Wickford) Ltd [1961] 2 All E.R. 46, [1962] 1 Q.B. 416 are notable examples. Parliament has given those who are aggrieved by refusals of planning permission or the serving of enforcement notices a right of appeal to the Secretary of State: see sections 36 and 88 of the 1971 Act. He can hear evidence as to the merits and take into account policy considerations. The courts can do neither. The application of the concept of estoppel because of what a planning officer had represented could result in a court adjudging that a planning authority was bound to allow a development which flouted its planning policy, with which the courts are not concerned.

There is another objection to any extension of the concept of estoppel which is illustrated by the facts of the *Lever (Finance) Ltd* case. If the modifications which were permitted by the planning officer in that case had been properly to be regarded as immaterial, no problem of general principle would arise. But the court regarded itself as competent to decide as to the materiality and, despite the submission to the contrary by the successful plaintiffs, held that the modifications were material. On what basis of evidence or judicial notice the court reached that conclusion, we need not stay to consider. We assume both that the court had jurisdiction to decide that question, and that, on the facts of that case, their decision as to materiality was right. But then comes the difficulty, and the real danger of injustice. To permit the estoppel no doubt avoided an injustice to the plaintiffs. But it also may fairly be regarded as having caused an injustice to one or more members of the public, the owners of adjacent houses who would be adversely affected by this wrong and careless decision of the planning officer that the modifications were not material. Yet they were not, and it would seem could not, be heard. How, in their absence, could the court balance the respective injustices according as the court did or did not hold that there was an estoppel in favour of the plaintiffs? What "equity" is there in holding, if such be the effect of the decision, that the potential injustice to a third party, as a result of the granting of the estoppel is irrelevant? At least it can be said that the less frequently this situation arises the better for justice.

In *Brooks and Burton Ltd. v. Secretary of State for the Environment* (1976) 75 L.G.R. 285 at 296 Lord Widgery C.J. adverted to extending the concept of estoppel. He said:

"There has been some advance in recent years of this doctrine of estoppel as applied to local authorities through their officers, and the most advanced case is the one referred to by the inspector, namely *Lever Finance Ltd v. Westminster (City) London Borough Council.* I do not propose to read it. It no doubt is correct on its facts, but I would deprecate any attempt to expand this doctrine because it seems to me, as I said a few minutes ago, extremely important that local government officers should feel free to help applicants who come and ask them questions without all the time having the shadow of estoppel hanging over them and without the possibility of their immobilising their authorities by some careless remark which produces such an estoppel."

We agree with what he said.

The statutory position

We turn now to "the statutory position". Counsel for the plaintiffs submits that besides their claims based on estoppel the plaintiffs have rights and remedies arising from the planning legislation and the decisions of the courts as to the exercise by statutory authorities of their powers and duties. The consideration of these rights and remedies overlaps at one point with the estoppel claim, but the plaintiffs could succeed on the "statutory position" even if they fail on estoppel. The essence of this part of the plaintiffs' case is that the decisions made by the defendant council on August 26, were invalid, a "nullity", an "abuse of their powers" and "unlawful". We have already said that there was no fraud or malice on the part of the defendant council or their officers. In this part of the case, therefore, the phrase "abuse of powers" means no more than that the defendant council have mistakenly acted in a way which was not permitted by their powers.

Sections 53 and 94 of the 1971 Act

In addition or in the alternative to their contention that the letter of April 26, is the foundation of an estoppel, the plaintiffs contend that it was a "determination" under section 53 of the 1971 Act, or alternatively an "established use certificate" under section 94 of that Act. Counsel for the defendant council accepts that if it was such a determination or certificate the council would be bound by it; under their standing orders the power to make such decisions is delegated to their officers.

Section 53(1) provides as follows:

"If any person who proposes to carry out any operations on land, or to make any change in the use of land, wishes to have it determined whether the carrying out of those operations, or the making of that change, would constitute or involve development of the land, and, if so, whether an application for planning permission in respect thereof is required under this Part of this Act, having regard to the provisions of the development order, he may, either as part of an application for planning permission, or without any such application, apply to the local planning authority to determine that question."

Section 53(2) applies in relation to applications and determinations under this section a number of other provisions of the 1971 Act, relating to development orders (ss.24 and 31(1)), determinations by local planning authorities (s.29 (1)), the power of the Secretary of State to give directions to local planning authorities (s.31(1)), the keeping of registers of applications which are open for inspection by the public (s.34(1) and (3)), the powers of the Secretary of State to call in applications (s.35) and the right of appeal to the Secretary of State (ss.35 and 36).

The Town and Country Planning General Development Order 1973 ... makes provision for the procedure to be followed on section 53 applications and determinations. Articles 6(2) and 7(2), (3) and (4) provide for the steps to be taken, the provision in each case being governed by the word "shall".

... Counsel for the plaintiffs does not contend that the letter of April 26, amounted to a determination that no planning permission was required in respect of the plaintiffs' building operations, but he contends that it was a determination either that the user contemplated by the plaintiffs' project did not constitute development or that no planning permission was required for such development.

It seems to us that section 53(2) of the 1971 Act and articles 6(2) and 7(2), (3) and (4) of the 1973 order contemplate a considerable degree of formality in applications and determinations under section 53. But counsel for the plaintiffs relied on the decision of the majority of this court in *Wells v. Minister of Housing and Local Government* [1967] 2 All E.R. 1041; [1967] 1 W.L.R. 1000 and on the judgment of Sachs L.J. in *Lever (Finance) Ltd v. Westminster Corp.* [1970] 3 All E.R. 496; [1971] 1 Q.B. 222 as establishing that no particular formalities are required.

In the *Wells* case the plaintiffs had applied for planning permission for the erection of a concrete batching plant 27′6″ in height. The council engineer and surveyor replied by letter saying: "I am now instructed to inform you that the works proposed can be regarded as 'permitted development' under Class VIII of the ... Development Order ... and it is therefore not proposed to take any further action on your application." The plaintiffs then changed their minds and decided to build a plant 48′ high. Their architect assumed that this new proposal would be covered by the council's letter in respect of the 27′6″ plant and applied for byelaw consent in respect of the 48′ plant. The council granted byelaw consent on a form which contained the words: "No action should be taken hereunder till the approval of the town planning and licensing authority have been obtained" (*sic*); these words had been struck out but were still legible. The majority of the court (Lord Denning M.R. and Davies L.J., Russell L.J. dissenting) held that there had been a valid application and determination under section 43 of the 1962 Act (now s.53) that planning permission was not required for the 27′ 6″ plant, but the court held unanimously that there had been no application for planning permission, nor any application or determination under section 43 in respect of the 48′ plant.

In the *Lever (Finance) Ltd* case (the facts of which have already been stated) Sachs L.J. took the view that what had happened could and should be treated as a valid application and determination under section 43 of the 1962 Act that no further planning permission was needed for the change in the position of the house (see [1970] 3 All E.R. 496 at 503–504, [1971] 1 Q.B. 222 at 234). But the majority of the court (Lord Denning M.R. and Megaw L.J.) put their decision on different grounds, which have been considered earlier in this judgment.

This court is, of course, bound by the ratio of the decision of the majority in the *Wells* case, though if we may respectfully say so we find the dissenting judgment of Russell L.J. very powerful. In our view, the ratio on which Lord Denning M.R. and Davies L.J. were agreed was that a formal written application for a determination under section 43 (now s.53) was not necessary and that an application for planning permission impliedly contains an invitation to determine under section 43 that planning permission is not required (see [1967] 2 All E.R. 1041 at 1045, 1046, [1967] 1 W.L.R. 1000 at 1008, 1010, *per* Lord Denning M.R. and Davies L.J.). But all three members of the court held that there was no application or determination under section 43 in respect of the 48′ plant, Lord Denning M.R. saying ([1967] 2 All E.R. 1041 at 1045, [1967] 1 W.L.R. 1000 at 1008):

> "Ready as I am to waive irregularities and procedural defects, I think that to satisfy section 43 there must be at least a positive statement in writing by or on behalf of the planning authority that no planning permission is necessary."

If we are right in our understanding of the ratio of the majority in the *Wells* case, it does not bind us to hold that there was in the present case an application under section 53: there was in April 1976 no application for planning permission. Although the judgment of Sachs L.J. in the *Lever (Finance) Ltd* case would, we think, greatly extend beyond the *Wells* case the permitted degree of informality in applications and determinations under section 53, it is, as we have already said, not binding on this court. In our judgment, the decision of the majority in the *Wells* case as to the 27′ 6″ plant should not be extended beyond cases in which there has been an application for planning permission; we feel supported in this view by the unanimous decision as to the 48′ plant.

But even if this is wrong, and some communications from a proposed developer to a planning authority other than an application for planning permission can constitute an application under section 53, we should find it impossible to hold as a matter of construction of the letters of April 8 and 26, that they constituted an application or a determination under section 53. . . .

We also reject the alternative contention that the letter of April 26, was an established use certificate under section 94 of the 1971 Act. . . . The purpose and effect of a section 94 certificate is that it is conclusive evidence "as respects any matters stated therein" for the purposes of an appeal to the Secretary of State against an enforcement notice served in respect of any land to which it relates (s.94(7)); the benefit of the certificate runs with the land. One would therefore expect that it would be required to be a formal document, and Sched. 14 to the 1971 Act and Article 18 of the Town and Country Planning General Development Order 1973 contain provisions to that effect as to the application and the certificate. We do not think we need refer to them in detail. But they include provisions that an application "shall not be entertained" unless it is accompanied by a certificate containing the prescribed particulars (see para. 3(1) of Sched. 14 and Art. 18(2)), which the letter of April 26, was not, and that established use certificates "shall be issued" in the form set out in Part II of Schedule 6 to the 1973 order, which of course does not bear the slightest resemblance to the letter of April 26. Even if these formal defects are not in themselves a complete answer to this contention, as in our view they are, we think it is impossible to construe the letter of April 26, as a certificate under section 94. We cannot see that it is capable of being conclusive evidence of anything. . . .

Appeal dismissed.

Notes

1. Contrast the judgment of the Court of Appeal in *Western Fish* with the following statements of Lord Denning M.R. in earlier cases. In *Robertson v. Minister of Pensions* [1949] 1 K.B. 227 at 232:

"In my opinion if a government department in its dealings with a subject takes it upon itself to assume authority upon a matter with which he is concerned, he is entitled to rely upon it having the authority which it assumes. He does not know, and cannot be expected to know, the limits of its authority."

In *Howell v. Falmouth Boat Construction Co.* [1950] 2 K.B. 16 at 26:

"The principle is this: whenever government officers, in their dealings with a subject, take on themselves to assume authority in a matter with which he is concerned, the subject is entitled to rely on their having the authority which they assume. He does not know and cannot be expected to know the limits of their authority, and ought not to suffer if they exceed it. That was the principle which I applied in *Robertson.* ..."

And in *Wells v. Minister of Housing and Local Government* [1967] 1 W.L.R. 1000 at 1007:

"... Now I know that a public authority cannot be estopped from doing its public duty, but I do think it can be estopped from relying on technicalities; and this is a technicality, to be sure. We were told that for many years the planning authorities ... have written letters on the same lines as [this] letter. ... It has been their practice to tell applicants that no planning permission is necessary. Are they now to be allowed to say that this practice was all wrong and their letters were of no effect? I do not think so. I take the law to be that a defect in the procedure can be cured, and an irregularity be waived, even by a public authority, so as to render valid that which would otherwise be invalid. Thus in *Robertson* ... an assurance (that Colonel Robertson's disability was accepted as attributable to war service) was held binding on the Crown, even though it was given independently by the War Office instead of the Ministry of Pensions. ..."

Note that Lord Denning's statement of principle in *Howell* was disapproved, obiter, when the House of Lords considered the case on appeal. Lord Simonds stated that "the illegality of an act is the same whether or not the actor has been misled by an assumption of authority on the part of a government officer however high or low in the hierarchy" [1951] A.C. 837 at 845.

In due course Lord Denning M.R. appeared to have relented. In *Co-operative Retail Services Ltd v. Taff-Ely B.C.* (1980) 39 P. & C.R. 1, he said in respect of a purported grant of planning permission by an unauthorised town clerk:

"... The protection of the public [*i.e.* as regards decisions as to planning permission] is entrusted to the representative bodies and to the minister. It would be quite wrong that it should be preempted by a mistaken issue by a clerk of a written form—without any authority in that behalf."

2. In *Norfolk County Council v. Secretary of State for the Environment* [1973] 1 W.L.R. 1400, the council resolved to refuse planning permission for a factory extension. By mistake, the planning officer sent a notice which contained all the details of a grant of planning permission to the applicants. The applicants ordered some machinery. 11 days later the council told the applicant of the mistake and sent them the refusal of permission. The applicant cancelled the machinery order without penalty, but claimed that the first communication constituted a grant of permission, and made a token start on the extension. The council's enforcement notice was quashed by the Secretary of State who held that there was a valid grant. The notice contained no apparent defect and it was acted on in good faith by the applicants. The Divisional Court allowed the council's appeal. The officer "had no authority himself to make such a decision [*i.e.* to grant permission]. His ostensible authority ... only went to his authority to transmit the decision which had been made ..." (*per* Lord Widgery C.J. at 1404). Therefore there was no planning permission. Moreover, the council was not estopped from denying that there was a grant of permission. Note also *Graham v. Secretary of State for the Environment* [1993] J.P.L. 353 (council could not be estopped by its officers from its duty to exercise unfettered discretion as regards enforcement of planning controls).

3. In *Rootkin v. Kent County Council* [1981] 1 W.L.R. 1186, the plaintiff's daughter was allocated a place at a school measured by the authority to be over three miles from her home. On that basis, the authority was under a duty either to provide transport or to reimburse travelling expenses, under section 39(2) of the Education Act 1944. It chose the latter course, and issued a bus pass, in the exercise of the discretionary power under section 55(2) of the 1944 Act. Shortly after, the authority made a more precise measurement and found the distance to be less than three miles. It then withdrew the bus pass. The plaintiff argued (i) that the authority was not entitled to rescind its determination that a bus pass should be issued, and (ii) that the authority was estopped from revoking its decision. The Court of Appeal held that the authority was entitled to withdraw the pass. On the first point it was stated that "if a citizen is entitled to payment in certain circumstances and a local authority is given the duty of deciding whether the circumstances exist and if they do exist of making the payment, then there is a determination which the local authority cannot rescind. That was established in *Livingston v. Westminster Corp.* [1904] 2 K.B. 109. But that line of authority does not apply ... to a case where the citizen has no right to a determination on certain facts being established, but only to the benefit of the exercise of a discretion by the local authority" (*per* Lawton L.J. at 1195; *cf.* Eveleigh L.J. at 1197 and Sir Stanley Rees at 1200). On the second point, it was held that an estoppel could not arise where that would prevent the exercise of a statutory discretion (*Southend-on-Sea Corporation v. Hodgson (Wickford) Ltd* [1961] 1 Q.B. 416), that there was here no exceptional situation of a kind contemplated in the *Western Fish* case, above, and that in any event the plaintiff had not altered her position so as to entitle her to rely on the doctrine of estoppel (see Lawton L.J. at 1196; Sir Stanley Rees expressed his agreement with these reasons at 1200).

4. On the *Lever Finance* case, see J.M. Evans (1971) 34 M.L.R. 335; J.E. Alder [1974] J.P.L. 447; B.C. Gould (1971) 87 L.Q.R. 15; A.W. Bradley [1971] C.L.J. 3. The principle in *Lever Finance* was recently applied in *Camden London Borough Council v. Secretary of State for the Environment* (1993) 67 P. & C.R. 59. An officer of the local authority responded to a developer's letter, indicating that a minor change to roof extension plans did not require planning permission. Subsequently the council served an enforcement notice. The occupier's appeal against the notice was upheld by an inspector and by the High Court. The latter held that the council was estopped by the letter from asserting that the extension as built was not within the planning permission granted. In view of the normal practice of delegating such decisions to officers, the council could be regarded as having conferred ostensible or apparent authority.

5. On the *Western Fish* case, see D.G.T. Williams [1981] C.L.J. 198; A.W. Bradley (1981) 34 C.L.P. 1; C. Crawford (1982) 45 M.L.R. 87.

6. Consider Craig's argument (*Craig*, Chap. 16) that it would be preferable if instead of adopting a general rule (either applying the estoppel principle to public authorities, or denying its applicability) the courts were to develop a balancing approach in which the court would enquire on the facts of the case whether:

"the disadvantages to the public interest by allowing estoppel to be pleaded really do outweigh the injustice to the individual" (p. 481).

7. It is clear from the *Western Fish* case and cases decided since then that it is only in exceptional circumstances that a public authority will be bound by an estoppel arising out of informal undertakings or representations made by itself or on its behalf, so as to preclude it altogether from making a decision inconsistent with that undertaking or representation. Instead, the courts have developed alternative mechanisms for reconciling the interests of public authorities with the legitimate interests and expectations of others arising from such informal undertakings or representations. Accordingly, an authority's subsequent failure to take account of such an undertaking or representation may constitute failure to take account of a relevant consideration, and thus an

abuse of discretion (see below, pp. 321–348). A decision to act inconsistently with a previous undertaking or representation may be held to be irrational or unreasonable in the *Wednesbury* sense (see below, pp. 349–379). The undertaking or representation may give rise to a legitimate expectation entitling the person affected to an opportunity to make representations before the authority can lawfully decide to act inconsistently (see below, pp. 379–397).

8. One issue raised in each of the *Wells*, *Western Fish* and *Rootkin* cases was whether the authority in question had made a formal "determination" which the authority had no power to revoke. This issue also arose in *Re 56 Denton Road, Twickenham* [1953] Ch. 51. The plaintiff's house was partly demolished by enemy action, and the local authority subsequently pulled down what was left. The War Damage Act 1943 provided that compensation was payable to cover the cost of works in repairing damage, unless the damage involved total loss in which case a "value payment" was payable, unless the War Damage Commission exercised its power to make a cost of works payment instead. For the plaintiff, a "value payment" would be much lower than "cost of works payment". The Commission initially made a "preliminary classification" of total loss, then told the plaintiff by letter dated November 12, 1945, that it had been "reclassified" as not a total loss, with a cost of works payment accordingly becoming payable. The Commission purported subsequently to change its mind again and revert to the original classification. Vaisey J. granted a declaration that the November 1945 letter constituted a final determination that the damage was one for which a cost of works payment ought to be awarded. His Lordship accepted the following proposition of the plaintiff's counsel:

> "that where Parliament confers upon a body such as the War Damage Commission the duty of deciding or determining any question, the deciding or determining of which affects the rights of the subject, such decision or determination made and communicated in terms which are not expressly preliminary or provision is final and conclusive, and cannot in the absence of express statutory power or the consent of the person or persons affected be altered or withdrawn by that body. I accept that proposition as well-founded, and applicable to the present case. It is, I think, supported by *Livingstone v. Westminster Corporation* [1904] 2 K.B. 109 and *Robertson v. Minister of Pensions* [1949] 1 K.B. 227.
>
> I think that the letter of November 12, 1945, was one upon which the plaintiff was invited to rely and was and is entitled to rely. It is, I think, admitted that if she had altered her position in reliance upon it, a case of estoppel would have been raised against the defendants. But I really cannot see that it ought to be denied its proper force and effect, quite apart from such a case.
>
> I think that the contrary view would introduce a lamentable measure of uncertainty, and so much disturbance in the minds of those unfortunate persons who have suffered war damage that the Act cannot have contemplated the possibility of such vacillations as are claimed to be permissible in such a case as the present."

See case notes at 214 L.T. 291; 69 L.Q.R. 13 (R.E.M.).

Compare this case with *R. v. Secretary of State for Education and Science, ex p. Hardy*, *The Times*, July 28, 1988. Proposals for the reorganisation of Ilkeston School were placed before the Parliamentary Under-Secretary for approval under section 12(6) of the Education Act 1980. He gave approval by ticking the word "Approve". Following a misunderstanding, an officer in the department informed the authority in confidence that the proposals had been approved. The Secretary of State subsequently decided that the proposals should be rejected. McNeill J. held that compliance with section 12(6) only occurred when there was a formal, precise and published decision. The initial approval was accordingly not an irrevocable decision, and could not be made so by a leak from the Minister's private office.

See generally G. Ganz, "Estoppel and *Res Judicata* in Administrative Law" [1965]

P.L. 237; M.B. Akehurst, "Revocation of Administrative Decisions" [1082] P.L. 613; D.C. Stanley, "*Res Judicata* in Administrative Law" (1983) 32 U.N.B. Law Journal 221.

Vaisey J. accepted in *Re 56 Denton Road* that a final decision could be reconsidered with the consent of the person affected. In *R. v. Hertfordshire County Council, ex p. Cheung, The Times,* April 4, 1986, the council in 1978 had refused C a student grant on the ground that he was not "ordinarily resident" in the United Kingdom. The test applied was shown to be erroneous by the House of Lords in *R. v. Barnet London Borough Council, ex p. Shah* [1982] 2 A.C. 309. Leave to challenge the 1978 decision was refused. The council refused C's request to reconsider the matter. McNeill J. at first instance held that the council did have power to reconsider the matter in the light of C's request; the Court of Appeal simply asserted that there was a discretion to reconsider. (The Court of Appeal held that C's case should have been reconsidered for the 1978/1979 academic year so as to be consistent with one of the students in the *Shah* case.) See C. Lewis [1987] P.L. 21, noting that the Court of Appeal had offered no guidance on the extent of the implied discretion to reconsider.

A decision on a planning appeal may give rise to issue estoppel (*Thrasyvoulou v. Secretary of State of the Environment* [1990] 2 A.C. 273; C. Crawford (1990) 53 M.L.R. 814).

(F) ERROR OF LAW IN CONSTRUING THE SCOPE OF A DISCRETION

R. v. VESTRY OF ST PANCRAS

(1890) 24 Q.B.D. 371 (Court of Appeal)

Mr R. Westbrook was appointed to the office of Collector of Rates for the parish of St Pancras in 1858. In 1888, he wished to retire on health grounds, "upon such superannuation allowance as the vestry are empowered to grant for long services". The Superannuation (Metropolis) Act 1866, s.1, provided that the vestry might "at their discretion, grant ... an annual allowance, not exceeding in any case two-thirds of his then salary, regard being had to the scale of allowances hereinafter contained...." The scale indicated that a man with W's length of service would receive £230 per annum. The vestry thought that they only had discretion as to whether the full allowance suggested by the statute should or should not be paid, and as they did not think W should have so large an allowance, they resolved to pay nothing. W sought mandamus to compel the vestry to consider his application in accordance with the statute.

LORD ESHER M.R.: ... I have no doubt that the vestry should take his application into their fair consideration, and do what they think fair to the man under the circumstances, and if they do this, I have equally no doubt that the legislature has entrusted the sole discretion to them, and that no mandamus could go to them to alter their decision. But they must fairly consider the application and exercise their discretion on it fairly, and not take into account any reason for their decision which is not a legal one. If people who have to exercise a public duty by exercising their discretion take into account matters which the Courts consider not to be proper for the guidance of their discretion, then in the eye of the law they have not exercised their discretion. ...

[T]he vestry of any parish and certain other bodies may in their discretion grant to any officer who satisfies the conditions an annual allowance. If the matter had stopped there, and in a subsequent part of the statute there had been found a fixed amount which was to be given, I should have thought that the discretion was limited to the question whether there should be an allowance or not. But the section goes on, "an annual allowance not exceeding two-thirds of his then salary". This by necessary implication involves that they may give less than the two-thirds. . . . Then there are the words in section 1, "regard being had to the scale of allowance hereinafter contained". That scale is set out in section 4, and is a rising scale according to the number of years' service. They are, therefore, to look at the scale to see the number of years' service, but that does not affect the power given by section 1 or the necessary implication from the words, "not exceeding", used in that section. It seems to me, therefore, that they have a discretion as to the amount though they cannot go beyond that set out in the scale. This interpretation takes away all difficulty in considering the meaning of section 4, for the word "shall" only applies to the use of the scale to ascertain the maximum, and not otherwise to the question of amount; and further it gives a reasonable, fair and sufficiently elastic power to the vestry, instead of a hard and fast rule which may work injustice in some cases. . . .

The result in this case seems to me to be that . . . the vestry did not bring their minds to the question which they had to decide, and took into account circumstances which they ought not to have taken into account, and so did not properly exercise their discretion. . . .

FRY L.J. delivered a concurring judgment.

Note
1. For an example of modern application of this ground of review, see, *e.g. R. v. Secretary of State for the Environment ex p. Dudley Metropolitan B.C., The Times*, June 14, 1989.

CHAPTER 7

ABUSE OF DISCRETION

IN this chapter we shall consider various grounds upon which it may be alleged that the manner of exercise of an admitted discretionary power amounts to an abuse of power. In this context the courts have consistently stated that their function is not to act as a "court of appeal" on the merits of the discretionary decision—their function is to intervene only if one or more of the established grounds of review, considered below, has been infringed. Consider, in reading the cases which follow, whether this distinction between "merits" and "legality" is tenable, and whether in all of the cases the courts have indeed been influenced only by the latter and not the former consideration.

The material which follows is divided into the following sections:

(i) Use of powers for an improper purpose;
(ii) Taking into account irrelevant considerations; failure to have taken into account relevant considerations;
(iii) Unreasonableness;
(iv) Inconsistency.

There then follows a section on "proportionality"—a ground of challenge which exists in the administrative law of a number of European countries and of the EEC, but which does not, at least as yet, appear to constitute a discrete ground of challenge under English law.

(A) USE OF POWERS FOR AN IMPROPER PURPOSE

A statutory power must only be used for the purposes expressed in, or to be implied from, the relevant statute. The *Municipal Council of Sydney* case (below, p. 301) provides an example of successful challenge where the statute expressly stated the purpose(s) for which the power had been conferred.

Where purposes are not explicitly stated, the courts look to the legislation as a whole and consider what "purpose limitations" are implicit. See *Padfield* (below, p. 303) and *Congreve* (below, p. 319).

In some cases it may appear that a decision has been motivated by a *mixture* of legitimate and illegitimate purposes. This issue will be treated after review for "relevant/irrelevant considerations" has been considered (see below).

MUNICIPAL COUNCIL OF SYDNEY v. CAMPBELL AND OTHERS

[1925] A.C. 338; 94 L.J.P.C. 65; 133 L.T. 63 (Privy Council: Viscount Cave, Lord Blanesborough, Duff J., Sir Adrian Knox)

(Appeal from the Supreme Court of New South Wales)

By section 16 of the Sydney Corporation Amendment Act 1905, the council was empowered to purchase compulsorily any land required for "carrying out improvements in or remodelling any portion of the city." The council resolved that certain land including the property of the respondents should be purchased. Their object was to get the benefit of the increase in the value of this land which would result from the proposed extension of a highway by the council. No plan for improvement or remodelling was at any time proposed to, or considered by, the council. The Chief Judge in Equity granted injunctions restraining the council from acting on their resolution (24 S.R. (N.S.W.) 179). The council appealed to the Privy Council. The opinion of their Lordships was delivered by Duff J.

Duff J.: ... Their Lordships think it not reasonably disputable that at the time of the passing of the resolution in June, the council conceived it to be within its powers to resume lands not needed for the extension itself, but solely for the purpose of appropriating the betterments arising from the extension; and that, as Street C.J.E. found, the council had not at that time applied itself to the consideration of any other object in connection with the resumption of the residual lands....

The legal principles governing the execution of such powers as that conferred by section 16, in so far as presently relevant, are not at all in controversy. A body such as the Municipal Council of Sydney, authorized to take land compulsorily for specified purposes, will not be permitted to exercise its powers for different purposes, and if it attempts to do so, the courts will interfere. As Lord Loreburn said, in *Marquess of Clanricarde v. Congested Districts Board* (1914) 79 J.P. 481: "Whether it does so or not is a question of fact." Where the proceedings of the council are attacked upon this ground, the party impeaching those proceedings must, of course, prove that the council, though professing to exercise its powers for the statutory purpose, is in fact employing them in furtherance of some ulterior object.

Their Lordships think that the conclusion of the learned Chief Judge in Equity upon this question of fact is fully sustained by the evidence.

Notes

1. The principles were stated more fully by the House of Lords in *Marquess of Clanricarde v. Congested Districts Board for Ireland* (1914) 79 J.P. 481. The Marquess claimed that the Board were exercising their powers of compulsory purchase (*inter alia*) for the reinstatement of evicted tenants, and not for the lawful purpose of the amalgamation or enlargement of smallholdings. The House held that there was no evidence to support the plaintiff's claims.

Per Earl Loreburn at 481:

"In form their [*i.e.* the Board's] proceedings were regular, but in substance, so the appellant contended, they were proceeding *ultra vires*. ... I believe the law is as follows. When an administrative body is authorised by statute to take land compulsorily for specified purposes, the court will interfere if it uses those powers for different purposes. Whether it does so or not is a question of fact. The administrative body must really intend to act for a statutory purpose, and the land they seek to take must be land which is capable of being made use of for a statutory purpose, by which I mean that, looking at the land as a whole, a man might in reason think the purchase could be utilised for any of the statutory purposes. That also is a question of fact. But anyone who objects to what is done on either of these grounds must prove his objection. In the one case he must prove that there was not such a purpose, and in the other case he must prove that the land was quite incapable of being so used. And the court will not interfere with the discretion or revise the opinion of the administrative body if there was anything on which it could in reason come to the conclusion it reached. Of course fraud or dishonesty stands on quite a different footing. A court will always defeat that under any shape, and quite regardless of all form. But when a board is set up with such compulsory powers as are possessed by the Congested Districts Boards, it is not intended that courts of law shall do what we have been invited to do, namely, dog its footsteps and peer into its minutes as if they were to be suspected of meaning more than they say, or trip it up upon the ground that it has not acted judiciously or has not kept proper minutes, or upon any other ground, dishonesty apart, than that it has in fact exceeded its powers."

2. In *Westminster Bank v. Beverley Borough Council* [1971] A.C. 509 the House of Lords held that the council as local planning authority could refuse planning permission for an extension to a bank on the ground that it "might prejudice the future widening" of the street, even though as highways authority the council could have prescribed an improvement line under the Highways Act 1959 to preserve a strip of land for the scheme. The improvement line procedure did, but refusal of planning permission did not, involve payment of compensation. It was held that it was not an "excess of power" to refuse planning permission on this ground. Section 118(1) of the Town and Country Planning Act 1947 provided "that the provisions of this Act ... apply ... in relation to any land notwithstanding that provision is made by any enactment in force at the passing of this Act ... for ... regulating any development of the land". The relevant Highways Act provisions were re-enacted from pre-1947 legislation. On the question as to whether there was an "abuse of power" in choosing the procedure where no compensation was payable:
Per Lord Reid (at 530):

"Parliament has chosen to set up two different ways of preventing development which would interfere with schemes for street widening. It must have been aware that one involved paying compensation but the other did not. Nevertheless it expressed no preference, and imposed no limit on the use of either. No doubt there might be special circumstances which make it unreasonable or an abuse of power to use one of these methods but here there were none. Even if the appellants' view of the facts is right, the authority had to choose whether to leave the appellants without compensation or to impose a burden on its ratepayers. One may think that it would be most equitable that the burden should be shared. But the Minister of Transport had made it clear in a circular sent to local authorities in 1954 that there would be no grant if a local authority proceeded in such a way that compensation would be payable, and there is nothing to indicate any disapproval of this policy by Parliament and nothing in any of the legislation to indicate that Parliament disapproved of depriving the subject of compensation. I cannot in these circumstances find any abuse of power in the local authority deciding that the appellants and not its ratepayers should bear the burden...."

cf. Asher v. Secretary of State for the Environment (above, p. 86); *Hoveringham Gravels Ltd v. Secretary of State for the Environment* [1975] Q.B. 754; *R. v. Exeter City Council, ex p. J.L. Thomas & Co. Ltd* [1991] 1 Q.B. 471.

PADFIELD AND OTHERS v. MINISTER OF AGRICULTURE, FISHERIES AND FOOD AND OTHERS

[1968] A.C. 997; [1968] 2 W.L.R. 924; 112 S.J. 171; [1968] 1 All E.R. 694 (House of Lords)

The Agricultural Marketing Act 1958 contained (*inter alia*) provisions relating to the milk marketing scheme. By section 19:

"(3) A committee of investigation shall— ... (b) be charged with the duty, if the Minister in any case so directs, of considering, and reporting to the Minister on, any ... complaint made to the Minister as to the operation of any scheme which, in the opinion of the Minister, could not be considered by a consumers' committee...

(6) If a committee of investigation report to the Minister that any provision of a scheme or any act or omission of a board administering a scheme is contrary to the interests of consumers of the regulated product, or is contrary to the interests of any persons affected by the scheme and is not in the public interest, the Minister, if he thinks fit to do so after considering the report—(a) may by order make such amendments in the scheme as he considers necessary or expedient for the purpose of rectifying the matter; (b) may by order revoke the scheme; (c) in the event of the matter being one which it is within the power of the board to rectify, may by order direct the board to take such steps to rectify the matter as may be specified in the order ..."

Under the scheme, producers had to sell their milk to the Milk Marketing Board, which fixed the different prices paid to the producers for milk in each of the 11 regions into which England and Wales were divided. The differentials reflected (*inter alia*) the varying costs of transporting milk from the producers to the consumers.

Had there been no controls, the profits of the south-eastern producers would have been the largest, as they were near to a very large market, and their transport costs would have been the lowest in the country. Under the scheme, transport costs were borne by the Board. Had a fixed price been paid to all producers, those in the south-east would have been treated unfairly. The current differentials had been fixed several years previously, when transport costs were much lower. For about 10 years, the south-eastern producers had unsuccessfully been urging the Board to increase the differentials. The differential between the south-east region and the far-west (where the lowest price was paid) was 1.19d. per gallon, and the south-eastern producers wanted this increased to 3.5d. Since the total sum available to the Board to pay for milk bought in all regions was fixed each year, giving effect to this claim would mean that the south-eastern producers and perhaps those in some other regions would get higher prices, but producers in the far-west and several other regions would get less.

The Board was constituted in such a way that the south-eastern producers could not hope to get a majority for their proposals. The present appellants, who were office bearers of the south-east regional committee, asked the Minister to appoint a committee of investigation under section 19. On May 1, 1964, they had been informed by letter that:

"3. In considering how to exercise his discretion the Minister would, amongst other things, address his mind to the possibility that if a complaint were so referred and the committee were to uphold it, he in turn would be expected to make a statutory order to give effect to the committee's recommendations. It is this consideration, rather than the formal eligibility of the complaint as a subject for investigation, that the Minister would have in mind in determining whether your particular complaint is a suitable one for reference to the committee. We were unable to hold out any prospect that the Minister would be prepared to regard it as suitable.

"4. The reasons which led us to this conclusion were explained to you as follows: (a) The guarantee given to milk producers under the Agriculture Acts is a guarantee given to the board on behalf of all producers. The Minister owes no duty to producers in any particular region, and this is a principle that would be seriously called into question by the making of an Order concerned with a regional price; (b) Such action would also bring into question the status of the Milk Marketing Scheme as an instrument for the self-government of the industry and such doubt would also, by extension, affect the other Marketing Schemes as well; and (c) It is by no means clear that the Minister could make an Order pertaining to the price of milk in the south-east without determining at least one of the major factors governing prices in the other regions, and he would therefore be assuming an inappropriate degree of responsibility for determining the structure of regional prices through England and Wales."

On March 23, 1965, the private secretary to the Minister wrote to inform the appellants that the Minister had decided not to refer the matter to the committee. The following reasons were given:

"The Minister's main duty in considering this complaint has been to decide its suitability for investigation by means of a particular procedure. He has come to the conclusion that it would not be suitable. The complaint is of course one that raises wide issues going beyond the immediate concern of your clients, which is presumably the prices they themselves receive. It would also affect the interests of other regions and involve the regional price structure as a whole. In any event the Minister considers that the issue is of a kind which properly falls to be resolved through the arrangements available to producers and the board within the framework of the scheme itself."

The appellants' solicitor by a letter of November 4, 1965, asked the Minister if he had excluded from his mind the considerations set out in the 1964 letter. The Minister did not give a direct answer to this question, merely stating: "I considered that the issue ... was one which in all the circumstances should be dealt with by the board rather than the committee of investigation."

In 1966, the Divisional Court granted an order of mandamus commanding the Minister (1) to refer the complaint to the committee or (2) to deal effectively with the complaints on relevant considerations only to the exclusion of irrelevant considerations (*The Times*, February 4, 1966). The Minister appealed successfully to the Court of Appeal (Diplock and Russell L.JJ., Lord Denning M.R. dissenting: [1968] A.C. 1003E–1015). The applicants appealed to the House of Lords.

LORD REID: ... The respondent contends that his only duty is to consider a complaint fairly and that he is given an unfettered discretion with regard to every complaint either to refer it or not to refer it to the committee as he may think fit. The appellants contend that it is his duty to refer every genuine and substantial complaint, or alternatively that his discretion is not unfettered and that in this case he failed to exercise his discretion according to law because his refusal was caused or influenced by his having misdirected himself in law or by his having taken into account extraneous or irrelevant considerations.

In my view, the appellants' first contention goes too far. There are a number of reasons which would justify the Minister in refusing to refer a complaint. For example, he might consider it more suitable for arbitration, or he might consider that in an earlier case the committee of investigation had already rejected a substantially similar complaint, or he might think the complaint to be frivolous or vexatious. So he must have at least some measure of discretion. But is it unfettered?

It is implicit in the argument for the Minister that there are only two possible interpretations of this provision—either he must refer every complaint or he has an unfettered discretion to refuse to refer in any case. I do not think that is right. Parliament must have conferred the discretion with the intention that it should be used to promote the policy and objects of the Act; the policy and objects of the Act must be determined by construing the Act as a whole and construction is always a matter of law for the court. In a matter of this kind it is not possible to draw a hard and fast line, but if the Minister, by reason of his having misconstrued the Act or for any other reason, so uses his discretion as to thwart or run counter to the policy and objects of the Act, then our law would be very defective if persons aggrieved were not entitled to the protection of the court. So it is necessary first to construe the Act.

When these provisions were first enacted in 1931 it was unusual for Parliament to compel people to sell their commodities in a way to which they objected and it was easily foreseeable that any such scheme would cause loss to some producers. Moreover, if the operation of the scheme was put in the hands of the majority of the producers, it was obvious that they might use their power to the detriment of consumers, distributors or a minority of the producers. So it is not surprising that Parliament enacted safeguards.

The approval of Parliament shows that this scheme was thought to be in the public interest, and in so far as it necessarily involved detriment to some persons, it must have been thought to be in the public interest that they should suffer it. But in sections 19 and 20 Parliament drew a line. They provide machinery for investigating and determining whether the scheme is operating or the board is acting in a manner contrary to the public interest.

The effect of these sections is that if, but only if, the Minister and the committee of investigation concur in the view that something is being done contrary to the public interest the Minister can step in. Section 20 enables the Minister to take the initiative. Section 19 deals with complaints by individuals who are aggrieved. I need not deal with the provisions which apply to consumers. We are concerned with other persons who may be distributors or producers. If the Minister directs that a complaint by any of them shall be referred to the committee of investigation, that committee will make a report which must be published. If they report that any provision of this scheme or any act or omission of the board is contrary to the interests of the complainers *and* is not in the public interest, then the Minister is empowered to take action, but not otherwise. He may disagree with the view of the committee as to public interest, and, if he thinks that there are other public interests which outweigh the public interest that justice should be done to the complainers, he would be not only entitled but bound to refuse to take action. Whether he takes action or not, he may be criticised and held accountable in Parliament but the court cannot interfere.

I must now examine the Minister's reasons for refusing to refer the appellants' complaint to the committee. I have already set out the letters of March 23 and May 3, 1965. I think it is right also to refer to a letter sent from the Ministry on May 1, 1964, because in his affidavit the Minister says he has read this letter and there is no indication that he disagrees with any part of it. It is as follows: [His Lordship read the letter and continued:]

The first reason which the Minister gave in his letter of March 23, 1965, was that this complaint was unsuitable for investigation because it raised wide issues. Here it appears to me that the Minister has clearly misdirected himself. Section 19(6) contemplates the raising of issues so wide that it may be necessary for the Minister to amend a scheme or even to revoke it. Narrower issues may be suitable for arbitration but section 19 affords the only method of investigating wide issues. In my view it is plainly the intention of the Act that even the widest issues should be investigated if the complaint is genuine and substantial, as this complaint certainly is.

Then it is said that this issue should be "resolved through the arrangements available to producers and the board within the framework of the scheme itself". This restates in a condensed form the reasons given in paragraph 4 of the letter of May 1, 1964, where it is said "the Minister owes no duty to producers in any particular region", and reference is made to the "status of the Milk Marketing Scheme as an instrument for the self-government of the industry", and to the Minister "assuming an inappropriate degree of responsibility". But, as I have already pointed out, the Act imposes on the Minister a responsibility whenever there is a relevant and substantial complaint that the board are acting in a manner inconsistent with the public interest, and that has been relevantly alleged in this case. I can find nothing in the Act to limit this responsibility or to justify the statement that the Minister owes no duty to producers in a particular region. The Minister is, I think, correct in saying that the board is an instrument for the self-government of the industry. So long as it does not act contrary to the public interest the Minister cannot interfere. But if it does act contrary to what both the committee of investigation and the Minister hold to be the public interest the Minister has a duty to act. And if a complaint relevantly alleges that the board has so acted, as this complaint does, then it appears to me that the Act does impose a duty on the Minister to have it investigated. If he does not do that he is rendering nugatory a safeguard provided by the Act and depriving complainers of a remedy which I am satisfied that Parliament intended them to have.

Paragraph 3 of the letter of May 1, 1964, refers to the possibility that, if the complaint were referred and the committee were to uphold it, the Minister "would be expected to make a statutory Order to give effect to the committee's recommendations". If this means that he is entitled to refuse to refer a complaint because, if he did so, he might later find himself in an embarrassing situation, that would plainly be a bad reason. I can see an argument to the effect that if, on receipt of a complaint, the Minister can satisfy himself from information in his possession as to the merits of the complaint, and he then chooses to say that, whatever the committee might recommend, he would hold it to be contrary to the public interest to take any action, it would be a waste of time and money to refer the complaint to the committee. I do not intend to express any opinion about that because that is not this case. In the first place it appears that the Minister has come to no decision as to the merits of the appellants' case and, secondly, the Minister has carefully avoided saying what he would do if the committee were to uphold the complaint.

It was argued that the Minister is not bound to give any reasons for refusing to refer a complaint to the committee, that if he gives no reasons his decision cannot be questioned, and that it would be very unfortunate if giving reasons were to put him in a worse position. But I do not agree that a decision cannot be questioned if no reasons are given. If it is the Minister's duty not to act so as to frustrate the policy and objects of the Act, and if it were to appear from all the circumstances of the case that that has been the effect of the Minister's refusal, then it appears to me that the court must be entitled to act. . . .

I have found no authority to support the unreasonable proposition that it must be all or nothing—either no discretion at all or an unfettered discretion. Here the words "if the Minister in any case so directs" are sufficient to show that he has some discretion but they give no guide as to its nature or extent. That must be inferred from a construction of the Act read as a whole, and for the reasons I have given I would infer that the discretion is not unlimited, and that it has been used by the Minister in a manner which is not in accord with the intention of the statute which conferred it.

As the Minister's discretion has never been properly exercised according to law, I would allow this appeal.

LORD HODSON: ... The reasons disclosed are not, in my opinion, good reasons for refusing to refer the complaint seeing that they leave out of account altogether the merits of the complaint itself. The complaint is, as the Lord Chief Justice pointed out, made by persons affected by the scheme and is not one for the consumer committee as opposed to the committee of investigation and it was eligible for reference to the latter. It has never been suggested that the complaint was not a genuine one. It is no objection to the exercise of the discretion to refer that wide issues will be raised and the interests of other regions and the regional price structure as a whole would be affected. It is likely that the removal of a grievance will, in any event, have a wide effect and the Minister cannot lawfully say in advance that he will not refer the matter to the committee to ascertain the facts because, as he says in effect, although not in so many words, "I would not regard it as right to give effect to the report if it were favourable to the appellants."

It has been suggested that the reasons given by the Minister need not and should not be examined closely for he need give no reason at all in the exercise of his discretion. True it is that the Minister is not bound to give his reasons for refusing to exercise his discretion in a particular manner, but when, as here, the circumstances indicate a genuine complaint for which the appropriate remedy is provided, if the Minister in the case in question so directs, he would not escape from the possibility of control by mandamus through adopting a negative attitude without explanation. As the guardian of the public interest he has a duty to protect the interests of those who claim to have been treated contrary to the public interest.

I would allow the appeal accordingly....

LORD PEARCE: ... It is quite clear from the Act in question that the Minister is intended to have *some* duty in the matter. It is conceded that he must properly consider the complaint. He cannot throw it unread into the waste-paper basket. He cannot simply say (albeit honestly) "I think that in general the investigation of complaints has a disruptive effect on the scheme and leads to more trouble than (on balance) it is worth; I shall therefore never refer anything to the committee of investigation." To allow him to do so would be to give him power to set aside for his period as Minister the obvious intention of Parliament, namely, that an independent committee set up for the purpose should investigate grievances and that their report should be available to Parliament. This was clearly never intended by the Act. Nor was it intended that he could silently thwart its intention by failing to carry out its purposes. I do not regard a Minister's failure or refusal to give any reasons as a sufficient exclusion of the court's surveillance. If all the *prima facie* reasons seem to point in favour of his taking a certain course to carry out the intentions of Parliament in respect of a power which it has given him in that regard, and he gives no reason whatever for taking a contrary course, the court may infer that he has no good reason and that he is not using the power given by Parliament to carry out its intentions. In the present case, however, the Minister has given reasons which show that he was not exercising his discretion in accordance with the intentions of the Act....

LORD UPJOHN: ... My Lords, I would only add this: that without throwing any doubt upon what are well known as the club expulsion cases, where the absence of reasons has not proved fatal to the decision of expulsion by a club committee, a decision of the Minister stands on quite a different basis; he is a public officer charged by Parliament with the discharge of a public discretion affecting Her Majesty's subjects; if he does not give any reason for his decision it may be, if circumstances warrant it, that a court may be at liberty to come to the conclusion that he had no good reason for reaching that conclusion and order a prerogative writ to issue accordingly.

The Minister in my opinion has not given a single valid reason for refusing to order an inquiry into the legitimate complaint (be it well founded or not) of the South-Eastern Region; all his disclosed reasons for refusing to do so are bad in law.

LORD MORRIS OF BORTH-Y-GEST dissented.

Appeal allowed.

The House of Lords ordered that the cause be remitted to the Divisional Court of the Queen's Bench Division to require the respondent, the Minister of Agriculture, Fisheries and Food, to consider the complaint of the appellants according to law.

Notes

1. After the House of Lords decision, the Minister "decided to refer the complaint to the Committee of Investigation".[1] The Committee reported on January 7, 1969, "that the acts and/or omissions of the Board in prescribing the terms on, and the prices at which, milk should be sold to the Board were contrary to the reasonable interests of the complainants and were not in the public interest".[2] The Minister (Mr Cledwyn Hughes having by then succeeded Mr Fred Peart) announced his decision in a written answer in the House of Commons[3]:

"... I have carefully considered the Committee's findings. I am satisfied that even if its recommendations were implemented within the framework of the regional pricing structure of the Milk Marketing Scheme, they would have a profound effect on incomes of milk producers in different parts of the country. Many of them, particularly those in the West of the country, would suffer significant losses. Moreover, if the principle that each and every producer should be paid according to his proximity to a liquid market were pursued to its logical conclusion, it would bring to an end the present system for the organised marketing of milk which has been so successful.

The Committee recognised that the wider questions of agricultural, economic and social policy involved in this matter were beyond the scope of its inquiry. These must, however, in my view be given full weight. After considering with great care all

[1] Report on Agricultural Marketing Schemes for 1966–67, p. 10 ([1967–1968] H.C.P. 423).
[2] Report for 1967–68, p. 12 ([1968–1969] H.C.P. 445).
[3] 780 H.C. Deb., cols. 46–47 (March 31, 1969).

the issues involved, and the very wide implications of the Committee's recommendations, I have concluded that it would not be in the public interest for me to direct the Board to implement the Committee's conclusions."

The Minister's decision was welcomed by dairy farmers in other parts of Britain, and by *The Times*, which pointed out in a leading article (April 1, 1969) that implementation of the Committee's recommendations could "easily reduce large tracts of the country, now relatively prosperous, to a condition where they were farmed on the 'dog-and-stick' methods of the inter-war years".

2. See case notes by J.F. Garner (1968) 31 M.L.R. 446; H.W.R. Wade (1968) 84 L.Q.R. 166; J.A. Farmer (and P.J. Evans) [1970] N.Z.L.J. 184. Note also the criticisms expressed by R.C. Austin (1975) C.L.P. 150, 167–173.

3. This case can be regarded as an example of the Minister taking irrelevant considerations into account (see following section) as well as a failure to exercise a power in accordance with the purpose for which the power was given.

4. *cf. British Oxygen Co. Ltd v. Minister of Technology* (above, p. 263) where it was held that Parliament had not given any guidance as to how the Ministry's power to give grants to eligible applicants was to be exercised.

5. In *Secretary of State for Employment v. ASLEF (No. 2)* [1972] 2 Q.B. 443, C.A., the Secretary of State could apply to the NIRC for a secret ballot order where it appeared to him (*inter alia*) that there were "reasons for doubting" whether workers would be taking part in industrial action in accordance with their wishes, and whether they had had an adequate opportunity of indicating their wishes. The Minister gave no reasons for his decision to apply for such an order. Lord Denning M.R. stated at 493–494:

"We have been referred to several recent cases, of which *Padfield v. Minister of Agriculture, Fisheries and Food* [1968] A.C. 997 is the best example, in which the courts have stressed that in the ordinary way a Minister should give reasons, and if he gives none the court may infer that he had no good reasons. Whilst I would apply that proposition completely in most cases, and particularly in cases which affect life, liberty or property, I do not think that it applies in all cases. Here we are concerned with a ballot to ascertain the wishes of 170,000 men. The executive committees of the unions consist, we are told, of 60 men. These 60 are, no doubt, fully convinced that the whole 170,000 will support them. It is the honourable tradition of the men to support their leaders. There are many messages and telegrams which have told of support from the branches. Yet there are times when even their leaders, in touch as they are, may be mistaken.

The Solicitor-General suggested to us some reasons for doubting whether the wishes of the individual men were behind this. The Minister, he suggested, might think that, as the dispute has been discussed and debated, before a chairman agreed by both sides, many of the workers would wish to accept his award rather than take part in industrial action. The Minister also had asked the leaders of the unions earnestly to consider holding a ballot of the workers so as to ascertain their wishes. The leaders were quite sure, and are quite sure, that the men are wholly in support of this industrial action. If so, there would seem to be no good reason why they should in any way not be content for a ballot to be held. I do not say that those reasons are right, but they are such as a reasonable Minister might entertain; and, if they are such—if the Minister could on reasonable grounds form the view and opinion that he did—as I read the law and the statute this court has no jurisdiction or power to interfere with his decision."

Per Roskill L.J. at 511:

"It has often been said that there must be a strong case before the court will interfere.

The court will, I apprehend, interfere in a case where there could in the nature of things be no evidence upon which a reasonable Secretary of State could have formed the reasons for the doubt claimed to exist and to justify an application. In my judgment, this point was effectively answered by the Solicitor-General yesterday afternoon. He was not giving the Secretary of State's actual reasons. Whether or not the Secretary of State gives those reasons is, as Buckley L.J. said, a matter of policy for him. It may be wise in some cases to give them, it may be unwise not to give them. That is not a matter with which this court is concerned. The Solicitor-General put forward, not as the Secretary of State's actual reasons, but as evidence before the court which was also available to the Secretary of State, evidence on which a reasonable Secretary of State could have formed the view that there were reasons to doubt whether the workers who were taking, or who were expected to take, part were or would be taking part in accordance with their wishes."

6. The *Padfield* dicta concerning the inferring of bad reasons for silence were applied in *R. v. Penwith District Council, ex p. May* (unreported, November 22, 1985). From about 1981, the Penzance and District Campaign for Nuclear Disarmament sold and distributed literature, badges and similar material in a pedestrian precinct in Penzance. The District Council resolved that as from April 1, 1984, Schedule 4 to the Local Government (Miscellaneous Provisions) Act 1982 would be applied in respect of this precinct and other streets. Accordingly, CND's activities in selling material now required street trading consent. The council refused consent, without giving reasons. (Schedule 4 did not impose a requirement to give reasons.) There had been no objections to C.N.D.'s activities over the years, no objections to their application for consent and the Environmental Services Committee had recommended that consent be given. Taylor J. held, applying the *Padfield* dicta, that he was prepared to infer that the council had no good reasons for refusal and granted certiorari to quash the refusal of consent.

The limits to this aspect of *Padfield* were brought out in the following case.

R. v. SECRETARY OF STATE FOR TRADE AND INDUSTRY
ex p. LONRHO plc.

[1989] 1 W.L.R. 525; [1989] 2 All E.R. 609 (House of Lords)

In March 1985 A.I.T. plc (which subsequently changed its name to House of Fraser plc ("Holdings")) acquired a majority of the share capital in House of Fraser plc, a company which owned a large number of department stores including Harrods. On March 14, 1985, before the acquisition had been completed, the Secretary of State for Trade and Industry announced that he had decided not to refer the proposed acquisition to the Monopolies and Mergers Commission. In April 1987 the Secretary of State appointed inspectors pursuant to section 432(2) of the Companies Act 1985 to investigate the affairs of Holdings in particular in relation to the acquisition of House of Fraser. The inspectors spent some 15 months pursuing their investigations and compiling their report, and during that time they received lengthy submissions from, *inter alios*, Lonrho plc, which had for several years been attempting to obtain a controlling interest in Harrods. On July 23, 1988 the inspectors submitted their report to the Secretary of State who by section 437 of the Act of 1985 had power to publish such a report "if he thinks fit". He did not publish it immediately upon receipt, but chose to submit the report to the Serious Fraud Office which was done by the end of July 1988. In August 1988 the Secretary of State also sent a copy of the report to the Director General of Fair Trading asking him to consider and to advise on whether the report disclosed the existence of material new facts and, if so, whether the merger of A.I.T. plc and House of Fraser plc should be referred to the Monopolies and Mergers Commission pursuant to section 64(4)(b) of the Fair Trading Act 1973, which empowered the Secretary of State to make such a reference if it appeared to him that there were new material facts about the merger and a reference was made within six months of the emergence of those facts. During that period, the Secretary of State received lengthy submissions from Lonrho urging him to publish the report. He indicated that his intention was to do so, and that the only question was the appropriate date for publication. On September 29, 1988, the Department of Trade and Industry issued a Press notice stating again the fact that the Secretary of State intended to publish the report. It added that he would not do so while the Serious Fraud Office was considering it. On November 25, 1988 the Department reiterated that the report would not be published while the prosecution authorities were conducting their inquiries. It also announced that although the report did indicate the existence of previously undisclosed material the Secretary of State had decided, in accordance with the advice of the Director General of Fair Trading, that a reference was not appropriate.

On applications by Lonrho for judicial review of both decisions, the Divisional Court of the Queen's Bench Division ((1989) 5 BCC 266) granted the applications and held (a) that the decision to delay publication of the report was *ultra vires* and unlawful and that mandamus should issue requiring reconsideration of the matter; (b) that the decision not to refer the 1984 and 1985 acquisition of the House of Fraser to the Monopolies and Mergers Commission was *ultra vires* and mandamus was issued requiring the Secretary of State to make that reference. On appeal by the Secretary of State, the Court of Appeal ((1989) 5 BCC 284) allowed the appeal. Lonrho appealed to the House of Lords.

LORD KEITH OF KINKEL: [held, first, that the challenge to the decision not to publish the report failed: on the facts, the Secretary of State had not delegated (unlawfully) the exercise of his discretion whether to publish to the S.F.O.; he had not acted on incorrect advice; and his decision was neither perverse nor irrational: he was entitled to take the view that early publication might be prejudicial to the S.F.O. and to a fair trial. His Lordship continued:]

It is true that the Divisional Court took a different view of the effect of early publication but the members of the Divisional Court had not read the report and knew nothing of the investigations of the S.F.O. The Divisional Court was also confident of the ability of a jury on the instructions of a judge to forget everything they had read and seen before the trial. But the Secretary of State who had read the report and was advised by the S.F.O. and officials and counsel of the DTI, who had also read the report, was obliged to consider the possible risks stemming from the early publication of this particular report relating to a notorious controversy which was bound to continue between Mr Rowland and the Al Fayed brothers.

The judgments of the Divisional Court illustrate the danger of judges wrongly though unconsciously substituting their own views for the views of the decision-maker who alone is charged and authorised by Parliament to exercise a discretion. The question is not whether the Secretary of State came to a correct solution or to a conclusion which meets with the approval of the Divisional Court but whether the discretion was properly exercised. The Secretary of State considered the advice he received from the S.F.O. about the effect of early publication and the contrary advice of counsel for Lonrho. The Secretary of State also considered the disadvantages urged by Lonrho of postponing publication. No fault can be found with the decision-making process of the Secretary of State and he was entitled and bound to make up his own mind to publish or postpone publication in the public interest. Any attack on the good faith of the Secretary of State was expressly disclaimed by counsel for Lonrho. The correspondence and memoranda of the negotiations between the DTI and Lonrho show a scrupulous anxiety on the part of the DTI to act fairly and to give proper consideration to the problems posed by the contents of the report.

The appeal in respect of the publication decision therefore fails.

The reference to the Monopolies and Mergers Commission

... Before arriving at [the decision not to make a reference to the Commission] the Secretary of State had not only received the inspectors' report and the advice of the director but had also had representations made to him on behalf of Lonrho by a legal team and by Mr Rowland personally at meetings with both the Secretary of State himself and with the officials of his department. The Secretary of State must have received a unique amount of advice upon the issue of whether or not he should exercise his discretion to refer the matter to the M.M.C.

Despite the fact that the Secretary of State has acted in accordance with the advice which Parliament has directed that he should receive from the director, Lonrho assert that he has acted unlawfully and in breach of his statutory duty under the Act. It is said that in following the advice of the director not to refer the bid to the M.M.C., the Secretary of State has acted so irrationally that his decision should be quashed and he should be ordered to make a reference. Irrationality is the sole ground upon which the Secretary of State's decision was challenged; there is no suggestion that the decision was taken in bad faith or for any improper reason such as a cover-up of political or departmental ineptitude.

The Divisional Court found in Lonrho's favour on this issue because they regarded it as the policy of the Act that there should be a reference to the M.M.C. on the ground that "when a merger situation is complicated by factors which are best understood by men rich in experience of the business world, their powers of investigation should be enlisted and their advice invited". I cannot accept this interpretation of the Act. The Act vests a discretion in the Secretary of State to decide whether to seek the advice of the M.M.C. which is one of the three statutory bodies created by the Act to give advice to the Secretary of State. The approach of the Divisional Court is to convert this discretion into a duty and it also ignores the expertise of the Director of Fair Trading and his department who are also rich in experience of merger situations and under a duty to give advice whether or not to make a reference to the M.M.C. If every complicated merger that qualified for a reference under section 64 and which potentially affected the public interest had to be referred to the M.M.C. the whole system would break down under the weight of the work. In 1988, 260 merger situations were considered in the office of the director of which only 11 were ultimately referred to the M.M.C. If all 260 mergers had been referred, the M.M.C. could not possibly have carried out their statutory duty to investigate and report within the time limit of six months required by the Act. The Secretary of State must exercise his discretion to decide which mergers to refer and it is clearly the policy of the Act that his discretion should be guided, although not fettered, by the advice of the director.

Padfield v. Minister of Agriculture, Fisheries and Food [1968] A.C. 997 was relied upon by Lonrho to support two limbs of their argument. First it was said to support a construction of the Act that imposed a duty on the Secretary of State to make a reference to the M.M.C., and secondly, the fact that the Secretary of State had given no reason for his decision not to make a reference led to the conclusion that no rational reason existed for his decision. In my view that case does not support either limb of the argument. The decision in *Padfield* turned on the construction of the Agricultural Marketing Act 1958.

[See above, pp. 303–309. His Lordship read the headnote, and continued:]

The Minister gave among his reasons for refusing to appoint a committee of investigation that the complaint was unsuitable for investigation because it raised "wide issues" and that the Minister owed no duty to producers in any particular region. It was held that these were bad reasons for refusing to appoint a committee and showed that the Minister had misunderstood the policy and intention of the Act which was that genuine and substantial complaints of this nature should be investigated by a committee of investigation. I can find no parallel between the appointment of a committee to investigate a specific complaint that individuals are suffering injustice and a reference to the M.M.C. to enable a wide-ranging inquiry to determine whether a commercial situation is or may be operating against the public interest. The two situations are entirely different and the construction placed upon the Agricultural Marketing Act 1958 throws no light on the construction of the Fair Trading Act 1973.

Turning now to the question of reasons, Sir Dingle Foot Q.C., instructed on behalf of the Minister, submitted in the course of his argument that the Minister can refuse to act on a complaint without giving any reasons and in such a case a complainant would have no remedy and his decision cannot be questioned. Not surprisingly this submission was rejected. Lord Pearce said, at 1053–1054:

> "I do not regard a Minister's failure or refusal to give any reasons as a sufficient exclusion of the court's surveillance. If all the prima facie reasons seem to point in favour of his taking a certain course to carry out the intentions of Parliament in respect of a power which it has given him in that regard and he gives no reason whatever for taking a contrary course, the court may infer that he has no good reason and that he is not using the power given by Parliament to carry out its intentions. In the present case, however, the Minister has given reasons which show that he was not exercising his discretion in accordance with the intentions of the Act."

See passages to the like effect in the speeches of Lord Reid, at 1032, Lord Hodson, at 1049 and Lord Upjohn, at 1061.

Although reference was made to the judgment of Sir John Donaldson M.R. in *R. v. Lancashire County Council, ex p. Huddleston* [1986] 2 All E.R. 941 in which he referred to the desirability of proceedings for judicial review being conducted with the cards face up on the table, it was not submitted to your Lordships that there was any general duty to give reasons for a decision in all cases, nor was it submitted that this Act imposed a particular duty on the Secretary of State to give reasons for his refusal to make a reference to the

M.M.C.; and it is not the practice of the Secretary of State to give reasons when he decides not to make a reference to the M.M.C.

The absence of reasons for a decision where there is no duty to give them cannot of itself provide any support for the suggested irrationality of the decision. The only significance of the absence of reasons is that if all other known facts and circumstances appear to point overwhelmingly in favour of a different decision, the decision-maker who has given no reasons cannot complain if the court draws the inference that he had no rational reason for his decision.

It is difficult to see what useful purpose would have been achieved by a reference to the M.M.C. other than as a step towards enabling the Secretary of State to exercise his powers under Schedule 8 to order Holdings to divest themselves of their shares in Fraser, in other words, to take Harrods away from the Al Fayed brothers which is, of course, Lonrho's principal objective in these proceedings. No competition or consumer issues are involved in the present situation and there is no indication that the particular expertise of the M.M.C. is required to advise the Secretary of State on any aspect of the public interest. It can of course be said that it is contrary to the public interest in its widest sense that the Director and the Secretary of State should be deceived during the investigation of a merger and that there is a public interest in pursuing and punishing those who do so. But on this aspect of the public interest the Secretary of State has already received the inspectors' report and further public resources are being committed in the investigation by the S.F.O. and the D.P.P. The Secretary of State does not need the assistance of the M.M.C. to clarify these aspects of the public interest about which he is already fully informed.

The measures that the Secretary of State can take under Schedule 8 pursuant to a finding by the M.M.C. that a merger is contrary to the public interest are designed to prevent or correct damage to the economy as a consequence of an undesirable merger rather than as punitive measures against individuals. If the director and the Secretary of State who has acted on his advice take the view that in the present circumstances it is unnecessary to take the power to order Holdings to divest themselves of their shares in Fraser and therefore unnecessary to have a reference to the M.M.C., I can see nothing irrational in such a decision. If the current investigation should warrant proceedings for serious fraud no doubt the criminal law will take its course. Furthermore, there are extensive powers available under the Company Directors Disqualification Act 1986 which would, if circumstances justified it, enable the Al Fayed brothers to be removed from control of Fraser. Looking at the matter from the point of view of the overall health of the economy, which is the manifest purpose for which the Secretary of State is given his powers under the Act of 1973, I find it impossible to say that it was irrational to decide not to launch the M.M.C. on an inquiry that would cover ground already investigated by the inspectors and which is being further investigated by the S.F.O. and the D.P.P. I . . . reach, without hesitation, the conclusion that Lonrho has not made a case that no reasonable Secretary of State could have refused to make a reference to the Monopolies and Mergers Commission.

For these reasons I would dismiss the appeal. . . .

LORDS TEMPLEMAN, GRIFFITHS, ACKNER and LOWRY agreed.

Notes

1. See D.G.T. Williams [1989] C.L.J. 161.

2. The inspectors' report was published in March 1990 (*House of Fraser Holdings plc*, HMSO), and concluded that the Fayeds had "won Government sanction of their £850 million bid for House of Fraser through the simple expedient of lying about their background and resources" (1990) 140 N.L.J. 349. The Government informed "an incredulous and angry House of Commons" that the available sanctions, which included prosecutions for obtaining by deception or perjury, or disqualification from holding directorships should not be invoked (*ibid.*). The Attorney-General said in the House of Commons that the evidence against the Fayeds was insufficient and hearsay (*The Independent*, March 13, 1990). The Divisional Court subsequently dismissed an application for judicial review of the decision not to apply to the court for an order under the Company Directors Disqualification Act 1986, s.8, disqualifying the Fayeds from being company directors (*R. v. Secretary of State for Trade and Industry, ex p. Lonrho plc, The Independent*, October 22, 1991). There were no grounds for saying that the Secretary of State had taken immaterial matters into account, or that his decision was perverse.

3. The reluctance of the courts to infer bad reasons from silence was confirmed in the context of dealings involving the Inland Revenue in *R. v. Inland Revenue Commissioners, ex p. T.C. Coombs & Co.* [1991] 2 A.C. 283, H.L., reversing the Court of Appeal. Lord Lowry said (at 301) that if "a strong case" was made for quashing a notice under the Taxes Management Act 1970, s.20(3) (requiring the production of documents), "it may be the duty of the revenue to meet that case with something more cogent than silence, however understandable or justifiable".

4. The *Lonrho* case confirmed that there is no general common law duty to give reasons for a decision. In *R. v. Civil Service Appeal Board, ex p. Cunningham* [1991] 4 All E.R. 310, Lord Donaldson M.R. stated that the contrary was "unarguable" (at 317), citing the decision of the High Court of Australia in *Public Service Board of New South Wales v. Osmond* (1986) 63 A.L.R. 559).

Such a duty may be imposed by statute (see, *e.g.* below, p. 582, note 4). Moreover, in certain circumstances, the courts will infer that a discretion has been abused (*cf.* the comments on *Padfield* in *Lonrho*) or fettered (see *Sagnata Investments Ltd v. Norwich Corporation*, below, pp. 543–550) unless reasons are forthcoming. Natural justice or the duty to act fairly may require the decision-maker to give prior notice and an opportunity to make representations before a decision is made, and this may require adequate disclosure of the evidence (see the discussion in *R. v. Gaming Board*, above, p. 472); moreover, a judicial tribunal may be required by the requirements of natural justice to give reasons (see pp. 509–515).

It has often been argued that there *should* be a general duty to give reasons. Strong support for this position was given by the JUSTICE/All Souls Review of Administrative Law in the United Kingdom, *Administrative Justice: Some Necessary Reforms* (1988), Chap. 3. The duty should be imposed by legislation; would arise on a demand being made; would make it incumbent to state not only the reasons but also the findings on material questions of fact with reference to the evidence or other material on which such findings were based; and could be subject to exemptions for specified categories of decision. Sir Harry Woolf has expressed the view that such a development would be "the most beneficial improvement which could be made to English administrative law" (*Protection of the Public—A New Challenge* (1990), p. 92).

5. Sir Harry Woolf has noted that once leave to apply for judicial review has been granted in respect of a decision of central government, it is the usual practice:

> "for the department to set out frankly in an affidavit the matters which were taken into account in reaching a decision. The decision-making process is fully disclosed"

(*Protection of the Public—A New Challenge* (1990), pp. 16–17, 92–97).

Indeed, he states that "most public bodies" adopt a "cards face up on the table" approach (*ibid.*, p. 97). This enables the court in most cases to dispense with any order for discovery and cross-examination on affidavits.

WHEELER v. LEICESTER CITY COUNCIL

[1985] A.C. 1054; [1985] 3 W.L.R. 335, [1985] 2 All E.R. 1106
(House of Lords)

The local authority purported to terminate the use which Leicester [Rugby] Football Club made of a recreation ground owned by the council. This action was taken following the club's refusal to comply fully with a number of requirements made of it by the local authority. The requirements were the council's response to the decision of three of the club's players to take part in a rugby tour of South Africa. The club was willing to condemn the tour but was not willing, and indeed doubted its powers, to put pressure on the players to induce them not to take part in the tour. The club applied for certiorari to quash the council's decision. In the proceedings the council argued that its policy was in accordance with its obligations under section 71 of the Race Relations Act 1976—"it shall be the duty of every local authority to make appropriate arrangements with a view to securing their various functions are carried out with due regard to the need—(a) to eliminate unlawful racial discrimination; and (b) to promote equality of opportunity, and good relations, between persons of different racial groups." The council was acting, it argued, in the interests of its local population, which consisted of 25 per cent persons of Asian or Afro-Caribbean origin.

The club was unsuccessful at first instance and in the Court of Appeal ([1985] 2 All E.R. 151). It then appealed to the House of Lords.

LORD ROSKILL: . . . None of the judges in the courts below have felt able to hold that the action of the club was unreasonable or perverse in the *Wednesbury* sense. They do not appear to have been invited to consider whether those actions, even if not unreasonable on *Wednesbury* principles, were assailable on the grounds of procedural impropriety or unfairness by the council in the manner in which . . . they took their decision to suspend for 12 months the use by the club of the Welford Road recreation ground.

I would greatly hesitate to differ from four learned judges on the *Wednesbury* issue but for myself I would have been disposed respectfully to do this and to say that the actions of the council were unreasonable in the *Wednesbury* sense. But even if I am wrong in this view, I am clearly of the opinion that the manner in which the council took that decision was in all the circumstances unfair within the third of the principles stated in *Council of Civil Service Unions v. Minister for the Civil Service*. [Editor's note: *i.e.* "procedural impropriety".] The council formulated those four questions in the manner of which I have spoken and indicated that only such affirmative answers would be acceptable. They received reasoned and reasonable answers which went a long way in support of the policy which the council had accepted and desired to see accepted. The views expressed in these reasoned and reasonable answers were lawful views and the views which, as the evidence shows, many people sincerely hold and believe to be correct. If the club had adopted a different and hostile attitude, different considerations might well have arisen. But the club did not adopt any such attitude.

In my view, therefore, this is a case in which the court should interfere because of the unfair manner in which the council set about obtaining its objective. I would not, with profound respect, rest my decision upon the somewhat wider ground which appealed to Browne-Wilkinson L.J. in his dissenting judgment.

Since preparing this speech I have had the advantage of reading in draft the speech of my noble and learned friend Lord Templeman with which I find myself in complete agreement. . . .

LORD TEMPLEMAN: My Lords, in my opinion the Leicester City Council were not entitled to withdraw from the Leicester Football Club the facilities for training and playing enjoyed by the club for many years on the council's recreation ground for one simple and good reason. The club could not be punished because the club had done nothing wrong.

The 1984 Rugby Tour of South Africa was organised by the Rugby Football Union which invited individuals, including three members of the club, to join the tour. There were two views about the tour amongst the opponents of apartheid. The view taken by the council, a view which I share, was that the tour would endorse the racist policies of the South African Government. The opposite view was expressed by Mr Dodge, who was one of the three members of the club who participated in the tour and who gave sworn evidence in these proceedings as follows:

"I personally deplore apartheid as being morally wrong. It is nevertheless my genuine belief that maintaining sporting links with South Africa does help break down the evil social barriers of apartheid, a personal belief which has been strengthened by observing in 1984 the improvement since 1980."

The council agreed that this belief was sincerely held not only by Mr Dodge but by other opponents of apartheid. The Government had subscribed to the Gleneagles agreement but did not take steps to ban the tour, leaving the decision to each individual invited to take part. The club does not practise racial discrimination, does not support apartheid, has not been guilty of any infringement of the Race Relations Act 1976, did not support the decision of the three members to join the tour and sought to discourage them from joining the tour by sending them copies of the reasoned memorandum published by the opponents of the tour. The council does not contend that the club should have threatened or punished the three club members who participated in the tour or that the club could properly have done so. Nevertheless, the club has been punished by the council according to Mr Soulsby for "failing to condemn the tour and to discourage its members from playing". My Lords, the laws of this country are not like the laws of Nazi Germany. A private individual or a private organisation cannot be obliged to display zeal in the pursuit of an object sought by a public authority and cannot be obliged to publish views dictated by a public authority.

The club having committed no wrong, the council could not use their statutory powers in the management of their property or any other statutory powers in order to punish the club. There is no doubt that the council intended to punish and have punished the club. When the club were presented by the council with four questions it was made clear that the club's response would only be acceptable if, in effect, all four questions were answered in the affirmative. . . .

... In my opinion, this use by the council of its statutory powers was a misuse of power. The council could not properly seek to use its statutory powers of management or any other statutory powers for the purposes of punishing the club when the club had done no wrong.

In *Congreve v. Home Office* [1976] Q.B. 629, the Home Secretary had a statutory power to revoke television licences. In exercise of that statutory power he revoked the television licences of individuals who had lawfully surrendered an existing licence and taken out a new licence before an increase in the licence fee was due to take effect. Lord Denning M.R. said, at 651:

"If the licence is to be revoked—and his money forfeited—the Minister would have to give good reasons to justify it. Of course, if the licensee had done anything wrong—if he had given a cheque for £12 which was dishonoured, or if he had broken the conditions of the licence—the Minister could revoke it. But when the licensee has done nothing wrong at all, I do not think the Minister can lawfully revoke the licence, at any rate, not without offering him his money back, and not even then except for good cause. If he should revoke it without giving reasons, or for no good reason, the courts can set aside his revocation and restore the licence. It would be a misuse of the power conferred on him by Parliament: and these courts have the authority—and, I would add, the duty—to correct a misuse of power by a Minister or his department, no matter how much he may resent it or warn us of the consequences if we do."

Similar considerations apply, in my opinion, to the present case. Of course this does not mean that the council is bound to allow its property to be used by a racist organisation or by any organisation which, by its actions or its words, infringes the letter or the spirit of the Race Relations Act 1976. But the attitude of the club and of the committee of the club was a perfectly proper attitude, caught as they were in a political controversy which was not of their making.

For these reasons and the reasons given by my noble and learned friend Lord Roskill, I would allow the appeal.

LORDS BRIDGE, BRIGHTMAN and GRIFFITHS expressed their agreement with both LORD ROSKILL and LORD TEMPLEMAN.

Notes

1. For *Wednesbury* unreasonableness as a ground of challenge, see below, p. 349. For challenge for "procedural impropriety" see below on procedural *ultra vires*, the *audi alteram partem* rule of natural justice, and the duty to "act fairly" (pp. 407–418, 418–516).

2. Do you agree with Lord Roskill's approach, basing his decision on unfair procedure?

3. Browne-Wilkinson L.J.'s dissent in the Court of Appeal was based on the view that the council's action was a violation of the fundamental right of free speech that Parliament could not have intended to authorise by section 71 of the 1976 Act.

4. For comments on *Wheeler*, see C. Turpin [1985] C.L.J. 333; T.R.S. Allan (1985) 48 M.L.R. 448 (on the Court of Appeal decision) and (1986) 49 M.L.R. 121 (expressing a preference for the judgment of Browne-Wilkinson L.J. in the Court of Appeal).

5. In *Congreve v. The Home Office* [1976] 1 Q.B. 629, Mr Congreve was one of over 20,000 people who took out a second colour television licence before the expiry of an

existing one, in anticipation of an increase in the licence fee, from £12 to £18, as from April 1, 1975. By section 1(2) of the Wireless Telegraphy Act 1949, "A licence . . . may be issued subject to such terms, provisions and limitations as the [Minister] may think fit." Section 1(4) provided that a licence "may be revoked . . . by a notice in writing served on the holder. . .". There were no other limitations expressed in the statute. The Home Office feared that a substantial part of the anticipated revenue from the issue of licences would be lost in view of the large estimated number of "overlappers". They initially demanded an extra £6 from each "overlapper" under threat of revocation, and subsequently modified their policy to one of revocation after eight months (£12 worth at an annual rate of £18). The Court of Appeal granted a declaration that the purported revocation of the plaintiff's licence was unlawful, invalid and of no effect. Lord Denning's somewhat extravagant reasoning, including the passage cited by Lord Templeman in *Wheeler*, was not echoed by the other judges in *Congreve*. Geoffrey Lane L.J., for example, put the matter more simply (at 662):

"... The licence was a valid one at the time of its issue. At that time the new regulation increasing the fee to £18 had not come into operation and therefore did not in law exist. There was no power to demand the extra £6 nor to receive it.... [The revocation] is illegal for two reasons. First, it is coupled with an illegal demand which taints the revocation and makes that illegal too. Secondly, or possibly putting the same matter in a different way, it is an improper exercise of a discretionary power to use a threat to exercise that power as a means of extracting money which Parliament has given the executive no mandate to demand: see *Attorney-General v. Wilts United Dairies* (1922) 91 L.J.K.B. 897...."

The Parliamentary Commissioner for Administration concluded that many members of the public had been caused needless distress and confusion through maladministration by the Home Office and their agents, the Television Licence Records Office, mainly in failing to make their policy officially and openly clear to the public (see his conclusions at para. 38 of his Report: the Seventh Report of the P.C.A. for Session 1974–1975, H.C.P. 680). However, on the assumption that it was lawful, he "found no ground for questioning the principle behind the arrangements" (para. 42).

The decision of the Court of Appeal was celebrated by Mr Bernard Levin in *The Times*, December 5, 1975 ("Blow the Loud Trumpets of Victory for Us over Them in the T.V. Licence War"). It was also welcomed by H.W.R. Wade (1976) 92 L.Q.R. 331. G. Ganz, however, was unenthusiastic ([1976] P.L. 14–15): "To elevate tax avoidance into a liberty of the subject protected by the Bill of Rights is a complete inversion of moral values.... The case epitomises the dangers of allowing the courts more scope to impose their values in this area of law as advocated by Scarman L.J. in *English Law— The New Dimension*. Their values have become fossilised so that they still see the individual battling against a hostile Executive once embodied in an autocratic King. They do not see the issue as one between the plaintiff and other taxpayers who will pay more whilst he pays less and that their judgment leads to an unequal sharing of burdens by the many for the benefit of a few."

6. In *R. v. Derbyshire County Council, ex p. The Times Supplements Ltd* (1990) 3 Admin.L.R. 241, the council resolved to remove all its advertising from newspapers owned by Mr Rupert Murdoch. Shortly before, *The Sunday Times* had published articles about the council which had led to the institution of libel proceedings by Councillor Bookbinder, the council leader. The decision involved switching advertising for teaching posts from *The Times Educational Supplement* to *The Guardian* notwithstanding that the cost was greater and the likely readership among teachers much smaller. The Divisional Court granted certiorari to quash the decision. The court was satisfied on the evidence (some councillors were cross-examined on their affidavits) that there was no educational ground for the decision (contrary to the claims of councillors) and that the majority Labour group on the council had been activated by bad faith or vindictiveness. The decision was "an abuse of power contrary to the public

good" (Watkins L.J. at 253). Had it been necessary to do so his Lordship was sure that the decision would have been held to be perverse, as having no sensible or justifiable basis (*ibid.*). cf. *R. v. Ealing London Borough Council, ex p. Times Newspapers* (1986) 85 L.G.R. 316 (successful challenge to division of three councils to ban certain newspapers from public libraries. Decisions taken to demonstrate support for former employees of those newspapers' publishers in a long, bitter and unresolved dispute: not taken with a view to fulfilling obligations to provide a "comprehensive ... library service".

(B) TAKING INTO ACCOUNT IRRELEVANT CONSIDERATIONS; FAILURE TO HAVE REGARD TO RELEVANT CONSIDERATIONS

Logically, this ground of challenge is wide enough to cover situations where powers are exercised for an improper purpose, given that desire to achieve that purpose will inevitably constitute the taking into consideration of an irrelevant consideration. However, the case law shows that a distinction between these grounds of challenge is commonly drawn.

As with "improper purposes", statutes sometimes are explicit as to the considerations which are to be taken into consideration in coming to a decision as to the exercise of a power; more usually, it is for the courts to determine what is implicit from the terms of the legislation as regards the relevance/irrelevance of particular matters. Even where a statute states certain matters which must be taken into consideration, it will be a matter of construction for the courts as to whether these are exhaustive of relevant considerations.

In addition to the cases extracted and discussed on the following pages note also the following recent illustrations of this ground of challenge: *R. v. Somerset County Council, ex p. Fewings* [1995] 1 W.L.R. 1037 (local authority, empowered to manage land for the benefit, improvement or development of area, banned deer hunting for ethical reasons. Held, decision tainted by irrelevant consideration); *R. v. Secretary of State for the Environment, ex p. Kingston upon Hull City Council, The Times,* January 31, 1996 (two local authorities successfully challenged Minister's decision as regards outer limits of the Humber and Severn estuaries, and his designation of "high dispersal areas" for the purposes of the Urban Waste Water Treatment (England and Wales) Regulations 1994). These regulations implement E.C. Directive 91/271 which indicates the considerations relevant in the exercise of such functions. Held, the Minister's admitted motivating consideration in reaching his decision—to minimise economic costs—was to have acted on the basis of a legally irrelevant consideration); *R. v. Gloucestershire County Council, ex p. Barry* [1996] 4 All E.R. 421, C.A. (local authority *not* entitled to take into account the availability of financial resources when determining whether it owed a duty to make provision for the needs of a disabled person under the Chronically Sick and Disabled Persons Act 1970. Once determination made that it was necessary to make provision, the availability of resources might well be a relevant consideration as regards the level and nature of provision made). Contrast, decision (by a majority of three to two) of the House of Lords that "cost of provision" is a relevant consideration, reversing the Court of Appeal [1997] 2 All E.R.1.

ROBERTS v. HOPWOOD AND OTHERS

[1925] A.C. 578; 94 L.J.K.B. 542; 133 L.T. 289; 41 T.L.R. 436; 89 J.P. 105; 69 S.J. 475; [1925] All E.R.Rep. 24; 23 L.G.R. 337
(House of Lords)

Poplar Borough Council had power under section 62 of the Metropolis Management Act 1855 to pay to their employees "such salaries and wages as ... [the council] may think fit". In 1914, the minimum wage for the lowest grade of worker was 30s. per week for men, and 22s. 6d. for women, these being in line with wages paid by the other metropolitan councils. By 1920, these figures had risen to 64s. and 49s. 9d. respectively. When auditing the 1920–1921 accounts the district auditor, Mr Carson Roberts, noted an increase to 80s. as the minimum for both men and women from May 1, 1920. He did not then raise any objection as the cost of living had greatly increased since 1914. In 1923, the auditor found that the rate of 80s. per week was still being maintained, although the cost of living had materially reduced. Indeed, he found that the total of the wage payments made by the council in 1921–1922 exceeded by about £17,000 the total amount that would have been paid if the trade union rates had been applicable; that wage increases since 1914 exceeded cost-of-living increases by between 85 per cent and 200 per cent depending upon the grade of worker; that working hours were considerably shorter in 1922 than in 1914; and that in the lower grades the new minimum rate varied from nearly three times to over four times the rate paid per hour in 1914.

The auditor heard representations from the Socialist councillors who controlled the council, led by George Lansbury, to the effect that they regarded themselves as bound to maintain these wage levels by a "mandate of the electors". He decided that the council had not paid due regard to the interests of the ratepayers, and had made payments far in excess of those necessary to obtain the service required and to maintain a high standard of efficiency, which were thus in reality gifts to their employees in addition to remuneration for their services. He was under a duty under section 247(7) of the Public Health Act 1875 to "disallow every item of account contrary to law, and surcharge the same on the person making or authorising the making of the illegal payment". Acting under this section he disallowed £5,000 and surcharged it on the councillors concerned.

The councillors applied for certiorari under the Public Health Act to quash the disallowance and surcharge. Section 247(8) enabled a person aggrieved to apply for a writ of certiorari to remove the disallowance to the King's Bench Division. As interpreted in earlier cases, *e.g. R. v. Roberts* [1908] 1 K.B. 407, this was regarded as giving in effect a right to appeal on fact and/or law.

The Divisional Court (Lord Hewart C.J., Sankey and Salter JJ.) rejected their application ([1924] 1 K.B. 514: *sub nom. R. v. Roberts, ex p. Scurr*).

The councillors appealed successfully to the Court of Appeal ([1924] 2 K.B. 695). The House of Lords unanimously allowed the auditor's appeal.

LORD BUCKMASTER: ... [T]he general rule applicable is that the council shall pay such wages as they may think fit, the discretion as to the reasonable nature of the wages being with them. The discretion thus imposed is a very wide one, and I agree with the principle enunciated by Lord Russell in the case of *Kruse v. Johnson* [1899] 2 Q.B. 91, 99 [below, p. 834], that when such a discretion is conferred upon a local authority the court ought to show great reluctance before they attempt to determine how, in their opinion, the discretion ought to be exercised.

Turning to what the borough council have done, the reason for their action is to be found in the affidavit sworn by Mr Scurr, Mr Key, Mr Lansbury and Mr Sumner. In para. 6 of that affidavit they make the following statement: "The council and its predecessors the district board of works have always paid such a minimum wage to its employees as they have believed to be fair and reasonable without being bound by any particular external method of fixing wages, whether ascertainable by Trade Union rate, cost of living, payments by other local or national authorities or otherwise." And if the matter ended there it would be my opinion that a decision so reached could not be impeached until it were shown that it was not *bona fide*, and absence of *bona fides* is not alleged in the present proceedings. Para. 9, however, of the same affidavit puts the matter in a different form. It is there said: "9.... The Council did not and does not take the view that wages paid should be exclusively related to the cost of living. They have from time to time carefully considered the question of the wages and are of the opinion, as a matter of policy, that a public authority should be a model employer and that a minimum rate of 4*l.* is the least wage which ought to be paid to an adult having regard to the efficiency of their workpeople, the duty of a public authority both to the rate-payers and to its employees, the purchasing power of the wages and other considerations which are relevant to their decisions as to wages."

Now it appears that on August 31, 1921, a resolution was passed by the borough council to the effect that no reduction of wage or bonus should be made during the ensuing four months, and this was acted upon for the following 12 months. It was, I think, well within their power to fix wages for a reasonable time in advance, and there are cogent reasons why this should be done, but that decision should be made in relation to existing facts, which they appear to have ignored. In August 1921, the cost of living had been continuously falling since November of the previous year, and it continued to fall, so that it is difficult to understand how, if the cost of living was taken into account in fixing the wages for adult workers at a minimum basis of 4*l.*, the sharp decline in this important factor should have been wholly disregarded by the borough council. But the affidavit contains another statement, which I think is most serious for the council's case. It states that 4*l.* a week was to be the minimum wage for adult labour, that is without the least regard to what that labour might be. It standardised men and women not according to the duties they performed, but according to the fact that they were adults. It is this that leads me to think that their action cannot be supported, and that in fact they have not determined the payment as wages, for they have eliminated the consideration both of the work to be done and of the purchasing power of the sums paid, which they themselves appear to regard as a relevant though not the dominant factor. Had they stated that they determined as a borough council to pay the same wage for the same work without regard to the sex or condition of the person who performed it, I should have found it difficult to say that that was not a proper exercise of their discretion. It was indeed argued that that is what they did, but I find it impossible to extract that from the statement contained in the affidavit. It appears to me, for the reasons I have given, that they cannot have brought into account the considerations which they say influenced them, and that they did not base their decision upon the ground that the reward for work is the value of the work reasonably and even generously measured, but that they took an arbitrary principle and fixed an arbitrary sum, which was not a real exercise of the discretion imposed upon them by the statute.

It is for these reasons that I think the appeal should succeed.

LORD ATKINSON: ... It is but right and natural that the rate of wages should rise if the cost of living rises, because this tends directly to keep the purchasing power of the labourer's wage at what it was before the cost of living increased. The principle apparently adopted by the council, however, is that wages should rise if the cost of living rises, but should never go down if the cost of living goes down....

In the sixth paragraph of Mr Scurr's affidavit he states that "the Council have always paid such a minimum wage as they have believed to be fair and reasonable without being bound by any particular external method of fixing wages, whether by trade union rates, cost of living, payments of other local or national authorities or otherwise". Nobody has contended that the council should be bound by any of these things, but it is only what justice and common sense demand that, when dealing with funds contributed by the whole body of the ratepayers, they should take each and every one of these enumerated things into consideration in order to help them to determine what was a fair, just and reasonable wage to pay their employees for the services the latter rendered. The council would, in my view, fail in their duty if, in administering funds which did not belong to their members alone, they put aside all these aids to the ascertainment of what was just and reasonable remuneration to give for the services rendered to them, and allowed themselves to be guided in preference by some eccentric principles of socialist philanthropy, or by a feminist ambition to secure the equality of the sexes in the matter of wages in the world of labour.

In para. 9 of Mr Scurr's affidavit he is good enough to disclose what the council did take into consideration in fixing the minimum rate of wages to be paid to their employees....

This system of procedure might possibly be admirably philanthropic, if the funds of the council at the time that they were thus administered belonged to the existing members of that body. These members would then be generous at their own expense.... A body charged with the administration for definite purposes of funds contributed in whole or in part by persons other than the members of that body, owes, in my view, a duty to those latter persons to conduct the administration in a fairly businesslike manner with reasonable care, skill and caution, and with a due and alert regard to the interest of those contributors who are not members of the body. Towards these latter persons the body stands somewhat in the position of trustees or managers of the property of others.

This duty is, I think, a legal duty as well as a moral one, and acts done in flagrant violation of it should, in my view, be properly held to have been done "contrary to law" within the meaning of section 247(7) of the Public Health Act of 1875.... It was strongly pressed in argument that the auditor believed the council acted *bona fide*; but what in this connection do the words "*bona fide*" mean? Do they mean, as apparently this gentleman thought, that no matter how excessive or illegal their scale of wages might be, they were bound to put it into force because their constituents gave them a mandate so to do, or again, do the words mean that as the payment of wages was a subject with which they had legally power to deal, the amount of their funds which they devoted to that purpose was their own concern which no auditor had jurisdiction to revise, or in reference to which he could surcharge anything? The whole system of audit to which the Legislature has subjected every municipal corporation or council is a most emphatic protest against such opinions as these....

[A]s wages are remuneration for services, the words "think fit" must, I think, be construed to mean "as the employer shall think fitting and proper" for the services rendered. It cannot, in my view, mean that the employer, especially an employer dealing with moneys not entirely his own, may pay to his employee wages of any amount he pleases. Still less does it mean that he can pay gratuities or gifts to his employees disguised under the name of wages....

What is a reasonable wage at any time must depend, of course, on the circumstances which then exist in the labour market. I do not say there must be any cheeseparing or that the datum line, as I have called it, must never be exceeded to any extent, or that employees may not be generously treated. But it does not appear to me that there is any rational proportion between the rates of wages at which the labour of these women is paid and the rates at which they would be reasonably remunerated for their services to the council.

I concur with the auditor in thinking that what has been given to the women as wages is really to a great extent gifts and gratuities disguised as wages, and is therefore illegal. The council have evidently been betrayed into the course they have followed by taking into consideration the several matters mentioned in Mr Scurr's affidavit, which they ought not properly to have taken into their consideration at all, and consequently did not properly exercise the discretion placed in them, but acted contrary to law: see *R. v. Adamson* (1875) 1 Q.B.D. 201; *R. v. St Pancras Vestry*, 24 Q.B.D. 371 [above, p. 299]; *R. v. Board of Education* [1910] 2 K.B. 165 at 179.

I think the appeal succeeds.

LORD SUMNER: ... The respondents conceded that for wages fixed *mala fide* no exemption from review could be claimed and that the mere magnitude of the wages paid, relatively to the wages for which the same service was procurable, might be enough in itself to establish bad faith. This admission, I am sure, was rightly made, but it leads to two conclusions. First, the final words of the section are not absolute, but are subject to an implied qualification of good faith—"as the board may *bona fide* think fit". Is the implication of good faith all? That is a qualification drawn from the general legal doctrine, that persons who hold public office have a legal responsibility towards those whom they represent—not merely towards those who vote for them—to the discharge of which they must honestly apply their minds. *Bona fide* here cannot simply mean that they are not making a profit out of their office or acting in it from private spite, nor is *bona fide* a short way of saying that the council has acted within the ambit of its powers and therefore not contrary to law. It must mean that they are giving their minds to the comprehension and their wills to the discharge of their duty towards that public, whose money and local business they administer.

The purpose, however, of the whole audit is to ensure wise and prudent administration and to recover for the council's funds money that should not have been taken out of them. If, having examined the expenditure and found clear proof of bad faith, which admittedly would open the account, the auditor further found that the councillors' evil minds had missed their mark, and the expenditure itself was right, then the expenditure itself would not be "contrary to law" and could not be disallowed. Bad faith admittedly vitiates the council's purported exercise of its discretion, but the auditor is not confined to asking, if the discretion, such as it may be, has been honestly exercised. He has to restrain expenditure within proper limits. His mission is to inquire if there is any excess over what is reasonable. I do not find any words limiting his functions merely to the case of bad faith, or obliging him to leave the ratepayers unprotected from the effects on their pockets of honest stupidity or unpractical idealism. The breach in the words "as they may think fit", which the admitted implication as to bad faith makes, is wide enough to make the necessary implication one both of honesty and of reasonableness. It might be otherwise if the express words were to be read as absolute and unqualified, but if they are to be read as subject to some qualification, I think that qualification must be derived from the purpose of the statutory audit, which is the protection of the ratepayers' pockets and not the immunity of spend-thrift administration. Next, in the case and for the purpose assumed, the auditor, when he reviews the accounts, is entitled and bound to use his own judgment as to the wages that would be reasonable under the circumstances. He must do so, in order to measure from that datum the excess of the wages paid, and to decide if the excess is so great as to evidence *mala fides*. So it will be also with the courts of law on appeal. If in the case of bad faith the auditor is capable of finding a reasonable amount and is bound to proceed to do so, I find no words in the section which, on a sound construction, preclude him from doing the same thing when good faith is present, and I think that in both cases the reasonableness of the amounts is a subject for his review. . . . I can find nothing in the Acts empowering bodies to which the Metropolis Management Act 1855 applies which authorizes them to be guided by their personal opinions on political, economic or social questions in administering the funds which they derive from levying rates.

Much was said at the Bar about the wide discretion conferred by the Local Government Acts on local authorities. In a sense this is true, but the meaning of the term needs careful examination. What has been said in cases which lie outside the provisions as to audit altogether is not necessarily applicable to matters which are concerned with the expenditure of public money. There are many matters which the courts are indisposed to question. Though they are the ultimate judges of what is lawful and what is unlawful to borough councils, they often accept the decisions of the local authority simply because they are themselves ill equipped to weigh the merits of one solution of a practical question as against another. This, however, is not a recognition of the absolute character of the local authority's discretion, but of the limits within which it is practicable to question it. There is nothing about a borough council that corresponds to autonomy. It has great responsibilities, but the limits of its powers and of its independence are such as the law, mostly statutory, may have laid down, and there is no presumption against the accountability of the authority. Everything depends on the construction of the sections applicable. In the present case, I think that the auditor was entitled to inquire into all the items of expenditure in question, to ask whether in incurring them the council had been guided by aims and objects not open to them or had disregarded considerations by which they should have been guided, and to the extent to which they had in consequence exceeded a reasonable expenditure, it was his duty to disallow the items.

LORD WRENBURY: . . . The cardinal word upon which emphasis is principally to be laid is the word "wages". Wages are the pecuniary return for services rendered. To determine the proper or true amount which in a given state of facts has been paid or is payable for services rendered is far from easy. It can never be determined with exactness. It is impossible to name in any particular case an amount which if diminished by 1s. a week would be too small, and if increased by 1s. a week would be too large. But it is possible to name an amount which would certainly be too large—as, for instance, if a charwoman were paid 2l. a day. Using my best endeavour to state the matter in general terms, I express it thus:

Wages in a particular service are such sum as a reasonable person, guiding himself by an investigation of the current rate in fact found to be paid in the particular industry, and acting upon the principle that efficient service is better commanded by paying an efficient wage, would find to be the proper sum. The figure to be sought is not the lowest figure at which the service could be obtained, nor is it the highest figure which a generous employer might, upon grounds of philanthropy or generosity, pay out of his own pocket. It is a figure which is not to be based upon or increased by motives of philanthropy nor even of generosity stripped of commercial considerations. It is such figure as is the reasonable pecuniary equivalent of the service rendered. Anything beyond this is not wages. It is an addition to wages, and is a gratuity. The authority is to pay not such sum but such wages as they think fit.

I pass from the word "wages" to the words "as [they] may think fit". We have heard argument upon the question whether these words are or are not to be understood as if the word "reasonable" or "reasonably" were inserted, so that the sentence would run "as they reasonably think fit" or "such reasonable wages as they may think fit". Is the verb "think" equivalent to "reasonably think"? My Lords, to my mind there is no difference in the meaning, whether the word "reasonably" or "reasonable" is in or out.... I rest my opinion upon higher grounds. A person in whom is vested a discretion must exercise his discretion upon reasonable grounds. A discretion does not empower a man to do what he likes merely because he is minded to do so—he must in the exercise of his discretion do not what he likes but what he ought. In other words, he must, by the use of his reason, ascertain and follow the course which reason directs. He must act reasonably.

Thirdly, and lastly, I point to the word "fit". That word means, I think, "fitting" or "suitable". The words "as they think fit" do not mean "as they choose". The measure is not the volition of the person vested with the discretion, it is the suitability or adequacy or fitness of the amount in the reasonable judgment of the person vested with the discretion.

[LORD CARSON delivered a short speech, concurring with some hesitancy. He held that it was "open to the auditor, upon coming to the conclusions as stated in his affidavit, to draw the inference that the council were not engaged in merely fixing a rate of wages, but were affected by considerations which could not be held to come within the ambit of the discretion entrusted to them."]

Appeal allowed.

Notes and Questions

1. One of the problems of interpretation considered by the House was that while the power under section 62 of the 1855 Act was a general power to employ officers and servants and to pay "such salaries and wages" as the authority "may think fit", other statutes which conferred on local authorities powers to employ persons for the purposes of the relevant statute often gave power to pay "reasonable" wages. Lord

Buckmaster (at 588) regarded section 62 as the dominant section. Lord Atkinson thought that "in each and every case the payment of all salaries and wages must be 'reasonable'. I see no difficulty in so construing the words of section 62" (at 599). Lord Wrenbury thought that "there is no difference in the meaning, whether the word 'reasonably' or 'reasonable' is in or out" (at 613). Nevertheless his Lordship did not rely on the presence of "reasonable" in some statutes—it was not obvious which provisions should give way. Lord Sumner and Lord Carson did not deal with the problem.

2. *Roberts v. Hopwood* also settled that the district auditor's power to disallow an "item" contrary to law was not limited to the situation where a complete item of account was *ultra vires* (as it would have been, for example, if the council had had no power to employ and pay any servants at all), but could be used in relation to *excessive* expenditure on an otherwise lawful item—the excess only being *ultra vires*. See further on local authority audit, above, p. 16.

3. Note the attitude of the majority in the Court of Appeal ([1924] 2 K.B. 695) who were willing to defer to the views of elected representatives of the people in such a matter as this, except in a clear case. Is the decision of the House of Lords correct, leaving aside the purple passages? Would the case have been decided differently had there been no stress on the quasi-fiduciary duty owed by local authorities to ratepayers? Can any general propositions of law concerning "reasonableness" in the exercise of discretions be derived from this case?

4. The leaders of Poplar Borough Council had recently been in conflict with central government on another issue: the payment of outdoor relief to the able-bodied poor. The story of "Poplarism" is told by B. Keith-Lucas [1962] P.L. 52, and further background information is given by G.W. Jones, "Herbert Morrison and Poplarism" [1973] P.L. 11 and N. Branson, *Poplarism* (1979). See also *Roberts v. Cunningham* (1925) 42 T.L.R. 162 and *Woolwich Corporation v. Roberts* (1927) 96 L.J.K.B. 757, where two other councils which paid "model" wages took their cases to the House of Lords.

5. At one stage in the events at Poplar, the councillors were imprisoned for their contempt of court in disobeying a writ of mandamus issued by the King's Bench Divisional Court. Some marched off to prison headed by the town band (at the cost of £10 which was subsequently disallowed by the District Auditor). Their imprisonment was a considerable political embarrassment for the Minister of Health.

6. In *Prescott v. Birmingham Corporation* [1955] 1 Ch. 210, the corporation, which had power to charge "such fares as they may think fit" on their public transport services resolved to introduce a scheme for free bus travel for old people. The corporation sought the consent of the traffic commissioners as required by the Road Traffic Act 1930. Consent was given, subject to the payment of £90,000 from the general rate fund to the account of the transport undertaking. A ratepayer brought an action for a declaration that the scheme was *ultra vires*. Vaisey J. and the Court of Appeal granted the declaration. Jenkins L.J. stated at 235–238 that if a trustee running a bus service allowed a class of persons whom he considered badly off to travel free or at reduced fares:

"it may be that passengers charged the full fare could not object on that account. But we apprehend that the *cestuis que trustent* certainly could....

Local authorities are not, of course, trustees for their ratepayers, but they do, we think, owe an analogous fiduciary duty to their ratepayers in relation to the application of funds contributed by the latter. Thus local authorities running an omnibus undertaking at the risk of their ratepayers, in the sense that any deficiencies must be met by an addition to the rates are not, in our view, entitled, merely on the strength of a general power, to charge different fares to different passengers or classes of passengers, to make a gift to a particular class of persons of rights of free travel on their vehicles, simply because the local authority concerned are of opinion that the favoured class of persons ought, on benevolent or philanthropic grounds, to be accorded that benefit. In other words, they are not, in our view, entitled to use their discriminatory power as proprietors of the transport undertaking in order to confer out of rates a special benefit on some particular class of inhabitants whom they, as the local authority for the town or district in question, may think deserving of such assistance. In the absence of clear statutory authority, for such a proceeding (which to our mind a mere general power to charge differential fares certainly is not) we would, for our part, regard it as illegal, on the ground that, to put the matter bluntly, it would amount simply to the making of a gift or present in money's worth to a particular section of the local community at the expense of the general body of ratepayers....

We are not persuaded by Mr Rowe's argument to the effect that the relevant legislation would allow the defendants to charge no fares at all to anyone and to finance their transport undertaking entirely out of the rates. We think it is clearly implicit in the legislation, that while it was left to the defendants to decide what fares should be charged within any prescribed statutory maxima for the time being in force, the undertaking was to be run as a business venture, or, in other words, that fares fixed by the defendants at their discretion, in accordance with ordinary business principles, were to be charged. That is not to say that in operating their transport undertaking the defendants should be guided by considerations of profit to the exclusion of all other considerations. They should, no doubt, aim at providing an efficient service of omnibuses at reasonable cost, and it may be that this objective is impossible of attainment without some degree of loss. But it by no means follows that they should go out of their way to make losses by giving away rights of free travel.

As to the instances of legitimate discrimination given by Mr Rowe, the concession in favour of workmen is enjoined by statute, and therefore does not advance his argument. The concessions in favour of children (who travel free or at half-fares according to age) are of a kind commonly, if not universally, accorded by transport undertakings, and, we should have thought, readily justifiable on business principles. The practice of allowing free travel to blind and disabled persons may, or may not, be strictly justifiable, but may perhaps be classed as a minor act of elementary charity to which no reasonable ratepayer would be likely to object.

In our opinion the scheme now in question goes beyond anything which can reasonably be regarded as authorized by the discretionary power of fixing fares and differentiation in the fares charged to different passengers or classes of passengers possessed by the defendants under the relevant legislation, and is, accordingly, *ultra vires* the defendants.

... [T]he scheme fares no better if its adoption is considered as a purported exercise by the defendants of their discretion in a matter not, on the face of it, necessarily outside the general ambit of the discretionary power of differentiation of fares conferred on them by the relevant legislation.... If we are right in thinking that, after all allowance is made for their special position as a local authority, the defendants owe a duty to their ratepayers to operate their transport undertaking substantially on business lines, we think it must necessarily follow that, in adopting the scheme, the defendants misapprehended the nature and scope of the discretion conferred on them, and mistakenly supposed that it enabled them to confer benefits, in the shape of rights of free travel, on any class or classes of the local inhabitants appearing to them to be deserving of such benefits by reason of their advanced age and limited means. Accordingly, if the case is to be regarded as turning upon the question whether the decision to adopt the scheme was a proper exercise of a discretion conferred on the defendants with respect to the differential treatment of passengers in the matter of fares, the answer, in our opinion, must be that it was not a proper exercise of such discretion. We think some support for this view is to be derived from the speeches in the House of Lords in *Roberts v. Hopwood* [1925] A.C. 578." [See above, pp. 321–327.]

See case notes at 72 L.Q.R. 237; 18 M.L.R. 159; [1955] C.L.J. 135. Parliament intervened to validate existing concessions by the Public Service Vehicles (Travel Concessions) Act 1955, and to give general powers to make such concessions by the Travel Concessions Act 1964. See now the Transport Act 1985, ss.93–105.

7. Consider the implications of Lord Sumner's suggestion that where bad faith is proved but the amount of expenditure is reasonable, the courts cannot interfere. See *Re Walker's Decision* [1944] K.B. 644; *Robins v. Minister of Health* [1939] 1 K.B. 520 at 537–538.

8. A modern analysis of *Roberts v. Hopwood* is provided by P. Fennell, "Roberts v. Hopwood: The Rule against Socialism" (1986) 13 J.L.S. 401. He comments (at 419):

> "In *Roberts v. Hopwood* the conduct of the councillors was stigmatised as unreasonable, irrational, arbitrary and eccentric. In subsequent cases the courts have ruled that to policies which require expenditure of the rates is attached the requirement that the interests of the ratepayers must be considered at every turn. The connection between socialism and irresponsibility is never made as explicitly as it was in Lord Atkinson's judgment, because it is neither politic nor necessary to do so. A party elected on a policy of reducing rates and charging for services is already doing its legal duty; a party elected on a policy of increasing welfare services has it yet to do."

See also A. Bradney, "Facade: The Poplar Case" (1983) 43 N.I.L.Q. 1, who examines the political background of the judges who heard the case.

9. *Roberts v. Hopwood* was distinguished by the Divisional Court in *Pickwell v. Camden London Borough Council* [1983] 1 Q.B. 962, above, p. 16.

10. The notion of a "fiduciary duty" owed to ratepayers (now also council taxpayers) was one of a number of grounds upon which the House of Lords ruled against the Greater London Council's introduction of its new "Fares Fair" public transport subsidy policy in 1981: *Bromley London Borough Council v. Greater London Council* [1982] 1 A.C. 768. As the extracts below show, the case is also an example of successful challenge on grounds (i) that the GLC intended to exercise its statutory power to make grants for purposes beyond those implicit in the legislation; and (ii) that the GLC had failed properly to retain discretion because the majority Labour group regarded itself as bound by its election manifesto to go ahead with the promised policy once elected.

BROMLEY LONDON BOROUGH COUNCIL v. GREATER LONDON COUNCIL

[1982] 1 A.C. 768; [1982] 2 W.L.R. 92; [1982] 1 All E.R. 129
(House of Lords)

The facts are given by Lord Wilberforce in his speech.

LORD WILBERFORCE: My Lords, this case concerns the validity of a supplementary precept issued by the Greater London Council to the London Borough of Bromley for the levying of a rate of 6.1p in the pound in respect of the period October 1, 1981, to March 31, 1982. The precept was issued pursuant to a resolution of the G.L.C. dated July 21, 1981. This resolution, in turn, was passed by way of implementation of a commitment, contained in an election manifesto for the election in May 1981, upon which the present majority in the G.L.C. was elected.

The supplementary precept went to all London boroughs. Bromley applied to the High Court for judicial review of the action of the G.L.C. by way of certiorari. They failed in the High Court but the Court of Appeal granted their application, quashed the supplementary precept and declared that it was *ultra vires*, null, void and of no effect.

The London Transport Executive is a party to the proceedings because the precept was issued in order to enable the G.L.C. to finance, by grant to the L.T.E., the cost of reducing L.T.E. fares overall by 25 per cent and of introducing a simplified zonal system. If the precept is set aside, the L.T.E. will not be able to maintain these changes, and to reverse them will cause considerable dislocation.

The precept is attacked on two main grounds: (1) That it is beyond the powers of the G.L.C. as defined by the Transport (London) Act 1969. (2) That even if the G.L.C. has the necessary statutory powers, the issuance of the precept was an invalid exercise of its discretion under the Act. This ground itself may be divisible into two contentions (a) that the exercise of the G.L.C.'s discretion was unreasonable, or (b) that the G.L.C. when deciding to issue the precept did not take relevant considerations into account, or did take into account irrelevant considerations or misdirected itself as to the law.

Both of these grounds depend upon the fact, which it is right to emphasise at the start, that the G.L.C., though a powerful body, with an electorate larger and a budget more considerable than those of many nation states, is the creation of statute and only has powers given to it by statute. The courts will give full recognition to the wide discretion conferred upon the council by Parliament and will not lightly interfere with its exercise. But its actions, unlike those of Parliament, are examinable by the courts, whether on grounds of vires, or on principles of administrative law (those two may overlap). It makes no difference on the question of legality (as opposed to reasonableness—see *Secretary of State for Education and Science v. Tameside Metropolitan Borough Council* [1977] A.C. 1014), whether the impugned action was or was not submitted to or approved by the relevant electorate: that cannot confer validity upon *ultra vires* action. Indeed, it forms part of Bromley's argument, that the G.L.C. in so far as it considered that it has a commitment to bring about the reduction in fares, regardless of other considerations, misdirected itself in law.

The first ground of attack involves a question of construction of the Act of 1969....

The general duty of the G.L.C. is stated, in section 1, as being to develop and encourage measures which will promote the provision of "integrated, efficient and economic transport facilities and services for Greater London".

There has been a good deal of argument as to the meaning of these words, particularly of "economic": no doubt they are vague, possibly with design. It has been strongly argued that the word means something like "on business principles" but for present purposes I will take it to mean "cost-effective", or "making the most effective use of resources in the context of an integrated system"—the meaning most favourable to the G.L.C.

Section 3 gives the G.L.C. power to make grants to the L.T.E. "for any purpose" and no doubt these words are wide enough to cover grants to revenue as well as for capital purposes. The section cannot, however, be read in isolation, and it is necessary to examine the rest of the Act in order to ascertain the framework in which this power is exercisable. Its extent and the manner in which it is to be exercised must be controlled by the fact that the G.L.C. owes a duty to two different classes. First, under its responsibility for meeting the needs of Greater London, it must provide for transport users: these include not only the residents of London, but persons travelling to and in London from outside (*e.g.* commuters) and tourists. Most of these will not pay rates to the G.L.C. Secondly, it owes a duty of a fiduciary character to its ratepayers who have to provide the money. These, it is said, represent 40 per cent only of the electorate and probably a smaller proportion of the travelling public: they would themselves, most likely, also be travellers. Most of the rates (62 per cent) have to be found from commercial ratepayers. For the extent of this fiduciary duty see *Prescott v. Birmingham Corporation* [1955] Ch. 210, a decision which remains valid in principle although free travel for selected categories has since been authorised by statute.

These duties must be fairly balanced one against the other: see *Roberts v. Hopwood* [1925] A.C. 578 and *Luby v. Newcastle-under-Lyme Corporation* [1964] 2 Q.B. 64, 72. *Roberts v. Hopwood*, which also remains authoritative as to principle although social considerations may have changed since 1925, was concerned with a case where there had been an election which, it was claimed, gave a mandate to the council to pay the wages in question, but Lord Atkinson at 596, emphatically rejected the proposition that however excessive or illegal their scale of wages might be, they were bound to put it into force—against the interests of ratepayers—because their constituents gave them a mandate so to do: see also *per* Lord Sumner, at 607, 609 and Lord Wrenbury at 613.

Part II of this Act, containing sections 4–15 is headed "The London Transport Executive". The executive is set up by section 4 "For the purpose of implementing the policies which it is the duty of the council under section 1 to develop." Sections 5 and 7 are critical for present purposes so I quote the relevant parts:

> "5—(1). Subject always to the requirements of section 7(3) of this Act, it shall be the general duty of the executive to exercise and perform their functions, in accordance with principles from time to time laid down or approved by the council, in such manner as, in conjunction with the railways board and the bus company, and with due regard to efficiency, economy and safety of operation, to provide or secure the provision of such public passenger transport services as best meet the needs for the time being of Greater London."

Here we find another triad of words with "economy" instead of "economic". Again, much fine argument has been given to them. If it makes any difference, I would read the words "of operation" as related only to "safety", but in any case I think that the triad must be taken as a whole. They seem to me to point rather more clearly than does section 1 in the direction of running on businesslike or commercial lines, but it would be reading "economy" too narrowly to treat it as requiring the executive to make, or try to make a profit. It does, on the other hand, prevent the L.T.E. from conducting its undertakings on other than economic considerations. . . .

[His Lordship set out the terms of s.7, and the rival arguments and continued:] In my opinion there are two clear provisions in the Act. The first is in section

7(3)(b). This states the obligation of the London Transport Executive to make good a deficit in the year following a deficit year. This is an obligation, the meeting of which the executive is to ensure as far as practicable. In my opinion this points to the taking of action which it is in the power of the executive to take. On the other hand, though I feel less confident about this ... I am willing to accept that, subject to the executive discharging the responsibilities cast upon it, it may make provision in its revenue account for grants in aid of revenue, actual or assumed. The corresponding provision as regards the G.L.C. is section 7(6) which dovetails with section 7(3). This recognises that the duty stated in section 7(3)(b) (to make up a deficit in year two) is one which "falls to be complied with by the executive", and then obliges the council in performing its functions to have regard to that duty and take action which will enable the executive to comply with those requirements. Such actions might take several forms: the council might direct fares to be raised or services to be adjusted. Or the council could decide to make a grant. But it can only do that after it has "had regard" to the executive's duty under section 7(3). The respective statutory obligations of the G.L.C. and London Transport Executive fit in with one another: the London Transport Executive must carry out its duty as defined in section 7(3): the G.L.C. cannot exercise its powers unless and until the London Transport Executive carries out that duty and must then do so with proper regard to its fiduciary duty to its ratepayers. If these constraints were not to exist, there would be no limit upon the power of the G.L.C. to make grants in aid of revenue, since the Act provides for no governmental control. I find it impossible, in the light of the previous history and of the far from definite language used, to accept that Parliament could have intended that this should be so. To say this is not to impose upon the London Transport Executive a rigid obligation to balance its accounts every year, nor, as it was at one time put in argument, to maximise fares. There is flexibility in the words "so far as practicable", and the obligatory establishment of a reserve gives room for manoeuvre (as indeed the London Transport Executive accounts from 1970 onwards show). But, given this, it appears to me clear that neither the executive in making its proposals, nor the G.L.C. in accepting them, could have power totally to disregard any responsibility for ensuring, so far as practicable, that outgoings are met by revenue, and that the London Transport Executive runs its business on economic lines....

This, then, being, as I interpret them, the effect of the applicable statutory provisions, it remains to ask whether the council and the executive acted in accordance with them. In my opinion they plainly did not. The L.T.E., as regards the year 1980, was running a deficit. Acting, as I am willing to accept, in accordance with their obligations under the Act of 1969, it submitted to the G.L.C., in November 1980, proposals to achieve a break-even by a possible increase in fare revenue, increased productivity, and an assumed G.L.C. grant of £80 million. Its budget contains a careful review of the measures taken, by way of economy and better fare collection, to keep the deficit down as far as practicable. Obviously this was not the only possible budget at the time, but in its preparation and structure it represents a serious attempt to comply with the Act. If a radical departure is made from that budget, that seems to suggest, strongly, that it is made outside the Act.

After the change in control in May 1981, the new leader of the G.L.C. immediately intimated to the L.T.E. that it should submit proposals involving a general reduction in fares of 25 per cent, proposals which would inevitably and greatly (to the extent of about £69 million) increase the operating deficit. This increased deficit would have to be borne by the G.L.C. ratepayers, and, as it soon appeared, would automatically bring about a loss of rate support grant (under central government legislation) involving an additional heavy burden on the ratepayers of an amount (approximately £50 million, attributable to the fare reduction) not far short of the whole cost of the 25 per cent reduction itself.

The L.T.E. submitted proposals, including in them a new zoning scheme. (This, in itself, may well be advantageous but is wholly ancillary to the 25 per cent reduction.) The G.L.C. approved them. In my opinion, both the G.L.C. and L.T.E. were in breach of their duties under the Act. The L.T.E. was, in its own words, meeting the G.L.C. requirement: it was not, and could not have thought that it was complying with its obligations under sections 5 and 7 of the Act of 1969. The G.L.C. could not have considered (as it was obliged to do before it could make a grant to revenue) that the L.T.E. was complying with its obligation under section 7(3). Furthermore, in deciding to proceed to make a grant to support the fare reduction, once it became apparent that the rate-payers' burden would be approximately doubled, it acted in breach of its fiduciary duty as defined above. It failed to hold the balance between the transport users and the ratepayers as it should have done.

I am therefore clearly of opinion that the actions of the G.L.C. and of the L.T.E. were *ultra vires* the Act of 1969....

LORD DIPLOCK: It cannot be too emphatically stated that your Lordships in this appeal are not concerned with the wisdom or, indeed, the fairness of the G.L.C.'s decision to reduce by 25 per cent the fares charged in Greater London by the London Transport Executive ("L.T.E.") which made it necessary to issue the supplementary precept, or the greater part of it. All that your Lordships are concerned with is the legality of that decision: was it within the limited powers that Parliament has conferred by statute upon the G.L.C.? ...

[Lord Diplock reviewed the relevant statutory provisions and concluded:] So I conclude that the mere fact that a grant on revenue account is made by the G.L.C. to the L.T.E. to enable it to comply with a direction to reduce fares to a level at which, in the absence of the grant, its revenue account could not be maintained in balance, is not *of itself* sufficient to render *ultra vires* either the grant or a precept issued by the G.L.C. to raise the money for the grant from rates.

This brings me back to the crucial section of the Act, section 1, to see what limitations (if any) it imposes upon the choice of policy by the G.L.C. as to the relative proportions in which the cost of running the passenger transport undertaking of the L.T.E. is to be met out of the fares paid by passengers or out of rates paid by ratepayers. Central to this question is the legal structure of the G.L.C. and the categories of persons to whom its duties, both generally and in particular in relation to public passenger transport, are owed.

When a statute speaks, as section 1 does, of a "duty" of a local authority composed of democractically elected members, it is speaking of the collective legal duty of all those members acting through the ordinary procedure of debate and resolution, to make choices of policy and of action that they believe to be in the best interests (weighing, where necessary, one against the other) of all those categories of persons to whom their collective duty is owed. This will involve identifying the persons to whom the particular duty is owed and in the event of a conflict of interest between one category and another deciding where the balance ought to lie. In the case of public passenger transport in Greater London those categories are: (1) potential passengers by bus and train in Greater London whether resident there or not; (2) residents in Greater London, who may be assumed to derive benefit from the general mobility of people living in or within commuting distance of Greater London resulting from the availability of a public passenger transport system, even though the particular resident may happen to make little or no use of it himself; and (3) ratepayers in Greater London, to the extent that they are required to contribute to the cost of the system. These three categories overlap but do not coincide. Most persons in category (2) will also be in category (1), and it will be convenient to refer to these as "passengers", but, as mentioned earlier, there is no such coincidence between either of these two categories and category (3), the ratepayers. They constitute only 40 per cent of residents and that 40 per cent bears only 38 per cent of the total burden borne by all ratepayers. The conflict of interest lies between passengers and the ratepayers.

I have left out electors as such, as constituting a separate category. A council member once elected is not the delegate of those who voted in his favour only; he is the representative of all the electors (*i.e.* adult residents) in his ward. If he fought the election on the basis of policies for the future put forward in the election manifesto of a particular political party, he presumably himself considered that in the circumstances contemplated in the manifesto those policies were in the best interest of the electors in his ward, and, if the democratic system as at present practised in local government is to survive, the fact that he received a majority of votes of those electors who took enough interest in the future policies to be adopted by the G.L.C. to cause them to cast their votes, is a factor to which considerable weight ought to be given by him when participating in the collective duty of the G.L.C. to decide whether to implement those policies in the circumstances that exist at the time that the decision falls to be made. That this may properly be regarded as a weighty factor is implicit in the speeches in the House in *Secretary of State for Education and Science v. Tameside Metropolitan Borough Council* [1977] A.C. 1014; although the issues dealt with in that case were very different from those arising in the present appeals. In this respect, I see no difference between those members of the G.L.C. who are members of what as a result of the election becomes the majority party and those who are members of a minority party. In neither case when the time comes to play their part in performing the collective duty of the G.L.C. to make choices of policy or action on particular matters, must members treat themselves as irrevocably bound to carry out pre-announced policies contained in election manifestos even though, by that time, changes of circumstances have occurred that were unforeseen when those policies were announced and would add significantly to the disadvantages that would result from carrying them out.

My Lords, the conflicting interests which the G.L.C. had to balance in deciding whether or not to go ahead with the 25 per cent reduction in fares, notwithstanding the loss of grant from central government funds that this would entail, were those of passengers and the ratepayers. It is well established by the authorities to which my noble and learned friend, Lord Wilberforce, has already referred, that a local authority owes a fiduciary duty to the

ratepayers from whom it obtains moneys needed to carry out its statutory
functions, and that this includes a duty not to expend those moneys thrift-
lessly but to deploy the full financial resources available to it to the best advantage; the financial resources of the G.L.C. that are relevant to the present
appeals being the rate fund obtained by issuing precepts and the grants from
central government respectively. The existence of this duty throws light upon
the true construction of the much-debated phrase in section 1(1) "integrated,
efficient and economic transport facilities and services". "Economic" in this
context must I think mean in the economic interests of passengers and the
ratepayers looked at together, *i.e.* keeping to a minimum the total financial
burden that the persons in these two categories have to share between them
for the provision by the L.T.E. in conjunction with the railways board and the
bus company of an integrated and efficient public passenger transport system
for Greater London. As I have already indicated I think that the G.L.C. had a
discretion as to the proportions in which that total financial burden should be
allocated between passengers and the ratepayers. What are the limits of that
discretion and whether those limits would have been exceeded if the only
effect of the G.L.C.'s decision to instruct the L.T.E. to lower its fares by 25 per
cent had been to transfer to the ratepayers the cost (amounting to some £69
million) of the financial relief that was afforded to the passengers by the lowering of the fares is a difficult question on which the arguments for and against
are by no means all one way. Fortunately I do not find it necessary to decide
that question in the present appeals. It does not, in my view, arise, because the
G.L.C.'s decision was not simply about allocating a total financial burden
between passengers and the ratepayers, it was also a decision to increase that
total burden so as nearly to double it and to place the whole of the increase on
the ratepayers. For, as the G.L.C. well knew when it took the decision to
reduce the fares, it would entail a loss of rate grant from central government
funds amounting to some £50 million, which would have to be made good by
the ratepayers as a result of the G.L.C.'s decision. So the total financial burden
to be shared by passengers and the ratepayers for the provision of an integrated and efficient public passenger transport system was to be increased by
an extra £50 million as a result of the decision, without any equivalent
improvement in the efficiency of the system, and the whole of the extra £50
million was to be recovered from the ratepayers. That would, in my view,
clearly be a thriftless use of moneys obtained by the G.L.C. from ratepayers
and a deliberate failure to deploy to the best advantage the full financial
resources available to it by avoiding any action that would involve forfeiting
grants from central government funds. It was thus a breach of the fiduciary
duty owed by the G.L.C. to the ratepayers. I accordingly agree with your
Lordships that the precept issued pursuant to the decision was *ultra vires* and
therefore void.

I would also have held the decision and the precept to be void upon another
ground ... the members of the majority party by whose votes the effective
resolutions were passed, acted upon an erroneous view ... that from first to
last they regarded the G.L.C. irrevocably committed to carry out the
reduction, whatever might be the additional cost to the ratepayers, because a
reduction of that amount had been pre-announced in the election manifesto
issued by the political party whose candidates formed a majority of the members elected. ...

LORD KEITH OF KINKEL: ... In my opinion the starting point for the consideration of this issue must be *Prescott v. Birmingham Corporation* [1955] Ch. 210. [His Lordship summarised this case, see above, p. 328, emphasising the requirement that fares be fixed "in accordance with ordinary business principles" and continued:]

The effect of the decision has been reversed by statute in relation to free travel for certain selected categories of persons, including the old (see section 138 of the Transport Act 1968, and, as regards London, section 40 of the Act of 1969), but the general principle laid down remains valid.

I turn to an examination of the Act of 1969 in order to determine whether that general principle has been statutorily departed from as regards London Transport. ...

[Lord Keith considered the terms of the legislation and concluded:] ... I have reached the conclusion that both the London Transport Executive and the G.L.C. acted *ultra vires* in relation to the proposed reduction of fares. It must follow that the supplementary precept issued for the purpose of financing the reduction was also *ultra vires* and must be quashed.

In these circumstances it is unnecessary to consider the second issue arising in the appeal, namely, whether the G.L.C., while not acting outwith its statutory powers, nevertheless exercised its discretion in a manner which was unreasonable and otherwise contrary to the principles laid down in *Associated Provincial Picture Houses Ltd v. Wednesbury Corporation* [1948] 1 K.B. 223....

LORD SCARMAN: [considered the statutory provisions and concluded:] ... I conclude, therefore, that the G.L.C. may make grants to provide not only for past, but for anticipated losses. It follows that the G.L.C. and the executive are entitled to anticipate a trading loss and to bring into their accounts grant to offset the resulting deficit.

It is the next step in the appellants' argument which I think is not authorised by the Act. They say that it follows that deficit on trading account is acceptable, even if it be, wholly or to some degree, avoidable, provided the G.L.C. judges it is justifiable on the ground of transport need. But, though revenue account may include grant income, it by no means follows that the Act entitles the G.L.C. and the executive to accept as an objective of policy a deficit upon trading account merely because it best meets what they regard as the interests of the travelling public and "transport need". So to interpret section 7(3) is, in my judgment, to disregard the duty owed to the ratepayers. The subsection is, however, capable of another interpretation which is consistent with that duty. This interpretation, which I accept, is that, while permitting advance budgeting, it, nevertheless requires the executive so to provide its services as to ensure, so far as practicable, that deficit is avoided. Though the executive may be compelled by circumstances to budget for a loss which will have to be made good by grant, the subsection requires them to avoid it, if they can. Their principal weapon is fares income. The subsection, though it envisages budgeting for a deficit, permits it not as an object of social or transport policy, but as a course of action which it may not be practicable or possible to avoid. Loss may be unavoidable: but it does not thereby become an acceptable object of policy.

To conclude ... I find nothing in section 7 which cuts down or modifies the fiduciary duty of the G.L.C. to its ratepayers—a duty which requires it to see that the services of this instrument, the executive, are provided on business principles so as to ensure, so far as practicable, that no avoidable loss falls on the ratepayers.

LORD BRANDON OF OAKBROOK [considered the statutory provisions and concluded:] . . . I am of opinion that it was beyond the powers of the L.T.E. to submit to the G.L.C. for their approval, and beyond the powers of the G.L.C. to approve proposals for an overall reduction of 25 per cent in the level of fares charged by the L.T.E. for the carriage of passengers in trains and buses operated by them.

It follows that I would dismiss these two appeals on that ground alone.

My Lords, as I indicated earlier, if the G.L.C. and the L.T.E. fail on the question of powers, as I consider for the reasons which I have given that they do, it is not necessary to go on to examine the further question of discretion. In case I am wrong about the question of powers, however, I propose to deal shortly also with the question of discretion.

In considering that question it is necessary to assume, contrary to the opinion which I have expressed above, that it is the intention of the Act that the provision by the L.T.E. of proper passenger services for Greater London is to be financed partly by fares paid by passengers and partly by income grants from the G.L.C. derived ultimately from rates levied on the ratepayers of the London boroughs; and further that the extent to which such provision is financed from the one source or the other is a matter for the administrative discretion of the G.L.C.

On those two assumptions the question is whether the G.L.C., in approving the mix of somewhat under 70 per cent and somewhat over 30 per cent, which they did approve, exercised their administrative discretion lawfully.

In my view it is plain for two reasons that the G.L.C. did not exercise their discretion lawfully. The first reason is that, if and in so far as they exercised their discretion at all, they considered themselves bound to exercise it in the way they did because they had promised to do so in their election manifesto. It is, of course, entirely appropriate for a council, the majority of whose members have been elected after setting out a particular policy in their election manifesto, to take into account, and give considerable weight to, that circumstance when exercising their discretion in relation to that policy after they have been elected and come to power. It is, however, entirely wrong for such a majority to regard themselves as bound to exercise their discretion in relation to that policy in accordance with their election promises, whatever the cost and other countervailing considerations may turn out to be. In my view it is an inevitable inference from the evidence taken as a whole that the majority on the G.L.C., when they approved the proposals for a 25 per cent overall reduction in fares, were motivated solely from the belief that, because they had promised such a reduction before their election, they were completely and irrevocably bound to implement it after being elected.

The second reason why I consider that the G.L.C. did not exercise their discretion lawfully is that they persisted in implementing their pre-election policy even after it had become apparent to them that, because of the withdrawal by central government of a large amount of block grant which they had expected to be available to them, the cost to the ratepayers of the London boroughs of their doing so, already very large, was going to be nearly doubled. On the assumptions made, it was the duty of the G.L.C. to balance fairly against each other the interests of the travelling public on the one hand and those of the ratepayers in the London boroughs on the other. In my view the decision of the G.L.C. to persist in the implementation of their election policy on public transport, after it had become apparent that the originally contemplated cost to the ratepayers of the London boroughs would be nearly doubled, was not a decision which the council, directing themselves properly in law, could reasonably have made....

Notes

1. The *Bromley* speeches adopted such a wide variety of reasoning that it is difficult, if not impossible, to extract a *ratio*. *Bromley* was distinguished in two subsequent cases in the Divisional Court. In *R. v. Merseyside County Council, ex p. Great Universal Stores Ltd* (1982) 80 L.G.R. 639, Woolf J. rejected a challenge to the validity of the council's policy of subsidising bus fares from the rates. Distinguishing factors included the point that the Transport Act 1968 required the county council to promote the provision of a "properly integrated and efficient" public passenger transport system with due regard, *inter alia*, to "economy and safety of operation", whereas the Transport (London) Act 1969 required the GLC to promote the provision of "integrated, efficient *and economic*" transport facilities; there was no question of an automatic loss of rate support grant; the council's policies were in accordance with the Merseyside Structure plan; and the proposal had been considered afresh after the elections.

There was also a sequel to the *Bromley* case in London: *R. v. London Transport Executive, ex p. Greater London Council* [1983] Q.B. 484; [1983] 2 All E.R. 262. Following the *Bromley* decision, fares were approximately doubled. Subsequently, the Divisional Court upheld the validity of a revised plan for London Transport fares, involving a reduction of about 25 per cent in the new fares and an increase in the deficit on the L.T.E.'s revenue account of about 17 per cent, to be made good by a grant from the GLC. The GLC was held to be entitled to make grants to the L.T.E. to meet continuing losses, provided there was no breach of the principles laid down in the *Wednesbury* and *Prescott* cases. Kerr L.J. expressed broad agreement with the submission on behalf of the GLC that the references in *Bromley* and *Prescott* to the requirement to conduct a transport system on business principles were primarily intended to exclude philanthropic considerations and to emphasise the need for the proper and cost-effective use of resources; they did not mean that fare revenue had to be maximised on ordinary business principles of profit and loss (see at 497, 499). The court granted declarations to the effect that the revised plan was within the powers of the GLC and the L.T.E. on the true construction of the Transport (London) Act 1969. It did not decide whether there was any breach of the *Wednesbury* and *Prescott* principles: both parties were agreed that there was no such breach and Kerr L.J. said that "nothing has emerged in the evidence and argument presented to us which has led us to think the contrary" (at 497).

2. The *Bromley* case is analysed critically by J. Dignan, "Policy-Making, Local Authorities and the Courts: The 'G.L.C. Fares' Case" (1983) 99 L.Q.R. 605. He concludes (at 643) that:

"It is strongly arguable that all the appellate judges in the 'G.L.C. Fares' case failed fully to appreciate the scale of the changes brought about in the sphere of public transport administration by the related Acts of 1968 and 1969. The new financial and administrative infrastructure set up under these Acts vested in local authorities greatly enlarged discretionary powers in order to discharge their weighty responsibilities for planning and policy making across a broad range of local transport issues, which extended far beyond the traditional parochial concerns of running municipal bus services on ordinary business principles. Both the need to protect the ratepayers' interests, and the presumption in favour of private property which was reflected in this, and in the retention of the notion of ordinary business principles, look anachronistic in the light of more recent conceptions of the role of the local state, as reflected in these two Acts."

See also J.L. Yelland [1982] P.L. 171; M. Loughlin, *Local Government in the Modern State* (1986), pp. 68–81; J.A.G. Griffith, "Judicial Decision-making in Public Law" [1985] P.L. 564, 575–579. The opinion of counsel for Bromley, Harry Sales, is reproduced at [1991] P.L. 499. The impact of *Bromley* on local authorities was the subject of an interdisciplinary study: L. Bridges *et al., Legality and Local Politics* (1987).

3. Compare the attitude of Lord Diplock and Lord Brandon on the significance to be attached to election manifesto commitments with that of the House of Lords in the *Tameside* case, below, p. 369.

In the cases so far considered in this chapter the question raised has been whether the purpose for which a power was exercised was a proper one, whether all relevant considerations were taken into account, or whether all irrelevant considerations were excluded from attention.

It may well be, however, that the issue is not so straightforward. What should be the position where a body is shown to have acted for a *plurality of purposes*, some of which are proper and some improper? Does the *mere fact* of having taken into consideration an irrelevant consideration taint the decision reached? Does failure to have taken into consideration *one of a number of relevant factors* necessarily have that invalidating effect?

The cases which follow address these various issues.

WESTMINSTER CORPORATION v. LONDON AND NORTH-WESTERN RAILWAY CO.

[1905] A.C. 426; 74 L.J.Ch. 629; 93 L.T. 143; 69 J.P. 425; 3 L.G.R. 1120 (House of Lords)

The Corporation, a sanitary authority, constructed public lavatories underground in the middle of Parliament Street. In the words of Lord Macnaghten:

"The plan of the construction is this: On each aside of the roadway there is an entrance, five feet nine inches wide, protected by railings and leading by a staircase of the same width to a passage or subway, ten feet wide and eight feet high, which runs the whole way across on a level with the underground conveniences. Out of this subway there are openings—two for men and one for women—into spacious chambers, where the usual accommodation (politely described as lavatories and cloakrooms) is provided on a large and liberal scale. All the arrangements seem to have been designed and carried out with due regard to decency, and with every possible consideration for the comfort of wayfarers in need of such accommodation."

The Railway Company owned a large block of buildings on the east side of Parliament Street. They objected to the sanitary works, and sought to have them removed, basing their claim alternatively on trespass, or obstruction to the highway causing special damage. The Corporation relied on their powers under the Public Health (London) Act 1891 to provide, make and maintain public lavatories and sanitary conveniences. The Company pointed out that both the Corporation and its predecessor, the Vestry of St Margaret's, Westminster, had exhibited a wish to have a subway constructed at that site. In September 1900 the Vestry's surveyor wrote to the Company referring to the construction of a "subway", and making no mention of the construction of the convenience. In December the acting town clerk of Westminster wrote that "the intention is the construction of a subway to facilitate pedestrians crossing ... a thoroughfare of great width and very considerable traffic.... Admission to the conveniences, which will be accessible from the subways, could otherwise have been provided from refuges above them."

The railway company claimed an injunction to prevent the corporation from continuing to trespass on their premises and to obstruct the footway opposite the premises and damages. When the parties came to trial, it was found that owing to some mistake, the corporation's works had encroached upon the footway. The trial judge, Joyce J. ([1902] 1 Ch. 269), ordered the corporation to remove the encroachment. On appeal, the Court of Appeal (Vaughan Williams, Stirling and Cozens-Hardy L.JJ. [1904] 1 Ch. 759) ordered the corporation to "pull down and remove the whole of the staircase, railings, and other works placed by the defendants upon the lands of the plaintiffs other than the conveniences in the pleadings mentioned, and such further portion of the construction as the court [might], upon application, sanction as a proper approach to the said conveniences". The order was suspended pending an appeal to the House of Lords. On appeal the corporation acquiesced in the order of Joyce J. but contended that the order of the Court of Appeal was wrong.

LORD MACNAGHTEN: ... There can be no question as to the law applicable to the case. It is well settled that a public body invested with statutory powers such as those conferred upon the corporation must take care not to exceed or abuse its powers. It must keep within the limits of the authority committed to it. It must act in good faith. And it must act reasonably. The last proposition is involved in the second, if not in the first. But in the present case I think it will be convenient to take it separately.

Now, looking merely at what has been done—at the work as designed and actually constructed—it seems to me that, apart from the encroachment on the footway, it is impossible to contend that the work is in excess of what was authorized by the Act of 1891. The conveniences themselves, extensive as the accommodation is, have not been condemned by the Court of Appeal or even attacked in the evidence.

[His Lordship then held that the entrance from the roadway was not excessively wide.]

Then I come to the question of want of good faith. That is a very serious charge. It is not enough to shew that the corporation contemplated that the public might use the subway as a means of crossing the street. That was an obvious possibility. It cannot be otherwise if you have an entrance on each side and the communication is not interrupted by a wall or a barrier of some sort. In order to make out a case of bad faith it must be shewn that the corporation constructed this subway as a means of crossing the street under colour and pretence of providing public conveniences which were not really wanted at that particular place. That was the view of their conduct taken by the Court of Appeal. "In my judgment," says Vaughan Williams L.J., "it is not true to say that the corporation have taken this land which they have taken with the object of using it for the purposes authorized by the Legislature." "You are acting *mala fide*," he added, "if you are seeking to acquire and acquiring lands for a purpose not authorized by the Act of Parliament." So you are; there can be no doubt of that. The other learned Lord Justices seem to take the same view of the conduct of the corporation. Now this, as I have said, is a very serious charge. A gross breach of public duty, and all for a mere fad! The learned judge who tried the case had before him the chairman of the works committee. That gentleman declared that his committee considered with very great care for a couple of years or more the question of these conveniences in Parliament Street. He asserted on oath that "the primary object of the committee was to provide these conveniences". Why is this gentleman not to be believed? The learned judge who saw and heard him believed his statement.

The learned judges of the Court of Appeal have discredited his testimony, mainly, if not entirely, on the ground of two letters about which he was not asked a single question.... The letter of the surveyor was a foolish letter, which the writer seems to have thought clever. The letter of the temporary representative of the acting town clerk, if you compare the two letters, seems to have derived its inspiration from the same source. I cannot conceive why the solemn statement of the chairman of the committee should be discredited on such a ground. I do not think there is anything in the minutes tending to disprove his testimony. I entirely agree with Joyce J. that the primary object of the council was the construction of the conveniences with the requisite and proper means of approach thereto and exit therefrom....

LORD JAMES (dissenting): ... [T]he question to be solved seems to be thus formulated: Was the so-called tunnel an approach to the conveniences only, or was it something more? (1) Was it a subway distinct from the approach, or (2) was it a subway in combination with the approach used for two distinct purposes?

In my judgment the construction in question comes within one or other of the two latter alternatives. Possibly within the first, certainly within the second.

If this finding on the facts is correct, the works, so far as they constitute the subway, are constructed without legal authority. The Legislature has not thought it right to confer on local bodies the power to compulsorily take land or impose rates for the purpose of constructing subways. In this case some land has been taken which would not have been required if the approach had not been enlarged into a subway, and an unauthorized burthen has been imposed upon the ratepayers in consequence of this enlargement.

Thus it is, in my opinion, that the appellants have acted beyond their powers and without justification.

THE EARL OF HALSBURY L.C. and LORD LINDLEY delivered speeches in favour of dismissing the appeal.

R. v. INNER LONDON EDUCATION AUTHORITY, ex p. WESTMINSTER CITY COUNCIL

[1986] 1 W.L.R. 28; [1986] 1 All E.R. 19 (Glidewell J.)

The ILEA, being opposed to central government public expenditure limitation policies, commenced a programme by which they sought to raise public awareness of those policies and of their implications. Under section 142(2) of the Local Government Act 1972 the ILEA had power to incur expenditure on publishing within its area "information on matters relating to local government". In July 1984 a sub-committee of the ILEA resolved to retain an advertising agency to mount a media and poster campaign, at a cost of some £651,000. The ILEA acknowledged that the purpose of the campaign was both to "inform" the public about government proposals and their effects (a lawful purpose) and to "persuade" the public to support the ILEA's stance on this matter (an unlawful purpose). The applicant council argued that the resolution was *ultra vires* the power in section 142(2), *inter alia*, because of the unlawful purpose and because the ILEA had taken into account an irrelevant consideration—its desire to persuade the public to oppose government policy.

GLIDEWELL J. [outlined the facts, reviewed the terms of section 142(2), and continued:] ... [T]he decision of July 23, 1984, was made with the two purposes of informing and persuading.

Two purposes

This brings me to what I regard as being the most difficult point in the case, namely: if a local authority resolves to expend its ratepayers' money in order to achieve two purposes, one of which it is authorised to achieve by statute but for the other of which it has no authority, is that decision invalid?

I was referred to the following authorities.

(i) *Westminster Corp. v. London and North Western Ry Co.* [1905] A.C. 426....

[His Lordship summarised this decision and concluded:] ... this suggests that a test for answering the question is, if the authorised purpose is the primary purpose, the resolution is within the power.

(ii) *Sydney Municipal Council v. Campbell* [1925] A.C. 338. This ... decision of the Privy Council ... does not really deal with the question that confronts me of a resolution passed with two purposes in mind.

(iii) More recently in *Hanks v. Minister of Housing and Local Government* [1963] 1 Q.B. 999, Megaw J. did have to deal with a case in which it was alleged that a compulsory purchase order had been made for two purposes, one of which did not fall within the empowering Act. At 1019, he quoted part of the dissenting judgment of Denning L.J. in *Earl Fitzwilliam's Wentworth Estates Co. Ltd v. Minister of Town and Country Planning* [1951] 2 K.B. 284, 307:

"If Parliament grants to a government department a power to be used for an authorised purpose, then the power is only validly exercised when it is used by the department genuinely for that purpose as its dominant purpose. If that purpose is not the main purpose, but is subordinated to some other purpose which is not authorised by law, then the department exceeds its powers and the action is invalid."

It had been submitted to Megaw J. that, although Denning L.J. had dissented from the decision of the majority, this passage in his judgment did not differ from the view of the majority.

Megaw J. went on ([1963] 1 Q.B. 999, 1020):

"I confess that I think confusion can arise from the multiplicity of words which have been used in this case as suggested criteria for the testing of the validity of the exercise of a statutory power. The words used have included 'objects', 'purposes', 'motives', 'motivation', 'reasons', 'grounds' and 'considerations'. In the end, it seems to me, the simplest and clearest way to state the matter is by reference to 'considerations'. A 'consideration', I apprehend, is something which one takes into account as a factor in arriving at a decision. I am prepared to assume, for the purposes of this case, that, if it be shown that an authority exercising a power has taken into account as a relevant factor something which it could not properly take into account in deciding whether or not to exercise the power, then the exercise of the power, normally at least, is bad. Similarly, if the authority fails to take into account as a relevant factor something which is relevant, and which is or ought to be known to it, and which it ought to have taken into account, the exercise of the power is normally bad. I say 'normally', because I can conceive that there may be cases where the factor wrongly taken into account, or omitted, is insignificant, or where the wrong taking-into-account, or omission, actually operated in favour of the person who later claims to be aggrieved by the decision...."

I have considered also the views of the learned authors of textbooks on this. Professor Wade in *Administrative Law* (5th ed., 1982), p. 388 under the heading "Duality of Purpose" says:

"Sometimes an act may serve two or more purposes, some authorised and some not, and it may be a question whether the public authority may kill two birds with one stone. The general rule is that its action will be lawful provided the permitted purpose is the true and dominant purpose behind the act, even though some secondary or incidental advantage may be gained for some purpose which is outside the authority's powers."

Professor Evans, in *de Smith's Judicial Review of Administrative Action* (4th ed., 1980), pp. 329–332, comforts me by describing the general problem of plurality of purpose as "a legal porcupine which bristles with difficulties as soon as it is touched". He distils from the decisions of the courts five different tests on which reliance has been placed at one time or another, including—

"(1) What was the *true purpose* for which the power was exercised? If the actor has in truth used his power for the purposes for which it was conferred, it is immaterial that he was thus enabled to achieve a subsidiary object.... (5) Was any of the purposes pursued an unauthorised purpose? If so, and if the unauthorised purpose has materially influenced the actor's conduct, the power had been invalidly exercised because irrelevant considerations have been taken into account."

These two tests, and Professor Evans' comment on them, seem to me to achieve much the same result and to be similar to that put forward by Megaw J. in *Hanks v. Minister of Housing and Local Government* [1963] 1 Q.B. 999 in the first paragraph of the passage I have quoted from his judgment. That is the part that includes the sentence: "In the end, it seems to me, the simplest and clearest way to state the matter is by reference to 'considerations'." I gratefully adopt the guidance of Megaw J., and the two tests I have referred to from *de Smith*.

It thus becomes a question of fact for me to decide, on the material before me, whether, in reaching its decision of July 23, 1984, the staff and general sub-committee of I.L.E.A. was pursuing an unauthorised purpose, namely that of persuasion, which has materially influenced the making of its decision. I have already said that I find that one of the sub-committee's purposes was the giving of information. But I also find that it had the purpose of seeking to persuade members of the public to a view identical with that of the authority itself, and indeed I believe that this was a, if not the, major purpose of the decision....

Adopting the test referred to above, I thus hold that I.L.E.A.'s sub-committee did, when making its decision of July 23, 1984, take into account an irrelevant consideration, and thus that decision was not validly reached.

If I am wrong on this, there would remain for consideration the last two arguments advanced by counsel for the city council. I will deal with these shortly. As to the alleged breach of fiduciary duty to the ratepayers, it is true that the cóst of employing AMV was very substantially greater than the sums which I.L.E.A. had already authorised to be expended on the "campaign". But this is a matter of discretion for the authority, which was advised that it had to take into account its duty to the ratepayers. It would be for Westminster City Council to show, if they could, that I.L.E.A. had disregarded that duty. In my view, Westminster City Council have failed to do this. Similarly, I cannot say on the material before me that I.L.E.A.'s decision was so unreasonable as to be perverse. If therefore the matter depended on either of these two grounds, Westminster City Council's challenge would fail.

Declaration granted.

R. v. BROADCASTING COMPLAINTS COMMISSION, ex p. OWEN

[1985] Q.B. 1153; [1985] 2 All E.R. 522, D.C. (Q.B.D.)

Under section 54 of the Broadcasting Act 1981 the B.C.C. had a statutory duty (subject to the terms of section 55(4)—discretion not to hear a complaint where, *inter alia,* "inappropriate") to consider and adjudicate upon complaints of, *inter alia,* "unjust or unfair treatment" in radio or television programmes. The applicant, Dr David Owen, was the leader of the Social Democratic Party. That party had entered into an alliance with the Liberal Party. Together these two parties had obtained only 2 per cent less of the votes at the 1983 election than had the main opposition party, the Labour Party. The number of seats won by Alliance candidates was, however, very much smaller than those won by Labour. In June 1984, Dr Owen wrote to the B.C.C. complaining of unjust and unfair treatment in that as a matter of policy the broadcasting organisations were giving considerably more attention in news and current affairs broadcasts to the views of the Labour Party than to the views of the alliance. In reply, the B.C.C. stated that (i) it had no jurisdiction to consider a complaint of such nature, and (ii) that, even if it had such jurisdiction, it would have declined to entertain the complaint for a variety of stated reasons.

May L.J. and Taylor J. held that the B.C.C. was wrong to have thought that it had no jurisdiction to have considered such a complaint. On the issue of whether it had properly exercised its discretion (under section 55(4)) to decline to hear complaints within jurisdiction:

MAY L.J.: ... I turn therefore to the commission's decision contained in their letter of November 13, 1984 that even if they did have jurisdiction to entertain the applicant's complaint under section 54 it would be inappropriate for them to do so under section 55(4) for the reasons they gave. I bear well in mind [the submission of counsel for Dr Owen] based on the decision in *Padfield's* case [1968] A.C. 997, that the discretion given to the commission to entertain or to refuse to entertain a complaint should be exercised to comply with the policy and objects of the Act of 1981. Nevertheless, the wording of section 55(4) is as wide as it could be....

On the general principles of law laid down in the cases to which I have referred the commission would of course not be entitled to decline to entertain or proceed with the consideration of the applicant's complaint merely at their own whim. They must be able to show that their declinature was founded upon what I can briefly describe as a relevant reason or reasons within the *Wednesbury* principles and they must be able to repel any suggestion that they have failed to take into account any other relevant reason which they ought to have done.

[His Lordship stated that he had heard argument upon each of the reasons given for the B.C.C.'s decision, and continued:]

In the end I am quite satisfied that there is no sufficient justification for the applicant's criticism of [certain of the] reasons in the commission's letter.... The essence of the applicant's complaint is political and within it lies the thorny problem whether the voting system of this country should be changed so as to introduce some form of proportional representation. In these circumstances I think that the stance taken by the commission as indicated by those reasons in their letter ... is that the applicant's complaint was to the effect that the broadcasting authorities have, as a matter of editorial policy, taken a decision about how they will treat the Alliance in comparison with the Labour Party. The complaint would, in effect, require the commission to decide whether its editorial policy, if it exists, is fair and just. But by what criteria? They would have to express a view about a fundamental issue of British politics, not merely about alleged unjust or unfair treatment in a broadcast or television programme about which there are quite clearly strongly different views held by both the Conservative and Labour Parties.

The applicant's real concern is not to have the broadcasting authorities required to publish a comment on the commission on past programmes but to achieve a change of what he contends is editorial policy on the part of the broadcasting authorities in the future. That is not the type of relief that the commission is empowered to grant.

In these circumstances, and on the above grounds, I think that [those] reasons ... given by the commission in their letter and the underlying thinking which they demonstrate were wholly justified in law and constituted an entirely relevant stance for the commission to take which cannot validly be criticised on, for instance, *Padfield's* principles....

In my opinion, however, reason 3 in their letter in support of their contention that to entertain the applicant's complaint was inappropriate cannot be justified in law. The mere fact that a task which it is their duty to carry out may be burdensome and require perhaps the employment of additional staff is not, I think, a sufficient reason to conclude that it would be inappropriate for them to proceed.

Contemplating the possibility that the court might reach the conclusion which I have, namely, that although four of the reasons given by the commission were valid in law, nevertheless the remaining fifth reason was not, [counsel for Dr Owen] referred us to the decision of Forbes J. in *R. v. Rochdale Metropolitan Borough Council, ex p. Cromer Ring Mill Ltd* [1982] 3 All E.R. 761, particularly the passage beginning at the foot of p. 768. Having considered a passage from *de Smith's Judicial Review of Administrative Action* (4th ed., 1980), pp. 339–340, and then the judgment of Denning L.J. in *Earl Fitzwilliam's Wentworth Estates Co. Ltd v. Minister of Town and Country Planning* [1951] 2 K.B. 284, 307 and of Megaw J. in *Hanks v. Minister of Housing and Local Government* [1963] 1 Q.B. 999, 1018–1019, Forbes J. said, at 769–770:

"Although it is fair to say that *Hanks'* case is not binding on me, it is a very persuasive authority and I would undoubtedly follow it, and do. It seems to me Megaw J. is there saying, having been apprised of the argument about dominant purpose, that the exercise of a power is bad if it is shown that an authority exercising that power has taken an irrelevant factor into account, one of many factors, as long as that irrelevant factor is not insignificant or insubstantial. To that extent, it seems to me, that that case wholly supports the formulation in Professor de Smith's book: 'If the influence of irrelevant factors is established, it does not appear to be necessary to prove that they were the sole or even the dominant influence; it seems to be enough to prove that their influence was substantial.' "

On this authority [counsel for Dr Owen] submitted that the invalidity of even only one of the reasons given by the commission invalidated their decision that it would be inappropriate for them to entertain or consider the applicant's complaint. In reply [counsel for B.C.C.] accepted that where reasons given by a statutory body are mixed and impossible to disentangle, as indeed was the situation in the *Rochdale* case, then the invalidity of one is sufficient to vitiate the whole of the decision based upon such reasons even if many of them are valid. He, nevertheless, submitted that where the reasons given are separate and alternative, then the mere fact that one can be criticised is not sufficient to vitiate a decision to which the statutory body would in any event have come had they left the invalid reason out of account.

For my part, I cannot accept [counsel for B.C.C.'s] entire submission on this point as he stated it. I respectfully agree that the material law is as was stated by Forbes J. but with one qualification. . . . Where the reasons given by a statutory body for taking or not taking a particular course of action are not mixed and can clearly be disentangled, but where the court is quite satisfied that even though one reason may be bad in law, nevertheless the statutory body would have reached precisely the same decision on the other valid reasons, then this court will not interfere by way of judicial review. In such a case, looked at realistically and with justice, such a decision of such a body ought not to be disturbed.

I am quite satisfied in this case on all the material before us that the commission would still have concluded that it would be inappropriate to entertain or consider the applicant's complaint if they had never thought about reason 3 in their letter of November 13, 1984.

Another approach to the same problem in such circumstances, which really reflects the same thinking is this: the grant of what may be the appropriate remedies in an application for judicial review is a matter for the discretion of this court. Where one is satisfied that although a reason relied on by a statutory body may not properly be described as insubstantial, nevertheless even without it the statutory body would have been bound to come to precisely the same conclusion on valid grounds, then it would be wrong for this court to exercise its discretion to strike down, in one way or another, that body's conclusion. . . .

[TAYLOR J. delivered a concurring judgment in which he expressed his agreement with May L.J., but did not deal specifically with the issues considered above.]

Notes

1. See H.F. Rawlings (1985) 48 M.L.R. 584. *cf. R. v. London Borough of Lewisham, ex p. Shell U.K. Ltd* [1988] 1 All E.R. 938, where the council passed a resolution to boycott Shell products. The Divisional Court found that it had two purposes: (1) a lawful purpose to promote good race relations in the borough in accordance with its duty under section 71 of the Race Relations Act 1976; and (2) an unlawful purpose to put pressure on Shell to withdraw from South Africa. The court held that where two reasons or purposes could not be disentangled, and one was bad, or, where they could be disentangled the bad reason demonstrably exerted the substantial influence, the court could interfere to quash the decision. Here, the two purposes were inextricably mixed up and the unlawful purpose had the effect of vitiating the decision as a whole. See T.R.S. Allan [1988] C.L.J. 334.

2. As *ex p. Owen* illustrates, the courts may be called upon to determine whether a particular consideration is or is not "relevant". It may be that the background legislation provides sufficient pointers to enable the courts to perform this task with some confidence. However, there is a danger that the courts become too ready to spell out relevant and irrelevant considerations based not so much on the statute as on their view as to what is and is not appropriate. Consider, for example, *Bristol District Council v. Clark* [1975] 1 W.L.R. 1443, where the Court of Appeal identified a number of factors as relevant to decisions to evict council tenants, which were found not in the statute but in a Department of the Environment circular: see the criticism of this approach by R.J. Buxton (1976) 39 M.L.R. 470; and *cf. Cannock Chase District Council v. Kelly* [1978] 1 W.L.R. 1. *cf.* the "fiduciary duty" considered in *Roberts v. Hopwood* and *Bromley*, above, pp. 321–339.

In *R. v. Secretary of State for the Environment, ex p. Bolton Metropolitan Borough Council* [1991] J.P.L. 32, Hodgson J. rejected an argument that unless a decision-maker was expressly required to take into account some matter, he was only "impliedly" required by law to take the matter into account if it was one which no reasonable decision-maker would fail to do so: his Lordship regarded this conflation of *Wednesbury* principles as illegitimate. The Court of Appeal dismissed an appeal on other grounds.

3. In some contexts, the courts have shown a disinclination to apply the considerations test. For example, it has been suggested that where the amount of expenditure by a local authority on a particular item is not unreasonable, the fact that irrelevant considerations may have been taken into account may not render the expenditure unlawful (*per* Lord Sumner in *Roberts v. Hopwood*, above, p. 321; *Re Walker's Decision* [1944] 1 K.B. 644). In *Pickwell v. Camden London Borough Council* [1983] 1 Q.B. 962, Ormrod L.J. held that a failure to take into account relevant matters, or the taking into account of irrelevant matters were in effect only evidence that the authority might have acted *ultra vires* (*cf.* the approach of Forbes J. who simply held that a breach of the *Wednesbury* principles was not established on the evidence). See above, p. 330.

A suggestion of the Court of Appeal that the full *Wednesbury* principles might not apply in relation to purely administrative decisions not affecting rights (*R. v. Barnet and Camden Rent Tribunal, ex p. Frey Investments Ltd* [1972] 2 Q.B. 342) has not found favour (see *Wade*, p. 417). In *R. v. Commission for Racial Equality, ex p. Hillingdon London Borough Council*, Griffiths L.J. in the Court of Appeal ([1982] Q.B. 276, 298–300) and Lord Diplock in the House of Lords ([1982] A.C. 779, 792) expressly affirmed that the *Wednesbury* principles apply to administrative functions.

It may be that suggestions that the considerations test does not apply in a particular context are simply a reflection of the point that there is no breach of the test where an authority considers but is not influenced by a particular legally irrelevant matter, or the same decision would have been reached by reference to other considerations (*ex p. Owen*, above).

(C) UNREASONABLENESS

The grounds of challenge considered in sections A and B, above, require evidence and proof of the purpose(s) of the body challenged, or the considerations which were or were not taken into account. In other words attention focuses in such cases on the "thought-processes" of the challenged body in exercising its discretionary power. Evidence of this may appear from any reasons, or explanation, it may give (or may be required to give) for its decision; or from affidavits (or, in exceptional cases, cross-examination) in the course of the legal challenge itself.

Challenge on the ground of "unreasonableness" proceeds on a rather different footing. It invites the court to hold that notwithstanding that there may be no firm evidence of improper purpose or relevant/irrelevant considerations, nevertheless the court should intervene on the basis that the decision as to the exercise of power is in substance one which no reasonable body, properly conversant with its legal obligations, could have come to.

The courts have consistently stated that in considering challenges on this ground they must preserve the distinction between review on the "merits" (is this the decision I would have come to?) and review of "legality" (is this a decision which a reasonable person could have come to?). The former may be appropriate in appeal proceedings, where such exist and permit the appellate body such a wide power of reconsideration; but is regarded by the judges as going beyond their proper remit in proceedings for judicial review. "Unreasonableness" is justified as a ground of review of legality on the basis that although Parliament may have intended to authorise a variety of, not unreasonable, ways in which a power might be exercised, and have intended to leave such choice to the body in question rather than to the judges, it can be assumed that Parliament had not intended its grant of that power to cover its "unreasonable" exercise.

(i) *Wednesbury* Unreasonableness

ASSOCIATED PROVINCIAL PICTURE HOUSES LTD v. WEDNESBURY CORPORATION

[1948] 1 K.B. 223; 177 L.T. 641; 63 T.L.R. 623; 112 J.P. 55; 92 S.J. 26; [1947] 2 All E.R. 680; 45 L.G.R. 635; [1948] L.J.R. 190 (Court of Appeal)

The plaintiff company, the owners and licensees of the Gaumont Cinema, Wednesbury, Staffordshire, were granted by the defendants who were the licensing authority for that borough under the Cinematograph Act 1909, a licence to give performances on Sundays under section 1(1) of the Sunday Entertainments Act 1932; but the licence was granted subject to a condition that "no children under the age of 15 years shall be admitted to any entertainment whether accompanied by an adult or not". In these circumstances the plaintiffs brought an action for a declaration that the condition was *ultra vires* and unreasonable.

Henn Collins J. ([1947] L.J.R. 678) dismissed the action, and the plaintiffs appealed to the Court of Appeal. Section 1(1) of the 1932 Act provided that the authority might attach to a licence "such conditions as the authority think fit to impose...."

LORD GREENE M.R.: ... Mr Gallop, for the plaintiffs, argued that it was not competent for the Wednesbury Corporation to impose any such condition and he said that if they were entitled to impose a condition prohibiting the admission of children, they should at least have limited it to cases where the children were not accompanied by their parents or a guardian or some adult.

His argument was that the imposition of that condition was unreasonable and that in consequence it was *ultra vires* the corporation. The plaintiffs' contention is based, in my opinion, on a misconception as to the effect of this Act in granting this discretionary power to local authorities. The courts must always, I think, remember this: first, we are dealing with not a judicial act, but an executive act; secondly, the conditions which, under the exercise of that executive act, may be imposed are in terms, so far as language goes, put within the discretion of the local authority without limitation. Thirdly, the statute provides no appeal from the decision of the local authority.

What, then, is the power of the courts? They can only interfere with an act of executive authority if it be shown that the authority has contravened the law. It is for those who assert that the local authority has contravened the law to establish that proposition. On the face of it, a condition of the kind imposed in this case is perfectly lawful. It is not to be assumed prima facie that responsible bodies, like the local authority in this case will exceed their powers; but the court, whenever it is alleged that the local authority have contravened the law, must not substitute itself for that authority. It is only concerned with seeing whether or not the proposition is made good. When an executive discretion is entrusted by Parliament to a body such as the local authority in this case, what appears to be an exercise of that discretion can only be challenged in the courts in a strictly limited class of case. As I have said, it must always be remembered that the court is not a court of appeal. When discretion of this kind is granted the law recognizes certain principles upon which that discretion must be exercised, but within the four corners of those principles the discretion, in my opinion, is an absolute one and cannot be questioned in any court of law. What then are those principles? They are well understood. They are principles which the court looks to in considering any question of discretion of this kind. The exercise of such a discretion must be a real exercise of discretion. If, in the statute conferring the discretion, there is to be found expressly or by implication matters which the authority exercising the discretion ought to have regard to, then in exercising the discretion it must have regard to those matters. Conversely, if the nature of the subject-matter and the general interpretation of the Act make it clear that certain matters would not be germane to the matter in question, the authority must disregard those irrelevant collateral matters. There have been in the cases expressions used relating to the sort of thing that authorities must not do, not merely in cases under the Cinematograph Act but, generally speaking, under the other cases where the powers of local authorities came to be considered. I am not sure myself whether the permissible grounds of attack cannot be defined under a single head. It has been perhaps a little bit confusing to find a series of grounds set out. Bad faith, dishonesty—those of course, stand by themselves—unreasonableness, attention given to extraneous circumstances, disregard of public policy and things like that have all been referred to, according to the facts of individual cases, as being matters which are relevant to the question. If they cannot all be confined under one head, they at any rate, I think, overlap to a very great extent. For instance, we have heard in this case a great deal about the meaning of the word "unreasonable".

It is true the discretion must be exercised reasonably. Now what does that mean? Lawyers familiar with the phraseology commonly used in relation to exercise of statutory discretions often use the word "unreasonable" in a rather comprehensive sense. It has frequently been used and is frequently used as a general description of the things that must not be done. For instance, a person entrusted with a discretion must, so to speak, direct himself properly in law. He must call his own attention to the matters which he is bound to consider. He must exclude from his consideration matters which are irrelevant to what he has to consider. If he does not obey those rules, he may truly be said, and often is said, to be acting "unreasonably". Similarly, there may be something so absurd that no sensible person could ever dream that it lay within the powers of the authority. Warrington L.J. in *Short v. Poole Corporation* [1926] Ch. 66, 90, 91, gave the example of the red-haired teacher, dismissed because she had red hair. That is unreasonable in one sense. In another sense it is taking into consideration extraneous matters. It is so unreasonable that it might almost be described as being done in bad faith; and, in fact, all these things run into one another.

In the present case, it is said by Mr Gallop that the authority acted unreasonably in imposing this condition. It appears to me quite clear that the matter dealt with by this condition was a matter which a reasonable authority would be justified in considering when they were making up their mind what condition should be attached to the grant of this licence. Nobody, at this time of day, could say that the well-being and the physical and moral health of children is not a matter which a local authority, in exercising their powers, can properly have in mind when those questions are germane to what they have to consider. Here Mr Gallop did not, I think, suggest that the council were directing their mind to a purely extraneous and irrelevant matter, but he based his argument on the word "unreasonable", which he treated as an independent ground for attacking the decision of the authority; but once it is conceded, as it must be conceded in this case, that the particular subject-matter dealt with by this condition was one which it was competent for the authority to consider, there, in my opinion, is an end of the case. Once that is granted, Mr Gallop is bound to say that the decision of the authority is wrong because it is unreasonable, and in saying that he is really saying that the ultimate arbiter of what is and is not reasonable is the court and not the local authority. It is just there, it seems to me, that the argument breaks down. It is clear that the local authority are entrusted by Parliament with the decision on a matter which the knowledge and experience of that authority can best be trusted to deal with. The subject-matter with which the condition deals is one relevant for its consideration. They have considered it and come to a decision upon it. It is true to say that, if a decision on a competent matter is so unreasonable that no reasonable authority could ever have come to it, then the courts can interfere. That I think, is quite right; but to prove a case of that kind would require something overwhelming, and, in this case, the facts do not come anywhere near anything of that kind. I think Mr Gallop in the end agreed that his proposition that the decision of the local authority can be upset if it is proved to be unreasonable, really meant that it must be proved to be unreasonable in the sense that the court considers it to be a decision that no reasonable body could have come to. It is not what the court considers unreasonable, a different thing altogether. If it is what the court considers unreasonable, the court may very well have different views to that of a local authority on matters of high public policy of this kind. Some courts might think that no children ought to be admitted on Sundays at all, some courts might think the reverse, and all over the country I have no doubt on a thing of that sort honest and sincere people hold different views. The effect of the legislation is not to set up the court as an arbiter of the correctness of one view over another. It is the local authority that are set in that position and, provided they act, as they have acted, within the four corners of their jurisdiction, this court, in my opinion, cannot interfere.

This case, in my opinion, does not really require reference to authority when once the simple and well known principles are understood on which alone a court can interfere with something prima facie within the powers of the executive authority, but reference has been made to a number of cases. ... [His Lordship referred to *Harman v. Butt* [1944] K.B. 491; *R. v. Burnley JJ.*, 85 L.J. (K.B.) 1565; and *Ellis v. Dubowski* [1921] 3 K.B. 621, the latter two being cases of unlawful delegation of powers.] Another case on which Mr Gallop relied is *Roberts v. Hopwood* [1925] A.C. 578, [above, p. 321]. That was a totally different class of case. The district auditor had surcharged the members of a council who had made payments of a minimum wage of 4*l.* a week to their lowest grade of workers. That particular sum had been fixed by the local authority not by reference to any of the factors which go to determine a scale of wages, but by reference to some other principle altogether, and the substance of the decision was that they had not fixed 4*l.* a week as wages at all and that they had acted unreasonably. When the case is examined, the word "unreasonable" is found to be used rather in the sense that I mentioned a short while ago, namely, that in fixing 4*l.* they had fixed it by reference to a matter which they ought not to have taken into account and to the exclusion of those elements which they ought to have taken into consideration in fixing a sum which could fairly be called a wage. That is no authority whatsoever to support the proposition that the court has power, a sort of overriding power, to decide what is reasonable and what is unreasonable. The court has nothing of the kind....

In the result, this appeal must be dismissed. I do not wish to repeat myself but I will summarize once again the principle applicable. The court is entitled to investigate the action of the local authority with a view to seeing whether they have taken into account matters which they ought not to take into account, or, conversely, have refused to take into account or neglected to take into account matters which they ought to take into account. Once that question is answered in favour of the local authority, it may still be possible to say that, although the local authority have kept within the four corners of the matters which they ought to consider, they have nevertheless come to a conclusion so unreasonable that no reasonable authority could ever have come to it. In such a case, again, I think the court can interfere. The power of the court to interfere in each case is not as an appellate authority to override a decision of the local authority, but as a judicial authority which is concerned, and concerned only, to see whether the local authority have contravened the law by acting in excess of the powers which Parliament has confided in them. The appeal must be dismissed with costs.

SOMERVELL L.J. and SINGLETON L.J. agreed.

Appeal dismissed.

Notes

1. In addition to the regularly quoted words of Lord Greene M.R. a number of other formulations of this test of "unreasonableness" have been suggested. In each case the

courts have been concerned to stress the distinction between review on this ground and reconsideration on the merits.

Thus, in *R. v. Greenwich London Borough Council, ex p. Cedar Holdings* [1983] R.A. 173, Griffiths L.J. warned that a court might "all to easily [be] lure[d] ... into substituting its own view of the way in which the ... council should have exercised its discretion for that of the council itself". This temptation was, at all costs, to be avoided: "Only in a case where the decision of the council had been so outrageous that no right thinking person could support it would it be right to interfere...."

In *Council of Civil Service Unions v. Minister for the Civil Service* [1985] A.C. 374, 410, Lord Diplock, having described the basis of this challenge as challenge for "irrationality", commented: "It applies to a decision which is so outrageous in its defiance of logic or of accepted moral standards that no sensible person who had applied his mind to the question to be decided could have arrived at it." See further on this case, above, p. 173 and below, pp. 460–464.

In *Nottinghamshire County Council v. Secretary of State for the Environment* [1986] A.C. 240, 247, Lord Scarman explained that for this ground of challenge to succeed a decision must be so absurd that the decision-maker "must have taken leave of his senses".

Concern that the principle might, if stated in overly extreme terms, prove "awkward" for courts to apply even in appropriate cases led Lord Donaldson to express a preference for the expression *Wednesbury unreasonable* rather than the term *irrational*. In a situation where a usually reliable body has in a particular instance taken an unjustifiable decision, His Lordship felt that courts would feel more willing to intervene, and would cast less in the way of unnecessary aspersion, applying the former label than the latter: see *R. v. Devon County Council, ex p. G* [1989] A.C. 573 at 577.

This ground of challenge has been argued, and referred to by the courts, on many occasions. Very often the courts have adverted to the test to be applied only then to hold that on the facts the test has not been satisfied. In other words, reference to the *Wednesbury* principle has commonly been in order to emphasise the limits to the functions of a court of *review* as distinct from *appeal*. See, *e.g. Re Lamplugh* (1968) 19 P. & C.R. 125; *Manchester Corporation v. Connolly* [1970] 1 Ch. 420.

For a general survey, see G.L. Peiris, "*Wednesbury* Unreasonableness: The Expanding Canvas" [1987] C.L.J. 53.

2. Notwithstanding the frequency with which the courts have noted this ground of challenge only to hold that, on the facts, the challenge did not succeed, there have been a number cases where this principle *has* formed the basis (sometimes together with other grounds) of successful challenge. Thus, in *Backhouse v. Lambeth London Borough Council, The Times*, October 14, 1972, the Labour-controlled council resolved to increase the rent of a three-bedroomed council house (unoccupied since May 1972 because of deficiencies in the damp course) from some £7 to the massive £18,000 per week. Section 62(1) of the Housing Finance Act 1972 provided that: "Every local authority shall ... make the increases [*i.e.* towards fair rents] required by sections 63 and 64...." Section 63(1) provided that such increases should not be made "If the authority made a general rent increase in the first half of 1972–73 which produces £26 or more per dwelling in 1972–73...". The council hoped to avoid a general rent increase of 55p per week by putting all the increase contemplated by section 63(1) on one house. Any tenant would get an "enormous" rebate. B, the leader of the council tenants, sought a declaration that the resolution was valid. Melford Stevenson J., however, held that it was *ultra vires*. His Lordship held that this was a resolution at which no reasonable local authority could have arrived. It was admittedly designed and only designed to avoid or evade obligations cast on the council by the 1972 Act. Counsel for the Secretary of State for the Environment, who defended the case instead of the council, also submitted that the council had obviously ignored all relevant considerations.

In *West Glamorgan County Council v. Rafferty* [1987] 1 W.L.R. 457, the Court of Appeal held that the council had acted unreasonably in the *Wednesbury* sense in seeking an order for possession against gypsies occupying a council-owned site and causing a nuisance. The council had for over 10 years been in breach of its duty under section 6 of the Caravan Sites Act 1968 to provide adequate accommodation for gypsies in its area, and had not on this occasion made any arrangements for alternative accommodation. Ralph Gibson L.J. said (at 477):

> "The court is not, as I understand the law, precluded from finding a decision to be void for unreasonableness merely because there are admissible factors on both sides of the question. If the weight of the factors against eviction must be recognised by a reasonable council, properly aware of its duties and its powers, to be overwhelming, then a decision the other way cannot be upheld if challenged. The decision upon eviction was a decision which required the weighing of the factors according to the personal judgment of the councillors but the law does not permit complete freedom of choice or assessment because legal duty must be given proper weight."

This decision was distinguished by Rose J. in *R. v. Avon County Council, ex p. Rexworthy* (1988) 87 L.G.R. 470, where the council was held not to have acted unlawfully in seeking to evict gypsies from an encampment on a public highway where there was evidence of substantial obstruction and danger on and damage to the highway. The council was aware of its shortcomings in providing sites, and had not abandoned the search for alternative sites and had to balance its responsibilities to gypsies against its duties to highway users. *West Glamorgan County Council v. Rafferty* was also distinguished in *R. v. London Borough of Camden, ex p. Maugham and McDonagh* [1990] C.O.D. 390, where Otton J. refused to quash the council's decision to seek possession of two areas of land where gypsies were residing: the applicants were trespassers, there was a manifest nuisance, the council was not under a statutory duty towards them and, on the facts, the applicants had no legitimate expectation of an opportunity to make representations.

Given that there were "admissible factors on both sides of the question" in *Rafferty*, can it be said that the council "must have taken leave of its senses" in coming to its decision? If not, the case suggests that the test for unreasonableness is not in practice as extreme as the dicta cited in note 1 suggests. For comments on *Rafferty*, see R. Ward [1987] C.L.J. 374.

For further examples of successful challenge on *Wednesbury* grounds, see, *e.g. Niarchos (London) Ltd v. Secretary of State for the Environment and Westminster City Council (No. 2)* (1981) 79 L.G.R. 264; *R. v. London Borough of Haringey, ex p. Barrs* [1983] J.P.L. 54; *R. v. Immigration Appeal Tribunal, ex p. Manshoora Begum* [1986] Imm.A.R. 385; *R. v. Bolton Metropolitan Borough, ex p. B* [1985] F.L.R. 343; *R. v. Norfolk County Council, ex p. M* [1989] 2 All E.R. 359; *R. v. Barnet London Borough Council, ex p. Johnson* (1990) 89 L.G.R. 581; *R. v. Lewisham London Borough Council, ex p. P* [1991] 1 W.L.R. 308; *R. v. London Borough of Newham, ex p. Gentle* (1993) 26 H.L.R. 466; *R. v. Wiltshire County Council, ex p. D* [1994] 1 F.C.R. 172. The ground was also a part of the reasoning in the speeches of Lord Brandon in the *Bromley* case (above, p. 338) and of Lord Roskill in the *Wheeler* case (above, p. 317).

3. Note that the *Wednesbury* formula is also used by the courts for certain other purposes in the context of judicial review and appeals. See, *e.g.* the "no evidence" rule (below, p. 574), and the scope of review of the exercise of powers conferred in "subjective" form (below, p. 369).

4. "Unreasonableness" constitutes a ground upon which the validity of byelaws may be challenged—see *Kruse v. Johnson* [1898] 2 Q.B. 91 (below, p. 834).

5. It has been held that "irrationality" is not available as a ground of challenge where the decision has been approved by one or both Houses of Parliament. This point has arisen in cases where the Secretary of State for the Environment has sought to "cap" the expenditure of designated local authorities. The most recent decision is *R. v. Secretary of State for the Environment, ex p. Hammersmith and Fulham London Borough Council* [1991] 1 A.C. 521, where the House of Lords rejected challenges by 19

of 21 designated authorities to the Secretary of State's decisions under the Local Government Finance Act 1988, s.100, to impose maximum budgets. (This would in turn require each authority to set a lower level of community charge.) Lord Bridge, having rejected arguments based on illegality, continued (at 594–597):

"The remaining grounds of challenge fall under the heads of irrationality or procedural impropriety. Before turning to these grounds it is appropriate to consider whether any limitations upon the scope of judicial review are imposed by the subject-matter of the legislation. In this we are not without authoritative guidance.

In *R. v. Secretary of State for the Environment, ex p. Nottinghamshire County Council* [1986] A.C. 240, the House had to consider an earlier challenge to the action of the Secretary of State under the Local Government, Planning and Land Act' 1980 which had this in common with the action here in question that the "expenditure guidance" which the Secretary of State had there issued to local authorities and which the authorities sought to challenge had a directly restraining effect on the authorities' conduct of their financial affairs but before it could take effect required the approval by resolution of the House of Commons. The appellant authorities in that case had challenged the Secretary of State's statutory expenditure guidance on the ground, *inter alia*, that it was unreasonable as contravening the principles expounded in the judgment of Lord Greene M.R. in *Associated Provincial Picture Houses Ltd v. Wednesbury Corporation* [1948] 1 K.B. 223, 229, which is the classic statement of the basis for a challenge to an administrative decision on the ground of irrationality. Adverting to this challenge in the *Nottinghamshire* case [1986] A.C. 240, 247, Lord Scarman said:

'The submission raises an important question as to the limits of judicial review. We are in the field of public financial administration and we are being asked to review the exercise by the Secretary of State of an administrative discretion which inevitably requires a political judgment on his part and which cannot lead to action by him against a local authority unless that action is first approved by the House of Commons.... I cannot accept that it is constitutionally appropriate, save in very exceptional circumstances, for the courts to intervene on the ground of "unreasonableness" to quash guidance framed by the Secretary of State and by necessary implication approved by the House of Commons, the guidance being concerned with the limits of public expenditure by local authorities and the incidence of the tax burden as between taxpayers and ratepayers. Unless and until a statute provides otherwise, or it is established that the Secretary of State has abused his power, these are matters of political judgment for him and for the House of Commons. They are not for the judges or your Lordships' House in its judicial capacity. For myself, I refuse in this case to examine the detail of the guidance or its consequences. My reasons are these. Such an examination by a court would be justified only if a prima facie case were to be shown for holding that the Secretary of State had acted in bad faith, or for an improper motive, or that the consequences of his guidance were so absurd that he must have taken leave of his senses.'

Later he added, at 250–251:

'To sum it up, the levels of public expenditure and the incidence and distribution of taxation are matters for Parliament, and, within Parliament, especially for the House of Commons. If Parliament legislates, the courts have their interpretative role: they must, if called upon to do so, construe the statute. If a minister exercises a power conferred on him by the legislation, the courts can investigate whether he has abused his power. But if, as in this case, effect cannot be given to the Secretary of State's determination without the consent of the House of Commons and the House of Commons has consented, it is not open to the courts to intervene unless the minister and the House must have misconstrued the statute or the minister has—to put it bluntly—deceived the House. The courts can properly rule that a minister has acted unlawfully if he has erred in law as to the limits of his power even when his action has the approval of the House of Commons, itself acting not legislatively but within the limits set by a statute. But, if a statute, as in this case, requires the House of Commons to approve a minister's decision before he can lawfully enforce it, and if the action proposed complies with the terms of the statute (as your Lordships, I understand, are convinced that it does in the present case), it is not for the judges to say that the action has such unreasonable consequences that the guidance upon which the action is based and of which the House of Commons had notice was perverse and must be set aside. For that is a question of policy for the minister and the Commons, unless there has been bad faith or misconduct by the minister. Where Parliament has legislated that the action to be taken by the Secretary of State must, before it is taken, be approved by the House of Commons, it is no part of the judges' role to declare that the action proposed is unfair, unless it constitutes an abuse of power in the sense which I have explained; for Parliament has enacted that one of its Houses is responsible. Judicial review is a great weapon in the hands of the judges: but the judges must observe the constitutional limits set by our parliamentary system upon the exercise of this beneficent power.'

Lord Scarman's speech commanded the agreement of all members of the Appellate Committee participating in the decision, of whom I was one. I regard the opinions expressed in the passages quoted as an accurate formulation of an important restriction on the scope of judicial review which is precisely in point in the instant case. There is here no suggestion that the Secretary of State acted in bad faith or for an improper motive or that his decisions to designate the appellant authorities or the maximum amounts to which he decided to limit their budgets were so absurd that he must have taken leave of his senses. Short of such an extreme challenge, and provided always that the Secretary of State has acted within the four corners of the Act, I do not believe there is any room for an attack on the rationality of the Secretary of State's exercise of his powers under Part VII of the Act.

This accords with the view expressed by the Divisional Court, though they went on to examine on their merits and to reject the grounds relied on by the applicant authorities including those challenging the rationality of the Secretary of State's decisions and orders. The Court of Appeal expressed a somewhat different view. Referring to irrationality as a ground for judicial review of the exercise of a statutory discretion they said, *ante*, 935D–E:

'This head is relevant if it is alleged that the decision taker has had regard to matters which are legally irrelevant or has failed to have regard to matters which are legally relevant or that his decision would frustrate the policy of the Act upon which he relies for his authority: see *Padfield v. Minister of Agriculture, Fisheries and Food* [1968] A.C. 997. There is nothing in the judgments in the *Nottinghamshire* case [1986] A.C. 240 to suggest that this aspect of the jurisdictional head of "irrationality" has no application to decisions concerning public financial administration, whether or not they are also subject to review by one or both Houses of Parliament and no principle dictates that this should be the case.'

I think there is a danger of confusion in terminology here. If the court concludes, as the House did in the *Padfield* case [1986] A.C. 997, that a minister's exercise of a statutory discretion has been such as to frustrate the policy of the statute, that conclusion rests upon the view taken by the court of the true construction of the statute which the exercise of the discretion in question is then held to have contravened. The administrative action or inaction is then condemned on the ground of illegality. Similarly, if there are matters which, on the true construction of the statute conferring discretion, the person exercising the discretion must take into account and others which he may not take into account, disregard of those legally relevant matters or regard of those legally irrelevant matters will lay the decision open to review on the ground of illegality.

The restriction which the *Nottinghamshire* case [1986] A.C. 240 imposes on the scope of judicial review operates only when the court has first determined that the ministerial action in question does not contravene the requirements of the statute, whether express or implied, and only then declares that, since the statute has conferred a power on the Secretary of State which involves the formulation and the implementation of national economic policy and which can only take effect with the approval of the House of Commons, it is not open to challenge on the grounds of irrationality short of the extremes of bad faith, improper motive or manifest absurdity. Both the constitutional propriety and the good sense of this restriction seem to me to be clear enough. The formulation and the implementation of national economic policy are matters depending essentially on political judgment. The decisions which shape them are for politicians to take and it is in the political forum of the House of Commons that they are properly to be debated and approved or disapproved on their merits. If the decisions have been taken in good faith within the four corners of the Act, the merits of the policy underlying the decisions are not susceptible to review by the courts and the courts would be exceeding their proper function if they presumed to condemn the policy as unreasonable."

[His Lordship concluded that an argument that the determination was *Wednesbury* unreasonable, which he rejected on its merits (in agreement with the Court of Appeal) was in any event "inadmissible".]

This restriction has been the subject of academic criticism: see *Wade*, pp. 404, 405; C.M.G. Himsworth 1985 S.L.T. 369 and [1986] P.L. 139; and A.I.L. Campbell 1986 S.L.T. 101 (on the similar approach of the Court of Session in the context of statutory instruments in *City of Edinburgh District Council v. Secretary of State for Scotland* 1985 S.L.T. 551; Himsworth [1986] P.L. 347; R. Ward, (1986) 49 M.L.R. 645 (on the *Nottinghamshire* decision) and [1991] P.L. 76 (on the *Hammersmith* decision). On the other hand, the point can be made that it is difficult to see what grounds of challenge are actually excluded by the terms of Lord Bridge's speech, given that a challenge to the *merits* of a "capping" decision would not in any event fall within the *ultra vires* doctrine.

A different perspective is provided by Lord Irvine of Lairg Q.C. ("Judges and Decision-makers: The Theory and Practice of *Wednesbury* Review" [1996] P.L. 59, 66):

"The danger with Lord Bridge's judgment is that it suggests that there is a level of 'irrationality' short of manifest absurdity which may found judicial review *in the ordinary case*. This encourages applications on a false basis."

Lord Diplock's formulation of *Wednesbury* unreasonableness in the *CCSU* case (above, p. 463):

"leaves no scope for 'super-*Wednesbury* irrationality'" (at 66–67)

(the term coined by Simon Brown L.J. in *R. v. Ministry of Defence, ex p. Smith* [1995] 4 All E.R. 427, 441, 445).

Note that the principle was held not to be applicable to the scope of review of social security regulations which were held to be *ultra vires* because they rendered nugatory rights of asylum-seekers provided under separate, asylum, legislation: *R. v. Secretary of State for Social Security, ex p. Joint Council for the Welfare of Immigrants* [1996] 4 All E.R. 385.

It was also held not to be applicable in *ex p. Smith*, below, p. 358.

6. J. Jowell and A. Lester ("Beyond *Wednesbury*: Substantive Principles of Administrative Law" [1987] P.L. 368) argue persuasively that as a concept *"Wednesbury*

unreasonableness" is unsatisfactory (at 372–374). It is "inadequate", providing insufficient justification for judicial intervention:

> "Intellectual honesty requires a further and better explanation as to *why* the act is unreasonable. The reluctance to articulate a principled justification naturally encourages suspicion that prejudice or policy considerations may be hiding underneath *Wednesbury's* ample cloak."

It is "unrealistic", the courts in practice being "willing to impugn decisions that are far from absurd and are indeed often coldly rational". It is "confusing, because it is tautologous".

Instead, the courts should develop substantive principles of review, that prohibit decisions that are " 'irrational' in the accepted sense of that term" or arbitrary; that violate accepted standards of administrative probity (*e.g.* fraudulent decisions or decisions in bad faith) or good administrative practice (*e.g.* decisions that are unjustifiably inconsistent or disproportionate); or that violate fundamental rights and freedoms.

The courts have in recent years developed the concept of unjustifiable inconsistency (below, pp. 379–397). However, in the *Brind* case (below, pp. 397–404) the House of Lords has limited the extent to which administrators are to be required to take account of the European Convention on Human Rights, and has put the brakes on any development of "proportionality" as an independent ground of challenge. Furthermore, Lord Irvine of Lairg, writing before he was appointed Lord Chancellor, has argued that any extension of the *Wednesbury* grounds to enable judges to interfere more readily with the decisions of elected public authorities would be inconsistent with the "constitutional imperative of judicial self restraint" ("Judges and Decision-makers: The Theory and Practice of *Wednesbury* Review" [1996] P.L. 59).

A modern example of judicial discussion and application of *Wednesbury* unreasonableness is to be found in the *Smith* case extracted below.

R. v. MINISTRY OF DEFENCE, ex p. SMITH

[1996] 1 All E.R. 257; (Court of Appeal)

The four appellants, a lesbian and three homosexual men, were administratively discharged from service in the armed forces pursuant to a Ministry of Defence policy. The policy related to sexual orientation. It mandated discharge even without there being any evidence of overt sexual conduct; nor any evidence of an individual's ability to discharge responsibilities having been impaired. In fact all four servicemen were accepted to have exemplary service records. The appellants sought judicial review of the Ministry of Defence policy. The Divisional Court held the Ministry policy to be lawful. The appellants appealed to the Court of Appeal.

SIR THOMAS BINGHAM M.R.: . . . The appellants challenge the lawfulness of their discharge and thus, indirectly, of the policy which required them to be discharged. They say that the policy is irrational, and in breach of the European Convention for the Protection of Human Rights and Fundamental Freedoms (Rome, November 4, 1950; T.S. 71 (1953); Cmd. 8969) and contrary to Council Directive (EEC) 76/207 on the implementation of the principle of equal treatment for men and women as regards access to employment, vocational training and promotion, and working conditions. They accept without reservation that any member of the armed services who acts inappropriately towards any other member, or who is guilty of any harassment, or who commits any offence or breach of service discipline, may be discharged administratively, if not on disciplinary grounds. So too, if a member's sexual orientation undermines that member's efficiency as a member of the service or is shown to cause demonstrable damage to the service. They claim no right or liberty to commit homosexual acts or to make homosexual advances on the mess-deck or in the barrack-room or in any other service setting. The accept that membership of a disciplined fighting force involves a curtailment of freedoms enjoyed by others in civilian employments, and recognise that the exigencies of service life may properly justify restrictions on homosexual activity and manifestations of homosexual orientation. Their challenge is, and is only, to the blanket, non-discretionary, unspecific nature of the existing policy.

Background

There can be no doubt that public attitudes to homosexuals and homosexuality have in the past varied widely from country to country, and within the same country at different times, and among different social groups in the same country. Almost any generalisation can be faulted. But there has in this country been a discernible trend, over the last half century or so, towards greater understanding and greater tolerance of homosexuals by heterosexuals, and towards greater openness and honesty by homosexuals. In part this trend has prompted, in part it may have been a result of, legislative change.

Section 1(1) of the Sexual Offences Act 1967 decriminalised homosexual acts between consenting adults in private. It only applied to males, since homosexual acts between women were not criminal anyway. This legislative change, now nearly 30 years ago, followed and gave effect to the *Report of the Committee on Homosexual Offences and Prostitution* (Cmnd. 247) (the Wolfenden Committee) in 1957. At that time very few European countries took cognisance of homosexual behaviour between consenting parties in private (see para. 59 and App III of the report). It does not appear that that committee addressed the issues with specific reference to the armed forces. But it is important to note that s.1(1) of the Act did not, by virtue of s.1(5), prevent a homosexual act being an offence (other than a civil offence) under the statutes governing the three services. Any person subject to those statutes remained liable to punishment for homosexual acts. So, by s.2 of the 1967 Act, did the crew of British merchant ships. Plainly, the view was then taken that to permit homosexual acts by or between members of the armed services, or in the special conditions pertaining aboard ship, would be subversive of discipline, efficiency and good order.

The routine quinquennial review of the statutes governing the armed forces has the effect that issues such as the treatment of homosexuals are reconsidered periodically. In 1986 a Select Committee of the House of Commons, despite argument that service law should be brought into line with civilian law, concluded that the law should remain as it then stood. But opinion did not stand still. In 1991 another House of Commons Select Committee returned to the subject. Submissions were then made that service law should be brought into line with civilian law and that homosexual orientation *alone* should not be a bar to membership of the armed forces. The Select Committee accepted the first of these submissions, seeing "no reason why Service personnel should be liable to prosecution under Service law for homosexual activity which would be legal in civilian law" (see *Special Report from the Select*

Committee on the Armed Forces Bill (H.C. Paper (1990–1991) No. 179, para. 41). But they rejected the second submission, concluding that there was "considerable force to MoD's argument that the presence of people known to be homosexual can cause tension in a group of people required to live and work sometimes under great stress and physically at very close quarters, and thus damage its cohesion and fighting effectiveness" (see para. 40). The Select Committee were not persuaded in 1991 that the time had yet come to permit the armed forces to accept homosexuals or homosexual activity.

In 1992 the responsible minister announced that in future individuals who engaged in homosexual activity that was legal in civilian law would not be prosecuted under service law. For want of parliamentary time, legislative effect was not given to this change until 1994, when s.146(1) of the Criminal Justice and Public Order Act 1994 was enacted. But s.146(4) provided that this change should not prevent a homosexual act (with or without other acts or circumstances) from constituting a ground for discharging a member of the armed forces.

In upholding the existing policy that homosexual activity or orientation should be an absolute bar to membership of the armed forces, the 1991 Select Committee undoubtedly reflected the overwhelming consensus of service and official opinion in this country. It does not appear that the Select Committee required or received any evidence of actual harm done by sexual orientation alone or by private homosexual activity outside the context of service life. Nor does the Select Committee appear to have considered whether the objectives of the existing policy could be met by a rule less absolute in its effect than that which was then applied.

In other areas of national life opinion has shifted. In July 1991 the Prime Minister announced that neither homosexual orientation nor private homosexual activity should henceforth preclude appointment even to sensitive posts in the home civil service and the diplomatic service. Lord Mackay of Clashfern L.C. has made similar announcements in relation to judicial office. In July 1994 the Royal Fleet Auxiliary introduced an equal opportunities policy stating that it did not discriminate on grounds of homosexuality. A majority of police forces now follow the same policy.

Outside the United Kingdom also, opinion has not stood still. Very few NATO countries bar homosexuals from their armed forces. This practice does not appear to have precluded the closest co-operation between such forces and our own. In the course of 1992–1993 Australia, New Zealand and Canada relaxed their ban on homosexuals in their armed services but, importantly, introduced codes of conduct which defined the forms of homosexual conduct which were judged to be unacceptable. In the United States, on the other hand, as an authoritative report in 1993 made plain, military opinion remained overwhelmingly against allowing homosexuals to serve. The lawfulness of the legislative compromise adopted in that country is in doubt (see *Able v. U.S.* (1995) 880 F. Supp 968 at 975). In arguing that case the U.S. government "recognized that a policy mandating discharge of homosexuals merely because they have a homosexual orientation or status could not withstand judicial scrutiny".

I regard the progressive development and refinement of public and professional opinion at home and abroad, here very briefly described, as an important feature of this case. A belief which represented unquestioned orthodoxy in Year X may have become questionable by Year Y, and unsustainable by Year Z. Public and professional opinion are a continuum. The four appellants were discharged towards the end of 1994. The lawfulness of their discharge falls to be judged as of that date.

Irrationality

(1)*The test*
Mr Davick Pannick Q.C. (who represented three of the appellants, and whose arguments were adopted by the fourth) submitted that the court should adopt the following approach to the issue of irrationality:

> "The court may not interfere with the exercise of an administrative discretion on substantive grounds save where the court is satisfied that the decision is unreasonable in the sense that it is beyond the range of responses open to a reasonable decision-maker. But in judging whether the decision-maker has exceeded this margin of appreciation the human rights context is important. The more substantial the interference with human rights, the more the court will require by way of justification before it is satisfied that the decision is reasonable in the sense outlined above."

This submission is in my judgment an accurate distillation of the principles laid down by the House of Lords in *Bugdaycay v. Secretary of State for the Home Dept* [1987] 1 All E.R. 940; [1987] A.C. 514 and *Brind v. Secretary of State for the Home Dept* [1991] 1 All E.R. 720, [1991] 1 AC 696. In the first of these cases Lord Bridge of Harwich said ([1987] 1 All E.R. 940 at 952; [1987] A.C. 514 at 531):

> "I approach the question raised by the challenge to the Secretary of State's decision on the basis of the law stated earlier in this opinion, *viz.* that the resolution of any issue of fact and the exercise of any discretion in relation to an application for asylum as a refugee lie exclusively within the jurisdiction of the Secretary of State subject only to the court's power of review. The limitations on the scope of that power are well known and need not be restated here. Within those limitations the court must, I think, be entitled to subject an administrative decision to the more rigorous examination, to ensure that it is in no way flawed, according to the gravity of the issue which the decision determines. The most fundamental of all human rights is the individual's right to life and, when an administrative decision under challenge is said to be one which may put the applicant's life at risk, the basis of the decision must surely call for the most anxious scrutiny."

Lord Templeman spoke to similar effect (see [1987] 1 All E.R. 940 at 956; [1987] A.C. 514 at 537). In the second case, having concluded that it was not open to an English court to apply the European Convention on Human Rights, Lord Bridge said ([1991] 1 All E.R. 720 at 723; [1991] 1 A.C. 696 at 748–749):

> "But I do not accept that this conclusion means that the courts are powerless to prevent the exercise by the executive of administrative discretions, even when conferred, as in the instant case, in terms which are on their face

unlimited, in a way which infringes fundamental human rights. Most of the rights spelled out in terms in the convention, including the right to freedom of expression, are less than absolute and must in some cases yield to the claims of competing public interests. Thus, art. 10(2) of the convention spells out and categorises the competing public interests by reference to which the right to freedom of expression may have to be curtailed. In exercising the power of judicial review we have neither the advantages nor the disadvantages of any comparable code to which we may refer or by which we are bound. But again, this surely does not mean that in deciding whether the Secretary of State, in the exercise of his discretion, could reasonably impose the restriction he has imposed on the broadcasting organisations, we are not perfectly entitled to start from the premise that any restriction of the right to freedom of expression requires to be justified and that nothing less than an important competing public interest will be sufficient to justify it. The primary judgment as to whether the particular competing public interest justifies the particular restriction imposed falls to be made by the Secretary of State to whom Parliament has entrusted the discretion. But we are entitled to exercise a secondary judgment by asking whether a reasonable Secretary of State, on the material before him, could reasonably make that primary judgment."

Again, Lord Templeman spoke to similar effect ([1991] 1 All E.R. 720 at 726; [1991] 1 A.C. 696 at 751):

"It seems to me that the courts cannot escape from asking themselves only whether a reasonable Secretary of State, on the material before him, could reasonably conclude that the interference with freedom of expression which he determined to impose was justifiable."

It was argued for the ministry, in reliance on *Nottinghamshire C.C. v. Secretary of State for the Environment* [1986] 1 All E.R. 199; [1986] A.C. 240 and *Hammersmith and Fulham London B.C. v. Secretary of State for the Environment* [1990] 3 All E.R. 589; [1991] 1 A.C. 521, that a test more exacting than *Wednesbury* was appropriate in this case (see *Associated Provincial Picture Houses Ltd v. Wednesbury Corp.* [1947] 2 All E.R. 680; [1948] 1 K.B. 223). The Divisional Court rejected this argument and so do I. The greater the policy content of a decision, and the more remote the subject matter of a decision from ordinary judicial experience, the more hesitant the court must necessarily be in holding a decision to be irrational. That is good law and, like most good law, common sense. Where decisions of a policy-laden, esoteric or security-based nature are in issue, even greater caution than normal must be shown in applying the test, but the test itself is sufficiently flexible to cover all situations.

The present cases do not affect the lives or liberty of those involved. But they do concern innate qualities of a very personal kind and the decisions of which the appellants complain have had a profound effect on their careers and prospects. The appellants' right as human beings are very much in issue. It is now accepted that this issue is justiciable. This does not of course mean that the court is thrust into the position of the primary decision-maker. It is not the constitutional role of the court to regulate the conditions of service in the armed forces of the Crown, nor has it the expertise to do so. But it has the constitutional role and duty of ensuring that the rights of citizens are not abused by the unlawful exercise of executive power. While the court must properly defer to the expertise of responsible decision-makers, it must not shrink from its fundamental duty to "do right to all manner of people".

(b) *The facts*

The reasons underlying the present policy were given in an affidavit sworn by Air Chief Marshall Sir John Willis K.C.B. C.B.E., the vice-chief of the defence staff, an officer of great seniority and experience. The relevant paragraphs of his affidavit have been recited in full by Simon Brown L.J. in his judgment in the Divisional Court, and it is unnecessary to duplicate that recital. Sir John advanced three reasons. The first related to morale and unit effectiveness, the second to the role of the services as guardian of recruits under the age of 18, and the third to the requirement of communal living in many service situations. Sir John described the ministry's policy as based not on a moral judgment but on a practical assessment of the implications of homosexual orientation on military life. By "a practical assessment" Sir John may have meant an assessment of past experience in practice, or he may have meant an assessment of what would be likely to happen in practice if the present policy were varied. His affidavit makes no reference to any specific past experience, despite the fact that over the years very many homosexuals must have served in the armed forces. He does, however, make clear the apprehension of senior service authorities as to what could happen if the existing policy were revoked or varied, and the grounds upon which he relies were the subject of consideration by the House of Commons Select Committees to which reference has already been made.

The first factor relied on by Sir John, morale and unit effectiveness, was the subject of searing criticism by Mr Pannick. He submitted that the effect of a homosexual member of any military unit would depend on the character, ability and personality of the member involved. He pointed out that many homosexuals had successfully served in the services over the years. He drew attention to the experience of other disciplined forces such as the police. He submitted that inappropriate behaviour by homosexual members of the armed forces could be effectively regulated. He submitted that the ministry should not be deterred from doing what fairness and good sense demanded by apprehensions of irrational and prejudiced behaviour on the part of others.

Mr Pannick also criticised the second factor relied on by Sir John. He pointed out that any service member behaving inappropriately towards an under-age member of the service could be disciplined and punished in the same way as in society at large. He rejected the suggestion that homosexuals were less able to control their sexual impulses than heterosexuals. Again he suggested that the policy of the ministry was pandering to ignorant prejudice.

Mr Pannick accepted, of course, that members of the services could in many situations find themselves living together in conditions of very close proximity, although he pointed out that one of the appellants (by reason of his seniority) and another of the appellants (by reason of her particular occupation) were in no foreseeable situation likely to share accommodation with anyone. The lack of privacy in service life was, he suggested, a reason for imposing strict rules and discipline, but not a reason for banning the membership of any homosexual. He drew attention to the experience of other disciplined services. He pointed out that each of the appellants had worked in the armed forces for a number of years without any concern being expressed or complaints made about inappropriate bnehaviour. Each of them had earned very favourable reports. The same, it was said, was true of many other homosexual members of the services.

Above all, Mr Pannick criticised the blanket nature of the existing rule. He placed great emphasis on the practice of other nations whose rules were framed so as to counter the particular mischiefs to which homosexual orientation or activity might give rise. He pointed out that other personal problems such as addiction to alcohol, or compulsive gambling, or marital infidelity were dealt with by the service authorities on a case by case basis and not on the basis of a rule which permitted no account to be taken of the peculiar features of the case under consideration.

The arguments advanced by Mr Pannick are in my opinion of very considerable cogency. They call to be considered in depth, with particular reference to specific evidence of past experience in this country, to the developing experience of other countries, and to the potential effectiveness or otherwise of a detailed prescriptive code along the lines adopted elsewhere in place of the present blanket ban. Such a reassessment of the existing policy is already, as I have noted, in train, and I note that the next Select Committee quinquennial review of the policy is to receive a departmental paper of evidence covering all the matters canvassed on this appeal. What the outcome of that review will be, I do not know.

The existing policy cannot in my judgment be stigmatised as irrational at the time when these appellants were discharged. It was supported by both Houses of Parliament and by those to whom the ministry properly looked for professional advice. There was, to my knowledge, no evidence before the ministry which plainly invalidated that advice. Changes made by other countries were in some cases very recent. The Australian, New Zealand and Canadian codes had been adopted too recently to yield much valuable experience. The ministry did not have the opportunity to consider the full range of arguments developed before us. Major policy changes should be the product of mature reflection, not instant reaction. The threshold of irrationality is a high one. It was not crossed in this case.

The European Convention

Article 8 of the European Convention on Human Rights provides:

"1. Everyone has the right to respect for his private and family life, his home and his correspondence.

2. There shall be no interference by a public authority with the exercise of this right except such as is in accordance with the law and is necessary in a democratic society in the interests of national security, public safety or the economic well-being of the country, for the prevention of disorder or crime, for the protection of health or morals, or for the protection of the rights and freedoms of others."

It is, inevitably, common ground that the United Kingdom's obligation, binding in international law, to respect and secure compliance with this article is not one that is enforceable by domestic courts. The relevance of the convention in the present context is as background to the complaint of irrationality. The fact that a decision-maker failed to take account of convention obligations when exercising an administrative discretion is not of itself a ground for impugning that exercise of discretion.

... I would dismiss these appeals.

HENRY L.J.: ... I agree with the judgment of Sir Thomas Bingham M.R. I will add some words of my own on the first and second topics.

Irrationality

On the evidence before us, our armed forces have had a long-standing absolute prohibition on those known to be homosexual joining or, once discovered, remaining in the armed forces. We are told that that policy existed throughout the years of conscription (1939 to 1960). This fact may surprise post-war national servicemen, whom I believe to have been generally unaware that a genuine homosexual orientation would have rendered them exempt from compulsory national service, but their ignorance is explained before us on the basis that the policy did not need to be publicised, committed to paper, or indeed specifically addressed until some time after male homosexual acts between consenting adults in private were decriminalised in civilian life (though not under military law) in 1967.

Despite this ban (and in the early years, perhaps as a result of ignorance of it) it seems to be realistically accepted on all sides that the reality is that many more homosexuals served in the armed forces than the relatively small numbers dismissed for it either on disciplinary grounds relating to their conduct (the minority) or on administrative grounds based on their status as homosexuals (the vast majority, at any rate in recent years). This suggests that the majority of serving homosexuals were undetected and had a useful and productive service life and that there had been nothing in their conduct which either disclosed their sexual orientation or threatened the cohesion of their units. This experience clearly should not be disregarded when considering the necessity for an absolute ban, especially as that experience is replicated in the case histories of the appellants before us.

Additionally, over the years since the passing of the Sexual Offences Act 1967, there can be no doubt that public opinion has moved a very long way towards toleration and acceptance of homosexuals (as Lord Wolfenden himself commented as long ago as 1976 in his autobiography *Turning Points*, pp. 144–146). We have seen a greater and greater public awareness and acceptance of homosexuality, together with a greater personal openness in acknowledging it. Consequently there has been a growing recognition of the specific human rights of homosexuals, including rights in the workplace.

But both sides of the argument as to acceptance of homosexuals in the armed forces accept first that the armed forces are quite unlike any other employer, that military life is quite different from civilian life, and second that the forces can properly demand (and those serving must unquestioningly accept) restriction on their liberty and behaviour that would not be acceptable if imposed on a citizen in civilian life. It is accepted that these personal sacrifices can be demanded and must be made in the interests of the overall goal of military effectiveness, based on high morale, good discipline and unit cohesion. It is accepted that certain conduct, whether homosexual or heterosexual, can threaten military effectiveness, and so can reasonably be proscribed by the armed forces where a civilian employer could not lawfully do so. For example, in America in 1993 the National Defense Research Institute (RAND), given by the Secretary of Defense the task of preparing a draft of an executive order "ending discrimination on the basis of sexual orientation in determining who may serve in the Armed Forces" in a way which was "practical and realistic, and consistent with the high standards of combat effectiveness and unit cohesion our Armed Forces must maintain", found that the only policy option to achieve that result was one conduct-based, commenting, "all personnel, including acknowledged homosexuals, must understand that the military environment is no place to advertise one's sexual orientation". (To like effect is the Australian Defence Force which in Annex B to its statement of policy on "Unacceptable Sexual Behaviour by Members of the Australian Defence Force" which may threaten operational effectiveness includes, for example "public flaunting and advocacy of a particular sexual proclivity".)

So the plaintiffs here accept the legitimacy of the armed forces achieving their aim by a non-discriminatory, conduct-based code restricting expression or other manifestation of their sexual orientation. What they challenge is the legitimacy of a status-based absolute proscription of all homosexuals in the armed forces, however exemplary their service conduct.

The sole question on the irrationality issue is, accepting the formulation as proposed by Mr Pannick Q.C. and accepted by Sir Thomas Bingham M.R., whether it was irrational at the end of 1994, when these appellants were discharged, for the defendants still to have in place an absolute proscription of all homosexuals.

I agree with Sir Thomas Bingham M.R. it was not. I would add only these remarks to his reasons. On the evidence before us, the issue between a conduct-based code or status-based ban was a relatively new one. It does not seem to have been raised before the Select Committee in 1986. It was raised in broad terms by the Stonewall Group in 1991. The Select Committee recognised that there was much more tolerance of differences in sexual orientation both without and (possibly) within the armed forces. But they were not persuaded that the time had yet come to require the armed forces to accept homosexuals.

But the clock did not stop there. Since then Canada, Australia and New Zealand all (in 1992 or 1993) moved away from an absolute ban, and the American middle position of "Don't ask, don't tell" is under powerful legal attack, with the last appellate word probably not yet said (see *Able v. U.S.* (1995) 880 F. Supp 968). All these were matters to be taken into consideration when the individual decision in these cases were taken.

It would seem that the movement in public opinion recognised by the Select Committee is continuing, and it might be that positions within the armed forces of Canada, Australia and New Zealand have shifted also—though the evidence does not make this clear. But the advice received from those with experience in our armed forces remained the same: that the absolute ban was necessary for the reasons stated. We know from the material before us the substance of that advice and the assertions contained in it, but we do not know details of the experience which informed that advice. Hence the lawyers' criticism that the advice is not based on evidence. I would not at this stage of the debate assume that the views of the armed forces are not based on evidence, though that evidence is not before us.

Those responsible for the policy were faced with a rapidly changing scene on a highly charged issue of great importance to both the armed forces and the individuals. That combination of circumstances points against precipitate action both by the policy maker with primary responsibility and, a fortiori, by the reviewing court in its secondary role. At the end of 1994 it could not be said that reasonable decision-makers must inevitably conclude that the existing policy was unlawful and so must be changed. It was not legally irrational to continue the policy. What was needed is what has now been set up—namely the ministry preparing a paper of evidence to assist the Select Committee. I am pleased to see that there are to be visits to overseas armed forces, as I was not persuaed by the bald submission in evidence that "comparison with other countries does not assist". In the balance, proper appreciation will have to be given both to the impact of a total ban on the human rights of the affected individuals, and to any practical justification for that ban and the evidence supporting it.

THORPE L.J.: I agree with both the preceding judgments . . .

Notes

1. See case note by M. Norris [1996] P.L. 590.

2. The case is of particular interest in its exploration of the applicability of *Wednesbury* principles in the context of the protection of human rights. Note (1) the recognition that the appellants' human rights were "very much in issue"; (2) the proposition that the

> "more substantial the interference with human rights, the more the court will require by way of justification before it is satisfied that the decison is reasonable";

and (3) the rejection of the Ministry's attempt to invoke the so-called "super-*Wednesbury*" standard of even greater deference to the decision-maker than the norm (based on the *Nottinghamshire* and *Hammersmith* cases, above, pp. 354–357). In the course of dealing with the third of these points, Sir Thomas Bingham M.R. stated that

> "The greater the policy content of a decision, and the more remote the subject matter of a decision from ordinary judicial experience, the more hesitant the court must necessarily be in holding the decison to be irrational."

Is this in fact reconcilable with proposition (2)? Does proposition (2) in reality involve "lowering the threshold of unreasonableness", a step rejected as impermissible by Neill L.J. in *R. v. Secretary of State for the Environment, ex p. NALGO* (1992) 5 Admin.L.R. 785, 798 and criticised by Lord Irvine of Lairg, in "Judges and Decision-makers: The Theory and Practice of *Wednesbury* Review" [1996] P.L. 59, 63–65 (see discussion by Norris [1996] P.L. 590, 593–597).

(ii) Express Requirements of Reasonableness

In some instances a grant of discretionary power may expressly provide that the power is only to be exercisable "reasonably," or is only to be exercisable where the body in question has "reasonable" grounds to consider that certain defined circumstances exist. In such cases the courts may consider whether the positive requirement of reasonableness has been satisfied. They will not be restricted to a consideration of whether the decision on the relevant issue is "so unreasonable...". The extent to which a reviewing court will be willing to substitute its own judgment of reasonableness for that of the statutorily designated body may depend on context. Compare the decisions in *Nakkuda Ali* and *Luby v. Newcastle-under-Lyme Corp.* [1965] 1 Q.B. 214 (requirement that rents be "reasonable": *per* Diplock L.J., "a matter with which the knowledge and experience of [the local] authority can best be trusted to deal": "reasonable" interpreted as "not unreasonable").

NAKKUDA ALI v. M.F. de S. JAYARATNE

[1951] A.C. 66; 66 T.L.R. (Pt 2) 214; 94 S.J. 516
sub nom. Ali v. Jayaratne
(Privy Council on appeal from the Supreme Court of Ceylon)

The respondent, the Controller of Textiles in Ceylon, exercised his power to cancel a textile dealer's licence "where the Controller has reasonable grounds to believe that any dealer is unfit to be allowed to continue as a dealer". The appellant sought a mandate in the nature of certiorari to quash the cancellation on the ground of breach of natural justice. The Privy Council held that there had been no breach, but that in any event certiorari would not lie as the Controller was not acting judicially but taking executive action to withdraw a privilege. This general aspect of the case is discussed by Lord Reid in *Ridge v. Baldwin* (below, p. 424). One specific point dealt with by the Privy Council was whether the requirement that the Controller have "reasonable grounds" indicated that he was acting judicially, which was the view of the Supreme Court.

LORD RADCLIFFE delivered the opinion of the Privy Council (LORDS PORTER, OAKSEY and RADCLIFFE, SIR JOHN BEAUMONT and SIR LIONEL LEACH): ... It would be impossible to consider the significance of such words as "Where the Controller has reasonable grounds to believe..." without taking account of the decision of the House of Lords in *Liversidge v. Sir John Anderson* [1942] A.C. 206. That decision related to a claim for damages for false imprisonment, the imprisonment having been brought about by an order made by the Home Secretary under the Defence (General) Regulations, 1939, reg. 18B, of the United Kingdom. It was not a case that had any direct bearing on the court's power to issue a writ of certiorari to the Home Secretary in respect of action taken under that regulation: but it did directly involve a question as to the meaning of the words "If the Secretary of State has reasonable cause to believe any person to be of hostile origin or associations..." which appeared at the opening of the regulation in question. And the decision of the majority of the House did lay down that those words in that context meant no more than that the Secretary of State had honestly to suppose that he had reasonable cause to believe the required thing. On that basis, granted good faith, the maker of the order appears to be the only possible judge of the conditions of his own jurisdiction.

Their Lordships do not adopt a similar construction of the words in reg. 62 which are now before them. Indeed, it would be a very unfortunate thing if the decision of *Liversidge's* case came to be regarded as laying down any general rule as to the construction of such phrases when they appear in statutory enactments. It is an authority for the proposition that the words "if A.B. has reasonable cause to believe" are capable of meaning "if A.B. honestly thinks that he has reasonable cause to believe" and that in the context and attendant circumstances of Defence Regulation 18B they did in fact mean just that. But the elaborate consideration which the majority of the House gave to the context and circumstances before adopting that construction itself shows that there is no general principle that such words are to be so understood; and the dissenting speech of Lord Atkin at least serves as a reminder of the many occasions when they have been treated as meaning "if there is in fact reasonable cause for A.B. so to believe". After all, words such as these are commonly found when a legislature or law-making authority confers powers on a minister or official. However read, they must be intended to serve in some sense as a condition limiting the exercise of an otherwise arbitrary power. But if the question whether the condition has been satisfied is to be conclusively decided by the man who yields the power the value of the intended restraint is in effect nothing. No doubt he must not exercise the power in bad faith: but the field in which this kind of question arises is such that the reservation for the case of bad faith is hardly more than a formality. Their Lordships therefore treat the words in reg. 62, "where the Controller has reasonable grounds to believe that any dealer is unfit to be allowed to continue as a dealer" as imposing a condition that there must in fact exist such reasonable grounds, known to the Controller, before he can validly exercise the power of cancellation....

Notes

1. This aspect of *Nakkuda Ali v. Jayaratne* is generally accepted as correct. See Lord Reid in *Ridge v. Baldwin*, below, p. 424, and *IRC v. Rossminster Ltd* [1980] A.C. 952—concession by IRC on this point. *Liversidge v. Anderson* was not relied upon by the Solicitor-General in *Secretary of State for Employment v. ASLEF (No. 2)* [1972] 2 Q.B. 443.

2. *Liversidge v. Anderson* [1942] A.C. 206 is a notorious case, but highly exceptional. For discussion, see *Garner*, pp. 321–323; *de Smith*, pp. 304 *et seq.*; R.F.V. Heuston, *Essays in Constitutional Law*, pp. 171–177; *Allen*, pp. 256, 297 and Appendix 1; R.F.V. Heuston, "*Liversidge v. Anderson* in Retrospect" (1970) 86 L.Q.R. 33, and "*Liversidge v. Anderson*, Two Footnotes" (1971) 87 L.Q.R. 161.

(iii) Reasonableness and Subjective Powers

The next issue to consider is the scope of review in situations where the grant of power is in "subjective" form—*i.e.* where it is power to act in circumstances which are "believed" to prevail, or to do such things as are considered appropriate in the judgment of the donee of the power (*e.g.* to impose such conditions as a body thinks fit). It might be argued that the intention of the legislation is, here, to exclude judicial review, or at least to restrict it to issues of "good faith" and actual honest belief. In fact the courts have been unwilling to accept such a limited power of review and have utilised the *Wednesbury* formula to strike down decisions based on honest but unreasonable subjective belief. This matter is considered fully in the extracts from the *Tameside* case (below).

SECRETARY OF STATE FOR EDUCATION AND SCIENCE v. METROPOLITAN BOROUGH OF TAMESIDE

[1977] A.C. 1014; [1976] 3 All E.R. 665; [1976] 3 W.L.R. 641
(Court of Appeal; House of Lords)

In March 1975, the defendant local education authority, then Labour-controlled, submitted a scheme to the Secretary of State under section 13 of the Education Act 1944, for the introduction of comprehensive education in schools in their area; these proposals were approved by the Secretary of State. In May 1976, the balance of political power was changed at the local government elections, and the authority came under the control of the Conservative party, who had promised in their election propaganda to reconsider the question of comprehensive education. The authority decided to modify the decision made in 1975 and to retain five grammar schools, at least for the school year commencing September, 1976, although arrangements to convert them to "comprehensives" were already in hand. The Secretary of State formed the opinion that the authority were acting unreasonably in so deciding, and accordingly he gave them a formal direction under section 68 of the Education Act 1944 (see below) to the effect that they were required to implement the 1975 scheme. The defendant authority refused to accept this, and the Secretary of State applied for an order of mandamus against the authority requiring them to comply with his direction. An order of mandamus was granted by the Divisional Court on July 12, 1976, but this order was quashed by the Court of Appeal (Lord Denning M.R., Scarman and Geoffrey Lane L.JJ.) on July 26, 1976, and the Court of Appeal's decision was upheld by the House of Lords on August 2, 1976.

Section 68 of the Education Act 1944 provides as follows:

"If the Secretary of State is satisfied, either on complaint by any person or otherwise, that any local education authority ... have acted or are proposing to act unreasonably with respect to the exercise of any power conferred or the performance of any duty imposed by or under this Act, he may ... give such directions as to the exercise of the power or the performance of the duty as appear to him to be expedient."

[In the Court of Appeal]

LORD DENNING M.R.: ... It was suggested in one place in the papers—on June 21, 1976 by the chief officers of the council—that once the Secretary of State said he was "satisfied", his decision could not be challenged in the courts unless it was shown to be made in bad faith. We were referred by counsel for the Secretary of State to *Liversidge v. Anderson* ([1942] A.C. 206, at 233) where Lord Atkin drew attention to cases where the Defence Regulations required the Secretary of State to be "satisfied" of something or other. Lord Atkin said: "In all these cases, it is plain that unlimited discretion is given to the Secretary of State assuming, as everyone does, that he acts in good faith" to which I would add a similar passage by Somervell L.J. in *Robinson v. Minister of Town and Country Planning* ([1947] K.B. 702, at 721). Those statements were made, however, in regard to regulations in war time or immediately after the war when the decisions of the executive had to be implemented speedily and without question. That was pointed out by Lord Radcliffe in *Nakkuda Ali v. M.F. de S. Jayaratne* ([1951] A.C. 66 at 77) and by Lord Reid in *Ridge v. Baldwin* ([1964] A.C. 40 at 73). Those statements do not apply today. Much depends on the matter about which the Secretary of State has to be satisfied. If he is to be satisfied on the matter of opinion, that is one thing. But if he has to be satisfied that someone has been guilty of some discreditable or unworthy or unreasonable conduct, that is another. To my mind, if a statute gives a Minister power to take drastic action if he is satisfied that a local authority have acted or are proposing to act improperly or unreasonably, then the Minister should obey all the elementary rules of fairness before he finds that the local authority are guilty or before he takes drastic action overruling them. He should give the party affected notice of the charge of impropriety or unreasonableness and a fair opportunity of dealing with it. I am glad to see that the Secretary of State did so in this case. He had before him the written proposals of the new council and he met their leaders. In addition, however, the Minister must direct himself properly in law. He must call his own attention to the matters he is bound to consider. He must exclude from his consideration matters which are irrelevant to that which he has to consider. And the decision to which he comes must be one which is reasonable in this sense, that it is, or can be, supported with good reasons or at any rate be a decision which a reasonable person might reasonably reach. Such is, I think, plain from *Padfield v. Minister of Agriculture, Fisheries and Food* ([1968] A.C. 997), which is a landmark in our administrative law and which we had in mind in *Secretary of State for Employment v. Associated Society of Locomotive Engineers and Firemen (No. 2)* ([1972] 2 Q.B. 455). So much for the requirements if the Minister is to be "satisfied"....

[His Lordship held that the Secretary of State must have misdirected himself on the interpretation of "unreasonableness", and that there was no evidence on which the Secretary of State could declare himself satisfied that the council were proposing to act unreasonably.]

SCARMAN L.J. [delivered a concurring judgment, which included the following passage]: ... I do not accept that the scope of judicial review is limited to quite the extent suggested by counsel for Secretary of State [*i.e.* to bad faith, misdirection in law, taking account of irrelevant matters, omitting to consider relevant matters, taking a view that no reasonable man could take]. I would add a further situation to those specified by him; misunderstanding or ignorance of an established and relevant fact. Let me give two examples. The fact may be either physical, something which existed or occurred or did not, or it may be mental, an opinion. Suppose that, contrary to the Secretary of State's belief, it was the fact that there was in the area of the authority adequate school accommodation for the pupils to be educated, and the Secretary of State acted under the section believing that there was not. If it were plainly established that the Secretary of State were mistaken, I do not think that he could substantiate the lawfulness of his direction under this section. Now, more closely to the facts of this case, taking a matter of expert professional opinion. Suppose that, contrary to the understanding of the Secretary of State, there does in fact exist a respectable body of professional or expert opinion to the effect that the selection procedures for school entry proposed are adequate and acceptable. If that body of opinion be proved to exist, and if that body of opinion proves to be available both to the authority and to the Secretary of State, then again I would have thought it quite impossible for the Secretary of State to invoke his powers under section 68. By adding this situation to situations more commonly described as occasions for judicial review, I can find no objection in principle.

Lord Denning M.R. has briefly referred to some of the case law on the matter; and in the short time available I have looked to see if there is authority which would belie what I believe to be the law, and there is none.

GEOFFREY LANE L.J. delivered a concurring judgment.

[In the House of Lords]

LORD WILBERFORCE: ... This section (s.68 of the Education Act 1944) does not say what the consequences of the giving of directions are to be, but I accept, for the purposes of the appeal, that the consequences are to impose on the authority a statutory duty to comply with them which can be enforced by an order of mandamus.

Analysis of the section brings out three cardinal points. 1. The matters with which the section is concerned are primarily matters of educational administration. The action, which the Secretary of State is entitled to stop, is unreasonable action with respect to the exercise of a power or the performance of a duty; the power and the duty of the authority are presupposed and cannot be interfered with. Local education authorities are entitled under the 1944 Act to have a policy, and this section does not enable the Secretary of State to require them to abandon or reverse a policy just because the Secretary of State disagrees with it. Specifically, the Secretary of State cannot use power under this section to impose a general policy of comprehensive education on a local education authority which does not agree with the policy. He cannot direct it to bring in a scheme for total comprehensive education in its area, and if it has done so he cannot direct it to implement it. If he tries to use a direction under section 68 for this purpose, his direction would be clearly invalid. A direction under section 68 must be justified on the ground of unreasonable action in doing what under the 1944 Act the local authority is entitled to do, and under the Act it has a freedom of choice. I do not think that there is any controversy on these propositions.

The critical question in this case, and it is not an easy one, is whether, on a matter which appears to be one of educational administration, namely whether the change of course proposed by the authority in May 1976 would lead to educational chaos or undue disruption, the Secretary of State's judgment can be challenged.

2. The section is framed in a subjective form—if the Secretary of State "is satisfied". This form of section is quite well known, and at first sight might seem to exclude judicial review. Sections in this form may, no doubt, exclude judicial review on what is or has become a matter of pure judgment. But I do not think that they go further than that. If a judgment requires, before it can be made, the existence of some facts, then, although the evaluation of those facts is for the Secretary of State alone, the court must enquire whether those facts exist, and have been taken into account, whether the judgment has been made on a proper self direction as to those facts, whether the judgment has not been made on other facts which ought not to have been taken into account. If these requirements are not met, then the exercise of judgment, however bona fide it may be, becomes capable of challenge: see *Secretary of State for Employment v. Associated Society of Locomotive Engineers and Firemen* (No. 2) ([1972] 2 Q.B. 455 at 493), *per* Lord Denning M.R.

3. The section has to be considered within the structure of the 1944 Act. In many statutes a Minister or other authority is given a discretionary power and in these cases the court's power to review any exercise of the discretion, though still real, is limited. In these cases it is said that the courts cannot substitute their opinion for that of the Minister; they can interfere on such grounds as that the Minister has acted right outside his powers or outside the purpose of the Act, or unfairly, or on an incorrect basis of fact. But there is no

universal rule as to the principles on which the exercise of a discretion may be reviewed: each statute or type of statute must be individually looked at. This Act of 1944, is quite different from those which simply create a ministerial discretion. The Secretary of State, under section 68, is not merely exercising a discretion; he is reviewing the action of another public body which itself has discretionary powers and duties. He, by contrast with the courts in the normal case, may substitute his opinion for that of the authority: this is what the section allows, but he must take account of what the authority, under the statute, is entitled to do. The authority—this is vital—is itself elected, and is given specific powers as to the kind of schools it wants in its area. Therefore two situations may arise. One is that there may be a difference of policy between the Secretary of State (under Parliament) and the local authority: the section gives no power to the Secretary of State to make his policy prevail. The other is that, owing to the democratic process involving periodic elections, abrupt reversals of policy make take place, particularly where there are only two parties and the winner takes all. Any reversal of policy if at all substantial must cause some administrative disruption; this was as true of the 1975 proposals as of those of Tameside. So the mere possibility, or probability, of disruption cannot be a ground for issuing a direction to abandon the policy. What the Secretary of State is entitled, by a direction if necessary, to ensure is that such disruptions are not "unreasonable", *i.e.* greater than a body, elected to carry out a new programme, with which the Secretary of State may disagree, ought to impose on those for whom it is responsible. After all, those who voted for the new programme, involving a change of course, must also be taken to have accepted some degree of disruption in implementing it.

The ultimate question in this case, in my opinion, is whether the Secretary of State has given sufficient, or any, weight to this particular factor in the exercise of the judgment.

I must now enquire what were the facts on which the Secretary of State expressed himself as satisfied that the council were acting or proposing to act unreasonably. The Secretary of State did not give oral evidence in the courts, and the facts on which he acted must be taken from the department's letters at the relevant time—*i.e.* on or about June 11, 1976—and from affidavits sworn by its officers. These documents are to be read fairly and in *bonam partem*, if reasons are given in general terms, the court should not exclude reasons which fairly fall within them: allowance must be fairly made for difficulties in expression. The Secretary of State must be given credit for having the background to this actual situation well in mind, and must be taken to be properly and professionally informed as to education practices used in the area and as to resources available to the local education authority. His opinion based as it must be on that of a strong and expert department, is not to be lightly overridden.

On June 11 the direction under section 68 was given in a letter of that date. The letter stated that the Secretary of State was satisfied that the authority was proposing to act unreasonably according to the formula used in section 68. A change of plan designed to come into effect in less than three months must, in the opinion of the Secretary of State, give rise to "considerable difficulties". It pointed out that over 3,000 pupils transferring from primary schools had already been allocated and allotted places. Then followed this paragraph (which I shall call "para. A"):

"The Authority's revised proposals *confront* the parents of children due to transfer in September *with the dilemma* of either adhering to secondary school allocations for their children which they may no longer regard as appropriate, or else *submitting* to an improvised selection procedure (the precise form of which the Secretary of State understands, has even now not been settled) carried out in circumstances and under a timetable which raise substantial doubts about its educational validity."

A further objection was taken to the proposed possible reallocation during or after the first year. . . . The change of plan at this time in the educational year threatened to give rise to practical difficulties in relation to the appointments of staff already made and the construction of buildings for the new comprehensive schools and to create a degree of confusion and uncertainty which could impair the efficient working of the schools.

These arguments were re-stated and expanded in the affidavit sworn on behalf of the Secretary of State in support of the application for mandamus. The affidavit stated three points. Point (i): that 653 of the 802 transfers, promotions and other appointments (of teachers) required to implement the reorganisation had been made. Point (ii): that contracts had been entered into for building work directly related to the change in character of two of the schools and work had started under the contracts. In the case of a third school, the authority had entered into commitments for such building work. Point (iii): that preparations were made for courses on the basis that the proposals communicated to the Secretary of State would be put into effect.

These points (i), (ii) and (iii) were dealt with fully by the authority and I need say no more about them than that they were completely exploded. They were held to have no substance in them by five of the six learned judges who have considered this matter: the sixth indicated general agreement without specific discussion and indeed point (ii) was criticised with some severity by one of the learned Lords Justices in the Court of Appeal.

Some attempt was made to rehabilitate these points in this House, but learned counsel decided, no doubt wisely, to concentrate on the allocation issue. But these three points cannot just be discarded as if they had never been made. They form part of a composite set of facts relied on as showing unreasonable conduct, and I am not at all sure that the disappearance of so many planks does not fatally weaken the stability of the platform. At the least—and I will give the department the benefit of this assumption—the remaining factual basis would need to be strong and clear if it alone were to be the basis for the Secretary of State's "satisfaction" as to unreasonable conduct.

So I come to the question of allocation, which was at the centre of the case as argued and it can best be approached via "para. A" above, a paragraph which I regard as revealing. It shows a very strange attitude toward the decision taken by the authority. After the electorate, including no doubt a large number of parents, had voted the new authority into office on the platform that some selective basis would be preserved, to say that this created "a dilemma" for the parents, with the undertone that this was something unreasonable, appears to me curious and paradoxical. Parents desired to have a chance of selective places. The new authority were giving it them. If they did not want selective places, they had no need and no obligation to apply for them. Unless the creation of freedom of choice, where no such freedom existed previously, is intrinsically an evil, it seems hard to understand how this so-called dilemma could be something unreasonably created. The impression which it gives of upsetting 3,000 places is entirely a false one since over 90 per cent of these would remain unaltered. Then, to refer to "submitting to an improvised selection procedure" hardly does justice to the authority's plan. Some selection procedure was inherent in what the electorate had voted for, a choice which, if it meant anything, must involve some change in allocation for the forthcoming school year and, unless exactly 240 parents applied for the 240 places, some selection. It would seem likely that in voting for this change in May 1976 the electors must have accepted, if not favoured, some degree of improvisation. The whole paragraph forces the conclusion that the Secretary of State was operating under a misconception as to what would be reasonable for a newly elected council to do, and that he failed to take into account that it was entitled—indeed in a sense bound—to carry out the policy on which it was elected, and failed to give weight to the fact that the limited degree of selection (for 240 places out of some 3,000), which was involved, though less than perfect, was something which a reasonable authority might accept and which the parents concerned clearly did accept.

What the Secretary of State was entitled to do, under his residual powers, was to say something to the effect that: "the election has taken place; the new authority may be entitled to postpone the comprehensive scheme: this may involve some degree of selection and apparently the parents desire it. Nevertheless from an educational point of view, whatever some parents may think, I am satisfied that in the time available this, or some part of it, cannot be carried out, and that no reasonable authority would attempt to carry it out." Let us judge him by this test, though I do not think that this was the test he himself applied. Was the procedure to be followed for choosing which of the applicants were to be allotted the 240 selective places such that no reasonable authority could adopt it? The authority's letter of June 7 said that selection would be by "a combination of reports, records and interviews". They had about three months in which to carry it out. The plan was lacking in specification, but it must have conveyed sufficient to the experts at the department to enable them to understand what was proposed. Selection by 11-plus examination was not the only selection procedure available. Lancashire, part of which was taken over by Tameside, had evolved and operated a method of selection by head teacher recommendation, ranking of pupils, reports and records, and standardised verbal reasoning tests. The Tameside authority had set up in May a panel of selection to operate a procedure of this kind, the chairman of which was experienced in the Lancashire method. He was, as he deposed in an affidavit before the Court of Appeal, of opinion that even though a verbal reasoning test might not be practicable in the time there would be no difficulty in selecting the number of places required. There were other opinions, expressed with varying degrees of confidence by experts, and no doubt the procedure could not be said to be perfect, but I do not think that such defects as there were could possibly, in the circumstances, having regard to the comparatively small number of places involved, enable it to be said that the whole of the authority's programme of which this was a part was such that no reasonable authority would carry it out.

But there is a further complication. The authority's selection plans were opposed by a number of the teachers' unions, and there was the likelihood of non-cooperation by some of the head teachers in the primary schools in production of records and reports. The department letters and affidavits do not rely on this matter, for understandable reasons, but they must be assumed to have had it in mind. Is this a fact on which the Secretary of State might legitimately form the judgment that the authority were acting unreasonably?

To rephrase the question: on June 11, 1976 (this is the date of the direction, and we are not entitled to see what happened thereafter) could it be said that the authority were acting unreasonably in proceeding with the selection procedure which was otherwise workable, in face of the possibility of persistent opposition by teachers' unions and individual teachers, or would *the only* (not "the more") reasonable course have been for the authority to abandon their plans? This is I think the ultimate factual question in the case. And I think that it must be answered in the negative, *i.e.* that it could not be unreasonable, in June 1976, and assuming that the Secretary of State did not interfere, for the authority to put forward a plan to act on their approved procedure. The teachers, after all, are public servants, with responsibility for their pupils. They were under a duty to produce reports. These reports and the records in the primary schools are public property. I do not think that it could be unreasonable (not "was unreasonable") for the authority to take the view that if the Secretary of State did not intervene under his statutory power, the teachers would cooperate in working the authority's procedure—a procedure which had, in similar form, been operated in part of this very area.

On the whole case, I come to the conclusion that the Secretary of State, real though his difficulties were, fundamentally misconceived and misdirected himself as to the proper manner in which to regard the proposed action of the authority after the local election of May 1976; that if he had exercised his judgment on the basis of the factual situation in which this newly elected authority were placed—with a policy approved by their electorate, and massively supported by the parents—there was no ground, however much he might disagree with the new policy, and regret such administrative dislocation as was brought about by the change, on which he could find that the authority were acting or proposing to act unreasonably. In my opinion, the judgments in the Court of Appeal were right and the appeal must be dismissed.

LORD DIPLOCK: ... A relevant question to which the Secretary of State should have directed his mind was the extent to which head teachers would be likely to persist in a policy of non-cooperation if he himself was known to have declined to stop the council from proceeding with their plan. There is no suggestion in the letter, nor in either of the affidavits sworn on his behalf by Mr Jenkins, that the Secretary of State ever directed his mind to this particular question or formed any view about it. Indeed, it is not until the second affidavit that it is disclosed that the teachers' trade unions had been writing directly to the department on the matter at all. It is not for a court of law to speculate how the Secretary of State would have answered that question had he directed his mind to it, although like others of your Lordships and members of the Court of Appeal, I find it difficult to believe that responsible head teachers, regardful of the interests of their pupils, would have persisted in a refusal to do their best to make the selection procedure work fairly and effectively if the Secretary of State had made it clear to them by his decision that he was not prepared himself to interfere with the council's proceeding with its plans. Assuming, however, that he had formed the view that cooperation by head teachers was likely to be only partial so that the selection process would be liable to greater possibility of error than where full cooperation could be obtained, the Secretary of State would have to consider whether the existence of such a degree of imperfection in the selection system as he thought would be involved was so great as to make it unreasonable conduct for the council to attempt to fulfil the mandate which they had so recently received from the electors. Again, there is no indication that the Secretary of State weighed these two considerations against one another.

Like all your Lordships, I would dismiss this appeal, although I prefer to put it on the ground that, in my view, the council have succeeded in establishing in these proceedings that the Secretary of State did not direct his mind to the right question: and so, since his good faith is not in question, he cannot have directed himself properly in law.

LORD SALMON: ... In my opinion, section 68, on its true construction, means that before the Secretary of State could lawfully issue directions under it, he must satisfy himself not only that he does not agree with the way in which the authority have acted or are proposing to act nor even that the authority are mistaken or wrong; the question he must ask himself is, could any reasonable local authority act in the way in which this authority have acted or are proposing to act? If, but only if, he is satisfied on any material capable of satisfying a reasonable man that the answer to the crucial question is No, he may lawfully issue directions under section 68....

I find it impossible ... to accept that any reasonable man could be satisfied that no reasonable authority on the evidence could take the view that a satisfactory selection of candidates for the 240 places in the grammar schools could have been made between June 11 and September 1, 1976. Therefore, either the Secretary of State must have erred in law by misconstruing s.68 and failing to ask himself the right question, or he asked himself that question and answered it No without any valid ground for doing so.

VISCOUNT DILHORNE and LORD RUSSELL OF KILLOWEN delivered concurring speeches.

Appeal dismissed.

Notes

1. See case notes by H.W.R. W[ade] (1977) 93 L.Q.R. 4 and D.G.T. Williams [1977] C.L.J. 1. The *Tameside* case was the subject of a talk by A.W. Bradley in the Radio 3 "Law in Action" series. See *The Listener*, May 5, 1977. The factual background is re-examined by D. Bull, "*Tameside* Revisited" (1987) 50 M.L.R. 307, noting inadequacies in the courts' appreciation of the schools admissions process.

2. In 1944, the following clause was added at the committee stage of the Education Bill, as clause 92(2):

"(2) Where the performance of any duty imposed by or for the purposes of this Act on a local education authority or on the managers or governors of any county school or auxiliary school is thereby made contingent upon the opinion of the authority or of the managers or governors, the Minister may nevertheless require the authority managers or governors to perform that duty if in his opinion the circumstances are such as to require the performance thereof."

This clause was withdrawn after objections were raised in the House of Lords (H.L. Deb., cols. 540–552, June 29, 1944). It was replaced by what became section 68 (H.L. Deb., cols. 862–864, July 12, 1944); (cols. 954–966 (July 18, 1944)). The Lord Chancellor (Viscount Simon) explained that the Minister would be able to act under section 68 to prevent "monstrous abuses" of discretion, or a "completely" or "utterly" unreasonable exercise of discretion, where mandamus would not be an appropriate remedy. The Earl of Selborne (who was in charge of the Bill in the House of Lords) stated that section 68 could be used to reverse an "unwise or unfortunate" decision. "The real purpose of the clause is to provide some court of appeal in cases where local authorities or managers have acted unreasonably" (col. 960).

3. The view taken by the ministry of their powers under section 68, as revealed in investigations by the P.C.A., is considered by D. Foulkes in "Tameside and the Education Act, 1944" (1976) 126 N.L.J. 649.

4. The *Tameside* case was discussed in the House of Commons on December 8, 1976. See H.C. Deb., Vol. 922, cols. 590–598 (1976/1977). The new Secretary of State (Mrs Shirley Williams) stated that the Department was advised in 1948 that "unreasonableness" in section 68 involved an element of perversity: indeed the judgments in the House of Lords contained nothing surprising on the interpretation of "unreasonable". However, the courts had "made judgments on issues and findings of fact ... in relation to matters which, as the law was previously understood, were regarded as entirely within the province of the Minister or Secretary of State", and some of the judgments and findings were "surprising" (col. 595). Overall, section 68 was used sparingly by successive Secretaries of State, almost invariably in relation to the allocation to schools of individual pupils or small groups of pupils.

Questions

1. Section 1 of the Education Act 1944 imposed on the Secretary of State the duty—

"to promote the education of the people of England and Wales and the progressive development of institutions devoted to that purpose, and to secure the effective execution by local authorities, under his control and direction, of the national policy for providing a varied and comprehensive educational service in every area".

Do you think that sufficient weight was given to this section?

2. Lord Wilberforce states that under section 68 the Secretary of State "by contrast with the courts in the normal case, may substitute his opinion for that of the authority". How far is this borne out in the *Tameside* case?

3. Where the Secretary of State considers an education authority to be acting unreasonably in what ways (if any) is the section 68 procedure more useful for the minister than an application to the High Court for one of the general administrative law remedies?

4. There was general agreement that matters had to be judged as at June 11, 1976. Lord Russell of Killowen did not "subscribe to the view that facts subsequently brought forward as then existing can be relied on as showing that the proposals were not unreasonable, unless those facts are of such a character that they can be taken to be within the knowledge of the department". Should "new evidence" of this sort be generally admissible?

5. Is this case authority for the proposition that a decision is *ultra vires* if it is

unsupported by any evidence? (See below, pp. 574 *et seq.*) Was the Secretary of State's decision that the authority were proposing to act unreasonably one of *jurisdictional* fact? (See above, pp. 193 *et seq.*)

(D) INCONSISTENCY

In the previous chapter we noted the unwillingness of the courts to utilise notions of estoppel in favour of applicants for review who claim to have been misled by a public body as to the scope of its powers, or by an official or a committee as to the extent of his or its authority. See above, pp. 283–299. The concern of the courts in these cases has been an unwillingness to allow the concept of estoppel to result in the enlargement of the powers actually conferred by the terms of the legislation, or of the powers actually delegable, or delegated, by the respondent body.

We now turn to consider a series of cases in which the applicants are making complaints broadly similar to those in the estoppel cases (*i.e.* that the respondent body has led them to expect something different from the course of action or decision actually taken, and that they have suffered loss or harm in consequence of relying on what they had been led to expect), but where conflict with the basic *ultra vires* doctrine is less apparent. In these cases there is no question of the courts being asked to "commit" a body to a decision which it had no power to make. The issue is whether in a situation where a body had a discretion to act in a variety of ways (or not to act at all) it may "commit" itself to a particular course of action because it had previously acted so as to engender in the applicant a legitimate expectation that it would exercise its discretion in that way. In other words, will the body be held no longer to retain its choice of alternatives, but be obliged to act so as to fulfil the expectations which its behaviour has aroused? It will be apparent that, just as in the "estoppel" cases, there are difficulties reconciling any such doctrine with the obligation (noted above, p. 266) that bodies possessing discretionary powers should retain an unencumbered discretion to exercise those powers as and how the public interest may from time to time require. In developing a doctrine of "unjustifiable inconsistency" we shall see that the courts have sought to achieve a compromise between this duty, and the notion that for a body to exercise discretionary power in a way which confounds expectations resulting from its own prior behaviour may itself be considered an abuse of the discretionary power.

Re PRESTON

[1985] A.C. 835; [1985] 2 All E.R. 327 (House of Lords)

In May 1978 an inspector of the Inland Revenue sought a meeting with the applicant taxpayer, to discuss his tax returns for the years 1975–1976 to 1976–1977, and in particular to discuss certain claims for reliefs in respect of losses and certain share transactions. The inspector requested full details of the share transactions. Bare details were furnished by the applicant. There followed an exchange of correspondence. In due course the applicant offered to withdraw his claim to reliefs if the Inland Revenue would settle his tax affairs for these years and raise no further questions about the share transactions. In July 1978 the inspector wrote to the applicant agreeing to this proposal. The taxpayer withdrew the claims and paid capital gains tax in respect of the shares. In October 1979 the Inland Revenue received information which led them to believe that the sale of the shares had been part of a tax avoidance scheme, thereby giving the applicant a "tax advantage". In July 1982, by which time it was too late for the applicant to make his claims for relief, the Inland Revenue issued a notice under section 465 of the Income and Corporation Taxes Act 1970 requiring the applicant to furnish information about the sale of the shares. The applicant supplied such information. The Inland Revenue, in September 1982, issued a further notice, under section 460 of the 1970 Act, cancelling the tax advantage gained by the applicant.

At first instance, Woolf J. held that the Revenue had failed to consider facts (*i.e.* the 1978 agreement) which were relevant to its exercise of discretion to issue the section 460 notice, and that it had in the circumstances exercised its discretion unreasonably ([1983] 2 All E.R. 300). The Court of Appeal allowed the Revenue's appeal, differing from the trial judge as to whether the Revenue had acted unreasonably. On appeal to the House of Lords:

LORD TEMPLEMAN: ... The court can only intervene by judicial review to direct the commissioners to abstain from performing their statutory duties or from exercising their statutory powers if the court is satisfied that "the unfairness" of which the applicant complains renders the insistence by the commissioners on performing their duties or exercising their powers an abuse of power by the commissioners.

In most cases in which the court has granted judicial review on grounds of "unfairness" amounting to abuse of power there has been some proven element of improper motive. In the leading case of *Padfield v. Minister of Agriculture, Fisheries and Food* [1968] A.C. 997 the Minister abstained from exercising his statutory discretion to order an investigation because he feared the consequences of the investigation might be politically embarrassing. In *Congreve v. Home Office* [1976] Q.B. 629 the Minister exercised his power to revoke television licences because he disapproved of the conduct of the licence holders, albeit they had acted lawfully. In *Laker Airways Ltd v. Department of Trade* [1977] Q.B. 643 the Minister exercised his statutory discretion to give directions with regard to civil airways with the ulterior motive of making it impossible for one of the airlines to pursue a course of which the Minister disapproved. In these cases judicial review was granted because the Ministers acted "unfairly" when they abused their powers by exercising or declining to exercise those powers in order to achieve objectives which were not the objectives for which the powers had been conferred. The question of "fairness" was considered in *H.T.V. Ltd v. Price Commission* [1976] I.C.R. 170.

In that case the Price Commission misconstrued the counter-inflation price code and changed its mind as to the treatment of exchequer levy as an item in the costs of television companies allowable for the purpose of increasing their advertising charges within the limits prescribed by the code. The effect of the change of mind of the Price Commission was to deprive the companies of an increase of advertising charges which they were plainly intended to enjoy and which they badly needed in order to remain financially viable. Lord Denning M.R. said, at 185–186:

"It has been often said, I know, that a public body, which is entrusted by Parliament with the exercise of powers for the public good, cannot fetter itself in the exercise of them. It cannot be estopped from doing its public duty. But that is subject to the qualification that it must not misuse its powers: and it is a misuse of power for it to act unfairly or unjustly towards a private citizen when there is no overriding public interest to warrant it...."

In the *H.T.V.* case [1976] I.C.R. 170 my noble and learned friend, then

Scarman L.J., ... after considering the Price Commission's change of mind, said, at 192, that "the commission's inconsistency has already resulted in unfairness, and, unless corrected, could cause further injustice. Firstly, it gives rise to a real possibility of an erosion of profit margin ..." Next, if, as the Price Commission contended, the Exchequer levy was excluded in 1976 but included in 1973 then the television companies would be unable to obtain a fair increase in advertising charges corresponding to increases in costs between 1973 and 1976:

> "The commission, to avoid being unfair, must either include or exclude Exchequer levy as a cost upon both sides of the comparison. Since it has made clear that, in the absence of a ruling to the contrary, it intends to exclude it when calculating current profit margins, the commission must also exclude it when calculating the profit margin at April 30, 1973. I am not completely sure that it intends so to do if it succeeds in this litigation. ... The commission has acted inconsistently and unfairly; and on this ground, were it necessary, I would think H.T.V. are also entitled to declaratory relief."

In the *H.T.V.* case [1976] I.C.R. 170, the "unfairness" of the decision was due not to improper motive on the part of the Price Commission but to an error of law whereby the Price Commission misconstrued the code they were intending to enforce. If the Price Commission had not misconstrued the code, they would not have acted "inconsistently and unfairly". Of course the inconsistent and unfair results to which Scarman L.J. drew attention were themselves powerful support for the contention that the Price Commission must have misconstrued the code.

In the present case, the appellant does not allege that the commissioners invoked section 460 for improper purposes or motives or that the commissioners misconstrued their powers and duties. However, the *H.T.V.* case and the authorities there cited suggest that the commissioners are guilty of "unfairness" amounting to an abuse of power if by taking action under section 460 their conduct would, in the case of an authority other than Crown authority, entitle the appellant to an injunction or damages based on breach of contract or estoppel by representation. In principle I see no reason why the appellant should not be entitled to judicial review of a decision taken by the commissioners if that decision is unfair to the appellant because the conduct of the commissioners is equivalent to a breach of contract or a breach of representation. Such a decision falls within the ambit of an abuse of power for which in the present case judicial review is the sole remedy and an appropriate remedy. There may be cases in which conduct which savours of breach of conduct or breach of representation does not constitute an abuse of power; there may be circumstances in which the court in its discretion might not grant relief by judicial review notwithstanding conduct which savours of breach of contract or breach of representation. In the present case, however, I consider that the appellant is entitled to relief by way of judicial review for "unfairness' amounting to abuse of power if the commissioners have been guilty of conduct equivalent to a breach of contract or breach of representations on their part.

[His Lordship reviewed the facts of the case and concluded that there had been no abuse of power in the above sense. In particular, the correspondence did not support the applicant's contention that the Revenue had agreed that there would be no further inquiries into the share transactions even on the Revenue becoming aware that the assessments, made in the light of the incomplete information supplied by the applicant, did not represent his full tax liability.]

LORD SCARMAN [agreeing with the reasons given by LORD TEMPLEMAN, said:] . . . It was the appellant's case that upon the true construction of the correspondence in 1978 . . . the commissioners purported to contract or to represent that they would not thereafter re-open the tax assessments . . . if he withdrew his claims for interest relief and capital loss. Had he made good this case, I do not doubt that he would have been entitled to relief by way of judicial review for unfairness amounting to abuse of the power. . . . But he failed upon the construction of the correspondence. . . .

LORDS EDMUND-DAVIES, KEITH OF KINKEL and BRIGHTMAN also agreed with the reasons given by LORD TEMPLEMAN.

Notes
1. See case note by C. Lewis (1986) 49 M.L.R. 251, and the articles cited below at p. 396, note 8.
2. For other examples of cases where the court has held representations to have been insufficient to have generated legitimate expectations, see *R. v. Secretary of State for the Home Department, ex p. Briggs, The Independent,* September 26, 1995; *R. v. Secretary of State for the Home Department, ex p. Edwards* [1994] C.O.D. 443: *R. v. Inland Revenue Commissioners, ex p. Matrix Securities* [1994] 1 W.L.R. 334; *R. v. Jockey Club, ex p. RAM Racecourses* [1993] 2 All E.R. 225; *R. v. Council of Legal Education, ex p. Eddis* (1995) 7 Admin.L.R. 357.

R. v. SECRETARY OF STATE FOR THE HOME DEPARTMENT, ex p. ASIF MAHMOOD KHAN

[1984] 1 W.L.R. 1337; [1985] 1 All E.R. 40 (Court of Appeal)

A Home Office circular letter stated that although the Immigration Rules did not permit a foreign child subject to immigration control to enter the United Kingdom for the purposes of adoption, the Secretary of State would permit such entry provided certain specified criteria were met. The criteria involved the adoption being genuine and not merely a device for obtaining entry, that the child's welfare in this country be assured, that the courts here would be likely to grant an adoption order, and that one of the intending adopters be domiciled in the United Kingdom. The letter then stated the procedure to be followed by would-be adopters. This was to obtain an entry clearance from an entry clearance officer abroad. That officer would have to be satisfied of the child's wishes and the wishes of the natural parents. The applicant and his wife wished to adopt a relative's child, living with its natural mother in Pakistan. Application for an entry clearance was made in Islamabad. All the various criteria listed above appeared to have been satisfied. However, in due course, following referral of the matter to the Home Office, entry clearance was refused. This was on the ground that there were no "serious and compelling family and other considerations", such as would make refusal of permission to enter undesirable. The entry clearance officer's report to the Home Office had made clear the fact that the child in question was living in good conditions with his natural mother. The applicant appealed against the decision of Stephen Brown J., dismissing his application for judicial review to quash the decision to refuse clearance.

PARKER L.J.: [His Lordship noted the policy actually applied by the Home Office in coming to its decision, and continued:] . . . If this was the policy, the "guidance" given in the Home Office letter is grossly misleading, as was frankly accepted by counsel on behalf of the Secretary of State. There is not a word [in the circular letter] to suggest that in exercising his discretion the Secretary of State requires to be satisfied that the natural parents are incapable of looking after the prospective adoptee, or even that their ability or inability to do so was considered relevant. Furthermore, there is no evidence that entry clearance officers were instructed to inquire as to this matter, which of course does not depend only on the standard of living enjoyed in the natural home. The whole tenor of the letter is that, if the application was genuine, if the child's welfare was assured, if a court would be likely to grant an order and if the natural parents gave a real consent, the child would be let in and its ultimate fate left to the court here. If an adoption order was made it would remain. If an order was refused it would be returned.

The applicant relies on three authorities on the basis of which he contends that the refusal of entry clearance should be quashed. The first of these cases is *R. v. Liverpool Corporation, ex p. Liverpool Taxi Fleet Operators' Association* [1972] 2 Q.B. 299. [See further, below, p. 448. His Lordship considered this decision and continued:]

In that case there was a specific undertaking, whereas here there is not; the corporation had a statutory power, whereas here the power of the Secretary of State is a common law power; and the matter complained of was a positive act, whereas here the complaint is a refusal to act. There can, however, be no doubt that the Secretary of State has a duty to exercise his common law discretion fairly. Furthermore, just as, in the case cited, the corporation was held not to be entitled to resile from an undertaking and change its policy without giving a fair hearing so, in principle, the Secretary of State, if he undertakes to allow in persons if certain conditions are satisfied, should not in my view be entitled to resile from that undertaking without affording interested persons a hearing and then only if the overriding public interest demands it.

The second of the authorities relied on by the applicant is *O'Reilly v. Mackman* [1983] 2 A.C. 237. The case is relied on solely for a statement of principle in the speech of Lord Diplock with which Lord Fraser of Tullybelton, Lord Keith of Kinkel, Lord Bridge of Harwich and Lord Brightman agreed. It is therefore necessary to state the facts only to the limited extent necessary to render that statement understandable. Four prisoners had been awarded forfeiture of remission by the board of visitors. They sought to challenge the decision of the board on the ground that there had been a failure to observe the rules of natural justice, the relief sought being declaratory only. [His Lordship set out the passage:

"It is not, and it could not be, contended that the decision of the board awarding him forfeiture of remission . . . which means no more than to act fairly towards him in carrying out their decision-making process, and I prefer so to put it" (below, p. 643).]

Here it is contended that the applicant, by virtue of the terms of the Home Office letter, had a legitimate expectation that the procedures set out in the letter would be followed and that such legitimate expectation gave him sufficient interest to challenge the admitted failure of the Secretary of State to observe such procedures. I agree and the contrary was not suggested by [counsel for the Secretary of State]. But to have a sufficient interest to afford a *locus standi* to challenge is a long way from being entitled to succeed in such challenge.

The applicant, however, contends that on the basis of the third authority on which he relies, coupled with his first which I have already considered, he is so entitled. That authority is a Privy Council case, *Att.-Gen. of Hong Kong v. Ng Yuen Shiu* [1983] 2 A.C. 629, which at the time of the hearing before the judge had been reported only in *The Times* newspaper. The advice of their Lordships were delivered by Lord Fraser of Tullybelton. The other members of the Judicial Committee were Lord Scarman, Lord Bridge of Harwich, Lord Brandon of Oakbrook and Sir John Megaw. For some years prior to October 23, 1980, the government of Hong Kong had adopted a policy under which illegal immigrants from China were not repatriated if they managed to reach the urban areas without being arrested. This was known as the "reached base" policy. On October 23, 1980, the government announced that this policy would be discontinued forthwith and at the same time issued a new ordinance which, *inter alia*, gave the Director of Immigration power to make removal orders in respect of illegal immigrants. There was no statutory provision for a hearing or inquiry before a removal order was made. Subsequent to the change of policy there were a series of television announcements stating that all illegal immigrants from China would be liable to be repatriated. Mr Ng, like many others in the colony, although they had entered illegally from Macau, was of Chinese origin. They were accordingly worried and on October 28, 1980, a group, not including Mr Ng, went to Government House and submitted a petition.

There, there were read out a series of questions and answers prepared in the office of the Secretary for Security which dealt with the position of such persons and the action they should take. One of such questions, with its answer, was:

"*Q*. Will we be given identity cards? *A*. Those illegal immigrants from Macau will be treated in accordance with procedures for illegal immigrants from anywhere other than China. They will be interviewed in due course. No guarantee can be given that you may not subsequently be removed. Each case will be treated on its merits."

Although Mr Ng was not present he did see a television programme on the subject on the evening of the same day.

On October 31 a removal order was made against him. This he challenged and eventually on May 13, 1981, the Court of Appeal of Hong Kong made an order of prohibition prohibiting the Director of Immigration from executing the removal order before an opportunity had been given to Mr Ng of putting all the circumstances of his case before the director. The Attorney-General appealed to the Privy Council.

The High Court and the Court of Appeal in Hong Kong had both held that Mr Ng had no general right to a fair hearing before a removal order was made against him and the Judicial Committee assumed, without deciding, that they had rightly so decided. It was concerned only with the narrow question whether what had been said outside Government House entitled Mr Ng to such a hearing. It is necessary to cite four passages from Lord Fraser's judgment:

(1) " 'Legitimate expectations' in this context are capable of including expectations which go beyond enforceable legal rights, *provided they have some reasonable basis.*" (at 636E–F)

(2) "The expectations may be based on some *statement* or undertaking by, or on behalf of, the public authority which has the duty of making the decision, if the authority has, through its officers, acted *in a way that would make it unfair or inconsistent with good administration for him to be denied such* an inquiry." (at 637C–D)

(3) "Their Lordships see no reason why the principle should not be applicable when the person who will be affected by the decision is an alien, just as much as when he is a British subject. The justification for it is primarily that, *when a public authority has promised to follow a certain procedure, it is in the interest of good administration that it should act fairly and should implement its promise, so long as implementation does not interfere with its statutory duty.* The principle is also justified by the further consideration that, when the promise was made, *the authority must have considered that it would be assisted in discharging its duty fairly* by any representations from interested parties and as a general rule that is correct. In the opinion of their Lordships the principle that a public authority is bound by its undertakings as to the procedure it will follow, provided they do not conflict with its duty, is applicable to the undertaking given by the government of Hong Kong to the respondent, along with other illegal immigrants from Macau, in the announcement outside Government House on October 28, 1980, that each case would be considered on its merits. The only ground on which it was argued before the Board that the undertaking had not been implemented was that the respondent had not been given an opportunity to put his case for an exercise of discretion, which the director undoubtedly possesses, in his favour before a decision was reached" (at 638E–H)

(4) "Their Lordships consider that this is a very narrow case on its facts, but they are not disposed to differ from the view expressed by both the courts below, to the effect that the government's promise to the respondent has not been implemented. Accordingly the appeal ought to be dismissed. But in the circumstances their Lordships are of opinion that the order made by the Court of Appeal should be varied. The appropriate remedy is not the conditional order of prohibition made by the Court of Appeal, but an order of certiorari to quash the removal order made by the director on October 31, against the respondent. That order of certiorari is of course entirely without prejudice to the making of a fresh removal order by the Director of Immigration after a fair inquiry has been held at which the respondent has

been given an opportunity to make such representations as he may see fit as to why he should not be removed" (at 639E–F).

The emphasis in each case is mine.

That case is, of course, not binding on this court but is of high persuasive authority. In my view it correctly sets out the law of England and should be applied.

I have no doubt that the Home Office letter afforded the applicant a reasonable expectation that the procedures it set out, which were just as certain in their terms as the question and answer in Mr Ng's case, would be followed, that if the result of the implementation of those procedures satisfied the Secretary of State of the four matters mentioned a temporary entry clearance certificate would be granted and that the ultimate fate of the child would then be decided by the adoption court of this country. I have equally no doubt that it was considered by the department at the time the letter was sent out that if those procedures were fully implemented they would be sufficient to safeguard the public interest. The letter can mean nothing else. This is not surprising. The adoption court will apply the law of this country and will thus protect all the interests which the law of this country considers should be protected. The Secretary of State is, of course, at liberty to change the policy but in my view, *vis-à-vis* the recipient of such a letter, a new policy can only be implemented after such recipient has been given a full and serious consideration whether there is some overriding public interest which justifies a departure from the procedures stated in the letter....

I would allow the appeal and quash the refusal of entry clearance. This will leave the Secretary of State free either to proceed on the basis of the letter or, if he considers it desirable to operate the new policy, to afford the applicant a full opportunity to make representations why, in his case, it should not be followed.

I would only add this. If the new policy is to continue in operation, the sooner the Home Office letter is redrafted and false hopes cease to be raised in those who may have a deep emotional need to adopt, the better it will be. To leave it in its present form is not only bad and grossly unfair administration but, in some instances at any rate, positively cruel.

[Dunn L.J. also delivered a judgment allowing the appeal. He took the view that "although the circular letter did not create an estoppel" it had indicated what were the relevant considerations as regards the exercise of this discretionary power, and the Secretary of State had therefore taken into account an *irrelevant* consideration. In so doing he had "misdirected himself according to his own criteria and acted unreasonably". Watkins L.J. dissented, taking the view that, properly construed, the circular letter only indicated factors which if not satisfied would certainly lead to refusal of clearance; it did not indicate that compliance with those factors would itself lead to grant of permission. The letter said that the Secretary "may exercise his discretion and exceptionally allow...". Parker L.J. had noted this formula, and had taken the view that a reader would have inferred that, provided the conditions were satisfied, permission to enter "would be the likely result".]

Appeal allowed

Notes

1. See case notes by C. Lewis (1986) 49 M.L.R. 251 and A.R. Mowbray [1985] P.L. 558.

2.—Although Dunn L.J. says that he is not applying an estoppel, the proposition that considerations other than the published criteria were legally irrelevant seems to come to the same thing (see P. Elias in J. Jowell and D. Oliver (eds.), *New Directions in Judicial Review* (1988), p. 48).

3. Mr Khan's application was subsequently reconsidered in accordance with the circular letter, and the letter was redrafted for the future, referring expressly to the policy requirement that the original parents must be incapable of looking after the child, but also stating that:

"... the Home Secretary may exceptionally exercise discretion to allow a child to come here for (adoption) if he is satisfied that this is appropriate in all the circumstances of the case".

Thus the Home Office had reacted "by reducing the specificity and precision of its administrative guidance" (see A.R. Mowbray [1985] P.L. 558 at 563).

4. *cf. Oloniluyi v. Secretary of State for the Home Department* [1989] Imm.A.R. 135, as explained in *R. v. Secretary of State for the Home Department, ex p. Mowla* [1991] Imm.A.R. 210. Compare *R. v. Secretary of State for the Home Department, ex p. Silva, The Times*, 1 April 1994; with *R. v. Secretary of State for the Home Department, ex p. Amnkwah* [1994] Imm.A.R. 240.

R. v. INLAND REVENUE COMMISSIONERS, ex p. MFK UNDERWRITING AGENTS LTD

[1990] 1 W.L.R. 1545; [1990] 1 All E.R. 90 (D.C. (Q.B.D.))

The applicants were Lloyd's underwriting agents. Under Lloyd's rules premiums had to be retained in trust funds for a period of two years after the close of an underwriting year. In order to produce a yield which was taxable as capital gain rather than as income Lloyd's syndicates invested in index-linked gilts or similar securities. Lloyd's rules also required that premiums paid in U.S./Canadian dollars be invested U.S./Canadian dollar accounts or securities. Until 1986 there were no index-linked dollar securities available in which to invest. A number of U.S. banks therefore proposed to issue such securities for the Lloyd's market. The banks and their solicitors and accountants each made approaches to the Revenue seeking assurances that the index-linked element payable on redemption would be regarded as capital and not income. The Revenue gave this assurance. Between April 1986 and October 1988 the applicants bought such bonds. In October 1988 the Revenue decided to tax the index-linked element as income. The applicants sought judicial review of this decision.

BINGHAM L.J.: ...

C. *The contentions of the parties*

... [Counsel for the applicants] submitted that decisions of the Revenue are subject to judicial review on the same grounds as those of any other public authority. These grounds include abuse or excess of power. The overriding criterion for deciding whether there has been an excess of abuse of power is to decide whether the authority's (here the Revenue's) conduct has been unfair. The Revenue's conduct was *prima facie* unfair if it conflicted with an undertaking or assurance of the Revenue which would (were the Revenue not a public body) give rise to an estoppel or breach of contract. If a public authority has a policy which it makes known or announces it may not act inconsistently with the policy without sufficient notice, and then not retrospectively. This rule applies even where, in private law, there might be no estoppel. It is a principle of public law that decisions of public bodies may not be internally inconsistent. A public body must recognise and give effect to the legitimate expectations of those who deal with it, in matters both of procedure and decision. For these propositions of law [counsel for the applicants] relied in particular on *R. v. Inland Revenue Commissioners, ex p. National Federation of Self-Employed and Small Businesses Ltd* [1982] A.C. 617 ("the *Fleet Street Casuals* case"); *R. v. Inland Revenue Commissioners, ex p. Preston* [1985] A.C. 835; *H.T.V. Ltd v. Price Commission* [1976] I.C.R. 170; *Att.-Gen. of Hong Kong v. Ng Yuen Shiu* [1983] 2 A.C. 629, *R. v. Secretary of State for the Home Department, ex p. Khan* [1984] 1 W.L.R. 1337 and *R. v. Secretary of State for the Home Department, ex p. Ruddock* [1987] 1 W.L.R. 1482.

On the facts [counsel for the applicants] submitted that the policy of the Revenue before March 1988 plainly was not to challenge as disguised interest the indexation uplift on bonds of this kind provided that the bonds paid a commercial rate of interest in addition to the indexation uplift. This policy was made known to potential investors and their advisers by answering the same sort of questions in the same way. The circumstances in which the answers were given were such that it was highly probable the answers would be passed to investors. On any view of the evidence the Revenue's statements were an effective inducement to these applicants to buy bonds.

The thrust of the applicants' argument was thus very simple. The Revenue had repeatedly made known its view of these bonds. It need not have done so, but it did. It would be grossly unfair to these applicants, and so an abuse of the Revenue's statutory powers, if the Revenue were now free to alter its position with retrospective effect to the prejudice of the applicants.

[Counsel for the Crown] accepted that his client was not immune from judicial review.... [Counsel] further accepted that unfairness might in principle amount to an abuse of power and that there could be an exceptional case where it would be unfair for the Revenue to resile from a representation made or undertaking given when the making of the representation or giving of the undertaking involved no breach of the Revenue's statutory duty. Judicial review could not, however, lie to oblige the Revenue to act contrary to its statutory duty. Such would be the case if these applications succeeded. It is for Parliament, and Parliament alone, to decide what taxes shall be paid. It is for the Inland Revenue to collect the tax Parliament has ordained. The Revenue has no general discretion to remit taxes Parliament has imposed: *Vestey v. Inland Revenue Commissioners (Nos 1 and 2)* [1980] A.C. 1148). While the Revenue has under the Inland Revenue Regulation Act 1890 and the Taxes Management Act 1970:

"a wide managerial discretion as to the best means of obtaining for the national exchequer from the taxes committed to their charge, the highest net return that is practicable having regard to the staff available to them and the cost of collection"

(*per* Lord Diplock in the *Fleet Street Casuals* case [1982] A.C. 617, 636G), this was a discretion which could only lawfully be exercised for the better, more efficient and more economical collection of tax and not otherwise. The taxing Acts provided for inspectors to make assessments on individual tax-payers year by year. One inspector could not bind another, nor one inspector bind himself from one year to another. When an assessment was disputed, a familiar and well-lubricated machinery existed to resolve the dispute. Special or General Commissioners, or on questions of law the courts, were the ulti-mate arbiters. The Revenue could not without breach of statutory duty agree or indicate in advance that it would not collect tax which, on a proper con-struction of the relevant legislation, was lawfully due.

In any event, [counsel for the Crown] argued, the Revenue had here done no such thing. Even if the Revenue might in principle be bound by clear and unqualified answers to questions put with reference to specific and fully detailed transactions, it could not be bound by general and qualified state-ments of its current thinking given in relation to different transactions. Such, he submitted, was the material on which the applicants relied. In contrast with *Att.-Gen. of Hong Kong v. Ng Yuen Shiu, ex p. Khan* and *ex p. Ruddock* the statements relied on fell far short of any statement of official policy.

[Counsel for the applicants] in reply accepted that the Revenue could not bind itself to act in conflict with its statutory duty. If its statutory duty left the Revenue no choice but to collect taxes then there was no scope for any binding representation. But the representations here were made in pursuance of the Revenue's duty to collect tax and fell within its reasonable area of managerial discretion....

D. *The correct approach in law*

I take as my starting point the following passage from Lord Templeman's speech in *ex p. Preston* [1985] A.C. 835, 866, expressly adopted by the other members of the House ... [His Lordships cited the passage "However, the *H.T.V.* case and the authorities there cited ... conduct equivalent to a breach of contract or breach of representations on their part."]

It was not suggested in *ex p. Preston* that the bargain allegedly made, if made, would have been a breach of the Revenue's statutory duty, but the applicants here accept that they must fail if the Revenue could not lawfully make the statements or representations which (it is said) it did. So if, in a case involving no breach of statutory duty, the Revenue makes an agreement or representation from which it cannot withdraw without substantial unfairness to the taxpayer who has relied on it, that may found a successful application for judicial review.

I cannot for my part accept that the Revenue's discretion is as limited as counsel for the Crown submitted. In the *Fleet Street Casuals* case the revenue agreed to cut past (irrecoverable) losses in order to facilitate collection of tax in future. In *ex p. Preston* the Revenue cut short an argument with the tax-payer to obtain an immediate payment of tax. In both cases the revenue acted within its managerial discretion. The present case is less obvious. But the Rev-enue's judgment on the best way of collecting tax should not lightly be cast aside. The Revenue might stick to the letter of its statutory duty, declining to answer any question when not statutorily obliged to do so (as it sometimes is: See, *e.g.* sections 464 and 488(11) of the Income and Corporation Taxes Act

1970) and maintaining a strictly arm's length relationship with the taxpayer. It is, however, understandable if the Revenue has not in practice found this to be the best way of facilitating collection of the public revenue. That this has been the Revenue's experience is, I think, made clear by Mr Beighton, who, having described the machinery for assessment and appeal, continues:

> "6. Notwithstanding this general approach in administering the tax system, the Board see it as a proper part of their function and contributing to the achievement of their primary role of assessing and collecting the proper amounts of tax and to detect and deter evasion, that they should when possible advise the public of their rights as well as their duties, and generally encourage co-operation between the Inland Revenue and the public."

I do not think that we, sitting in this court, have any reason to dissent from this judgment. It follows that I do not think the assurances the Revenue are here said to have given are in themselves inconsistent with the Revenue's statutory duty.

I am, however, of opinion that in assessing the meaning, weight and effect reasonably to be given to statements of the Revenue the factual context, including the position of the Revenue itself, is all important. Every ordinarily sophisicated taxpayer knows that the Revenue is a tax-collecting agency, not a tax-imposing authority. The taxpayers' only legitimate expectation is, prima facie, that he will be taxed according to statute, not concession or a wrong view of the law (see *R. v. Attorney-General, ex p. Imperial Chemical Industries plc* (1986) 60 T.C. 1, 64 *per* Lord Oliver). Such taxpayers would appreciate, if they could not so pithily express, the truth of the aphorism of "One should be taxed by law, and not be untaxed by concession". See *Vestey v. Inland Revenue Commissioners, per* Walton J. [1979] Ch. 177, 197. No doubt a statement formally published by the Revenue to the world might safely be regarded as binding, subject to its terms, in any case falling clearly within them. But where the approach to the Revenue is of a less formal nature a more detailed inquiry is, in my view, necessary. If it is to be successfully said that as a result of such an approach the Revenue has agreed to forgo, or has represented that it will forgo, tax which might arguably be payable on a proper construction of the relevant legislation it would in my judgment, be ordinarily necessary for the taxpayer to show that certain conditions had been fulfilled. I say "ordinarily" to allow for the exceptional case where different rules might be appopriate, but the necessity in my view exists here. First, it is necessary that the taxpayer should have put all his cards face upwards on the table. This means that he must give full details of the specific transaction on which he seeks the Revenue's ruling, unless it is the same as an earlier transaction on which a ruling has already been given. It means that he must indicate to the Revenue the ruling sought. It is one thing to ask an official of the Revenue whether he shares the taxpayer's view of a legislative provision, quite another to ask whether the Revenue will forgo any claim to tax on any other basis. It means that the taxpayer must make plain that a fully considered ruling is sought. It means, I think, that the taxpayer should indicate the use he intends to make of any ruling given. This is not because the Revenue would wish to favour one class of taxpayers at the expense of another but because knowledge that a ruling is to be publicised in a large and important market could affect the person by whom and the level at which a problem is considered and, indeed, whether it is appropriate to give a ruling at all. Second, it is necessary that the ruling or statement relied on should be clear, unambiguous and devoid of relevant qualification.

In so stating these requirements I do not, I hope, diminish or emasculate the valuable developing doctrine of legitimate expectation. If a public authority so conducts itself as to create a legitimate expectation that a certain course will be followed it would often be unfair if the authority were permitted to follow a different course to the detriment of one who entertained the expectation, particularly if he acted on it. If in private law a body would be in breach of contract in so acting or estopped from so acting a public authority should generally be in no better position. The doctrine of legitimate expectation is rooted in fairness. But fairness is not a one-way street. It imports the notion of equitableness, of fair and open dealing, to which the authority is as much entitled as the citizen. The Revenue's discretion, while it exists, is limited. Fairness requires that its exercise should be on a basis of full disclosure. Counsel for the applicants accepted that it would not be reasonable for a representee to rely on an unclear or equivocal representation. Nor, I think, on facts such as the present, would it be fair to hold the Revenue bound by anything less than a clear, unambiguous and unqualified representation.

E. *Conclusions*

Against that legal background I return to the representations relied on here to consider whether they meet the conditions specified. . . .

[Bingham L.J. considered the correspondence in detail and concluded:] The materials before us in this case make plain how strongly the applicants feel that the Revenue's conduct, in taxing the indexation uplift on these bonds as income, is unfair. I do not, however, think that in the disputed cases the Revenue has promised to follow or indicated that it would follow a certain course so as to render any departure from that course unfair. I do not accordingly find any abuse of power. I would therefore refuse relief. Had I found that there was unfairness, significant enough to be an abuse of power, I would not exercise my discretion to refuse relief.

JUDGE J.: . . . In the present case the Revenue promulgated a number of guidelines and answered questions by or on behalf of taxpayers about the likely approach to a number of given problems. The Revenue is not bound to give any guidance at all. If however the taxpayer approaches the Revenue with clear and precise proposals about the future conduct of his fiscal affairs and receives an unequivocal statement about how they will be treated for tax purposes if implemented, the Revenue should in my judgment be subject to judicial review on grounds of unfair abuse of power if it peremptorily decides that it will not be bound by such statements when the taxpayer has relied on them. The same principle should apply to revenue statements of policy. In those cases where the taxpayer has approached the Revenue for guidance the court will be unlikely to grant judicial review unless it is satisfied that the taxpayer has treated the revenue with complete frankness about his proposals. Applying private law tests the situation calls for utmost good faith on the part of the taxpayer. He should make full disclosure of all the material facts known to him.

For the reasons given by Bingham L.J. the evidence in the present case does not establish abuse of power by the Revenue. Accordingly, I agree that these applications should be refused.

Notes

1. See A.R. Mowbray (1990) 106 L.Q.R. 568; S. Tidball [1991] B.T.R. 48 and W. Hinds, "Estopping the Taxman" [1991] B.T.R. 191.

2. The concept of "legitimate expectation" is at the heart of this developing ground of challenge for "inconsistency". This concept emerged first as a factor relevant to the question whether the *audi alteram partem* rule of natural justice applied in a particular context. To defeat a person's legitimate expectation was to do to that person an act which should in ordinary circumstances be preceded by warning and the giving of an opportunity to make representations. A stock example of such a situation is the person who, having had the benefit of a licence or permission seeks its renewal. See further, below, p. 454.

Subsequently, the notion of legitimate expectation was utilised to assist an applicant who complained—(i) that he had been adversely affected by a decision or action taken, (ii) that although in ordinary circumstances this was not a situation in which he was entitled to any "hearing" under the *audi alteram partem* rule, (iii) on the facts he had been given a legitimate expectation to expect such a "hearing" prior to the decision or action being taken. Such expectation might arise either from a settled practice of affording such opportunities or from statements or assurances given. Where such complaints have been substantiated the courts have been willing to quash decisions taken without the expected procedure being complied with. See further, below, pp. 448 *et seq.*

Both these applications of the notion of legitimate expectation relate to procedural obligations prior to taking decisions. The cases considered above have used the concept of legitimate expectation to impose restrictions on the substance of decisions or action that a body may take.

3. An important issue is whether the doctrine of inconsistency, in addition to giving rise to a right to a hearing—(i) prohibits any decision being taken which confounds the expectation which the body in question has engendered; or (ii) prohibits such decisions except where some countervailing facet of the public interest so requires, this being judged in the light of the harm being done to the applicant; or (iii) prohibits such decisions except in the circumstances referred to in (ii) above, but with the added requirement that the affected individual be notified of the intended change of policy, and be given an opportunity to offer his thoughts against the new policy and/or its application to himself. On this issue see the various statements of principle in the cases extracted above, and note also the *Laker* case (below).

In *Laker Airways Ltd v. Department of Trade* [1977] Q.B. 643, C.A. (the *Skytrain* case) the plaintiffs were granted a licence by the Civil Aviation Authority in 1972 for a cheap passenger air service between London and New York, a licence confirmed on appeal by the (Conservative) Secretary of State. The Government also "designated" the plaintiffs under the Bermuda Agreement of 1946 between the United Kingdom and the United States of America, with the result under the Agreement that the United States Government were under a duty to grant a permit for operations over United States territory "without undue delay", provided the plaintiffs came up to the required standards. The Government worked closely with the plaintiffs in exerting pressure on the United States authorities. The plaintiffs, with the active help and encouragement of the Government, spent over £6 million on the project. In 1975, the Labour Government reversed its predecessor's policy, and decided that not more than one United Kingdom airline should be licensed for any given long-haul route. The Secretary of State instructed the Civil Aviation Authority to revoke the plaintiff's licence (see above, p. 237) and withdrew the "designation". Mocatta J. ([1976] 3 W.L.R. 537) held, *inter alia*, that the government were estopped by their previous conduct from withdrawing the designation, but was reversed on this point by the Court of Appeal. Lawton Ł.J. said, at 271:

"Whatever representations the Secretary of State in office between 1972 and 1974 may have made to Laker Airways Ltd he made them pursuant to his public duty and in good faith. If in 1976 his successor was of the opinion that the public interest required him to go back on those representations, he was in duty bound to go back on them. The fact that Laker Airways Ltd. suffered loss ás a result of the change is unfortunate: they have been the victims of a change of government policy. This often happens. Estoppel cannot be allowed to hinder the formation of government policy."

Roskill L.J. stated, at 254, that the doctrine of estoppel cannot be allowed to hinder the constitutional result of a general election.

Lord Denning M.R. said (at 252):

"The underlying principle is that the Crown cannot be estopped from exercising its powers, whether given in a statute or by common law, when it is doing so in the proper exercise of its duty to act for the public good, even though this may work some injustice or unfairness to a private individual: see *Maritime Electric Co. Ltd v. General Dairies Ltd* [above, p. 285] where the Privy Council, unfortunately, I think, reversed the Supreme Court of Canada [1935] S.C.R. 519. It can, however, be estopped when it is not properly exercising its powers, but is misusing them; and it does misuse them if it exercises them in circumstances which work injustice or unfairness to the individual without any countervailing benefit for the public...."

Applying this principle Lord Denning M.R. took the view that the claim of "estoppel" had not been made out.

4. A further authority that supports the view that a legitimate expectation can give rise to substantive as well as procedural rights is *R. v. Secretary of State for the Home Department, ex p. Ruddock and Others* [1987] 2 All E.R. 518. One of the three applicants, John Cox, a Vice-President of the Campaign for Nuclear Disarmament, sought judicial review of a warrant issued by the Secretary of State authorising the tapping of his telephone, alleging that the intercept fell outside the criteria for the interception of communications, which required, *inter alia,* that there was reasonable cause to believe that major subversive activity was being carried out, and that interception was not to be used for party political purposes. These criteria had been published and successive Secretaries of State had acknowledged their binding effect. The Secretary of State argued that the doctrine of legitimate expectation related only to cases where the applicant's expectation was of being consulted or given the opportunity to make representations before a certain decision adverse to him was made, and that as here there could be no question of his being consulted or heard before a warrant was issued, the legitimate expectation doctrine could not reply. Taylor J. considered *Schmidt v. Home Secretary,* the *CCSU, Ng Yuen Shiu, Findlay* and *ex p. Khan* cases, concluded that while most of the cases concerned the right to be heard, the doctrine could not be so confined:

"Indeed, in a case where ex hypothesi there is no right to be heard, it may be thought the more important to fair dealing that a promise or undertaking by the minister as to how he will proceed should be kept. Of course such promise or undertaking must

not conflict with his statutory duty or his duty, as here, in the exercise of a prerogative power. I accept ... that the respondent cannot fetter his discretion. By declaring
a policy he does not preclude any possible need to change it. But then if the practice
has been to publish the current policy, it would be incumbent on him in dealing fairly
to publish the new policy, unless again that would conflict with his duties" (at 531).

Here a legitimate expectation that the published criteria would be applied arose from
both an express promise and a regular practice. The Secretary of State did not argue
that the criteria had been changed or that an exception had been made for security
reasons; his contention was that the intercept fell within the published criteria. Taylor
J. concluded on the evidence that the Secretary of State had not deliberately flouted the
criteria and that his decision that the warrant fell within them was not irrational.

5. *Ex p. Ruddock* can be compared with two cases where legitimate expectations
could not prevent changes in policy. In *Re Findlay* [1985] A.C. 318, the Secretary of
State for the Home Department announced changes of parole policy in respect of certain categories of prisoners. Prisoners sentenced for the murder of police or prison
officers, terrorist offences, sexual or sadistic murder of children, or murder by a fire-
arm in the course of robbery would henceforth normally serve at least 20 years; prisoners serving determinate sentences of over five years for offences of violence or drug
trafficking would, save in exceptional circumstances, be granted parole only when
release under supervision for a few months before the end of their sentence was likely
to reduce the long-term risk to the public. Four prisoners who were affected by the
changes sought judicial review on a variety of grounds. One ground in respect of the
two life sentence prisoners was that they had good reason under the old policy to
expect release much earlier than was likely under the new policy. Lord Scarman commented (at 338):

> "The doctrine of legitimate expectation has an important place in the developing
> law of judicial review. It is however, not necessary to explore the doctrine in this
> case, it is enough merely to note that a legitimate expectation can provide a sufficient
> interest to enable one who cannot point to the existence of a substantive right to
> obtain the leave of the court to apply for judicial review. These two appellants
> obtained leave. But their submission goes further. It is said that the refusal to except
> them from the new policy was an unlawful act on the part of the Secretary of State in
> that his decision frustrated their expectation. But what was their *legitimate* expec-
> tation? Given the substance and purpose of the legislative provisions governing par-
> ole, the most that a convicted prisoner can legitimately expect is that his case will be
> examined individually in the light of whatever policy the Secretary of State sees fit to
> adopt provided always that the adopted policy is a lawful exercise of the discretion
> conferred upon him by the statute. Any other view would entail the conclusion that
> the unfettered discretion conferred by the statute upon the minister can in some
> cases be restricted so as to hamper, or even prevent, changes of policy. Bearing in
> mind the complexity of the issues which the Secretary of State has to consider and
> the importance of the public interest in the administration of parole I cannot think
> that Parliament intended the discretion to be restricted in this way."

Subsequently, in *R. v. Secretary of State for Health, ex p. United States Tobacco
International Inc.* [1992] 1 Q.B. 353 the Divisional Court considered a challenge to
the Secretary of State's change of policy in deciding to make regulations banning oral
snuff (a smokeless tobacco product). The applicants marketed "Skoal Bandits",
porous sachets containing oral snuff. In 1984 they had discussed with various government departments the possibility of opening a factory in Scotland to manufacture their
product. On the advice of a committee that advised the Secretary of State for Health,
the government negotiated an agreement whereby the applicants undertook not to
market oral snuff to persons under 18. The applicants opened their factory in 1985,

with the help of a government grant. The agreement was revised in 1986 and subsequently extended to April 1988. In June 1986, however, the committee advised the Secretary of State to ban oral snuff; in February 1988, the Secretary of State announced a proposal for such a ban. The Divisional Court quashed the regulations on the ground of a lack of consultation with the applicants (see below, p. 412). However, the court rejected an argument based on legitimate expectation. Taylor L.J. noted that the:

"applicants are understandably aggrieved that after leading them on, the government should then strike them a mortal blow by totally banning their products" (at 368).

They contended that they had

"a legitimate expectation that, provided they continued to perform their obligations under the voluntary agreement and absent the emergence of stronger evidence as to the risk to health, their operators would be permitted to continue" (*ibid.*).

This was not based on any express promise, but was implied by the course of conduct. Taylor L.J. cited, *inter alia*, the passages from Lord Scarman's judgment in *Re Findlay* and his own judgment in *ex p. Ruddock* set out above. He then said (at 369):

"In the present case, if the Secretary of State concluded on rational grounds that a policy change was required and oral snuff should be banned in the public interest, his discretion could not be fettered by moral obligations to the applicants deriving from his earlier favourable treatment of them. It would be absurd to suggest that some moral commitment to a single company should prevail over the public interest."

Morland J. said (at 372):

"The applicants were entitled to expect that their commercial operations would be allowed to continue and expand subject to their compliance with the voluntary agreement unless there were good and substantial reasons for a change in Government policy. However, they must have been aware that their expectations could never fetter the Secretary of State's duty to promote and safeguard the health of the public. That is a duty which must ... override private commercial expectations and interests. The right of government to change its policy in the field of health must be unfettered. This is so even if the basic scientific evidence remains unchanged or substantially unchanged. Reconsideration and re-evaluation of that evidence may call for a change of policy."

See B. Schwehr and P. Brown [1991] P.L. 163, who criticise the decision on this aspect of the case as diluting an "otherwise healthy and beneficial doctrine" (at 167). In holding that there was no legitimate expectation, the court had conflated two distinct issues: first, whether there was a legitimate expectation and, secondly, if there was, whether there was good ground for it to be overridden in the public interest:

"The relevant question for the court is not, 'is there a legitimate expectation?' but, 'has the minister shown a good reason for changing his mind?' " (at 166).

The court had failed to address the second question directly (although the answer might still have been in the affirmative). See, to similar effect, P.P. Craig (1992) 108 L.Q.R. 79, 97.

6. The Court of Appeal has recently held that unfairness amounting to abuse of power may be found notwithstanding the absence of "an unqualified and

unambiguous representation." In *R. v. IRC, ex p. Unilever plc* [1996] S.T.C. 681, for over 20 years, tax computations by the applicants has been accepted by the Revenue notwithstanding that relief in respect of trading losses was not expressly sought; such an express claim was required by section 393 of the Income and Corporation Taxes Act 1988 as the computations were submitted more than two years after the accounting period to which they related. The Court of Appeal concluded that on these "unique facts" the Revenue's actions in rejecting the claims in reliance on the two year time limit, without clear and general advance notice, were so unfair as to amount to an abuse of power, and irrational. Sir Thomas Bingham M.R. stated (at 690):—

"The categories of unfairness are not closed, and precedent should act as a guide not a cage."

The arrangements that had been followed had been entirely sufficient to meet the needs of both the Revenue and the applicants; the enforcement of the two-year time limit was demonstrably pointless. It is also of interest that Simon Brown L.J. (at 695) regarded "the *MFK* category of legitimate expectation as essentially but a head of *Wednesbury* unreasonableness, not necessarily exhaustive of the grounds upon which a successful substantive unfairness challenge may be based". Sir Thomas Bingham M.R. (at 691–692) followed the trial judge in treating the argument based on unfairness as distinct from that based on irrationality, although he did not "think that in truth this raises a new point". See N. Bamforth [1997] C.L.J. 1.

7. Applying the principles which emerge from the cases in this section it may be necessary for a determination to be reached as to whether or not the "public interest" in a change of policy should be regarded as sufficient to override the interests of those with legitimate expectations of that policy's continuance. Who should judge this matter? The administration? The reviewing court? The administration, subject to its decision on the matter being *Wednesbury* reviewable? In *R. v. Ministry of Agriculture, Fisheries and Food, ex p. Hamble (Offshore) Fisheries Ltd* [1995] 2 All E.R. 714, Sedley J. indicated favour for the second of these three possibilities. However, more recently, in *R. v. Secretary of State for the Home Department, ex p. Hargreaves,* [1997] 1 W.L.R. 906 the Court of Appeal has overruled *Hamble* on this point. Sedley J.'s ratio does not represent the proper approach, in so far as it involved a balancing exercise to be undertaken by the court: shades of "proportionality" (see below, p. 397). The approach favoured by the Court of Appeal was to apply the *Wednesbury* test to the administrator's exercise of judgment on this matter of public interest. Hirst L.J. commented in *Hargreaves,* "Mr Beloff characterised Sedley J.'s approach as heresy, and in my judgment he was right to do so. On matters of substance (as contrasted with procedure) *Wednesbury* provides the correct test. It follows that while Sedley J.'s actual decision in the *Hamble* case stands, his ratio in so far as it propounds a balancing exercise to be undertaken by the the court should in my judgment be overruled." In similar vein Pill L.J. said, "The court can quash the decision only if, in relation to the expectation and in all the circumstances, the decision to apply the new policy in the particular case was unreasonable in the *Wednesbury* sense ... The claim to a broader power to judge the fairness of a decision of substance ... is in my view wrong in principle." The approach adopted in *Hargreaves* seems consistent with the stance adopted by Laws J. in *R. v. Secretary of State for Transport, ex p. Richmond LBC* [1994] 1 W.L.R. 74 at 94.

8. The legitimate expectation concept, in both its procedural and substantive aspects, has given rise to a considerable literature. See G. Ganz, "Legitimate Expectation: A Confusion of Concepts" in C. Harlow (ed.), *Public Law and Politics* (1986), Chap. 8; R. Baldwin and D. Horne, "Expectations in a Joyless Landscape" (1986) 49 M.L.R. 685; P. Elias, "Legitimate Expectation and Judicial Review" in J. Jowell and D. Oliver (eds.), *New Directions in Judicial Review* (1988), pp. 37–50; C.F. Forsyth, "The Provenance and Protection of Legitimate Expectations" [1988] C.L.J. 238; B. Hadfield, "Judicial Review and the Concept of Legitimate Expectation" (1988) 39

N.I.L.Q. 103; P.P. Craig, "Legitimate Expectations: A Conceptual Analysis" (1992) 108 L.Q.R. 79 and "Substantive Legitimate Expectations in Domestic and Community Law" [1996] C.L.J. 289. Some commentators are sceptical of the soundness of the substantive dimension to the concept, arguing that it can lead to conflict with the rule against the fettering of discretion (*e.g.* Ganz); others have welcomed the development (*e.g.* Forsyth, Craig).

(E) NOTE ON "PROPORTIONALITY" AS A GROUND OF REVIEW

In this chapter, and in the one which preceded it, we have considered the case law depicting the scope of review of discretionary powers. We have done so on the basis of categories and subdivisions which have, over the last three decades, partly as a result of the language of the judges and partly as a result of the rationalisations of commentators, acquired a familiarity and consistency of usage. This had had beneficial consequences in terms of the development and refinement of doctrine.

It does not follow, however, that the various categories are mutually exclusive as to their operation—indeed we have had cause to note areas of overlap and actual or potential conflict. Moreover, it does not follow that the categories are exhaustive of the ways in which a body may fail to retain or may abuse its discretionary powers.

In this latter regard there has been, and remains, some uncertainty as to the extent to which the notion of "proportionality" may or should be considered to be a ground of review. This concept is a common feature of the jurisprudence of civil law countries, and has become a regularly used tool of legal reasoning in the European Court of Justice and the European Court of Human Rights. In essence the doctrine provides that a court of review may intervene if it considers that the harms attendant upon a particular exercise of power are disproportionate to the benefits sought to be achieved.

It will be evident that in many cases where a plea of disproportionality might succeed the applicant would succeed also under one of the established grounds of challenge—for example, improper purpose or relevant/irrelevant considerations or unreasonableness. To this extent incorporation of proportionality as an accepted ground of review would add little beyond new vocabulary to the language of review.

Proponents of the doctrine would argue that it would, in fact, permit the courts a scope of review which goes beyond the existing categories, whilst still preserving the important distinction between review of legality and appeal on merits. These issues as to the scope of review (if any) on grounds of disproportionality was quite recently considered by the House of Lords in the *Brind* case (below).

R. v. SECRETARY OF STATE FOR THE HOME DEPARTMENT, ex p. BRIND

[1991] 1 A.C. 696; [1991] 2 W.L.R. 588; [1991] 1 All E.R. 721 (House of Lords)

In October 1988 the Home Secretary, exercising powers under the Broadcasting Act 1981 (in respect of independent broadcasting) and the BBC's licence and agreement (in respect of that body), issued a directive prohibiting the broadcasting of "words spoken" by any person representing or purporting to represent certain organisations. The organisations were those proscribed under the Northern Ireland (Emergency Provisions) Act 1978, the Prevention of Terrorism (Temporary Provisions) Act 1984, and Sinn Féin, Republican Sinn Féin and the Ulster Defence Association.

The powers under the 1981 Act and the licence/agreement authorised the Home

Secretary to require the broadcasting authorities to "refrain from broadcasting any matter or classes of matter specified in the notice".

The applicants, who were journalists, sought judicial review of the Home Secretary's decision. They were unsuccessful in the Divisional Court and the Court of Appeal ([1990] 1 A.C. 700). On appeal to the House of Lords:

LORD BRIDGE OF HARWICH: My Lords, this appeal has been argued primarily on the basis that the power of the Secretary of State ... to impose restrictions ... may only be lawfully exercised in accordance with art. 10 of the European Convention on Human Rights.... Any exercise by the Secretary of State of the power in question necessarily imposes some restriction on freedom of expression. The obligations of the United Kingdom, as a party to the convention, are to secure to every one within its jurisdiction the rights which the convention defines, including both the right to freedom of expression under art. 10 and the right under art. 13 to "an effective remedy before a national authority" for any violation of the other rights secured by the convention. It is accepted, of course, by the appellants that, like any other treaty obligations which have not been embodied in the law by statute, the convention is not part of the domestic law, that the courts accordingly have no power to enforce convention rights directly and that, if domestic legislation conflicts with the convention, the courts must nevertheless enforce it. But it is already well settled that, in construing any provision in domestic legislation which is ambiguous in the sense that it is capable of a meaning which either conforms to or conflicts with the convention, the courts will presume that Parliament intended to legislate in conformity with the convention, not in conflict with it. Hence, it is submitted, when a statute confers upon an administrative authority a discretion capable of being exercised in a way which infringes any basic human right protected by the convention, it may similarly be presumed that the legislative intention was that the discretion should be exercised within the limitations which the convention imposes. I confess that I found considerable persuasive force in this submission. But in the end I have been convinced that the logic of it is flawed. When confronted with a simple choice between two possible interpretations of some specific statutory provision, the presumption whereby the courts prefer that which avoids conflict between our domestic legislation and our international treaty obligations is a mere canon of construction which involves no importation of international law into the domestic field. But where Parliament has conferred on the executive an administrative discretion without indicating the precise limits within which it must be exercised, to presume that it must be exercised within convention limits would be to go far beyond the resolution of an ambiguity. It would be to impute to Parliament an intention not only that the executive should exercise the discretion in conformity with the convention, but also that the domestic courts should enforce that conformity by the importation into domestic administrative law of the text of the convention and the jurisprudence of the European Court of Human Rights in the interpretation and application of it. If such a presumption is to apply to the statutory discretion exercised by the Secretary of State ... in the instant case, it must also apply to any other statutory discretion exercised by the executive which is capable of involving an infringement of convention rights. When Parliament has been content for so long to leave those who complain that their convention rights have been infringed to seek their remedy in Strasbourg, it would be surprising suddenly to find that the judiciary had, without Parliament's aid, the means to incorporate the convention into such an important area of domestic law and I cannot escape the conclusion that this would be a judicial usurpation of the legislative function.

But I do not accept that this conclusion means that the courts are powerless to prevent the exercise by the executive of administrative discretions, even when conferred, as in the instant case, in terms which are on their face unlimited, in a way which infringes fundamental human rights. Most of the rights spelled out in terms in the convention, including the right to freedom of expression, are less than absolute and must in some cases yield to the claims of competing public interests. Thus, art. 10(2) of the convention spells out and categorises the competing public interests by reference to which the right to freedom of expression may have to be curtailed. In exercising the power of judicial review we have neither the advantages nor the disadvantages of any comparable code to which we may refer or by which we are bound. But again, this surely does not mean that in deciding whether the Secretary of State, in the exercise of his discretion, could reasonably impose the restriction he has imposed on the broadcasting organisations, we are not perfectly entitled to start from the premise that any restriction of the right to freedom of expression requires to be justified and that nothing less than an important competing public interest will be sufficient to justify it. The primary judgment as to whether the particular competing public interest justifies the particular restriction imposed falls to be made by the Secretary of State to whom Parliament has entrusted the discretion. But we are entitled to exercise a secondary judgment by asking whether a reasonable Secretary of State, on the material before him, could reasonably make that primary judgment.

Applying these principles to the circumstances of the case.... I find it impossible to say that the Secretary of State exceeded the limits of his discretion. In any civilised and law-abiding society the defeat of the terrorist is a public interest of the first importance. That some restriction on the freedom of the terrorist and his supporters to propagate his cause may well be justified in support of that public interest is a proposition which I apprehend the appellants hardly dispute. Their real case is that they, in the exercise of their editorial judgment, may and must be trusted to ensure that the broadcasting media are not used in such a way as will afford any encouragement or support to terrorism and that any interference with that editorial judgment is necessarily an unjustifiable restriction on the right to freedom of expression. Accepting, as I do, their complete good faith, I nevertheless cannot accept this proposition. The Secretary of State, for the reasons he made so clear in Parliament, decided that it was necessary to deny to the terrorist and his supporters the opportunity to speak directly to the public through the most influential of all the media of communication and that this justified some interference with editorial freedom. I do not see how this judgment can be categorised as unreasonable. What is perhaps surprising is that the restriction imposed is of such limited scope. There is no restriction at all on the matter which may be broadcast, only on the manner of its presentation. The viewer may see the terrorist's face and hear his words provided only that they are not spoken in his own voice. I well understand the broadcast journalist's complaint that to put him to the trouble of dubbing the voice of the speaker he has interviewed before the television camera is an irritant which the difference in effect between the speaker's voice and the actor's voice hardly justifies. I well understand the political complaint that the restriction may be counter-productive in the sense that the adverse criticism it provokes outweighs any benefit it achieves. But these complaints fall very far short of demonstrating that a reasonable Secretary of State could not reasonably conclude that the restriction was justified by the important public interest of combating terrorism. I should add that I do not see how reliance on the doctrine of "proportionality" can here advance the appellants' case. But I agree with what my noble and learned friend, Lord Roskill, says in his speech about the possible future development of the law in that respect.

I would dismiss the appeal.

LORD TEMPLEMAN: ... The English courts must, in conformity with the *Wednesbury* principles ... consider whether the Home Secretary has taken into account all relevant matters and has ignored irrelevant matters. These conditions are satisfied by the evidence in this case, including evidence by the Home Secretary that he took the convention into account. If these conditions are satisfied, then it is said on *Wednesbury* principles the court can only interfere by way of judicial review if the decision of the Home Secretary is "irrational" or "perverse".

The subject-matter and date of the *Wednesbury* principles cannot in my opinion make it either necessary or appropriate for the courts to judge the validity of an interference with human rights by asking themselves whether the Home Secretary has acted irrationally or perversely. It seems to me that the courts cannot escape from asking themselves only whether a reasonable Secretary of State, on the material before him, could reasonably conclude that the interference with freedom of expression which he determined to impose was justifiable. In terms of the convention, as construed by the European Court of Human Rights, the interference with freedom of expression must be necessary and proportionate to the damage which the restriction is designed to prevent.

My Lords, applying these principles I do not consider that the court can conclude that the Home Secretary has abused or exceeded his powers. The broadcasting authorities and journalists are naturally resentful of any limitation on their right to present a programme in such manner as they think fit. But the interference with freedom of expression is minimal and the reasons given by the Home Secretary are compelling.

I, too, would dismiss this appeal.

LORD ACKNER: ... The Secretary of State's reasons for taking the action complained of are set out in the Hansard Reports of those debates and were before your Lordships. The four matters which influenced the Secretary of State were ... (1) offence had been caused to viewers and listeners by the appearance of the apologists for terrorism, particularly after a terrorist outrage; (2) such appearances had afforded terrorists undeserved publicity which was contrary to the public interest; (3) these appearances had tended to increase the standing of terrorist organisations and to create a false impression that support for terrorism is itself a legitimate political opinion; (4) broadcast statements were intended to have, and did in some cases have, the effect of intimidating some of those at whom they were directed.

The challenge
I now turn to the bases upon which it is contended that the Secretary of State exceeded his statutory powers.

(1) ...

(2)*The directives were unlawful on "Wednesbury" grounds*

Save only in one respect, namely the European Convention for the Protection of Human Rights and Fundamental Freedoms ... which is the subject-matter of a later heading, it is not suggested that the minister failed to call his attention to matters which he was bound to consider, nor that he included in his considerations matters which were irrelevant. In neither of those senses can it be said that the minister acted unreasonably. The failure to mount such a challenge in this appeal is important. In a field which concerns a fundamental human right, namely that of free speech, close scrutiny must be given to the reasons provided as justification for interference with that right. Your Lordships' attention was drawn to *R. v. Secretary of State for Transport, ex p. de Rothschild* [1989] 1 All E.R. 933, a case which concerned compulsory purchase and therefore involved, albeit somewhat indirectly, another fundamental human right—the peaceful enjoyment of one's possessions: see art. 1 of the First Protocol to the Convention. In that case Slade L.J. said, at 939:

> "Given the obvious importance and value to land owners of their property rights, the abrogation of those rights in the exercise of his discretionary power to confirm a compulsory purchase order would, in the absence of what he perceived to be a sufficient justification on the merits, be a course which surely no reasonable Secretary of State would take."

Slade L.J. was in no sense increasing the severity of the *Wednesbury* test.... He was applying that part of it which requires the decision-maker to call his attention to matters that he is obliged to consider. He was emphasising the Secretary of State's obligation to identify the factors which had motivated his decision so as to ensure that he had overlooked none which a reasonable Secretary of State should have considered.

There remains however the potential criticism under the *Wednesbury* grounds ... that the conclusion was "so unreasonable that no reasonable authority could ever have come to it". This standard of unreasonableness, often referred to as "the irrationality test", has been criticised as being too high. But it has to be expressed in terms that confine the jurisdiction exercised by the judiciary to a supervisory, as opposed to an appellate, jurisdiction. Where Parliament has given to a minister or other person or body a discretion, the court's jurisdiction is limited, in the absence of a statutory right of appeal, to the supervision of the exercise of that discretionary power, so as to ensure that it has been exercised lawfully. It would be a wrongful usurpation of power by the judiciary to substitute its view, the judicial view, on the merits and on that basis to quash the decision. If no reasonable minister properly directing himself would have reached the impugned decision, the minister has exceeded his powers and thus acted unlawfully and the court, in the exercise of its supervisory role, will quash that decision. Such a decision is correctly, though unattractively, described as a "perverse" decision. To seek the court's intervention on the basis that the correct or objectively reasonable decision is other than the decision which the minister has made, is to invite the court to adjudicate as if Parliament had provided a right of appeal against the decision, that is to invite an abuse of power by the judiciary.

So far as the facts of this case are concerned it is only necessary to read the speeches in the Houses of Parliament, ... to reach the conclusion, that whether the Secretary of State was right or wrong to decide to issue the directives, there was clearly material which would justify a reasonable minister making the same decision. In the words of Lord Diplock in *Secretary of State for Education and Science v. Tameside Metropolitan Borough* [1977] A.C. 1014, 1064:

> "The very concept of administrative discretion involves a right to choose between more than one possible course of action on which there is room for reasonable people to hold differing opinions as to which is to be preferred."

... I entirely agree with McCowan L.J. [in the Court of Appeal] when he said that he found it quite impossible to hold that the Secretary of State's political judgment that the appearance of terrorists on programmes increases their standing and lends them political legitimacy is one that no reasonable Home Secretary could hold....

Mr Lester has contended that in issuing these directives the Secretary of State has used a sledgehammer to crack a nut. Of course that is a picturesque way of describing the *Wednesbury* "irrational" test. The Secretary of State has in my judgment used no sledgehammer. Quite the contrary is the case.

I agree with Lord Donaldson M.R. who, when commenting on how limited the restrictions were, said in his judgment ...:

> "They have no application in the circumstances mentioned in para. 3 (proceedings in the United Kingdom Parliament and elections) and, by allowing reported speech either verbatim or in paraphrase, in effect put those affected in no worse a position than they would be if they had access to newspaper publicity with a circulation equal to the listening and viewing audiences of the programmes concerned. Furthermore, on the applicants' own evidence, if the directives had been in force during the previous 12 months, the effect would have been minimal in terms of air time. Thus, [ITN] say that 8 minutes 20 seconds (including repeats) out of 1,200 hours, or 0.01%, of air time would have been affected. Furthermore, it would not have been necessary to omit these items. They could have been recast into a form which complied with the directives."

Thus the extent of the interference with the right to freedom of speech is a very modest one....

(3)*The minister failed to have proper regard to the European Convention for the Protection of Human Rights and Fundamental Freedoms and in particular art. 10*

Article 10 reads as follows:

> "(1) Everyone has the right to freedom of expression. This right shall

include freedom to hold opinions and to receive and impart information and ideas without interference by public authority and regardless of frontiers. This Article shall not prevent States from requiring the licensing of broadcasting, television or cinema enterprises.

(2) The exercise of these freedoms, since it carries with it duties and responsibilities, may be subject to such formalities, conditions, restrictions or penalties as are prescribed by law and are necessary in a democratic society, in the interests of national security, territorial integrity or public safety, for the prevention of disorder or crime, for the protection of health or morals, for the protection of the reputation or rights of others, for preventing the disclosure of information received in confidence, or for maintaining the authority and impartiality of the judiciary."

[His Lordship noted that the Convention is a treaty to which the United Kingdom is a party but which has not been incorporated by legislation into English domestic law. He also noted that the terms of a treaty may be used to resolve an ambiguity in an Act, but held that there was no such ambiguity in the terms of the 1981 Act. He then referred to a further argument of counsel for the applicants, and continued:]

... Mr Lester ... claims that the Secretary of State before issuing his directives should have considered not only the convention (it is accepted that he in fact did so) but that he should have properly construed it and correctly taken it into consideration. It was therefore a relevant, indeed a vital, factor to which he was obliged to have proper regard pursuant to the *Wednesbury* doctrine, with the result that his failure to do so rendered his decision unlawful. The fallacy of this submission is, however, plain. If the Secretary of State was obliged to have proper regard to the convention, *i.e.* to conform with art. 10, this inevitably would result in incorporating the convention into English domestic law by the back door. It would oblige the courts to police the operation of the convention and to ask itself in each case, where there was a challenge, whether the restrictions were "necessary in a democratic society ..." applying the principles enunciated in the decisions of the European Court of Human Rights. The treaty, not having been incorporated in English law, cannot be a source of rights and obligations and the question—did the Secretary of State act in breach of art. 10?—does not therefore arise....

(4) *The Secretary of State has acted ultra vires because he has acted "in a disproportionate manner"*

This attack is not a repetition of the *Wednesbury* "irrational" test under another guise. Clearly a decision by a minister which suffers from a total lack of proportionality will qualify for the "*Wednesbury* unreasonable" epithet. It is, ex hypothesi, a decision which no reasonable minister could make. This is, however, a different and severer test.

Mr Lester is asking your Lordships to adopt a different principle: the principle of "proportionality" which is recognised in the administrative law of several members of the European Economic Community. What is urged is a further development in English administrative law, which Lord Diplock viewed as a possibility in *Council of Civil Service Unions v. Minister for the Civil Service* [1985] A.C. 374, 410.

In his written submissions, Mr Lester was at pains to record "that there is a clear distinction between an appeal on the merits and a review based on whether the principle of proportionality has been satisfied". He was prepared to accept that to stray into the realms of appellate jurisdiction involves the courts in a wrongful usurpation of power. Yet in order to invest the proportionality test with a higher status than the *Wednesbury* test, an inquiry into and a decision upon the merits cannot be avoided. Mr Pannick's (Mr Lester's junior) formulation—could the minister reasonably conclude that his direction was necessary?—must involve balancing the reasons, pro and con, for his decision, albeit allowing him "a margin of appreciation" to use the European concept of the tolerance accorded to the decision-maker in whom a discretion has been vested. The European test of "whether the 'interference' complained of corresponds to a 'pressing social need' " (*The Sunday Times v. United Kingdom* (1979) 2 E.H.R.R. 245 at 277) must ultimately result in the question—is the particular decision acceptable?—and this must involve a review of the merits of the decision. Unless and until Parliament incorporates the convention into domestic law, a course which it is well known has a strong body of support, there appears to me to be at present no basis upon which the proportionality doctrine applied by the European Court can be followed by the courts of this country.

I would accordingly dismiss this appeal. . . .

Appeal dismissed.

Notes

1. Lord Roskill agreed with the reasons given by Lord Bridge. On the issue of proportionality he referred to Lord Diplock's statement in the *Council of Civil Service Unions* case about the "possible adoption in future" of this principle of review, and noted Lord Diplock's view that any such development would be on a case by case basis. Lord Roskill continued (at 750):

"I am clearly of the view that the present is not a case in which the first step can be taken for the reason that to apply the principle in the present case would be for the court to substitute its own judgment of what was needed to achieve a particular objective for the judgment of the Secretary of State upon whom that duty has been laid by Parliament. But so to hold in the present case is not to exclude the possible future development of the law in this respect..."

Lord Lowry agreed with Lord Ackner. On the issue of "proportionality" as a ground of challenge, he said (at 766–767):

"In my opinion proportionality and the other phrases are simply intended to move the focus of discussion away from the hitherto accepted criteria for deciding whether the decision-maker has abused his power and into an area in which the court will feel more at liberty to interfere.

The first observation I would make is that there is *no* authority for saying that proportionality in the sense in which the appellants have used it is part of the English common law and a great deal of authority the other way. This, so far as I am concerned, is not a cause for regret for several reasons. (1) The decision-makers, very often elected, are those to whom Parliament has entrusted the discretion and to interfere with that discretion beyond the limits as hitherto defined would itself be an abuse of the judges' supervisory jurisdiction. (2) The judges are not, generally speaking, equipped by training or experience, or furnished with the requisite knowledge and advice, to decide the answer to an administrative problem where the scales are evenly balanced, but they have a much better chance of reaching the right answer where the question is put in a *Wednesbury* form. The same applies if the judges' decision is appealed. (3) Stability and relative certainty would be jeopardised if the new doctrine held sway, because there is nearly always something to be said against any administrative decision and parties who felt aggrieved would be even more likely than at present to try their luck with a judicial review application both at first instance and on appeal. (4) The increase in applications for judicial review of administrative action (inevitable if the threshold of unreasonableness is lowered) will lead to the expenditure of time and money by litigants, not to speak of the prolongation of uncertainty for all concerned with the decisions in question, and the taking up of court time which could otherwise be devoted to other matters. The losers in this respect will be members of the public, for whom the courts provide a service.

1(1) *Halsbury's Laws of England* (4th ed., vol. 1(1) reissue, 1989) recognises proportionality in the context of administrative law as follows:

> '78. Proportionality. The courts will quash exercise of discretionary powers in which there is not a reasonable relationship between the objective which is sought to be achieved and the means used to that end, or where punishments imposed by administrative bodies or inferior courts are wholly out of proportion to the relevant misconduct. The principle of proportionality is well established in European law, and will be applied by English courts where European law is enforceable in the domestic courts. The principle of proportionality is still at a stage of development in English law; lack of proportionality is not usually treated as a separate ground of review in English law, but is regarded as one indication of manifest unreasonableness.'

(The High Court's decision in the instant case (see *The Times*, May 30, 1989) is cited in the copious footnotes to this paragraph as the authority for the concluding statement.)

It finally occurs to me that there can be very little room for judges to operate an independent judicial review proportionality doctrine in the space which is left between the conventional judicial review doctrine and the admittedly forbidden appellate approach. To introduce an intermediate area of deliberation for the court seems scarcely a practical idea, quite apart from the other disadvantages by which, in my opinion, such a course would be attended."

2. See comments by C. Lewis [1991] C.L.J. 211; B. Thompson [1989] P.L. 527 (on *Brind* in the Divisional Court) and [1991] P.L. 346; J. Jowell [1990] P.L. 149 (on *Brind* in the Court of Appeal); and M. Halliwell (1991) 42 N.I.L.Q. 246.

3. As mentioned in the extract from *Halsbury's Laws* cited by Lord Lowry, proportionality is well established as a ground of review in European Community Law, with its origins in continental administrative law: see D. Wyatt and A. Dashwood, *The Substantive Law of the E.E.C.* (3rd ed., 1993), pp. 89–91; and T.C. Hartley, *The Foundations of European Community Law* (3rd ed., 1994), pp. 155–156. Note also the comments of F. Stroink in *Judicial Control: Comparative Essays on Judicial Review* (1995), pp. 81–100. In Case 181/84, *R. v. Intervention Board for Agricultural Produce, ex p. E.D. & F. Man (Sugar) Ltd* [1985] ECR 2889; [1985] 3 CMLR 759; [1986] 2 All E.R. 115, the Court of Justice of the European Communities stated that "in order to establish whether a provision of Community law is in conformity with the principle of proportionality it is necessary to ascertain whether the means which it employs are appropriate and necessary to attain the objective sought" (at 124). Where a question of Community law arises for consideration in an English court, the court may be required to give effect to the proportionality principle as it is understood in Community law: see, *e.g. Thomas v. Adjudication Officer* [1991] 3 All E.R. 315; *cf.*

Hoffmann J. in *Stoke-on-Trent v. B&Q plc* [1991] 4 All E.R. 221. (Note, however, the argument of A. Arnull (1991) 16 E.L.Rev. 112) that Hoffmann J.'s formulation of the proportionality test in community law was incorrect. Hoffmann J., in reviewing the proportionality of the Sunday trading legislation, was prepared only to inquire whether the "compromise adopted by the United Kingdom Parliament" was "one which a reasonable legislative could have reached" (at 235); his Lordship refused to carry out a balancing exercise himself or to form his own view on whether the legislative objective (the arrangement of working hours "so as to accord with national or regional socio-cultural characteristics": Case 145/88 *Torfaen Borough Council v. B&Q plc* [1989] E.C.R. 3851; [1990] 1 C.M.L.R. 337; [1990] 2 Q.B. 19) could be achieved by other means. Arnull argues that Community law requires the latter approach to be adopted.

CHAPTER 8

ERRORS OF PROCEDURE

(A) FAILURE TO OBSERVE STATUTORY REQUIREMENTS

ACTION taken by a public authority may be void if it offends against procedural conditions laid down, expressly or by necessary implication, in the enabling statute. This principle may be applied in a variety of situations, including the procedure by which a decision is taken, the timing of the decision and the identity of the persons taking the decision. In the latter instance, there may be a breach of the rule against delegation (*delegatus non potest delegare*) (above, p. 239) or an authority may be found to have been improperly constituted (above, p. 192).

A distinction has traditionally been drawn in the case law between procedural requirements which are *mandatory*, breach of which renders the ultimate decision *ultra vires*, and those which are *directory*. In the latter case, the requirements should be observed, but if they are not there is at most a mere *intra vires* error. "[I]n each case you must look to the subject matter; consider the importance of the provision that has been disregarded, and the relation of that provision to the general object intended to be secured by the Act . . ." (*per* Lord Penzance in *Howard v. Bodington* (1877) 2 P.D. 203, 211). *de Smith, Woolf and Jowell* consider that the terms mandatory and directory: ". . . often cause more problems than they solve. The law relating to the effect of failure to comply with statutory requirements thus resembles an inextricable tangle of loose ends and judges have often stressed the impracticability of specifying exact rules for the assignment of a provision to the appropriate category" (p. 266). In recent times the senior judiciary have been adopting a more flexible approach (see below, p. 413).

AGRICULTURAL, HORTICULTURAL AND FORESTRY INDUSTRY TRAINING BOARD v. AYLESBURY MUSHROOMS LTD

[1972] 1 W.L.R. 190; (1971) 116 S.J. 57; [1972] 1 All E.R. 280; [1972] I.T.R. 16 (Donaldson J.)

The Industrial Training Act 1964 provided for the establishment by Order of industrial training boards. Each board arranged training for those employed in the industries concerned, and was supported by levies imposed on the employers in those industries. Section 1(4) of the Act provided:

"Before making an industrial training order the Minister shall consult any organisation or association of organisations appearing to him to be representative of substantial numbers of employers engaging in the activities concerned and any organisation or association of organisations appearing to him to be representative of substantial numbers of persons employed in those activities; and if those activities are carried on to a substantial extent by a body established for the purpose of carrying on under national ownership any industry or part of an industry or undertaking, shall consult that body."

407

In 1965, the Ministry of Labour was minded to set up the plaintiff board. Consultations were held between Ministry officials and the largest representative body concerned, the National Farmers' Union. By April 1966 a draft Order had been prepared. An advance copy of the schedule to the Order, which defined the industry to which the order related, was sent to the National Farmers' Union on April 15, 1966. On April 26, 1966, copies of this document were circulated to a large number of addresses, including the Mushroom Growers' Association, inviting comments. Simultaneously there was a press notice summarising the activities which it was proposed should be covered by the new board and advising any organisation which considered that it had an interest in the draft schedule and which had not received a copy to apply to the Ministry of Labour. No comments were received from the Mushroom Growers' Association and no application was made by them for a copy of the schedule.

The Order was made on August 2, 1966, laid before Parliament on August 11, and came into operation on August 15. The Mushroom Growers' Association applied in May 1968 for complete exemption from the Order on various grounds. They had never received a copy of the draft schedule, and had no knowledge of the consultations between the Ministry and the National Farmers' Union, or of the press notice. The Mushroom Growers' Association was a specialist branch of the National Farmers' Union, although largely autonomous. It represented about 85 per cent of all mushroom growers in England and Wales, who were responsible for about 80 per cent of mushroom production.

The Board sought a determination as to whether the Minister had complied with his duty of consultation, and if not, what were the consequences. The real defendants were the Mushroom Growers' Association, but as that was an unincorporated association, it was thought more convenient that the nominal defendants should be Aylesbury Mushrooms Ltd, who were representative of the Mushroom Growers' Association membership.

DONALDSON J.: . . . Both parties are agreed that under the terms of section 1(4) of the Act, some consultation by the Minister is mandatory and that in the absence of any particular consultation which is so required, the persons who should have been but were not consulted are not bound by the Order, although the Order remains effective in relation to all others who were in fact consulted or whom there was no need to consult. Both parties are further agreed that if consultation with the Mushroom Growers' Association was mandatory and there was no sufficient consultation the Order takes effect according to its terms subject to a rider that it does not apply to the growing of mushrooms or to persons engaged in this activity solely by reason of their being so engaged. They may, of course, come within the scope of the Order in some other capacity.

Both parties are also agreed that the organisations required to be consulted are those which appear to the Minister, or to his alter ago who in this case was a Mr Devey, to be representative of substantial numbers of employers engaging in the activities concerned or persons employed therein and nationalised industries which engage in those activities to a substantial extent. Thus whether any particular organisation has to be consulted depends upon a subjective test, subject always to *bona fides* and reasonableness which are not in question.

Against this background Mr Bradburn, for the association, submits that the court must see what organisations appeared to the Minister to fall into the specified categories, and that the Minister clearly sought to consult the Mushroom Growers' Association thereby showing that he regarded it as being within the class of organisation which had to be consulted. It follows, as he submits, that neither the board nor the Minister can now turn round and say that consùltation with the National Farmers' Union constituted a sufficient discharge of his duties. Mr Bradburn goes on to submit that there can be no consultation without at least unilateral communication and that no such communication occurred.

Mr Gettleson for the board submitted that "any" in the phrase "the Minister shall consult any organisation" imposed a duty to consult not more than one organisation, that posting the letter of April 26, 1966, constituted consultation with 'the Mushroom Growers' Association despite the fact that it was never received, that the Mushroom Growers' Association was not an organisation which had to be consulted and that consultation with the National Farmers' Union involved consultation with all its branches including the Mushroom Growers' Association.

I have no doubt that Mr Gettleson's first point is without foundation. "Any" must mean "every" in the context of section 1(4). There is a little more to be said for his submission that the mere sending of the letter of April 26, 1966, constituted consultation in that the Shorter Oxford English Dictionary gives as one definition of the verb "to consult" "to ask advice of, seek counsel from; to have recourse to for instruction or professional advice". However, in truth the mere sending of a letter constitutes but an attempt to consult and this does not suffice. The essence of consultation is the communication of a genuine invitation, extended with a receptive mind, to give advice: see *per* Bucknill L.J. approving a dictum of Morris J. in *Rollo v. Minister of Town and Country Planning* [1948] 1 All E.R. 13, 17. If the invitation is once received, it matters not that it is not accepted and no advice is proffered. Were it otherwise organisations with a right to be consulted could, in effect, veto the making of any order by simply failing to respond to the invitation. But without communication and the consequent opportunity of responding, there can be no consultation.

This leaves only the related questions of whether the Mushroom Growers' Association did in fact appear to the Minister to be an organisation falling within the categories set out in section 1(4) with the consequence that he was under an obligation to consult them and whether in any event his consultations with the National Farmers' Union constituted consultation with the Mushroom Growers' Association as a branch of the N.F.U. This is the heart of the problem.

Mr Devey has deposed in paragraph 5 of his affidavit:

"In accordance with practice the circulation of the draft schedule was not restricted to organisations that appeared to me to be representative of substantial numbers of employers engaging in activities specified in the draft schedule. This will appear sufficiently from a persual of the document. In particular the Mushroom Growers' Association was listed, although it was, and remains, a specialist branch of the National Farmer's Union. The listed address of the association is the same as that of the union which is Agriculture House, Knightsbridge, London, S.W.1."

In each case he sent a covering letter in one of three forms. The addresses on the first list, such as the National Farmers' Union, the Trades Union Congress, the Confederation of British Industry, and major government departments received special letters from Mr Devey. Those on the second list received letters which were in standard form but were sent personally to named officials of the organisation concerned. These included the Local Government Examinations Board which clearly is an organisation which should have been consulted, but not one which in the terms of the Act had to be consulted. Those on the third list, including the Mushroom Growers' Association, received or should have received letters in standard form addressed to the organisation impersonally. I can find no clue in the form of the covering letter to whether any particular addressee appeared to the Minister to be a section 1(4) organisation and examples can be found in each list of organisations which plainly fall outside this category. I am thus thrown back on Mr Devey's affidavit coupled with a letter dated January 20, 1969, signed by a Mr Thomson of the Department of Employment and Productivity which states that a copy of the draft schedule was sent to the National Farmers' Union of which it is understood that the Mushroom Growers' Association is a specialist branch "and also as a matter of courtesy to that association". Bearing in mind the importance which attaches to consultation in the scheme of the Industrial Training Act 1964, which seems to be based upon the healthy principle of "no taxation without consultation", and the fact that Mr Devey has not in terms said that the association did not appear to him to fall within the scope of section 1(4), I feel obliged to conclude that it was an organisation which had to be consulted, although its small membership in the context of the number of persons employed in agriculture, horticulture and forestry, and the specialised nature of their activities could well have led the Minister to take a different view.

This only leaves the question of whether it was consulted vicariously, and it may be accidentally, by means of the consultations with the National Farmers' Union. This is a nice point. *Prima facie* consultation with the parent body undoubtedly constitutes consultation with its constituent parts, but I think that this general rule is subject to an exception where, as here, the Minister has also attempted and intended direct consultation with a branch. The association's complaint has very little merit, because it seems to have been completely blind to all that was going on around it. Nevertheless it is important that statutory powers which involve taxation shall strictly construed and, so construed, I consider that the association should have been consulted and was not consulted.

I therefore answer the questions in the originating summons as follows: "Whether before making an order establishing a training board for the agricultural, horticultural and forestry industry, the Minister was under a duty to consult the Mushroom Growers' Association"—yes.

"Whether the consultations held by the Minister with the National Farmers' Union constituted a sufficient consultation with an organisation or association of organisations representative of those engaged in the activity of horticulture"—no.

"If it be held that the Minister was under a duty to consult the Mushroom Growers' Association, whether on the facts such consultation took place"—no.

"If it be held that the Minister was under a duty to consult the Mushroom Growers' Association and failed to do so, what effect such failure had upon the provisions of the Industrial Training (Agricultural, Horticultural and Forestry Board) Order 1966 (S.I. 1966 No. 969)"—the Order has no application to mushroom growers as such.

Order accordingly.

Notes

1. See case note by D. Foulkes (1972) 35 M.L.R. 647.

2. The question of consultation was raised in *R. v. Secretary of State for the Environment, ex p. Association of Metropolitan Authorities* [1986] 1 W.L.R. 1. The Secretary had power under the Housing Benefits Act 1982 to make regulations constituting the housing benefit scheme. Section 36(1) of the Act provided that before making regulations (including amending regulations) "the Secretary of State shall consult with organisations appearing to him to be representative of the authorities concerned" (*i.e.* local authorities). The Secretary of State habitually consulted the local authority associations, including the AMA, before making regulations, and it was common ground that the AMA was one of the organisations contemplated by s.36(1). On November 16, 1984, the DHSS wrote to the AMA requesting their views on proposals to make certain amendments to the regulations designed to close a "loophole". The letter was received on November 22 and a response was sought by November 30. The AMA requested an extension of time but no answer was forthcoming. Further proposed amendments were summarised in a letter of December 4, which sought a response by December 12. No draft of the proposed amendments was enclosed, and no mention was made of a material feature (which would require local authorities to investigate the background to the creation of joint tenancies by claimants so as to satisfy themselves that the tenancies had not been contrived to take advantage of the housing benefit scheme). The AMA replied on December 13 with brief comments. The amending regulations were made on December 17 and became law on December 19. Webster J. granted a declaration that the Secretary of State had failed to comply with s.36(1), but refused, in the exercise of his discretion, to quash the regulations. Webster J. said (at 4–5):

"There is no general principle to be extracted from the case law as to what kind or amount of consultation is required before delegated legislation, of which consultation is a precondition, can validly be made. But in any context the essence of consultation is the communication of a genuine invitation to give advice and a genuine receipt of that advice. In my view it must go without saying that to achieve consultation sufficient information must be supplied by the consulting to the consulted party to enable it to tender helpful advice. Sufficient time must be given by the consulting to the consulted party to enable it do to that, and sufficient time must be available for such advice to be considered by the consulting party. Sufficient, in that context, does not mean ample, but at least enough to enable the relevant purpose to be fulfilled. By helpful advice, in this context, I mean sufficiently informed and considered information or advice about aspects of the form or substance of the proposals, or their implications for the consulted party, being aspects material to the implementation of the proposal as to which the Secretary of State might not be fully informed or advised and as to which the party consulted might have relevant information or advice to offer.

These propositions, as it seems to me, can partly be derived from, and are wholly consistent with, the decisions and various dicta, which I need not enumerate, in *Rollo v. Minister of Town and Country Planning* [1948] 1 All E.R. 13 and *Port Louis Corporation v. Attorney-General of Mauritius* [1965] A.C. 1111."

Webster J. noted that as the day-to-day administration of the scheme was in the hands of local authorities, who bore 10 per cent of the scheme's cost, the obligation to consult was mandatory and not directory. In considering whether the consultation required by s.36(1) was in substance carried out, the court:

"should have regard not so much to the actual facts which preceded the making of the regulations as to the material before the Secretary of State when he made the regulations, that material including facts or information as it appeared or must have appeared to him acting in good faith, and any judgments made or opinions expressed to him before the making of the regulations about those facts which appeared to could have appeared to him to be reasonable."

The effect of this approach was:

"to give a certain flexibility to the notions of sufficiency, sufficient information, sufficient time and sufficiently informed and consider information and advice in my homespun attempt to define proper consultation. Thus, it can have the effect that what would be sufficient information or time in one case might be more or less than sufficient in another, depending on the relative degrees of urgency and the nature of the proposed regulation. There is no degree of urgency, however, which absolves the Secretary of State from the obligation to consult at all."

His Lordship concluded that while the department was entitled to expect a quick response, the urgency of the situation was not such as to justify requiring views within such a short period that they might be insufficiently informed or considered.

However, the regulations were not quashed. Only one of six local authority associations had challenged the regulations; authorities would by then have adapted to the difficulties created by the regulations; revocation would mean that applicants refused benefit under the amended regulations would be entitled to make fresh claims, but this advantage would only last for six months as the challenged regulations had subsequently been consolidated in the Housing Benefits Regulations 1985, and the consolidation was not challenged.

3. In *R. v. Secretary of State for Health, ex p. United States Tobacco International Inc.* [1992] 1 Q.B. 353 (the "Skoal Bandits" case, above, p. 394), the regulations were quashed on the ground of inadequate consultation. Section 11(5)(a) of the Consumer Protection Act 1987 provided that before making safety regulations the Secretary of State was under a duty to consult "such organisations as appear to him to be representative of interests substantially affected by the proposal". Taylor L.J. stated (at 369–372) that there were three reasons why consultation under s.11(5)(a) in the present case "required a high degree of fairness and candour to be shown by the Secretary of State". First, the history.

"Although the applicants cannot successfully rely on the doctrine of legitimate expectation, the fact is that they were led up the garden path."

Secondly, although the regulations were of general application, they impinged almost exclusively on the applicants as the sole manufacturers and packagers of oral snuff in the United Kingdom. Thirdly, the effect of the regulations was likely to be catastrophic to the applicants' United Kingdom business. Accordingly:

"it was important that the Secretary of State ... should give the applicants a full opportunity to know and respond to the material and evaluations which led him to such a striking change of policy".

The Secretary of State was not obliged to let the applicants see the 300 other representations received given his undertaking to apprise the applicants of any fresh point arising from them to which he was minded to have regard (this point had already been settled in *R. v. Secretary of State for Social Security, ex p. United States Tobacco International Inc.*, unreported, July 21, 1988). However, his refusal to disclose the text of the professional advice received from his advisory committee could not be justified. His claim that otherwise committee members might feel inhibited in expressing their views was "unconvincing." The committee members were "scientific experts of integrity and standing.... I cannot believe that they would be affected by the suggested inhibitions."

"One cannot help feeling that the denial of the applicants' request was due to an inbuilt reluctance to give reasons or disclose advice lest it give opponents fuel for argument.... To conceal from them the scientific advice which directly led to the ban was ... unfair and unlawful."

WANG v. COMMISSIONER OF INLAND REVENUE

[1994] 1 W.L.R. 1286; [1995] 1 All E.R. 367 (Privy Council)

In 1987 the Hong Kong Commissioner of Inland Revenue raised three assessments to profits tax on the taxpayer, Mrs Wang, as (1) agent for a specified company, (2) in her personal capacity and (3) as trustee for the company. The assessments related to complicated financial transactions with foreign companies involving many millions of U.S. dollars. The taxpayer objected to the assessments. In 1988 the Deputy Commissioner confirmed the assessment issued against the taxpayer as trustee. The taxpayer appealed against the assessment. In 1990 the Deputy Commissioner confirmed the earlier assessments made against Mrs Wang as an agent and in her personal capacity. The Revenue proposed that her appeals against the three assessments should be heard together. Mrs Wang sought an order of certiorari to quash the latter assessments on the ground that they had not been confirmed "within a reasonable time" as required by s.64 of the Inland Revenue Ordinance. The High Court of Hong Kong held that s.64 established a mandatory requirement and that, as the department had failed to comply with it, the 1990 decisions of confirmation were *ultra vires*. The Court of Appeal in Hong Kong allowed an appeal by the Commissioner. The taxpayer then appealed to the Privy Council.

LORD SLYNN OF HADLEY: ... The distinction between "mandatory" and "directory" or between "imperative" and "mandatory", the latter in that context being the same as "directory", has a long history and has led to much litigation and on occasion to somewhat refined distinctions.

The starting point, however, upon which both appellant and respondent rely is the well-known case of *Howard v. Bodington* (1877) 2 P.D. 203. Under s.9 of the Public Worship Regulation Act 1874 a bishop to whom a representation was made of an illegal act by an incumbent, unless he thought that no proceeding should be taken—

"shall within twenty-one days after receiving the representation transmit a copy thereof to the person complained of ... the bishop shall forthwith transmit the representation ... to the archbishop [who] shall forthwith require the judge to hear the matter of the representation ...".

In that case the bishop did not send a copy of the representation; the archbishop did so but only some seven weeks after the bishop had received the representation. The archbishop required the judge to hear the matter. The Court of Arches held that the proceedings were void and must be dismissed since the time within which the representation should be sent to the party complained of was "imperative", and had not been complied with. Lord Penzance said (at 210–211):

"Well, then, secondly, it was contended that, although it is a positive provision of the Act that a copy of the representation shall be transmitted to the respondent within twenty-one days from the time the bishop received it, yet that that provision is only what has been called in the law courts 'directory'.

Now the distinction between matters that are directory and matters that are imperative is well known to us all in the common language of the courts at Westminster. I am not sure that it is the most fortunate language that could have been adopted to express the idea that it is intended to convey; but still that is the recognised language, and I propose to adhere to it. The real question in all these cases is this: A thing has been ordered by the legislature to be done. What is the consequence if it is not done? In the case of statutes that are said to be imperative, the Courts have decided that if it is not done the whole thing fails, and the proceedings that follow upon it are all void. On the other hand, when the Courts hold a provision to be mandatory or directory, they say that, although such provision may not have been complied with, the subsequent proceedings do not fail. Still, whatever the language, the idea is a perfectly distinct one. There may be many provisions in Acts of Parliament which, although they are not strictly obeyed, yet do not appear to the Court to be of that material importance to the subject-matter to which they refer, as that the legislature could have intended that the non-observance of them should be followed by a total failure of the whole proceedings. On the other hand, there are some provisions in respect of which the Court would take an opposite view, and would feel that they are matters which must be strictly obeyed, otherwise the whole proceedings that subsequently follow must come to an end. Now the question is, to which category does the provision in question in this case belong? . . . I believe, as far as any rule is concerned, you cannot safely go further than that in each case you must look to the subject-matter; consider the importance of the provision that has been disregarded, and the relation of that provision to the general object intended to be secured by the Act; and upon a review of the case in that aspect decide whether the matter is what is called imperative or only directory."

Illustrations of the application of this principle are to be found in both directions. Thus on the one hand in *Cullimore v. Lyme Regis Corp.* [1961] 3 All E.R. 1008; [1962] 1 Q.B. 718 a borough council, as coastal protection authority, prepared a works scheme for carrying out coast protection under s.6 of the Coast Protection Act 1949. The scheme provided pursuant to s.7(1) and (4)(b) of the Act that "The Council will within six months after the completion of the works determine the interest in the contributory land by reference to which coast protection charges are to be levied" and the amount of the charge. The council did not determine these matters until almost two years after the completion of the works. Edmund Davies J. held that the council was exercising statutory power (for which they had fixed the period themselves) and that since they did not act in time he could not "accordingly regard their purported action as having any validity at all" (see [1961] 3 All E.R. 1008 at 1012–1013; [1962] 1 Q.B. 718 at 728). In the alternative he said:

"It is undisputed that, if these be mere duties and if, accordingly, the provisions as to their exercise are to be regarded as directory only, it is sufficient if there has been substantial compliance with those directions."

He underlined, however, that the issue turned on the construction of the particular Act in question and this was stressed in *Grunwick Processing Laboratories Ltd v. Advisory Conciliation and Arbitration Service* [1978] 1 All E.R. 338 at 367; [1978] A.C. 655 at 698 by Lord Salmon:

"The result of this appeal turns solely on whether that part of s.14(1) [of the Employment Protection Act 1975] which I have cited is mandatory or directory. Prima facie the word 'shall' suggests that it is mandatory but that word has often been rightly construed as being directory. Everything turns on the context in which it is used: the subject-matter, the purpose and effect of the section in which it appears."

The commissioner points on the other hand to *R. v. H.M. Inspector of Taxes, ex p. Clarke* [1972] 1 All E.R. 545; [1974] Q.B. 220 and *Hughes (Inspector of Taxes) v. Viner* [1985] 3 All E.R. 40, where procedural provisions in the United Kingdom tax statutes were held to be merely directory.

In *London and Clydeside Estates Ltd v. Aberdeen D.C.* [1979] 3 All E.R. 876 at 883; [1980] 1 W.L.R. 182 at 190 Lord Hailsham of St Marylebone L.C., having stressed that statutory requirements can be of many different kinds with different degrees of obligation and different results flowing from a failure to comply with the obligation, concluded:

"In such cases, though language like 'mandatory', 'directory', 'void', 'voidable', 'nullity' and so forth may be helpful in argument, it may be misleading in effect if relied on to show that the courts, in deciding the consequences of a defect in the exercise of power, are necessarily bound to fit the facts of a particular case and a developing chain of events into rigid legal categories or to stretch or cramp them on a bed of Procrustes invented by lawyers for the purposes of convenient exposition. As I have said, the case does not really arise here, since we are in the presence of total non compliance with a requirement which I have held to be mandatory. Nevertheless I do not wish to be understood in the field of administrative law and in the domain where the courts apply a supervisory jurisdiction over the acts of subordinate authority purporting to exercise statutory powers, to encourage the use of rigid legal classifications. The jurisdiction is inherently discretionary and the court is frequently in the presence of differences of kind."

Having reviewed the authorities cited by the taxpayer in this appeal, not all of which are referred to in this opinion, their Lordships consider that when a question like the present one arises—an alleged failure to comply with a time provision—it is simpler and better to avoid these two words "mandatory" and "directory" and to ask two questions. The first is whether the legislature intended the person making the determination to comply with the time provision, whether a fixed time or a reasonable time. Secondly, if so, did the legislature intend that a failure to comply with such a time provision would deprive the decision-maker of jurisdiction and render any decision which he purported to make null and void?

In the present case the legislature did intend that the commissioner should make his determination within a reasonable time. At the same time it is no less plain that the legislation imposed on the Revenue authorities, including the commissioner, the duty of assessing and collecting profits tax from 'every person carrying on a trade, profession or business in Hong Kong' (see s.14). If the commissioner failed to act within a reasonable time he could be compelled to act by an order of mandamus. It does not follow that his jurisdiction to make a determination disappears the moment a reasonable time has elapsed. If the court establishes the time by which a reasonable time is to be taken as having expired, which will depend on all the circumstances, including factors affecting not only the taxpayer but also the Revenue, it would be surprising if the result was that the commissioner had jurisdiction to make the determination just before but not just after that time. Their Lordships do not consider that that is the effect of a failure to comply with the obligation to act within a reasonable time in the present legislation. Such a result would not only deprive the government of revenue, it would also be unfair to other taxpayers who need to shoulder the burden of government expenditure; the alternative result (that the commissioner continues to have jurisdiction) does not necessarily involve any real prejudice for the taxpayer in question by reason of the delay.

Their Lordships accordingly consider that in the context of this legislation a failure to act within a reasonable time (had it occurred) would not have deprived the commissioner of jurisdiction or made any determination by him null and void.

Appeal dismissed.

Notes

1. The abandonment of the traditional mandatory/directory dichotomy has been supported by a number of judgments in other cases. For example, in *Main v. Swansea City Council* (1984) 49 P. & C.R. 26, the Court of Appeal held that in principle the grant of outline planning permission for the residential development of certain land was vitiated: first, the necessary certificate that all the other owners of the land had been notified was incorrect, in that a small part of the land was in fact owned by a third party whose identity was known; secondly, as the land included land within 67 metres of the middle of a highway, the Secretary of State should have been given notice of the application under art. 11 of the Town and Country Planning General Development Order 1973. The Court of Appeal cited the *London and Clydeside* case both on the point that an invalid certificate could nevertheless have some legal effect, and on Lord Hailsham's preference for a flexible approach. Parker L.J. said (at 37):

> "In our judgment, the most significant observation in Lord Hailsham's speech, indeed in the whole of the *Clydesdale* [*sic*] case, is that the court must consider the consequences in the light of a concrete state of facts and a continuing chain of events. This recognises that the court looks not only at the nature of the failure but also at such matters as the identity of the applicant for relief, the lapse of time, the effect on other parties and on the public and so on."

The court, however, declined to quash the permission, in the exercise of its discretion. The outline permission had been granted in 1977; reserved matters were approved in 1980, and during this period no objections had been made to the outline permission; the actual development would not take place on the land owned by the unidentified person; and the Secretary of State had for a very long time been aware of the position and had not sought relief.

In *R. v. London Borough of Lambeth, ex p. Sharp* (1986) 55 P. & C.R. 232, notice of a proposed development published in a local newspaper failed to specify the period during which objections should be made, and failed to state that objections should be in writing. The Court of Appeal upheld the trial judge's decision to quash the subsequent grant of planning permission. Stephen Brown L.J. said (at 238):

R.T.C. LIBRARY, LETTERKENNY

"It seems to me that it is not necessary to consider whether these requirements are 'mandatory' or 'directory', or whether they go to powers or duties. One has to look at the terms of the regulations, and a breach of them, in my judgment, clearly provides a basis upon which the court can be seized of an application for judicial review. It is of course material to consider the nature of such a breach—that is to say, its gravity and relevance—when considering whether relief shall be granted. For my part, I am satisfied that the breach in question, which I find the judge was right to hold established, was fundamental, bearing in mind that it is a provision which requires notification of proposed development to members of the public. This was in a conservation area and is obviously a matter of general local public interest. Public notification of the proposed grant of planning permission must accordingly be of fundamental public importance. I would hold that this is not a mere procedural technicality but rather it is a requirement fundamental to the operation of this particular planning procedure."

His Lordship also rejected an argument that the court should decline to quash the permission on the basis that there had been substantial compliance with the requirement of the regulation as a whole, and that no one had been prejudiced. This was a fundamental flaw; it was impossible to say that the applicant had not been prejudiced (he had not seen the site notice); and it was a matter of intense public interest in the locality.

Woolf L.J. said (at 239–240):

"The regulations are but an example of the numerous different statutory regulations which lay down procedures which have to be followed by public authorities in carrying out their functions. When the provisions of such regulations are contravened, almost invariably it is unhelpful to consider what are the consequences of non-compliance with the regulations by classifying them as containing mandatory or directory provisions, or as containing a condition precedent, or as containing a provision which renders a decision void or voidable, or by considering whether they contain a provision which goes to jurisdiction. What has to be considered is: what is the particular provision designed to achieve? If, as here, it is designed to give the public an opportunity to make objections to what is proposed, then the court is bound to attach considerable importance to any failure to comply with the requirements.

However, the breach of the requirements cannot be considered alone. It has to be considered in the context of the particular circumstances in relation to which the matter comes before the court."

(His Lordship stated that he adopted the approach of Parker L.J. in *Main v. Swansea City Council*, which in turn was based upon Lord Hailsham's speech in the *London and Clydeside* case.)

"In adopting that approach to the circumstances in this case, I would come to the same conclusion as the learned judge and my Lord, Stephen Brown L.J. I appreciate that it may be said that this approach introduces an element of uncertainty as to what will be the consequences of a breach of regulations of this nature. However, while accepting that this may be the position, I observe that the attempts which have been made in the past to categorise breaches, and therefore their consequences, have not in fact achieved any degree of continuity and, indeed, have in themselves been a source of considerable litigation as to the particular category in relation to which a particular breach could be said to fall."

Sir John Donaldson M.R. agreed with both judgments.

For further examples of the adoption of the flexible approach, see Woolf J. in *R. v. Chester City Council,` ex p. Quietlynn Ltd, The Times*, October 19, 1983, and *R. v. Secretary of State for the Environment, ex p. Leicester City Council* (1985) 25 R.V.R. 31; Schiemann J. in *R. v. Doncaster Metropolitan Borough Council* [1987] J.P.L. 444 and M.T. Pill Q.C. in *Robbins v. Secretary of State for the Environment* (1987) 56 P. & C.R. 416 and *Porritt v. Secretary of State for the Environment* [1988] J.P.L. 414.

2. In *R. v. London Borough of Tower Hamlets, ex p. Tower Hamlets Combined Traders Association* [1994] C.O.D. 325, Sedley J. emphasised that it was important to distinguish between two separate issues when considering the judicial response to a public authority's breach of statutory procedural requirements. First, that the legal consequences of non-compliance were variable and secondly, that the grant of relief by the courts is discretionary. (See further, below, pp. 679–690.) Here, the council had failed to give street traders notice of a designated statutory period of time in which they could make representations concerning a proposed large increase in fees charged by the authority. Sedley J. concluded that the notice condition was a fundamental aspect of the statutory scheme and therefore the Council's failure to observe it meant that the ensuing decision, to increase the fees by 90 per cent, was a nullity. However, financial circumstances required that some increase in fees be allowed, consequently his Lordship quashed the decision to the extent that it exceeded a 35 per cent increase in fees.

(B) NATURAL JUSTICE: THE DUTY TO ACT FAIRLY[1]

In administrative law the "rules of natural justice" have traditionally been regarded as comprising the rules *audi alteram partem* and *nemo judex in causa sua*. Respectively, these apply to require the maker of a decision to give prior notice of the decision to persons affected by it, and an opportunity for those persons to make representations; and also to disqualify the decision-maker from acting if he or she has a direct pecuniary or proprietary interest, or where there is a real danger that he or she might otherwise be biased. The rules are historically closely tied to judicial decision-making in the courts, but they have been extended to apply to administrative authorities and to administrative decision-making, and it is here that the main difficulties have arisen. It is not clear how far the rules of natural justice apply to decisions which do not have a significant judicial element. Here, the courts have increasingly prescribed a basic duty to act fairly, which may include some aspects of "natural justice", but which may simply amount to a duty to refrain from any abuse of discretion.

In the case of each of the twin rules of natural justice two basic issues are involved:

(a) Does the rule apply to the particular situation; and
(b) if so, what is the precise content of the rule in that situation?

Finally, of course, if it applies, has the rule been observed?

(i) The Right to a Fair Hearing

In the twentieth century, the application of this rule (historically termed *audi alteram partem*) has been considered by the House of Lords in a series of cases including *Board of Education v. Rice* [1911] A.C. 179, *Local Government Board v. Arlidge* [1915] A.C. 120, *Ridge v. Baldwin* (1963) (below, p. 424), *Bushell v. Secretary of State for the Environment* (1980) (below, p. 496), *Lloyd v. McMahon* (1987) (below, p. 487), *R. v. Board of Visitors of H.M. Prison, The Maze, ex p. Hone* (1988) (below, p. 491) and

---

[1] See generally P. Jackson, *Natural Justice* (2nd ed., 1979); G.A. Flick, *Natural Justice* (2nd ed., 1984); *de Smith, Woolf and Jowell*, Chap. 8; *Craig*, Chap. 8; *Wade and Forsyth*, Part V; and *Garner*, pp. 240–278.

Al-Mehdawi v. Secretary of State for the Home Department (1990) (below, p. 479). The pivotal decision is that of *Ridge v. Baldwin.* This removed some restrictions on the rule's application that had developed since 1914 in lower courts, and led to an "explosion" of natural justice cases.

Briefly stated, the traditional basic principle is that the *audi alteram partem* rule must be observed by anyone who is making a judicial or quasi-judicial, as distinct from an administrative, decision. Since *Ridge v. Baldwin,* a wider variety of decisions have been regarded as "judicial" or "quasi-judicial" for this purpose (note the discussion of these categories in Chapter 1 of the previous edition of this work). In turn this has led some judges to argue that it is no longer necessary to distinguish between the "judicial" or "quasi-judicial" and the "administrative" (*e.g.* Lord Denning in *Schmidt v. Secretary of State for Home Affairs* [1969] 2 Ch. 149). If a decision seriously affects individual interests, natural justice or fairness must be observed irrespective of the label applicable to that decision, all the legal argument being about the appropriate content of the rule in the particular situation. Another approach that has been taken is to require observation of "natural justice" in the making of judicial or quasi-judicial decisions, and of a "duty to act fairly" in the making of administrative decisions (*e.g.* Lord Parker C.J. in *Re H.K. (An Infant)* (1967) (below, p. 442). This will usually lead to the same result as the previous approach, but it preserves the need to label decisions, a task that properly should be redundant.

Each of these approaches may be contrasted with the previous situation where judges adopted an "analytical" approach, denying the relevance of natural justice to non-judicial decisions. This led either to injustice, where natural justice was held not to apply to decisions that substantially prejudiced individual interests (as in *Nakkuda Ali v. Jayaratne* [1951] A.C. 66 (below, p. 433) (discussed in *Ridge v. Baldwin*), where a decision to revoke a trader's licence and thereby to deprive him of his livelihood was held to be non-judicial), or strained analysis, where clearly administrative decisions were classified as "judicial" (as in *Cooper v. Wandsworth Board of Works,* below p. 420).

de Smith, Woolf and Jowell assert that:

"The term 'natural justice' is being increasingly replaced by a general duty to act fairly, which is a key element of procedural propriety.

Whichever term is used, the time has come to make a break with the artificial constraints surrounding the situations in which natural justice or the duty to act fairly are required. The previous distinctions were already comatose and should be formally declared moribund. . . . The law has moved on; not to the state where the entitlement to procedural protection can be extracted with certainty from a computer, but to where the courts are able to insist upon some degree of participation in reaching most official decisions by those whom the decisions will affect in widely different situations, subject only to well-established exceptions" (p. 401).

In the following subsections we consider (1) the types of decision-making which have been subject to some form of fair hearing obligations, (2) factors which have induced the judiciary to limit the application of the right to a fair hearing, and (3) the content of the right to a fair hearing in particular decision-making contexts.

(a) *When does the "right to a fair hearing" apply?*

COOPER v. THE BOARD OF WORKS FOR THE WANDSWORTH DISTRICT

(1863) 14 C.B.(N.S.) 180; 32 L.J.C.P. 185; 8 L.T. 278; 2 New Rep. 31; 9 Jur.(N.S.) 1155; 11 W.R. 646; 143 E.R. 414 (Court of Common Pleas)

The Metropolis Local Management Act 1855, s.76, provided that: "before beginning to lay or dig out the foundation of any new house or building ... seven days notice in writing shall be given to the ... board by the person intending to build ... such house or building...". This ensured that the board had opportunity to give directions under the Act as to the drains. Section 76 also provided that "in default of such notice ... it shall be lawful for ... the board to cause such house or building to be demolished or altered ... and to recover the expenses thereof from the owner...". The plaintiff, a builder, was employed to build a house in Wandsworth. He claimed that he sent a notice under section 76 to the board, but this was denied. He admitted, however, that he had commenced digging out the foundations within five days of the day on which he claimed to have sent the notice. The house had reached the second storey when the board, without giving any notice, sent round their surveyor and a number of workmen at a late hour in the evening. The men razed the house to the ground.

The plaintiff sued for damages for trespass. Willes J. found for the plaintiff. The defendants obtained a rule nisi for a nonsuit. They argued (*inter alia*) (1) that "the great safeguard against abuses ... is that the members of which these boards are composed are elected by the rate-payers of the district". (2) "What necessity can there be for giving the party notice, when he well knows that he is doing an illegal act, and that the board have power to prostrate his house?" (3) "It is not like the case where a judicial discretion is to be exercised. An arbitrary power is conferred upon the board, which is necessarily to be exercised without any control."

ERLE C.J.: ... The contention on the part of the plaintiff has been, that, although the words of the statute, taken in their literal sense, without any qualification at all, would create a justification for the act which the district board has done, the powers granted by that statute are subject to a qualification which has been repeatedly recognised, that no man is to be deprived of his property without his having an opportunity of being heard. ... I think that the power which is granted by the 76th section is subject to the qualification suggested. It is a power carrying with it enormous consequences. The house in question was built only to a certain extent. But the power claimed would apply to a complete house. It would apply to a house of any value, and completed to any extent; and it seems to me to be a power which may be exercised most perniciously, and that the limitation which we are going to put upon it is one which ought, according to the decided cases, to be put upon it, and one which is required by a due consideration for the public interest. I think the board ought to have given notice to the plaintiff, and to have allowed him to be heard. The default in sending notice to the board of the intention to build, is a default which may be explained. There may be a great many excuses for the apparent default. The party may have intended to conform to the law. He may have actually conformed to all the regulations which they would wish to impose, though by accident his notice may have miscarried; and, under those circumstances, if he explained how it stood, the proceeding to demolish, merely because they had ill-will against the party, is a power that the legislature never intended to confer. I cannot conceive any harm that could happen to the district board from hearing the party before they subjected him to a loss so serious as the demolition of his house; but I can conceive a great many advantages which might arise in the way of public order, in the way of doing substantial justice, and in the way of fulfilling the purposes of the statute, by the restriction which we put upon them, that they should hear the party before they inflict upon him such a heavy loss. I fully agree that the legislature intended to give the district board very large powers indeed: but the qualification I speak of is one which has been recognised to the full extent. It has been said that the principle that no man shall be deprived of his property without an opportunity of being heard, is limited to a judicial proceeding, and that a district board ordering a house to be pulled down cannot be said to be doing a judicial act. I do not quite agree with that; neither do I undertake to rest my judgment solely upon the ground that the district board is a court exercising judicial discretion upon the point: but the law, I think, has been applied to many exercises of power which in common understanding would not be at all more a judicial proceeding than would be the act of the district board in ordering a house to be pulled down. The case of the corporation of the University of Cambridge, who turned out Dr Bentley, in the exercise of their assumed power of depriving a member of the University of his rights, and a number of other cases which are collected in the *Hammersmith Rent-Charge* Case, 4 Exch. 96, in the judgment of Parke B., show that the principle has been very widely applied. The district board must do the thing legally; there must be a resolution; and, if there be a board, and a resolution of that board, I have not heard a word to show that it would not be salutary that they should hear the man who is to suffer from their judgment before they proceed to make the order under which they attempt to justify their act. It is said that an appeal from the district board to the metropolitan board (under s.211) would be the mode of redress. But, if the district board have the power to do what is here stated, I am not at all clear that there would be a right of redress in that way. The metropolitan board may not have a right to give redress for that which was done under the provisions of the statute. I think the appeal clause would evidently indicate that many exercises of the power of a district board would be in the nature of judicial proceedings; because, certainly when they are appealed from, the appellant and the respondent are to be heard as parties, and the matter is to be decided at least according to judicial forms. I take that to be a principle of very wide application, and applicable to the present case; and I think this board was not justified under the statute, because they have not qualified themselves for the exercise of their power by hearing the party to be affected by their decision.

WILLES J.: I am of the same opinion. I apprehend that a tribunal which is by law invested with power to affect the property of one of Her Majesty's subjects, is bound to give such subject an opportunity of being heard before it proceeds: and that that rule is of universal application, and founded upon the plainest principles of justice. Now, is the board in the present case such a tribunal? I apprehend it clearly is, whether we consider it with reference to the discretion which is vested in it, or whether we look at the analogy which exists between it and other recognised tribunals (and no one ever doubted that such tribunals are bound by the rules which a court of justice is bound by), or whether you look at it with reference to the estimation in which it is held by the legislature, as appears from the language used in the statute....

... With respect to nuisances, the board exercises the power of a criminal court of high jurisdiction, because it has a discretion as to whether it will abate that which is a nuisance altogether, or whether it will simply direct that there shall be a modification of the works which in its opinion are necessary for the health of the neighbourhood. I apprehend it is clear that the powers thus exercised by the board under the Act are powers which have always been considered judicial, and which could not be exercised without giving notice to the party who is to be proceeded against. In this very section, 76, the legislature speaks of coming "under the jurisdiction of the vestry or board"; and it is clear that these boards do exercise judicial powers. The power here is one that, probably more than any, requires that the party to be affected by it should be heard, because of its extent, and because the board may be satisfied with a modification of that which has been done....

[His Lordship summarised section 76.]

The matter to be considered by the board before they make that order [*i.e.* an order giving directions] is, first of all, has any notice been given? And then the party clearly ought to be allowed to show, either that he has given a notice which may have been overlooked, or, if the notice has not been received by the board, to show that he did his best towards doing so, in order to induce them to look on the case favourably—not to demolish the house, but to seen whether any and what qualification is necessary for the purpose of bringing it within what should be done if the notice had been regularly served. In either of those cases, I apprehend, it is clear that it would be the right of the party to be heard. But there is a third case; and that is where, by wilfully disregarding the order, or by the act of some third person, whom he did his best to control, the owner of the house may have subjected his house to demolition by the board, or to be dealt with severely by reason of its defects. That is a case in which judicial power is to be exercised, and in which clearly the party sought to be affected should be heard. Then, as to the appeal section, 211, what light does that throw upon the matter? There is an appeal from the district board, not to any judicial tribunal in the sense of any tribunal more judicial in its form than the local board of works, but to the metropolitan board of works, which is just as much and just as little judicial in its acts as the board whose conduct we are now considering. What is to take place upon such appeal? "And all such appeals shall stand referred to the committee appointed by such board for hearing appeals, as herein provided; and such committee shall *hear and determine* all such appeals." Nothing can be more clear than that the legislature thought that the matters which might come before the board upon appeal, that is, the same matters which came before the local board of works in the first instance, were proper, not only to be determined, but also to be heard; and, if fit to be heard upon an appeal, a *fortiori* fit to be heard in the first instance, before a wrongful decision can make an appeal lie....

... There is another remark to be made with reference to these parties' proceedings. The board are not only to do the work of demolishing the house, if they think proper, or modifying it, but they are to charge the expenses on the person who has erred against the Act. His property is affected and his purse is further affected. What happens upon that? and how is the money to be got? That is a proceeding under the 225th section, which is a section giving jurisdiction to the justices before whom the costs are to be ascertained and recovered; and it is clear that under that section the justices could not proceed without having before them the person against whom the expenses are to be adjudged. And it does seem an absurdity to say, that, in determining the amount of expenses, the party shall be heard, but that, in determining whether proceedings should be taken, his mouth should be closed. I cannot help thinking that a board exercising this large power should follow the ordinary rule, that the party sought to be affected should be heard; and I think that the verdict for the plaintiff ought to stand.

BYLES J.: I am of the same opinion. This is a case in which the Wandsworth district board have taken upon themselves to pull down a house, and to saddle the owner with the expenses of demolition, without notice of any sort. There are two sorts of notice which may possibly be required, and neither of them has been given: one, a notice of a hearing, that the party may be heard if he has anything to say against the demolition; the other is a notice of the order, that he may consider whether he can mitigate the wrath of the board, or in any way modify the execution of the order. Here they have given him neither opportunity. It seems to me that the board are wrong whether they acted judicially or ministerially. I conceive they acted judicially, because they had to determine the offence, and they had to apportion the punishment as well as the remedy. That being so, a long course of decisions, beginning with Dr Bentley's case,[2] and ending with some very recent cases, establish, that, although there are no positive words in a statute requiring that the party shall be heard, yet the justice of the common law will supply the omission of the legislature. The judgment of Mr Justice Fortescue, in Dr Bentley's case, is somewhat quaint, but it is very applicable, and has been the law from that time to the present. He says, "The objection for want of notice can never be got over. The laws of God and man both give the party an opportunity to make his defence, if he has any. I remember to have heard it observed by a very learned man, upon such an occasion, that even God himself did not pass sentence upon Adam before he was called upon to make his defence. 'Adam' (says God), 'where art thou? Hast thou not eaten of the tree whereof I commanded thee that thou shouldest not eat?' And the same question was put to Eve also." If, therefore, the board acted judicially, although there are no words in the statute to that effect, it is plain they acted wrongly. But suppose they acted ministerially—then it may be they were not bound to give the first sort of notice, *viz.* the notice of the hearing; but they were clearly bound, as it seems to me, by the words of the statute, to give notice of their order before they proceeded to execute it. Section 76 contains these words: "The vestry or district board shall make their order in relation to the matters aforesaid, and cause the same to be notified" (observe what follows) "to the person from whom such notice was received, within seven days after the receipt of the notice." The plain construction of those words, as it seems to me, is this: the order is to be notified, and, in the case of a person who has given a notice, that notification is to be conveyed to

---

[2] *The King v. The Chancellor, &c., of Cambridge*, 1 Stra. 557; 2 Ld.Raym. 1334; 8 Mod. 148; Fortescue 202.

him within seven days from the date of his notice.. That has not been done. There has been neither notice of the one sort nor of the other; and it seems to me, therefore, that, whether the board acted judicially or ministerially, they have acted against the whole current of authorities, and have omitted to do that which justice requires, and contravened the words of the statute. I entirely agree with what my Brother Willes has said about section 211, which clearly shows, that, if the board acted ministerially, they ought to give notice of the latter character. I cannot entertain any doubt that in this case the board have exercised their power wrongfully.

KEATING J. delivered a concurring judgment.

Rule discharged.

Notes

1. A wide variety of arguments are advanced by the judges; note in particular their avowed aim of promoting good administration. They do not simply incant "no man shall be deprived of his property without a hearing".

2. Note the willingness of Byles J. to read words requiring a hearing into the statute. Compare the views of the Privy Council in *Furnell v. Whangarei School Board* [1973] 1 All E.R. 400, P.C. The majority (Lords Morris of Borth-y-Gest, Simon of Glaisdale and Kilbrandon) were of the opinion that where a detailed and elaborate disciplinary code was prescribed by statutory regulations, as it was for the investigation of complaints against teachers in New Zealand, it was "not lightly to be affirmed" that it was unfair "when it has been made on the advice of the responsible Minister and on the joint recommendation of organisations representing teachers employed and those employing. Nor is it the function of the court to redraft the code" (at 411). The approach of the minority (Viscount Dilhorne and Lord Reid) was to ask first whether the nature of the powers exercised gave rise to a presumption that they were to be exercised only after the person affected had been given a fair hearing. If a fair hearing was necessary but had not been given, the burden shifted to the authority to establish that the regulations "clearly show an intention to exclude that which natural justice would otherwise require" (at 417). Which approach is preferable? See case note by J.M. Evans (1973) 36 M.L.R. 439 and article by J.F. Northey [1972] N.Z.L.J. 307. For the contemporary view of the House of Lords, see Lord Bridge's speech in *Lloyd v . McMahon* (below, p. 489).

RIDGE v. BALDWIN AND OTHERS

[1964] A.C. 40; [1963] 2 W.L.R. 935; 127 J.P. 295; 107 S.J. 313; [1963] 2 All E.R. 66; 61 L.G.R. 369 (House of Lords)

The Municipal Corporations Act 1882 provided by section 191: "(4) The Watch Committee, ... may at any time dismiss, any borough constable whom they think negligent in the discharge of his duty, or otherwise unfit for the same." The Police Act 1919 provided by section 4(1): "It shall be lawful for the Secretary of State to make regulations as to the ... conditions of service of the members of all police forces within England and Wales, and every police authority shall comply with the regulations so made." It was accepted that the 1919 Act did not impliedly repeal the relevant provisions of the 1882 Act. The relevant regulations contained detailed provisions as to the procedure to be followed where a report or allegation was received by the police authority from which it appeared that a chief constable might have committed an offence against the "Discipline Code" (set out in the regulations).

According to the regulations, the detailed procedure, which involved a formal hearing before a specially constituted tribunal, could only be dispensed with if the chief constable admitted that he had committed an offence against the code.

Charles Ridge was appointed chief constable of the County Borough of Brighton in 1956. The appointment was "subject to the Police Act and Regulations". In 1957, Ridge, two police officers and two others were indicted for conspiracy to obstruct the course of justice between 1949 and 1957. Ridge was acquitted, but the other two police officers were convicted. On February 28, in passing sentence, the trial judge, Donovan J., made certain observations as to the chief constable's conduct. In the words of Lord Evershed: "As I understand the language of Donovan J.... the appellant had been shown not to possess a sense of probity or of responsibility sufficient for the office which he held, and so had been unable to provide the essential leadership and example to the police force under his control which his office properly required." On March 6, no evidence was offered against R on a further charge of corruption. Here Donovan J. referred to the police force's need for a leader "who will be a new influence and who will set a different example from that which has lately obtained." The following day, the Watch Committee, purporting to act under section 191(4) of the 1882 Act summarily dismissed R on the ground that in their opinion he had been negligent in the discharge of his duty, and was unfit for the same. He was given neither any notice of the meeting, nor any opportunity to make representations. The regulations were in no way operated. On March 18, the committee heard representations from R's solicitor, but gave no further particulars of the case against him. On July 5, the Home Secretary dismissed R's appeal under the Police (Appeals) Act 1927 (as amended), holding "that there was sufficient material on which the Watch Committee could properly exercise their power of dismissal under section 191(4)". The appeal had been made expressly without prejudice to any rights to contend that the purported dismissal was bad in law as being contrary to natural justice and not in accordance with the regulations.

R then brought an action in the High Court for a declaration that the dismissal was illegal, *ultra vires* and void, and for damages. His main purpose was to obtain the opportunity to resign voluntarily, his pension rights thus being preserved.

Eight significant issues arose:

1. Did the regulations apply? If they did, there had been a clear non-compliance.
2. If they did not, did the *audi alteram partem* rule of natural justice nevertheless apply?
3. If it applied, was it complied with?
4. If the decision to dismiss was bad under either of the foregoing heads, was it void or voidable?
5. If the initial dismissal was bad, was it cured by the second meeting of the committee on March 18?
6. Did the exercise of the right of appeal cure any invalidity?
7. Was the invalidity cured by the Police (Appeals) Act 1927, s.2(3), which stated that the Secretary of State's decision should be final and binding on all parties?
8. Should the invalidity be ignored, on the ground that the case was "as plain as a pikestaff?"

Streatfeild J. at first instance ([1961] 2 W.L.R. 1054), held that natural justice had to be observed, and that the Watch Committee had done so. The Court of Appeal ([1963] 1 Q.B. 539) held that natural justice did not have to be observed as the action of the committee was "administrative" or "executive". They were not deciding a question between two contending parties. Ridge's appeal to the House of Lords was allowed. The leading speeches were those of Lord Reid, who dealt mainly with natural justice at common law, and Lord Morris of Borth-y-Gest, who dealt mainly with the regulations. Lord Hodson came to the same conclusions as both Lord Reid and Lord Morris. Lord Devlin's speech was based solely on the regulations. Lord Evershed dissented.

LORD REID: ... The appellant's case is that in proceeding under the Act of 1882 the watch committee were bound to observe what are commonly called the principles of natural justice. Before attempting to reach any decision they were bound to inform him of the grounds on which they proposed to act and give him a fair opportunity of being heard in his own defence. The authorities on the applicability of the principles of natural justice are in some confusion, and so I find it necessary to examine this matter in some detail. The principle *audi alteram partem* goes back many centuries in our law and appears in a multitude of judgments of judges of the highest authority. In modern time opinions have sometimes been expressed to the effect that natural justice is so vague as to be practically meaningless. But I would regard these as tainted by the perennial fallacy that because something cannot be cut and dried or nicely weighed or measured therefore it does not exist. The idea of negligence is equally insusceptible to exact definition, but what a reasonable man would regard as fair procedure in particular circumstances and what he would regard as negligence in particular circumstances are equally capable of serving as tests in law, and natural justice as it has been interpreted in the courts is much more definite than that. It appears to me that one reason why the authorities on natural justice have been found difficult to reconcile is that insufficient attention has been paid to the great difference between various kinds of cases in which it has been sought to apply the principle. What a minister ought to do in considering objections to a scheme may be very different from what a watch committee ought to do in considering whether to dismiss a chief constable. So I shall deal first with cases of dismissal. These appear to fall into three classes: dismissal of a servant by his master, dismissal from an office held during pleasure, and dismissal from an office where there must be something against a man to warrant his dismissal.

The law regarding master and servant is not in doubt. There cannot be specific performance of a contract of service, and the master can terminate the contract with his servant at any time and for any reason or for none. But if he does so in a manner not warranted by the contract he must pay damages for breach of contract. So the question in a pure case of master and servant does not at all depend on whether the master has heard the servant in his own defence: it depends on whether the facts emerging at the trial prove breach of contract. But this kind of case can resemble dismissal from an office where the body employing the man is under some statutory or other restriction as to the kind of contract which it can make with its servants, or the grounds on which it can dismiss them. The present case does not fall within this class because a chief constable is not the servant of the watch committee or indeed of anyone else.

Then there are many cases where a man holds an office at pleasure. Apart from judges and others whose tenure of office is governed by statute, all servants and officers of the Crown hold office at pleasure, and this has been held even to apply to a colonial judge (*Terrell v. Secretary of State for the Colonies* [1953] 2 Q.B. 482). It has always been held, I think rightly, that such an officer has no right to be heard before he is dismissed, and the reason is clear. As a person having the power of dismissal need not have anything against the officer, he need not give any reason. That was stated as long ago as 1670 in *R. v. Stratford-on-Avon Corporation* (1809) 11 East 176 where the corporation dismissed a town clerk who held office *durante bene placito*. The leading case on this matter appears to be *R. v. Darlington School Governors* (1844) 6 Q.B. 682 although that decision was doubted by Lord Hatherley L.C. in *Dean v. Bennett* (1870) L.R. 6 Ch. 489 and distinguished on narrow grounds in *Willis v. Childe* (1851) 13 Beav. 117. I fully accept that where an office is simply held at pleasure the person having power of dismissal cannot be bound to disclose his reasons. No doubt he would in many cases tell the officer and hear his explanation before deciding to dismiss him. But if he is not bound to disclose his reason and does not do so, then, if the court cannot require him to do so, it cannot determine whether it would be fair to hear the officer's case before taking action. But again that is not this case. In this case the Act of 1882 only permits the watch committee to take action on the grounds of negligence or unfitness. Let me illustrate the difference by supposing that a watch committee who had no complaint against their present chief constable heard of a man with quite outstanding qualifications who would like to be appointed. They might think it in the public interest to make the change, but they would have no right to do it. But there could be no legal objection to dismissal of an officer holding office at pleasure in order to put a better man in his place.

So I come to the third class, which includes the present case. There I find an unbroken line of authority to the effect that an officer cannot lawfully be dismissed without first telling him what is alleged against him and hearing his defence or explanation. An early example is *Bagg's Case* (1615) 11 Co.Rep. 93b though it is more properly deprivation of the privilege of being a burgess of Plymouth. *R. v. Gaskin* (1799) 8 Term Rep. 209 arose out of the dismissal of a parish clerk, and Lord Kenyon C.J. referred to *audi alteram partem* as one of the first principles of justice. *R. v. Smith* (1844) 5 Q.B. 614 was another case of dismissal of a parish clerk, and Lord Denman C.J. held that even personal knowledge of the offence was no substitute for hearing the officer: his explanation might disprove criminal motive or intent and bring forward other facts in mitigation, and in any event delaying to hear him would prevent yielding too hastily to first impressions. *Ex parte Ramshay* (1852) 18 Q.B. 173 is important. It dealt with the removal from office of a county court judge, and the form of the legislation which authorised the Lord Chancellor to act is hardly distinguishable from the form of section 191, which confers powers on the watch committee. The Lord Chancellor was empowered if he should think fit to remove on the ground of inability or misbehaviour, but Lord Campbell C.J. said (*ibid.*, 190) that this was "only on the implied condition prescribed by the principles of eternal justice". In *Osgood v. Nelson* (1872) L.R. 5 H.L. 636 at 649, H.L., objection was taken to the way in which the Corporation of the City of London had removed the clerk to the Sheriff's Court, and Lord Hatherley L.C. said: "I apprehend, my Lords, that, as has been stated by the learned Baron who has delivered, in the name of the judges, their unanimous opinion, the Court of Queen's Bench has always considered that it has been open to that court, as in this case it appears to have considered, to correct any court, or tribunal, or body of men who may have a power of this description, a power of removing from office, if it should be found that such persons have disregarded any of the essentials of justice in the course of their inquiry, before making that removal, or if it should be found that in the place of reasonable cause those persons have acted obviously upon mere individual caprice."

That citation of authority might seem sufficient, but I had better proceed further. In *Fisher v. Jackson* [1891] 2 Ch. 84 three vicars had power to remove the master of an endowed school. But, unlike the *Darlington* case, 6 Q.B. 682 the trust deed set out the grounds on which he could be removed—briefly, inefficiency or failing to set a good example. So it was held that they could not remove him without affording him an opportunity of being heard in his own defence. Only two other cases of this class were cited in argument, *Cooper v. Wilson* [1937] 2 K.B. 309 and *Hogg v. Scott* [1947] K.B. 759. Both dealt with the dismissal of police officers and both were complicated by consideration of regulations made under the Police Acts. In the former the majority at least recognised that the principles of natural justice applied, and in deciding the latter Cassels J. in deciding that a chief constable could dismiss without hearing him an officer who had been convicted of felony, appears to have proceeded on a construction of the regulations. Of course, if the regulations authorised him to do that and were *intra vires* in doing so, there would be no more to be said. I do not think it necessary to consider whether the learned judge rightly construed the regulations, for he did not expressly or, I think, by implication question the general principle that a man is not to be dismissed for misconduct without being heard.

Stopping there, I would think that authority was wholly in favour of the appellant, but the respondent's argument was mainly based on what has been said in a number of fairly recent cases dealing with different subject-matter. Those cases deal with decisions by ministers, officials and bodies of various kinds which adversely affected property rights or privileges of persons who had had no opportunity or no proper opportunity of presenting their cases before the decisions were given. And it is necessary to examine those cases for another reason. The question which was or ought to have been considered by the watch committee on March 7, 1958, was not a simple question whether or not the appellant should be dismissed. There were three possible courses open to the watch committee—reinstating the appellant as chief constable, dismissing him, or requiring him to resign. The difference between the latter two is that dismissal involved forfeiture of pension rights, whereas requiring him to resign did not. Indeed, it is now clear that the appellant's real interest in this appeal is to try to save his pension rights.

It may be convenient at this point to deal with an argument that, even if as a general rule a watch committee must hear a constable in his own defence before dismissing him, that case was so clear that nothing that the appellant could have said could have made any difference. It is at least very doubtful whether that could be accepted as an excuse. But, even if it could, the respondents would, in my view, fail on the facts. It may well be that no reasonable body of men could have reinstated the appellant. But as between the other two courses open to the watch committee the case is not so clear. Certainly on the facts, as we know them, the watch committee could reasonably have decided to forfeit the appellant's pension rights, but I could not hold that they would have acted wrongly or wholly unreasonably if they had in the exercise of their discretion decided to take a more lenient course.

I would start an examination of the authorities dealing with property rights and privileges with *Cooper v. Wandsworth Board of Works* (1863) 14 C.B.(N.S.) 180.

[His Lordship summarised this case, and *Hopkins v. Smethwick Local Board of Health* (1890) 24 Q.B.D. 712; *Smith v. The Queen* (1878) L.R. 3 App.Cas. 614, P.C.; and *De Verteuil v. Knaggs* [1918] A.C. 557.]

I shall now turn to a different class of case—deprivation of membership of a professional or social body. In *Wood v. Woad* (1874) L.R. 9 Ex. 190 the committee purported to expel a member of a mutual insurance society without hearing him, and it was held that their action was void, and so he was still a member. Kelly C.B. said of *audi alteram partem* (*ibid.* 196): "This rule is not confined to the conduct of strictly legal tribunals, but is applicable to every tribunal or body of persons invested with authority to adjudicate upon matters involving civil consequences to individuals." This was expressly approved by Lord Macnaghten giving the judgment of the Board in *Lapointe v. L'Association de Bienfaisance et de Retraite de la Police de Montréal* [1906] A.C. 535, P.C. In that case the board of directors of the association had to decide whether to give a pension to a dismissed constable—the very point the watch committee had to decide in this case—and it was held (*ibid.* p. 539) that they had to observe "the elementary principles of justice".

Then there are the club cases, *Fisher v. Keane* (1878) 11 Ch.D. 353 and *Dawkins v. Antrobus* (1879) 17 Ch.D. 615, C.A. In the former, Jessel M.R. said of the committee, 11 Ch.D. 353 at 362–363: "They ought not, as I understand it, according to the ordinary rules by which justice should be administered by committees of clubs, or by any other body of persons who decide upon the conduct of others, to blast a man's reputation for ever—perhaps to ruin his prospects for life, without giving him an opportunity of either defending or palliating his conduct." In the latter case it was held that nothing had been done contrary to natural justice. In *Weinberger v. Inglis* [1919] A.C. 606, H.L., a member of enemy birth was excluded from the Stock Exchange, and it was held that the committee had heard him before acting. Lord Birkenhead L.C. said (*ibid.* at 616): "... if I took the view that the appellant was condemned upon grounds never brought to his notice, I should not assent to the legality of this course, unless compelled by authority". He said this although the rule under which the committee acted was in the widest possible terms—that the committee should each year re-elect such members as they should deem eligible as members of the Stock Exchange.

I shall not at present advert to the various trade union cases because I am deliberately considering the state of the law before difficulties were introduced by statements in various fairly recent cases. It appears to me that if the present case had arisen 30 or 40 years ago the courts would have had no difficulty in deciding this issue in favour of the appellant on the authorities which I have cited. So far as I am aware none of these authorities has ever been disapproved or even doubted. Yet the Court of Appeal have decided this issue against the appellant on more recent authorities which apparently justify that result. How has this come about?

At least three things appear to me to have contributed. In the first place there have been many cases where it has been sought to apply the principles of natural justice to the wider duties imposed on Ministers and other organs of government by modern legislation. For reasons which I shall attempt to state in a moment, it has been held that those principles have a limited application in such cases and those limitations have tended to be reflected in other decisions on matters to which in principle they do not appear to me to apply. Secondly, again for reasons which I shall attempt to state, those principles have been held to have a limited application in cases arising out of war-time legislation; and again such limitations have tended to be reflected in other cases. And, thirdly, there has, I think, been a misunderstanding of the judgment of Atkin L.J. in *R. v. Electricity Commissioners, ex p. London Electricity Joint Committee Co.* [1924] 1 K.B. 171.

In cases of the kind I have been dealing with the Board of Works or the Governor or the club committee was dealing with a single isolated case. It was not deciding, like a judge in a lawsuit, what were the rights of the person before it. But it was deciding how he should be treated—something analogous to a judge's duty in imposing a penalty. No doubt policy would play some part in the decision—but so it might when a judge is imposing a sentence. So it was easy to say that such a body is performing a quasi-judicial task in considering and deciding such a matter, and to require it to observe the essentials of all proceedings of a judicial character—the principles of natural justice.

Sometimes the functions of a minister or department may also be of that character, and then the rules of natural justice can apply in much the same way. But more often their functions are of a very different character. If a minister is considering whether to make a scheme for, say, an important new road, his primary concern will not be with the damage which its construction will do to the rights of individual owners of land. He will have to consider all manner of questions of public interest and, it may be, a number of alternative schemes. He cannot be prevented from attaching more importance to the fulfilment of his policy than to the fate of individual objectors, and it would be quite wrong for the courts to say that the minister should or could act in the same kind of way as a board of works deciding whether a house should be pulled down. And there is another important difference. As explained in *Local Government Board v. Arlidge* [1915] A.C. 120 a minister cannot do everything himself. His officers will have to gather and sift all the facts, including objections by individuals, and no individual can complain if the ordinary accepted methods of carrying on public business do not give him as good protection as would be given by the principles of natural justice in a different kind of case.

We do not have a developed system of administrative law—perhaps because until fairly recently we did not need it. So it is not surprising that in dealing with new types of cases the courts have had to grope for solutions, and have found that old powers, rules and procedure are largely inapplicable to cases which they were never designed or intended to deal with. But I see nothing in that to justify our thinking that our old methods are any less applicable today than ever they were to the older types of case. And if there are any dicta in modern authorities which point in that direction, then, in my judgment, they should not be followed.

And now I must say something regarding war-time legislation. The older authorities clearly show how the courts engrafted the principles of natural justice on to a host of provisions authorising administrative interference with private rights. Parliament knew quite well that the courts had an inveterate habit of doing that and must therefore be held to have authorised them to do it unless a particular Act showed a contrary intention. And such an intention could appear as a reasonable inference as well as from express words. It seems to me to be a reasonable and almost an inevitable inference from the circumstances in which Defence Regulations were made and from their subject-matter that, at least in many cases, the intention must have been to exclude the principles of natural justice. War-time secrecy alone would often require that, and the need for speed and general pressure of work were other factors. But it was not to be expected that anyone would state in so many words that a temporary abandonment of the rules of natural justice was one of the sacrifices which war conditions required—that would have been almost calculated to create the alarm and despondency against which one of the regulations was specifically directed. And I would draw the same conclusion from another fact. In many regulations there was set out an alternative safeguard more practicable in war time—the objective test that the officer must have reasonable cause to believe whatever was the crucial matter. (I leave out of account the very peculiar decision of this House in *Liversidge v. Anderson* [1942] A.C. 206.) So I would not think that any decision that the rules of natural justice were excluded from war-time legislation should be regarded as of any great weight in dealing with a case such as this case, which is of the older type, and which involves the interpretation of an Act passed long before modern modifications of the principles of natural justice became necessary, and at a time when, as Parliament was well aware, the courts habitually applied the principles of natural justice to provisions like section 191(4) of the Act of 1882.

The matter has been further complicated by what I believe to be a misunderstanding of a much-quoted passage in the judgment of Atkin L.J. in *R. v. Electricity Commissioners, ex p. London Electricity Joint Committee Co.* [1924] 1 K.B. 171 at 205. He said: "... the operation of the writs [of prohibition and certiorari] has extended to control the proceedings of bodies which do not claim to be, and would not be recognised as, courts of justice. Wherever any body of persons having legal authority to determine questions affecting the rights of subjects, and having the duty to act judicially, act in excess of their legal authority, they are subject to the controlling jurisdiction of the King's Bench Division exercised in these writs."

A gloss was put on this by Lord Hewart C.J. in *R. v. Legislative Committee of the Church Assembly, ex p. Haynes-Smith* [1928] 1 K.B. 411. There it was sought to prohibit the Assembly from proceeding further with the Prayer Book Measure 1927. That seems to me to have no resemblance to a question whether a person should be deprived of his rights or privileges, and the case was decided on the ground that this was a deliberative or legislative body and not a judicial body. Salter J. put it in a few lines (*ibid.* at 419): "The person or body to whom these writs are to go must be a judicial body in this sense, that it has power to determine and to decide; and the power carries with it, of necessity, the duty to act judicially. I think that the Church Assembly has no such power, and therefore no such duty." But Lord Hewart said (*ibid.* at 415) having quoted the passage from Atkin L.J.'s judgment: "The question, therefore, which we have to ask ourselves in this case is whether it is true to say in this matter, either of the Church Assembly as a whole, or of the Legislative Committee of the Church Assembly, that it is a body of persons having legal authority to determine questions affecting the rights of subjects, and having the duty to act judicially. It is to be observed that in the last sentence which I have quoted from the judgment of Atkin L.J. the word is not 'or', but 'and'. In order that a body may satisfy the required test it is not enough that it should have legal authority to determine questions affecting the rights of subjects; there must be superadded to that characteristic the further characteristic that the body has the duty to act judicially. The duty to act judicially is an ingredient which, if the test is to be satisfied, must be present. As these writs in the earlier days were issued only to bodies which without any harshness of construction could be called, and naturally would be called courts, so also today these writs do not issue except to bodies which act or are under the duty to act in a judicial capacity."

I have quoted the whole of this passage because it is typical of what has been said in several subsequent cases. If Lord Hewart meant that it is never enough that a body simply has a duty to determine what the rights of an individual should be, but that there must always be something more to impose on it a duty to act judicially before it can be found to observe the principles of natural justice, then that appears to me impossible to reconcile with the earlier authorities.... And, as I shall try to show, it cannot be what Atkin L.J. meant.

In *R. v. Electricity Commissioners, ex p. London Electricity Joint Committee Co.* [1924] 1 K.B. 171, the commissioners had a statutory duty to make schemes with regard to electricity districts and to hold local inquiries before making them. They made a draft scheme which in effect allocated duties to one body which the Act required should be allocated to a different kind of body. This was held to be *ultra vires*, and the question was whether prohibition would lie. It was argued that the proceedings of the commissioners were purely executive and controllable by Parliament alone. Bankes L.J. said (*ibid.* at 198): "On principle and on authority it is in my opinion open to this court to hold, and I consider that it should hold, that powers so far-reaching, affecting as they do individuals as well as property, are powers to be exercised judicially, and not ministerially or merely, to use the language of Palles C.B., as proceedings towards legislation." So he inferred the judicial element from the nature of the power. And I think that Atkin L.J. did the same. Immediately after the passage which I said has been misunderstood, he cited a variety of cases and in most of them I can see nothing "superadded" (to use Lord Hewart's word) to the duty itself. Certainly Atkin L.J. did not say that anything was superadded. And a later passage in his judgment convinces me that he, like Bankes L.J., inferred the judicial character of the duty from the nature of the duty itself. Although it is long I am afraid I must quote it [1924] 1 K.B. 171 at 206–207: "In the present case the Electricity Commissioners have to decide whether they will constitute a joint authority in a district in accordance with law, and with what powers they will invest that body. The question necessarily involves the withdrawal from existing bodies of undertakers of some of their existing rights, and imposing upon them of new duties, including their subjection to the control of the new body, and new financial obligations. It also provides in the new body a person to whom may be transferred rights of purchase which at present are vested in another authority. The commissioners are proposing to create such a new body in violation of the Act of Parliament, and are proposing to hold a possibly long and expensive inquiry into the expediency of such a scheme, in respect of which they have the power to compel representatives of the prosecutors at attend and produce papers. I think that in deciding upon the scheme, and in holding the inquiry, they are acting judicially in the sense of the authorities I have cited."

There is not a word in Atkin L.J.'s judgment to suggest disapproval of the earlier line of authority which I have cited. On the contrary, he goes further than those authorities. I have already stated my view that it is more difficult for the courts to control an exercise of power on a large scale where the treatment to be meted out to a particular individual is only one of many matters to be considered. This was a case of that kind, and, if Atkin L.J. was prepared to infer a judicial element from the nature of the power in this case, he could hardly disapprove such an inference when the power relates solely to the treatment of a particular individual.

The authority chiefly relied on by the Court of Appeal in holding that the watch committee were not bound to observe the principles of natural justice was *Nakkuda Ali v. Jayaratne* [1951] A.C. 66. In that case the Controller of Textiles in Ceylon made an order cancelling the appellant's licence to act as a dealer, and the appellant sought to have that order quashed. The controller acted under a Defence Regulation which empowered him to cancel a licence "where the controller has reasonable grounds to believe that any dealer is unfit to be allowed to continue as a dealer".

The Privy Council regarded that (*ibid.* at 77) as "imposing a condition that there must in fact exist such reasonable grounds, known to the controller, before he can validly exercise the power of cancellation." But according to their judgment certiorari did not lie, and no other means was suggested whereby the appellant or anyone else in his position could obtain redress even if the controller acted without a shred of evidence. It is quite true that the judgment went on, admittedly unnecessarily, to find that the controller had reasonable grounds and did observe the principles of natural justice, but the result would have been just the same if he had not. This House is not bound by decisions of the Privy Council, and for my own part nothing short of a decision of this House directly in point would induce me to accept the position that, although an enactment expressly requires an official to have reasonable grounds for his decision, our law is so defective that a subject cannot bring up such a decision for review however seriously he may be affected and however obvious it may be that the official acted in breach of his statutory obligation.

The judgment proceeds: "But it does not seem to follow necessarily from this that the controller must be acting judicially in exercising the power. Can one not act reasonably without acting judicially? It is not difficult to think of circumstances in which the controller might, in any ordinary sense of the words, have reasonable grounds of belief without having ever confronted the licence holder with the information which is the source of his belief. It is a long step in the argument to say that because a man is enjoined that he must not take action unless he has reasonable ground for believing something he can only arrive at that belief by a course of conduct analogous to the judicial process. And yet, unless that proposition is valid, there is really no ground for holding that the controller is acting judicially or quasi-judicially when he acts under this regulation. If he is not under a duty so to act then it would not be according to law that his decision should be amenable to review and, if necessary, to avoidance by the procedure of certiorari."

I would agree that in this and other Defence Regulation cases the legislature has submitted an obligation not to act without reasonable grounds for the ordinary obligation to afford to the person affected an opportunity to submit his defence. It is not necessary in this case to consider whether by so doing he has deprived the courts of the power to intervene if the officer acts contrary to his duty. The question in the present case is not whether Parliament substituted a different safeguard for that afforded by natural justice, but whether in the Act of 1882 it excluded the safeguard of natural justice and put nothing in its place.

So far there is nothing in the judgment of the Privy Council directly relevant to the present case. It is the next paragraph which causes the difficulty and I must quote the crucial passage (*ibid.* at 78): "But the basis of the jurisdiction of the courts by way of certiorari has been so exhaustively analysed in recent years that individual instances are now only of importance as illustrating a general principle that is beyond dispute. That principle is most precisely stated in the words of Atkin L.J. in *R. v. Electricity Commissioners, ex p. London Electricity Joint Committee Co.* [1924] 1 K.B. 171 at 205"—and then follows the passage with which I have already dealt at length. And then there follows the quotation from Lord Hewart, which I have already commented on, ending with the words—"there must be superadded to that characteristic the further characteristic that the body has the duty to act judicially". And then it is pointed out: "It is that characteristic that the controller lacks in acting under regulation 62."

Of course, if it were right to say that Lord Hewart's gloss of Atkin L.J. stated "a general principle that is beyond dispute", the rest would follow. But I have given my reasons for holding that it does no such thing, and in my judgment the older cases certainly do not "illustrate" any such general principle—they contradict it. No case older than 1911 was cited in *Nakkuda's* case on this question, and this question was only one of several difficult questions which were argued and decided. So I am forced to the conclusion that this part of the judgment in *Nakkuda's* case was given under a serious misapprehension of the effect of the older authorities and therefore cannot be regarded as authoritative.

I would sum up my opinion in this way. Between 1882 and the making of police regulations in 1920 section 191(4) had to be applied to every kind of case. The respondents' contention is that, even where there was a doubtful question whether a constable was guilty of a particular act of misconduct, the watch committee were under no obligation to hear his defence before dismissing him. In my judgment it is abundantly clear from the authorities I have quoted that at that time the courts would have rejected any such contention. In later cases dealing with different subject-matter, opinions have been expressed in wide terms so as to appear to conflict with those earlier authorities. But learned judges who expressed those opinions generally had no power to overrule those authorities, and in any event it is a salutary rule that a judge is not to be assumed to have intended to overrule or disapprove of an authority which has not been cited to him and which he does not even mention. So I would hold that the power of dismissal in the Act of 1882 could not then have been exercised and cannot now be exercised until the watch committee have informed the constable of the grounds on which they propose to proceed and have given him a proper opportunity to present his case in defence.

Next comes the question whether the respondents' failure to follow the rules of natural justice on March 7 was made good by the meeting on March 18. I do not doubt that if an officer or body realises that it has acted hastily and reconsiders the whole matter afresh, after affording to the person affected a proper opportunity to present his case, then its later decision will be valid. An example is *De Verteuil's* case. But here the appellant's solicitor was not fully informed of the charges against the appellant and the watch committee did not annul the decision which they had already published and proceed to make a new decision. In my judgment, what was done on that day was a very inadequate substitute for a full rehearing. Even so, three members of the committee changed their minds, and it is impossible to say what the decision of the committee would have been if there had been a full hearing after disclosure to the appellant of the whole case against him. I agree with those of your Lordships who hold that this meeting of March 18 cannot affect the result of this appeal.

The other ground on which some of your Lordships prefer to proceed is the respondents' failure to act in accordance with the Police Regulations. I have had an opportunity of reading the speech about to be delivered by my noble and learned friend, Lord Morris of Borth-y-Gest, and I agree with his view about this.

Then there was considerable argument whether in the result the watch committee's decision is void or merely voidable. Time and again in the cases I have cited it has been stated that a decision given without regard to the principles of natural justice is void, and that was expressly decided in *Wood v. Woad*. I see no reason to doubt these authorities. The body with the power to decide cannot lawfully proceed to make a decision until it has afforded to the person affected a proper opportunity to state his case.

Finally, there is the question whether by appealing to the Secretary of State the appellant is in some way prevented from now asserting the nullity of the respondents' decision. A person may be prevented from asserting the truth by estoppel, but it is not seriously argued that that doctrine applies here. Then it is said that the appellant elected to go to the Secretary of State and thereby waived his right to come to the court. That appears to me to be an attempt to set up what is in effect estoppel where the essential elements for estoppel are not present. There are many cases where two remedies are open to an aggrieved person, but there is no general rule that by going to some other tribunal he puts it out of his power thereafter to assert his right in court; and there was no express waiver because in appealing to the Secretary of State the appellant reserved his right to maintain that the decision was a nullity.

But then it was argued that this case is special because by statute the decision of the Secretary of State is made final and binding. I need not consider what the result would have been if the Secretary of State had heard the case for the appellant and then given his own independent decision that the appellant should be dismissed. But the Secretary of State did not do that. He merely decided "that there was sufficient material on which the watch committee could properly exercise their power of dismissal under section 191(4)". So the only operative decision is that of the watch committee, and, if it was a nullity, I do not see how this statement by the Secretary of State can make it valid.

Accordingly, in my judgment, this appeal must be allowed. There appears to have been no discussion in the courts below as to remedies which may now be open to the appellant, and I do not think that this House should do more than declare that the dismissal of the appellant is null and void and remit the case to the Queen's Bench Division for further procedure. But it is right to put on record that the appellant does not seek to be reinstated as chief constable: his whole concern is to avoid the serious financial consequences involved in dismissal as against being required or allowed to resign.

ʃLORD EVERSHED (dissenting) held that:

(1) "the shortcomings of the appellant as chief constable" did not fall within the Discipline Code;

(2) therefore, the Watch Committee were entitled to exercise their residual powers under section 191(4) of the 1882 Act without observing the regulations;

(3) there was no "report or allegation" before the Watch Committee. Those words suggested "something in the nature of an accusation as distinct from a conclusion reached after proper inquiry" (*i.e.* Donovan J.'s conclusion);

(4) that "this was a special and entirely exceptional case outside the scope of the regulations, and, as a matter of public notoriety, requiring instant action by the Watch Committee";

(5) that if natural justice ought to have been observed, a decision in breach of natural justice would normally be voidable, not void, in that the body would be "acting within its jurisdiction." A decision would only be void if based on "frivolous or futile" grounds or if there had been "a real substantial miscarriage of justice";

(6) that apart from the prejudice to pension rights, the Watch Committee need not have given the plaintiff any opportunity to state points he had already made before Donovan J. The committee also had to act urgently. However, his Lordship was prepared to assume that the plaintiff should have had an opportunity to state his case for being allowed to resign;

(7) that justice had been done as representations had been made to the Watch Committee on March 18;

(8) that if he (his Lordship) was wrong on the last point, any defect was cured by the appeal to the Secretary of State, whose decision was rendered "final and binding" by section 2(3) of the Police (Appeals) Act 1927. ＇

Therefore his Lordship would have dismissed the appeal.

LORD MORRIS OF BORTH-Y-GEST held that:

(1) there was a "report or allegation" before the Watch Committee. There were, for example, a transcript of the judge's remarks, and "certain statements made ... by members of the committee and the town clerk";

(2) the regulations should have been applied. As there was no admission of the commission of an offence, the regulations required a hearing;

(3) as the regulations had been ignored, the dismissal was void. (*Andrews v. Mitchell* [1905] A.C. 78, *Lapointe v. L'Association de Bienfaisance et de Retraite de la Police de Montréal* [1906] A.C. 535, and *Annamunthodo v. Oilfield Workers' Trade Union* [1961] A.C. 945 applied);

(4) the defect was not cured by the second hearing on March 18, as the plaintiff was never given notice of the allegations against him;

(5) the defect was not cured by the appeal to the Secretary of State as the original decision was a nullity, and the plaintiff so maintained during the appeal;

(6) apart from the regulations, natural justice should have been observed. The dismissal was not an "executive or administrative act" as it was based on a "suggestion of neglect of duty";
(7) a decision in breach of natural justice was void not voidable.

LORD HODSON delivered a speech concurring substantially with LORD REID and LORD MORRIS.

LORD DEVLIN held that the regulations applied and should have been observed. Any decision in breach of the regulations would be voidable unless any regulation laid down a "condition precedent to the conferment of authority on the committee which had not been fulfilled". Article 11(1) of the 1882 regulations allowed the police authority to act only on receipt of a report from the tribunal set up under the regulations to hear the evidence and make recommendations. The committee's decision was therefore void *ab initio*.

His Lordship held that a decision in breach of natural justice was voidable only.]

Appeal allowed.

Notes

1. There are many points of interest, including the scope of natural justice, the ways in which defective decisions may or may not be cured, whether such decisions are void or voidable, the application of statutory procedural requirements, and the proper approach that should be taken to cases decided in wartime. The case has been followed and cited in many subsequent cases. See case notes and articles by A.W. Bradley [1964] C.L.J. 83; G.H.L. Fridman (1963) 113 L.J. 716; A. L. Goodhart (1964) 80 L.Q.R. 105 and (1963) 26 M.L.R. 543; D.G. Benjafield and H. Whitmore (1963) 37 A.L.J. 140; D. Paterson [1966] N.Z.L.J. 107; P. Brett 16 Malaya L.R. 100; K.J. Keith, "*Ridge v. Baldwin*—Twenty Years On" (1983) 13 V.U.W.L.R. 239.

2. The dismissal of police officers is now regulated by the Police Act 1996, and regulations made thereunder.

3. In *Durayappah v. Fernando* [1967] 2 A.C. 337, a minister had power to order the dissolution of a municipal council if it appeared to him that it "is not competent to perform, or persistently makes default in the performance of, any duty or duties imposed upon it, or persistently refuse or neglects to comply with any provision of law...". Such an order was made in respect of Jaffna Municipal Council, and challenged by the mayor on the ground that no hearing had been given. The Privy Council rejected the view of the Supreme Court of Ceylon, that the subjective wording automatically excluded a duty to act judicially. They pointed out that words could be implied into a statute, as in *Cooper v. Wandsworth Board of Works*, and that if the law were otherwise, *Capel v. Child* (1832) 2 Cromp. & Jer. 558 would have been decided differently. It would be wrong to attempt to give an exhaustive classification of the cases where the *audi alteram partem* principle should be applied. *Per* Lord Upjohn at 349:

"Outside the well-known classes of cases, no general rule can be laid down as to the application of the general principle in addition to the language of the provision. In their Lordships' opinion there are three matters which must always be borne in mind when considering whether the principle should be applied or not. These three matters are: first, what is the nature of the property, the office held, status enjoyed or services to be performed by the complainant of injustice. Secondly, in what circumstances or upon what occasions is the person claiming to be entitled to exercise the measure of control entitled to intervene. Thirdly, when a right to intervene is proved, what sanctions in fact is the latter entitled to impose upon the other. It is only upon a consideration of all these matters that the question of the application of the principle can properly be determined."

These matters were considered in turn. First, the Council was by statute a public corporation entrusted with the administration of a large area and the discharge of important duties. It enjoyed a considerable measure of independence from the central government. The responsibility of the Minister to the legislature did not exclude the possibility of "responsibility to the courts under the principle *audi alteram partem*". Secondly, it was a most serious charge to allege persistent default or refusal or neglect to comply with a provision of law. It was not possible to distinguish these from the ground actually alleged here, namely incompetence. It would not be right to hold that whether or not natural justice had to be observed depended on the ground on which the order was eventually made. Thirdly, the sanction was "as complete as could be imagined", the dissolution of the Council and the confiscation of all its properties. The Council owned large areas of land, had a municipal fund, and levied rates. So, on the principle of *Cooper v. Wandsworth Board of Works* "that no man is to be deprived of his property without a hearing", in addition to the other grounds, the Minister should have observed natural justice.

Nevertheless, the Mayor of Jaffna was refused a remedy, on the grounds that he had insufficient *locus standi*.

See J.M. Eekelaar (1967) 30 M.L.R. 701; G. Nettheim (1967) 2 Federal L.R. 215.

4. Subsequently, in *Chief Constable of North Wales v. Evans* [1982] 1 W.L.R. 1155, the House of Lords held that a Chief Constable is subject to the rules of natural justice when exercising his statutory powers to discharge a probationer constable. In that case inaccurate rumours regarding the private life of probationary Constable Evans were conveyed to senior officers. The Chief Constable briefly interviewed Constable Evans and gave him the opportunity or resigning or being dismissed. Evans resigned and sought judicial review of the Chief Constable's actions. Lord Brightman (with whom the other Law Lords agreed) referred to *Ridge* and then concluded:

"it was the duty of the Chief Constable to deal fairly with the respondent in relation to the adverse factors upon which he was proposing to act. The Chief Constable failed in his performance of that duty because these supposedly adverse factors were never put to the respondent. He was given no opportunity to offer one word of explanation.... The decision-making process was therefore defective" (at 1174).

Their Lordships granted a declaration to the effect that the Chief Constable had acted unlawfully in threatening to dismiss Evans unless he resigned, but they did not order his reinstatement as to have done so would have "usurped" the powers of the Chief Constable.

Sir William Wade believed, "[Evans's] correct remedy, it would appear, was an action for damages for the tort of intimidation, having been forced to act to his detriment under threat of unlawful injury" (1983) 99 L.Q.R. 171 at 172. See also J. McMullen (1984) 47 M.L.R. 234.

5. The tripartite classification of employment relationships articulated by Lord Reid in *Ridge* was further refined by his Lordship in *Malloch v. Aberdeen Corporation* [1971] 1 W.L.R. 1578. In that case Mr Malloch was a teacher employed by the corporation. Regulations made under the Education (Scotland) Act 1946, required all teachers employed by education authorities to register with a new statutory body—the General Teaching Council for Scotland. Malloch was entitled to be registered with the

Teaching Council, but he refused on a point of principle. Aberdeen Corporation were advised that they could no longer employ Malloch and they informed him (as they were obliged to do under the Education (Scotland) Act 1962) that the education committee would be meeting to pass a resolution for his dismissal. Malloch was permitted to attend the committee's meeting, but he was not allowed to address the meeting. The committee resolved to dismiss him. Malloch then sought judicial review of that decision arguing that it had been made in breach of the rules of natural justice. In the House of Lords, Lord Reid stated (at 1582):

"An elected public body is in a very different position from a private employer. Many of its servants in the lower grades are in the same position as servants of a private employer. But many in higher grades or "offices" are given special statutory status or protection. The right of a man to be heard in his own defence is the most elementary protection of all and, where a statutory form of protection would be less effective if it did not carry with it a right to be heard, I would not find it difficult to imply this right."

His Lordship then went on to find that despite Malloch's employment status, as an office holder dismissable at pleasure, legislation had impliedly given him a right to be heard before being dismissed. Therefore, the Corporation had acted unlawfully (Lords Guest and Morris and Borth-y-Gest dissented).

Since the 1980s the courts have displayed a reluctance to allow employment disputes to be litigated through the judicial review procedure of R.S.C. Ord. 53, see the example the Court of Appeal's decision in *R. v. East Berkshire Health Authority, ex p. Walsh* [1985] Q.B. 152 (below, p. 625).

Today employees who are categorised as "servants" may be able to take proceedings against their employer (before an Industrial Tribunal) for unfair dismissal if, *inter alia*, they have not been accorded a fair procedure before being dismissed (see the Employment Rights Act 1996).

Moreover, the courts are now more prepared to hold that an obligation to observe natural justice is to be implied into the contract of employment, and more willing to grant the remedies of a declaration or injunction. See *Stevenson v. United Road Transport Union* [1977] I.C.R. 893 (trade union official); *R. v. British Broadcasting Corporation, ex p. Lavelle* [1983] 1 W.L.R. 23 (BBC employee); F.P. Davidson, "Judicial Review of Decisions to Dismiss" (1984) 35 N.I.L.Q. 121.

6. Note Lord Reid's dismissal of the argument that nothing the chief constable could have said would have made any difference. The same point arose in *Malloch v. Aberdeen Corporation* (above, n. 5). The Corporation argued that a hearing was unnecessary as they were bound by the regulations to dismiss Mr Malloch. Lord Wilberforce said (at 1595):

"The appellant has first to show that his position was such that he had, in principle, a right to make representations before a decision against him was taken. But to show this is not necessarily enough, unless he can also show that if admitted to state his case he had a case of substance to make. A breach of procedure, whether called a failure of natural justice, or an essential administrative fault, cannot give him a remedy in the courts, unless behind it there is something of substance which has been lost by the failure. The court does not act in vain."

His Lordship accepted Lord Reid's view that something of substance was at stake. Lord Reid said (at 1582–1583):

"Then it was argued that to have afforded a hearing to the appellant before dismissing him would have been a useless formality because whatever he might have said could have made no difference. If that could be clearly demonstrated it might be a good answer. But I need not decide that because there was here, I think, a substantial possibility that a sufficient number of the committee might have been persuaded not to vote for the appellant's dismissal. The motion for dismissal had to be carried by a two-thirds majority of those present, and at the previous meeting of the committee there was not a sufficient majority to carry a similar motion. Between these meetings the committee had received a strong letter from the Secretary of State urging them to dismiss the teachers who refused to register. And it appears that they had received some advice which might have been taken by them to mean that those who failed to vote for dismissal might incur personal liability. The appellant might have been able to persuade them that they need not have any such fear.

Then the appellant might have argued that on their true construction the regulations did not require the committee to dismiss him and that, if they did require that, they were *ultra vires*. The question of *ultra vires* was not argued before us and on that I shall say no more than that it is not obvious that the Secretary of State had power under any statute to make regulations requiring the dismissal of teachers who failed to acquire and pay for a new qualification such as registration. But the question of the proper construction of the regulations was argued and there I think that the appellant had at least an arguable case...."

These speeches accordingly both recognised the possibility that the court might not have intervened if a hearing would have made no difference, and rejected the argument on the facts.

Two possibilities should be noted. The law could be that as a matter of substance there is no *breach* of natural justice unless something of substance has been lost (D.H. Clark [1975] P.L. 27, 48, argues that this is what Lord Wilberforce meant in *Malloch*). Alternatively, this factor could simply be considered by the court in deciding, in the exercise of its discretion, whether to grant a remedy. This approach is illustrated by the following case. In *Glynn v. Keele University* [1971] 1 W.L.R. 487, Pennycuick V.-C. held that the university vice-chancellor was "acting in a quasi-judicial capacity" in exercising his disciplinary power to suspend a student who had "appeared naked" on the campus. This could not be regarded as a matter merely of "internal discipline" (which would not "lie within the purview of the court in its control over quasi-judicial acts") because it was "so fundamental to the position of the student in the university" (at 495). The student had been given no prior notice of the decision, and no opportunity to make representations, and his Lordship held this to be a clear breach of natural justice. Nevertheless, an injunction was refused in the exercise of the court's discretion:

"I recognise that this particular discretion should be very sparingly exercised in that sense where there has been some failure in natural justice. On the other hand, it certainly should be exercised in that sense in an appropriate case, and I think this is such a case. There is no question of fact involved, as I have already said. I must plainly proceed on the footing that the plaintiff was one of the individuals concerned. There is no doubt that the offence was one of a kind which merited a severe penalty according to any standards current even today. I have no doubt that the sentence of exclusion of residence in the campus was a proper penalty in respect of that offence. Nor has the plaintiff in his evidence put forward any specific justification for what he did. So the position would have been that if the vice-chancellor had accorded him a hearing before making his decision, all that he, or anyone on his behalf, could have done would have been to put forward some plea by way of mitigation. I do not disregard the importance of such a plea in an appropriate case, but I do not think the mere fact he was deprived of throwing himself on the mercy of the vice-chancellor in that way is sufficient to justify setting aside a decision which was intrinsically a perfectly proper one.

In all the circumstances, I have come to the conclusion that the plaintiff has suffered no injustice...."

(See case notes by M.H. Matthews [1971] C.L.J. 181; H.W.R. W[ade] (1971) 37 L.Q.R. 320.)

In either form, the argument needs to be viewed with caution. Where, *ex hypothesi*, the adjudicating body has failed to observe natural justice, *its* protestations that a hearing would have made no difference must be in principle viewed with scepticism (see further D.H. Clark [1975] P.L. 27, 43–60). In *John v. Rees* [1970] Ch. 345, Megarry J. said (at 402):

> "As everybody who has anything to do with the law well knows, the path of the law is strewn with examples of open and shut cases which, somehow, were not; of unanswerable charges which, in the event, were completely answered; of inexplicable conduct which was fully explained; of fixed and unalterable determinations that, by discussion suffered a change."

For further examples of cases where this argument has been rejected on the facts, see *R. v. Secretary of State for the Environment, ex p. Brent London Borough Council* [1982] Q.B. 593, 645–646 (in respect of the discretion to refuse a remedy) and *Lloyd v. McMahon* [1987] A.C. 625, 669, where Woolf L.J. (in the Court of Appeal) said in respect of the submission that the result would have inevitably been the same even if there had not been such a defect in procedure:

> "I recognise that there can be cases where such a submission will have to be considered by the court. However, I regard the authorities on which [counsel] relies, including *George v. Secretary of State for the Environment* [see below] and *Malloch v. Aberdeen Corporation* ... as having application in very limited circumstances, and certainly I would not regard them as applying here."

(On the House of Lords decision, see below, p. 487.)

In *R. v. Secretary of State for Education, ex p. Prior* [1994] I.C.R. 877, Brooke J. required the Secretary to reconsider his decision, reached after an unlawful and unfair hearing by a grant-maintained school's committee; because, " ... nothing is certain and in my judgment the applicant is entitled to a decision on his complaint which is not seriously flawed as a matter of law" (at 896).

Lord Denning has also doubted the validity of this kind of argument. In *Annamunthodo v. Oilfield Workers Trade Union* [1961] A.C. 945, he said (at 956):

> "Mr Lazarus did suggest that a man could not complain of a failure of natural justice unless he could show that he had been prejudiced by it. Their Lordships cannot accept this suggestion.... It is a prejudice to any man to be denied justice.... [H]e can always ask for the decision to be set aside."

Then, in *Kanda v. Government of Malaya* [1962] A.C. 322, he said (at 337):

> "The court will not go into the likelihood of prejudice. The risk of it is enough."

However, in *George v. Secretary of State for the Environment* (1979) 77 L.G.R. 689, Lord Denning M.R. stated, equally firmly, in the context of a statutory application to quash (see below, pp. 552–564), that:

> " ... there is no such thing as a technical breach of natural justice ... the position under the first limb is almost indistinguishable from that under the second limb. You should not find a breach of natural justice unless there has been substantial prejudice to the applicant as a result of the mistake or error which has been made" (at 695).

[Under the second limb, the ground of challenge was that the applicant had been substantially prejudiced by a failure to comply with a (procedural) requirement.] On the facts, the court seemed justified in holding that Mrs George was not prejudiced where the council failed to serve her with notice of a compulsory purchase order: the council mistakenly thought that Mr George was the sole owner (whereas they were joint owners); Mr George had been served, had appeared at the local public inquiry, and "took every objection that was open to either of them.... She was not prejudiced, either substantially or at all" (*per* Lord Denning M.R. at 694). (*cf. Cheall v. A.P.E.X.* [1983] 2 A.C. 180 and Brandon L.J. in *Cinnamond v. British Airports Authority,* below, p. 466.)

The question cannot, accordingly, be regarded as wholly settled.

Re H.K. (AN INFANT)

[1967] 2 Q.B. 617; [1967] 2 W.L.R. 962; 111 S.J. 296; *sub nom. Re K. (H.) (An Infant)* [1967] 1 All E.R. 226 D.C. (Queen's Bench Division)

Until the Commonwealth Immigrants Act 1962 came into force, Commonwealth subjects were entitled as of right to come to the United Kingdom. Thereafter, under section 2(1) of that Act, an immigration officer had a discretion to refuse admission to Commonwealth citizens, or to admit them subject to conditions. However, under section 2(2), that discretion could not be exercised in respect of "any person who satisfies an immigration officer that he ... (a) is ordinarily resident in the United Kingdom or was so resident at any time within the past two years; or (b) is the ... child under 16 years of age, of a Commonwealth citizen who is resident in the United Kingdom...". Paragraph 2(4) of Schedule 1 to that Act gave an immigration officer power to cancel a notice refusing a person admission.

Abdul Rehman Khan, a native of Pakistan, settled in Bradford in 1961. He claimed that he had left in Pakistan a wife and five children. In 1966, he went to Pakistan and returned with H.K., whom he said was his son aged 15½. On arrival at London Airport they were interviewed by an immigration officer. Abdul Rehman appeared to be within s.2(2)(a). However, the officer's suspicions were aroused because H.K. appeared to be well over 15. The officer sent H.K. to the port medical officer, who estimated the boy's age at "17 years". The officer then interviewed A.R. and H.K. separately, with the aid of interpreters. His suspicions were increased, and he referred the matter to the Chief Immigration Officer, Mr Collison. As a result of further interviews Mr Collison made up his mind that he was not satisfied that H.K. was under 16, and a notice refusing admission was served on November 21. H.K. was to be removed at noon on the following day. The following morning, further inquiries were made concerning a school certificate which gave as a date of birth February 29, 1951 (a non-existent date). Abdul Rehman applied for a writ of habeas corpus, and H.K.'s departure was delayed. During the course of the hearing by the Divisional Court he was given leave to move also for an order of certiorari to quash the decision to refuse H.K. admission.

LORD PARKER C.J.: ... Mr Gratiaen [counsel] submits that in deciding whether or not he is satisfied as to the matter set out in the subsection—in this case whether he is satisfied that the boy is under 16—an immigration officer is acting in a judicial or quasi-judicial capacity and must conform to the rules of natural justice. Subject to there being due compliance with those rules, Mr Gratiaen admits that the decision of the immigration officer cannot be challenged and that this court could not interfere. He does, however, maintain that the rules of natural justice require that before reaching his decision the immigration officer must give the immigrant an opportunity to satisfy him and if, as in this case, he has formed an impression that the immigrant is 16 or more, he must give the immigrant an opportunity to remove that impression. He claims that if that opportunity had been given, evidence would have been provided such as has been produced before us in these proceedings and that such evidence would have satisfied the officer. Having regard to the course which these proceedings have taken, it is unnecessary and, I think, indeed inadvisable to comment on that further evidence.... One thing I myself am quite clear on and that is that even if an immigration officer is required to act judicially or quasi-judicially, even if that is so, he is not under any duty to hold a full-scale inquiry or to adopt judicial process and procedure. The burden here under the Act is on the immigrant to satisfy the immigration officer and the provisions of the Schedule to which I have referred quite clearly show that it is impossible and therefore not contemplated that an immigration officer should hold any inquiry of that sort.... I doubt whether it can be said that the immigration authorities are acting in a judicial or quasi-judicial capacity as those terms are generally understood. But at the same time, I myself think that even if an immigration officer is not in a judicial or quasi-judicial capacity, he must at any rate give the immigrant an opportunity of satisfying him of the matters in the subsection, and for that purpose let the immigrant know what his immediate impression is so that the immigrant can disabuse him. That is not, as I see it, a question of acting or being required to act judicially, but of being required to act fairly. Good administration and an honest or bona fide decision must, as it seems to me, require not merely impartiality, nor merely bringing one's mind to bear on the problem, but acting fairly; and to the limited extent that the circumstances of any particular case allow, and within the legislative framework under which the administrator is working, only to that limited extent do the so-called rules of natural justice apply, which in a case such as this is merely a duty to act fairly. I appreciate that in saying that it may be said that one is going further than is permitted on the decided cases because heretofore at any rate the decisions of the courts do seem to have drawn a strict line in these matters according to whether there is or is not a duty to act judicially or quasi-judicially. It has sometimes been said that if there is no duty to act judicially or quasi-judicially there is no power in the court whatever to interfere. I observe that in the well-known case of *Nakkuda Ali v. M.F. de S. Jayaratne* [1951] A.C. 66 again a decision of the Privy Council, the court were considering this kind of case. There the Controller of Textiles in Ceylon was empowered to revoke licences where the controller had reasonable grounds to believe that any dealer was unfit to be allowed to continue as a dealer. Those were the words to be considered in that case which are of course different in the present case. But Lord Radcliffe, when giving the advice of the Judicial Committee, began by distinguishing that case from the well-known case of *Liversidge* [1942] A.C. 206 and went on to consider the position of the controller in law. He said [1951] A.C. 66 at 78:

> "In truth, when he cancels a licence he is not determining a question: he is taking executive action to withdraw a privilege because he believes, and has reasonable grounds to believe, that the holder is unfit to retain it."

He goes on to say that:

"the power conferred on the controller ... stands by itself on the bare words
of the regulation and, if the mere requirement that the controller must have
reasonable grounds of belief is insufficient to oblige him to act judicially,
there is nothing else in the context or conditions of his jurisdiction that
suggests that he must regulate his action by analogy to judicial rules."

Having come to that decision, Lord Radcliffe then went on in effect to deal
with the position if that was wrong, and if the controller was acting in a
judicial capacity. He said (*ibid.* at 81):

"It is impossible to see in this any departure from natural justice. The
respondent had before him ample material that would warrant a belief that
the appellant had been instrumental in getting the interpolations made and
securing for himself a larger credit at the bank than he was entitled to. Nor
did the procedure adopted fail to give the appellant the essentials that justice would require, assuming the respondent to have been under a duty to
act judicially."

That might be understood as saying that if there was no duty to act judicially,
then it would be impossible to interfere, even if the applicant had not been
given the essentials that justice requires. I very much doubt, however, whether
it was intended to say any more than that there is no duty to invoke judicial
process unless there is a duty to act judicially. I do not understand him to be
saying that if there is no duty to act judicially, then there is no duty even to be
fair.

When, however, that has been said, it seems to me impossible in the present
case to say that the decision made on the evening of November 21, 1966, was
not arrived at, as I put it, fairly. It is impossible to believe other than that both
father and son knew full well of what they had to satisfy the authorities. They
were, as it seems to me, given ample opportunity to do so, and the fact that the
officer was not satisfied is not, as is admitted, a matter for this court.

[His Lordship then held that any question as to whether the authorities
should have taken any further steps in the light of evidence adduced after the
decision had been taken was not a matter for certiorari or habeas corpus.
Furthermore the matter was now having the personal attention of the Home
Secretary. "Accordingly, it seems to me that Mr Gratiaen has had even more
that he hoped for, and that there is no reason why this court should retain any
further control over it.... I would dismiss both the application for habeas
corpus and the application for certiorari."]

SALMON L.J.: ... I have no doubt at all that ... the immigration officer is
obliged to act in accordance with the principles of natural justice. That does
not of course mean that he has to adopt judicial procedures or hold a formal
inquiry, still less than he has to hold anything in the nature of a trial, but he
must act, as Lord Parker C.J. has said, fairly in accordance with the ordinary
principles of natural justice. If, for example, and this I am sure would never
arise, it could be shown that when he made an order refusing admission he
was biased or had acted capriciously or dishonestly, this court would have
power to intervene by the prerogative writ. There are, as my Lord has said, a

good many cases in which the view has been expressed that unless a person exercising a power is acting in a judicial or quasi-judicial capacity the courts cannot intervene. Of course, an immigration officer is acting in an administrative rather than in a judicial capacity. What, however, is a quasi-judicial capacity has, so far as I know, never been exhaustively defined. It seems to me to cover at any rate a case where the circumstances in which a person who is called upon to exercise a statutory power and make a decision affecting basic rights of others are such that the law impliedly imposes upon him a duty to act fairly. When Parliament passed the Commonwealth Immigrants Act 1962, it deprived Commonwealth citizens of their right of unrestricted entry into the United Kingdom. It laid down conditions under which they might enter and left it to the immigration officers to decide whether such conditions existed. Their decision is of vital importance to the immigrants since their whole future may depend upon it. In my judgment it is implicit in the statute that the authorities in exercising these powers and making decisions must act in accordance with the principles of natural justice.

Mr Gratiaen has not suggested, nor would it be possible to suggest on the evidence before this court, that when on November 21, 1966, the immigration officer refused admission to H.K. to enter the United Kingdom, he acted otherwise than in accordance with the rules of natural justice. It is quite plain that no one could say that on the material then before him as a fair man he must have been satisfied that this boy was under 16 years of age. The material before him did not satisfy him and I for one am not at all surprised. Therefore the refusal made and the notice served on November 21, 1966, are unimpeachable. It follows that the boy's detention pending his removal abroad was lawful.

Accordingly, the application in this case is quite hopeless.

BLAIN J.: ... I would only say that an immigration officer having assumed the jurisdiction granted by those provisions [*i.e.* to cancel a notice refusing admission, under Sched. 1, para. 2(4)] is in a position where it is his duty to exercise that assumed jurisdiction, whether it be administrative, executive or quasi-judicial, fairly, by which I mean applying his mind dispassionately to a fair analysis of the particular problem and the information available to him in analysing it. If in any hypothetical case, and in any real case, this court was satisfied that an immigration officer was not so doing, then in my view mandamus would lie. That is not the position in this case, nor indeed is the court in this case moved for leave to issue a writ of mandamus.

I need say no more other than that I agree with what has fallen from my Lords.

Applications refused.

Notes

1. The modern "duty to act fairly" is sometimes said to originate in this case. There are no authorities cited to support such a duty. There are dicta in earlier cases which indicate that certain decisions by administrative authorities must be taken "fairly". In *L.G.B. v. Arlidge* [1915] A.C. 120, Viscount Haldane L.C. said (at 133) that the board should act "judicially and fairly" although they need not observe the procedures of a court. Lord Shaw said that they must "do their best to act justly, and to reach just ends by just means". In *Board of Education v. Rice* [1911] A.C. 179, Lord Loreburn L.C.

indicated that the Board was "under a duty to act in good faith, and to listen fairly to both sides". Many other judgments stress that natural justice does not require the scrupulous procedures of courts to be imposed on administrative authorities. The concepts of "fairness", "just means", "substantial justice" are indistinguishable, and require elaboration in decided cases to be properly understood.

2. The "duty to act fairly" has been implied by the courts in many cases outside immigration law. See, for example, *R. v. Birmingham City Justice, ex p. Chris Foreign Foods (Wholesalers) Ltd*, [1970] 1 W.L.R. 1428 (proceedings for the condemnation of unfit food); *Cinnamond v. British Airports Authority* [1980] 1 W.L.R. 582 (exercise of the power to ban specific persons from Heathrow airport; see below, p. 466); and *Bushell v. Secretary of State for the Environment* (below, p. 496) (public inquiry proceedings). For further discussions of "fairness", see D.J. Mullan, "Fairness: The New Natural Justice?" (1975) 25 U.T.L.J. 281, the response by M. Loughlin at (1978) 28 U.T.L.J. 215 and D.J. Mullan, "Natural Justice and Fairness— Substantive as well as Procedural Standards for the Review of Administrative Decision-Making?" (1982) 27 McGill L.J. 250.

3. The modern approach was summarised as follows by Taylor L.J. in *R. v. Army Board of the Defence Council, ex p. Anderson* [1992] 1 Q.B. 169. A, the only black soldier in his platoon, went absent without leave after various incidents of racial harassment and abuse. He was subsequently arrested and returned to his unit. His commanding officer called in the Special Investigation Branch of the Royal Military Police to inquire into his allegations of racial discrimination. A copy of the SIB's report was not made available to A despite his request. A pleaded guilty at his court-martial to going AWOL, and was sentenced to detention. After the court-martial, the Ministry of Defence gave him a summary of the SIB report, which stated that his complaints of verbal abuse, but not assault, had been borne out by the admissions of other soldiers, but also alleged that A had sought to exploit the racial issue. A made a formal complaint of racial discrimination, which under the Race Relations Act 1976 was referred to his C.O. rather than an industrial tribunal. The C.O. rejected the complaint and informed him that disciplinary action had been taken against two soldiers who had admitted racial abuse. A then complained to the Army Board. His requests for disclosure of the SIB report and other documents and for an oral hearing were rejected. The complaint was dealt with by two members of the board, who considered the papers separately and reached their individual conclusions without meeting to discuss the matter. The board stated that appropriate action had been taken against those responsible for the abuse, but refused compensation or apology and gave no reasons for that refusal.

The Court of Appeal quashed the board's decision. On the question of what procedural requirements were necessary, Taylor L.J. said (at 185–186):

"What procedural requirements are necessary to achieve fairness when the Army Board considers a complaint of this kind? In addressing this issue, counsel made much of the distinction between judicial and administrative functions. Were it necessary to decide in those terms the functions of the Army Board when considering a race discrimination complaint, I would characterise it as judicial rather than administrative. The board is required to adjudicate on an alleged breach of a soldier's rights under the 1976 Act and, if it be proved, to take any necessary steps by way of redress. It is accepted that the board has the power, *inter alia*, to award compensation. A body required to consider and adjudicate upon an alleged breach of statutory rights and to grant redress when necessary seems to me to be exercising an essentially judicial function. It matters not that the body has other functions which are non-judicial: see *R. v. Secretary of State for the Home Dept, ex p. Tarrant* [1985] Q.B. 251, 268.

However, to label the board's function either 'judicial' or 'administrative' for the purpose of determining the appropriate procedural regime is to adopt too inflexible an approach. We were referred to many decided cases, but the principles laid down in *Ridge v. Baldwin* [1964] A.C. 40 are well summarised by Sir William Wade in his *Administrative Law* (6th ed., 1988), pp. 518–519, as follows:

> '[Lord Reid] attacked the problem at its root by demonstrating how the term "judicial" had been misinterpreted as requiring some superadded characteristic over and above the characteristic that the power affected some person's rights. The mere fact that the power affects rights or interests is what makes it "judicial", and so subject to the procedures required by natural justice. In other words, a power which affects rights must be exercised "judicially", *i.e.* fairly, and the fact that the power is administrative does not make it any the less "judicial" for this purpose. Lord Hodson put his point very clearly ([1964] A.C. 40 at 130): "... the answer in a given case is not provided by the statement that the giver of the decision is acting in an executive or administrative capacity as if that were the antithesis of a judicial capacity. The cases seem to me to show that persons acting in a capacity which is not on the face of it judicial but rather executive or administrative have been held by the Courts to be subject to the principles of natural justice." '

This approach was echoed by Lord Lane C.J. in *R. v. Commission for Racial Equality, ex p. Cottrell & Rothon* [1980] 1 W.L.R. 1580, 1587. He said:

> 'It seems to me that there are degrees of judicial hearing, and those degrees run from the borders of pure administration to the borders of the full hearing of a criminal cause or matter in the Crown Court. It does not profit one to try to pigeon-hole the particular set of circumstances either into the administrative pigeon-hole or into the judicial pigeon-hole. Each case will inevitably differ, and one must ask oneself what is the basic nature of the proceeding which was going on here.' "

His Lordship also referred to *Lloyd v. McMahon*, below, p. 487. He accepted the arguments of counsel for the board that by deliberately excluding soldiers' complaints from industrial tribunals, it could not be axiomatic that all the tribunal's procedures had to be made available by the board. On the other hand, he rejected the argument that the board's duty of fairness required no more than that it should act *bona fide*, not capriciously or in a biased manner, and that it should afford the complainant a chance to respond to the basic points put against him. This did not go far enough:

> "The Army Board as the forum of last resort, dealing with an individual's fundamental statutory rights, must by its procedures achieve a high standard of fairness."

The requirements were:

(1) There must be a proper hearing "in the sense that the board must consider, as a single adjudicating body, all the relevant evidence and contentions before reaching its conclusions": accordingly, the board should meet.

(2) The hearing did not necessarily have to be an oral hearing in all cases:

> "Whether an oral hearing is necessary will depend upon the subject matter and circumstances of the particular case and upon the nature of the decision to be made. It will also depend upon whether there are substantial issues of fact which cannot be

satisfactorily resolved on the available written evidence. This does not mean that, whenever there is a conflict of evidence in the statements taken, an oral hearing must be held to resolve it. Sometimes such a conflict can be resolved merely by the inherent unlikelihood of one version or the other. Sometimes the conflict is not central to the issue for determination and would not justify an oral hearing. Even when such a hearing is necessary, it may only require one or two witnesses to be called and cross-examined."

There did not have to be oral hearings in all discrimination cases. On the other hand the board here had fettered its discretion by having an inflexible policy never to hold oral hearings.

(3) The board had a discretion whether to have the evidence tested by cross-examination.

(4) "Whether oral or not, there must be what amounts to a hearing of any complaint under the 1976 Act. This means that the Army Board must have such a complaint investigated, consider all the material gathered in the investigation, give the complainant an opportunity to respond to it and consider his response.
   But what is the board obliged to disclose to the complainant to obtain his response? Is it sufficient to indicate the gist of any material adverse to his case or should he be shown all the material seen by the board? Mr Pannick submits that there is no obligation to show all to the complainant. He relies upon three authorities, *R. v. Secretary of State for the Home Department, ex p. Mughal* [1974] Q.B. 313; *R. v. Secretary of State for the Home Department, ex p. Santillo* [1981] Q.B. 778 and *R. v. Monopolies and Mergers Commission, ex p. Matthew Brown plc* [1987] 1 W.L.R. 1235. However, in each of those cases, the function of the decision-making body was towards the administrative end of the spectrum. Because of the nature of the Army Board's function pursuant to the Race Relations Act 1976, already analysed above, I consider that a soldier complainant under that Act should be shown all the material seen by the board, apart from any documents for which public interest immunity can properly be claimed. The board is not simply making an administrative decision requiring it to consult interested parties and hear their representations. It has a duty to adjudicate on a specific complaint of breach of a statutory right. Except where public interest immunity is established, I see no reason why on such an adjudication the board should consider material withheld from the complainant."

Here, A's response had been hampered by the lack of full information.
   On point (2), see also *R. v. Department of Health, ex p. Gandhi* [1991] 4 All E.R. 547 (Secretary of State not obliged to hold an oral hearing when dealing with an appeal against a decision of a Medical Practices Committee raising a complaint of racial discrimination).

R. v. LIVERPOOL CORPORATION, ex p. LIVERPOOL TAXI FLEET OPERATORS' ASSOCIATION

[1972] 2 Q.B. 299; [1972] 2 W.L.R. 1262; 116 S.J. 201; 71 L.G.R. 387; *sub nom. Re Liverpool Taxi Owners' Association* [1972] 2 All E.R. 589 (Court of Appeal)

From 1948 onwards, Liverpool Corporation, in the exercise of its powers under section 37, of the Town Police Clauses Act 1847, to "license ... such number of hackney coaches or carriages ... as they think fit" in their area, limited the number of taxi cabs to 300. In 1970 and 1971 there were many private cars operating for hire in Liverpool. These did not have to be licensed. To meet this competition, the taxi cab drivers wanted the number of licenses increased. The taxi cab owners wanted the number to remain at 300. All the 300 existing owners were represented by two associations, the Liverpool Taxi Fleet Operators' Association and the Liverpool Taxi Owners' Association. On July 24, 1970, the town clerk wrote to the associations, saying:

"No decision has been taken on the number of hackney carriage plates and, before any such decision was taken, you have my assurance that interested parties would be fully consulted."

That was reaffirmed on October 28, 1970, when the town clerk wrote:

"I have no doubt that your clients will be given an opportunity to make representations, at the appropriate time, should they wish to do so."

In July 1971 the matter was considered by a sub-committee of the corporation. The taxicab owners were represented by counsel. The sub-committee recommended an increase above 300, to the extent that there should be 50 more in the year beginning in January 1972 (making 350) and a further 100 in the year beginning January 1973 (making 450), and thereafter an unlimited number.

On August 4, 1971, that recommendation came up for consideration by the city council itself. The minutes were approved subject to some matters being sent back. In addition the chairman of the committee, Alderman Craine, gave an undertaking (which was put into writing by the town clerk in a letter on August 11, 1971):

"The chairman of the committee gave an undertaking in council that no plates in addition to the existing 300 would be issued until proposed legislation had been enacted and had come into force."

After the meeting on August 4 the alderman came out to the representatives of the taxicab proprietors. The treasurer of the association asked:

"It is right, Alderman Craine, that no licenses will be issued until legislation controlling private hire vehicles is in force?" The alderman replied: "I have just stated that publicly. I have just made an announcement to that effect."

At that time it was expected that the Bill promoted by the corporation would be introduced towards the end of 1971, passed in 1972, and in force early in 1973.

The corporation was then advised that the undertaking was not lawful and that they ought not to hold themselves bound by it. Without informing the owners or their associations, a sub-committee met on November 16, 1971. They rescinded the earlier resolution and put forward a new recommendation, namely, that from January 1, 1972, a further 50 licences would be issued bringing the total to 350: and that from July 1, 1972, a further 50, bringing the total to 400; and no limit from January 1, 1973.

The taxicab owners indirectly got to hear of that recommendation. (They were never told officially). So their solicitors asked for a further hearing. They asked if there were any new facts and requested that their clients should be given an opportunity of making further representations. On December 7, 1971, the town clerk replied:

"There are no new important material facts. if there are any new material facts of which you have become aware, please let me have details of them by return."

The meeting was to be on the next day, December 8. It was impossible for the owners to make any reply by return.

The sub-committee recommendation was confirmed at the committee meeting on December 8, and at a meeting of the city council on December 22. The associations applied to the Divisional Court of the Queen's Bench Division (Lord Widgery C.J., Phillimore L.J. and Lawson J.) for leave to apply for:

(1) an order of prohibition prohibiting the corporation from issuing more than 300 licences:
(2) an order of mandamus requiring the corporation to hear and determine in their discretion the question whether or not the 300 limit should be increased;
(3) an order of certiorari to quash the city council's resolution of December 22, and the sub-committee's resolution of November 16.

They were refused leave, and then appealed to the Court of Appeal, who heard full argument on whether the orders should be granted.

LORD DENNING M.R.: ... That Act was explained by Lord Goddard C.J., in *R. v. Weymouth Borough Council, ex p. Teletax (Weymouth) Ltd* [1947] K.B. 583, 589:

"It also seems reasonably clear that what Parliament had in mind was that it was desirable that the commissioners should be able to control the number of carriages which applied for hire in a given area, and should also be entitled to prescribe the kind and the description of the carriages.... I have no doubt they ... certainly could take into consideration the number of cabs which were already licensed, so that there would not be an undue number or, on the other hand, if they found there were not enough for the reasonable requirements of the public, they would be able to license more from time to time as they thought fit."

The licence is a licence for the vehicle. It is not a licence for the owner or the driver. Accordingly the owner of a vehicle can transfer his vehicle during the year to a buyer. The buyer can use it under the licence for the rest of the year. When the owner applies for the licence to be renewed for another year, the corporation can take into consideration not only the then proprietor, but also any new applicant. We were referred to an unreported case on that point: *R. v. Southampton Corporation, ex p. Lankford* on October 27, 1960....

First I would say this: when the corporation consider applications for licences under the Town Police Clauses Act 1847, they are under a duty to act fairly. This means that they should be ready to hear not only the particular applicant but also any other persons or bodies whose interests are affected. In *R. v. Brighton Corporation, ex p. Thomas Tilling Ltd* (1916) 85 L.J.K.B. 1552, 1555, Sankey J. said:

"Persons who are called upon to exercise the functions of granting licences for carriages and omnibuses are, to a great extent, exercising judicial functions; and although they are not bound by the strict rules of evidence and procedure observed in a court of law, they are bound to act judicially. It is their duty to hear and determine according to law, and they must bring to that task a fair and unbiased mind."

It is perhaps putting it a little high to say they are exercising judicial functions. They may be said to be exercising an administrative function. But even so, in our modern approach, they must act fairly: and the court will see that they do so.

To apply that principle here: suppose the corporation proposed to reduce the number of taxicabs from 300 to 200, it would be their duty to hear the taxicab owners' association: because their members would be greatly affected. They would certainly be persons aggrieved. Likewise suppose the corporation propose to increase the number of taxicabs from 300 to 350 or 400 or more: it is the duty of the corporation to hear those affected before coming to a decision adverse to their interests. The Town Clerk of Liverpool was quite aware of this and acted accordingly. His letters of July 24, 1970, and October 28, 1970, were perfectly proper.

The other thing I say is that the corporation were not at liberty to disregard their undertaking. They were bound by it so long as it was not in conflict with their statutory duty.

It is said that a corporation cannot contract itself out of its statutory duties. In *Birkdale District Electric Supply Co. Ltd v. Southport Corporation* [1926] A.C. 355 Lord Birkenhead said, at 364, that it was

"a well established principle of law, that if a person or public body is entrusted by the legislature with certain powers and duties expressly or impliedly for public purposes, those persons or bodies cannot divest themselves of these powers and duties. They cannot enter into any contract or take any action incompatible with the due exercise of their powers or the discharge of their duties."

But that principle does not mean that a corporation can give an undertaking and break it as they please. So long as the performance of the undertaking is compatible with their public duty, they must honour it. And I should have thought that this undertaking was so compatible. At any rate they ought not to depart from it except after the most serious consideration and hearing what the other party has to say: and then only if they are satisfied that the overriding public interest requires it. The public interest may be better served by honouring their undertaking than by breaking it. This is just such a case. It is better to hold the corporation to their undertaking than to allow them to break it. Just as it was in *Robertson v. Minister of Pensions* [1949] 1 K.B. 227 and *Lever Finance Ltd v. Westminster (City) London Borough Council* [1971] 1 Q.B. 222.

Applying these principles, it seems to me that the corporation acted wrongly at their meetings in November and December 1971. In the first place, they took decisions without giving the owners' association an opportunity of being heard. In the second place, they broke their undertaking without any sufficient cause or excuse.

The taxicab owners' association here have certainly a locus standi to apply for relief.

We have considered what the actual relief should be. On the whole we think it is sufficient in this case to let prohibition issue. The order should prohibit the corporation or their committee or sub-committee from acting on the resolutions of November 16, 1971, December 8, 1971, and December 22, 1971; in particular, from granting any further number of licences pursuant to section 37 of the Town Police Clauses Act 1847 over and above the 300 currently existing, without first hearing any representations which may be made by or on behalf of any persons interested therein, including the applicants in this case and any other matters relevant thereto, including the undertaking recorded in the town clerk's letter of August 11. If prohibition goes in those terms, it means that the relevant committee, sub-committee and the corporation themselves can look at the matter afresh. They will hear all those interested and cóme to a right conclusion as to what is to be done about the number of taxicabs on the streets of Liverpool....

RUSSELL L.J.: ... I do not think this court is under any duty to protect the interests of either rival group of licensees or would-be licensees. Its duty is to see that in dealing with the conflicting interests the council acts fairly between them. It is for the council and not for this court to determine what the future policy should be in relation to the number of taxi licences which are to be issued in the City of Liverpool.... This court is concerned to see that whatever policy the corporation adopts is adopted after due and fair regard to all the conflicting interests. The power of the court to intervene is not limited, as once was thought, to those cases where the function in question is judicial or quasi-judicial. The modern cases show that this court will intervene more widely than in the past. Even where the function is said to be administrative, the court will not hesitate to intervene in a suitable case if it is necessary in order to secure fairness. It has been said by Mr Morland that there is no precedent for this court to intervene and enforce an undertaking which he claims to be of no legal effect and thus prevent the council giving effect to delegated legislation of the validity of which there is not doubt. For my part, I am not prepared to be deterred by the absence of precedent if in principle the case is one in which the court should interfere.

If I thought that the effect of granting to the applicants the relief sought was to prevent the council validly using those powers which Parliament has conferred upon it, I would refuse relief. But that is not the present case. It seems to me that the relief claimed will in the end, as Mr Morland in effect ultimately conceded, assist the council to perform rather than inhibit the performance of its statutory duties. Lord Denning M.R. has referred to *Birkdale District Electric Supply Co. Ltd v. Southport Corporation* [1926] A.C. 355. The decision of this court in *William Cory & Son Ltd v. London Corporation* [1951] 2 K.B. 476, shows that a local authority such as the council cannot contractually fetter the performance of its statutory duties. But the present case is not such a case. The principle applicable is plain. In matters of this kind, such as the granting of licences for hackney carriages, the local authority concerned is required to act fairly, as well as, as Lord Denning M.R. has said, in a quasi-judicial capacity. It has been said that the council and its relevant committee and sub-committee were never under any duty to hear any representations from the applicants. That may or may not be correct. In the light of what has happened, I do not think it necessary to express any opinion upon that question. The relevant sub-committee had the advantage of hearing representations made on behalf of the applicants. Subsequently, having heard those representations, they made the recommendation which led up to the resolution of August 4, 1971, as well as, of course, to the undertaking of the breach of which complaint is made. It seems to me, therefore, that now to allow the council to resile from that undertaking without notice to and representations from the applicants is to condone unfairness in a case where the duty was to act fairly. To stop temporarily action on the resolution of December 22, 1971, is not in any way to perpetuate that undertkaing; nor should it embarrass the council in carrying out its statutory duties. The council must make up its own mind what policy it wishes to follow; but before doing so it must act fairly to all concerned, to present licensees and to would-be licensees and to others also who may be interested. In the end it may adhere to its present policy or it may not; but in my view this court should not allow the undertaking given by Alderman Craine on August 4 and repeated by the town clerk with the council's authority in the letter of August 11 to be set at naught. The council can at some future date, if it wishes, depart from that undertaking; but if it does so, it must do so after due and proper consideration of the representations of all those interested. I am not persuaded that any such due and proper consideration has yet been given. On the contrary, the evidence before this court shows that the passing of the resolution of December 22 was—as I have said—a flagrant breach of the undertaking....

SIR GORDON WILLMER delivered a concurring judgment.

Application for prohibition granted.
Applications for certiorari and mandamus refused.

Notes

1. See case note by J.M. Evans (1973) 36 M.L.R. 93.

2. See above, Chap. 6 on undertakings and estoppel.

3. Note that neither Russell L.J. nor Sir Gordon Willmer was prepared to go as far as Lord Denning M.R. so as to hold the authority bound by the assurance unless it was satisfied that the overriding public interest required departure from it. All the judges were agreed that in the light of the assurance, fairness required that the Association be given a further opportunity to make representations (note the form of the relief granted). Lord Denning's broader view has, however, helped form the basis of a development whereby assurances can in certain circumstances give rise to substantive effects (see above, pp. 379–397).

4. Which "undertaking" is the real foundation of this case: the undertakings that the association would be consulted or the undertaking that the limit on licences would not be raised above 300 until the proposed private legislation was in force? David Widdicombe Q.C. (sitting as a deputy High Court judge), considered it to be the latter: see *Pelham Homes Ltd v. Secretary of State for the Environment and Runnymede Borough Council* (1994) 69 P. & C.R. 64 at 75. Does it matter?

5. Compare the cases on legitimate expectations (below, pp. 460–468). Although the expression "legitimate expectation" is not used in the judgments, could it have been?

6. *cf. R. v. Gravesham Borough Council, ex p. Gravesham Association of Licensed*

Hackney Carriage Owners, The Independent, January 14, 1987, where Hodgson J. held that taxi drivers had no legitimate expectation to be consulted before the council decided to adopt a policy of placing no numerical ceiling on the number of hackney carriage licences which it issued under section 16 of the Transport Act 1985. There had been no promise of consultation, no prior consultation with them and no right of theirs was being infringed.

7. In *R. v. Blackpool Borough Council, ex p. Red Cab Taxis Ltd and Others* [1994] R.T.R. 402, the council was faced with rivalry between private hire vehicles and hackney carriage operators. The council consulted both groups, but following complaints from the hackney carriage operators the authority unilaterally amended the licences of private hire vehicles to prevent them from standing their vehicles at any "public place". Judge J. was highly critical of the decision-making process followed by the local authority because:

"At the lowest the effect was to create a perception within one group that they had been disadvantaged at the behest of the other. Another view of the condition imposed on the second group was that they were in fact disadvantaged and that greater difficulties had been created for them in the conduct of their business. . . . In my judgment this process was inappropriate and unfair and therefore flawed" (at 406).

However, his Lordship refused the application for judicial review as the private hire vehicle operators had a statutory right of appeal against the new condition to the local justices.

McINNES v. ONSLOW-FANE AND ANOTHER

[1978] 1 W.L.R. 1520; [1978] 3 All E.R. 211 (Chancery Division, Megarry V.-C.)

The plaintiff had held a promoter's licence for boxing matches issued in the 1950s by the British Boxing Board of Control (a voluntary self-regulatory organisation). In 1971 the board granted him a trainer's licence and in 1973 a master of ceremonies' licence. After an incident at a boxing match in 1973, the Board withdrew all the plaintiff's licences. Subsequently, he applied to the Board for a manager's licence on five occasions, but his applications were rejected. The plaintiff sought a declaration against the Board (represented by two of its members) that it had acted contrary to the rules of natural justice/or unfairly by (1) failing to inform the plaintiff of the case against him so that he could answer those concerns and (2) by not granting him an oral hearing prior to rejecting his last licence application.

MEGARRY V.-C.: . . . It was common ground between Mr Beloff [counsel for the plaintiff] and Mr Moses [counsel for the defendants] that the point before me was the subject of no direct authority: although expulsion from clubs and other bodies is the subject of an ample range of authorities, the refusal of applications for membership is much less richly endowed. It was also accepted that the point is of considerable general importance. There are many bodies which, though not established or operating under the authority of statute, exercise control, often on a national scale, over many activities which are important to many people, both as providing a means of livelihood and for other reasons. Sometimes that control is exercised, as by the board, by means of a system of granting or refusing licences, and sometimes it is operated by means of accepting or rejecting applications for membership. One particular aspect of this is membership of a trade union, without which it is impossible to obtain many important forms of work. In such cases it is plainly important, both to the body and the applicant, for them to know whether, before the application is rejected, the applicant is entitled to prior notice of any case against granting him a licence or admitting him to membership, and whether he is entitled to an oral hearing.

I think that I should take the matter by stages. First, there is the question of whether the grant or refusal of a licence by the board is subject to any requirements of natural justice or fairness which will be enforced by the courts. The question is not one that is governed by statute or contract, with questions of their true construction or the implication of terms; for there is no statute, and there is no contract between the plaintiff and the board. Nevertheless, in recent years there has been a marked expansion of the ambit of the requirements of natural justice and fairness reaching beyond statute and contract. A striking example is *Nagle v. Feilden* [1966] 2 Q.B. 633. There, a woman sought a declaration and injunctions against the Jockey Club to enforce her claim that she ought not to be refused a trainer's licence for horse-racing merely because she was a woman. At first instance her claim had been struck out, but the Court of Appeal reversed this decision. Lord Denning M.R. accepted that social clubs could refuse to admit an applicant for membership as they wished; but the Jockey Club exercised "a virtual monopoly in an important field of human activity", and what gave the courts jurisdiction was "a man's right to work": see 644, 646. In reaching his conclusion, Lord Denning M.R. observed that being a jockey could be regarded as being an unsuitable occupation for a woman, whereas being a trainer could not: see 647.

... [W]here the court is entitled to intervene, I think it must be considered what type of decision is in question. I do not suggest that there is any clear or exhaustive classification; but I think that at least three categories may be discerned. First, there are what may be called the forfeiture cases. In these, there is a decision which takes away some existing right or position, as where a member of an organisation is expelled or a licence is revoked. Second, at the other extreme there are what may be called the application cases. These are cases where the decision merely refuses to grant the applicant the right or position that he seeks, such as membership of the organisation, or a licence to do certain acts. Third, there is an intermediate category, which may be called the expectation cases, which differ from the application cases only in that the applicant has some legitimate expectation from what has already happened that his application will be granted. This head includes cases where an existing licence-holder applies for a renewal of his licence, or a person already elected or appointed to some position seeks confirmation from some confirming authority: see, for instance, *Weinberger v. Inglis* [1919] A.C. 606; *Breen v. Amalgamated Engineering Union* [1971] 2 Q.B. 175; and see *Schmidt v. Secretary of State for Home Affairs* [1969] 2 Ch. 149, 170, 173 and *R. v. Barnsley Metropolitan Borough Council, ex p. Hook* [1976] 1 W.L.R. 1052, 1058.

It seems plain that there is a substantial distinction between the forfeiture cases and the application cases. In the forfeiture cases, there is a threat to take something away for some reason: and in such cases, the right to an unbiased tribunal, the right to notice of the charges and the right to be heard in answer to the charges (which in *Ridge v. Baldwin* [1964] A.C. 40, 132, Lord Hodson said were three features of natural justice which stood out) are plainly apt. In the application cases, on the other hand, nothing is being taken away, and in all normal circumstances there are no charges, and so no requirement of an opportunity of being heard in answer to the charges. Instead, there is the far wider and less defined question of the general suitability of the applicant for membership or a licence. The distinction is well-recognised, for in general it is clear that the courts will require natural justice to be observed for expulsion from a social club, but not on an application for admission to it. The intermediate category, that of the expectation cases, may at least in some respects be regarded as being more akin to the forefeiture cases than the application cases; for although in form there is no forfeiture but merely an attempt at acquisition that fails, the legitimate expectation of a renewal of the licence or confirmation of the membership is one which raises the question of what it is that has happened to make the applicant unsuitable for the membership or licence for which he was previously thought suitable.

I pause there. I do not think that I need pursue the expectation cases, for in the present case I can see nothing that would bring the plaintiff within them....

... In my judgment, the case is plainly an application case in which the plaintiff is seeking to obtain a licence that he has never held and had no legitimate expectation of holding; he had only the hope (which may be confident or faint or anything between) which any applicant for anything may always have.

...[T]here is the question of the requirements of natural justice or fairness that have to be applied in an application case such as this. What are the requirements where there are no provisions of any statute or contract either conferring a right to the licence in certain circumstances, or laying down the procedure to be observed, and the applicant is seeking from an unofficial body the grant of a type of licence that he has never held before, and, though hoping to obtain it, has no legitimate expectation of receiving?

I do not think that much help is to be obtained from discussing whether "natural justice" or "fairness" is the more appropriate term. It one accepts that "natural justice" is a flexible term which imposes different requirements in different cases, it is capable of applying appropriately to the whole range of situations indicated by terms such as "judicial", "quasi-judicial" and "administrative". Nevertheless, the further the situation is away from anything that resembles a judicial or quasi-judicial situation, and the further the question is removed from what may reasonably be called a justiciable question, the more appropriate it is to reject an expression which includes the word "justice" and to use instead terms such as "fairness", or "the duty to act fairly": see *Re H.K. (An Infant)* [1967] 2 Q.B. 617, 630, *per* Lord Parker C.J.; *Re Pergamon Press Ltd* [1971] Ch. 388, 399, *per* Lord Denning M.R.; *Breen's* case [1971] 2 Q.B. 175, 195, *per* Edmund Davies L.J. ("fairly exercised"); *Pearlberg v. Varty* [1972] 1 W.L.R. 534, 545, *per* Viscount Dilhorne, and at 547, *per* Lord Pearson. The suitability of the term "fairness" in such cases is increased by the curiosities of the expression "natural justice". Justice is far from being a "natural" concept. The closer one goes to a state of nature, the less justice does one find. Justice, and with it "natural justice", is in truth an elaborate and artificial product of civilisation which varies with different civilisations: see *Maclean v. Workers' Union* [1929] 1 Ch. 602, 624, *per* Maugham J. To Black J., "natural justice" understandably meant no more than "justice" without the adjective: see *Green v. Blake* [1948] I.R. 242, 268. However, be that as it may, the question before me is that of the content of "the duty to act fairly" (or of "natural justice") in this particular case. What does it entail? In particular, does it require the board to afford the plaintiff not only information of the "case against him" but also an oral hearing? . . .

I think it is clear that there is no general obligation to give reasons for a decision. Certainly in an application case, where there are no statutory or contractual requirements but a simple discretion in the licensing body, there is no obligation on that body to give their reasons. . . .

As I have said, Mr Moses accepted that the board were under a duty to reach an honest conclusion without bias and not in pursuance of any capricious policy. That, I think, is right: and if the plaintiff showed that any of these requirements had not been complied with, I think the court would intervene. Mr Beloff accepted that the burden of proof would have been on him if any such questions had arisen. But assume a board acting honestly and without bias or caprice: why should a duty to act fairly require them to tell an applicant the gist of the reasons (which may vary from member to member) why they think he ought not to be given a licence? Is a college or university, when selecting candidates for admission or awarding scholarships, or a charity when making grants to the needy, acting "unfairly" when it gives no reason to the unsuccessful? Are editors and publishers "unfair" when they send out unreasoned rejection slips? Assume that they are under no enforceable duty to act fairly, and it may still be a matter of concern to them if they are to be told that they are acting "unfairly" in not giving the gist of their reasons to the rejected. Again, do judges act unfairly when, without any indication of their reasons, they refuse leave to appeal, or decide questions of costs? . . .

Looking at the case as whole, in my judgment there is no obligation on the board to give the plaintiff even the gist of the reasons why they refused his application, or proposed to do so. This is not a case in which there has been any suggestion of the board considering any alleged dishonesty or morally culpable conduct of the plaintiff. A man free from any moral blemish may nevertheless be wholly unsuitable for a particular type of work. The refusal of the plaintiff's application by no means necessarily puts any slur on his character, nor does it deprive him of any statutory right. There is no mere narrow issue as to his character, but the wide and general issue whether it is right to grant this licence to this applicant. In such circumstances, in the absence of anything to suggest that the board have been affected by dishonesty or bias or caprice, or that there is any other impropriety, I think that the board are fully entitled to give no reasons for their decision, and to decide the application without any preliminary indication to the plaintiff of those reasons. The board are the best judges of the desirability of granting the licence, and in the absence of any impropriety the court ought not to interfere.

There is a more general consideration. I think that the courts must be slow to allow any implied obligation to be fair to be used as a means of bringing before the courts for review honest decisions of bodies exercising jurisdiction over sporting and other activities which those bodies are far better fitted to judge than the courts. This is so even where those bodies are concerned with the means of livelihood of those who take part in those activities. The concepts of natural justice and the duty to be fair must not be allowed to discredit

themselves by making unreasonable requirements and imposing undue burdens. Bodies such as the board which promote a public interest by seeking to
maintain high standards in a field of activity which otherwise might easily
become degraded and corrupt ought not to be hampered in their work without good cause. Such bodies should not be tempted or coerced into granting
licences that otherwise they would refuse by reason of the courts having
imposed on them a procedure for refusal which facilitates litigation against
them. As Lord Denning M.R. said in *Re Pergamon Press Ltd* [1971] Ch. 388,
400, "No one likes to have an action brought against him, however
unfounded." The individual must indeed be protected against impropriety;
but any claim of his for anything more must be balanced against what the
public interest requires.

That brings me to the fifth point, the contention that the board are obliged
to afford the plaintiff a hearing. This, I think, has in large part been disposed
of by what I have said in rejecting the contention that the plaintiff has a right to
be told the gist of the reasons for proposing to reject his application. The contention that the plaintiff ought to be given a hearing seems to have been put
forward mainly as an ancillary to the alleged obligation to inform him of the
gist of the reasons for provisionally deciding not to grant him the licence, and
so as to enable him to meet what is said. However, if one treats the right to a
hearing as an independent requirement, I would say that I cannot see how the
obligation to be fair can be said in a case of this type to require a hearing. I do
not see why the board should not be fully capable of dealing fairly with the
plaintiff's application without any hearing. The case is not an expulsion case
where natural justice confers the right to know the charge and to have an
opportunity of meeting it at a hearing. I cannot think that there is or should be
any rule that an application for a licence of this sort cannot properly be
refused without giving the applicant the opportunity of a hearing, however
hopeless the application, and whether it is the first or the fifth or the fiftieth
application that he has made. Certainly Mr Beloff has not referred me to any
authority which appears to me to give any real support to such a proposition
in a case such as this. I therefore reject the contention that the board should be
required to give the plaintiff a hearing or interview.

In my judgment, therefore, the plaintiff's claim fails. It is easy to understand
a very natural curiosity and, doubtless, anxiety on his part to know what it is
that stands between him and the grant of the licence that he seeks. He may
wonder whether it is something that endeavour on his part may put right, or
whether it is something beyond cure. It may be that it would be considerate of
the board if they were to give him at least some indication of what stands in his
way. I for one would not be surprised if his previous career as a licence-holder
had played a substantial part in this, although no details of the various epi-
sodes have been put before me. At the same time, I can well see that the board
would be reluctant to adopt a more elaborate and time-consuming procedure
for determining applications for licences, and even more reluctant to be
required to give reasons (whether in full or in outline) which might provide
ammunition for litigation against the board. The board's regulations seem to
me to make fair and reasonable provisions for disciplinary cases which may
lead to the suspension or withdrawal of a licence and so on, and the distinction
under the regulations between such cases and applications for the grant of
licences seems to me to be proper and generally in accordance with the law.
Furthermore, the offer of a hearing made by the board's solicitors after the

originating summons had been issued seems to me to have been reasonable and benign; I regret that the plaintiff's solicitors should have been insistent upon the board paying the plaintiff's costs. My duty, however, is simply to apply the law as I understand it; and for the reasons that I have given, I hold that on the questions that are before me the plaintiff's claims fail and will be dismissed.

Summons dismissed.

Notes

1. 11 years after the above decision, Michael Beloff Q.C. (who had been counsel for Mr McInnes) expressed the following view regarding the judicial attitude towards legal actions brought against the governing bodies of different sports:

"no less than three Vice-Chancellors of different generations and jurisdictions have taken the view that the courts should abstain where possible from interfering with the decisions of bodies controlling sporting spheres. ... It is, I suspect, the floodgates argument that is the unspoken premise of the Vice-Chancellarial observations, the fear that limited court time will be absorbed by a new and elastic category of case with much scope for abusive or captious litigation. It is an argument which intellectually has little to commend it, and pragmatically is usually shown to be ill-founded. For it is often the case that, once the courts have shown the willingness to intervene, the standards of the bodies at risk of their intervention tend to improve. The threat of litigation averts its actuality" "(Pitch, Pool, Rink, ... Court? Judicial Review in the Sporting World" [1989] P.L. 95 at 109–110).

See also E. Grayson, *Sport and the Law* (2nd ed., 1994), and below, pp. 617–622.

In *Jones v. Welsh Rugby Football Union, The Times*, March 6, 1997, Ebsworth J. granted the plaintiff, a player with Ebbw Vale RFC, an injunction lifting a four-week suspension imposed on him by the defendants for allegedly fighting during a match. Her Ladyship considered that the plaintiff had an arguable case that the defendants had not followed a fair disciplinary procedure by, *inter alia*, preventing the plaintiff effectively challenging the allegations against him. Her Ladyship observed that:

"sport was now big business; many people earned their living from it in one way or another. It would be naïve to pretend that the modern world of sport could be conducted as it used to be not very many years ago."

2. Where licensing decisions under statutory powers do have an effect on livelihood, the court have generally been willing to imply procedural standards. In *R. v. Huntingdon District Council, ex p. Cowan* [1984] 1 W.L.R. 501., Glidewell J. held that when dealing with an application for an entertainment licence under Part I of the Local Government (Miscellaneous Provisions) Act 1982 a local authority must inform the applicant of the substance of any objection or representation in the nature of an objection (not necessarily the whole of it, nor to say necessarily who has made it); and give the applicant an opportunity to make representations in reply. (See also *R. v. Preston Borough Council, ex p. Quietlynn Ltd* and other cases (1984) 83 L.G.R. 308, C.A.). In *R. v. Bristol City Council, ex p. Pearce* (1984) 83 L.G.R. 711, the same judge held that when considering an application for a street trading consent under para. 7 of Schedule 4 to the Local Government (Miscellaneous Provisions) Act 1982, a local authority was obliged to tell the applicants of the content of any objection (other than from its own officers or the police) and to give them some opportunity to comment. However, an oral hearing need not be held, and reasons need not be given. (His Lordship held that the applicant here did not have a legitimate expectation, but that nevertheless some procedural standards were applicable.) In *R. v. Wear Valley District Council, ex p. Binks* [1985] 2 All E.R. 699, the council decided to terminate the applicant's contractual licence to station a caravan on the council's land (in a market place). The applicant used the caravan to earn her living by selling take away food. Taylor J. held that the council was obliged to give notice of and the reasons for the proposed termination, and an opportunity to be heard, notwithstanding that the licence was contractual and not statutory.

Question
Is Megarry V.-C.'s explanation of the relationship between natural justice and procedural fairness convincing?

COUNCIL OF CIVIL SERVICE UNIONS v. MINISTER FOR THE CIVIL SERVICE

[1985] A.C. 374; [1985] I.C.R. 14; [1984] 3 W.L.R. 1174; [1984] 3 All E.R. 935 (House of Lords)

The main functions of Government Communications Headquarters ("GCHQ") were to ensure the security of military and official communications and to provide the Government with signals intelligence; they involved the handling of secret information vital to national security. Since 1947, staff employed at GCHQ had been permitted to belong to national trade unions, and most had done so. There was a well-established practice of consultation between the official and trade union sides about important alterations in the terms and conditions of service of the staff. On December 22, 1983, the Minister for the Civil Service gave an instruction, purportedly under article 4 of the Civil Service Order in Council 1982, for the immediate variation of the terms and conditions of service of the staff with the effect that they would no longer be permitted to belong to national trade unions. There had been no consultation with the trade unions or with the staff at GCHQ prior to the issuing of that instruction. The applicants, a trade union and six individuals, sought judicial review of the minister's instruction on the ground that she had been under a duty to act fairly by consulting those concerned before issuing it. In an affidavit, the Secretary to the Cabinet deposed to disruptive industrial action in support of national trade unions that had taken place at GCHQ as part of a national campaign by the unions designed to damage government agencies and that it had been considered that prior consultation about the minister's instruction would have involved a risk of precipitating further disruption and would moreover have indicated vulnerable areas of GCHQ's operations. Glidewell J. granted the applicants a declaration that the instruction was invalid and of no effect. The Court of Appeal allowed an appeal by the minister, and a further appeal was dismissed.

The House of Lords held (1) that the Government's action was not immune from judicial review merely because it was in pursuance of a common law or a prerogative power; (2) that the applicants would apart from national security considerations have had a legitimate expectation that unions and employees would have been consulted before the instruction was issued; but (3) that the Minister had shown that her decision had in fact been based on considerations of national security that outweighed the applicant's legitimate expectation.

The following extracts concern the second issue:

LORD FRASER OF TULLYBELTON: . . .

The duty to consult
Mr Blom-Cooper submitted that the Minister had a duty to consult the CCSU, on behalf of employees at GCHQ, before giving the instruction on December 22, 1983, for making an important change in their conditions of service. His main reason for so submitting was that the employees had a legitimate, or reasonable, expectation that there would be such prior consultation before any important change was made in their conditions.

It is clear that the employees did not have legal right to prior consultation.

The Order in Council confers no such right, and article 4 makes no reference at all to consultation. The Civil Service handbook (*Handbook for the New Civil Servant*, 1973 ed. as amended 1983) which explains the normal method of consultation through the departmental Whitley Council, does not suggest that there is any legal right to consultation; indeed it is careful to recognise that, in the operational field, considerations of urgency may make prior consultation impracticable. The Civil Service Pay and Conditions of Service Code expressly states:

"The following terms and conditions also apply to your appointment in the Civil Service. It should be understood, however, that in consequence of the constitutional position of the Crown, the Crown has the right to change its employees' conditions of service at any time, and that they hold their appointments at the pleasure of the Crown."

But even where a person claiming some benefit or privilege has no legal right to it, as a matter of private law, he may have a legitimate expectation of receiving the benefit or privilege, and, if so, the courts will protect his expectation of judicial review as a matter of public law. This subject has been fully explained by my noble and learned friend, Lord Diplock, in *O'Reilly v. Mackman* [1983] 2 A.C. 237 and I need not repeat what he has so recently said. Legitimate, or reasonable, expectation may arise either from an express promise given on behalf of a public authority or from the existence of a regular practice which the claimant can reasonably expect to continue. Examples of the former type of expectation are *R. v. Liverpool Corporation, ex p. Liverpool Taxi Fleet Operators' Association* [1972] 2 Q.B. 299 and *Attorney-General of Hong Kong v. Ng Yuen Shiu* [1983] 2 A.C. 629. (I agree with Lord Diplock's view, expressed in the speech in this appeal, that "legitimate" is to be preferred to "reasonable" in this context. I was responsible for using the word "reasonable" for the reason explained in *Ng Yuen Shiu*, but it was intended only to be exegetical of "legitimate.") An example of the latter is *R. v. Board of Visitors of Hull Prison, ex p. St Germain* [1979] Q.B. 425 approved by this House in *O'Reilly*, at 274D. The submission on behalf of the appellants is that the present case is of the latter type. The test of that is whether the practice of prior consultation of the staff on significant changes in their conditions of service was so well established by 1983 that it would be unfair or inconsistent with good administration for the Government to depart from the practice in this case. Legitimate expectations such as are now under consideration will always relate to a benefit or privilege to which the claimant has no right in private law, and it may even be to one which conflicts with his private law rights. In the present case the evidence shows that, ever since GCHQ began in 1947, prior consultation has been the invariable rule when conditions of service were to be significantly altered. Accordingly in my opinion if there had been no question of national security involved, the appellants would have had a legitimate expectation that the minister would consult them before issuing the instruction of December 22, 1983.

LORD DIPLOCK: ... Judicial review, now regulated by R.S.C., Ord. 53, provides the means by which judicial control of administrative action is exercised. The subject-matter of every judicial review is a decision made by some person (or body of persons) whom I will call the "decision-maker" or else a refusal by him to make a decision.

To qualify as a subject for judicial review the decision must have consequences which affect some person (or body of persons) other than the decision-maker, although it may affect him too. It must affect such other person either:

(a) by altering rights or obligations of that person which are enforceable by or against him in private law; or

(b) by depriving him of some benefit or advantage which either (i) he had in the past been permitted by the decision-maker to enjoy and which he can legitimately expect to be permitted to continue to do until there has been communicated to him some rational grounds for withdrawing it on which he has been given an opportunity to comment; or (ii) he has received assurance from the decision-maker will not be withdrawn without giving him first an opportunity of advancing reasons for contending that they should not be withdrawn. (I prefer to continue to call the kind of expectation that qualifies a decision for inclusion in class (b) a "legitimate expectation" rather than a "reasonable expectation," in order thereby to indicate that it has consequences to which effect will be given in public law, whereas an expectation or hope that some benefit or advantage would continue to be enjoyed, although it might well be entertained by a "reasonable" man, would not necessarily have such consequences. The recent decision of this House in *Re Findlay* [1985] A.C. 318 presents an example of the latter kind of expectation. "Reasonable" furthermore bears different meanings according to whether the context in which it is being used is that of private law or of public law. To eliminate confusion it is best avoided in the latter.)

For a decision to be susceptible to judicial review the decision-maker must be empowered by public law (and not merely, as in arbitration, by agreement between private parties) to make decisions that, if validly made, will lead to administrative action or abstention from action by an authority endowed by law with executive powers, which have one or other of the consequences mentioned in the preceding paragraph. The ultimate source of the decision-making power is nearly always nowadays a statute or subordinate legislation made under the statute; but in the absence of any statute regulating the subject-matter of the decision the source of the decision-making power may still be the common law itself, *i.e.* that part of the common law that is given by lawyers the label of "the prerogative". Where this is the source of decision-making power, the power is confined to executive officers of central as distinct from local government and in constitutional practice is generally exercised by those holding ministerial rank.

It was the prerogative that was relied on as the source of the power of the Minister for the Civil Service in reaching her decision of December 22, 1983, that membership of national trade unions should in future be barred to all members of the home civil service employed at GCHQ....

My Lords, I see no reason why simply because a decision-making power is derived from a common law and not a statutory source, it should *for that reason only* be immune from judicial review. Judicial review has I think developed to a stage today when without reiterating any analysis of the steps by which the development has come about, one can conveniently classify under three heads the grounds upon which administrative action is subject to control by judicial review. The first ground I would call "illegality", the second "irrationality" and the third "procedural impropriety". That is not to say that further development on a case by case basis may not in course of time add further grounds. I have in mind particularly the possible adoption in the future of the principle of "proportionality" which is recognised in the administrative law of several of our fellow members of the European Economic Community; but to dispose of the instant case the three already well-established heads that I have mentioned will suffice.

By "illegality" as a ground for judicial review I mean that the decision-maker must understand correctly the law that regulates his decision-making power and must give effect to it. Whether he has or not is par excellence a justiciable question to be decided, in the event of dispute, by those persons, the judges, by whom the judicial power of the state is exercisable.

By "irrationality" I mean what can by now be succinctly referred to as "*Wednesbury* unreasonableness" (*Associated Provincial Picture Houses Ltd v. Wednesbury Corporation* [1948] 1 K.B. 223). It applies to a decision which is so outrageous in its defiance of logic or of accepted moral standards that no sensible person who had applied his mind to the question to be decided could have arrived at it. Whether a decision falls within this category is a question that judges by their training and experience should be well equipped to answer, or else there would be something badly wrong with our judicial system. To justify the court's exercise of this role, resort I think is today no longer needed to Viscount Radcliffe's ingenious explanation in *Edwards v. Bairstow* [1956] A.C. 14 of irrationality as a ground for a court's reversal of a decision by ascribing it to an inferred though unidentifiable mistake of law by the decision-maker. "Irrationality" by now can stand upon its own feet as an accepted ground on which a decision may be attacked by judicial review.

I have described the third head as "procedural impropriety" rather than failure to observe basic rules of natural justice or failure to act with procedural fairness towards the person who will be affected by the decision. This is because susceptibility to judicial review under this head covers also failure by an administrative tribunal to observe procedural rules that are expressly laid down in the legislative instrument by which its jurisdiction is conferred, even where such failure does not involve any denial of natural justice. But the instant case is not concered with the proceedings of an administrative tribunal at all. . . .

[His Lordship concluded that it was well established that decisions whose ultimate source of power was the common law (whether or not labelled as "the prerogative") could be the subject of judicial review on the grounds of illegality or procedural impropriety. There was no *a priori* reason to rule out challenge on the ground of irrationality, he found it difficult to envisage cases where such a challenge would be justifiable.]

Prima facie ... civil servants employed at GCHQ who were members of national trade unions had, at best, in December 1983, a legitimate expectation that they would continue to enjoy the benefits of such membership and of representation by those trade unions in any consultations and negotiations with representatives of the management of that government department as to changes in any term of their employment. So, but again *prima facie* only, they were entitled, as a matter of public law under the head of "procedural propriety", before administrative action was taken on a decision to withdraw that benefit, to have communicated to the national trade unions by which they had theretofore been represented the reason for such withdrawal, and for such unions to be given an opportunity to comment on it. . . .

LORD ROSKILL: . . . The particular manifestation of the duty to act fairly which is presently involved is that part of the recent evolution of our administrative law which may enable an aggrieved party to evoke judicial review if he can show that he has "a reasonable expectation" of some occurrence or action preceding the decision complained of and that that "reasonable expectation" was not in the event fulfilled.

The introduction of the phrase "reasonable expectation" into this branch of our administrative law appears to show its origin to Lord Denning M.R. in *Schmidt v. Secretary of State for Home Affairs* [1969] 2 Ch. 149, 170 (when he used the phrase "legitimate expectation"). Its judicial evolution is traced in the opinion of the Judicial Committee delivered by my noble and learned friend, Lord Fraser of Tullybelton, in *Attorney-General of Hong Kong v. Ng Yuen Shiu* [1983] 2 A.C. 629, 636–638. Though the two phrases can. I think, now safely be treated as synonymous for the reasons there given by my noble and learned friend, I prefer the use of the adjective "legitimate" in this context and use it in this speech even though in argument it was the adjective "reasonable" which was generally used. The principle may now be said to be firmly entrenched in this branch of the law. As the cases show, the principle is closely connected with "a right to be heard". Such an expectation may take many forms. One may be an expectation of prior consultation. Another may be an expectation of being allowed time to make representations especially where the aggrieved party is seeking to persuade an authority to depart from a lawfully established policy adopted in connection with the exercise of a particular power because of some suggested exceptional reasons justifying such a departure. . . .

My Lords, if no question of national security were involved I cannot doubt that the evidence and the whole history of the relationship between management and staff since 1919 shows that there was a legitimate expectation of consultation before important alterations in the conditions of service of civil servants were made. No doubt in strict theory civil servants are dismissible at will and the various documents shown to your Lordships seek to preserve the strict constitutional position. But in reality the management-staff relationship is governed by an elaborate code to which it is unnecessary to refer in detail. I have little doubt that were management to seek to alter without prior consultation the terms and conditions of civil servants in a field which had no connection whatever with national security or perhaps, though the matter does not arise in this appeal, with urgent fiscal emergency, such action would in principle be amenable to judicial review.

LORDS SCARMAN and BRIGHTMAN delivered concurring speeches.

Notes

1. The important decision in *Attorney-General of Hong Kong v. Ng Yeun Shui* [1983] 2 A.C. 629 is summarised in *R. v. Secretary of State for the Home Department,*

ex p. Khan, above, p. 384. Although cited by Lord Fraser, the *Liverpool Taxi* case (above p. 448) does not actually use the term "legitimate expectation".

2. The literature on legitimate expectations is listed above at p. 396, n. 8. The argument that a legitimate expectation gives rise to procedural rights has been less controversial than the notion it can also place substantive restrictions on the powers of the decision-maker (see above, pp. 382–397).

3. Simon Brown L.J. has distinguished four broad categories in the use of the phrase "legitimate expectation" (*R. v. Devon County Council, ex p. Baker and Another; R. v. Durham County Council, ex p. Curtis and Another* [1995] 1 All E.R. 73 at 88–89):

"(1) Sometimes the phrase is used to denote a substantive right: an entitlement that the claimant asserts cannot be denied him. It was used in this sense and the assertion upheld in cases such as *R. v. Secretary of State for the Home Dept, ex p. Khan* [1985] 1 All E.R. 40; [1984] 1 W.L.R. 1337 and *R. v. Secretary of State for the Home Dept, ex p. Ruddock* [1987] 2 All E.R. 518; [1987] 1 W.L.R. 1482. It was used in the same sense but unsuccessfully in, for instance, *R. v. Board of Inland Revenue, ex p. MFK Underwriting Agencies Ltd* [1990] 1 All E.R. 91; [1990] 1 W.L.R. 1545 and *R. v. Jockey Club, ex p. RAM Racecourses Ltd* (1990) [1993] 2 All ER 225. These various authorities show that the claimant's right will only be found established when there is a clear and unambiguous representation upon which it was reasonable for him to rely. Then the administrator or other public body will be held bound in fairness by the representation made unless only its promise or undertaking as to how its power would be exercised is inconsistent with the statutory duties imposed upon it. The doctrine employed in this sense is akin to an estoppel. In so far as the public body's representation is communicated by way of a stated policy. this type of legitimate expectation falls into two distinct sub-categories: cases in which the authority are held entitled to change their policy even so as to affect the claimant, and those in which they are not. An illustration of the former is *R. v. Torbay B.C., ex p. Cleasby* [1991] C.O.D. 142; of the latter, *ex p. Khan*.

(2) Perhaps more conventionally the concept of legitimate expectation is used to refer to the claimant's interest in some ultimate benefit which he hopes to retain (or, some would argue, attain). Here, therefore, it is the interest itself rather than the benefit that is the substance of the expectation. In other words the expectation arises not because the claimant asserts any specific right to a benefit but rather because his interest in it is one that the law holds protected by the requirements of procedural fairness; the law recognises that the interest cannot properly be withdrawn (or denied) without the claimant being given an opportunity to comment and without the authority communicating rational grounds for any adverse decision. Of the various authorities drawn to our attention, *Schmidt v. Secretary of State for Home Affairs* [1969] 1 All E.R. 904; [1969] 2 Ch. 149, *O'Reilly v. Mackman* [1982] 3 All E.R. 1124; [1983] 2 A.C. 237 and the recent decision of Roch J. in *R. v. Rochdale Metropolitan B.C., ex p. Schemet* [1993] 1 F.C.R. 306 are clear examples of this head of legitimate expectation.

(3) Frequently, however, the concept of legitimate expectation is used to refer to the fair procedure itself. In other words it is contended that the claimant has a legitimate expectation that the public body will act fairly towards him. As was pointed out by Dawson J. in *Att.-Gen. for New South Wales v. Quin* (1990) 93 A.L.R. 1 at 39 this use of the term is superfluous and unhelpful: it confuses the interest which is the basis of the requirement of procedural fairness with the requirement itself:

'No doubt people expect fairness in their dealings with those who make decisions affecting their interests, but it is to my mind quite artificial to say that this is the reason why, if the expectation is legitimate in the sense of well founded, the law imposes a duty to observe procedural fairness. Such a duty arises, if at all, because the circumstances call for a fair procedure and it adds nothing to say that they also are such as to lead to a legitimate expectation that a fair procedure will be adopted.'

(4) The final category of legitimate expectation encompasses those cases in which it is held that a particular procedure, not otherwise required by law in the protection of an interest, must be followed consequent upon some specific promise or practice. Fairness requires that the public authority be held to it. The authority is bound by its assurance, whether expressly given by way of a promise or implied by way of established practice. *Re Liverpool Tax Owners' Association* [1972] 2 All E.R. 589; [1972] 2 Q.B. 299 and *Att.-Gen. of Hong Kong v. Ng Yuen Shiu* [1983] 2 All E.R. 346; [1983] 2 A.C. 629 are illustrations of the court giving effect to legitimate expectations based upon express promises; *Council of Civil Service Unions v. Minister for the Civil Service* an illustration of a legitimate expectation founded upon practice albeit one denied on the facts by virtue of the national security implications."

4. A legitimate expectation of being consulted may arise simply from the nature of the applicant's interests, as distinct from past practice or an express undertaking. In *R. v. Brent London Borough Council, ex p. Gunning* (1985) 84 L.G.R. 168, Hodgson J. held that while there was no statutory duty placed upon local education authorities to consult parents of pupils before making proposals for the closure or amalgamation of schools, parents nevertheless had a legitimate expectation that they would be consulted. "The interest of parents in the educational arrangements in the area in which they lived is self-evident. It is explicitly recognised in the legislation (see, *e.g.* section 6 of the Education Act 1980). The legislation places clear duties upon parents, backed by draconian criminal sanctions." Local authorities (including Brent) habitually consulted on these matters, and were exhorted to do so by the Secretary of State. On the facts here, the consultative document was wholly inadequate and misleading as to the cost of the proposals and the period allowed for consultation was unreasonably short. Furthermore, as the proposals ultimately adopted were materially different from those on which consultation had taken place, the parents of schoolchildren in the area should have been given a further opportunity to be consulted. The authority's decision to make the proposals was quashed.

(Hodgson J. stated (at 187) that their legitimate expectation gave them the same right as if it had been specifically given by statute. In *R. v. Gwent County Council, ex p. Bryant, The Independent*, April 19, 1988, his Lordship stated that he had gone too far in equating a legitimate expectation with a statutory right. In the former case, a defect in consultation could be rectified by the Secretary of State, in the latter, it could not; *R. v. Northampton County Council, ex p. Tebbutt*, unreported, June 26, 1986, applied. See also *R. v. Haberdashers' Aske's Hatcham School Governors, ex p. Inner London Education Authority, The Times*, March 7, 1989.) See P. Meredith [1988] P.L. 4. The Court of Appeal has expressed the view that the duty of public authorities to consult affected persons is an aspect of the general duty of fairness. In the context of local authorities' decisions to close residential homes for the elderly that are owned and operated by the councils, the Court held that the duty of consultation required: "(1) that the residents should have known that closure of the homes was under consideration well before the final decision to close them was made, (2) that the residents should have had a reasonable time to put to the council their objections to the closure of the homes and (3) that the residents' objections should have been considered by the council" (*per* Dillon L.J. at 83 in *Devon County Council*, above, note 3).

5. There is some authority than a person's misconduct may deprive him or her of a *legitimate* expectation. In *Cinnamond v. British Airports Authority* [1980] 1 W.L.R. 582, the authority exercised its power under byelaws to prohibit six car-hire drivers from entering Heathrow airport (save as a *bona fide* passenger), until further notice.

Each of the six had many convictions under the byelaws for loitering and offering services to passengers, and all had unpaid fines outstanding. The authority had received many complaints that car hire drivers charged exorbitant fares in comparison with the licensed taxis. The drivers sought a declaration that the notices were invalid. One ground was that they had not been given an opportunity to make representations. Lord Denning M.R. said (at 590–591) that the drivers had no legitimate expectation:

"... suppose that these car-hire drivers were of good character and had for years been coming into the airport under an implied licence to do so. If in that case there was suddenly a prohibition order preventing them from entering, then it would seem only fair that they should be given a hearing and a chance to put their case. But that is not this case. These men have a long record of convictions. They have large fines outstanding. They are continuing to engage in conduct which they must know is unlawful and contrary to the byelaws. When they were summonsed for past offences, they put their case, no doubt, to the justices and to the Crown Court. Now when the patience of the authority is exhausted, it seems to me that the authority can properly suspend them until further notice—just like the police officer I mentioned. In the circumstances they had no legitimate expectation of being heard. It is not a necessary preliminary that they should have a hearing or be given a further chance to explain. Remembering always this: that it must have been apparent to them why the prohibition was ordered: and equally apparent that, if they had a change of heart and were ready to comply with the rules, no doubt the prohibition would be withdrawn. They could have made representations immediately, if they wished, in answer to the prohibition order. That they did not do."

Shaw L.J. said (at 592):

"As to the suggestion of unfairness in that the drivers were not given an opportunity of making representations, it is clear on the history of this matter that the drivers put themselves so far outside the limits of tolerable conduct as to disentitle themselves to expect that any further representations on their part could have any influence or relevance. The long history of contraventions, of flouting the regulations, and of totally disregarding the penalties demonstrate that in this particular case there was no effective deterrent. The only way of dealing with the situation was by excluding them altogether.

It does not follow that the attitude of the authority may not change if they can be persuaded by representations on behalf of the drivers that they are minded in future to comply with the regulations."

Brandon L.J. agreed with Lord Denning and Shaw L.J. on the natural justice point, and then said (at 593):

"If I am wrong in thinking that some opportunity should have been given, then it seems to me that no prejudice was suffered by the minicab drivers as a result of not being given that opportunity. It is quite evident that they were not prepared then, and are not even prepared now, to give any satisfactory undertakings about their future conduct. Only if they were would representations be of any use. I would rely on what was said in *Malloch v. Aberdeen Corporation* [1971] 1 W.L.R. 1578, first *per* Lord Reid at 1582 and secondly *per* Lord Wilberforce at 1595. [See above, p. 438.] The effect of what Lord Wilberforce said is that no one can complain of not being given an opportunity to make representations if such an opportunity would have availed him nothing."

de Smith, Woolf and Jowell disagree with Lord Denning's approach: "... it is wrong to suggest that a legitimate expectation can be forfeited, for example by unmeritorious conduct on the part of the applicant. Unless the expectation were expressly made conditional upon the applicant's 'good behaviour', the decision whether to rely on the expectation or to waive it lies with the applicant alone. It would also seem wrong to prejudge the merits of the applicant's present case on his previous wrongdoing" (at pp. 429–430).

6. One of the first actions of the new Labour Government in May 1997 was to undertake to restore trade union membership rights for staff employed at GCHQ.

(b) *Limitations on the right to a fair hearing*

(1) *National security*

R v. SECRETARY OF STATE FOR HOME AFFAIRS, ex p. HOSENBALL

[1977] 1 W.L.R. 766; [1977] 3 All E.R. 452. (Court of Appeal)

The appellant was a United States citizen who worked as a journalist in the United Kingdom. At first he worked for the weekly journal *Time Out* and was responsible for an article entitled "The Eavesdroppers" about communications monitoring by the Government, which appeared in May 1976. During July 1976, Hosenball moved to the *Evening Standard* as a general news reporter. In November 1976, he was informed that the Home Secretary had decided to deport him on the grounds that Hosenball's "departure from the United Kingdom would be conducive to the public good as being in the interests of national security". The Home Secretary considered that Hosenball had sought and obtained for publication information harmful to the security of the United Kingdom and prejudicial to the safety of Crown servants. Hosenball had no right of appeal against the decision under the terms of the Immigration Act 1971. However, he was given a non-statutory hearing before "three advisers" (appointed by the Home Secretary) who reported back in confidence to the Secretary of State. The Home Secretary later made a deportation against Hosenball. Hosenball then applied for an order of certiorari to quash the deportation order on the ground, *inter alia*, that the principle of *audi alteram partem* had been breached by the failure to supply him with details of the case against him prior to his appearance before the "three advisers". The High Court dismissed Hosenball's application and he then appealed to the Court of Appeal.

LORD DENNING M.R.: ... Now I would like to say at once that if this were a case in which the ordinary rules of natural justice were to be observed, some criticism could be directed upon it. For one thing, the Home Secretary himself, and I expect the advisory panel also, had a good deal of confidential information before them of which Mr Hosenball knew nothing and was told nothing: and which he had no opportunity of correcting or contradicting; or of testing by cross-examination. In addition, he was not given sufficient information of the charges against him so as to be able effectively to deal with them or answer them. All this could be urged as a ground for upsetting any ordinary decision of a court of law or of any tribunal, statutory or domestic: see *Kanda v. Government of Malaya* [1962] A.C. 322, 337.

But this is no ordinary case. It is a case in which national security is involved: and our history shows that, when the state itself is endangered, our cherished freedoms may have to take second place. Even natural justice itself may suffer a set-back. Time after time Parliament has so enacted and the courts have loyalty followed. In the first world war in *R. v. Halliday* [1917]

A.C. 260, 270 Lord Finlay L.C. said: "The danger of espionage and of damage by secret agents ... had to be guarded against." In the second world war in *Liversidge v. Sir John Anderson* [1942] A.C. 206, 219 Lord Maugham said:

> "... there may be certain persons against whom no offence is proved nor any charge formulated, but as regards whom it may be expedient to authorise the Secretary of State to make an order for detention."

That was said in time of war. But times of peace hold their dangers too. Spies, subverters and saboteurs may be mingling amongst us, putting on a most innocent exterior. They may be endangering the lives of the men in our secret service, as Mr Hosenball is said to do.

If they are British subjects, we must deal with them here. If they are foreigners, they can be deported. The rules of natural justice have to be modified in regard to foreigners here who prove themselves unwelcome and ought to be deported....

So it seems to me that when the national security is at stake even the rules of natural justice may have to be modified to meet the position. I would refer in this regard to the speech of Lord Reid in *R. v. Lewes JJ., ex p. Secretary of State for the Home Department* [1973] A.C. 388, 402....

The information supplied to the Home Secretary by the Security Service is, and must be, highly confidential. The public interest in the security of the realm is so great that the sources of the information must not be disclosed— nor should the nature of the information itself be disclosed—if there is any risk that it would lead to the sources being discovered. The reason is because, in this very secretive field, our enemies might try to eliminate the sources of information. So the sources must not be disclosed. Not even to the House of Commons. Nor to any tribunal or court of inquiry or body of advisers, statutory or non-statutory. Save to the extent that the Home Secretary thinks safe. Great as is the public interest in the freedom of the individual and the doing of justice to him, nevertheless in the last resort it must take second place to the security of the country itself....

There is a conflict here between the interests of national security on the one hand and the freedom of the individual on the other. The balance between these two is not for a court of law. It is for the Home Secretary. He is the person entrusted by Parliament with the task. In some parts of the world national security has on occasions been used as an excuse for all sorts of infringements of individual liberty. But not in England. Both during the wars and after them, successive ministers have discharged their duties to the complete satisfaction of the people at large. They have set up advisory committees to help them, usually with a chairman who has done everything he can to ensure that justice is done. They have never interfered with the liberty or the freedom of movement of any individual except where it is absolutely necessary for the safety of the state. In this case we are assured that the Home Secretary himself gave it his personal consideration, and I have no reason whatever to doubt the care with which he considered the whole matter. He is answerable to Parliament as to the way in which he did it and not to the courts here.

I would dismiss the appeal.

GEOFFREY LANE L.J.: There are occasions, though they are rare, when what are more generally the rights of an individual must be subordinated to the protection of the realm. When an alien visitor to this country is believed to have used the hospitality extended to him so as to present a danger to security, the Secretary of State has the right and, in many cases, has the duty of ensuring that the alien no longer remains here to threaten our security. It may be that the alien has been in the country for many years. It may be that he has built a career here in this country, and that consequently a deportation order made against him may result in great hardship to him. It may be that he protests that he has done nothing wrong so far as this country's security is concerned. It may be that he protests that he cannot understand why any action of this sort is being taken against him. In ordinary circumstances common fairness—you can call it natural justice if you wish—would demand that he be given particulars of the charges made against him; that he be given the names of the witnesses who are prepared to testify against him and, indeed, probably the nature of the evidence which those witnesses are prepared to give should also be delivered to him. But there are counter-balancing factors....

It may well be that if an alien is told with particularity what it is said he has done it will become quite obvious to him from whence that information has been received. The only person who can judge whether such a result is likely is the person who has in his possession all the information available. That, in this case, is the Secretary of State himself. If he comes to the conclusion that for reasons such as those which I have just endeavoured to outline he cannot afford to give the alien more than the general charge against him, there one has the dilemma. The alien certainly has inadequate information upon which to prepare or direct his defence to the various charges which are made against him, and the only way that could be remedied would be to disclose information to him which might probably have an adverse effect on the national security. The choice is regrettably clear: the alien must suffer, if suffering there be, and this is so on whichever basis of argument one chooses....

Different principles and strict principles apply where matters of the safety of the realm are at stake. What is fair cannot be decided in a vacuum: it has to be determined against the whole background of any particular case. The advisory panel system is an effort to ensure fairness as far as possible in these difficult circumstances, but in the end it is the Secretary of State who must in those circumstances be trusted to speak the last word....

I would dismiss the appeal.

CUMMING-BRUCE L.J. I agree with all that has fallen from Lord Denning M.R. and Geoffrey Lane L.J....

Appeal dismissed.

Notes

1. After the above legal action Hosenball returned to the United States from where he contributed to the *Sunday Times*.

2. The general public became aware of the existence of Government Communications Headquarters ("GCHQ") in Cheltenham during January 1984, when the Government announced that its employees would no longer be able to join national trade unions. This action led to the famous *CCSU* case, see above (p. 460).

3. Lord Denning's contented view of the relationship between the legitimate needs of national security and individual liberty has not been endorsed by either the European Commission of Human Rights or the Committee of Ministers of the Council of Europe. In the case of *Hewitt and Harman and N. v. U.K.* (1989) 67 D.R. 88, the Commission reached the opinion that the Security Service had violated the applicants' right to privacy (under Article 8 of the European Convention on Human Rights) by means of secret surveillance and information gathering directed at the applicants. As a consequence of this case the Government secured the passage of the Security Service Act 1989, which places the Service on a statutory basis and creates a Tribunal to deal with complaints against the organisation. Further institutional reforms, including the creation of an oversight committee composed of Parliamentarians, were introduced by the Intelligence Services Act 1994.

4. In *Chahal v. U.K.* (1997) 23 E.H.R.R. 413, the European Court of Human Rights, unanimously, found the limited processes of review offered by the High Court and the "three advisers" to a potential national security deportee did not meet the requirements of Article 5(4) of the ECHR (right rö review by a court of the lawfulness of detention). During the Gulf War of early 1991, the Home Secretary decided to deport a number of Iraqis and other Arab persons living in the United Kingdom, on the grounds that their continued presence was not conducive to national security. In one instance a Lebanese citizen, who had lived in the United Kingdom for 15 years, sought judicial review of the Home Secretary's decision arguing, *inter alia*, that the denial of legal representation before the three advisers and the provision of less than full particulars of the allegations against him violated natural justice. Lord Donaldson M.R. emphasised the limited role of the courts in reviewing matters of national security: "... the responsibility is exclusively that of the government of the day, but its powers are limited by statute and the courts will intervene if it is shown that the minister responsible has acted otherwise than in good faith or has in any way overstepped the limitations upon his authority which are imposed by the law" (at 334). His Lordship rejected the appellant's contentions by noting that, "... natural justice has to take account of realities and something which would otherwise constitute a breach is not to be so considered if it is unavoidable" (at 335): *R. v. Secretary of State for the Home Department, ex p. Cheblak* [1991] 2 All E.R. 319. See I. Leigh [1991] P.L. 331.

5. An Irish national, Gallagher, who had been imprisoned in Ireland for possession of firearms for an unlawful purpose, came to work in the United Kingdom. The Home Secretary made an exclusion order against Gallagher, under the Prevention of Terrorism (Temporary Provisions) Act 1989, because he was satisfied that Gallagher was or had been involved in acts of terrorism concerned with Northern Ireland. Gallagher consented to his removal to Ireland where he was granted an interview, at the British Embassy in Dublin, before an unnamed person appointed by the Home Secretary, who listened to Gallagher's contentions but was unable to give further particulars regarding the reasons for the exclusion order. The Home Secretary reconsidered his decision in the light of the person's report and determined not to revoke the order. Gallagher challenged his actions in the British courts alleging, *inter alia*, a breach of his European Community law rights. The majority of the Court of Appeal held that the procedure followed had infringed Gallagher's rights under Article 9 of Council Directive 64/221 and that the interpretation of those provisions should be referred to the European Court of Justice: *R. v. Secretary of State for the Home Department, ex p. Gallagher, The Times*, February 16, 1994. Subsequently, the ECJ ruled that Article 9 did not prevent the person (called "the competent authority") hearing the representations of the E.U. Member State national from being appointed by the Home Secretary, provided that the competent authority was able to perform his/her duties in absolute independence. Except in cases of urgency, the competent authority should be able to give an opinion on the proposed expulsion before such an order is made by the Home Secretary. However, the Directive did not require the competent authority to identify its members to those making representations: *R. v. Secretary of State for the Home Department, ex p. Gallagher*, Case C–175/94, *The Times*, December 12, 1995. For a related case see also *R. v. Secretary of State for the Home Department, ex p. McQuillan* [1995] 4 All E.R. 400.

(2) *Withholding of confidential information*

R. v. GAMING BOARD FOR GREAT BRITAIN, ex p. BENAIM AND KHAIDA

[1970] 2 Q.B. 417; [1970] 2 W.L.R. 1009; 114 S.J. 266; [1970] 2 All E.R. 528 (Court of Appeal)

The Gaming Act 1968 prohibited gaming except in premises licensed for this purpose by the justices. Before any person could apply for a licence he had to obtain a "certificate of consent" from the Gaming Board, a body set up by the 1968 Act. The present applicants, the joint managing directors of Crockford's gaming club, applied unsuccessfully for a certificate. The board declined to give reasons for the refusal. In particular they refused to specify the matters which troubled them. The applicants sought certiorari to quash the refusal, and mandamus to compel the board to give sufficient information to enable them to answer the case against them.

LORD DENNING M.R.: ... To what extent are the board bound by the rules of natural justice? That is the root question before us. Their jurisdiction is country wide. They have to keep under review the extent and character of gaming in Great Britain: see s.10(3). Their particular task in regard to Crockford's is to see if the applicants are fit to run a gaming club: and if so, to give a certificate of consent.

Their duty is set out in Schedule 2, para. 4(5) and (6):

"... (5) ... the board shall have regard only to the question whether, in their opinion, the applicant is likely to be capable of, and diligent in, securing that the provisions of this Act and of any regulations made under it will be complied with, that gaming on those premises will be fairly and properly conducted, and that the premises will be conducted without disorder or disturbance.

(6) For the purposes of sub-paragraph (5) ... the board shall in particular take into consideration the character, reputation and financial standing— (a) of the applicant, and (b) of any person (other than the applicant) by whom ... the club ... would be managed, or for whose benefit ... that club would be carried on, but may also take into consideration any other circumstances appearing to them to be relevant in determining whether the applicant is likely to be capable of, and diligent in, securing the matters mentioned in that sub-paragraph."

Note also that Schedule 1, paragraph 7, gives the board power to regulate their own procedure. Accordingly the board have laid down an outline procedure which they put before us. It is too long to read in full. So I will just summarise it. It says that the board will give the applicant an opportunity of making representations to the board, and will give him the best indications possible of the matters that are troubling them. Then there are these two important sentences:

"In cases where the *source* or *content* of this *information* is *confidential*, the board accept that they are obliged to withhold particulars of the disclosure of which would be a breach of confidence inconsistent with their statutory duty and the public interest. . . ."

"In the course of the interview the applicant will be made aware, to the greatest extent to which this is consistent with the board's statutory duty and the public interest, of the matters that are troubling the board."

Mr Quintin Hogg criticised that outline procedure severely. He spoke as if Crockford's were being deprived of a right of property or of a right to make a living. He read his client's affidavit saying that "Crockford's has been established for over a century and is a gaming club with a worldwide reputation for integrity and respectability", with assets and goodwill valued at £185,000. He said that they ought not to be deprived of this business without knowing the case they had to meet. He criticised especially the way in which the board proposed to keep that confidential information. He relied on some words of mine in *Kanda v. Government of Malaya* [1962] A.C. 322, 337, when I said "that the judge or whoever has to adjudicate must not hear evidence or receive representations from one side behind the back of the other".

Mr Hogg put his case, I think, too high. It is an error to regard Crockford's as having any right of which they are being deprived. They have not had in the past, and they have not now, any right to play these games of chance—roulette, chemin-de-fer, baccarat and the like—for their own profit. What they are really seeking is a privilege—almost, I might say, a franchise—to carry on gaming for profit, a thing never hitherto allowed in this country. It is for them to show that they are fit to be trusted with it.

If Mr Hogg went too far on his side, I think Mr Kidwell went too far on the other. He submitted that the Gaming Board are free to grant or refuse a certificate as they please. They are not bound, he says, to obey the rules of natural justice any more than any other executive body, such as, I suppose, the Board of Trade, which grant industrial development certificates, or the Television Authority, which awards television programme contracts. I cannot accept this view. I think the Gaming Board are bound to observe the rules of natural justice. The question is: What are those rules?

It is not possible to lay down rigid rules as to when the principles of natural justice are to apply: nor as to their scope and extent. Everything depends on the subject-matter: see what Tucker L.J. said in *Russell v. Norfolk (Duke of)* [1949] 1 All E.R. 109, 118 and Lord Upjohn in *Durayappah v. Fernando* [1967] 2 A.C. 337, 349. At one time it was said that the principles only apply to judicial proceedings and not to administrative proceedings. That heresy was scotched in *Ridge v. Baldwin* [1964] A.C. 40. At another time it was said that the principles do not apply to the grant or revocation of licences. That too is wrong. *R. v. Metropolitan Police Commissioner, ex p. Parker* [1953] 1 W.L.R. 1150 and *Nakkuda Ali v. Jayaratne* [1951] A.C. 66 are no longer authority for any such proposition. See what Lord Reid and Lord Hodson said about them in *Ridge v. Baldwin* [1964] A.C. 40, 77–79, 133.

So let us sheer away from those distinctions and consider the task of this Gaming Board and what they should do. The best guidance is, I think, to be found by reference to the cases of immigrants. They have no right to come in, but they have a right to be heard. The principle in that regard was well laid down by Lord Parker C.J. in *Re H.K. (An Infant)* [1967] 2 Q.B. 617. He said, at 630:

"... even if an immigration officer is not in a judicial or quasi-judicial capacity, he must at any rate give the immigrant an opportunity of satisfying him of the matters in the subsection, and for that purpose let the immigrant know what his immediate impression is so that the immigrant can disabuse him. That is not, as I see it, a question of acting or being required to act judicially, but of being required to act fairly."

Those words seem to me to apply to the Gaming Board. The statute says in terms that in determining whether to grant a certificate, the board "shall have regard only" to the matters specified. It follows, I think, that the board have a duty to act fairly. They must give the applicant an opportunity of satisfying them of the matters specified in the subsection. They must let him know what their impressions are so that he can disabuse them. But I do not think that they need quote chapter and verse against him as if they were dismissing him from an office, as in *Ridge v. Baldwin* [1964] A.C. 40; or depriving him of his property, as in *Cooper v. Wandsworth Board of Works* (1863) 14 C.B.N.S. 180. After all, they are not charging him with doing anything wrong. They are simply inquiring as to his capability and diligence and are having regard to his character, reputation and financial standing. They are there to protect the public interest, to see that persons running the gaming clubs are fit to be trusted.

Seeing the evils that have led to this legislation, the board can and should investigate the credentials of those who make application to them. They can and should receive information from the police in this country or abroad who know something of them. They can, and should, receive information from any other reliable source. Much of it will be confidential. But that does not mean that the applicants are not to be given a chance of answering it. They must be given the chance, subject to this qualification: I do not think they need tell the applicant the source of their information, if that would put their informant in peril or otherwise be contrary to the public interest. Even in a criminal trial, a witness cannot be asked who is his informer. The reason was well given by Lord Eyre C.J. in *Hardy's* case [*R. v. Hardy*] 24 *State Trials* 199, 808:

"... there is a rule which has universally obtained on account of its importance to the public for the detection of crimes, that those persons who are the channel by means of which that detection is made, should not be unnecessarily disclosed."

And Buller J. added, at 818: "... if you call for the name of the informer in such cases, no man will make a discovery, and public justice will be defeated." That rule was emphatically reaffirmed in *Attorney-General v. Briant* (1846) 15 M. & W. 169 and *Marks v. Beyfus* (1890) 25 Q.B.D. 494. That reasoning applies with equal force to the inquiries made by the Gaming Board. That board was set up by Parliament to cope with disreputable gaming clubs and to bring them under control. By bitter experience it was learned that these clubs had a close connection with organised crime, often violent crime, with protection rackets and with strong-arm methods. If the Gaming Board were bound to disclose their sources of information, no one would "tell" on those clubs, for fear of reprisals. Likewise with the details of the information. If the board were bound to disclose every detail, that might itself give the informer away and put him in peril. But, without disclosing every detail, I should have thought that the board ought in every case to be able to give to the applicant sufficient indication of the objections raised against him such as to enable him to answer them. That is only fair. And the board must at all costs be fair. If they are not, these courts will not hesitate to interfere.

Accepting that the board ought to do all this when they come to give their decision, the question arises, are they bound to give their reasons? I think not. Magistrates are not bound to give reasons for their decisions: see *R. v. Northumberland Compensation Appeal Tribunal, ex p. Shaw* [1952] 1 K.B. 338, at 352. Nor should the Gaming Board be bound. After all, the only thing that they have to give is their *opinion* as to the capability and diligence of the applicant. If they were asked by the applicant to give their reasons, they could answer quite sufficiently: "In our opinion, you are not likely to be capable of or diligent in the respects required of you." Their opinion would be an end of the matter.

Tested by those rules, applying them to this case, I think that the Gaming Board acted with complete fairness. They put before the applicants all the information which led them to doubt their suitability. They kept the sources secret, but disclosed all the information. Sir Stanley Raymond said so in his affidavit: and it was not challenged to any effect. The board gave the applicants full opportunity to deal with the information. And they came to their decision. There was nothing whatever at fault with their decision of January 9, 1970. They did not give their reasons. But they were not bound to do so.

But then complaint is made as to what happened afterwards. It was said that the board did not pin-point the matters on which they thought the explanations were not satisfactory. They did not say which of the matters (a) to (e) they were not satisfied about. But I do not see anything unfair in that respect. It is not as if they were making any charges against the applicants. They were only saying they were not satisfied. They were not bound to give any reasons for their misgivings. And when they did give some reasons, they were not bound to submit to cross-examination on them.

Finally, complaint was made that the board refused to consider a new or amended application in respect of these premises of Crockford's in the current round. They refused to consider applications in other names or in new names. But here again I see nothing unfair. Crockford's had full opportunity of putting their application in the first instance. If there had been a technical defect in it, I feel sure that the board would have allowed an amendment. But if the application fails in matters of substance, that should be the end of it. There must be an end to the claim to "cut and come again".

In all the circumstances I think that all the criticisms of the board's conduct fail, and in my opinion the application should be dismissed.

LORD WILBERFORCE and PHILLIMORE L.J. agreed.

Application dismissed.

Notes

1. See comments by H.W.R. Wade (1970) 86 L.Q.R. 309 and S.A. de Smith [1970]

C.L.J. 177. The decision was applied by Glidewell J. in *R. v. Bristol City Council, ex p. Pearce*, above, p. 459.

2. The doctrine of Public Interest Immunity may also be invoked by bodies performing some public function, to justify the withholding of confidential information during the course of legal proceedings. For an account of this doctrine, see E.C.S. Wade and A.W. Bradley, *Constitutional and Administrative Law* (11th ed. by A.W. Bradley and K.D. Ewing, 1993), p. 753; and for the application of this doctrine to the work of the Gaming Board, see *R. v. Lewes J.J., ex p. Secretary of State for Home Department* [1973] A.C. 388. In recent times the doctrine has been applied in the context of national security matters in *Balfour v. Foreign and Commonwealth Office* [1994] 2 All E.R. 588, and the House of Lords has considered its relevance to the police complaints system in *R. v. Chief Constable of the West Midlands, ex p. Wiley* [1995] A.C. 274.

(3) *Emergency action*

R. v. SECRETARY OF STATE FOR TRANSPORT, ex p. PEGASUS HOLDINGS (LONDON) LTD AND ANOTHER

[1988] 1 W.L.R. 990; [1989] 2 All E.R. 481 (Schiemann J.)

The applicant companies provided foreign holidays from the United Kingdom and used aircraft chartered from a Romanian organisation and flown by a Romanian crew. In order for the Romanian aircraft and crew to be allowed to operate such holiday flights from the United Kingdom they had received a permit from the Secretary of State granted under the authority of the Air Navigation Order 1985, Article 83. Article 62 of the Order empowered the Transport Secretary to provisionally suspend permits if he thought fit, pending a full investigation of the matter. During the middle of July 1987, five Romanian pilots voluntarily undertook flying tests conducted by the British Civil Aviation Authority; all these pilots failed the test (four displayed an inability to manoeuvre the aircraft). On July 29 at midday, the Department of Transport received a letter from the CAA, informing them of these test results. During the ensuing afternoon the Department alerted the applicants to the concerns of the CAA. On July 30 the Secretary of State signed provisional suspension orders (made under Article 62) regarding the Romanians' permit to operate the holiday charter flights from the United Kingdom. This decision caused the applicant package holiday company great difficulties in transporting its customers. The applicants sought a judicial review of the decision of the Transport Secretary, claiming, *inter alia*, that the suspension orders had been made in breach of the requirements of natural justice.

SCHIEMANN J.: ... So far as the law is concerned, I do not think that there is anything between the parties as to the principles to be applied. These are conveniently set out in the leading case of *Wiseman v. Borneman* [1971] A.C. 297, where Lord Guest, at 311, cites an earlier judgment by Tucker L.J. in *Russell v. Duke of Norfolk* [1949] 1 All E.R. 109, 118 in which Tucker L.J. opined:

"There are, in my view, no words which are of universal application to every kind of inquiry and every kind of domestic tribunal. The requirements of natural justice must depend on the circumstances of the case, the nature of the inquiry, the rules under which the tribunal is acting, the subject-matter that is being dealt with, and so forth. Accordingly, I do not derive much assistance from the definitions of natural justice which have been from time to time used, but, whatever standard is adopted, one essential is that the person concerned should have a reasonable opportunity of presenting his case."

Mr Flint accepts that the opportunity to state a case can in certain circumstances be excluded in relation to such provisional matters as those with which I am concerned but says that they should not be excluded unless the situation genuinely demands it.

Mr Pannick referred me to a Court of Appeal case, *Lewis v. Heffer* [1978] 1 W.L.R. 1061, where there are discussions in the various unreserved judgments delivered by the court that are not precisely to the same effect in what they say. In particular, he drew my attention to the following comments of Lord Denning M.R., at 1073. After having quoted Megarry J. in *John v. Rees* [1970] Ch. 345 where he had said, at 397:

"suspension is merely expulsion *pro tanto*. Each is penal, and each deprives the member concerned of the enjoyment of his rights of membership or office. Accordingly, in my judgment the rules of natural justice *prima facie* apply to any such process of suspension in the same way that they apply to expulsion."

Lord Denning M.R. went on to say:

"Those words apply, no doubt, to suspensions which are inflicted by way of punishment: as for instance when a member of the Bar is suspended from practice for six months, or when a solicitor is suspended from practice. But they do not apply to suspensions which are made, as a holding operation, pending inquiries. Very often irregularities are disclosed in a government department or in a business house: and a man may be suspended on full pay pending inquiries. Suspicion may rest on him: and so he is suspended until he is cleared of it. No one, so far as I know, has ever questioned such a suspension on the ground that it could not be done unless he is given notice of the charge and an opportunity of defending himself and so forth. The suspension in such a case is merely done by way of good administration. A situation has arisen in which something must be done at once. The work of the department or the office is being affected by rumours and suspicions. The others will not trust the man. In order to get back to proper work, the man is suspended. At that stage the rules of natural justice do not apply: ..."

It is right to point out that the other Lords Justices tend not to go quite as far as Lord Denning M.R. in that formulation.

In the present case, I am content to proceed on the basis that the rules of natural justice do apply but that, in the words chosen by Mr Pannick, in such an emergency as the present, with a provisional suspension being all that one is concerned with, one is at the low end of the duties of fairness. Mr Pannick referred me in the course of his submissions on this point to *R. v. Civil Aviation Authority, ex p. Northern Air Taxis Ltd* [1976] 1 Lloyd's Rep. 344. That case, which was a Divisional Court case, was concerned with matters not dissimilar in some ways to the present. Natural justice as such was not argued;

the matters were dealt with on the basis of the statutory requirements, but undoubtedly the result does lend some support to the view that, when one is dealing with this type of situation, not much is required of the Secretary of State in order to act fairly.

The way the case is put by Mr Flint is this. He says that in the present case the Secretary of State could not reasonably decline to afford Tarom[3] a short period to put its case as to why the permit should not be suspended, having regard to a number of matters that Mr Flint identified. One of these is the lack of action on the letter of July 14, which I have read. As I have indicated, I regard that letter as irrelevant. A second matter to which Mr Flint drew my attention in this context was the time that the CAA took to refer the matter, which he said was some indication as to its view of the urgency. I have set out the relevant dates. It is clear that the failing of the tests took place on July 17, and the Secretary of State was not informed until July 29. That may or may not be a legitimate criticism of the CAA, but in my judgment, so far as the action of the Secretary of State is concerned, it cannot be regarded as unfair in the circumstances of this case that he acted in the speedy way in which he did act. One has in the context of unfairness to bear in mind, on the one hand, the no doubt substantial economic damage to the applicants and perhaps the irritation and inconvenience that I do not doubt the passengers suffered. On the other hand, one has to bear in mind the magnitude of the risk, by which I mean not so much the high percentage chance of it happening but the disastrous consequences of what would happen if something did happen. It is the old problem that one has with installations of nuclear power, or vehicles such as aeroplanes carrying a large number of people, that, if something goes wrong, then very many lives will be lost. While I do not doubt that different people, and maybe different Secretaries of State, would react differently to the same basic material, I am not prepared to say that the failure of the Secretary of State to permit more by way of representations than I have indicated took place was a breach of the rules of natural justice....

Application dismissed.

Notes

1. Apart from the need to take emergency action, another factor present in the above case was the nature of the decision being taken—*i.e.* to suspend *provisionally* the Romanians' permit. Other cases indicate that where the challenged decision is a preliminary determination, which will be subject to a more detailed later consideration, then the full rigour of the *audi alteram partem* principle may not be invoked against the procedures leading up to the preliminary decision. For example in *Pearlberg v. Varty* [1972] 1 W.L.R. 534, a taxpayer asserted that the Inland Revenue were obliged to give him a fair hearing prior to seeking to make tax assessments on him. The House of Lords rejected his claims and Lord Hailsham L.C. stated:

"the third factor which affects my mind is the consideration that the decision, once made, does not make any final determination of the rights of the taxpayer. It simply enables the inspector to raise an assessment, by satisfying the commissioner that there are reasonable grounds for suspecting loss of tax resulting from neglect, fraud,

[3] The Romanian organisation which owned and operated the aircraft.

or wilful default, that is that there is a *prima facie* probability that there has been neglect, etc., and that the Crown may have lost by it. When the assessment is made, the taxpayer can appeal against it, and, on the appeal, may raise any question, (*inter alia*) which would have been relevant on the application for leave, except that the leave given should be discharged."

2. The Court of Appeal has held that local authority trading standards officers are not under a general duty to consult businesses prior to issuing them with a suspension notice prohibiting the supply of unsafe products for up to six months under the terms of the Consumer Protection Act 1987. The Court believed that to impose such a duty would frustrate the statutory purpose of protecting consumer safety. Also, affected business have a right of appeal to the magistrates' court and to compensation where an order has been wrongly issued: *R. v. Birmingham City Council, ex p. Ferrero Ltd* [1993] 1 All E.R. 530.

3. In the field of financial services the Court of Appeal has determined that a self-regulatory body, exercising statutory powers, is not under a duty to hear the representations of affected businesses prior to urgent intervention action carried out with the objective of safeguarding the interests of investors. But Glidewell L.J. considered that "if a decision-making body is to exercise powers such as those of serving an intervention notice without giving anybody the opportunity to make representations beforehand, its procedures should provide that those who might otherwise expect to have been allowed to make representations should at least be allowed to make immediate application to set the decision aside and to appeal against it" (at 560). See *R. v. Life Assurance and Unit Trust Regulatory Organisation Ltd, ex p. Ross* [1993] 1 All E.R. 545.

Question
In what other decision-making contexts should emergency action be permitted to limit the right to a fair hearing?

(4) *Failings of the individual's legal advisers*

AL-MEHDAWI v. SECRETARY OF STATE FOR THE HOME DEPARTMENT

[1990] 1 A.C. 876; [1989] 3 All E.R. 843 (House of Lords)

The respondent was an Iraqi citizen who was refused a further extension of his leave to remain in the United Kingdom during May 1984. In March 1985 the respondent was notified that the Home Secretary had decided to make a deportation order against him. The respondent instructed solicitors to appeal against the deportation decision. The solicitors were notified of the hearing date for the appeal before an immigration adjudicator; however, neither they nor the respondent attended the appeal. Consequently, the adjudicator determined the appeal on the basis of the documents before him and dismissed the appeal. There was no appeal lodged against the adjudicator's decision within the statutory time limits. Subsequently, it emerged that the respondent's solicitors had sent notice of the hearing date and the adjudicator's decision to a previous address of the respondent (even though they knew his current one) with the result that he had received no information regarding the appellate proceedings. The respondent sought judicial review of the adjudicator's decision on the ground that there had been a breach of the rules of natural justice in that he had been denied a hearing. The High Court granted his application and the Court of Appeal affirmed that decision. The Home Secretary appealed to the House of Lords.

LORD BRIDGE OF HARWICH: ... The appeal raises a question of great importance with respect to the scope of the remedy by order of certiorari to quash the decision of an inferior tribunal. Does certiorari lie to quash a decision given without hearing the applicant for certiorari when the tribunal giving the decision has acted correctly in the procedure adopted but the applicant was deprived of the opportunity to put his case by the negligence of his own legal advisers or otherwise without personal fault on the part of the applicant. This question had been considered once before by the Court of Appeal in *R. v. Diggines, ex p. Rahmani* [1985] 1 Q.B. 1109. That was another case relating to the decision of an adjudicator under the Act of 1971 who was mistakenly informed by the United Kingdom Immigrants Advisory Service ("U.K.I.A.S."), acting for the appellant, that they had no instructions. The Court of Appeal quashed the decision on the ground of a denial of natural justice to the appellant arising from the fault of the U.K.I.A.S. The Court of Appeal proceeded on the assumption that there had been no error of procedure by the adjudicator. However, when *ex p. Rahmani* came before your Lordships' House on appeal the House held that the question decided by the Court of Appeal did not arise and dismissed the appeal on the ground that the adjudicator had erred in determining the appeal without a hearing in reliance on rule 12(c) of the Immigration Appeals (Procedure) Rules 1972 (S.I. 1972 No. 1684), the rules then in force, since there was no material before the adjudicator which justified him in finding under that sub-rule that no person was authorised to represent the appellant at the hearing. In the instant case, by contrast, no criticism is, nor could be, made of the procedure adopted by the adjudicator in hearing and determining the appeal in the absence of the appellant in the exercise of the express discretion conferred on him by rule 34(2) of the Rules of 1984....

The central submission made by Mr Laws, for the Secretary of State, is that the so-called rules of natural justice are concerned solely with the propriety of the procedure adopted by the decision maker. In particular, the rule expressed in the Latin maxim *audi alteram partem* requires no more than that the decision maker should afford to any party to a dispute an opportunity to present his case. This view certainly receives support from many classic statements of the doctrine. The duty "fairly to hear both sides" is described by Lord Loreburn L.C. in *Board of Education v. Rice* [1911] A.C. 179, 182 as "a duty lying upon every one who decides anything". In *Ridge v. Baldwin* [1964] A.C. 41, 64, Lord Reid said of the watch committee who had dismissed the chief constable without a hearing:

"Before attempting to reach any decision they were bound to inform him of the grounds on which they proposed to act and give him a fair opportunity of being heard in his own defence."

... Mr Laws submits that the very concept of impropriety in the procedure by which a decision is reached necessarily connotes an irregularity in the conduct of the proceedings by the decision maker. Conversely, a failure by the legal adviser or any other agent to whom a party to any proceedings has entrusted the conduct of his case, being beyond the knowledge and control of the decision maker, cannot involve either any procedural impropriety or the breach of any duty which the decision maker owes to that party.

However, the authority on which Sir Charles Fletcher-Cooke [counsel for the respondent] relies, and which persuaded the Court of Appeal that the procedural impropriety involved in a breach of the rules of natural justice could not be confined to errors on the part of the decision-making body, is *R. v. Leyland Justices, ex p. Hawthorn* [1979] Q.B. 283. In that case the driver of one of two cars involved in a collision had been prosecuted and convicted for driving without due care and attention. The police had taken statements from two witnesses of the accident, but these witnesses were not called by the prosecution and their existence was not disclosed to the defence. The driver successfully applied for an order of certiorari to quash the conviction. Delivering the first judgment Lord Widgery C.J. said, at 286:

"There is no doubt that an application can be made by certiorari to set aside an order on the basis that the tribunal failed to observe the rules of natural justice. Certainly if it were the fault of the justices that this additional evidentiary information was not passed on, no difficulty would arise. But the problem—and one can put it in a sentence—is that certiorari in respect of breach of the rules of natural justice is primarily a remedy sought on account of an error of the tribunal, and here, of course, we are not concerned with an error of the tribunal; we are concerned with an error of the police prosecutors. Consequently, amongst the arguments to which we have listened an argument has been that this is not a certiorari case at all on any of the accepted grounds.

"We have given this careful thought over the short adjournment because it is a difficult case in that the consequences of the decision either way have their unattractive features. However, if fraud, collusion, perjury and such-like matters not affecting the tribunal themselves justify an application for certiorari to quash the conviction, if all those matters are to have that effect, then we cannot say that the failure of the prosecution which in this case has prevented the tribunal from giving the defendant a fair trial should not rank in the same category.

"We have come to the conclusion that there was here a clear denial of natural justice. Fully recognising the fact that the blame falls on the prosecutor and not on the tribunal, we think that it is a matter which should result in the conviction being quashed. In my judgment, that is the result to which we should adhere."

This decision was followed in *R. v. Blundeston Prison Board of Visitors, ex p. Fox-Taylor* [1982] 1 All E.R. 646.

Though I do not question the correctness of the decision in *ex p. Hawthorn* [1979] Q.B. 283, I do question whether it is correctly classified as a case depending on either procedural impropriety or a breach of the rules of natural justice. Certainly there was unfairness in the conduct of the proceedings, but this was because of a failure by the prosecutor, in breach of a duty owed to the court and to the defence, to disclose the existence of witnesses who could have given evidence favourable to the defence. Although no dishonesty was suggested, it was this *suppressio veri* which had the same effect as a *suggestio falsi* in distorting and vitiating the process leading to conviction, and it was, in my opinion, the analogy which Lord Widgery C.J. drew between the case before him and the cases of fraud, collusion and perjury which had been relied on in-counsel's argument, which identified the true principle on which the decision could be justified.

In any event, *ex p. Hawthorn*, if it is relied on as an authority to support the conclusion of the Court of Appeal in *ex p. Rahmani* [1985] Q.B. 1109 and the instant case, proves too much. If unfairness resulting from a failure by the prosecutor to disclose the names of witnesses, so that the defence is deprived of their evidence, is taken as a precedent for allowing certiorari on the ground of a failure in the conduct of proceedings by the defendant's own legal advisers, the logic of the argument would lead to the conclusion that a negligent failure by the defendant's own legal advisers to secure the attendance of necessary defence witnesses would entitle the defendant to have his conviction quashed if he was personally free of blame for the failure. But this was a conclusion which Sir Charles Fletcher-Cooke rightly declined to support....

But there are many familiar situations where one party to litigation will effectively lose the opportunity to have his case heard through the failure of his own legal advisers, but will be left with no remedy at all except against those legal advisers. I need only instance judgments signed in default, actions dismissed for want of a prosecution and claims which are not made within a fixed time limit which the tribunal has no power to extend. In each of these situations a litigant who wishes his case to be heard and who has fully instructed his solicitor to take the necessary steps may never in fact be heard because of his solicitor's neglect and through no fault of his own. But in any of these cases it would surely be fanciful to say that there had been a breach of the *audi alteram partem* rule. Again, take the case of a county court action where a litigant fails to appear at the hearing because his solicitor has neglected to inform him of the date and consequently judgment is given against him. He can at best invite the court in its discretion to set aside the judgment and it is likely to do so only on the terms that he should pay the costs thrown away. Yet, if it can be said that he has been denied natural justice, he ought in principle to be able to apply for certiorari to quash the judgment which, if he is personally blameless, should be granted as a matter of course.

These considerations lead me to the conclusion that a party to a dispute who has lost the opportunity to have his case heard through the default of his own advisers to whom he has entrusted the conduct of the dispute on his behalf cannot complain that he has been the victim of a procedural impropriety or that natural justice has been denied to him, at all events when the subject-matter of the dispute raises issues of private law between citizens. Is there any principle which can be invoked to lead to a different conclusion where the issue is one of public law and where the decision taken is of an administrative character rather than the resolution of a *lis inter partes*? I cannot discover any such principle and none has been suggested in the course of argument....

But I would add that, if once unfairness suffered by one party to a dispute in consequence of some failure by his own advisers in relation to the conduct of the relevant proceedings was admitted as a ground on which the High Court in the exercise of its supervisory jurisdiction over inferior tribunals could quash the relevant decision, I can discern no principle which could be invoked to distinguish between a "fundamental unfairness", which would justify the exercise of the jurisdiction, and a less than fundamental unfairness, which would not. Indeed, Sir Charles Fletcher-Cooke was constrained to rest on the proposition that, in the last analysis, it was all a matter of discretion and the court could be trusted only to exercise its discretion in extreme cases where justice demanded a remedy. I am of the opinion that the decision of the Court of Appeal can only be supported at the cost of opening such a wide door which would indeed seriously undermine the principle of finality in decision making.

The effect of this conclusion in a deportation case may appear harsh, though no harsher than the perhaps more common case when an immigrant's solicitor fails to give notice of appeal under section 15 within the time limited by rule 4 of the Rules of 1984. But it is perhaps worth pointing out that in neither case is the immigrant left wholly without a remedy. In the case of a notice of appeal served out of time, the Secretary of State has a discretion under rule 5 to extend the time "if he is of the opinion that, by reason of special circumstances, it is just and right so to do". In the case where the immigrant has failed to attend the hearing of his appeal to the adjudicator and the appeal has been heard and dismissed in his absence, the Secretary of State has the discretion conferred on him by section 21 of the Act whereby he "may at any time refer for consideration under this section any matter relating to the case which was not before the adjudicator". If such a reference is made, the adjudicator is required by section 21(2) to "consider the matter which is the subject of the reference and report to the Secretary of State the opinion of the adjudicator ... thereon". It would, as it seems to me, certainly be open to the Secretary of State, if persuaded that the merits of a case required it, to invite an adjudicator to hear the oral evidence of an appellant whose appeal had, through no fault of his own, been dismissed in his absence, and to report his opinion whether this evidence would have affected the outcome of the appeal.

I would allow the appeal, set aside the orders of MacPherson J. and the Court of Appeal and restore the determination of the adjudicator.

LORDS ROSKILL, BRANDON OF OAKBROOK, OLIVER OF AYLMERTON and GOFF OF CHIEVELEY agreed with the speech given by LORD BRIDGE.

Appeal allowed.

Notes
1. The above decision has been criticised for unduly circumscribing the application of the *audi alteram partem* principle. One critic has suggested the following approach:

> "By drawing on the theory that natural justice—and judicial review as a whole—is vitally concerned with setting standards for public authorities and structuring the exercise of public power, it is suggested that the House of Lords should have held that certiorari for breach of natural justice could lie although a tribunal was not responsible for the defect, but only where responsibility for the procedural impropriety can be attributed to a body exercising public authority: either the prosecutor (in a criminal case) or a party to an adversarial process with a public law function (for example, the Home Office in proceedings before the immigration adjudicator). Such a view recognises the strong argument in favour of finality of litigation, but holds that finality should not override the importance of natural justice in 'policing' public power ..."

(J. Herberg, "The Right to a Hearing: Breach Without Fault?" [1990] P.L. 467 at 474–475).

2. *Ex p. Hawthorn* was applied, and *Al-Mehdawi* distinguished, in *R. v. Bolton JJ., ex p. Scally* [1991] 2 All E.R. 619, where the Divisional Court quashed convictions for driving with excess alcohol based on scientific evidence subsequently shown to be flawed. There had been no dishonesty, but the prosecutor had "corrupted the process leading to conviction in a manner which was unfair". A later Divisional Court held that only where a prosecutor's conduct was "analogous to fraud" would it quash a conviction in the magistrates' court. The notification, by the Crown Prosecution Service, after the completion of a trial of defects in the procedure by which a blood sample had been obtained from a suspected drink driver did not fall into this category of conduct: *R. v. Burton Upon Trent JJ., ex p. Woolley* [1995] R.T.R. 139. This approach was endorsed in *R. v. Dolgellau JJ., ex p. Cartledge, The Times*, August 4, 1995, where the High Court dismissed an application for judicial view because there was no evidence that the prosecution had falsified or suppressed evidence that might have led to an acquittal.

(5) *The making of legislation*

BATES v. LORD HAILSHAM OF ST MARYLEBONE AND OTHERS

[1972] 1 W.L.R. 1373; 116 S.J. 584; [1972] 2 All E.R. 1019 (Megarry J.)

Mr Bates was a solicitor and a leading member of the British Legal Association, to which about 2,900 of the 26,000 solicitors with practising certificates belonged. On May 1, 1972, the Lord Chancellor announced at a press conference that the scale fees for conveyancing work prescribed under Schedule 1 to the Solicitors' Remuneration Order 1883, would be replaced by a *quantum meruit* system. The British Legal Association sent a circular to all solicitors opposing the changes. The Law Society received a draft order for the implementation of the changes from the Lord Chancellor's department as required by the Solicitors' Act 1957, s.58(3). A period of one month was prescribed by section 56 for observations to be submitted to the statutory committee which would make the new order. The date of the meeting of the committee was fixed for July 19, at 4.30 p.m. On June 21, the draft order was published in the Law Society's Gazette. The British Legal Association sent submissions and letters to the committee on July 11 and 14, requesting postponement of the changes "for perhaps two months", and further consultations. On July 18, the Lord Chancellor wrote to the British Legal Association refusing their requests. The plaintiff the same day served a writ against the members of the committee. He contended that the draft order had been prepared by the Lord Chancellor's department and had not been considered by the committee. He claimed: (i) a declaration that any order made by the committee under section 56 would be *ultra vires* and void unless the draft had been considered by the committee and an opportunity had been given for representations on the order to be made by the British Legal Association and others; (ii) an injunction restraining the committee from making an order until these steps had been taken. At 2.00 p.m. on July 19, the plaintiff moved *ex parte* for an injunction to stop the committee making an order at its 4.30 p.m. meeting.

MEGARRY J.: ... His [*i.e.* Counsel for the plaintiff's] two main points were, first, that if the order was made at the meeting of the committee, the committee would not be complying with its duty to act fairly. The committee, he said, would be exercising not judicial or quasi-judicial functions, but administrative functions; and where, as here, so vast a change was going to be made as the overturn of the entire basis of charging in conveyancing transactions, a basis that had lasted for nearly 90 years and affected a profession of some 26,000 spread throughout the country, it was not fair to make it without a substantially longer period for consultation and representations. His second point was one which he accepted as being technical; but in effect he said that it was advanced in a good cause. It was that it was implicit in section 56(3) that the draft of the order which was to be sent to the council of the Law Society must be a draft prepared or approved by the committee, and not, as appeared to be the case here, a draft prepared by or on behalf of the Lord Chancellor's department, without previous consultation with the committee.

On the first point, Mr Nicholls relied on *R. v. Liverpool Corporation, ex p. Liverpool Taxi Fleet Operators' Association* [1972] 2 Q.B. 299 [above, p. 448]; and he read me some passages from the judgments of Lord Denning M.R. and Roskill L.J. It cannot often happen that words uttered by a judge in his judicial capacity will, within six months, be cited against him in his personal capacity as defendant; yet that is the position here. The case was far removed from the present case. It concerned the exercise by a city council of its powers to license hackney carriages, and a public undertaking given by the chairman of the relevant committee which the council soon proceeded to ignore. The case supports propositions relating to the duty of a body to act fairly when exercising administrative functions under a statutory power: see at 307, 308 and 310. Accordingly, in deciding the policy to be applied as to the number of licences to grant, there was a duty to hear those who would be likely to be affected. It is plain that no legislation was involved: the question was one of the policy to be adopted in the exercise of a statutory power to grant licences.

In the present case, the committee in question has an entirely different function: it is legislative rather than administrative or executive. The function of the committee is to make or refuse to make a legislative instrument under delegated powers. The order, when made, will lay down the remuneration for solicitors generally; and the terms of the order will have to be considered and construed and applied in numberless cases in the future. Let me accept that in the sphere of the so-called quasi-judicial the rules of natural justice run, and that in the administrative or executive field there is a general duty of fairness. Nevertheless, these considerations do not seem to me to affect the process of legislation, whether primary or delegated. Many of those affected by delegated legislation, and affected very substantially, are never consulted in the process of enacting that legislation; and yet they have no remedy. Of course, the informal consultation of representative bodies by the legislative authority is a commonplace; but although a few statutes have specifically provided for a general process of publishing draft delegated legislation and considering objections (see, for example, the Factories Act 1961, Schedule 4), I do not know of any implied right to be consulted or make objections, or any principle upon which the courts may enjoin the legislative process at the suit of those who contend that insufficient time for consultation and consideration has been given. I accept that the fact that the order will take the form of a statutory instrument does not *per se* make it immune from attack, whether by injunction or otherwise; but what is important is not its form but its nature, which is plainly legislative.

There is a further point. The power in question in the *Liverpool Corporation* case [1972] 2 Q.B. 299 was a general power to "license ... such number of hackney coaches or carriages ... as they think fit" under section 37 of the Town Police Clauses Act 1847, with no special procedure laid down for the process of licensing. Here, Parliament has laid down the procedure to be followed. *Expressum facit cessare tacitum.* It is easier to imply procedural safeguards when Parliament has provided none than where Parliament has laid down a procedure, however inadequate its critics may consider it to be. Parliament has here provided that the committee must, before making any order, consider any observations in writing submitted to it by the council of the Law Society within one month of the draft having been sent to the council. What in effect the plaintiff is seeking to do is to add by implication a further requirement that if the draft will make momentous changes, more than a month must be allowed, and opportunities must be given for representations to be made by bodies other than the council of the Law Society. Mr Nicholls understandably shrank from asserting that the process of consultation need go beyond any substantial organised body of solicitors, or that the committee need accede to a request for further time from any other body or persons. My difficulty is to see how even the organised bodies that he postulated can be implied into the subsection or imposed upon it. If the procedure laid down by Parliament is fairly and substantially followed, I cannot see that the committee need do more; and I see nothing in the evidence to suggest that the committee has not fully and fairly complied with the statutory requirements....

[His Lordship then rejected the plaintiff's second point.]

Notes

1. The unwillingness of the judiciary to place common law procedural obligations upon legislative processes has been alluded to by the House of Lords. In a case involving the disciplinary powers of prison governors, Lord Oliver stated:

"it is a public function which affects the liberty and, to a degree, the status of the persons affected by it. As such it must, as it seems to me, be subject to the general common law principle which imposes a duty of procedural fairness when a public authority makes a decision *not of a legislative nature* affecting the rights, privileges and interests of individuals" (emphasis added): *Leech v. Parkhurst Prison Deputy Governor* [1988] 1 All E.R. 485 at 509.

2. On consultation and delegated legislation see J.F. Garner [1976] P.L. 307 and A. Jergesen [1978] P.L. 290. More generally see the chapter on delegated legislation below, p. 811, and above, pp. 407 *et seq.*

3. Similarly, a local authority need not give an opportunity for persons to be heard before making a decision that is universal in its application such as the fixing by the authority of the rates for the year (now the level of council tax) or the scale on which fees are to be charged (*R. v. Greater London Council, ex p. The Rank Organisation Ltd, The Times*, February 19, 1982).

(c) *Specific aspects of the right to a fair hearing in particular decision-making contexts*

(1) *Oral or written representations?*

LLOYD AND OTHERS v. McMAHON

[1987] 1 A.C. 625; [1987] 1 All E.R. 1118 (House of Lords)

During 1984 Liverpool Council had delayed making a rate until July of that year. In April of 1985 the district auditor sent a report to the council expressing concern that a rate had not yet been made for 1985. On May 21 the district auditor sent a further report to the council in which he stated that unless a rate was made by the end of May he would commence action under the Local Government Act 1982, s.20, to recover any financial losses occasioned by the failure to make a rate from the members responsible for incurring them. On June 6 the Audit Commission ordered that an extraordinary audit of the council be carried out. The council made a rate on June 14. On June 26 the district auditor sent a notice to 42 councillors (who by their voting or absence might have failed to discharge their duties as councillors) stating that he had to consider whether to certify the sum of £106,103 as lost by their wilful misconduct. The individual councillors were informed that they could make written representations to the district auditor before he reached a decision. The councillors (assisted by the chief executive of the council) made a collective written response to the district auditor. They did not seek an oral hearing before the district auditor. In September 1985 the district auditor certified that the named councillors were jointly and severally liable for the above sum. The councillors appealed to the High Court (under section 20(3) of the Act) against the district auditor's decision. The High Court dismissed their appeal and that decision was confirmed by the Court of Appeal. The councillors then appealed to the House of Lords.

LORD KEITH OF KINKEL: ... The argument by counsel for the appellants did not invite your Lordships to enter deeply into the merits of the question whether or not they had been guilty of wilful misconduct, nor was attention drawn to any details of the affidavits and other material placed before the Divisional Court. The substance of the argument was that the district auditor's decision had been vitiated by his failure to offer the appellants an oral hearing before reaching it, and should therefore have been quashed. The argument was supported by an examination of earlier legislation in regard to local government audits, starting with the Poor Law Amendment Act 1844 (7 & 8 Vict. c. 101), where oral hearings were the order of the day, and by reference to the Code of Local Government Audit Practice for England and Wales, made under section 14 of the Act of 1982 and approved by resolution of both Houses of Parliament. The code, by paragraphs 16 to 20, contemplates that an oral hearing will be held where the auditor is dealing with a notice of objection given under section 17(3) of the Act of 1982, which itself refers to the objector attending before the auditor. The code does not deal with the procedure to be followed where the auditor takes action under section 20(1). Counsel produced a list of all instances since 1972 where a district auditor had occasion to consider an issue of wilful misconduct, indicating that in all but one of them an oral hearing had been offered. This had the effect, so it was maintained, of creating a legitimate expectation on the part of the appellants that they would be offered an oral hearing before the district auditor arrived at his decision.

My Lords, if the district auditor had reached a decision adverse to the appellants without giving them any opportunity at all of making representations to him, there can be no doubt that his procedure would have been contrary to the rules of natural justice and that, subject to the question whether the defect was capable of being cured on appeal to the Divisional Court, the decision would fall to be quashed. In the event, written representations alone were asked for. These were duly furnished, in very considerable detail, and an oral hearing was not requested, though that could very easily have been done, and there is no reason to suppose that the request would not have been granted. None of the appellants stated, in his or her affidavit before the Divisional Court, that they had an expectation that an oral hearing, though not asked for, would be offered. The true question is whether the district auditor acted fairly in all the circumstances. It is easy to envisage cases where an oral hearing would clearly be essential in the interests of fairness, for example where an objector states that he has personal knowledge of some facts indicative of wilful misconduct on the part of a councillor. In that situation justice would demand that the councillor be given an opportunity to depone to his own version of the facts. In the present case the district auditor had arrived at his provisional view upon the basis of the contents of documents, minutes of meetings and reports submitted to the council from the auditor's department and their own officers. All these documents were appended to or referred to in the notice of June 26 sent by the district auditor to the appellants. Their response referred to other documents, which were duly considered by the district auditor, as is shown by his statement of reasons dated September 6, 1985. No facts contradictory of or supplementary to the contents of the documents were or are relied on by either side. If the appellants had attended an oral hearing they would no doubt have reiterated the sincerity of their motives from the point of view of advancing the interests of the inhabitants of Liverpool. It seems unlikely, having regard to the position adopted by their counsel on this matter before the Divisional Court, that they would have been willing to reveal or answer questions about the proceedings of their political caucus. The sincerity of the appellants' motives is not something capable of justifying or excusing failure to carry out a statutory duty, or of making reasonable what is otherwise an unreasonable delay in carrying out such a duty. In all the circumstances I am of opinion that the district auditor did not act unfairly, and that the procedure which he followed did not involve any prejudice to the appellants....

Upon the view which I take, that the district auditor's decision was not vitiated by procedural unfairness, the question whether such unfairness, had it existed, was capable of being cured by the appeal to the High Court does not arise directly for decision. It is, however, my opinion that the particular appeal mechanism provided for by section 20(3) of the Act of 1982, considered in its context, is apt to enable the court, notwithstanding that it finds some procedural defect in the conduct of an audit which has resulted in a certificate based on wilful misconduct, to inquire into the merits of the case and arrive at its own decision thereon. Section 20(3)(b) empowers the court to "confirm the decision or quash it and give any certificate which the auditor could have given". The relevant rules of court enable a rehearing of the broadest possible scope to take place. Evidence may be given on oath, which is not possible before the auditor, and there is no limit to the further material which may be introduced so as to enable the whole merits to be fully examined. There is no question of the court being confined to a review of the evidence which was available to the auditor....

I may add that I agree entirely with all that is said upon this aspect of the appeal in the speech of my noble and learned friend Lord Bridge of Harwich.

LORD BRIDGE OF HARWICH: My Lords, the so-called rules of natural justice are not engraved on tablets of stone. To use the phrase which better expresses the underlying concept, what the requirements of fairness demand when any body, domestic, administrative or judicial, has to make a decision which will affect the rights of individuals depends on the character of the decision-making body, the kind of decision it has to make and the statutory or other framework in which it operates. In particular, it is well-established that when a statute has conferred on any body the power to make decisions affecting individuals, the courts will not only require the procedure prescribed by the statute to be followed, but will readily imply so much and no more to be introduced by way of additional procedural safeguards as will ensure the attainment of fairness....

I followed with interest Mr Blom-Cooper's [counsel for the appellants] carefully researched review of the history of local government audit legislation, but I did not find that it threw any light on what, in particular, is required to provide such an opportunity in the circumstances of any particular case under the statute presently in force. Still less do I attach any significance to the fact that since 1972, when provisions substantially to the like effect as those which we find in the Act of 1982 first reached the Statute Book, auditors have, as a matter of practice, always invited oral representations from members of local authorities before certifying the amount of any loss or deficiency as due from them. When a single individual is thought to have failed to bring a sum into account or by his wilful misconduct to have caused a loss or deficiency, it is no doubt a very appropriate practice to invite his explanation orally. But I fail to understand how that practice can constrain the courts to construe the statute as requiring an auditor proposing to act under section 20 to invite oral representations as a matter of law in every case....

The proposition that it was, *per se*, in breach of the rules of natural justice not to invite oral representations in this case is quite untenable....

These conclusions would be sufficient to dispose of the appeals. But I return to the question of more general importance whether, if there had been any unfairness in the procedure followed by the auditor, this would necessarily have led, as the Divisional Court thought, to the quashing of the certificate or whether, as the Court of Appeal concluded, the full hearing of the appeal to the court on the merits was in law able to make good any deficiency in the auditor's procedure. It was in order to set this question in its proper context that I thought it necessary, earlier in this opinion, to set out the relevant statutory provisions *in extenso*. The question how far in domestic and administrative two-tier adjudicatory systems a procedural failure at the level of the first tier can be remedied at the level of the second tier was considered by the Privy Council in *Calvin v. Carr* [1980] A.C. 574 in which all the relevant previous authorities on the subject are reviewed. I do not find it necessary in this case to examine the general principles there discussed, nor would I think it appropriate in this case to seek to lay down any principles of general application. This is because the question arising in the instant case must be answered by considering the particular statutory provisions here applicable which establish an adjudicatory system in many respects quite unlike any that has come under examination in any of the decided cases to which we were referred. We are concerned with a point of statutory construction and nothing else....

In every case it must be for the court, as a matter of discretion, to decide how in all the circumstances its jurisdiction under section 20(3) can best be exercised to meet the justice of the case. But I am clearly of opinion that when the court has, as here, in fact conducted a full hearing on the merits and reached a conclusion that the issue of a certificate was justified, it would be an erroneous exercise of discretion nevertheless to quash the certificate on the ground that, before the matter reached the court, there had been some defect in the procedure followed.

LORDS BRANDON and GRIFFITHS agreed. LORD TEMPLEMAN delivered a concurring speech.

Appeal dismissed.

Notes

1. The background to the process of district audit is considered above Chapter 1(B)(ii).

2. A local fund was established to raise the moneys needed to discharge the councillors' legal liabilities. By 1990 the fund had collected such an amount.

3. The second limb of their Lordships' decision concerned the issue of "curative appeals" which is examined below (pp. 506–509) in the case of *Calvin v. Carr*.

4. On the oral hearing point see also *R. v. Army Board of the Defence Council, ex p. Anderson*, above, p. 446, applied in *R. v. Secretary of State for Health, ex p. Gandhi* [1991] 4 All E.R. 547, 556–577. The High Court decided, following *Anderson*, that a committee of the Legal Aid Board acted unlawfully by circulating documents to each of the members individually; rather than reconvening a meeting with all the members attending in person for group deliberation: see *R. v. Legal Aid Board, ex p. Donn & Co.* [1996] 3 All E.R. 1.

5. Sir Louis Blom-Cooper Q.C., sitting as a Deputy High Court Judge, has held that fairness may require the Secretary of State to convene a public inquiry to hear conflicting testimony on the status of a footpath when the issue cannot be resolved by documentation alone. In his judgment, "the court's intrusion in a case of judicial review will not be to build into the statute [the Wildlife and Countryside Act 1981] a blanket procedure of fairness, but only to inject its notion of fairness, as and when conflicting documentary material in a particular case compels a means of testing the evidence in a public inquiry": *R. v. Secretary of State for Wales, ex p. Emery* [1996] 4 All E.R. 1 at 15. For an analysis of this statutory provision see A.R. Mowbray, "Rights of Way and Highways" in A.A. Lennon (ed.), *Agricultural Law, Tax & Finance*.

6. The Court of Appeal has held that a convicted prisoner does not have a right in all circumstances to be present in court to argue every civil case he or she may initiate. It was, therefore, lawful for the Home Secretary to require prisoners to make a formal application for permission to be allowed to attend such proceedings and for the Secretary of State to require the prisoners to pay the costs incurred in producing them in court: *R. v. Secretary of State for the Home Department, ex p. Wynne* [1992] 1 Q.B. 406. Staughton L.J. said:

"Finally, I turn to considerations of natural justice. There are two aspects of this which cause me concern. The first is that, if a prisoner is not allowed to be present in court when his case is heard, he will not be able to answer new arguments put forward by the other side or to rebut new evidence which is produced against him. The importance of this point depends on the nature of the case. When, as here, it is a prisoner's application for judicial review, the judge at the hearing should be careful to allow no new evidence and no new arguments, beyond those which the prisoner has already had the opportunity to answer in writing. Then no injustice can arise. In other types of case it may be an important factor for the Home Office to have in mind when deciding whether to allow production and if so on what terms" (at 428).

Question
How significant was it that none of the councillors asked for an oral hearing before the district auditor?

(2) *A right to legal representation?*

R. v. BOARD OF VISITORS OF H.M. PRISON, THE MAZE, ex p. HONE

[1988] 1 A.C. 379; [1988] 1 All E.R. 321 (House of Lords)

The appellant was a prisoner serving a life sentence in Northern Ireland. He was charged with an offence against discipline of assaulting a prison officer contrary to rule 31(5) of the Prison Rules (Northern Ireland) 1982. Because of the seriousness of the charge it was referred to the board of visitors for determination. The board found the charge proved (the appellant had pleaded not guilty) and sentenced him to 30 days' cellular confinement and a concurrent loss of privileges for 60 days. The appellant sought judicial review of the board's decision arguing, *inter alia*, that it was unlawful as he had been denied the right to legal representation before the board. The High Court dismissed the application and this decision was confirmed by the Court of Appeal. The appellant then appealed to the House of Lords.

This case was dealt with as a consolidated appeal together with a similar action brought by another prisoner, McCartan.

LORD GOFF OF CHIEVELEY: ... Before your Lordships' House, the submissions on behalf of the appellants were as follows. The basic submission was that a convicted prisoner retains all his civil rights, except those which are taken away from him expressly or by necessary implication; and that an ordinary citizen charged with a criminal offence is entitled to legal representation before the tribunal which hears the charge against him. It was, however, accepted that, on an inquiry by the governor of a prison, a prisoner has no right to legal representation; such a right, it was submitted, applied only to hearings before boards of visitors, when the prisoner is charged with a criminal offence or the equivalent of a criminal offence.

... The first of the authorities is the decision of the Court of Appeal in *R. v. Assessment Committee of St Mary Abbotts, Kensington* [1891] 1 Q.B. 378. In that case it was held that a householder who objected to a valuation list and wished his objection to be advanced before the assessment committee need not appear in person before the committee but could depute another person to do so on his behalf. This decision has been invoked on subsequent occasions in support of the proposition that any person appearing before a disciplinary tribunal is entitled to legal representation. The decision of the Court of Appeal in *Pett v. Greyhound Racing Association Ltd* [1969] 1 Q.B. 125 appeared, at first sight, to give some credence to that proposition. In that case the plaintiff claimed the right to legal representation at an inquiry by the association into a disciplinary matter, concerned with a serious charge against the plaintiff relating to the circumstances in which a greyhound of his was withdrawn from a race, it being alleged that traces of barbiturates were found in the dog's urine. On an interlocutory appeal Lord Denning M.R., in holding that natural justice required that in matters affecting a man's reputation or livelihood or any matters of serious purport he should, if he wished, be legally represented, relied upon the *St Mary Abbotts* case; and Russell L.J., at 135, referred to his "common law right" to be so represented. However, on the substantive hearing (*Pett v. Greyhound Racing Association Ltd (No. 2)* [1970] 1 Q.B. 46), Lyell J. concluded that the only duty on the association was to observe the rules of natural justice, and distinguished the *St Mary Abbotts* case as being concerned not with legal representation before a tribunal but with a man employing an agent to communicate with a body performing an administrative act. He said, at 63:

"It appears to me that the Court of Appeal regarded the overseers as performing an administrative act in preparing the valuation lists ... It has, so far as I am aware, never been suggested that the valuation officer in considering such objections is acting otherwise than in an administrative capacity. In view of the many authorities that domestic tribunals are subject only to the duty of observing what are called the rules of natural justice and any procedure laid down or necessarily to be implied from the instrument that confers their power, I am unable to follow the views expressed by the Court of Appeal, that the plaintiff is entitled to appear by an agent unless such right was expressly negatived by the rules of the club."

Subsequent cases have proceeded on the same basis. Thus in *Enderby Town Football Club Ltd v. Football Association Ltd* [1971] Ch. 591, Lord Denning M.R. rejected the suggestion that a man who is charged before a domestic tribunal is entitled as of right to be legally represented; on the contrary, he regarded that matter as being within the discretion of the tribunal. A similar suggestion was rejected by the Court of Appeal in *Fraser v. Mudge* [1975] 1 W.L.R. 1132, which is very much in point in the present case. There a prisoner asked for an injunction to restrain a board of visitors from inquiring into a charge against him of assaulting a prison officer unless he was represented by a solicitor and counsel of his choice. The case therefore raised the question whether, in such circumstances, the prisoner was entitled to legal representation as of right. Chapman J. refused to grant the injunction, and his decision was affirmed by the Court of Appeal. Roskill L.J. said, at 1134:

"The argument of Mr Sedley, as I follow it, really involves that justice cannot be done or cannot at least be seen to be done by the defendants, the visitors, in this case unless there is legal representation of the plaintiff. I wish to make it plain that I do not subscribe to the view that in every type of case, irrespective of the nature or jurisdiction of the body in question, justice can neither be done nor be seen to be done without legal representation of the party or parties appearing before that body. Such a proposition to my mind is untenable. There are many bodies before which a party or parties can be required to appear but who can do justice and can be seen to do justice without the party against whom complaint is made being legally represented. Further, as Lord Denning M.R. has said, if the argument in relation to rule 49(2) of the Prison Rules 1964 were well founded, it would equally apply to complaints heard by the governor to which the same language applies, a proposition which I think is also untenable. One looks to see what are the broad principles underlying these rules. They are to maintain discipline in prison by proper, swift and speedy decisions, whether by the governor or the visitors; and it seems to me that the requirements of natural justice do not make it necessary that a person against whom disciplinary proceedings are pending should as of right be entitled to be represented by solicitors or counsel or both."

Subsequently, in *R. v. Secretary of State for the Home Department, ex p. Tarrant* [1985] Q.B. 251, a Divisional Court (consisting of Kerr L.J. and Webster J.) accepted *Fraser v. Mudge* as binding authority that, before a board of visitors, a prisoner charged with a disciplinary offence has no right to legal representation, though it was held that a board of visitors has a discretion to grant representation; and, in his full and careful judgment, Webster J. referred to considerations which he considered that every board of visitors should take into account when exercising its discretion whether to allow legal representation, or indeed the assistance of a friend or adviser, to a prisoner appearing before it on a disciplinary charge....

In advancing his submissions for the appellants in the present case before your Lordships' House, Mr Hill had of necessity to submit that the decision of the Court of Appeal in *Fraser v. Mudge* was wrong. In support of his submissions, which I have already summarised, he relied upon rule 30(2) of the Rules of 1982, which provides that at an inquiry into a charge against a prisoner he shall be given a full opportunity of presenting his own case. He stressed that a hearing before a board of visitors is a sophisticated hearing. In particular, he submitted, there is an oral hearing; a formal plea is entered; cross-examination is allowed and witnesses are called; the onus and standard of proof are the same as in a criminal trial; free legal aid is available; punishments are imposed; a plea in mitigation can be entered; and the board has greater powers of punishment than those exercised by magistrates' courts. He also, like others before him, invoked the *St Mary Abbotts* case [1891] 1 Q.B. 378 as authority for the proposition that each appellant had a common law right to appoint a lawyer as his agent to appear before the board of visitors on his behalf.

I am unable to accept these submissions. I would first of all reject the argument founded upon the *St Mary Abbotts* case as misconceived, for the very reasons given by Lyell J. in *Pett v. Greyhound Racing Association Ltd (No. 2)* [1970] 1 Q.B. 46, 63, quoted above, that the case is not in point since it was concerned only with the making of a communication to an administrative body. But, so far as Mr Hill's wider submissions are concerned, I am unable to accept his second proposition that any person charged with a crime (or the equivalent thereof) and liable to punishment is entitled as a matter of natural justice to legal representation. No doubt it is true that a man charged with a crime before a criminal court is entitled to legal representation—both before the Crown Court and (as a matter of statute) before a magistrates' court: see section 122 of the Magistrates' Courts Act 1980.... No doubt it is also correct that a board of visitors is bound to give effect to the rules of natural justice. But it does not follow that, simply because a charge before a disciplinary tribunal such as a board of visitors relates to facts which in law constitute a crime, the rules of natural justice require the tribunal to grant legal representation. Indeed, if this were the case, then, as Roskill L.J. pointed out in *Fraser v. Mudge* [1975] 1 W.L.R. 1132, exactly the same submission could be made in respect of disciplinary proceedings before the governor of a prison. Mr Hill was at pains to escape from this conclusion by attempting to distinguish between a governor and a board of visitors, on the basis that there was no right of legal representation before the governor but an absolute right to legal representation before the board of visitors. I for my part am unable to accept this distinction. Each, both governor and board of visitors, is exercising a disciplinary jurisdiction; and, as the Rules of 1982 clearly demonstrate, each may do so in respect of offences against discipline which could in law constitute criminal offences. Each must also be bound by the rules of natural justice. The difference between them is not so much a legal as a practical difference. The jurisdiction exercised by the governor is of a more summary nature, and should properly be exercised with great expedition; furthermore the punishments which he can award are limited to those set out in rule 32 of the Rules of 1982, though he can refer the matter to the Secretary of State (and, through him, to a board of visitors) under rule 33(1)(e) if he considers that it may be desirable that a more severe punishment should be awarded. In the nature of things, it is difficult to imagine that the rules of natural justice would ever require legal representation before the governor. But though the rules of natural justice may require legal representation before a board of visitors, I can see no basis for Mr Hill's submission that they should do so in every case as of right. Everything must depend on the circumstances of the particular case, as is amply demonstrated by the circumstances so carefully listed by Webster J. in *R. v. Secretary of State for the Home Department, ex p. Tarrant* [1985] Q.B. 251 as matters which boards of visitors should take into account. But it is easy to envisage circumstances in which the rules of natural justice do not call for representation, even though the disciplinary charge relates to a matter which constitutes in law a crime, as may well happen in the case of a simple assault where no question of law arises, and where the prisoner charged is capable of presenting his own case. To hold otherwise would result in wholly unnecessary delays in many cases, to the detriment of all concerned including the prisoner charged, and to wholly unnecessary waste of time and money, contrary to the public interest. Indeed, to hold otherwise would not only cause injustice to prisoners; it would also lead to an adventitious distinction being drawn between disciplinary offences which happen also to be crimes and those which happen not to be so, for the punishments liable to be imposed do not depend upon any such distinction....

LORD MACKAY OF CLASHFERN L.C., LORD BRIDGE OF HARWICH, LORD ACKNER and LORD OLIVER OF AYLMERTON agreed with the above speech.

Appeals dismissed.

Notes

1. The criteria articulated by Webster J. in *R. v. Secretary of State for the Home Department, ex p. Tarrant* [1985] Q.B. 251, were the following:

(a) The seriousness of the charge and of the potential penalty;
(b) Whether any points of law are likely to arise in the proceedings;
(c) The capacity of the prisoner to present his/her own case (*i.e.* their intellectual and educational abilities);
(d) Procedural difficulties (*e.g.* whether the prisoner has been able to interview relevant witnesses prior to the hearing);
(e) The need for reasonable speed in making an adjudication;
(f) The need for fairness between prisoners and between prisoners/prison officers.

2. In *Tarrant* it was reported that, nationally, boards of visitors reached approximately 3,000 adjudications per year. Woolf L.J. (as he then was) recommended the abolition of the disciplinary powers of boards of visitors, because of the difficulty of combining that role with the boards' responsibility for protecting the interests of prisoners, in his report *Prison Disturbances* (Cm. 1456) (examining the Strangeways and other subsequent prison riots). He favoured increasing the role of the ordinary criminal courts in dealing with serious misbehaviour inside prisons. The Government accepted this recommendation and from April 1992 boards of visitors ceased to have a role in disciplinary adjudication.

3. M.J. Dixon is critical of Lord Goff's speech in *Hone* because:

"It is unfortunate that the House of Lords in *Hone* did not seize the opportunity to examine the whole matter in closer detail. As it is, they were content to rely on general propositions about the flexible nature of natural justice and on previous decisions which are not altogether satisfactory. The jurisdiction of a board of visitors is non-voluntary, and it is not enough to rely on cases that deny the right of legal representation before tribunals whose jurisdiction depends wholly on the consent of the parties ... However, not only has the decision in *Hone* extinguished any possibility of a prisoner being entitled to legal representation as of right, Lord Goff's emphasis on administrative efficiency may encourage visitors to exercise that discretion against a prisoner in all but the most extreme cases" ((1989) 40 N.I.L.Q. 71 at 77).

4. Parties to proceedings in the ordinary courts have a right to be advised, in court, by a lay person who is not a qualified lawyer. The court can only exclude such an adviser:

"... if it becomes apparent that the 'assistance' is unreasonable in nature or degree or if it becomes apparent that the 'assistance' is not being provided bona fide, but for an improper purpose or is being provided in a way which is inimical to the proper and efficient administration of justice, by for example, causing the party to waste time, advising the introduction of irrelevant issues or the asking of irrelevant or repetitious questions" (at 946).

The Court of Appeal, therefore, held that justices had acted unlawfully in denying a defendant the right to be assisted by an adviser during proceedings for a liability order in respect of failure to pay the community charge ("poll tax"), when there was no reason to exclude the adviser: see *R. v. Leicester City JJ., ex p. Barrow and another* [1991] 3 All E.R. 935.

5. The European Court of Human Rights has held that Article 6(3)(c) of the ECHR obliges the United Kingdom to provide legal assistance at a magistrates' court hearing (at no cost to the defendant if he/she cannot afford to pay) for a defendant facing a sentence of imprisonment for failing to pay the community charge: see *Benham v. U.K.* (1996) 22 E.H.R.R. 293.

Question
To what extent can the reasoning in *Tarrant* and *Hone* be applied outside the context of adjudications by boards of visitors?

(3) *A right to cross-examine opponents?*

BUSHELL AND ANOTHER v. SECRETARY OF STATE FOR THE ENVIRONMENT

[1981] A.C. 75; [1980] 3 W.L.R. 22; [1980] 2 All E.R. 608; (1980) 78 L.G.R. 269 (House of Lords)

The Department had proposed the construction of two adjoining stretches of motorway in the West Midlands. Local residents, and other amenity groups, objected to the proposals. Under the terms of the Highways Act 1959, the Secretary of State was obliged to hold a local public inquiry into such objections. One local inquiry was convened to hear the above objections (100 different parties were present at the inquiry which lasted for 100 working days). The respondents were objectors who sought to challenge the statistical methods used by the department to predict future traffic needs. The inspector allowed the respondents to criticise the department's methodology (contained in the "Red Book") and to call expert witnesses to support their criticisms, but he would not permit them to cross-examine the department's representatives upon this matter. The inspector noted the respondents' criticisms in his report which was generally favourable to the department's proposals. The Secretary of State accepted the inspector's recommendations and made schemes for the construction of these sections of motorway. The respondents applied, under Schedule 2 to the 1959 Act, to the High Court to quash the schemes on the ground, *inter alia*, that the inspector had been wrong in law to disallow them from cross-examining departmental representatives on the "Red Book". The High Court dismissed their application, but the Court of Appeal (Templeman L.J. dissenting) allowed their appeal. The Secretary of State appealed to the House of Lords.

LORD DIPLOCK: The provision and improvement of a national system of routes for through traffic for which a government department and not a local authority should be the highway authority has formed a part of national transport policy since the passing of the Trunk Roads Act in 1936. As part of this national network, or superimposed upon it, there have been constructed by stages during the course of the last 30 years special roads familiarly known as motorways which were first authorised by the Special Roads Act 1949. The construction of motorways is a lengthy and expensive process and it has been the policy of successive governments, which would in any event have been dictated by necessity, to construct the network by stages. The order in which the various portions of the network are to be constructed thus becomes as much a matter of government transport policy as the total extent and configuration of the motorway network itself. It also has the consequence that schemes for the provision of special roads which the Minister proposes to make under section 11 of the Highways Act 1959 deal with comparatively short stretches in a particular locality of what, when the other stretches are completed, will be integral parts of the national network. It follows, therefore, that there will be a whole series of schemes relating to successive stretches of the national network of motorways each of which may be the subject of separate local inquiries under Schedule 1, paragraph 9, to the Act.

... So from the publication of the draft scheme to the actual construction of the stretch of motorway which is authorised the process is necessarily a long one in the course of which circumstances may alter and even government policy may change.

Where it is proposed that land should be acquired by a government department or local authority and works constructed on it for the benefit of the public either as a whole or in a particular locality, the holding of a public inquiry before the acquisition of the land and the construction of the works are authorised has formed a familiar part of the administrative process ever since authorisation by ministerial order of compulsory acquisition of land for public purposes began to be used to replace parliamentary authorisation by Private Bill procedure in the nineteenth century. The essential characteristics of a "local inquiry", an expression which when appearing in a statute has by now acquired a special meaning as a term of legal art, are that it is held in public in the locality in which the works that are the subject of the proposed scheme are situated by a person appointed by the Minister upon whom the statute has conferred the power in his administrative discretion to decide whether to confirm the scheme. The subject-matter of the inquiry is the objections to the proposed scheme that have been received by the Minister from local authorities and from private persons in the vicinity of the proposed stretch of motorway whose interests may be adversely affected, and in consequence of which he is required by Schedule 1, paragraph 9, to hold the inquiry. The purpose of the inquiry is to provide the Minister with as much information about those objections as will ensure that in reaching his decision he will have weighed the harm to local interests and private persons who may be adversely affected by the scheme against the public benefit which the scheme is likely to achieve and will not have failed to take into consideration any matters which he ought to have taken into consideration.

... The Highways Act 1959 being itself silent as to the procedure to be followed at the inquiry, that procedure, within such limits as are necessarily imposed by its qualifying for the description "local inquiry", must necessarily be left to the discretion of the Minister or the inspector appointed by him to hold the inquiry on his behalf, or partly to one and partly to the other. In exercising that discretion, as in exercising any other administrative function, they owe a constitutional duty to perform it fairly and honestly and to the best of their ability, as Lord Greene M.R. pointed out in his neglected but luminous analysis of the quasi-judicial and administrative functions of a Minister as confirming authority of a compulsory purchase order made by a local authority, which is to be found in *B. Johnson & Co. (Builders) Ltd v. Minister of Health* [1947] 2 All E.R. 395, 399–400. That judgment contains a salutary warning against applying to procedures involved in the making of administrative decisions concepts that are appropriate to the conduct of ordinary civil litigation between private parties. So rather than use such phrases as "natural justice" which may suggest that the prototype is only to be found in procedures followed by English courts of law, I prefer to put it that in the absence of any rules made under the Tribunals and Inquiries Act 1971, the only requirement of the Highways Act 1959, as to the procedure to be followed at a local inquiry held pursuant to Schedule 1, paragraph 9, is that it must be fair to all those who have an interest in the decision that will follow it whether they have been represented at the inquiry or not. What is a fair procedure to be adopted at a particular inquiry will depend upon the nature of its subject-matter.

What is fair procedure is to be judged not in the light of constitutional fictions as to the relationship between the Minister and the other servants of the Crown who serve in the government department of which he is the head, but in the light of the practical realities as to the way in which administrative decisions involving forming judgments based on technical considerations are reached. To treat the Minister in his decision-making capacity as someone separate and distinct from the department of government of which he is the political head and for whose actions he alone in constitutional theory is accountable to Parliament is to ignore not only practical realities but also Parliament's intention. Ministers come and go; departments, though their names may change from time to time, remain. Discretion in making administrative decisions is conferred upon a Minister not as an individual but as the holder of an office in which he will have available to him in arriving at his decision the collective knowledge, experience and expertise of all those who serve the Crown in the department of which, for the time being, he is the political head. The collective knowledge, technical as well as factual, of the civil servants in the department and their collective expertise is to be treated as the Minister's own knowledge, his own expertise. It is they who in reality will have prepared the draft scheme for his approval; it is they who will in the first instance consider the objections to the scheme and the report of the inspector by whom any local inquiry has been held and it is they who will give to the Minister the benefit of their combined experience, technical knowledge and expert opinion on all matters raised in the objections and the report. This is an integral part of the decision-making process itself; it is not to be equiparated with the Minister receiving evidence, expert opinion or advice from sources outside the department after the local inquiry has been closed. . . .

It is evident that an inquiry of this kind and magnitude is quite unlike any civil litigation and that the inspector conducting it must have a wide discretion as to the procedure to be followed in order to achieve its objectives. These are to enable him to ascertain the facts that are relevant to each of the objections, to understand the arguments for and against them and, if he feels qualified to do so, to weigh their respective merits, so that he may provide the Minister with a fair, accurate and adequate report on these matters.

Proceedings at a local inquiry at which many parties wish to make representations without incurring the expense of legal representation and cannot attend the inquiry throughout its length ought to be as informal as is consistent with achieving those objectives. To "over-judicialise" the inquiry by insisting on observance of the procedures of a court of justice which professional lawyers alone are competent to operate effectively in the interests of their clients would not be fair. It would, in my view, be quite fallacious to suppose that at an inquiry of this kind the only fair way of ascertaining matters of fact and expert opinion is by the oral testimony of witnesses who are subjected to cross-examination on behalf of parties who disagree with what they have said. Such procedure is peculiar to litigation conducted in courts that follow the common law system of procedure; it plays no part in the procedure of courts of justice under legal systems based upon the civil law, including the majority of our fellow Member States of the European Community; even in our own Admiralty Court it is not availed of for the purpose of ascertaining expert opinion on questions of navigation—the judge acquires information about this by private inquiry from assessors who are not subject to cross-examination by the parties. So refusal by an inspector to allow a party to cross-examine orally at a local inquiry a person who has made statements of facts or has expressed expert opinions is not unfair *per se.*

Whether fairness requires an inspector to permit a person who has made statements on matters of fact or opinion, whether expert or otherwise, to be cross-examined by a party to the inquiry who wishes to dispute a particular statement must depend on all the circumstances. In the instant case, the question arises in connection with expert opinion upon a technical matter. Here the relevant circumstances in considering whether fairness requires that cross-examination should be allowed include the nature of the topic upon which the opinion is expressed, the qualifications of the maker of the statement to deal with that topic, the forensic competence of the proposed cross-examiner, and, most important, the inspector's own views as to whether the likelihood that cross-examination will enable him to make a report which will be more useful to the Minister in reaching his decision than it otherwise would be is sufficient to justify any expense and inconvenience to other parties to the inquiry which would be caused by any resulting prolongation of it.

The circumstances in which the question of cross-examination arose in the instant case were the following. Before the inquiry opened each objector had received a document containing a statement of the Minister's reasons for proposing the draft scheme. It was itself a long and detailed document, and was accompanied by an even longer and more detailed one called "Strategic Studies Information", which gave an account of various traffic studies that had been undertaken between 1964 and 1973 in the area to be served by M42 Bromsgrove and M40 Warwick, the methodology used for those studies and the conclusions reached. The second paragraph of the Minister's statement of reasons said: "The Government's policy to build these new motorways" (*sc.* for which the two schemes provided) "will not be open to debate at the forthcoming inquiries [*sic*]: the Secretary of State is answerable to Parliament for this policy."

"Policy" as descriptive of departmental decisions to pursue a particular course of conduct is a protean word and much confusion in the instant case has, in my view, been caused by a failure to define the sense in which it can properly be used to describe a topic which is unsuitable to be the subject of an investigation as to its merits at an inquiry at which only persons with local interests affected by the scheme are entitled to be represented. A decision to construct a nationwide network of motorways is clearly one of government policy in the widest sense of the term. Any proposal to alter it is appropriate to be the subject of debate in Parliament, not of separate investigations in each of scores of local inquiries before individual inspectors up and down the country upon whatever material happens to be presented to them at the particular inquiry over which they preside. So much the respondents readily concede.

At the other extreme the selection of the exact line to be followed through a particular locality by a motorway designed to carry traffic between the destinations that it is intended to serve would not be described as involving government policy in the ordinary sense of that term. It affects particular local interests only and normally does not affect the interests of any wider section of the public, unless a suggested variation of the line would involve exorbitant expenditure of money raised by taxation. It is an appropriate subject for full investigation at a local inquiry and is one on which the inspector by whom the investigation is to be conducted can form a judgment on which to base a recommendation which deserves to carry weight with the Minister in reaching a final decision as to the line the motorway should follow.

Between the black and white of these two extremes, however, there is what my noble and learned friend, Lord Lane, in the course of the hearing described as a "grey area". Because of the time that must elapse between the preparation of any scheme and the completion of the stretch of motorway that it authorises, the department, in deciding in what order new stretches of the national network ought to be constructed, has adopted a uniform practice throughout the country of making a major factor in its decision the likelihood that there will be a traffic need for that particular stretch of motorway in 15 years from the date when the scheme was prepared. This is known as the "design year" of the scheme. Priorities as between one stretch of motorway and another have got to be determined somehow. Semasiologists may argue whether the adoption by the department of a uniform practice for doing this is most appropriately described as government policy or as something else. But the propriety of adopting it is clearly a matter fit to be debated in a wider forum and with the assistance of a wider range of relevant material than any investigation at an individual local inquiry is likely to provide; and in that sense at least, which is the relevant sense for present purposes, its adoption forms part of government policy.

The "need" for a new road to carry traffic between given destinations is an imprecise concept. If it is to be used as an important factor in comparing one situation with another for the purpose of determining priorities, there must be uniform criteria by which that need in each locality is to be measured. The test of future needs in the design year which the department has adopted is: whether, if the new stretch of motorway is not constructed, there will be undue congestion of traffic on existing roads, either in the locality or forming other parts of the national network of motorways, for which the new stretch of motorway would provide an alternative route. To apply this test of need to a design year 15 years ahead involves, among other things, estimating (1) the amount of traffic that the existing roads in the locality are capable of bearing without becoming so congested as to involve unacceptable delays; and (2) the amount of traffic that in the absence of the new stretch of motorway would in the design year be using those existing roads which the motorway is intended to relieve.

The methods used by the department for arriving at these estimates are very complicated. So far as I am capable of understanding them as one who is by now (I hope) a reasonably well-informed layman, it is obvious to me that no one who is not an expert in this esoteric subject could form a useful judgment as to their merits. The methods used are kept under periodical review by the department's own experts as a result of which they are revised from time to time. They are described in published documents. One which it will be necessary to mention dealt with the capacity of rural roads; but that which is most relevant to the respondents' complaint about refusal to permit cross-examination in the instant case has been referred to as the "Red Book". It was published in 1968 under the title *Traffic Prediction for Rural Roads (Advisory Manual on)* and described the method that had been used for predicting the growth of traffic up to the design year on the roads which the M42 Bromsgrove and M40 Warwick were intended to relieve. Important features of the method set out in the Red Book for predicting traffic that will be using the roads in a particular locality are the assumptions (1) that in general, traffic on rural roads throughout the country will grow at the same rate in all areas, except where exceptional changes can be foreseen as likely to take place in a particular locality; and (2) that the annual rate of growth will fall off as vehicle ownership in the country approaches saturation point; and that the best way of predicting what the growth will have been up to a particular design year is by assuming that it can be graphically represented by a curve that is asymptotic (*i.e.* broadly "S"-shaped) and whose shape where it represents future years can be extrapolated (*i.e.* predicted) from the shape of the curve which represents the observed annual increase in vehicle registrations over past years. It was recognised that predictions as applied to individual roads could only be very approximate and were subject to margins of error as high as 10 per cent to 20 per cent.

The decisions to make these two assumptions for the purpose of calculating and comparing what traffic needs will be in all localities throughout the country in which it is proposed to construct future stretches of the national network of motorway might not, in a general context, be most naturally described as being government policy; but if a decision to determine priorities in the construction of future stretches of the national network of motorways by reference to their respective traffic needs in a design year 15 years ahead can properly be described as government policy, as I think it can, the definition of "traffic needs" to be used for the purposes of applying the policy, *viz.* traffic needs as assessed by methods described in the Red Book and the departmental publication on the capacity of rural roads, may well be regarded as an essential element in the policy. But whether the uniform adoption of particular methods of assessment is described as policy or methodology, the merits of the methods adopted are, in my view, clearly not appropriate for investigation at individual local inquiries by an inspector whose consideration of the matter is necessarily limited by the material which happens to be presented to him at the particular inquiry which he is holding. It would be a rash inspector who based on that kind of material a positive recommendation to the Minister that the method of predicting traffic needs throughout the country should be changed and it would be an unwise Minister who acted in reliance on it.

At the local inquiry into the M42 Bromsgrove and the M40 Warwick, objectors including the respondents, whose property would be affected by the scheme, and the M42 Action Committee, a "pressure group" which supported them primarily upon environmental grounds, had studied in advance the Minister's reasons for the schemes, the "Strategic Studies Information" and the Red Book. They came to the inquiry prepared to criticise the methods used to predict the traffic needs in the design year on local roads in the localities of the M42 Bromsgrove and M40 Warwick and to call evidence of witnesses with professional qualifications to testify to their unreliability. The circumstances in which the inspector was induced to give an early ruling as to what evidence he would admit and what cross-examination he would allow are recounted in the speeches of my noble and learned friends. In the result— and when one is considering natural justice it is the result that matters—the objectors were allowed to voice their criticisms of the methods used to predict traffic needs for the purposes of the two schemes and to call such expert evidence as they wanted to in support of their criticisms. What they were not allowed to do was to cross-examine the department's representatives upon the reliability and statistical validity of the methods of traffic prediction described in the Red Book and applied by the department for the purpose of calculating and comparing traffic needs in all localities throughout the country. This is the only matter in relation to the conduct of the inquiry by the inspector of which complaint is made.

Was this unfair to the objectors? For the reasons I have already given and in full agreement with the minority judgment of Templeman L.J. in the Court of Appeal, I do not think it was. I think that the inspector was right in saying that the use of the concept of traffic needs in the design year *assessed by a particular method* as the yardstick by which to determine the order in which particular stretches of the national network of motorways should be constructed was government policy in the relevant sense of being a topic unsuitable for investigation by individual inspectors upon whatever material happens to be presented to them at local inquiries held throughout the country....

VISCOUNT DILHORNE: ... It is clear that the objectors at this inquiry had every opportunity of putting forward their case. An inspector at an inquiry has a wide discretion as to its conduct. He may, in my view, properly disallow a particular line of cross-examination if it is not likely to serve any useful purpose. An admission or expression of view in the course of cross-examination at a trial may well affect the result, but the views of departmental witnesses as to the comparative merits of different methods of forecasting traffic elicited in the course of cross-examination are not likely to affect the ultimate outcome.

In the lengthy and detailed report of the inspector the evidence of the expert witnesses called by objectors was faithfully recorded. It was there for the Secretary of State to see and consider, no doubt in the light of advice he received from the civil servants in his department. I cannot think that the expression of views at the inquiry by civil servants as to methods of forecasting traffic would have assisted him or have served any useful purpose.

In my opinion the inspector was fully entitled in the exercise of his discretion to refuse to allow that cross-examination and only if one treats proceedings at an inquiry as a trial—which they are not—can any ground be found for saying that in disallowing this cross-examination there was a denial of natural justice or unfairness. In my opinion there was not....

LORD EDMUND-DAVIES (dissenting): ... My Lords, for the present I defer considering whether the outcome of the inquiry would, or might have been, different had cross-examination been allowed. The topic now under consideration relates solely to the propriety of its refusal. I have natural diffidence in differing from your Lordships in regarding that refusal as clearly wrong, but such is my considered view. It is beyond doubt that the inspector could—and should—disallow questions relating to the merits of government policy. But matters of policy are matters which involve the exercise of political judgment, and matters of fact and expertise do not become "policy" merely because a department of government relies on them. And, as the Franks committee had put it in 1957: "We see no reason why the factual basis for a departmental view should not be explained and its validity tested in cross-examination." (*Report of the Committee on Administrative Tribunals and Inquiries* (Cmnd. 218), para. 316.)

Then, if the Red Book is not "government policy," on what basis can the cross-examination of departmental witnesses relying on its methodology be properly refused? Sir Douglas Frank Q.C. surprisingly asserted, 76 L.G.R. 460, 472–473 (a) that its *authors* "were the only persons competent to answer questions on it", and (b) that "it seems to me necessarily to follow that the inspector was entitled to disallow cross-examination on it of a person who had had nothing to do with its preparation". But expert witnesses frequently quote and rely upon the publications of others and are regularly cross-examined upon the works so relied upon even though they played no part in their preparation. Nor, my Lords, is it right to assume, as was suggested in the course of the inquiry and as some of your Lordships appear to accept, that Mr Brooks, the highly qualified and experienced traffic engineer, would have been incompetent to deal in cross-examination with questions directed to establishing the unreliability of the Red Book methodology upon which he himself heavily relied, albeit not without some emendations. Indeed, in paragraph 567 of this report the inspector described the witness as "thoroughly competent".

Pausing there, I conclude that the grounds hitherto considered for refusing cross-examination are unacceptable. But is it the case that, in an inquiry such as that with which this House is presently concerned, some special rule prevails which renders regular a procedure which in other circumstances would undoubtedly have been condemned as irregular? The general law may, I think, be summarised in this way: (a) In holding an administrative inquiry (such as that presently being considered), the inspector was performing quasi-judicial duties. (b) He must therefore discharge them in accordance with the rules of natural justice. (c) Natural justice requires that objectors (no less than departmental representatives) be allowed to cross-examine witnesses called for the other side on all relevant matters, be they matters of fact or matters of expert opinion. (d) In the exercise of jurisdiction outside the field of criminal law, the only restrictions on cross-examination are those general and well-defined exclusionary rules which govern the admissibility of relevant evidence (as to which reference may conveniently be had to *Cross on Evidence*, (5th ed., 1979), p. 17); beyond those restrictions there is *no* discretion on the civil side to exclude cross-examination on relevant matters.

There is ample authority for the view that, as Professor H.W.R. Wade Q.C. puts it (*Administrative Law* (4th ed., 1977), p. 418): "... it is once again quite clear that the principles of natural justice apply to administrative acts generally." And there is a massive body of accepted decisions establishing that natural justice requires that a party be given an opportunity of challenging by cross-examination witnesses called by another party on relevant issues; see, for example, *Marriott v. Minister of Health* (1935) 52 T.L.R. 63, *per* Swift J., at 67—compulsory purchase orders inquiry; *Errington v. Minister of Health* [1935] 1 K.B. 249, *per* Maugham L.J., at 272—clearance order; *R. v. Deputy Industrial Injuries Commissioner, ex p. Moore* [1965] 1 Q.B. 465, *per* Diplock L.J., at 488A, 490E–G; and *Wednesbury Corporation v. Ministry of Housing and Local Government (No. 2)* [1966] 2 Q.B. 275, *per* Diplock L.J., at 302G–303A—local government inquiry.

Then is there any reason why those general rules should have been departed from in the present case? We have already seen that the parameters of the inquiry, as agreed to by the department representatives, embraced *need* as a topic relevant to be canvassed and reported upon. We have already considered the unacceptable submission that the Red Book was "government policy". And, while I am alive to the inconvenience of different inspectors arriving at different conclusions regarding different sections of a proposed trunk road, the risk of that happening cannot, in my judgment, have any bearing upon the question whether justice was done at this particular inquiry, which I have already explained was, in an important respect, unique of its kind.

There remains to be considered the wholly novel suggestion, which has found favour with your Lordships, that there is a "grey area"—existing, as I understand, somewhere between government policy (which admittedly may not be subjected to cross-examination) and the exact "line" of a section of a motorway (which may be)—and that in relation to topics falling within the "grey area" cross-examination is a matter of discretion. I find that suggestion to be too nebulous to be grasped. Furthermore, *why* such an area should exist has not been demonstrated—certainly not to my satisfaction—nor have its boundaries been defined, unlike those existing restrictions on cross-examination to which I have already referred. And I confess to abhorrence of the notion that any such area exists. For the present case demonstrates that its adoption is capable of resulting in an individual citizen denied justice nevertheless finding himself with no remedy to right the wrong done to him.

My Lords, it is for the foregoing reasons that I find myself driven to the conclusion that the refusal in the instant case to permit cross-examination on what, by common agreement, was evidence of cardinal importance was indefensible and unfair and, as such, a denial of natural justice....

LORD LANE: ... The objectors submit that by depriving them of the opportunity of cross-examining the department's witnesses as to how they came to the conclusion that the motorway was necessary the inspector in short did not accord them a fair hearing.

There can be no doubt that the obligation to hold an inquiry comprises the requirement that the inquiry should be fair. If the inquiry is not fair then there has been a "failure to comply" within the terms of paragraph 3 of Schedule 2 to the Act of 1959. If that failure has resulted in the objectors' interests being substantially prejudiced, then the court may quash the order....

It is clear that all the material was before the Secretary of State and his staff.

The only things missing were the replies which Mr Brooks might have made to questions put to him by the objectors and their representatives. I find it difficult to see how in the circumstances the inability to cross-examine can be described as unfair. There are some occasions when cross-examination may be vital, for example, when at trial a witness's accuracy of recollection or observation is in question. But this was not a trial, nor was the witness's accuracy being challenged. It was a local inquiry convened because there had been objections to proposals in respect of one stretch of a proposed motorway. The obligation on the Secretary of State under paragraph 10 of Schedule 1 to the Act of 1959 was simply to consider any objections which were not withdrawn and to consider the report of the person holding the inquiry before coming to his conclusion about the scheme. To say, as the objectors do, that because cross-examination would have been allowed at a trial it was wrong to disallow it here is to misunderstand the nature of the inquiry. The refusal of cross-examination did not *ipso facto* result in unfairness. If cross-examination had been permitted, the result would have been, as is apparent from the extract from the report I have quoted, an even lengthier hearing without any appreciable advantage. . . .

Appeal allowed.

Questions

How does Lord Diplock's elaboration of the concept of "policy" differ from that articulated by Lord Edmund-Davies? Is it significant that Lord Diplock subjects local inquiries to the requirements of "fairness", whereas Lord Edmund-Davies applies the rules of natural justice to the holding of such inquiries?

Notes

1. For a fuller consideration of inquiries see above, Chapter 2(C).

2. The statutory provisions regulating highway inquiries are now contained in the Highways Act 1980 and the Highways (Inquiries Procedure) Rules 1994, S.I. 1994 No. 3263.

3. Professor Jackson concludes:

"Dicta abound for, and against the view that natural justice (or fairness) requires a right to cross-examine. To take them out of context as authority for an absolute rule is misleading. *Bushell* demonstrates, in an unusually full discussion of the problem, that the answer depends on a number of factors including the purpose of the hearing, the issue involved, the nature of the evidence" ((1980) 96 L.Q.R. 497).

4. Giving the opinion of the Privy Council, Lord Diplock stated that in the context of a New Zealand Royal Commission (a body analogous to a Tribunal of Inquiry in the United Kingdom):

"The technical rules of evidence applicable to civil or criminal litigation form no part of the rules of natural justice. What is required . . . is that the decision to make the finding must be based upon *some* material that tends logically to show the existence of facts consistent with the finding and that the reasoning supportive of the finding, if it be disclosed, is not logically self-contradictory"

(*Mahon v. Air New Zealand Ltd and Others* [1984] A.C. 808 at 821).

(4) Can a breach of the right to a fair hearing be cured by a later rehearing or appeal?

CALVIN v. CARR AND OTHERS

[1980] A.C. 574; [1979] 2 All E.R. 440 (Privy Council)

The appellant was the part-owner of a racehorse which competed in a race organised under the auspices of the Australian Jockey Club. The horse did not run as well as expected and his performance was subject to a stewards' inquiry. The stewards interviewed, *inter alios*, the jockey, the trainer and the appellant. They also saw film of the horse running in other races. 13 days after the race, the stewards determined that the jockey was guilty of an offence under the Club's Rules of Racing (namely not running a horse on its merits) and that the appellant was a party to that breach. They disqualified the appellant from membership of the Club for one year, which prevented him from entering any horse in a race organised by the Club for that period. The appellant exercised his right, under the Rules, to appeal against the stewards' decision to a committee of the Club. Before the committee he was represented by counsel and had full opportunity to call witnesses and subject others to cross-examination. The committee dismissed his appeal. The appellant then brought an action in the Supreme Court of New South Wales for a declaration that his disqualification from the Club was unlawful and an injunction to restrain the Club from acting on the purported disqualification. The major argument advanced by the appellant was that the stewards had acted in breach of the right to a fair hearing, consequently their decision was invalid, and this defect could not be cured by a lawful hearing before the appellate committee. The action was dismissed by the Australian court, so the appellant brought this appeal before the Privy Council.

LORD WILBERFORCE: ... The plaintiff's second argument can be stated, for purposes of description, as being that such defects of natural justice as may have existed as regards the proceedings before the stewards were not capable of being cured by the appeal proceedings before the committee, even though, as was not contested before this Board, these were correctly and fairly conducted. The defendants contend the contrary. This part of the argument involved consideration of a wide range of authorities of this Board, and in Australia, Canada, England and New Zealand. As regards decisions of this Board a conflict was said to exist between *Annamunthodo v. Oilfields Workers' Trade Union* [1961] A.C. 945 and *Pillai v. Singapore City Council* [1968] 1 W.L.R. 1278, each of which has been followed by other decisions. There was also said to be a conflict between *Annamunthodo's* case, and the High Court in *Australian Workers' Union v. Bowen* (No. 2) (1948) 77 C.L.R. 601, a conflict giving rise to difficulties for Australian state courts. Other individual decisions were cited which it appears difficult to reconcile.

Although, as will appear, some of the suggested inconsistencies of decisions disappear, or at least diminish, on analysis, their Lordships recognise and indeed assert that no clear and absolute rule can be laid down on the question whether defects in natural justice appearing at an original hearing, whether administrative or quasi-judicial, can be "cured" through appeal proceedings. The situations in which this issue arises are too diverse, and the rules by which they are governed so various, that this must be so. There are, however, a number of typical situations as to which some general principle can be stated. First there are cases where the rules provide for a rehearing by the original body, or some fuller or enlarged form of it. This situation may be found in relation to social clubs. It is not difficult in such cases to reach the conclusion that the first hearing is superseded by the second, or, putting it in contractual terms, the parties are taken to have agreed to accept the decision of the hearing body, whether original or adjourned. Examples of this are *De Verteuil v. Knaggs* [1918] A.C. 557, 563; *Posluns v. Toronto Stock Exchange and Gardiner* (1965) 53 D.L.R. (2d) 193; *Re Clark and Ontario Securities Commission* (1966) 56 D.L.R. (2d) 585; *Re Chromex Nickel Mines Ltd* (1970) 16 D.L.R. (3d) 273; and see also *Ridge v. Baldwin* [1964] A.C. 40, 79, *per* Lord Reid.

At the other extreme are cases, where, after examination of the whole hearing structure, in the context of the particular activity to which it relates (trade union membership, planning, employment, etc.) the conclusion is reached that a complainant has the right to nothing less than a fair hearing both at the original and at the appeal stage. This was the result reached by Megarry J. in *Leary v. National Union of Vehicle Builders* [1971] Ch. 34. In his judgment in that case the judge seems to have elevated the conclusion thought proper in that case into a rule of general application. In an eloquent passage he said, at 49:

> "If the rules and the law combine to give the member the right to a fair trial and the right of appeal, why should he be told that he ought to be satisfied with an unjust trial and a fair appeal? ... As a general rule ... I hold that a failure of natural justice in the trial body cannot be cured by a sufficiency of natural justice in an appellate body."

In their Lordships' opinion this is too broadly stated. It affirms a principle which may be found correct in a category of cases: these may very well include trade union cases, where movement solidarity and dislike of the rebel, or renegade, may make it difficult for appeals to be conducted in an atmosphere of detached impartiality and so make a fair trial at the first—probably branch—level an essential condition of justice. But to seek to apply it generally overlooks, in their Lordships' respectful opinion, both the existence of the first category, and the possibility that, intermediately, the conclusion to be reached, on the rules and on the contractual context, is that those who have joined in an organisation, or contract, should be taken to have agreed to accept what in the end is a fair decision, notwithstanding some initial defect.

In their Lordship's judgment such intermediate cases exist. In them it is for the court, in the light of the agreements made, and in addition having regard to the course of proceedings, to decide whether, at the end of the day, there has been a fair result, reached by fair methods, such as the parties should fairly be taken to have accepted when they joined the association. Naturally there may be instances when the defect is so flagrant, the consequences so severe, that the most perfect of appeals or rehearings will not be sufficient to produce a just result. Many rules (including those now in question) anticipate that such a situation may arise by giving power to remit for a new hearing. There may also be cases when the appeal process is itself less than perfect: it may be vitiated by the same defect as the original proceedings: or short of that there may be doubts whether the appeal body embarked on its task without predisposition or whether it had the means to make a fair and full inquiry, for example where it has no material but a transcript of what was before the original body. In such cases it would no doubt be right to quash the original decision. These are all matters (and no doubt there are others) which the court must consider. Whether these intermediate cases are to be regarded as exceptions from a general rule, as stated by Megarry J., or as a parallel category covered by a rule of equal status, is not in their Lordships' judgment necessary to state, or indeed a matter of great importance. What is important is the recognition that such cases exist, and that it is undesirable in many cases of domestic disputes, particularly in which an inquiry and appeal process has been established, to introduce too great a measure of formal judicialisation. While flagrant cases of injustice, including corruption or bias, must always be firmly dealt with by the courts, the tendency in their Lordships' opinion in matters of domestic disputes should be to leave these to be settled by the agreed methods without requiring the formalities of judicial processes to be introduced....

It remains to apply the principles above stated to the facts of the present case. In the first place, their Lordships are clearly of the view that the proceedings before the committee were in the nature of an appeal, not by way of an invocation, or use, of whatever original jurisdiction the committee may have had....

In addition to these formal requirements, a reviewing court must take account of the reality behind them. Races are run at short intervals; bets must be disposed of according to the result. Stewards are there in order to take rapid decisions as to such matters as the running of horses, being entitled to use the evidence of their eyes and their experience. As well as acting inquisitorially at the stage of deciding the result of a race, they may have to consider disciplinary action: at this point rules of natural justice become relevant. These require, at the least, that persons should be formally charged, heard in their own defence, and know the evidence against them. These essentials must always be observed but it is inevitable, and must be taken to be accepted, that there may not be time for procedural refinements. It is in order to enable decisions reached in this way to be reviewed at leisure that the appeal procedure exists. Those concerned know that they are entitled to a full hearing with opportunities to bring evidence and have it heard. But they know also that this appeal hearing is governed by the Rules of Racing, and that it remains an essentially domestic proceeding, in which experience and opinions as to what is in the interest of racing as a whole play a large part, and in which the standards are those which have come to be accepted over the history of this sporting activity. All those who partake in it have accepted the Rules of Racing, and the standards which lie behind them: they must also have accepted to be bound by the decisions of the bodies set up under those rules so long as when the process of reaching these decisions has been terminated, they can be said, by an objective observer, to have had fair treatment and consideration of their case on its merits.

In their Lordships' opinion precisely this can, indeed must, be said of the present case. The plaintiff's case has received, overall, full and fair consideration, and a decision, possibly a hard one, reached against him. There is no basis on which the court ought to interfere, and his appeal must fail....

Appeal dismissed.

Notes

1. Elliott considers that the most significant aspect of this judgment was "the way it eschews statements of abstract principle". Instead, he approves of Lord Wilberforce's pragmatic attitude towards the tailoring of procedural obligations to different decision-making contexts. But, Elliott wonders whether "an administrative law adversarial action before judges with necessarily limited knowledge may not be the best place to assess the procedures that particular situations require ...": M. Elliott, "Appeals, Principles and Pragmatism in Natural Justice" (1980) 43 M.L.R. 66.

Do the views of Elliott represent a fundamental attack upon the process of procedural review undertaken by the courts? What other institutions might be better suited to this task?

2. Although *Calvin v. Carr* concerns the decision of a sporting body, it is clear that the principles stated by Lord Wilberforce may apply to administrative bodies exercising statutory powers. See *R. v. Oxfordshire Local Valuation Panel, ex p. Oxford City Council* (1981) 79 L.G.R. 432; the Court of Appeal decision in *Lloyd v. McMahon* [1987] A.C. at 655, 669 (above, p. 487); *cf. R. v. Brent London Borough Council, ex p. Gunning* (1985) 84 L.G.R. 168 (above, p. 466). In *ex p. Gunning* it was argued that any defects in the local council's consultation process could be cured by the procedure in the Education Act 1980, s.12(3), (4) and (6), under which objections could be made to the Secretary of State. Hodgson J. doubted whether the principles of fairness "developed in the quasi-judicial field of domestic disciplinary proceedings", could apply to "purely administrative procedures of the sort with which we are concerned". If he was wrong on that, he expressed a preference for the approach of Megarry J. in *Leary v. National Union of Vehicle Builders* [1971] Ch. 34, 49 (cited by Lord Wilberforce in *Calvin v. Carr*, above, p. 507), and the approach of the Privy Council in *Calvin v. Carr* itself (see at 192–193). Here:

"in any event, in the circumstances of this case, the statutory procedures are themselves fatally flawed by the inadequacies of the previous consultation." (at 193).

3. In the context of criminal cases determined by magistrates' courts a procedurally unfair conviction can be cured by a fair appeal, involving a complete rehearing, before the Crown court. Turner L.J. held that; "in the field of criminal law, their Lordships knew of no principle, let alone authority, to suggest that a person was entitled to more than one fair trial". However, following *Calvin v. Carr*, other considerations might apply when examining the effect of appeals within domestic or specialist tribunal systems. See *R. v. Peterborough JJ., ex p. Dowler, The Times*, 3 May, 1996. In the subsequent High Court case of *R. v. Hereford Magistrates' Court, ex p. Rowlands, The Times*, February 17, 1997, Lord Bingham L.C.J. emphasised that a defendant's right to fairness was stronger in criminal proceedings before magistrates than in administrative or domestic tribunals.

"It was not doubted that *Dowler* was correctly decided but the decision was not to be treated as authority that a party complaining of procedural unfairness or bias in the magistrates' court should be denied leave to move for judicial review and left to whatever rights he might have in the crown court."

(5) Does fairness require the decision-maker to give reasons?

DOODY v. SECRETARY OF STATE FOR THE HOME DEPARTMENT AND OTHER APPEALS

[1994] 1 A.C. 531; [1993] 3 All E.R. 92 (House of Lords)

The respondents, Doody and three others, were prisoners who had been convicted of murder and sentenced to a mandatory term of life imprisonment. After consulting the trial judge and the Lord Chief Justice, the Home Secretary (or another Minister at the Home Office) determined the period of imprisonment (the tariff or penal element) that the respondents should serve before the Parole Board would consider whether to recommend, to the Home Secretary, that the prisoner could be released on life licence. The respondents sought judicial review of the Home Secretary's decisions regarding the penal elements of their sentences on the ground that he had followed an unfair procedure. One significant element in the respondents' challenge was their argument that fairness required the Home Secretary to give reasons where he decided to impose a different penalty element from that recommended by the judiciary. The High Court dismissed the application, but on appeal the Court of Appeal decided in part in favour of the respondents. The Home Secretary appealed to the House of Lords.

LORD MUSTILL: My Lords, the sentencing of a convicted murderer according to English law is a unique formality. Although it is a very grave occasion it is a formality in this sense, that the task of the judge is entirely mechanical. Once a verdict of guilty is returned the outcome is preordained. No matter what the opinion of the judge on the moral quality of the act, no matter what circumstances there may be of mitigation or aggravation, there is only one course for him to take, namely to pass a sentence of life imprisonment.

This purely formal character of the sentencing proces is unique in more than one respect. Thus, whilst it is true that there are other, comparatively unimportant, offences where a particular sentence, or component of a sentence, is prescribed by law, there is in practice no other offence besides murder for which a custodial sentence is mandatory. This singularity is not to be accounted for by the fact that the crime has resulted in the death of the victim, since although the offence of manslaughter carries a maximum penalty of life imprisonment the sentence is discretionary and the maximum is rarely imposed; and other offences in which the death of the victim is an element are subject to maximum fixed terms. Nor can the uniqueness of the mandatory sentence of murder be ascribed to the uniquely wicked quality of the intent which accompanies the fatal act, since as every law student knows, although many who speak in public on the subject appear to overlook, it is possible to commit murder without intending to kill, and many of those convicted of murder have intended to do no more than commit grievous bodily harm, In truth the mandatory life sentence for murder is symbolic.

The sentence of life imprisonment is also unique in that the words which the judge is required to pronounce do not mean what they say. Whilst in a very small minority of cases the prisoner is in the event confined for the rest of his natural life, this is not the usual or the intended effect of a sentence of life imprisonment, as a judge faced with a hard case will take pains to explain to the offender before sentence is passed. But although everyone knows what the words do not mean, nobody knows what they do mean, since the duration of the prisoner's detention depends on a series of recommendations to, and executive decisions by, the Home Secretary, some made at an early stage and others much later, none of which can be accurately forecast at the time when the offender is sent to prison.

There is, however, another form of life sentence, of which the philosophy, statutory framework and executive practice are quite different even though the words pronounced by the judge are the same. This is the discretionary life sentence. . . .

The discretionary life sentence may thus be regarded as the sum of two sentences, to be served consecutively. First, a determinate number of years appropriate to the nature and gravity of the offence. This is often called the "tariff" element of the sentence. For my part, although I recognise that this is not inappropriate in the context of a discretionary life sentence, I consider that for reasons which I will later develop it is illogical and misleading when the usage is transferred to a mandatory sentence. I therefore prefer to avoid this terminology and will instead call the first component of the life sentence the "penal element". The second component is an undeterminate period, which the offender begins to serve when the penal element is exhausted. I will call this the "risk element". . . .

My Lords, I believe that this summary has shown how, in contrast with the position as regards discretionary life sentences, the theory and the practice for convicted murderers are out of tune. The theory—and it is the only theory which can justify the retention of the mandatory life sentence—was restated by Mrs Rumbold[4] less than two years ago. It posits that murder is an offence so grave that the proper "tariff" sentence is invariably detention for life, although as a measure of leniency it may be mitigated by release on licence. Yet the practice established by Mr Brittan[5] in 1983 and still in force founds on the proposition that there is concealed within the life term a fixed period of years, apt to reflect not only the requirements of deterrence, but also the moral quality of the individual act (retribution). These two philosophies of sentencing are inconsistent. Either may be defensible, but they cannot both be applied at the same time.

I make this point, not to argue for one regime rather than another, nor to suggest that each of them is unsatisfactory. This is a question for Parliament and we must take the law as it stands. The importance of the inconsistency for present purposes is that the choice of the theory goes a long way towards determining the requirements of fairness with which the practice should conform. . . .

For this reason I believe it impossible to proceed any distance towards determining the present appeal without deciding which of the two competing philosophies is to form the starting point. As it seems to me, the only possible choice is the regime installed by Mr Brittan, as later modified. This is the regime by which successive Home Secretaries have chosen to exercise the wide powers conferred by Parliament, and the arguments have throughout assumed that the regime is firmly in place, and that the task of the courts is to decide what the elements of fairness demand as to the working out of that regime, in the light of the sentencing philosophy which is expressed to underlie it. This being so, I think it essential not to cloud the discussion by introducing the inconsistent theory enunciated by the Minister of State, and I shall leave this entirely out of account. . . .

What does fairness require in the present case? My Lords, I think it unnecessary to refer by name or to quote from, any of the often-cited authorities in which the courts have explained what is essentially an intuitive judgment. They are far too well known. From them, I derive the following. (1) Where an Act of Parliament confers an administrative power there is a

---

[4] Minister of State at the Home Office in 1991 (ed.).
[5] Home Secretary in 1983 (ed.).

presumption that it will be exercised in a manner which is fair in all the circumstances. (2) The standards of fairness are not immutable. They may change with the passage of time, both in the general and in their application to decisions of a particular type. (3) The principles of fairness are not to be applied by rote identically in every situation. What fairness demands is dependent on the context of the decision, and this is to be taken into account in all its aspects. (4) An essential feature of the context is the statute which creates the discretion, as regards both its language and the shape of the legal and administrative system within which the decision is taken. (5) Fairness will very often require that a person who may be adversely affected by the decision will have an opportunity to make representations on his own behalf either before the decision is taken with a view to producing a favourable result, or after it is taken, with a view to procuring its modification, or both. (6) Since the person affected usually cannot make worthwhile representations without knowing what factors may weigh against his interests fairness will very often require that he is informed of the gist of the case which he has to answer.

My Lords, the Secretary of State properly accepts that whatever the position may have been in the past these principles apply in their generality to prisoners, including persons serving life sentences for murder, although their particular situation and the particular statutory regime under which they are detained may require the principles to be applied in a special way. Convesely, the respondents acknowledge that it is not enough for them to persuade the court that some procedure other than the one adopted by the decision-maker would be better or more fair. Rather, they must show that the procedure is actually unfair. The court must constantly bear in mind that it is to the decision-maker, not the court, that Parliament has entrusted not only the making of the decision but also the choice as to how the decision is made.

I accept without hesitation, and mention it only to avoid misunderstanding, that the law does not at present recognise a general duty to give reasons for an administrative decision. Nevertheless, it is equally beyond question that such a duty may in appropriate circumstances be implied, and I agree with the analyses by the Court of Appeal in *R. v. Civil Service Appeal Board, ex p. Cunningham* [1991] 4 All E.R. 310 of the factors which will often be material to such an implication.

Turning to the present dispute I doubt the wisdom of discussing the problem in the contempoary vocabulary of "prisoner's rights", given that as a result of his own act the position of the prisoner is so forcibly distanced from that of the ordinary citizen, nor is it very helpful to say that the Home Secretary should out of simple humanity provide reasons for the prisoner, since any society which operates a penal system is bound to treat some of its citizens in a way which would, in the general, be thought inhumane. I prefer simply to assert that within the inevitable constraints imposed by the statutory framework, the general shape of the administrative regime which ministers have lawfully built around it, and the imperatives of the public interest, the Secretary of State ought to implement the scheme as fairly as he can. The giving of reasons may be inconvenient, but I can see no ground at all why it should be against the public interest: indeed, rather the reverse. This being so, I would ask simply: is a refusal to give reasons fair? I would answer without hesitation that it is not. As soon as the jury returns its verdict the offender knows that he will be locked up for a very long time. For just how long immediately becomes the most important thing in the prisoner's life. When looking at statistics it is easy to fall into the way of thinking that there is not really very much difference between one extremely long sentence and another: and there may not be, in percentage terms. But the percentage reflects a difference of a year or years: a long time for anybody, and longer still for a prisoner. Where a defendant is convicted of, say, several armed robberies he knows that he faces a stiff sentence: he can be advised by reference to a public tariff of the range of sentences he must expect; he hears counsel address the judge on the relationship between his offences and the tariff; he will often hear the judge give an indication during exchanges with counsel of how his mind is working; and when sentence is pronounced he will always be told the reasons for it. So also when a discretionary life sentence is imposed, coupled with an order under s.34. Contrast this with the position of the prisoner sentenced for murder. He never sees the Home Secretary; he has no dialogue with him: he cannot fathom how his mind is working. There is no true tariff, or at least no tariff exposed to public view which might give the prisoner an idea of what to expect. The announcement of his first review date arrives out of thin air, wholly without explanation. The distant oracle has spoken, and that is that.

My Lords, I am not aware that there still exists anywhere else in the penal system a procedure remotely resembling this. The beginnings of an explanation for its unique character might perhaps be found if the Executive had still been putting into practice the theory that the tariff sentence for murder is confinement for life, subject only to a wholly discretionary release on licence: although even in such a case I doubt whether in the modern climate of administrative law such an entirely secret process could be justified. As I hope to have shown, however, this is no longer the practice, and can hardly be sustained any longer as the theory. I therefore simply ask, is it fair that the mandatory life prisoner should be wholly deprived of the information which all other prisoners receive as a matter of course. I am clearly of the opinion that it is not.

My Lords, I can moreover arrive at the same conclusion by a different and more familiar route, of which *ex p. Cunningham* [1991] 4 All E.R. 310 provides a recent example. It is not, as I understand it, questioned that the decision of the Home Secretary on the penal element is susceptible to judicial review. To mount an effective attack on the decision, given no more material than the facts of the offence and the length of the penal element, the prisoner has virtually no means of ascertaining whether this is an instance where the decision-making process has gone astray. I think it important that there should be an effective means of detecting the kind of error which would entitle the court to intervene, and in practice I regard it as necessary for this purpose that the reasoning of the Home Secretary should be disclosed. If there is any difference between the penal element recommended by the judges and actually imposed by the Home Secretary, this reasoning is bound to include, either explicitly or implicitly, a reason why the Home Secretary has taken a different view. Accordingly, I consider that the respondents are entitled to an affirmative answer on the third issue. . . .

"It is declared that: (1) The Secretary of State is required to afford to a prisoner serving a mandatory life sentence the opportunity to submit in writing representations as to the period he should serve for the purposes of retribution and deterrence before the Secretary of State sets the date of the first review of the prisoner's sentence. (2) Before giving the prisoner the opportunity to make such representations, the Secretary of State is required to inform him of the period recommended by the judiciary as the period he should serve for the purposes of retribution and deterrence, and of any other opinion expressed by the judiciary which is relevant to the Secretary of State's decision as to the appropriate period to be served for these purposes. (3) Secretary of State is obliged to give reasons for departing from the period recommended by the judiciary as the period which he should serve for the purposes of retribution and deterrence."

LORDS KEITH, LANE, TEMPLEMAN and BROWNE-WILKINSON agreed with the speech given by Lord Mustill.

Appeal dismissed. Cross-appeal allowed in part and further declaration granted.

Notes

1. Whilst the House of Lords was not willing in *Doody* to impose a general duty on all administrative decision-makers to give reasons for their decisions (presumably because such a requirement might be seen as a judicial usurpation of Parliament's legislative function; and the public administration costs could outweigh the benefits to the public), the judgment represents a watershed in the judicial attitude towards the giving of reasons by public persons and bodies. As Lord Mustill noted in the above case, "I find in the more recent cases on judicial review a perceptible trend towards an insistence on greater openness, or if one prefers the contemporary jargon 'transparency', in the making of administrative decisions" (at 561). By recognising that in certain decision-making contexts fairness necessitated the giving of reasons, their Lordships have opened up the possibility for the lower courts to apply the *Doody* principle in other areas of administration. For commentaries see A.R. Mowbray (1994) *Journal of Forensic Psychiatry* 137 and N.R. Campbell [1994] P.L. 184.

2. The High Court elaborated upon the extent of the duty to give reasons in *R. v. Higher Education Funding Council, ex p. Institute of Dental Surgery* [1994] 1 All E.R. 651. There the applicant Institute had its research output assessed by the Funding Council. The Council awarded a lower grade to the Institute's work, compared with the previous grade allocated. As a consequence of this lower grade, the Institute received £270,000 less in research funds from the Council. The Council refused to give any reasons for the lower grade as it considered that the assessment had been made by a peer group of experts using their collective professional judgment. The applicant sought judicial review of the assessment decision, claiming that it violated the concept of fairness in that reasons had not been given for the decision. The judgment of the Divisional Court (Mann L.J. and Sedley J.) was delivered by Sedley J.:

"... each case will come to rest between two poles, or possibly at one of them: the decision which cries out for reasons, and the decision for which reasons are entirely inapposite. Somewhere between the two poles comes the dividing line separating those cases in which the balance of factors calls for reasons from those where it does not. At present there is no sure indication of where the division comes. . . . No doubt the common law will develop, as the common law does, case by case. It is not entirely satisfactory that this should be so, not least because experience suggests that in the absence of a prior principle irreconcilable or inconsistent decisions will emerge. But from the tenor of the decisions principles will come, and if the common law's pragmatism has a virtue it is that these principles are likely to be robust. At present, however, this court cannot go beyond the proposition that, there being no general obligation to give reasons, there will be decisions for which fairness does not demand reasons" (at 666).

Following on from *Doody* his Lordship concluded that:

"(1) There is no general duty to give reasons for a decision, but there are classes of case where there is such a duty. (2) One such class is where the subject matter is an interest so highly regarded by the law—for example personal liberty—that fairness requires that reasons, at least for particular decisions, be given as of right. (3)(a) Another such class is where the decision appears aberrant. Here fairness may require reasons so that the recipient may know whether the aberration is in the legal sense real (and so challengeable) or apparent. (b) It follows that this class does not include decisions which are themselves challengeable by reference only to the reasons for them. A pure exercise of academic judgment is such a decision" (at 672–673).

Consequently, the application was dismissed. From this judgment we can see the court beginning the refinement of *Doody* by starting to explain the different situations where fairness does require the provision of reasons for decisions.

3. In *R. v. The Mayor and Commonalty and Citizens of the City of London and Another, ex p. Matson*, *The Times*, October 20, 1995, the Court of Appeal held that the Court of Aldermen was required by fairness to give reasons for its decision to refuse to accept Mr Matson's election as an Alderman of the City. Matson had been elected by 54 votes to 15, but by virtue of ancient custom his election was subject to approval by the Court of Aldermen. He appeared before the Court of Aldermen and was subject to "somewhat hostile" questioning about his career and alleged support for another person in a separate contest for a council seat. By a secret ballot the Court of Aldermen refused to endorse Matson by 17 votes to 1. No reasons were given for the decision. Neill L.J. considered that Matson's election to a public office, the fact that the Court of Aldermen was a court of record, and the effect on Matson's reputation of his rejection by the Court of Aldermen, were factors which meant that fairness required the provision of reasons by the latter body. Swinton-Thomas L.J. also noted the nature of the office concerned, the effect on Matson's reputation and the absence of justification for the Court of Aldermen's refusal to give reasons. Waite L.J. agreed with the judgments of his brethren. These factors suggest that the courts are engaged in a balancing exercise when determining if reasons are required in a particular decision-making context. For a commentary upon this case which is critical of the Court of Appeal's reasoning, see R. Thomas [1996] 1 Web JCLI.

4. Fairness did not require a local authority to provide reasons for its decision to refuse an application for a housing renovation grant: *R. v. Bristol County Council, ex p. Bailey and Another* (1994) 27 H.L.R. 307.

5. The Home Secretary is obliged to give reasons, because of fairness, where he refuses entry clearance for an alien to enter the United Kingdom on the ground that entry would not be conducive to the public good. Sedley J. considered that this requirement was especially relevant in the context of an application for leave to enter the United Kingdom made by an unpopular person. The judgment was given in the case of the "Rev." Sun Myung Moon, the Korean leader of "the Unification Church" (frequently called the "Moonies" by the media): *R. v. Secretary of State for the Home Department, ex p. Moon*, *The Times*, December 8, 1995. This decision would appear to fall within Sedley J.'s class of cases involving highly regarded interests; see *Institute of Dental Surgery* (above). In *R. v. Secretary of State for the Home Department, ex p. Mohammed Al Fayed*, *The Times*, November 18, 1996, Lord Woolf M.R. similarly concluded that, in principle, the decision to refuse an application for naturalisation (as a British citizen) was subject to a duty to give reasons. However, that common law requirement was overridden by s.44(2) of the British Nationality Act 1981, which

expressly stated that the Home Secretary was not obliged to supply reasons for such decisions.

6. There is no general duty on local planning authorities to give reasons for granting planning permission, neither is there such a duty when an authority changes its mind and grants permission after an earlier refusal: *R. v. Aylesbury Vale District Council and Another, ex p. Chaplin and others, The Times*, July 23, 1996.

7. Where fairness requires the provision of reasons the courts will also examine the adequacy of any reasons given by the decision-maker. The Court of Appeal has stated that: "the question the court has to decide, therefore, is whether the reasons in fact given by the minister enable the reader to know what conclusions he has reached on the principal important controversial issues" (*per* Brooke L.J. in *R. v. Secretary of State for Transport, ex p. Richmond upon Thames LBC and Others (No. 4)* [1996] 4 All E.R. 903 at 919). In that case it was held that the brief reasons given by the Secretary, for his promulgation of a statutory order imposing new night flight restrictions at London's major airports, were acceptable as they had been preceded by a detailed consultation paper. More generally on the adequacy of reasons see *Save Britain's Heritage* (above, p. 77) and Appeals, Chapter 9.

(ii) The Rule Against Bias or Interest

This rule (historically termed *nemo judex in causa sua potest*) has the objective of ensuring that decision-makers do not participate in decisions where they have a prohibited financial interest in the matter or where there is a real danger of bias on their part because of some other pre-existing connection with the issue (*e.g.* a friendship with one party to a legal dispute). As *de Smith, Woolf and Jowell* state: "the decision-maker should not be biased or prejudiced in a way that precludes fair and genuine consideration being given to the arguments advanced by the parties. Although perfect objectivity may be an unrealisable objective, the rule against bias thus aims at preventing a hearing from being a sham or a ritual or a mere exercise in 'symbolic reassurance', due to the fact that the decision-maker was not in practice persuadable" (p. 521).

The rule is primarily concerned with the appearance of regulated public decision-making. Thus, the courts take no account of the fact that a decision-maker with a direct pecuniary interest did not allow himself to be influenced by it in any way; such an interest disqualifies automatically. Also, it is generally easier to establish an improper appearance than actual impropriety. Confusion in the case law regarding the correct test to be applied by the courts when determining if apparent bias has been established (*i.e.* the existence of "a reasonable suspicion of bias" or "a real likelihood of bias": see the previous edition of this book at pp. 576–585) has now been resolved by the House of Lords in the momentous case of *R. v. Gough* (below).

Traditionally, the rule against bias or interest applied only to decision-making processes which the courts classified as "judicial" or "quasi-judicial" (see below: *Franklin v. Minister of Town and Country Planning* and *R. v. Kent Police Authority, ex p. Godden*). However, as we have seen above, the idea of procedural fairness has resulted in the extension of a right to a fair hearing being applied to a much broader range of decision-making. The recent judgment of the High Court in *R. v. Secretary of State for the Environment, ex p. Kirkstall Valley Campaign Ltd* (below) opens up the dramatic possibility of a similar extension in the ambit of the rule against bias or interest.

For general readings see: *Garner*, p. 242–250, *de Smith, Woolf and Jowell*, Chap. 12, *Craig*, Chap. 9, *Wade and Forsyth*, Chap. 14.

(a) *The rule against interest*

DIMES v. GRAND JUNCTION CANAL PROPRIETORS

(1852) 3 H.L.Cas. 759; 8 State Tr. N.S. 85; 19 L.T.O.S. 317; 17 Jur. 73; 10 E.R. 301 (House of Lords)

In 1796, the canal proprietors, a company incorporated under statute, purchased some land, part of which was used for the canal and tow-path. This land was the subject of litigation between the proprietors and Dimes, an attorney who was the Lord of the Manor, which dragged on from 1831 to 1852. In 1838, 1848 and 1850 Lord Chancellor Cottenham affirmed decrees made by the Vice-Chancellor in favour of the proprietors, including an injunction to restrain Dimes from obstructing the canal (for example, by throwing bricks into it), and an order subsequently committing him to prison for contempt in disobeying the injunction. In 1849, Dimes discovered that the Lord Chancellor had for over 10 years held several thousand pounds worth of shares in the canal company, some in his own right and the others as trustee. The Lord Chancellor continued to hear matters concerned with the litigation, relying on the advice of the Master of the Rolls with whom he sat. Dimes appealed to the House of Lords against all the decrees and orders made in the litigation. He was represented by the Solicitor-General and other counsel, who argued that the whole proceedings were void in that the Lord Chancellor was disqualified by interest, and that his incompetency affected his deputy, the Vice-Chancellor. On the other hand, it was accepted that the formal act of enrolling the order to enable an appeal to be brought to the House of Lords had to be performed by the Lord Chancellor: "The enrolment of this order is a matter of necessity, but it is also a matter of form, and is not an act which decides the case, but only enables the party to make the decision the subject of an appeal. The House cannot say to an appealing party who complains of the wrongful exercise of an unwarranted jurisdiction, that he cannot come here to make the complaint without getting the Lord Chancellor's signature, and yet, when he gets it, that he thereby admits the jurisdiction. That would be to make the wrong itself a reason for refusing the remedy." This was not to say that it was necessary for the Lord Chancellor to hear the main issues. "There might have been a bill of complaint addressed to the Sovereign in the High Court of Chancery, and it would have been referred to the Master of the Rolls. . . ." (3 H.L.Cas. at 770).

The House of Lords took the advice of the Judges:

Mr Baron Parke: In answer to the first question proposed by your Lordships, I have to state the unanimous opinion of the Judges, that, in the case suggested, the order or decree of the Lord Chancellor was not absolutely *void*, on account of his interest, but *voidable* only.

If this had been a proceeding in an inferior court, one to which a prohibition might go from a court in Westminster Hall, such a prohibition would be granted, pending the proceedings, upon an allegation that the presiding Judge of the court was interested in the suit: whether a prohibition could go to the Court of Chancery, it is unnecessary to consider.

If no prohibition should be applied for, and in cases where it could not be granted, the proper mode of taking the objection to the interest of the Judge would be, in courts of common law, by bringing a writ of error. . . .

The former course was stated to be proper in the case of *Brooks v. Earl of Rivers* (Hardr. 503), it being suggested that the Earl of Derby, who was

Chamberlain of Chester, had an interest in the suit; and the Court held that, where the Judge had an interest, neither he nor *his deputy* can determine a cause or sit in court; and if he does, a prohibition lies.

The latter course was adopted in the case of *The Company of Mercers and Ironmongers of Chester v. Bowker* (1 Stra. 639), where it was assigned for error in fact, on the record of a judgment for the Company of Mercers in the Mayor's Court at Chester, that after verdict, and before judgment, one of the Company of Mercers became mayor; and for that reason the judgment was reversed in the Court of Quarter Sessions, and that judgment of reversal affirmed in the King's Bench.

In neither of these cases was the judgment held to be absolutely void. Till prohibition had been granted in one case, or judgment reversed in the other, we think that the proceedings were valid, and the persons acting under the authority of the Court would not be liable to be treated as trespassers.

The many cases in which the Court of King's Bench has interfered (and may have gone to a great length), where interested parties have acted as magistrates, and quashed the orders made by the Court of which they formed part, afford an analogy.

None of these orders is absolutely void; it would create great confusion and inconsequence if it was. The objection might be one of which the parties acting under these orders might be totally ignorant till the moment of the trial of an action of trespass for the act done (see, with relation to this point, the observations of the Lord Chancellor in the case of *Scadding v. Lorant, ante,* at 447); but these orders may be quashed after being removed by *certiorari,* and the Court shall do complete justice in that respect.

We think that the order of the Chancellor is not void; but we are of opinion, that as he had an interest which would have disqualified a witness under the old law, he was disqualified as a Judge; that it was a voidable order, and might be questioned and set aside by appeal or some application to the Court of Chancery, if a prohibition would not lie.

[The Judges also advised that the Vice-Chancellor was not the mere deputy of the Lord Chancellor, but exercised an independent jurisdiction; that his decrees took effect unaffected by the Lord Chancellor's disqualification; and that as the latter's signature was required by statute for the enrolment of the decrees the disqualification did not affect that act.]

For this is a case of necessity, and where that occurs the objection of interest cannot prevail. Of this the case in the Year Book (Year Book, 8 Hen. 6, 19; 2 Roll. Abr. 93) is an instance, where it was held that it was no objection to the jurisdiction of the Common Pleas that an action was brought against all the Judges of the Common Pleas, in a case in doubt which could only be brought in that court....

[Their Lordships then heard arguments on the merits, in form acting as if on an appeal directly from the Vice-Chancellor. At its conclusion, their Lordships expressed their views on the disqualification issue.]

LORD ST LEONARDS L.C. and LORD BROUGHAM concurred in the opinion of the Judges, and said that it was proper to reverse the orders of Lord Cottenham L.C.

LORD CAMPBELL: I take exactly the same view of this case as do my noble and learned friends, and I have very little to add to their observations. With respect to the point upon which the learned Judges were consulted, I must say that I entirely concur in the advice which they have given to your Lordships. No one can suppose that Lord Cottenham could be, in the remotest degree, influenced by the interest that he had in this concern; but, my Lords, it is of the last importance that the maxim that no man is to be a judge in his own cause should be held sacred. And that is not to be confined to a cause in which he is a party, but applies to a cause in which he has an interest. Since I have had the honour to be Chief Justice of the Court of Queen's Bench, we have again and again set aside proceedings in inferior tribunals because an individual, who had an interest in a cause, took a part in the decision. And it will have a most salutary influence on these tribunals when it is known that this high Court of last resort, in a case in which the Lord Chancellor of England had an interest, considered that his decree was on that account a decree not according to law, and was set aside. This will be a lesson to all inferior tribunals to take care not only that in their decrees they are not influenced by their personal interest, but to avoid the appearance of labouring under such an influence....

[The Vice-Chancellor's decrees and orders were upheld on the merits.]

Notes

1. A pecuniary interest in order to disqualify may be trivial in amount, but it must not be "too remote". In *R. v. Rand* (1866) L.R. 1 Q.B. 230, Bradford Corporation were empowered by statute to take water flowing into Harden Beck. They could do so without the consent of the mill-owners on that beck, if they obtained first a justices' certificate that a certain reservoir was completed, of a given capacity, and filled with water. Two of the justices who granted this certificate were trustees of institutions which held Bradford corporation bonds. The Court of Queen's Bench held that these justices were not disqualified by interest, even though "the security of their *cestui que trusts* would be improved by anything improving the borough fund, and anything improving the waterworks ... would produce that effect". The two justices might have been disqualified by interest had they been "liable to costs, or to other pecuniary loss or gain" in consequence of being trustees (*per* Blackburn J. at 232).

2. In more recent times, the Court of Appeal (Criminal Division) has held that an Old Bailey judge who owned 1,600 shares in a major clearing bank did not have such a prohibited interest when he presided over the trial of a defendant who was convicted of robbing a branch of that bank, together with similar robberies committed against other banks and building societies: *R. v. Mulvihill* [1990] 1 All E.R. 436. The Privy Council has considered the application of the prohibition on direct pecuniary interests in the post-*Gough* era: *Eves v. Hambros Bank (Jersey) Ltd* [1996] 1 W.L.R. 251. In that case the appellant, Eves, had borrowed money from the bank and they had obtained a charge over his house. When he defaulted on his payments the bank began legal proceedings and eventually the Royal Court of Jersey was asked to grant the bank an order for possession of the property. The application was granted by the deputy bailiff and two jurats. One of the jurats, Jurat Coutanche, was a director of the bank. Eves appealed against the decision to the Jersey Court of Appeal, but he was unsuccessful. He then appealed to the Privy Council arguing, *inter alia*, that the participation of Jurat Coutanche violated the prohibition on decision-makers having direct pecuniary interests. Lord Hoffmann held that:

"in order for a litigant to be able to complain that a member of the tribunal has made himself a judge in his own cause, there must be a question which has to be decided as between the litigant and another party. In this case there was none. . . . It follows that the order of confirmation was not vitiated by the interest of Jurat Coutanche. Their Lordships recognise the importance of the rule that no person sitting in a judicial capacity should have a pecuniary interest in the outcome of the proceedings. As Lord Goff of Chieveley said in *R. v. Gough*, public confidence in the administration of justice requires that a decision made in such circumstances should not stand. But this statement was made with reference to proceedings in which the party objecting was legitimately concerned. On the other hand, public confidence in the administration of justice also requires that the process should not be abused and the rights of litigants frustrated by technical objections to proceedings in which Mr Eves has no legal interest" (at 255–256).

Therefore, the appeal was dismissed. Thus it seems that an applicant will only be able to successfully invoke the rule against direct pecuniary interests in regard to proceedings in which he is a formal party. Sedley J. has characterised the decision as being primarily concerned with the issue of *locus standi*. "The judgment in *Eves* is not in my view authorityfor the proposition that it is only in a *lis inter partes* that the rule against sitting as judge in one's own cause operates. The decision is simply that a person who had no right in any event to be heard (no doubt because the proceeding was a routine step not open to disputation) has no *locus* from which to contest the consequent order on any ground, including alleged bias in a member of the court. By contrast, once the sufficiency of the interest of an applicant is established . . . the decision in the *Eves* case has no bearing": *R. v. Secretary of State for the Environment and another, ex p. Kirkstall Valley Campaign Ltd* [1996] 3 All E.R. 304 at 323.

(b) *The rule against bias*

R. v. GOUGH

[1993] A.C. 647; [1993] 2 All E.R. 724 (House of Lords)

The appellant, Gough, was indicted on a count of conspiring with his brother to rob a betting shop. Proceedings were dropped against his brother at the committal hearing. During the trial of the appellant, his brother's name had been given and a police photograph (a "mug shot") of him had been presented to the jury. The appellant was convicted and sentenced to 15 years' imprisonment. Thereupon, the brother began shouting in protest from the public gallery of the court. At this time one of the jurors realised that the brother was in fact her next door neighbour. Subsequently, the juror swore an affidavit that, *inter alia*, she had never seen the appellant before his trial and the fact that his brother was her neighbour did not influence her thinking as a juror. Nevertheless, Gough appealed against his conviction arguing that the presence of his brother's neighbour on the jury amounted to a serious irregularity in the conduct of the trial. That contention was rejected by the Court of Appeal and Gough appealed to the House of Lords.

LORD GOFF OF CHIEVELEY: ... In considering the subject of the present appeal, your Lordships have been faced with a series of authorities which are not only large in number, but bewildering in their effect. It is only too clear how great a difficulty courts of first instance, and indeed Divisional Courts and the Court of Appeal, must face in cases which come before them; and there is a compelling need for your Lordships' House to subject the authorities to examination and analysis in the hope of being able to extract from them some readily understandable and easily applicable principles, thus obviating the necessity of conducting on each occasion a trawl through authorities which are by no means easy to reconcile. It is on that exercise that I now propose to embark.

A layman might well wonder why the function of a court in cases such as these should not simply be to conduct an inquiry into the question whether the tribunal was in fact biased. After all it is alleged that, for example, a justice or a juryman was biased, *i.e.* that he was motivated by a desire unfairly to favour one side or to disfavour the other. Why does the court not simply decide whether that was in fact the case? The answer, as always, is that it is more complicated than that. First of all, there are difficulties about exploring the actual state of mind of a justice or juryman. In the case of both, such an inquiry has been thought to be undesirable; and in the case of the juryman in particular, there has long been an inhibition against, so to speak, entering the jury room and finding out what any particular juryman actually thought at the time of decision. But there is also the simple fact that bias is such an insidious thing that, even though a person may in good faith believe that he was acting impartially, his mind may unconsciously be affected by bias—a point stressed by Devlin L.J. in *R. v. Barnsley Licensing Justices, ex p. Barnsley and District Licensed Victuallers' Association* [1960] 2 Q.B. 167, 187. In any event, there is an overriding public interest that there should be confidence in the integrity of the administration of justice, which is always associated with the statement of Lord Hewart C.J. in *R. v. Sussex Justices, ex p. McCarthy* [1924] 1 K.B. 256, 259, that it is "of fundamental importance that justice should not only be done, but should manifestly and undoubtedly be seen to be done". I shall return to that case in a moment, for one of my tasks is to place the actual decision in that case in its proper context. At all events, the approach of the law has been (save on the very rare occasion where actual bias is proved) to look at the relevant circumstances and to consider whether there is such a degree of possibility of bias that the decision in question should not be allowed to stand.

. . . The argument before the Appellate Committee was presented on the basis that there were two rival, alternative tests for bias to be found in the authorities, and that the result in the present case depended on the choice made by your Lordships' House between them. The first test, favoured by Mr Hytner for the appellant, was whether a reasonable and fair minded person sitting in the court and knowing all the relevant facts would have had a reasonable suspicion that a fair trial by the defendant was not possible. The second test, favoured by Mr Leveson for the Crown, was whether there was a real likelihood of bias. I shall for convenience refer to these two tests respectively as the reasonable suspicion test, and the real likelihood test. It was recognised by Mr Hytner before the Appellate Committee, as before the Court of Appeal, that if the real likelihood test is to be preferred, the appeal must fail.

In fact, examination of the authorities reveals that selection of the appropriate test does not simply involve a choice between the two tests formulated by counsel in the present case. Thus, when the appropriate test in cases concerned with juries fell to be considered by your Lordships' House in *R. v. Spencer* [1987] A.C. 128, a variant of the real likelihood test, *viz.* whether there was a real danger of bias, was adopted, as it was by the Court of Appeal in the present case. There are also to be found in the authorities variants of the reasonable suspicion test; and sometimes the two tests seem to have been combined . . .

. . . I wish to draw attention to the fact that there are certain cases in which it has been considered that the circumstances are such that they must inevitably shake public confidence in the integrity of the administration of justice if the decision is to be allowed to stand. Such cases attract the full force of Lord Hewart C.J.'s requirement that justice must not only be done but manifestly be seen to be done. These cases arise where a person sitting in a judicial capacity has a pecuniary interest in the outcome of the proceedings. In such a case, as Blackburn J. said in *R. v. Rand* (1866) L.R. 1 Q.B. 230, 232: "any direct pecuniary interest, however small, in the subject of inquiry, does disqualify a person from acting as a judge in the matter." The principle is expressed in the maxim that nobody may be judge in his own cause (*nemo judex in sua causa*). Perhaps the most famous case in which the principle was applied is *Dimes v. Proprietors of Grand Junction Canal* (1852) 3 H.L.Cas. 759, in which decrees affirmed by Lord Cottenham L.C. in favour of a canal company in which he was a substantial shareholder were set aside by this House, which then proceeded to consider the matter on its merits, and in fact itself affirmed the decrees. Lord Campbell said, at 793:

> "No one can suppose that Lord Cottenham could be, in the remotest degree, influenced by the interest that he had in this concern; but, my Lords, it is of the last importance that the maxim that no man is to be a judge in his own cause should be held sacred."

In such a case, therefore, not only is it irrelevant that there was in fact no bias on the part of the tribunal, but there is no question of investigating, from an objective point of view, whether there was any real likelihood of bias, or any reasonable suspicion of bias, on the facts of the particular case. The nature of the interest is such that public confidence in the administration of justice requires that the decision should not stand.

I turn next to the broader question of bias on the part of a member of the relevant tribunal. Here it is necessary first to put on one side the very rare case where actual bias is shown to exist. Of course, if actual bias is proved, that is an end of the case; the person concerned must be disqualified. But it is not necessary that actual bias should be proved; and in practice the inquiry is directed to the question whether there was such a degree of possibility of bias on the part of the tribunal that the court will not allow the decision to stand. Such a question may arise in a wide variety of circumstances. These include, but are by no means limited to, cases in which a member of the tribunal has an interest in the outcome of the proceedings, which falls short of a direct pecuniary interest. Such interests may vary widely in their nature, in their effect, and in their relevance to the subject matter of the proceedings; and there is no rule, as there is in the case of a pecuniary interest, that the possession of such an interest automatically disqualifies the member of the tribunal from sitting. Each case falls to be considered on its own facts. . . .

In conclusion, I wish to express my understanding of the law as follows. I think it possible, and desirable, that the same test should be applicable in all cases of apparent bias, whether concerned with justices or members of other inferior tribunals, or with jurors, or with arbitrators. Likewise I consider that, in cases concerned with jurors, the same test should be applied by a judge to whose attention the possibility of bias on the part of a juror has been drawn in the course of a trial, and by the Court of Appeal when it considers such a question on appeal. Furthermore, I think it unnecessary, in formulating the appropriate test, to require that the court should look at the matter through the eyes of a reasonable man, because the court in cases such as these personifies the reasonable man; and in any event the court has first to ascertain the relevant circumstances from the available evidence, knowledge of which would not necessarily be available to an observer in court at the relevant time. Finally, for the avoidance of doubt, I prefer to state the test in terms of real danger rather than real likelihood, to ensure that the court is thinking in terms of possibility rather than probability of bias. Accordingly, having ascertained the relevant circumstances, the court should ask itself whether, having regard to those circumstances, there was a real danger of bias on the part of the relevant member of the tribunal in question, in the sense that he might unfairly regard (or have unfairly regarded) with favour, or disfavour, the case of a party to the issue under consideration by him; though, in a case concerned with bias on the part of a justices' clerk, the court should go on to consider whether the clerk has been invited to give the justices advice and, if so, whether it should infer that there was a real danger of the clerk's bias having infected the views of the justices adversely to the applicant.

It follows from what I have said that the Court of Appeal applied the correct test in the present case. On that test, it was accepted by Mr Hytner that there was no ground for disturbing the jury's verdict. I would therefore dismiss the appeal.

LORD WOOLF: My Lords, I have had the advantage of reading in draft the speech of Lord Goff of Chieveley and I agree that this appeal should be dismissed for the reasons which he gives. In particular, I agree that the correct test to adopt in deciding whether a decision should be set aside on the grounds of alleged bias is that given by Lord Goff, namely, whether there is a real danger of injustice having occurred as a result of the alleged bias.

.   .   .

It must be remembered that except in the rare case where actual bias is alleged, the court is not concerned to investigate whether or not bias has been established. Whether it is a judge, a member of the jury, justices or their clerk, who is alleged to be biased, the courts do not regard it as being desirable or useful to inquire into the individual's state of mind. It is not desirable because of the confidential nature of the judicial decision making, process. It is not useful because the courts have long recognised that bias operates in such an insidious manner that the person alleged to be biased may be quite unconscious of its effect.

It is because the court in the majority of cases does not inquire whether actual bias exists that the maxim that justice must not only be done but seen to be done applies. When considering whether there is a real danger of injustice, the court gives effect to the maxim, but does so by examining all the material available and giving its conclusion on that material. If the court having done so is satisfied there is no danger of the alleged bias having created injustice, then the application to quash the decision should be dismissed. ....

... There is only one established special category and that exists where the tribunal has a pecuniary or proprietary interest in the subject matter of the proceedings as in *Dimes v. Proprietors of Grand Junction Canal*, 3 H.L.Cas. 759. The courts should hesitate long before creating any other special category since this will immediately create uncertainty as to what are the parameters of that category and what is the test to be applied in the case of that category. The real danger test is quite capable of producing the right answer and ensure that the purity of justice is maintained across the range of situations where bias may exist.

LORDS ACKNER, MUSTILL and SLYNN OF HADLEY agreed with the reasoning of Lord Goff.

Appeal dismissed.

Notes

1. The above decision clarifies the law by enunciating the real danger of bias test (often termed the unitary test) as the standard by which courts engaged in judicial review will determine if decision-making is unlawful through allegations of bias (other than cases involving proof of actual bias on the part of the decision-maker or where it can be shown that the decision-maker had a direct pecuniary interest in the decision). The real danger test has subsequently been applied in a number of significant cases.

2. In *Rees and Others v. Crane* [1994] A.C. 173, the respondent, Crane, was a senior High Court judge in Trinidad and Tobago who had been withdrawn from judicial work by the Chief Justice. The latter had received complaints about Crane's performance in court and he had doubts about Crane's state of health. The Judicial and Legal Service Commission, of which the Chief Justice was a member, affirmed the latter's decision. Subsequently, the Commission decided to recommend to the President that a formal investigation should be established to consider whether Crane ought to be removed from office. Crane sought judicial review of these decisions alleging, *inter alia*, bias on the part of the Chief Justice and the Commission. Lord Slynn, on behalf of the Privy Council, noted that there was evidence of hostility by the Chief Justice towards Crane. However, his Lordship believed that "it is not lightly to be assumed that he would allow personal hostility to colour his decision". Likewise, regarding the Commission, "their professional backgrounds are such that an assumption of bias should not lightly be made". Hence the Privy Council was not satisfied that there had been a real danger of bias on the part of the Chief Justice or the Commission (although the Council upheld other claims of unfairness made by the respondent). This decision suggest that the real danger of bias test may be a high standard for applicants to surmount, but the Privy Council was undoubtedly influenced by the positions occupied by the appellants when applying the test to the facts in this case.

3. The Court of Appeal elaborated upon the test and applied it to the actions of a coroner in *R. v. Inner West London Coroner, ex p. Dellagio and Another* [1994] 4 All E.R. 139. During the protracted inquest into the deaths of 51 young persons, caused when the "Bowbelle" dredger collided with the passenger launch "Marchioness" in the river Thames, several of the victims' parents contacted the press to protest at the way in which matters had been dealt with by officials. In response the coroner, Dr Knapman, held a meeting with two journalists during which they reported that he stated that one of the parents was "unhinged". Subsequently, the relevant parents

sought judicial review of the coroner's refusal to remove himself on the grounds of alleged bias. Simon Brown L.J. derived a number of propositions from *Gough* including: (i) "a decision-maker may have unfairly regarded with disfavour one party's case either consciously or unconsciously. Where, as here, the applicants expressly disavow any suggestion of actual bias, it seems to me that the court must necessarily be asking itself whether there is a real danger that the decision-maker was unconsciously biased" and (ii) "what must be established is the real danger of bias having affected the decision in the sense of having caused the decision-maker, albeit unconsciously, to weigh the competing contentions, and so decide the merits, unfairly". His Lordship concluded that:

> "for a judicial officer to say publicly of someone that they are unreliable because 'unhinged' shows, I have no doubt, an appearance of bias: such a description is not merely injudicious and insensitive but bound to be interpreted as a gratuitous insult. . . . I find myself in the last analysis unable to discount the real possibility that the coroner unconsciously allowed himself to be influenced against the applicants and other members of the action group by a feeling of hostility towards them. . . . I just add this footnote. No one should interpret this judgment as a condemnation of Dr Knapman. Almost without exception he handled the many difficulties he faced not merely with sensitivity but with an evident sympathy for the bereaved families. Understandably, and indeed justifiably, riled by an unfair article in the *Mail on Sunday*, he was guilty of but a single intemperate comment. The case should serve as a reminder to all judicial officers of the almost invariable unwisdom of every talking to the press about any aspect of current legal proceedings" (at 153 and 156).

Therefore, the Court ordered that another coroner should assume responsibility for the inquest.

4. A black person sued the police for alleged malicious prosecution. During her summing up the judge referred to certain police officers as "the niggers in the woodpile", she immediately apologised for her comments. The jury dismissed the plaintiff's claim. He appealed to the Court of Appeal contending that the judge and jury had been biased. Beldam L.J. stated that no tribunal should use that expression in the light of our multi-racial society. However, the judge had realised her mistake, the comment had not been directed at the plaintiff, and her summing up showed an even balance between the parties. His Lordship, applying the unitary test, concluded that there was not a real danger that the jury was biased by the judge's comment; therefore, the appeal was rejected: see *Reid v. Chief Constable of Merseyside, The Times*, February 5, 1996.

5. The extra-statutory practice of the Parole Board confirming the decision of the Home Secretary to recall a discretionary life prisoner to prison did not create a real danger that the Board would be biased against the prisoner when it subsequently held a formal statutory review of the case. The Court of Appeal noted that different members of the Board would sit for the formal review, they would have a wider range of information at their disposal and the prisoner would be entitled to representation at the review: *R. v. Parole Board, ex p. Watson* [1996] 2 All E.R. 641.

6. The Privy Council has held that the unitary test is not violated where an appellate court has to rule on whether a defendant should be retried, even if some members of the court have formed a view as to the guilt of the defendant: see *Berry v. DPP (No. 2), The Times*, October 28, 1996.

(c) *The types of decision-making processes subject to the rule against bias or interest*

FRANKLIN AND OTHERS v. MINISTER OF TOWN AND COUNTRY PLANNING

[1948] A.C. 87; [1947] L.J.R. 1440; 63 T.L.R. 446; 111 J.P. 497; [1947] 2 All E.R. 289; 45 L.G.R. 581 (House of Lords)

In January 1946, a committee appointed in 1945 by the Minister and the Secretary of State for Scotland (the "Reith Committee") made an interim report (Cmd. 6759) which pointed out that Stevenage was suggested in the Greater London Plan 1944 as one of the new towns in the outer ring round London. The committee had been informed that this development was urgently needed, and they recommended that a Government-sponsored corporation should be established in advance of legislation. The Minister, Lewis Silkin, introduced the New Towns Bill in the House of Commons in April.

On May 6, 1946, Mr Silkin spoke at a public meeting in Stevenage Town Hall, called to consider a proposal for the designation of land near Stevenage as the site of a new town. The meeting was lively. Mr Silkin explained the plans for the development of new towns to relieve London's population density. His speech included the following passages:

"In anticipation of the passage of the Bill—and I have no doubt that it will go through—certain preliminary steps have been taken regarding Stevenage by way of discussion with some of the local authorities concerned—(*Voice*: There has been no discussion with the Stevenage Local Authority)—and the preparation of a plan, and the giving of notices for the acquisition of land under powers which I already have in pursuance of the Town and Country Planning Act, 1932 . . . I think you will agree that if we are to carry out our policy of creating a number of new towns to relieve congestion in London we could hardly have chosen for the site of one of them a better place than Stevenage. Now I know that many objections have been raised by the inhabitants of Stevenage, perhaps not unnaturally. . . . The project will go forward. It will do so more smoothly and more successfully with your help and co-operation. Stevenage will in a short time become world famous—(*Laughter*). . . In answer to a question as to whether the rates would be increased by the development, the respondent said: No, in due course Stevenage will gain. Local authorities will be consulted all the way through. But we have a duty to perform, and I am not going to be deterred from that duty. While I will consult as far as possible all the local authorities, at the end, if people are fractious and unreasonable, I shall have to carry out my duty—(*Voice*: Gestapo!)."

The New Towns Bill received the Royal Assent on August 1, 1946. On August 3, the Minister prepared the draft Stevenage New Town (Designation) Order 1946 under paragraph 1 of Schedule 1 to the Act. The draft order was publicised as required by the Act. Objections to the designation were received from the appellants and others. A public local inquiry was held on behalf of the Minister in October. The inspector's report to the Minister summarised the objector's submissions and evidence.

In November, the Minister wrote to the objectors that he had decided to make the order, "after giving careful consideration to the various submissions made to him . . .". He dealt with the main objections raised. The order was made on November 11. The following month, the present appellants who owned houses and land in the area, applied to the High Court to have the order quashed on the grounds that: (1) The order was not within the powers of the Act, or alternatively that the Act's requirements had not been complied with to the substantial prejudice of the appellants' interests, in that—(a) before considering the objections the Minister stated that he would make the order and was thereby biased in any consideration of the order; and (b) the Minister did not before making the order cause a public local inquiry to be held with respect thereto; and (2) That the Act impliedly required that the appellants' objections should be fairly and properly considered by the Minister and that the Minister should give fair and proper effect to the result of such consideration in deciding whether the order should be made, and that such implied requirements were not complied with.

The Minister swore an affidavit which was not challenged, stating (*inter alia*): "Before causing the said order to be made, I personally carefully considered all the objections made by the objectors including the present [appellants] together with the submissions made and evidence given on their behalf as appearing in the said transcript" (of the inquiry proceedings). He also stated that he carefully considered the inspector's report.

Henn Collins J. (63 T.L.R. 143) held that the Minister had not fulfilled his duty to act judicially in considering the objections.

The Court of Appeal (63 T.L.R. 187) reversed this decision, holding that the appellants had not discharged the onus of proving that the Minister was biased when he made the order.

The appellants appealed to the House of Lords.

LORD THANKERTON: [stated the facts, expressed agreement with the Court of Appeal's views that the appellant had not proved that the Minister was biased, and continued:] My Lords, I agree with the decision of the Court of Appeal, but I am of opinion that an incorrect view of the law applicable in this case was taken by the learned judge, and I feel bound, despite the assumption of its correctness by the Court of Appeal, to examine the correctness of the learned judge's view as to the proper inference from the respondent's speech of May 6, 1946. While the fact that the speech was made just before the second reading of the Bill, and some months before the statutory duties as to designation of new towns was imposed on the respondent has some bearing on the fair construction of the speech, I am prepared to assume in favour of the appellants that, under the Bill as introduced, it was proposed to impose these duties on the respondent, as Minister of Town and Country Planning, and that these duties presented no material difference from those contained in the Bill when passed into law. It could hardly be suggested that, prior to its enactment, he was subject to any higher duty than is to be found in the statute. In my opinion, no judicial, or quasi-judicial, duty was imposed on the respondent, and any reference to judicial duty, or bias, is irrelevant in the present case. The respondent's duties under section 1 of the Act and Sched. I thereto are, in my opinion, purely administrative, but the Act prescribes certain methods of or steps in, discharge of that duty. It is obvious that, before making the draft order, which must contain a definite proposal to designte the area concerned as the site of a new town, the respondent must have made elaborate inquiry into the matter and have consulted any local authorities who appear to him to be concerned, and obviously other departments of the Government, such as the Minister of Health, would naturally require to be consulted. It would seem, accordingly, that the respondent was required to satisfy himself that it was a sound scheme before he took the serious step of issuing a draft order. It seems clear also, that the purpose of inviting objections, and, where they are not withdrawn, of having a public inquiry, to be held by someone other than the respondent, to whom that person reports, was for the further information of the respondent, in order to the final consideration of the soundness of the scheme of the designation; and it is important to note that the development of the site, after the order is made, is primarily the duty of the development corporation established under section 2 of the Act. I am of opinion that no judicial duty is laid on the respondent in discharge of these statutory duties, and that the only question is whether he has complied with the statutory directions to appoint a person to hold the public inquiry, and to consider that person's report. On this contention of the appellants no suggestion is made that the public inquiry was not properly conducted, nor is there any criticism of the report by Mr Morris. In such a case the only ground of challenge must be either that the respondent did not in fact consider the report and the objections, of which there is here no evidence, or that his mind was so foreclosed that he gave no genuine consideration to them, which is the case made by the appellants. Although I am unable to agree exactly with the view of the respondent's duty expressed by the learned judge, or with some of the expressions used by the Court of Appeal in regard to that matter, it does appear to me that the issue was treated in both courts as being whether the respondent had genuinely considered the objections and the report, as directed by the Act.

My Lords, I could wish that the use of the word "bias" should be confined to its proper sphere. Its proper significance, in my opinion, is to denote a departure from the standard of even-handed justice which the law requires from those who occupy judicial office, or those who are commonly regarded as holding a quasi-judicial office, such as an arbitrator. The reason for this clearly is that, having to adjudicate as between two or more parties, he must come to his adjudication with an independent mind, without any inclination or bias towards one side or other in the dispute. . . . But, in the present case, the respondent having no judicial duty, the only question is what the respondent actually did, that is, whether in fact he did genuinely consider the report and the objections.

Coming now to the inference of the learned judge from the respondent's speech on May 6, that he had not then a mind open to conviction, the learned judge states it thus (1947) 176 L.T. 200 at 203: "If I am to judge by what he said at the public meeting which was held very shortly before the Bill, then published, became an Act of Parliament, I could have no doubt but that any issue raised by objectors was forejudged. The Minister's language leaves no doubt about that. He was not only saying there must and shall be satellite towns, but he was saying that Stevenage was to be the first of them." It seems probable that the learned judge's mind was influenced by his having already held that the respondent's function was quasi-judicial, which would raise the question of bias, but, in my view, I am clearly of opinion that nothing said by the respondent was inconsistent with the discharge of his statutory duty, when subsequently objections were lodged, and the local public inquiry took place, followed by the report of that inquiry, genuinely to consider the report and the objections. . . .

[His Lordship referred to the contentious passages from the Minister's speech.]

My Lords, these passages in a speech, which was of a political nature, and of the kind familiar in a speech on second reading, demonstrate (1) the speaker's view that the Bill would become law, that Stevenage was a most suitable site and should be the first scheme in the operation, and that the Stevenage project would go forward, and (2) the speaker's reaction to the hostile interruptions of a section of the audience. In my opinion, these passages are not inconsistent with an intention to carry out any statutory duty imposed on him by Parliament, although he intended to press for the enactment of the Bill, and thereafter to carry out the duties thereby involved, including the consideration of objections which were neither fractious nor unreasonable. I am, therefore of opinion that the first contention of the appellants fails, in that they have not established either that in the respondent's speech he had forejudged any genuine consideration of the objections or that he had not genuinely considered the objections at the later stage when they were submitted to him. . . .

[His Lordship went on to hold that the Act did not require evidence to be led at the public inquiry in support of the order. Paragraph 3 of Schedule 1 to the 1946 Act required that, if objections were made, "the Minister shall, before making the order, cause a public local inquiry to be held with respect thereto. . . . The last three words were held to mean "with respect to the objections". Thus the inquiry was properly held.]

LORDS PORTER, UTHWATT, DU PARCQ and NORMAND concurred.

Appeal dismissed.

Notes

1. This case was decided at a time when the courts tied the label "judicial" only to *lis inter partes* situations. In the context of planning, a minister was held to be acting in a judicial capacity only after objections had been received and an inquiry was necessary. See *Errington v. Minister of Health* [1935] 1 K.B. 249.

2. Over more recent years the lower courts have expressed divergent views as to the extent to which the rule against bias applies to the decision-making of local planning authorities. In *Steeples v. Derbyshire County Council* [1985] 1 W.L.R. 256, the council owned an area of parkland and entered into an agreement with a company to jointly develop the site. The agreement provided that the council would take reasonable steps to obtain planning permission for the proposed development. The planning committee of the council considered the application and granted permission for the development. A member of a local amenity group sought a declaration that the permission was unlawful having been made in breach of the rule against bias. Webster J. sought to judge the legality of the council's actions according to a modified version of the test in *Metropolitan Properties Ltd v. Lannon* [1969] 1 Q.B. 577:

"In conclusion ... it is probable that a reasonable man, not having been present at the meeting when the decision was made, and not knowing of my conclusion as to the actual fairness of it, knowing of the existence and of all the terms of the contract (but without regard to the question whether they would in law have been enforceable), would think that there was a real likelihood that those provisions in the contract which require the county council, and for that matter the joint venture committee, to use their best endeavours to obtain planning permission, and the contract as a whole in the light of its provision to which I have referred, had had a material and significant effect on the planning committee's decision to grant the permission; and accordingly, on that ground, I hold that that decision was either voidable or void" (at 288).

Whereas, in *R. v. Amber Valley District Council, ex p. Jackson* [1985] 1 W.L.R.

298, Woolf J. doubted the applicability of the *Lannon* principle to administrative decisions of planning committees. This case was a sequel to *Steeples* in that subsequently the development company applied to the local district council (Amber Valley), whose area covered the parkland, for planning permission to develop the site. Prior to Amber Valley's planning committee considering the application, the majority Labour party group on the council resolved to support the development (this policy was in accordance with the views of the Labour controlled Derbyshire County Council). A member of the local amenity group opposed to the development sought an order of prohibition against Amber Valley District Council to prevent the council considering the planning application on the grounds that any determination was likely to be biased in the light of the earlier policy decision of the controlling Labour group. The learned judge considered:

> "The rules of fairness or natural justice cannot be regarded as being rigid. They must alter in accordance with the context. Thus in the case of highways, the department can be both the promoting authority and the determining authority. When this happens, of course any reasonable man would regard the department as being pre-disposed towards the outcome of the inquiry. The department is under an obligation to be fair and carefully to consider the evidence given before the inquiry but the fact that it has a policy in the matter does not entitle a court to intervene. So in this case I do not consider the fact that there is a declaration of policy by the majority group can disqualify a district council from adjudicating on a planning application" (at 307–308).

Consequently, the application for an order of prohibition was dismissed.

In *R. v. Sevenoaks District Council, ex p. Terry* [1985] 3 All E.R. 226, the High Court disagreed with the *Steeples* test for bias and proposed its own formula. The case concerned a piece of land owned by the council. In the summer of 1981 the council accepted an offer from a development company to lease the site in order to construct a supermarket. Then in early 1982 the council granted the developers planning permission to develop the site. A local ratepayer sought an order of certiorari to quash the planning grant on the ground that the council was biased in favour of the application because of its previous dealings with the developers. Glidewell J. determined that the *Lannon* principle did not apply to this decision-making function:

> "Of course, the council must act honestly and fairly, but it is not uncommon for a local authority to be obliged to make a decision relating to land or other property in which it has an interest. In such a situation, the application of the rule designed to ensure that a judicial officer does not appear to be biased would, in my view, often produce an administrative impasse.... the correct test to be applied in the present case is for the court to pose to itself the question: had the district council before [determining the planning application] acted in such a way that it is clear that, when the committee came to consider [the developers'] application for planning permission, it could not exercise proper discretion? Of course, in asking that question, it may appear that the answer is Yes, even though an individual councillor says quite genuinely and honestly that he personally was able to approach the decision without bias. But, if the answer to the question is No, it is in my judgment neither necessary nor desirable for the court to go further and consider what the opinion of a reasonable man would be. In so far as this formulation differs from that adopted by Webster J. in *Steeples v. Derbyshire C.C.*, I respectfully disagree with him" (at 233).

Applying this test the learned judge found that the council had not unlawfully fettered the exercise of its discretion to grant or refuse planning permission for the site in

January 1982; therefore, he dismissed the application. This test was also endorsed and applied by Stocker J. in *R. v. St Edmundsbury Borough Council, ex p. Investors in Industry Commercial Properties Ltd* [1985] 3 All E.R. 234.

In *R. v. City of Wakefield Metropolitan District Council and British Coal Corporation, ex p. Warmfield Co. Ltd* [1994] J.P.L. 341, the applicant challenged several grants of planning permission made by the council on the grounds, *inter alia*, that the council had a pre-existing policy favouring open-cast mining and that the council had commercial relationships with British Coal (who were the beneficiaries of some of the impugned planning decisions). Tucker J. held that:

> "he did not regard the House of Lords in *Gough* as having overruled the decision of Glidewell J. (as he then was) in *Terry*, which was apparently not cited to them. In his view it was open to him to look at and to derive assistance from the judgment of Glidewell J. in that case. . . . But whether one applied the *Gough* test or (if there was any significant difference between them) the *Terry* test, he was bound to say that he did not detect any hint of bias in the present case" (at 354–355).

Therefore, the application was dismissed.

For the latest judicial view, see *Kirkstall Valley Campaign* (below).

R. v. KENT POLICE AUTHORITY, ex p. GODDEN

[1971] 2 Q.B. 662; [1971] 3 W.L.R. 416; 115 S.J. 640; 69 L.G.R. 533; *sub nom. Re Godden* [1971] 3 All E.R. 20 (Court of Appeal)

In 1969 the applicant, a police chief inspector, was transferred to administrative duties. He made accusations of unjust treatment against his superiors. A chief constable held an inquiry and reported in May 1970 that there was no evidence of malpractice. The applicant was told the result of the inquiry but was not shown the report.

On July 4, 1970, the applicant's desk was searched by a senior officer. Erotic documents including a draft letter said to be in the applicant's handwriting were removed. The applicant denied knowledge of the documents. It was arranged for the applicant to be seen by the chief medical officer of the force, who was supplied with a copy of the report of May 1970 and the documents. He saw the applicant and on July 23, 1970, reported that after reading the reports he formed the opinion that the applicant was "suffering from a mental disorder of paranoid type". On July 31, 1970, he certified that the applicant was unfit for police duty on the same ground. The applicant was put on sick leave.

The applicant saw his own doctor, who sent him to a consultant psychiatrist. The consultant psychiatrist reported on August 18, 1970, that the applicant was "psychiatrically completely normal" and on May 17, 1971, that in his opinion he was "normal psychiatrically and in good mental and physical health". The police would not allow the consultant psychiatrist to see the report of May 1970.

The police authority took steps compulsorily to retire the applicant. On January 22, 1971, they notified the applicant that they had selected the same chief medical officer as their "duly qualified practitioner" to determine whether the applicant was "permanently disabled" under regulation 70(2) of the Police Pensions Regulations 1971.

The applicant sought orders of prohibition and mandamus. The Divisional Court dismissed the applications. The applicant appealed.

LORD DENNING M.R.: . . . I am clearly of opinion that the decisions leading to compulsory retirement are of a judicial character and must conform to the rules of natural justice. They are, first, decision by the medical practitioner or on appeal by the medical referee, and, secondly, the inquiry by the police authority themselves. We have been referred to two cases where medical certificates were required which affected the rights of individuals. One is *R. v. Postmaster-General, ex p. Carmichael* [1928] 1 K.B. 291. The other is *R. v. Boycott, ex p. Keasley* [1939] 2 K.B. 641. In each of those cases certiorari was granted.

When a medical practitioner is making a decision which may lead to a man being compulsorily retired, he must act fairly. He is not acting simply as doctor to patient. He is not diagnosing illness or prescribing treatment. He is not saying merely whether a man is fit or unfit for duty. He is doing something which affects the man's whole future. He must beyond doubt act fairly. Take this very case. A man's mental state is at issue. It affects not only his pension rights and payments to him. It affects his standing in the community, his ability to get other work and the like. It is quite plain to me that the person concerned is entitled to have a fair opportunity of correcting or contradicting any statements made to his prejudice, and a fair opportunity of calling in his own medical consultant and getting him to give his opinion to the deciding person. His own medical consultant should be entitled to have before him all material which the other doctors have.

That brings me to the first question: was it proper for the Kent police authorities to refer for decision this question to Dr Crosbie Brown? I must say I think it was not. Dr Crosbie Brown was disqualified from acting. He had already expressed an opinion adverse to Chief Inspector Godden. As early as July 23, 1970, Dr Crosbie Brown had said that the chief inspector was suffering from a mental disorder. Dr Crosbie Brown acted on that opinion by putting him on sick leave. He has put his opinion on affidavit. He has committed himself to a view in advance of the inquiry. I think it would be impossible for Dr Crosbie Brown—who is just a general medical practitioner and not a consultant—to bring a completely impartial mind to bear upon the matter. In any event, to the person affected by it, Chief Inspector Godden, it must inevitably appear that Dr Crosbie Brown cannot bring an impartial judgment to bear upon the matter. If he was to decide the matter justice would not be seen to be done. In view of the additional material before us (which was not before the Divisional Court) I hold that Dr Crosbie is disqualified. For that reason in my opinion the first request for prohibition should go "to prohibit Dr Crosbie Brown from determining whether Chief Inspector Godden was permanently disabled within the police pensions regulations for the time being in force".

If the police authority determine further to consider the matter, they should refer it for decision to somebody else. I would suggest that it would be better to have someone quite outside this case altogether—not even any of the names which have been men tioned, such as Dr Pollitt or Dr Hierons—but some duly qualified medical practitioner who has had no part in the case hitherto. Then the question arises, what material may or should be put before such a person? Is it to include the Pratt report and all such other matters? I am inclined to think it should. Whoever is entrusted with the decision should have before him all material relative to the state of mind of Chief Inspector Godden, whether it is for him or against him.

The next question is whether Chief Inspector Godden's own medical advisers should see the material. In my opinion they should. Dr Hordern (or whatever medical consultant Chief Inspector Godden engages) should have the selfsame material before him upon which to give his opinion as that which is placed before any other doctor who is considering the matter.

One word more. Although the medical advisers on each side should be fully informed, I do not see that justice requires that Chief Inspector Godden should himself be able to roam through this Pratt report. One does not want to keep anything back from him, but in a matter of this kind it seems to me that justice can well be done by his own consultant seeing it. No doubt his own consultant will have to ask him many questions on it, and he is bound to get to know a good deal about it. But for myself I do not see that justice requires that Chief Inspector Godden should see it all himself. I do not suggest that he would use it as a basis for an action for libel, but it would be most deplorable if it were used for that purpose. Rather than risk such a thing, it seems to me justice can fairly be done by letting his medical consultant see everything that any other doctor sees on the matter and give his advice accordingly. I would therefore issue an order of mandamus to the police authority telling them that, if at any time consideration is given as to whether Chief Inspector Godden is permanently disabled within the police pensions regulations, they should supply to the medical consultant of Chief Inspector Godden all letters and other material which is placed by them before any duly qualified practitioner selected by them under police pensions regulation 70. I would therefore allow the appeal and let prohibition and mandamus issue in the terms which I have stated.

SALMON L.J.: . . . It seems to me that the duly qualified medical practitioner selected by the authority to give a decision as to whether a police officer is disabled, and, if so, whether the disablement is likely to be permanent, is undoubtedly performing a quasi-judicial function in reaching that decision. The relationship between him and the officer concerned is not an ordinary relationship of patient and doctor. Now, when I say he is exercising a quasi-judicial function, I certainly do not mean that he should conduct anything in the nature of a trial or hear the officer's legal advisers; nor that he is bound by the rules of evidence. He must, however, act fairly. . . .

KARMINSKI L.J. delivered a concurring judgment.

Appeal allowed.

R. v. SECRETARY OF STATE FOR THE ENVIRONMENT AND ANOTHER, ex p. KIRKSTALL VALLEY CAMPAIGN LTD

[1996] 3 All E.R. 304 (Queen's Bench Division)

The applicant amenity organisation sought an order of certiorari to quash decisions made in 1995 by Leeds Development Corporation, an urban development corporation created under the Local Government Planning and Land Act 1980 and dissolved later in 1995, granting outline planning permission for the construction of a superstore in the Kirkstall valley near the centre of Leeds. The applicants contended that the decisions were unlawful because of alleged bias on the part of the chairman of the

Corporation and two fellow board members together with the commercial director of the Corporation. The alleged bias resulted from a number of different interests including: property interests, membership of a political party and membership of a rugby club whose playing fields were subject to the disputed planning permissions. The application was contested by the Secretary of State, in his capacity as the residual authority for the dissolved Corporation, and by a grocery company which had paid over £2 million to purchase the relevant land and planning permissions from the rugby club.

SEDLEY J.: . . . Although Mr Drabble [counsel for the Secretary of State] in his submissions for the Secretary of State was content to accept Mr Hobson's [counsel for the applicant company] governing proposition that the law on apparent bias is now to be found in unitary form in the decision of the House of Lords in *R. v. Gough* [1993] 2 All E.R. 724; [1993] A.C. 646, as developed in *R. v. Inner West London Coroner, ex p. Dallaglio* [1994] 4 All E.R. 139, Mr Ryan [counsel for the superstore developers/owners] has advanced a radical alternative: that non-judicial bodies such as an urban development corporation are governed by a different set of principles, to be found in a succession of cases beginning with the decision of Glidewell J. in *R. v. Sevenoaks D.C., ex p. Terry* [1985] 3 All E.R. 226. If Mr Ryan is right, the question to be asked in relation to an impugned decision of a body such as the Leeds Development Corporation, is not whether on the facts now known to the court there was a real danger of bias in one or more members of the decision-making body, but whether the body as a whole can be shown to have gone beyond mere predisposition in favour of a particular course and to have predetermined it. . . .

. . . there is, in my judgment, nothing in the jurisprudence of *R. v. Gough* which necessarily limits to judicial or quasi-judicial tribunals the rule against the participation of a person with a personal interest in the outcome. The line of authority relied upon by Mr Ryan represents, in my view, a different although equally important principle: that the decision of a body, albeit composed of disinterested individuals, will be struck down if its outcome has been predetermined whether by the adoption of an inflexible policy or by the effective surrender of the body's independent judgment. The decision of the House of Lords in *Franklin v. Minister of Town and Country Planning* [1947] 2 All E.R. 289; [1948] A.C. 87 cannot now be regarded as diluting this principle. . . .

Not only is there, therefore, no authority which limits the *Gough* principle to judicial or quasi-judicial proceedings; there are sound grounds of principle in modern public law for declining so to limit it. The concrete reason, which is not always given the attention it deserves, is that in the modern state the interests of individuals or of the public may be more radically affected by administrative decisions than by the decisions of courts of law and judicial tribunals. The individual who has just been tried for a minor road traffic infraction will not be much comforted by the fact that he was tried with the full safeguards of the criminal law if on returning home he finds that an administrative decision in which he had no say is going to take away his home or his job. Nothing in the years since the publication of Robson's *Justice and Administrative Law* (2nd ed., 1947) has diminished the accuracy of what Robson wrote (pp. 4–5):

". . . it is probably the fact that some functions of government are not capable of classification into legislative, executive and judicial powers. It is very difficult to discover any adequate method by which, in a highly developed country like England, judicial functions can be clearly distinguished from administrative functions. Mere names are of no avail, for, as we shall see, judges often administer, and administrators often judge. It is easy enough to take a typical example of each kind of function, and to identify it as belonging to a particular category. But that does not get us out of the difficulty, unless we can extract from it some characteristics essential to its nature. A further difficulty arises from the fact that many of the features which once belonged almost exclusively to activities that were carried on only in courts of law, are now to be observed as attaching also, to a greater or less extent, to activities carried on by other departments of government. Furthermore, what we may call the judicial attitude of mind has spread from the courts of law, wherein it originated, to many other fields, with the result that an increasingly large number of governmental activities bear the marks of both the administrative process *and* the judicial process, and cannot be distinguished by any simple test. 'The changing combinations of events will beat upon the walls of ancient categories', a distinguished American judge has observed; and that is precisely what has occurred in the classification of governmental functions in England."

This is why modern public law, since the landmark decision in *Ridge v. Baldwin* [1963] 2 All E.R. 66; [1964] A.C. 40, has set its face against the partitioning of proceedings into judicial, administrative and something in between. The distinctions are not only increasingly hard to make in the variety of adjudicative processes in the modern state; they were historically mistaken. The celebrated chapter of Professor Wade's *Administrative Law* on the right to a fair hearing (currently Chap. 15 in *Wade and Forsyth's Administrative Law* (7th ed., 1994)) shows how the centuries-old jurisdiction of this court over both administrative and judicial acts was mistakenly collapsed into a notion of control over judicial acts only, followed by an artificial expansion of the concept of the judicial to include much that was in truth administrative. Since *Ridge v. Baldwin*, although not without occasional deviations, public law has returned to the broad highway of due process across the full range of justiciable decision-making. . . .

I hold, therefore, that the principle that a person is disqualified from participation in a decision if there is a real danger that he or she will be influenced by a pecuniary or personal interest in the outcome, is of general application in public law and is not limited to judicial or quasi-judicial bodies or proceedings.

How then will the principle apply to a body exercising town and country planning powers? In the case of an elected body the law recognises that members will take up office with publicly stated views on a variety of policy issues. In the case of an urban development corporation the Secretary of State will have had regard, in making his appointments, to "the desirability of securing the services of people having special knowledge of the locality" (para. 2(2) of Sched. 26 to the 1980 Act), as well as to the pro-active purpose of the corporation set out in s.136(1) "to secure the regeneration of its area". In both cases, where predetermination of issues or forfeiture of judgment is alleged, the court will be concerned to distinguish, within the statutory framework, legitimate prior stances or experience from illegitimate ones. But such issues will be governed by the separate line of authority on predetermination. So far as concerns apparent bias, there can be little if any difference between an elected and an appointed planning authority. In both cases there is a constant risk that the body will have to decide matters in which a member happens to have pecuniary or personal interest. In such cases, as the Secretary of State's successive codes for urban development corporations and for local government recognise, unless it is too remote or insignificant to matter, the interest must be declared and the member concerned must not participate in the decision. The likelihood that some such conflict of interest will sooner or later arise for a member appointed to an urban development corporation pursuant to the provisions of the 1980 Act, is no more an excuse for non-observance of the principle of disqualification than it would be for a member elected to a planning authority on a platform of planning issues. The *Gough* test of bias will be uniformly applied: what will differ from case to case is the significance of the interest and its degree of proximity or remoteness to the issue to be decided and whether, if it is not so insignificant or remote as to be discounted, the disqualified member has violated his disqualification by participating in the decision.

. . . the next issue which the present case raises: what should a member of a body do or refrain from doing when a conflict of interest arises? . . .

. . . as Mr Hobson submits with some force, the need to be rigorous about non-participation is even greater in a body such as an urban development corporation which does not necessarily or ordinarily meet in public or publish its proceedings, as compared with an elected local authority which is required by law to sit in public and to publish its proceedings, save only in relation to confidential items.

It is accordingly Mr Hobson's submission, and one which is important in relation to the facts of this case, that any member of a decision-making body who has an interest requiring to be declared must not only refrain from voting on the issue but must absent himself or herself from the meeting while the issue is discussed. Mr Drabble submits that there is no such rule. For the reasons explained by the House of Lords in *R. v. Gough*, I accept that there is no such rule—but this is a long way from concluding that a member with an interest to declare has no need to do more than refrain from voting. The applicable principle is not a matter of form but of substance: it is that an individual with a personal, pecuniary or proprietary interest in the subject matter of the decision is disqualified from participating in it. Mr Drabble has accepted, subject to possible questions of discretion, that the participation of a single member who is disqualified by bias vitiates the decision. . . .

It is thus distinctly possible that the mere declaration of a disqualifying interest, followed by abstention from discussion or voting, will not be enough to negate participation in the decision. This is why the courts, like the Secretary of State, have repeatedly counselled caution, not only for the sake of appearances, but because the line between participation and abstention is in many cases a fine one.

Application dismissed.

Notes

1. His Lordship found: (1) that the chairman of the Corporation had either a prohibited direct pecuniary interest or interests which created a real danger of bias in the

early years of the Corporation's activities concerning the redevelopment of the Kirkstall valley. But, those interests did not "contaminate" the later decisions granting planning permission. (2) One board member's only interest with the land was as an honorary vice-president of the rugby club and that this did not create a real danger of bias. (3) Another board member, who was a surveyor, had a professional relationship with the rugby club and Sedley J. concluded that this person's presence (although he had declared his interests and did not vote) at early meetings of the Corporation created a real danger of bias. However, this person did not attend any of the later meetings where the impugned decision were taken. (4) The commercial director's vice-presidency of the rugby club and his membership of the same ward association of the Conservative party as the chairman did not amount to a real danger of bias in the advice that he provided to the Corporation.

2. The democratically elected Leeds City Council wanted the Kirkstall valley to remain a public open space and an area of sporting facilities.

Question

Does Sedley J.'s extension of the *Gough* unitary test for apparent bias to all categories of public decision-making simplify the law?

CHAPTER 9

APPEALS

IN law, an appeal against a decision is possible only if it has been established by statute. In the context of administrative law Parliament has not been consistent in the creation of rights of appeal. There are considerable variations in the type of decision appealable, the possible grounds of appeal, and the body to which an appeal may be made. Appeals in the context of tribunals and inquiries were considered by the Franks Committee (below) and appeals to the High Court by the Law Commission (*Administrative Law: Judicial Review and Statutory Appeals*, Consultation Paper No. 126 (1993) and Report, Law Com. No. 226 (1994)). Suggestions have been made for rationalisation of appeal rights and procedures, but the Law Commission ultimately proposed limited changes (below, p. 541).

Because appeals depend on a statutory, as distinct from a common law, origin, the grounds of appeal will be confined to those specified in, or to be deduced from, the statute. These appeals must be distinguished from *review* by the courts under their common law powers. A key difference is that on an appeal to the High Court, as distinct from an application for judicial review, the Court may commonly substitute a different decision for that originally reached.

See *de Smith C.A.*, pp. 587–589; *Lewis*, Chap. 13; R. Gordon, *Crown Office Proceedings*, Parts E, F and G.

(A) WHEN SHOULD AN APPEAL BE AVAILABLE?

REPORT OF THE FRANKS COMMITTEE ON ADMINISTRATIVE TRIBUNALS AND ENQUIRIES 1957

(HMSO Cmnd. 218)

Part II: Tribunals in General

103. Most of the evidence which we have received has stressed the desirability of some form of appeal from tribunals of first instance, and many witnesses have advocated that at some stage there should be an appeal to the courts.

The merits of a right of appeal

104. The existence of a right of appeal is salutary and makes for right

adjudication. Provision for appeal is also important if decisions are to show reasonable consistency. Finally, the system of adjudication can hardly fail to appear fair to the applicant if he knows that he will normally be allowed two attempts to convince independent bodies of the soundness of his case.

An appeal structure for tribunals

105. The first question is the extent to which appeals should lie to the courts or to further appellate tribunals. An appeal to the courts on matters of fact would not, we think, be desirable since it would constitute an appeal from a body expert in the particular subject to a relatively inexpert body. In the absence of special consideration we consider that the ideal appeal structure for tribunals should take the form of a general appeal from a tribunal of first instance to a second or appellate tribunal. By a general appeal we mean an appeal on fact, law or merits. We do not think that it is necessary for appeals to the second or appellate tribunal always to be heard orally. As a matter of general principle we consider that appeal should not lie from a tribunal to a Minister.

106. It is not essential to set up an appellate tribunal when the tribunal of first instance is so exceptionally strong and well qualified that an appellate tribunal would be no better qualified to review its decisions. Thus, for example, we see no need to provide for appeal to a further tribunal from decisions of Pensions Appeal Tribunals or the General Claims Tribunal. The evidence indicates no dissatisfaction with the absence of such appeal in these cases.

Appeals to the courts on points of law

107. We are firmly of the opinion that all decisions of tribunals should be subject to review by the courts on points of law. This review could be obtained either by proceedings for certiorari or by appeal. [The Committee noted that an appeal on points of law was wider in scope than an application for certiorari to quash for error of law on the fact of the record (above, p. 174) and recommended:] that review by the courts of decisions of tribunals should in general be provided by making the decisions subject to appeal on points of law. We think, however, that special considerations arise in connection with the National Insurance Commissioner, the Industrial Injuries Commissioner and National Assistance Appeal Tribunals. . . .

109. The reasons which lead us to think that appeals on merits from National Assistance Appeal Tribunals are unnecessary (see paragraph 182) apply equally to appeals on points of law from these Tribunals. Accordingly we think that an exception to the general rule should also be made in the case of these Tribunals, leaving any review by the courts to be exercised by certiorari. . . .

115. There remains the question of the court to which appeals on points of law should lie. The possible alternatives are the Court of Appeal, the Divisional Court of the Queen's Bench Division, a nominated judge of the High Court or the County Court. We think that there would be some advantage in concentrating appeals in the Divisional Court. . . . Nevertheless we think that it would be wrong to lay down a hard and fast rule. In the case of the Lands

Tribunal and the Transport Tribunal there seems no cogent reason for disturbing the present practice by which appeals lie to the Court of Appeal. In certain cases it may, as the Law Society suggests, be cheaper and simpler for appeals to lie to County Courts. Where a number of new tribunals is set up and there is likely to be a large volume of appeals on technical matters there is much to be said in favour of the appeals being decided by a nominated judge, as are appeals from Pensions Appeal Tribunals.

116. We do not necessarily intend that in every case there should be unrestricted recourse through the Supreme Court and up to the House of Lords. To permit this would in many cases be inconsistent, by reason of the expense and delay involved, with the purposes for which tribunals are established. We suggest that in each case there should be one further appeal on law, by leave, and no more.

Notes

1. The recommendation that there always be a right of appeal on the merits from a tribunal of first instance to an appellate tribunal has not been implemented, no doubt at least in part for reasons of cost. However, the Tribunals and Inquiries Act 1958 provided for appeals on points of law; see now the 1992 Act, s.11, above, p. 53.

2. Paragraph 182, in relation to National Assistance Appeal Tribunals stated:

"182. Although in form [National Assistance Appeal] Tribunals hear and determine appeals against decisions of local officers of the National Assistance Board and therefore exercise adjudicating functions, in practice their task much resembles that of an assessment or case committee, taking a further look at the facts and in some cases arriving at a fresh decision on the extent of need. For this reason and also because by their very nature questions of assistance require to be finally determined as quickly as possible, we do not think that the provision of a further appeal on merits from the Tribunals is appropriate. We have already recommended, in paragraph 109, that decisions of these Tribunals should be subject to review by certiorari but not subject to appeal on points of law."

This recommendation is discussed by A.W. Bradley in *Justice, Discretion and Poverty* (ed. by Adler and Bradley) (1975), pp. 45–46. There were many suggestions that there should be a right of further appeal from the decisions of these tribunals, subsequently renamed Supplementary Benefit Appeal Tribunals. See Ruth Lister (in Adler and Bradley (eds.), *ibid.*, p. 181); H. Calvert (*ibid.*, Chap. xiv); and Adler and Bradley (*ibid.*, pp. 213–216). Rights of appeal on a point of law to the High Court were established in 1978 (S.I. 1977 No. 1735) and replaced by an appeal on a point of law to the Social Security Commissioners (Supplementary Benefits Act 1976, s.15A, inserted by the Social Security Act 1979, s.6), with a further appeal on a point of law to the Court of Appeal (Social Security Act 1980, s.14).

Controversially, on the replacement of supplementary benefit by income support and payments from the social fund, under Part III of the Social Security Act 1986, appeals were only established in respect of income support. Payments from the cash-limited social fund (replacing single payments and urgent needs payment under the supplementary benefit legislation), mostly in the form of loans, are made by social fund officers appointed by the Secretary of State. These are, in theory, discretionary payments, but the detailed directions given to the officers by the Secretary of State operate very much in the manner of regulations. Instead of an appeal, there is provision for internal review by social fund inspectors, who are DSS officials appointed as inspectors by the Social Fund Commissioner. The Commissioner is appointed by the Secretary of State. The lack of a proper appeal to an independent tribunal was criticised (to no avail) by the Council on Tribunals: Special Report, *Social Security—Abolition of*

Independent Appeals under the Proposed Social Fund, Cmnd. 9722 (1986), above, pp. 110–111. See H. Bolderson (1988) 15 J.L.S. 279; R. Drabble and T. Lynes [1989] P.L. 297.

The Council for many years pressed for the introduction of a right of appeal from the Immigration Appeal Tribunal to the courts, on a point of law, replacing applications for judicial review (Annual Report, 1990–1991 (1991–1992 H.C. 97), pp. 8–9). The Asylum and Immigration Appeals Act 1993, s.9, now provides for such an appeal.

Rather more unusually, an appeal on a point of law to the *county court* in respect of decisions made under the remodelled homelessness legislation (Part VII of the Housing Act 1996) has been created by section 204 of the 1996 Act. This is designed to curtail the stream of applications for judicial review to the High Court in homelessness cases. See annotations by A. Arden and C. Hunter in *Current Law Statutes Annotated 1996.*

3. Sir Harry Woolf has argued cogently that order needs to be introduced into the chaos of appeals to the High Court and Court of Appeal from inferior tribunals and other judicial and quasi-judicial bodies ("A Hotchpotch of Appeals—The Need for a Blender" (1988) 7 C.J.Q. 44). Appeals from a court should go to the Court of Appeal direct, normally with a requirement of leave, and with the same time limits applying to all appeals. Appeals from other bodies should only lie to the Court of Appeal if the sole issue turns on the construction of a statute or document or involves a conflict between previous decisions of the court; or the appeal is from an appellate body such as the E.A.T. Otherwise, the sole method of application should be by way of an application for judicial review.

The Law Commission's Report on *Administrative Law: Judicial Review and Statutory Appeals* (Law Com. No. 226, 1994), contained modest reform proposals in respect of appeals (Part XII, pp. 102–115). These included recommendations that all public law procedures should be consolidated into one set of Crown Office Rules; that no new case stated provisions should be created in the future (although abolition of existing procedures was not proposed); that a model application to quash (Appendix E) be used in future (although it was not suggested that existing provisions should be altered); that the test for standing under statutory appeals ("person aggrieved") should not be widened; that intervention by third parties should be permitted; and that the orders available on statutory appeals (apart from applications to quash) be harmonised. There was no proposal to standardise time-limits, to establish a general judicial discretion to extend time or to introduce a general leave requirement. The cautious nature of the proposals perhaps reflects scepticism as to whether the benefits of rationalisation would justify the cost.

Part IV: Administrative Procedures Involving an Inquiry or Hearing—General Questions

355. Under present legislation the Minister's decision in the various procedures relating to land is final, subject in most cases to a right of appeal to the High Court, exercisable generally within six weeks of the decision, on the ground that the order in question (the compulsory purchase order, clearance order, etc.) is *ultra vires* or that the prescribed procedure has not been followed. It is provided that the decision shall not otherwise be questioned in any legal proceedings whatsoever. This right of appeal thus replaces any remedy by way of an order of certiorari. Where this right of appeal is not given, for example in the case of decisions on planning appeals, the action of the Minister could presumably be challenged in certiorari proceedings.

Appeal on fact or merits

356. Several proposals have been submitted to us, particularly by organisations representing members of the legal profession, for extending the scope of recourse to the courts against the Minister's decision. We do not propose to describe them in detail; it is fair to say that for the most part their broad effect would be to enable appeals to be brought additionally on the ground either that the inspector's report or the Minister's letter of decision contained errors of fact or that, in one respect or another, the Minister's decision was not "reasonably" based upon the evidence at the inquiry and the facts found by the inspector.

357. Many of these proposals, particularly those which seek to apply a test of "reasonableness" to the basis of the Minister's decision, would have the effect of introducing an appeal on merits against the decision. We cannot regard such an appeal as appropriate. If, as we have already recommended, the parties are enabled to propose corrections to the inspector's findings of fact and the Minister is required to submit new factual evidence to the parties, there seems no need for an appeal beyond the Minister on fact.

358. Most of the witnesses who in their memoranda of evidence had proposed a wider scope of appeal to the courts agreed in oral evidence that, provided that the findings of fact were properly open to challenge before the decision and that the procedure was improved in other respects—notably by making inspectors independent of the deciding Minister and by requiring from the Minister, whenever possible, a statement of policy before the inquiry and full reasons for his eventual decision—then appeals to the courts against the Minister's decision could be restricted, as at present, to the two grounds of *ultra vires* and procedural defect.

Appeal on law

359. There remains the question of an appeal on law. It is difficult to see how any question of law could arise other than a question of jurisdiction or procedure. The present form of appeal, covering these two matters, seems to us adequate, particularly since the scope for bringing appeals on grounds of alleged procedural irregularity will be wider if the various recommendations which we have made for strengthening and improving the procedure are adopted and, where appropriate, given statutory effect. This form of appeal should, however, be applied to decisions on planning appeals in the same way as it applies to decisions in other cases relating to land. We think that it would be reasonable to reduce, for example from six to four weeks, the limit of time for lodging appeals to the courts if a period of 14 days were allowed at an earlier stage for challenging the inspector's findings of fact. It is for consideration whether, following the lines of our suggestions concerning tribunals, all such appeals could not with advantage be made to the Divisional Court. There should then be one further appeal, by leave.

Note
See further pp. 552 *et seq.*, below, on the form of appeal described in paragraph 355.

(B) Appeals on Questions of Fact or Merits

SAGNATA INVESTMENTS LTD v. NORWICH CORPORATION

[1971] 2 Q.B. 614; [1971] 3 W.L.R. 133; [1971] 2 All E.R. 1441; 69 L.G.R. 471 (Court of Appeal)

The Betting, Gaming and Lotteries Act 1963, Sched. 6, para. 2 provided that the grant of a permit for amusements with prizes should be "at the discretion of the local authority". Schedule 6, para. 6, provided that where a local authority refused an application for a permit, the applicant could "appeal in accordance with the provisions of the Quarter Sessions Act 1849" to quarter sessions. Section 1 of the 1849 Act provided that "In every case of appeal ... to any court of quarter sessions 14 clear days' notice of appeal ... shall be given ... and such notice of appeal shall be in writing, ... and the grounds of appeal shall be specified in every such notice: Provided always, that it shall not be lawful for the appellant or appellants, on the trial of any such appeal, to go into or give evidence of any other ground of appeal besides those set forth in such notice."

In March 1969, Sagnata Investments Ltd applied under the Act of 1963 for a permit for amusements with prizes at an amusement arcade to be built at a site known as Old Post Office Court in Norwich. That application was in due course refused by the Fire Service and Licensing Committee of Norwich Corporation, and their written grounds of refusal were in the following terms:

> "(a) The use of these premises as an amusement place would be likely to have undesirable social effects on the young people expected to frequent them; (b) the making available of gaming facilities in Norwich which could be used by children was something which the committee are not prepared to permit; (c) the number of amusements with prizes machines legally available elsewhere in Norwich for the use of adults was sufficient to meet all reasonable needs."

The unsuccessful applicants appealed from that refusal to Norwich City Quarter Sessions, their stated ground of appeal being, "that the decision ... was unreasonable, having regard to the information available to the committee and contrary to natural justice".

The recorder, Michael Havers Q.C., found the following facts to be either proved or admitted: that no objection was made to the company, the premises or the site, the last named being particularly suitable; that the council as a whole had by an overwhelming majority of 41 to 1 taken a general policy decision not to grant permits for amusements with prizes for any such amusement places in Norwich and that decision had been applied to the application by the committee; that whilst it was likely that a certain number of children and young people would use the amusement arcade there was no evidence either way as to whether or not they would do so to a considerable extent and/or whether or not such a use would be socially undesirable. In that respect evidence was called before the recorder in the form of the committee chairman—a Norwich city councillor since 1934 and a former Lord Mayor who expressed his fears in that matter. Whilst accepting his evidence, the recorder did not find that it amounted to anything more than the expression of a realistic and honest opinion; that the committee's decision was reached fairly and honestly with a genuine belief in the socially harmful result of setting up such an amusement arcade; that there were not sufficient facilities of that nature in Norwich at the present time.

The recorder was of the opinion that the committee had so fettered its discretion by following the policy decisions of the council that no application for such a permit could succeed before it and the committee had therefore failed to exercise its discretion at all; that it was for the corporation to prove that the provision of an amusement arcade would be socially undesirable; that having regard to the exclusion of amusement places from section 3 of the Betting, Gaming and Lotteries Act 1964 neither the committee nor quarter sessions were entitled to take into consideration the fact that by reason of the purpose for which or the persons by whom the premises were to be used it was undesirable that such a permit be granted; that the *obiter dictum* of Lord Parker C.J. in *R. v. Essex Quarter Sessions, ex p. Thomas* [1966] 1 W.L.R. 359, 362, that:

"Speaking for myself, I would hesitate, and I would expect any chairman of quarter sessions to hesitate, long before differing from the local justices who had dealt with the matter in their locality with the greatest care,"

had no bearing on such an appeal as the recorder was hearing. In the result the recorder felt he had no alternative but to allow the appeal.

The Corporation appealed unsuccessfully to the Divisional Court, and then to the Court of Appeal. The grounds of appeal were that the recorder (1) misdirected himself that his appellate discretion was absolute and unfettered, with the result that he substituted his own discretion for that of the Fire Service and Licensing Committee notwithstanding the fact that the committee were not shown to have erred in fact or law; (2) misdirected himself in holding as a matter of law and/or fact that the committee had fettered its own discretion by implementing a general policy decision of the whole council; (3) misdirected himself in holding that the views of the councillors who sat on the committee were irrelevant and/or of no evidential value to him as appellate tribunal in deciding the issue as to the desirability and need for the provision of such an amusement arcade; (4) failed to take into consideration the evidence of the chairman of the committee; (5) erred in fact and in law in holding that there was no sufficient evidence before him to establish that the provision of such facilities in the locality was socially undesirable or harmful; (6) failed to deal adequately or at all with the third and final ground on which the committee based its refusal, namely, that such new facilities were not required since there were adequate amusement with prizes machines already available elsewhere in Norwich.

LORD DENNING M.R.: (dissenting) [His Lordship summarised the facts, the legislative history and the relevant statutory provisions, and continued:]

4. *The Hearing by the Local Authority*
On May 2, 1969, the licensing committee of the City of Norwich heard the application. The applicants were represented by a solicitor, who put their case fully. The committee asked pertinent questions which the solicitor answered. At the end of the committee thanked him for presenting a clear case and he, in his turn, thanked the committee for listening to him. We were given a note of the proceedings before the committee. I append it herewith (*post*, p. 628G). It shows that the committee acted with the utmost fairness and discretion. They explored questions of policy and of detail, and, at the end, reserved their decision....

5. *The Appeal to the Recorder*
[His Lordship summarised the reasons of the recorder in allowing the appeal, and pointed out that no evidence was given in support of the stated

ground of appeal.] The recorder was not even told of the "information available to the committee". And I see no possible justification for the assertion that the decision was "unreasonable" or "contrary to natural justice...".

6. *The General Policy Decision*

There has been much discussion lately on the right of a licensing body to lay down for itself a general policy to guide its decisions. In the past, recourse has been had to the words of Bankes L.J. in *R. v. Port of London Authority, ex p. Kynoch Ltd* [1919] 1 K.B. 176, 182–186, and to the judgment of Lord Goddard C.J. in *R. v. Torquay Licensing Justices, ex p. Brockman* [1951] 2 K.B. 784, 788–792; but these cases have now to be read in the light of the decisions of Cooke J. in *Stringer v. Minister of Housing and Local Government* [1970] 1 W.L.R. 1281, 1297–1298 and of the House of Lords in *British Oxygen Co. Ltd v. Board of Trade* [1971] A.C. 610, and of this court in *Cumings v. Birkenhead Corporation* [1971] 2 W.L.R. 1458. I take it to be perfectly clear now that an administrative body, including a licensing body, which may have to consider numerous applications of a similar kind, is entitled to lay down a general policy which it proposes to follow in coming to its individual decisions, provided always that it is a reasonable policy which it is fair and just to apply. Once laid down, the administrative body is entitled to apply the policy in the individual cases which come before it. The only qualification is that the administrative body must not apply the policy so rigidly as to reject an applicant without hearing what he has to say. It must not "shut its ears to an application": see [1971] A.C. 610, 625, *per* Lord Reid. The applicant is entitled to put forward reasons urging that the policy should be changed, or saying that in any case it should not be applied to him. But, so long as the administrative body is ready to hear him and consider what he has to say, it is entitled to apply its general policy to him as to others.

The local authority at Norwich fulfilled every one of these requirements. If you read the note of the proceedings before the committee, it is apparent that, although the city council laid down a general policy, the licensing committee did not regard that policy as inflexible or as binding on them: that they listened to everything that the applicants had to say: and yet decided against them.

The recorder seems to have thought that the local authority were not entitled to have a general policy at all: or, at any rate, not to be able to apply it in any individual case. He said:

"I have sympathy with the committee who feel that the well-being and protection of the young people of this city is part of their general responsibility, and I am absolutely certain that they have acted fairly, honestly and fearlessly in forming their policy. It may be that their policy is right, but unless and until Parliament provides for a local authority in this type of application the right to make the kind of policy rule that does exist in respect of other premises, each application must be treated on its merits...."

I think that, in these words, the recorder misdirected himself in law. By his very words, he acknowledges that the policy was fairly and honestly formed and was a reasonable policy. If so, the local authority were entitled to have the policy and to apply it in this individual case, provided that they listened to all the applicant had to say—which they most clearly did.

7. *Evidence de Novo*
The recorder said:

"... this being an appeal to quarter sessions, I must consider the matter de novo.... I must now approach the matter afresh with a complete and unfettered discretion. What is the evidence? As I have said, no objection is taken to the applicant, the premises or the site. The objection for which I have some sympathy is really the risk of providing easily accessible gambling facilities to children and young persons. On the facts there seems to be very little evidence of this; ... I would require some evidence not only that such a place would be used to a considerable extent by young people, but also that such a use would be socially undesirable."

Those were the grounds of the recorder's judgment.

Mr Boreham Q.C. [counsel for the company] supported this view. He submitted that the recorder ought to hear the evidence afresh, and exercise his own discretion, quite uninfluenced by what the local authority had done. He relied on *Godfrey v. Bournemouth Corporation* [1969] 1 W.L.R. 47, 52. I do not think this is correct. It is plain from the Act of 1849 that the recorder must hear evidence on all matters raised by the notice of appeal: and is not to travel outside on to other matters, because that might prejudice the respondent. It is also plain that the recorder ought to give great weight to the decision of the local authority. Lord Parker C.J. said so in *R. v. Essex Quarter Sessions, ex p. Thomas* [1966] 1 W.L.R. 359, 361–362, and repeated it in this very case.

In this case the local authority formed the opinion that it was socially undesirable to have amusement arcades in Norwich. That is why they laid down their general policy. But the recorder put their views on one side. He was not prepared, he said, to act on "unproved general principles of social undesirability and potential danger to young people", but wanted evidence on it.

I think that, in so holding, the recorder misdirected himself in law. Seeing that Parliament has entrusted the discretion to the local authority, it must intend then that their views should carry great weight. They are elected by the people to do all things proper to be done for the good administration of their city. They know their locality. They know its needs. They respond to the feelings of the citizens. If they think that an amusement arcade is socially undesirable, they are entitled to say so. They do not require evidence for the purpose. It is a matter of opinion on which their views are worth as much as those of any other person: and, indeed, worth more than those of a stranger. In any case, their views coincide with those of the Churches' Committee on Gambling: and that goes a long way. Their views should not be pushed on one side by the courts as worth nothing. Just as with their power to make by-laws, so also with their power to grant licences for amusement arcades. Their decision "ought to be supported if possible": see *Kruse v. Johnson* [1898] 2 Q.B. 91, 99, *per* Lord Russell C.J. In rejecting their views, the recorder was in error.

8. *Conclusion*
In my opinion the recorder erred in law in the two respects which I have stated. I would therefore allow the appeal and uphold the decision of the local authority.

My brethren disagree. Together with the recorder, and all the other judges, they hold that the views of the citizens of Norwich must be overruled. They must grant the freedom of their city to this amusement arcade, even though they believe it to be socially undesirable. I do not think this is right. This, in my opinion, is a matter for local self-government. Parliament intentionally made this a matter for the discretion of the local authority and there is no good reason for overruling their decision.

EDMUND DAVIES L.J.: ... This litigation is said to raise in an acute form the question as to the nature of appeals to quarter sessions in such cases as the present. At one stage, Lord Denning M.R. summarised the issue in this way:

"Is the hearing to be treated as a new trial to be determined on evidence de novo, without being influenced by what the local authority has done? Or is the hearing to be treated as an appeal proper, in which the local authority's decision is to be regarded as of considerable weight, and is not to be reversed unless their decision is shown to be wrong?"

With profound respect, however, I do not think that this is the proper antithesis, and I shall seek to show that there is a half-way house between these two approaches.

It is well established that no right of appeal exists apart from statute. As already observed, the only statutory provision relevant to the present case is that "the applicant may appeal in accordance with the provisions of the Quarter Sessions Act 1849". In *Drover v. Rugman* [1951] 1 K.B. 380, dealing with a case stated by quarter sessions on an appeal from the juvenile court, Lord Goddard C.J. said, at 382:

"When a case goes to a quarter sessions it is reheard; the person seeking an order proves his case over again. That only means that quarter sessions are taking the place, as it may be expressed, of petty sessions; but the proceedings are none the less an appeal."

This, he explained, was due to the fact that there was no formal record of proceedings before justices, an observation equally true of proceedings before the licensing committee of this local authority, which (as Lord Denning M.R. has observed) are wholly dissimilar to those conducted by a body exercising judicial functions.

For my part, I cannot see how it is practicable in cases such as the present for an appeal to quarter sessions to be other than by way of a complete rehearing. Having no record before him of what transpired before the local authority, how could the recorder otherwise begin to judge the cogency of the written reasons placed before him? ...

As it appears to me, Mr Tapp [counsel for the corporation] has attached excessive weight to the fact that the granting or renewal of a permit under the Act of 1963 is expressed to be "at the discretion of the local authority" when he concludes therefrom that quarter sessions are bound by the decision of the local authority and its stated reasons unless it can be demonstrated that they were wrong. A similar contention was raised—and rejected—in *Stepney*

Borough Council v. Joffe [1949] 1 K.B. 599, where street traders' licences to trade were revoked by the borough council. This they had done pursuant to a statutory provision where "the applicant or licensee is on account of misconduct or for any other sufficient reason in their opinion unsuitable to hold such licence ...". Section 25(1) of the London County Council (General Powers) Act 1947 provided that persons aggrieved by such refusal "may appeal to a petty sessional court and on any such appeal the court may confirm, reverse or vary the decision of the borough council ...". The traders accordingly appealed to a magistrate, whereupon the council contended (1) that the magistrate was not entitled to substitute his own opinion as to the suitability of the traders to hold licences for that of the council; (2) that he was not empowered to review the merits; and (3) that his jurisdiction was limited to considering whether or not there was any material on which the council could reasonably have arrived at their decisions to revoke the licences. (One may note, in parenthesis, the close similarity of those submissions to that advanced by the present appellant.) But the magistrate would have none of this. He held that he was bound to consider the whole matter de novo, and he allowed the appeals. Upholding that decision in the Divisional Court, and referring to the submission that the magistrate had not been entitled to substitute his opinion for that of the borough council and that all he could decide was whether there was evidence upon which the council could arrive at their conclusion, Lord Goddard C.J. said, at 602:

> "If that argument be right, the right of appeal, ... would be purely illusory. Such an appeal would ... really be only an appeal on the question of law whether there was any evidence upon which the borough council could have formed an opinion. If their decision were a mere matter of opinion and that opinion were to be conclusive, I do not know that the borough council would be obliged to have any evidence. They could simply say: 'In our opinion this person is unsuitable to hold a licence.' It is true that they must give a sufficient reason, but they could give any reason they liked and say: 'That is sufficient in our opinion.' I do not know how a court could then say on appeal that that was not a sufficient reason. If the reason need only be one which is sufficient in the opinion of the borough council, it is difficult to see how any court of appeal could set aside their decision. It seems to me that [section 25(1)] gives an unrestricted right of appeal, and if there is an unrestricted right of appeal, it is for the court of appeal to substitute its opinion for the opinion of the borough council."

I would apply those words in full measure to the present case. The provision for an appeal to quarter sessions seems to me largely, if not entirely, "illusory" if the contention of the appellant council is right. If it is, I am at a loss to follow how the recorder would set about discharging his appellate function. Lacking all information as to what had happened before the local authority, save the bare knowledge that they had refused the application and their written grounds for refusal, he would be powerless, as I think, to make any effective examination of the validity of those reasons. Furthermore, unless he is free to embark on a complete consideration of all the relevant material presented to him, how can he in due course proceed to state a case for the Divisional Court if called upon to do so? The customary (and preferable) way of doing this is *inter alia* to set out in separate paragraphs those facts found by the lower court to have been "proved or admitted", and indeed we were shown a copy of the draft case prepared (but ultimately not used) by the local authority in the present case which was in that form. But how could the recorder proceed to state what *his* findings of fact were if he was not free to receive evidence and assess it? No satisfactory answer to this question has, in my judgment, been advanced, and for this reason, among others, I am forced to the conclusion that the appellants are wrong in their main contention. I hold that the proceedings before this recorder were by way of a complete rehearing.

But, contrary to what has been contended, this conclusion does *not* involve that the views earlier formed by the local authority have to be entirely disregarded by quarter sessions. It is true that in *Godfrey v. Bournemouth Corporation* [1969] 1 W.L.R. 47, after observing that an appeal to quarter sessions under Schedule 6 to this same Act was by way of a complete rehearing, Lord Parker C.J. said, at 52, "the discretion is a discretion which the recorder in the present case had to arrive at himself uninfluenced by what the local authority had done". But with respect, I do not accept this. It went much too far, it was in direct conflict with the view which Lord Parker C.J. had earlier expressed in *R. v. Essex Quarter Sessions, ex p. Thomas* [1966] 1 W.L.R. 359, 363, it was contrary to the approach adopted both by the recorder and by Lord Parker C.J. himself in the instant case, and it was, with deference, an uncalled-for observation. Here again, *Stepney Borough Council v. Joffe* [1949] 1 K.B. 599 establishes what I regard as the proper approach, for, having made the point that there was in that case an unrestricted appeal, Lord Goddard C.J. continued, at 602, 603:

"That does not mean to say that the court of appeal, in this case the metropolitan magistrate, ought not to pay great attention to the fact that the duly constituted and elected local authority have come to an opinion on the matter, and ought not lightly, of course, to reverse their opinion. It is constantly said (although I am not sure that it is always sufficiently remembered) that the function of a court of appeal is to exercise its powers when it is satisfied that the judgment below is wrong, not merely because it is not satisfied that the judgment was right."

I find no reason for thinking that the recorder in the present case failed in any degree to pay proper regard to the decision arrived at by an overwhelming majority of the local authority. On the contrary, he manifestly entertained considerable sympathy with their attitude. But, as he said, he was ultimately obliged to act on the totality of the material placed before him, balancing that called for the appellants against that presented by the local authority and paying due regard to the existing decision being appealed from. Having done so, he concluded that the appellants had made out their case, the Divisional Court in its turn have upheld him, and for my part I have to say that it was not established to my satisfaction that either erred in law. I therefore find myself compelled to hold that this appeal should be dismissed and that the order of the recorder granting the permit be upheld.

PHILLIMORE L.J.: ... [T]here is no need for authority for the proposition that a council and its committees are entitled to agree on a policy provided always that they do not impose it inflexibly. In this case, however, we were told that the chairman of the committee—a former Mayor of Norwich—gave evidence before the recorder to the effect that they had rejected the application solely on the basis of the policy decision taken by the General Purposes Committee....

[The recorder said:]

> "I am forced to the conclusion that in this case, where the application met with all the ordinary requirements as to suitability of site, premises and management, the general policy must have been applied. In other words, no application to the local authority, however suitable, would succeed."

In other words the council had *not* exercised any form of discretion. They had simply dismissed this application after going through the necessary motions without regard to its individual merits or demerits. I take this to be a finding of fact with which this court is in no position to interfere.

Incidentally, I cannot see that the recorder could avoid this decision. Apparently no evidence was called to support either ground (a) or ground (b). Nobody came forward to say that this sort of arcade had resulted in disastrous damage to the morality of the young in Great Yarmouth or any other seaside place or was likely to prove particularly harmful to the young of Norwich. Indeed, as I think, the Act of 1964 by section 3 tends to suggest that in regard to premises such as this it is wrong to refuse a licence on the ground that some particular class such as young persons may be injuriously affected....

I think that the recorder was clearly right and that his judgment should not be disturbed. This is a case where he was satisfied that the council's committee had failed to keep an open mind and had applied their policy without regard to the facts of the individual case.

[His Lordship agreed with EDMUND DAVIES L.J. that the appeal to Quarter Sessions was by way of rehearing.]

Appeal dismissed.

Notes and Questions

1. See case note by J. Prophet [1971] P.L. 162.

2. The recorder said: "In my view ... the licensing committee have decided that they will not grant a permit for *any* amusement place with prizes in the City of Norwich, and the reasons they give for *this* refusal would apply to *any* application" (italics added by Edmund Davies L.J.). What are the implications of this view?

3. Where should the right to decide such a question as that raised in *Sagnata* lie, with the courts or with the local authority?

4. Appeals which formerly lay to quarter sessions now lie to the Crown Court: the Courts Act 1971, ss.8, 9, Scheds. 1, 9; I.R. Scott, *The Crown Court* (1972), paras. 204–233.

5. The grant of permits in respect of the provision of amusements with prizes is now governed by Part III of the Gaming Act 1968 (gaming by means of machines) and the Lotteries and Amusements Act 1976 (see C. Milner Smith and S.P. Monkcom, *The Law of Betting, Gaming and Lotteries* (1987), Chaps. 10 and 11; *R. v. Chichester Crown Court, ex p. Forte* [1995] 160 J.P. 285.

The *Sagnata* approach applies also to appeals to the Crown Court concerning general gaming club licences (*i.e.* casino and bingo club licences) (*R. v. Crown Court at*

Knightsbridge, ex p. Aspinall Curzon Ltd, The Times, December 16, 1982; Smith and Monkcom, *op. cit.*, pp. 218–220). See also *Sutton London Borough Council v. Davis* [1994] Fam. 241, where Wilson J. held that the justices on an appeal under the Children Act 1989, s.77, against the local authority's refusal to register the applicant as a childminder, had to look at the matter *de novo* and decide for themselves whether she was a fit person. The justices were not obliged to accept the local authority's policy that any person who declined to give an undertaking not to smack the children was unfit.

6. In the fact that an appeal is by way of rehearing enables the court to consider evidence of matters arising between the original decision appealed against and the appeal: *Rushmoor Borough Council v. Richards, The Times,* February 5, 1996 (appeal against refusal to extend licensing hours of a nightclub under the Local Government (Miscellaneous Provisions) Act 1982, Sched. 1; court entitled to hear evidence that the nightclub was badly run.

7. In certain situations, local authorities have express statutory power to pass "blanket" resolutions that would otherwise be impermissible under the rule against the fettering of discretion. A local authority is empowered by the Gaming Act 1968, Sched. 9, para. 3, to resolve not to grant or renew permits under Part III in respect of "a class of premises specified in the resolution". However, the power cannot apply to premises used or to be used wholly or mainly for the provision of amusements by means of machines to which Part III applies (para. 4), thus requiring applications in respect of amusement centres, arcades and the like to be considered on their merits. The policy behind this power was:

"parliament's view that local consideration should be given considerable weight in determining in which types of premises amusements with prizes generally, and machines in particular, should be available to the general public for gaming. A particular factor which influenced parliament . . . was the availability of such machines to persons under the age of 18" (Smith and Monkcom, *op. cit.*, p. 325).

It is uncertain whether a local authority's resolution not to grant or renew permits in respect of *all* premises in its area other than those exempted by para. 4 would be *intra vires* (see Smith and Monkcom, *op. cit.*, pp. 326–328, noting the view of Woolf J. in *Westminster City Council v. Lunepalm Ltd, The Times,* December 10, 1985, that it would be, but dicta to the contrary in *Walker v. Leeds City Council* [1978] A.C. 403, 421 at 422, *per* Lords Simon and Kilbrandon).

Similarly, the Lotteries and Amusements Act 1976, Sched. 3, para. 2 enables a local authority to pass a resolution that it will not grant, or will neither grant nor renew, any permits for the commercial provision of amusements with prizes in respect of premises of a class specified in the resolution. By para. 3, such a resolution may not be passed in respect of premises used or to be used wholly or mainly for the purposes of a pleasure fair consisting wholly or mainly of amusements. These provisions, which formerly appeared in the Betting, Gaming and Lotteries Act 1963, Sched. 6 (as amended), were considered in *R. v. Herrod, ex p. Leeds City Council* [1976] Q.B. 540, C.A.; affirmed, *sub nom. Walker v. Leeds County Council* [1978] A.C. 403, H.L. The Court of Appeal emphasised that the courts should construe the power to pass "blanket" resolutions strictly, as the refusal or non-renewal of a licence without a hearing seemed contrary to natural justice and a non-renewal might cause serious economic loss (see Lord Denning M.R. at 560, James L.J. at 566 and Shaw L.J. at 570–571). Accordingly, the term "pleasure fair" in the para. 3 exemption was to be given a wide meaning as including premises used for the purposes of playing prize bingo. An appeal to the House of Lords was dismissed. Lord Wilberforce stated at 417 that if the term "pleasure fair" was to be interpreted restrictively as meaning "fun fair," bingo hall owners in areas where the appropriate "blanket" resolutions were passed would be "unable even to present a case on the merits to the local authorities. They are automatically resolved out of business. This, in relation to a comparatively innocuous form of activity, seems rather draconian, and at least justifies the courts looking to see whether there is possible alternative."

8. In other contexts, a narrow interpretation has been given to the scope of an appeal notwithstanding that no grounds have been specified in the statute. Thus, in *John Dee Ltd v. Customs and Excise Commissioners* [1995] S.T.C. 941, the Court of Appeal held that a Value Added Tax Tribunal on an appeal under the Value Added Tax Act 1983, s.40(1)(n), against a decision of the Commissioners where it appeared requisite for the protection of the revenue to provide security for the payment of VAT, could not exercise a fresh discretion in the matter. The protection of the revenue was not a matter for a tribunal or a court. The tribunal merely had to consider whether the commissioners had acted in a way in which no reasonable panel of commissioners could have acted or whether they had taken into account some irrelevant matter or had disregarded something to which they should have given weight. Rather confusingly, the court was also at pains to emphasise that the jurisdiction was appellate and not supervisory and that "references in this context to *Wednesbury* principles are capable of being a source of confusion" (*per* Neill L.J. at 952)(!).

(C) Statutory *Ultra Vires*

ACQUISITION OF LAND ACT 1981

Part IV: Validity and Date of Operation of Orders and Certificates

Grounds for application to High Court

23.—(1) If any person aggrieved by a compulsory purchase order desires to question the validity thereof, or of any provision contained therein, on the ground that the authorisation of a compulsory purchase thereby granted is not empowered to be granted under this Act or any such enactment as is mentioned in section 1(1) of this Act, he may make an application to the High Court.

(2) If any person aggrieved by—
  (a) a compulsory purchase order, or
  (b) a certificate under Part III of, or Schedule 3 to, this Act.
desires to question the validity thereof on the ground that any relevant requirement has not been complied with in relation to the order or certificate he may make an application to the High Court.

(3) In subsection (2) above, "relevant requirement" means—
  (a) any requirement of this Act, or of any regulation under section 7(2) above, or
  (b) any requirement of the Tribunals and Inquiries Act [1992] or of any rules made, or having effect as if made, under that Act.

(4) An application to the High Court under this section shall be made within six weeks.
  (a) in the case of a compulsory purchase order to which the Statutory Orders (Special Procedure) Act 1945 applies (and which is not excluded by section 27 below), from the date on which the order becomes operative under that Act,

(b) in the case of a compulsory purchase order to which the said Act of 1945 does not apply, from the date on which notice of the confirmation or making of the order is first published in accordance with this Act,

(c) in the case of a certificate, the date on which notice of the giving of the certificate is first published in accordance with this Act.

Powers of the court

24.—(1) On an application under section 23 above the court may by interim order suspend the operation of the compulsory purchase order or any provision contained therein, or of the certificate, either generally or in so far as it effects any property of the applicant, until the final determination of the proceedings.

(2) If on the application the court is satisfied that—

(a) the authorisation granted by the compulsory purchase order is not empowered to be granted under this Act or any such enactment as is mentioned in section 1(1) of this Act, or

(b) the interests of the applicant have been substantially prejudiced by any relevant requirement (as defined in section 23(3) above) not having been complied with,

the court may quash the compulsory purchase order or any provision contained therein, or the certificate, either generally or in so far as it affects any property of the applicant.

Restriction on other court proceedings

25. Subject to the preceding provisions of this Part of this Act, a compulsory purchase order, or a certificate under Part III of, or Schedule 3 to, this Act, shall not, either before or after it has been confirmed, made or given, be questioned in any legal proceedings whatsoever.

Date of operation

26.—(1) Subject to section 24 above, a compulsory purchase order, other than one to which the Statutory Orders (Special Procedure) Act 1945 applies, shall become operative on the date on which notice of the confirmation or making of the order is first published in accordance with this Act.

(2) Subject to section 24 above, a certificate under Part III of, or Schedule 3 to, this Act shall become operative on the date on which notice of the giving of the certificate is first published in accordance with this Act.

Exclusion of orders confirmed by Act of Parliament

27. This Part of this Act shall not apply to an order which is confirmed by Act of Parliament under section 6 of the Statutory Orders (Special Procedure) Act 1945.

Notes

1. An appeal provision in this form was first introduced in section 11 of the Housing Act 1930, which Act gave greater slum clearance powers to local authorities. The

limitations both as to the grounds and the period allowed for appeals were thought necessary in view of the chaos that had been caused by the availability of the prerogative writs to challenge improvement schemes under earlier legislation. In *R. v. Minister of Health, ex p. Davis*,[1] the Divisional Court had granted a writ of prohibition to restrain the Minister from confirming a scheme for a site in the centre of Derby. The scheme was held to be *ultra vires* on the ground that some of the land was to be purchased compulsorily for the purpose of resale, and not for any purpose of rearrangement or reconstruction as authorised by the Act. It was alleged that no scheme confirmed by the Minister up to 1929 was valid.[2] Counsel for the property owners in the *Davis* case said that he had examined about 100 schemes, all of which were invalid.[3] As a result new schemes and schemes in progress were held up[4]; "and ... it was decided that the whole purpose of the Act had been frustrated by the slum landlords and the Court, and that nothing substantial could be done until new legislation was passed."[5]

From 1930, provisions similar to section 11 of the Housing Act 1930 were included in many statutes, perhaps too often as a matter of course.[6] The need for finality is rarely as compelling as it is for large scale slum clearance schemes, compulsory purchase orders and the like. The main examples of "statutory *ultra vires*" clauses are: the Acquisition of Land Act 1981, Part IV (compulsory purchase orders: see *Smith v. East Elloe RDC* below, p. 799); the New Towns Act 1981, Sched. 1 (orders designating the site of a new town: see *Franklin v. Minister of Town and Country Planning*, above, p. 526); the Highways Act 1980, Sched. 2 (orders designating a highway as a trunk road, motorway schemes, etc.); *ibid.*, Sched. 7 (public path creation extinguishment and diversion orders); the Town and Country Planning Act 1990, s.287 (structure or local plans, etc.); *ibid.*, s.288 (a large variety of planning matters including decisions of the Secretary of State on appeals against a refusal of planning permission; *cf.* section 289 of the 1990 Act which give rights of appeal on a point of law to the High Court, against decisions of the Secretary of State (*inter alia*) to uphold an enforcement notice.

The attitude the courts should take to statutory *ultra vires* clauses has been restated by Lord Denning M.R. (in the *Ashbridge* and *Coleen* cases, below, pp. 555 and 560). Other examples of challenges under these procedures given in this book are *Lavender v. M.H.L.G.* (p. 258); *Stringer v. M.H.L.G.* (p. 262 (note)); *Hanks v. M.H.L.G.* (p. 343) and *Franklin v. Minister of Town and Country Planning* (p. 526). The question of the exclusion of judicial review by procedures other than that laid down in the relevant clause are considered in *Smith v. East Elloe RDC* (p. 799) and *ex p. Ostler* (p. 804).

2. The line between decisions and orders that are protected by a statutory *ultra vires* clause, and decisions that remain subject to judicial review can be complex, and depends on the exact wording of the clause in question. For example, the special appeal provisions apply to a decision by the Secretary of State to confirm a compulsory purchase order, but not a refusal to confirm an order, or a decision to exclude land from an order (*Islington London Borough Council v. Secretary of State for the Environment*; *Stockport Metropolitan Borough Council v. Secretary of State for the Environment* (1980) 43 P. & C.R. 300; *R. v. Secretary of State for the Environment, ex p. Melton Borough Council* [1986] J.P.L. 190); or a question whether implementation of an order would be unconscionable (*R. v. Carmarthenshire District Council, ex p. Blewin*

---

[1] [1929] 1 K.B. 619.

[2] Sir John Lorden, *Minutes of Evidence of the Donoughmore Committee* (1932), p. 68, para. 1010.

[3] Mr H.A. Hill, *ibid.*, p. 72, para. 1027.

[4] The Minister of Health (Mr Arthur Greenwood): oral answer, H.C.Deb., Vol. 234, col. 1164 (January 30, 1930); Second Reading of the Housing Bill, H.C.Deb., Vol. 237, cols. 1805–1807 (April 7, 1930).

[5] W.I. Jennings, "Local Government Law" (1935) 51 L.Q.R. 180, at 193.

[6] B. Schwartz lists 18 examples from 1930 to 1948 in *Law and the Executive in Britain* (1949), p. 209, n. 138.

Trust (1989) 59 P. & C.R. 379). On the position under the Town and Country Planning Act 1990, see annotations to section 284 in the *Encyclopedia of Planning Law and Practice.*

ASHBRIDGE INVESTMENTS LTD v. MINISTER OF HOUSING AND LOCAL GOVERNMENT

(Re Stalybridge (Castle Hall No. 7) and (Acres Lane and Lawton Street) Compulsory Purchase Order 1963)

[1965] 1 W.L.R. 1320; 129 J.P. 580; 109 S.J. 595; [1965] 3 All E.R. 371; 63 L.G.R. 400 (Court of Appeal)

Stalybridge Borough Council declared an area to be a clearance area for the purposes of section 42(1) of the Housing Act 1957, on the ground that the houses therein were unfit for human habitation. This area included two adjoining terrace houses of similar appearance, numbers 17 and 19, Grosvenor Street, owned by the respondents. Subsequently the local authority made a compulsory purchase order in respect of the clearance area, which was coloured pink on the map of the order, and of certain adjoining land which was coloured grey on the map. The compensation payable in respect of the pink area (unfit houses) was less than that payable in the grey area. Following objections by the owners, a local inquiry was held. The Minister confirmed the order with modifications. One modification was the transfer of number 19 from the pink area to the grey area on the ground that it had lost its identity as a dwelling, and so was not a "house". The owners applied under Schedule 4, para. 2, to the Housing Act 1957, for an order quashing the compulsory purchase order in so far as it affected number 17, on the ground that it was not a "house", or alternatively was not unfit for human habitation.

Mocatta J. (1965) 109 S.J. 474, held that the question whether number 17 was a "house" was a question going to the jurisdiction of the Minister and that the court should receive evidence of the facts and reach its own conclusion thereon, and was not confined to the question whether the Minister, on the evidence before him could properly conclude that number 17 was a house. The Minister appealed.

LORD DENNING M.R.: [outlined the facts and continued:] Now the owners make application to the High Court asking for the order to be quashed in regard to No. 17. They say that the Minister has gone outside his jurisdiction because No. 17 is not a house. It is no more a house than No. 19. The owners say that the court should receive evidence afresh on this point and should come to its own conclusion as to whether or no No. 17 is a house or not.

The Minister objects. He says: "This is not a matter on which the court should receive fresh evidence at all, or go into the matter afresh. It is simply a case for the court to ask: Did the Minister have reasonable grounds or no for determining No. 17 to be a house?" The Minister concedes that, if he had no evidence before him such as to justify that finding, or if the materials before him were such that he could not reasonably come to the conclusion that it was a house then, of course, the court could interfere. The Minister also concedes that if he has erred in point of law the court can inquire into and quash his decision. But he says that this should be determined on the materials which he had before him, and not on fresh evidence. Mocatta J. has held that the court can look into the matter afresh and receive fresh evidence.

Section 42 of the Housing Act 1957, says: "(1) Where a local authority, upon consideration of an official representation or other information in their possession, are satisfied as respects any area in their district—(a) that the houses in that area are unfit for human habitation ... the authority shall cause that area to be defined on a map", and so on. It is apparent that the question "fit or unfit?" is essentially one for the inspector and the Minister, and the courts would not ordinarily admit fresh evidence on it. But the owners say that, on the question of "house or not a house", the court can and should look into the whole matter itself afresh.

In order to decide this question it is helpful to look at Schedule 3, para. 4(3). It says that "If the Minister is of opinion that any land included by the local authority in a clearance area should not have been so included, he shall ... modify it so as to exclude that land for all purposes from the clearance area." It is clear, therefore, that the Minister can move the land from the pink into the grey if he thinks that it should not have been originally included in the pink area. It seems to me that, in order to determine this matter, the Minister must himself decide the question of "house or not a house", just as he must decide "fit or unfit". The legislature has entrusted it to the Minister for decision. If it is not unfit, he can remove it from the pink to the grey. If it is not a house, he can likewise remove it from the pink to the grey.

Seeing that that decision is entrusted to the Minister, we have to consider the power of the court to interfere with his decision. It is given in Schedule 4, para. 2. The court can only interfere on the ground that the Minister has gone outside the powers of the Act or that any requirement of the Act has not been complied with. Under this section it seems to me that the court can interfere with the Minister's decision if he has acted on no evidence; or if he has come to a conclusion to which on the evidence he could not reasonably come; or if he has given a wrong interpretation to the words of the statute; or if he has taken into consideration matters which he ought not to have taken into account, or vice versa; or has otherwise gone wrong in law. It is identical with the position when the court has power to interfere with the decision of a lower tribunal which has erred in point of law.

We have to apply this to the modern procedure whereby the inspector makes his report and the Minister gives his letter of decision, and they are made available to the parties. It seems to me that the court should look at the material which the inspector and the Minister had before them just as it looks at the material before an inferior court, and see whether on that material the Minister has gone wrong in law. We were referred to two cases: *Re Butler, Camberwell (Wingfield Mews) No. 2 Clearance Order, 1936* [1939] 1 K.B. 570 and *Re Ripon (Highfield) Housing Confirmation Order, 1938, White and Collins v. Minister of Health* [1939] 2 K.B. 838 [above, p. 193]. They were decided at a time when the report of the inspector was not open to the parties. There was no letter of decision. There was nothing but the formal order of the Minister. It was necessary, therefore, for affidavits to be received showing what was the material available before the Minister. They were received in those cases for that purpose. Nowadays, when the material is available, it seems to me that the court should limit itself to that material. Fresh evidence should not be admitted save in exceptional circumstances. It is not correct for the court to approach the case absolutely do novo as though the court was sitting to decide the matter in the first instance. The court can receive evidence to show what material was before the Minister; but it cannot receive evidence of the kind which was indicated in the present case so as to decide the whole matter afresh.

I think that the preliminary point taken on behalf of the Minister, namely, that this is not a matter for fresh evidence, ought to be upheld, and I would allow the appeal accordingly.

HARMAN L.J.: ... The judge before whom this matter came was, I think, misled by the two cases to which we have been referred. In *Re Ripon*, which on the face of it looks the nearest to this one, the decision eventually was that there was no evidence on which the Minister could have come to his conclusion. The terms of the Act were that if the land in question was part of a park it could not be included; that was not a matter for the opinion of the Minister or the satisfaction of the local authority, but was a statutory prohibition.

Therefore, it was necessary to see on what grounds the Minister had come to this conclusion, and as he had not been bound to give any reasons, nor to publish the report of his inspector, it was absolutely necessary to have some evidence to show what must have been the materials on which he so decided. Once they came out, it was seen that this was in fact part of a park and could not have been anything else. Therefore, there was no evidence on which the Minister could reach the conclusion which he did, and the order was quashed.

Now that does not seem to me to be an authority which involves anything here. It is true that the headnote states that the Court of Appeal held that a motion of this sort was a new and independent proceeding, and not a rehearing or a retrial. That, of course, we accept. But the fact that it is a new and independent proceeding does not mean that everything is necessarily open to the court. Some of the matters are left to the Minister, some are not. It is left to his opinion to decide whether a house is a house or another building, and it is left to his opinion also to decide whether it is or is not unfit for human habitation. In both those matters he relies on his inspector's view, and it is quite clear from the inspector's report in this case that he did take both those matters into his consideration.... That being so, and it appearing from paragraph 4(3) of Schedule 3 that those matters are for the Minister's opinion, it would not be right for this court to substitute its opinion for that of the Minister; and I do not think there is any case which involves us in doing so....

We can interfere if the decision of the Minister was perverse and could not have been properly arrived at on the facts which his inspector gathered for him, but otherwise it seems to me that the legislature has entrusted that part of it to him, and not to us, and we should not interfere....

WINN L.J. delivered a concurring judgment.

Appeal allowed.

Notes

1. Clearance area compulsory purchase orders made under the Housing Act 1985, s.290, on or after April 1, 1990, are regulated by the Acquisition of Land Act 1981 (see above, p. 552, for the applicable appeal provisions).

2. Differing views had previously been expressed *obiter* in *Smith v. East Elloe Rural District Council* [1956] A.C. 736, (below, p. 799) on the permissible scope of challenges under a statutory *ultra vires* clause. A majority (Lords Morton (at 754–755), Reid (at 763) and Somervell (at 772) held that it only covered claims that an order was *ultra vires* in the narrow sense of non-compliance with some requirement (substantive or procedural) to be found in the relevant statute, and not allegations of bad faith or

improper motives or (in Lord Reid's formulation, at 762–763) the *Wednesbury* grounds of challenge. Lord Radcliffe disagreed, stating that they covered "any case in which the complainant sought to say that the order in question did not carry the statutory authority which it purported to" (at 768). Viscount Simonds inclined to the same view as Lord Radcliffe but preferred to leave the point open (at 752). These observations were *obiter* given that the issue was whether any form of challenge could be made *after* the six week period. Subsequently, in *Webb v. Minister of Housing and Local Government* [1965] 1 W.L.R. 755, Lord Denning M.R. stated *obiter* (in the course of a dissenting judgment) that the "differing voices" in the House of Lords on the scope of the paragraph were "so differing that they give no clear guidance or, at any rate, no guidance that binds us" (at 770). He preferred Lord Radcliffe's approach. Danckwerts and Davies L.JJ. did not mention the point in the course of quashing a compulsory purchase order held not to be made for the purposes set out in the enabling statute. In a discussion of the *Ashbridge* case in *The Discipline of Law* (1979), pp. 106–108, Lord Denning described the rejection of the narrow approach of the *Smith v. East Elloe RDC* majority as a "remarkable turn of events. . . . The one who did it—strange to relate—was the Minister himself; through his mouthpiece—the Treasury Devil" (at 106). What makes the matter rather less "strange" is the fact that in argument in *Smith v. East Elloe RDC* the Attorney-General, counsel for the respondents, who included the Ministry of Housing and Local Government, accepted the broader interpretation that the ground of challenge extended to "fraud, or bad faith, or on any other ground showing that [the order] was not within the powers conferred by the Act" (at 743).

3. The Minister has not in any reported case taken the point that the error of law alleged does not take him beyond his powers. See, for example, *Chelmsford Corporation v. Secretary of State for the Environment* (1971) 22 P. & C.R. 880 at 881 (Browne J.; a planning case). Lord Denning's *Ashbridge* formula has been applied in *Crabtree v. M.H.L.G.* (1965) 64 L.G.R. 104 (Paull J.; a planning case); *Howard v. M.H.L.G.* (1967) 65 L.G.R. 257 (John Stephenson J.; a housing case); the *Coleen* case (below, p. 560); *British Dredging (Services) Ltd v. Secretary of State for Wales* [1975] 1 W.L.R. 687 (Park J.; a case under the Coast Protection Act 1949); *R. v. Medicines Commission, ex p. Organon Laboratories Ltd* [1989] C.O.D. 479 (a case under the Medicines Act 1968, s.107); and *R. v. Secretary of State for Transport, ex p. de Rothschild* [1989] 1 All E.R. 933, C.A. In *Brookdene Investments Ltd v. M.H.L.G.* (1970) 21 P. & C.R. 545, counsel for the Minister expressly reserved the point whether the court could intervene for a non-jurisdictional error of law. Fisher J. also thought that counsel would have conceded that if a non-jurisdictional error of law involved a failure to comply with a relevant requirement, and substantial prejudice were established, a decision could be quashed. Such arguments would seem obsolete in the light of *ex p. Page* (above, p. 225).

4. In *Bradley v. Secretary of State for the Environment* (1982) 47 P. & C.R. 374 Glidewell J. stated (at 388) that, in his view, Lord Denning in the *Ashbridge* case was "expressing in somewhat different form exactly the same principles as those formulated by Lord Greene" in *Associated Provincial Picture Houses Ltd v. Wednesbury Corporation* [1948] 1 K.B. 223. It is submitted that the wording of the *Ashbridge* case is on its face significantly wider: this being made clear by the equation with interference with decisions of an inferior tribunal for error of law. In *R. v. Secretary of State for Transport, ex p. de Rothschild* [1989] 1 All E.R. 933, Slade L.J. stated that the conventional grounds for challenging a compulsory purchase order were those set out in the *Ashbridge* case taken together with those derived from *Wednesbury*, thus indicating that they are distinct.

5. Four further points may be noted. First, where a "requirement" of the Act is not fulfilled, and there is "substantial prejudice", then a decision may be quashed whether the error is jurisdictional or non-jurisdictional (*per* Fisher J., *obiter*, in *Brookdene Investments v. Minister of Housing and Local Government* (1970) 21 P. & C.R. 545, 553).

Secondly, a literal interpretation of the statutory formula would limit the need to show "substantial prejudice" to cases of non-compliance with procedural requirements under the second limb of the statutory formula. Moreover, in some cases, such non-compliance would be so serious as to render the decision *ultra vires* and so open to attack under the first limb (see *Wade and Forsyth*, pp. 750–751, where it is suggested that the second limb may well be intended to cover cases of non-compliance with directory procedural requirements: see pp. 407–418). It has been suggested, however, that it is necessary to establish "substantial prejudice" under both limbs of the statutory formula (*Re Manchester (Ringway Airport) Compulsory Purchase Order* (1935) 153 L.T. 219, Branson J.) although this view is difficult to reconcile with the terms of the relevant provisions (*cf.* Forbes J. in *Seddon Properties v. Secretary of State for the Environment* (1978) 248 E.G. 950, (1978) 42 P. & C.R. 26 (Note) and in *Bell and Colvill Ltd v. Secretary of State for the Environment* [1980] J.P.L. 823, 828). Establishing that there has been a breach of the rules does not *per se* discharge the onus of showing substantial prejudice (*Bell and Colvill*, above.)

Thirdly, the view has been taken that the provision under the statutory formula that the court "may" quash an order on one or other of the stated grounds gives the court a discretion whether to intervene even where one of the grounds is clearly established (*Errington v. Minister of Health* [1935] 1 K.B. 249, 279 *per* Maugham L.J.; *Miller v. Weymouth and Melcombe Regis Corporation* (1974) 27 P. & C.R. 468, 478–480, Kerr J., criticised by J.E. Alder (1975) 91 L.Q.R. 10; *Preston Borough Council v. Secretary of State for the Environment* [1978] J.P.L. 548; *Peak Park Joint Planning Board v. Secretary of State for the Environment* (1979) 39 P. & C.R. 361; *London Borough of Richmond upon Thames v. Secretary of State for the Environment* [1984] J.P.L. 24).

In the *Peak Park* case, Sir Douglas Frank said (at 385) that the discretion not to quash should in general only be exercised if the point is technical and there is no possible detriment to the applicant. In the *Richmond* case, Glidewell J. declined to quash a grant of planning permission by an inspector, where the inspector was wrong to hold that a policy in the development plan had been overridden, but where there had been other considerable advantages in the proposed development, and where it would be a waste of time to send the matter back to the Secretary of State.

Fourthly, affidavit evidence may be received if designed to establish "no evidence" on a point in issue (*H. Sabey & Co. v. Secretary of State for the Environment* [1978] 1 All E.R. 586); or to establish that proper procedures have not been complied with or that a particular matter of real importance had been left out of the inspector's report (*East Hampshire District Council v. Secretary of State for the Environment* [1978] J.P.L. 182).

6. "Statutory *ultra vires*" clauses are discussed by J. Alder (1975) 38 M.L.R. 274; Sir Frederick Corfield and R.J.A. Carnwath, *Compulsory Acquisition and Compensation* (1978), pp. 52–66; M. Grant, *Urban Planning Law* (1982), pp. 633–644, and annotations to the Town and Country Planning Act 1990, ss.284–288, in the *Encyclopedia of Planning Law and Practice*; *Wade and Forsyth*, pp. 742–756; M. Purdue, E. Young and J. Rowan-Robinson, *Planning Law and Procedure* (1989), pp. 564–581.

Questions

Lord Denning M.R. equates the catalogue of errors which cause a Minister to act outside his powers "with the position when the court has power to interfere with the decision of a tribunal which has erred in point of law."

1. How obvious is it that the concept of "not within the powers of the Act" is the same as that of "error of law"?

2. If Lord Denning is right, is there any point in Parliament's drawing a distinction between appeals on points of law, and applications to quash as under Schedule 2 to the Housing Act? Compare sections 287 and 288 of the Town and Country Planning Act 1990 (applications to quash structure plans, etc.) with section 289 (appeals on points of law against enforcement notices, etc.).

COLEEN PROPERTIES LTD v. MINISTER OF HOUSING AND LOCAL GOVERNMENT

[1971] 1 W.L.R. 433; 115 S.J. 112; [1971] 1 All E.R. 1049; 69 L.G.R. 175; 22 P. & C.R. 417 (Court of Appeal)

Tower Hamlets London Borough Council declared two rows of houses, on Clark Street and Sidney Street, to be clearance areas under the Housing Act 1957. By section 43(2) of that Act they had power to purchase compulsorily "any adjoining land the acquisition of which is reasonably necessary for the satisfactory development or use of the cleared area". They wished to exercise this power in respect of Clark House, a good property owned by Coleen Properties Ltd and situated on the corner of the two streets. The owners objected, and an inspector held a public local inquiry and inspected the properties. The council called witnesses (the Medical Officer of Health, Housing Officer and Public Health Housing Inspector) to show that the old houses in the clearance areas were in a bad condition. They did not call any witnesses as to the planning merits, in particular to show that it was necessary to acquire Clark House. They merely asserted, through the mouth of their advocate, the Deputy Town Clerk, that:

"the acquisition of such properties (*i.e.* the added lands including Clark House) is reasonably necessary for the purpose of the satisfactory development or use of the clearance areas (*i.e.* the old houses)".

The objectors called a qualified surveyor and architect to give evidence on the planning merits.
The inspector reported to the Minister as to Clark House:

"This is a first class property and I am of the opinion that its acquisition by the council is not reasonably necessary for the satisfactory development or use of the cleared area."

However, his recommendation that Clark House be excluded from the compulsory purchase order was rejected by the Minister:

"The Minister disagrees with the inspector's recommendation with regard to Reference No. 13 (*i.e.* Clark House). It appears to him that by the very nature of its position, the exclusion of this property must seriously inhibit the future redevelopment of the rectangular block of land between Sidney Street and Damien Street in which it stands. He has decided, therefore, that the acquisition of Reference 13 (Clark House) is reasonably necessary for the satisfactory development or use of the cleared area...."

The owners applied to the High Court for the order to be quashed in so far as it affected Clark House under Schedule 4, para. 2 to the Housing Act 1957.

LORD DENNING M.R.: ... [referred to his statement in the *Ashbridge* case (above, p. 556) "the court can interfere ... lower tribunal which has erred in point of law".] ...
In my opinion the Minister was in error in reversing the inspector's recommendation. The Minister had before him only the report of the inspector. He did not see the premises himself. To my mind there was no material on which the Minister could properly overrule the inspector's recommendation. Clark House is a first class new property. It has shops with flats over. In order to acquire it compulsorily, the local authority must show that the acquisition

"is reasonably necessary for the satisfactory development or use of the cleared area". In order to show it, they ought to have produced some evidence to the inspector as to what kind of development would be a "satisfactory development" of the area, and to show how the acquisition of Clark House is "reasonably necessary". I do not say that they ought to have produced a detailed plan of the proposed development. I realise well enough that in many cases that may not be practicable. For instance, when an area is to be developed for industrial purposes, you cannot go into details until you have the businessmen wanting the factories. But, when an area is to be developed for residential purposes—for the council's own housing plans—it ought to be possible to give an outline plan of the proposed development. I cannot myself see that the council could get any more dwellings on to the site of Clark House than the six flats which are already there. The council may desire to make a neat and tidy development of these two streets, including Clark House, but this may well be possible whilst leaving Clark House standing. At any rate, I am quite clear that the mere *ipse dixit* of the local council is not sufficient. There must be some evidence to support their assertion. And here there was none.

Then there is the report of the inspector. He was clearly of opinion that the acquisition of Clark House was not reasonably necessary. I can see no possible justification for the Minister in overruling the inspector. There was no material whatever on which he could so do. I know that on matters of planning policy the Minister can overrule the inspector, and need not send it back to him, as happened in *Luke v. Minister of Housing and Local Government* [1968] 1 Q.B. 172. But the question of what is "reasonably necessary" is not planning policy. It is an inference of fact on which the Minister should not overrule the inspector's recommendation unless there is material sufficient for the purpose. There was none here. In my judgment the Minister was wrong and this court should intervene and overrule him. . . .

SACHS L.J.: . . . [Counsel's] submission raised the question as to whether there was any evidence before the Minister upon which he could properly come to a conclusion which would enable him to exercise the powers that stem from the provisions of Part III of the Act of 1957—clearance and redevelopment: was he entitled to reverse the finding contained in paragraph 37 of the inspector's report to the effect that it was not reasonably necessary for the satisfactory development or use of the cleared area to acquire the property at the corner known as Clark House? The need for evidence to be available to a Minister before he can act has been the subject of earlier decisions. The question before him was not, to my mind, one of policy: it was in essence a question of fact that had to be established as a condition precedent to the exercise of the powers to take away the subject's property. It was no less a question of fact because it involved forming a judgment on matters on which expert opinion can and indeed ought to be given. (I rather doubt whether there is much material difference between the view I have just expressed and that of Mr Slynn [counsel for the Minister] who has argued that the question was simply a matter of planning judgment which had to be based on evidence.) As long ago as the *Sheffield* case (*Sheffield Burgesses v. Minister of Health* (1935) 52 T.L.R. 171 at 173) Swift J. said:

"... it is for the court, if the matter is brought before it, to say whether there is any material on which the Minister could have come to the conclusion that it was reasonably necessary. If the court comes to the conclusion that there is no such material, then it will not hesitate to quash the Minister's order."

That passage coincides with those passages in the judgment of Lord Denning M.R. in the *Ashbridge* case [1965] 1 W.L.R. 320 to which he has referred.

The Minister, therefore, cannot come to a conclusion of fact contrary to that which the inspector found in this case unless there was evidence before the latter on which he (the Minister) could form that contrary conclusion. Upon the inquiry, an inspector is, of course, entitled to use the evidence of his own eyes, evidence which he as an expert, in this case he was an architect, can accept. The Minister, on the other hand, can only look at what is on the record. He cannot, as against the subject, avail himself of other expert evidence from within the Ministry—at any rate, without informing the subject and giving him an opportunity to deal with that evidence on the lines which are set out in regard to a parallel matter in the Compulsory Purchase by Local Authorities (Inquiries Procedure) Rules 1962.[7] Whilst the inspector, even if not an architect, may well be looked on as an expert for the purpose of forming an opinion of fact, the Minister is in a different position. It is by no means intended as a criticism to say with all respect that no Minister can personally be an expert on all matters of professional opinion with which his officers deal from day to day.

Before turning to the report and examining the evidence, there is a further observation to be made. When seeking to deprive a subject of his property and cause him to move himself, his belongings and perhaps his business to another area, the onus lies squarely on the local authority to show by clear and unambiguous evidence that the order sought for should be granted. What then is the state of the evidence here? Mr Slynn has properly pressed us to look at plan B. . . . From that plan it is quite plain that when developing the rectangle it may well be convenient to have the corner site included in the development, so as perhaps to make it more homogeneous. It is plain that to get possession of it and include it in the development may well be "a tidy idea" according to the canons of Whitehall. It may be that it is better from the point of view of looks. But all that is not enough. It must be reasonably *necessary* for the satisfactory development or use under consideration.

The nature of the development or use under consideration in this case is to be found in paragraph 20 of the report, which refers to "the area zoned in the development plan for residential use" and again in the Minister's own phraseology in his letter of October 25: "The council proposed to redevelop the two clearance areas for housing purposes." That then is the object of the proposed development and use: but what materially serious obstacle to that objective is constituted by the existence of Clark House, a first class property reconstructed in 1956 at public expense and described in paragraphs 29 and 36 as containing, *inter alia*, six self-contained flats with four shops?

On the evidence, there is nothing on which to suggest that there was any material, far less a materially serious obstacle. There is no evidence that the

[7] [Editor's note] S.I. 1962 No. 1424: see now S.I. 1990 No. 512.

demolition of Clark House would result in even a single extra family being housed. There is no evidence that any addition to the costs of the redevelopment scheme because Clark House was not acquired would approach or exceed the value of the buildings. There was no evidence that some amenity to the community to be housed on the redeveloped site would be lost: thus there was no question of any gardens of Clark House being needed to such purpose—so far as I can see, it had none. There is no suggestion that Clark House or any portion of the area it occupied was needed for road widening: indeed the contrary was established. Thus there was no evidence whatsoever establishing that Clark House fell within the ambit of section 43(2).

The architect inspector came to his conclusion after an inspection. His conclusions are certainly no help to the submission on behalf of the Minister that this site did fall within the subsection: on the contrary, on the facts of this particular case, one would have thought that his opinion—the only expert opinion—was almost conclusive the other way. Having already made plain that the Minister was not entitled in this case to find as a fact that the premises were reasonably necessary for the purpose mentioned except on evidence before the inspector, and it being clear that there was no such evidence, he had no power to make the order, and in my judgment the appeal should be allowed.

BUCKLEY L.J.: ... The crucial consideration here I think is whether there was material before the Minister in this case which justified him in the course which he took ... Mr Slynn, appearing before us on behalf of the Minister, has submitted that that decision is a matter of planning judgment; but he concedes that the judgment must be based upon some evidence. That evidence must be, I take it, evidence of a kind which would justify a reasonable man in reaching the conclusion which the Minister reached.... As I think that the Minister had no sufficient material upon which to reach the decision which he did reach, it follows that he acted *ultra vires* the section and that his decision is one which should not be permitted to stand. I therefore agree that this appeal should be allowed.

Appeal allowed.

Notes

1. See case notes by J.M. Evans (1971) 34 M.L.R. 561 and H.W.R. W[ade] (1971) 87 L.Q.R. 318.

2. In *Migdal Investments Ltd v. Secretary of State for the Environment* [1976] J.P.L. 365, Bristow J. distinguished *Coleen* on the ground that evidence of fact and opinion given by a qualified expert (a Senior Planning Officer of the City of Manchester) was not the "mere *ipse dixit*" of the local authority. The statute did not require the authority to place before the Minister a plan of some degree of precision showing why the acquisition of neighbouring land was reasonably necessary for the satisfactory development or use of the relevant clearance areas. In *Banks Horticultural Products Ltd v. Secretary of State for the Environment* (1979) 252 E.G. 811, Banks appealed against a refusal of permission to extract peat from certain land. At the inquiry, it became clear that the question turned on whether there were other reasonable sources of supply. By agreement, it was left to the Ministry of Agriculture's witness to supply written evidence on the point after the inquiry. This was done, and the appeal was rejected. Phillips J. held that this evidence provided a wholly insufficient basis for the inspector to

reach a conclusion on this point, as it dealt only with the physical characteristics of the alternative supply of peat and not with such questions as availability, suitability and cost. There was either no evidence, or no evidence upon which the inspector could have properly have reached his conclusion.

3. In *R. v. Secretary of State for the Environment, ex p. Powis* [1981] 1 W.L.R. 584, the applicant challenged the decision of the Secretary of State to certify under section 57(1) of the Landlord and Tenant Act 1954 that land held by a county council as landlord was requisite for the purposes of the authority, and that its use or occupation be changed. One ground was that the only evidence before the Minister was the bald assertion of the council that no alternative sites were available for its purposes, and that therefore there was no evidence upon which the Secretary of State was entitled to rely, under the *Coleen* principle. The Court of Appeal rejected this argument. Unlike the situation in *Coleen*, section 57 did not envisage a hearing or inquiry. As there was no public hearing, it was for the Minister to weigh the statements submitted to him, and reach a conclusion based on that material.

Question

Is the *Coleen* case an example of judicial review for lack of evidence to support a finding of jurisdictional fact (*cf. White & Collins v. Minister of Health*, above, p. 193, or is it authority for a general proposition that all determinations unsupported by any evidence are *ultra vires* (*contra R. v. Nat Bell Liquors Ltd* [1922] 2 A.C. 128, below, p. 575)?

(D) Appeals on Questions of Law

This is the typical ground upon which Parliament has granted rights of appeal to the High Court. See for example section 289 of the Town and Country Planning Act 1990, and note the extension of rights of appeal from the decisions of tribunals by section 9 of the Tribunals and Inquiries Act 1958 (now s.11 of the 1992 Act, above, p. 53), following recommendations of the Franks Committee (above, p. 539).

(E) The Distinction Between Questions of Law and Questions of Fact[8]

It is necessary to draw this distinction where an appeal is limited to a question of law and where there is an application for certiorari to quash for error of law on the face of the record. The distinction may also be relevant where there is an allegation of jurisdictional error, as the courts are less likely to find that there has been an error of fact than an error of law.[9]

The line between law and fact has been drawn differently in different contexts. The distinction has generated much case law, but the courts have generally been unwilling to adopt a consistent approach. Areas of administrative law which have been particu-

---

[8] See W.A. Wilson, "A Note on Fact and Law" (1963) 26 M.L.R. 609; W.A. Wilson, "Questions of Degree" (1969) 32 M.L.R. 361; C. Morris, "Law and Fact" (1941–1942) 55 Harv.L.R. 1303; L.B. Jaffe, "Judicial Review—Questions of Law" (1955–1956) 69 Harv.L.R. 239; H.W.R. W[ade] (1969) 85 L.Q.R. 18–20; H. Whitmore [1967] 2 *Federal Law Review* 159; *de Smith, Woolf and Jowell*, pp. 277–286; E. Mureinik, "The Application of Rules: Law or Fact" (1982) 98 L.Q.R. 587; J. Beatson, "The Scope of Judicial Review for Error of Law" (1984) 4 O.J.L.S. 22; *Emery and Smythe*, Chap. 3 (based on (1984) 100 L.Q.R. 612); G.J. Pitt, "Law, Fact and Casual Workers" (1985) 101 L.Q.R. 217.
[9] See *ex p. Honig*, above, p. 202.

larly fertile include revenue law,[10] workmen's compensation,[11] national insurance,[12] town and country planning[13] and rating.[14] In the wider context, the distinction has been before the courts in connection with magisterial law (particularly appeals by way of case stated to the Divisional Court from decisions of the justices[15]), and appeals to the Court of Appeal on a point of law from decisions of county court judges.[16]

It is clear that an issue is one of fact where its resolution depends on the reliability or credibility (but not the admissibility in law) of direct evidence such as a witness's testimony. A finding based on an admission is equivalent to a fact proved by direct evidence. An issue whose resolution depends on probabilities, for example on an inference from circumstantial evidence, is also one of fact. An issue which depends on whether the facts found fall within a statutory description does not fall clearly into either category of fact or law. In different contexts such an issue has been characterised as one of "law", "fact", "mixed law and fact", "fact and degree", "degree", or as *sui generis*.[17] Which view is taken seems to depend on how much control an appellate court wishes to exercise over an inferior court or tribunal, rather than by reference to principle. There may occasionally be a tendency for an appellate court to classify an issue as one of law merely because it thinks the decision below wrong or unjust. Other factors which may be influential include whether the word or phrase in the statute can be said to be an "ordinary English expression" (see *R. v. National Insurance Commissioner, ex p. Secretary of State*, below, p. 568), or a "question of degree" (see the *Bendles* case, below, p. 563).

BRITISH LAUNDERERS' ASSOCIATION v. BOROUGH OF HENDON RATING AUTHORITY

[1949] 1 K.B 462; [1949] L.J.R. 416; 65 T.L.R. 103; 93 S.J. 58; *sub nom. British Launderers' Research Association v. Central Middlesex Assessment Committee and Hendon Rating Authority*, 113 J.P. 72; [1949] 1 All E.R. 21; 47 L.G.R. 113; 41 R. & I.T. 564 (Court of Appeal)

The Association was established to promote research and other scientific work in connection with the laundry and cleaning trades. It owned a site in Hendon with a laboratory block, an experimental laundry, a boiler house and other buildings. The rating authority demanded rates in respect of the site in 1946 for the first time in 20 years. The Association claimed they were exempt from rates by reason of section 1 of the Scientific Societies Act 1843. They appealed successfully on this point to quarter sessions. The Divisional Court reversed the decision of quarter sessions, on an appeal by case

[10] "The issue, upon cases stated by the Commissioners ... has been *directly* before the courts in well over two hundred cases." A. Farnsworth (1946) 62 L.Q.R. at 248. See *Simon's Direct Tax Service*, para. A3.703.
[11] See *Willis's Workmen's Compensation* (notes to s.1(1)–(3) of the Workmen's Compensation Act 1925).
[12] See, *e.g. R. v. National Insurance Commissioner, ex p. Secretary of State* (below, p. 568).
[13] See, *e.g. Bendles Ltd v. Bristol Corporation* (below, p. 563); *Encyclopedia of Planning Law and Practice*, notes to s.289 of the Town and Country Planning Act 1990.
[14] See *Ryde on Rating and the Community Charge* (1991), paras. F410–F415.
[15] See the Magistrates' Courts Act 1980, s.111.
[16] See *Halsbury's Laws of England* (4th ed.), Vol. 10, "County Courts", para. 658; *The County Court Practice* (1991), pp. 68–72.
[17] See Whitmore, *op. cit.* pp. 170–177. As a matter of *theory* it is difficult to resist the conclusion that this is really a question of law: Mureinik, *op. cit.*; *Wade and Forsyth*, pp. 950–952.

stated on a point of law, holding that the Association was not instituted "for the purposes of science ... exclusively", as required by section 1, but also for commercial purposes which were not merely incidental to the purposes of science. The Association argued that this was a question of fact from which there was no appeal to the Divisional Court.

DENNING L.J.: ... Mr Rowe says, however, that quarter sessions came to a conclusion of fact in his favour with which the Divisional Court should not have interfered. On this point it is important to distinguish between primary facts and the conclusions from them. Primary facts are facts which are observed by witnesses and proved by oral testimony or facts proved by the production of a thing itself, such as original documents. Their determination is essentially a question of fact for the tribunal of fact, and the only question of law that can arise on them is whether there was any evidence to support the finding. The conclusions from primary facts are, however, inferences deduced by a process of reasoning from them. If, and in so far as, those conclusions can as well be drawn by a layman (properly instructed on the law) as by a lawyer, they are conclusions of fact for the tribunal of fact: and the only questions of law which can arise on them are whether there was a proper direction in point of law; and whether the conclusion is one which could reasonably be drawn from the primary facts: see *Bracegirdle v. Oxley* [1947] K.B. 349 at 358. If, and in so far, however, as the correct conclusion to be drawn from primary facts requires, for its correctness, determination by a trained lawyer—as, for instance, because it involves the interpretation of documents or because the law and the facts cannot be separated, or because the law on the point cannot properly be understood or applied except by a trained lawyer—the conclusion is a conclusion of law on which an appellate tribunal is as competent to form an opinion as the tribunal of first instance.

... The question is whether the association was instituted for the purposes of science exclusively. That is, a conclusion of law to be drawn from the primary facts, particularly, but not exclusively, from the memorandum and articles of association, and involves questions of interpretation of those documents and of the Act. The Divisional Court were able, and indeed bound, to form their own opinion as to the proper conclusion to be drawn from those primary facts, and I find myself in entire agreement with them. ...

BUCKNILL L.J. and JENKINS J. agreed.

Appeal dismissed.

BENDLES MOTORS LTD v. BRISTOL CORPORATION AND ANOTHER

[1963] 1 W.L.R. 247; 127 J.P. 203; 107 S.J. 77; [1963] 1 All E.R. 578; 14 P. & C.R. 128; 61 L.G.R. 205 D.C. (Queen's Bench Division)

Bendles Ltd permitted the installation by one J. Allcock, a veterinary surgeon and poultry farmer, of an egg-vending machine, free-standing on a base two feet seven inches square, on their garage and petrol filling station forecourt, which had a frontage of 120 feet and a depth of 15 feet. The local planning authority served an enforcement

notice stating that it appeared that development had been carried out without permission and the site-owners appealed to the Minister of Housing and Local Government who ordered an inquiry. The Minister considered the evidence and arguments on
the issues of law put forward at the inquiry, and concluded that the stationing on the
site involved a change of use of the land on which the machine stood; that, while a
petrol filling station was not a shop, the machine standing in part of the forecourt of the
petrol filling station was of the nature of shop use; and, being satisfied on the facts that
the introduction of the machine involved a material change of use, dismissed the
appeal and upheld the enforcement notice.

Bendles Ltd appealed to the Divisional Court on a point of law.

Section 12(1) of the Town and Country Planning Act 1962 (now s.55(1) of the 1990
Act) provided that development (for which planning permission was required) "means
the carrying out of building, engineering, mining or other operations in, on, over or
under land, or the making of any material change in the use of any buildings or other
land ...".

LORD PARKER C.J.: ... The Minister in his decision of August 31, 1962,
recited the relevant parts of the inspector's report, and went on: "3. The
Minister has considered the evidence and the arguments put forward at the
inquiry on the issues of law. He notes that the machine is not attached to the
freehold and is movable, though it is of substantial size and construction
and is not normally intended to be moved about the site. It appears to the
Minister that its stationing on the site involves a change of use of the land on
which it stands. It is now necessary to consider whether the change of use is
material."

In the next paragraph he says: "As to this it is to be observed that a petrol
filling station is excepted from the definition of 'shop' in the Town and
Country Planning (Use Classes) Order 1950, by article 2(2) of the Order. The
machine stands in part of the forecourt of the petrol filling station and is of the
nature of a 'shop' use. Moreover, although the space occupied by the machine
is small in comparison with the total area of the forecourt, it attracts
customers not necessarily concerned with the motoring service provided by
the establishment and introduces a noticeably different element of use of the
premises. The Minister is satisfied, on the facts, that the introduction of the
machine on the site involves a material change of use of the land, for which the
grant of planning permission is required."

As this court has said on more than one occasion, the question of whether a
change of use is a material change of use is largely a matter of degree and fact.
In *East Barnet Urban District Council v. British Transport Commission*
[1962] 2 Q.B. 484 after referring to this matter, I said (*ibid.* at 492): "It is a
question of fact and degree in every case and, when the matter comes before
this court by way of case stated, the court is unable to interfere with a finding
of the justices on such a matter unless it must be said that they could not
properly have reached that conclusion." That was dealing with a case
stated from justices, but in my judgment the same is true of an appeal from
the Minister himself. This court can only interfere if satisfied that it is a
conclusion that he could not, properly directing himself as to the law, have
reached.

That being so, one has to examine his decision with some care. Counsel for
the site-owners has stated first that there is a fatal error at the very outset in
that the Minister is only considering the nine square feet, or whatever it may

be, upon which the machine stands. Quite clearly, if one is looking at those nine square feet alone, there would be a change of use and undoubtedly a material change of use. Counsel says, and in my judgment rightly, that that is the wrong approach, and that in considering materiality one ought to consider the premises as a whole. It seems to me, however, that that is exactly what the Minister has done. It is true that he was referring to the fact that the stationing of this machine involves a change of use of the land upon which this machine stands, but he then goes on to deal with the matter of whether it is a material change, and for the purposes of deciding the material change it is clear that he is going beyond the nine square feet upon which the machine stands and is considering, if not the whole of the premises, at any rate the forecourt because he says in the next paragraph: "Moreover, although the space occupied by the machine is small in comparison with the total area of the forecourt, it attracts customers not necessarily concerned with the motoring service" and so on.

The Minister having, therefore, properly directed himself on the law, this court could in my judgment only interfere if satisfied that the judgment was perverse in the sense that the evidence could not support it. That is going a very long way when one is dealing with planning considerations. I confess that at first sight, and indeed at last sight, I am somewhat surprised that it can be said that the placing of this small machine on this large forecourt can be said to change the use of these premises in a material sense from that of a garage and petrol filling station by the addition of a further use. It is surprising, and it may be, if it was a matter for my own personal judgment, that I should feel inclined to say that the egg-vending machine was *de minimis*; but it is not a question of what my opinion is on that matter, it is for the Minister to decide.

I cannot say that he was wrong in law in holding that the undoubted change of use of part of the premises did not amount to a material change of use of the whole. The Minister, in this case, has given a very careful decision, to which I find it unnecessary to refer in detail, but it is quite clear that with this type of machine coming on to the market it may well be that premises like garage premises may become used as shopping centres. The Minister in this case has not considered this as a case of *de minimis* and, that being so, I find it impossible to interfere. I would dismiss the appeal.

ASHWORTH and LYELL JJ. agreed.

Appeal dismissed.

Notes

1. *Bendles* may be compared with *Birmingham Corporation v. M.H.L.G. and Habib Ullah* [1964] 1 Q.B. 178 where the Divisional Court held that the Minister had erred in law in holding that the intensification of a use of land could not constitute a material change of use, and remitted the case to him to determine whether on the facts there had been such a change.

2. See further on the meaning of "development": Sir Desmond Heap, *An Outline of Planning Law* (11th ed., 1996), Chap. 7; A.E. Telling and N. Duxbury, *Planning Law and Procedure* (9th ed., 1993), Chap. 5; M. Purdue, E. Young and J. Rowan-Robinson, *Planning Law and Procedure* (1989), Chap. 5.

EDWARDS (INSPECTOR OF TAXES) v. BAIRSTOW AND ANOTHER

[1956] A.C. 14 (House of Lords)

In 1946, Harold Bairstow and Fred Harrison, neither of whom had previously under-taken any transactions in machinery, purchased for £12,000 a complete spinning plant, agreeing not to hold it but to make a quick resale. Between then and February 1948, and after various negotiations, the plant was sold in separate lots at a profit of over £18,000. The General Commissioners of Income Tax found that this was not "an adventure . . . in the nature of trade" so as to justify an assessment to income tax under Case I of Schedule D of the Income Tax Act 1918. The Inspector of Taxes appealed by case stated on a point of law to the High Court. The High Court and Court of Appeal (1954) 33 A.T.C. 131 rejected the appeal, treating the matter as a "pure question of fact", but a further appeal was allowed by the House of Lords.

VISCOUNT SIMONDS: . . . [I]n my opinion, whatever test is adopted, that is, whether the finding that the transaction was not an adventure in the nature of trade is to be regarded as a pure finding of fact or as the determination of a question of law or of mixed law and fact, the same result is reached in this case. The determination cannot stand: this appeal must be allowed and the assess-ments must be confirmed. For it is universally conceded that, though it is a pure finding of fact, it may be set aside on grounds which have been stated in various ways but are, I think, fairly summarized by saying that the court should take that course if it appears that the commissioners have acted with-out any evidence or upon a view of the facts which could not reasonably be entertained.

. . . [H]aving read and re-read [the facts found by the commissioners] with every desire to support the determination if it can reasonably be supported, I find myself quite unable to do so. The primary facts, as they are sometimes called, do not, in my opinion, justify the inference or conclusion which the commissioners have drawn: not only do they justify it but they lead irresistibly to the opposite inference or conclusion. It is therefore a case in which, whether it be said of the commissioners that their finding is perverse or that they have misdirected themselves in law by a misunderstanding of the statutory lan-guage or otherwise, their determination cannot stand. I venture to put the matter thus strongly because I do not find in the careful and, indeed, exhaus-tive statement of facts any item which points to the transaction not being an adventure in the nature of trade. Everything pointed the other way. . . .

LORD RADCLIFFE: . . . My Lords, I think that it is a question of law what meaning is to be given to the words of the Income Tax Act "trade, manufac-ture, adventure or concern in the nature of trade" and for that matter what constitute "profits or gains" arising from it. Here we have a statutory phrase involving a charge of tax, and it is for the courts to interpret its meaning, having regard to the context in which it occurs and to the principles which they bring to bear upon the meaning of income. But, that being said, the law does not supply a precise definition of the word "trade": much less does it prescribe as detailed or exhaustive set of rules for application to any particular set of circumstances. In effect it lays down the limits within which it would be permissible to say that a "trade" as interpreted by section 237 of the Act does or does not exist.

But the field so marked out is a wide one and there are many combinations of circumstances in which it could not be said to be wrong to arrive at a conclusion one way or the other. If the facts of any particular case are fairly capable of being so described, it seems to me that it necessarily follows that the determination of the Commissioners, Special or General, to the effect that a trade does or does not exist is not "erroneous in point of law"; and, if a determination cannot be shown to be erroneous in point of law, the statute does not admit of its being upset by the court on appeal. I except the occasions when the commissioners, although dealing with a set of facts which would warrant a decision either way, show by some reason they give or statement they make in the body of the case that they have misunderstood the law in some relevant particular.

All these cases in which the facts warrant a determination either way can be described as questions of degree and therefore as questions of fact. . . .

. . . If a party to a hearing before commissioners expresses dissatisfaction with their determination as being erroneous in point of law, it is for them to state a case and in the body of it to set out the facts that they have found as well as their determination. I do not think that inferences drawn from other facts are incapable of being themselves findings of fact, although there is value in the distinction between primary facts and inferences drawn from them. When the case comes before the court it is its duty to examine the determination having regard to its knowledge of the relevant law. If the case contains anything ex facie which is bad law and which bears upon the determination, it is, obviously, erroneus in point of law. But, without any such misconception appearing ex facie, it may be that the facts found are such that no person acting judicially and properly instructed as to the relevant law could have come to the determination under appeal. In those circumstances, too, the court must intervene. It has no option but to assume that there has been some misconception of the law and that this has been responsible for the determination. So there, too, there has been error in point of law. I do not think that it much matters whether this state of affairs is described as one in which there is no evidence to support the determination or as one in which the evidence is inconsistent with and contradictory of the determination, or as one in which the true and only reasonable conclusion contradicts the determination. Rightly understood, each phrase propounds the same test. For my part, I prefer the last of the three, since I think that it is rather misleading to speak of there being no evidence to support a conclusion when in cases such as these many of the facts are likely to be neutral in themselves, and only to take their colour from the combination of circumstances in which they are found to occur.

If I apply what I regard as the accepted test to the facts found in the present case, I am bound to say, with all respect to the judgments under appeal, that I can see only one true and reasonable conclusion. The profit from the set of operations that comprised the purchase and sales of the spinning plant was the profit of an adventure in the nature of trade. . . .

Lord Tucker agreed with both speeches.

Lord Somervell agreed with Lord Radcliffe.

Appeal allowed.

Notes

1. The *Edwards v. Bairstow* approach has been adopted in many other cases in administrative law. See *Emery and Smythe*, pp. 114–121, citing, *inter alia, R. v. Industrial Injuries Commissioner, ex p. A.E.U. (No. 2)* [1966] 2 Q.B. 31, where the Court of Appeal, including Lord Denning M.R., considered the question whether an employee was injured "in the course of employment" (note Lord Denning's comments on this case in *R. v. Preston S.B.A.T., ex p. Moore* [1975] 1 W.L.R. 624, 631–632); *Global Plant Ltd v. Secretary of State for Social Services* [1972] 1 Q.B. 139; *O'Kelly v. Trusthouse Forte plc* [1984] Q.B. 90 (question whether a contract was "for services" or "of service" held not to be a pure question of law); *I.R.C. v. Scottish and Newcastle Breweries Ltd* [1982] 1 W.L.R. 322 (application of the term "plant" for income tax purposes); and *A.C.T. Construction Ltd v. Customs and Excise Commissioners* [1982] 1 All E.R. 84 (below, note 4). For a defence of the approach against charges of uncertainty (Beatson (1984) 4 O.J.L.S. 22) and that it "smacks of abdication of responsibility" and fails to take rights seriously (Pitt (1985) 101 L.Q.R. 217, 233), see *Emery and Smythe*, pp. 121–127.

2. See *R. v. National Insurance Commissioner, ex p. Secretary of State for Social Services* [1974] 1 W.L.R. 1290, D.C., where the court held the question whether the functions related to going to bed were attributable to the "night" or the "day", for the purposes of entitlement to attendance allowance, was a question of fact for the attendance allowance board (an expert board of medical practitioners). The national insurance commissioner, hearing an appeal limited to points of law, could only interfere with the board's decision that these functions were attributable to the day "if the construction of the statute drove one to the conclusion that preparations for bed were necessarily part of the night", or "if the conclusion of the board is so unreasonable that no properly instructed board could have reached it" (*per* Lord Widgery C.J. at 1295). Neither of these alternatives was established, and so the court granted certiorari to quash the commissioner's decision to allow an appeal from the board. The court also gave some guidance on the proper construction of "night" and "day" in this context (which settled a divergence of view among the commissioners: see Sir Robert Mickelthwait, *The National Insurance Commissioners* (1976), pp. 136, 146 (nn. 40, 41)). In this Lord Widgery noted the words of Lord Reid in *Cozens v. Brutus* [1973] A.C. 854 at 861, to the effect that the giving of a meaning to an ordinary English word is not a question of law at all, although the construction of a statute is a question of law. "However, though 'night' is one of the commonest English words in its ordinary usage, it does have different shades of meaning and the decision of the correct shade of meaning to give to the word in a particular context requires consideration of the context, and thus becomes a matter of construction and therefore a matter of law" (at 1296). His Lordship thought that in this context "night" meant "the coming of night according to the domestic routine of the household".

3. In *Cozens v. Brutus* [1973] A.C. 854, Lord Reid stated at 861 (in relation to the meaning of "insulting" in section 5 of the Public Order Act 1936):

"The meaning of an ordinary word of the English language is not a question of law. The proper construction of a statute is a question of law. If the context shows that a word is used in an unusual sense the court will determine in other words what that unusual sense is. But here there is in my opinion no question of the word 'insulting' being used in any unusual sense. It appears to me, for reasons which I shall give later, to be intended to have its ordinary meaning. It is for the tribunal which decides the case to consider, not as law but as fact, whether in the whole circumstances the words of the statute do or do not as a matter of ordinary usage of the English language cover or apply to the facts which have been proved. If it is alleged that the tribunal has reached a wrong decision then there can be a question of law but only of a limited character. The question would normally be whether their decision was unreasonable in the sense that no tribunal acquainted with the ordinary use of language could reasonably reach that decision.

Were it otherwise we should reach an impossible position. When considering the meaning of a word one often goes to a dictionary. There one finds other words set out. And if one wants to pursue the matter and find the meaning of those other words the dictionary will give the meaning of those other words in still further words which often include the word for whose meaning one is searching.

No doubt the court could act as a dictionary. It could direct the tribunal to take some word or phrase other than the word in the statute and consider whether that word or phrase applied to or covered the facts proved. But we have been warned time and again not to substitute other words for the words of a statute. And there is very good reason for that. Few words have exact synonyms. The overtones are almost always different.

Or the court could frame a definition. But then again the tribunal would be left with words to consider. No doubt a statute may contain a definition—which incidentally often creates more problems than it solves—but the purpose of a definition is to limit or modify the ordinary meaning of a word and the court is not entitled to do that."

cf. Lord Denning's remarks in the *British Launderers' Association* case, above, p. 565. Do you think this approach results in the classification of too many matters as questions of fact? *cf.* the discussion in the criminal law context by Glanville Williams [1976] Crim.L.R. 472 and 532. The "ordinary English word" argument has in the criminal law context been ignored more often in practice than applied: D.W. Elliott, "*Brutus v. Cozens*: Decline and Fall" [1989] Crim.L.R. 323.

4. Lord Denning was not always consistent on this question. In *A.C.T. Construction Ltd v. Customs and Excise Commissioners* [1981] 1 All E.R. 324, the question was whether work done in underpinning a house with inadequate foundations constituted "maintenance". If it did, the work was positive-rated for VAT; if not, the work was zero-rated. Lord Denning said (at 327–328):

"The great contest in the case is whether it is 'maintenance' or not. Counsel for the Crown said that the question whether a particular work is 'maintenance' or not is a matter on which two opinions can easily be held without either being unreasonable at all. Quite reasonably one person might say that underpinning is 'maintenance'. Another person might equally reasonably say that it is not 'maintenance'. So he said there is a band in which either view is reasonable. He said that in such a case the courts should not interfere with the decision of a tribunal, whichever way it decided. He said the courts should not interfere with the decision of a tribunal unless it was right outside the band of reasonableness, so unreasonable that no reasonable man could come to that conclusion. He sought to find some support for this argument in some observations of Lord Diplock in the recent case of *Re Racal Communications Ltd* [1980] 2 All E.R. 634 at 639, [1980] 3 W.L.R. 181 at 187–188. But I cannot accept that submission. Once you have the primary facts established, as you have here, about the underpinning, then the question whether the work comes within the word 'maintenance' or not is a question of law for the judges to decide. Brandon and Ackner L.JJ. pointed out that in hundreds of arbitrations in the City of London the arbitrators state their findings of fact and then ask the court whether on the true construction of the document (the charterparty or whatever it may be) they came to the right conclusion. In everyday practice, once the primary facts are found, the interpretation of a word is a question of law for the judges to decide.

Many a time we have expressly so held. We so held in a value added tax case, *British Railways Board v. Customs and Excise Comrs* [1977] 2 All E.R. 873; [1977] S.T.C. 221; and we so held in an analogous case not involving value added tax but structural alterations, *Pearlman v. Keepers and Governors of Harrow School* [1979] 1 All E.R. 365, [1979] Q.B. 56. With regard to the latter case, I would say that the whole court were unanimous in thinking that the county court judge below was wrong in his construction of the words 'structural alterations', and that accordingly he had made a mistake of law. The only ground on which Geoffrey Lane L.J. dissented was that he thought it was an error within their jurisdiction which was not subject to correction. But, on whether it was a point of law, Geoffrey Lane L.J. agreed with the rest of us.

I would add that this is especially important in work which is repetitive, and frequently arising, as in this case of underpinning. Throughout the industry it is essential that the contractors and their employers should know whether the work is to be positive-rated or zero-rated. It would be intolerable if one tribunal were to give one view and another tribunal were to give another view, and that no one could decide between them. You would have different rulings in relation to similar work in different parts of the country, according to which tribunal happened to be hearing the case. That cannot be right. I would ask: if there are two tribunals giving different decisions, what are the commissioners to do? Are they to be the arbitrators between the differing views? I hope not. Tax gatherers should not be judges in their own cases. Surely not. When a definite ruling is needed for the guidance of builders and customers everywhere, it must be for the courts of law to give a definite and final ruling as to the meaning of a word such as 'maintenance'."

Brandon L.J. stated (at 329) that the question of law was whether the work was "capable of coming within the expression 'maintenance' ". Ackner L.J. said that:

"To my mind this appeal raises a short question of law, *viz.* whether on the true construction of the relevant section of and schedule to the Finance Act 1972, as applied to the undisputed facts in this case, there was a zero-rated supply of service" (at 330).

(To what extent are these formulations different ways of saying the same thing?)

All three members of the Court of Appeal were agreed that the underpinning was a work of alteration and not maintenance. The decision was affirmed by the House of Lords ([1982] 1 All E.R. 84). The sole speech was delivered by Lord Roskill, who regarded the case as raising "a single short point of construction" (at 87), and endorsed Brandon L.J.'s approach (at 88). He concluded:

"My Lords, I decline to attempt to define 'repair or maintenance' when the 1972 Act and the 1972 order do not do so, but leave those ordinary words which are in common use to be given their ordinary meaning. In some cases, there may be room for dispute which side of the line particular work falls. If so, that would be a question of fact or degree for the tribunal of fact concerned to determine. The problem should not prove difficult of solution if their task is approached by applying the facts as that tribunal finds them to the relevant statutory provisions interpreted as I have endeavoured to state" (at 88).

This seems to endorse the *Edwards v. Bairstow* approach rather than Lord Denning's (see *Emery and Smythe*, pp. 120–121).

5. An illustration of the difficulties in drawing the line between law and fact is provided by the decision of the House of Lords in *Fitzpatrick v. I.R.C.; Smith (Inspector of Taxes) v. Abbott* [1994] 1 W.L.R. 306. Here, a majority of the House of Lords, led by Lord Templeman, held that the question whether expenditure by journalists on the purchase of newspapers and periodicals was incurred "in the performance of the duties" of the employment so as to qualify as deductible expenses was a question of law. This enabled the House to reconcile different decisions made by Income Tax

Commissioners in separate cases in Scotland and England by overturning the English Commissioners' decision in favour of the taxpayers. Lord Browne-Wilkinson dissented, arguing that the issue was essentially one of fact which could only be overturned on *Edwards v. Bairstow* principles, which were not established. See A.A. Olowofoyeku [1996] B.T.R. 28, who argues persuasively that Lord Browne-Wilkinson's approach is to be preferred.

6. The approach adopted in distinguishing questions of law from questions of fact becomes crucial if it is accepted that all errors of *law* go to jurisdiction (above, pp. 210–233). The adoption of Lord Denning's approach in the *A.C.T.* case would give the courts a wide power to intervene; the adoption of the *Edwards v. Bairstow* approach (or that of Lord Denning himself in *ex p. A.E.U. (No. 2)*), a narrower power. This point is made forcefully by J. Beatson at (1984) 4 O.J.L.S. 22, 39–45, noting that Lord Diplock in *Re Racal Communications* seemed to prefer the *Edwards v. Bairstow* approach (see above, p. 569).

(F) Error of Law

The courts have used many different phrases to describe errors of law, and it is usually possible to describe a particular error in more than one of these ways. Examples include "misinterpreting a statute" (*e.g. R. v. Northumberland Compensation Appeal Tribunal, ex p. Shaw* [1952] 1 K.B. 338 (the leading case on the doctrine of error of law on the face of the record)); "taking irrelevant considerations into account" (*e.g. R. v. Southampton JJ., ex p. Green* [1976] Q.B. 11, *cf.* pp. 321–349 on abuse of discretion); "applying the wrong legal test" (*e.g.* in determining the "planning unit" relevant to the question whether there has been a material change of use under s.55 of the Town and Country Planning Act 1990: see *Burdle v. Secretary of State for the Environment* [1972] 1 W.L.R. 1207; M. Purdue, E. Young and J. Rowan-Robinson, *Planning Law and Procedure* (1989), pp. 94–101. Note that Lord Denning equates the grounds for statutory applications to quash with error of law in the *Ashbridge* case (above, p. 555).

Three particularly important problems are (a) whether lack of evidence for a decision renders it erroneous in point of law (below), (b) whether failure to give reasons constitutes error of law (below, p. 577) and (c) whether a point as to *vires* may be raised on an appeal on a point of law (below, p. 584).

(i) Lack of Evidence[18]

Notes and Questions

1. The following cases illustrate the rule that a decision based on "no evidence" is erroneous in law: *Bendles Ltd v. Bristol Corporation* (above, p. 566); *Edwards v. Bairstow* (above, p. 569); *Ashbridge Investments Ltd v. M.H.L.G.* (above, p. 560); *Coleen Properties Ltd v. M.H.L.G.* (above, p. 560).

2. The powers of the Divisional Court in dealing with appeals by way of case stated on a point of law from decisions of magistrates' courts were summarised as follows by Lord Goddard C.J. in *Bracegirdle v. Oxley* [1947] 1 K.B. 349, at 353:

"... [Counsel] concedes that if magistrates come to a decision to which no reasonable bench of magistrates, applying their minds to proper considerations and giving themselves proper directions, could come, then this court can interfere, because the position is exactly the same as if the magistrates had come to a decision of fact without evidence to support it. Sometimes it has been said of the verdict of a jury given in those circumstances, that it is perverse, and I should have no hesitation in applying

---

[18] See *de Smith, Woolf and Jowell*, pp. 282–283, 286, 561; J.M. Evans (1971) 34 M.L.R. 561 (case note on *Coleen Properties Ltd v. M.H.L.G.*); R.R.S. Tracey (1976) 50 A.L.J. 568.

that term to the decisions of magistrates which are arrived at without evidence to support them."

Humphreys J. stated at 357:

"... [F]or a very great number of years, whenever justices have found facts from which only one conclusion can be drawn by reasonable persons honestly applying their minds to the question, and have refused to draw that only conclusion, this court has invariably upset the decision of the justices in the appropriate manner."

Denning J. (as he then was) stated at 358:

"In a case under s.11 of the Road Traffic Act 1930, the question whether a speed is dangerous is a question of degree and a conclusion on a question of degree is a conclusion of fact. The court will only interfere if the conclusion cannot reasonably be drawn from the primary facts, but that is the case here. In my opinion, the conclusion drawn by these justices from the primary facts was not one that could reasonably be drawn from them."

Will these formulations invariably lead to the same result? Which of them are used in the cases cited in note 1?

3. Does the "no evidence" rule apply in the same way to (i) a primary finding of fact; (ii) the application of a statutory description to facts where this is regarded as a question of fact; and (iii) the final determination in a case of all the relevant questions of law and fact?

4. If a body acts on "no evidence" has it "failed to take into account relevant considerations" or acted "irrationally"? The question whether a decision unsupported by any evidence could be *ultra vires* was considered in *R. v. Nat Bell Liquors Ltd* [1922] 2 A.C. 128, P.C.: the defendant firm was convicted of selling liquor contrary to the Liquor Act 1916. The only evidence of the fact of sale was furnished by a police *agent provocateur*. The firm sought certiorari to quash the conviction (*inter alia*) on the ground of lack of evidence.

Per Lord Sumner at 143–144, 151–152:

"[Their Lordships] ... have not been referred to any decisive authority which applies to certiorari the same considerations as apply to testing a jury's verdict, when challenged on a motion for a new trial or on an appeal; nor, apart from a few expressions, here and there, not very carefully considered, can any judicial dicta be found to support it. Whether the verdict was one which 12 reasonable men could have found, whether the evidence was such that 12 reasonable men could find on it otherwise than in one way, whether the evidence was such that a jury could safely confict upon it, and whether it was such that a court of criminal appeal should refuse to interfere with the conviction, are questions which, though fully argued, have no relation to the functions of a superior court on certiorari. They all imply that there was evidence, but not much; they all ask whether that little evidence was enough; they are all applied to a body of men who are not the absolute judges of fact, but only judges whose decision may, though rarely, be disturbed. On certiorari, so far as the presence or absence of evidence becomes material, the question can at most be whether any evidence at all was given on the essential point referred to. Its weight is entirely for the inferior court....

It has been said that the matter may be regarded as a question of jurisdiction, and that a justice who convicts without evidence is acting without jurisdiction to do so. Accordingly, want of essential evidence, if ascertained somehow, is on the same footing as want of qualification in the magistrate, and goes to the question of his right to enter on the case at all. Want of evidence on which to convict is the same as want of jurisdiction to take evidence at all. This, clearly, is erroneous. A justice who convicts without evidence is doing something that he ought not to do, but he is doing it as a judge, and if his jurisdiction to entertain the charge is not open to impeachment, his subsequent error, however grave, is a wrong exercise of a jurisdiction which he has, and not a usurpation of a jurisdiction which he has not. How a magistrate, who has acted within his jurisdiction up to the point at which the missing evidence should have been, but was not given, can, thereafter, be said by a kind of relation back to have had no jurisdiction over the charge at all, it is hard to see. It cannot be said that his conviction is void, and may be disregarded as a nullity, or that the whole proceeding was *coram non judice*. To say that there is no jurisdiction to convict without evidence is the same thing as saying that there is jurisdiction if the decision is right, and none if it is wrong; or that jurisdiction at the outset of a case continues so long as the decision stands, but that, if it is set aside, the real conclusion is that there never was any jurisdiction at all."

Can this be reconciled with *Coleen Properties Ltd* v. *M.H.L.G.*? Consider Lord Sumner's reasoning in the light of the *Anisminic* case, above, p. 210.

5. A finding of a preliminary or jurisdictional fact which is unsupported by any evidence will presumably cause the decision on the main question to be *ultra vires*. See above, pp. 193–209. Was *Re Ripon; White and Collins v. Minister of Health* (above, p. 193) decided on this ground? (See *Ashbridge Investments Ltd v. M.H.L.G.*, above, p. 555). Is this the proper explanation of *R. v. Secretary of State for the Home Department, ex p. Zamir* (above, p. 197)?

6. Wade and Forsyth argue (*Administrative Law* (7th ed.), pp. 312–319), that "this ground of review ought now to be regarded as established on a general basis . . . as part of the judicial policy of preventing abuse of discretionary power." It is recognised in habeas corpus cases (see *Wade and Forsyth*, pp. 621–623); in cases under the Housing Acts (*e.g.* the *Coleen* case, above); in jurisdictional fact cases (see note 5); and by Lord Diplock as an aspect of natural justice (see p. 505).

7. In *R. v. London Residuary Body, ex p. Inner London Education Authority, The Times*, July 24, 1987, the Divisional Court held that:

"a mistake as to fact can vitiate a decision as where the fact is a condition precedent to an exercise of jurisdiction, or where the fact was the only evidential basis for a decision or whether the fact was as to a matter which expressly or impliedly had to be taken into account. Outside those categories we do not accept that a decision can be flawed in this court, which is not an appellate tribunal, upon the ground of mistake of fact."

A dictum in the *Tameside* case by Lord Wilberforce ([1977] A.C. 1014, 1047) that the court's power of judicial review enable it to interfere with an exercise of discretion "on such grounds as that the minister has acted right outside his powers or outside the purpose of the Act, or unfairly, or upon an incorrect basis of fact", cannot have been intended "to introduce a new and independent head of challenge". (The view that a decision could be held invalid on the ground of mistake of fact was, however, expressed by Cooke J. in *Daganayasi v. Minister of Immigration* [1980] 2 N.Z.L.R. 130.)

The passage from *ex p. ILEA* was cited with apparent approval by Sedley J. in *R. v. Secretary of State for Education, ex p. Stitt* (unreported, April 15, 1995). Sedley J. noted that:

"As can be seen, there remains a question whether a matter which does not have to be but has legitimately been taken into account by the decision maker . . . if it is entertained on a radically flawed basis of fact, may equally vitiate a decision. The Divisional Court seems to have thought not, and it is not necessary to decide for the present purposes whether such a case can be logically distinguished from the third of the classes of case in which it has held error of fact to be a ground of review."

8. The equivalent rule in the United States allows a "reviewing court to determine whether an administrative determination made after a formal hearing is supported by substantial evidence on the record taken as a whole" (*Schwartz and Wade*, p. 228, referring to s.10(e)(B)5 of the Federal Administrative Procedure Act 1946, and Article 78 of the New York Civil Practice Law and Rules, which are based on case law).

The rule is useful in relation to formal decision-making processes where there is a full record of the proceedings, including the evidence, and it enables the courts to exercise a greater measure of control than the British "no evidence" rule. While a much smaller proportion of decisions in this country are supported by a full record than in the United States, that does not mean that the "substantial evidence" rule should not be applied where a full record is available, for example, in planning appeals with the inspector's report, and Minister's letter.

(ii) Failure to Give Adequate Reasons

CRAKE v. SUPPLEMENTARY BENEFITS COMMISSION; BUTTERWORTH v. SUPPLEMENTARY BENEFITS COMMISSION

[1982] 1 All E.R. 498 (Woolf J.)

In two separate cases the Commission decided that the respective applicants were not entitled to a supplementary allowance on the ground that their resources and require-ments were to be aggregated with those of a man with whom they were residing as they were "living together as husband and wife" within Sched. 1, para. 3(1)(b) to the Sup-plementary Benefits Act 1976. In each case the decision was upheld by a Supplemen-tary Benefits Appeal Tribunal. In the case of Mrs Crake the tribunal did not make any findings of fact, but merely summarised the history of the case and the parties' sub-missions, and gave as its reasons that most of the criteria specified in a supplementary benefit handbook for determining this question had been satisfied and that therefore C and the man were to be treated as living together as husband and wife. The tribunal did not state whether it accepted C's evidence that she was merely a housekeeper. C appealed, *inter alia*, on the ground that the tribunal had failed to give adequate reasons in accordance with its duties under r.12(1) of the Supplementary Benefit (Appeal Tri-bunal) Rules 1971 or s.12 of the Tribunals and Inquiries Act 1971.

WOOLF J.: . . . There was no formal request for reasons in this case and so perhaps the better approach is to look at it as if only the rule was applicable. However, whether one looks at the matter in the light of the rules or the Act, the situation is the same and there is an obligation on the tribunal to give reasons; and those must be reasons which are sufficient to indicate to the per-son who is in receipt of its decision why the tribunal came to the conclusion which it did.

It has got to be borne in mind, particularly with tribunals of this sort, that they cannot be expected to give long and precise accounts of their reasoning; but a short and concise statement in clear language should normally be poss-ible which fairly indicates to the recipient why his appeal was allowed or dis-missed; and it seems to me quite clear that when one looks at the findings of this tribunal together with the reasons for its decision, it falls far short of the standard which the Act requires.

First of all, when one analyses what are meant to be the findings of the tribunal on questions of fact, one finds that they are not any such thing. They are a citation of the history of the matter together with the submissions of the parties, and the reasons for the decision are not as clear as they should be. Where a question whether a person is entitled to benefit or not arises which involves the issue whether persons are living together as husband and wife, it is important that a decision of that nature should grapple with the real issues which are before the tribunal. Frequently there will be a question of who the tribunal believes and it may be possible to give the very shortest reasons to make it clear that the decision has been reached because, notwithstanding what the appellant said before the tribunal, her evidence is not accepted and the tribunal prefers the other evidence which indicates the relationship as husband and wife went beyond, for example, that of mere housekeeper.

It is right to say that useful guidance is again given to tribunals on this precise matter in the Supplementary Benefits Appeal Tribunals Guide to Procedure, and having looked at that handbook it seems to me that if tribunals pay attention to what is said in that handbook they will not go very far wrong.

Having said that, the reasons here are, in my view, inadequate. It is next necessary to consider what the consequences of that are. I am afraid that here one enters into a position where the law is somewhat confused. The latest edition, which has just recently come out, of *de Smith's Judicial Review of Administrative Action* (4th ed., 1980), p. 151 deals with what are the consequences of the reasons not being in accordance with a statutory requirement in these terms:

"Unfortunately it is still far from clear what are the other legal effects of non-compliance with a statutory duty to give reasons for decisions. There is authority for the proposition that failure to give reasons, or to give adequate reasons, is not in itself an error of law entitling the court to set the decision aside."

And then there is a reference to two cases in particular. One is *Re Allen and Matthews's Arbitration* [1971] 2 All E.R. 1259; [1971] 2 Q.B. 518 and the other is *Mountview Court Properties Ltd v. Devlin* (1970) 21 P. & C.R. 689 to which I will have to come back in a moment. The editor continues:

". . . if good and bad reasons for a decision are given, the decision should stand provided that the reasons are independent and severable. There is also authority (which it is submitted, is to be preferred) for treating material omissions as errors of law or as a failure to comply with the requirements of the legislation in question, and for regarding the adduction of legally irrelevant reasons as an excess of jurisdiction."

In support of the alternative way of approaching the matter the editor relies in particular on *Re Poyser and Mills's Arbitration* [1963] 1 All E.R. 612; [1964] 2 Q.B. 467, *Givaudan & Co. Ltd v. Minister of Housing and Local Government* [1966] 3 All E.R. 696; [1967] 1 W.L.R. 250 and *United*

Kingdom Association of Professional Engineers v. Advisory, Conciliation and Arbitration Service [1979] 2 All E.R. 478; [1979] 1 W.L.R. 570.

Those authorities have been cited to me together with a number of other authorities, and it seems to me that in approaching this question one must pay particular regard first of all to the *Mountview* decision. The facts of that case do not matter because it is a case involving a failure of the rent assessment committee to give reasons. In the course of his judgment Lord Parker C.J. said (21 P. & C.R. 689 at 695):

"For my part, I find it impossible to say that a failure to provide sufficient reasons of itself gives rise to the right of this court on an appeal to quash the decision of the committee. Secondly, it is to be observed that, quite apart from that, *Re Poyser and Mills' Arbitration* was really a case where, on the reasons stated, the proper inference was that there had been an error of law and that the arbitrator had misdirected himself. Of course, if the very insufficiency of the reason gives rise to a proper inference that there has been an error of law in arriving at the decision, then clearly it would be a case for quashing the decision."

Cooke J. agreed with that judgment. Bridge J. said (at 695–696):

"It seems to me that there was here a lack of adequate reason for the decision, but I fully agree with my Lord and I add a word on this point because it seems to me to be a point of some importance: that a failure to give reasons pursuant to the duty imposed by section 12 of the Tribunals and Inquiries Act 1958 is not *per se* a ground on which the court could properly allow an appeal under section 9, the right of appeal being conferred upon a person who is dissatisfied in point of law with a decision. That language, and, indeed, any analogous language found in the statutes giving a right of appeal on a point of law, to my mind connotes that a successful appellant must demonstrate that the decision with which he is dissatisfied is itself vitiated by reason of the fact that it has been reached by an erroneous process of legal reasonsing. Mr Slynn [as *amicus curiae*] concedes that there may in theory be cases where from a failure to give reasons one may legitimately infer, on a balance of probabilities, that the tribunal's process of legal reasoning must have been defective."

And the judge goes on to say that at one stage in the argument he thought that was a case falling within that concession.

That decision of the Divisional Court has never been overruled and, in my view, it is binding on me. There are a number of cases where decisions have been set aside, among those being the decisions referred to by the editor of *de Smith* in the passage to which I have made reference, but when one looks at those cases they are in no way inconsistent with the *Mountview* case because they either turn on the particular statutory provision which gave the grounds for bringing the matter before the High Court in that case, or they turned on a statutory provision which was very different from the statutory provision which is under consideration here.

If there is a statutory right to have the decision quashed where statutory procedures have not been complied with and a person has been prejudiced, as in the *Givaudan* case, then of course once it is shown that those statutory requirements for the giving of reasons have not been complied with and an applicant has been prejudiced, it follows that the decision will be quashed.

Likewise, the *UKAPE* case was a case which contained a statutory provision which made it fundamental that there should be reasons for the decision of ACAS. Such an obligation cannot be implied here so as to make the tribunal's decision automatically a nullity if proper reasons are not given.

I would therefore still regard the *Mountview* case as being the main authority to be applied. However, it has to be applied in the light of the ten years which have elapsed since that case was decided. Over that period of ten years the approach of the courts with regard to the giving of reasons has been much more definite than they were at that time and courts are now much more ready to infer that because of inadequate reasons there has been an error of law, than perhaps they were prepared to at the time that the *Mountview* case was decided.

In other spheres there are numerous cases which have been before the courts where tribunals of all sorts have had to reconsider their decisions because the reasoning was inadequate. Therefore in practice I think that there will be few cases where it will not be possible, where the reasons are inadequate, to say one way or another whether the tribunal has gone wrong in law. In some cases the absence of any reasons would indicate that the tribunal had never properly considered the matter (and it must be part of the obligation in law to consider the matter properly) and that the proper thought processes have not been gone through.

In other cases it will be seen from the reasons given that there has been a failure to take into account something which should have been taken into account or that something which should not have been taken into account has in fact been taken into account. Again, in that situation, there will be an error of law which will justify this court interfering on an appeal on a point of law.

In the rare case where it is not possible to decide either way whether or not there is an error of law, then, in my view, this court has got a jurisdiction, as was indicated in the *Mountview* case, to remit the matter to the tribunal for reconsideration. That power arises because of the very wide terms of s.13 of the Tribunals and Inquiries Act 1971, which is the Act which brings the matter before this court; and also because of the wording of R.S.C. Ord. 55, r. 7. There are great practical disadvantages in that course, as was stressed in argument before me, in relation to tribunals of this nature, because tribunals of this nature are informal bodies which cannot readily be reconvened and, indeed, if they are reconvened, may well have no recollection of the case which they herd; and so obviously the situations where it will be necessary to remit the matter will be limited. They can be limited if it is borne in mind that, as I have already stressed, this sort of tribunal cannot be expected to give the fullest and most detailed reasons, and a short and succinct statement is all that is required. . . .

[His Lordship then held that the reasons given suggested that the tribunal had misunderstood its role and was regarding itself as sitting as a review body rather than hearing an appeal on the merits. However, the Chairman's notes, admitted by virtue of R.S.C. Ord. 55, r. 7, made it clear that the tribunal was "clearly concerned about the question of the merits". Furthermore, it was open on the evidence for the tribunal to find that C was living with the man as husband and wife.]

Having approached the matter with the notes in mind I have come to the conclusion that notwithstanding the inadequacy of the reasoning of the tribunal, it would be wrong to allow this appeal on the grounds that the tribunal were approaching the matter in the wrong way.

Appeal dismissed.

Notes

1. The whole question of the giving of reasons is discussed by M.B. Akehurst (1970) 33 M.L.R. 154. See also *de Smith*; *Woolf and Jowell*, pp. 457–473; G. Richardson [1986] P.L. 437. On the development of requirements to give reasons based on fairness rather than statutory requirements, see above, pp. 509–516.

2. *Crake* was followed in respect of reasons given by a rent assessment committee in *R. v. London Rent Assessment Committee, ex p. St George's Court Ltd* (1983) 265 E.G. 984, and the same approach has been adopted in the contexts of road transport licences (*R. v. Secretary of State for Transport, ex p. Cumbria County Council* [1983] R.T.R. 88), immigration appeals (*R. v. Immigration Appeal Tribunal, ex p. Khan* [1983] Q.B. 790) and Legal Aid Appeal Committees (*R. v. Legal Aid Area No. 8 (Northern) Appeal Committee, ex p. Angell* (1990) 3 Admin.L.R. 189. In *South Glamorgan County Council v. Long* (unreported, December 21, 1995), Carnwath J. stated that where reasons were inadequately expressed by a Special Educational Needs Tribunal, the parties could seek elaboration or clarification by asking the Tribunal to exercise its power itself to review its decision under reg. 32 of the Special Educational Needs Tribunal Regulations 1994. His Lordship continued:

> "I . . . doubt very much whether the authorities relating to other statutory provisions in other contexts are really applicable in the context of this statutory scheme. A prime concern when one is dealing with the eduction of a child, particularly one who is disadvantaged in some way, must be to determine his future as quickly as possible and with as little anxiety for the parents and the child, and for others involved (including the authority). I think it would only be in a very extreme case that the court would wish to prolong this process by remitting a matter simply for clarification of reasons, which may have been inadequately expressed but which at least arrive at a clear final decision."

On this last point, his Lordship disagreed with the view of Latham J. in *S. v. Special Educational Needs Tribunal* [1996] 1 All E.R. 171, that a failure to give reasons would normally lead to the matter being remitted for a rehearing by the same or a differently constituted tribunal.

3. There are, by contrast, a number of situations where a failure to give adequate reasons will be regarded as an error of law leading to the quashing of the decision in question. Examples include the decisions of the National Industrial Relations Court and the Employment Appeal Tribunal (*Alexander Machinery (Dudley) Ltd v. Crabtree* [1974] I.C.R. 120; *Levy v. Marrable & Co.* [1984] I.C.R. 583; decisions of mental health review tribunals (*R. v. Mental Health Review Tribunal, ex p. Pickering* [1986] 1 All E.R. 99) and decisions of local authorities under the homelessness legislation (*R. v. Westminster City Council, ex p. Ermakov* [1996] 2 All E.R. 302). In *ex p. Ermakov*, the Court of Appeal quashed a decision of the council that E was intentionally homeless on the ground that the reason given in pursuance of the duty to give reasons under section 64 of the Housing Act 1985 was, by mistake, not the real reason. The Court held that it would only allow evidence to be adduced to elucidate, or, exceptionally,

correct or add to the reasons given under section 64. Here the reason given was completely different from the real reason. Furthermore, the Court would normally (as here) quash the decision by certiorari, requiring the matter to be reconsidered, and not merely issue mandamus requiring reasons to be given. It was not necessary for the applicant to show he had been prejudiced. Allowing reasons to be amended or reversed would "encourage a sloppy approach by the decision-maker" (*per* Hutchison L.J. at 316). *Ex p. Ermakov* has been applied to decisions of a housing benefit review board (*R. v. Lambeth London Borough Council Housing Benefit Review Board, ex p. Harrington, The Times*, December 10, 1996) and the Parole Board (*R. v. Secretary of State for the Home Department, ex p. Lillycrop, The Times*, December 13, 1996).

It is difficult to discern a principled basis for the distinction between these cases and those summarised in the preceding note: see G. Richardson [1986] P.L. 437, 447–469.

4. In planning cases, by the Town and Country Planning (Inquiries Procedure) Rules 1992, r. 17(1), the Secretary of State is required to give reasons for his decisions in determining appeals. The same duty applies where an appeal is determined by an inspector. A failure to give adequate and intelligible reasons may lead to the decision being quashed under section 288 of the Town and Country Planning Act 1990 on the ground that the applicant's interests have been substantially prejudiced by a failure to comply with a relevant requirement. The reasons must be proper, adequate and intelligible and deal with the substantial points raised (*Re Poyser and Mills' Arbitration* [1964] 2 Q.B. 467, 478, approved by the House of Lords in *Westminster City Council v. Great Portland Estates plc* [1985] 661, 673) and enable

> "the appellant to understand on what grounds the appeal has been decided and be in sufficient detail to enable him to know what conclusions the inspector has reached on the principal important controversial issues"

(*per* Phillips J. in *Hope v. Secretary of State for the Environment* (1975) 31 P. & C.R. 120, 123, approved by Lord Bridge for the House of Lords in *Save Britain's Heritage v. Number 1 Poultry Ltd* [1991] 1 W.L.R. 153, 165). Decision letters should not be construed as statutes and should be read as a whole (*ibid.*). However, Lord Bridge in the *Save Britain's Heritage* case emphasised that the courts could not set a general standard as to the adequacy of reasons. Commenting on a passage from Woolf L.J.'s judgment in the Court of Appeal (60 P. & C.R. 539, 545), he said (at 166–167):

> "I certainly accept that the reasons should enable a person who is entitled to contest the decision to make a proper assessment as to whether the decision should be challenged. But I emphatically reject the proposition that in planning decisions the 'standard', 'threshold' or 'quality' of the reasons required to satisfy the statutory requirement varies according to who is making the decision, how much time he has to reflect upon it, and whether or not he had legal assistance, or depends upon the degree of importance which attaches to the matter falling to be decided. The obligation, being imposed on the Secretary of State and his inspectors in identical terms, must be construed in the same sense.
>
> The three criteria suggested in the dictum of Megaw J. in *Re Poyser and Mills' Arbitration* [1964] 2 Q.B. 467, 478 are that the reasons should be proper, intelligible and adequate. The application of the first two of these presents no problem. If the reasons given are improper they will reveal some flaw in the decision-making process which will be open to challenge on some ground other than the failure to give reasons. If the reasons given are unintelligible, this will be equivalent to giving no reasons at all. The difficulty arises in determining whether the reasons given are adequate, whether, in the words of Megaw J., they deal with the substantial points that have been raised or, in the words of Phillips J. in *Hope v. Secretary of State for the Environment* 31 P. & C.R. 120, 123, enable the reader to know what conclusion the decision-maker has reached on the principal controversial issues. What degree of

particularity is required? It is tempting to think that the Court of Appeal or your Lordships' House would be giving helpful guidance by offering a general answer to this question and thereby "setting the standard" but I feel no doubt that the temptation should be resisted, precisely because the court has no authority to put a gloss on the words of the statute, only to construe them. I do not think one can safely say more in general terms than that the degree of particularity required will depend entirely on the nature of the issues falling for decision.

Whatever may be the position in any other legislative context, under the planning legislation, when it comes to deciding in any particular case whether the reasons given are deficient, the question is not to be answered *in vacuo*. The alleged deficiency will only afford a ground for quashing the decision if the court is satisfied that the interests of the applicant have been substantially prejudiced by it. This reinforces the view I have already expressed that the adequacy of reasons is not to be judged by reference to some abstract standard. There are in truth not two separate questions: (1) were the reasons adequate? (2) if not, were the interests of the applicant substantially prejudiced thereby? The single indivisible question, in my opinion, which the court must ask itself whenever a planning decision is challenged on the ground of a failure to give reasons is whether the interests of the applicant have been substantially prejudiced by the deficiency of the reasons given. Here again, I disclaim any intention to put a gloss on the statutory provisions by attempting to define or delimit the circumstances in which deficiency of reasons will be capable of causing substantial prejudice, but I should expect that normally such prejudice will arise from one of three causes. First, there will be substantial prejudice to a developer whose application for permission has been refused or to an opponent of development when permission has been granted where the reasons for the decision are so inadequately or obscurely expressed as to raise a substantial doubt whether the decision was taken within the powers of the Act. Secondly, a developer whose application for permission is refused may be substantially prejudiced where the planning considerations on which the decision is based are not explained sufficiently clearly to enable him reasonably to assess the prospects of succeeding in an application for some alternative form of development. Thirdly, an opponent of development, whether the local planning authority or some unofficial body like Save, may be substantially prejudiced by a decision to grant permission in which the planning considerations on which the decision is based, particularly if they relate to planning policy, are not explained sufficiently clearly to indicate what, if any, impact they may have in relation to the decision of future applications."

(The House held, reversing the Court of Appeal, that the reasons given by the Secretary of State in granting planning permission for the demolition of listed buildings and their replacement by a modern building were adequate. See above, p. 77 and Sir Desmond Heap and M. Thomas [1991] J.P.L. 207). Subsequently, in *Bolton Metropolitan District Council v. Secretary of State for the Environment* (1995) 71 P. & C.R. 309, the House of Lords made it clear that while the Secretary of State had to have regard to all material considerations, it was not necessary for every such consideration to be dealt with specifically in the reasons for the ultimate decision to grant or withhold planning consent.

5. In *French Kier Developments Ltd v. Secretary of State for the Environment* [1977] 1 All E.R. 296, Willis J. quashed the Minister's decision to dismiss an appeal against a refusal of planning permission. One ground was that the Minister had not given a clear and intelligible statement of the reasons for his decision. The inspector had recommended that the appeal be allowed. The Minister agreed with all his findings of fact, but expressed "some disagreement with him about the degree of emphasis which he has put" on certain factors. Per Willis J. at 304: "One is entitled to ask, where has he gone wrong? What is the nature of the disagreement? Where should the emphasis have been put? Nothing could be vaguer on these matters than the decision letter."

This approach may be compared with that of the Divisional Court in *Guppys (Bridport) Ltd v. Sandoe* (1975) 30 P. & C.R. 69. Here, a rent assessment committee decided to assess the fair rent for a house on the basis suggested by the tenant, and not on any of the bases suggested by the landlord. In the statement of reasons required by the Tribunals and Inquiries Act 1971, the committee explained *which* basis they adopted, but not *why* they rejected those suggested by the landlord. The court held that the committee had complied with their duty to give reasons. Lord Widgery C.J. (at 74–75) stated that where a judge has two conflicting opinions put before him in evidence, it is not possible to explain why one is preferable to the other. "Such explanations are not possible. They are matters of judgment, impression and sometimes even instinct, and it is quite impossible to give detailed reasons to explain how the system of decision has worked, and so with a rent assessment committee."

cf. Metropolitan Property Holdings Ltd v. Laufer (1974) 29 P. & C.R. 172.

(iii) Questions of *Vires*

Notes

There are a number of authorities that suggest or hold that a question of *vires* cannot be raised on an appeal on a point of law. In some, this has been on the doubtful basis that if a decision is *ultra vires* and void there is nothing to appeal against (*Metropolitan Properties Co. (F.G.C.) Ltd v. Lannon* [1968] 1 W.L.R. 815, D.C., and *Chapman v. Earl* [1968] 1 W.L.R. 1315, D.C., below, p. 766). In *Henry Moss Ltd v. Customs and Excise Commissioners* [1981] 2 All E.R. 86, Lord Denning M.R. stated (at 90) that the proper way to challenge the validity of regulations and administrative directions made under the authority of a statute was by way of an application for judicial review under Order 53, and not by an appeal on a point of law. The other members of the Court of Appeal did not mention the point expressly. Each of them prefaced his judgment by the words "I agree" but it is possible that these words merely indicated agreement with the order allowing the appeal, and not necessarily with all the reasons given in the judgment of Lord Denning M.R. Counsel for the Commissioners invited the court to deal with the case as if there had been an application for judicial review, and the court acceded to that invitation. This approach was criticised as unduly restrictive by A.W. Bradley [1981] P.L. 476, as apparently regarding the introduction of Order 53 as outlawing collateral review.

There are certainly other authorities which accept that a question of *vires can* be raised on an appeal. See, *e.g. Elliott v. Brighton Borough Council* (1980) 79 L.G.R. 506: a general right to "appeal"; *Nolan v. Leeds City Council* (1990) 23 H.L.R. 135 (Housing Act 1985, ss.353 and 367, 362 and 371, which, respectively, provided for an appeal on the ground of an "informality, defect or error in or in connection with the notice", no specified ground, and that "the making of the order was unnecessary"). In *R. v. Inland Revenue Commissioners, ex p. Preston* [1985] A.C. 835, Lord Templeman stated (at 862) that on an appeal by case stated on a point of law from the General or Special Commissioners to the High Court, the court:

"can ... correct all kinds of errors of law including errors which might otherwise be the subject of judicial review proceedings: see *Edwards (Inspector of Taxes) v. Bairstow* [1956] A.C. 14".

In *Chief Adjudication Officer v. Foster* [1993] A.C. 754, the House of Lords (reversing the Court of Appeal on this point) held that a question of the validity of the income support regulations could be raised through the statutory appellate structure, including the appeal from a social security appeal tribunal to the Social Security

Commissioner on the ground that the tribunal's decision was "erroneous in point of law" (Social Security Act 1975, s.101, now the Social Security Administration Act 1992, s.23). See D. Feldman (1992) 108 L.Q.R 5 and A.W. Bradley [1992] P.L. 185 on the decision of the Court of Appeal and D. Feldman and N.J. Wikeley (1993) 109 L.Q.R. 544 and N. Harris (1993) 56 M.L.R. 710 on the decision of the House of Lords. It is certainly arguable that this broader approach is convenient as it enables cases which raise points of *vires* as well as legality or (if appropriate) merits to be fully disposed of on appeal: *Wade and Forsyth*, p. 954.

These cases strictly concern the *jurisdiction* of the appellate court to consider questions of *vires*. The relationship between appeals and judicial review is further complicated by the separate principles (1) that it may be held to be an abuse of process for a point as to *vires* to be raised other than on an application for judicial review (*O'Reilly v. Mackman*, below, pp. 642–662); and (2) that judicial review will not lie, as a matter of discretion, if there is another more appropriate remedy, such as an appeal (below, pp. 687–689). It will be noted that these principles pull in different directions. The former was considered in *R. v. Oxford Crown Court, ex p. Smith, The Independent*, January 19, 1990, where Simon Brown J. held that it was not an abuse of process for a point as to *vires* to be raised on an appeal to the Crown Court against a clearance notice served under section 65 of the Town and Country Planning Act 1971 (now s.215 of the 1990 Act); his Lordship dealt with the matter as raising the *O'Reilly v. Mackman* principle rather than as a question of the proper interpretation of the statutory grounds of appeal. Similarly, in *Nolan v. Leeds City Council* (1990) 23 H.L.R. 135, the Court of Appeal held that it was not an abuse of process to raise a matter of *vires* on appeals under the Housing Act 1985. The latter principle was emphasised by Lord Templeman in *Preston* (above), although in that case the allegation was that the conduct of the commissioners in initiating proceedings was unlawful, in which case the relevant appeal procedure could not begin to operate.

Finally, it may be noted that Parliament may expressly provide that certain matters shall not be challenged *except* by judicial review: see, *e.g.* the Local Government Finance Act 1992, s.66, in respect of the setting of the council tax and related matters.

(G) "Persons Aggrieved"

Many appeals established by statute may only be brought by a "person aggrieved". This term has been considered by the courts on many occasions. The view most commonly relied on as to its meaning is that expressed by James L.J. in *ex p. Sidebotham* (1880) 14 Ch.D. 458 at 465:

> "... [T]he words 'person aggrieved' do not really mean a man who is disappointed of a benefit which he might have received if some other order had been made. A 'person aggrieved' must be a man who has suffered a legal grievance, a man against whom a decision has been pronounced which has wrongfully deprived him of something, or wrongfully refused him something, or wrongfully affected his title to something."

The attitude of the court has, however, varied according to the context.

In many areas of local government law, a local authority is empowered to serve a notice requiring a private person to have works done on his property, and a person aggrieved by the notice may appeal to a court. That private person is a "person aggrieved" by the notice, and by a decision of a court upholding a notice. Is the local authority a "person aggrieved" by a decision of the justices against them? A series of decisions of the Divisional Court established that it was not, unless a legal burden was placed upon them as a result of the decision. This was clear where the justices' decision threw a financial burden on the authority (beyond the costs of the magistrates' court proceedings), as in *Phillips v. Berkshire County Council* [1967] 2 Q.B. 991, where justices decided that a street was not a private street, and thus was maintainable at the public expense. Where the authority was seeking to enforce a restriction on activities, it was unlikely that they would be placed under a burden if the private person appealed successfully to the court. The cases where it was held that a local authority was not a "person aggrieved" by the quashing of an enforcement notice served by the authority had to be overruled by statute (see now s.289 of the Town and Country Planning Act 1990, and *cf.* s.288(2) (*ibid.*)). The obligation to pay costs was in some cases held to be sufficient to render the authority a "person aggrieved" (*e.g.* under section 301 of the Public Health Act 1936: *R. v. Surrey Quarter Sessions, ex p. Lilley* [1951] 2 K.B. 749, applied in *Cook v. Southend Borough Council* (1987) 151 J.P. 641, D.C.), but not in others (*e.g. R. v. Dorset Quarter Sessions Appeals Committee, ex p. Weymouth Corporation* [1960] 2 Q.B. 230, in relation to the Town and Country Planning Act 1947, s.23).

Another common situation was where the local authority could grant a licence for an activity. A person refused a licence was a "person aggrieved" for the purposes of an appeal (*e.g. Stepney B.C. v. Joffe* [1949] 1 K.B. 599); but it was held that the local authority might not be a "person aggrieved" by the reversal of their decision (*e.g. R. v. London Q.S., ex p. Westminster Corporation* [1951] 2 K.B. 508, applied in *R. v. Southwark London Borough Council, ex p. Watts* (1989) 88 L.G.R. 86; but *cf. Penwith District Council v. McCartan-Mooney, The Times*, October 20, 1984).

The courts showed a less rigid attitude where the question concerned persons affected by the decisions of public authorities (*Turner v. Secretary of State for the Environment*, below). The cases concerning public authorities as "persons aggrieved" were reconsidered by the Court of Appeal in *Cook v. Southend Borough Council*, below, p. 593, and a broader view was adopted.

TURNER AND ANOTHER v. SECRETARY OF STATE FOR THE ENVIRONMENT AND OTHERS

(1973) 72 L.G.R. 380; 28 P. & C.R. 123; 228 E.G. 335 (Ackner J.)

In February 1967 the local planning authority gave outline planning permission, with details reserved, for the erection of two houses in the grounds of Rutland Lodge, Petersham. In October 1967 they gave permission on a detailed application to carry out that development (two two-storey houses). Further alternative applications were made to erect two larger houses on the land. The Secretary of State decided to hold a local inquiry to consider whether he should exercise his default powers under section 207 of the Town and Country Planning Act 1962 (now s.100 of the 1992 Act) in respect of the first two permissions. He "called in" the second two applications under section 22 (now s.77) for his own determination and these too were considered at the inquiry. In July 1971, after the inquiry, the Secretary of State refused permission on the second two applications, and gave notice of his intention to revoke the original permissions (*inter alia*) because of the detrimental effect the development would have on the view from Richmond Hill.

In August 1971 the landowner applied for permission to erect two single-storey houses on the land. The local planning authority regarded this as a fresh application. The Secretary of State called this application in for consideration in conjunction with the proposed revocation order. In June 1972 a second inquiry was held. The inspector exercised his discretion to allow certain opponents of any grant of planning permission in relation to the land to be represented at the inquiry. These were the Petersham Society (a local preservation society), and other amenity societies. At the inquiry the landowner maintained, and the local council did not contest, that the August 1971 application was not a fresh application, but an application for approval of the details reserved in the February 1967 outline permission. If this contention were correct, the only relevant considerations would concern whether the detailed design was acceptable, and not whether development was acceptable in principle. The inspector recommended that if the landowner's contention were correct, permission should be granted, as the proposed design was reasonable, and compensation would be payable for revocation of permission. On the other hand, if the proper view were that this was a fresh application, permission should be refused, as a wider range of considerations could properly be considered. The Secretary of State accepted the landowner's view of the legal status of the application, and approved the plan to erect two single-storey houses. The October 1967 detailed permission [*i.e.* for two two-storey houses] was revoked.

The Petersham Society sought to have this decision quashed under section 245(1)(b) of the 1971 Act [see now s.288 of the 1990 Act]. They pointed out that the site of the August 1971 application overlapped and exceeded the area subject to the February 1967 outline permission. Counsel for the Secretary of State, and for the landowner, argued that Ackner J. had no jurisdiction to hear the appeal, on the ground that the Society was not a "person aggrieved".

ACKNER J.: . . . The first point taken by Mr Frank and Mr Rich is the familiar one, that the applicants are not persons aggrieved by any action on the part of the Secretary of State. Both counsel rely, essentially, on the decision of this court in *Buxton v. Minister of Housing and Local Government* [1961] 1 Q.B. 278; 59 L.G.R. 45, a decision of Salmon J. In that case the owners and occupiers of certain land (the operators) applied under section 14 of the Town and Country Planning Act 1947, to the local planning authority for permission to develop their land by digging chalk. The local planning authority refused the application, and the operators appealed to the Minister of Housing and Local Government pursuant to section 16 of the Act of 1947. The Minister caused a local inquiry to be held by an inspector appointed by him under sections 15 and 16 of the Act into the refusal of permission by the local planning authority. Amongst those who appeared at the inquiry, called evidence and were heard were the operators, the local authority, and the applicants, four substantial landowners whose land was adjacent to that of the operators and was being used for agricultural and residential purposes. The inspector in his report recommended that the operators' appeal should be dismissed. The Minister rejected the inspector's report and allowed the appeal; hence, the application by the landowners against the decision. The preliminary point was taken on behalf of the Minister that the landowners were not persons aggrieved within the meaning of section 31 of the Act, which was in identical terms to section 245 of the Act of 1971 so far as is relevant to this case. In his judgment the judge stated that the case raised the perennial question as to what the legislature meant when it used the words "aggrieved person". . . .

Later in his judgment Salmon J. said, at 283 and 47:

"Superficially, there is much to be said for the view that the applicants are aggrieved by the Minister's action. For example, Mr Buxton, one of the applicants, as the inspector's report shows, has an estate of about 250 acres adjoining the operators' land. He is interested in landscape gardening and ornithology and has spent large sums of money for these purposes on his land. Moreover, he has a herd of pedigree pigs and some breeding mares very close indeed to the site from which the chalk is to be won. I can well understand his annoyance at the Minister's decision to reject recommendations which the Minister's inspector has made after a thorough inspection of the site and careful investigation of a considerable body of evidence. If I could approach this problem free from authority, without regard to the scheme of the Town and Country Planning legislation and its historical background, the arguments in favour of the applicants on the preliminary point would be most persuasive, if not compelling, for in the widest sense of the word the applicants are undoubtedly aggrieved. In my judgment, however, I am compelled to restrict the meaning of the words 'person aggrieved' to a person with a legal grievance."

He then dealt in some detail with the legislation and ended by saying, at 285 and 48:

"The Minister's action which these applicants seek to challenge infringed none of their common law rights. They have no rights as individuals under the statutes. Accordingly, in my judgment, none of their legal rights has been infringed, and in these circumstances it could not, in my view, have been the intention of the legislature to enable them to challenge the Minister's decision in the courts. Ever since the judgment of James L.J. in the well-known case of *Re Sidebotham* (1880) 14 Ch.D. 458, it has been generally accepted that the words 'person aggrieved' in a statute connote the person with a legal grievance, that is to say, someone whose legal rights have been infringed. James L.J. said: 'the words "person aggrieved" do not really mean a man who is disappointed of a benefit which he might have received if some other order had been made. A "person aggrieved" must be a man who has suffered a legal grievance, a man against whom a decision has been pronounced which has wrongfully deprived him of something, or wrongfully refused him something, or wrongfully affected his title to something.' "

Salmon J. considered that the guiding principle was that laid down by James L.J. in that case, and which, as far as he knew, had never been challenged.

At the time when that decision was made, July 1960, there was not then in existence the Town and Country Planning (Inquiries Procedure) Rules 1962, which have been re-enacted with various amendments until they are now to be found in the Town and Country Planning (Inquiries Procedure) Rules 1969. The Rules of 1962, as continued to be provided, made provision for appearances at the inquiry and in their present form they are to be found in rule 5 which deals with notification of inquiry, and rule 7 with appearances at the inquiry. Rule 7 provides:

"(1) The persons entitled to appear at the inquiry shall be"—and then it sets out obvious categories such as the applicant and the local planning authority, and ends with—"(g) any persons on whom the Minister has required notice to be served under rule 5(2)(b). (2) Any other person may appear at the inquiry at the discretion of the appointed person."

The part of the judgment in *Buxton's* case (*supra*) upon which the respondents, including, of course, the owner, relied is found on 285 and 48 and reads:

> "In my judgment, anyone given a statutory right to have his representations considered by the Minister impliedly has the right that the Minister, in considering those representations, shall act within the powers conferred upon him by the statute and shall comply with the relevant requirements of the statute."

It is accepted by Mr Frank and Mr Rich that a rule 7(1)(g) person is a person given a statutory right to have his representations considered by the Minister and is covered by what follows in that part of the judgment, but they each contend that a rule 7(2) person, a person who appears at the inquiry at the discretion of the appointed person, is a "second-class citizen" for the purpose of rights of appeal from which it must follow that Salmon J.'s judgment should be adopted in regard to them to read as follows:

> "In my judgment, anyone given a right to appear at the inquiry at the discretion of the appointed person has impliedly no right that the Minister in considering his representations shall act within the powers conferred upon him by the statute and shall comply with the relevant requirements of the statute."

I must say that I find that a particularly unattractive proposition and I am sure Salmon J. would have felt the same if that submission had been made to him. In further support of the proposition that the rule 7(2) person has no entitlement to appeal my attention was drawn to the decision of Paull J. in *Gregory v. Camden London Borough Council* [1966] 1 W.L.R. 899; 64 L.G.R. 215....

A number of cases were referred to in argument and in the judgment, and there was a reference to the decision of Salmon J. The decision in *Buxton's* case (*supra*) was on the fringe of the issues there being decided because there the issue was the right to bring an action for a declaration direct against the owner and did not raise the question as to what were the statutory rights of appeal given against the decision of the Minister following an inquiry held at his instance and at which parties seeking to appeal had been allowed to appear and make representations. I do not, therefore, find it of any assistance in this case and, significantly, neither of the extremely experienced counsel who appeared and who were praised for their interesting and detailed arguments thought fit to invite the judge's attention to two recent authorities which clearly have a direct bearing upon the extent to which Salmon J.'s decision should now be followed. Those two cases are, first, *Attorney-General of the Gambia v. N'Jie* [1961] A.C. 617, a decision of the Privy Council. In that case section 7 of the Supreme Court Ordinance of the Gambia provided:

> "... it shall be lawful for the Governor to appoint a deputy judge to represent the judge of the Supreme Court of the Colony of the Gambia [the Chief Justice] in the exercise of his judicial powers..."

and Order IX, r. 7 of the Rules of the Supreme Court of the Gambia provided:

"The judge shall have power, for reasonable cause, to suspend any barrister or solicitor from practising within the jurisdiction of the court ... or order his name to be struck off the Roll of Court."

The name of the respondent, a member of the English Bar who had been admitted to practise as a barrister and solicitor of the Supreme Court of the Gambia, was, after due inquiry into allegations of professional misconduct by a deputy judge appointed under section 7 of the Supreme Court Ordinance, ordered by him to be struck off the roll of the Supreme Court of the Gambia. On his appeal, the West African Court of Appeal set aside the deputy judge's order on the ground that he had only jurisdiction to represent the Chief Justice "in the exercise of his judicial powers", and that the power to strike a legal practitioner off the roll was not a judicial power. On appeal by the Attorney-General of the Gambia by special leave the Privy Council held:

"... that the Attorney-General, representing the Crown as guardian of the public interest, was a 'person aggrieved'—words of wide import—by the decision of the West African Court of Appeal within the meaning of section 31 of the West African (Appeal to Privy Council) Order in Council, 1949, and accordingly had a *locus standi* to petition for special leave to appeal."

In that case Lord Denning in giving the opinion of the Board made a specific reference to James L.J.'s judgment in *Re Sidebotham (supra)* which was much relied upon by Salmon J. in the manner in which I have already indicated. Lord Denning said at 634:

"If this definition were to be regarded as exhaustive, it would mean that the only person who could be aggrieved would be a person who was a party to a *lis*, a controversy *inter partes*, and had had a decision given against him. The Attorney-General does not come within this definition, because, as their Lordships have already pointed out, in these disciplinary proceedings there is no suit between parties, but only action taken by the judge, *ex mero motu* or at the instance of the Attorney-General or someone else, against a delinquent practitioner. But the definition of James L.J. is not to be regarded as exhaustive. Lord Esher M.R. points that out in *ex p. Official Receiver, Re Reed, Bowen & Co.* (1887) 19 Q.B.D. 174 at 178. The words 'person aggrieved' are of wide import and should not be subjected to a restrictive interpretation. They do not include, of course, a mere busybody who is interfering in things which do not concern him; but they do include a person who has a genuine grievance because an order has been made which prejudicially affects his interests."

That case was referred to in a decision of the Court of Appeal in *Maurice v. London County Council* [1964] 2 Q.B. 362; 62 L.G.R. 241. The owner of premises situated within 100 yards of a proposed block of flats more than 100 feet high appealed under section 52(2)(a) of the London Building Act 1930, as a person who deemed herself aggrieved, against a consent granted by the London County Council under section 51 of the Act of 1930 as amended by section 5 of the London County Council (General Powers) Act 1954. In the course of his judgment Lord Denning M.R. said, on the subject of "person aggrieved", at 377–378 and 243–244:

"Miss Maurice now appeals to this court. The first point argued before us is whether she can complain of loss of amenity. On this point I am afraid I have come to a decision different from that of the Divisional Court. The material words in section 52(2)(a) give a right of appeal 'to the owner or lessee of any land within 100 yards who may deem himself aggrieved' by the grant of consent. It is quite clear that the person must be aggrieved in respect of his interest in a building or land within 100 yards. But there is no limitation whatever as to the kind of grievance. I can see no reason whatever for excluding loss of amenities. I know that at one time the words 'person aggrieved' (which I regard as the same as 'person who shall deem himself aggrieved') were given in these courts a very narrow and restricted interpretation. It was said that the words 'person aggrieved' in a statute only meant a person who had suffered a legal grievance. Indeed in *Buxton v. Minister of Housing and Local Government (supra)*, which I mentioned in the course of the argument, Salmon J. declined to go into the question of loss of amenities. But that narrow view should now be rejected. In the more recent case of *Attorney-General of the Gambia v. N'Jie (supra)*, the Privy Council had to consider these words 'person aggrieved' once again. On behalf of the Board, I ventured to say there"—he then sets out that part of the opinion of the Board which I have cited—"so here in this case they do include a person who has a genuine grievance because a consent has been given which prejudicially affects his interests. His interests may be prejudicially affected, not only in regard to light and air, but in regard to amenities also. The one requisite must be that his grievance must be in respect of his interest as an owner or lessee of a building within 100 yards."

Pearson L.J. agreed with Lord Denning M.R. He said, at 381 and 246:

"It is clear that in order to qualify for appealing under section 52(2)(a) the appellant must be the owner or lessee of a building or land within 100 yards of the site of the intended building, and must also deem herself to be aggrieved by the grant of the consent. Evidently the word 'deem' is used because, when she launches her appeal, she can only have an opinion that she is aggrieved. In my view (and Mr Megarry does not dispute this) there is an implication that the appellant, in order to establish a prima facie case in her appeal, must prove that she is, by reason of the height of the intended building, likely to suffer damage in her capacity as owner or lessee of her property."

Wilberforce J. said, at 384 and 248: "I entirely agree with the judgments which have been delivered." . . .

There is a firm, fixed, immutable time limit provided in the appeal provisions. The appeal can only be based on very limited and restricted grounds, as the section clearly reveals. I see no merit in the proposition that a person who has merely been given notice of the existence of the inquiry at the request of and not by the requirement of the Secretary of State and whose right to attend and make his representations has resulted from the exercise of the inspector's discretion, should be obliged to sit by and accept the decision which, *ex hypothesi*, is bad in law. I can see no compelling matter of policy which requires this form of silence to be imposed upon a person who has, again *ex hypothesi*, a clear grievance in law. On the other hand, I see good reason, so long as the grounds of appeal are so restricted, for ensuring that any person who, in the ordinary sense of the word, is aggrieved by the decision, and certainly any person who has attended and made representations at the inquiry, should have the right to establish in the courts that the decision is bad in law because it is *ultra vires* or for some other good reason. It is true that the would-be developer may be held up while the appeal is made but, as the dates in this case indicate, the procedure is a reasonably expeditious one, and I have no doubt that an application for special expedition, where justified, would be listened to sympathetically by the court.

In his report the inspector classifies the applicants, *inter alios*, as "interested persons", a classification which is clearly justified by the facts. They were persons whom the appointed person in his discretion had allowed to appear at the inquiry and make representations in relation to the subject-matter of the inquiry, which representations had to be recorded by the inspector and transmitted with the inspector's findings of fact and conclusions to the Secretary of State with a view to the Secretary of State accepting or rejecting those findings of fact and conclusions. Such persons have, in my judgment, impliedly the right that the Secretary of State, in considering those representations, shall act within the powers conferred upon him by the statute and shall comply with the relevant requirements of the statute, in just the same way (as is conceded to be the case) as a person who makes representations at the inquiry being a person on whom the Secretary of State has required notice of the inquiry to be served. I thus conclude that no valid differentiation can be made between a person who appears at an inquiry and makes his representations having had notice of the inquiry at the insistence of the Secretary of State and a person who appears and makes his representations by permission of the appointed person. This question was not before Salmon J. in *Buxton's* case (*supra*), the Inquiry Procedure Rules of 1962 having not then been passed. Moreover, I derive from the recommendation of the Court of Appeal that the narrow construction should now be rejected, just sufficient fortitude for not following the decision in the *Buxton* case so reluctantly reached by the judge. I therefore reject the first proposition that there is no jurisdiction in this court because I am obliged to impose a very restricted meaning upon the words "aggrieved person...."

[His Lordship nevertheless held that he had no jurisdiction, on the ground that sections 242(3) and 245(3) of the 1971 Act gave a right of appeal against "any decision of the Secretary of State on an application for planning permission referred to him under section 35 of this Act", and not against a decision on an application for approval of reserved details.]

Notes

1. See articles by J.E. Trice [1973] J.P.L. 580 (written before *Turner's* case was reported); and H.M. Purdue and Trice [1974] J.P.L. 20 (on *Turner's* case); W. Parkes [1978] J.P.L. 739; B. Hough [1992] J.P.L. 319.

2. Full materials on the *Chalkpit* affair, of which *Buxton's* case was a part, are given

in J.A.G. Griffith and H. Street, *A Casebook of Administrative Law* (1964). See also [1961] P.L. 121; [1962] P.L. 362.

3. *Turner* has been followed in *Bizony v. Secretary of State for the Environment* [1976] J.P.L. 306; *Hollis v. Secretary of State for the Environment* (1982) 47 P. & C.R. 351; *Morbaine Ltd v. Secretary of State for the Environment* (1993) 68 P. & C.R. 525 (company chosen to develop appeal site and with an option to purchase it was a "person aggrieved" notwithstanding that it had not appeared at the inquiry); *Bannister v. Secretary of State for the Environment* [1994] 2 E.G.L.R. 197 (owner of land adjoining appeal site across which the site had access, and who attended the inquiry and made written representations was a "person aggrieved") and approved by the Court of Appeal in *Times Investment Ltd v. Secretary of State for the Environment* (1990) 61 P. & C.R. 98, where it was held that a successor in title to land subject to a planning appeal can be a person aggrieved.

Questions

1. How satisfactory is the reasoning of Ackner J. (1) on the general approach to *locus standi*; (2) on the question whether the present applicants were "persons aggrieved" on the assumption that the narrow approach of Salmon J. in *Buxton* is not followed?

2. Compare this decision with the case law on applications for judicial review (below, pp. 663–679).

COOK v. SOUTHEND BOROUGH COUNCIL

[1990] 2 Q.B. 1; [1990] 2 W.L.R. 61; [1990] 1 All E.R. 243;
(1990) 88 L.G.R. 408 (Court of Appeal)
(*Pet. dis.*, [1990] 1 W.L.R. 1, H.L.)

C's hackney carriage vehicle and driver's licences were revoked by the council under sections 60 and 61 of the Local Government (Miscellaneous Provisions) Act 1976. C successfully appealed to the magistrates' court, which made an order for costs against the council. The council appealed to the Crown Court, claiming to be a "person aggrieved" and therefore entitled to appeal by virtue of section 77(1) of the 1976 Act and section 301 of the Public Health Act 1936. The Crown Court allowed the appeal. C appealed by case stated to the High Court, and the judge dismissed the appeal, holding that he was constrained by authority to hold that the council was a person aggrieved on the ground that an order for costs had been made against it by the magistrates. The Court of Appeal dismissed C's appeal, but was free to reconsider the basis of the council's standing.

WOOLF L.J.: ... The question of who is "a person aggrieved" for the purpose of giving a right to make an application to a court or other judicial or quasi-judicial body has been the subject of a great many reported decisions of the courts going back from the present day to the nineteenth century. However, the majority of the decisions are at first instance and not binding on this court. They draw arbitrary and unsatisfactory distinctions between different statutes and situations and lead to needless highly technical arguments as to *locus standi*.

In these circumstances it is, I hope, useful if I set out certain general propositions which I would expect to apply where the expression "a person aggrieved" is used in relation to a right of appeal in the absence of a clear contrary intention in a particular statutory context. (1) A body corporate including a local authority is just as capable of being a person aggrieved as an individual. (2) Any person who has a decision decided against him (particularly in adversarial proceedings) will be a person aggrieved for the purposes of appealing against that decision unless the decision amounts to an acquittal of a purely criminal offence. In the latter case the statutory context will be all-important. (3) The fact that the decision against which the person wishes to appeal reverses a decision which was originally taken by that person and does not otherwise adversely affect that person does not prevent that person being a person aggrieved. On the contrary it indicates that he is a person aggrieved who is entitled to exercise the right of appeal in order to have the original decision restored.

Turning to the circumstances giving rise to this appeal, in the absence of authority I would have no hesitation in coming to the conclusion that irrespective of whether or not the justices had made an order for costs, the council had a right of appeal under section 301. The purpose of entrusting the council with the power of granting licences to drivers of hackney carriages and in respect of hackney carriages is so that the public in the locality will be provided with a suitable taxi service. This involves proper standards being maintained as to drivers and vehicle licence holders. Although there is an appeal to justices, and that appeal is a rehearing, the justices are entitled to take into account the policy of the council. As Lord Goddard C.J. said in *Stepney Borough Council v. Joffe* [1949] 1 K.B. 599, 602–603:

> "if there is an unrestricted right of appeal, it is for the court of appeal to substitute its opinion for the opinion of the borough council. That does not mean to say that the court of appeal, in this case the metropolitan magistrate, ought not to pay great attention to the fact that the duly constituted and elected local authority have come to an opinion on the matter, and it ought not lightly, of course, to reverse their opinion."

Where, as for example here, the justices have departed from a policy which the council has in relation to who is an appropriate person to hold a licence, I consider the council can justifiably feel aggrieved. Furthermore, the council would, in the context of the statutory provisions here being considered, clearly be a "person" because of the application of the Interpretation Act 1978 (previously the Interpretation Act 1889) which provides [by section 5 and Schedule 1] that unless a contrary intention appears " 'person' includes a body of persons corporate or unincorporate". There is nothing in the context of section 301 or the other provisions of the Act of 1936 which indicates a contrary intention, and the contrast between the language of section 301 of the Act of 1936 and sections 60(3) and 61(3) of the Act of 1976 which have to be treated as part of the Act of 1936, referring as they do specifically to a "driver" and "proprietor", emphasise that this is the position.

However, there are the authorities, to which I must now turn, the majority of which indicate that in the past the courts have adopted an unduly restrictive approach to who is a person aggrieved, unlike the approach on an application for judicial review under R.S.C., Ord. 53, where the test is whether the applicant "has a sufficient interest in the matter to which the application relates" (see Ord. 53, r. 3(7)), a test which was deliberately substituted for that of a person aggrieved, which was the test which applied to applications for the prerogative orders prior to the introduction of judicial review in 1977.

[His Lordship reviewed the authorities (see above, pp. 585–586), which fell into three groups: pre-1951 (the *Westminster* case, above); 1951–1960 (the *Weymouth* case, above); and the post-1960 cases.]

. . . [H]aving analysed those authorities against the background of the first and last groups of decisions to which I have referred, I am quite satisfied that the Divisional Court took a wrong turning in the *Westminster Corporation* case both in relation to the question as to whether the council was a "person" and as to whether it was "aggrieved". This wrong turn has resulted in the decisions which have occurred since that time deviating from the right road.

As the present case illustrates, the question of who is a "person aggrieved" is still very much alive in many statutory situations. It therefore appears to me to be important for this court to intervene so that in future the decisions in the 1950s will not continue to cause the courts unduly to restrict the right of local authorities to appeal. I have therefore come to the conclusion that *R. v. London Quarter Sessions, ex p. Westminster Corporation* [1951] 2 K.B. 508 should be regarded as having been wrongly decided and should no longer be followed. There is no need for a legal burden to be placed on a party to proceedings to give a right of appeal. A decision against the party suffices. Furthermore, all the later cases in which the *Westminster Corporation* case has been followed should be treated with considerable reserve and re-examined. Whether or not they are correctly decided will depend upon their individual circumstances. However, I suggest that, except for criminal cases which come within a special category, and where the decision against which a local authority seeks to appeal can be regarded as being an acquittal, the normal result of that re-examination should be that a public authority which has an adverse decision made against it in an area where it is required to perform public duties, is entitled to be treated as a person aggrieved. As to whether a local authority is in this context a "person", the Interpretation Act 1978 will normally be decisive. It should not be forgotten that frequently the body against which the public authority will take action will itself be a body corporate and if this body is a person there are difficulties in treating a public authority in a different way.

In *R. v. Dorset Quarter Sessions Appeal Committee, ex p. Weymouth Corporation* [1960] 2 Q.B. 230, Lord Parker C.J. regarded the question as being by no means easy and he was clearly influenced in coming to his conclusion by the absurd result which would follow if the planning authority was "a person aggrieved" only because of the order for costs. In the ordinary situation, where the special considerations which apply to criminal proceedings do not exist, it is clearly in the public interest that if a wrong decision has been made against a public authority, that public authority should be entitled to seek to have the position remedied in a higher court. Its interest in the issues is much greater than those of an ordinary member of the public, as was made clear in *Stepney Borough Council v. Joffe* [1949] 1 K.B. 599. Those interests justify the public authority in that situation being regarded as a person aggrieved.

The desirability of this approach is in my view emphasised by the fact that many of the statutory provisions which give a right of appeal to a person aggrieved are doing little more than giving a statutory right to judicial review. The approach of the courts on the appeal is the same: see, for example, section 245 of the Town and Country Planning Act 1971. In the case of such a statutory provision, it would be nonsense to regard the public authority as not being a person aggrieved since it would in any event be entitled to obtain the same relief by applying for judicial review. In the case of the present appeal provision the position is not the same. While the council would be entitled to apply for judicial review if it had no right to appeal, the court's powers on the appeal are much more extensive than they would be on an application for judicial review since the appeal is a rehearing. In general, if Parliament intends the person against whom action is taken by the public authority to have a right of appeal, I cannot see any reason why Parliament should not also intend that the public authority should have a right of appeal.

I would therefore dismiss this appeal on the basis that the council was a person aggrieved by the decision of the Southend justices quite apart from the order for costs which was made against the council. However, even if this is not the position, the effect of the order for costs is to make this case indistinguishable from the decision of the House of Lords in *Jennings v. Kelly* [1940] A.C. 206.

It follows that in my view this appeal must be dismissed.

Sɪʀ Jᴏʜɴ Mᴇɢᴀᴡ and Dɪʟʟᴏɴ L.J. agreed.

Appeal dismissed.

CHAPTER 10

REMEDIES[1]

(A) INTRODUCTION

THE position as to remedies in administrative law was materially affected by the introduction of the "application for judicial review", with effect from January 11, 1978, by a revised version of R.S.C. Order 53. Prior to that date, the position was as follows.

There was a series of prerogative remedies available against public authorities: *Certiorari* lay to quash a decision that was *ultra vires* or in breach of natural justice, that was affected by an error of law that was apparent on the face of the record or that was procured by fraud. *Prohibition* lay to prevent action or continuing action in excess of jurisdiction or contrary to natural justice. *Mandamus* lay to compel performance of a public duty. Certiorari and prohibition traditionally lay:

"wherever any body of persons having legal authority to determine questions affecting the rights of subjects, and having the duty to act judicially, act in excess of their legal authority..." (*per* Atkin L.J. in *R. v. Electricity Commissioners, ex p. London Electricity Joint Committee Co.* [1924] 1 K.B. 411, 415).

Mandamus was never limited to judicial or quasi-judicial functions. The remedies originally took the form of prerogative writs but, by virtue of the Administration of Justice (Miscellaneous Provisions) Act 1938, they had become prerogative orders.

Apart from these public law remedies, from the 1950s in particular, increasing use had been made against public authorities of the private law remedies of *injunction* and *declaration*. A prohibitory injunction might be granted to restrain the performance of *ultra vires* acts. A mandatory injunction might (rarely) be available to compel performance of a public duty. A declaration would simply declare authoritatively the law on a disputed point.

Other remedies that might be available when appropriate included *damages*, where a public authority was held liable in contract or tort, and the prerogative writ of *habeas corpus*, available to test the legality of the actions of the respondent (whether or not a public authority) in holding a person in detention.

Applications for certiorari, prohibition and mandamus were governed by the unreformed R.S.C. Order 53 and were heard in the Divisional Court of the Queen's Bench Division, usually by a court presided over by the Lord Chief Justice. Proceedings for a declaration or injunction were ordinary civil proceedings in the High Court, and could be commenced in the Queen's Bench Division or the Chancery Division, in practice according to the preference of counsel for the plaintiff.

The remedies were discretionary, and there were particular rules governing not only

---

[1] See G. Aldous and J. Alder, *Applications for Judicial Review: Law and Practice of the Crown Office* (2nd ed., 1993); R. Gordon, *Judicial Review: Law and Procedure* (2nd ed., 1996); Public Law Project, *The Applicant's Guide to Judicial Review* (1995); J. Manning, *Judicial Review Proceedings: A Practitioner's Guide* (1995); *de Smith, Woolf and Jowell*, Chaps. 2, 3, 14–20; *Wade and Forsyth*, Chaps. 16–19; *Craig*, Chaps. 13–16.

the kinds of decisions or acts that could be reached by each remedy, but also such matters as *locus standi*, whether interlocutory relief was available and the grounds on which the remedy could be refused. Some of these rules were by no means settled.

The Law Commission in its Report on Remedies in Administrative Law (Cmnd. 6407, 1976, Law Com. 73) highlighted the defects in the existing arrangements. For example, declarations were available in respect of a wide range of acts and omissions, and proceedings for a declaration could be initiated without leave, with no fixed limit of time and with the advantages of full discovery. However, declarations did not order or prohibit any action and were not available in a provisional form, and there was considerable doubt as to the requirements of standing. Applications for a prerogative order could be made by a wide range of applicants, but leave was necessary, discovery was not in practice available and there was a six month time-limit for applications for certiorari. A claim for damages or injunction could be joined with an application for a declaration but not an application for a prerogative order. The revised version of R.S.C. Order 53 (below) was largely based on this report, although there was no provision as recommended by the Law Commission for an interim declaration. Express statutory authority for the application for judicial review was subsequently enshrined in the Supreme Court Act 1981, s.31 (see below, p. 604).

Under the new Order 53, any of the remedies summarised above (except *habeas corpus*, which is governed by R.S.C. Ord. 52), may be granted on an application for judicial review. This is indeed the exclusive procedure by which one of the prerogative orders may be obtained. An injunction or declaration may still be obtained against a public authority in ordinary proceedings, but the House of Lords in *O'Reilly v. Mackman* (below, p. 642) held that in certain circumstances it will be an abuse of process to attempt to secure an injunction or declaration against a public authority other than on an application for judicial review.

Proposals for further reforms of judicial review procedure are contained in the Law Commission's Report on *Administrative Law: Judicial Review and Statutory Appeals* (Law Com. No. 226, 1994) and Lord Woolf's Report, *Access to Justice: Final Report* (1996), which are considered below, pp. 700–708.

(B) R.S.C. ORDER 53; SUPREME COURT ACT 1981, ss.29–31

R.S.C. ORDER 53: APPLICATIONS FOR JUDICIAL REVIEW

(Introduced by S.I. 1977 No. 1955 and as amended by S.I. 1980 No. 2000, S.I. 1982 No. 111, S.I 1987 No. 1423, S.I. 1989 No. 177 and S.I. 1992 No. 1907)

Cases appropriate for application for judicial review
1.—(1) An application for—

(a) an order of mandamus, prohibition or certiorari, or
(b) an injunction under Section [30 of the Act][2] restraining a person from acting in any office in which he is not entitled to act,

shall be made by way of an application for judicial review in accordance with the provisions of this Order.

[2] [Editor's note] *i.e.* the Supreme Court Act 1981.

(2) An application for a declaration or an injunction (not being an injunction mentioned in paragraph (1)(b)) may be made by way of an application for judicial review, and on such an application the Court may grant the declaration or injunction claimed if it considers that, having regard to—

(a) the nature of the matters in respect of which relief may be granted by way of an order of mandamus, prohibition or certiorari,
(b) the nature of the persons and bodies against whom relief may be granted by way of such an order, and
(c) all the circumstances of the case,

it would be just and convenient for the declaration or injunction to be granted on an application for judicial review.

Joinder of claims for relief

2. On an application for judicial review any relief mentioned in rule 1(1) or (2) may be claimed as an alternative or in addition to any other relief so mentioned if it arises out of or relates to or is connected with the same matter.

Grant of leave to apply for judicial review

3.—(1) No application for judicial review shall be made unless the leave of the Court has been obtained in accordance with this rule.

[(2) An application for leave must be made *ex parte* to a judge by filing in the Crown Office—

(a) a notice in Form No. 86A containing a statement of
  (i) the name and description of the applicant,
  (ii) the relief sought and the grounds upon which it is sought,
  (iii) the name and address of the applicant's solicitors (if any), and
  (iv) the applicant's address for service; and
(b) an affidavit verifying the facts relied on.

(3) The judge may determine the application without a hearing, unless a hearing is requested in the notice of application, and need not sit in open court; in any case, the Crown Office shall serve a copy of the judge's order on the applicant.

(4) Where the application for leave is refused by the judge, or is granted on terms, the applicant may renew it by applying—

(a) in any criminal cause or matter, to a Divisional Court of the Queen's Bench Division;
(b) in any other case, to a single judge sitting in open court or, if the Court so directs, to a Divisional Court of the Queen's Bench Division:

Provided that no application for leave may be renewed in any non-criminal cause or matter in which the judge has refused leave under paragraph (3) after a hearing.

(5) In order to renew his application for leave the applicant must, within 10 days of being served with notice of the judge's refusal, lodge in the Crown Office notice of his intention in Form No. 86B.]

(6) Without prejudice to its powers under Order 20, rule 8, the Court

hearing an application for leave may allow the applicant's statement to be amended, whether by specifying different or additional grounds or relief or otherwise, on such terms, if any, as it thinks fit.

(7) The Court shall not grant leave unless it considers that the applicant has a sufficient interest in the matter to which the application relates.

(8) Where leave is sought to apply for an order of certiorari to remove for the purpose of its being quashed any judgment, order, conviction or other proceeding which is subject to appeal and a time is limited for the bringing of the appeal, the Court may adjourn the application for leave until the appeal is determined or the time for appealing has expired.

(9) If the Court grants leave, it may impose such terms as to costs and as to giving security as it thinks fit.

(10) Where leave to apply for judicial review is granted, then—

    (a) if the relief sought is an order of prohibition or certiorari and the Court so directs, the grant shall operate as a stay of the proceedings to which the application relates until the determination of the application or until the Court otherwise orders;

    (b) if any other relief is sought, the Court may at any time grant in the proceedings such interim relief as could be granted in an action begun by writ.

[4.—(1) [An application for leave to apply for judicial review] shall be made promptly and in any event within three months from the date when grounds for the application first arose unless the Court considers that there is good reason for extending the period within which the application shall be made.

(2) Where the relief sought is an order of certiorari in respect of any judgment, order, conviction or other proceeding, the date when grounds for the application first arose shall be taken to be the date of that judgment, order, conviction or proceeding.

(3) Paragraph (1) is without prejudice to any statutory provision which has the effect of limiting the time within which an application for judicial review may be made.]

Mode of applying for judicial review

5.—[(1) In any criminal cause or matter where leave has been granted to make an application for judicial review, the application shall be made by originating motion to a Divisional Court of the Queen's Bench Division.

(2) In any other such cause or matter, the application shall be made by originating motion to a judge sitting in open court, unless the Court directs that it shall be made—

    (a) by originating summons to a judge in chambers; or

    (b) by originating motion to a Divisional Court of the Queen's Bench Division.

Any direction under sub-paragraph (a) shall be without prejudice to the judge's powers under Order 32, rule 13.]

(3) The notice of motion or summons must be served on all persons directly affected and where it relates to any proceedings in or before a court and the object of the application is either to compel the court or an officer of the court

to do any act in relation to the proceedings or to quash them or any order made therein, the notice or summons must also be served on the clerk or registrar of the court and, where any objection to the conduct of the judge is to be made, on the judge.

(4) Unless the Court granting leave has otherwise directed, there must be at least 10 days between the service of the notice of motion or summons and ... the hearing.

(5) A motion must be entered for hearing within 14 days after the grant of leave.

(6) An affidavit giving the names and addresses of, and the places and dates of service on, all persons who have been served with the notice of motion or summons must be filed before the motion or summons is entered for hearing and, if any person who ought to be served under this rule has not been served, the affidavit must state that fact and the reason for it; and the affidavit shall be before the Court on the hearing of the motion or summons.

(7) If on the hearing of the motion or summons the Court is of opinion that any person who ought, whether under this rule or otherwise, to have been served has not been served, the Court may adjourn the hearing on such terms (if any) as it may direct in order that the notice or summons may be served on that person.

Statements and affidavits

6.—(1) Copies of the statement in support of an application for leave under rule 3 must be served with the notice of motion or summons and, subject to paragraph (2), no grounds shall be relied upon or any relief sought at the hearing except the grounds and relief set out in the statement.

[(2) The Court may on the hearing of the motion or summons allow the applicant to amend his statement, whether by specifying different or additional grounds or relief or otherwise, on such terms, if any, as it thinks fit and may allow further affidavits to be used by him.]

(3) Where the applicant intends to ask to be allowed to amend his statement or to use further affidavits, he shall give notice of his intention and of any proposed amendment to every other party.

[(4) Any respondent who intends to use an affidavit at the hearing shall file it in the Crown Office, and give notice thereof to the applicant, as soon as practicable and in any event, unless the Court otherwise directs, within 21 days after the service upon him of the documents required to be served by paragraph (1).]

(5) Each party to the application must supply to every other party on demand and on payment of the proper charges copies of every affidavit which he proposes to use at the hearing including, in the case of the applicant, the affidavit in support of the application for leave under rule 3.

Claim for damages

7.—(1) On an application for judicial review the Court may, subject to paragraph (2), award damages to the applicant if—

(a) he has included in the statement in support of his application for leave under rule 3 a claim for damages arising from any matter to which the application relates, and

(b) the Court is satisfied that, if the claim had been made in an action begun by the applicant at the time of making his application, he could have been awarded damages.

(2) Order 18, rule 12, shall apply to a statement relating to a claim for damages as it applies to a pleading.

Application for discovery, interrogatories, cross-examination, etc.

8.—(1) Unless the Court otherwise directs, any interlocutory application in proceedings on an application for judicial review may be made to any judge or a master of the Queen's Bench Division, notwithstanding that the application for judicial review has been made by motion and is to be heard by a Divisional Court.

In this paragraph "interlocutory application" includes an application for an order under Order 24 or 26 or Order 38, rule 2(3), or for an order dismissing the proceedings by consent of the parties.

(2) In relation to an order made by a master pursuant to paragraph (1), Order 58, rule 1, shall, where the application for judicial review is to be heard by a Divisional Court, have effect as if a reference to that Court were substituted for the reference to a judge in chambers.

(3) This rule is without prejudice to any statutory provision or rule of law restricting the making of an order against the Crown.

Hearing of application for judicial review

9.—(1) On the hearing of any motion or summons under rule 5, any person who desires to be heard in opposition to the motion or summons, and appears to the Court to be a proper person to be heard, shall be heard, notwithstanding that he has not been served with notice of the motion or the summons.

(2) Where the relief sought is or includes an order of certiorari to remove any proceedings for the purpose of quashing them, the applicant may not question the validity of any order, warrant, commitment, conviction, inquisition or record unless before the hearing of the motion or summons he has lodged in the Crown Office a copy thereof verified by affidavit or accounts for his failure to do so to the satisfaction of the Court hearing the motion or summons.

(3) Where an order of certiorari is made in any such case as is referred to in paragraph (2), the order shall, subject to paragraph (4), direct that the proceedings shall be quashed forthwith on their removal into the Queen's Bench Division.

(4) Where the relief sought is an order of certiorari and the Court is satisfied that there are grounds for quashing the decision to which the application relates, the Court may, in addition to quashing it, remit the matter to the court, tribunal or authority concerned with a direction to reconsider it and reach a decision in accordance with the findings of the Court.

(5) Where the relief sought is a declaration, an injunction or damages and the Court considers that it should not be granted on an application for judicial review but might have been granted if it had been sought in an action begun by writ by the applicant at the time of making his application, the Court may, instead of refusing the application, order the proceedings to continue as if they

had been begun by writ; and Order 28, rule 8, shall apply as if, in the case of an application made by motion, it had been made by summons.

Saving for person acting in obedience to mandamus
10. No action or proceeding shall be begun or prosecuted against any person in respect of anything done in obedience to an order of mandamus. . . .

[Appeal from judge's order
13. No appeal shall lie from an order made under paragraph (3) of rule 3 on an application for leave which may be renewed under paragraph (4) of that rule.]

Meaning of "Court"
14. In relation to the hearing by a judge of an application for leave under rule 3 or of an application for judicial review, any reference in this Order to "the Court" shall, unless the context otherwise requires, be construed as a reference to the judge.

SUPREME COURT ACT 1981

Orders of mandamus, prohibition and certiorari

29.—(1) The High Court shall have jurisdiction to make orders of mandamus, prohibition and certiorari in those classes of cases in which it had power to do so immediately before the commencement of this Act.

(2) Every such order shall be final, subject to any right of appeal therefrom.

(3) In relation to the jurisdiction of the Crown Court, other than its jurisdiction in matters relating to trial on indictment, the High Court shall have all such jurisdiction to make orders of mandamus, prohibition or certiorari as the High Court possesses in relation to the jurisdiction of an inferior court.

(4) The power of the High Court under any enactment to require justices of the peace or a judge or officer of a county court to do any act relating to the duties of their respective offices, or to require a magistrates' court to state a case for the opinion of the High Court, in any case where the High Court formerly had by virtue of any enactment jurisdiction to make a rule absolute, or an order, for any of those purposes, shall be exercisable by order of mandamus.

(5) In any enactment—

(a) references to a writ of mandamus, of prohibition or of certiorari shall be read as references to the corresponding order; and
(b) references to the issue or award of any such writ shall be read as references to the making of the corresponding order.

Injunctions to restrain persons from acting in offices in which they are not entitled to act

30.—(1) Where a person not entitled to do so acts in an office to which this section applies, the High Court may—

(a) grant an injunction restraining him from so acting; and

(b) if the case so requires, declare the office to be vacant.

(2) This section applies to any substantive office of a public nature and permanent character which is held under the Crown or which has been created by any statutory provision or royal charter.

Application for judicial review

31.—(1) An application to the High Court for one or more of the following forms of relief, namely—

(a) an order of mandamus, prohibition or certiorari;

(b) a declaration or injunction under subsection (2); or

(c) an injunction under section 30 restraining a person not entitled to do so from acting in an office to which that section applies,

shall be made in accordance with rules of court by a procedure to be known as an application for judicial review.

(2) A declaration may be made or an injunction granted under this subsection in any case where an application for judicial review, seeking that relief, has been made and the High Court considers that, having regard to—

(a) the nature of the matters in respect of which relief may be granted by orders of mandamus, prohibition or certiorari;

(b) the nature of the persons and bodies against whom relief may be granted by such orders; and

(c) all the circumstances of the case,

it would be just and convenient for the declaration to be made or the injunction to be granted, as the case may be.

(3) No application for judicial review shall be made unless the leave of the High Court has been obtained in accordance with rules of court; and the court shall not grant leave to make such an application unless it considers that the applicant has a sufficient interest in the matter to which the application relates.

(4) On an application for judicial review the High Court may award damages to the applicant if—

(a) he has joined with his application a claim for damages arising from any matter to which the application relates; and

(b) the court is satisfied that, if the claim had been made in an action begun by the applicant at the time of making his application, he would have been awarded damages.

(5) If, on an application for judicial review seeking an order of certiorari, the High Court quashes the decision to which the application relates, the High

Court may remit the matter to the court, tribunal or authority concerned, with a direction to reconsider it and reach a decision in accordance with the findings of the High Court.

(6) Where the High Court considers that there has been undue delay in making an application for judicial review, the court may refuse to grant—

(a) leave for the making of the application; or
(b) any relief sought on the application,

if it considers that the granting of the relief sought would be likely to cause substantial hardship to, or substantially prejudice the rights of, any person or would be detrimental to good administration.

(7) Subsection (6) is without prejudice to any enactment or rule of court which has the effect of limiting the time within which an application for judicial review may be made.

Note

For initial comments on the introduction of the new Order 53, see J.F. Garner (1982) 1 C.J.Q. 292; V. Moore [1980] P.L. 349 and [1981] P.L. 28; J. Beatson and M. Matthews (1978) 41 M.L.R. 419; L. Blom-Cooper [1982] P.L. 250.

(C) SCOPE OF THE APPLICATION FOR JUDICIAL REVIEW

Traditionally, judicial review remedies have been available against public bodies, established by statute or under the royal prerogative. The decision of the Court of Appeal in the following case showed that the application for judicial review can extend to all bodies exercising public functions.

R. v. PANEL ON TAKEOVERS AND MERGERS, ex p. DATAFIN plc AND ANOTHER

[1987] Q.B. 815; [1987] 2 W.L.R. 699; [1987] 1 All E.R. 564 (Court of Appeal)

The applicants, Datafin plc and Prudential Bache Securities Inc., who were bidding in competition with Norton Opax plc to take over another company, McCorquodale plc, complained to the Panel of Takeovers and Mergers that N plc had acted in concert with other parties in breach of the City Code on Takeovers and Mergers. The panel dismissed the complaint and the applicants applied to the High Court for leave to apply for judicial review by way, *inter alia*, of certiorari to quash the panel's decision and of mandamus to compel the panel to reconsider the complaint. Hodgson J. refused leave on the ground that the panel's decision was not susceptible to judicial review.

On the renewed application before the Court of Appeal, the court granted leave in order itself to consider both the substantive application and the question of jurisdiction.

SIR JOHN DONALDSON M.R.: The Panel on Take-overs and Mergers is a truly remarkable body. Perched on the 20th floor of the Stock Exchange building in the City of London, both literally and metaphorically it oversees and regulates a very important part of the United Kingdom financial market. Yet it performs this function without visible means of legal support.

The panel is an unincorporated association without legal personality and, so far as can be seen, has only about twelve members. But those members are appointed by and represent the Accepting Houses Committee, the Association of Investment Trust Companies, the Association of British Insurers, the Committee of London and Scottish Bankers, the Confederation of British Industry, the Council of the Stock Exchange, the Institute of Chartered Accountants in England and Wales, the Issuing Houses Association, the National Association of Pension Funds, the Financial Intermediaries Managers and Brokers Regulatory Association, and the Unit Trust Association; the chairman and deputy chairman being appointed by the Bank of England. Furthermore, the panel is supported by the Foreign Bankers in London, the Foreign Brokers in London and the Consultative Committee of Accountancy Bodies.

It has no statutory, prerogative or common law powers and it is not in contractual relationship with the financial market or with those who deal in that market. According to the introduction to the City Code on Take-overs and Mergers, which it promulgates:

"The code has not, and does not seek to have, the force of law, but those who wish to take advantage of the facilities of the securities markets in the United Kingdom should conduct themselves in matters relating to take-overs according to the code. Those who do not so conduct themselves cannot expect to enjoy those facilities and may find that they are withheld. The provisions of the code fall into two categories. On the one hand, the code enunciates general principles of conduct to be observed in take-over transactions: these general principles are a codification of good standards of commercial behaviour and should have an obvious and universal application. On the other hand, the code lays down a series of rules, some of which are no more than examples of the application of the general principles whilst others are rules of procedure designed to govern specific forms of take-over. Some of the general principles, based as they are upon a concept of equity between one shareholder and another, while readily understandable in the City and by those concerned with the securities markets generally, would not easily lend themselves to legislation. The code is therefore framed in non-technical language and is, primarily as a measure of self-discipline, administered and enforced by the panel, a body representative of those using the securities markets and concerned with the observance of good business standards, rather than the enforcement of the law. As indicated above, the panel executive is always available to be consulted and where there is doubt this should be done in advance of any action. Taking legal or other professional advice on matters of interpretation under the code is not an appropriate alternative to obtaining a view or a ruling from the executive."

"Self-regulation" is an emotive term. It is also ambiguous. An individual who voluntarily regulates his life in accordance with stated principles, because he believes that this is morally right and also, perhaps, in his own long term interests, or a group of individuals who do so, are practising self-regulation. But it can mean something quite different. It can connote a system whereby a group of people, acting in concert, use their collective power to force themselves and others to comply with a code of conduct of their own devising. This is not necessarily morally wrong or contrary to the public interest, unlawful or even undesirable. But it is very different.

The panel is self-regulating body in the latter sense. Lacking any authority *de jure*, it exercises immense power *de facto* by devising, promulgating, amending and interpreting the City Code on Take-overs and Mergers, by waiving or modifying the application of the code in particular circumstances, by investigating and reporting upon alleged breaches of the code and by the application or threat of sanctions. These sanctions are no less effective because they are applied indirectly and lack a legally enforceable base. Thus, to quote again from the introduction to the code:

> "If there appears to have been a material breach of the code, the executive invites the person concerned to appear before the panel for a hearing. He is informed by letter of the nature of the alleged breach and of the matters which the director general will present. If any other matters are raised he is allowed to ask for an adjournment. If the panel finds that there has been a breach, it may have recourse to private reprimand or public censure or, in a more flagrant case, to further action designed to deprive the offender temporarily or permanently of his ability to enjoy the facilities of the securities markets. The panel may refer certain aspects of a case to the Department of Trade and Industry, the Stock Exchange or other appropriate body. No reprimand, censure or further action will take place without the person concerned having the opportunity to appeal to the appeal committee of the panel."

The unspoken assumption, which I do not doubt is a reality, is that the Department of Trade and Industry or, as the case may be, the Stock Exchange or other appropriate body would in fact exercise statutory or contractual powers to penalise the transgressors. Thus, for example, rules 22 to 24 of the Rules of the Stock Exchange (1984) provide for the severest penalties, up to and including expulsion, for acts of misconduct and by rule 23.1:

> "Acts of misconduct may consist of any of the following... (g) Any action which has been found by the Panel on Take-overs and Mergers (including where reference has been made to it, the appeal committee of the panel) to have been in breach of the City Code on Take-overs and Mergers. The findings of the panel, subject to any modification by the appeal committee of the panel, shall not be re-opened in proceedings taken under rules 22 to 24."

The principal issue in this appeal, and only issue which may matter in the longer term, is whether this remarkable body is above the law. Its respectability is beyond question. So is its *bona fides*. I do not doubt for one moment that it is intended to, and does, operate in the public interest and that the enormously wide discretion which it arrogates to itself is necessary if it is to function efficiently and effectively. Whilst not wishing to become involved in the political controversy on the relative merits of self-regulation and governmental or statutory regulation, I am content to assume for the purposes of this appeal that self-regulation is preferable in the public interest. But that said, what is to happen if the panel goes off the rails? Suppose, perish the thought, that it were to use its powers in a way which was manifestly unfair. What then? Mr Alexander [counsel for the panel] submits that the panel would lose the support of public opinion in the financial markets and would be unable to continue to operate. Further or alternatively, Parliament could and would intervene. Maybe, but how long would that take and who in the meantime could or would come to the assistance of those who were being oppressed by such conduct?...

It will be seen that there are three principal issues, *viz.*: (a) Are the decisions of the panel susceptible to judicial review? This is the "jurisdictional" issue. (b) If so, how in principle is that jurisdiction to be exercised given the nature of the panel's activities and the fact that it is an essential part of the machinery of a market in which time is money in a very real sense? This might be described as the "practical" issue. (c) If the jurisdictional issue is answered favourably to the applicants, is this a case in which relief should be granted and, if so, in what form?

As the new Norton Opax ordinary shares have been admitted to the Official Stock Exchange List and so can be traded, subject to allotment, any doubt as to the outcome of the present proceedings could affect the price at which these shares are or could be traded and thus the rights of those entitled to trade in them. Accordingly we thought it right to announce at the end of the argument that the application for judicial review would be refused. However, I propose to explain my reasons for reaching this conclusion by considering the three issues in the order in which I have set them out.

The jurisdictional issue

As I have said, the panel is a truly remarkable body, performing its function without visible means of legal support. But the operative word is "visible", although perhaps I should have used the word "direct". Invisible or indirect support there is in abundance. Not only is a breach of the code, so found by the panel, *ipso facto* an act of misconduct by a member of the Stock Exchange, and the same may be true of other bodies represented on the panel, but the admission of shares to the Official List may be withheld in the event of such a breach. This is interesting and significant for listing of securities is a statutory function performed by the Stock Exchange in pursuance of the Stock Exchange (Listing) Regulations 1984 (S.I. 1984 No. 716), enacted in implementation of EEC directives. And the matter does not stop there, because in December 1983 the Department of Trade and Industry made a statement explaining why the Licensed Dealers (Conduct of Business) Rules 1983 (S.I. 1983 No. 585) contained no detailed provisions about take-overs. It said:

"There are now no detailed provisions in these statutory rules about take-overs and the following paragraphs set out the provisions as regards public companies and private companies respectively. 2. As regards public companies (as well as private companies which have had some kind of public involvement in the ten years before the bid) the department considers it better to rely on the effectiveness and flexibility of the City Code on Take-overs and Mergers, which covers bids made for public companies and certain private companies which have had some past public involvement. The City code has the support of, and can be enforced against, professional security dealers and accordingly the department expects, as a matter of course, that those making bids for public companies (and private companies covered by the code) to use the services of a dealer in securities authorised under the Prevention of Fraud (Investments) Act 1958 (such as a stockbroker, exempt dealer, licensed dealer, or a member of a recognised association), in which case the Secretary of State's permission for the distribution of take-over documents is not required. This is seen as an important safeguard for the shareholders of the public company (of which there may be several hundreds or thousands) and as a means of ensuring that such take-overs are conducted properly and fully in accordance with the provisions of the City code. It would only be in exceptional cases that the Secretary of State would consider removing this safeguard by granting permission under section 14(2) of the Act for the distribution of take-over documents in these circumstances."

The picture which emerges is clear. As an act of government it was decided that, in relation to take-overs, there should be a central self-regulatory body which would be supported and sustained by a periphery of statutory powers and penalties wherever non-statutory powers and penalties were insufficient or non-existent or where EEC requirements called for statutory provisions.

No one could have been in the least surprised if the panel had been instituted and operated under the direct authority of statute law, since it operates wholly in the public domain. Its jurisdiction extends throughout the United Kingdom. Its code and rulings apply equally to all who wish to make take-over bids or promote mergers, whether or not they are members of bodies represented on the panel. Its lack of a direct statutory base is a complete anomaly, judged by the experience of other comparable markets world wide. The explanation is that it is an historical "happenstance", to borrow a happy term from across the Atlantic. Prior to the years leading up to the "Big Bang", the City of London prided itself upon being a village community, albeit of an unique kind, which could regulate itself by pressure of professional opinion. As government increasingly accepted the necessity for intervention to prevent fraud, it built on City institutions and mores, supplementing and reinforcing them as appeared necessary. It is a process which is likely to continue, but the position has already been reached in which central government has incorporated the panel into its own regulatory network built up under the Prevention of Fraud (Investments) Act 1958 and allied statutes, such as the Banking Act 1979.

The issue is thus whether the historic supervisory jurisdiction of the Queen's courts extends to such a body discharging such functions, including some which are quasi-judicial in their nature, as part of such a system. Mr Alexander, for the panel, submits that it does not. He says that this jurisdiction only extends to bodies whose power is derived from legislation or the exercise of the prerogative. Mr Lever for the applicants, submits that this is too narrow a view and that regard has to be had not only to the source of the body's power, but also to whether it operates as an integral part of a system which has a public law character, is supported by public law in that public law sanctions are applied if its edicts are ignored and performs what might be described as public law functions.

In *R. v. Criminal Injuries Compensation Board, ex p. Lain* [1967] 2 Q.B. 864, 882, Lord Parker C.J., who had unrivalled experience of the prerogative remedies both on the Bench and at the Bar, said that the exact limits of the ancient remedy of certiorari had never been and ought not to be specifically defined. I respectfully agree and will not attempt such an exercise. He continued, at 882:

"They have varied from time to time being extended to meet changing conditions. At one time the writ only went to an inferior court. Later its ambit was extended to statutory tribunals determining a *lis* inter partes. Later again it extended to cases where there was no lis in the strict sense of the word but where immediate or subsequent rights of a citizen were affected. The only constant limits throughout were that it was performing a public duty. Private or domestic tribunals have always been outside the scope of certiorari since their authority is derived solely from contract, that is, from the agreement of the parties concerned.... We have as it seems to me reached the position when the ambit of certiorari can be said to cover every case in which a body of persons of a public as opposed to a purely private or domestic character has to determine matters affecting subjects provided always that it has a duty to act judicially. Looked at in this way the board in my judgment comes fairly and squarely within the jurisdiction of this court. It is, as Mr Bridge said, 'a servant of the Crown charged by the Crown, by executive instruction, with the duty of distributing the bounty of the Crown'. It is clearly, therefore, performing public duties."

Diplock L.J., who later was to make administrative law almost his own, said, at 884–885:

"The jurisdiction of the High Court as successor of the Court of Queen's Bench to supervise the exercise of their jurisdiction by inferior tribunals has not in the past been dependent upon the source of the tribunal's authority to decide issues submitted to its determination, except where such authority is derived solely from agreement of parties to the determination. The latter case falls within the field of private contract and thus within the ordinary civil jurisdiction of the High Court supplemented where appropriate by its statutory jurisdiction under the Arbitration Acts. The earlier history of the writ of certiorari shows that it was issued to courts whose authority was derived from the prerogative, from Royal Charter, from franchise or custom as well as from Act of Parliament. Its recent history shows that as new kinds of tribunals have been created, orders of certiorari have been extended to them too and to all persons who under authority of the Government have exercised quasi-judicial functions. True, since the victory of Parliament in the constitutional struggles of the 17th century, authority has been, generally if not invariably, conferred upon new kinds of tribunals by or under Act of Parliament and there has been no recent occasion for the High Court to exercise supervisory jurisdiction over persons whose ultimate authority to decide matters is derived from any other source. But I see no reason for holding that the ancient jurisdiction of the Court of Queen's Bench has been narrowed merely because there has been no occasion to exercise it. If new tribunals are established by acts of government, the supervisory jurisdiction of the High Court extends to them if they possess the essential characteristics upon which the subjection of inferior tribunals to the supervisory control of the High Court is based. What are these characteristics? It is plain on the authorities that the tribunal need not be one whose determinations give rise directly to any legally enforceable right or liability. Its determination may be subject to certiorari notwithstanding that it is merely one step in a process which may have the result of altering the legal rights or liabilities of a person to whom it relates. It is not even essential that the determination must have that result, for there may be some subsequent condition to be satisfied before the determination can have any effect upon such legal rights or liabilities. That subsequent condition may be a later determination by another tribunal (see *R. v. Postmaster-General, ex p. Carmichael* [1928] 1 K.B. 291; *R. v. Boycott, ex p. Keasley* [1939] 2 K.B. 651). Is there any reason in principle why certiorari should not lie in respect of a determination, where the subsequent condition which must be satisfied before it can affect any legal rights or liabilities of a person to whom it relates is the exercise in favour of that person of an executive discretion, as distinct from a discretion which is required to be exercised judicially?"

Ashworth J., who like Lord Parker C.J. had served as junior counsel to the Treasury and as such had vast experience in this field, said, at 891–892:

"It is a truism to say that the law has to adjust itself to meet changing circumstances and although a tribunal, constituted as the board, has not been the subject of consideration or decision by this court in relation to an order of certiorari, I do not think that this court should shrink from entertaining this application merely because the board had no statutory origin. It cannot be suggested that the board had unlawfully usurped jurisdiction: it acts with lawful authority, albeit such authority is derived from the executive and not from an Act of Parliament. In the past this court has felt itself able to consider the conduct of a minister when he is acting judicially or quasi-judicially and while the present case may involve an extension of relief by way of certiorari I should not feel constrained to refuse such relief if the facts warranted it."

The Criminal Injuries Compensation Board, in the form which it then took, was an administrative novelty. Accordingly it would have been impossible to find a precedent for the exercise of the supervisory jurisdiction of the court which fitted the facts. Nevertheless the court not only asserted its jurisdiction, but further asserted that it was a jurisdiction which was adaptable thereafter. This process has since been taken further in *O'Reilly v. Mackman* [1983] 2 A.C. 237, 279 (*per* Lord Diplock) by deleting any requirement that the body should have a duty to act judicially; in *Council of Civil Service Unions v. Minister for the Civil Service* [1985] A.C. 374 by extending it to a person exercising purely prerogative power; and in *Gillick v. West Norfolk and Wisbech Area Health Authority* [1986] A.C. 112, where Lord Fraser of Tullybelton, at 163F and Lord Scarman, at 178F–H expressed the view obiter that judicial review would extend to guidance circulars issued by a department of state without any specific authority. In all the reports it is possible to find enumerations of factors giving rise to the jurisdiction, but it is a fatal error to regard the presence of all those factors as essential or as being exclusive of other factors. Possibly the only essential elements are what can be described as a public element, which can take many different forms, and the exclusion from the jurisdiction of bodies whose sole source of power is a consensual submission to its jurisdiction.

In fact, given its novelty, the panel fits surprisingly well into the format which this court had in mind in the *Criminal Injuries Compensation Board* case. It is without doubt performing a public duty and an important one. This is clear from the expressed willingness of the Secretary of State for Trade and Industry to limit legislation in the field of take-overs and mergers and to use the panel as the centrepiece of his regulation of that market. The rights of citizens are indirectly affected by its decisions, some, but by no means all of whom, may in a technical sense be said to have assented to this situation, *e.g.* the members of the Stock Exchange. At least in its determination of whether there has been a breach of the code, it has a duty to act judicially and it asserts that its raison d'etre is to do equity between one shareholder and another. Its source of power is only partly based upon moral persuasion and the assent of institutions and their members, the bottom line being the statutory powers exercised by the Department of Trade and Industry and the Bank of England. In this context I should be very disappointed if the courts could not recognise the realities of executive power and allowed their vision to be clouded by the subtlety and sometimes complexity of the way in which it can be exerted.

Given that it is really unthinkable that, in the absence of legislation such as affects trade unions, the panel should go on its way cocooned from the attention of the courts in defence of the citizenry, we sought to investigate whether it could conveniently be controlled by established forms of private law, *e.g.* torts such as actionable combinations in restraint of trade, and, to this end, pressed Mr Lever to draft a writ. Suffice it to say that the result was wholly unconvincing and, not surprisingly, Mr Alexander did not admit that it would be in the least effective. . . .

[His Lordship held on the *practical issue* that there were insufficient reasons for excluding judicial review altogether (see note 1, below), and rejected the applicants' arguments on the substance of their claim.]

LLOYD L.J.: . . . Mr Alexander . . . argues (i) that the sole test whether the body of persons is subject to judicial review is the source of its power, and (ii) that there has been no case where that source has been other than legislation, including subordinate legislation, or the prerogative.

I do not agree that the source of the power is the sole test whether a body is subject to judicial review, nor do I so read Lord Diplock's speech [in *Council of Civil Service Unions v. Minister for the Civil Service* [1985] A.C. 374, 409]. Of course the source of the power will often, perhaps usually, be decisive. If the source of power is a statute, or subordinate legislation under a statute, then clearly the body in question will be subject to judicial review. If, at the other end of the scale, the source of power is contractual, as in the case of private arbitration, then clearly the arbitrator is not subject to judicial review: see *R. v. National Joint Council for the Craft of Dental Technicians (Disputes Committee), ex p. Neate* [1953] 1 Q.B. 704.

But in between these extremes there is an area in which it is helpful to look not just at the source of the power but at the nature of the power. If the body in question is exercising public law functions, or if the exercise of its functions have public law consequences, then that may, as Mr Lever submitted, be sufficient to bring the body within the reach of judicial review. It may be said that to refer to "public law" in this context is to beg the question. But I do not think it does. The essential distinction, which runs through all the cases to which we referred, is between a domestic or private tribunal on the one hand and a body of persons who are under some public duty on the other. Thus in *R. v. Criminal Injuries Compensation Board, ex p. Lain* [1967] 2 Q.B. 864 Lord Parker C.J., after tracing the development of certiorari from its earliest days, said, at 882:

> "The only constant limits throughout were that [the tribunal] was performing a public duty. Private or domestic tribunals have always been outside the scope of certiorari since their authority is derived solely from contract, that is, from the agreement of the parties concerned."

To the same effect is a passage from a speech of Lord Parker C.J. in an earlier case, to which we were not, I think, referred, *R. v. Industrial Court, ex p. A.S.S.E.T.* [1965] 1 Q.B. 377, 389:

> "It has been urged on us that really this arbitral tribunal is not a private arbitral tribunal but that in effect it is undertaking a public duty or a quasi-public duty and as such is amenable to an order of mandamus. I am quite unable to come to that conclusion. It is abundantly clear that they had no duty to undertake the reference. If they refused to undertake the reference they could not be compelled to do so. I do not think that the position is in any way different once they have undertaken the reference. They are clearly doing something which they are not under any public duty to do and, in those circumstances, I see no jurisdiction in this court to issue an order of mandamus to the industrial court."

More recently, in *R. v. British Broadcasting Corporation, ex p. Lavelle* [1983] 1 W.L.R. 23, Woolf J. had to consider an application for judicial review where the relief sought was an injunction under R.S.C., Ord. 53, r. 1(2). The case was brought by an employee of the BBC. In refusing relief, Woolf J. said, at 31:

> "Ord. 53, r. 1(2) does not strictly confine applications for judicial review to cases where an order for mandamus, prohibition or certiorari could be granted. It merely requires that the court should have regard to the nature of the matter in respect of which such relief may be granted. However, although applications for judicial review are not confined to those cases where relief could be granted by way of prerogative order, I regard the wording of Ord. 53, r. 1(2) and section 31(2) of the Act of 1981 as making it clear that the application for judicial review is confined to reviewing activities of a public nature as opposed to those of a purely private or domestic character. The disciplinary appeal procedure set up by the BBC depends

purely upon the contract of employment between the applicant and the BBC, and therefore it is a procedure of a purely private or domestic character."

So I would reject Mr Alexander's argument that the sole test whether a body is subject to judicial review is the source of its power. So to hold would in my judgment impose an artificial limit on the developing law of judicial review. That artificiality is well illustrated in the present case by reference to the listing regulations issued by the Council of the Stock Exchange. As the foreword to the current edition makes clear, a new edition of the regulations became necessary as the result of the Stock Exchange (Listing) Regulations 1984. Those Regulations were made as the result of a requirement of an EEC Council directive. Mr Alexander conceded that the listing regulations are now the subject of public law remedies. By contrast (if his submission is correct) the code, which is the subject not of a Council directive, but of a Commission recommendation, is not.

I now turn to the second of Mr Alexander's two arguments under this head. He submits that there has never been a case when the source of the power has been other than statutory or under the prerogative. There is a certain imprecision in the use of the term "prerogative" in this connection, as Professor Sir William Wade makes clear in another Child & Co. Oxford Lecture, "Procedure and Prerogative in Public Law" (1985) 101 L.Q.R. 180. Strictly the term "prerogative" should be confined to those powers which are unique to the Crown. As Professor Wade points out, there was nothing unique in the creation by the government, out of funds voted by Parliament, of a scheme for the compensation of victims of violent crime. Any foundation or trust, given sufficient money, could have done the same thing. Nor do I think that the distinction between the Criminal Injuries Compensation Board and a private foundation or trust for the same purposes lies in the source of the funds. The distinction must lie in the nature of the duty imposed, whether expressly or by implication. If the duty is a public duty, then the body in question is subject to public law.

So once again one comes back to what I regard as the true view, that it is not just the source of the power that matters, but also the nature of the duty. I can see nothing in *R. v. Criminal Injuries Compensation Board, ex p. Lain* [1967] 2 Q.B. 864 which contradicts that view, or compels us to decide that, in non-statutory cases, judicial review is confined to bodies created under the prerogative, whether in the strict sense, or in the wider sense in which that word has now come to be used. Indeed, the passage from Diplock L.J.'s judgment, at 884, which Sir John Donaldson M.R. has already read, points in the opposite direction.

But suppose I am wrong: suppose that the courts are indeed confined to looking at the source of the power, as Mr Alexander submits. Then I would accept Mr Lever's submission that the source of the power in the present case is indeed governmental, at least in part. Mr Alexander argued that, so far from the source of the power being governmental, this is a case where the government has deliberately abstained from exercising power. I do not take that view. I agree with Mr Lever when he says that there has been an implied devolution of power. Power exercised behind the scenes is power nonetheless. The express powers conferred on inferior tribunals were of critical importance in the early days when the sole or main ground for intervention by the courts was that the inferior tribunal had exceeded its powers. But those days are long since past. Having regard to the way in which the panel came to be established, the fact that the Governor of the Bank of England appoints both the chairman and the deputy chairman, and the other matters to which Sir John Donaldson M.R. has referred, I am persuaded that the panel was established "under authority of the Government", to use the language of Diplock L.J. in *Lain's* case. If in addition to looking at the source of the power we are entitled to look at the nature of the power, as I believe we are, then the case is all the stronger.

Before leaving Mr Alexander's second argument, I should mention one last point. The jurisdiction of the court to grant relief by way of judicial review is now, of course, recognised by section 31 of the Supreme Court Act 1981. Section 31(1)(a) refers specifically to the old prerogative writs, namely mandamus, prohibition and certiorari. Section 31(1)(b) and (2) provide that in an application for judicial review, the court may grant a declaration or injunction if it is just or convenient to do so, having regard to various matters. I have already referred to the passage in Woolf J.'s judgment in *R. v. British Broadcasting Corporation, ex p. Lavelle* [1983] 1 W.L.R. 23, 31, in which he says that applications for judicial review under R.S.C., Ord. 53, r. 1(2) are not confined to those cases where relief could be granted by way of prerogative order. As at present advised, I would agree with that observation. I would only add as a rider that section 31(1) of the Supreme Court Act 1981 should not be treated as having put a stop to all further development of the law relating to the prerogative remedies. I do not accept Mr Alexander's submission that we are here extending the law. But if we were, I would not regard that as an insuperable objection. The prerogative writs have always been a flexible instrument for doing justice. In my judgment they should remain so.

NICHOLLS L.J. delivered a concurring judgment.

Notes

1. In relation to the *practical issue*, counsel for the panel argued that the court having and exercising jurisdiction to review the decisions of the panel would have disastrous consequences. Even unmeritorious applications for judicial review would dislocate the operation of the market during the pendency of proceedings; rulings by the panel were required to have speed and certainty.

In response, Sir John Donaldson noted (1) that a panel decision would remain effective unless set aside; (2) the court retained a discretion whether to grant a remedy; (3) the courts were aware of the need for speed; and (4) an applicant needed leave to make an application. The panel and those affected by its decisions should treat them as valid and binding, unless and until they were set aside.

There would be little scope for complaint that the panel had promulgated rules that were *ultra vires*, save in the unlikely eventuality that they violated the principle, proclaimed by the panel, of being based on the concept of doing equity between one shareholder and another. In interpreting the rules, considerable latitude would be given to the panel, both because they were the legislators, and because the rules laid down principles to be applied in spirit as much as in letter. Moreover, the court might well decline to quash an interpretative decision, instead granting a declaration as to the true meaning of the rule, and leaving it to the panel to promulgate a new rule accurately expressing its intentions.

As regards the panel's disciplinary function, the internal right of appeal should be exercised before the court could consider intervening. The only circumstances where the use of certiorari would be anticipated would be where there was a breach of natural justice.

Sir John Donaldson concluded (at 842) that the limitations in practice to the scope of intervention by the courts would lead to "a workable and valuable partnership between the courts and the panel in the public interest and would avoid all of the perils to which Mr Alexander alluded".

The Court of Appeal returned to some of these issues in *R. v. Panel on Takeovers and Mergers, ex p. Guinness plc* [1990] 1 Q.B. 146. Here the court rejected applications for declarations that the panel had acted unfairly in refusing to adjourn a hearing into allegations that Guinness, under its previous management, had acted "in concert" with a third party in purchasing shares in Distillers, a take-over target, this being contrary to the City Code. Lord Donaldson referred to the point he made in *Datafin* that he would expect the relationship between the panel and the court to be historic rather than contemporaneous (above, p. 615), said that this had been "misunderstood, at least by academic writers", and commented (at 158–159):

"When the take-over is in progress the time scales involved are so short and the need of the markets and those dealing in them to be able to rely on the rulings of the panel so great, that contemporary intervention by the court will usually either be impossible or contrary to the public interest. Furthermore it is important that this should be known, as otherwise attempts would undoubtedly be made to undermine the authority of the panel by tactical applications for judicial review. On the other hand, once the immediate problem has been dealt with by the panel, no similar objections would apply to a retrospective review of its actions designed to avoid the repetition of error, if error there has been. And when it comes to disciplinary action by the panel, which necessarily will be taken in retrospect and with all due deliberation, the court will find itself in its traditional position of protecting the individual from any abuse of power."

As to the *grounds* of challenge,

"Illegality would certainly apply if the panel acted in breach of the general law, but it is more difficult to apply in the context of an alleged misinterpretation of its own rules by a body which under the scheme is both legislator and interpreter. Irrationality, at least in the sense of failing to take account of relevant factors or taking account of irrelevant factors, is a difficult concept in the context of a body which is itself charged with the duty of making a judgment on what is and what is not relevant, although clearly a theoretical scenario could be constructed in which the panel acted on the basis of considerations which on any view must have been irrelevant or ignored something which on any view must have been relevant. And similar problems arise with procedural impropriety in the narrow sense of failing to follow accepted procedures, given the nature of the panel and of its functions and the lack of any statutory or other guidance as to its procedures which are intended to be of its own devising. Similarly, in the broad sense of breach of the rules of natural justice, what is or is not fair may depend on underlying value judgments by the panel as to the time scale which is appropriate for decision, the consequences of delay and matters of that kind. Approaching the problem on the basis of separate grounds for relief may at once bring several interlocking and mutually inconsistent considerations into play—were the underlying judgments tainted by illegality or irrationality? If not, accepting those judgments, was the action unfair? If the underlying judgments were so tainted, was the action unfair on the basis of judgments which might reasonably have been made? The permutations, if not endless, are considerable and confusing.

It may be that the true view is that in the context of a body whose constitution, functions and powers are sui generis, the court should review the panel's acts and omissions more in the round than might otherwise be the case and, whilst basing its decision on familiar concepts, should eschew any formal categorisation" (at 159–160).

On *Datafin*, see P. Cane, "Self Regulation and Judicial Review" (1987) 6 C.J.Q. 324; L. Hilliard (1987) 50 M.L.R. 372; H.W.R. Wade (1987) 103 L.Q.R. 323; C.F. Forsyth [1987] P.L. 356; C.J. Kinsella [1987] C.L.J. 200; J. Beatson, "The Courts and the Regulators" (1987) 3 P.N. 121. More generally on the Panel, see Lord Alexander of Weedon, "Judicial Review and City Regulators" (1989) 52 M.L.R. 640, J. Jowell, "The Take-over Panel: Autonomy, Flexibility and Legality" [1991] P.L. 149 and G.K. Morse "The City Code on Takeovers and Mergers—Self-Regulation or Self Protection" [1991] J.B.L. 509.

2. Prior to the establishment of the application for judicial review, the analogous issue to that considered in *Datafin* was the scope of the prerogative orders of prohibition and certiorari. It was held that these orders lay to bodies performing a public duty, such as inferior courts (*e.g.* an election court: *R. v. Cripps, ex p. Muldoon* [1984] Q.B. 686), statutory tribunals, individuals exercising public functions (*e.g. R. v. Kent Police Authority, ex p. Godden*: above, p. 531), Ministers of the Crown, Government bodies and bodies established under the royal prerogative (*e.g. R. v. Criminal Injuries Compensation Board, ex p. Lain*: considered in *Datafin*, above, p. 609). They did not lie against the Crown; to a body which had no legal authority (*Re Clifford and O'Sullivan* [1921] 2 A.C. 570: a military court acting under martial law, and not under statute law or the common law, which was to be regarded as a body of military officers advising the military commander); to a non-statutory arbitrator (*R. v. Disputes Committee of Dental Technicians* [1953] 1 Q.B. 704); to a legislative assembly (*R. v. Church Assembly, ex p. Haynes-Smith* [1928] 1 K.B. 411) or to a body exercising authority by virtue of a contract (*R. v. Post Office, ex p. Byrne* [1975] I.C.R. 221).

3. Initially, a similar approach was adopted as regards the scope of the application for judicial review. In particular, bodies exercising jurisdiction by virtue of a contract were held not to be subject to judicial review (*cf.* Lloyd L.J. in *Datafin*, above, p. 612). In *R. v. British Broadcasting Corporation, ex p. Lavelle* [1983] 1 W.L.R. 23, Miss Lavelle, a BBC employee, was charged with the theft of tapes from the BBC. Pending her trial at the Crown Court, the BBC instituted disciplinary proceedings against her, leading to a decision that she be dismissed. Only one hour's notice of the initial disciplinary interview was given, and she was unable to arrange to be accompanied by a union or other representative, as allowed by the BBC's disciplinary procedure. Although she still had the right to appeal to the Director General of the BBC, she applied for judicial review of the decision to dismiss. Woolf J. was clear that this procedure was inappropriate (see the passage cited in Lloyd L.J.'s judgment, above, p. 613). With the consent of the parties, Woolf J. proceeded, under Ord. 53, r. 9(5), to consider the case on the basis that the action had been begun by writ. He concluded (1) that the court did have jurisdiction to grant an injunction or declaration in an employment situation of the kind involved here; but (2) that on the facts, no relief would be granted (*cf.* above, p. 439).

Moreover, in *Law v. National Greyhound Racing Club Ltd* [1983] 1 W.L.R. 1302, the Court of Appeal refused to strike out claims for declaration against the NGRC, a company limited by guarantee which acted as the judicial body for the discipline and conduct of greyhound racing in Great Britain. The stewards suspended the plaintiff's trainer's licence for six months because he had in his charge a greyhound that had been doped. The plaintiff issued an originating summons seeking declarations that this decision was ultra vires. The court rejected the NGRC's argument that the plaintiff should have applied for judicial review, holding that the NGRC was not in any event amenable to judicial review. The pre-1978 authorities such as *R. v. Criminal Injuries Compensation Board, ex p. Lain* [1967] 2 Q.B. 864, 882 and *R. v. Post Office, ex p.*

Byrne [1975] I.C.R. 221 were clear that the prerogative orders did not lie to domestic tribunals. The position had not been changed by the new Order 53, and, in particular, the enactment of section 31 of the Supreme Court Act 1981. Section 31 was not intended to extend the jurisdiction of the court on an application for judicial review to grant an injunction or declaration in respect of a private contractual dispute simply on the basis that it might be considered "just and convenient" so to do (see Lawton L.J. at 1308 and Slade L.J. at 1313–1315).

4. The decision in *Law* has been accepted as good law in post-*Datafin* cases concerning sporting bodies. Decisions of the Jockey Club and the Football Association have been held not to be amenable to judicial review (*R. v. Disciplinary Committee of the Jockey Club, ex p. Massingberd-Mundy,* [1993] 2 All E.R. 207, D.C.; *R. v. Jockey Club, ex p. RAM Racecourses Ltd* [1993] 2 All E.R. 225, D.C.; *R. v. Disciplinary Committee, of the Jockey Club, ex p. Aga Khan* [1993] 1 W.L.R. 909, C.A.; *R. v. Football Association of Wales, ex p. Flint Town United Football Club* [1991] C.O.D. 44; *R. v. Football Association Ltd, ex p. The Football League Ltd* [1993] 2 All E.R. 833. In *ex p. Massingberd-Mundy*, the Divisional Court stated that if the matter had been free from authority it might (Neill L.J.) or would (Roch J.) have concluded that at least some decisions of the Jockey Club related to quasi-public functions amenable to judicial review; however, the point was concluded by the decision of the Court of Appeal in *Law*. Particularly important is the decision of the Court of Appeal in *ex p. Aga Khan*. Here, the Aga Khan's filly, Aliysa, won the Oaks (a classic race), but was then found to have a prohibited substance in its urine. The Jockey Club's Disciplinary Committee disqualified the filly and fined the trainer. (It was not suggested that either the Aga Khan or the trainer was party to the doping.) The Aga Khan sought leave to apply for judicial review of this decision. It was accepted that the Jockey Club, a body established by Royal Charter but with no prerogative or statutory powers, exercised *de facto* control over the racing industry. Nevertheless, the Court of Appeal held unanimously that judicial review did not lie in this case, although the reasoning varied. Sir Thomas Bingham M.R. said (at 923–924):

"I have little hesitation in accepting the applicant's contention that the Jockey Club effectively regulates a significant national activity, exercising powers which affect the public and are exercised in the interest of the public. I am willing to accept that if the Jockey Club did not regulate this activity the government would probably be driven to create a public body to do so.

But the Jockey Club is not in its origin, its history, its constitution or (least of all) its membership a public body. While the grant of a Royal Charter was no doubt a mark of official approval, this did not in any way alter its essential nature, functions or standing. Statute provides for its representation on the Horserace Betting Levy Board, no doubt as a body with an obvious interest in racing, but it has otherwise escaped mention in the statute book. It has not been woven into any system of government control of horseracing, perhaps because it has itself controlled horseracing so successfully that there has been no need for any such government system and such does not therefore exist. This has the result that while the Jockey Club's powers may be described as, in many ways, public they are in no sense governmental. The discretion conferred by section 31(6) of the Supreme Court Act 1981 to refuse the grant of leave or relief where the appellant has been guilty of delay which would be prejudicial to good administration can scarcely have been envisaged as applicable in a case such as this.

I would accept that those who agree to be bound by the Rules of Racing have no effective alternative to doing so if they want to take part in racing in this country. It also seems likely to me that if, instead of Rules of Racing administered by the Jockey Club, there were a statutory code administered by a public body, the rights and obligations conferred and imposed by the code would probably approximate to those conferred and imposed by the Rules of Racing. But this does not, as it seems to me, alter the fact, however anomalous it may be, that the powers which the Jockey Club exercises over those who (like the applicant) agree to be bound by the Rules of Racing derive from the agreement of the parties and give rise to private rights on which effective action for a declaration, an injunction and damages can be based without resort to judicial review. It would in my opinion be contrary to sound and long-standing principle to extend the remedy of judicial review to such a case.

It is unnecessary for purposes of this appeal to decide whether decisions of the Jockey Club may ever in any circumstances be challenged by judicial review and I do not do so. Cases where the applicant or plaintiff has no contract on which to rely may raise different considerations and the existence or non-existence of alternative remedies may then be material. I think it better that this court should defer detailed consideration of such a case until it arises. I am, however, satisfied that on the fact of this case the appeal should be dismissed."

Farquharson L.J. noted that it was conceded that there was a contractual relationship between the club and the applicant both as a registered owner and arising out of the entry of Aliysa for the Oaks:

"By entering into those agreements the applicant was expressly submitting to the Rules of Racing and acknowledging that he was governed by the disciplinary powers of the Jockey Club. Mr Kentridge has referred to the lack of reality of describing such a relationship as consensual. The fact is that if the applicant wished to race his horses in this country he had no choice but to submit to the club's jurisdiction. This may be true but nobody is obliged to race his horses in this country and it does not destroy the element of consensuality" (at 928).

His Lordship stated that the decision in *Law* was not affected by *Datafin*:

"there has never been any doubt that public law remedies do not lie against domestic bodies, as they derive solely from the consent of the parties. In *Law*'s case the court was applying well established principles. The question remains whether the Jockey Club or this particular decision of it, can properly be described as a domestic body acting by consent" (at 929).

His Lordship could discern no relevant distinction between the Jockey Club and the Greyhound Racing Club. Nor could he find

"any public element in the Jockey Club's position and powers within the meaning of that term as explained in ... *Datafin* .... No doubt ... many of the decisions of the Jockey Club through its committees will affect members of the public who have no connection with it, but there is a difference between what may affect the public and what amounts to a public duty. It is difficult to see that the disqualification of this particular filly—important though the race was—could transform the role of the Jockey Club from a domestic to a public one. The courts have always been reluctant to interfere with the control of sporting bodies over their own sports and I do not detect in the material available to us any grounds for supposing that, if the Jockey Club were dissolved, any governmental body would assume control of racing. Neither in its framework nor its rules nor its function does the Jockey Club fulfil a governmental role.

I understand the criticism made by Mr Kentridge of the reality of the consent to the authority of the Jockey Club. The invitation to consent is very much on a take it or leave it basis. But I do not consider that this undermines the reality of the consent. Nearly all sports are subject to a body of rules to which an entrant must subscribe. These are necessary, as already observed, for the control and integrity of the sport concerned. In such a large industry as racing has become, I would suspect that all those actively and honestly engaged in it welcome the control of licensing and discipline exerted by the Jockey Club.

For these reasons I would hold that the decision of the Disciplinary Committee of the Jockey Club to disqualify Aliysa from the 1989 Oaks is not susceptible to judicial review.

As to Mr Milmo's assertion that the question of the Jockey Club's susceptibility to judicial review must be answered on an all or nothing basis, I can only say as at present advised that I do not agree. In *R. v. Jockey Club, ex p. R.A.M. Racecourses Ltd* [1993] 2 All E.R. 225 Simon Brown J. had similar reservations. In both that case and *R. v. Disciplinary Committee of the Jockey Club, ex p. Massingberd-Mundy* [1993] 2 All E.R. 207, the applicants had no contractual relationship with the Jockey Club. While I do not say that particular circumstances would give a right to judicial review I do not discount the possibility that in some special circumstances the remedy might lie. If for example the Jockey Club failed to fulfil its obligations under the charter by making discriminatory rules, it may be that those affected would have a remedy in public law.

In the present appeal there is no hardship to the applicant in his being denied judicial review. If his complaint that the disciplinary committee acted unfairly is well-founded there is no reason why he should not proceed by writ seeking a declaration and an injunction. Having regard to the issues involved it may be a more convenient process" (at 929–930).

Hoffmann L.J. held that

"however impressive its powers may be, the Jockey Club operates entirely in the private sector and its activities are governed by private law ... [T]here is no public source for any of its powers. It operates directly or indirectly by consent" (at 931).

While the absence of a formal public source of power was not conclusive, the power "needs to be identified as governmental in nature" (at 931). The Jockey Club was not "integrated into a system of statutory regulation" (at 931–932). There was

"nothing to suggest that, if the Jockey Club had not voluntarily assumed the regulation of racing, the government would feel obliged or inclined to set up a statutory body for the purpose ... I would ... accept that a body such as the Take-over Panel or IMRO which exercises governmental powers is not any the less amenable to publc law because it has contractual relations with its members. In my view, however, neither the National Greyhound Racing Club Ltd nor the Jockey Club is exercising governmental powers and therefore the decision in *Law*'s case remains binding in this case" (at 932).

His Lordship continued:

"All this leaves is the fact that the Jockey Club has power. But the mere fact of power, even over a substantial area of ecnomic activity, is not enough. In a mixed economy, power may be private as well as public. Private power may affect the public interest and the livelihoods of many individuals. But that does not subject it to the rules of public law. If control is needed, it must be found in the law of contract, the doctrine of restraint of trade, the Restrictive Practices Act 1976, Articles 85 and 86 of the EEC Treaty and all the other instruments available in law for curbing the excesses of private power.

It may be that in some cases the remedies available in private law are inadequate. For example, in cases in which power is exercised unfairly against persons who have no contractual relationship with the private decision-making body, the court may not find it easy to fashion a cause of action to provide a remedy. In *Nagle v. Feilden*

[1996] 2 Q.B. 633, for example, this court had to consider the Jockey Club's refusal on grounds of sex to grant a trainer's licence to a woman. She had no contract with the Jockey Club or (at that time) any other recognised cause of action, but this court said that it was arguable that she could still obtain a declaration and injunction. There is an improvisatory air about this solution and the possibility of obtaining an injunction has probably not survived *Siskina (Owners of cargo lately laden on board) v. Distos Compania Naviera S.A.* [1979] A.C. 210.

It was recognition that there might be gaps in the private law that led Simon Brown J. in *R. v. Jockey Club, ex p. R.A.M. Racecourses Ltd* [1993] 2 All E.R. 225 to suggest that cases like *Nagle v. Feilden* [1966] 2 Q.B. 633, as well as certain others involving domestic bodies like the Football Association in *Eastham v. Newcastle United Football Club Ltd* [1964] Ch. 413 and a trade union in *Breen v. Amalgamated Engineering Union* [1971] 2 Q.B. 175, "had they arisen today and not some years ago, would have found a natural home in judicial review proceedings". For my part, I must respectfully doubt whether this would be true. Trade unions have now had obligations of fairness imposed upon them by legislation, but I doubt whether, if this had not happened, the courts would have tried to fill the gap by subjecting them to public law. The decision of Rose J. in *R. v. Football Association Ltd ex p. Football League Ltd, The Times*, August 22, 1991, which I found highly persuasive, shows that the same is probably true of the Football Association. I do not think that one should try to patch up the remedies available against domestic bodies by pretending that they are organs of government.

In the present case, however, the remedies in private law available to the Aga Khan seem to me entirely adequate. He has a contract with the Jockey Club, both as a registered owner and by virtue of having entered his horse in the Oaks. The club has an implied obligation under the contract to conduct its disciplinary proceedings fairly. If it has not done so, the Aga Khan can obtain a declaration that the decision was ineffective (I avoid the slippery word void) and, if necessary, an injunction to restrain the club from doing anything to implement it. No injustice is therefore likely to be caused in the present case by the denial of a public law remedy" (at 932–933).

D. Pannick ([1992] P.L. 1) argues that the courts have taken an unduly restrictive approach to the scope of judicial review. The key question should be whether a body exercises monopolistic powers. If it does, judicial review should not be ruled out on the basis of a consensual submission to jurisdiction, as the individual in question has "no effective choice but to comply with their rules, regulations and decisions in order to operate in that area" (p. 3). Moreover, it should not be necessary to speculate as to what Parliament would do but for the existence of the body in question; the fact that powers are monopolistic is sufficient itself to justify the imposition of minimum standards on the substance and procedure of decision-making in that context (p. 6).

The Court of Appeal in *ex p. Aga Khan* clearly took a different view. However, there are difficulties in the reasoning. First, it seems difficult to conclude that powers are not governmental if it is the case that a public body would be established were the private organisation not already in operation; yet this is the position taken by Sir Thomas Bingham M.R. (Farquharson and Hoffmann L.JJ. were agreed that government would not necessarily establish a public regulatory body in the absence of the Jockey Club). Secondly, any argument that because powers are expressed directly or indirectly by contract therefore they cannot be governmental cannot stand with Hoffmann L.J.'s point that a body that exercises governmental powers is "not any the less amenable to public law because it has contractual relations with its members". It is submitted that Hoffmann L.J.'s view is to be preferred. Thirdly, the position of persons significantly affected by Jockey Club decisions (*e.g.* warning them off racecourses) but who are not in a contractual relationship with the Jockey Club is particularly unfortunate. On the one hand, there are hints from Sir Thomas Bingham M.R. and Farquharson L.J. that judicial review may be available in such a case (although it is difficult to see how the powers would suddenly become "governmental": *cf.* Hoffmann L.J., above, p. 621). On the other hand, private law may not provide an appropriate remedy, for the reasons given by Hoffmann L.J. Fourthly, the extent of the *de facto* monopoly exercised by the Jockey Club provides a good illustration of Pannick's criticism of reliance by the courts on the technicality that jurisdiction is conferred by consent in circumstances where there is "no effective choice".

Much of the comment on *ex p. Aga Khan* has been critical: see M.J. Beloff Q.C. and T. Kerr, "Judicial Control of Sporting Rules: The Commonwealth Jurisprudence" *Sports and the Law Journal*, vol. 3, issue 1 (Spring 1995), p. 5, and "Why *Aga Khan* is Wrong" [1996] J.R. 30. See also N. Bamforth [1993] P.L. 239; R. Gordon and C. Barlow (1993) 143 N.L.J. 158. (The Aga Khan responded to the Court of Appeal's decision by withdrawing all his horses from British racing for several years.)

5. Outside the sporting field, it has been held that a decision of the Chief Rabbi in respect of the dismissal of a Rabbi was not subject to judicial review (*R. v. The Chief Rabbi, ex p. Wachmann* [1992] 1 W.L.R. 1036). To attract the court's supervisory jurisdiction there had to be not merely a public but potentially a governmental interest in the decision-making power in question. It could not be suggested that but for the office of the Chief Rabbi, the Government would impose a statutory regime. By contrast, decisions of the Rabbinical Commission, chaired by the Chief Rabbi, in the exercise of statutory licensing functions under the Slaughterhouses Act 1974, Sched. 1, were subject to judicial review (*R. v. Rabbinical Commission, ex p. Cohen*, unreported, December 14, 1987, C.A.). Similarly, in *R. v. Imam of Bury Park Jame Masjid, Luton, ex p. Sulaiman Ali* [1994] C.O.D. 142, the Imam's decision that the applicants were not eligible to vote in the election of the executive committee of a mosque was held not to be subject to judicial review. It lacked the requisite public element and involved matters intimate to a religious community.

Other matters and bodies falling outside the scope of judicial review include the decision of an independent school to expel a pupil (*R. v. Headmaster of Fernhill Manor School, ex p. Brown* [1992] C.O.D. 446); Lloyd's of London (*R. v. Lloyd's of London, ex p. Briggs* [1993] 1 Lloyds L.R. 176, D.C.); the Insurance Ombudsman (*R. v. Insurance Ombudsman Bureau, ex p. Aegon Life Assurance Ltd*, D.C., *The Times*, January 7, 1994); and the actions of a developer not exercising public functions (*R. v. Eurotunnel Developments Ltd, ex p. Stephens* (1995) 73 P. & C.R. 1). The cases concerning Lloyd's and the Insurance Ombudsman are of particular interest. In *R. v. Lloyd's of London, ex p. Briggs* certain Lloyd's Names sought judicial review of decisions to make cash calls. The Divisional Court held *inter alia* that even if the Corporation of Lloyd's did perform public functions, for example the protection of policyholders, the rights relied on in the present case related exclusively to the contracts between Names and their Agents. Furthermore, it was noted that Lloyd's was

"not a public law body which regulates the insurance market .... [T]he Department of Trade and Industry does that. Lloyd's operates within one section of the market. Its powers are derived from a private Act which does not extend to any persons in the insurance business other than those who wish to operate in the section of the market governed by Lloyd's and who, in order to do so, have to commit themselves by entering into the uniform contract prescribed by Lloyd's" (*per* Leggatt L.J. at 85).

Accordingly there was not such a public law element as to bring the relationship between the Names and Lloyd's within the public domain.

R. v. Insurance Ombudsman Bureau, ex p. Aegon Life Assurance Ltd, above, concerned the Insurance Ombudsman Bureau, which was set up in 1981 by three insurance companies and which by 1993 had over 350 members. Membership was voluntary and the Bureau's powers were conferred exclusively by the contracts of membership. Companies could opt for regulation by LAUTRO's complaints sub-committee. Complainants could choose between a court action and a reference to the ombudsman. For Rose L.J., it did not necessarily follow that because regulatory decisions of LAUTRO were subject to judicial review, the decision of bodies (including the Complaints Sub-committee) set up by, or bodies (such as the IOB) recognised by LAUTRO under its statutory powers conferred by the Financial Services Act 1986 were in the same position. The Bureau was established as a "free standing independent body whose jurisdiction was dependent on the contractual consent of its members". Its status was not changed by the 1986 Act. Furthermore, the judgments in *Aga Khan* and *Datafin* could not

> "be constructed as contemplating that such a body as the IOB, even if it became interwoven into a governmental system, would be susceptible to judicial review".

Here, the

> "IOB's power over its membership is . . . still, despite the Act, solely derived from contract and it simply cannot be said that it exercises governmental functions . . . . [E]ven if it can be said that it has now been woven into a governmental system, the source of the IOB's power is still contractual, its decisions are of an arbitrative nature in private law and those decisions are not, save very remotely, supported by any public law sanction."

Given that the Bureau's jurisdiction depended upon the consent of both insurance company and complainant, the decision in this case is unsurprising. Furthermore, any "interweaving" into the governmental system of regulation appeared to be of a limited nature. Rose L.J.'s comments concerning "interweaving" must be read in that context. Any suggestion that a body exercising jurisdiction by virtue of a contract can never become so interwoven into a governmental system of regulation as to be regarded as exercising governmental functions would be inconsistent with *Datafin* itself.

On the extent to which private law remedies may be available in cases falling outside the scope of judicial review, it is interesting to note the decision of Carnwath J. and the Court of Appeal in *Stevenage Borough Football Club Ltd v. The Football League Ltd*, *The Times*, August 1, 9, 1996. Here, Stevenage Borough F.C. finished top of the GM Vauxhall Conference in May 1996 but failed to obtain promotion to the Third Division of the Football League as they did not comply with the admission criteria as to ground capacity and finance specified at the beginning of the 1995–96 season by the League. Stevenage sought to challenge the criteria as being in restraint of trade and unreasonable and sought an injunction to prevent the League applying the criteria so as to refuse membership to Stevenage. Carnwath J. held that the League was not simply an independent body but an important part of the elaborate structure established for the control of professional football in the interests of the participants and the public generally. As such, if admission criteria were shown to be arbitrary or capricious in effect, either as formulated or as applied, they were open to challenge. The judge found that two of the criteria were indeed open to objection on the ground of restraint of trade, although it was doubtful whether they were "arbitrary or capricious". However, the present challenge was dismissed as it had come too late. The criteria had been accepted for the 1995–1996 season not only by Stevenage itself but by the representative bodies at all levels of the hierarchy of football, and it was no excuse that Stevenage had waited until they had won the Conference Championship before instituting proceedings. An appeal to the Court of Appeal was dismissed, the Court placing particular emphasis on the delay in instituting proceedings.

6. The position is more difficult where the institution is a statutory body, which is clearly amenable to judicial review in respect of its statutory functions, but which is dealing with what is arguably a contractual matter. This situation was considered in *R. v. East Berkshire Health Authority, ex p. Walsh* (below, p. 625). Cases near the borderline where a public authority has been held to be performing a public function

include R. v. *Secretary of State for the Home Department, ex p. Benwell* [1985] Q.B. 554, where the dismissal of a prison officer was held to be subject to judicial review; the officer had no private law rights that could be enforced in civil proceedings. (See M. Stokes (1985) 14 I.L.J. 117 and Y. Cripps [1985] C.L.J. 177.) However, in *McClaren v. Home Office* [1990] I.C.R. 824, the Court of Appeal held that it was at least arguable that the relationship between the Home Office and prison officers was a contractual one. See further, below, p. 632. Another example is R. v. *Kidderminster District Valuer, ex p. Powell, The Times,* July 23, 1991, where the Divisional Court held that the valuation by the district valuer of a particular house for the purpose of determining the maximum limit of rent allowance payable to a police officer under the Police Regulations 1987 (S.I. 1987 No. 851), reg. 49(4)(b), was a public function subject to judicial review. It was a function performed within the statutory framework of the regulations and had important public elements.

7. Other non-statutory bodies which have been held to be amenable to judicial review include the following: a hospital ethics committee (R. v. *Ethical Committee of St Mary's Hospital, ex p. Harriott* [1988] 1 F.L.R. 512 (see A. Grubb and D. Pearl [1988] C.L.J. 167)); the Civil Service Appeal Board, which is a non-statutory body established under the royal prerogative to hear appeals against the dismissal of civil servants (R. v. *Civil Service Appeal Board, ex p. Bruce* [1979] I.C.R. 171); the Advertising Standards Authority, a non-statutory body that regulates advertisers (R. v. *Advertising Standards Authority Ltd, ex p. The Insurance Service plc* [1990] C.O.D. 42); the Professional Conduct Committee of the General Council of the Bar (R. v. *General Council of the Bar, ex p. Percival* [1991] 1 Q.B. 212); the Code of Practice Committee of the Association of the British Pharmaceutical Industry, a voluntary self-regulating body whose Code of Practice had emerged in its present form as a result of consultation with the Department of Health (R. v. *Code of Practice Committee of the Association of the British Pharmaceutical Industry, ex p. Professional Counselling Aids Ltd* [1991] C.O.D. 228); LAUTRO (R. v. *Life Assurance Trust Regulatory Organisation, ex p. Ross* [1992] 1 All E.R. 422); FIMBRA (R. v. *Financial Intermediaries Managers and Brokers Regulatory Association, ex p. Cochrane* [1991] BCLC 106: concession by counsel for FIMBRA); a university visitor (R. v. *Visitor of the University of Hull, ex p. Page* [1991] 1 W.L.R. 1277); the judges of the High Court sitting as Visitors to the Inns of Court (R. v. *Visitors to the Inns of Court, ex p. Calder* [1993] Q.B. 1); ICSTIS (an independent body set up by agreement between British Telecom and other network operators to supervise premium rate telephone services, exercising jurisdiction by virtue of contracts between the service providers and the network operators) (R. v. *Independent Committee for the Supervision of Telephone Information Services, ex p. Firstcode Ltd* [1993] C.O.D. 325); a company that administers a scheme established by the Securities and Investments Board in the exercise of statutory powers (R. v. *Investors Compensation Scheme, ex p. Weyell Ltd* [1994] Q.B. 749; here, the company accepted that it was subject to judicial review); a city technology college (R. v. *Haberdashers' Aske's Hatcham College Trust, ex p. T* [1995] C.O.D. 399; and (possibly) the BBC as regards the allocation of party political broadcasts (R. v. *BBC, ex p. Referendum Party, The Times,* April 29, 1997).

8. Where a function falls in general within the scope of judicial review, there must still normally be a *decision* in the exercise of that function if an application is to be entertained. In R. v. *London Waste Regulation Authority, ex p. Specialist Waste Management Ltd, The Times,* November 1, 1988, an expression of opinion, to a person using plant to dispose of "controlled waste" within the meaning of the Control of Pollution Act 1974, to the effect that he required a disposal licence, was held not to be amenable to judicial review. It was not a decision to which the applicant had to conform. Similarly, in R. v. *Devon County Council, ex p. L* [1991] 2 F.L.R. 541, Eastham J. held that a letter from the council responding to a request that social workers refrained from disseminating the belief that L was a child sex abuser, in the absence of a case conference or other proceedings, was not a "decision" amenable to judicial

review: the letter dealt solely with what had occurred in the past and did not deal with the assurance requested. *cf. R. v. Secretary of State for the Environment, ex p. London Borough of Greenwich, The Times*, May 17, 1989 (decision to issue leaflet on the community charge potentially open to judicial review for abuse of discretion: see C.R. Munro [1990] P.L. 1, 7–9); *R. v. Secretary of State for Employment, ex p. Equal Opportunities Commission* [1995] 1 A.C. 1 (Secretary of State's letter expressing the view that provisions of the Employment Protection (Consolidation) Act 1978 were compatible with Community law not a "decision" amenable to the supervisory jurisdiction; a declaration stating that the provisions were incompatible was nevertheless available (see further below, p. 699)).

9. For general surveys of the scope of judicial review post-*Datafin*, see M.J. Beloff, "The Boundaries of Judicial Review"; D. Pannick, "What is a Public Authority for the Purposes of Judicial Review" in J. Jowell and D. Oliver, *New Directions in Judicial Review* (1988), pp. 5 and 23; *Lewis*, Chap. 2; *de Smith, Woolf and Jowell*, Chap. 3.

R. v. EAST BERKSHIRE HEALTH AUTHORITY, ex p. WALSH

[1985] Q.B. 152; [1985] 3 W.L.R. 818; [1984] I.C.R. 743; [1984] 3 All E.R. 425 (Court of Appeal) (*pet. dis.*, [1984] 1 W.L.R. 1357, H.L.)

The applicant, a senior nursing officer employed by the health authority under a contract which incorporated the Whitley Council agreement on conditions of service in the health service, was dismissed by a district nursing officer for misconduct. He applied for judicial review under R.S.C., Ord. 53, for an order of certiorari to quash the dismissal on the grounds that the district nursing officer had no power to dismiss him and that there had been a breach of the rules of natural justice in the procedure which led up to his dismissal. The health authority raised the preliminary point whether the subject matter of the application entitled the applicant to apply for judicial review. The judge held that, although the public might have no interest in an ordinary master and servant case, the public was concerned to see that a great public service acted lawfully and fairly to its officers and the remedy of an order of certiorari would be an appropriate remedy. Alternatively, the judge held that it would be appropriate to allow the proceedings to continue under Ord. 53, r. 9(5), as if they had been begun by writ. The Court of Appeal allowed an appeal by the health authority.

SIR JOHN DONALDSON M.R.: ... I now return to the main issue, namely whether the applicant's complaints give rise to any right to judicial review. They all relate to his employment by the health authority and the purported termination of his employment and of his contract of employment. Essentially they fall into two distinct categories. The first relates to Miss Cooper's power to act on behalf of the authority in dismissing him. The second relates to the extent to which there was any departure from the rules of natural justice in the procedures which led up to that dismissal. Both fall well within the jurisdiction of an industrial tribunal. The first goes to whether or not the applicant was dismissed at all within the meaning of section 55 of the Employment Protection (Consolidation) Act 1978. The second goes to whether the dismissal, if such there was, was unfair. Furthermore, both are issues which not uncommonly arise when the employer is a company or individual, as contrasted with a statutory authority. However, this only goes to the exercise of the court's discretion, whether or not to give leave to apply for and whether or not to grant judicial review. As the authority seek to have the proceedings dismissed in limine, if they are to succeed they can only do so on the basis that, accepting all the applicant's complaints as valid, the remedy of judicial review is nevertheless wholly inappropriate and the continuance of the application for judicial review would involve a misuse—the term "abuse" has offensive overtones—of the procedure of the court under R.S.C., Ord. 53.

The remedy of judicial review is only available where an issue of "public law" is involved, but, as Lord Wilberforce pointed out in *Davy v. Spelthorne Borough Council* [1984] A.C. 262, 276, the expressions "public law" and "private law" are recent immigrants and, whilst convenient for descriptive purposes, must be used with caution, since English law traditionally fastens not so much upon principles as upon remedies. On the other hand, to concentrate on remedies would in the present context involve a degree of circularity or levitation by traction applied to shoe-strings, since the remedy of certiorari might well be available if the health authority is in breach of a "public law" obligation, but would not be if it is only in breach of a "private law" obligation.

The judge referred carefully and fully to *Vine v. National Dock Labour Board* [1957] A.C. 488; *Ridge v. Baldwin* [1964] A.C. 40 and *Malloch v. Aberdeen Corporation* [1971] 1 W.L.R. 1578. He seems to have accepted that there was no "public law" element in an "ordinary" relationship of master and servant and that accordingly in such a case judicial review would not be available. However, he held, on the basis of these three cases and, in particular, *Malloch's* case, that the applicant's relationship was not "ordinary". He said:

> "The public may have no interest in the relationship between servant and master in an 'ordinary' case, but where the servant holds office in a great public service, the public is properly concerned to see that the authority employing him acts towards him lawfully and fairly. It is not a pure question of contract. The public is concerned that the nurses who serve the public should be treated lawfully and fairly by the public authority employing them. . . . It follows that if in the exercise of my discretion I conclude that the remedy of certiorari is appropriate, it can properly go against the respondent authority."

The judge then said that if he was wrong in this conclusion, it would be appropriate to allow the proceedings to continue as if they had been begun by writ: see R.S.C., Ord. 53, r. 9(5).

None of the three decisions of the House of Lords to which I have referred was directly concerned with the scope of judicial review under R.S.C., Ord. 53. Two, *Ridge v. Baldwin* [1964] A.C. 40 and *Malloch v. Aberdeen Corporation* [1971] 1 W.L.R. 1578, were concerned with whether or not the plaintiff had a right to be heard before being dismissed and the third, *Vine v. National Dock Labour Board* [1957] A.C. 488, with whether the body purporting to dismiss was acting *ultra vires*. *Vine's* case and *Ridge's* case were actions begun by writ. *Malloch's* case was a Scottish proceeding in which the remedy of "production and reduction" was claimed. This is indeed akin to certiorari, but it is available whether or not the claim involves "public" or "administrative" law. There are, however, dicta, particularly in the speech of Lord Wilberforce in *Malloch's* case, which may be thought to point the way in which we should go.

[His Lordship then considered passages by Lord Reid in *Ridge v. Baldwin* (above, p. 426), and by Lords Reid and Wilberforce in *Malloch* (above, p. 439).)]

In all three cases there was a special statutory provision bearing directly upon the right of a public authority to dismiss the plaintiff. In *Vine v. National Dock Labour Board* [1957] A.C. 488 the employment was under the statutory dock labour scheme and the issue concerned the statutory power to dismiss given by that scheme. In *Ridge v. Baldwin* [1964] A.C. 40 the power of dismissal was conferred by statute: section 191(4) of the Municipal Corporations Act 1882 (45 & 46 Vict. c. 50). In *Malloch v. Aberdeen Corporation* [1971] 1 W.L.R. 1578 again it was statutory: section 3 of the Public Schools (Scotland) Teachers Act 1882 (45 & 46 Vict. c. 18). As Lord Wilberforce said, at 1595–1596, it is the existence of these statutory provisions which injects the element of public law necessary in this context to attract the remedies of administrative law. Employment by a public authority does not *per se* inject any element of public law. Nor does the fact that the employee is in a "higher grade" or is an "officer". This only makes it more likely that there will be special statutory restrictions upon dismissal, or other underpinning of his employment: see *per* Lord Reid in *Malloch v. Aberdeen Corporation*, at 1582. It will be this underpinning and not the seniority which injects the element of public law. Still less can I find any warrant for equating public law with the interest of the public. If the public through Parliament gives effect to that interest by means of statutory provisions, that is quite different, but the interest of the public *per se* is not sufficient.

I have therefore to consider whether and to what extent the applicant's complaints involve an element of public law sufficient to attract public law remedies, whether in the form of certiorari or a declaration. That he had the benefit of the general employment legislation is clear, but it was not contended that this was sufficient to attract administrative law remedies. What is relied upon are statutory restrictions upon the freedom of the authority to employ senior and other nursing officers on what terms it thought fit. This restriction is contained in the National Health Service (Remuneration and Conditions of Service) Regulations 1974 (S.I. 1974 No. 296), which provides by regulation 3(2):

"Where conditions of service, other than conditions with respect to remuneration, of any class of officers have been the subject of negotiations by a negotiating body and have been approved by the Secretary of State after considering the result of those negotiations, the conditions of service of any officer belonging to that class shall include the conditions so approved."

The conditions of service of, *inter alios*, senior nursing officers were the subject of negotiations by a negotiating body, namely the Whitley Council for the Health Service (Great Britain) and the resulting agreement was approved by the Secretary of State. It follows, as I think, that if the applicant's conditions of service had differed from those approved conditions, he would have had an administrative law remedy by way of judicial review enabling him to require the authority to amend the terms of service contained in his contract of employment. But that is not the position. His notification of employment dated May 12, 1975, which is a memorandum of his contract of employment, expressly adopted the Whitley Council agreement on conditions of service.

When analysed, the applicant's complaint is different. It is that *under* those conditions of service Miss Cooper had no right to dismiss him and that *under* those conditions he was entitled to a bundle of rights which can be collectively classified as "natural justice". Thus he says, and I have to assume for present purposes that he is correct, that under section XXXIV of the Whitley Council's agreement on conditions of service, his position as a senior nursing officer is such that his employment can only be terminated by a decision of the full employing authority and that this power of dismissal cannot be delegated to any officer or committee of officers. I do not think that he relies upon any express provision of those conditions when claiming the right to natural justice, but if he has such a right, apart from the wider right not to be unfairly dismissed which includes the right to natural justice, it clearly arises out of those conditions and is implicit in them.

The ordinary employer is free to act in breach of his contracts of employment and if he does so his employee will acquire certain private law rights and remedies in damages for wrongful dismissal, compensation for unfair dismissal, an order for reinstatement or re-engagement and so on. Parliament can underpin the position of public authority employees by directly restricting the freedom of the public authority to dismiss, thus giving the employee "public law" rights and at least making him a potential candidate for administrative law remedies. Alternatively it can require the authority to contract with its employees on specified terms with a view to the employee acquiring "private law" rights under the terms of the contract of employment. If the authority fails or refuses to thus create "private law" rights for the employee, the employee will have "public law" rights to compel compliance, the remedy being mandamus requiring the authority so to contract or a declaration that the employee has those rights. If, however, the authority gives the employee the required contractual protection, a breach of that contract is not a matter of "public law" and gives rise to no administrative law remedies....

I therefore conclude that there is no "public law" element in the applicant's complaints which could give rise to any entitlement to administrative law remedies. I confess that I am not sorry to have been led to this conclusion, since a contrary conclusion would have enabled *all* National Health Service employees to whom the Whitley Council agreement on conditions of service apply to seek judicial review. Whilst it is true that the judge seems to have thought that this right would be confined to senior employees, I see no grounds for any such restriction in principle. The most that can be said is that only senior employees could complain of having been dismissed in the exercise of delegated authority, because it is only senior employees who are protected from such dismissal. *All* employees would, however, have other rights based upon the fact that Parliament had intervened to specify and, on this view, protect those conditions of service as a matter of "public law".

In my judgment, this is not therefore a case for judicial review.

There remains the alternative of allowing the matter to proceed pursuant to R.S.C., Ord. 53, r. 9(5) as "if it had been sought in an action begun by writ". This is an anti-technicality rule. It is designed to preserve the position of an applicant for relief, who finds that the basis of *that relief* is private law rather than public law. It is not designed to allow him to amend and to claim different relief.

Only two species of relief are claimed by the notice of application, namely certiorari and prohibition. Prohibition is no longer sought and certiorari is a purely public law remedy. If R.S.C., Ord. 53, r. 9(5) is to be applied in the applicant's case, it can only be on the basis that the passing reference in his affidavit to "a declaration" is sufficient to justify the court in ordering the proceedings to continue as if a declaration had been sought in an action begun by writ. But if a declaration had been so sought, its terms would have been defined, if not in the writ, at least in the statement of claim. Yet in the 592 pages of documentation before Hodgson J. the terms of the declaration are never mentioned. Even in this court all that has been achieved, under pressure from the court, is a few lines indicating the type of declarations which might be sought if leave were given to amend to seek declarations. Furthermore, it seems likely that the applicant will want to claim damages, although there is no hint of that in the papers, and may also want to claim accrued wages, *i.e.* to have a judgment in debt, but that is outside the scope of R.S.C., Ord. 53. Accordingly I would not allow the applicant to continue the proceedings under R.S.C., Ord. 53, r. 9(5) and claim declaratory relief. I consider that costs will be saved and the issues emerge much more clearly if the applicant issues a writ and properly formulates what relief, if any, he is really seeking in addition or in the alternative to his claim for unfair dismissal....

I would allow the appeal and order that the applicant's application for judicial review be dismissed.

MAY and PURCHAS L.JJ. delivered concurring speeches.

Appeal allowed.

Notes

1. See H. Collins (1984) 13 I.L.J. 174; Y. Cripps [1984] C.L.J. 214; K.D. Ewing and A. Grubb (1987) 16 I.L.J. 145, 146–155; B. Walsh [1989] P.L. 131; S. Fredman and G.S. Morris [1988] P.L. 58, *The State as Employer* (1989), Chaps. 3 and 7, (1991) 107 L.Q.R. 298 and [1991] P.L. 485; M.R. Freedland (1990) 19 I.L.J. 199 and (1991) 20 I.L.J. 72.

2. Note the fine distinction drawn between questions concerning the *incorporation* of Whitley Council conditions and the *application* of the approved conditions. Is this distinction workable? Is it perhaps explained by the variant of the familiar "floodgates" argument that appears later in Sir John Donaldson's judgment?

3. In *McClaren v. Home Office* [1990] I.C.R. 824, a prison officer was suspended without pay for refusing to work a new shift system. The officer brought a private law action claiming, *inter alia*, a declaration that he was still employed on the basis of the previous shift system and the payment of salary withheld. He contended that the new system was in breach of the Fresh Start collective agreement between the Home Office and the Prison Officers' Association and a local agreement, and that these agreements were incorporated into his contract or his conditions of service. The Court of Appeal refused to strike out the claim, rejecting the Home Office's argument that the officer could only apply for judicial review, and holding that it was at least arguable that the officer had a contractual claim. A helpful analysis was provided by Woolf L.J. (at 836–837):

"There are two issues on this appeal. (1) Is the plaintiff required to bring his claim against the Home Office by way of judicial review? (2) If he is not required to bring his proceedings by way of judicial review has he a reasonable cause of action or was his claim correctly struck out as being clearly unsustainable?

The first issue

In resolving this issue the following principles have to be borne in mind.

(1) In relation to his personal claims against an employer, an employee of a public body is normally in exactly the same situation as other employees. If he has a cause of action and he wishes to assert or establish his rights in relation to his employment he can bring proceedings for damages, a declaration or an injunction (except in relation to the Crown) in the High Court or the county court in the ordinary way. The fact that a person is employed by the Crown may limit his rights against the Crown but otherwise his position is very much the same as any other employee. However, he may, instead of having an ordinary master and servant relationship with the Crown, hold office under the Crown and may have been appointed to that office as a result of the Crown exercising a prerogative power or, as in this case, a statutory power. If he holds such an appointment then it will almost invariably be terminable at will and may be subject to other limitations, but whatever rights the employee has will be enforceable normally by an ordinary action. Not only will it not be necessary for him to seek relief by way of judicial review, it will normally be inappropriate for him to do so: see *Kodeeswaran v. Attorney-General of Ceylon* [1970] A.C. 1111; *R. v. East Berkshire Health Authority, ex p. Walsh* [1984] I.C.R. 743 and *R. v. Derbyshire County Council, ex p. Noble* [1990] I.C.R. 808.

(2) There can however be situations where an employee of a public body can seek judicial review and obtain a remedy which would not be available to an employee in the private sector. This will arise where there exists some disciplinary or other body established under the prerogative or by statute to which the employer or the employee is entitled or required to refer disputes affecting their relationship. The procedure of judicial review can then be appropriate because it has always been part of the role of the court in public law proceedings to supervise inferior tribunals and the court in reviewing disciplinary proceedings is performing a similar role. As long as the 'tribunal' or other body has a sufficient public law element, which it almost invariably will have if the employer is the Crown, and it is not domestic or wholly informal, its proceedings and determination can be an appropriate subject for judicial review. An example is provided here by the decision of the Divisional Court in *R. v. Civil Service Appeal Board, ex p. Bruce* [1988] I.C.R. 649. If there had not been available the more effective alternative remedy before an industrial tribunal, the Divisional Court would have regarded the decision of the Civil Service Appeal Board in that case as reviewable upon judicial review. The decision of this court which has just been given in *R. v. Secretary of State for the Home Department, ex p. Attard, The Times,* March 14, 1990 [[1990] C.O.D. 261] is another example of the same situation. There what was being considered by this court were the powers of a prison governor in connection with disciplinary proceedings in respect of prison officers. The prison governor's disciplinary powers in relation to prisoners are reviewable only on judicial review (see *Leech v. Deputy Governor of Parkhurst Prison* [1988] A.C. 533) and they can also be reviewed on judicial review where they affect a prison officer on the application of that officer.

(3) In addition if an employee of the Crown or other public body is adversely affected by a decision of general application by his employer, but he contends that that decision is flawed on what I loosely describe as *Wednesbury* grounds (*Associated Provincial Picture Houses Ltd v. Wednesbury Corporation* [1948] 1 K.B. 223), he can be entitled to challenge that decision by way of judicial review. Within this category comes *Council of Civil Service Unions v. Minister for the Civil Service* [1985] I.C.R. 14. In the House of Lords there was no dispute as to whether the case was appropriately brought by way of judicial review. The House of Lords assumed that it was and I would respectfully suggest that they were right to do so. The decision under challenge was one affecting employees at GCHQ generally. The action which was being challenged was the instruction by the Minister for the Civil Service in the interests of national security to vary the terms and conditions of service

of the staff so that they would no longer be permitted to belong to trade unions. Although the decision affected individual members of the staff, it was a decision which was taken as a matter of policy, not in relation to a particular member of staff, but in relation to staff in general and so it could be the subject of judicial review.

(4) There can be situations where although there are disciplinary procedures which are applicable they are of a purely domestic nature and therefore, albeit that their decisions might affect the public, the process of judicial review will not be available. However this does not mean that a particular employee who is adversely affected by those disciplinary proceedings will not have a remedy. The existence of the disciplinary proceedings may be highly material to indicate that the category of employee concerned, unlike an ordinary employee, is not limited to a claim for damages but can in the appropriate circumstances in an ordinary action seek a declaration or an injunction to ensure that the proceedings are conducted fairly. (As to dismissal see *Ridge v. Baldwin* [1964] A.C. 40, 65, *per* Lord Reid; *Law v. National Greyhound Racing Club Ltd* [1983] 1 W.L.R. 1302 and *R. v. British Broadcasting Corporation, ex p. Lavelle* [1983] I.C.R. 99.)"

Woolf L.J. concluded that the proceedings here fell with the first of these categories, and that concluded the first issue in favour of the plaintiff. (See also his judgment in *R. v. Derbyshire County Council, ex p. Noble* [1990] I.C.R. 808. For comments on *McClaren* and *ex p. Noble*, see H. Carty (1991) 54 M.L.R. 129.)

4. *Ex p. Walsh* has been applied by Macpherson J. in *R. v. Trent Regional Health Authority, ex p. Jones, The Times*, June 19, 1986 (refusal to appoint consultant surgeon not subject to judicial review; no statutory underpinning); by Russell J. in *R. v. South Glamorgan Health Authority, ex p. Phillips, The Times*, November 21, 1986 (disciplinary decision of the health authority declared to be of no effect as the disciplinary tribunal had applied the wrong standard of proof; the judge allowed an application for judicial review to be continued as if begun by writ under r. 9(5)); by the Court of Appeal in *R. v. Derbyshire County Council, ex p. Noble* [1990] I.C.R. 808 (termination of appointment as deputy police surgeon held not to have a sufficient public law element to attract judicial review); by Otton J. in *R. v. Secretary of State for the Home Department, ex p. Hebron* (unreported, January 18, 1991) (challenge to dismissal of prison officer held to be a private law matter; leave to apply for judicial review set aside); by the Court of Appeal in *R. v. City of London Polytechnic, ex p. Amir Ali Majid* (unreported, November 1, 1993) (failure to appoint lecturer in constitutional and administrative law to principal lectureship, allegedly on racial grounds, held to be a "private matter" although it was "not a question of contract because... it was open to anyone to apply"); and by the Court of Appeal in *R. v. Crown Prosecution Service v. Hogg, The Times*, March 14, 1994 (dismissal of Crown Prosecutor; however, the Court indicated that had action been based on the exercise of a discretion as prosecutor, there would have been a sufficient public element given the "cardinal importance of maintaining the total independence and impartiality" of the CPS (Hirst L.J.)). These seem to fall into Woolf L.J.'s category (1).

5. Other examples of Woolf L.J.'s category (3) include the following. In *R. v. Liverpool City Council, ex p. Ferguson, The Times*, November 20, 1985, the council's decision to dismiss all teachers in order to alleviate the consequences of its failure to set a rate sufficient to balance its budget was declared *ultra vires* as it (1) was the direct consequence of setting an illegal rate; (2) was not made for proper educational purposes; and (3) would lead to a breach of the council's duties under the Education Act 1944, s. 8, to secure the provision of sufficient schools (see G. Morris (1986) 15 I.L.J. 194). In further proceedings involving most of the same parties, *R. v. Liverpool City Council, ex p. Ferguson and Ferguson* [1985] I.R.L.R. 501, the council's decision to refuse to pay teachers who presented themselves for work on a "day of action", but who were unable to work because of the actions of other trade unionists, was quashed on the grounds of unreasonableness. Mann J., applying a statement by Sir John

Donaldson M.R. in *R. v. Herefordshire County Council, ex p. N.U.P.E.* [1985] I.R.L.R. 258, 260, held that the allegation of *Wednesbury* unreasonableness rendered the matter justiciable by way of judicial review. This broad approach is criticised by Bernadette Walsh at [1989] P.L. 131, 149–152, noting that this:

"puts the cart before the horse. The primary question is surely whether the public authority in the performance of a particular function is subject to judicial review. If it is subject to judicial review, then an applicant may challenge the performance of the particular function on the grounds of unreasonableness. The approach advocated by Donaldson M.R. is rather to ask whether the challenge is based on unreasonableness and, if it is, to conclude that the applicant is entitled to judicial review....It is most unlikely that Donaldson M.R intended that the principles in *Walsh* should be subverted by the simple expedient of basing a challenge on this ground." (See also M. Stokes (1985) 14 I.L.J. 117, 119–120.)

This comment is perhaps echoed by the Divisional Court in *R. v. London Borough of Hammersmith and Fulham, ex p. NALGO* [1990] I.R.L.R. 249, where Nolan L.J. stated (at 256):

"I do not believe that Woolf L.J. was saying [in his category (3)] that every policy decision of a public authority affecting its employees as a whole is automatically justiciable as a matter of public law."

Nevertheless, he went on to hold that an allegation, as in the present case, that the adoption by a local authority of an employment or redeployment policy that was in breach of the Sex Discrimination Act or the Race Relations Act or was otherwise unlawful on *Wednesbury* grounds, could be challenged by way of judicial review. On the facts, it could not be shown that the policy as a whole was unlawful. The most that could be said was that the implementation of the policy might offend the law in individual cases, depending on how the implementation was carried out. This could only properly be tested on a case by case basis in pursuance of the applicants' private law remedies.

A further example is provided by *R. v. Walsall Metropolitan Borough Council, ex p. Yapp* (1993) 92 L.G.R. 110 where the Court of Appeal entertained (but rejected on its merits) an application for judicial review of the council's resolution to seek fresh competitive tenders for building work, brought by employees in the council's Building Works Division. The applicants contended that this resolution interfered with their legitimate expectations arising out of a resolution passed three months earlier by which the work was given to the Building Works Division; the council argued in its defence that acceptance of these claims would fetter its discretion under the relevant statutory powers. Nolan L.J. (at 113) was

"satisfied...that the conduct of the council falls to be judged by public law principles. The statutory element, if nothing else, brings the case within the scope of our public law jurisdiction".

6. The question of the availability (and possible exclusivity) of judicial review has also arisen in cases concerning civil servants. Here, the long-standing view that civil servants are not employed under a contract of employment has come increasingly into question (see S. Fredman and G.S. Morris, *The State as Employer* (1989), pp. 61–71 and [1988] P.L. 58). It is no longer thought that there is any constitutional bar to the contractual employment of civil servants (*Kodeeswaren v. Attorney-General of Ceylon* [1970] A.C. 1111, P.C.), and in *R. v. Lord Chancellor's Department, ex p. Nangle* [1992] 1 All E.R. 897, the Divisional Court held that there could be, and was, the necessary intention to create legal relations (not following the decision to the contrary

of the Divisional Court in *R. v. Civil Service Appeal Board, ex p. Bruce* [1988] I.C.R. 649). In *ex p. Nangle*, the court concluded that as the applicant was employed by the Crown under a contract of service, then, applying *ex p. Walsh*, he had no remedy in public law. Furthermore, the court concluded that if they were wrong on that point, and there was no contract between the Crown and the civil servant, there was still not a sufficient public law element to attract judicial review: the case arose out of "internal disciplinary proceedings" which were "of a domestic nature" and "informal". (The court seemed to doubt the decision in *R. v. Secretary of State for the Home Department, ex p. Benwell* [1985] Q.B. 554, above, p. 624.) (This is alarming. It is one thing to say that a person must pursue contractual remedies rather than judicial review (or vice versa); on this argument the applicant is left without any external remedy.) See S. Fredman and G.S. Morris [1991] P.L. 485. For further developments, see M.R. Freedland [1995] P.L. 224.

7. The recent spate of cases in this area is reviewed by S. Fredman and G.S. Morris, "Public or Private? State Employees and Judicial Review" (1991) 107 L.Q.R. 298. They argue that the state as employer:

"has characteristics which mean that the exercise of its employment function cannot simply be regarded as a matter for regulation by private law" (p. 315).

These include (pp. 309–312) the source of its power to employ from statute or the prerogative; in the case of central government, its power to endow managerial decisions with the force of law; the exclusive power of the executive to decide issues of national security; the weak arrangements for political accountability to which the state is subject; and the fact that the Government derives its revenue to pay employees primarily from taxation, rather than profits. These points require recognition of a public law dimension. However, they argue that current attempts to establish a clear dividing line between the private law and public law dimensions:

"are haphazard, unpredictable and produce illogical results.... It is high time that the quest for the ephemeral dividing line was abandoned. Employment decisions relating to public employees should be considered in a single forum which would enable the public interest in good administration to be secured without prejudice to individual rights" (pp. 315–316).

8. Outside the field of employment, there are a number of cases where the commercial or business decisions of a public body have been held not to be subject to judicial review. In *R. v. National Coal Board, ex p. National Union of Mineworkers* [1986] I.C.R. 791, Macpherson J. held that the Board's decision to close a colliery contrary to a recommendation of an independent review body established by itself and the union, was not the subject of judicial review. This was:

"an executive, or business, or management decision in exactly the same category as a decision in similar circumstances made by a public company" (at 795).

It was not a decision in the exercise of powers or duties under the Coal Industry Nationalisation Act 1946, which would have been subject to judicial review. (*cf. R. v. British Coal Corp., ex p. Vardy* [1993] I.C.R. 720, where decisions to close 10 collieries were quashed on the ground of non-compliance with statutory consultation procedures; after consultation, the closures proceeded lawfully: *R. v. British Coal Corp., ex p. Price (No. 3), The Times*, May 28, 1993). Similarly, in *R. v. Independent Broadcasting Authority, ex p. Rank Organisation plc, The Times*, March 14, 1986, Mann J. held that the IBA's decision not to permit Rank to exercise voting rights in respect of shares constituting in excess of 5 per cent of the issued voting shares of Granada, was not subject to judicial review. The power arose under Granada's articles of association and not in the exercise of any function under the Broadcasting Act 1981. Of particular concern is the decision of the Divisional Court in *R. v. Lord Chancellor, ex p. Hibbitt and Sanders (A Firm), The Times*, March 12, 1993, that the process whereby the Lord Chancellor sought tenders and awarded contracts for the supply of court reporting services was not subject to judicial review. The judges expressly found that the LCD's approach had been, in part at least, unfair. The LCD had advertised for tenders on the basis that bids could be "clarified" in subsequent discussions. In fact it entered discussions with the companies who had submitted the four lowest tenders for services at Chelmsford leading to further reductions in the tenders, and one of these was then accepted. The applicants, who had supplied reporting services at Chelmsford for many years, were not one of the four, and would have responded to the opportunity to submit a lower bid, particularly as there had been some confusion as to the treatment of staff costs. On the jurisdiction point, the court found that there was no evidence to support the applicant's argument that the LCD enjoyed a near-monopoly status as shorthand writers were also needed for arbitrations and professional disciplinary proceedings; although employed pursuant to statutory requirements for shorthand notes to be taken of court proceedings, there was no statutory underpinning to the employment itself; the absence of any alternative remedy was immaterial to the question of the existence of a public law remedy; and it was "not appropriate to equate tendering conditions attendant on a common law right to contract with a statement of policy or practice or policy decisions in the spheres of Inland Revenue, immigration and the like, control of which is in the especial province of the State" (Rose L.J.). See D. Oliver [1993] P.L. 214.

In other contexts, the exercise of the contractual powers of public authorities has been held to be subject to judicial review principles. The courts have sometimes, but not always taken the view that this only follows where there is a public law element in the decision (*cf.* the *East Berkshire* case). See the survey by S. Arrowsmith, "Judicial Review and the Contractual Powers of Public Authorities" (1990) 106 L.Q.R. 277. Judicial review has been held to be applicable to the termination of market trader's licences (*R. v. Barnsley Metropolitan Borough Council, ex p. Hook* [1976] 1 W.L.R. 1052: the council's powers were held to regulate the trader's common law rights to trade in the market; *R. v. Basildon District Council, ex p. Brown* (1981) 79 L.G.R. 655: Lord Denning M.R. here regarded all the council's powers as derived from statute and therefore reviewable, Templeman L.J. simply asserted that judicial review was applicable, Dunn L.J. disagreed on this point (see R. Ward (1982) 45 M.L.R. 588); *R. v. Wear Valley District Council, ex p. Binks* [1985] 2 All E.R. 699, above, p. 459: Taylor J. found that there was a public law element as the public had access to the land (see P. Jackson (1986) 102 L.Q.R. 24); *R. v. Durham City Council, ex p. Robinson, The Times*, January 31, 1992). Decisions of local authorities as landlords have been held to be subject to judicial review without the courts seeking to identify a public law element: *Cannock Chase District Council v. Kelly* [1978] 1 W.L.R. 1; *Sevenoaks District Council v. Emmett* (1979) 79 L.G.R. 346; *Wheeler v. Leicester City Council*, above, p. 317; as have procurement decisions: *R. v. Lewisham London Borough Council, ex p. Shell U.K. Ltd*, above, p. 348; *R. v. Enfield London Borough Council, ex p. Unwin* [1989] C.O.D. 466.

Arrowsmith (*op. cit.*, p. 291) argues that the courts should "adopt the same approach to the judicial review of contractual powers as they do to the review of other activities of government"; review could be negated or limited by special policy factors, but there would be no need to identify a public law element. The *East Berkshire* case is the main obstacle to such a development. Can it be limited to employment cases?

9. A private law action cannot be brought under Order 53 by agreement (see below, p. 661).

(D) Procedure

Notes

The application for leave

1. The procedure on an application for judicial review is a two-stage process, modelled on the previous practice in relation to the prerogative orders. The application for leave is made *ex parte* to a judge, although it may be renewed to a Divisional Court (in a criminal case or, otherwise, if the court directs) or to a judge sitting in open court. A statement of the applicant's name and description, the relief sought, the grounds and certain other matters, and an affidavit verifying the facts relied on must be filed. The statement can be amended with the court's consent.

The courts require *uberrima fides* on the part of an applicant. If material facts are suppressed by the applicant in his affidavit, the court may dismiss the application without going into the merits (*R. v. Kensington Income Tax Commissioners, ex p. de Polignac* [1917] 1 K.B. 486 (prohibition); *R. v. Stevens, ex p. Callender* [1956] C.L.Y. 2160, *The Times*, October 26, 1956; *O'Reilly v. Mackman* [1983] 2 A.C. 237, 280; *R. v. Secretary of State for the Home Department, ex p. Nachatter Singh, The Times,* August 2, 1985; *R. v. British Coal Corporation and Roo Management Ltd, ex p. G.C. Whittaker (Properties) Ltd* [1989] C.O.D. 528). All matters must be disclosed which are likely to affect the court in exercising its discretion to grant leave. r. 3(2)(b) is not limited only to facts of advantage to the applicant's case (*R. v. Greenwich JJ., ex p. Aikens, The Times*, July 3, 1982, C.A.; *R. v. Secretary of State for the Home Department, ex p. Mannan, The Times*, March 29, 1984). Where an extension of time is granted on the basis of incomplete disclosure of the material facts the court on the *inter partes* application may reconsider the extension and dismiss the application (*R. v. British Railways Board, ex p. Great Yarmouth Borough Council, The Times*, March 15, 1983).

The grant of leave

2. Leave may be refused where the applicant has no reasonable case to put forward: *R. v. Hammersmith and Fulham Borough Council, ex p. People Before Profit Ltd* (1981) 80 L.G.R. 322. In *Inland Revenue Commissioners v. National Federation of Self-Employed and Small Businesses Ltd* [1982] A.C. 617, Lord Diplock suggested at 644 that it should be sufficient for an applicant to show that he has an "arguable case" for him to be given leave. Lord Scarman stated at 655 that the applicants in that case should have been granted leave had they been able to show reasonable grounds for believing that the board had abused its discretion "or that there was a case to that effect which merited investigation and examination by the court". In *R. v. Inspector of Taxes, ex p. Kissane* [1986] 2 All E.R. 37, Nolan J. said (at 39) that on an application for leave "it is not for me to delve too deeply into the arguments. I have to be satisfied, before giving leave, that there is at any rate an arguable case. The threshold, if one excludes obviously hopeless claims, is fairly low." In *R. v. Secretary of State for the Home Department, ex p. Swati* [1986] 1 W.L.R. 477, Sir John Donaldson M.R. stated (at 485) that "an applicant must show more than that it is not impossible that grounds for judicial review exist. To say that he must show a prima facie case that such grounds do in fact exist may be putting it too high, but he must at least show that it is a real, as opposed to a theoretical, possibility. In other words, he must have an arguable case."

If on the papers in support of the *ex parte* application the judge remains uncertain whether there is an arguable case, he should invite the putative respondent to attend and make representations as to the grant or refusal of leave: only brief arguments should be submitted at such a hearing (*R. v. Secretary of State for the Home Department, ex p. Angur Begum* [1990] Imm.A.R. 1, C.A.).

If leave is granted on one ground but refused on others, the court at the substantive hearing is entitled not to permit those other grounds to be reopened (*R. v. Staffordshire County Council ex p. Ashworth, The Times*, October 18, 1996).

The existence of the leave requirement has been controversial. The JUSTICE/All Souls Review of Administrative Law recommended that it should be abolished as a matter of principle:

> "The citizen does not require leave to sue a fellow citizen and we do not think that he should have to obtain leave in order to proceed against the state and administrative bodies"

(*Administrative Justice: Some Necessary Reforms* (1988), pp. 152–155). However, it has been defended by Sir Harry Woolf as a useful filter in respect of vexatious and frivolous applications, as being an inexpensive and simple procedure, and as it "enables a litigant expeditiously and cheaply to obtain the view of a High Court judge on the merits of his application" (*Protection of the Public—A New Challenge* (1990), pp. 19–23). A review of the law and practice of the leave requirement by A.P. Le Sueur and M. Sunkin ("Applications for Judicial Review: The Requirement of Leave" [1992] P.L. 102) concluded that the political reality seemed to be that the requirement would remain for the foreseeable future. However, there should be a presumption in favour of the grant of leave; "the exercise of judicial discretion at the leave stage should be more clearly confined, structured and checked"; the "arguability" test should be replaced by a test whether there is a "serious case to be tried"; and consideration should be given to a mechanism to dispense with the leave requirement where both parties agree there is a triable case. See further the proposals of the Law Commission and Lord Woolf, below, pp. 700, 706.

Setting aside a grant of leave

3. An application may be made under the general inherent jurisdiction of the court (R.S.C., Ord. 32, r. 6) to set aside leave which has been granted *ex parte* (*R. v. Governor of Pentonville Prison, ex p. Herbage (No. 2)* [1987] Q.B. 1077; *R. v. District Auditor, No. 10 Audit District, ex p. Judge* [1989] C.O.D. 390; *R. v. Arthur Young (A Firm), ex p. Thamesdown Borough Council* [1989] C.O.D. 392; *R. v. Secretary of State for the Home Department, ex p. Angur Begum* [1989] Imm.A.R. 302; *R. v. British Coal Corporation and Roo Management Ltd, ex p. G.G. Whittaker (Properties) Ltd* [1989] C.O.D. 528); *R. v. Secretary of State for the Home Department, ex p. Grazyna Beecham* [1996] Imm.A.R. 87. An application to set aside may also be made in respect of leave granted at an *inter partes* hearing (*R. v. Secretary of State for the Home Department, ex p. Sita Kamara Vafi (No. 2)* [1995] Imm.A.R. 528 (issue on which leave had been granted now academic; other points academic or unarguable; appeal to the Court of Appeal dismissed: [1996] Imm.A.R. 169).

If the judge is satisfied that the substantive motion has no reasonable prospect of success and must accordingly fail, then the leave, whether granted by himself or another judge, must be set aside; otherwise he would be aiding and abetting a waste of time and money (*per* McCowan J. in *ex p. Angur Begum*, above; the Court of Appeal subsequently granted leave: [1990] Imm.A.R. 1). It may, for example, be clear that the proceedings are prevented by an ouster clause (*R. v. Secretary of State for the Environment, ex p. Upton Brickworks Ltd* [1992] C.O.D. 301).

Non-disclosure of material facts (*cf.* p. 635, above) may lead to the court setting aside the grant of leave (*R. v. Jockey Club Licensing Committee, ex p. Wright* [1991] C.O.D. 306: leave to apply for judicial review of refusal on medical grounds to renew jockey's licence was set aside once it emerged that the applicant had failed to disclose that the refusal was based on a neurological condition and not, as suggested in the papers in support of the application, a stigmatism (the Jockey Club reserved its position as to jurisdiction); *R. v. Bromsgrove District Council, ex p. Kennedy* [1992] C.O.D. 129; *R. v. Lloyd's of London, ex p. Briggs* [1993] 1 Lloyd's L.R. 176

non-disclosure of overlap between the judicial review proceedings and other private law proceedings). The courts apply the principles set out in *Brink's Mat Ltd v. Elcombe* [1988] 1 W.L.R. 1350, 1356 in respect of the effect of non-disclosure on the making of a *Mareva* injunction. These, *inter alia*, require the applicant to make proper inquiries before making the application and state that the court will be astute to deprive the applicant of any advantage from non-disclosure. However, dismissal of the application does not automatically follow: the matter is one for the court's discretion, taking account of the importance of the non-disclosed fact to the issues to be decided.

The jurisdiction set aside is not, however, limited to cases of non-disclosure or new factual developments (*per* Bingham L.J. in *R. v. Secretary of State for the Home Department, ex p. Chinoy* [1991] C.O.D. 381).

The application

4. Applications for judicial review are entered in the Crown Office list, along with other public law matters, including proceedings for committal for contempt of court, applications for *habeas corpus* and a variety of statutory appeals. See *Practice Direction (Trials in London)* [1981] 1 W.L.R. 1296; *Practice Direction (Crown Office list)* [1987] 1 W.L.R. 232; *Practice Direction (Crown Office list) (No. 2)* [1991] 1 W.L.R. 280. There are over 20 High Court judges nominated by the Lord Chief Justice to hear Crown Office proceedings, and the Deputy Chief Justice exercises particular responsibility in Crown Office matters (R. Gordon, *Crown Office Proceedings* (1990), para. A1–004; Law Com. No. 226, p. 13). Criminal cases are heard by a Divisional Court; other cases normally by a single judge (see Order 53, r. 5(1)(2)).

Third parties

5. Order 53 r. 5(3) requires notice of motion to be served on all persons directly affected; r. 9(1) provides that apart from this the court may hear any person who desires to be heard and appears to be a proper person to be heard. Only the former will make the person a party with a subsequent right of appeal (*per* Lord Keith of Kinkel in *R. v. Rent Officer Service, ex p. Muldoon* [1996] 3 All E.R. 498, 500). The House of Lords in *ex p. Muldoon* held that the fact that the Secretary of State for Social Security was required to meet up to 95 per cent of the cost of housing benefit did not mean that he was "directly affected" by an application for judicial review of a decision by a local authority to refuse benefit. This test connoted that a person "was affected without the intervention of an intermediate agency" (*per* Lord Keith at 500). Here the Secretary of State would not pay the disputed benefit to the applicants whether directly or through the local authority; instead the amount would be added to the subsidy paid to the local authority at the end of the financial year. See A. Lidbetter (1997) 113 L.Q.R. 40, who argues that while the decision appears to be correct on its own facts, an unduly restrictive approach will not be appropriate in other contexts (*e.g.* neighbours in environmental cases and other unsuccessful bidders in franchising cases). It is submitted, however, that the approach in the case itself is unduly narrow. What if a large sum of money were at stake depending on a disputed question of interpretation of the regulations? (Would the Secretary of State have standing as applicant to challenge a local authority's decision to pay housing benefit in a particular case?)

A joint report by JUSTICE and the Public Law Project (*A Matter of Public Interest* (1996)) recommends that r. 9(1) be extended to cover third parties who wish to intervene in support of an application, and that the court should have a discretion to give leave for a person to intervene in proceedings if "satisfied that the proceedings raise a matter of public interest and the intervention is likely to assist the court". Such intervention would be by a written submission not exceeding 20 pages, unless otherwise ordered. For discussion, see Lord Justice Schiemann [1996] P.L. 240, noting that the Report did address the implications for cost and delay, but did not "set out any awareness of the dangers of judges becoming more and more explicitly involved in making judgments of social policy" (at 243). Lord Woolf (below, p. 705) proposes that further consideration should be given to this matter.

Discovery

6. Order 53 r. 8(1) enables an application for discovery under Order 24 to be made in judicial review proceedings. There is no *right* to discovery; the matter lies in the discretion of the judge. In *I.R.C. v. National Federation of Self-Employed and Small Businesses Ltd* [1982] A.C. 617, Lord Scarman said (at 654):

> "... Upon general principles, discovery should not be ordered unless and until the court is satisfied that the evidence reveals reasonable grounds for believing that there has been a breach of public duty; and it should be limited strictly to documents relevant to the issue which emerges from the affidavits."

However, this view may be too restrictive. In *O'Reilly v. Mackman* [1983] 2 A.C. 237, Lord Diplock stated simply that discovery should be ordered "whenever, and to the extent that, the justice of the case so requires" (below, p. 649).

These views were discussed by Hodgson J. in *R. v. Governor of Pentonville Prison, ex p. Herbage (No. 2)*, *The Times*, May 29, 1986. Hodgson J. held that in deciding whether to grant discovery in judicial review proceedings the court should apply a standard no higher than that applied when considering whether or not leave to apply for judicial review should be granted (appeal dismissed: [1987] Q.B. 1077, *sub. nom. R. v. Secretary of State for the Home Department, ex p. Herbage (No. 2)*). See also Simon Brown J. in *R. v. Inland Revenue Commissioners, ex p. J. Rothschild Holdings* [1986] S.T.C. 410 (appeal dismissed: [1987] S.T.C. 163); *R. v. Secretary of State for the Home Department, ex p. Harrison*, *The Independent*, December 21, 1987, considered in *R. v. Inland Revenue Commissioners, ex p. Taylor* [1988] S.T.C. 832; *R. v. Parole Board, ex p. Bradley* [1990] C.O.D. 375; *R. v. Secretary of State for the Environment, ex p. Doncaster Borough Council* [1990] C.O.D. 441. Discovery will only be ordered to go behind the contents of an affidavit if there is some material before the court which suggests that the affidavits of the party are not accurate: *R. v. Secretary of State for the Environment, ex p. Doncaster Borough Council* [1990] C.O.D. 441; *R. v. Secretary of State for the Home Department, ex p. B.H. et al.* [1990] C.O.D. 445; *R. v. Secretary of State for the Environment, ex p. Islington London Borough Council, The Independent*, September 6, 1991; *R. v. Governors and Appeals Committee of Bishop Challenor R.C. Comprehensive School, ex p. C and P* (1991) 90 L.G.R. 1037. It will not be ordered merely "in the hope that something might turn up" (characterised by Henry J. in *Re CEMI Ltd* (unreported, February 18, 1987) as "contingent" or "Micawber" discovery): *ex p. Doncaster Borough Council*, above.

Cross-examination on affidavits

7. Evidence in judicial review proceedings is normally given by way of affidavits.

Rule 8(1), by virtue of the express reference to Order 38, r. 1(3), makes it clear that cross-examination on affidavits may be allowed. Previously, cross-examination under Order 38, r. 2(3) on applications for a prerogative order was possible but permitted only in very exceptional circumstances (*R. v. Kent JJ., ex p. Smith* [1928] W.N. 137; *R. v. Stokesley, Yorkshire, JJ., ex p. Bartram* [1956] 1 W.L.R. 254). At first, at least, it seemed unlikely that the practice would be more liberal even though express provision had now been made (*George v. Secretary of State for the Environment* (1979) 77 L.G.R. 689: statutory application to quash; *R. v. Home Secretary, ex p. Zamir* [1980] A.C. 930, 949). In *R. v. Secretary of State for the Home Department, ex p. Khawaja* [1984] A.C. 74, Lord Bridge stated (at 124–125): "It may be that the express discretion conferred on the court to permit cross-examination by the new procedure for judicial review under R.S.C. Ord. 53 has been too sparingly exercised when deponents could readily attend court. But, however that may be, the discretion to allow cross-examination should only be exercised when justice so demands." The House of Lords in *O'Reilly v. Mackman* [1983] 2 A.C. 237 made it clear that "the grant of leave to cross-examine deponents on applications for judicial review is governed by the same principles as it is in actions begun by originating summons; it should be allowed whenever the justice of the particular case so requires" (*per* Lord Diplock at 282–283). See also *R. v. Board of Visitors, Nottingham Prison, ex p. Moseley, The Times,* January 23, 1981 (conflict of affidavit evidence resolved without recourse to cross-examination); *R. v. Secretary of State for the Environment, ex p. Manuel, The Times,* March 21, 1984 (cross-examination ordered on the application of the Secretary of State where the applicant, Manuel, had offered himself for cross-examination); *R. v. Waltham Forest London Borough Council, ex p. Baxter* [1988] Q.B. 419 (councillors cross-examined as to whether they had fettered their discretion in voting); *R. v. Derbyshire County Council, ex p. The Times Supplements, The Times,* July 19, 1990 (above, p. 320).

On cross-examination and discovery in judicial review, see M. Purdue, "The scope for fact finding in judicial review" in G. Hand and J. McBride (eds.), *Droit Sans Frontieres: Essays in Honour of L. Neville Brown* (1991), pp. 193–201. The approach of the courts to these matters has been criticised as too restrictive (below, p. 662), but the Law Commission and Lord Woolf (below, pp. 700–708) have no proposals for change.

Interim relief

8. Rule 3(10) provides for interim relief on an application for judicial review.

The normal principles on which an interim injunction may be awarded are set out by the House of Lords in *American Cyanamid Co. v. Ethicon Ltd* [1975] A.C. 396. Lord Diplock stated at 407–408 that the court should consider, first, whether there is "a serious question to be tried", and, if satisfied that there is, proceed to consider the "balance of convenience":

> "As to that, the governing principle is that the court should first consider whether, if the plaintiff were to succeed at the trial in establishing his right to a permanent injunction, he would be adequately compensated by an award of damages for the loss he would have sustained as a result of the defendant's continuing to do what was sought to be enjoined between the time of the application and the time of the trial. If damages in the measure recoverable at common law would be adequate remedy and the defendant would be in a financial position to pay them, no interlocutory injunction should normally be granted, however strong the plaintiff's claim appeared to be at that stage. If, on the other hand, damages would not provide an adequate remedy for the plaintiff in the event of his succeeding at the trial, the court should then consider whether, on the contrary hypothesis that the defendant were to succeed at the trial in establishing his right to do that which was sought to be enjoined, he would be adequately compensated under the plaintiff's undertaking as to damages for the loss he would have sustained by being prevented from doing so between the time of the application and the time of the trial. If damages in the measure recoverable under such an undertaking would be an adequate remedy and the plaintiff would be in a financial position to pay them, there would be no reason upon this ground to refuse an interlocutory injunction.
>
> It is where there is doubt as to the adequacy of the respective remedies in damages available to either party or to both, that the question of balance of convenience arises. It would be unwise to attempt even to list all the various matters which may need to be taken into consideration in deciding where the balance lies, let alone to suggest the relative weight to be attached to them. These will vary from case to case.
>
> Where other factors appear to be evenly balanced it is a counsel of prudence to take such measures as are calculated to preserve the status quo."

Examples of the application of these principles include the following. In *Smith v. Inner*

London Education Authority [1978] 1 All E.R. 411, the Court of Appeal discharged interlocutory injunctions restraining the authority from closing a grammar school: the applicants had "no real prospect of . . . succeeding at the trial" (*per* Lord Denning M.R. at 418). In *R. v. Westminster City Council, ex p. Sierbien, The Times*, March 30, 1987, the Court of Appeal approved the refusal of Otton J. to grant interlocutory injunctions to restrain the council from enforcing the Local Government (Miscellaneous Provisions) Act 1982. The applicants sought the injunctions pending the outcome of their application for judicial review of the council's refusal to grant them a licence to carry on a sex encounter establishment. The court held that the ordinary financial considerations in *American Cyanamid*, although relevant, had to be qualified by a recognition of the public interest. The grant of an injunction would have the effect of preventing a public body from carrying out its duty and of trespassing on a matter in the domain of the criminal law.

On the availability of a mandatory injunction on an interlocutory application see *De Falco v. Crawley Borough Council* [1980] Q.B. 460; *Locabail International Finance Ltd v. Agroexport* [1986] 1 W.L.R. 657.

An application for interim relief can be made *ex parte* or on notice to the other side. Nevertheless, the giving of notice is an advisable step in all cases (see *R. v. Kensington and Chelsea Royal London Borough Council, ex p. Hammell* [1989] Q.B. 518, 539, *per* Parker L.J.).

On the question of undertakings in damages and interim relief, see below, pp. 767 and 775.

Interim declaratory relief

9. An interim declaration may not be granted (see *Underhill v. Minister of Food* [1950] 1 All E.R. 593, *International General Electric Co. of New York Ltd v. Customs and Excise Commissioners* [1962] Ch. 784, *R. v. Inland Revenue Commissioners, ex p. Rossminster Ltd* [1980] A.C. 952, and *Riverside Mental Health NHS Trust v. Fox, The Times*, October 28, 1993). Note, however, that the point was left open by the House of Lords in *M. v. Home Office* [1994] 1 A.C. 327 and *R. v. Secretary of State for the Environment, ex p. Royal Society for the Protection of Birds, The Times*, February 10, 1995 (where the House held that an appropriate case for the grant of such relief had not been made out, assuming that such a remedy was available in law).

A final declaration may exceptionally be awarded in interlocutory proceedings (see *Wallersteiner v. Moir* [1974] 1 W.L.R. 991, 1030; *Meade v. Haringey London Borough Council* [1979] 1 W.L.R. 637, 648–649, 657; *Malone v. Metropolitan Police Commissioner* [1979] Ch. 344, 382; *Clarke v. Chadburn* [1985] 1 W.L.R. 78; *cf. Ashby v. Ebdon* [1984] 3 All E.R. 869, 872).

The general absence of interim declaratory relief causes particular difficulty in respect of proceedings against the Crown. Section 21(2) of the Crown Proceedings Act 1947 provides that "The court shall not in any civil proceedings grant any injunction or make any order against an officer of the Crown if the effect of granting the injunction or making the order would be to give any relief against the Crown which could not have been obtained in proceedings against the Crown." However, the extent of difficulty has been moderated by the ruling in the House of Lords in *M. v. Home Office* [1994] 1 A.C. 327 that injunctions, including interim injunctions, may be awarded against ministers or other officers of the Crown.

The House of Lords had previously ruled that English courts may be required by European Community law to award interim relief against the Crown, where a point of Community law is involved: Case C-213/89, *R. v. Secretary of State for Transport, ex p. Factortame Ltd (No. 2)* [1991] 1 A.C. 603, ECJ and H.L.

See generally on the *Factortame* litigation, N.P. Gravells [1989] P.L. 568, [1991] P.L. 180 and [1996] P.L. 567. For other comments on interim relief against the Crown, see J. Alder (1987) 50 M.L.R. 10; M. Matthews (1988) 8 O.J.L.S. 154; Sir William Wade (1991) 107 L.Q.R. 4.

There seems no good reason why interim declaratory relief should not be made available. The Law Commission so recommended in its Report on Remedies in Administrative Law (Law Com. No. 73), para. 51 and Administrative Law: Judicial Review and Statutory Appeals (Law Com. No. 226), para. 6.27 . This was supported by Lord Diplock in the *Rossminster* case ([1980] A.C. at 1015), but opposed by Lords Wilberforce, Dilhorne and Scarman in the same case (at 1001, 1007, 1027). Lord Scarman said:

> "For myself, I find absurd the posture of a court declaring one day in interlocutory proceedings that an applicant has certain rights and upon a later day that he has not" (at 1027).

On the other hand, it can be argued that it is not self-evidently absurd for a court at an interim stage to express a *provisional* or *prima facie* view, where that would be helpful for one or both of the parties.

The Crown is not, but Departments and Ministers acting in a personal or official capacity are, amenable to the contempt jurisdiction (*M. v. Home Office* [1994] 1 A.C. 327, H.L.)

Availability of declarations

10. In *Inland Revenue Commissioners v. National Federation of Self-Employed and Small Businesses Ltd* [1982] A.C. 617 Lord Diplock (at 639) and Lord Scarman (at 648) expressed the view that a declaration could only be granted under Order 53 in circumstances where one or other of the prerogative orders could issue. Otherwise, r. 1(2) would have been *ultra vires* in that it would have purported to effect a substantive and not merely a procedural change in the law. (See P. Cane, [1981] P.L. 322, 325–329.) The subsequent enactment of the basic features of Order 53 in the Supreme Court 1981 could be regarded as overcoming any such difficulty. Nevertheless, Lord Diplock's view was accepted by Fox and Slade L.JJ. in *Law v. National Greyhound Racing Club Ltd* [1983] 1 W.L.R. 1302, 1310, 1313 (see further, above, p. 618); and the views of both Lords Diplock and Scarman were accepted by Lord Wilberforce in *Davy v. Spelthorne Borough Council* [1984] A.C. 262, 277–278.

On the other hand, in *R. v. Bromley London Borough Council, ex p. Lambeth London Borough Council, The Times,* June 16, 1984, Hodgson J. held that the court had jurisdiction to grant a declaration that the proposed payment of a subscription to the Association of London Authorities would be *intra vires,* notwithstanding that there was as yet no judgment, order or decision to be reviewed, and that there was no claim in the application for one of the prerogative orders. His Lordship accepted the argument that the enactment of section 31 of the Supreme Court Act 1981 meant that it was no longer necessary to consider whether one of the prerogative orders would have been available on the facts. A similar view was expressed by Kennedy J. in *R. v. Secretary of State for the Environment, ex p. Nottinghamshire County Council, The Independent,* November 13, 1986 (but *cf.* McNeill J. in *R. v. Secretary of State for the Home Department, ex p. Dew* [1987] 1 W.L.R. 881).

In *R. v. Secretary of State for Employment, ex p. Equal Opportunities Commission* [1995] 1 A.C. 1, Lord Browne-Wilkinson held that the view adopted by Lords Diplock and Scarman was no longer applicable in view of the 1981 Act (see below, p. 699). However, none of the other authorites on the point were cited.

Appeals

11. Rule 13 provides that no appeal lies from an order on an application for leave which may be renewed to a Divisional Court or judge sitting in open court under r. 3(4).

In a criminal cause or matter, a renewed application is made to a Divisional Court (r. 3(4)(a)). It is uncertain whether an appeal can lie to the House of Lords against a refusal of leave by the Divisional Court (see G. Aldous and J. Alder, *Applications for Judicial Review* (2nd ed., 1993) p. 177, who point out that such a refusal would be unlikely in practice to raise a point of law of general public importance).

In a non-criminal cause or matter, the application may be renewed either to a judge in open court or to a Divisional Court (if the Court so directs) (r. 3(4)(b)) except that if the decision to refuse leave is made by a judge after an oral hearing, the application for leave may not be renewed in the High Court under r. 3(4) (see the proviso to r. 3(4) in conjunction with r. 13). In such a cause or matter, where an application for leave may not be further renewed in the High Court, a renewed application may be made to the Court of Appeal (*R. v. Commissioner for the Special Purposes of the Income Tax Acts, ex p. Stipplechoice Ltd* [1985] 2 All E.R. 465; *R. v. Secretary of State for the Home Department, ex p. Swati* [1986] 1 W.L.R. 477; *Re Dhillon, The Times,* January 28, 1987). This is not technically an appeal against the refusal of leave (*per* Sir John Donaldson M.R. in *Re Dhillon,* above). Renewed applications made to the Court of Appeal are treated as a priority category (*In re Bakole, The Times,* March 25, 1988). If the Court of Appeal grants leave it may hear the substantive motion (*R. v. Industrial Injuries Commissioner, ex p. A.E.U.* [1966] 2 Q.B. 21), but this will now not normally be done unless the court below is bound by authority or for some other reason an appeal to the Court of Appeal is inevitable (*Practice Direction (Judicial Review: Appeals)* [1982] 1 W.L.R. 1375): the application is normally to be heard by a single judge in the High Court, unless a judge directs that the application is to be heard by a Divisional Court (*Practice Note* [1990] 1 W.L.R. 51). In *British Airways Board v. Laker Airways Ltd* [1984] 1 Q.B. 142, the Court of Appeal, exceptionally, ordered the substantive application for judicial review to be made direct to the Court of Appeal after granting a renewed application for leave: this was to enable the matter to be considered in conjunction with other appeals pending before that court (see 184–185). Similarly, in *R. v. Secretary of State for Education, ex p. Avon County Council (No. 2)* (1990) 88 L.G.R. 737, the hearing of a substantive application for judicial review was reserved to the Court of Appeal with the agreement of both parties: this was to secure the early hearing of a challenge to decisions rejecting proposals for the reorganisation of secondary education in Bath and approving the acquisition by one school of grant maintained status.

There is no further appeal in a civil case, in respect of a refusal of leave, to the House of Lords (*Re Poh* [1983] 1 W.L.R. 2; *Practice Direction (House of Lords: Petitions: Judicial Review)* [1983] 1 W.L.R. 404).

Where in a civil case a full application has been heard in the High Court, further appeals may lie (with leave, except in cases involving nationality or immigration) to the Court of Appeal and the House of Lords. In a criminal case, an appeal lies from the Divisional Court to the House of Lords under the Administration of Justice Act 1960, ss.1 and 19, Sched. 3.

(E) Exclusivity of the Application for Judicial Review

O'REILLY AND OTHERS v. MACKMAN AND OTHERS

[1983] 2 A.C. 237; [1983] 3 W.L.R. 1096; [1982] 3 All E.R. 1124
(House of Lords)

The four plaintiffs, prisoners in Hull Prison, were charged with disciplinary offences before the board of visitors to the prison, arising out of riots in December 1976 (in the case of three of the plaintiffs) and 1979 (in the case of the fourth). In the case of each plaintiff the board held an inquiry, found the charges proved and imposed penalties. In

1980, three of the plaintiffs brought actions by writ in the Queen's Bench Division of the High Court against the board alleging that it had acted in breach of the Prison Rules and the rules of natural justice and claiming a declaration that the board's findings against them and the penalties awarded were void and of no effect. The fourth plaintiff started proceedings by originating summons in the Chancery Division against the Home Office and the board of visitors alleging bias by a member of the board and claiming a declaration that the board's adjudication was void for want of natural justice. In all four cases the defendants applied to strike out the proceedings. Peter Pain J. dismissed the applications. The Court of Appeal reversed that decision and struck out the proceedings on the ground that they were an abuse of the process of the court and that the plaintiffs' only proper remedy was by way of judicial review under R.S.C. Ord. 53. The House of Lords (Lords Diplock, Fraser, Keith, Bridge and Brightman) unanimously dismissed the plaintiffs' appeals. The leading speech was delivered by Lord Diplock.

LORD DIPLOCK: .... [N]o question arises as to the "jurisdiction" of the High Court to grant to each of the appellants relief by way of a declaration in the terms sought, if they succeeded in establishing the facts alleged in their respective statements of claim or originating summons and the court considered a declaration to be an appropriate remedy. All that is at issue in the instant appeal is the procedure by which such relief ought to be sought. Put in a single sentence the question for your Lordships is: whether in 1980 after R.S.C., Ord. 53 in its new form, adopted in 1977, had come into operation it was an abuse of the process of the court to apply for such declarations by using the procedure laid down in the Rules for proceedings begun by writ or by originating summons instead of using the procedure laid down by Order 53 for an application for judicial review of the awards of forfeiture of remission of sentence made against them by the board which the appellants are seeking to impugn?

In their respective actions, the appellants claim only declaratory relief. It is conceded on their behalf that, for reasons into which the concession makes it unnecessary to enter, no claim for damages would lie against the members of the board of visitors by whom the awards were made. The only claim was for a form of relief which it lies within the discretion of the court to grant or to withhold. So the first thing to be noted is that the relief sought in the action is discretionary only.

It is not, and it could not be, contended that the decision of the board awarding him forfeiture of remission had infringed or threatened to infringe any right of the appellant derived from private law, whether a common law right or one created by a statute. Under the Prison Rules remission of sentence is not a matter of right but of indulgence. So far as private law is concerned all that each appellant had was a legitimate expectation, based upon his knowledge of what is the general practice, that he would be granted the maximum remission, permitted by rule 5(2) of the Prison Rules, of one-third of his sentence if by that time no disciplinary award of forfeiture of remission had been made against him. So the second thing to be noted is that none of the appellants had any remedy in private law.

In public law, as distinguished from private law, however, such legitimate expectation gave to each appellant a sufficient interest to challenge the legality of the adverse disciplinary award made against him by the board on the ground that in one way or another the board in reaching its decision had acted outwith the powers conferred upon it by the legislation under which it was acting; and such grounds would include the board's failure to observe the rules of natural justice: which means no more than to act fairly towards him in carrying out their decision-making process, and I prefer so to put it.

The power of boards of visitors of a prison to make disciplinary awards is conferred upon them by subordinate legislation: the Prison Rules 1964 made by the Secretary of State under sections 6 and 47 of the Prison Act 1952. The charges against the appellants were of grave offences against discipline falling within rule 51. They were referred by the governor of the prison to the board under rule 51(1). It thereupon became the duty of the board under rule 51(3) to inquire into the charge and decide whether it was proved and if so to award what the board considered to be the appropriate punishment. Rule 49(2) is applicable to such inquiry by the board. It lays down expressly that the prisoner "shall be given a full opportunity of hearing what is alleged against him and of presenting his own case". In exercising their functions under rule 51 members of the board are acting as a statutory tribunal, as contrasted with a domestic tribunal upon which powers are conferred by contract between those who agree to submit to its jurisdiction. Where the legislation which confers upon a statutory tribunal its decision-making powers also provides expressly for the procedure it shall follow in the course of reaching its decision, it is a question of construction of the relevant legislation, to be decided by the court in which the decision is challenged, whether a particular procedural provision is mandatory, so that its non-observance in the process of reaching the decision makes the decision itself a nullity, or whether it is merely directory, so that the statutory tribunal has a discretion not to comply with it if, in its opinion, the exceptional circumstances of a particular case justify departing from it. But the requirement that a person who is charged with having done something which, if proved to the satisfaction of a statutory tribunal, has consequences that will, or may, affect him adversely, should be given a fair opportunity of hearing what is alleged against him and of presenting his own case, is so fundamental to any civilised legal system that it is to be presumed that Parliament intended that a failure to observe it should render null and void any decision reached in breach of this requirement. What is alleged by the appellants other than Millbanks would amount to an infringement of the express rule 49; but even if there were no such express provision a requirement to observe it would be a necessary implication from the nature of the disciplinary functions of the board. In the absence of express provision to the contrary Parliament, whenever it provides for the creation of a statutory tribunal, must be presumed not to have intended that the tribunal should be authorised to act in contravention of one of the fundamental rules of natural justice or fairness: *audi alteram partem.*

In Millbanks's case, there is no express provision in the Prison Rules that the members of the board who inquire into a disciplinary offence under rule 51 must be free from personal bias against the prisoner. It is another fundamental rule of natural justice or fairness, too obvious to call for express statement of it, that a tribunal exercising functions such as those exercised by the board in the case of Millbanks should be constituted of persons who enter upon the inquiry without any pre-conceived personal bias against the prisoner. Failure to comply with this implied requirement would likewise render the decision of the tribunal a nullity. So the third thing to be noted is that each of the appellants, if he established the facts alleged in his action, was entitled to a remedy in public law which would have the effect of preventing the decision of the board from having any adverse consequences upon him.

My Lords, the power of the High Court to make declaratory judgments is conferred by what is now R.S.C., Ord. 15, r. 16. The language of the rule which was first made in 1883 has never been altered, though the numbering of the rule has from time to time been changed. It provides:

> "No action or other proceeding shall be open to objection on the ground that a merely declaratory judgment or order is sought thereby, and the court may make binding declarations of right whether or not any consequential relief is or could be claimed."

This rule, which is in two parts separated by "and", has been very liberally interpreted in the course of its long history, wherever it appeared to the court that the justice of the case required the grant of declaratory relief in the particular action before it. Since "action" is defined so as to have included since 1938 an originating motion applying for prerogative orders, Ord. 15, r. 16 says nothing as to the appropriate procedure by which declarations of different kinds ought to be sought. Nor does it draw any distinction between declarations that relate to rights and obligations under private law and those that relate to rights and obligations under public law. Indeed the appreciation of the distinction in substantive law between what is private law and what is public law has itself been a latecomer to the English legal system. It is a consequence of the development that has taken place in the last 30 years of the procedures available for judicial control of administrative action. This development started with the expansion of the grounds upon which orders of certiorari could be obtained as a result of the decision of the Court of Appeal in *R. v. Northumberland Compensation Appeal Tribunal, ex p. Shaw* [1952] 1 K.B. 338; it was accelerated by the passing of the Tribunals and Inquiries Act 1958, and culminated in the substitution in 1977 of the new form of R.S.C., Ord. 53 which has since been given statutory confirmation in section 31 of the Supreme Court Act 1981.

[His Lordship referred to the re-discovery in *ex p. Shaw* of the power to grant certiorari to quash for error of law on the face of the record (above, p. 174); and the provisions in the 1958 Act, now replaced by the 1971 Act, requiring most statutory tribunals to give reasons, and repealing most clauses purporting to exclude judicial review.]

[Section 14(1) of the Act (now s.12(1) of the 1992 Act, above, p. 54)] it is to be observed, says nothing about any right to bring civil actions for declarations of nullity of orders or determinations of statutory bodies where an earlier Act of Parliament contains a provision that such order or determination "shall not be called into question in any court". Since actions begun by writ seeking such declarations were already coming into common use in the High Court so as to provide an alternative remedy to orders of certiorari, the section suggests a parliamentary preference in favour of making the latter remedy available rather than the former. I will defer consideration of the reasons for this preference until later.

Fortunately for the development of public law in England, section 14(3) contained express provision that the section should not apply to any order or determination of the Foreign Compensation Commission, a statutory body established under the Foreign Compensation Act 1950, which Act provided by section 4(4) an express provision: "The determination by the commission of any application made to them under this Act shall not be called in question in any court of law." It was this provision that provided the occasion for the landmark decision of this House in *Anisminic Ltd v. Foreign Compensation Commission* [1969] 2 A.C. 147, and particularly the leading speech of Lord Reid, which has liberated English public law from the fetters that the courts had theretofore imposed upon themselves so far as determinations of inferior courts and statutory tribunals were concerned, by drawing esoteric distinctions between errors of law committed by such tribunals that went to their jurisdiction, and errors of law committed by them within their jurisdiction. The breakthrough that the *Anisminic* case made was the recognition by the majority of this House that if a tribunal whose jurisdiction was limited by statute or subordinate legislation mistook the law applicable to the facts as it had found them, it must have asked itself the wrong question, *i.e.* one into which it was not empowered to inquire and so had no jurisdiction to determine. Its purported "determination", not being a "determination" within the meaning of the empowering legislation, was accordingly a nullity.

Anisminic Ltd v. Foreign Compensation Commission was an action commenced by writ for a declaration, in which a minute of the commission's reasons for their determination adverse to the plaintiff company did not appear upon the face of their determination, and had in fact been obtained only upon discovery: but, as appears from the report of my own judgment when the *Anisminic* case was in the Court of Appeal ([1968] 2 Q.B. 862, 893), the case had been argued up to that stage as if it were an application for certiorari in which the minute of the commission's reasons formed part of the "record" upon which an error of law appeared. In the House of Lords the question of the propriety of suing by writ for a declaration instead of applying for certiorari and mandamus played no part in the main argument for the commission. It appears for the first time in the report of the commission's counsel's reply, where an argument that the court had no "jurisdiction" to make the declaration seems to have been put forward upon the narrow ground, special to the limited functions of the commission, alluded to at pp. 910–911 of my own judgment in the Court of Appeal that the House overruled; but I did not purport to decide the question because, in the view that I had (erroneously) taken of the effect of section 4(4) of the Act, it appeared to me to be unnecessary to do so.

My Lords, *Anisminic Ltd v. Foreign Compensation Commission* [1969] 2 A.C. 147 was decided by this House before the alteration was made to R.S.C., Ord. 53 in 1977. The order of the Supreme Court dealing with applications for the prerogative orders of mandamus, certiorari and prohibition in force at the time of the *Anisminic* case was numbered Order 53 and had been made in 1965. It replaced, but in substance only repeated, the first 12 rules of what had been Order 59 and which had in 1938 itself replaced the former Crown Office Rules of 1906. The pre-1977 Order 53, like its predecessors, placed under considerable procedural disadvantage applicants who wished to challenge the lawfulness of a determination of a statutory tribunal or any other body of persons having legal authority to determine questions affecting the common law or statutory rights or obligations of other persons as individuals. It will be noted that I have broadened the much-cited description by Atkin L.J. in *R. v. Electricity Commissioners, ex p. London Electricity Joint Committee Co. (1920) Ltd* [1924] 1 K.B. 171, 205 of bodies of persons subject to the supervisory jurisdiction of the High Court by prerogative remedies (which in 1924 then took the form of prerogative writs of mandamus, prohibition, certiorari, and quo warranto) by excluding Atkin L.J.'s limitation of the bodies of persons to whom the prerogative writs might issue, to those "having the duty to act judicially". For the next 40 years this phrase gave rise to many attempts, with varying success, to draw subtle distinctions between decisions that were quasi-judicial and those that were administrative only. But the relevance of arguments of this kind was destroyed by the decision of this House in *Ridge v. Baldwin* [1964] A.C. 40, where again the leading speech was given by Lord Reid. Wherever any person or body of persons has authority conferred by legislation to make decisions of the kind I have described, it is amenable to the remedy of an order to quash its decision either for error of law in reaching it or for failure to act fairly towards the person who will be adversely affected by the decision by failing to observe either one or other of the two fundamental rights accorded to him by the rules of natural justice or fairness, *viz.* to have afforded to him a reasonable opportunity of learning what is alleged against him and of putting forward his own case in answer to it, and to the absence of personal bias against him on the part of the person by whom the decision falls to be made. In *Ridge v. Baldwin* it is interesting to observe that Lord Reid said at 72 "We do not have a developed system of administrative law—perhaps because until fairly recently we did not need it." By 1977 the need had continued to grow apace and this reproach to English law had been removed. We did have by then a developed system of administrative law, to the development of which Lord Reid himself, by his speeches in cases which reached this House, had made an outstanding contribution. To the landmark cases of *Ridge v. Baldwin* and *Anisminic Ltd v. Foreign Compensation Commission* [1969] 2 A.C. 147 I would add a third, *Padfield v. Minister of Agriculture, Fisheries and Food* [1968] A.C. 997, another case in which a too-timid judgment of my own in the Court of Appeal was (fortunately) overruled.

Although the availability of the remedy of orders to quash a decision by certiorari had in theory been widely extended by these developments, the procedural disadvantages under which applicants for this remedy laboured remained substantially unchanged until the alteration of Order 53 in 1977. Foremost among these was the absence of any provision for discovery. In the case of a decision which did not state the reasons for it, it was not possible to challenge its validity for error of law in the reasoning by which the decision had been reached. If it had been an application for certiorari those who were the plaintiffs in the *Anisminic* case would have failed; it was only because by pursuing an action by writ for a declaration of nullity that the plaintiffs were entitled to the discovery by which the minute of the commission's reasons which showed that they had asked themselves the wrong question, was obtained. Again under Order 53 evidence was required to be on affidavit. This in itself is not an unjust disadvantage; it is a common feature of many forms of procedure in the High Court, including originating summonses; but in the absence of any express provision for cross-examination of deponents, as your Lordships who are familiar with the pre-1977 procedure will be aware, even *applications* for leave to cross-examine were virtually unknown—let alone the grant of leave itself—save in very exceptional cases of which I believe none of your Lordships has ever had actual experience. Lord Goddard C.J., whose experience was at that time unrivalled, had so stated in *R. v. Stokesley, York-shire, J.J., ex p. Bartram* [1956] 1 W.L.R. 254, 257.

On the other hand as compared with an action for a declaration commenced by writ or originating summons, the procedure under Order 53 both before and after 1977 provided for the respondent decision-making statutory tribunal or public authority against which the remedy of certiorari was sought protection against claims which it was not in the public interest for courts of justice to entertain.

First, leave to apply for the order was required. The application for leave which was *ex parte* but could be, and in practice often was, adjourned in order to enable the proposed respondent to be represented, had to be supported by a statement setting out, *inter alia*, the grounds on which the relief was sought and by affidavits verifying the facts relied on: so that a knowingly false statement of fact would amount to the criminal offence of perjury. Such affidavit was also required to satisfy the requirement of *uberrima fides*, with the consequence that failure to make on oath a full and candid disclosure of material facts was of itself a ground for refusing the relief sought in the substantive application for which leave had been obtained on the strength of the affidavit. This was an important safeguard, which is preserved in the new Order 53 of 1977. The public interest in good administration requires that public authorities and third parties should not be kept in suspense as to the legal validity of a decision the authority has reached in purported exercise of decision-making powers for any longer period than is absolutely necessary in fairness to the person affected by the decision. In contrast, allegations made in a statement of claim or an indorsement of an originating summons are not on oath, so the requirement of a prior application for leave to be supported by full and candid affidavits verifying the facts relied on is an important safeguard against groundless or unmeritorious claims that a particular decision is a nullity. There was also power in the court on granting leave to impose terms as to costs or security.

Furthermore, as Order 53 was applied in practice, as soon as the application for leave had been made it provided a very speedy means, available in urgent cases within a matter of days rather than months, for determining whether a disputed decision was valid in law or not. A reduction of the period of suspense was also effected by the requirement that leave to apply for certiorari to quash a decision must be made within a limited period after the impugned decision was made, unless delay beyond that limited period was accounted for to the satisfaction of the judge. The period was six months under the pre-1977 Order 53; under the current Order 53 it is further reduced to three months.

My Lords, the exclusion of all right to discovery in application for certiorari under Order 53, particularly before the passing of the Tribunal and Inquiries Act 1958, was calculated to cause injustice to persons who had no means, if they adopted that procedure, of ascertaining whether a public body, which had made a decision adversely affecting them, had done so for reasons which were wrong in law and rendered their decision invalid. It will be within the knowledge of all of your Lordships that, at any rate from the 1950s onwards, actions for declarations of nullity of decisions affecting the rights of individuals under public law were widely entertained, in parallel to applications for certiorari to quash, as means of obtaining an effective alternative remedy. I will not weary your Lordships by reciting examples of cases where this practice received the express approval of the Court of Appeal, though I should point out that of those cases in this House in which this practice was approved, *Vine v. National Dock Labour Board* [1957] A.C. 488 and *Ridge v. Baldwin* [1964] A.C. 40 involved, as well as questions of public law, contracts of employment which gave rise to rights under private law. In *Anisminic Ltd v. Foreign Compensation Commission* [1969] 2 A.C. 147 the procedural question was not seriously argued, while *Pyx Granite Ltd v. Ministry of Housing and Local Government* [1960] A.C. 260, which is referred to in the notes to Order 19 appearing in the *Supreme Court Practice* (1982) as an instance of the approval by this House of the practice of suing for a declaration instead of applying for an order of certiorari, appears on analysis to have been concerned with declaring that the plaintiffs had a legal right to do what they were seeking to do without the need to obtain any decision from the Minister. Nevertheless I accept that having regard to disadvantages, particularly in relation to the absolute bar upon compelling discovery of documents by the respondent public authority to an applicant for an order of certiorari, and the almost invariable practice of refusing leave to allow cross-examination of deponents to affidavits lodged on its behalf, it could not be regarded as an abuse of the process of the court, before the amendments made to Order 53 in 1977, to proceed against the authority by an action for a declaration of nullity of the impugned decision with an injunction to prevent the authority from acting on it, instead of applying for an order of certiorari; and this despite the fact that, by adopting this course, the plaintiff evaded the safeguards imposed in the public interest against groundless, unmeritorious or tardy attacks upon the validity of decisions made by public authorities in the field of public law.

Those disadvantages, which formerly might have resulted in an applicant's being unable to obtain justice in an application for certiorari under Order 53, have all been removed by the new Order introduced in 1977. There is express provision in the new rule 8 for interlocutory applications for discovery of documents, the administration of interrogatories and the cross-examination of deponents to affidavits. Discovery of documents (which may often be a time-consuming process) is not automatic as in an action begun by writ, but otherwise Order 24 applies to it and discovery is obtainable upon application whenever, and to the extent that, the justice of the case requires; similarly Order 26 applies to applications for interrogatories; and to applications for cross-examination of deponents to affidavits Ord. 28, r. 2(3) applies. This is the rule that deals with evidence in actions begun by originating summons and permits oral cross-examination on affidavit evidence wherever the justice of the case requires. It may well be that for the reasons given by Lord Denning M.R. in *George v. Secretary of State for the Environment* (1979) 77 L.G.R. 689, it will only be upon rare occasions that the interests of justice will require that leave be given for cross-examination of deponents on their affidavits in applications for judicial review. This is because of the nature of the issues that normally arise upon judicial review. The facts, except where the claim that a decision was invalid on the ground that the statutory tribunal or public authority that made the decision failed to comply with the procedure prescribed by the legislation under which it was acting or failed to observe the fundamental rules of natural justice or fairness, can seldom be a matter of relevant dispute upon an application for judicial review, since the tribunal or authority's findings of fact, as distinguished from the legal consequences of the facts that they have found, are not open to review by the court in the exercise of its supervisory powers except on the principles laid down in *Edwards v. Bairstow* [1956] A.C. 14, 36; and to allow cross-examination presents the court with a temptation, not always easily resisted, to substitute its own view of the facts for that of the decision-making body upon whom the exclusive jurisdiction to determine facts has been conferred by Parliament. Nevertheless having regard to a possible misunderstanding of what was said by Geoffrey Lane L.J. in *R. v. Board of Visitors of Hull Prison, ex p. St Germain (No. 2)* [1979] 1 W.L.R. 1401, 1410 your Lordships may think this an appropriate occasion on which to emphasise that whatever may have been the position before the rule was altered in 1977 in all proceedings for judicial review that have been started since that date the grant of leave to cross-examine deponents upon applications for judicial review is governed by the same principles as it is in actions begun by originating summons; it should be allowed whenever the justice of the particular case so requires.

Another handicap under which an applicant for a prerogative order under Order 53 formerly laboured (though it would not have affected the appellants in the instant cases even if they had brought their actions before the 1977 alteration to Order 53) was that a claim for damages for breach of a right in private law of the applicant resulting from an invalid decision of a public authority could not be made in an application under Order 53. Damages could only be claimed in a separate action begun by writ; whereas in an action so begun they could be claimed as additional relief as well as a declaration of nullity of the decision from which the damage claimed had flowed. Rule 7 of the new Order 53 permits the applicant for judicial review to include in the statement in support of his application for leave a claim for damages and empowers the court to award damages on the hearing of the application if satisfied that such damages could have been awarded to him in an action begun by him by writ at the time of the making of the application.

Finally rule 1 of the new Order 53 enables an application for a declaration or an injunction to be included in an application for judicial review. This was not previously the case; only prerogative orders could be obtained in proceedings under Order 53. Declarations or injunctions were obtainable only in actions begun by writ or originating summons. So a person seeking to challenge a decision had to make a choice of the remedy that he sought at the outset of the proceedings, although when the matter was examined more closely in the course of the proceedings it might appear that he was not entitled to that remedy but would have been entitled to some other remedy available only in the other kind of proceeding.

This reform may have lost some of its importance since there have come to be realised that the full consequences of the *Anisminic* case, in introducing the concept that if a statutory decision-making authority asks itself the wrong question it acts without jurisdiction, have been virtually to abolish the distinction between errors within jurisdiction that rendered voidable a decision that remained valid until quashed, and errors that went to jurisdiction and rendered a decision void *ab initio* provided that its validity was challenged timeously in the High Court by an appropriate procedure. Failing such challenge within the applicable time limit, public policy, expressed in the maxim *omnia praesumuntur rite esse acta*, requires that after the expiry of the time limit it should be given all the effects in law of a valid decision.

Nevertheless, there may still be cases where it turns out in the course of proceedings to challenge a decision of a statutory authority that a declaration of rights rather than certiorari is the appropriate remedy. *Pyx Granite Co. Ltd v. Ministry of Housing and Local Government* [1960] A.C. 260 provides an example of such a case.

So Order 53 since 1977 has provided a procedure by which every type of remedy for infringement of the rights of individuals that are entitled to protection in public law can be obtained in one and the same proceeding by way of an application for judicial review, and whichever remedy is found to be the most appropriate in the light of what has emerged upon the hearing of the application, can be granted to him. If what should emerge is that his complaint is not of an infringement of any of his rights that are entitled to protection in public law, but may be an infringement of his rights in private law and thus not a proper subject for judicial review, the court has power under rule 9(5), instead of refusing the application, to order the proceedings to continue as if they had begun by writ. There is no such converse power under the R.S.C. to permit an action begun by writ to continue as if it were an application for judicial review; and I respectfully disagree with that part of the judgment of Lord Denning M.R. which suggests that such a power may exist; nor do I see the need to amend the rules in order to create one.

My Lords, at the outset of this speech, I drew attention to the fact that the remedy by way of declaration of nullity of the decisions of the board was discretionary—as are all the remedies available upon judicial review. Counsel for the plaintiffs accordingly conceded that the fact that by adopting the procedure of an action begun by writ or by originating summons instead of an application for judicial review under Order 53 (from which there have now been removed all those disadvantages to applicants that had previously led the courts to countenance actions for declarations and injunctions as an alternative procedure for obtaining a remedy for infringement of the rights of the individual that are entitled to protection in public law only) the plaintiffs had thereby been able to evade those protections against groundless, unmeritorious or tardy harassment that were afforded to statutory tribunals or decision-making public authorities by Order 53, and which might have resulted in the summary, and would in any event have resulted in the speedy disposition of the application, is among the matters fit to be taken into consideration by the judge in deciding whether to exercise his discretion by refusing to grant a declaration; but, it was contended, this he may only do at the conclusion of the trial.

So to delay the judge's decision as to how to exercise his discretion would defeat the public policy that underlies the grant of those protections: *viz.*, the need, in the interests of good administration and of third parties who may be indirectly affected by the decision, for speedy certainty as to whether it has the effect of a decision that is valid in public law. An action for a declaration or injunction need not be commenced until the very end of the limitation period; if begun by writ, discovery and interlocutory proceedings may be prolonged and the plaintiffs are not required to support their allegations by evidence on oath until the actual trial. The period of uncertainty as to the validity of a decision that has been challenged upon allegations that may eventually turn out to be baseless and unsupported by evidence on oath, may thus be strung out for a very lengthy period, as the actions of the first three appellants in the instant appeals show. Unless such an action can be struck out summarily at the outset as an abuse of the process of the court the whole purpose of the public policy to which the change in Order 53 was directed would be defeated.

My Lords, Order 53 does not expressly provide that procedure by application for judicial review shall be the exclusive procedure available by which the remedy of a declaration or injunction may be obtained for infringement of rights that are entitled to protection under public law; nor does section 31 of the Supreme Court Act 1981. There is great variation between individual cases that fall within Order 53 and the Rules Committee and subsequently the legislature were, I think, for this reason content to rely upon the express and the inherent power of the High Court, exercised upon a case to case basis, to prevent abuse of its process whatever might be the form taken by that abuse. Accordingly, I do not think that your Lordships would be wise to use this as an occasion to lay down categories of cases in which it would necessarily always be an abuse to seek in an action begun by writ or originating summons a remedy against infringement of rights of the individual that are entitled to protection in public law.

The position of applicants for judicial review has been drastically ameliorated by the new Order 53. It has removed all those disadvantages, particularly in relation to discovery, that were manifestly unfair to them and had, in many cases, made applications for prerogative orders an inadequate remedy if justice was to be done. This it was that justified the courts in not treating as an abuse of their powers resort to an alternative procedure by way of action for a declaration or injunction (not then obtainable on an application under Order 53), despite the fact that this procedure had the effect of depriving the defendants of the protection to statutory tribunals and public authorities for which for public policy reasons Order 53 provided.

Now that those disadvantages to applicants have been removed and all remedies for infringements of rights protected by public law can be obtained upon an application for judicial review, as can also remedies for infringements of rights under private law if such infringements should also be involved, it would in my view as a general rule be contrary to public policy, and as such an abuse of the process of the court, to permit a person seeking to establish that a decision of a public authority infringed rights to which he was entitled to protection under public law to proceed by way of an ordinary action and by this means to evade the provisions of Order 53 for the protection of such authorities.

My Lords, I have described this as a general rule; for though it may normally be appropriate to apply it by the summary process of striking out the action, there may be exceptions, particularly where the invalidity of the decision arises as a collateral issue in a claim for infringement of a right of the plaintiff arising under private law, or where none of the parties objects to the adoption of the procedure by writ or originating summons. Whether there should be other exceptions should, in my view, at this stage in the development of procedural public law, be left to be decided on a case to case basis—a process that your Lordships will be continuing in the next case in which judgment is to be delivered today [*Cocks v. Thanet District Council* [1983] 2 A.C. 286].

In the instant cases where the only relief sought is a declaration of nullity of the decisions of a statutory tribunal, the Board of Visitors of Hull Prison, as in any other case in which a similar declaration of nullity in public law is the only relief claimed, I have no hesitation, in agreement with the Court of Appeal, in holding that to allow the actions to proceed would be an abuse of the process of the court. They are blatant attempts to avoid the protections for the defendants for which Order 53 provides.

I would dismiss these appeals.

Notes

1. Lord Diplock makes it clear that this was not a case where the applicants had any claim to a remedy as a matter of private law. In the 1950s, 1960s and 1970s the courts had taken a generous view of the availability of private law remedies against public authorities. The orthodox view of the requirement of *locus standi* for an injunction or declaration was that, as private law remedies, they were only available to protect an applicant's private law rights, or where an applicant suffered special damage from interference with a public right. Occasionally, judges adopted this strict approach (*e.g. Gregory v. Camden London Borough Council* [1966] 1 W.L.R. 899). More commonly, declarations and injunctions were awarded against public authorities in circumstances where it did not seem that the applicant's private law rights were at stake, or that he had suffered special damage, but where no point was taken by the public authority as to the plaintiff's standing on the availability of the remedy (see, *e.g. Prescott v. Birmingham Corporation* [1955] Ch. 210; *Lee v. Department of Education and Science* [1967] 66 L.G.R. 211).

The House of Lords in *Gouriet v. Union of Post Office Workers* [1978] A.C. 435, in a case where the plaintiff was seeking an injunction to restrain a threatened breach of the criminal law by the respondent trade union, reaffirmed that the proper test for *locus standi* was whether the plaintiff's legal rights were at stake, or he had suffered special damage. The position where the respondent was a public authority was not tested before the introduction of the new Order 53.

In the light of this, *O'Reilly v. Mackman* can be interpreted simply as repudiating the generous, but unsoundly based, approach to standing in injunction and declaration cases that was in any event under a cloud following *Gouriet*. As Laws J. stated in *British Steel plc v. Customs and Excise Commissioners* [1996] 1 W.L.R. 1002, 1012–1013:

"Where a complaint sought to be raised in litigation touches only a public law issue, there being no question of a private right involved, the complainant must generally seek his remedy by way of judicial review in the public law court. This is the basic *O'Reilly* principle. Though it looks like a rule of procedure (and has been castigated as a bad one by Sir William Wade), it is in fact a rule of substance, for reasons explained by Lord Diplock in *O'Reilly* itself and underlined by Lord Slynn in *Mercury* [below, p. 657]: namely it would be an abuse of process to litigate such claims by ordinary private law means. The concept of abuse of process is not a function of mere procedural regulation; it is a necessary safeguard against manipulation of court process."

What might have given rise to cause for concern would have been if the new approach had made it more difficult for plaintiffs to vindicate their private law rights where the defendant was a public authority. Subsequent case law has provided some reassurance on the point.

2. The decision of the House of Lords in *Cocks v. Thanet District Council* [1983] 2

A.C. 286 was delivered on the same day as that in *O'Reilly v. Mackman*. In this case, the plaintiff applied to the council, as the local housing authority, for permanent accommodation for himself and his family. The council provided temporary accommodation. The plaintiff commenced proceedings in the county court for a declaration that the council owed and was in breach of its duty under the Housing (Homeless Persons) Act 1977, for consequential mandatory injunctions and for damages. The matter was removed by consent into the High Court, where Milmo J. decided, as a preliminary question, that the plaintiff was entitled to proceed as he was doing, and not limited to proceeding by way of an application for judicial review. In this, the judge was bound by the decision of the Court of Appeal in *De Falco v. Crawley Borough Council* [1980] Q.B. 460. The council appealed directly to the House of Lords, and the House unanimously allowed the appeal. The council's duty to provide accommodation under the housing legislation (the "full housing duty") arose where an applicant was (1) homeless or threatened with homelessness; (2) had a priority need; and (3) had not become homeless intentionally. The issue here was likely ultimately to turn on the question of intentional homelessness. The only speech was delivered by Lord Bridge, who stated that the functions of housing authorities under the legislation fell into two distinct categories.

First, it was for the housing authority to inquire into and decide whether it was satisfied as to the matters that gave rise to the full housing duty. Its decision on these points could only be challenged under the *ultra vires* doctrine on such grounds as, for example, procedural unfairness or abuse of discretion. Once a decision had been reached which gave rise to the full housing duty (or any of the other duties under the legislation),

> "rights and obligations are immediately created in the field of private law. Each of the duties referred to, once established, is capable of being enforced by injunction and the breach of it will give rise to a liability in damages. But it is inherent in the scheme of the Act that an appropriate public law decision of the housing authority is a condition precedent to the establishment of the private law duty" (at 292–293).

The Court of Appeal in *De Falco* (of which Lord Bridge had been a member) had "failed to appreciate the significance" of this dichotomy of functions. Lord Bridge then held that the *O'Reilly v. Mackman* principle was applicable to challenges to decisions as to the existence or otherwise of the "condition precedent" to the private law duty.

Following amendments effected by the Housing and Planning Act 1986, s.14(3), the full housing duty became a duty, *inter alia*, to make available or secure that the applicant obtains "suitable accommodation" (Housing Act 1985, ss.65, 69). In *Mohram Ali v. Tower Hamlets London Borough Council* [1993] Q.B. 407, the Court of Appeal held that the question of whether accommodation was "suitable" fell on the "decision-making" side of the line enunciated by Lord Bridge. This judgement had to be made "before the executive act of securing the suitable accommodation for the applicant can be performed" (Nolan L.J. at 413). The council's public law duties were not complete until it had decided upon the suitable accommodation which it was obliged to secure for the applicant; if this process was properly carried out as a matter of public law, then the consequential private law right "was simply a right to the accommodation which [the council] had decided to be suitable" (at 415). Accordingly, the court struck out proceedings in the county court alleging a breach of statutory duty and claiming an injunction requiring the council to fulfil its duty under the 1985 Act, ss.65 and 69. This was followed by the Court of Appeal in a series of cases.

First, in *London Borough of Tower Hamlets v. Abdi* (1992) 25 H.L.R. 80 a defence and counterclaim to proceedings for the possession of temporary accommodation following refusal of offer of permanent accommodation were struck out; the defence alleged that the refusal of the accommodation was reasonable; the counterclaim sought that the council was in breach of its duty under the 1985 Act. Then in *London*

Borough of Hackney v. Lambourne (1992) 25 H.L.R. 172 a defence to proceedings for the possession of temporary accommodation following refusal of offer of permanent accommodation was struck out; the defence alleged, *inter alia*, that the notice to quit the temporary accommodation was invalid as the council had failed to provide suitable alternative accommodation and was thus in breach of its duties under the 1985 Act. (There had been no challenge to the validity of the notice to quit in *Abdi*.) The decision of the Court of Appeal in *Lambourne* can be supported on the grounds (1) that there was no necessary link between the notice to quit and the Council's decision as to the suitability of the permanent accommodation (Ralph Gibson L.J. at 181; Sir Roger Parker at 187), and (2) that the *Wednesbury* grounds had not been pleaded with sufficient particularity. However, suggestions that the applicants had no private law rights at stake (Ralph Gibson L.J. at 179; Evans L.J. at 186) cannot be supported. As Ralph Gibson L.J. himself stated elsewhere in his judgment (at 179–180), if it could be shown that the notice to quit was unlawful and void, the defendants "could claim to remain in right of the unterminated weekly tenancy of the temporary accommodation". *cf. Wandsworth London Borough Council. v. Winder*, below, p. 658.

Finally, in *R. v. Northavon District Council, ex p. Palmer* (1995) 27 H.L.R. 576, the Court of Appeal carried the logic of *Cocks v. Thanet District Council* to the length of holding that no action for damages for breach of statutory duty lay in respect of a period of time when (it was alleged) the council should have been satisfied as to the existence of the condition precedent but in fact had failed even to recognise the case as one requiring consideration under Part III of the 1985 Act.

> "The applicant cannot...overcome the difficulty...that she cannot recover damages save for breach of a private law duty, that she cannot establish a private law duty until the local authority's public law decision-making function has been concluded and that that (in the absence of a concession) is a function which only it can perform" (*per* Bingham M.R. at 581).

The Court rejected the applicant's argument that the situation—that the council, had it directed itself to the relevant matters, must have concluded that the condition precedent had been satisfied—was to be equated with an actual decision to that effect.

The possibility of an action for damages has now been excluded altogether (see below, pp. 732–733).

3. In *Davy v. Spelthorne Borough Council* (1983) 81 L.G.R. 580, the plaintiff was the owner of premises used to produce precast concrete. In November 1979, he entered an agreement with the defendant (the local planning authority) whereby he undertook not to appeal against an enforcement notice in respect of the use of the premises provided that the notice was not enforced by the authority for a period of three years from the date of service of the notice. In October 1980, a notice was served as contemplated by the agreement, and, *inter alia*, required the removal of buildings. The plaintiff did not appeal against the notice and the time for appealing against it expired. In August 1982, the plaintiff brought an action in the Chancery Division claiming (1) an injunction restraining the council from implementing the enforcement notice, (2) damages for negligent advice alleged to have been given by the council resulting in a failure to appeal against the notice and (3) an order that the enforcement notice be set aside. The Court of Appeal held that claims (1) and (3) should be struck out as an abuse of process as in substance they involved an attack on the validity of the notice and were designed to have the same effect as would be obtained by an order of certiorari or a declaration under Order 53. However, the claim for damages should not be struck out as it was a claim at common law for a breach of duty owned in private law, notwithstanding that it related to the exercise of statutory functions and notwithstanding that in order to obtain a substantial award of damages, he would have to demonstrate that he had lost at least a chance of making out a good defence to the enforcement notice. While such a claim could be brought under Order 53, this would only be permitted at the discretion of the Queen's Bench Division. If there was a successful application out of time for judicial review, all the proceedings should continue

in the Queen's Bench Division; otherwise, the action for damages should proceed in the Chancery Division. The local authority appealed against the refusal of the Court of Appeal to strike out the claim for damages. The House of Lords unanimously dismissed the appeal ([1984] A.C. 262). Lord Fraser of Tullybelton (with whose speech Lords Roskill, Brandon and Brightman agreed) stated that "[i]n the present case ... the respondent does not impugn or wish to overturn the enforcement notice. His whole case on negligence depends on the fact that he has lost his chance to impugn it. In my opinion therefore the general rule stated in *O'Reilly v. Mackman* is inapplicable" (*ibid.*, at 274). The respondent's claim was concerned with the alleged infringement of his rights at common law. Other considerations were (1) that as the notice itself was not now challenged, no public authority or third party was being kept in suspense on that matter and there was accordingly no requirement for a speedy decision; (2) that in any event procedure under Order 53 would be "entirely inappropriate in this case" (*ibid.*, at 274); (3) that if the claim were to be struck out, "the blow to the respondent's chances of recovering damages might well be mortal" (*ibid.*, at 274): the court had no power to order the proceedings to continue as if they had been made under Order 53 and so the respondent would have to seek leave to start proceedings for judicial review, now long out of time; and (4) it was impossible to hold that the true purpose of the claim for damages was only to put pressure on the local authority not to enforce the notice. In his concurring speech, Lord Wilberforce emphasised the point that "[b]efore a proceeding at common law can be said to be an abuse of process, it must, at least, be shown (1) that the claim in question *could* be brought by way of judicial review (2) that it *should* be brought by way of judicial review" (*ibid.*, at 751). In *O'Reilly v. Mackman*, above, it was not argued that the prisoners would not have had a remedy by way of judicial review, and "indeed, as I understand the case, they would not have had a remedy in private law at all" (*ibid.*). The claim in the present case neither could nor should be brought by way of judicial review.

The case is of significance at two levels. First, the House of Lords' decision to refuse to strike out claim (2) made it clear that the courts would be reluctant to apply the principle of *O'Reilly v. Mackman* to interfere with what was one of the classic forms of a private right of action: an action for damages in tort. However, could it not also be said that the authority's decision to serve an enforcement notice involved at least a potential interference with private rights? If the plaintiff did not comply with the notice, he could be prosecuted for a criminal offence. Moreover, the local authority could have entered the land and itself undertaken the work necessary for compliance with the notice. Can it be argued that the Court of Appeal's decision in this case takes matters one step beyond *O'Reilly v. Mackman*?

The decision of the House of Lords was echoed in *Roy v. Kensington and Chelsea and Westminster Family Practitioner Committee* [1992] 1 A.C. 624 where the House of Lords refused to strike out part of an action based on the plaintiff's private law rights to be paid for work done. Lord Lowry (at 653) expressed a preference for a "broad approach" under which *O'Reilly v. Mackman* "merely required the aggrieved person to proceed by judicial review only when private law rights were not at stake"; however, the case was decided on a "narrow approach", under which it was to be regarded as an exception to the principle. His Lordship concluded (at 654–655):

"Whichever approach one adopts, the arguments for excluding the present case from the ambit of the rule or, in the alternative, making an exception of it are similar and to my mind convincing.
(1) Dr Roy has either a contractual or a statutory private law right to his remuneration in accordance with his statutory terms of service.
(2) Although he seeks to enforce performance of a public law duty under paragraph 12.1, his private law rights dominate the proceedings.
(3) The type of claim and other claims for remuneration (although not this particular claim) may involve disputed issues of fact.

(4) The order sought (for the payment of money due) could not be granted on judicial review.

(5) The claim is joined with another claim which is fit to be brought in an action (and has already been successfully prosecuted.)

(6) When individual rights are claimed, there should not be a need for leave or a special time limit, nor should the relief be discretionary.

(7) The action should be allowed to proceed unless it is plainly an abuse of process.

(8) The cases... show that the rule in *O'Reilly v. Mackman* [1983] 2 A.C. 237, assuming it to be a rule of general application, is subject to many exceptions based on the nature of the claim and on the undesirability of erecting procedural barriers. ...

In conclusion, my Lords, it seems to me that, unless the procedure adopted by the moving party is ill suited to dispose of the question at issue, there is much to be said in favour of the proposition that a court having jurisdiction ought to let a case be heard rather than entertain a debate concerning the form of the proceedings."

See I. Hare [1992] C.L.J. 203; S. Fredman and G. Morris (1992) 108 L.Q.R. 353; P. Cane [1992] P.L. 193; A. Tanney (1993) 56 M.L.R. 575. Note the helpful interpretation of *Roy* by Laws J. in *Bristol Steel plc v. Customs and Excise Commissioners* [1996] 1 All E.R. 1002, 1013:

"Where a claimant enjoys a private right whose existence is not contingent upon the making of a prior public law decision in his favour (in Lord Bridge's words in *Cocks*, where there is no such 'condition precedent' to the right), the claimant may sue at private law even though he must assault an administrative or discretionary decision on the way (see *Roy*). Here again, the concept at the root of this jurisprudence, abuse of process, is in play. If the plaintiff stands in a relationship with the defendant whereby he enjoys a settled and existing private right, it cannot be abusive that he should seek to make it good by ordinary action merely because its value or quantification depends upon the defendant's opinion as to certain aspects given to him to decide."

(The Court of Appeal ([1997] 2 All E.R. 366) subsequently allowed on appeal, but did not criticise this statement.)

Similarly, in *Mercury Communications Ltd v. Director General of Communications* [1995] 1 W.L.R. 48, the House of Lords refused to strike out an originating summons seeking a declaration as to the true construction of phrases in a condition attached to BT's licence to run a telecommunications system granted by the Secretary of State under section 7 of the Telecommunications Act 1984. The dispute in substance and in form was as to the effect of the terms of a contract between Mercury and BT even if it could also be expressed as a dispute as to the terms of the licence. Lord Slynn stated (at 57) that "It is of particular importance... to retain some flexiblity as the precise limits of what is called 'public law', and what is called 'private law' are by no means worked out." The procedure by way of originating summons in the Commercial Court was at least as well and might be better suited to the determination of these issues as judicial review. In any event, in dealing with the summons, the trial judge could "have regard to, even if he is not strictly bound by, the procedural protection which would be available to a public authority under the provisions of Order 53" (*per* Lord Slynn at 58). See A. McHarg [1995] P.L. 539.

4. In *O'Reilly v. Mackman*, Lord Diplock stated (at 285) that an exception might be made "where the invalidity of the decision arises as a collateral issue in a claim for infringement of a right of the plaintiff arising under private law". Subsequent case law has shown that the *O'Reilly v. Mackman* principle does not apply to prevent the

invalidity of a decision being raised as a defence to enforcement proceedings. The point
has arisen in both civil and criminal cases.

The leading authority in civil cases in *Wandsworth London Borough Council v.
Winder* [1985] A.C. 461. W occupied a flat let by the council on a secure tenancy. In
1981 and 1982 the council, in exercise of its powers under the Housing Act 1957,
resolved to increase council rents. On each occasion, W regarded the increase as
unreasonable and paid only such rent as he considered reasonable. The council took
proceedings in the county court claiming arrears of rent, and also claiming possession
of the premises on the ground that the rent lawfully due had not been paid. W defended
the action on the ground that the decisions increasing the rent were *ultra vires* and void
as being unreasonable. He also counterclaimed for a declaration that the notices of
increases of rent were *ultra vires* and void, and for a declaration that the rent payable
was the old rent. The registrar dismissed the council's application to strike out the
paragraphs of the defence and counterclaim that asserted that the decisions were void.
The county court judge allowed the council's appeal, but stayed the proceedings to
allow W to seek leave to apply for judicial review out of time. (W's application for
leave was refused.) The Court of Appeal (Robert Goff and Parker L.JJ., Ackner L.J.
dissenting) then allowed W's appeal against the order of the county court judge. The
council's further appeal to the House of Lords was dismissed.

The sole speech was delivered by Lord Fraser. His Lordship noted that there were
two important differences between the facts of *O'Reilly v. Mackman* and the present
case. First, the plaintiffs in *O'Reilly v. Mackman* "had not suffered any infringement
of their rights in private law" whereas here "what the respondent complains of is the
infringement of a contractual right in private law" (at 507). Until April 6, 1981, W
"had a contractual right to occupy the flat, provided he paid the rent of £12.06 and
complied with the other terms of the tenancy" (at 505). The terms could only be varied
by a notice that, *inter alia*, was not unreasonable in the *Wednesbury* sense. The second
difference was that "in *O'Reilly* the prisoners had initiated the proceedings . . . while in
the present case the respondent is the defendant" (at 507). *Cocks v. Thanet District
Council* was also distinguishable: the impugned decision in that case "did not deprive
the plaintiff of a pre-existing private law right; it prevented him from establishing a
new private law right", moreover "the party complaining of the decision was the
plaintiff" (at 508).

Lord Fraser did *not*, however, regard the case as falling with any of the exceptions
mentioned by Lord Diplock in *O'Reilly v. Mackman*. In particular, the invalidity of
the council's decision was not "truly collateral to the issue between the parties . . . [I]t is
the whole basis of the respondent's defence and it is the central issue which has to be
decided."

Nevertheless, the principle underlying *O'Reilly v. Mackman* and *Cocks v. Thanet
District Council* was not applicable (at 510–511):

"The main argument urged on behalf of the appellants was that this is a typical case
where there is a need for speedy certainty in the public interest. I accept, of course,
that the decision in this appeal will indirectly affect many third parties including
many of the appellants' tenants, and perhaps most if not all of their ratepayers
because if the appellants' impugned decisions are held to be invalid, the basis of their
financial administration since 1981 will be upset. That would be highly inconvenient from the point of view of the appellants, and of their ratepayers, and it
would be a great advantage to them if persons such as the respondent who seek to
challenge their decision were limited to doing so by procedure under Order 53. It
may well be that such protection to public authorities tends to promote good administration. But there may be other ways of obtaining speedy decisions; for example in
some cases it may be possible for a public authority itself to initiate proceedings for
judicial review. In any event, the arguments for protecting public authorities against
unmeritorious or dilatory challenges to their decisions have to be set against the

arguments for preserving the ordinary rights of private citizens to defend themselves against unfounded claims.

It would in my opinion be a very strange use of language to describe the respondent's behaviour in relation to this litigation as an abuse or misuse by him of the process of the court. He did not select the procedure to be adopted. He is merely seeking to defend proceedings brought against him by the appellants. In so doing he is seeking only to exercise the ordinary right of any individual to defend an action against him on the ground that he is not liable for the whole sum claimed by the plaintiff. Moreover he puts forward his defence as a matter of right, whereas in an application for judicial review, success would require an exercise of the court's discretion in his favour. Apart from the provisions of Order 53 and section 31 of the Supreme Court Act 1981, he would certainly be entitled to defend the action on the ground that the plaintiff's claim arises from a resolution which (on his view) is invalid: see for example *Cannock Chase District Council v. Kelly* [1978] 1 W.L.R. 1, which was decided in July 1977, a few months before Order 53 came into force (as it did in December 1977). I find it impossible to accept that the right to challenge the decision of a local authority in course of defending an action for non-payment can have been swept away by Order 53, which was directed to introducing a procedural reform. As my noble and learned friend Lord Scarman said in *R. v. Inland Revenue Commissioners, ex p. Federation of Self Employed and Small Businesses Ltd* [1982] A.C. 617, 647G, 'The new R.S.C., Ord. 53 is a procedural reform of great importance in the field of public law, but it does not—indeed, cannot—either extend or diminish the substantive law. Its function is limited to ensuring "ubi jus, ibi remedium." ' Lord Wilberforce spoke to the same effect at 631A. Nor, in my opinion, did section 31 of the Supreme Court Act 1981 which refers only to "an application" for judicial review have the effect of limiting the rights of a defendant sub silentio. I would adopt the words of Viscount Simonds in *Pyx Granite Co. Ltd v. Ministry of Housing and Local Government* [1960] A.C. 260, 286 as follows:

'It is a principle not by any means to be whittled down that the subject's recourse to Her Majesty's courts for the determination of his rights is not to be excluded except by clear words.'

The argument of the appellants in the present case would be directly in conflict with that observation.

If the public interest requires that persons should not be entitled to defend actions brought against them by public authorities, where the defence rests on a challenge to a decision by the public authority, then it is for Parliament to change the law."

(Having been allowed to raise it, Mr Winder's defence was in the event unsuccessful: *Wandsworth London Borough Council v. Winder (No. 2)* (1987) 19 H.L.R. 204.)

Wandsworth London Borough Council v. Winder was distinguished by the Court of Appeal in *Avon County Council v. Buscott and Others* [1988] 2 Q.B. 656. Here, the respondents to eviction proceedings brought by the council were held not to be entitled to resist them on the ground that the council's decision to institute them was unreasonable in the *Wednesbury* sense. The respondent conceded that they were trespassers and that they had no defence on the merits. Accordingly they were not seeking to protect their legal rights and it was this factor that distinguished the case from *Winder*. *Winder* was also distinguished in *Waverley Borough Council v. Hilden* [1988] 1 W.L.R. 246, where Scott J. held that where a defendant to proceedings for an injunction commenced by a local authority under section 222 of the Local Government Act 1972 sought to argue that the decision to proceed under section 222 was *ultra vires*, that challenge had to be by way of an application for judicial review. It did not amount to a substantive defence to the enforcement proceedings.

5. The principle of *O'Reilly v. Mackman*, above, does not prevent the defendant in a criminal case relying on the *ultra vires* doctrine in conducting his defence. For example, in *R. v. Jenner* [1983] 1 W.L.R. 873 the Court of Appeal (Criminal Division) quashed the appellant's conviction for contravention of a stop notice issued under section 90 of the Town and Country Planning Act 1971 on the ground that he had not been permitted to argue in his defence that the stop notice was invalid. The Court rejected the prosecution's argument that the only way by which the appellant could challenge the validity of the notice was by applying for judicial review. *Per* Watkins L.J. at 877:

> "The process of judicial review, which rarely allows of the reception of oral evidence, is not suited to resolving the issues of fact involved in deciding whether activity said to be prohibited by it is caught by section 90. These issues could not possibly be decided upon the contents of affidavits which is the form of evidence usually received by the Divisional Court."

However, recent cases have held that apart from any question of abuse of process, courts other than the High Court on an application for judicial review may not have *jurisdiction* to deal with allegations that an act is *ultra vires* unless the act is bad on its face ("substantively invalid"): see below, pp. 778–788.

6. The position where it is the public authority asserting the defence of statutory authority was considered by the Court of Appeal in *The Great House of Sonning Ltd v. Berkshire County Council* [1996] R.T.R. 407. The Court (Hutchison and Nourse L.J., Saville L.J. dissenting) held that where the council relied on an order temporarily closing a road made under the Road Traffic Regulation Act 1984, as a defence to claims in public nuisance brought by businesses affected by the closure, the matter had to proceed by judicial review. *Per* Hutchison L.J. (at 412):

> "The order prevents that obstruction from being a nuisance, unless and until it is set aside. There is, thus, ... no private law right that, so long as this order stands, the plaintiffs can assert."

It is submitted that the dissent of Saville L.J. (at 413) is to be preferred:

> "The plaintiffs' claim does not depend on proving that the local authority was unauthorised by statute to obstruct the highway, but merely requires proof that the public authority is threatening to obstruct the highway so as to cause them ... serious damage."

It was then for the local authority to establish the defence of statutory authority "if it can".

7. Other cases decided after *O'Reilly v. Mackman*, where private actions have been struck out as an abuse of process include: *Luxclose Ltd v. London Borough of Hammersmith and Fulham* [1983] J.P.L. 662; *London Borough of Wandsworth v. Orakpo* (1986) 19 H.L.R. 57; *G. v. Hounslow London Borough Council* (1987) 86 L.G.R. 186; *Allen v. Chief Constable of Cheshire, The Times*, July 18, 1988 (injunction set aside by the Court of Appeal).

Cases where private actions have not been struck out include: *An Bord Bainne Co-operative Ltd (Irish Dairy Board) v. Milk Marketing Board* [1984] 1 C.M.L.R. 519 (decisions in the public law field alleged to constitute infringements of directly effective

EEC regulations which created direct rights in private law: these rights could be protected in the same way as an individual could in certain cases sue for breach of statutory duty) affirmed: [1984] 2 CMLR 584, C.A.; *Ettridge v. Morrell* (1986) 85 L.G.R. 100 (candidate's right to use of school room under s.96(1) of the Representation of the People Act 1983 enforceable in private law); *Doyle v. Northumbria Probation Committee* [1991] 4 All E.R. 294 (action for breach of contract not struck out where the respondent raised a public law defence at a time when the plaintiff was out of time to proceed by judicial review).

8. In *O'Reilly v. Mackman*, Lord Diplock indicated (above, p. 652) that ordinary proceedings might be brought by agreement. In *Inner London Education Authority v. Department of the Environment* (1983) 82 L.G.R. 322, Woolf J. heard proceedings for a declaration commenced by originating summons, in respect of the issue whether I.L.E.A. was a "local authority" for the purpose of Part III of the Local Government, Planning and Land Act 1980. No objection was taken to this course and the matter was set down in the Crown Office list. See also *Gillick v. West Norfolk and Wisbech Area Health Authority* [1986] A.C. 112, *per* Lord Scarman at at 177–178. (Conversely, a private law matter cannot be brought under Order 53 by agreement: *R. v. Durham County Council, ex p. Robinson, The Times*, January 31, 1992.)

9. Academic reaction to the *O'Reilly v. Mackman* principle has generally been critical. There are several themes. On the assumption that both a civil action and an application for judicial review were technically available, for

> "a complainant, whether against a public authority or not, to find his complaint dismissed without an investigation of its merits, not on the ground that it is without substance ... not even on the ground that he lacks *locus standi*, but purely and simply because he selected the wrong form of action is a singularly unfortunate step back to the technicalities of a bygone age."

(J.A. Jolowicz [1983] C.L.J. 15, 18). (*cf.* H.W.R. Wade (1995) 101 L.Q.R. 180, 187: "The overall picture is one of waste of time and money on litigation merely about procedure"; S. Fredman and G.S. Morris [1994] P.L. 69, 80: "[L]itigants are tempted to use the confusion for tactical advantage.")

The line between "public law" and "private law" is widely recognised as difficult to draw, the cases summarised in the previous notes failing to provide clear and convincing guidance. See the discussion by J. Beatson, " 'Public' and 'Private' in Administrative Law" (1987) 103 L.Q.R. 34; C.F. Forsyth, "Beyond *O'Reilly v. Mackman*: The Foundations and Nature of Procedural Exclusivity" [1985] C.L.J. 415; G.L. Peiris, "The Exclusivity of Judicial Review Procedure: The Growing Boundary Dispute" (1986) 15 Anglo-Am.L.R. 83; *Lewis*, Chap. 3; S. Fredman and G.S. Morris, "The Costs of Exclusivity: Public and Private Re-examined" [1994] P.L. 69. The point is well illustrated by the cases in the section on the scope of Order 53 (above, pp. 605–634).

A third line of criticism addresses the twin assumptions that underlie the present state of the law: (1) that public authorities need the special safeguards inherent in the Order 53 procedure; but (2) that the vindication of private rights ought not to be encumbered by the restrictions that apply in consequence to litigants. If the safeguards are really necessary in the public interest why should they not apply also to private actions against public authorities (*cf. Craig*, p. 583). Why should interests protected by public law be regarded as less important than private law rights?

> "... [W]hen one considers the subject-matter of some of the public law interests which have generated litigation (*e.g.* remission of sentence, obtaining council housing) this assumption appears absurd" (*Cane*, p. 95).

The present difficulties have been said to be the "inevitable" result of the recommendations of the Law Commission: a new procedure with safeguards for public authorities was to be set up, but was not to be exclusive (Wade (1985) 101 L.Q.R. 180, 187.

If the differences between public law and private law had been exaggerated the appropriate move would presumably be towards greater assimilation of public law and private law procedures. It has been argued that the proper approach would be:

> "to fit the prerogative remedies into the mechanism of an ordinary action, so that there would be no dichotomy and no dilemma for the litigant" (Wade (1985) 101 L.Q.R. 180, 189).

There would then be one single form of action covering both public and private law; there would be no leave requirement, but the respondent authority could apply for an expedited procedure incorporating the appropriate Order 53 safeguards, such as the time limits (Wade, *op. cit.* pp. 189–190, *cf. Craig*, pp. 590–591). A variant of this is suggested by Cane. On the assumption that public bodies need special protection (which is itself questionable), every applicant for a remedy against a public body or in relation to the exercise of public functions would need first to obtain leave. If no public law issues were raised, private law procedure would then be followed and the *litigant* would choose whether to proceed by writ (where there were substantial disputes of fact) or originating summons (otherwise). If public law issues were involved the *court* would choose which of two procedural tracks should apply, one suitable for cases raising substantial factual disputes, the other for cases where there were no such disputes (*Cane*, pp. 101–102).

The JUSTICE/All Souls Review of Administrative Law in the United Kingdom (*Administrative Justice: Some Necessary Reforms* (1988), Chap. 6) concluded that *O'Reilly v. Mackman* was an unfortunate decision. "All" the disadvantages associated with the prerogative orders had not been removed; objectionable features survived (the need to obtain leave, the shortness of the time-limit, little change in the old attitudes unfavourable to discovery and cross-examination on affidavit evidence (see pp. 638–639)); a clear-cut distinction could not be drawn between public law and private law rights. The Committee also recommended that the leave requirement should be abandoned; that the three-month time-limit should be repealed, and matter of delay left on the more general basis provided by the Supreme Court Act 1981, s.31(6) (above, p.605, below, pp.679–687); discovery of documents, interrogatories and cross-examination should be permitted more liberally; provision should be made enabling the court to order that proceedings wrongly commenced by writ should continue as if they were an application for judicial review. Only some of these have subsequently been endorsed by the Law Commission (see below, pp. 706–708).

10. For other comments see J. McBride (1983) 2 C.J.Q. 268; M. Sunkin (1983) 46 M.L.R. 645; H.W.R. Wade (1983) 99 L.Q.R. 199; A. Grubb [1983] P.L. 190; P. Cane [1983] P.L. 202 (on *O'Reilly* and *Cocks*); A. Grubb [1983] C.L.J. 16; P. Cane [1984] P.L. 16 (on *Davy v. Spelthorne*); C.F. Forsyth [1985] P.L. 355; A. Grubb (1985) 101 L.Q.R. 486 (on *Winder*); C.T. Emery [1992] C.L.J 308; Sir Henry Woolf [1992] P.L. 221; J. Alder, "Hunting the Chimera—The End of *O'Reilly v. Mackman*" (1993) 13 L.S. 183 (arguing that the decision in *Roy* renders the *O'Reilly v. Mackman* principle "virtually meaningless. Ord. 53 is exclusive only where no private rights are involved at all, that is in cases where no ordinary action would be possible anyway" (at 202); A. Tanney, "Procedural Exclusivity in Administrative Law" [1994] P.L. 51 (disagreeing with Alder on the basis that Lord Lowry in *Roy* actually adopted the narrow approach to *O'Reilly v. Mackman* "leaving the possibility that Ord. 53 is compulsory even in some cases involving a mixture of public and priate rights" (at 61)).

(F) STANDING

R. v. INLAND REVENUE COMMISSIONERS, ex p. NATIONAL FEDERATION OF SELF-EMPLOYED AND SMALL BUSINESSES LTD

[1982] A.C. 617; [1981] 2 W.L.R. 722; [1981] 2 All E.R. 93
(House of Lords)

Some 6,000 casual workers in Fleet Street were nominated by their trade unions to work for newspapers on specified occasions. They were given call slips and then collected pay dockets to enable them to draw their pay from their employers but a substantial number of them gave false names and addresses (*e.g.* "Mickey Mouse of Sunset Boulevard" and "Sir Gordon Richards of Tattenham Corner") so that it was impossible for the Inland Revenue to collect the tax which was due from them. The consequent loss to the revenue was estimated at £1 million a year. In view of the frauds, the Inland Revenue after discussions with the employers and the unions, introduced a special arrangement which would ensure that for the future tax would either be deducted at source or be properly assessed and made it clear that, if the arrangement were generally accepted, and subject to certain other conditions, investigation into tax lost in certain previous years would not be carried out. A federation representing the self-employed and small businesses, who contrasted the attitude taken by the revenue to the tax evasions of the Fleet Street casuals with that adopted by the revenue in other cases where tax evasions were suspected, applied for judicial review and claimed a declaration that the Inland Revenue acted unlawfully in granting the amnesty and an order of mandamus directed to the revenue to assess and collect income tax from the casual workers.

The Divisional Court granted leave *ex parte*, but at the hearing *inter partes*, on the Inland Revenue's objection that the federation had no *locus standi*, the Divisional Court held that the federation had not "sufficient interest" within R.S.C., Ord. 53, r. 3(5), to claim the declaration and order sought.

On the federation's appeal, which proceeded on the assumption that the Inland Revenue had no power to grant such a tax "amnesty", the Court of Appeal (by a majority) allowed the appeal ([1980] Q.B. 407) holding that the body of taxpayers represented by the federation could reasonably assert that they had a genuine grievance in the alleged failure of the Inland Revenue to do its duty and the granting of an unlawful tax indulgence to the casual workers, and accordingly they had a "sufficient interest" within the meaning of R.S.C., Ord. 53, r. 3(5) to apply for judicial review under that order.

The Inland Revenue appealed to the House of Lords and the House unanimously allowed their appeal.

LORD WILBERFORCE: . . . [noted that the question of *locus standi* had been taken as a preliminary point of law, and continued:] I think that it is unfortunate that this course has been taken. There may be simple cases in which it can be seen at the earliest stage that the person applying for judicial review has no interest at all, or no sufficient interest to support the application: then it would be quite correct at the threshold to refuse him leave to apply. The right to do so is an important safeguard against the courts being flooded and public bodies harassed by irresponsible applications. But in other cases this will not be so. In these it will be necessary to consider the powers or the duties in law of those against whom the relief is asked, the position of the applicant in relation to those powers or duties, and to the breach of those said to have been committed. In other words, the question of sufficient interest can not, in such cases, be considered in the abstract, or as an isolated point: it must be taken together with the legal and factual context. The rule requires sufficient interest *in the matter to which the application relates*. This, in the present case, necessarily involves the whole question of the duties of the Inland Revenue and the breaches or failure of those duties of which the respondents complain.

Before proceeding to consideration of these matters, something more needs to be said about the threshold requirement of "sufficient interest". The courts in exercising the power to grant prerogative writs, or, since 1938, prerogative orders, have always reserved the right to be satisfied that the applicant had some genuine *locus standi* to appear before it. This they expressed in different ways. Sometimes it was said, usually in relation to certiorari, that the applicant must be a person aggrieved; or having a particular grievance (*R. v. Thames Magistrates' Court, ex p. Greenbaum* (1957) 55 L.G.R. 129); usually in relation to mandamus, that he must have a specific legal right (*R. v. Lewisham Union Guardians* [1897] 1 Q.B. 498 and *R. v. Russell, ex p. Beaverbrook Newspapers Ltd* [1969] 1 Q.B. 342); sometimes that he must have a sufficient interest (*R. v. Cotham* [1898] 1 Q.B. 802, 804 (mandamus), *ex p. Stott* [1916] 1 K.B. 7 (certiorari)). By 1977, when R.S.C., Ord. 53 was introduced, the courts, guided by Lord Parker C.J., in cases where mandamus was sought, were moving away from the *Lewisham Union* test of specific legal right, to one of sufficient interest. In *R. v. Russell* Lord Parker had tentatively adhered to the test of legal specific right but in *R. v. Customs and Excise Commissioners, ex p. Cook* [1970] 1 W.L.R. 450 he had moved to sufficient interest. Shortly afterward the new rule (R.S.C., Ord. 53, r. 3) was drafted with these words.

R.S.C., Ord. 53 was, it is well known, introduced to simplify the procedure of applying for the relief formerly given by prerogative writ or order—so the old technical rules no longer apply. So far as the substantive law is concerned, this remained unchanged: the Administration of Justice (Miscellaneous Provisions) Act 1938 preserved the jurisdiction existing before the Act, and the same preservation is contemplated by legislation now pending. The Order, furthermore, did not remove the requirement to show *locus standi*. On the contrary, in rule 3, it stated this in the form of a threshold requirement to be found by the court. For all cases the test is expressed as one of sufficient interest in the matter to which the application relates. As to this I would state two negative propositions. First, it does not remove the whole—and vitally important—question of *locus standi* into the realm of pure discretion. The matter is one for decision, a mixed decision of fact and law, which the court must decide on legal principles. Secondly, the fact that the same words are used to cover all the forms of remedy allowed by the rule does not mean that the test is the same in all cases. When Lord Parker C.J. said that in cases of mandamus the test may well be stricter (sc. than in certiorari)—the *Beaverbrook Newspapers* case [1969] 1 Q.B. 342 and in *Cook's* case [1970] 1 W.L.R. 450, 455F, "on a very strict basis", he was not stating a technical rule—which can now be discarded—but a rule of common sense, reflecting the different character of the relief asked for. It would seem obvious enough that the interest of a person seeking to compel an authority to carry out a duty is different from that of a person complaining that a judicial or administrative body has, to his detriment, exceeded its powers. Whether one calls for a stricter rule than the other may be a linguistic point: they are certainly different and we should be unwise in our enthusiasm for liberation from procedural fetters to discard reasoned authorities which illustrate this. It is hardly necessary to add that recognition of the value of guiding authorities does not mean that the process of judicial review must stand still.

In the present case we are in the area of mandamus—an alleged failure to perform a duty. It was submitted by the Lord Advocate that in such cases we should be guided by the definition of the duty, in this case statutory, and inquire whether expressly, or by implication, this definition indicates—or the contrary—that the complaining applicant is within the scope or ambit of the duty. I think that this is at least a good working rule though perhaps not an exhaustive one.

The Inland Revenue Commissioners are a statutory body. Their duties are, relevantly, defined in the Inland Revenue Regulation Act 1890 and the Taxes Management Act 1970.

... [I]t is clear that the Inland Revenue Commissioners are not immune from the process of judicial review. They are an administrative body with statutory duties, which the courts, in principle, can supervise. They have indeed done so—see *R. v. Income Tax Special Commissioners* (1881) 21 Q.B.D. 313 (mandamus) and *Income Tax Special Commissioners v. Linsleys (Established 1894) Ltd* [1958] A.C. 569, where it was not doubted that a mandamus could be issued if the facts had been right. It must follow from these cases and from principle that a taxpayer would not be excluded from seeking judicial review if he could show that the revenue had either failed in its statutory duty toward him or had been guilty of some action which was an abuse of their powers or outside their powers altogether. Such a collateral attack—as contrasted with a direct appeal on law to the courts—would no doubt be rare, but the possibility certainly exists.

The position of other taxpayers—other than the taxpayers whose assessment is in question—and their right to challenge the revenue's assessment or non-assessment of that taxpayer, must be judged according to whether, consistently with the legislation, they can be considered as having sufficient interest to complain of what has been done or omitted. I proceed thereto to examine the revenue's duties in that light.

These duties are expressed in very general terms and it is necessary to take account also of the framework of the income tax legislation. This establishes that the commissioners must assess each individual taxpayer in relation to his circumstances. Such assessments and all information regarding taxpayers' affairs are strictly confidential. There is no list or record of assessments which can be inspected by other taxpayers. Nor is there any common fund of the produce of income tax in which income taxpayers as a whole can be said to have any interest. The produce of income tax, together with that of other inland revenue taxes, is paid into the consolidated fund which is at the disposal of Parliament for any purposes that Parliament thinks fit.

The position of taxpayers is therefore very different from that of ratepayers. As explained in *Arsenal Football Club Ltd v. Ende* [1979] A.C. 1, the amount of rates assessed upon ratepayers is ascertainable by the public through the valuation list. The produce of rates goes into a common fund applicable for the benefit of the ratepayers. Thus any ratepayer has an interest, direct and sufficient, in the rates levied upon other ratepayers; for this reason, his right as a "person aggrieved" to challenge assessments upon them has long been recognised and is so now in section 69 of the General Rate Act 1967. This right was given effect to in the *Arsenal* case.

The structure of the legislation relating to income tax, on the other hand, makes clear that no corresponding right is extended to be conferred upon taxpayers. Not only is there no express or implied provision in the legislation upon which such a right could be claimed, but to allow it would be subversive of the whole system, which involves that the commissioners' duties are to the Crown, and that matters relating to income tax are between the commissioners and the taxpayer concerned. No other person is given any right to make proposals about the tax payable by any individual: he cannot even inquire as to such tax. The total confidentiality of assessments and of negotiations between individuals and the revenue is a vital element in the working of the system. As a matter of general principle I would hold that one taxpayer has no sufficient interest in asking the court to investigate the tax affairs of another taxpayer or to complain that the latter has been under-assessed or over-assessed: indeed, there is a strong public interest that he should not. And this principle applies equally to groups of taxpayers: an aggregate of individuals each of whom has no interest cannot of itself have an interest.

That a case can never arise in which the acts or abstentions of the revenue can be brought before the court I am certainly not prepared to assert, nor that, in a case of sufficient gravity, the court might not be able to hold that another taxpayer or other taxpayers could challenge them. Whether this situation has been reached or not must depend upon an examination, upon evidence, of what breach of duty or illegality is alleged. Upon this, and relating it to the position of the complainant, the court has to make its decision.

[His Lordship examined the evidence and concluded that the arrangements in question had been entered by the Inland Revenue, acting genuinely in the care and management of the taxes, under the powers entrusted to them.]

Looking at the matter as a whole, I am of opinion that the Divisional Court, while justified on the *ex parte* application in granting leave, ought, having regard to the nature of "the matter" raised, to have held that the federation had shown no sufficient interest in that matter to justify its application for relief. I would therefore allow the appeal and order that the originating motion be dismissed.

LORD DIPLOCK: . . . The whole purpose of requiring that leave should first be obtained to make the application for judicial review would be defeated if the court were to go into the matter in any depth at that stage. If, on a quick perusal of the material then available, the court thinks that it discloses what might on further consideration turn out to be an arguable case in favour of granting to the applicant the relief claimed, it ought, in the exercise of a judicial discretion, to give him leave to apply for that relief. The discretion that the court is exercising at this stage is not the same as that which it is called upon to exercise when all the evidence is in and the matter has been fully argued at the hearing of the application.

The analysis to which . . . the relevant legislation has been subjected by some of your Lordships, . . . mean that occasions will be very rare on which an individual taxpayer (or pressure group of taxpayers) will be able to show a sufficient interest to justify an application for judicial review of the way in which the revenue has dealt with the tax affairs of any taxpayer other than the applicant himself.

Rare though they may be, however, if, in the instant case, what at the threshold stage was suspicion only had been proved at the hearing of the application for judicial review to have been true in fact (instead of being utterly destroyed), I would have held that this was a matter in which the federation had a sufficient interest in obtaining an appropriate order, whether by way of declaration or mandamus, to require performance by the board of statutory duties which for reasons shown to be *ultra vires* it was failing to perform.

It would, in my view, be a grave lacuna in our system of public law if a pressure group, like the federation, or even a single public-spirited taxpayer, were prevented by outdated technical rules of *locus standi* from bringing the matter to the attention of the court to vindicate the rule of law and get the unlawful conduct stopped. The Attorney-General, although he occasionally applies for prerogative orders against public authorities that do not form part of central government, in practice never does so against government departments. It is not, in my view, a sufficient answer to say that judicial review of the actions of officers or departments of central government is unnecessary because they are accountable to Parliament for the way in which they carry out their functions. They are accountable to Parliament for what they do so far as regards efficiency and policy, and of that Parliament is the only judge; they are responsible to a court of justice for the lawfulness of what they do, and of that the court is the only judge.

I would allow this appeal upon the ground upon which, in my view, the Divisional Court should have dismissed it when the application came to be heard, instead of singling out the lack of a sufficient interest on the part of the federation, *viz.* that the federation completely failed to show any conduct by the board that was *ultra vires* or unlawful.

LORD FRASER: .... I agree with the reasoning of Lord Wilberforce and Lord Roskill but I wish to explain my reasons in my own words.... The rules of court give no guidance as to what is a sufficient interest for this purpose. I respectfully accept from my noble and learned friends who are so much more familiar than I am with the history of the prerogative orders that little assistance as to the sufficiency of the interest can be derived from the older cases. But while the standard of sufficiency has been relaxed in recent years, the need to have an interest has remained and the fact that R.S.C., Ord. 53, r. 3 requires a sufficient interest undoubtedly shows that not every applicant is entitled to judicial review as of right.

The new Order 53, introduced in 1977, no doubt had the effect of removing technical and procedural differences between the prerogative orders, and of introducing a remedy by way of declaration or injunction in suitable cases, but I do not think it can have had the effect of throwing over all the older law and of leaving the grant of judicial review in the uncontrolled discretion of the court. On what principle, then, is the sufficiency of interest to be judged? All are agreed that a direct financial or legal interest is not now required, and that the requirement of a legal specific interest laid down in *R. v. Lewisham Union Guardians* [1897] 1 Q.B. 488 is no longer applicable. There is also general agreement that a mere busybody does not have a sufficient interest. The difficulty is, in between those extremes, to distinguish between the desire of the busybody to interfere in other people's affairs and the interest of the person affected by or having a reasonable concern with the matter to which the application relates. In the present case that matter is an alleged failure by the appellants to perform the duty imposed upon them by statute.

The correct approach in such a case is, in my opinion, to look at the statute under which the duty arises, and to see whether it gives any express or implied right to persons in the position of the applicant to complain of the alleged unlawful act or omission. On that approach it is easy to see that a ratepayer would have a sufficient interest to complain of unlawfulness by the authorities responsible for collecting the rates.... The position of the taxpayer is entirely different...

[I]f the class of persons with a sufficient interest is to include all taxpayers it must include practically every individual in the country who has his own income, because there must be few individuals, however frugal their requirements, who do not pay some indirect taxes including value added tax. It would, I think, be extravagant to suggest that every taxpayer who believes that the Inland Revenue or the Commissioners of Customs and Excise are giving unlawful preference to another taxpayer, and who feels aggrieved thereby, has a sufficient interest to obtain judicial review under Order 53. It may be that, if he was relying on some exceptionally grave or widespread illegality, he could succeed in establishing a sufficient interest, but such cases would be very rare indeed and this is not one of them.

LORD SCARMAN:... In your Lordships' House the Lord Advocate, who now appears for the appellants, the Inland Revenue Commissioners,... has put at the forefront of his argument a reasoned analysis of the statutory duties of the revenue, and has invited the House to hold that the statutory code neither recognises nor imposes upon the revenue a duty such as the federation alleges to the general body, or any group of taxpayers.

Before I consider this submission, it is necessary to deal with a subsidiary point taken by the Lord Advocate. He submitted that, notwithstanding the language of R.S.C., Ord. 53, r. 1(2), the court has no jurisdiction to grant to a private citizen a declaration save in respect of a private right or wrong: and he relied on the House's decision in *Gouriet v. Union of Post Office Workers* [1978] A.C. 435. Declaration is, of course, a remedy developed by the judges in the field of private law. *Gouriet's* case is authority for the proposition that a citizen may not issue a writ claiming a declaration or other relief against another for the redress of a public wrong unless he can persuade the Attorney-General, on his "relation", to bring the action. The case has nothing to do with the prerogative jurisdiction of the High Court; and it was decided before the introduction of the new Order 53, at a time when a declaration could not be obtained by a private citizen unless he could show (as in a claim for injunction) that a private right of his was threatened or infringed. The new Order has made the remedy available as an alternative, or an addition, to a prerogative order. Its availability has, therefore, been extended, but only in the field of public law where a prerogative order may be granted. I have already given my reasons for the view that this extension is purely a matter of procedural law, and so within the rule-making powers of the Rules Committee. I therefore reject this submission of the Lord Advocate.

I pass now to the two critical issues: (1) the character of the duty upon the revenue and the persons to whom it is owed. Is it legal, political, or merely moral? (2) The nature of the interest which the applicant has to show. It is an integral part of the Lord Advocate's argument that the existence of the duty is a significant factor in determining the sufficiency of an applicant's interest.

The duty

[His Lordship concluded:]

[A] legal duty of fairness is owed by the revenue to the general body of taxpayers. It is, however, subject to the duty of sound management of the tax which the statute places upon the revenue.

The interest

The sufficiency of the interest is, as I understand all your Lordships agree, a mixed question of law and fact. The legal element in the mixture is less than the matters of fact and degree: but it is important, as setting the limits within which, and the principles by which, the discretion is to be exercised. At one time heresy ruled the day. The decision of the Divisional Court in *R. v. Lewisham Union Guardians* [1897] 1 Q.B. 498 was accepted as establishing that an applicant must establish "a legal specific right to ask for the interference of the court" by order of mandamus: *per* Wright J. at 500. I agree with Lord Denning M.R. in thinking this was a deplorable decision. It was at total variance with the view of Lord Mansfield C.J. Yet its influence has lingered on, and is evident even in the decision of the Divisional Court in this case. But the tide of the developing law has now swept beyond it, as the Court of Appeal's decision in *R. v. Greater London Council, ex p. Blackburn* [1976] 1 W.L.R. 550 illustrates. In the present case the House can put down a marker buoy warning legal navigators of the danger of the decision. As Professor Wade pointed out in *Administrative Law* (4th ed., 1977), p. 610, if the *Lewisham* case were correct, mandamus would lose its public law character, being no more than a remedy for a private wrong.

My Lords, I will not weary the House with citation of many authorities. Suffice it to refer to the judgment of Lord Parker C.J. in *R. v. Thames Magistrates' Court, ex p. Greenbaum*, 55 L.G.R. 129, a case of certiorari; and to words of Lord Wilberforce in *Gouriet v. Union of Post Office Workers* [1978] A.C. 435, 482, where he stated the modern position in relation to prerogative orders: "These are often applied for by individuals and the courts have allowed them liberal access under a generous conception of *locus standi*." The one legal principle, which is implicit in the case law and accurately reflected in the rule of court, is that in determining the sufficiency of an applicant's interest it is necessary to consider the matter to which the application relates. It is wrong in law, as I understand the cases, for the court to attempt an assessment of the sufficiency of an applicant's interest without regard to the matter of his complaint. If he fails to show, when he applies for leave, a *prima facie* case, or reasonable grounds for believing that there has been a failure of public duty, the court would be in error if it granted leave. The curb represented by the need for an applicant to show, when he seeks leave to apply, that he has such a case is an essential protection against abuse of legal process. It enables the court to prevent abuse by busybodies, cranks, and other mischief-makers. I do not see any further purpose served by the requirement for leave.

But, that being said, the discretion belongs to the court: and, as my noble and learned friend, Lord Diplock, has already made clear, it is the function of the judges to determine the way in which it is to be exercised. Accordingly I think that the Divisional Court was right to grant leave *ex parte*. Mr Payne's affidavit of March 20, 1979, revealed a prima facie case of failure by the Inland Revenue to discharge its duty to act fairly between taxpayer and taxpayer. But by the time the application reached the Divisional Court for a hearing, *inter partes*, of the preliminary issue, two very full affidavits had been filed by the revenue explaining the "management" reasons for the decision not to seek to collect the unpaid tax from the Fleet Street casuals. At this stage the matters of fact and degree upon which depends the exercise of the discretion whether to allow the application to proceed or not became clear. It was now possible to form a view as to the existence or otherwise of a case meriting examination by the court. And it was abundantly plain upon the evidence that the applicant could show no such case. But the Court of Appeal, misled into thinking that, at that stage and notwithstanding the evidence available, *locus standi* was to be dealt with as a preliminary issue, assumed illegality (where in my judgment none was shown) and, upon that assumption, held that the applicant had sufficient interest. Were the assumption justified, which on the evidence it was not, I would agree with the reasoning of Lord Denning M.R. and Ackner L.J. I think the majority of the Court of Appeal, in formulating a test of genuine grievance reasonably asserted, were doing no more than giving effect to the general principle which Lord Mansfield C.J. had stated in the early days on the remedy. Any more stringent test would, as Wade, *Administrative Law* (4th ed.), p. 612 observes, open up "a serious gap in the system of public law"....

Lord Roskill: ... It is clear that the respondents are seeking to intervene in the affairs of individual taxpayers, the Fleet Street casual workers, and to require the appellants to assess and collect tax from them which the appellants have clearly agreed not to do. Theoretically, but one trusts only theoretically, it is possible to envisage a case when because of some grossly improper pressure or motive the appellants have failed to perform their statutory duty as respects a particular taxpayer or class of taxpayer. In such a case, which emphatically is not the present, judicial review might be available to other taxpayers. But it would require to be a most extreme case for I am clearly of the view, having regard to the nature of the appellants' statutory duty and the degree of confidentiality enjoined by statute which attaches to their performance, that in general it is not open to individual taxpayers or to a group of taxpayers to seek to interfere between the appellants and other taxpayers, whether those other taxpayers are honest or dishonest men, and that the court should, by refusing relief by way of judicial review, firmly discourage such attempted interference by other taxpayers. It follows that, in my view, taking all those matters into account, it cannot be said that the respondents had a "sufficient interest" to justify their seeking the relief claimed by way of judicial review....

[His Lordship also expressed agreement with Lord Wilberforce and Lord Fraser.]

Notes

1. For comments, see P. Cane [1981] P.L. 322; D. Feldman (1982) 45 M.L.R. 92;

and *Lewis*, Chap. 10. The old law of standing was highly complex, varying according to the remedy sought, and with uncertainty if not conflicting authorities on many points. See generally S.M. Thio, *Locus Standi and Judicial Review* (1971); P. Cane, "The Function of Standing Rules in Administrative Law" [1980] P.L. 303. In theory, the old law was not entirely swept away by the new Order 53 or the *Fleet Street Casuals* case. Nevertheless, references to the old authorities when points as to standing are considered are now unusual. Points that emerge from the *Fleet Street Casuals* case (also sometimes known as "Mickey Mouse" case) include (1) that the question of *locus standi* cannot be considered in isolation from the legal and factual context of the application; (2) that it is one of mixed law and fact to be decided on legal principles and not simply a matter of discretion; (3) that a decision that an applicant has sufficient interest to be granted leave does not preclude the matter being raised at the full hearing; (4) that the question is inappropriate to be taken on appeal as a preliminary issue; and (5), most significantly, that the courts should not take an unduly restrictive approach to questions of standing. There are a number of difficulties.

On point (1), their Lordships indicate that the court must consider both whether on the facts it is established that the decision is *ultra vires*, and, if so, the nature of the illegality. If this means that no person has standing without a good case on the merits and, conversely, that every person with a good case on the merits has standing, then standing has disappeared as a separate concept. Wade and Forsyth accept that the "House of Lords' new criterion would seem virtually to abolish the requirement of standing" as a distinct concept (*Administrative Law* (7th ed.), p. 711). However, this seems to put it too high. Schiemann J., writing extra-judicially, states that:

> "wherever someone is ... excluded by reason of *locus standi* rules, the law regards it as preferable that an illegality should continue than that the person excluded should have access to the courts" ([1990] P.L. at 342).

(*cf.* his Lordship's comments in the *Rose Theatre* case, below, p. 672).

Too much cannot be read into point (2). While Lords Wilberforce, Scarman and Roskill make this point, it is clear from Lord Scarman's speech that the "legal element is less than the matters of fact and degree" (see above, p. 669). In other words the test of sufficient interest is so broadly expressed as to leave considerable leeways for choice on the part of the judges; whether this is to be labelled "law and fact" or "discretion" is of less significance. Only Lord Diplock was prepared to say that the court has an "unfettered discretion to decide what in its own good judgment it considers to be 'a sufficient interest' on the part of an applicant in the particular circumstances of the case before it" (at 642). Subsequent judges have used the term "discretion" (see, *e.g.* Watkins L.J. in *R. v. Felixstowe JJ., ex p. Leigh* [1987] Q.B. 582, 597 and Otton J. in *ex p. Greenpeace (No. 2)*, below, p. 674; *cf.* Schiemann J. in the *Rose Theatre* case, below, p. 672 (at 520), where he stated that the matter is "not purely a matter of discretion in the courts").

It is clear from point (3) that the question of standing arises at two stages. One difficulty is that the statutory test in Ord. 53, r. 3(7), and the Supreme Court Act 1981, s.31(3), refers expressly to the leave stage; the House of Lords acted on the assumption that this was also the appropriate test on the hearing of the full application. While *formally* the same test applies at both stages, its application differs in that at the leave stage the court is only forming a "provisional" or "*prima facie*" view on the question (see the extracts from Lord Diplock's and Lord Scarman's speeches (above, pp. 666 and 670)). A final view can only properly be expressed at the second stage, when the merits of the complaint can be considered. Accordingly, it is only in the clearest of cases that an application will be ruled out at the leave stage on the ground that the applicant lacks *locus*.

2. *Ratepayers and taxpayers*
The House of Lords confirmed, *obiter*, that a ratepayer has *locus standi* to challenge

rating decisions concerning other ratepayers in the same area (*cf. Arsenal Football Club Ltd v. Ende* [1979] A.C. 1). It is likely that ratepayers and council tax payers will have standing to challenge decisions of local authorities that involve expenditure (and possibly other decisions or acts, though not necessarily all; a council tax is unlikely, for example, automatically to have *locus standi* to challenge a decision in the field of child care).

The general principle that one taxpayer does not have *locus standi* to challenge decisions concerning other taxpayers is not an absolute rule. No member of the House of Lords was willing to say that a taxpayer would *never* have *locus standi* in such a case. Then, in *R. v. Attorney-General, ex p. Imperial Chemical Industries plc* [1985] 1 CMLR 588, Woolf J. held that ICI had *locus standi* to challenge a valuation of ethane for the purposes of calculating Petroleum Revenue Tax that would be unduly favourable to its rivals, Esso, Shell and BP. ICI's interests were adversely affected by the approach of the Revenue, and was the only body whose interests were likely to be so affected. They were not complaining about a particular assessment in relation to another taxpayer's affairs but about an approach which, but for the judicial review proceedings, would presumably have continued for a substantial time and was in certain respects wrong in law. Woolf J.'s judgment on this point was endorsed by the Court of Appeal ([1987] 1 CMLR 72).

The position of a taxpayer is stronger when he wishes to challenge unlawful expenditure. In *R. v. H.M. Treasury, ex p. Smedley* [1985] 1 Q.B. 657, Slade L.J. said that he did not "feel much doubt" that Mr Smedley, "if only in his capacity as a taxpayer" had sufficient interest to raise a "serious question" as to the *vires* of an Order in Council, which would have led to the expenditure of substantial sums from the Consolidated Fund for the purpose of the European Community budget.

3. *Pressure groups and planning*

Since the House of Lords' decision, *locus standi* has been accorded to persons and bodies such as amenity societies who, for example, oppose grants of planning permission. In *Covent Garden Community Association Ltd v. Greater London Council* [1981] J.P.L. 183, Woolf J. held that the applicant company, formed to represent and safeguard the interests of Covent Garden residents, had *locus standi* to seek certiorari to quash a decision of the council to grant "deemed planning permission" in respect of premises in the Covent Garden area owned by the council. Certiorari was, however, refused on the merits. (*cf. R. v. Sheffield City Council, ex p. Mansfield* (1979) 37 P. & C.R. 1 and *R. v. Stroud District Council, ex p. Goodenough* [1982] J.P.L. 246 (mandamus); *R. v. Royal County of Berkshire, ex p. Mangnall* [1985] J.P.L. 258; *R. v. Castle Point District Council, ex p. Brooks* [1985] J.P.L. 473.). In *R. v. Hammersmith and Fulham Borough Council, ex p. People Before Profit Ltd* (1981) 80 L.G.R. 322, an unincorporated association of persons called "People Before Profit" took an active part at a public inquiry in objecting to the Hammersmith Local Plan. After the inquiry, but before the report came out, the planning policy committee of the borough council resolved to grant planning permission to London Transport in respect of a proposed development which was an aspect of the plan to which objections had been made. The subsequent report favoured the objectors. The association was formed into a company limited by guarantee and sought leave to bring an application for judicial review seeking an order quashing the resolution. Comyn J. held (1) that the organisation had *locus standi*: any person was entitled to object in a planning matter if he had a legitimate *bona fide* reason—he did not have to be a ratepayer or a resident, but was not to be an officious bystander or busybody; (2) that the mere fact of a different legal entity was not alone sufficient to defeat them having fulfilled all the other qualifications as objectors; but (3) that they had no reasonable case to put forward. Leave to bring the application was accordingly refused.

An apparently less liberal approach was adopted by Schiemann J. in *R. v. Secretary of State for the Environment, ex p. Rose Theatre Trust Co.* [1990] 1 Q.B. 504. In the course of development of a site in central London, some remains of an historical theatre, the Rose Theatre, were discovered. A trust company was set up with the objects of preserving the remains and making them accessible to the public. Its members included persons of expertise and distinction in archaeology, the theatre and literature, local residents and the local M.P. The company applied to the Secretary of State for the Environment for the theatre to be listed in the Schedule of monuments made under section 1 of the Ancient Monuments and Archaeological Areas Act 1979. The Secretary of State, whilst accepting that the remains were of national importance, declined to list them and, in his decision letter, gave as reasons, *inter alia*, his view that the site was not under threat, that scheduling might give rise to claims for compensation, the need to balance the desirability of preservation against the need for a city to thrive, and the likelihood of co-operation by the developers. The company applied for judicial review. Schiemann J. held that the Secretary of State had lawfully exercised his discretion, but that in any event, the company lacked *locus standi*. His Lordship stated that "the decision not to schedule is one of those governmental decisions in respect of which the ordinary citizen does not have a sufficient interest to enable him to obtain leave to move for judicial review" (at 521). A person could not aquire a sufficient interest by writing to the Secretary of State on the matter, or receiving a reply. A number of individuals without standing could not acquire it by getting together to form a company. If this approach meant that unlawful decisions might be left unchallenged, then that followed from Parliament's failure to enact a wide right of access for every individual who is interested in having the legality of an administrative action litigated.

This decision has been criticised as unduly restrictive and out of line with other authorities (R. Gordon, *Crown Office Proceedings* (1990), para. C3–031; *cf.* P. Cane [1991] P.L. 307, who criticises the reasoning rather than the result). Perhaps the main difficulty with the reasoning is the assumption made without discussion that "an individual of acknowledged distinction in the field of archaeology, of which the company has several among its members", which Schiemann J. took as a test case for the claim to standing, had no greater interest than an "ordinary citizen". The other points made by his Lordship are, however, difficult to resist. On the other hand, the decision must also be seen in its context. A decision to approve a local plan or to grant planning permission for a significant development is, for example, likely to have a greater impact on the locality than a decision not to schedule an ancient monument, particularly given the absence of evidence that the monument was under any threat. Had the remains been under a threat that could have been removed by a decision in favour of scheduling, the decision's impact would have been greater and, accordingly, the interests of such persons as distinguished archaeologists and local residents would arguably have been "sufficient". It is submitted that this line of reasoning is more acceptable than the argument that the company should have been accorded standing if the decision had been shown to be *ultra vires* (*Wade and Forsyth*, p. 717) which would seem to empty standing requirements of all content. Note also Cane's view that the specification of the Historic Buildings and Monuments Commission (English Heritage) as the only body the Secretary of State was expressly required to consult might alone have given grounds for the decision. Here, English Heritage were satisfied that adequate arrangements had been made by the developers for the protection of the remains.

This decision may be compared with another by the same judge in *R. v. Poole Borough Council, ex p. Beebee and Others* [1991] C.O.D. 264, where his Lordship held that the British Herpetological Society had *locus standi* to seek judicial review of the council's decision to grant planning permission to itself for the development of part of a heath. The Society had a long association with the site in connection with rare species found on it, and had been named in a condition attached to the permission. On the other hand, the Worldwide Fund for Nature, which had made grants to the Society and had been involved in conservation of the Dorset heathlands for 15 years, would not in principle have had a sufficient interest, had there been no consent order to its being joined as an applicant after leave had been granted.

Subsequent cases in the planning and related contexts have confirmed that the *Rose*

Theatre case has not stemmed the general tide in favour of a liberal approach. For example, in *R. v. Inspectorate of Pollution, ex p. Greenpeace Ltd (No. 2)* [1994] 4 All E.R. 329 Otton J. held that Greenpeace had *locus standi* to challenge variations of authorisations under the Radioactive Substances Act 1960 to permit testing of British Nuclear Fuels plc's new thermal oxide processing plant (THORP) at Sellafield, Cumbria, although the application was dismissed on its merits. His Lordship took into account the nature of Greenpeace, the extent of its interest in the issues raised and the nature of the relief sought. Greenpeace International had nearly 5 million supporters worldwide; Greenpeace U.K. had over 400,000 supporters with about 2,500 in the Cumbria region. It was a campaigning organisation with the protection of the natural environment as its prime object. His Lordship continued (at 350–351):

> "BNFL rightly acknowledges the national and international standing of Greenpeace and its integrity. So must I. I have not the slightest reservation that Greenpeace is an entirely responsible and respected body with a genuine concern for the environment. That concern naturally leads to a bona fide interest in the activities carried on by BNFL at Sellafield and in particular the discharge and disposal of radioactive waste from its premises and to which the respondents' decision to vary relates. The fact that there are 400,000 supporters in the United Kingdom carries less weight than the fact that 2,500 of them come from the Cumbria region. I would be ignoring the blindingly obvious if I were to disregard the fact that those persons are inevitably concerned about (and have a genuine perception that there is) a danger to their health and safety from any additional discharge of radioactive waste even from testing. I have no doubt that the issues raised by this application are serious and worthy of determination by this court.
>
> It seems to me that if I were to deny standing to Greenpeace, those it represents might not have an effective way to bring the issues before the court. There would have to be an application either by an individual employee of BNFL or a near neighbour. In this case it is unlikely that either would be able to command the expertise which is at the disposal of Greenpeace. Consequently, a less well-informed challenge might be mounted which would stretch unnecessarily the court's resources and which would not afford the court the assistance it requires in order to do justice between the parties. Further, if the unsuccessful applicant had the benefit of legal aid it might leave the respondents and BNFL without an effective remedy in costs. Alternatively, the individual (or Greenpeace) might seek to persuade Her Majesty's Attorney General to commence a relator action which (as a matter of policy or practice) he may be reluctant to undertake against a government department (see the learned commentary by Schiemann J on "Locus Standi" [1990] P.L. 342). Neither of these courses of action would have the advantage of an application by Greenpeace, who, with its particular experience in environmental matters, its access to experts in the relevant realms of science and technology (not to mention the law), is able to mount a carefully selected, focused, relevant and well-argued challenge. It is not without significance that in this case the form 86 contains six grounds of challenge but by the time it came to the substantive hearing before me, the Greenpeace 'team' (if I may call them that) had been able to evaluate the respondents' and BNFL's evidence and were able to jettison four grounds and concentrate on two. This responsible approach undoubtedly had the advantage of sparing scarce court resources, ensuring an expedited substantive hearing and an early result (which it transpires is helpful to the respondents and to BNFL).
>
> I also take into account the nature of the relief sought. In *I.R.C. v. National Federation of Self-Employed and Small Businesses Ltd* the House of Lords expressed the view that if mandamus were sought that would be a reason to decline jurisdiction. Here, the primary relief sought is certiorari (less stringent) and, if granted, the question of an injunction to stop the testing pending determination of the main applications would still be in the discretion of the court. I also take into account the fact

that Greenpeace has been treated as one of the consultees during the consultation process and that they were invited (albeit with other non-consultees) to comment on the 'minded to vary' letter.

It follows that I reject the argument that Greenpeace is a 'mere' or 'meddlesome busybody'. I regard the applicant as eminently respectable and responsible and its genuine interest in the issues raised is sufficient for it to be granted locus standi....

... [I]t must not be assumed that Greenpeace (or any other interest group) will automatically be afforded standing in any subsequent application for judicial review in whatever field it (and its members) may have an interest. This will have to be a matter to be considered on a case by case basis at the leave stage and if the threshold is crossed again at the substantive hearing as a matter of discretion.

I also bear this consideration in mind when I respectfully decline to follow the decision of Schiemann J. in *R. v. Secretary of State for the Environment, ex p. Rose Theatre Trust Co.* [1990] 1 All E.R. 754; [1990] 1 Q.B. 504. Suffice it to say that the circumstances were different, the interest group had been formed for the exclusive purpose of saving the Rose Theatre site and no individual member could show any personal interest in the outcome. In any event his decision on the locus standi point (as indeed is mine) was not central to his decision...."

See also *R. v. Canterbury City Council, ex p. Springimage* (1994) 68 P. & C.R. 171 (a rival developer may have *locus standi* to challenge a grant of planning permission); *R. v. Sheffield City Council, ex p. Power, The Times,* June 7, 1994 (Action Group formed for the purposes of the proceedings in question had sufficient interest to apply for judicial review of an established use certificate issued in terms wider than the existing use; as no application had been made for planning permission, there was no other way in which the decision could be made the subject of effective challenge).

The cases in this area are analysed by C. Hilson and I. Cram, "Judicial Review and Environmental Law—Is There a Coherent View of Standing?" (1996) 16 L.S. 1. They conclude that there is not.

4. *Legitimate expectation*

A person with a "legitimate expectation" protected by public law will have *locus standi* to seek judicial review (see Lord Diplock in *O'Reilly v. Mackman* (above, p. 643) and pp. 392–397).

5. *Other contexts*

Other cases indicative of a broad approach to questions of standing include the following. In *R. v. Secretary of State for the Environment, ex p. Ward* [1984] 1 W.L.R. 834, Woolf J. held that a gypsy had *locus* to challenge a decision of the Secretary of State not to exercise his powers under section 9 of the Caravan Sites Act 1968 to direct local authorities to provide caravan sites for gypsies. The same judge held that the Child Poverty Action Group (although not the Greater London Council) had *locus* to challenge the manner in which the Secretary of State was administering the law concerning social security payments (*R. v. Secretary of State for Social Services, ex p. Greater London Council, The Times,* August 16, 1984; appeal dismissed, *The Times,* August 8, 1985; *cf. R. v. Secretary of State for Social Services, ex p. Child Poverty Action Group* [1990] 2 Q.B. 540, where the Court of Appeal stated that the question of standing went to the jurisdiction of the court and could not be conferred by the consent of the respondent; the court was satisfied on the evidence, but without the advantage of argument, that the CPAG had standing to challenge the interpretation by the Secretary of State and the Chief Adjudication Officer of their duties under the Social Security Act 1975 (the application for judicial review was rejected on its merits). In *R. v. Liverpool City Corporation, ex p. Ferguson* [1985] I.R.L.R. 501, it was held that the secretary of a branch of a teachers' union (the branch having no corporate status) had *locus standi* to challenge the decision of a council sub-committee to refuse to pay teachers who presented themselves for work on a "day of action", but who were unable to work because of the actions of the other trade unionists.

In *R. v. Felixstowe JJ., ex p. Leigh* [1987] Q.B. 582, a journalist was granted a declaration that the justices had erred in law in deciding as a matter of policy that their identities should not be disclosed. The journalist had not been covering the case in respect of which the decision challenged had been made, but was a "public spirited citizen" acting as "guardian of the public interest in the maintenance and preservation of open justice in magistrates' courts, a matter of vital concern in the administration of justice". This was "a matter of national importance" as a policy of routine non-disclosure was being adopted by a growing number of justices elsewhere: "No one has contended that he has acted as a mere busybody in coming to this court to ask for the relief he seeks. The seriousness of his purpose is apparent. I think he has a sufficient interest..." (*per* Watkins L.J. at 598). However, he had insufficient standing to be granted mandamus to order disclosure in the case in question, as his aim "was not to report the case; it was to comment on various issues arising out of reports by others of the case" (*per* Watkins L.J. at 597). This reinforces Lord Wilberforce's point that the application of the test may *differ* according to the remedy sought, although Watkins L.J. was "inclined to think" that the test was not *stricter* for mandamus (at 597). *cf.* however, Olton J. in *ex p. Greenpeace (No. 2)* (above).

In *R. v. Manchester City Council, ex p. Baragrove Properties Ltd* (1991) 23 H.L.R. 337, the Divisional Court held that a property management company had *locus* to challenge the council's interpretation of a housing benefit regulation, which directly affected the rents receivable by the applicants; the company would not, however, have had *locus* to challenge a determination made in relation to the particular circumstances of a tenant.

Particularly interesting is the decision of the Divisional Court in *R. v. Secretary of State for Foreign and Commonwealth Affairs, ex p. World Development Movement Ltd* [1996] 1 W.L.R. 386 that WDM, an internationally recognised non-partisan pressure group, had standing to challenge (successfully) the legality of the payment of what would have totalled £234 million from the Aid and Trade Provision budget to support the project to build the Pergau Dam in Malaysia. Under section 1 of the Overseas Development and Co-operation Act 1980, the Secretary of State had power to provide such funding "for the purpose of promoting the development" of a country outside the United Kingdom. The grant was unlawful in the light of advice to the Secretary of State that the project was uneconomic; the 1980 Act only authorised grants in respect of economically sound developments. Rose L.J. (at 395–396) found that there was nothing in the *National Federation of Self-Employed* case to deny standing to WDM. The authorities seemed "to indicate an increasingly liberal approach to standing on the part of the courts during the last 12 years". Relevant factors included "the importance of vindicating the rule of law", the likely absence of any other responsible challenger, the nature of the breach of duty and the prominent role of WDM in giving advice, guidance and assistance with regard to aid. Furthermore,

> "... if the Divisional Court in *Ex parte Rees-Mogg* [1994] Q.B. 552, ... was able to accept that the applicant in that case had standing in the light of his 'sincere concerns for constitutional issues', *a fortiori*, it seems to me that the present applicants, with the national and international expertise and interest in promoting and protecting aid to underdeveloped nations, should have standing in the present application."

The sum at stake would presumably have afforded standing to any taxpayer. (*cf.* above, p. 671). See I. Hare [1995] C.L.J. 227 and (on the wider background to the case), F. White, I. Harden and K. Donnelly, "Audit, Accounting Officers and Accountability: The Pergau Dam Affair" [1994] P.L. 526 and I. Harden, F. White and K. Hollingsworth, "Value for Money and Administrative Law" [1996] P.L. 661.

6. In *R. v. Secretary of State for Employment, ex p. Equal Opportunities Commission* [1995] 1 A.C. 1, the House of Lords (Lord Jauncey of Tullichettle dissenting) held that the EOC had standing to challenge the compatibility with Community law of

legislation concerning the rights of part-time employees, on the grounds of sex discrimination (see further below, p. 699). Under the Sex Discrimination Act 1975, s.53(1), the EOC's duties included those of working towards the elimination of discrimination and promoting equality of opportunity between men and women generally. It would be a "very retrograde step now to hold that the EOC has no *locus standi* to agitate in judicial review questions related to sex discrimination which are of public importance and affect a large section of the population" (*per* Lord Keith of Kinkel at 26). The EOC had been joined as an applicant by a Mrs Day, a part-time worker made redundant by a public authority in circumstances such that she did not qualify for redundancy pay under the U.K. legislation. Lord Keith held that hers was a purely private claim against her employer, in which she would be able to raise before an industrial tribunal arguments based on Community law. Indeed, such proceedings had been started and adjourned. She was not properly joined in the present proceedings as "the Divisional Court was not the appropriate forum to adjudicate upon . . . her private law claim". The basis of this is unclear. If all Mrs Day were pursuing was her private law claim, it would fall outside the scope of judicial review under the *East Berkshire* principle (above, pp. 625–634). However, she surely had sufficient interest to pursue the general question of the validity of the legislation alongside the EOC (see P. Cane [1995] P.L. 276, 284–285; C. Harlow and E. Szyszczak (1995) 32 C.M.L.Rev. 641, 644–645). The explanation may be that, as Mrs Day had been employed by a public authority, she could assert her directly effective rights under the directive against her employer. Accordingly, the statute did not "adversely affect" her at all.

7. Standing outside Order 53

Prior to the introduction of the application for judicial review, the issue of *locus standi* was considered separately in respect of each administrative law remedy, the courts generally being stricter in respect of the private law remedies of declaration or injunction (see above, p. 668). The orthodox approach in respect of private law remedies was set out in *Boyce v. Paddington Corporation* [1903] 1 Ch. 109. The plaintiff, shortly before the action, erected buildings on land abutting on an open space under the control of the borough council. The council resolved to erect a hoarding which would obstruct the access of light to the plaintiff's windows. The plaintiff brought an action to restrain the council from doing this. It was held that as the plaintiff was suing in respect of an alleged private right to the access of light, or in respect of an alleged interference with a public right from which he personally sustained special damage, he could sue without joining the Attorney-General as plaintiff (see below, p. 694). The action failed on grounds unconnected with the right to sue. The House of Lords in *Gouriet v. Union of Post Office Workers* [1978] A.C. 435 affirmed that this was the correct approach in respect of a private action for an injunction to restrain a threatened breach of the criminal law by a trade union.

Different views have been expressed on the test for *locus standi* where a private action is brought against a public authority. In *Steeples v. Derbyshire County Council* [1985] 1 W.L.R. 256, Webster J. held that the plaintiff had the necessary *locus standi* to challenge the grant of planning permission by the council for two interrelated developments, which involved the establishment of a leisure complex at Shipley Park, near Ilkeston, Derbyshire. The plaintiff alleged, *inter alia*, breach of procedural requirements and the breach of the *nemo judex* principle of natural justice. Webster J. held that the plaintiff had the necessary *locus standi* under *Boyce v. Paddington Borough Council* [1903] 1 Ch. 109. As regards one of the two interrelated developments ("the ancillary development") the plaintiff's private right was affected as a small part of his land was to be taken for it. The other development ("the leisure development") would take place on land adjacent to his own and would result in his view being impaired, in the ambient noise level being increased, in some interference with his use of a lane which bisected land farmed by him and in a risk of his land being invaded by litter and possibly by vandals or trespassers. This would amount to special damage resulting from interference with a public right:

"If the Plaintiff can show that a proprietary interest of his, reasonably and probably to be affected by the act in question, will probably be prejudiced by it then, even in the absence of authority, I would hold that he suffers in respect of that act damage under a head recognised by the law."

The judge also held that the plaintiff had *locus standi* in respect of the leisure development by virtue of his undoubted *locus* in respect of the ancillary development, as the two developments were closely connected.

The judge further stated that if it had been necessary to decide the point, he would have held that a person with sufficient interest for the purpose of an application for judicial review, and having thereby *locus standi* to apply for an injunction, would have a similar *locus standi* to seek an injunction in ordinary proceedings. Any difference in substance between the two forms of proceeding could, if necessary, be given effect to when the discretion of the court arose as to the relief to be given. The *Gouriet* case was distinguished on the grounds that the plaintiff here was not attempting to enforce the criminal law but to challenge the decision of a public body which he said was wrongly made, and claimed to be threatened by damage special to himself resulting from that decision.

However, in *Barrs v. Bethell* [1982] Ch. 294, three ratepayers of Camden London Borough Council issued a writ and statement of claim in the Chancery Division against the members of the majority group on the council and the council itself claiming certain declarations and other orders. It was alleged that there had been various abuses of discretion, and that the councillors had breached the fiduciary duty owed to the ratepayers, *inter alia*, by failing to make cuts in services and to raise council house rents. Warner J. held that a ratepayer was not entitled to sue a local authority or its members, without the leave of the Attorney-General, unless he could show that he had *locus standi* under the rules laid down in *Boyce v. Paddington Borough Council* [1903] 1 Ch. 109. His Lordship disagreed with the view expressed by Webster J. in the *Steeples* case, above, that a person with "sufficient interest" under Order 53 would have *locus standi* in ordinary proceedings.

8. The precise *purposes* of the requirement of standing in respect of public law remedies are rarely discussed by the judges, including the law lords in the *Fleet Street Casuals* case. The distinctions between standing for remedies in private law and in public law is explained as follows by Cane ([1980] P.L. 303):

"In private law entitlement to a remedy and the right to apply for that remedy merge; the two issues are not treated separately—the former entails the latter" (p. 303).

For example, the law of tort limits the range of plaintiffs who may sue for economic loss:

"By limiting entitlement to the remedy of damages, entitlement to institute proceedings is *ipso facto* also limited" (*ibid.*).

The position in public law is different:

"... the public law litigant is required to show that the respondent public body has infringed one of the values embodied in the substantive heads of judicial review and *also* that some personal interest of his has been thereby infringed thus giving a reason why *he* should be allowed to complain in court of the abuse of power" (p. 304).

The literature generally is clearer on the purposes that are or should *not* be served by standing rules. For example, in discussing these rules in the context of American constitutional law, K.C. Davis wrote, in a passage cited by Cane:

"The law of standing is the wrong tool to accomplish judicial objectives unrelated to the task of deciding whether a particular interest asserted is deserving of judicial protection. The courts should avoid hypothetical or remote questions—through the law of ripeness,[3] not through the law of standing. The courts should decline to enter political areas—through the law of political questions, not through the law of standing. The courts should limit themselves to issues 'appropriate for judicial determination'—through the law of case or controversy, but not through that part of the law of case or controversy pertaining to standing. The courts should avoid taking over functions of government that are committed to executives or administrators—through the law of scope of review, not through the law of standing. The courts should virtually stay away from some governmental activities, such as foreign affairs and military operations—through the law of unreviewability,[4] not through the law of standing. The courts should insist upon competent presentation of cases—through refusals to respond to inadequate presentations, not through the law of standing." (37 Univ. of Chicago L.R. 450, 469).

What is clear is that rules that confined access to judicial review to those whose private law rights were at stake would not be appropriate. One of the clear purposes of judicial review is to secure the public interest that governmental institutions act within the law, and this would not be served if standing rules were unduly restrictive. There is much to be said for Lord Denning's statement in *R. v. Greater London Council, ex p. Blackburn* [1976] 1 W.L.R. 550 at 556:

"I regard it as a matter of high constitutional principle that if there is good ground for supposing that a government department or a public authority is transgressing the law, or is about to transgress it, in a way which offends or injures thousands of Her Majesty's subjects, then any one of those offended or injured can draw it to the attention of the courts of law and seek to have the law enforced, and the courts in their discretion can grant whatever remedy is appropriate."

This was endorsed by Lord Diplock in the *Fleet Street Casuals* case (at 641), but rejected by Lord Roskill (at 661) and by Lord Wilberforce (in the context of relator actions) in the *Gouriet* case ([1978] A.C. 435, 483). Note, however, the further broadening of the requirements for standing proposed by the Law Commission and Lord Woolf (below, pp. 704–705).

9. The issue of standing must be distinguished from that of the capacity of an unincorporated association to apply for judicial review. In *R. v. Darlington Borough Council, ex p. Association of Darlington Taxi Owners, The Times,* January 21, 1994, it was held that such an association did not have capacity (costs were, however, awarded against the members of the applicant associations). A different view was taken by Sedley J. in *R. v. London Borough of Tower Hamlets, ex p. Tower Hamlets Combined Traders Association* [1994] C.O.D. 325 and by Turner J. in *R. v. Traffic Commissioners for the North Western Traffic Area, ex p. "Brake"* [1996] C.O.D. 248. The Law Commission (Law Com. 226, p. 51) has recommended that express provision should be made in respect of unincorporated associations: see below, p. 707. See also K. Gledhill [1996] J.R. 67.

(G) DISCRETIONARY REFUSAL OF A REMEDY

(i) Delay

Delay was an established ground on which, prior to the introduction of the application for judicial review, the court might, in the exercise of its discretion, refuse one of the

---

[3] [Editor's note] *cf.* below, p. 700.
[4] [Editor's note] *cf.* above, p. 699.

prerogative remedies or an injunction or declaration. The new Ord. 53 made express provision concerning delay. However, as the following case shows, there have been difficulties arising from the defective drafting of the relevant provisions.

R. v. DAIRY PRODUCE QUOTA TRIBUNAL, ex p. CASWELL

[1990] 2 A.C. 738; [1990] 2 W.L.R. 1320; [1990] 2 All E.R. 434
(House of Lords)

The applicants, Mr and Mrs Caswell, having failed to qualify for a wholesale quota in respect of milk production, claimed relief under the exceptional hardship provisions set out in the Dairy Produce Quotas Regulations 1984. In February 1985 the Dairy Produce Quota Tribunal, on their construction of the Regulations, dismissed the claim. Initially unaware of a remedy, the applicants took no step to challenge the tribunal's decision until 1987 when they applied for and obtained *ex parte* leave to move for judicial review. On the hearing of the substantive application the applicants conceded before the judge that there had been "undue delay" within the meaning of section 31(6) of the Supreme Court Act 1981 and R.S.C., Ord. 53, r. 4(1), but they resisted an assertion by the tribunal that since there had been a number of other unsuccessful applications to which the same provisions applied, the grant of relief would be detrimental to good administration. The judge held that the tribunal had erred in their construction of the Regulations but, accepting the tribunal's evidence, he declined to grant relief. The Court of Appeal and the House of Lords dismissed the applicants' appeal. In the House, the sole speech was delivered by Lord Goff.

LORD GOFF:... [stated the facts, read Ord. 53, r. 4 and s.31(6), (7), of the Supreme Court Act 1981 (above pp. 600, 605), and continued:]

When Order 53 was redrawn in 1977, rule 4(1) then provided that, where there had been undue delay in making an application for judicial review, the court might refuse to grant leave for the making of the application, or any relief sought on the application:

"if, in the opinion of the court, the granting of the relief sought would be likely to cause substantial hardship to, or substantially prejudice the rights of, any person or would be detrimental to good administration."

Rule 4(2) then provided that, for an order of certiorari to remove any proceeding for the purpose of quashing it, the relevant period for the purpose of paragraph (1) was three months after the date of the relevant proceeding. In 1980, however, that rule was replaced by the present rule, save only that rule 4(1) referred to "An application for judicial review...". Following critical comment by the Court of Appeal in *R. v. Stratford-on-Avon District Council, ex p. Jackson* [1985] 1 W.L.R. 1319, in which it was held that those words must be read as referring to an application for leave to apply for judicial review, the rule was amended to give express effect to that interpretation. Despite the change in Ord. 53, r. 4, made in 1980, section 31(6) of the Supreme Court Act 1981 mirrored the old rule 4, which had by then been replaced. In 1985, clause 43 of the Administration of Justice Bill of that year contained a provision which would have repealed section 31(6) of the Act of 1981; but the clause was abandoned for other reasons, and the proposed repeal fell with it.

In the result, the courts have been left with the task of giving effect to two provisions relating to delay, which at first sight are not easy to reconcile. First, in Ord. 53, r. 4(1), undue delay is defined, whereas in section 31(6) it is not. Secondly, rule 4(1) applies only to applications for leave to apply for judicial review, whereas section 31(6) applies both to applications for leave to apply and to applications for substantive relief. Thirdly, rule 4(1) looks to the existence of good reason for extending the specified period, whereas section 31(6) looks to certain effects of delay as grounds for refusing leave, or substantive relief, as the case may be. A further twist is provided by the fact that rule 4(1) and (2) are expressed to be without prejudice to any statutory provision which has the effect of limiting the time within which an application for judicial review may be made; and that section 31(6) is expressed to be without prejudice to any enactment or rule of court which had that effect. These two provisions were said by Lloyd L.J., in the Court of Appeal, to produce a *circulus inextricabilis*: [1989] 1 W.L.R. 1089, 1094F.

The relationship between Ord. 53, r. 4, and section 31(6) was considered by the Court of Appeal in *R. v. Stratford-on-Avon District Council, ex p. Jackson* [1985] 1 W.L.R. 1319 (to which I have already referred) with particular reference to the meaning of the expression "undue delay". It was there submitted that, where good reason had been held to exist for the failure to act promptly as required by Ord. 53, r. 4(1), and the time for applying for leave had therefore been extended, the effect of section 31(7) was that in such circumstances there was no power to refuse either leave to apply or substantive relief under section 31(6) on the ground of undue delay, because an extension of time under Ord. 53, r. 4, itself negatives the existence of undue delay. That submission was rejected by the Court of Appeal. Ackner L.J., who delivered the judgment of the court, said, at 1325:

> "This is not an easy point to resolve, but we have concluded that whenever there is a failure to act promptly or within three months there is 'undue delay'. Accordingly, even though the court may be satisfied in the light of all the circumstances, including the particular position of the applicant, that there is good reason for that failure, nevertheless the delay, viewed objectively, remains 'undue delay'. The court therefore still retains a discretion to refuse to grant leave for the making of the application or the relief sought on the substantive application on the grounds of undue delay if it considers that the granting of the relief sought would be likely to cause substantial hardship to, or substantially prejudice the rights of, any person or would be detrimental to good administration."

With this conclusion, I respectfully agree. First, when section 31(6) and (7) refer to "an application for judicial review", those words must be read as referring, where appropriate, to an application for leave to apply for judicial review. Next, as I read rule 4(1), the effect of *the rule* is to limit the time within which an application for leave to apply for judicial review may be made in accordance with its terms, *i.e.* promptly and in any event within three months. The court has, however, power to grant leave to apply despite the fact that an application is late, if it considers that there is good reason to exercise that power; this it does by extending the period. This, as I understand it, is the reasoning upon which the Court of Appeal reached its conclusion in *R. v.*

Stratford-on-Avon District Council, ex p. Jackson. Furthermore, the combined effect of section 31(7) and of rule 4(1) is that there is undue delay for the purposes of section 31(6) whenever the application for leave to apply is not made promptly and in any event within three months from the relevant date.

It follows that, when an application for leave to apply is not made promptly and in any event within three months, the court may refuse leave on the ground of delay unless it considers that there is good reason for extending the period; but, even if it considers that there is such good reason, it may still refuse leave (or, where leave has been granted, substantive relief) if in its opinion the granting of the relief sought would be likely to cause hardship or prejudice (as specified in section 31(6)) or would be detrimental to good administration. I imagine that, on an *ex parte* application for leave to apply before a single judge, the question most likely to be considered by him, if there has been such delay, is whether there is good reason for extending the period under rule 4(1). Questions of hardship or prejudice, or detriment, under section 31(6) are, I imagine, unlikely to arise on an *ex parte* application, when the necessary material would in all probability not be available to the judge. Such questions could arise on a contested application for leave to apply, as indeed they did in *R. v. Stratford-on-Avon District Council, ex p. Jackson*; but even then, as in that case, it may be thought better to grant leave where there is considered to be good reason to extend the period under rule 4(1), leaving questions arising under section 31(6) to be explored in depth on the hearing of the substantive application.

In this way, I believe, sensible effect can be given to these two provisions, without doing violence to the language of either. Unlike the Court of Appeal, I do not consider that rule 4(3) and section 31(7) lead to a *circulus inextricabilis*, because 31(6) does not limit "the time within which an application for judicial review may be made" (the words used in rule 4(3)). Section 31(6) simply contains particular grounds for refusing leave or substantive relief, not referred to in rule 4(1), to which the court is bound to give effect, independently of any rule of court.

Accordingly, in the present case, the fact that the single judge had granted leave to the appellants to apply for judicial review despite the lapse (long before) of three months from the date when the ground for their application first arose, did not preclude the court from subsequently refusing substantive relief on the ground of undue delay in the exercise of its discretion under section 31(6). This was the approach adopted by both courts below, applying (as they were bound to do) the decision of the Court of Appeal in *R. v. Stratford-on-Avon District Council, ex p. Jackson* [1985] 1 W.L.R. 1319. Before your Lordships Mr Gordon for the appellants submitted that the principles stated in *ex p. Jackson* were erroneous; but, for the reasons I have already given, I am unable to accept that submission.

It follows that there is no doubt that, in the present case, there was undue delay within section 31(6). No suggestion has been made that substantial hardship or substantial prejudice were likely to be caused by the grant of the relief sought. The only questions which remained on the appeal were (1) whether the Court of Appeal should reject the judge's conclusion that the grant of such relief would be detrimental to good administration; and (2) if not, whether it should interfere with the judge's exercise of his discretion to refuse such relief. The Court of Appeal decided against the appellants on both of these points.

On the question of detriment to good administration, the judge reviewed with care the evidence before him. This consisted of an affidavit sworn by Mr Newton, who was secretary of D.P.Q.T. until September 1988, and two affidavits submitted by the appellants in answer to that affidavit, one sworn by Mr May of the legal department of the National Farmers' Union, and the other by Mr Collinson, a partner in the solicitors acting for the appellants. It appeared from the evidence that the essence of the quota system is that there is a finite amount of milk quota available, so that a quota given to one producer is not available to others. In fact, about 4,000 exceptional hardship appeals were heard by D.P.Q.T. Of these, about 600 were successful, additional quota being granted; so about 3,400 producers failed in their applications for additional quota on this ground. In a large number of these latter cases, the end of the final quota year was stated to be the major consideration. Next, the fact that judicial review was the remedy available to a milk producer aggrieved by a decision of D.P.Q.T. must have become well known at least after September 1985, when the first hearing of an application for judicial review in such a case received wide publicity in the dairy trade.[5] Consideration was given to the possibility of other producers seeking judicial review of adverse decisions of D.P.Q.T. if the appellants' application for substantive relief was successful. It was accepted that sufficient provision had been made to deal with the appellants' claim for extra quota. But, in Mr Newton's opinion, a small but administratively substantial number of milk producers could be encouraged to make applications for judicial review relying on the same point as the appellants, or a variation of it; and that could mean re-opening the quota for the year 1984–85, and for each succeeding year. Further allocations of quota could only be made at the expense of all other producers whose quotas would have to be reduced accordingly. Mr Collinson, in his affidavit, questioned whether other milk producers would be likely to follow the appellants' lead and seek judicial review or whether, if they did so, they would obtain leave to apply after such a long delay.

Having reviewed the evidence, the judge expressed his conclusion on this point in the following passage in his judgment:

> "It is obvious that if there are a number of applications the problem of re-opening these claims, going back now three years, is going to be very great. It arises out of events in 1985. The evidential problems are self-evident, leaving aside the question of being able fairly to deal with claims now in relation to matters in 1985. I think there is likely to be a very real problem in relation to a number of cases. I do not think the number of cases is *de minimis*. I have concluded that the fact that hitherto there have been only these two applications is not a matter which is of very great help in determining what the effect will be of the particular decision in this case. I have come to the clearest view that there will be a detriment to good administration if this application were granted."

The judge's conclusion, on the evidence before him, that there was likely to

---

[5] *R. v. Dairy Produce Quota Tribunal for England and Wales, ex p. Atkinson* (unreported), September 25, 1985, Macpherson J.

be a very real problem in relation to a number of cases, was a finding of fact with which I can see no reason to interfere. Once that conclusion was reached, it seems to me inevitable that to grant the relief sought in the present case would cause detriment to good administration. As Lloyd L.J. pointed out in his judgment [1989] 1 W.L.R. 1089, 1099, two things emerged from the evidence with sufficient clarity: first that, if the appellants' application for substantive relief were to be successful, there would be a significant number of further applications, and secondly that, if a significant number of applications were granted, then all previous years back to 1984 would have to be reopened. These facts disclose, in my opinion, precisely the type of situation which Parliament was minded to exclude by the provision in section 31(6) relating to detriment to good administration. Lord Diplock pointed out in *O'Reilly v. Mackman* [1983] 2 A.C. 237, 280–281:

> "The public interest in good administration requires that public authorities and third parties should not be kept in suspense as to the legal validity of a decision the authority has reached in purported exercise of decision-making powers for any longer period than is absolutely necessary in fairness to the person affected by the decision."

I do not consider that it would be wise to attempt to formulate any precise definition or description of what constitutes detriment to good administration. This is because applications for judicial review may occur in many different situations, and the need for finality may be greater in one context than in another. But it is of importance to observe that section 31(6) recognises that there is an interest in good administration independently of hardship, or prejudice to the rights of third parties, and that the harm suffered by the applicant by reason of the decision which has been impugned is a matter which can be taken into account by the court when deciding whether or not to exercise its discretion under section 31(6) to refuse the relief sought by the applicant. In asking the question whether the grant of such relief would be detrimental to good administration, the court is at that stage looking at the interest in good administration independently of matters such as these. In the present context, that interest lies essentially in a regular flow of consistent decisions, made and published with reasonable dispatch; in citizens knowing where they stand, and how they can order their affairs in the light of the relevant decision. Matters of particular importance, apart from the length of time itself, will be the extent of the effect of the relevant decision, and the impact which would be felt if it were to be re-opened. In the present case, the court was concerned with a decision to allocate part of a finite amount of quota, and with circumstances in which a re-opening of the decision would lead to other applications to re-open similar decisions which, if successful, would lead to re-opening the allocation of quota over a number of years. To me it is plain, as it was to the judge and to the Court of Appeal, that to grant the appellants the relief they sought in the present case, after such a lapse of time had occurred, would be detrimental to good administration. It is, in my opinion, unnecessary to deal expressly with the detailed arguments advanced by Mr Gordon on behalf of the appellants on this point. They were substantially the same as the arguments canvassed by him before the Court of Appeal, which considered and dismissed each argument seriatim. None of them, in my opinion, made any impact upon the essential matters, which I have identified.

Finally, I can, like the Court of Appeal, see no basis for interfering with the judge's exercise of his discretion. The judge took into account the relevant factors, including in particular the financial hardship suffered by the appellants by reason of the erroneous approach adopted by D.P.Q.T., and in particular the imposition upon them of substantial superlevy in the years 1986–87 and 1987–88. He then balanced the various factors and, as he said, came down firmly against the view of the appellants. I can perceive no error here which would justify interference with the judge's conclusion.

For these reasons, I would dismiss the appeal.

LORDS BRIDGE, GRIFFITHS, ACKNER and LOWRY agreed with LORD GOFF.

Appeal dismissed.

Notes

1. A number of points emerge from the relevant provisions, and their interpretation in *Caswell*:

• The three-month limit is not an *entitlement*; an application for leave must in any event be made promptly. In *Re Friends of the Earth Ltd* (unreported, July 6, 1987) an application for leave to apply for judicial review of the decision of the Secretary of State for Energy to grant consent for the construction of Sizewell B nuclear power station, made just within the three-month period, was rejected. Kennedy J. held that it had not been made promptly, there were no good reasons for the delay, and there would be considerable prejudice to good administration if leave were granted. The applicants had been aware that time was of the essence. This view was endorsed by the Court of Appeal in respect of two of the grounds: the others were unarguable: [1988] J.P.L. 93. See also *R. v. ITC, ex p. TVNI Ltd and TVS Television Ltd, The Times,* December 30, 1991.

• A finding on an *inter partes* hearing of an application for leave that the application, brought within three months, has been made promptly, does not prevent the court at the substantive hearing finding that there has been undue delay, and exercising its discretion under section 31(6)(b) of the Supreme Court Act 1981 to refuse to grant any relief: *R. v. Swale Borough Council, ex p. Royal Society for the Protection of Birds* [1991] J.P.L. 39.

• The applicant must, in the application, give reasons for any delay (*Practice Direction (Crown Office List: Criminal Proceedings)* [1983] 1 W.L.R. 925, para. 3); *R. v. Elmbridge Borough Council, ex p. Health Care Corporation* (1991) 63 P. & C.R. 260, 264–265.

• The fact that a respondent to a hearing for judicial review indicates that no point will be taken on delay is no bar to the court considering the matter of its own motion (*R. v. Dairy Produce Quota Tribunal, ex p. Wynn Jones* (1987) 283 E.G. 463).

• An extension of time granted on an *ex parte* application for leave is not final, but is open to consideration on the *inter partes* application (*R. v. British Railways Board, ex p. Great Yarmouth Borough Council, The Times,* March 15, 1983; *R. v. Tavistock General Commissioners, ex p. Worth* [1985] S.T.C. 565; *Patterson v. London Borough of Greenwich* (1994) 26 H.L.R. 159). This view is criticised by A. Lindsay ([1995] P.L. 417, 419–420) on the basis that such an order should properly be reviewed on an application to set aside.

• Cases where an extension of time has been granted include the following:

R. v. Stratford-on-Avon District Council, ex p. Jackson [1985] 1 W.L.R. 1319 concerned a challenge to a grant of planning permission to a third party. Among the reasons for delay, which the court regarded as legitimate, were that time was taken in an attempt made, on the advice of counsel, to persuade the Secretary of State to "call in" the planning application, and that time was taken in obtaining legal aid. In *R. v. Hertfordshire County Council, ex p. Cheung; R. v. Sefton Metropolitan Borough Council, ex p. Pau, The Times,* April 4, 1986, Sir John Donaldson M.R. stated, *obiter,* that where a test case was in progress in the public law court, others in the same position as the applicant should not be expected themselves to begin proceedings in order to protect their positions. That would strain the resources of that court to breaking point. More importantly, it was a cardinal principle of good administration that all persons who were in a similar position should be treated similarly. Accordingly, they could assume that the result of the case would be applied to them without the need for proceedings, and if that did not occur, the court would regard that as a complete justification for a late application for judicial review. In *R. v. Port Talbot Borough Council, ex p. Jones, The Independent,* January 5, 1988, the applicant commenced proceedings on December 11 for judicial review of a decision, taken in April, to grant a divorced councillor the tenancy of a house (rather than a flat). Nolan J. granted certiorari and a declaration, holding that the applicant could not reasonably be expected to come to court before an internal inquiry had been held by the council. There was therefore no culpable delay of any significance and there were good grounds for extending the time limit. In *R. v. Commissioner for Local Administration, ex p. Croydon London Borough Council* [1989] 1 All E.R. 1033, the Commissioner in October 1985 notified the council that a complaint against the council had been received, and sought further information. His jurisdiction was challenged by the council in November 1985, but he proceeded with the investigation and reported in October 1986. The council then applied for judicial review. The Divisional Court granted a declaration that the report was void, holding that there had been no undue delay: it had been reasonable for the council to wait until the report had been made. Woolf L.J. stated that r. 4 and s.31(6) of the 1981 Act "are not intended to be applied in a technical manner. As long as no prejudice is caused . . ., the courts will not rely on those provisions to deprive a litigant who has behaved sensibly and reasonably of relief to which he is otherwise entitled" (at 1046). In *R. v. Chichester JJ. and Another, ex p. Chichester District Council* (1990) 88 L.G.R. 707, the council sought judicial review of the decision of magistrates on November 30, 1988, to dismiss committal proceedings. The Divisional Court held that there had not been undue delay in applying: counsel's opinion had had to be obtained, then the authority of the appropriate committee; in addition, Christmas and New Year had intervened. No substantial hardship had been caused.

In many more cases, such as the *Caswell* case, applications are refused on the ground of delay.

● As *Caswell* shows, where an extension of time is granted, relief may still ultimately be refused on the ground of delay.
● Even where an application for leave is brought promptly, a delay before the hearing of the application for leave may give rise to an argument that the discretion to refuse relief under s.31(6) should be exercised (*R. v. South Hertfordshire District Council, ex p. Felton* [1991] J.P.L. 633, where the argument was rejected on the facts: the hearing of an application for leave to challenge a grant of planning permission was adjourned by agreement, while an alternative site was considered; there was no risk to good administration).
● On the language of s.31(6) there is no requirement for a causal connection between prejudice and undue delay; what is required is a connection between prejudice and the grant of the relief sought: *R. v. Secretary of State for Health, ex p. Furneaux* [1994] 2 All E.R. 652, C.A. Here, an application by doctors for judicial review of the Secretary of State's decision to refuse them permission to provide pharmaceutical services was brought after six months. Relief was refused, as to grant it would prejudice a person who had bought a rival pharmacy in reliance on the Secretary of State's decision. The fact that no *additional* prejudice was caused by the delay could be relevant to the exercise of discretion, but on the facts here was an "insignificant point" (*per* Mann L.J. at 658).

2. The case law on delay is considered by A. Lindsay, "Delay in Judicial Review Cases: A Conundrum Solved?" [1995] P.L. 417; and R. Leiper [1996] J.R. 201.

(ii) Effect of Alternative Remedies

It is well established that the court will not entertain an application for judicial review where there is some equally convenient and beneficial remedy, such as an appeal to a specialised tribunal, or to the High Court by case stated, or to a more appropriate Division of the High Court. For example, in *R. v. Hillingdon London Borough, ex p. Royco Homes Ltd* [1974] 1 Q.B. 720, Lord Widgery C.J. held that a planning condition that was invalid in law on its face could be challenged directly by an application for certiorari, notwithstanding the existence of the statutory appeal structure; in such circumstances it might well be "more efficient, cheaper and quicker to proceed by certiorari". In *R. v. Paddington Valuation Officer, ex p. Peachey Property Ltd* [1966] 1 Q.B. 380, Lord Denning M.R. stated (at 400) that where it was alleged that a whole valuation list was invalid, the statutory procedure for proposing alterations in a valuation list would be "nowhere near so convenient, beneficial and effectual as certiorari or mandamus". In *R. v. Huntingdon District Council, ex p. Cowan* [1984] 1 All E.R. 58, Glidewell J. stated that the question was which remedy was "the most effective and convenient in all the circumstances" (at 63). In *ex p. Waldron* [1986] Q.B. 824 Glidewell L.J. said (at 852):

> "Whether the alternative statutory remedy will resolve the question at issue fully and directly, whether the statutory procedure would be quicker or slower, than procedure by way of judicial review, whether the matter depends on some particular or technical knowledge which is more readily available to the alternative appellate body, these are amongst the matters which a court should take into account when deciding whether to grant relief by way of judicial review when an alternative remedy is available."

More recently, it has been emphasised that where there is a statutory remedy, the mere fact that an application for judicial review might be more convenient and effective may not be sufficient for the court to intervene by way of judicial review: judicial review in such circumstances will only be granted in exceptional cases. In *R. v. Chief Constable of the Merseyside Police, ex p. Calveley* [1986] Q.B. 424, complaints were made in 1981 against five police officers in respect of an incident in which the officers had arrested the complainants. An investigating officer was appointed, but the officers were not notified of the complaints until November 1983; the Police (Discipline) Regulations 1977 (S.I. 1977 No. 580), reg. 7, required this to be done "as soon as is practicable". In September 1984, following a disciplinary hearing, the chief constable found the offences proved, required three officers to resign and dismissed the others. The officers gave notice of appeal to an appeal tribunal constituted under the Police (Appeal) Rules 1977 (S.I. 1977 No. 759), but also sought certiorari to quash the chief constable's decisions, in particular on the ground that the non-compliance with reg. 7 had prejudiced the officers. The Court of Appeal granted certiorari, holding that the officers were not required to exhaust the appeal procedures first. Sir John Donaldson M.R. (with whom Glidewell L.J. agreed) stated that the court would only "very rarely" make judicial review available where there was an alternative remedy by way of appeal. Moreover, the appeal tribunal did possess specialist expertise, which the chief constable had argued rendered it better than a court to assess the prejudice. Nevertheless, here there had been "so serious a departure from the police disciplinary procedure" that judicial review should be granted.

In *R. v. Secretary of State for the Home Department, ex p. Swati* [1986] 1 W.L.R. 477, the Master of the Rolls stated that the *Calveley* case decided that:

"the jurisdiction would not be exercised where there was an alternative remedy by way of appeal, save in exceptional circumstances" (at 485).

Note that in this formulation there is no requirement that the alternative remedy be "equally convenient and beneficial". In *Calveley,* May L.J. expressly denied (at 436–437) that the judgment in the *Royco Homes* and *Peachey Properties* cases supported the view that judicial review would be granted merely because it might be more effective and convenient to do so. In *ex p. Swati* itself, a person refused leave to enter the United Kingdom was refused leave to apply for judicial review, and left to his statutory right of appeal. From the applicant's point of view the latter was certainly less "convenient" as it could only be exercised from outside the United Kingdom, but that consideration did not sway the court, Parker L.J. stating that this did not, even arguably, constitute an "exceptional circumstance". Sir John Donaldson M.R. stated that:

"...where Parliament provides an appeal procedure, judicial review will have no place unless the applicant can distinguish his case from the type of case for which the appeal procedure was provided" (at 485).

(Can this be right? If the point *cannot* be raised on the statutory appeal, then that ceases to be an "alternative remedy.") These new, restrictive, dicta are criticised by Wade and Forsyth (*Administrative Law* (7th ed.), pp. 721–726) who argue that "if an applicant can show illegality, it is wrong in principle to require him to exercise a right of appeal. Illegal action should be stopped in its tracks as soon as it is shown" (p. 725). Factors such as convenience and speed are in principle irrelevant. However, he also notes that "the normal rule is...still working, but behind a camouflage of discouraging dicta" (p. 724), noting that there was nothing really exceptional in the *Calveley* case, and that the applicant in *ex p. Swati* had no arguable case. "When genuine grounds for judicial review are alleged, it is the refusal rather than the grant of review which is the exceptional course" (p. 725).

The dicta in *ex p. Calveley* have been endorsed by the Court of Appeal, notwithstanding Wade's reservations, in *R. v. Birmingham City Council, ex p. Ferrero* [1993] 1 All E.R. 530. More reassuringly, in *R. v. Devon County Council, ex p. Baker* [1995] 1 All E.R. 73, Simon Brown L.J. reverted to the formula that which of two available avenues of redress is to be preferred "will depend ultimately upon which is the more convenient, expeditious and effective" (at 92). On the other hand, Dillon L.J. found *Calveley* and *Swait* "particularly helpful" (at 87). They were agreed that judicial review was more appropriate than a ministerial default power to resolve an issue of law. Farquharson L.J. agreed with both judgments.

For further examples of the many cases where judicial review has been refused on this ground, see *R. v. Westminster City Council, ex p. Hilditch* [1991] C.O.D. 434 (complaint already under investigation by the auditor under the Local Government Finance Act 1982); *R. v. Blackpool Borough Council, ex p. Red Cab Taxis Ltd* [1994] R.T.R. 402 (unreasonable licence condition not quashed on judicial review as rectification was possible by statutory appeal to magistrates' court); *R. v. Royal Borough of Kingston upon Thames, ex p. X* [1993] C.O.D. 470 (complaints procedure under Part III of the Children Act 1989 more convenient and effective than judicial review); *R. v. Secretary of State for the Home Department, ex p. Capti-Mehmet* [1997] C.O.D. 61.

Where a party complains of procedural irregularity or bias on the part of a magistrates' court in a criminal case, an application for judicial review may be brought; there is no requirement that an appeal is first taken to the Crown Court: *R. v. Hereford Magistrates' Court, ex p. Rowlands* [1997] 2 W.L.R. 854. Parliament was to be taken to have intended that a defendent is entitled to both a fair trail and a fair retrial on appeal to the Crown Court (*Calvin v. Carr*, above, pp. 506–509, distinguished).

See generally N. Collar (1991) 10 C.J.Q. 138; S. Juss [1986] C.L.J. 372 (on *Swati*); and C. Lewis, "The Exhaustion of Alternative Remedies in Administrative Law" [1992] C.L.J. 138 and *Lewis*, pp. 297–309. Compare the cases where the courts have held, exceptionally, that the court's supervisory jurisdiction is excluded by the existence of an alternative remedy (below, p. 700); exclusion is normally regarded as a matter of discretion, not jurisdiction: *R. v. Deputy Governor of Parkhurst Prison, ex p. Leech* [1988] A.C. 533, 562 (Lord Bridge).

(iii) Other Grounds

Even where an applicant for judicial review establishes one of the grounds for review, the court retains a discretion whether to grant a remedy. Relevant factors that have already been mentioned include the nature of the applicant's standing, any delay and the existence of alternative remedies. See *R. v. Secretary of State for Social Services, ex p. Association of Metropolitan Authorities* [1986] 1 W.L.R. 1, above, p. 411.

In *R. v. Monopolies and Mergers Commission, ex p. Argyll Group plc* [1986] 1 W.L.R. 763, Sir John Donaldson M.R. stated (at 774) that in exercising this discretion the court should approach its duties with a proper awareness of the needs of public administration. Among the factors relevant there were that good public administration is concerned with substance rather than form, and with the speed of decision, particularly in the financial field; it requires a proper consideration of the public interest and of the legitimate interest of individual citizens; and requires decisiveness and finality unless there are compelling reasons to the contrary. The court declined to quash a decision of the chairman of the commission to lay aside a reference of a takeover bid to the commission, which decision should have been made by a group of members and not by the chairman alone (see also Dillon L.J. at 778–779 and Neill L.J. at 782–783). In *R. v. Secretary of State for Education and Science, ex p. London Borough of Lewisham* [1990] C.O.D. 31, the Divisional Court declined to quash a decision of the Secretary of State to give leave to school governors to serve a notice discontinuing two schools as voluntary schools under Part II of the Education Act 1944, prior to their becoming City Technology Colleges; the Secretary of State's consultation process had been flawed, but the applications were not made with the promptness that the situation demanded, it was virtually certain that the Secretary of State would, after reconsideration, reach the same decision, and granting relief would merely lead to a further year's uncertainty which would be likely to cause substantial hardship to all concerned. (The last two cases were applied in *R. v. Warwickshire City Council, ex p. Boyden* [1991] C.O.D. 31.) In *Dorot Properties Ltd v. London Borough of Brent* [1990] C.O.D. 378, the Court of Appeal declined to quash a flawed decision to refuse overpaid rates: the ratepayer had wrongfully delayed in paying rates it was obliged to pay, and the sum in question represented no more than fair compensation for the council's loss of interest.

In older cases, certiorari was refused where the applicant had behaved unreasonably. In *ex p. Fry* [1954] 1 W.L.R. 730, a fireman disobeyed an order (to clean a superior officer's uniform) which he claimed was unlawful. He subsequently sought certiorari to quash the decision to caution him for a disciplinary offence, alleging breach of natural justice. Singleton L.J. thought his disobedience "extraordinarily foolish conduct". He should have obeyed the order and made a complaint later through the procedures laid down by regulations.

See generally, Sir Thomas Bingham, "Should Public Law Remedies be Discretionary?" [1991] P.L. 64; *Lewis*, Chap. 11.

(H) PARTICULAR REMEDIES

(i) Certiorari and Prohibition

(a) *Scope*

An order of certiorari quashes a decision that had already been made. Prohibition restrains a body from acting unlawfully in the future or from completing an act already begun. They were formerly limited to cases where a public authority was under a duty to act judicially (see *Ridge v. Baldwin* [1964] A.C. 40 (above, p. 424)). They now extend generally to administrative acts and are not limited to cases where there is a duty to act judicially (*R. v. Hillingdon London Borough Council, ex p. Royco Homes Ltd* [1974] 1 Q.B. 720 (certiorari granted to quash a grant of planning permission); *O'Reilly v. Mackman* [1983] 2 A.C. 237, 279, *per* Lord Diplock (above, p. 646)). Certiorari has been granted, for example, to quash a decision to refuse a mandatory grant to a student (*R. v. Barnet London Borough Council, ex p. Nilish Shah* [1983] 2 A.C. 309) and a decision to abolish corporal punishment in schools (*R. v. Manchester City Council, ex p. Fulford* (1982) 81 L.G.R. 292). Certiorari has also been granted to quash subordinate legislation, although legislative acts have traditionally been challenged by proceedings for a declaration. See *R. v. Secretary of State for Social Security, ex p. Association of Metropolitan Authorities* [1986] 1 W.L.R. 1 (certiorari assumed to be available to quash statutory instrument for lack of consultation but refused in the exercise of discretion); *R. v. Secretary of State for Health, ex p. U.S. Tobacco International* [1992] 1 Q.B. 353 (above, p. 412, certiorari granted).

(b) *Grounds*

Certiorari may be granted (i) if a decision is *ultra vires* or in breach of natural justice; (ii) if there is an error of law in the face of the record (above, p. 174); this doctrine is now obsolete); or (iii) if a decision has been procured by assertions shown clearly to be fraudulent or deliberately misleading. Ground (iii) is illustrated by *R. v. Ashford JJ.* [1956] 1 Q.B. 167; *R. v. Wolverhampton Crown Court, ex p. Crofts* [1983] 1 W.L.R. 204 (order quashing conviction procured by perjured evidence); *cf. R. v. Knightsbridge Crown Court, ex p. Goonatilleke* [1986] Q.B. 1 (conviction based on evidence of a witness who concealed his previous bad character quashed for breach of natural justice rather than fraud; it was not *certain* that the magistrate would have acquitted but for the fraud or perjury).

In *R. v. West Sussex Quarter Sessions, ex p. Albert and Maud Johnson Trust Ltd* [1973] Q.B. 188, the Court of Appeal (Lord Denning M.R. dissenting) held that certiorari would not lie to quash a decision merely on the ground that fresh evidence, relevant to the issue in the case, had been discovered after the trial. Lord Denning suggested that as evidence was admissible by affidavit to prove fraud or collusion, then it should also be admissible to prove mistake, but the majority (Orr and Lawton L.JJ.) held that the limits of certiorari were well established, and did not extend beyond defects or irregularities at the trial.

Prohibition prevents action or continuing action in excess of jurisdiction or contrary to natural justice: see, *e.g. Dimes v. Grand Junction Canal Co.* (above, p. 517); *R. v. Kent Police Authority, ex p. Godden* (above, p. 531).

Disobedience to certiorari or prohibition may lead to proceedings for contempt of court (*cf.* below, p. 692).

(ii) Mandamus[6]

(a) *Scope*

Mandamus lies to compel the performance of a public duty. There has never been any limitation of mandamus to judicial or quasi-judicial acts. Alternative methods of enforcing public or statutory duties include an action for damages (below, Chap. 11); for a mandatory injunction (below, p. 693); or for a declaration (below, p. 696); criminal prosecution or a statutory default power (above, pp. 85–90).

(b) *Statutory duties*

A statutory duty must be couched in fairly precise terms if it is to be enforceable. For example, section 10 of the Education Act 1996 provides that: "The Secretary of State shall promote the education of the people of England and Wales." This is pitched at such a high level of generality that there is no question of its being a legally enforceable duty, although no doubt a failure to fulfil the "duty" will be the subject of political criticism.

The most straightforward situation is where statute requires a specific act to be done, and it is not done. This may be because the person entrusted with the duty believes that the statute gives him a discretion whether or not to act, and so the main issue before the court is the proper interpretation of the statute.

Where the statute gives a discretion rather than imposes a duty, mandamus may still be available to compel the exercise of discretion according to law, for example, where a power is used for an improper purpose (*Padfield v. Minister of Agriculture*, above, p. 303); where irrelevant considerations are taken into account (see *R. v. P.L.A., ex p. Kynoch Ltd*, above, p. 256, where mandamus was refused on the facts); where a discretion is fettered by reliance on a fixed rule of policy (*R. v. Torquay JJ., ex p. Brockman* [1951] 2 K.B. 784); or where there is an error of law in construing the scope of a discretion (*R. v. Vestry of St Pancras*, above, p. 299). Indeed, mandamus is available wherever an inferior tribunal wrongfully declines to exercise a discretion or jurisdiction that in law it possesses. It would be unusual (although possible) for Parliament to entrust powers to a named body and at the same time to allow them to decline to *consider* whether those powers should be exercised. The courts emphasise in these circumstances that they do not seek to control the merits of an exercise of discretion or jurisdiction, but the circumstances may be such that the inferior tribunal is left with little alternative but to exercise the discretion, or their jurisdiction to determine a dispute, in a particular way (See *R. v. Justices of Kingston, ex p. Davey* (1902) 86 L.T. 589; and note the form of the order in *Padfield's* case, above, p. 309).

The following cases illustrate situations where mandamus lies. *R. v. Braintree District Council, ex p. Willingham* (1982) 81 L.G.R. 70 concerned section 71 of the Shops Act 1950, which provides that it is the duty of every local authority to enforce the Act. The council decided not to prosecute the operators of a Sunday Market for offences under the Act. The Divisional Court found that they had taken into account the expense of prosecuting and the fact that the market was popular in the locality. The court held that these were irrelevant considerations, and mandamus should go, requiring the council to perform its duty under section 71. The council had no general

---

[6] See A.J. Harding, *Public Duties and Public Law* (1989); *Lewis*, pp. 164–173.

discretion not to enforce the Act; the only scope for discretion was whether any particular proceedings were necessary to secure observance, and, as an aspect of that, the council could take account of the likelihood of failure. Then, in *R. v. Camden London Borough Council, ex p. Gillan* (1988) 21 H.L.R. 114, the council was held to be in breach of its statutory duty to hear and adjudicate upon applications regarding homelessness under Part III of the Housing Act 1985 where the homeless persons unit was only open between 9.30 a.m. and 12.30 p.m. on weekdays. Furthermore, applications had to be made by telephone and not face-to-face. A shortage of money arising from rate capping was not an adequate excuse. Orders of mandamus and declarations were granted.

(c) *Particular grounds for the refusal of mandamus*

● The defendant is the Crown. See *de Smith, Woolf and Jowell*, pp. 203–204, 217–218. *cf. R. v. Customs and Excise Commissioners, ex p. Cook* [1970] 1 W.L.R. 450.
● *Per* Scarman L.J. in *R. v. Bristol Corporation, ex p. Hendy* [1974] 1 W.L.R. 498, C.A., at 503: "I[f] there is evidence that a local authority is doing all that it honestly and honourably can to meet the statutory obligation, and that its failure, if there be failure, to meet that obligation arises really out of circumstances over which it has no control, then I would think it would be improper for the court to make an order of mandamus compelling it to do that which either it cannot do or which it can only do at the expense of other persons not before the court who may have equal rights with the applicant and some of whom would certainly have equal moral claims."

The court held that the local authority had complied with their duty under section 39(1) of the Land Compensation Act 1973 to secure that the applicant was provided with "suitable alternative residential accommodation on reasonable terms" after he had been displaced from his flat by a closing order under the Housing Act 1957. They had offered him temporary accommodation until a council house was available. Section 39(1) was held not to require the authority to give the applicant priority over other persons on the housing list.

cf. R. v. Secretary of State for the Environment, ex p. Smith [1988] C.O.D. 3.

(d) *Effect of disobedience*

If a local authority disobeys an order of mandamus, whether derived from the prerogative writ or statute, proceedings for contempt of court may be taken against the council. Local councils in Northern Ireland which disobeyed orders of mandamus requiring the holding of meetings for the proper dispatch of business have been fined: *Re Cook's Application* [1986] 3 N.I.J.B. 64 (Belfast City Council, £25,000); *Re Morrow's Application* [1987] 3 N.I.J.B. 16 (Castlereagh Borough Council, £10,000); *Re Cook's Application* [1987] 4 N.I.J.B. 42 (Belfast City Council, £25,000 fine reimposed). In addition, contempt proceedings may be taken against the individual councillors concerned: *R. v. Worcester Corporation* (1903) 68 J.P. 130; (1905) 69 J.P. 269; *R. v. Poplar Borough Council (No. 2)* [1922] 1 K.B. 95. In the latter case most of the Poplar councillors were imprisoned for a period for contempt: B. Keith-Lucas, "Poplarism" [1962] P.L. 52, 60–62.

(iii) Injunction

"An injunction is an order of a court addressed to a party requiring that party to do or to refrain from doing a particular act" (*de Smith, Woolf and Jowell*, p. 705). A prohibitory injunction may be appropriate to restrain the performance of *ultra vires* acts. A mandatory injunction may (rarely) be available to compel performance of a public duty. See generally, *Lewis*, Chap. 8.

Proceedings for an injunction may include an application for interlocutory relief to maintain the status quo pending trial of the main action. (See above, pp. 639–640.)

An injunction may be granted in one of several different forms. It may be expressed to last for a fixed period, or for ever, or indefinitely until some condition is fulfilled. It may be suspended to give reasonable time for compliance.

(a) *Examples of the use of injunctions in administrative law*

An example of a case where a mandatory injunction was granted is *Att.-Gen. v. Bastow* [1957] 1 Q.B. 514 where the Attorney-General at the relation of a local planning authority obtained an order requiring (*inter alia*) the removal of caravans placed on land in breach of planning control. An example of a refusal of an injunction in the exercise of the court's discretion on grounds peculiar to the mandatory form is *Dowty Boulton Paul Ltd v. Wolverhampton Corporation (No. 1)*, above, p. 275; and see *Morris v. Redland Bricks* [1970] A.C. 652.

Prohibitory injunctions may lie as follows:

● To restrain breaches of statutory duty (*e.g. Att.-Gen. ex rel. McWhirter v. I.B.A.* (The "Warhol" case) [1973] 1 Q.B. 629.
● To restrain *ultra vires* acts (*e.g. Att.-Gen. v. Fulham Corporation*, above, p. 182; *Att.-Gen. v. Crayford U.D.C.*, above, p. 184; especially where the *ultra vires* act involves unlawful payments from public funds (*e.g. Att.-Gen. v. De Winton* [1906] 2 Ch. 106, and *cf.* the functions of the district auditor discussed above, pp. 16–21). See also *Municipal Council of Sydney v. Campbell*, above, p. 301.
● To restrain repeated breaches of the criminal law, such as breaches of planning control and disobedience to enforcement notices (see *Att.-Gen. v. Bastow*, above). Compare *Att.-Gen. v. Harris* [1961] 1 Q.B. 74, where Mr and Mrs Harris were restrained by injunction from selling flowers outside Southern Cemetery, Manchester, contrary to the Manchester Police Regulation Act 1844. Mr Harris had been convicted and fined for offences against the Act on 142 occasions, his wife on 95. Further proceedings were taken against them, subsequently, for contempt of court: see *The Times*, September 21, 1960; February 15 and 28, 1961. *cf. Gouriet v. Union of Post Office Workers* [1978] A.C. 435, where the House of Lords refused to grant G a declaration that it would be unlawful for the union to seek to interrupt mail between this country and South Africa, on the ground that G lacked *locus standi*. See D. Feldman, "Injunctions and the Criminal Law" (1979) 42 M.L.R. 369; *Imperial Tobacco Ltd v. Att.-Gen.* [1981] A.C. 718 and *Att.-Gen. v. Able* [1984] Q.B. 795 (declarations and the criminal law).
● To restrain a public nuisance (*e.g. Pride of Derby Angling Association v. British Celanese and Others* [1953] Ch. 149).

(b) Locus standi *in relation to injunctions*

Apart from on an application for judicial review (see above, pp. 663–679), proceedings for an injunction may be brought:
● by the Attorney-General, on behalf of the Crown as *parens patriae* for "the protection of public rights or public interests as opposed to matters of a private character" (*Thio*, p. 134). He may for example seek to restrain a public although not a private

nuisance (*Att.-Gen. v. P.Y.A. Quarries* [1957] 2 Q.B. 169); to restrain public bodies from exceeding their powers; and to restrain repeated breaches of the criminal law;
• by a private individual "in two cases: first, where the interference with the public right is such that some private right of his is at the same time interfered with...; and, secondly, where no private right is interfered with, but the plaintiff, in respect of his public right, suffers special damage peculiar to himself from the interference with the public right" (*per* Buckley J. in *Boyce v. Paddington B.C.* [1903] 1 Ch. 109, 114). These principles were first established in private actions for public nuisance, but are of wider application, and it is normally a pre-condition for *locus standi* for an injunction for a plaintiff to be in a position to sue for damages for a tort or other wrong. If the execution of an *ultra vires* act would be an actionable tort, then the person affected clearly has *locus standi* to obtain an injunction (*e.g. Westminster Corporation v. L.N.W. Ry*, above, p. 340). These principles were reaffirmed by the House of Lords in *Gouriet v. Union of Post Office Workers* [1978] A.C. 435 (see above, pp. 653 and 668).
• by the Attorney-General in a relator action. See *Att.-Gen. v. Crayford U.D.C.*, above, p. 184; *Att.-Gen. v. I.B.A.* [1973] Q.B. 629.
• by a local authority. Section 222(1) of the Local Government Act 1972 provides that:

> "Where a local authority consider it expedient for the promotion or protection of the interests of the inhabitants of their area—
>> (a) they may prosecute or defend or appear in any legal proceedings and, in the case of civil proceedings, may institute them in their own name, and
>> (b) they may, in their own name, make representations in the interests of the inhabitants at any public inquiry held by or on behalf of any Minister or public body under any enactment."

This has altered the previous rule that local authorities were subject to the same *locus standi* requirements as private individuals (*Thio*, pp. 206–215). Now authorities are able to commence *any* civil proceedings in their own name—not just actions for an injunction. Local authorities have frequently relied on section 222 to seek injunctions to restrain breaches of the tree preservation orders (*e.g. Kent County Council v. Batchelor (No. 2)* [1979] 1 W.L.R. 213); enforcement and stop notices (*e.g. Westminster City Council v. Jones* (1981) 80 L.G.R. 241; *Runnymede Borough Council v. Ball* [1986] 1 W.L.R. 353; see S. Tromans [1986] C.L.J. 374); unlicensed street trading (*Westminster City Council v. Freeman* (1985) 135 N.L.J. 1232); the operation of an unlicensed sex shop (*Portsmouth City Council v. Richards* [1989] 1 CMLR 673); breaches of a noise control notice (*City of London Corporation v. Bovis Construction Ltd* (1988) 86 L.G.R. 660). Most difficulties have arisen in respect of injunctions to restrain breaches of the Sunday trading law, particularly on the question of the compatibility of that law with European Community law (see *Stoke-on-Trent City Council v. B & Q (Retail) Ltd* [1984] A.C. 754; *Wychavon District Council v. Midland Enterprises (Special Events) Ltd* (1987) 86 L.G.R. 83; Case 145/88 *Torfaen Borough Council v. B & Q plc* [1989] ECR 3851; [1990] 1 CMLR 337; [1990] 2 Q.B. 19; *W.H. Smith Do-It-All Ltd v. Peterborough City Council* [1991] 1 Q.B. 304; *Stoke-on-Trent City Council v. B & Q plc* [1991] Ch. 48). See P. Diamond, "Dishonourable Defences: The Use of Injunctions and the E.E.C. Treaty—Case Study of the Shops Act 1950" (1991) 54 M.L.R. 72. Restrictions on Sunday trading were substantially lifted by the Sunday Trading Act 1994.

The local authority must consider whether the institution of civil proceedings is in the interests of the inhabitants of their area (*Stoke-on-Trent City Council v. B & Q (Retail) Ltd* [1984] A.C. 754). After some uncertainty, the House of Lords has held that a local authority is not necessarily to be required to give an undertaking in damages (*Kirklees Metropolitan Borough Council v. Wickes Building Supplies Ltd.* [1993] A.C. 227 (below, p. 775)).

Apart from section 222, local authorities may be given specific powers to seek injunctions. Recent examples include the Environmental Protection Act 1990, s.81(5) (statutory nuisances); the Town and Country Planning Act 1990, s.187B (inserted by the Planning and Compensation Act 1991, s.3) (breaches of planning control): see M. Phillips [1992] J.P.L. 407.

The enactment of section 222 of the Local Government Act 1972 and the extension of specific powers to seek injunctions means that local authorities are unlikely to have to use relator proceedings. See generally on section 222, B. Hough, "Local Authorities as Guardians of the Public Interest" [1992] P.L. 130.

(c) *Relator actions*

Notes

1. Relator actions are proceedings for a declaration or injunction brought by the Attorney-General at the relation of (*i.e.* on the information of) a private individual. In theory, the Attorney has entire control over the proceedings; in practice, once he has given his consent to the proceedings, it is the relator who conducts them and is liable for costs. Where consent is given, no point can be taken as to the relator's standing or motives. The Attorney's approach is to grant consent if a *prima facie* case is shown of an infringement of a public right and there is no countervailing public interest (*de Smith, Woolf and Jowell*, p. 153).

2. The House of Lords in *Gouriet v. Union of Post Office Workers* [1978] A.C. 435 confirmed that the refusal of the Attorney-General to grant his consent to relator proceedings was not subject to review by the courts; and rejected the dictum by Lord Denning M.R. in *Att.-Gen. v. I.B.A.* [1973] Q.B. 629 at 649 that an individual member of the public can apply for an injunction "if the Attorney-General refuses leave in a proper case, or improperly or unreasonably delays in giving leave, or his machinery works too slowly." On *Gouriet*, see H.W.R. Wade (1978) 94 L.Q.R. 4; D.G.T. Williams [1977] C.L.J. 201 and [1977] Crim.L.R. 703; D. Lunny (1978) 12 U.B.C. Law Rev. 320; D. Feldman (1979) 42 M.L.R. 369. The same principle applies in respect of the Attorney-General's refusal to prosecute for an offence under the Shops Act 1950 (*R. v. Att-Gen., ex p. Edey*, unreported, February 26, 1992, C.A.); to authorise an application under the Coroners Act 1988, s.13 for the High Court to order an inquest (*R. v. Att.-Gen., ex p. Ferrante*, unreported, July 1, 1994); or to bring proceedings for contempt of court (*R. v. Solicitor-General, ex p. Taylor, The Times*, August 14, 1995, D.C.; see D.J. Feldman and C.J. Miller (1997) 113 L.Q.R. 36, who note that "it is time to ask whether [the Law Officers'] privileged position can be justified on principled or practical grounds" (at 40).

3. For an argument that the House of Lords decision in the *CCSU* case extending the scope of judicial review in respect of prerogative powers (above, p. 180) should lead to a reconsideration of the Attorney-General's immunity to review, see B. Hough, "Judicial Review Where the Attorney General Refuses to Act: Time for a Change" (1988) 8 L.S. 189.

4. The continued value of the relator action as a mechanism for obtaining a remedy against a public authority is uncertain (see S. Nott [1984] P.L. 22). The broader the approach to *locus standi* under Order 53 (see above, pp. 663–679), the less the need to seek the Attorney-General's consent to relator proceedings. One substantial limitation is that the Attorney in practice does not give consent where the proceedings are brought against a minister or a central government department (see *de Smith, Woolf and Jowell*, p. 149, who note that if he considered a department was not observing the law, he would presumably advise accordingly and resign if his advice were ignored). Relator proceedings have become something of a rarity (*ibid.*, p. 153).

For examples, see *Att.-Gen. ex rel. Tilley v. Wandsworth London Borough Council* [1981] 1 W.L.R. 854; *Att.-Gen. ex rel. Yorkshire Derwent Trust Ltd v. Brotherton* [1992] 1 A.C. 270 (assertion of a public right of way). *cf. Att.-Gen. ex rel. Scotland v. Barratt Manchester Ltd* (1991) 63 P. & C.R. 179 (remedy refused as no public right was involved). Relator proceedings presumably constitute an exception to the principle of *O'Reilly v. Mackman* (above, pp. 642–662). See A. Grubb [1983] P.L. 190, 200.

5. Lord Woolf has argued the case for the establishment of an office of Director of Civil Proceedings. The D.C.P. would take over from the Attorney-General responsibility for instituting or intervening in proceedings in the public interest, having the advantage of being outside politics and holding office independently and irrespective of the government of the day. The Attorney-General would retain responsibility for advising, and instituting proceedings on behalf of, the Government. The D.C.P. would also be able to authorise a member of the public to bring proceedings, his decision being subject to the supervision of the courts, and would have general responsibility for the development of the civil law and, in particular, public law. See "Public Law—Private Law: Why the Divide? A Personal View" [1986] P.L. 220, 236–238; *Protection of the Public—A New Challenge* (1990), pp. 103–113.

6. See generally on relator actions, *de Smith, Woolf and Jowell*, pp. 150–154; *Wade and Forsyth*, pp. 601–6102; J.Ll.J. Edwards, *The Law Officers of the Crown* (1964), pp. 186–195, and *The Attorney-General, Politics and the Public Interest* (1984), pp. 129–153; The JUSTICE/All Souls Review of Administrative Law, *Administrative Justice: Some Necessary Reforms* (1988), pp. 186–190, 203–204.

(d) *Grounds on which an injunction may be refused*

The injunction is an equitable remedy, and so, like the prerogative remedies, is discretionary. It may be refused in accordance with various recognised principles such as waiver, acquiescence, delay or unmeritorious conduct (see, *e.g. Bates v. Lord Hailsham*, above, p. 484; but *cf. Islington Vestry v. Hornsey UDC*, above, p. 284 (note)). Similarly, an injunction may be refused if it is unnecessary in view of the availability of an alternative remedy, an undertaking by the defendant, or the triviality of the injury to the plaintiff (*cf. Glynn v. Keele University*, above, p. 440 (note)).

A court cannot grant an injunction or an order for specific performance against the Crown (Crown Proceedings Act 1947, s.21(1)(a)); or against an officer of the Crown "if the effect of granting the injunction or making the order would be to give any relief against the Crown which could not have been obtained in proceedings against the Crown" (*ibid*. s.21(2)). (See above, p. 640.)

(iv) Declaration[7]

(a) *General Principles*

R.S.C. Order 15, r. 16 provides that:

"16. No action or other proceeding shall be open to objection on the ground that a merely declaratory judgment or order is sought thereby, and the court may make

---

[7] See *Zamir and Woolf*; G. Borrie (1955) 18 M.L.R. 138; P. W. Young, *Declaratory Orders* (2nd ed., 1984); *Lewis*, Chap. 7.

binding declarations of right whether or not any consequential relief is or should be claimed."

cf. the procedure by way of originating summons under R.S.C. Ord. 5, r. 2, where a question arises on an instrument. In *Dyson v. Att.-Gen.* [1911] 1 K.B. 410, it was established that "in a civil action brought by a competent plaintiff, the court could grant declaratory relief against the Crown as to the legality of actions which the Crown proposed to take" (*per* Lord Browne-Wilkinson in *R. v. Secretary of State for Employment, ex p. Equal Opportunities Commission* [1995] 1 A.C. 1, 34).

The declaration is the most useful of the remedies in administrative law in situations where a coercive order, disobedience of which constitutes a contempt, is not required, or where no wrongful act has as yet been committed. In some situations, for example in an action against the Crown, it is the only possible remedy (see above, p. 640). Where the defendant is a public authority, there is usually no question but that the law will be obeyed, once the precise legal position has been established authoritatively. Moreover, a declaratory order will be *res judicata* between the parties. For example, a planning condition declared to be *ultra vires* by a court can not be the subject of enforcement proceedings. There are additional advantages in the considerable flexibility in the form that a declaration may take, and the wide variety of situations in which a declaration may be made. A basic feature is that it is a discretionary remedy.

It is now available on an application for judicial review or in private law proceedings. In proceedings for a declaration, the court's jurisdiction may be *supervisory* or *original.* the former involves the review by the court of a decision by another person or body; the latter involves a decision by the court itself as to the "contested legal rights, subsisting or future, of the parties represented in the litigation before it" (see Lord Diplock in *Gouriet v. Union of Post Office Workers* [1978] A.C. 435, 501). The role of the court on an application for judicial review is almost invariably supervisory (*de Smith, Woolf and Jowell,* p. 738). The principle of *O'Reilly v. Mackman* (above, p. 642), taken together with the decision in *Gouriet,* generally prevents applicants whose private law rights are not at stake from seeking declarations under the supervisory jurisdiction in private law proceedings. There are, however, some cases where, perhaps anomalously, this appears to have been permitted (see below).

(b) Locus standi *for a declaration*

Outside the application for judicial review, the principles applicable to injunctions are generally applicable also to declarations (see pp. 693–696). There have, however, been cases that are difficult to fit within the traditional *locus standi* principles where the courts have given guidance on difficult and contentious issues of law in proceedings for a declaration. In *Royal College of Nursing v. Department of Health and Social Security* [1981] A.C. 800, the House of Lords (by 3:2) granted the College a declaration that advice in a DHSS circular that no offence was committed by nurses who terminated a pregnancy by medical induction if a doctor decided on the termination, initiated it, and remained responsible throughout for its overall conduct and control, did not involve the performance of unlawful acts by members of the College. Woolf J. at first instance noted that neither party desired to take any points as to the jurisdiction of the court to grant a declaration; stated that, nevertheless, questions of *locus standi* could not be overcome by consent of the parties; and concluded that he had jurisdiction, accepting the Solicitor General's argument that the case should be regarded as exceptional because of the College's special responsibilities in providing advice and insurance for its members, and the relationship between the department and the nurses, many of whom were employed by bodies acting under the department's supervision. It would, however, have been much better for proceedings to have been brought under Order

53. This aspect of the case was not mentioned by the Court of Appeal or the House of Lords.

Then, in *Gillick v. West Norfolk and Wisbech Area Health Authority* [1986] A.C. 112, the House of Lords held (by 3:2) that a DHSS memorandum of guidance, which stated that in exceptional cases it was a matter for the doctor's clinical judgment to decide whether to prescribe contraception for a child under 16 without the knowledge and consent of the parents, did not contain advice that was an infringement of parents' rights or was unlawful. As in the *RCN* case, it was not suggested that Mrs Gillick was acting inappropriately in instituting proceedings for a declaration. The writ and statement of claim was issued three months before the decision in *O'Reilly v. Mackman* (above, pp. 642–662) (see Lord Fraser at 163). Lord Scarman stated (at 178) that Mrs Gillick's action was "essentially to protect what she alleges to be her rights as a parent under private law". He did not see her claim "as falling under the embargo imposed by *O'Reilly's* case"; if he was wrong on that he would nevertheless think "that the private law content of her claim was so great as to make her case an exception to the general rule" (at 178). Both the "collateral issue" and "consent" exceptions recognised by Lord Diplock in *O'Reilly* (above, p. 652) could be said to apply. Lord Fraser agreed with Lord Scarman (at 163). Lord Bridge, in contrast, said that Mrs Gillick "had no private right which she is in a position to assert" against the second respondent, the DHSS. Nevertheless, no objection had been or could now be raised on the "procedural technicality that the proceedings were commenced by writ rather than by application for judicial review" (at 192). Lords Brandon and Templeman did not discuss the procedural question. Lord Bridge expressed concern on another point. He did not agree with Lords Scarman and Fraser that the issue of a memorandum with guidance that would result in unlawful acts would be challengeable as an *ultra vires* abuse of discretion on *Wednesbury* grounds. "Here there is no specific statutory background by reference to which the appropriate *Wednesbury* questions would be formulated" (at 192). Instead, it had to be recognised that the *RCN* case

"does effect a significant extension of the court's power of judicial review. We must now say that if a government department, in a field of administration in which it exercises responsibility, promulgates in a public document, albeit non-statutory in form, advice which is erroneous in law, then the court, in proceedings in appropriate form commenced by an applicant or plaintiff who possesses the necessary *locus standi*, has jurisdiction to correct the error of law by an appropriate declaration. Such an extended jurisdiction is no doubt a salutary and indeed a necessary one in certain circumstances, as the *Royal College of Nursing* case [1981] A.C. 800 itself well illustrates. But the occasions of a departmental non-statutory publication raising, as in that case, a clearly defined issue of law, unclouded by political, social or moral overtones, will be rare. In cases where any proposition of law implicit in a departmental advisory document is interwoven with questions of social and ethical controversy, the court should, in my opinion, exercise its jurisdiction with the utmost restraint, confine itself to deciding whether the proposition of law is erroneous and avoid either expressing *ex cathedra* opinions in areas of social and ethical controversy in which it has no claim to speak with authority or proferring answers to hypothetical questions of law which do not strictly arise for decision" (at 193–194).

Lord Templeman echoed Lord Bridge's warning "against the involvement of the courts in areas of social and ethical controversy or hypothetical questions. Nevertheless the questions raised by this appeal must now be answered" (at 206).

The willingness of the House of Lords to entertain the case is strongly criticised by C. Harlow (1986) 49 M.L.R. 768, who argues that Mrs Gillick lacked *locus standi* to be granted a private law declaration, and that *O'Reilly v. Mackman* should have applied. See also H.W.R. Wade (1986) 102 L.Q.R. 173; Sir Harry Woolf, *Protection of the Public—A New Challenge* (1990), pp. 43–44.

Following these cases, the courts have been prepared to grant declarations as to the lawfulness of proposed medical treatment (see *Re F (Mental Patient: Sterilisation)* [1990] 2 A.C. 1, H.L. (sterilisation operation on mentally handicapped adult); *Airedale NHS Trust v. Bland* [1993] A.C.789 (artificial discontinuance of life sustaining treatment and support from patient in a persistent vegetative state).

As regards the court's *original* jurisdiction, by contrast, the Court of Appeal has confirmed Lord Diplock's statement in *Gouriet* (above) that it is confined to declarations as to the private law rights of the parties (see *Meadows Indemnity Co. v. The Insurance Corporation of Ireland plc and the International Commercial Bank plc* [1989] 2 Lloyd's Rep. 298; discussed in *Zamir and Woolf*, pp. 45–48, which notes that the House of Lords decision in *RCN* and *Gillick* were not cited in *Meadows*, and that in those cases the House was not referred to *Gouriet*). See also Knox J. in *Mid Kent Holdings plc v. General Utilities plc* [1996] 3 All E.R. 132, holding that a private person had no right to seek a declaration that G was in breach of undertakings given to the Secretary of State under the Fair Trading Act 1973 following a report by the Monopolies and Mergers Commission. On analysis, the breach of statutory duty was not intended to give rise to a civil remedy, whether by damages, injunction or declaration.

Conversely, Lord Browne-Wilkinson in *R. v. Secretary of State for Employment, ex p. Equal Opportunities Commission* [1995] 1 A.C. 1, 34–37, emphasised that it was still possible for a "declaration as to public rights" to be granted on an application for judicial review. Order 53, r. 1(2) and s.31 of the Supreme Court Act 1981 (above, pp. 599, 604) did not limit the grant of declarations to cases where one of the prerogative orders was available. A dictum to the contrary by Lord Scarman in *R. v. I.R.C., ex p. National Federation of Self-Employed and Small Businesses Ltd.* [1982] A.C. 617, 648, was based on the argument that "to do otherwise would be to condemn [r. 1(2)] as *ultra vires*" and could not survive the enactment of section 31. Lords Jauncey and Lowry agreed with Lord Browne-Wilkinson's remarks on these points. (But see above, p. 641). Thus, the way was open for the House of Lords to grant declarations that the provisions of the Employment Protection (Consolidation) Act 1978 which prescribed less favourable conditions with respect to qualification for redundancy pay and compensation for unfair dismissal for part-time as compared with full-time workers were "incompatible with" European Community law (respectively, Art. 119/EEC and the Equal Pay Directive (Dir. 75/117) and the Equal Treatment Directive (Dir. 76/207)). Lord Keith of Kinkel noted that at no stage in the *Factortame* litigation (above, p. 640) was it suggested "that judicial review was not available for the purpose of obtaining an adjudication upon the validity of the legislation in so far as it affected the applicants" (at 27). Whether this is in truth the exercise of the original or the supervisory jurisdiction is, however, uncertain. Perhaps the proper analysis is that this is *sui generis*, a hybrid situation where the court is in reality exercising a supervisory jurisdiction (reviewing the validity of an Act of Parliament in a way similar to that by which it might review the validity of a byelaw) while purporting, out of deference to Parliamentary sensibilities, merely to exercise an original jurisdiction to declare rights.

(c) *Some grounds on which a declaration may be refused*

A declaration may be refused because the matter is non-justiciable, for example, because it is a question of morality rather than law (see *Cox v. Green* [1966] 1 Ch. 216: medical ethics); or because it is a question of the Crown's treaty-making power which the court's decline to consider for policy reasons (see *Blackburn v. Att.-Gen.* [1971] 1 W.L.R. 1037 and *McWhirter v. Att.-Gen.* [1972] CMLR 882); or because there is an attempt to challenge the validity of Parliamentary proceedings (see *British Railways*

Board v. Pickin [1974] A.C. 765; *cf. R. v. H.M. Treasury, ex p. Smedley* [1985] Q.B. 657).

Moreover, there must be a real and not a hypothetical question in dispute between two parties (see Lord Sumner in *Russian Commercial and Industrial Bank v. British Bank for Foreign Trade Ltd* [1921] 2 A.C. 438 at 452); J. Jaconelli (1985) 101 L.Q.R. 587. In *Blackburn v. Att.-Gen.* [1971] 1 W.L.R. 1037, the Court of Appeal declined to make a declaration on the hypothetical question whether by signing the Treaty of Rome, Her Majesty's Government would irreversibly surrender in part the sovereignty of Parliament. In *R. v. Secretary of State for the Environment, ex p. Nottinghamshire County Council, The Independent*, November 13, 1986, declarations were refused where they related to determinations subsequently validated by retrospective legislation (*cf. R. v. Local Commissioner, ex p. Eastleigh Borough Council* (above, p. 154)). Then, in *R. v. Secretary of State for Education and Science, ex p. Birmingham City Council* (unreported, May 14, 1991), Brooke J. set aside the grant of leave to the council to seek a declaration that revised arrangements for its secondary schools would enable the council to comply with its obligations under the Sex Discrimination Act 1975. (In *Birmingham City Council v. Equal Opportunities Commission* [1989] A.C. 1155, the House of Lords had held the council to be in breach of its obligations under the 1975 Act). The Secretary of State had expressed no view on the question and was not a proper contradictor. It may be noted that, while the courts continue to be reluctant to pronounce on issues that are now academic, they are increasingly prepared to give what are in effect advisory declarations concerning the legality of forthcoming measures (see Sir John Laws, "Judicial Remedies and the Constitution" (1994) 57 M.L.R. 213, citing the *RCN*, *Gillick* and *Bland* cases and *ex p. Smedley* (above); Sir John favours the development of this practice).

The original *jurisdiction* of the court to grant a declaration may be regarded as excluded where Parliament creates new rights and duties and by the same enactment appoints a specific tribunal for their enforcement (*Barraclough v. Brown* [1987] A.C. 615, H.L., distinguished in *Pyx Granite Co. Ltd v. Ministry of Housing and Local Government* [1960] A.C. 260, H.L.). Where this principle does not apply in respect of the original jurisdiction, and in cases involving the supervisory jurisdiction, the existence of an alternative remedy may instead give rise to a *discretion* to refuse a remedy (above, pp. 687–689; *Leech v. Deputy Governor of Parkhurst Prison* [1988] A.C. 533, H.L.). See discussion in *Zamir and Woolf* pp. 67–74; *Lewis*, pp. 309–315.

(I) Proposals for Reform

A full review of remedies was undertaken by the Law Commission, which reported in 1994 (*Administrative Law: Judicial Review and Statutory Appeals*, Law Com. No. 226, 1994–1995 H.C. 669). Many of its proposals were subsequently endorsed by Lord Woolf in the course of his review of the whole civil justice system (*Access to Justice: Final Report*, HMSO, 1996, Chap. 18). At the time of writing (January 1997), the Government had not announced its position on these reports, although a number of Lord Woolf's more central proposals on reform of civil procedure have been accepted (*Access to Justice:"The Way Forward"*, the *Lord Chancellor's Strategy for Implementing Lord Woolf's Review of the Procedure for the Civil Courts*, LCD, October 1996).

LORD WOOLF, ACCESS TO JUSTICE: FINAL REPORT, JULY 1996

Chapter 18: Crown Office List

Introduction

1. Many of the public law proceedings which are administered by the Crown Office are of considerable constitutional significance, since they are the means whereby the lawfulness of decisions of public bodies can be examined by the courts and individuals who have been improperly detained can secure their liberty. As has so often been stated, the growth of public law and, in particular, of judicial review has been one of the most significant developments in the English legal system in the last 25 years. It is therefore important to consider how the procedure and management of these proceedings are to be absorbed into the reformed civil justice system which I am advocating.

2. My objective is to secure greater uniformity of procedure among those cases which are dealt with by the Crown Office, which can at present be bedevilled by disputes as to procedure, notably where there may be an option as to what remedy to seek. For the same reason, there also needs to be greater uniformity between the procedures in public law cases and those in private law cases. The procedural exclusivity rule, whereby it is normally an abuse of process not to use judicial review when it is the appropriate procedure, has led to wholly undesirable procedural wrangles and has been much criticised by distinguished commentators. It continues to cause problems, notwithstanding some clarification by the House of Lords in the *Roy* case (*Roy v. Kensington and Chelsea and Westminster FPC* [1992] 1 A.C. 624).

3. The Law Commission, in its 1994 report, *Administrative Law: Judicial Review and Statutory Appeals*, has made a series of recommendations for procedural reform which for the most part I warmly endorse....

4. Cases administered by the Crown Office List rarely involve determining factual evidence or hearing witnesses. Any necessary evidence is nearly always given by affidavit. Discovery, too, is rare. Crown Office proceedings are therefore on the whole free of the excesses that plague other proceedings. They can proceed rapidly to a hearing which will usually be quite short. They should involve relatively modest expenditure by the parties.

Nominated judges

5. The use of judges specially nominated to hear Crown Office cases is one of the strengths of the Crown Office List. I hope, however, that in the future more judges from other Divisions can be nominated to hear Crown Office cases where their experience in a specialist area would be valuable.

Local disposal

6. There is also a real need for the resolution of some Crown Office List cases on Circuit....

Judicial review

7. Some of the general recommendations which I am making apply as much to Crown Office cases as to private law cases. Some apply even more strongly. Among these is the recommendation that applicants should be encouraged to resolve their complaints without resorting to litigation. There is an increasing number of grievance procedures and ombudsmen available for this purpose. Applicants should normally use these procedures first. Judicial review ought to be conserved as a remedy of last resort. Before an application is made to initiate proceedings for judicial review, the proposed applicant should have taken advantage of any system of dispute resolution available, unless it would be unreasonable to do so, for example because the complaints procedure is too slow. If there is no satisfactory system of ADR the applicant should notify the proposed defendant of the claim, giving sufficient information to enable a response to be made rapidly so that the applicant could still comply with the three month time limit within which the claim must usually be brought. The defendant would not be obliged to respond, but should notify the applicant that there was to be no response. The fact that the court can extend time should avoid an applicant who waits for a reasonable period for a response from being prejudiced. This will put on a slightly more formal basis the growing practice of writing a letter before commencing proceedings, which was strongly urged by Brooke J. in *R. v. Horsham D.C., ex p. Wenman* [1994] 4 All E.R. 681.

The form of application

8. Rather than being a completely separate form, as at present, an application for judicial review should follow the standard claim form. In other words, it must include a summary of the facts relied on and its contents must be verified. It will therefore replace the application and principal affidavit in support. I hope that it will also overcome the current problem of excessively lengthy applications and affidavits. There will, of course, be particular requirements for claims for judicial review, for example that a copy of the decision which is the subject matter of the claim and any response by the defendant to the pre-application process must be attached.

The remedies which should be available

9. I see no reason why any remedies which could be obtained in a private law action, or a writ of *habeas corpus*, should not also be included in a claim for judicial review, so long as it is not inconvenient to do so. The court should be able to direct that additional claims should be disposed of separately or made the subject of a separate claim if their inclusion would interfere with the disposal of the claim for judicial review. When considering whether to grant relief the court should be able to take into account any offer by the defendant to pay compensation.

10. I recommend that the court should have an express power to grant advisory declarations when it is in the public interest to do so. However, this should be limited to cases where the issue was of public importance and was defined in insufficiently precise terms, and where the appropriate parties were before the court.

11. Litigants will be encouraged to issue their claims for judicial review at the Crown Office, since it will continue to administer them. However, the originating process will not be invalidated if the claimant issues a claim in another court and it will be for that court to transmit the claim to the Crown Office.

Preliminary consideration

12. I agree with the Law Commission that the leave stage should be renamed the preliminary consideration stage. This will also demonstrate that the initial filtering process is very much the same as that which will take place in private law proceedings. It should, however, take place on the application being made, before any defence is filed, rather than after the defence has been filed, as usually happens in private law proceedings. The same criteria should also be applied in determining whether the case should proceed, namely whether there is a realistic prospect of success or some other reason why the case ought to be disposed of at a substantive hearing. The judge should give brief reasons where he refuses permission to proceed.

13. After a written refusal there should be a right of renewal to a single judge at an oral hearing and a further right of appeal to the Court of Appeal, but only with the leave of the judge or a Lord Justice, from a refusal at the oral hearing. In my view it would be sensible if this procedure applied in criminal causes and matters as well as civil causes. I recognise, however, that it raises questions of judicial deployment in criminal cases and further consultation will be needed to ensure that any difficulties can be overcome.

14. The preliminary consideration should be in writing, as the Law Commission proposes, unless the court directs an oral hearing. The judge conducting the preliminary consideration should be able to call upon the defendant to provide information, in a standard questionnaire, or to make representations, although I hope that greater use of the pre-application process will mean that this is not normally necessary. It would not be obligatory for the defendant to respond but failure to do could be taken into account in the decision whether the application should proceed.

15. The court should be able to grant interim relief before the preliminary consideration of the claim, although interim relief on an *ex parte* basis would only be granted in a very clear and urgent case. The rules should also make it clear that any appropriate remedy, including a stay, an interim declaration and bail, can be granted. The provisions on bail will be clarified, as recommended by the working group.

16. Case management is applicable to judicial review claims as well as to private law claims. At the preliminary consideration the judge should consider giving directions for the future conduct of the proceedings and the claimant should be able to indicate on a *pro forma* or standard form what directions should be given. The judge should also be able to ask the defendant for his views, although in most cases it will be preferable to make the directions subject to any written representations by him. Directions could be given as to:

(a) the persons on whom the claim should be served (the court should consider whether any public body other than the proposed defendant will be affected by the decision);

  (b) whether there should be a defence;
  (c) what, if any, further evidence is required and the form it should take (usually witness statements but exceptionally affidavits);
  (d) the form which the hearing should take.

The judge should lay down a timetable, with as precise a date for the hearing as can be given. By giving directions the court should be able to limit the number of interlocutory hearings.

Defence

17. If the issues are sufficiently clear from the claim the judge may decide to inform the defendant that he need only provide a skeleton argument. Otherwise, he will indicate that there should be a defence, although the defendant will have the option of saying on the notice of intention to defend that he will not file a defence. The defence should be in the standard form of a defence to the claim. Like the claim, it will not be a lengthy and complex document but should be restricted to a succinct statement of the facts (so far as they differ from those set out in the claim) relied on by the defendant and his contentions. It should have annexed to it any documents relied on. It would replace the present principal affidavit, since there will be a requirement that the defendant verify the truth of its contents.

18. The defendant should be able to counterclaim for a declaration or other appropriate remedy which arises out of the matters to which the claim relates, unless the counterclaim could not be dealt with conveniently with the claim, as might happen where it would add extra parties. In certain cases it may be appropriate to impose a condition that a public authority should not seek the costs of the counterclaim.

Further evidence

19. The parties will be allowed to put in additional evidence, but they will have to justify the costs of doing so, since judicial review is not the normal way of resolving issues of fact.

Standing

20. I support the Law Commission's recommendation that the present generous practice of the courts in interpreting the requirement that the applicant must have a "sufficient interest" in the matter to which the application relates should be incorporated in the new rules. This should be in general terms, although a practice guide could indicate relevant factors. I agree with the Commission that the applicant will have standing if he has been or will be adversely affected or if it is in the public interest that the proceedings should be brought. This is the test which I consider should be of general application: in appropriate private law cases, such as claims for a declaration, the courts

should on occasion be able to allow proceedings to continue if it is in the interests of justice or in the public interest that they should do so. As the Justice/Public Law Project paper points out, the question of the applicant's standing can ultimately be treated as secondary to the merits of the case.

21. Consideration should be given to conferring on the court a discretion to allow third party intervention, both in the applicant's interest and in the public interest. If this is thought desirable, it should be a principle of general application, although the courts' approach should be more cautious when considering whether to allow intervention in proceedings concerning private rather than public law rights.

Costs

22. I agree with the Law Commission that legislation should confer a discretion on the court to order costs to be paid out of public funds where it is in the public interest that proceedings should be brought. If this recommendation is not implemented I recommend that the court should have a discretion not to order an unsuccessful party to pay the other party's costs, on the grounds that the proceedings have been brought in the public interest. Initially the discretion should only be exercised where there would otherwise be substantial hardship.

Written determination

23. As judicial review and some statutory applications in the Crown Office List do not usually involve oral evidence, they are susceptible to disposal in writing. This would not be appropriate for cases involving a point of principle, but it could sometimes be a valuable option for a straightforward case where the parties agreed on its use. Arrangements would need to be made for the documents and the judgement to be inspected by the public. Subject to these points I recommend that the judge should have a discretion to direct that there should be no hearing.

Divisional Court and appeals

24. At present judicial review in criminal causes and in the heaviest civil cases are heard by a Divisional Court of at least two judges. The justification in criminal causes is the restricted right of appeal to the House of Lords. In my view all cases of judicial review should be heard by a single judge unless there are exceptional circumstances. The proposals in paragraph 13 as to renewal at the preliminary consideration stage should be applied to appeals from substantive decisions. In criminal causes the appeal should be to the Criminal Division of the Court of Appeal and in non-criminal causes to the Civil Division. In both cases leave from the judge or the appeal court would be required. The requirement of leave is justified because of the need for certainty in criminal matters; it already exists in most civil appeals. As with the proposals on renewal of applications, there should be further consultation about this.

The prerogative orders

25. Although I am an enthusiast for adopting modern English, I am not in favour of the Law Commission's proposal to replace the names *certiorari*, prohibition and *mandamus* with a quashing, prohibiting and mandatory order. The Latin names are used throughout the common law world and have become synonymous with the duty of superior courts to protect the public against the abuse of power. I am not sure that the proposed alternatives are that much easier to comprehend. On the other hand I agree with the Treasury Solicitor that the title of judicial review proceedings, *R. v. A ex parte B*, is outmoded and should be changed to *A v. B*.

Bridging the divide

26. The recommendations which I have made are intended to bridge the divide between public law and private law claims by bringing the two procedures together. The same statements of case will be used in both, so that there will be no need for a claim in one area to be treated as though it had been begun by another procedure. It is nevertheless important that the safeguards of the three month time limit and of standing, which are necessary in judicial review claim, should not be bypassed, but these can be retained without making it an abuse of process to adopt the wrong procedure.

27. If a question arises as to whether the proceedings should have been brought by judicial review it will be possible to transfer the claim to the Crown Office for a case management conference, at which the same filtering process, without the court having to consider whether the issues are ones of public or private law, will apply, unless the answer is obvious or unless the issue needs to be resolved for substantive as opposed to procedural reasons. If the case is without merit, it can be dismissed irrespective of whether it raises public or private law issues; if it has merit the judge can direct it to proceed without determining whether it is a public or private law case. Furthermore, if the court thinks this is the best course to adopt in all the circumstances, it will be possible to leave consideration of standing and time limits until the final hearing. This is often necessary at present because the merits can affect both questions of standing and delay. . . .

Notes

1. The Law Commission stated in their 1994 report (Law Com. No. 226) that in making their recommendations they had to form a view about the proper balance among "(a) the importance of vindicating the rule of law, so that public law bodies take lawful decisions and are prevented from relying on invalid decisions; (b) the need for speed and certainty in administrative decision-making in cases where the whole community, or large sections of it, will be affected by the decisions of public law bodies; (c) the private interest of individual litigants in obtaining a remedy for their grievances." There was also a public interest in the prompt adjudication of disputes through the courts (p. 7). Of particular concern was the increase in case load and delays in recent years (pp. 10–16). One measure which would assist would be the creation of a right of appeal to a court or independent tribunal in homelessness cases (p. 15) (a recommendation subsequently implemented: see above, p. 541).

Many of their specific recommendations were endorsed by Lord Woolf, and with that endorsement appear to stand a good chance of implementation. One advantage for Lord Woolf was that as his remit extended to the whole of the civil justice process he was able to make more radical proposals to address the problems caused by the relationship between public and private law. On the issue of procedural exclusivity, the Law Commission did not favour proposals for a unified procedure for public and private law cases, with provision for striking out rather than a leave requirement. Such a procedure would "prevent the expeditious disposal of public law cases by specialist judges and could increase complexity and costs." It was "essential to filter out hopeless applications" (p. 20). Reform should be by a combination of "building on the restrictive approach to the exclusivity principle taken in *Roy v. Kensington and Chelsea and Westminster FPC*" (above, p. 656 (note)), and facilitating the transfer of cases into as well as out of Order 53 (pp. 21–30). Lord Woolf favours a greater assimilation of procedures, while retaining the three-month time-limit and standing requirement for public law cases.

The Law Commission noted the evidence of the wide disparity in the rates at which different judges granted leave (see above, p. 636). Its response was to propose that the Rules should state that "unless the application discloses a serious issue which ought to be determined it should not be allowed to proceed to a substantive hearing" (p. 41); and should direct the judge to consider whether the application complies with the requirement as to standing and time-limits and "whether the applicant has, or the reasons why he has not, pursued alternative legal remedies" (pp. 40–50). As to standing, the modern liberal approach should be taken further by the express recognition of a judicial discretion to entertain cases where that is considered to be in the public interest. Time-limits should be governed by the Rules rather than the Supreme Court Act 1980. Section 31(6) (above, p. 605) should be repealed; the Rules should provide for a three-month limit, a power to refuse an application if it is not "sufficiently prompt" *and* if the grant of ultimate relief "would be likely to cause substantial hardship to, or substantially prejudice the rights of, any person or be detrimental to good administration" and a power to extend time if there is "good reason for the application not having been made" within three months *and* it is not likely to cause hardship, etc. Applicants must either exhaust alternative legal remedies or demonstrate that "despite the existence of such a remedy, judicial review is an appropriate procedure". The court should take account of the pursuit of an alternative remedy as a good reason for extending time. Lord Woolf's position on some of these details is not stated.

Other points in Lord Woolf's proposals largely endorse Law Commission recommendations. However, some are not mentioned, including (a) that the court should be empowered to substitute its own decision for that of an inferior court or tribunal where there was only one lawful decision that could be arrived at and the ground for review arose out of an error of law; (b) that unincorporated associations should be permitted to apply in their own name through one or more members applying in a representative capacity, where the court is satisfied that the members have been or would be adversely affected or are raising an issue of public interest warranting judicial review, and that the members are appropriate persons to bring that challenge; (c) that the legal regulations be amended to enable the Legal Aid Board to consider the wider public interest in having the case heard. Unlike the Commission, Lord Woolf appears to favour access to the Court of Appeal being by appeal rather than renewal of the application. Other points (reference to alternative grievance procedures, the possible availability of all private law remedies, directions and case management, the filing of a defence, written disposition of some cases) are based more on the wider work of the *Access to Justice* project than Law Commission proposals. It is notable that neither Lord Woolf nor the Commission have any proposal to widen the use of discovery in judicial review (*cf.* above, p. 638).

2. On the Law Commission Report, see R. Gordon [1995] P.L. 11; N.J. Bamforth (1995) 58 M.L.R. 722; I. Hare [1995] C.L.J. 268; C.T. Emery [1995] P.L. 450

considering the advantages of a unified civil procedure and public law challenge outside the civil justice system).

3. Overall, both sets of proposals involve the further evolution of judicial review procedure rather than radical change, in a number of respects in parallel to developments by the judges. A central feature is that the case for retaining special protection for public authorities has been accepted notwithstanding the views of the sceptics. Indeed, given the recent problems of case load and delay this outcome is wholly unsurprising. Furthermore, the time-limits protection can be seen as all the more necessary with the proposed further relaxation in standing.

CHAPTER 11

CIVIL LIABILITY OF PUBLIC AUTHORITIES

(A) CONTRACT[1]

POWERS to contract may be conferred specifically by statute (see *Cross*, paras. 7–02–7–06; Turpin, *Government Procurement and Contracts* (1989), p. 84), generally by such statutory provisions as section 111 of the Local Government Act 1972 (above, p. 188), and by the common law, such as the general contractual capacity of the Crown apart from statute (Turpin, *op. cit.* pp. 83–84). If an authority enters into a contract when it has no power to do so, the contract is null and void—neither party may sue on it (see *Rhyl U.D.C. v. Rhyl Amusements Ltd*, above, p. 283; *Credit Suisse v. Allerdale Borough Council*, below, p. 776) and the authority will not be estopped from denying its validity (*ibid.*). There may, however, be rights conferred by the law of restitution (below, pp. 760–764). Moreover, a public authority may not disable itself by contract from discharging its primary purposes (see cases given above, at pp. 266 *et seq.*). This principle is closely related to, if not identical with, the doctrine of *The Amphitrite* (see Turpin, *op. cit.* pp. 85–90, above, p. 277). In general, the courts have shown some reluctance to apply judicial review principles to the exercise of contractual powers (see S. Arrowsmith (1990) 106 L.Q.R. 277; (1990) 10 L.S. 231, arguing that "the contractual nature of a power should in itself generally be irrelevant to the scope of review" (at 239)). See above, pp. 605–634 on the scope of the application for judicial review. The exercise of contractual powers is also normally excluded from review by the P.C.A. or the Local Government Ombudsman.

Parliament has recently imposed express restrictions on the power of local authorities to take account of non-commercial considerations (see above, pp. 94–97); cf. the use of contracting powers by central government to achieve policy goals (above, pp. 90–94). In addition, Parliament has imposed requirements as to compulsory competitive tendering across an increasing range of the activities of local government, seeking to move local authorities from being the providers of services to the "enablers" of service provision (see *Cross*, Chap. 7; S. Arrowsmith, *The Law of Public and Utilities Procurement* (1996), Chaps. 12–14, 18; S. Cirell and J. Bennett, *Compulsory Competitive Tendering: Law and Practice*; Local Government, Planning and Land Act 1980, Part III; Local Government Act 1988, Part I).

Public procurement is now increasingly regulated by European Community law. Article 30 of the E.C. Treaty prohibits quantitative restrictions on the free movement of goods between Member States, which would include decisions that discriminate against goods from other Member States. Public supply and works contracts with an estimated value above the prevailing threshold were made subject to common advertising procedures and award criteria (Directives 77/62, as amended, and 71/305, as amended; DoE Circulars 6/89 and 16/90). Other Directives (70/32 and 71/304)

[1] See C. Turpin, *Government Procurement and Contracts* (1989); H. Street, *Governmental Liability* (1953), Chap. 3; J.D.B. Mitchell, *The Contracts of Public Authorities* (1954); M. Aronson and H. Whitmore, *Public Torts and Contracts* (1982); S. Arrowsmith, *Government Procurement and Judicial Review* (1988), (1990) 10 L.S. 231, *Civil Liability and Public Authorities* (1992) and *The Law of Public and Utilities Procurement* (1996); P.W. Hogg, *Liability of the Crown* (2nd ed., 1989), Chap. 8.

required the abolition of discriminatory practices which might prevent contractors from other Member States from participating in public contracts on equal terms. The enforcement of these obligations was left to the E.C. Commission to take action in the European Court against a Member State under Art. 169/EEC. Directive 89/665 introduced new requirements for the establishment of review procedures in national courts or tribunals in respect of alleged infringement of Community law in the field of public procurement or national rules implementing that law. See S. Weatherill, "National Remedies and Equal Access to Public Procurement" (1990) 10 Y.E.L. 243. The Public Supply Contracts Regulations 1991 (S.I. 1991 No. 2679) and the Public Works Contracts Regulations 1991 (S.I. 1991 No. 2680) enacted the relevant E.C. procurement directives. Directive 92/50 introduced provisions regulating public services contracts and was implemented by the Public Services Contracts Regulations 1993 (S.I. 1993 No. 3228). Directive 93/36 consolidated the provisions applicable to supply contracts and was implemented by the Public Supply Contracts Regulations 1995 (S.I. 1995 No. 201).

The Supply, Works and Services regulations, as amended, apply, respectively, to (1) certain contracts for the supply of goods; (2) certain building and engineering works; and (3) certain contracts under which an authority engages a person to provide services, but excluding a contract of employement or other contract of service, and contracts that come under the regime of the other regulations. The current thresholds are 5,000,000 ECU under the works regulations, and 200,000 ECU for the supply (subject to exceptions) and services regulations. The regulations apply to contracts placed by "contracting authorities", a term that includes Ministers, government departments, local authorities and many other specified bodies. The regulations make provision in respect of technical specifications in contract documents, procedures leading to the award of contracts, the selection of suppliers or contractors, and the award of contracts. The obligation on a contracting authority to comply with the Regulations and any enforceable Community obligation in relation to the award of a contract is a duty owed to suppliers, contractors and services providers and is actionable by any such person "who, in consequence, suffers, or risks suffering, loss or damage". Proceedings may not be brought unless the supplier, etc., has notified the authority of the breach and of his intention to bring proceedings; and must be brought promptly and in any event within three months from the date when grounds for proceedings first arose unless the court considers there is good reason for extending the period. (*cf.* the position on judicial review, above, pp. 679–687.) The court may by an interim order (which may include an injunction against the Crown; *cf.* above, p. 640) and may set aside a decision or action taken or award damages. If the contract has been entered into, the only remedy is damages. (For the enforcement provisions, see S.I. 1995 No. 201, reg. 29, S.I. 1991 No. 2680, reg. 31 and S.I. 1993 No. 3228, reg. 32. These regulations are fully analysed by S. Arrowsmith, *The Law of Public and Utilities Procurement* (1996), Chaps. 5–11. On the relationship between the Works Directive and the Public Works Contracts Regulations, see *R. v. Portsmouth City Council, ex p. Coles* (1997) 16 Tr.L.R. 83.

(B) Tort[2]

Public authorities may both sue and be sued in tort (see section 222 of the Local Government Act 1972, above, p. 694). The liability of public authorities in tort is of

---

[2] See A. Rubinstein, *Jurisdiction and Illegality* (1965), Chap. VI; G.E. Robinson, *Public Authorities and Legal Liability* (1925); H. Street, *Governmental Liability* (1953), Chap. 2; P.W. Hogg, *Liability of the Crown* (2nd ed.), Chaps. 5–7; B.C. Gould, "Damages as a Remedy in Administrative Law" (1972) 5 N.Z.U.L.R. 105; C. Harlow, "Fault Liability in French and English Public Law" (1976) 39 M.L.R. 516 and *Compensation and Government Torts* (1982); M. Aronson and H. Whitmore, *Public Torts and Contracts* (1982); A.W. Bradley (1989) 23 L.T. 109; T. Weir [1989] P.L. 40; *Lewis*, pp. 374–414.

particular interest to administrative lawyers in so far as the ordinary principles of liability are modified, or should be modified, to take account of the special position of those authorities in law and society. In many respects a public authority is in no different position from that of any other plaintiff or defendant. For example, if a local authority van is carelessly driven, and injury is caused, ordinary tort principles apply. (Did the driver fall below the standard of the reasonable driver? Was the driver in the course of his employment, or was he taking the van on a frolic of his own?) It makes no difference that the van was publicly rather than privately owned.

On the other hand, the position of public authorities is complicated by the facts that their powers and duties are usually derived from statute, and that they must act *intra vires*. Statutory authority may be pleaded as a defence to an action in tort. Conversely, the grounds of an action may be failure to perform a statutory power or duty, the negligent performance of a power or duty, or malicious performance of a power (the malicious performance of a duty presumably merely adds insult to "injury"). Difficult questions of statutory interpretation may arise. It is a matter of debate how far, if at all, the legitimate interests of public authorities can be sufficiently protected by the application of ordinary tort principles.

It should be noted that the particular officer who commits the tortious act is personally liable, in addition to the vicarious liability of the authority (see *Ministry of Housing and Local Government v. Sharp* [1970] 2 Q.B. 223). Moreover, exemplary damages may be awarded in cases of oppressive, arbitrary or unconstitutional action in the exercise of public powers (*Rookes v. Barnard* [1964] A.C. 1129 at 1226, *per* Lord Devlin; *Broome v. Cassell & Co.* [1972] A.C. 1027). However, the tort must be one in respect of which such an award of damages was made prior to 1964, when *Rookes v. Barnard* was decided (*A.B. v. South West Water Services Ltd* [1993] Q.B. 507, C.A.: exemplary damages cannot be awarded in public nuisance; previous cases in which such damages had been awarded in respect of race and sex discrimination (*Bradford Metropolitan City Council v. Arora* [1991] 2 Q.B. 50) and private nuisance had not considered this point.) Accordingly, such awards may be made for trespass to the person or to land or false imprisonment (*e.g.* against police officers), malicious prosecution and defamation, but not negligence, deceit, public nuisance and (anomalously) misfeasance in a public office (see *de Smith, Woolf and Jowell*, p. 790)). £50,000 is the maximum appropriate for an award of exemplary damages against the police, and then only where officers of at least the rank of superintendent are involved in the unlawful conduct (*Thompson v. Commissioner of Police of the Metropolis* [1997] 2 All E.R. 762, C.A.).

Outside the law of tort, a finding of maladministration by an ombudsman may commonly lead to an *ex gratia* award of compensation. See A.W. Bradley (1989) 23 L.T. 109, 126–127.

(i) The Defence of Statutory Authority[3]

It is a good defence to an action in tort that the act alleged to constitute, for example, nuisance or trespass is expressly or impliedly authorised by statute.

Where the act of a public authority would be a tort if committed by a private person, and it is *ultra vires* the authority, the defence obviously fails. For example, in *Smith v. East Elloe RDC and John Champion & Son Ltd* (1952) 160 E.G. 148 ([1952] C.P.L. 738; 103 L.J. 108) Devlin J. (sitting with a jury) gave judgment for the plaintiff for £850, as damages for trespass. The council had continued the requisition of the plaintiff's property although the lawful purposes of the requisition (to house evacuees, and then to help to relieve the consequences of the housing shortage) had ceased because dilapidations (see the sequel, below, p. 799). Another example is *Cooper v.*

---

[3] See J. Fleming, *The Law of Torts* (8th ed.), pp. 439–441; *Cross*, pp. 10-15–10-19; G. Kodilinye (1990) 19 Anglo-Am.L.R. 72.

Wandsworth Board of Works (above, p. 420 (trespass)). *A fortiori*, a public authority may not argue in its *defence* that the act alleged to be tortious was *ultra vires*, and therefore not one which they had a legal power to perform (*Campbell v. Paddington Corporation* [1911] 1 K.B. 869, where the corporation authorised its employees to erect a stand in the street opposite the plaintiff's house. This was held to be a public nuisance). Rather more difficult are those cases where it it not clear whether the statute authorises the specific act that has been done. There must be a power or duty to perform the specific act in the particular manner complained of (*Metropolitan Asylum District v. Hill* (1881) 6 App.Cas. 193: general power to build a smallpox hospital did not confer a defence of statutory authority to a claim in nuisance). Alternatively the infringement of legal rights must be the inevitable or unavoidable result of authorised acts (*Hammersmith Ry v. Brand* (1869) L.R. 4 H.L. 171). The key factor is the precision of the statutory authorisation, and not necessarily whether that authorisation is a power or a duty. Thus, on the assumption that the provision of a smallpox hospital can constitute a nuisance to neighbours (*cf. Metroplitan Asylum District v. Hill*), a duty to build such a hospital on a particular site negatives liability to the neighbours; a power to build on that site (*i.e.* a choice whether or not to build) presumably also negatives liability *c.f. Allen v. Gulf Oil Refining Ltd* [1981] A.C. 1001); a power to build with no site specified will not negative liability, unless it is impossible to build without infringing someone's rights. On the defence of statutory authority and the rule in *Rylands v. Fletcher*, see *Dunne v. N.W. Gas Board* [1964] 2 Q.B. 806, C.A. See further *Marriage v. E. Norfolk Rivers Catchment Board* [1950] 1 K.B. 284 and *Department of Transport v. North West Water Authority* [1984] A.C. 336, 344, 359–360.

(ii) Negligent Exercise of Powers and Duties[4]; Breach of Statutory Duty[5]

Public authorities may clearly be liable for failures to perform statutory duties and for the negligent exercise of powers and duties. The main difficulties have arisen in respect of some of the specialised activities of public authorities—in particular in determining whether a duty of care is owed. The House of Lords provided a survey of the principles in the following case.

X (MINORS) v. BEDFORDSHIRE COUNTY COUNCIL

[1995] 2 A.C. 633; [1995] 3 W.L.R. 152; [1995] 3 All E.R. 353
(House of Lords)

The House of Lords heard appeals in five cases on the question whether claims for negligence or for breach of statutory duty should be struck out. Two (*X (Minors) v.*

---

[4] There is now an extensive body of literature on the negligence liability of public authorities—see, *e.g.* W. Friedmann (1944) 8 M.L.R. 31; H. Street, *Governmental Liability* (1953), pp. 40, 56–80; C.J. Hamson [1969] C.L.J. 273 (on the Court of Appeal decision in *Home Office v. Dorset Yacht Co.*); G. Ganz, "Compensation for Negligent Administrative Action" [1973] P.L. 84; C.S. Phegan, (1976) 22 McGill L.J. 605; C. Harlow, "Fault Liability in French and English Public Law" (1976) 39 M.L.R. 516, (1980) 43 M.L.R. 241, and *Compensation and Government Torts* (1982); P.P. Craig (1978) 94 L.Q.R. 428 and *Craig*, pp. 618–632; D. Oliver (1980) 33 C.L.P. 269; M.J. Bowman and S.H. Bailey [1984] P.L. 277; S.H. Bailey and M.J. Bowman [1986] C.L.J. 430; S. Todd, "The Negligence Liablity of Public Authorities: Divergence in the Common Law" (1986) 102 L.Q.R. 370 and "Public Authorities' Liability: The New Zealand Dimension" (1987) 103 L.Q.R. 19; P.W. Hogg, *Liability of the Crown* (2nd ed., 1989) Chap. 6; S. Arrowsmith, *Civil Liability and Public Authorities* (1992), pp. 176–185; *de Smith, Woolf and Jowell*, pp. 774–782.
[5] See W.V.H. Rogers, *Winfield & Jolowicz on Tort* (14th ed., 1994), Chap. 7; R.A. Buckley (1984) 100 L.Q.R. 204; K.M. Stanton, *Breach of Statutory Duty in Tort* (1986).

Bedfordshire County Council and *M (a Minor) v. Newham London Borough Council*)
concerned powers and duties in relation to the protection of children from abuse; three
(*E (a Minor) v. Dorset County Council, Christmas v. Hampshire County Council* and
Keating v. Bromley London Borough Council) concerned powers and duties in
relation to children with educational needs.

The five plaintiffs in the *Bedfordshire* case claimed damages for personal injury arising out of breach of statutory duty and negligence by the council in failing to protect
them from parental abuse. In the *Newham* case, the plaintiff M and her mother
claimed damages for personal injuries (psychiatric injury specified as anxiety neurosis)
arising out of breach of statutory duty and negligence by the local authority, the area
health authority and a consultant psychiatrist employed by the latter. They alleged
that the psychiatrist and a social worker employed by the local authority had concluded that M had been sexually abused, but then mistakenly identified the abuser as
the mother's cohabitee (who shared the same first name as the cousin whom M
intended to identify). This led to the authority's obtaining court orders removing M
from her mother, placing her in foster care and restricting the mother's access to her.

In the *Dorset* case, the plaintiff, E claimed damages for breach of statutory duty and
negligence by the council, alleging that it had initially wrongly advised his parents and
failed to diagnose that he suffered from a special learning disorder, and subsequently,
after his difficulties were acknowledged, failed to take the appropriate steps. In the
Hampshire case, the plaintiff (born in 1973) claimed damages against the council for
negligence in the assessment of his educational needs. He alleged that his primary
school headmaster had failed to refer him to the council for formal assessment or to an
educational psychologist for diagnosis, notwithstanding his exhibiting learning difficulties consistent with dyslexia and behavioural problems. Furthermore, the council's
teachers' advisory centre, to which he had been referred, had also failed to ascertain his
difficulty. The failure to treat his condition had disadvantaged him in realising his
potential and significantly restricted his vocational prospects. In the *Bromley* case, the
plaintiff (born in 1971) claimed damages for breach of statutory duty and negligence
against the council, alleging failure to place him at a reasonably appropriate school
and to identify him as a child with special needs. He claimed damages for the alleged
consequent impairment of his development and the disadvantage at which he was
placed in seeking employment.

All the claims were struck out at first instance. The Court of Appeal allowed appeals
against striking out as regards the claims in the education cases based on negligence.
The House of Lords held that all the causes of action should be struck out except those
in respect of allegations of professional negligence against one authority directly in
respect of its provision of a psychological advice service and against teachers and educational psychologists for whom defendant authorities were vicariously liable.

The leading speech was given by Lord Browne-Wilkinson, with whom Lords Jauncey of Tullichettle, Lane, Acker and (subject to one point) Nolan agreed.

LORD BROWNE-WILKINSON: ...

General approach

Introductory—public law and private law

The question is whether, if Parliament has imposed a statutory duty on an
authority to carry out a particular function, a plaintiff who has suffered damage in consequence of the authority's performance or non-performance of
that function has a right of action in damages against the authority. It is
important to distinguish such actions to recover damages, based on a private
law cause of action, from actions in public law to enforce the due performance
of statutory duties, now brought by way of judicial review. The breach of a

public law right by itself gives rise to no claim for damages. A claim for damages must be based on a private law cause of action. . . .

Private law claims for damages can be classified into four different categories, *viz*: (A) actions for breach of statutory duty simpliciter (*i.e.* irrespective of carelessness); (B) actions based solely on the careless performance of a statutory duty in the absence of any other common law right of action; (C) actions based on a common law duty of care arising either from the imposition of the statutory duty or from the performance of it; (D) misfeasance in public office, *i.e.* the failure to exercise, or the exercise of, statutory powers either with the intention to injure the plaintiff or in the knowledge that the conduct is unlawful.

Category (D) is not in issue in this case. I will consider each of the other categories but I must make it clear that I am not attempting any general statement of the applicable law: rather I am seeking to set out a logical approach to the wide ranging arguments advanced in these appeals.

(A) *Breach of statutory duty simpliciter*
This category comprises those cases where the statement of claim alleges simply (a) the statutory duty, (b) a breach of that duty, causing (c) damage to the plaintiff. The cause of action depends neither on proof of any breach of the plaintiffs' common law rights nor on any allegation of carelessness by the defendant.

The principles applicable in determining whether such statutory cause of action exists are now well established, although the application of those principles in any particular case remains difficult. The basic proposition is that in the ordinary case a breach of statutory duty does not, by itself, give rise to any private law cause of action. However a private law cause of action will arise if it can be shown, as a matter of construction of the statute, that the statutory duty was imposed for the protection of a limited class of the public and that Parliament intended to confer on members of that class a private right of action for breach of the duty. There is no general rule by reference to which it can be decided whether a statute does create such a right of action but there are a number of indicators. If the statute provides no other remedy for its breach and the Parliamentary intention to protect a limited class is shown, that indicates that there may be a private right of action since otherwise there is no method of securing the protection the statute was intended to confer. If the statute does provide some other means of enforcing the duty that will normally indicate that the statutory right was intended to be enforceable by those means and not by private right of action: *Cutler v. Wandsworth Stadium Ltd* [1949] A.C. 398; *Lonrho Ltd v. Shell Petroleum Co. Ltd (No. 2)* [1982] A.C. 173. However, the mere existence of some other statutory remedy is not necessarily decisive. It is still possible to show that on the true construction of the statute the protected class was intended by Parliament to have a private remedy. Thus the specific duties imposed on employers in relation to factory premises are enforceable by an action for damages, notwithstanding the imposition by the statutes of criminal penalties for any breach: see *Groves v. Wimborne (Lord)* [1898] 2 Q.B. 402.

Although the question is one of statutory construction and therefore each case turns on the provisions in the relevant statute, it is significant that your Lordships were not referred to any case where it had been held that statutory provisions establishing a regulatory system or a scheme of social welfare for the benefit of the public at large had been held to give rise to a private right of action for damages for breach of statutory duty. Although regulatory or welfare legislation affecting a particular area of activity does in fact provide protection to those individuals particularly affected by that activity, the legislation is not to be treated as being passed for the benefit of those individuals but for the benefit of society in general. Thus legislation regulating the conduct of betting or prisons did not give rise to a statutory right of action vested in those adversely affected by the breach of the statutory provisions, *i.e.* bookmakers and prisoners: see *Cutler's* case [1949] A.C. 398; *R. v. Deputy Governor of Parkhurst Prison, ex p. Hague* [1992] 1 A.C. 58. The cases where a private right of action for breach of statutory duty have been held to arise are all cases in which the statutory duty has been very limited and specific as opposed to general administrative functions imposed on public bodies and involving the exercise of administrative discretions.

(B) *The careless performance of a statutory duty—no common law duty of care*

This category comprises those cases in which the plaintiff alleges (a) the statutory duty and (b) the "negligent" breach of that duty but does not allege that the defendant was under a common law duty of care to the plaintiff. It is the use of the word "negligent" in this context which gives rise to confusion: it is sometimes used to connote mere carelessness (there being no common law duty of care) and sometimes to import the concept of a common law duty of care. In my judgment it is important in considering the authorities to distinguish between the two concepts: as will appear, in my view the careless performance of a statutory duty does not in itself give rise to any cause of action in the absence of either a statutory right of action (Category (A) above) or a common law duty of care (Category (C) below).

Much of the difficulty can be traced back to the confusion between the ability to rely on a statutory provision as a defence and the ability to rely on it as founding a cause of action. The source of the confusion is to be found in the dictum of Lord Blackburn in *Geddis v. Proprietors of Bann Reservoir*, 3 App.Cas. 430, 455–456:

> "For I take it, without citing cases, that it is now thoroughly well established that no action will lie for doing that which the legislature has authorised, if it be done without negligence, although it does occasion damage to anyone; but an action does lie for doing that which the legislature has authorised, if it be done negligently. And I think that if by a reasonable exercise of the powers, either given by statute to the promoters, or which they have at common law, the damage could be prevented it is, within this rule, 'negligence' not to make such reasonable exercise of their powers."

This dictum, divorced from its context, suggests that the careless performance of a statutory duty in itself gives rise to a cause of action for damages. But it has to be read in context.

In *Geddis* the defendants were authorised to construct and maintain a reservoir the water from which was discharged, via a new artificial watercourse, into an old watercourse which the defendants were authorised by the statute to widen and maintain. Water originating from the reservoir flooded from the old watercourse onto the plaintiff's adjoining land, such flooding being due to the "negligent" failure of the defendants to maintain the old watercourse adequately. The cause of action relied upon by the plaintiff is not clear from the report: it could have been either nuisance (including *Rylands v. Fletcher* (1868) L.R. 3 H.L. 330) or negligence. If the cause of action founded upon was in nuisance, the question was whether the statutory power to construct and maintain the works provided a defence to what would otherwise constitute an actionable wrong. It is well established that statutory authority only provides a defence to a claim based on a common law cause of action where the loss suffered by the plaintiff is the inevitable consequence of the proper exercise of the statutory power or duty: *Metropolitan Asylum District v. Hill*, 6 App.Cas. 193; *Allen v. Gulf Oil Refining Ltd* [1981] A.C. 1001. Therefore the careless exercise of a statutory power or duty cannot provide a defence to a claim based on a freestanding common law cause of action, whether in trespass, nuisance or breach of a common law duty of care. If Lord Blackburn's dictum in *Geddis*'s case, 3 App.Cas. 430, 455–456, merely refers to the circumstances in which statutory authority can be used as a defence it raises no problems.

In my judgment *Geddis*'s case is best treated as a decision that the careless exercise by the defendant of a statutory duty or power provides no defence to a claim by the plaintiff based on a freestanding common law cause of action. It was so treated by Lord Wilberforce in the *Gulf Oil* case who said [1981] A.C. 1001, 1011:

> "It is now well settled that where Parliament by express direction or by necessary implication has authorised the construction and use of an undertaking or works, that carries with it an authority to do what is authorised with immunity from any action based on nuisance. The right of action is taken away: *Hammersmith and City Railway Co. v. Brand* (1869) L.R. 4 H.L. 171, 215 *per* Lord Cairns. To this there is made the qualification, or condition, that the statutory powers are exercised without 'negligence'— that word here being used in a special sense so as to require the undertaker, as a condition of obtaining immunity from action, to carry out the work and conduct the operation with all reasonable regard and care for the interests of other persons: *Geddis* . . ."

See also *Sutherland Shire Council v. Heyman* (1985) 157 C.L.R. 424, 458 and the article by Sir Gerard Brennan "Liability in Negligence of Public Authorities: The Divergent Views" (1990) 48 *The Advocate* 842, 844–846.

[His Lordship then stated that the same position had been taken by the majority of the House of Lords in *Home Office v. Dorset Yacht Co. Ltd* [1970] A.C. 1004 (Lords Morris, Pearson and Reid) although Lord Diplock had adopted a different approach.]

In my judgment the correct view is that in order to found a cause of action flowing from the careless exercise of statutory powers or duties, the plaintiff has to show that the circumstances are such as to raise a duty of care at common law. The mere assertion of the careless exercise of a statutory power or duty is not sufficient.

(C) *The common law duty of care*

In this category, the claim alleges either that a statutory duty gives rise to a common law duty of care owed to the plaintiff by the defendant to do or refrain from doing a particular act or (more often) that in the course of carrying out a statutory duty the defendant has brought about such a relationship between himself and the plaintiff as to give rise to a duty of care at common law. A further variant is a claim by the plaintiff that, whether or not the authority is itself under a duty of care to the plaintiff, its servant in the course of performing the statutory function was under a common law duty of care for breach of which the authority is vicariously liable.

Mr Munby, in his reply in the *Newham* case, invited your Lordships to lay down the general principles applicable in determining the circumstances in which the law would impose a common law duty of care arising from the exercise of statutory powers or duties. I have no doubt that, if possible, this would be most desirable. But I have found it quite impossible either to detect such principle in the wide range of authorities and academic writings to which we were referred or to devise any such principle de novo. The truth of the matter is that statutory duties now exist over such a wide range of diverse activities and take so many different forms that no one principle is capable of being formulated applicable to all cases. However, in my view it is possible in considering the problems raised by these particular appeals to identify certain points which are of significance.

1. *Co-existence of statutory duty and common law duty of care*

It is clear that a common law duty of care may arise in the performance of statutory functions. But a broad distinction has to be drawn between: (a) cases in which it is alleged that the authority owes a duty of care in the manner in which it exercises a statutory discretion; (b) cases in which a duty of care is alleged to arise from the manner in which the statutory duty has been implemented in practice.

An example of (a) in the educational field would be a decision whether or not to exercise a statutory discretion to close a school, being a decision which necessarily involves the exercise of a discretion. An example of (b) would be the actual running of a school pursuant to the statutory duties. In such latter case a common law duty to take reasonable care for the physical safety of the pupils will arise. The fact that the school is being run pursuant to a statutory duty is not necessarily incompatible with a common law duty of care arising from the proximate relationship between a school and the pupils it has agreed to accept. The distinction is between (a) taking care in exercising a statutory discretion whether or not to do an act and (b) having decided to do that act, taking care in the manner in which you do it.

2. *Discretion: justiciability and the policy operational test*
(a) *Discretion*

Most statutes which impose a statutory duty on local authorities confer on the authority a discretion as to the extent to which, and the methods by which, such statutory duty is to be performed. It is clear both in principle and from the decided cases that the local authority cannot be liable in damages for doing that which Parliament has authorised. Therefore if the decisions complained of fall within the ambit of such statutory discretion they cannot be actionable in common law. However if the decision complained of is so unreasonable that it falls outside the ambit of the discretion conferred upon the local authority, there is no a priori reason for excluding all common law liability.

That this is the law is established by the decision in the *Dorset Yacht* case [1970] A.C. 1004 and by that part of the decision in *Anns v. Merton London Borough Council* [1978] A.C. 728 which, so far as I am aware, has largely escaped criticism in later decisions. In the *Dorset Yacht* case Lord Reid said [1970] A.C. 1004, 1031:

> "Where Parliament confers a discretion the position is not the same. Then there may, and almost certainly will, be errors of judgment in exercising such a discretion and Parliament cannot have intended that members of the public should be entitled to sue in respect of such errors. But there must come a stage when the discretion is exercised so carelessly or unreasonably that there has been no real exercise of the discretion which Parliament has conferred. The person purporting to exercise his discretion has acted in abuse or excess of his power. Parliament cannot be supposed to have granted immunity to persons who do that."

See also *per* Lord Morris, at 1037F.

Lord Diplock, . . . took a rather different line, making it a condition precedent to any common law duty arising that the decision impugned should be shown to be ultra vires in the public law sense. For myself, I do not believe that it is either helpful or necessary to introduce public law concepts as to the validity of a decision into the question of liability at common law for negligence. In public law a decision can be *ultra vires* for reasons other than *Wednesbury* unreasonableness (*Associated Provincial Picture Houses Ltd v. Wednesbury Corporation* [1948] 1 K.B. 223) (*e.g.* breach of the rules of natural justice) which have no relevance to the question of negligence. Moreover it leads, in my judgment mistakenly, to the contention that claims for damages for negligence in the exercise of statutory powers should for procedural purposes be classified as public law claims and therefore, under *O'Reilly v. Mackman* [1983] 2 A.C. 237 should be brought in judicial review proceedings: see *Lonrho plc v. Tebbit* [1992] 4 All E.R. 280. However, although I consider that the public law doctrine of *ultra vires* has, as such, no role to play in the subject under discussion, the remarks of Lord Diplock were plainly directed to the fact that the exercise of a statutory discretion cannot be impugned unless it is so unreasonable that it falls altogether outside the ambit of the statutory discretion. He said [1970] A.C. 1004, 1068:

> "These considerations lead me to the conclusion that neither the intentional release of a Borstal trainee under supervision, nor the unintended escape of a Borstal trainee still under detention which was the consequence of the application of a system of relaxed control intentionally adopted by the Home Office as conducive to the reformation of trainees, can have been intended by Parliament to give rise to any cause of action on the part of any private citizen unless the system adopted was so unrelated to any purpose of reformation that no reasonable person could have reached a bona fide conclusion that it was conducive to that purpose. Only then would the decision to adopt it be *ultra vires* in public law."

Exactly the same approach was adopted by Lord Wilberforce in *Anns v.*

Merton London Borough Council [1978] A.C. 728 who, speaking of the duty of a local authority which had in fact inspected a building under construction, said, at 755:

> "But this duty, heavily operational though it may be, is still a duty arising under the statute. There may be a discretionary element in its exercise—discretionary as to the time and manner of inspection, and the techniques to be used. A plaintiff complaining of negligence must prove, the burden being on him, that action taken was not within the limits of a discretion bona fide exercised, before he can begin to rely upon a common law duty of care."

It follows that in seeking to establish that a local authority is liable at common law for negligence in the exercise of a discretion conferred by statute, the first requirement is to show that the decision was outside the ambit of the discretion altogether: if it was not, a local authority cannot itself be in breach of any duty of care owed to the plaintiff.

In deciding whether or not this requirement is satisfied, the court has to assess the relevant factors taken into account by the authority in exercising the discretion. Since what are under consideration are discretionary powers conferred on public bodies for public purposes the relevant factors will often include policy matters, for example social policy, the allocation of finite financial resources between the different calls made upon them or (as in *Dorset Yacht*) the balance between pursuing desirable social aims as against the risk to the public inherent in so doing. It is established that the courts cannot enter upon the assessment of such "policy" matters. The difficulty is to identify in any particular case whether or not the decision in question is a "policy" decision.

(b) *Justiciability and the policy operational dichotomy*

In English law the first attempt to lay down the principles applicable in deciding whether or not a decision was one of policy was made by Lord Wilberforce in *Anns v. Merton London Borough Council* [1978] A.C. 728, 754:

> "Most, indeed probably all, statutes relating to public authorities or public bodies, contain in them a large area of policy. The courts call this 'discretion' meaning that the decision is one for the authority or body to make, and not for the courts. Many statutes also prescribe or at least presuppose the practical execution of policy decisions: a convenient description of this is to say that in addition to the area of policy or discretion, there is an operational area. Although this distinction between the policy area and the operational area is convenient, and illuminating, it is probably a distinction of degree; many 'operational' powers or duties have in them some element of 'discretion'. It can safely be said that the more 'operational' a power or duty may be, the easier it is to superimpose upon it a common law duty of care."

As Lord Wilberforce appreciated, this approach did not provide a hard and fast test as to those matters which were open to the court's decision. In *Rowling v. Takaro Properties Ltd* [1988] A.C. 473 the Privy Council reverted to the problem. In that case the trial judge had found difficulty in applying the policy/operational test, but having classified the decision in question as being operational, took the view that as a result there was a common law duty of care. Commenting on the judge's view, Lord Keith of Kinkel said, at 501:

"Their Lordships feel considerable sympathy with Quilliam J.'s difficulty in solving the problem by reference to this distinction. They are well aware of the references in the literature to this distinction (which appears to have originated in the United States of America), and of the critical analysis to which it has been subjected. They incline to the opinion, expressed in the literature, that this distinction does not provide a touchstone of liability, but rather is expressive of the need to exclude altogether those cases in which the decision under attack is of such a kind that a question whether it has been made negligently is unsuitable for judicial resolution, of which notable examples are discretionary decisions on the allocation of scarce resources or the distribution of risks: see especially the discussion in *Craig on Administrative Law* (1983), pp. 534–538. If this is right, classification of the relevant decision as a policy or planning decision in this sense may exclude liability; but a conclusion that it does not fall within that category does not, in their Lordships' opinion, mean that a duty of care will *necessarily* exist." (Emphasis added.)

From these authorities I understand the applicable principles to be as follows. Where Parliament has conferred a statutory discretion on a public authority, it is for that authority, not for the courts, to exercise the discretion: nothing which the authority does within the ambit of the discretion can be actionable at common law. If the decision complained of falls outside the statutory discretion, it *can* (but not necessarily will) give rise to common law liability. However, if the factors relevant to the exercise of the discretion include matters of policy, the court cannot adjudicate on such policy matters and therefore cannot reach the conclusion that the decision was outside the ambit of the statutory discretion. Therefore a common law duty of care in relation to the taking of decisions involving policy matters cannot exist.

3. If justiciable, the ordinary principles of negligence apply
If the plaintiff's complaint alleges carelessness, not in the taking of a discretionary decision to do some act, but in the practical manner in which that act has been performed (*e.g.* the running of a school) the question whether or not there is a common law duty of care falls to be decided by applying the usual principles, *i.e.* those laid down in *Caparo Industries plc v. Dickman* [1990] 2 A.C. 605, 617–618. Was the damage to the plaintiff reasonably foreseeable? Was the relationship between the plaintiff and the defendant sufficiently proximate? Is it just and reasonable to impose a duty of care? See *Rowling v. Takaro Properties Ltd* [1988] A.C. 473; *Hill v. Chief Constable of West Yorkshire* [1989] A.C. 53.

However the question whether there is such a common law duty and if so its ambit, must be profoundly influenced by the statutory framework within which the acts complained of were done. The position is directly analogous to that in which a tortious duty of care owed by A to C can arise out of the performance by A of a contract between A and B. In *Henderson v. Merrett Syndicates Ltd* [1994] 3 W.L.R. 761 your Lordships held that A (the managing agent) who had contracted with B (the members' agent) to render certain services for C (the Names) came under a duty of care to C in the performance of those services. It is clear that any tortious duty of care owed to C in those circumstances could not be inconsistent with the duty owed in contract by A to B. Similarly, in my judgment a common law duty of care cannot be imposed on a statutory duty if the observance of such common law duty of care would be inconsistent with, or have a tendency to discourage, the due performance by the local authority of its statutory duties.

4. *Direct liability and vicarious liability*
In certain of the appeals before the House, the local authorities are alleged to be under a direct duty of care to the plaintiff not only in relation to the exercise of a statutory discretion but also in relation to the operational way in which they performed that duty.

This allegation of a direct duty of care owed by the authority to the plaintiff is to be contrasted with those claims which are based on the vicarious liability of the local authority for the negligence of its servants, *i.e.* for the breach of a duty of care owed by the servant to the plaintiff, the authority itself not being under any relevant duty of care to the plaintiff. Thus, in the *Newham* case the plaintiffs' claim is wholly based on allegations that two professionals, a social worker and a psychiatrist, individually owed professional duties of care to the plaintiff for the breach of which the authorities as their employers are vicariously liable. It is not alleged that the authorities were themselves under a duty of care to the plaintiff.

This distinction between direct and vicarious liability can be important since the authority may not be under a direct duty of care at all or the extent of the duty of care owed directly by the authority to the plaintiff may well differ from that owed by a professional to a patient. However, it is important not to lose sight of the fact that, even in the absence of a claim based on vicarious liability, an authority under a direct duty of care to the plaintiff will be liable for the negligent acts or omissions of its servant which constitute a breach of that direct duty. The authority can only act through its servants.

The position can be illustrated by reference to the hospital cases. It is established that those conducting a hospital are under a direct duty of care to those admitted as patients to the hospital (I express no view as to the extent of that duty). They are liable for the negligent acts of a member of the hospital staff which constitute a breach of that duty, whether or not the member of the staff is himself in breach of a separate duty of care owed by him to the plaintiff: *Gold v. Essex County Council* [1942] 2 K.B. 293, 301, *per* Lord Green; *Cassidy v. Ministry of Health* [1951] 2 K.B. 343, *per* Denning L.J.; *Roe v. Minister of Health* [1954] 2 Q.B. 66; see also *Wilsons & Clyde Coal Co. Ltd v. English* [1938] A.C. 57; *McDermid v. Nash Dredging & Reclamation Co. Ltd* [1987] A.C. 906. Therefore in the cases under appeal, even where there is no allegation of a separate duty of care owed by a servant of the authority to the plaintiff, the negligent acts of that servant are capable of constituting a breach of the duty of care (if any) owed directly by the authority to the plaintiff.

Striking out
In all these cases the defendants are seeking to strike out the claims at an early stage, before discovery has taken place and before the facts are known. It is therefore necessary to proceed on the basis that the facts alleged in the various

statements of claim are true. It must be stressed that these allegations are not admitted by the defendants.

Actions can only be struck out under R.S.C., Ord. 18, r. 19 where it is clear and obvious that in law the claim cannot succeed....

THE ABUSE CASES

[His Lordship stated the facts of the *Bedfordshire* and *Newham* cases. He then summarised the powers and duties of local authorities to take children into care where, *inter alia*, they are at risk of being harmed (Children and Young Persons Act 1969, ss.1, 2; Child Care Act 1980, ss.1, 2; Children Act 1989, ss.17, 20(1), 47, Sched. 2). He noted that from April 1, 1991, there had been a statutory complaints procedure applicable to the Children Act provisions (Local Authority Social Services Act 1970, s.7B; Local Authority Social Services (Complaints Procedure) Order 1990 (S.I. 1990 No. 2244). His Lordship also referred to the Secretary of State's powers to give guidance and directions under the 1970 Act, ss.7, 7A, which were to be found in the publication *Working Together* (1991).]

The claim for breach of statutory duty: Category (A)

The Court of Appeal were unanimous in striking out these claims in both actions. I agree. My starting point is that the Acts in question are all concerned to establish an administrative system designed to promote the social welfare of the community. The welfare sector involved is one of peculiar sensitivity, involving very difficult decisions how to strike the balance between protecting the child from immediate feared harm and disrupting the relationship between the child and its parents. Decisions often have to be taken on the basis of inadequate and disputed facts. In my judgment in such a context it would require exceptionally clear statutory language to show a parliamentary intention that those responsible for carrying out these difficult functions should be liable in damages if, on subsequent investigation with the benefit of hindsight, it was shown that they had reached an erroneous conclusion and therefore failed to discharge their statutory duties.

It is true that the legislation was introduced primarily for the protection of a limited class, namely children at risk, and that until April 1991 the legislation itself contained only limited machinery for enforcing the statutory duties imposed. But in my view those are the only pointers in favour of imputing to Parliament an intention to create a private law cause of action. When one turns to the actual words used in the primary legislation to create the statutory duties relied upon in my judgment they are inconsistent with any intention to create a private law cause of action.

Thus, the duty imposed by section 2(2) of the Act of 1969 to bring care proceedings is made conditional upon the subjective judgment of the local authority that there are grounds for so doing. Similarly, the duty to receive a child into care under section 2(1) of the Act of 1980 only arises "where it appears to a local authority" that the parents are prevented from providing properly for the child *and* that its intervention is necessary in the interest of the child. So far as the Act of 1989 is concerned, the duty relied on in section 17 is described as "a general duty" which has two parts: (a) to safeguard the children and (b) "so far as is consistent" with (a) to promote the upbringing of the children by their families. Thus not only is the duty not a specific one but the section itself points out the basic tension which lies at the root of so much child protection work: the decision whether to split the family in order to protect the child. I find it impossible to construe such a statutory provision as demonstrating an intention that even where there is no carelessness by the authority it should be liable in damages if a court subsequently decided with hindsight that the removal, or failure to remove, the child from the family either was or was not "consistent with" the duty to safeguard the child.

All the duties imported by Schedule 2 to the Act of 1989 are to "take reasonable steps" to do certain things. The duty to make inquiries under section 47 is limited to "such inquiries as they consider necessary". Thus all the statutory provisions relied upon in the *Bedfordshire* case are, as one would expect, made dependent upon the subjective judgment of the local authority. To treat such duties as being more than public law duties is impossible. . . .

In the *Newham* case, the claim by the plaintiffs for damages for breach of statutory duty (Category (A)) was founded solely on sections 1 and 18 of the Act of 1980: the Act of 1989 was not in force at the relevant time. The claim was only faintly pursued by Mr Munby and, for the reasons given by Peter Gibson L.J. in the Court of Appeal [1994] 2 W.L.R. 554, 590,[6] in my judgment it is ill founded.

For these reasons (which are in substance the same as those of the Court of Appeal), the claims in both abuse cases to the extent that they are based on a claim for damages for breach of statutory duty simpliciter were rightly struck out.

Direct common law duty of care owed by the local authorities

In the *Newham* case it is not alleged that the borough council was under any direct duty of care to the plaintiffs: the case is based solely on the vicarious liability of the council and the health authority for the negligence of their servants.

In the *Bedfordshire* case, Mr Jackson formulated the common law duty of care owed by the county council as being "a duty to children in respect of whom they receive reports of neglect or ill-treatment to take reasonable care to protect such children". The first question is whether the determination by the court of the question whether there has been a breach of that duty will involve unjusticiable policy questions. The alleged breaches of that duty relate for the most part to the failure to take reasonable practical steps, *e.g.* to remove the children, to allocate a suitable social worker or to make proper investigations. The assessment by the court of such allegations would not require the court to consider policy matters which are not justiciable. They do not necessarily involve any question of the allocation of resources or the determination of general policy. There are other allegations the investigation of which by a court might require the weighing of policy factors, *e.g.* allegations that the county council failed to provide a level of service appropriate to the plaintiffs' needs. If the case were to go to trial, the trial judge might have to rule

---

[6] [Editor's note] The duties were general duties couched in imprecise terms: a duty to make available such advice, guidance and assistance as would have promoted the welfare of the child by diminishing the need to receive her or keep her in care (s.1) or a duty to give first consideration to the need to promote the welfare of the child (s.18). Peter Gibson L.J. held that neither could have been intended by Parliament to give rise to a private law action.

out these issues as not being justiciable. But since some of the allegations are justiciable, it would not be right to strike out the whole claim on this ground.

Next, do the allegations of breach of duty in the operational field all relate to decisions the power to make which Parliament has conferred on the local authority, *i.e.* are they all decisions within the ambit of the local authority's statutory discretion? I strongly suspect that, if the case were to go to trial, it would eventually fail on this ground since, in essence, the complaint is that the local authority failed to take steps to remove the children from the care of their mother, i.e. negligently failed properly to exercise a discretion which Parliament has conferred on the local authority. But again, it would not be right to strike out the claim on this ground because it is possible that the plaintiffs might be able to demonstrate at trial that the decisions of the local authority were so unreasonable that no reasonable local authority could have reached them and therefore, for the reasons given by Lord Reid in the *Dorset Yacht* case [1970] A.C. 1004, 1031 fall outside the ambit of the discretion conferred by Parliament.

I turn then to consider whether, in accordance with the ordinary principles laid down in the *Caparo* case [1990] 2 A.C. 605, the local authority in the *Bedfordshire* case owed a direct duty of care to the plaintiffs. The local authority accepts that they could foresee damage to the plaintiffs if they carried out their statutory duties negligently and that the relationship between the authority and the plaintiffs is sufficiently proximate. The third requirement laid down in *Caparo* is that it must be just and reasonable to impose a common law duty of care in all the circumstances. It was submitted that this third requirement is only applicable in cases where the plaintiffs' claim is for pure economic loss and that it does not apply where, as in the child abuse cases, the claim is for physical damage. I reject this submission: although *Caparo* and many other of the more recent cases were decisions where only pure economic loss was claimed, the same basic principles apply to claims for physical damage and were applied in, for example, *Hill v. Chief Constable of West Yorkshire* [1989] A.C. 53.

Is it, then, just and reasonable to superimpose a common law duty of care on the local authority in relation to the performance of its statutory duties to protect children? In my judgment it is not. Sir Thomas Bingham M.R. took the view, with which I agree, that the public policy consideration which has first claim on the loyalty of the law is that wrongs should be remedied and that very potent counter considerations are required to override that policy [1994] 2 W.L.R. 554, 572F. However, in my judgment there are such considerations in this case.

First, in my judgment a common law duty of care would cut across the whole statutory system set up for the protection of children at risk. As a result of the ministerial directions contained in "Working Together" the protection of such children is not the exclusive territory of the local authority's social services. The system is inter-disciplinary, involving the participation of the police, educational bodies, doctors and others. At all stages the system involves joint discussions, joint recommendations and joint decisions. The key organisation is the Child Protection Conference, a multi-disciplinary body which decides whether to place the child on the Child Protection Register. This procedure by way of joint action takes place, not merely because it is good practice, but because it is required by guidance having statutory force binding on the local authority. The guidance is extremely detailed and extensive: the current edition of "Working Together" runs to 126 pages. To introduce into such a system a common law duty of care enforceable against only one of the participant bodies would be manifestly unfair. To impose such liability on all the participant bodies would lead to almost impossible problems of disentangling as between the respective bodies the liability, both primary and by way of contribution, of each for reaching a decision found to be negligent.

Second, the task of the local authority and its servants in dealing with children at risk is extraordinarily delicate. Legislation requires the local authority to have regard not only to the physical wellbeing of the child but also to the advantages of not disrupting the child's family environment: see, for example, section 17 of the Act of 1989. In one of the child abuse cases, the local authority is blamed for removing the child precipitately: in the other, for failing to remove the children from their mother. As the Report of the Inquiry into Child Abuse in Cleveland 1987 (Cm. 412) said, at p. 244:

> "It is a delicate and difficult line to tread between taking action too soon and not taking it soon enough. Social services whilst putting the needs of the child first must respect the rights of the parents; they also must work if possible with the parents for the benefit of the children. These parents themselves are often in need of help. Inevitably a degree of conflict develops between those objectives."

Next, if a liability in damages were to be imposed, it might well be that local authorities would adopt a more cautious and defensive approach to their duties. For example, as the Cleveland Report makes clear, on occasions the speedy decision to remove the child is sometimes vital. If the authority is to be made liable in damages for a negligent decision to remove a child (such negligence lying in the failure properly first to investigate the allegations) there would be a substantial temptation to postpone making such a decision until further inquiries have been made in the hope of getting more concrete facts. Not only would the child in fact being abused be prejudiced by such delay: the increased workload inherent in making such investigations would reduce the time available to deal with other cases and other children.

The relationship between the social worker and the child's parents is frequently one of conflict, the parent wishing to retain care of the child, the social worker having to consider whether to remove it. This is fertile ground in which to breed ill feeling and litigation, often hopeless, the cost of which both in terms of money and human resources will be diverted from the performance of the social service for which they were provided. The spectre of vexatious and costly litigation is often urged as a reason for not imposing a legal duty. But the circumstances surrounding cases of child abuse make the risk a very high one which cannot be ignored.

If there were no other remedy for maladministration of the statutory system for the protection of children, it would provide substantial argument for imposing a duty of care. But the statutory complaints procedures contained in section 76 of the Act of 1980 and the much fuller procedures now available under the Act of 1989 provide a means to have grievances investigated, though not to recover compensation. Further, it was submitted (and not controverted) that the local authorities Ombudsman would have power to investigate cases such as these.

Finally, your Lordships' decision in the *Caparo* case [1990] 2 A.C. 605 lays down that, in deciding whether to develop novel categories of negligence the court should proceed incrementally and by analogy with decided categories. We were not referred to any category of case in which a duty of care has been held to exist which is in any way analogous to the present cases. Here, for the first time, the plaintiffs are seeking to erect a common law duty of care in relation to the administration of a statutory social welfare scheme. Such a scheme is designed to protect weaker members of society (children) from harm done to them by others. The scheme involves the administrators in exercising discretions and powers which could not exist in the private sector and which in many cases bring them into conflict with those who, under the general law, are responsible for the child's welfare. To my mind, the nearest analogies are the cases where a common law duty of care has been sought to be imposed upon the police (in seeking to protect vulnerable members of society from wrongs done to them by others) or statutory regulators of financial dealings who are seeking to protect investors from dishonesty. In neither of those cases has it been thought appropriate to superimpose on the statutory regime a common law duty of care giving rise to a claim in damages for failure to protect the weak against the wrongdoer: see *Hill v. Chief Constable of West Yorkshire* [1989] A.C. 53 and *Yuen Kun Yeu v. Attorney-General of Hong Kong* [1988] A.C. 175. In the latter case, the Privy Council whilst not deciding the point said, at 198, that there was much force in the argument that if the regulators had been held liable in that case the principles leading to such liability "would surely be equally applicable to a wide range of regulatory agencies, not only in the financial field, but also, for example, to the factory inspectorate and social workers, to name only a few". In my judgment, the courts should proceed with great care before holding liable in negligence those who have been charged by Parliament with the task of protecting society from the wrongdoings of others.

Vicarious liability
[His Lordship then dealt with arguments that the defendant authorities were vicariously liable for the negligence of their staff.]

The claim based on vicarious liability is attractive and simple. The normal duty of a doctor to exercise reasonable skill and care is well established as a common law duty of care. In my judgement, the same duty applies to any other person possessed of special skills, such as a social worker. It is said, rightly, that in general such professional duty of care is owed irrespective of contract and can arise even where the professional assumes to act for the plaintiff pursuant to a contract with a third party: *Henderson v. Merrett Syndicates Ltd* [1994] 3 W.L.R. 761; *White v. Jones* [1995] 2 W.L.R. 187. Therefore, it is said, it is nothing to the point that the social workers and psychiatrist only came into contact with the plaintiffs pursuant to contracts or arrangements made between the professionals and the local authority for the purpose of the discharge by the local authority of its statutory duties. Once brought into contact with the plaintiffs, the professionals owed a duty properly to exercise their professional skills in dealing with their "patients", the plaintiffs. This duty involved the exercise of professional skills in investigating the circumstances of the plaintiffs and (in the *Newham* case) conducting the interview with the child. Moreover, since the professionals could foresee that negligent advice would damage the plaintiffs, they are liable to the plaintiffs for tendering such advice to the local authority.

Like the majority in the Court of Appeal, I cannot accept these arguments. The social workers and the psychiatrists were retained by the local authority to advise the local authority, not the plaintiffs. The subject matter of the advice and activities of the professionals is the child. Moreover the tendering of any advice will in many cases involve interviewing and, in the case of doctors, examining the child. But the fact that the carrying out of the retainer involves contact with and relationship with the child cannot alter the extent of the duty owed by the professionals under the retainer from the local authority. The Court of Appeal drew a correct analogy with the doctor instructed by an insurance company to exaine an applicant for life insurance. The doctor does not, by examining the applicant, come under any general duty of medical care to the applicant. He is under a duty not to damage the applicant in the course of the examination: but beyond that his duties are owed to the insurance company and not to the applicant.

The position is not the same as in the case of the purchaser of property who is owed a duty of care by a surveyor instructed by the building society which is going to advance the money: see *Smith v. Eric S. Bush* [1990] 1 A.C. 831. In such a case the surveyor is only liable to the purchaser in negligence because he is aware that the purchaser will regulate his (the purchaser's) conduct by completing the purchase in reliance on the survey report. In the child abuse cases, even if the advice tendered by the professionals to the local authority comes to the knowledge of the child or his parents, they will not regulate their conduct in reliance on the report. The effect of the report will be reflected in the way in which the local authority acts.

Nor is the position the same as in *Henderson v. Merrett Syndicates Ltd* where, pursuant to a contract with the members' agents, the managing agents undertook the management of the insurance business of the indirect Names. The managing agents were held to be under a tortious duty of care to the indirect Names, notwithstanding that the managing agents were operating under the terms of a contract with a third party. But the duty of care to the Names in that case arose from, and fell within the ambit of, the terms of the retainer contained in the contract between the managing agents and the members' agents. The Names were not seeking to impose on the managing agents any obligation beyond that which the retainer itself required to be performed. So also in *White v. Jones* [1995] 2 W.L.R. 187.

In my judgment in the present cases, the social workers and the psychiatrist did not, by accepting the instructions of the local authority, assume any general professional duty of care to the plaintiff children. The professionals were employed or retained to advise the local authority in relation to the well being of the plaintiffs but not to advise or treat the plaintiffs. . . .

Even if, contrary to my view, the social workers and psychiatrist would otherwise have come under a duty of care to the plaintiffs, the same considerations which have led me to the view that there is no direct duty of care owed by the local authorities apply with at least equal force to the question whether it would be just and reasonable to impose such a duty of care on the individual social workers and the psychiatrist.

For these reasons, in my judgment the professionals involved were under no separate duty of care to the plaintiffs for breach of which the local authorities could be vicariously liable.

Witness immunity
[His Lordship then held that the psychiatrist in the *Newham* case was entitled to witness immunity from civil liability under *Watson v. M'Ewan; Watson v. Jones* [1905] A.C. 480 and *Evans v. London Hospital Medical College (University of London)* [1981] 1 W.L.R. 184.]

In the present case, the psychiatrist was instructed to carry out the examination of the child for the specific purpose of discovering whether the child had been sexually abused and (if possible) the identity of the abuser. The psychiatrist must have known that, if such abuse was discovered, proceedings by the local authority for the protection of the child would ensue and that her findings would be the evidence on which those proceedings would be based. It follows in my judgment that such investigations having such an immediate link with possible proceedings in pursuance of a statutory duty cannot be made the basis of subsequent claims.

Although anyone would have great sympathy for the plaintiffs in both these cases (if the allegations which they make are true), for these reasons I agree with the Court of Appeal that they have no private law claim in damages. I would dismiss both appeals.

THE EDUCATION CASES

The legislation
[His Lordship summarised the relevant statutory provisions. The Education Act 1944 as originally enacted imposed duties on local education authorities to provide sufficient schools having regard to the need to secure the provision of special educational treatment for pupils with any disability of mind or body, and to ascertain what children in their area require such treatment (ss.7, 8, 33, 34, 36). The Education Act 1981 introduced new arrangements whereby authorities were to have regard to the need for securing that special educational provision was made for pupils with special educational needs. Such pupils were to be identified and assessed and, if the authority was of the opinion that it should determine the special educational provision that should be made for them, it was to make a statement of educational needs. If the authority decided not to determine such provision, an appeal lay to the Secretary of State. Similarly, there was a right to appeal against the provision specified in a statement to an appeal committee and then to the Secretary of State (see the 1981 Act, ss.2, 4, 5, 7–9).]

The Dorset case
[His Lordship summarised the facts.]

Common law duty of care—direct
... As to the claim based on the negligent failure to comply with the statutory requirements of the Act of 1981, it is in essence a claim that the authority was negligent in the exercise of the statutory discretions conferred on the defendant authority by the Act of 1981. The claim cannot be struck out as being not justiciable. Although it is very improbable, it may be that the exercise of the

statutory discretions involved in operating the special needs machinery of the Act of 1981 involved policy decisions. The decision as to what should be included in the statement and what provisoin should be made is, by statute, a decision conferred on the defendant authority. Therefore, even if such decisions were made carelessly, the claim will fail unless the plaintiff can show that the decisions were so careless that no reasonable education authority could have reached them. Again, although it seems most improbable that this requirement can be satisfied, it is impossible to be certain until all the facts are known. Therefore the claim cannot be struck out at this stage on the grounds that it is not justiciable or the acts complained of fell within the statutory discretion.

The question, then, is whether it is right to superimpose on the statutory machinery for the investigation and treatment of the plaintiff's special educational needs a duty of care to exercise the statutory discretions carefully? I find this a difficult question on which my views have changed from time to time. In favour of imposing a duty of care is the fact that it was plainly foreseeable that if the powers were exercised carelessly a child with special educational needs might be harmed in the sense that he would not obtain the advantage that the statutory provisions were designed to provide for him. Further, for the reasons that I have given, a common law duty of care in the exercise of statutory discretions can only arise in relation to an authority which has decided an issue so carelessly that no reasonable authority could have reached that decision. Why, it may be asked, should such a grossly delinquent authority escape liability? However, I have reached the conclusion that, powerful though those considerations may be, they are outweighed by other factors.

First, in relation to the special statutory duties imposed by sections 2, 4, 5 and 7 of the Act of 1981, the exercise of the discretions involves the close participation of the parents who are themselves under a duty to cause the child to receive "efficient full-time education suitable to his . . . ability and aptitude": section 36 of the Education Act 1944. The parents are themselves involved in the process of decision making and can appeal against decisions which they think to be erroneous. Although in the *Dorset* case the parents availed themselves of all the advantages of the statutory machinery, in the generality of cases to allow either the parents (on behalf of the child) or the child when he attains his majority to bring a claim alleging negligence by the authority in the making of the decision would be to duplicate remedies. Although in the present case this factor is not directly in point, if a duty of care is to be held to exist it must apply as much in relation to actions brought by a parent or child who has not used the statutory machinery as in the case of parents or a child who have.

Next, the number of cases which could successfully be brought for breach of such a duty of care would be very small since, as I have said, it would have to be shown that the decision impugned was taken so carelessly that no authority could have reached it. Yet, if a common law duty of care is held to exist, there is a very real risk that many hopeless (and possibly vexatious) cases will be brought, thereby exposing the authority to great expenditure of time and money in their defence. If there were no other remedy open, this is a price which might have to be paid in the interests of justice. But, in almost every case which could give rise to a claim for the negligent exercise of the statutory discretions, it is probable that, as in the present case, there will be an alternative remedy by way of a claim against the authority on the grounds of its vicarious liability for the negligent advice on the basis of which it exercises its discretion: as to which see below.

We were not referred to any category of case by analogy with which, in accordance with the *Caparo* principles [1990] 2 A.C. 605, it would be right to impose a direct duty of care on the authority in the exercise of its statutory discretions. . . .

In my judgment, as in the child abuse cases, the courts should hesitate long before imposing a common law duty of care in the exercise of discretionary powers or duties conferred by Parliament for social welfare purposes. The aim of the Act of 1981 was to provide, for the benefit of society as a whole, an administrative machinery to help one disadvantaged section of society. The statute provides its own detailed machinery for securing that the statutory purpose is performed. If, despite the complex machinery for consultation and appeals contained in the Act, the scheme fails to provide the benefit intended that is a matter more appropriately remedied by way of the Ombudsman looking into the administrative failure than by way of litigation.

For these reasons I reach the conclusion that an education authority owes no common law duty of care in the exercise of the powers and discretions relating to children with special educational needs specifically conferred on them by the Act of 1981.

I turn then to the other duty of care which, it is alleged, the defendant authority owes directly to the plaintiff. There the position is wholly different. The claim is based on the fact that the authority is offering a service (psychological advice) to the public. True it is that, in the absence of a statutory power or duty, the authority could not offer such a service. But once the decision is taken to offer such a service, a statutory body is in general in the same position as any private individual or organisation holding itself out as offering such a service. By opening its doors to others to take advantage of the service offered, it comes under a duty of care to those using the service to exercise care in its conduct. The position is directly analogous with a hospital conducted, formerly by a local authority now by a health authority, in exercise of statutory powers. In such a case the authority running the hospital is under a duty to those whom it admits to exercise reasonable care in the way it runs it: see *Gold v. Essex County Council* [1942] 2 K.B. 293.

For these reasons, I can see no ground on which it can be said at this stage that the defendant authority, in providing a psychology service, could not have come under a duty of care to the plaintiff who, through his parents, took advantage of that service. It may well be that when the facts are fully investigated at trial it may emerge that, for example, the alleged psychology service was merely part and parcel of the system established by the defendant authority for the discharge of its statutory duties under the Act of 1981. If so, it may be that the existence and scope of the direct duty owed by the defendant authority will have to be excluded or limited so as not to impede the due performance by the authority of its statutory duties. But at this stage it is impossible to say that the claim under this head must fail.

Common law duty of care—vicarious
The claim is that the educational psychologists and other members of the staff of the defendant authority owed a duty to use reasonable professional skill

and care in the assessment and determination of the plaintiff's educational needs. It is further alleged that the plaintiff's parents relied on the advice of such professionals. The defendant authority is vicariously liable for any breach of such duties by their employees.

Again, I can see no ground for striking out this claim at least in relation to the educational psychologists. Psychologists hold themselves out as having special skills and they are, in my judgment, like any other professional bound both to possess such skills and to exercise them carefully. Of course, the test in *Bolam v. Friern Hospital Management Committee* [1957] 1 W.L.R. 582 will apply to them, *i.e.* they are only bound to exercise the ordinary skill of a competent psychologist and if they can show that they acted in accordance with the accepted views of some reputable psychologist at the relevant time they will have discharged the duty of care, even if other psychologists would have adopted a different view. In the context of advice on the treatment of dyslexia, a subject on which views have changed over the years, this may be an important factor. But that said, I can see no ground on which, at this stage, the existence of a professional duty of care can be ruled out. The position of other members of the defendant's staff is not as clear, but I would not at this stage strike out the claims relating to them.

The position of the psychologists in the education cases is quite different from that of the doctor and social worker in the child abuse cases. There is no potential conflict of duty between the professional's duties to the plaintiff and his duty to the educational authority. Nor is there any obvious conflict between the professional being under a duty of care to the plaintiff and the discharge by the authority of its statutory duties. If, at trial, it emerges that there are such conflicts, then the trial judge may have to limit or exclude any duty of care owed by the professional to the plaintiff. But at this stage no obvious conflict has been demonstrated.

Finally, the defendant authority submitted that the damage claimed, being the cost of providing alternative fee paying education for the plaintiff, is not recoverable. In my view it is not appropriate to decide this point at the striking out stage: the matter will be better resolved at trial when the true facts are known.

My conclusion therefore in the *Dorset* case is that the defendant authority is under no liability at common law for the negligent exercise of the statutory discretions conferred on them by the Education Acts 1944 to 1981, but could be liable, both directly and vicariously, for negligence in the operation of the psychology service and negligent advice given by its officers.

The Hampshire case

The facts

[His Lordship stated the facts and held that the common law recognised a duty of care owed by a head teacher and an educational advisor to a pupil. There was no incompability between such a duty and the existence of the statutory special educational needs scheme. The authority would be vicariously liable for the negligence of such teachers in advising on and meeting the educational needs of pupils. The claim would be amended to allege that the failure to treat the plaintiff's dyslexia cause psychological damage sufficiently serious to constitute an identifiable mental illness. The claim should not be struck out.]

The Bromley case

[His Lordship stated the facts and held (1) that breaches of section 8 of the Education Act 1944 (duty to provide sufficient schools) or the 1944 Act provisions concerning special educational treatment and the 1981 Act provisions (summarised above at p. 724) did not give rise to a civil action; (2) as in the *Dorset* case, there was no common law duty of care in relation to the exercise of statutory discretions under the 1944 and 1981 Acts; and (3) possible claims based on vicarious liability for the negligence of one or more professionals employed by the authority should not be struck out.]

Appeals in the Bedfordshire and Newham cases dismissed; appeals in the Dorset and Bromley cases allowed in part; appeal in the Hampshire case and cross-appeal in the Bromley case dismissed.

Notes and Questions

1. This landmark decision on the liability of public authorities for breach of statutory duty and negligence throws much light on the relevant issues. At the same time, some parts of the picture remain clouded or are plunged further into darkness. Particularly helpful are the discussion of breach of statutory duty, the point that liability in negligence must be based on a common law duty of care and the open and full discussion of the policy arguments for and against imposition of a duty of care. More problematic are the failure to consider the point that some of the matters of which complaint were made were omissions and the dicta concerning the approach to be made to discretionary decisions. It is remarkable that a short time later these matters received the full attention of a differently composed House of Lords in *Stovin v. Wise, Norfolk County Council (Third Party)* (below, pp. 737–752) (only Lord Jauncey of Tullichettle sat on both appeals). The task of reconciling the two decisions is not straightforward (see below, pp. 751–752).

2. *Breach of statutory duty.* Following *X. v. Bedfordshire County Council* the potential scope of civil liability for breaches of statutory duties placed on public authorities is extremely narrow. There are a few situations where a duty is recognised. For example, in *Refell v. Surrey County Council* [1964] 1 W.L.R. 358, Veale J. held the council liable both at common law and for breach of its duty under the Education Act 1944, s.10, to secure that school premises complied with standards prescribed by regulations, and under the relevant regulation[7] that required the design, construction and properties of materials to be such that the health and safety of the occupants "shall be reasonably assured", where a pupil put her hand through a glass panel in a cloakroom door made of ⅛-inch non-toughened glass. This can be seen to be closely analogous to cases where breach of health and safety regulations made for the protection of factory workers and the like have been held to give rise to civil actions, and the decision is not inconsistent with the principles stated in *X v. Bedfordshire County Council*. The Court of Appeal has held that breach of the duties of a local authority under the homelessness legislation gives rise to a civil action (*Thornton v. Kirklees Metropolitan Borough Council* [1979] Q.B. 626). However, in *X v. Bedfordshire County Council* Lord Browne-Wilkinson said that the point had been conceded, and that the decision was "in some respects a puzzling one and may need to be reconsidered at a future date" (at 181). In any event, the courts have adopted a narrow view, holding that the possibility of a civil action only arises where there has been a decision of the local authority on the preconditions for entitlement under the legislation in the applicant's favour; up to that point, the only avenue of challenge is through an application for judicial review (see

---

[7] Standards for School Premises Regulations 1959 (S.I. 1959 No. 890), reg. 51.

above, pp. 653–655. *Thornton* has now been overruled by the House of Lords in *O'Rourke v. Camden L.B.C.* [1997] 3 W.L.R. 86.[8]

Even before *X v. Bedfordshire County Council*, the clear tendency was against finding that breaches of duties placed on public authorities gave rise to civil actions. See, *e.g. Wyatt v. Hillingdon London Borough Council* (1978) 76 L.G.R. 727 (duty under the Chronically Sick and Disabled Persons Act 1970; remedy for breach provided by ministerial default power); *R. v. Deputy Governor of Parkhurst Prison, ex p. Hague* [1992] 1 A.C. 58 (breach of Prison Rules held not to give rise to action for breach of statutory duty).

3. *Negligence: policy.* Lord Browne-Wilkinson advances a series of policy arguments against imposition of a duty of care in both the child abuse and the education cases. Are you convinced? How many of them could apply as arguments justifying an immunity from negligence liability for doctors (whether employed publicly or privately)? Do you agree that these arguments are not valid as regards the teachers and psychologists against whom actions are proceeding?

The argument in *Home Office v. Dorset Yacht Co. Ltd* [1970] A.C. 1004 in support of an immunity based on policy grounds received short shrift from Lord Reid (at 1032–1033):

> "Finally I must deal with public policy. It is argued that it would be contrary to public policy to hold the Home Office or its officers liable to a member of the public for this carelessness— or, indeed, any failure of duty on their part. The basic question is: who shall bear the loss caused by that carelessness—the innocent respondents or the Home Office, who are vicariously liable for the conduct of their careless officers? I do not think that the argument for the Home Office can be put better than it was put by the Court of Appeals of New York in *Williams v. State of New York* (1955) 127 N.E. 2d 545, 550:
>
>> '. . . public policy also requires that the State be not held liable. To hold otherwise would impose a heavy responsibility upon the State, or dissuade the wardens and principal keepers of our prison system from continued experimentation with "minimum security" work details—which provide a means for encouraging better-risk prisoners to exercise their senses of responsibility and honor and so prepare themselves for their eventual return to society. Since 1917, the legislature has expressly provided for out-of-prison work, Correction Law, § 182, and its intention should be respected without fostering the reluctance of prison officials to assign eligible men to minimum security work, lest they thereby give rise to costly claims against the State, or indeed inducing the State itself to terminate this "salutary procedure" looking toward rehabilitation.'
>
> It may be that public servants of the State of New York are so apprehensive, easily dissuaded from doing their duty and intent on preserving public funds from costly claims that they could be influenced in this way. But my experience leads me to believe that Her Majesty's servants are made of sterner stuff. So I have no hesitation in rejecting this argument. I can see no good ground in public policy for giving this immunity to a government department."

Notwithstanding this, the decision here that there were sufficient policy reasons to exclude a duty of care is echoed in much of the recent case law. Examples include the following:

(a) regulatory authorities: *Yuen Kun Yeu v. Att.-Gen. of Hong Kong* [1988] A.C. 175 (Commissioner of Deposit-taking Companies in Hong Kong held not to owe a duty of care to potential depositors); *Minories Finance Ltd v. Arthur Young (a Firm) (Bank of*

---

[8] Note that significant changes to the homelessness legislation are to be made by the Housing Act 1996.

England, Third Party) [1989] 2 All E.R. 105 (Bank of England held not to be under a legal obligation to an individual commercial bank to exercise reasonable care and skill in carrying out its function of supervising the operation of commercial banks); *Davies v. Radcliffe* [1990] 1 W.L.R. 821, P.C.). See H. McLean, "Negligent Regulatory Authorities and the Duty of Care" (1988) 8 O.J.L.S. 442.

(b) local authorities: *Ephraim v. Newham London Borough Council* (1992) 25 H.L.R. 207 (council not liable in respect of injuries suffered by E in a fire at a bed and breakfast establishment; E was homeless and had been advised to go there by the council as housing authority, but the essence of the complaint was a failure to inspect the premises and it was not fair, just and reasonable for a duty of care to be owed); *Barrett v. Enfield London Borough Council, The Times*, April 22, 1997 (no duty of care owed by authority to child in its care as regards decisions as to his future which would normally have been made by a parent);

(c) health authority: *Martine v. South East Kent Health Authority, The Times*, March 8, 1993 (authority owed no duty of care in respect of an investigation into a registered nursing home);

(d) police: *Hill v. Chief Constable of West Yorkshire* [1989] A.C. 59 (House of Lords held that the police did not owe a duty of care to individual members of the public to identify and apprehend an unknown criminal, even though it was reasonably foreseeable that harm was likely to be caused); *Calveley v. Chief Constable of the Merseyside Police* [1989] A.C. 1228 (the House held that police investigating a possible crime did not owe a duty of care to the suspect):

> "... it would plainly be contrary to public policy, in my opinion, to prejudice the fearless and efficient discharge by police officers of their vitally important public duty of investigating crime by requiring them to act under the shadow of a potential action for damages for negligence by the suspect" (*per* Lord Bridge at 1238);

Clough v. Bussan [1990] 1 All E.R. 431 (claim in respect of alleged police failure to respond quickly where traffic lights became defective struck out); *Ancell v. McDermott* [1993] 4 All E.R. 355 (claim in respect of alleged police failure to deal adequately with traffic hazard resulting from spillage of oil leading to fatal accident struck out); *Alexandrou v. Oxford* [1993] 4 All E.R. 328 (claim in respect of allegedly negligent response to burglar alarm dismissed); *Osman v. Ferguson* [1993] 4 All E.R. 344 (claim in respect of alleged police failure to prevent a person known to have threatened P from injuring him struck out; see J. Steele and D.S. Cowan [1994] P.L.4). But *cf. Swinney v. Chief Constable of the Northumbria Police* [1996] 3 All E.R. 449 (arguable that police owe a duty of care to informant to keep the confidential information supplied, including the informant's identity, secure);

(e) fire service: *John Munroe (Acrylics) Ltd v. London Fire and Civil Defence Authority* [1996] 4 All E.R. 318 (no sufficient proximity between fire brigade and owner of premises which might be ablaze to give rise to a duty to respond to a call for assistance; also contrary to public policy for such a duty to be recognised; once the fire brigade did respond, it would only be liable if it undertook a personal responsibility to some individual during the course of its activity); *Church of Jesus Christ of Latter-Day Saints (Great Britain) v. Yorkshire Fire and Civil Defence Authority, The Times*, May 9, 1996 (contrary to public policy for duty of care to be recognised arising out of failure to take reasonable steps to ensure an adequate supply of water at the scene of a fire); *cf. Capital and Counties plc v. Hampshire County Council* [1996] 4 All E.R. 336 (fire brigade liable where officer negligently ordered sprinkler system in a burning building to be turned off; no public policy immunity); *Duff v. Highlands and Islands Fire Board, The Times*, November 3, 1995. In *Stovin v. Wise* (below, p. 747), Lord

Hoffmann doubted whether a duty should be owed. The Court of Appeal dismissed appeals in the *London, Yorkshire* and *Hampshire* cases: [1997] 2 All E.R. 865.

(f) others: *Jones v. Department of Employment* [1989] Q.B. 1 (adjudication officer owes no duty of care to benefit claimant); *Philcox v. Civil Aviation Authority, The Times*, June 8, 1995 (CAA owes no duty of care to owners of aircraft to ensure they maintained them properly); *Skinner v. Secretary of State for Transport, The Times*, January 3, 1995 (coastguard owes no duty of care to mariner); *Elguzouli-Daf v. Commissioner of Police of the Metropolis* [1995] 1 All E.R. 833 (Crown Prosecution Service owed no duty of care to defendant save where it assumes by conduct responsibility to a particular person); *W v. Home Office, The Times*, March 14, 1997 (no duty of care owed by immigration officer as regards detention decisions).

It will be noted that many of these cases concern alleged failures to protect the plaintiff from harm caused by third parties or (sometimes) by themselves. As explained by Lord Hoffmann in *Stovin v. Wise (Norfolk County Council (Third Party)* (below, pp. 737–739), there are good reasons why it is less appropriate for such omissions to lead to civil liability than positive acts which cause harm.

Recurrent themes in the reasoning to justify the exclusion of a duty include fears that actual litigation would divert officials and resources from more useful tasks and that the fear of litigation would inappropriately inhibit proper decision-making; the existence of alternative remedies; and the fact that if a public authority (with a bottomless purse) is always available as a defendant, it may end up footing the entire bill notwithstanding that the major cause of harm to the plaintiff is another party (now bankrupt).

4. *Negligence: discretion*. It is widely accepted that the courts should be particularly cautious before holding that an exercise (or non-exercise) of a statutory discretionary power should lead to liability in negligence for damages. In particular, decisions as to the allocation of limited resources may be made by elected bodies (or by expert agencies accountable to such bodies) with the appropriate mechanism for redress for those injured or disadvantaged by such decisions being through the ballot box rather than through an action for damages. This has given rise to two broad schools of thought. The first sees the need for there to be an immunity in respect of those acts or omissions that can be said to be *policy* decisions; the *operational* implementation of a policy decision then may or may not give rise to liability depending on the circumstances. The second regards this distinction as unworkable and unnecessary, the ordinary principles governing the imposition of the duty of care and, equally importantly, breach of duty are sufficiently sensitive and flexible to ensure that full account is taken of the legitimate interests of public authorities. Curiously, the first of these schools of thought is exemplified by the dicta of Lord Browne-Wilkinson in *X v. Bedfordshire County Council*, and the second by the House of Lords (both majority and minority) in *Stovin v. Wise (Norfolk County Council)* (below, pp. 737–750). For further discussion, see below, pp. 750–752.

5. *Negligence: recognised areas of liability*. There are, of course, many situations where the existence of a duty of care is well established and applied to public authorities without more ado. Accidents involving vehicles owned by public authorities are dealt with by the application of ordinary principles (which may admittedly include in the consideration of whether there is a breach of duty reference to the nature of the object to be achieved (*Watt v. Hertfordshire County Council* [1954] 1 W.L.R. 835)). Local authorities and teachers may owe a duty of care in respect of the physical safety of children in their schools (*Carmarthenshire County Council v. Lewis* [1955] A.C. 549). Public authorities as occupiers of land are subject to the Occupiers' Liability Acts 1957 and 1984 (see M. Jones, *Textbook on Torts* (4th ed., 1996), Chap. 6). Public

authorities may be liable directly or vicariously for negligence in the performance of professional services, as discussed in *X v. Bedfordshire County Council* itself (above, pp. 730–731; n. 6 below). They may by their conduct assume responsibility towards individuals, a possibility discussed by Lord Hoffmann in *Stovin v. Wise (Norfolk County Council, Third Party)*, below, pp. 738, 746–747. Nevertheless, identifying the line between areas where negligence is actionable and those where it is not is problematic. It is not, for example, possible to identify situations where a public authority acts in a private capacity as candidates for the application of ordinary principles. First, all the powers of public authorities other than the Crown must be referable expressly or impliedly to statute. Secondly, legal burdens placed by ordinary law on the supposedly *private* activities of a public authority will have at least an indirect impact on the way it performs its *public* functions (*ex hypothesi*, the authority's *raison d'être*). Thirdly, the case law on the ambit of judicial review (pp. 605–634) demonstrates the difficulty of drawing a line between "public" and "private" at both the institutional and functional levels, especially given the context where apparently public functions are increasingly discharged by bodies independent of Government.

It is also not the case that the distinction between acts and omissions (discussed in *Stovin v. Wise (Norfolk County Council (Third Party)*, below, pp. 737–739 is the touchstone of liability. On the one hand, the public policy arguments against liability may apply in cases where an authority's acts have caused harm as (on the assumed facts) in *X v. Bedfordshire County Council*). Conversely, there are some situations where the common law of negligence recognises positive obligations to act for the benefit of another (see Lord Hoffmann, below, pp. 738, 746). Ultimately, one is left with a sea of individual decisions where any developments are to be incremental only and where there is no attempt to identify an organising theme. Some clarity is being achieved slowly at the expense of a mass of otherwise unproductive litigation.

6. *Negligent misstatement.* Negligent misstatements that give rise to physical damage may lead to liability on ordinary principles (see the discussion in *X v. Bedfordshire County Council* (above, pp. 726–728, 730–731). The House of Lords in *Hedley Byrne & Co. Ltd v. Heller and Partners Ltd* [1964] A.C. 465 recognised that a duty of care could arise in respect of such misstatements that caused economic loss. However, the defendant will only be liable where he knows that his statement will be communicated to the plaintiff, either as an individual or as a member of an identifiable class, specifically in connection with a particular transaction or kind of transaction, and that the plaintiff would be very likely to rely on it for the purpose of deciding whether to enter that transaction or kind of transaction (Lord Bridge in *Caparo Products plc v. Dickman* [1990] 1 All E.R. 568, 576. In *Henderson v. Merrett Syndicates* [1994] 3 W.L.R. 761, the House stated that the *Hedley Byrne* principle extended beyond the provision of information and advice to cover assumptions of responsibility for the performance of services for the plaintiff.

Public authorities have been held liable for negligent statements and other acts that cause economic loss to the plaintiff (*Coats Paton (Retail) Ltd v. Birmingham Corporation* (1971) 69 L.G.R. 356 (negligent answer to enquiries before purchase of a shop); *Ministry of Housing and Local Government v. Sharp* [1970] 2 Q.B. 223 (negligent search of local land charges register); *Harris v. Wyre Forest District Council* [1990] 1 A.C. 831 (negligent house survey); *Welton v. North Cornwall District Council* [1997] 1 W.L.R. 570 (environmental health officer negligently required owners of food premises to undertake works which were, in fact, unnecessary); *Lambert v. West Devon Borough Council, The Times*, March 27, 1997 (negligent advice by building control officer that L could proceed with building works). By contrast, in *Tidman v. Reading Borough Council, The Times*, November 10, 1994, Buxton J. held that a response by council officers to an *informal*, telephoned planning inquiry by a member of the public did not give rise to a duty of care.

STOVIN v. WISE, NORFOLK COUNTY COUNCIL (THIRD PARTY)

[1996] A.C. 923; [1996] 3 W.L.R. 388; [1996] 3 All E.R. 801
(House of Lords)

In December 1988, the plaintiff, Thomas Stovin, was riding a motorcycle along Station Road, Wymondham, Norfolk, when he collided with a motorvehicle which was driven by the defendant, Rita Wise, out of a junction on his left. He was seriously injured. Although the junction was not a busy one, the county council as highway authority knew it to be dangerous because the view of road users turning out of the junction was restricted by a bank of earth on adjoining land. There had been accidents in 1976 and 1982 at the spot. In January 1988 the council wrote to the owner of the land, British Rail, suggesting that part of the bank should be removed and that the council would meet the cost of about £1,000. There was a third accident in March 1988. However, there was no response to the letter and the matter had not been followed up by the council by December.

The trial judge found that Mrs Wise was 70 per cent responsible and the council, brought in as a third party, 30 per cent. The council's appeal to the Court of Appeal was dismissed ([1994] 1 W.L.R 1124). The council's appeal to the House of Lords was allowed by 3:2 (Lords Hoffmann, Goff of Chievely and Jauncey of Tullichettle; Lords Nicholls of Birkenhead and Slynn of Hadley dissenting). The major speeches of the majority and minority were given, respectively, by Lords Hoffmann and Nicholls of Birkenhead.

LORD HOFFMANN: . . .

4. *Acts and omissions*
The judge made no express mention of the fact that the complaint against the council was not about anything which it had done to make the highway dangerous but about its omission to make it safer. Omissions, like economic loss, are notoriously a category of conduct in which Lord Atkin's generalisation in *Donoghue v. Stevenson* [1932] A.C. 562 offers limited help. In the High Court of Australia in *Hargrave v. Goldman* (1963) 110 C.L.R. 40, 66, Windeyer J. drew attention to the irony in Lord Atkin's allusion, in formulating his "neighbour" test, to the parable of the Good Samaritan [1932] A.C. 562, 580:

> "The priest and the Levite, when they saw the wounded man by the road, passed by on the other side. He obviously was a person whom they had in contemplation and who was closely and directly affected by their action. Yet the common law does not require a man to act as the Samaritan did."

A similar point was made by Lord Diplock in *Dorset Yacht Co. Ltd v. Home Office* [1970] A.C. 1004, 1060. There are sound reasons why omissions require different treatment from positive conduct. It is one thing for the law to say that a person who undertakes some activity shall take reasonable care not to cause damage to others. It is another thing for the law to require that a person who is doing nothing in particular shall take steps to prevent another from suffering harm from the acts of third parties (like Mrs Wise) or natural causes. One can put the matter in political, moral or economic terms. In political terms it is less of an invasion of an individual's freedom for the law to require him to consider the safety of others in his actions than to impose upon him a duty to rescue or protect. A moral version of this point may be called the "why pick on me?" argument. A duty to prevent harm to others or to render assistance to a person in danger or distress may apply to a large and indeterminate class of people who happen to be able to do something. Why should one be held liable rather than another? In economic terms, the efficient allocation of resources usually requires an activity should bear its own costs. If it benefits from being able to impose some of its costs on other people (what economists call "externalities"), the market is distorted because the activity appears cheaper than it really is. So liability to pay compensation for loss caused by negligent conduct acts as a deterrent against increasing the cost of the activity to the community and reduces externalities. But there is no similar justification for requiring a person who is not doing anything to spend money on behalf of someone else. Except in special cases (such as marine salvage) English law does not reward someone who voluntarily confers a benefit on another. So there must be some special reason why he should have to put his hand in his pocket.

In *Hargrave v. Goldman*, 110 C.L.R. 40, 66, Windeyer J. said:

> "The trend of judicial development in the law of negligence has been . . . to found a duty to take care either in some task undertaken, or in the ownership, occupation, or use of land or chattels."

There may be a duty to act if one has undertaken to do so or induced a person to rely upon one doing so. Or the ownership or occupation of land may give rise to a duty to take positive steps for the benefit of those who come upon the land and sometimes for the benefit of neighbours. In *Hargrave v. Goldman* the High Court of Australia held that the owner and occupier of a 600-acre grazing property in Western Australia had a duty to take reasonable steps to extinguish a fire, which had been started by lightning striking a tree on his land, so as to prevent it from spreading to his neighbour's land. This is a case in which the limited class of persons who owe the duty (neighbours) is easily identified and the political, moral and economic arguments which I have mentioned are countered by the fact that the duties are mutual. One cannot tell where the lightning may strike and it is therefore both fair and efficient to impose upon each landowner a duty to have regard to the interests of his neighbour. In giving the advice of the Privy Council affirming the decision (*Goldman v. Hargrave* [1967] 1 A.C. 645) Lord Wilberforce underlined the exceptional nature of the liability when he pointed out that the question of whether the landowner had acted reasonably should be judged by reference to the resources he actually had at his disposal and not by some general or objective standard. This is quite different from the duty owed by a person who undertakes a positive activity which carries the risk of causing damage to others. If he does not have the resources to take such steps as are objectively reasonable to prevent such damage, he should not undertake that activity at all.

5. Omissions in the Court of Appeal

[His Lordship rejected views adopted by members of the Court of Appeal (1) that this was an omission in the context of a positive decision to act analogous to the failure of a car driver to apply the brakes (*per* Kennedy L.J. [1994] 1

W.L.R. 1124, 1138); and (2) that the highway authority's position was analogous to that of the occupier of premises in relation to visitors (Roch L.J.
[1994] 1 W.L.R. 1124, 1139). As to (1), S's injuries "were not caused by the
negotiations between the council and British Rail or anything else which the
council did". As to (2), the analogy was insufficient given that an occupier
could normally take steps to keep out unwanted entrants; and where he could
not, as where a public right of way lay across his land, it was established that
there was no duty to take reasonable steps to make the way safe for users
(*McGeown v. Northern Ireland Housing Executive* [1995] 1 A.C. 233,
H.L.).]

6. Public authorities

The argument that the council had a positive duty to take action giving rise to
a claim for compensation in tort must therefore depend, as the judge and the
Court of Appeal recognised, upon the public nature of its powers, duties and
funding. The argument is that while it may be unreasonable to expect a private
landowner to spend money for the benefit of strangers who have the right to
cross his land, the very purpose of the existence of a public authority like the
council is to spend its resources on making the roads convenient and safe. For
that purpose it has a large battery of powers in the Highways Act 1980. These
do not actually include a power which would have enabled the council to go
upon the land of British Rail and remove the bank of earth. But there is power
under section 79 to serve a notice requiring the bank to be removed. The
power is conferred for the purpose of "the prevention of danger arising from
obstruction to the view of persons using the highway". Although the allegation is not that the council failed to use this power (it probably would not
have been necessary to do so), its existence shows that one of the purposes for
which Parliament contemplated that the highway authority would spend its
money was the removal of exactly the kind of obstructions which caused the
accident in this case.

It is certainly true that some of the arguments against liability for omissions
do not apply to public bodies like a highway authority. There is no "why pick
on me?" argument: as Kennedy L.J. said, at 1139, the highway authority
alone had the financial and physical resources, as well as the legal powers, to
eliminate the hazard. But this does not mean that the distinction between acts
and omissions is irrelevant to the duties of a public body or that there are not
other arguments, peculiar to public bodies, which may negative the existence
of a duty of care.

(a) Negligent conduct in the exercise of statutory powers

Since *Mersey Docks and Harbour Board Trustees v. Gibbs* (1866) L.R. 1 H.L.
93 it has been clear law that in the absence of express statutory authority, a
public body is in principle liable for torts in the same way as a private person.
But its statutory powers or duties may restrict its liability. For example, it may
be authorised to do something which necessarily involves committing what
would otherwise be a tort. In such a case it will not be liable: *Allen v. Gulf Oil
Refining Ltd* [1981] A.C. 1001. Or it may have discretionary powers which
enable it to do things to achieve a statutory purpose notwithstanding that they
involve a foreseeable risk of damage to others. In such a case, a bona fide
exercise of the discretion will not attract liability: *X (Minors) v. Bedfordshire*

County Council [1995] 2 A.C. 633 and *Dorset Yacht Co. Ltd v. Home Office* [1970] A.C. 1004.

In the case of positive acts, therefore, the liability of a public authority in tort is in principle the same as that of a private person but may be *restricted* by its statutory powers and duties. The argument in the present case, however, is that whereas a private person would have owed no duty of care in respect of an omission to remove the hazard at the junction, the duty of the highway authority is *enlarged* by virtue of its statutory powers. The existence of the statutory powers is said to create a "proximity" between the highway authority and the highway user which would not otherwise exist.

(b) *Negligent omission to use statutory powers*

Until the decision of this House in *Anns v. Merton London Borough Council* [1978] A.C. 728, there was no authority for treating a statutory power as giving rise to a common law duty of care. Two cases in particular were thought to be against it. In *Sheppard v. Glossop Corporation* [1921] 3 K.B. 132 the council had power to light the streets of Glossop. But their policy was to turn off the lamps at 9 p.m. The plaintiff was injured when he fell over a retaining wall in the dark after the lamps had been extinguished. He sued the council for negligence. The Court of Appeal said that the council owed him no duty of care. Atkin L.J. said, at 150:

> "[The local authority] is under no legal duty to act reasonably in deciding whether it shall exercise its statutory powers or not, or in deciding to what extent, over what particular area, or for what particular time, it shall exercise its powers . . . The real complaint of the plaintiff is not that they caused the danger, but that, the danger being there, if they had lighted it he would have seen and avoided it."

In *East Suffolk Rivers Catchment Board v. Kent* [1941] A.C. 74, 102 the facts of which are too well known to need repetition,[9] Lord Romer cited *Sheppard v. Glossop Corporation* and stated the principle which he said it laid down, at 102:

> "Where a statutory authority is entrusted with a mere power it cannot be made liable for any damage sustained by a member of the public by reason of a failure to exercise that power."

There are two points to be made about the *East Suffolk* case by way of anticipation of what was said about it in the *Anns* case. First, Lord Wilberforce said [1978] A.C. 728, 757:

> "only one of their Lordships [Lord Atkin] considered [the case] in relation to a duty of care at common law . . . I believe that the conception of a general duty of care, not limited to particular accepted situations, but extending generally over all relations of sufficient proximity, and even pervading the sphere of statutory functions of public bodies, had not at that time become fully recognised."

---

[9] [Editor's note] see below, p. 752.

I must say with great respect that I do not think that this is a fair description of the reasoning of the majority. As a claim of breach of statutory duty had expressly been abandoned, it is hard to imagine what the majority could have thought was the alleged cause of action unless it was breach of a duty of care at common law. What the majority found impossible was to derive such a duty from the existence of a statutory power: to turn a statutory "may" into a common law "ought".

The second point about the *East Suffolk* case is that Lord Atkin, who dissented, does not appear to have founded a duty of care solely upon the existence of the board's statutory powers. He appears to have held that by going upon the plaintiff's land to do work which the plaintiff himself could have done (see at 91–92) the board accepted a duty to execute the work with due dispatch. On this argument, the only relevance of the board's statutory powers was that it could have done the work. It had no statutory defence which would not have been available to a private contractor who had gone upon the land in similar circumstances. Whether Lord Atkin's reasoning is good or bad, it does not support the proposition that statutory powers can generate a duty of care which would not otherwise have existed.

The equally well known case of *Dorset Yacht Co. Ltd v. Home Office* [1970] A.C. 1004 also cast no doubt upon the general principle stated by Lord Romer in *East Suffolk*. The only reference to the case is by Viscount Dilhorne, at 1050G–H, in a dissenting speech. All members of the House plainly did not regard the case as one in which the alleged breach of duty was merely an omission to use a statutory power. The negligence was caused by something which the Borstal officers did, namely to use their statutory powers of custody to bring the trainees onto the island, where they constituted a foreseeable risk to boat owners, and then take no care to prevent them from escaping in the night. The case was therefore prima facie within *Mersey Docks and Harbour Board Trustees v. Gibbs*, L.R. 1 H.L. 93, and their Lordships were concerned only with whether the Crown had a defence on the grounds that the alleged breach of duty involved the exercise of a statutory discretion or whether the fact that the damage was caused by the criminal act of the Borstal trainees negatived the causal link with the Crown's breach of duty. Both these defences were rejected.

7. *Anns v. Merton London Borough Council*

This brings me to the *Anns* case [1978] A.C. 728. As this case is the mainstay of Mrs Wise's argument, I must examine it in some detail. The plaintiffs were lessees of flats in a new block which had been damaged by subsidence caused by inadequate foundations. They complained that the council had been negligent in the exercise of its statutory powers to inspect the foundations of new buildings. The council said that it owed no duty to inspect and therefore could not be liable for negligent inspection. The House rejected this argument. So far as it held that the council owed a duty of care in respect of purely economic loss, the case has been overruled by *Murphy v. Brentwood District Council* [1991] 1 A.C. 398. The House left open the question of whether the council might have owed a duty in respect of physical injury, although I think it is fair to say that the tone of their Lordships' remarks on this question was somewhat sceptical. Nevertheless, it is now necessary to ask whether the reasoning can support the existence of a duty of care owed by a public authority in respect of foreseeable physical injury which is founded upon the existence of statutory powers to safeguard people against that injury.

Lord Wilberforce, who gave the leading speech, first stated the well known two-stage test for the existence of a duty of care. This involves starting with a prima facie assumption that a duty of care exists if it is reasonably foreseeable that carelessness may cause damage and then asking whether there are any considerations which ought to "negative, or to reduce or limit the scope of the duty or the class of person to whom it is owed or the damages to which a breach of it may arise". Subsequent decisions in this House and the Privy Council have preferred to appoach the question the other way round, starting with situations in which a duty has been held to exist and then asking whether there are considerations of analogy, policy, fairness and justice for extending it to cover a new situation: see for example Lord Bridge of Harwich in *Caparo Industries plc v. Dickman* [1990] 2 A.C. 605, 617–618. It can be said that, provided that the considerations of policy etc. are properly analysed, it should not matter whether one starts from one end or the other.

On the other hand the assumption from which one starts makes a great deal of difference if the analysis is wrong. The trend of authorities has been to discourage the assumption that anyone who suffers loss is prima facie entitled to compensation from a person (preferably insured or a public authority) whose act or omission can be said to have caused it. The default position is that he is not.

This does not of course mean that the actual analysis in the *Anns* case was wrong. It has to be considered on its own merits. Lord Wilberforce had to deal with an argument by the council which was based upon two propositions. The first was that if the council owed no duty to inspect in the first place, it could be under no liability for having done so negligently. The second relied upon Lord Romer's principle in the *East Suffolk* case [1941] A.C. 74, 97: a public authority which has a mere statutory powr cannot on that account owe a duty at common law to exercise the power. Lord Wilberforce did not deny the first proposition. This, if I may respectfully say so, seems to me to be right. If the public authority was under no duty to act, either by virtue of its statutory powers or on any other basis, it cannot be liable because it has acted but negligently failed to confer a benefit on the plaintiff or to protect him from loss. The position is of course different if the negligent action of the public authority has left the plaintiff in a worse position than he would have been in if the authority had not acted at all. Lord Wilberforce did however deny the council's second proposition. His reasoning was as follows, at 755:

> "I think that this is too crude an argument. It overlooks the fact that local authorities are public bodies operating under statute with a clear responsibility for public health in their area. They must, and in fact do, make their discretionary decision responsibly and for reasons which accord with the statutory purpose; ... If they do not exercise their discretion in this way they can be challenged in the courts. Thus, to say that councils are under no duty to inspect, is not a sufficient statement of the position. They are under a duty to give proper consideration to the question whether they should inspect or not. Their immunity from attack, in the event of failure to inspect, in other words, though great is not absolute. And because it is not absolute, the necessary premise for the proposition 'if no duty to inspect, then no duty to take care in inspection' vanishes."

The duty of care at common law is therefore derived from the council's duty in public law to "give proper consideration to the question whether they should inspect or not". It is clear, however, that this public law duty cannot in itself give rise to a duty of care. A public body almost always has a duty in public law to consider whether it should exercise its powers, but that does not mean that it necessarily owes a duty of care which may require that the power should actually be exercised. As Mason J. said in *Sutherland Shire Council v. Heyman*, 157 C.L.R. 424, 465:

"although a public authority may be under a public duty, enforceable by mandamus, to give proper consideration to the question whether it should exercise a power, this duty cannot be equated with, or regarded as a foundation for imposing, a duty of care on the public authority in relation to the exercise of the power. Mandamus will compel proper consideration of the authority of its discretion, but that is all."

A mandamus can require future consideration of the exercise of a power. But an action for negligence looks back to what the council ought to have done. Upon what principles can one say of a public authority that not only did it have a duty in public law to consider the exercise of the power but that it would thereupon have been under a duty in private law to act, giving rise to a claim in compensation against public funds for its failure to do so? Or as Lord Wilberforce puts it in the *Anns* case [1978] A.C. 728, 754:

"The problem which this kind of action creates, is to define the circumstances in which the law should impose, over and above, or perhaps alongside, these public law powers and duties, a duty in private law towards individuals such that they may sue for damages in a civil court."

The only tool which the *Anns* case provides for defining these circumstances is the distinction between policy and operations. Lord Wilberforce said:

"Most, indeed probably all, statutes relating to public authorities or public bodies, contain in them a large area of policy. The courts call this 'discretion' meaning that the decision is one for the authority or body to make, and not for the courts. Many statutes also prescribe or at least presuppose the practical execution of policy decisions: a convenient description of this is to say that in addition to the area of policy or discretion, there is an operational area. Although this distinction between the policy area and the operational area is convenient, and illuminating, it is probably a distinction of degree; many 'operational' powers or duties have in them some element of 'discretion'. It can safely be said that the more 'operational' a power or duty may be, the easier it is to superimpose upon it a common law duty of care."

The *East Suffolk* case [1941] A.C. 74 and *Sheppard v. Glossop Corporation* [1921] 3 K.B. 132 were distinguished as involving questions of policy or discretion. The inspection of foundations, on the other hand, was "heavily operational" and the power to inspect could therefore give rise to a duty of care. Lord Romer's statement of principle in *East Suffolk* was limited to cases in which the exercise of the power involved a policy decision.

8. Policy and operations

Since *Anns v. Merton London Borough Council*, there have been differing views, both in England and the Commonwealth, over whether it was right to breach the protection which the *East Suffolk* principle gave to public authorities. In *Sutherland Shire Council v. Heyman*, 157 C.L.R. 424, 483, Brennan J. thought that it was wrong: one simply could not derive a common law "ought" from a statutory "may". But I think that he was the only member of the court to adhere to such uncompromising orthodoxy. What has become clear, however, is that the distinction between policy and operations is an inadequate tool with which to discover whether it is appropriate to impose a duty of care or not. In *Rowling v. Takaro Properties Ltd* [1988] A.C. 473, 501 Lord Keith of Kinkel said:

> "[Their Lordships] incline to the opinion, expressed in the literature, that this distinction does not provide a touchstone of liability, but rather is expressive of the need to exclude altogether those cases in which the decision under attack is of such a kind that a question whether it has been made negligently is unsuitable for judicial resolution, of which notable examples are discretionary decisions on the allocation of scarce resources or the distribution of risks. . . . If this is right, classification of the relevant decision as a policy or planning decision in this sense may exclude liability; but a conclusion that it does not fall within that category does not, in their Lordships' opinion, mean that a duty of care will necessarily exist."

There are at least two reasons why the distinction is inadequate. The first is that, as Lord Wilberforce himself pointed out, the distinction is often elusive. This is particularly true of powers to provide public benefits which involve the expenditure of money. Practically every decision about the provision of such benefits, no matter how trivial it may seem, affects the budget of the public authority in either timing or amount. The *East Suffolk* case, about which Lord Wilberforce said in the *Anns* case [1978] A.C. 728, 757, that the activities of the board, though "operational", were "well within a discretionary area, so that the plaintiff's task in contending for a duty of care was a difficult one" is a very good example. But another reason is that even if the distinction is clear cut, leaving no element of discretion in the sense that it would be irrational (in the public law meaning of that word) for the public authority not to exercise its power, it does not follow that the law should superimpose a common law duty of care. This can be seen if one looks at cases in which a public authority has been under a statutory or common law *duty* to provide a service or other benefit for the public or a section of the public. In such cases there is no discretion but the courts have nevertheless not been willing to hold that a member of the public who has suffered loss because the service was not provided to him should necessarily have a cause of action, either for breach of statutory duty or for negligence at common law.

There are many instances of this principle being applied to statutory duties, but perhaps the most relevant example of the dissociation between public duty and a liability to pay compensation for breach of that duty was the ancient common law duty to repair the highway. The common law imposed this financial burden upon the inhabitants of the parish. But it saw no need to impose upon them the additional burden of paying compensation to users of the highway who suffered injury because the highway surveyor had failed to repair. The duty could be enforced only by indictment. This rule continued to apply when the duty to maintain was transferred by statute to highway authorities and was only abolished by section 1 of the Highways (Miscellaneous Provisions) Act 1961. Likewise in *Hill v. Chief Constable of West Yorkshire* [1989] A.C. 53 it was held that the public duty of the police to catch criminals did not give rise to a duty of care to a member of the public who was injured because the police had negligently failed to catch one. The decision was mainly based upon the large element of discretion which the police necessarily have in conducting their operations, but the judgment excludes liability even in cases in which the alleged breach of duty would constitute public law irrationality.

In terms of public finance, this is a perfectly reasonable attitude. It is one thing to provide a service at the public expense. It is another to require the public to pay compensation when a failure to provide the service has resulted in loss. Apart from cases of reliance, which I shall consider later, the same loss would have been suffered if the service had not been provided in the first place. To require payment of compensation increases the burden on public funds. Before imposing such an additional burden, the courts should be satisfied that this is what Parliament intended.

Whether a statutory duty gives rise to a private cause of action is a question of construction: see *R. v. Deputy Governor of Parkhurst Prison, ex p. Hague* [1992] 1 A.C. 58. It requires an examination of the policy of the statute to decide whether it was intended to confer a right to compensation for breach. Whether it can be relied upon to support the existence of a common law duty of care is not exactly a question of construction, because the cause of action does not arise out of the statute itself. But the policy of the statute is nevertheless a crucial factor in the decision. As Lord Browne-Wilkinson said in *X (Minors) v. Bedfordshire County Council* [1995] 2 A.C. 633, 739C in relation to the duty of care owed by a public authority performing statutory functions:

> "the question whether there is such a common law duty and if so its ambit, must be profoundly influenced by the statutory framework within which the acts complained of were done".

The same is true of omission to perform a statutory duty. If such a duty does not give rise to a private right to sue for breach, it would be unusual if it nevertheless gave rise to a duty of care at common law which made the public authority liable to pay compensation for foreseeable loss caused by the duty not being performed. It will often be foreseeable that loss will result if, for example, a benefit or service is not provided. If the policy of the act is not to create a statutory liability to pay compensation, the same policy should ordinarily exclude the existence of a common law duty of care.

In the case of a mere statutory power, there is the further point that the legislature has chosen to confer a discretion rather than create a duty. Of course there may be cases in which Parliament has chosen to confer a power because the subject matter did not permit a duty to be stated with sufficient precision. It may nevertheless have contemplated that in circumstances in which it would be irrational not to exercise the power, a person who suffered loss because it had not been exercised, or not properly exercised, would be entitled to compensation. I therefore do not say that a statutory "may" can never give rise to a common law duty of care. I prefer to leave open the question of whether the *Anns* case was wrong to create any exception to Lord Romer's statement of principle in the *East Suffolk* case and I shall go on to consider the circumstances (such as "general reliance") in which it has been suggested that such a duty might arise. But the fact that Parliament has conferred a discretion must be some indication that the policy of the act conferring the power was not to create a right to compensation. The need to have regard to the policy of the statute therefore means that exceptions will be rare.

In summary, therefore, I think that the minimum preconditions for basing a duty of care upon the existence of a statutory power, if it can be done at all, are, first, that it would in the circumstances have been irrational not to have exercised the power, so that there was in effect a public law duty to act, and secondly, that there are exceptional grounds for holding that the policy of the statute requires compensation to be paid to persons who suffer loss because the power was not exercised.

9. Particular and general reliance

In *Sutherland Shire Council v. Heyman*, 157 C.L.R. 424, 483, Brennan J., as I have mentioned, thought that a statutory power could never generate a common law duty of care unless the public authority had created an expectation that the power would be used and the plaintiff had suffered damage from reliance on that expectation. A common example is the lighthouse authority which, by the exercise of its power to build and maintain a lighthouse, creates in mariners an expectation that the light will warn them of danger. In such circumstances, the authority (unlike the Glossop Corporation in *Sheppard v. Glossop Corporation* [1921] 3 K.B. 132) owes a duty of care which requires it not to extinguish the light without giving reasonable notice. This form of liability, based upon representation and reliance, does not depend upon the public nature of the authority's powers and causes no problems.

In the same case, however, Mason J. suggested a different basis upon which public powers might give rise to a duty of care. He said, at 464:

> "there will be cases in which the plaintiff's reasonable reliance will arise out of a general dependence on an authority's performance of its function with due care, without the need for contributing conduct on the part of a defendant or action to his detriment on the part of a plaintiff. Reliance or dependence in this sense is in general the product of the grant (and exercise) of powers designed to prevent or minimise a risk of personal injury or disability, recognised by the legislature as being of such magnitude or complexity that individuals cannot, or may not, take adequate steps for their own protection. This situation generates on one side (the individual) a general expectation that the power will be exercised and on the other side (the authority) a realisation that there is a general reliance or dependence on its exercise of the power. . . . The control of air traffic, the safety inspection of aircraft and the fighting of a fire in a building by a fire authority . . . may well be examples of this type of function."

This ground for imposing a duty of care has been called "general reliance". It has little in common with the ordinary doctrine of reliance; the plaintiff does not need to have relied upon the expectation that the power would be used or even known that it existed. It appears rather to refer to general expectations in the community, which the individual plaintiff may or may not have shared. A widespread assumption that a statutory power will be exercised may affect the general pattern of economic and social behaviour. For example, insurance premiums may take into account the expectation that statutory powers of inspection or accident prevention will ordinarily prevent certain kinds of risk from materialising. Thus the doctrine of general reliance requires an inquiry into the role of a given statutory power in the behaviour of members of the general public, of which an outstanding example is the judgment of Richardson J. in *Invercargill City Council v. Hamlin* [1994] 3 N.Z.L.R. 513, 526.

It appears to be essential to the doctrine of general reliance that the benefit or service provided under statutory powers should be of a uniform and routine nature, so that one can describe exactly what the public authority was supposed to do. Powers of inspection for defects clearly fall into this category. Another way of looking at the matter is to say that if a particular service is provided as a matter of routine, it would be irrational for a public authority to provide it in one case and arbitrarily withhold it in another. This was obviously the main ground upon which this House in the *Anns* case considered that the power of the local authority to inspect foundations should give rise to a duty of care.

But the fact that it would be irrational not to exercise the power is, as I have said, only one of the conditions which has to be satisfied. It is also necessary to discern a policy which confers a right to financial compensation if the power has not been exercised. Mason J. thought in *Sutherland Shire Council v. Heyman*, 157 C.L.R. 424, 464, that such a policy might be inferred if the power was intended to protect members of the public from risks against which they could not guard themselves. In the *Invercargill* case, as I have said, the New Zealand Court of Appeal [1994] 3 N.Z.L.R. 513 and the Privy Council [1996] 2 W.L.R. 367 found it in general patterns of socio-economic behaviour. I do not propose to explore further the doctrine of general reliance because, for reasons which I shall explain, I think that there are no grounds upon which the present case can be brought within it. I will only note in passing that its application may require some very careful analysis of the role which the expected exercise of the statutory power plays in community behaviour. For example, in one sense it is true that the fire brigade is there to protect people in situations in which they could not be expected to be able to protect themselves. On the other hand they can and do protect themselves by insurance against the risk of fire. It is not obvious that there should be a right to compensation from a negligent fire authority which will ordinarily ensure by right of subrogation to an insurance company. The only reason would be to provide a general deterrent against inefficiency. But there must be better ways of doing this than by compensating insurance companies out of public funds. And while premiums no doubt take into account the existence of the fire brigade and the likelihood that it will arrive swiftly upon the scene, it is not clear that they would be very different merely because no compensation was paid in the rare cases in which the fire authority negligently failed to perform its public duty. . . .

11. *Duties of a highway authority*
I return to consider whether the council owed a duty of care which required it to take steps to improve the junction. Since the only basis for such a duty is the

authority's statutory powers, both specifically under section 79 of the Act of 1980 and generally to carry out works of improvement with the consent of British Rail, I will start by asking whether in the light of what the council knew or ought to have known about the junction, it would have had a duty in public law to undertake the work. This requires that it would have been irrational not to exercise its discretion to do so. The trial judge did not address himself to this question. He thought it was sufficient that, as he put it, "a decision had already been taken to deal with the situation" in which "budgetary considerations were not a restraint".

The fact that Mr Longhurst and Mr Deller had agreed to do the work does not show that it would have been unreasonable or irrational for the council not to have done it. That is simply a non sequitur. The Court of Appeal seems to have reasoned that the "decision" to do the work disposed of any question of policy or discretion and left only the operational question of when the work should have been done. But this too seems to me fallacious. The timing of the work and the budgetary year in which the money is spent is surely as much a matter of discretion as the decision in principle to do it. And why should the council be in a worse position than if Mr Longhurst had left Mr Deller's report at the bottom of his in-tray and forgotten about it? In that case, it is said, the council would have been in breach of its duty in public law to give due consideration to the exercise of its powers. Perhaps it would, but that does not advance the case far enough. It would still be necessary to say that if the council had considered the matter, it would have been bound to decide to do the work. One comes back, therefore, to the question of whether it would have been irrational to decide not to do it.

Furthermore, to say that a decision had been taken oversimplifies the situation. Mr Longhurst had not committed himself to any particular time within which the work would be done. There was, as Mr Deller said, a "nil time scale involved"; he did not think it mattered whether the work took one, two or three years. At the time when the letter to British Rail was sent, the March 1988 accident with the police car had not yet happened. Nor was it notified to Mr Longhurst or Mr Deller when it did. The judge found that they would have displayed a greater sense of urgency if they had known about it. But the judge made no finding that the council should have had a system by which Mr Longhurst was notified of every accident on the roads of South Norfolk. Such a system would have been quite impractical. There were 3,500 personal injury accidents in Norfolk every year and their particulars were simply entered on a computer from which the Accident Studies Section in Norwich identified "cluster sites" for special attention. No firm decision had been taken on expenditure either. Mr Deller thought that the work would cost less than £1,000, in which case it would have come within Mr Longhurst's discretionary budget for small works. But he said he could not be sure of the cost until he had consulted a design engineer: "it could be lots and lots more". This caution was justified by events. After Mr Stovin's accident, Mr Brian Meadows, who worked for the Accident Studies Section, inspected the junction and said that the bank could not be regraded within the budget for a low cost remedial scheme.

The judge, as I say, made no finding as to whether it would have been irrational for the council not to have done the work. The unchallenged evidence of Mr Reid, who was head of the Accident Studies Office, would have made it very difficult to do so. In evidence in chief, he was asked about the March 1988 accident:

> "Q. So far as you are concerned, what difference, if any, would the signficance of this accident have made in relation to priority given to carrying out work at this site, against the background of what had happened with British Rail? A. In practical terms, it would have made no difference at all to the priority within the accident remedial budget, because our attention and resources would have been directed to those many sites in the county which already had much higher accident records."

There was no suggestion in cross-examination that this was an unreasonable, let alone irrational, attitude to take.

It seems to me therefore that the question of whether anything should be done about the junction was at all times firmly within the area of the council's discretion. As they were therefore not under a public law duty to do the work, the first condition for the imposition of a duty of care was not satisfied.

But even if it were, I do not think that the second condition would be satisfied. Assuming that the highway authority ought, as a matter of public law, to have done the work, I do not think that there are any grounds upon which it can be said that the public law duty should give rise to an obligation to compensate persons who have suffered loss because it was not performed. There is no question here of reliance on the council having improved the junction. Everyone could see that it was still the same. Mr Stovin was not arbitrarily denied a benefit which was routinely provided to others. In respect of the junction, he was treated in exactly the same way as any other road user. The foundation for the doctrine of general reliance is missing in this case, because we are not concerned with provision of a uniform identifiable benefit or service. Every hazardous junction, intersection or stretch of road is different and requires a separate decision as to whether anything should be done to improve it. It is not without significance that the Canadian cases in which a duty of care has been held to exist have all involved routine inspection and maintenance rather than improvements.

I have mentioned earlier that maintenance of the highway was, until 1961, a striking example of a public duty which involved no obligation to compensate a person who had suffered damage because of its breach. The power in section 79 of the Highways Act 1980, upon which the plaintiff principally relies to generate a duty of care, was first enacted as section 4 of the Roads Improvement Act 1925. It seems to me impossible to discern a legislative intent that there should be a duty of care in respect of the use of that power, giving rise to a liability to compensate persons injured by a failure to use it, when there was at the time no such liability even for breach of the statutory duty to maintain the highway.

In my view the creation of a duty of care upon a highway authority, even on grounds of irrationality in failing to exercise a power, would inevitably expose the authority's budgetary decisions to judicial inquiry. This would distort the priorities of local authorities, which would be bound to try to play safe by increasing their spending on road improvements rather than risk enormous liabilities for personal injury accidents. They will spend less on education or social services. I think that it is important, before extending the duty of care owed by public authorities, to consider the cost to the community of the defensive measures which they are likely to take in order to avoid liability. It would not be surprising if one of the consequences of the *Anns* case and the spate of cases which followed was that local council inspectors tended to insist upon stronger foundations than were necessary. In a case like this, I do not think that the duty of care can be used as a deterrent against low standards in improving the road layout. Given the fact that the British road network largely antedates the highway authorities themselves, the court is not in a position to say what an appropriate standard of improvement would be. This must be a matter for the discretion of the authority. On the other hand, denial of liability does not leave the road user unprotected. Drivers of vehicles must take the highway network as they find it. Everyone knows that there are hazardous bends, intersections and junctions. It is primarily the duty of drivers of vehicles to take due care. And if, as in the case of Mrs Wise, they do not, there is compulsory insurance to provide compensation to the victims. There is no reason of policy or justice which requires the highway authority to be an additional defendant. I would therefore allow the appeal.

Appeal allowed.

Notes and Questions

1. *The dissent.* In his dissenting speech, Lord Nicholls of Birkenhead's statement of the relevant principles was very similar to Lord Hoffmann's. Thus the distinction between acts and omissions was "fundamentally sound" (at 393); the facts here constituted an omission, the failure to remove a source of danger not created by the council (at 393); and a common law duty "must not be inconsistent with the performance by the authority of its statutory duties and powers in the manner intended by Parliament, or contrary in any other way to the presumed legislative intention" (at 398); there was here no general or particular reliance based on the previous conduct of the council (at 398). However, a concurrent common law duty could be recognised where that did not impose a greater burden than the public law duty not to act irrationally (*i.e.* so unreasonably that no reasonable authority could have so acted), and there was a special circumstance rendering it fair and reasonable for the authority to be under a common law duty (at 399); policy decisions should not be regarded as a "no-go" area, given that the distinction between policy and other areas is artificial and elusive and that no statutory power is inherently immune from judicial review, where no difficulty is found in recognising "that reasonable people can reach widely differing conclusions when making decisions based on social, political or economic grounds (at 401). The crucial difference was that the minority thought that on the facts the council had behaved irrationally (at 399) and that it was fair and reasonable for a duty to be owed (at 402–403). On the latter point, key elements were that the risk here was of physical injury; that the authority *knew* of the danger; if the council had acted "rationally" the accident would not have happened; the council was made liable by statute for an omission if it failed to take reasonable care to keep the highway itself safe (Highways Act 1980, s.58); the purpose of the relevant statutory powers under the Act was to protect road users; there was some analogy with the liability of an occupier to entrants; it was clearly fair to a "hapless" injured road user unable to sue another insured party to recover from the highway authority and it should not make any difference that (as here) a claim did lie against another insured defendant.

2. *The relevance of irrationality.* Both Lord Hoffmann and Lord Nicholls regard a finding of irrationality to be a prerequisite of liability for failure to exercise a power. This raises a number of difficulties. First, there needs to be clarity as to what exactly is the "decision" that has to be shown to be irrational. Lord Nicholls concentrated on the actual chain of events (at 399):

"With knowledge of the danger the council decided to act. It then failed to proceed with reasonable diligence. The failure to proceed was not an exercise of discretion by the council. The council did not change its mind. The matter was overlooked. Given the decision to act, the only proper course was to proceed to implement the decision. Had the council acted as any reasonable authority would, that is what would have happened. The council failed to fulfil its public law obligations just as much as if it were in breach of a statutory duty."

For Lord Hoffmann (at 415) the issue was more the hypothetical one whether

"it would in the circumstances have been irrational not to have exercised the power, so that there was in effect a public law duty to act".

It is submitted that the latter approach is to be preferred. Whether or not there has been maladministration in the way a matter is handled cannot be decisive. If, had the matter been considered "properly", it was still open to the council to make a rational decision not to act (*e.g.* because other more pressing priorities intervened), then the equivalent of a statutory duty to act just does not exist. Lord Nicholls' conclusion that the "only" proper course was for the council to proceed with the matter is not borne out by the facts (see Lord Hoffmann's discussion at the end of his speech).

Secondly, there also needs to be clarity about what is meant by "irrationality". Consideration of the cases at pp. 349–367, above, should demonstrate that this is not straightforward.

In the present context it seems that a decision not to exercise a statutory power would only count as "irrational" where the council *in effect had no choice but to exercise the power*; *i.e.* that no reasonable authority could have decided not to exercise it. This is the equivalent of a situation where, on an application for judicial review, mandamus would lie not merely to have the matter reconsidered by the council (which assumes that the council would have liberty to decide not to exercise the power at the end of its reconsideration) but *to require the power to be exercised*. This is highly unusual. However, the fact that such a narrow approach is adopted perhaps explains why Lord Browne-Wilkinson in *X v. Bedfordshire County Council* was at pains to emphasise that the full ramifications of the *ultra vires* doctrine had no part to play in the determination of these issues as to tort liability.

3. *Justiciability and the policy operational dichotomy.* Compare the views of Lord Browne-Wilkinson in *X v. Bedfordshire County Council* and Lord Hoffmann in the present case. Lord Browne-Wilkinson's approach certainly makes it necessary to ask additional complex questions. Perhaps the most telling argument against the identification of a "no go" area on the basis of "non-justiciability" or "policy" is that this raises questions that are so difficult to resolve that they cannot be employed effectively at the striking-out stage, as amply demonstrated by *X v. Bedfordshire County Council* itself and its associated cases.

Following *Anns*, the lower courts in a number of cases sought to apply the distinction between policy and operational matters expounded by Lord Wilberforce, but encountered difficulties in doing so; see, *e.g. Bird v. Pearce* [1978] R.T.R. 290 and [1979] R.T.R. 369; *Haydon v. Kent County Council* [1978] Q.B. 343; *Vicar of Writtle v. Essex County Council* (1979) 77 L.Q.R. 656, discussed by D. Oliver (1980) 33 C.L.P. 269 and S.H. Bailey and M.J. Bowman [1986] C.L.J. 430. Commentators were divided on the question whether the concept of "policy" or "discretion" would cover any situation where the authority had an element of choice, or whether it only applied where the issues involved were not suitable for consideration by a court of law (see M. Aronson and H. Whitmore, *Public Torts and Contracts* (1982), pp. 69–73; Bailey and Bowman [1986] C.L.J. 430, 437–439).

As time went on, the courts tended simply to rely directly on a variety of public policy arguments in rejecting duties of care (see above, pp. 733–735) and did not reach or rely on the policy operational dichotomy (but with some exceptions; see, *e.g.* Sir Nicolas Browne-Wilkinson V.-C. (as he then was) in *Lonrho plc v. Tebbitt* [1991] 4 All E.R. 973; *cf.* Dillon L.J. in the Court of Appeal, [1992] 4 All E.R. 280, 287).

4. *The status of the East Suffolk and Anns cases.* In *East Suffolk Catchment Board v. Kent* [1941] A.C. 74, an exceptionally high spring tide caused the River Deben to overflow its banks and many pastures were flooded. The trial judge found that the Board's staff had so inefficiently carried out repair works that it took them 178 days, whereas with reasonable skill the gap should have been closed in 14 days. The Board has no statutory *duty* to repair the breach but had a statutory *power* to do this. It was held that the Board could not be made liable in damages. Lord Romer said (at 102):

> "Where a statutory authority is entrusted with a mere power it cannot be made liable for any damage sustained by a member of the public by reason of a failure to exercise that power. If in the exercise of their discretion they embark upon an execution of that power, the only duty they owe to any member of the public is not thereby to add to the damages that he would have suffered had they done nothing. So long as they exercise their discretion honestly, it is for them to determine the method by which and the time within which and the time during which the power shall be exercised; and they cannot be made liable, except to the extent that I have just mentioned, for any damage that would have been avoided had they exercised their discretion in a more reasonable way."

Given that the duty was limited to the avoidance of extra damage there was no causal link between any breach of that duty and the damage of which the plaintiff complained, namely the continuance of the inundation for 164 extra days.

This decision has been the subject of much criticism, not least by Lord Wilberforce in the *Anns* case. However, it has in a large measure been rehabilitated by Lord Hoffmann's speech in *Stovin v. Wise (Norfolk County Council (Third Party))*, but subject to the qualification that an irrational failure to exercise a power may lead to liability in damages. It is submitted that it should be regarded as good law. There seems no good reason why the Board, a body with limited resources, should be liable in negligence to the plaintiffs for inefficiency in rescuing their land from the effects of flooding given that (1) the Board were under no duty to act; (2) that on the facts as found, neither the plaintiffs themselves nor any third party would have been in a position to do the necessary work; and (3) that the plaintiffs had not secured the Board's services under a contract (for which they would have provided consideration). See further, Bowman and Bailey [1984] P.L. 277. If the Board's employees had through negligence caused additional physical damage to the plaintiff's land, the Board would have been held liable on ordinary principles. In this situation, the Board's *actions* would have caused distinct damage.

The decision in *Anns* was overruled by the House of Lords in *Murphy v. Brentwood District Council* [1991] 1 A.C. 398, mainly on the ground that the loss suffered by the plaintiff in repairing a house that was inherently defective was properly characterised as pure economic loss. This left open the possibility that an action might lie where a failure to inspect or a faulty inspection of a building led to a collapse that caused property damage or physical injury. Do you think an action could lie here in the light of the principles stated in *X v. Bedfordshire County Council* and *Stovin v. Wise, Norfolk County Council (Third Party)*? Can a local authority whose inspector carelessly inspects foundations be said to have assumed responsibility towards the plaintiff? Is there particular or general reliance?

(iii) Misfeasance in a Public Office

BOURGOIN S.A. v. MINISTRY OF AGRICULTURE, FISHERIES AND FOOD

[1986] Q.B. 716; [1985] 3 W.L.R. 1027; [1985] 3 All E.R. 585
(Mann J. and C.A.)

The plaintiffs, who were variously concerned in the production in France of frozen turkeys and turkey parts and in their sale and distribution within the United Kingdom, imported frozen turkeys and turkey parts into the United Kingdom under a general licence granted by the defendant. On September 1, 1981, the defendant, purporting to act in the interests of preventing the spread of Newcastle disease into the United Kingdom, revoked the licence and replaced it with one which had the effect of prohibiting the importation of turkeys and turkey parts from France. The Court of Justice of the European Communities subsequently held that the withdrawal of the licence had constituted a contravention of Article 30 of the EEC Treaty and had therefore been *ultra vires*, and in consequence of that decision the defendant issued a licence which permitted the resumption of such importation from November 1982. The plaintiffs claimed damages, alleging (by paragraph 23 of the amended statement of claim) that the withdrawal of the licence and the defendant's refusal subsequently to permit turkeys or turkey parts to be imported into the United Kingdom from France had caused the plaintiffs substantial loss and damage; (by paragraph 24) that such loss and damage had been caused by the defendant's breach of his statutory duty under Article 30 and that such a breach sounded in damages; (by paragraph 25) that such loss and damage had been caused by the commission by the defendant of an innominate tort by so breaching Article 30, or acting contrary to its provisions, as to cause them injury; and (by paragraph 26) that the withdrawal of the licence had amounted to misfeasance in public office, in that the defendant had exercised its power to withdraw the licence for a purpose which, as it had known, was contrary to Article 30 and/or was calculated to, and did, damage unlawfully the plaintiffs and/or was not the purpose for which those powers had been conferred on the defendant.

On the trial of the preliminary issue whether paras. 23–26 disclosed any causes of action, Mann J. found for the plaintiffs, holding that since Article 30 of the Treaty had direct effect, it conferred on persons injured by a contravention, even though arising from a breach of statutory duty, a cause of action in damages and that the defendant was liable to the plaintiffs for any damage which had flowed from the withdrawal of the licence as pleaded in paragraphs 23 and 24, but, since the commission of an innominate tort as a formulation of a cause of action was obsolete, the claim in paragraphs 23 and 25 did not disclose any cause of action; that in order to establish the tort of misfeasance in public office it was not necessary to prove that the defendant had been actuated by malice towards the plaintiff or had acted in bad faith but it was sufficient to show that the officer knew that he had no power to do that which he did and that his action would injure the plaintiff and subsequently did injure him and that paragraphs 23 and 26 did disclose a cause of action.

The Court of Appeal allowed an appeal in part, holding (Oliver L.J. dissenting) that breach of Article 30 did not give rise to a cause of action in damages (although it would give rise to a right to judicial review). On the other points, the Court of Appeal agreed with Mann J.

OLIVER L.J.: ... The third way in which the case is formulated on the pleadings is as a claim for damages against the Minister for misfeasance in public office, a tort which was described by Lord Diplock in *Dunlop v. Woollahra Municipal Council* [1982] A.C. 158, 173E, as "well-established". That is not in dispute. The difference between the parties rests only in their respective appreciations of the essential ingredients of the tort. For the purposes only of the preliminary issue, it was accepted that the Minister's purpose in revoking the general licence was to protect English turkey producers, and that he knew at the time (i) that this involved a failure to perform the United Kingdom's obligations under Article 30; (ii) that the revocation would cause damage to the plaintiffs in their business; and (iii) that the protection of English producers from foreign competition was not one for the achievement of which powers were conferred on him by the enabling legislation or the Importation of Animal Products and Poultry Products Order 1980. The Solicitor-General's submission, however, was that it was an essential allegation, and one not made on the pleadings, that the Minister acted with the purpose of inflicting harm upon the plaintiffs. This has been referred to conveniently as an allegation of "targeted malice".

The court has been referred to a large number of cases both in this country and in Canada and Australia from which, it is said, the inference can be drawn that in order to constitute the tort it is necessary to show an improper motive specifically aimed at the plaintiff. The authorities were extensively reviewed by the judge and it would, I think, be a work of supererogation to repeat the exercise here. There are in certain of the older cases phrases in the judgments or pleadings which might be taken to suggest that "targeted malice" was regarded as essential. I say "might", because in my judgment they are entirely inconclusive. There are also strong indications in the other direction, particularly in the older election cases. For instance in *Cullen v. Morris* (1819) 2 Stark. 577, 587, Abbott C.J. observed:

"On the part of the defendant it has been contended, that an action is not maintainable for merely refusing the vote of a person who appears afterwards to have really had a right to vote, unless it also appears that the refusal resulted from a malicious and improper motive, and that if the party act honestly and uprightly according to the best of his judgment, he is not amenable in an action for damages. I am of opinion, that the law, as it has been stated by the counsel for the defendant, is correct."

Again, he said, at 589:

"If a vote be refused with a view to prejudice either the party entitled to vote, or the candidate for whom he tenders his vote, the notice is an improper one, and an action is maintainable."

Coming to more modern times there is the Privy Council case of *Dunlop v. Woollahra Municipal Council* [1982] A.C. 158, where the allegation was one of damage caused to the plaintiff by passing planning resolutions, which were in fact invalid, restricting the height of his proposed building. Paragraph 15A of the pleading was (so far as material) in these terms, at 169–170:

"the defendant was a public corporate body which occupied office and was incorporated by a public statute ... and the defendant abused its said office and public duty under the said statute by purporting to pass each of the said resolutions with the consequence that damage was occasioned to the plaintiff."

In delivering the judgment of the Board, Lord Diplock said, at 172:

> "In pleading in paragraph 15A of the statement of claim that the council abused their public office and public duty the plaintiff was relying upon the well-established tort of misfeasance by a public officer in the discharge of his public duties ... [Their Lordships] agree with [the trial judge's] conclusion that, in the absence of malice, passing without knowledge of its invalidity a resolution which is devoid of any legal effect is not conduct that of itself is capable of amounting to such 'misfeasance' as is a necessary element in this tort."

Of this case Wade in his book on *Administrative Law* (5th ed., 1982), pp. 672–673, comments that the Privy Council held that the tort "required as a necessary element either malice or knowledge ... of the invalidity" a view which is in line with that expressed by Smith J. in *Farrington v. Thomson and Bridgland* [1959] V.R. 286, which was carefully considered by Mann J. in the course of his judgment in the instant case. Having concluded his review of the authorities, Mann J. concluded, *ante*, 740D–G:

> "I do not read any of the decisions to which I have been referred as precluding the commission of the tort of misfeasance in public office where the officer actually knew that he had no power to do that which he did, and that his act would injure the plaintiff as subsequently it does. I read the judgment in *Dunlop v. Woollahra Municipal Council* [1982] A.C. 158 in the sense that malice and knowledge are alternatives. There is no sensible reason why the common law should not afford a remedy to the injured party in circumstances such as are before me. There is no sensible distinction between the case where an officer performs an act which he has no power to perform with the object of injuring A (which the defendant accepts is actionable at the instance of A) and the case where an officer performs an act which he knows he has no power to perform with the object of conferring a benefit on B but which has the foreseeable and actual consequence of injury to A (which the defendant denies is actionable at the instance of A). In my judgment each case is actionable at the instance of A and, accordingly, I determine that paragraphs 23 and 36 of the amended statement of claim do disclose a cause of action."

For my part, I too can see no sensible distinction between the two cases which the judge mentions.

If it be shown that the Minister's motive was to further the interests of English turkey producers by keeping out the produce of French turkey producers—an act which must necessarily injure them—it seems to me entirely immaterial that the one purpose was dominant and the second merely a subsidiary purpose for giving effect to the dominant purpose. If an act is done deliberately and with knowledge of its consequences, I do not think that the actor can sensibly say that he did not 'intend" the consequences or that the act was not "aimed" at the person who, it is known, will suffer them. In my judgment, the judge was right in his conclusion also on this point.

PARKER and NOURSE L.JJ. agreed with OLIVER L.J. on this point.

Notes

1. On this tort, see A. Rubinstein, *Jurisdiction and Illegality* (1965), pp. 128–33; B. Gould (1972) 5 N.Z.U.L.R. 105; J. McBride [1979] C.L.J. 323; M. Aronson and H. Whitmore, *Public Torts and Contracts* (1982), pp. 120–131.

2. The parties in *Bourgoin* settled for £3.5 million (H.C. Deb., Vol. 102, col. 116 (July 23, 1986), written answer).

3. So far as the first limb of the tort is concerned (deliberate and dishonest wrongful abuse of powers by a public officer with the intention of injuring the plaintiff or a person in a class of which the plaintiff is a member: the formulation of Clarke J. in *Three Rivers District Council v. Bank of England (No. 3)* [1996] 3 All E.R. 558, 632), there must be proof of an intent to injure and not merely recklessness: *Bennett v. Metropolitan Police Commissioner* [1995] 1 W.L.R. 488. Another case on the first limb is *Jones v. Swansea City Council*, n. 6, below. See also *Elliott v. Chief Constable of Wiltshire, The Times*, December 5, 1996 (disclosure by police officer of P's previous convictions with intent to injure could amount to the tort, notwithstanding that this did not constitute the exercise of a particular power or authority).

4. The exact parameters of the second limb of the misfeasance tort were analysed by Clarke J. in *Three Rivers District Council v. Bank of England (No. 3)* [1996] 3 All E.R. 558. The plaintiffs were depositors with a deposit-taker, BCCI, licensed by the Bank of England. They lost the amounts deposited when BCCI went into liquidation. They sued the Bank, alleging that the Bank was liable for misfeasance in a public office in the performance of its public duty to supervise banking operations in the United Kingdom in that it had either wrongly granted a licence to BCCI or had wrongly failed to revoke BCCI's licence. Certain preliminary issues were tried, including (i) whether the Bank was capable of being liable to the plaintiffs for the misfeasance tort, and (ii) whether the plaintiff's alleged losses were caused in law or capable of being caused by the Bank's acts or omissions. Clarke J. considered the case law at some length. He held (at 568) that where Mann J. used the word "foreseeable" in the passage cited in Oliver L.J.'s judgment,

> "I think that he must have meant 'foreseen'. That is partly because there are three previous references either to 'foreseen' or to knowledge of the consequences and partly because it was an agreed fact (for the purposes of the issue to be determined) that the minister knew that his act would injure the plaintiffs in their business and the plaintiffs' case was that such knowledge was sufficient for liability. No one was suggesting that foreseeability of damage was enough. Thus, I do not think that Mann J. was applying his mind separately to that question. He was principally concerned with whether malice (in the sense of targeted malice) was required or whether knowledge of absence of power would in certain circumstances be sufficient."

On the other hand, Clarke J. also held (at 569) that Oliver L.J.'s judgment was not to be interpreted as requiring under the *second* limb of the tort that the plaintiff prove both (a) that injuring the plaintiff was at least a subsidiary actual purpose of the defendant and (b) that the defendant must know that his act will necessarily cause the loss suffered by the plaintiff:

> "There is nothing in the judgment of Oliver L.J. which limits the requirements in that way. It appears to me that he was expressly approving the judgment and reasoning of Mann J. . . . Mann J. at no stage defined the second limb of the tort in terms of purpose, intention or 'aiming at'."

The issue then addressed was whether under the second limb of the tort it might be sufficient for the plaintiff to establish something less than *knowledge* that the act *was* unlawful and that it *would* cause damage to him or her. This had not arisen for consideration in any of the post-*Bourgoin* cases except by the High Court of Australia in

Northern Territory v. Mengel (1995) 69 A.L.J.R. 527 (see at 570–578). There the plaintiffs were owners of cattle stations who suffered loss because of the actions of two government stock inspectors. There was no statutory or other authority for their actions, but the inspectors neither knew this, nor did they intend to injure the plaintiffs. The High Court concluded that there cannot be liability merely on the basis that the officer *ought to have known* that he or she lacked power to do what he or she did. The majority (Mason C.J., Dawson, Toohey, Gaudron and McHugh JJ.) thought that the test should extend to the case where the officer "recklessly disregards the means of ascertaining his or her power" and where there is "reckless indifference to the harm that is likely to ensue" (see Clarke J. at 575–576). Brennan and Deane JJ., who delivered minority judgments, did not dissent on this point (at 576–578). Clarke J.'s conclusions were as follows:

"(1) The tort of misfeasance in public office is concerned with a deliberate and dishonest wrongful abuse of the powers given to a public officer. It is not to be equated with torts based on an intention to injure, although, as suggested by the majority in *Mengel*, it has some similarities to them.

(2) Malice, in the sense of an intention to injure the plaintiff or a person in a class of which the plaintiff is a member, and knowledge by the officer both that he has no power to do the act complained of and that the act will probably injure the plaintiff or a person in a class of which the plaintiff is a member are alternative, not cumulative, ingredients of the tort. To act with such knowledge is to act in a sufficient sense maliciously (see *Mengel* (1995) 69 A.L.J.R. 527 at 554 *per* Deane J.).

(3) For the purposes of the requirement that the officer knows that he has no power to do the act complained of, it is sufficient that the officer has actual knowledge that the act was unlawful or, in circumstances in which he believes or suspects that the act is beyond his powers, that he does not ascertain whether or not that is so, or fails to take such steps as would be taken by an honest and reasonable man to ascertain the true position.

(4) For the purposes of the requirement that the officer knows that his act will probably injure the plaintiff or a person in a class of which the plaintiff is a member it is sufficient if the officer has actual knowledge that his act will probably damage the plaintiff or such a person or, in circumstances in which he believes or suspects that his act will probably damage the plaintiff or such a person, if he does not ascertain whether or not that is so, or if he fails to make such inquiries as an honest and reasonable man would make as to the probability of such damage.

(5) If the states of mind in (4) and (5) do not amount to actual knowledge, they amount to recklessness which is sufficient to support liability under the second limb of the tort.

As I see it, those propositions are capable of applying to omissions as well as acts on the part of a public officer, although a careful scrutiny of each alleged omission would be required. It is to be observed that in propositions (2) and (4) I have described the relevant knowledge as either actual knowledge that the act will *probably* cause damage not that it will *necessarily* or *inevitably* do so or as turning a blind eye to the *probability* of such damage not to its *necessity* or *inevitability*. I have also described the knowledge as knowledge that the act will probably cause damage to the plaintiff or to a person in a class of which the plaintiff is a member.

I recognise that to do so is to reject the submission of the Bank that only knowledge that the plaintiff will inevitably suffer damage is sufficient. I entirely understand that if this is a tort which depends upon intention to injure the plaintiff or aiming at the plaintiff, then such a requirement would be necessary. However, once it is accepted that there are two alternative limbs of the tort as discussed above, and as it seems to me that the cases suggest, the necessity for such a requirement no longer exists. It would in my judgment unnecessarily restrict the tort. The purpose of the tort as I see it is to give compensation to those who have suffered loss as a result of improper abuse of power. That being so, knowledge that the relevant person will probably suffer damage is surely sufficient. Equally it is surely sufficient if the relevant person is not the plaintiff himself, but a person within a class of which the plaintiff is one. I shall return to this point under issue (3).

In arriving at the above conclusions I have not made a detailed comparison between the ingredients of this tort and those of other torts such as conspiracy and interference with contractual relations. Those are torts which can be and ordinarily are committed by private individuals or entities. They therefore lack the essential feature of the tort with which I am concerned, namely that it can only be committed by a public officer and then only when he has been guilty of an abuse of power. In these circumstances it appears to me that little if any assistance is to be gained by a comparison between misfeasance in public office and the intentional torts which were referred to in argument."

Although this position represented a development of the law, there was nothing in the previous case law that required his Lordship to reach any other conclusions (see at 584–593).

Other points dealt with by Clarke J. were as follows:

(1) There is no need for the plaintiff to identify a legal right which is being infringed on a particular duty owed to him or her, beyond the right not to be damaged or injured by a deliberate abuse of power by a public officer (at 583–584, 593–594).

(2) The Bank of England's powers and duties were conferred by the Banking Act 1979, implementing Council Directive 77/780 (the 1977 Banking Directive). Neither the Act nor the Directive were to be interpreted as conferring enforceable rights on savers or depositors. Thus the plaintiffs could not rely on provisions of the Directive as directly effective. There was also no liability in damages under the principle of Cases C–6/90 & C–9/90, *Francovich v. Italy* [1991] E.C.R. I–5357; [1993] C.M.L.R. 66, given the requirement that the provisions of the Directives concerned be sufficiently precise and unconditional as to "the identity of the persons entitled to the guarantee provided, the content of the guarantee and the identity of the person liable to provide the guarantee" [1991] E.C.R. I–5357 at 5408, para. 12 (at 594–622).

(3) Although the point did not arise for determination, the better view is that a claim for damages under the *Francovich* principle (as developed by the Court of Justice in Cases C–46/93 & C–48/93, *Brasserie du Pêcheur SA v. Germany; R. v. Secretary of State for Transport, ex p. Factortame Ltd (Factortame III)* [1996] Q.B. 404):

"should not be regarded as a claim for damages for the tort of misfeasance in a public office, but rather as a claim of a different type not known to the common law, namely a claim for damages for breach of a duty imposed by Community Law or for the infringement of a right conferred by Community Law" (at 623–624).

(4) If the defendants were shown to have known that his act would probably injure the plaintiff or a person in the class of which the plaintiff is a member (see point 4 in Clarke J.'s summary, above), there is no reason why

"it should not follow that the loss was caused by the act or omission complained of. Common sense suggests that in those circumstances there would be a direct and effective causal link between the act or omission and the loss. That would in my opinion be so even on the basis (as is the case on the facts) that another cause of the loss was fraud on the part of the managers" (at 626–631).

In the light of these observations, His Lordship made certain rulings on the pleadings. The litigation is proceeding.

5. It will always be necessary to show a causal link between the misfeasance and the loss. In *Wood v. Blair and the Helmsley RDC, The Times*, July 3, 4, 5, 1957, [1956–1957] Admin.L.R. 343, the manageress of the plaintiff's dairy farm was found to be suffering from typhoid. The plaintiff was ill in hospital at the same time, and had had typhoid in the past. The medical officer of health (B) served a notice under regulation 20 of the Milk and Dairies Regulations 1949[10] forbidding the sale of milk for human consumption. He later served a notice forbidding the sale of unpasteurised milk from the farm. The plaintiff obeyed the notices, and for six weeks poured the milk produced down the drain. His business as a retailer of bottled milk came to a standstill. The notices were subsequently held to be nullities. Hallett J. held that if the plaintiff could show that he had suffered damage by complying with the notices he had a good cause of action, but that he had not suffered any loss because he would have had to leave the farm anyway because of troubles with the landlords, and the cancellation of his registration as a dairy farmer and the revocation of his T.T. licence. On appeal, the Court of Appeal held that the plaintiff had not proved any of his claims for general or special damages, apart from one item in respect of a lost milk subsidy of £99 from the Milk Marketing Board. His claim for exemplary damages failed because the defendants acted from the highest motives. (On the facts, it did not seem that either defendant knew that the notices were invalid, but liability was conceded.)

6. The misfeasance tort is applicable in respect of the abuse of any powers exercisable by a public authority or officer, whether private powers or powers with a statutory or public origin (*Jones v. Swansea City Council* [1990] 1 W.L.R. 54: where the Court of Appeal held that the alleged abuse of a contractual power would give rise to the tort; the court left open whether it could in any event properly be regarded as a purely "private" power. This question was left open on appeal to the House of Lords: [1990] 1 W.L.R. 1453, 1458). In *Jones v. Swansea City Council* [1990] 1 W.L.R. 1453, the House of Lords upheld the decision of the trial judge to dismiss the plaintiff's claim for damages for misfeasance arising out of the council's decision as landlord to refuse consent for the change of use of certain premises leased by the plaintiff. The decision had been taken by 28 to 15, the majority being formed by Labour councillors. The plaintiff's husband was a political opponent of the Labour group. Lord Lowry stated that in such circumstances "generally speaking, if a plaintiff proves that a majority of the councillors present, having voted for a resolution, did so with the object of damaging the plaintiffs, he thereby proves against the council misfeasance in a public office" (at 1458–1459). This apparently would mean 22 out of the 43 councillors present (at 1470). However, the plaintiff's pleadings alleged that all the 28 councillors had been infected by malice, and the judge had rightly found this not to be made out on the evidence.

7. If an officer commits the tort of misfeasance, the employing authority may be vicariously liable unless the unauthorised acts are so unconnected with the officer's authorised duties as to be quite independent of and outside those duties: *Racz v. Home Office* [1994] 2 A.C. 45, H.L.

8. The widening of the scope of the second limb of the tort can be justified by the argument that "the absence of an honest attempt to perform the functions of the office ... constitutes the abuse of the office" and that compensation should be payable in respect of loss thereby caused (Brennan J. in *Northern Territory v. Mengel* (1995) 69 A.L.J.R. 527, 546–547, cited by Clarke J. in *Three Rivers District Council v. Bank of England (No. 3)* [1996] 3 All E.R. 558, 577). All are agreed that negligence is

[10] S.I. 1949 No. 1588.

insufficient to establish the misfeasance tort. In the *Bourgoin* and *Three Rivers* cases, the plaintiffs were obliged to pursue the misfeasance tort given, respectively, the ruling in *Bourgoin* itself that no action lay for breach of statutory duty, and authorities that prevented the plaintiffs in the *Three Rivers* case from instituting claims for negligence or breach of statutory duty against the Bank of England (*Yuen Kun Yeu v. Att.-Gen. of Hong Kong* [1988] A.C. 175, P.C.; *Davis v. Radcliffe* [1990] 1 W.L.R. 821, P.C.). There may, however, be cases where loss is caused by a public officer to the plaintiff in circumstances where a duty of care is recognised, as where there is a special relationship between the plaintiff and defendant derived, for example, from a voluntary assumption of responsibility (see p. 738).

9. Given the widening in scope of the second limb of the misfeasance tort, in what circumstances will it be profitable or necessary for a plaintiff to seek to establish liability under the first limb?

(C) RESTITUTION

In recent years the law of restitution has had an increasing impact on public authorities. On the one hand, the House of Lords in *Woolwich Equitable Building Society v. Inland Revenue Commissioners* [1993] A.C. 70 expanded the citizen's right to recover money paid to a public authority pursuant to an unlawful demand. On the other, the decision in *Hazell v. Hammersmith and Fulham London Borough Council* [1992] 2 A.C. 1, above, p. 188, that interest rate swap transactions entered by local authorities were *ultra vires*, has given rise to litigation in which local authorities have recovered money paid to banks in the course of such transactions (and vice versa).

Notes

1. In the *Woolwich Equitable* case, the Building Society paid some £57 million in response to a Revenue demand. The demand was based on regulations subsequently held by the House of Lords to be *ultra vires* (*Woolwich Equitable Building Society v. Inland Revenue Commissioners* [1990] 1 W.L.R. 1400 (below, p. 795)). The Revenue had repaid the money when the judicial review proceedings had been decided against them at first instance. The Society now claimed the payment of interest on the capital from the date of payment until judgment was given at first instance. The House of Lords (Lords Goff of Chieveley, Browne-Wilkinson and Slynn of Hadley, Lords Keith of Kinkel and Jauncey of Tullichettle dissenting) upheld the Building Society's claim. Prior to this decision, it was established, *inter alia*, that (1) as a general rule, while money paid under a mistake of fact was recoverable, money paid under a mistake of law was not; (2) that money paid under compulsion might be recoverable; and (3) that money is irrecoverable where the payer has the opportunity to contest liability but instead gives way and pays (see Lord Goff at 164–165).

Depending on the circumstances, a claim to recover money paid to a public authority in response to an unlawful demand might fail on the grounds that there was a mistake of law, an absence of compulsion or, otherwise, a voluntary payment. The House of Lords recognised a separate principle that

"the subject who makes a payment in response to an unlawful demand of tax acquires forthwith a prima facie right in restitution to the repayment of the money" (Lord Goff at 171).

This development was justified by Lord Goff in the following terms:

"The justice underlying Woolwich's submission is, I consider, plain to see. Take the present case. The revenue has made an unlawful demand for tax. The taxpayer is convinced that the demand is unlawful, and has to decide what to do. It is faced with the revenue, armed with the coercive power of the state, including what is in practice a power to charge interest which is penal in its effect. In addition, being a reputable society which alone among building societies is challenging the lawfulness of the demand, it understandably fears damage to its reputation if it does not pay. So it decides to pay first, asserting that it will challenge the lawfulness of the demand in litigation. Now, Woolwich having won that litigation, the revenue asserts that it was never under any obligation to repay the money, and that it in fact repaid it only as a matter of grace. There being no applicable statute to regulate the position, the revenue has to maintain this position at common law.

Stated in this stark form, the revenue's position appears to me, as a matter of common justice, to be unsustainable; and the injustice is rendered worse by the fact that it involves, as Nolan J. pointed out [1989] 1 W.L.R. 137, 140, the revenue having the benefit of a massive interest-free loan as the fruit of its unlawful action. I turn then from the particular to the general. Take any tax or duty paid by the citizen pursuant to an unlawful demand. Common justice seems to require that tax to be repaid, unless special circumstances or some principle of policy require otherwise; prima facie, the taxpayer should be entitled to repayment as of right.

To the simple call of justice, there are a number of possible objections. The first is to be found in the structure of our law of restitution, as it developed during the 19th and early 20th centuries. That law might have developed so as to recognise a *condictio indebiti*—an action for the recovery of money on the ground that it was not due. But it did not do so. Instead, as we have seen, there developed common law actions for the recovery of money paid under a mistake of fact, and under certain forms of compulsion. What is now being sought is, in a sense, a reversal of that development, in a particular type of case; and it is said that it is too late to take that step. To that objection, however, there are two answers. The first is that the retention by the state of taxes unlawfully exacted is particularly obnoxious, because it is one of the most fundamental principles of our law—enshrined in a famous constitutional document, the Bill of Rights 1688—that taxes should not be levied without the authority of Parliament; and full effect can only be given to that principle if the return of taxes exacted under an unlawful demand can be enforced as a matter of right. The second is that, when the revenue makes a demand for tax, that demand is implicitly backed by the coercive powers of the state and may well entail (as in the present case) unpleasant economic and social consequences if the taxpayer does not pay. In any event, it seems strange to penalise the good citizen, whose natural instinct is to trust the revenue and pay taxes when they are demanded of him."

The situation would not appropriately be dealt with by developing the common law concept of compulsion, an approach adopted by the High Court of Australia in *Mason v. New South Wales*, 102 C.L.R. 108. Here, Woolwich:

"was in reality suffering from no mistake at all, so much so that it was prepared to back its conviction that the revenue was acting *ultra vires* by risking a very substantial amount of money in legal costs in establishing that fact; and, since the possibility of distraint by the revenue was very remote, the concept of compulsion would have to be stretched to the utmost to embrace the circumstances of such a case as this. It is for this reason that Woolwich's alternative claim founded upon compulsion did not loom large in the argument, and is difficult to sustain. In the end, logic appears to demand that the right of recovery should require neither mistake nor compulsion, and that the simple fact that the tax was exacted unlawfully should prima facie be enough to require its repayment." (Lord Goff at 173).

Furthermore, the recognition of this principle constituted a legitimate development of the law, although the "armoury of common law defences" might have to be extended, for example by imposing short time-limits within which claims had to be advanced (at 173–177). His Lordship concluded:

"I would therefore hold that money paid by a citizen to a public authority in the form of taxes or other levies paid pursuant to an *ultra vires* demand by the authority is prima facie recoverable by the citizen as of right. As at present advised, I incline to the opinion that this principle should extend to embrace cases in which the tax or other levy has been wrongly exacted by the public authority not because the demand was *ultra vires* but for other reasons, for example because the authority has misconstrued a relevant statute or regulation. It is not however necessary to decide the point in the present case, and in any event cases of this kind are generally the subject of statutory regimes which legislate for the circumstances in which money so paid either must or may be repaid. Nor do I think it necessary to consider for the purposes of the present case to what extent the common law may provide the public authority with a defence to a claim for the repayment of money so paid; though for the reasons I have already given, I do not consider that the principle of recovery should be inapplicable simply because the citizen has paid the money under a mistake of law. It will be a matter for consideration whether the fact that the plaintiff has passed on the tax or levy so that the burden has fallen on another should prove a defence to his claim."

The exact scope of the *Woolwich* principle is uncertain. The Law Commission (Law Com. No. 227; see note 3) has expressed the view that it "may well be held to apply to all taxes, levies, assessments, tolls or charges, whether for the provision of services or not, collected by any person or body under a statutory provision which is the sole source of the authority to charge". It is not

"limited to payments of tax or to Governmental or quasi-Governmental exactions, or to payments made in accordance with a demand. We believe that the crucial element is that the payment is collected by any person or body which is operating outside its statutory authority, that is, it is acting *ultra vires*. The requirement of *ultra vires* is not in our view confined to the excess of statutory power but also extends to procedural abuses, abuse of power and error of law on the part of the charging authority" (paras. 6.32–6.42).

2. There are some statutory provisions which expressly authorise the repayment of overpaid taxes, etc. See *R. v. Tower Hamlets London Borough Council, ex p. Chetnik Developments Ltd* [1988] A.C. 858, considering the General Rate Act 1967, s.9. Here, the House of Lords upheld an application for judicial review of the council's refusal to exercise the discretion under s.9 in favour of the application on the grounds that the council had had regard to irrelevant considerations (the financial circumstances of the overpaying ratepayer or the general body of ratepayers, and the internal finances of the council and the financial constraints to which it was subject). In the *Woolwich* case, it was held that the Building Society's claim fell outside the statutory framework for the repayment of overpaid tax, as it was not the case of an assessment that was erroneously excessive, but of a demand that was *ultra vires* and a nullity (see Lord Goff at 168–169).

3. At the time the *Woolwich* case was decided, the issues of mistakes of law and *ultra vires* receipts and payments were under consideration by the Law Commission (see Law Commission Working Paper No. 120, *Restitution of Payments Made Under a Mistake of Law* (1991). The Law Commission's subsequent Report (*Restitution: Mistakes of Law and* Ultra Vires *Public Authority Receipts and Payments*, Law Com. No. 227, 1994) proposed (1) that the rule precluding restitution of payments made, services rendered and benefits conferred under a mistake of law be abolished and (2) that

there should be a series of specific amendments to the statutory provisions governing recovery of overpaid tax to reflect the *Woolwich* principle. See L. Flynn [1995] B.T.R. 15. One consequence has been the introduction of a statutory right to recover overpaid excise duty (Finance Act 1995, s.20), inserting a new s.137A in the Customs and Excise Management Act 1979; this provision is modelled on section 80 of the Value Added Tax Act 1994.

4. On restitution and public authorities, see P. Birks (1980) 33 C.L.P. 191 and "Restitution from the Executive" in P. Finn (ed.), *Essays on Restitution* (1990); W. Cornish [1987] J.M.C.L. 41; A. Burrows, "Public Authorities, *Ultra Vires* and Restitution" in Burrows (ed.), *Studies on the Law of Restitution* (1991); G. Jones, *Restitution in Public and Private Law* (1991). On the *Woolwich* case, see J. Beatson (1993) 109 L.Q.R. 1, and "Restitution of Taxes, Levies and other Imposts: Defining the Extent of the *Woolwich* Principle" (1993) 109 L.Q.R. 401; G. Virgo, "The Law of Taxation is not an Island—Overpaid Taxes and the Law of Restitution" [1993] B.T.R. 442; P. Birks [1992] P.L. 580 and (1993) 46 C.L.P. 157; T. Hill (1993) 56 M.L.R. 856.

For an argument that a right to recover tax should be based not on restitution but on an action in tort against the Crown for breach of statutory duty under article 4 of the Bill of Rights (1689), see D. Wilde "A 'Revolutionary' Approach to Unlawful Taxation" [1995] B.T.R. 137.

5. Following the decision in the *Hazell* case that interest rate swap agreements were *ultra vires* and void *ab initio*, claims for restitution have been brought variously by banks and local authorities who were parties to such transactions. Thus, in *Westdeutsche Landesbank Girozentrale v. Islington London Borough Council* [1994] 1 W.L.R. 938 the Court of Appeal held that the council receiving payments from a bank under such transactions was obliged at common law to repay the balance of the money on the ground of unjust enrichment at the expense of the bank since there had been no consideration for the bank's payments; in equity it was to be regarded as holding the money on a resulting trust for the bank since the purpose of the payments had wholly failed. There was an appeal to the House of Lords only on the question of the basis of an award for interest ([1996] 2 All E.R. 961), the House holding by 3 to 2 that the bank was entitled only to simple and not compound interest. However, the House held unanimously in the course of deciding this point that there was no basis for the imposition of a resulting trust, the claim properly being based solely on the common law. (See M. Cope (1996) 112 L.Q.R. 521; G. Jones [1996] C.L.J. 432.) Suggestions by Hobhouse J. at first instance and the Court of Appeal that the common law claim arose from the *absence* rather than the *total failure* of consideration have been strongly criticised (P. Birks (1993) 23 U.W.A.L.R. 195; W.J. Swadling [1994] R.L.R. 73; A. Burrows [1995] R.L.R. 15) and doubted by Lord Goff *obiter* in the House of Lords [1996] 2 All E.R. 961, 968. (The point was not argued in the House of Lords.)

See also *Kleinwort Benson Ltd v. South Tyneside Metropolitan Borough Council* [1994] 4 All E.R. 972 (Hobhouse J.: bank entitled to recover payments made within the six-year limitation period notwithstanding they had hedged their liabilities under parallel transactions); *Morgan Grenfell & Co. Ltd v. Welwyn Hatfield District Council; Islington London Borough Council (Third Party)* [1995] 1 All E.R. 1 (Hobhouse J.: bank entitled to repayments; swap deals were not wagering contracts); *South Tyneside Metropolitan Borough Council v. Svenska International plc* [1995] 1 All E.R. 545 (Clarke J.: local authority entitled to recover net payments from bank; no defence of change of position); *Kleinwort Benson Ltd v. Birmingham City Council* [1996] 4 All E.R. 733 (C.A.: no defence to bank's claim that it had or might have entered independent hedging arrangements so as to suffer no loss).

6. It is established law that any payment made out of the Consolidated Fund without Parliamentary authority is *ultra vires* and may be recovered by the Crown if it can be traced: *Auckland Harbour Board v. R.* [1924] A.C. 318, 327, *per* Viscount

Haldane. The Law Commission (Law Com. No. 227, see note 3, above, paras. 17.1–17.21) proposed no change in this rule, on the understanding that the common law defences of change of position and submission or compromise would apply in this context.

7. A claim for restitution (unlike a claim for damages) may not at present be added to an application for judicial review (above, p. 601). The Law Commission and Lord Woolf have recommended that this anomaly be rectified (above. p. 702).

Chapter 12

VALIDITY OF UNLAWFUL ADMINISTRATIVE ACTION[1]

(A) Principles

What is the exact status and effect of an *ultra vires* act? This question has caused considerable academic controversy and some difficulty in the case law. Attempts to find answers to it have been side-tracked by a debate as to whether all (or some) *ultra vires* acts are to be regarded as "void" or "voidable", concepts or labels borrowed from private law. Employing these labels, it could be argued that an *ultra vires* act should be regarded as null and void for all purposes ("void", a "nullity"). On the other hand, an act which may be set aside only on an appeal, or on an application to quash for non-jurisdictional error of law on the face of the record, could be said to be "voidable"; it is valid until set aside. See *Wade and Forsyth*, pp. 339–340. This formulation is, however, deceptively simple and increasingly unhelpful. First, now that all errors of law are normally regarded as jurisdictional errors and the concept of error of law on the face of the record as a dead letter (above, pp. 174–175) this line now merely marks the divide between decisions challengeable on an application for judicial review and those challengeable on appeal. Secondly, and more importantly, it is now firmly established that "voidness" in administrative law is a *relative* and not an *absolute* concept. An *ultra vires* act is not totally devoid of legal effect:

(i) In some situations it can simply be ignored (see note (a) below). However, it will often be advisable, or even necessary, for the person affected to obtain a court ruling that the act is *ultra vires*. At this point, it must be remembered that the courts will not always be prepared to intervene. A direct challenge may only be brought by a person with the appropriate *locus standi* and within the relevant time-limit. Even if the applicant makes out a good case as a matter of substance, the court may decline to grant a remedy in the exercise of its discretion. These matters are considered in Chapter 10. In consequence, if an act is not challenged by the only persons with *locus standi* to do so then the courts will treat it as valid. For example, only the Chief Constable in *Ridge v. Baldwin* would be regarded as having standing to challenge the lawfulness of his own dismissal (*cf.* the discussion of this point in *Durayappah v. Fernando*, below, p. 768). This point is also illustrated by the *Rose Theatre Trust* case (above, p. 672), on the assumption that English Heritage would have had standing to challenge the Secretary of State's decision (unlike the applicants in that case), but chose not to do so. Similarly, once a statutory time-limit for challenging an act has expired, it may be regarded as valid (see *Smith v. East Elloe R.D.C.*, below, p. 799; *cf.* the cases on undue delay on an application for judicial review (above, pp. 679–687)).

---

[1] See: H.W.R. Wade (1967) 83 L.Q.R. 499 and (1968) 84 L.Q.R. 95; M.B. Akehurst (1968) 31 M.L.R. 2, 138; *de Smith, Woolf and Jowell*, pp. 256–265, 355–357; A. Rubinstein, *Jurisdiction and Illegality* (1965); P. Cane, "A Fresh Look at Punton's Case" (1980) 43 M.L.R. 266; D. Oliver (1981) C.L.P. 43; G.L. Peiris [1983] P.L. 634; M. Taggart, "Rival Theories of Invalidity in Administrative Law" in Taggart (ed.), *Judicial Review of Administrative Action in the 1980s* (1986), pp. 70–103; *Craig*, pp. 447–475; *Wade and Forsyth*, pp. 339–344.

(ii) If an act is not invalid on its face, the courts will act on the assumption that it is valid, unless and until it is set aside (see *F. Hoffmann-La Roche v. Secretary of State for Trade and Industry*, below, p. 767).

(iii) In exceptional circumstances, an act may be regarded as partially invalid only (see below, pp. 788–795).

In some cases, judges have taken the view that the fact that an *ultra vires* act is not totally devoid of legal effects in the senses already discussed means that "voidable" is the only appropriate label. See the speech of Lord Evershed in *Ridge v. Baldwin* [1964] A.C. 40, 86–94; the Privy Council in *Durayappah v. Fernando* [1967] 2 A.C. 337; and the views of Lord Denning M.R. (below, pp. 774–775). More recently, the judges have preferred to label *ultra vires* acts as void, given that once a court rules that an act is *ultra vires* and grants a remedy, the act is regarded as void *ab initio*. At the same time, they have accepted that unless and until there has been such a ruling, a challenged act may have substantive legal effects. They have sought to analyse those effects directly without worrying too much about conceptual labels that might be attached.

Where an act is *void*, in the relative sense in which the term is properly understood, several consequences follow:

(a) It may, if appropriate, be ignored by the person affected. If the public authority takes enforcement proceedings, the voidness of the act can be raised as a defence. See, for example, *Maltglade Ltd v. St Albans R.D.C.* [1972] 1 W.L.R. 1230, *Allingham v. Minister of Agriculture* [1948] 1 All E.R. 780 (where a notice requiring farmers to grow sugar beet on certain fields was held to be invalid because the task of specifying the fields had been delegated unlawfully by a county agricultural committee to an officer). A person with the appropriate standing is normally permitted to raise a question as to *vires* as a collateral question, by way of an exception to the principle of *O'Reilly v. Mackman* (see pp. 642–662). However, there have been attempts to limit the permissible scope of collateral challenge (pp. 778–788). Furthermore, in many situations collateral challenge will be of no use to the person affected. For example, where a decision refuses an applicant some licence or other benefit, he or she will normally have to take direct action to have the decision set aside.

(b) A statutory provision purporting to prohibit recourse to the courts to challenge the validity of an act will normally be interpreted as effective to prevent challenges to voidable acts only. A void act is not an "act", "order", or "decision" protected by the privative clause at all. See below, pp. 799 *et seq.* and *Anisminic Ltd v. Foreign Compensation Commission* (above, p. 210).

(c) The courts may refuse to hear an appeal against a void decision, on the basis that there is nothing to appeal against. See *Metropolitan Properties Co. (F.G.C.) Ltd v. Lannon* [1969] 1 Q.B. 577, and *Chapman v. Earl* [1968] 1 W.L.R. 1315. In the latter case the Divisional Court, on an appeal on a point of law against the decision of a rent assessment committee, gave leave for the plaintiff to apply for certiorari on the ground that a mandatory procedural step had not been observed by the committee. Certiorari was granted, and the appeal dismissed.

Statute may expressly provide for an appeal on the ground that the act impugned is *ultra vires*: see above, pp. 552 *et seq.*; and the Magistrates' Courts Act 1980, s.111 (appeals by way of case stated).

(d) The exercise of a right of appeal to a higher administrative body will not necessarily cure the defect of a void act (*Ridge v. Baldwin*, above, p. 424). If the proceedings on appeal are by way of a complete rehearing, then the invalidity of the original decision may be irrelevant. The appellate body makes its own, independent, valid decision. (See *Stringer v. Minister of Housing and Local Government*, above, pp. 262 and 274; *Calvin v. Carr*, above, p. 506.)

(e) There is a general rule that a void act cannot be validated by the consent, waiver or acquiescence of the person affected by it. In *Mayes v. Mayes* [1971] 1 W.L.R. 679, justices dismissed a wife's complaint of desertion after hearing her evidence, without giving her solicitor the opportunity of addressing them on her behalf. This was held to be a breach of natural justice, which was not cured by the fact that the right to address was not asserted at the time. Sir Jocelyn Simon P. stated at 684: "I am inclined to think that the general principle is that a rule of natural justice which goes to the very basis of judicature (as I think this does) cannot be waived. You cannot by waiver convert a nullity into a validity."

The general principle that an *ultra vires* act is void, and that a breach of natural justice renders an act void, was stated unequivocally in *Anisminic Ltd v. Foreign Compensation Commission* [1969] 2 A.C. 147 (above, p. 210), by Lord Reid at 171 (p. 213), Lord Pearce at 195 (p. 220) and Lord Wilberforce at 207–208. The speeches of Lord Morris and Lord Pearson contained nothing against that principle. The majority in *Ridge v. Baldwin* [1964] A.C. 40 similarly had held that breach of the *audi alteram partem* rule of natural justice rendered the decision void. See Lord Reid at 80 (above, p. 435), Lord Morris at 125 and Lord Hodson at 136. Lord Morris at 117, Lord Hodson at 135 and Lord Devlin at 139, expressly held that the decision was also void for breach of mandatory procedural requirements. Similarly, in *O'Reilly v. Mackman* (above, p. 644), Lord Diplock confirmed that breach of natural justice renders the decision void. The Court of Appeal in *Cooper v. Wilson* [1937] 2 K.B. 309 held that a decision tainted by bias or interest under the *nemo judex* principle of natural justice (see pp. 516–537) was void (dicta to the contrary by Baron Parke in *Dimes v. Grand Junction Canal Proprietors* (1852) 3 H.L.C. 759, 786, were not cited, but have been cogently criticised by H.W.R. Wade (1968) 84 L.Q.R. 95, 107–108.

The materials in the remainder of the chapter concentrate on the issues of the presumption of validity, the permissible extent of collateral challenge and partial invalidity.

(B) The Presumption of Validity

F. HOFFMANN-LA ROCHE & CO. A.G. AND OTHERS v. SECRETARY OF STATE FOR TRADE AND INDUSTRY

[1975] A.C. 295; [1974] 3 W.L.R. 104; 118 S.J. 500; [1974] 2 All E.R. 1128 (House of Lords)

Hoffmann-La Roche and some associated companies held a patent for two tranquillising drugs, "Librium" and "Valium". They were widely used in the United Kingdom and most were paid for by the Department of Health and Social Security. The Department of Health and Social Security felt that the price charged was too high. The Secretary of State for Trade and Industry referred the matter to the Monopolies Commission for investigation and report under the Monopolies, etc., Act 1948. The Commission reported that the prices were excessive, and should be reduced substantially. The report was laid before Parliament as required by the Act. Under the 1948 Act, and the Monopolies and Mergers Act 1965, this reduction could be ordered by statutory instrument approved by both Houses of Parliament. An Order was made and, after debate and investigation by a special orders committee of the House of Lords, the Order was approved by Parliament. The companies alleged that the Monopolies Commission report had been prepared in breach of natural justice and was therefore invalid. The power to make the statutory instrument depended on the existence of a valid report, and so the Order was invalid. They threatened to ignore the order and continue to charge the old prices. The Secretary of State then sought an injunction restraining the companies from charging prices in excess of the figures fixed by the Order. On a motion for an interim injunction, the Secretary of State refused to give an undertaking in damages so as to recompense the companies if at the trial of the action the Order was held to be invalid. On July 13, 1973, Walton J. refused to grant the interim injunction on the companies' undertaking to pay the difference between the prices being charged and those specified in the Order into a bank account in the joint names of the parties' solicitors. The Court of Appeal ([1975] A.C. 308) allowed the Secretary of State's appeal.

LORD DENNING M.R.: [held at 318–319 that although there might be many situations where it would be proper for the Crown to give an undertaking in damages, as was the usual practice in the case of ordinary litigants, this was not a proper case for an undertaking as the Crown was coming to court "to enforce the law". On the plaintiff's submission that the report of the Monopolies Commission was void for breach of natural justice his Lordship stated:]
... I will assume for present purposes that the Monopolies Commission did act contrary to the rules of natural justice—though I would not wish to imply that it was in fact the case. Mr Yorke says that their report would be void. He referred us to passages from *Ridge v. Baldwin* [1964] A.C. 40, 80; *Durayappah v. Fernando* [1967] 2 A.C. 337, 355 and *Anisminic Ltd v. Foreign Compensation Commission* [1969] 2 A.C. 147, 171.

I have always understood the word "void" to mean that the transaction in question is absolutely void—a nullity incapable of any legal consequences—not only bad but incurably bad—so much so that all the world can ignore it and that nothing can be founded on it: see *MacFoy v. United Africa Co. Ltd* [1962] A.C. 152, 160.

If the word "void" is used in that sense, the report of the Monopolies Commission was certainly not void. A failure to observe the rules of natural justice does not render a decision or order or report absolutely void in the sense that it is a nullity. The legal consequences are best told by recounting the remedies available in respect of it. A person who has been unfairly treated (by reason of the breach of natural justice) can go to the courts and ask for the decision or order or report, or whatever it is, to be quashed, or for a declaration that it is invalid, that it has not and never has had any effect as against him. But it is a personal remedy, personal to him. If he does not choose himself to query it and seek a remedy, no one else can do so: see *Durayappah v. Fernando* [1967] 2 A.C. 337, 353. But it is within the discretion of the court whether to grant him such a remedy or not. He may be debarred from relief if he has acquiesced in the invalidity or has waived it. If he does not come with due diligence and ask for it to be set aside, he may be sent away with nothing: see *R. v. Aston University Senate, ex p. Roffey* [1969] 2 Q.B. 538. If his conduct has been disgraceful and he has in fact suffered no injustice, he may be refused relief: see *Glynn v. Keele University* [1971] 1 W.L.R. 487 and *Ward v. Bradford Corp.* (1971) 70 L.G.R. 27. If it is a decision or order or report which affects many other persons besides him, the court may not think it right to declare it invalid at his instance alone: see *Maxwell v. Department of Trade and Industry* (unreported), December 20, 1972, a decision of Wien J., of which we were supplied with a transcript. Moreover, pending a decision by the courts as to its validity, other persons may be justified in acting on the footing that it is valid. If the decision or order or report is good on the face of it, and there is no good reason for supposing it to be invalid, other persons can treat it as valid. To it would apply the words of Lord Radcliffe in *Smith v. East Elloe Rural District Council* [1956] A.C. 736, 769–770:

"An order, ... is still an act capable of legal consequences. It bears no brand of invalidity upon its forehead. Unless the necessary proceedings are taken at law to establish the cause of invalidity and to get it quashed or otherwise upset, it will remain as effective for its ostensible purpose as the most impeccable of orders."

So here, the report of the Monopolies Commission, even if it was made in breach of the rules of natural justice, is still capable of legal consequence. The question, therefore, is of what legal consequences is it capable? In my opinion, when the Secretary of State received the report of the Monopolies Commission, he was entitled to treat it as valid and to act as he did on the faith of it. It was perfectly good on the face of it. . . .

BUCKLEY and LAWTON L.JJ. delivered concurring judgments.

The company appealed to the House of Lords.

LORD REID: . . . An interim injunction against a party to a litigation may cause him great loss if in the end he is successful. In the present case it is common ground that a long time—it may be years—will elapse before a decision can be given. During that period if an interim injunction is granted the appellants will only be able to make the charges permitted by the Order. So if in the end the Order is annulled that loss will be the difference between those charges and those which they could have made if the Order had never been made. And they may not be able to recover any part of that loss from anyone. It is said that the loss might amount to £8m. The appellants' case is that justice requires that such an injunction should not be granted without an undertaking by the respondent to make good that loss to them if they are ultimately successful.

The respondent's first answer is that when an interim injunction is granted to the Crown no undertaking can be required as a condition of granting it. It is not in doubt that in an ordinary litigation the general rule has long been that no interim injunction likely to cause loss to a party will be granted unless the party seeking the injunction undertakes to make good that loss if in the end it appears that the injunction was unwarranted. He cannot be compelled to give an undertaking but if he will not give it he will not get the injunction.

But there is much authority to show that the Crown was in a different position. In general no undertaking was required of it. But whatever justification there may have been for that before 1947 I agree with your Lordships that the old rule or practice cannot be justified since the passing of the Crown Proceedings Act of that year. So if this had been a case where the Crown were asserting a proprietary right I would hold that the ordinary rule should apply and there should be no interlocutory injunction unless the Crown chose to give the usual undertaking.

But this is a case in a different and novel field. No doubt it was thought that criminal penalties were inappropriate as a means of enforcing Orders of this kind, and the only method of enforcement is by injunction. Dealing with alleged breaches of the law is a function of the Crown (or of a department of the executive) entirely different in character from its function in protecting its proprietary right. It has more resemblance to the function of prosecuting those who are alleged to have committed an offence. A person who is prosecuted and found not guilty may have suffered serious loss by reason of the prosecution but in general he has no legal claim against the prosecutor. In the absence of special circumstances I see no reason why the Crown in seeking to enforce Orders of this kind should have to incur legal liability to the person alleged to be in breach of the Order.

It must be borne in mind that an Order made under statutory authority is as much the law of the land as an Act of Parliament unless and until it has been found to be *ultra vires*. No doubt procedure by way of injunction is more flexible than procedure by prosecution and there may well be cases when a court ought to refuse an interim injunction or only to grant it on terms. But I think that it is for the person against whom the interim injunction is sought to show special reason why justice requires that the injunction should not be granted or should only be granted on terms.

The present case has a special feature which requires anxious consideration. As I have already indicated, the Crown has a very large financial interest in obtaining an interim injunction. The Department of Health will reap a large immediate benefit from the lower prices set out in the Order at the expense of the appellants. If in the end it were decided that the order was *ultra vires* those prices ought never to have been enforced, the department ought never to have had that benefit and the appellants would have suffered a large loss. So why should the respondent not be required to give the undertaking which the appellants seek as a condition of getting the interim injunction?

But, on the other hand, the Order which the appellants seek to annul is the law at present and if an interim injunction is refused that means that the law is not to be enforced and the appellants are to be at liberty to disregard it by charging forbidden prices. And the matter does not stop there. Doctors will continue to prescribe these drugs. Chemists will have to pay the forbidden prices if the public are to be provided with drugs which doctors think they ought to have. And chemists cannot be expected to pay the appellants' prices unless the department is willing to reimburse them. So the department will have to acquiesce in and indeed aid and abet the appellants' breaches of the law if the medical profession and the public are to get what they are entitled to.

It is true that the appellants have proposed an ingenious scheme which they would undertake to operate if an interim injunction is refused. The effect of it would be that they would continue to charge the forbidden prices but that if the Order were ultimately held to be *intra vires* they would repay the difference between the forbidden charges which they had made and the lower charges which they ought to have made. The scheme would involve considerable practical difficulties and would probably not be fully effective, but I shall not discuss those difficulties because the serious objection would remain that the law laid down in the Order is to be disregarded until the case is decided.

My Lords, if I thought that the appellants had a strong case on the merits I would try to stretch a point in their favour to protect them from obvious injustice though I would find difficulty in doing so. It is true that although we heard a good deal of argument on the merits we are not in a position to express any firm opinion as to the appellants' prospects of success. But if it is for them to show us at this stage that their case is so strong that they are entitled to some special consideration, I can say that they have completely failed to convince me that they have a strong prima facie case.

I would therefore dismiss this appeal.

LORD WILBERFORCE: (dissenting) [stated that the discretion as exercised by

Walton J.] seems to be well within the area permitted to the judge and should not be displaced except for some error in law. The result appears both "just and convenient". The contrary course, approved by the Court of Appeal, of granting an injunction *tout court* (as if the DTI had already won the action) potentially creates a serious injustice.

The position so stated—and there is I believe no over-simplification about it—is for me decisive of this appeal: I think that the judge's approach was right.

[His Lordship added "brief observations" on some of the other arguments heard, holding first that an undertaking in damages could be required of the Crown. His Lordship continued:] 2. . . . I regard [the argument that the Crown was "enforcing the law"] as fallacious. To say that the Crown is enforcing the law is a *petitio principii*, since the very issue in the action is whether what is alleged to be law (and denied to be law by the appellants) is law or not. The answer given to this is, I understand, that there is a presumption of validity until the contrary is shown. The consequence drawn from this is that unconditional obedience must be required by the court: "obey first and argue afterwards" in Lord Denning M.R.'s graphic phrase [1973] 3 W.L.R. 805, 821. I think that there is a confusion here. It is true enough that a piece of subordinate legislation is presumed to be valid against persons who have no *locus standi* to challenge it—the puzzling case of *Durayappah v. Fernando* [1967] 2 A.C. 337 can be understood as exemplifying this. But it is quite another matter to say, and I know of no supporting authority, that such a presumption exists when the validity of the subordinate legislation is legitimately in question before a court and is challenged by a person who has *locus standi* to challenge it. Certainly no support for any such proposition is to be found in the passage, so often partially quoted, from the speech of Lord Radcliffe in *Smith v. East Elloe Rural District Council* [1956] A.C. 736. One has only to read what he said, at 769–770:

> "At one time the argument was shaped into the form of saying that an order made in bad faith was in law a nullity and that, consequently, all references to compulsory purchase orders in paragraphs 15 and 16 must be treated as references to such orders only as had been made in good faith. But this argument is in reality a play on the meaning of the word nullity. An order, even if not made in good faith, is still an act capable of legal consequences. It bears no brand of invalidity upon its forehead. Unless the necessary proceedings are taken at law to establish the cause of invalidity and to get it quashed or otherwise upset, it will remain as effective for its ostensible purpose as the most impeccable of orders."

How this can be said to support an argument that when proceedings *are* taken at law the impugned Order must be given full legal effect against the challenger before the proceedings are decided I am unable to comprehend.

In any event the argument proves too much, for, if it were right, the court would have no discretion to refuse an injunction whatever the consequences, however irreparably disastrous, to the object. Such rigidity of power seems to be contrary to section 45 of the Supreme Court of Judicature (Consolidation) Act 1925. Further, if one considers some of the Orders which, under this Act, can be made under section 3 the injustice of this can be easily perceived.... If, then, it is said that there must always remain a residual discretion the argument vanishes: we are back on discretion.

3. It is said that no undertaking should be insisted on unless the effect of the appellants' eventual success were to make the order "void *ab initio*"—the argument being that otherwise no injustice would result. Buckley L.J. ([1973] 3 W.L.R. 805, 827–828) made this the conclusion of a judgment with the rest of which I respectfully concur. The phrase "void *ab initio*" has engendered many learned distinctions and much confused thinking—unnecessarily, in my opinion. There can be no doubt in the first place that an *ultra vires* act is simply void—see in confirmation *Ridge* v. *Baldwin* [1964] A.C. 40. In truth when the court says that an act of administration is voidable or void but not *ab initio* this is simply a reflection of a conclusion, already reached on unexpressed grounds, that the court is not willing *in casu* to give compensation or other redress to the person who establishes the nullity. Underlying the use of the phrase in the present case, and I suspect underlying most of the reasoning in the Court of Appeal, is an unwillingness to accept that a subject should be indemnified for loss sustained by invalid administrative action. It is this which requires examination rather than some supposed visible quality of the order itself.

In more developed legal systems this particular difficulty does not arise. Such systems give indemnity to persons injured by illegal acts of the administration. Consequently, where the prospective loss which may be caused by an order is pecuniary, there is no need to suspend the impugned administrative act: it can take effect (in our language an injunction can be given) and at the end of the day the subject can, if necessary, be compensated. On the other hand, if the prospective loss is not pecuniary (in our language "irreparable") the act may be suspended pending decision—in our language, interim enforcement may be refused.

... [T]he combination of section 11 of the Act of 1948 with section 45 of the Supreme Court of Judicature (Consolidation) Act 1925 gives to the court a practical instrument by which injustice to private individuals, faced with possibly invalid action, may be avoided. If this is not possible in every case, it should not be rejected in a case, however special, where justice to both sides can be done....

LORD DIPLOCK: ...

The legal status of the Order

Under our legal system ... the courts as the judicial arm of government do not act on their own initiative. Their jurisdiction to determine that a statutory instrument is *ultra vires* does not arise until its validity is challenged in proceedings *inter partes* either brought by one party to enforce the law declared by the instrument against another party or brought by a party whose interests are affected by the law so declared sufficiently directly to give him *locus standi* to initiate proceedings to challenge the validity of the instrument. Unless there is such challenge and, if there is, until it has been upheld by a judgment of the court, the validity of the statutory instrument and the legality of acts done pursuant to the law declared by it are presumed. It would, however, be inconsistent with the doctrine of *ultra vires* as it has been developed in English law as a means of controlling abuse of power by the executive arm of government if the judgment of a court in proceedings properly constituted that a statutory instrument was *ultra vires* were to have any lesser consequence in law than to render the instrument incapable of ever having had any legal effect upon the rights or duties of the parties to the proceedings (*cf. Ridge v. Baldwin* [1964] A.C. 40). Although such a decision is directly binding only as between the parties to the proceedings in which it was made, the application of the doctrine of precedent has the consequence of enabling the benefit of it to accrue to all other persons whose legal rights have been interfered with in reliance on the law which the statutory instrument purported to declare.

The presumption of validity of the Order

My Lords, I think it leads to confusion to use such terms as "voidable," "voidable *ab initio*", "void" or "a nullity" as descriptive of the legal status of subordinate legislation alleged to be *ultra vires* for patent or for latent defects, before its validity has been pronounced on by a court of competent jurisdiction. These are concepts developed in the private law of contract which are ill-adapted to the field of public law. All that can usefully be said is that the presumption that subordinate legislation is *intra vires* prevails in the absence of rebuttal, and that it cannot be rebutted except by a party to legal proceedings in a court of competent jurisdiction who has *locus standi* to challenge the validity of the subordinate legislation in question.

All *locus standi* on the part of anyone to rebut the presumption of validity may be taken away completely or may be limited in point of time or otherwise by the express terms of the Act of Parliament which conferred the subordinate legislative power, though the courts lean heavily against a construction of the Act which would have this effect (*cf. Anisminic Ltd v. Foreign Compensation Commission* [1969] 2 A.C. 147). Such was the case, however, in the view of the majority of this House in *Smith v. East Elloe Rural District Council* [1956] A.C. 736, at any rate as respects invalidity on the ground of latent defects, so the compulsory purchase order sought to be challenged in the action had legal effect notwithstanding its potential invalidity. Furthermore, apart from express provision in the governing statute, *locus standi* to challenge the validity of subordinate legislation may be restricted, under the court's inherent power to control its own procedure, to a particular category of persons affected by the subordinate legislation, and if none of these persons chooses to challenge it the presumption of validity prevails. Such was the case in *Durayappah v. Fernando* [1967] 2 A.C. 337 where on an appeal from Ceylon, although the Privy Council was of opinion that an order of the Minister was *ultra vires* owing to a latent defect in the procedure prior to its being made, they nevertheless treated it as having legal effect because the party who sought to challenge it had, in their view, no *locus standi* to do so.

The legal status of the Regulation of Prices (Tranquillising Drugs) (No. 3) Order 1973 which the appellants seek to challenge in the instant case is aptly stated in the words of Lord Radcliffe in *Smith v. East Elloe Rural District Council* [1956] A.C. 736, 769–770:

> "An order, . . ., is still an act capable of legal consequences. It bears no brand of invalidity upon its forehead. Unless the necessary proceedings are taken at law to establish the cause of invalidity and to get it quashed or otherwise upset, it will remain as effective for its ostensible purpose as the most impeccable of orders."

The instant case is not one where the appellants contend that what they are threatening to do would not be a contravention of the Order—as was the case in *Post Office v. Estuary Radio Ltd* [1967] 1 W.L.R. 847, [1968] 2 Q.B. 740. Different considerations would apply to that. Their only answer to the application for an interim injunction to enforce the Order against them is that they intend to challenge its validity. It is not disputed that they have *locus standi* to do so, but this does not absolve them from their obligation to obey the Order while the presumption in favour of its validity prevails—as it must so long as there has been no final judgment in the action to the contrary.

So in this type of law enforcement action if the only defence is an attack on the validity of the statutory instrument sought to be enforced the ordinary position of the parties as respects the grant of interim injunctions is reversed. The duty of the Crown to see that the law declared by the statutory instrument is obeyed is not suspended by the commencement of proceedings in which the validity of the instrument is challenged. Prima facie the Crown is entitled as of right to an interim injunction to enforce obedience to it. To displace this right or to fetter it by the imposition of conditions it is for the defendant to show a strong prima facie case that the statutory instrument is *ultra vires*.

Even where a strong prima facie case of invalidity has been shown upon the application for an interim injunction it may still be inappropriate for the court to impose as a condition of the grant of the injunction a requirement that the Crown should enter into the usual undertaking as to damages. For if the undertaking falls to be implemented, the cost of implementing it will be met from public funds raised by taxation and the interests of members of the public who are not parties to the action may be affected by it....

Accordingly, I agree with the majority of your Lordships that the Secretary of State is entitled to the interim injunction that he claimed without giving any undertaking as to damages unless the appellants have succeeded in showing a strong prima facie case that the Order sought to be enforced by the injunction is *ultra vires*. It is not for the Secretary of State to show that the appellant's case cannot possibly succeed as Walton J. thought it was. It is for the appellants to show that their defence of *ultra vires* is likely to be successful.

I agree with the majority of your Lordships that they have signally failed to do this....

LORDS MORRIS OF BORTH-Y-GEST and CROSS OF CHELSEA delivered speeches in favour of dismissing the appeal.

Appeal dismissed.

Notes

1. See the notes by H.W.R. W[ade] (1974) 90 L.Q.R. 436; P. Wallington [1974] C.L.J. 26, 194.

2. Lord Denning's views on this question have varied over the years. His statement in *Hoffmann-La Roche* (above, p. 768) seems consistent with the principles stated at the start of the chapter, save for his preference for the use of the word "void" in the, inappropriate, absolute sense. *cf.* his Lordship's remarks in *D.P.P. v. Head* [1959] A.C. 83, 111–112 and *R. v. Paddington Valuation Officer, ex p. Peachey Property Corporation Ltd* [1966] 1 Q.B. 380.

Subsequently, Lord Denning accepted *Firman v. Ellis* [1978] Q.B. 886 and extra-judicially (*The Discipline of Law* (1979), p. 77) that a decision in breach of natural justice, on being set aside, is void *ab initio* and not voidable. However, in *Lovelock v.*

Minister of Transport (1980) 40 P. & C.R. 336, it was alleged that compulsory purchase orders affecting green belt land made by the Minister for a motorway scheme were invalid, *inter alia*, on the ground that the necessary consent of the Secretary of State for the Environment to encroachment on the green belt had not validly been given. Lord Denning M.R. said (at 345):

"Assuming that [the Secretary of State] did fail to take into account a relevant consideration, the result is that, in point of legal theory, his consent was 'void'. It was made without jurisdiction. It was a nullity. Just as if he had failed to observe the rules of natural justice. But, in point of practice, it was 'voidable'. I have got tired of all the discussion about 'void' and 'voidable'. It seems to me to be a matter of words—of semantics—and that is all. The plain fact is that, even if such a decision as this is 'void' or a 'nullity', it remains in being unless and until some steps are taken before the court to have it declared void. As Lord Radcliffe said long ago in *Smith v. East Elloe Rural District Council* [1956] A.C. 736, 769–770: 'It bears no brand of invalidity upon its forehead. Unless the necessary proceedings are taken at law to establish the cause of invalidity and to get it quashed or otherwise upset, it will remain as effective for its ostensible purpose as the most impeccable of orders.' That point of view was adopted by the House of Lords in *F. Hoffman-La Roche & Co. A.G. v. Secretary of State for Trade and Industry* [1975] A.C. 295 by Lord Reid (at 341) and by Lord Morris of Borth-y-Gest (at 350).

So, even if there was anything wrong in what the Secretary of State did—even if he did fail to take into account a relevant consideration—even if there was any failure of natural justice in that or any other regard—this consent remained valid and effective for all purposes, and for people to act on it, unless and until steps were taken to call it in question. No steps were taken until the appeal was opened in this court.

Meanwhile, what has happened? As a result of the consent having been given, the Minister of Transport has gone through all the machinery leading to the making of the compulsory purchase orders. He has given all the notices in the newspapers. He has held an inquiry lasting for many, many days. Eventually, he made the orders. We are told that tenders have been put out for the work to be done. All this has been done in the belief that the consent was valid—as, indeed, it was unless and until it was set aside.

That having been done, it seems to me impossible now to challenge the orders on the ground that the statutory procedures or requirements have not been satisfied."

(*cf.* Waller L.J. to similar effect at 350; Dunn L.J. agreed with both Lord Denning and Waller L.J.: see at 353). See Comment [1980] J.P.L. 821.

3. Local authorities when seeking an injunction by virtue of the Local Government Act 1972, s.222, to enforce the criminal law are not necessarily to be required to give an undertaking in damages: *Kirklees Metropolitan Borough Council v. Wickes Building Supplies Ltd* [1993] A.C. 227. They are entitled to the special exemption enjoyed by the Crown. The House accepted that if the grant of an injunction was subsequently held to be in breach of Community Law, the United Kingdom might be obliged to make good damage caused to individuals by the breach. However, that obligation would arise irrespective of any undertaking in damages.

4. In *London and Clydeside Estates Ltd v. Aberdeen District Council*, above, p. 415, Lord Hailsham deprecated the use of the terms "void" and "voidable" (just as he disapproved of the terms "mandatory" and "directory" in respect of procedural requirements). See *Craig*, pp. 462–466, for an argument that Lord Hailsham's view that matters should largely be left to the discretion of the court goes too far:

"That the concept of retrospective nullity can give rise to awkward problems is no doubt true. But to infer that therefore it ought to be totally discarded is a *non sequitur*."

See also Sedley J. in *R. v. London Borough of Tower Hamlets, ex p. Tower Hamlets Combined Traders Association* [1994] C.O.D. 325 (above, p. 418). His Lordship held that the *ratio decidendi* of the *London & Clydeside* case was to be found in the speech of Lord Keith, and included the proposition that the question whether non-compliance with a procedural requirement rendered a decision invalid was a question of judgment according to legal criteria and not discretion, and depended on the general significance of the requirement and not the effect of its omission on the particular applicant. It was also clear that the court retained a discretion to refuse to grant a remedy even in respect of a breach of a requirement of fundamental importance. His Lordship had difficulty with Lord Hailsham's speech in so far as it could be interpreted as conflating these separate points:

> "This passage, which contains general reflections on a developing area of jurisprudence in public law, is manifestly not intended . . . to qualify the uniform reasoning of the whole House on the issue before it. This reasoning ran to a conclusion that the nature of the breach was such that no question of discretionary refusal on relief arose, so that the 'legal consequence of a non-compliance on the rights of the subject' did not in the event have to be 'viewed in the light of a concrete state of facts and continuing chain of events'. Their Lordships unanimously held the legal consequence of non-compliance in the case before them to be determined by an appraisal of the importance of the statutory purpose without regard to consequent facts or subsequent events. Correspondingly, the "spectrum of possibilities" which Lord Hailsham describes is a range of situations dependent upon the intrinsic importance of the provision and not its extrinsic effect on the complainant. Where, in the final sentence of the passage, Lord Hailsham returns to the question of discretion, I confess that I find his formulation problematical. The differences of degree, meaning presumably the degree of significance of the provision and of the breach of it, can readily be said to merge into differences of kind because their effect has ultimately to be judged to be either fatal or non-fatal to the measure concerned. This is unproblematical. But the prefatory remark ("The jurisdiction is inherently discretionary . . .") has no obvious link with the proposition that follows and is moreover puzzling in itself; for while the exercise of the jurisdiction may ultimately bring a court to discretionary considerations, the entire exercise which the House was carrying out, including the gauging of differences of degree which Lord Hailsham was here describing, was visibly a matter of judgment according to the legal principles and not to discretion."

Furthermore, the adoption of Lord Hailsham's remarks by the Court of Appeal in *Main v. Swansea City Council* (1985) 49 P. & C.R. 26 and *R. v. London Borough of Lambeth, ex p. Sharp* (1986) 55 P. & C.R. 232, was to be regarded as relating to the exercise of discretion whether to grant a remedy and not to the prior question of the legal effect of the failure to comply with a procedural requirement.

5. The judgment of Hobhouse L.J. in *Credit Suisse v. Allerdale Borough Council* [1996] 4 All E.R. 129, 162–175, contains the valuable reminder that the principles applicable in determining the legal consequences of an *ultra vires* act in public law are not necessarily the same as those applicable as a matter of private law:

> "*The relationship of public, private and administrative law*
> Where a statutory corporation purports to enter into a contract which it is not empowered by the relevant statute to enter into, the corporation lacks the capacity to make the supposed contract. This lack of capacity means that the document and the agreement it contains does not have effect as a legal contract. It exists in fact but not in law. It is legal nullity. The purported contract which is in truth not a contract does not confer any legal rights on either party. Neither party can sue upon it. This conclusion gives rise to no conflict between public law and private law principles.

The role of public law is to answer the question: what is the capacity of the local authority to contract? The role of private law is to answer the question: when one of the parties to a supposed contract lacks contractual capacity, does the supposed contract give rise to legal obligations? When a plaintiff is asserting a private law right—a private law cause of action, typically a claim for damages for breach of contract or tort—the plaintiff must establish his cause of action. Any defence raised by the defendant must be one which is recognised by private law. Lack of capacity to contract is a defence recognised by private law" (at 165).

Furthermore, it must be recognised

"that terms are used differently in administrative law and other branches of the law. Before using the phrase 'ultra vires' or the words 'void' and 'nullity', it is necessary to pause and consider the breadth of the meaning which one is given them. It is not correct to take terminology from administrative law and apply it without the necessary adjustment and refinement of meaning to private law. Where private law rights are concerned, as in the present case, the terminology must be used in the sense which is appropriate to private law....

In resolving a private law issue it is always necessary to have regard to who are the actual parties to the issue. This may affect the analysis of the issue and the answer which private law gives to it. Some improper conduct of the decision-making body may be material within the broader spectrum of administrative law, but it will not necessarily be material as between the parties to a private law dispute. A want of natural justice is specifically material to the respective private law rights of the aggrieved party and the decision-maker or a person who asserts rights based upon the decision. The private law rights of a third party who himself has not been a victim of any want of natural justice will not be affected.

Similarly, if the abuse of power by one party can properly be categorised as a 'fault' of that party, it cannot on private law principles be used as a basis for conferring rights which would not otherwise exist upon the party at fault against another party, who would otherwise have rights against the party at fault or would not be liable to the party at fault. Again, similarly, considerations of the knowledge of, or degree of notice to, a party who is asserting a private law right may be relevant to the question whether the right is enforceable against another where there has been some irregularity in the transaction which is alleged to have given rise to the right.

Private law issues must be decided in accordance with the rules of private law. The broader and less rigorous rules of administrative law should not without adjustment be applied to the resolution of private law disputes in civil proceedings. Public law, that is to say, the law governing public law entities and their activities, is a primary source of the principles applied in administrative law proceedings. The decisions of such entities are the normal subject matter of applications for judicial review. When the activities of a public law body (or individual) are relevant to a private law dispute in civil proceedings, public law may in a similar way provide answers which are relevant to the resolution of the private law issue. But after taking into account the applicable public law, the civil proceedings have to be decided as a matter of private law. The issue does not become an administrative law issue; administrative law remedies are irrelevant" (at 170–171).

The Court of Appeal held unanimously that Credit Suisse could not enforce an *ultra vires* contract of guarantee, entered by the local authority in connection with the establishment of a limited liability company to assist with the financing of a leisure pool complex. Hobhouse L.J. (at 171) rejected the bank's argument that any defence should be regarded as discretionary and approached in the same way as the decision whether to grant a remedy in judicial review proceedings (*cf*. above, pp. 679–690). The local authority could simply rely on the private law defence of want of capacity. Neill L.J. (at

152–159) came to the same conclusion but without the same emphasis on the distinction between the concepts of public law and private law. His Lordship simply rejected the bank's argument that in private law proceedings the court could exercise a discretion not to grant a remedy where a decision was *ultra vires* "not for lack of statutory capacity, but because of some procedural impropriety" (the latter including here irrationality and use of power for an improper purpose):

> "I know of no authority for the proposition that the *ultra vires* decisions of local authorities can be classified into categories of invalidity. I do not think that it is open to this court to introduce such a classification. Where a public authority acts outside its jurisdiction in any of the ways indicated by Lord Reid in *Anisminic*, the decision is void. In the case of a decision to enter into a contract of guarantee, the consequences in private law are those which flow where one of the parties to a contract lacks capacity" (at 159).

Peter Gibson L.J. (at 162) preferred not to express a view. Is the difference of approach between Hobhouse L.J. and Neill L.J. anything more than one of terminology?

(C) COLLATERAL CHALLENGE

The extent to which an act or decision may be challenged collaterally in civil or criminal proceedings, as distinct from directly on an application for judicial review, raises a number of difficult issues. One is whether to proceed collaterally is an abuse of process under the principle of *O'Reilly v. Mackman* (above, pp. 642–662). The following case shows that the extent to which collateral challenge is available depends on the context, and in particular the construction of the relevant legislation.

R. v. WICKS

[1997] 2 W.L.R. 876; [1997] 2 All E.R. 801 (House of Lords)

W was charged at the Crown Court with failing to take steps required by an enforcement notice under section 179 of the Town and Country Planning Act 1990 (as unamended). He raised as a defence an allegation that the decision to serve the notice had been *ultra vires*. The trial judge ruled that unless the notice was invalid on its face a challenge to the decision to issue such a notice could not be raised as a defence in the Crown Court. W changed his plea to guilty. He now appealed to the Court of Appeal on the ground that he should have been allowed to argue that the notice was *ultra vires* on grounds of *Wednesbury* unreasonableness and bad faith. The Court of Appeal (Criminal Division) ((1995) 93 L.G.R. 377) dismissed the appeal. W's further appeal to the House of Lords was dismissed unanimously.

LORD HOFFMANN: [stated the facts and summarised the powers of a local planning authority to serve an enforcement notice (Town and Country Planning Act 1990, ss. 172–175). Under these provisions, the local planning authority may issue an enforcement notice where it appears to the authority that there has been a breach of planning control, and the authority considers it expedient to do so having regard to the provisons of the development plan and to any other material considerations. The notice must, *inter alia*, specifiy the matters alleged to constitute a breach of planning control, the steps the authority requires to be taken and the period within which any such step is to be taken. There is a right to appeal to the Secretary of State on eight specified grounds, including (a) that planning permission ought to be granted; (b) that the matters alleged in the notice do not constitute a breach of planning control; (c) that the breach of planning control alleged in the notice has not taken place; (d) that copies of the notice were not properly served; and (e) that the specified steps exceed what is necessary. Section 285(1) provides that:

"subject to the provisions of this section, the validity of an enforcement notice shall not, except by way of an appeal under Part VII, be questioned in any proceedings whatsoever on any of the grounds on which such an appeal may be brought".]

The Court of Appeal (Lord Taylor of Gosforth C.J., Mantell and Keene JJ.) dismissed the appeal. Keene J., who gave the judgment of the court, referred to the well-known distinction which Upjohn L.J. had made in *Miller-Mead v. Minister of Housing and Local Government* [1963] 2 Q.B. 196, 226 between an enforcement notice which was a nullity ("waste paper") and one which was invalid only in the sense of being liable to be quashed. A notice which on its face failed to comply with some requirement of the Act was a nullity. A notice which could be quashed on the basis of extrinsic facts (for example, because in fact no breach of planning control had taken place) was invalid but not a complete nullity.

Miller-Mead v. Minister of Housing and Local Government concerned the power of the Secretary of State to amend or vary an enforcement notice under what is now section 176(2) of the Act of 1990. The Court of Appeal decided that he could amend a notice which was otherwise invalid but not one which was upon its face a nullity. The purpose for which the distinction was used was therefore different from the issue in this case. But, as Keene J. observed, a very similar distinction was employed by the Divisional Court in *Bugg v. Director of Public Prosecutions* [1993] Q.B. 473 to describe the grounds upon which a defendant to a prosecution under a local byelaw could challenge the validity of the byelaw in the criminal proceedings.

Mr Bugg was prosecuted for breach of a byelaw made under the Military Lands Act 1892 (55 & 56 Vict. c. 43). He claimed that on various grounds the byelaw was *ultra vires* and the question was whether he could raise these points before the magistrates. Woolf L.J. drew a distinction between "substantive invalidity," where, as he put it, the byelaw is

"on its face invalid because either it is outwith the power pursuant to which it was made because, for example, it seek to deal with matters outside the scope of the enabling legislation, or it is patently unreasonable",

and "procedural invalidity," in which the complaint is of some impropriety in the way the byelaw was made. Substantive invalidity could be raised as a defence before the magistrates but procedural invalidity could not. If the byelaw was valid on its face, it should be treated as valid until set aside by judicial review proceedings in the Divisional Court.

Keene J. said that the distinction between substantive and procedural invalidity corresponded with Upjohn L.J.'s distinction between nullity and invalidity. Defects on the face of the enforcement notice could be relied upon in the criminal proceedings but (procedural) invalidity was a matter either for the Secretary of State on appeal or the Divisional Court on judicial review. The judge went on to give reasons why it was appropriate to apply this distinction in the case of an enforcement notice, to which I shall in due course return.

Before your Lordships' House Mr Speaight, on behalf of the appellant, launched a sustained attack on the principle formulated in *Bugg v. Director of Public Prosecutions*. He said, by reference to cases on prosecutions under byelaws going back many years, that the distinction between substantive and procedural invalidity was an entirely new invention, retrospectively imposed upon cases which had said in perfectly general terms that a defendant in criminal proceedings was entitled to challenge the vires of the byelaw under which he was being prosecuted. The most recent such general statement was by Lloyd L.J in the Divisional Court in *R. v. Reading Crown Court, ex p. Hutchinson* [1988] Q.B. 384, another prosecution for breach of byelaws made under the Act of 1892. The Act provided, in section 14(1), that "no byelaws promulgated under this section shall authorise the Secretary of State to take away or prejudicially affect any right of common" and the defendants claimed that a byelaw prohibiting access to a military base at Greenham Common infringed this proviso. The Crown Court decided that as this was not a defect appearing upon the face of the byelaw and would have to be proved by evidence, it could not be raised as a defence to criminal proceedings. Lloyd L.J. disagreed and said in robust and general terms that:

> "justices have always had jurisdiction to inquire into the validity of a byelaw. They are not only entitled, but bound to do so when the defendant relies on the invalidity of the byelaw by way of defence".

Woolf L.J., in *Bugg's* case, at 498, distinguished *R. v. Reading Crown Court, ex p. Hutchinson* on the ground that there the defence was one of substantive invalidity and could therefore properly be raised. The distinction between substantive and procedural invalidity had not been argued. However, if substantive invalidity means a defect apparent on the face of the byelaw, I confess to some difficulty in seeing how the Greenham Common defence came within this category. Evidence must have been needed to establish the existence and nature of the common rights which were prejudicially affected. It is true that in subsequent litigation (*Director of Public Prosecutions v. Hutchinson* [1990] 2 A.C. 783, 812) Lord Bridge of Harwich said that certain of the byelaws were "*ultra vires* as they stand". But "as they stand" was being contrasted with what might be their effect if they were modified by some form of severence. It was necessary to have evidence from the commons register of the common rights which would be prejudicially affected.

On the other hand, it is certainly true that the Greenham Common defence cannot be said to have concerned a procedural matter. This suggests, as do some other authorities, that the line between the substantive and procedural in the normal sense of those words does not necessarily coincide with the distinction between matters which appear on the face of the instrument and those which need to be established from extrinsic facts.

Woolf L.J. in *Bugg's* case, at 500, appears to have been conscious of this difficulty: he conceded the existence of a "grey area" occupied in particular by:

> "cases where it is suggested that there has been an abuse of power because

of mala fides on the part of the byelaw maker. In the case of bad faith, there may be an issue which the criminal court can determine and if so, evidence will be required."

The breadth of the principle, which did not appear to be confined to bye-laws, was also said to be inconsistent with the reasoning in cases like *Wandsworth London Borough Council v. Winder* [1985] A.C. 461. There a tenant was sued for non-payment of rent. He was held entitled to raise as a defence in the county court an allegation that the council's decision to increase rents had been *Wednesbury* unreasonable (*Associated Provincial Picture Houses Ltd v. Wednesbury Corporation* [1948] 1 K.B. 223). In *Bugg v. Director of Public Prosecutions* [1993] Q.B. 473, 496, this case was also said to have involved substantive invalidity. As a matter of ordinary language, this seems to be right: the tenant's complaint was that "the [council's] decisions to increase the rent were such as no reasonable man could consider justifiable": [1985] A.C. 461, 506. This appears concerned with the decision itself and not the way it was made. But the ground of invalidity would not have appeared upon the face of the resolution fixing the new rents. A good deal of detailed evidence would probably have been required.

Woolf L.J., in *Bugg's* case, at 495–496, also said that *Winder's* case was concerned with civil proceedings. He may have had in mind that a circuit judge could probably cope rather better with difficult questions of administrative law than magistrates. But there are other matters to be taken into account. Lord Fraser of Tullybelton said of the defendant in *Winder's* case [1985] A.C. 461, 509–510:

"He did not select the procedure to be adopted. He is merely seeking to defend proceedings brought against him by the appellants. In so doing he is seeking only to exercise the ordinary right of any individual to defend an action against him on the ground that he is not liable for the whole sum claimed by the plaintiff. Moreover he puts forward his defence as a matter of right, whereas in an application for judicial review, success would require an exercise of the court's discretion in his favour. . . . I would adopt the words of Viscount Simonds in *Pyx Grantie Co. Ltd v. Ministry of Housing and Local Government* [1960] A.C. 260, 286 as follows: 'It is a principle not by any means to be whittled down that the subject's recourse to Her Majesty's courts for the determination of his rights is not to be excluded except by clear words.'"

It is reasonable to suppose that Lord Fraser would have regarded these sentiments as applying with even greater force to a defendant to a criminal prosecution.

There are two statements in cases in this House which are often cited in this context. One is by Lord Radcliffe in *Smith v. East Elloe Rural District Council* [1956] A.C. 736, 769–770, and the other by Lord Diplock in *F. Hoffmann-La Roche & Co. A.G. v. Secretary of State for Trade and Industry* [1975] A.C. 295, 366. In the former, Lord Radcliffe said of a compulsory purchase order:

"An order, even if not made in good faith, is still an act capable of legal consequences. It bears no brand of invalidity upon its forehead. Unless the necessary proceedings are taken at law to establish the cause of invalidity

and get it quashed or otherwise upset, it will remain as effective for its ostensible purpose as the most impeccable of orders."

These remarks were made specifically about the effect of a compulsory purchase order. They are not capable of being generalised so as to have any bearing on the question of whether, and to what extent, an *ultra vires* defence may
be raised in criminal proceedings. All that can be gained from this citation is
that it is conceptually possible to have an act which is entirely valid and effective until quashed in appropriate proceedings. Whether a particular exercise
of statutory power should be regarded as such an act is an altogether different
question.

In the other passage, Lord Diplock, [1975] A.C. 295, 366 deprecated the
use of terms like "voidable", "void" or "a nullity" as useful descriptions of the
status of subordinate legislation:

> "before its validity has been pronounced on by a court of competent juris-
> diction ... All that can usefully be said is that the presumption that subordi-
> nate legislation is *intra vires* prevails in the absence of rebuttal, and that it
> cannot be rebutted except by a party to legal proceedings in a court of com-
> petent jurisdiction who has *locus standi* to challenge the validity of the sub-
> ordinate legislation in question."

The context of these remarks was the question of whether the Crown
should be obliged to give a cross-undertaking in damages in return for an
interlocutory injunction enforcing a statutory instrument which was alleged
by the defendant to be *ultra vires*. The presumption of validity to which Lord
Diplock referred was in my view an evidential matter at the interlocutory
stage and the presumption existed pending a final decision by the court. Lord
Diplock was not putting forward the sweeping proposition that subordinate
legislation must be treated for all purposes as valid until set aside. He did not
distinguish between substantive and procedural invalidity and such a proposition would have gone far beyond anything said in *Bugg v. Director of Public
Prosecutions* [1993] Q.B. 473.

As your Lordships will have gathered, I think that there is considerable
force in Mr Speaight's criticisms of the principle enunciated in *Bugg's* case. It
is not necessary in these proceedings to express any concluded opinion on its
application to byelaws. It does however seem to be the case, as Lloyd L.J. said
in *R. v. Reading Crown Court, ex p. Hutchinson* [1988] Q.B. 384, 391, that
defendants prosecuted for breaches of local byelaws have always in the past
been allowed to challenge their vires without discrimination as to the grounds
upon which they were doing so. I have some doubt as to whether this ancient
jurisdiction of the local justices can be cut back in the manner suggested or
whether it would be wise to do so. Like Lloyd L.J., I am impressed by the
submission of the defendant before him in *R. v. Reading Crown Court ex p.
Hutchinson*, which he recorded as follows, at 392:

> "Coming to London to the High Court is inconvenient and expensive. Bye-
> laws are generally local laws which have been made for local people to do
> with local concerns. Magistrates' courts are local courts and there is one in
> every town of any size in England. The cost of proceedings in a magistrates'

court are far less than in the High Court. I believe this egalitarian aspect of seeking recourse to the law in a magistrates' court to be an important sign of the availability of justice for all."

I recognise that there is a good deal in the point that the issues which arise in modern judicial review proceedings are sometimes unsuited for decision by a magistrates' court. *Ultra vires* was a relatively unsophisticated doctrine in the days of *Kruse v. Johnson* [1898] 2 Q.B. 91; today it requires a good deal of specialised legal knowledge and a sensitivity to the proper boundaries between legislative, executive and judicial power. The distinction between substantive and procedural invalidity is presumably intended to confine magistrates' courts to points of law on which the justices can be advised by their clerk. It is meant to avoid them having to apply complicated rules of administrative law to their findings of fact. But, as the cases show, the distinction between substantive and procedural invalidity appears to cut across the distinction between grounds of invalidity which require no extrinsic evidence and those which do.

If the argument is that developments in judicial review have brought about a change in the old law about challenging byelaws, there is great difficulty in identifying when the change took place. I agree with Lloyd L.J. that it could hardly have been as a result of changes in the procedure for judicial review or the practice introduced by *O'Reilly v. Mackman* [1983] 2 A.C. 237. It may be that the problem cannot be solved by judicial creativity and that, as Lord Fraser of Tullybelton said in *Wandsworth London Borough Council v. Winder* [1985] A.C. 461, 510, if it is thought inconvenient to have questions of *ultra vires* decided by magistrates, Parliament must change the law.

Furthermore, I have read in draft the speech of my noble and learned friend, Lord Nicholls of Birkenhead, and I agree that the implications of *Bugg v. Director of Public Prosecutions* [1993] Q.B. 473, in particular its generalisation of the passages from the speeches of Lord Radcliffe and Lord Diplock to which I have referred, go wider than questions of procedure. They suggest that someone who contravenes a byelaw commits an offence even if the byelaw is afterwards quashed for procedural invalidity. For my part, I would (in the absence of specific legislation) find their conclusion unacceptable.

But, my Lords, while I am willing for the sake of argument to accept Mr Speaight's submission that there is a wide right for anyone prosecuted under a local byelaw to challenge its validity, the point at which we absolutely part company is when he submits that this right can be extrapolated to enable a defendant to challenge the vires of every act done under statutory authority if its validity forms part of the prosecutions's case or its invalidity would constitute a defence. In my view no such generalisation is possible. The question must depend entirely upon the construction of the statute under which the prosecution is brought. The statute may require the prosecution to prove that the act in question is not open to chllenge on any ground available in public law, or it may be a defence to show that it is. In such a case, the justices will have to rule upon the validity of the act. On the other hand, the statute may upon its true construction merely require an act which appears formally valid and has not been quashed by judicial review. In such a case, nothing but the formal validity of the act will be relevant to an issue before the justices. It is in my view impossible to construct a general theory of the *ultra vires* defence which applies to every statutory power, whatever the terms and policy of the statute.

The correct approach is in my view illustrated by the decision of the Divisional Court in *Quietlynn Ltd v. Plymouth City Council* [1988] Q.B. 114....

In my view the question in this case is likewise one of construction. What is meant by "enforcement notice" in section 179(1) of the Act of 1990? Does it mean a notice which is not liable to be quashed on any of the standard grounds in public law? Or does it mean a notice issued by the planning authority which complies with the formal requirements of the Act and has not actually been quashed on appeal or judicial review? The words "enforcement notice" are in my view capable of either meaning. The correct one must be ascertained from the scheme of the Act and the public law background against which it was passed.

In my view, when one examines Part VII of the Town and Country Planning Act 1990, the scheme of enforcement of planning control which it exhibits and the history of its provisions, one is driven to the conclusion that "enforcement notice" means a notice issued by the planning authority which is formally valid and has not been quashed.

I start with a brief history of the enforcement notice provisions. These have been recast by Parliament on several occasions since they were first introduced in sections 23 and 24 of the Town and Country Planning Act 1947. Originally there was a right of appeal on limited grounds to the local justices and from them to quarter sessions. In some cases the method of dealing with non-compliance was for the planning authority to do the work and claim the cost from the owner. In others, non-compliance was a summary offence. At that time there was plainly no restriction on the way in which the validity of an enforcement notice could be challenged by an owner in criminal proceedings.

A radical change was made by the Caravan Sites and Control of Development Act 1960, when the right of appeal to the justices was abolished and a right of appeal to the minister on wider grounds was substituted. Section 33(8) of that Act provided for the first time that, save by means of the appeal procedure, the validity of an enforcement notice could not be questioned in any proceedings on certain of the grounds on which an appeal could be brought.

The enforcement notice code was further amended and re-enacted by the Town and Country Planning Act 1968 which was consolidated in the Town and Country Planning Act 1971. The latter Act also for the first time made the offence of failure to comply triable on indictment. The code was again amended and re-enacted in the Local Government and Planning (Amendment) Act 1981. It is the provisions substituted by this last Act which are now consolidated in the Town and Country Planning Act 1990.

The history shows that over the years there has been a consistent policy of progressively restricting the kind of issues which a person served with an enforcement notice can raise when he is prosecuted for failing to comply. The reasons for this policy of restriction are clear: they relate, first, to the unsuitability of the subject matter for decision by the criminal court; secondly, to the need for the validity of the notice to be conclusively determined quickly enough to enable planning control to be effective and to allow the timetable for service of such notices in the Act to be operated; and thirdly, to the fact that the criminal proceedings are part of the mechanism for securing the enforcement of planning control in the public interest.

First, then, the suitability of the subject matter. The Act of 1960 recognised that the planning merits of the enforcement notice were unsuitable for decision by a magistrates' court. It not only transferred the right of appeal to the minister (now the Secretary of State) but excluded challenge on most such grounds in any other proceedings. The present position is that no challenge is possible on any ground which can form the subject matter of an appeal.

On the other hand, there remain residual grounds of challenge lying outside the grounds of appeal in section 174(2) of the Act of 1990, such as mala fides, bias or other procedural impropriety in the decision to issue the notice. I shall call these "the residual grounds". Mr Speaight says that the fact that the residual grounds were not swept up in the appeal procedure supports his argument. If section 285(1) says that the notice cannot be questioned on certain grounds, it follows that it *can* be questioned on any other grounds. But the fact that the residual grounds are not altogether excluded does not necessarily mean that they can be raised as a defence to a prosecution. They may be available only by some other means. One has to ask why they were not included in the appeal procedure. The reason, as it seems to me, is obvious. Questions of whether the planning authority was motivated by mala fides or bias or whether the decision to issue the notice was based upon irrelevant or improper grounds are quite unsuitable for decision by a planning inspector. The question then is whether Parliament regarded them as suitable for decision by a criminal court.

In deciding this question one is (and here I echo the words of Webster J. in *Quietlynn Ltd v. Plymouth City Council* [1988] Q.B. 114) entitled to take into account the complexity and sophistication of the law relating to the residual grounds; a matter of which Parliament would have been aware when the legislation last received substantive consideration in 1981. I think it no criticism of lay justices to say that many would not find it easy to apply the distinction, which comes so easily to the Divisional Court, between the legality of an administrative act and its substantive merits. It would in practice be difficult to prevent the hearing from turning into a reassessment of the planning merits and thereby subverting the whole scheme of the Act.

In the case of a trial on indictment, which was first introduced by the Act of 1971, Mr Speaight submits that these questions would have to be decided by the jury after being given proper directions as to the law. Although on my view of the construction of section 179(1) the question does not arise for decision, I think that this is probably wrong. The vires of the enforcement notice is a question of law and should be decided by the judge, even if he has to hear evidence on the point: compare *R. v. Goldstein* [1982] 1 W.L.R. 804; [1983] 1 W.L.R. 151. But if Mr Speaight is right, the point about the unsuitability of the subject matter gains added force.

Then there is the question of timing. The enforcement of planning control obviously does not have the same urgency as the measures to prevent the spread of infectious diseases considered in *R. v. Davey* [1899] 2 Q.B. 301. But one is entitled to say that the institution and extension of the appeal procedure shows a policy of having challenges to enforcement notices decided as soon as possible after they have been served. It is not only a question of avoiding undue delay. The policy must be seen against the background of the time-tables laid down by the Act. An enforcement notice in respect of a breach of planning control by carrying out building operations without planning permission (such as occurred in this case) must be served within four years from the date of the breach: section 172(4). That may seem a long time but the facts of this case show that if the validity of the enforcement notice is left to be determined in the criminal prosecution, there may not be time to serve another. The breach took place in January or February 1990 and the notice was served with commendable rapidity on March 13, 1990. Despite the case being a relatively simple one and the waiver of any public inquiry, the appeal was not determined until May 10, 1991. There were then negotiations and the summons was not issued until June 11, 1992. Election for trial on indictment had the effect of delaying the trial until September 27, 1993. By that time there would have been less than six months in which to serve a fresh notice and if Mr Wicks's appeal had been allowed by the Court of Appeal on April 11, 1995 it would have been too late. This was, as a I say, an extremely straightforward case and (apart from the period of negotiation in 1991–1992) there is nothing to show that the planning authority could have progressed the matter more quickly. Thus the exclusion of the residual grounds from the appeal procedure in section 174(2) would harmonise better with the scheme of the Act if they had to be raised by judicial review within the time limits prescribed for that procedure than if they could be relied upon in a criminal prosecution.

Thirdly, there is the purpose of the provisions for enforcement by criminal proceedings. The provisions of section 179(5), by which failure to comply after a first conviction gives rise to a fresh offence punishable by a daily fine, show that the criminal law is being used not merely to punish for a past act but as an instrument of coercion to encourage compliance in the future. The criminal proceedings thus form part of the general scheme of enforcement of planning control contained in Part VII of the Act and should in my view be interpreted to give effect to the overall policy of the enforcement procedures.

I do not think that construing the Act in this way involves any inroad upon the principle that criminal statutes should be clear and in case of ambiguity construed in favour of the defendant. The duty of the landowner is perfectly clear: if the enforcement notice has not been quashed, he must obey it. It was submitted that the power of the Divisonal Court to quash an enforcement notice is discretionary and that criminal liability should not depend upon judicial discretion. As Sir William Wade has said in a passage in his book on *Administrative Law*, 6th ed. (1988), p. 354, which was cited in *Bugg v. Director of Public Prosecutions* [1993] Q.B. 473, 499–500:

> "There are grave objections to giving the courts discretion to decide whether governmental action is lawful or unlawful: the citizen is entitled to resist unlawful action as a matter of right, and to live under the rule of law, not the rule of discretion. 'To remit the maintenance of constitutional right to the region of judicial discretion is to shift the foundations of freedom from rock to sand:' *Scott v. Scott* [1913] A.C. 417, 477. The true scope for discretion is in the law of remedies, where it operates within narrow and recognised limits and is far less objectionable. If the courts were to undermine the principle of *ultra vires* by making it discretionary, no victim of an excess or abuse of power could be sure that the law would protect him."

In my view this passage, with which I entirely agree, has no application to the present case. The fact that the decision not to quash the notice was an exercise of discretion (for example, because the court was satisfied that although one councillor should not have taken part in the decision, the notice would certainly have been served in any case) does not mean that any discretion enters into the question of whether the owner has committed an offence. The original decision to serve the notice was also a matter of discretion. But the offence is to disobey an enforcement notice which has not been quashed and the fact that the decision to issue it or not to quash it involved the exercise of discretion is irrelevant. On the contrary, it seems to me that the discretion which the Divisional Court has to refuse to quash when it is satisfied that a procedural impropriety would have made no difference is a reason why Parliament would not have intended this question to go to the justices or jury, who would obviosuly have no such discretion.

I do not think that in practice hardship will be caused by requiring the residual grounds to be raised in judicial review proceedings. The statutory grounds of appeal are so wide that they include every aspect of the merits of the decision to serve an enforcement notice. The residual grounds will in practice be needed only for the rare case in which enforcement is objectively justifiable but the decision that service of the notice is "expedient" (section 172(1)(b)) is vitiated by some impropriety. As Keene J. said in the Court of Appeal, the owner has been served with the notice and knows that he has to challenge it or comply with it. His position is quite different from that of a person who has contravened a byelaw, who may not have heard of the byelaw until he contravened it.

All these reasons lead me to conclude that "enforcement notice" in section 179(1) means a notice issued by a planning authority which on its face complies with the requirements of the Act and has not been quashed on appeal or by judicial review. There was no dispute that Mr Wicks had failed to comply with such an enforcement notice and he was therefore guilty of the offence. The matters which he proposed to raise at his trial were irrelevant. ...

Appeal dismissed.

Notes and Questions

1. *Bugg v. D.P.P.* has been followed in a number of cases decided before the decision of the House of Lords in *R. v. Wicks*: see *R. v. Bovis Construction Ltd* [1994] Crim.L.R. 938; *R. v. Ettrick Trout Co. Ltd* [1994] Env.L.R. 165 (not open to defendant prosecuted for contravening the conditions of a consent to discharge trade effluent to argue that the condition had been imposed for an improper purpose); *Boddington v. British Transport Police, The Times,* July 23, 1996 (not open to defendant convicted under byelaws for smoking on a train, where that had been prohibited by a notice exhibited under the byelaws and not bad on its face, to argue that the decision to introduce the prohibition was *ultra vires* or irrational). Can these cases survive the decision in *Wicks*?

2. While the establishing that a byelaw is *ultra vires* will entitle a defendant convicted for breach of it to have the conviction quashed, this will not have the further effect of making that person's arrest unlawful so as to give rise to an action in tort against the arresting officer: *Percy v. Hall* [1996] 4 All E.R. 523.

3. On collateral challenge generally, see C.T. Emery, "The Vires Defence—'Ultra Vires' as a Defence to Criminal or Civil Proceedings" [1992] C.L.J. 308 (predating *Bugg*), and "Collateral Attack—Attacking Ultra Vires Action Indirectly in Courts and Tribunals" (1993) 56 M.L.R. 643. Emery proposes that any court or tribunal in which a collateral *vires* issue is raised should have jurisdiction to entertain the *vires* argument

and should have discretion to pronounce on the point or refer it to the High Court for a ruling.

(D) Partial Invalidity

D.P.P. v. HUTCHINSON

[1990] 2 A.C. 783; [1990] 3 W.L.R. 196; [1990] 2 All E.R. 836; (1990) 89 L.G.R. 281 (House of Lords)

Section 14(1) of the Military Lands Act 1892 provides:

> "Where any land belonging to a Secretary of State ... is for the time being appropriated by ... a Secretary of State for any military purpose, a Secretary of State may make byelaws for regulating the use of the land for the purposes for which it is appropriated, and for securing the public against dangers arising from that use, with power to prohibit all intrusion on the land and all obstruction of the use thereof. Provided that no byelaws promulgated under the section shall authorise the Secretary of State to take away or prejudicially affect any right of common."

The Secretary of State for Defence, acting under section 14 of the Act of 1892, made the R.A.F. Greenham Common Byelaws 1985 in respect of common land appropriated for military purposes. Byelaw (2)(b) provided that no person should, *inter alia*, enter or remain in the protected area without the authority or permission of an authorised person. The defendants, who were not commoners, entered the land and were charged with and convicted by the justices of entering it contrary to byelaw 2(b). The Crown Court allowed their appeals, holding that the byelaws were *ultra vires* in that they prejudicially affected rights of common. The Divisional Court of the Queen's Bench Division allowed an appeal by case stated by the Director of Public Prosecutions. The defendants appealed to the House of Lords.

LORD BRIDGE: ... The Divisional Court (Mann L.J. and Schiemann J.) [1989] Q.B. 583 allowed the Crown's appeal and restored the convictions. They held that the Greenham byelaws, although *ultra vires* on their face, could be severed, so that they might be upheld and enforced as against all except persons entitled to exercise rights of common over the protected area. It mattered not that the severance could only be achieved by reading into the byelaws, where necessary, appropriate exceptions and exemptions, provided that the court was satisfied, as Schiemann J. stated, at 599, that it was, that the Secretary of State, if he had appreciated the limitation on his powers would:

> "nevertheless have gone on to make the byelaws in such a way that the proviso to section 14(1) was given effect but that all the world save commoners would still have been within their ambit...".

When a legislative instrument made by a law-maker with limited powers is challenged, the only function of the court is to determine whether there has been a valid exercise of that limited legislative power in relation to the matter which is the subject of disputed enforcement. If a law-maker has validly exercised his power, the court may give effect to the law validly made. But if the court sees only an invalid law made in excess of the law-maker's power, it has no jurisdiction to modify or adapt the law to bring it within the scope of the law-maker's powers. These, I believe, are the basic principles which have always to be borne in mind in deciding whether legislative provisions which on their face exceed the law-maker's power may be severed so as to be upheld and enforced in part.

The application of these principles leads naturally and logically to what has traditionally been regarded as the test of severability. It is often referred to inelegantly as the "blue pencil" test. Taking the simplest case of a single legislative instrument containing a number of separate clauses of which one exceeds the law-maker's power, if the remaining clauses enact free-standing provisions which were intended to operate and are capable of operating independently of the offending clause, there is no reason why those clauses should not be upheld and enforced. The law-maker has validly exercised his power by making the valid clauses. The invalid clause may be disregarded as unrelated to, and having no effect upon, the operation of the valid clauses, which accordingly may be allowed to take effect without the necessity of any modification or adaptation by the court. What is involved is in truth a double test. I shall refer to the two aspects of the test as textual severability and substantial severability. A legislative instrument is textually severable if a clause, a sentence, a phrase or a single word may be disregarded, as exceeding the law-maker's power, and what remains of the text is still grammatical and coherent. A legislative instrument is substantially severable if the substance of what remains after severance is essentially unchanged in its legislative purpose, operation and effect.

The early English authorities take it for granted, I think, that if byelaws are to be upheld as good in part notwithstanding that they are bad in part, they must be both textually and substantially severable. Thus, Lord Kenyon C.J. said in *R. v. Company of Fishermen of Faversham* (1799) 8 Durn. & E. 352, 356:

"With regard to the form of the byelaw indeed, though a byelaw may be good in part and bad in part, yet it can be so only where the two parts are entire and distinct from each other."

[His Lordship also cited *R. v. Lundie* (1862) 8 Jur.N.S. 640 and *Strickland v. Hayes* [1896] 1 Q.B. 290. He then referred to United States and Australian authorities that emphasised the need for both textual and substantial severability.]

Our attention has been drawn to a number of more recent English authorities on the severability of provisions contained in various documents of a public law character. I doubt if these throw much light on the specific problem of severance in legislative instruments. The modern authority most directly in point and that on which the Divisional Court relied is *Dunkley v. Evans* [1981] 1 W.L.R. 1522. The West Coast Herring (Prohibition of Fishing) Order 1978 (S.I. 1978 No. 930) prohibited fishing for herring in an area defined in the Schedule to the Order as within a line drawn by reference to co-ordinates and coastlines. The Order was made by the Minister of Agriculture, Fisheries and Food under the Sea Fish (Conservation) Act 1967. The prohibited area included a stretch of sea adjacent to the coast of Northern Ireland, representing 0.8 per cent of the total area covered by the Order, to which the enabling power in the Act of 1967 did not extend. The defendants admitted fishing in part of the prohibited area to which the enabling power did extend but submitted that, by including the area to which the enabling power did not extend, the Minister had acted *ultra vires* and, since textual severance was not possible, the whole Order was invalid. The justices accepted this submission and dismissed the informations. The Divisional Court allowed the prosecutor's appeal. Delivering the judgment of the court, Ormrod L.J. cited, at 1524–1525, the following passage from the judgment of Cussen J. in the Supreme Court of Victoria in *Olsen v. City of Camberwell* [1926] V.L.R. 58, 68:

> " 'If the enactment, with the invalid portion omitted, is so radically or substantially different a law as to the subject-matter dealt with by what remains from what it would be with the omitted portions forming part of it as to warrant a belief that the legislative body intended it as a whole only, or, in other words, to warrant a belief that if all could not be carried into effect the legislative body would not have enacted the remainder independently, then the whole must fail.' "

It is to be noted that this quotation is from the judgment in a case where textual severance was possible. Following the quotation the judgment of Ormrod L.J. continued:

> "We respectfully agree with and adopt this statement of the law. It would be difficult to imagine a clearer example than the present case of a law which the legislative body would have enacted independently of the offending portion and which is so little affected by eliminating the invalid portion. This is clearly, therefore, an order which the court should not strive officiously to kill to any greater extent than it is compelled to do.... We can see no reason why the powers of the court to sever the invalid portion of a piece of subordinate legislation from the valid should be restricted to cases where the text of the legislation lends itself to judicial surgery, or textual emendation by excision. It would have been competent for the court in an action for a declaration that the provisions of the Order in this case did not apply to the area of the sea off Northern Ireland reserved by section 23(1) of the Act of 1967, as amended, to make the declaration sought, without in any way affecting the validity of the Order in relation to the remaining 99·2 per cent. of the area referred to in the Schedule to the Order. Such an order was made, in effect, by the House of Lords in *Hotel and Catering Industry Training Board v. Automobile Proprietary Ltd* [1969] 1 W.L.R. 697, and by Donaldson J. in *Agricultural, Horticultural and Forestry Industry Training Board v. Aylesbury Mushrooms Ltd* [1972] 1 W.L.R. 190."

I do not think any light is thrown on the point at issue by the last two cases referred to by Ormrod L.J. In *Hotel and Catering Industry Training Board v. Automobile Proprietary Ltd* the subordinate legislation in question was textually severable. In *Agricultural, Horticultural and Forestry Industry Training Board v. Aylesbury Mushrooms Ltd* the text was not severable but the issue of severance was never canvassed in argument and I cannot help thinking that the outcome might have been different if it had been....
The modern English authority to which I attach most significance is

Daymond v. Plymouth City Council [1976] A.C. 609, where severability was not in issue, but where it appears to have been taken for granted without question that severance was possible. Section 30(1) of the Water Act 1973 gave power to water authorities:

> "to fix, and to demand, take and recover such charges for the services performed, facilities provided or rights made available by them including separate charges for separate services, facilities or rights or combined charges for a number of services, facilities or rights) as they think fit."

The subsection was silent as to who was liable to pay the charges. The Water Authorities (Collection of Charges) Order 1974 (S.I. 1974 No. 448) embodied provisions which required a rating authority to collect on behalf of a water authority a "general services charge" (article 7(2)) referable to sewerage services "from every person who is liable to pay the general rate in respect of a hereditament..." (article 10(1)). A householder whose property was not connected to a sewer, the nearest sewer being 400 yards away from his house, refused to pay the charge and brought an action for a declaration that the Order could not properly apply to him. This House held, by a majority of three to two, that on the true construction of the enabling legislation there was no power to impose a charge for sewerage services upon occupiers of property not connected to a sewer. As I have said, the question of severability was not raised, but there is no hint in the speeches that the invalidation of the charging provision in relation to properties not connected to sewers would affect their validity in relation to properties which were so connected.

The test of textual severability has the great merit of simplicity and certainty. When it is satisfied the court can readily see whether the omission from the legislative text of so much as exceeds the law-maker's power leaves in place a valid text which is capable of operating and was evidently intended to operate independently of the invalid text. But I have reached the conclusion, though not without hesitation, that a rigid insistence that the test of textual severability must always be satisfied if a provision is to be upheld and enforced as partially valid will in some cases, of which *Dunkley v. Evans* and *Daymond v. Plymouth City Council* are good examples, have the unreasonable consequence of defeating subordinate legislation of which the substantial purpose and effect was clearly within the law-maker's power when, by some oversight or misapprehension of the scope of that power, the text, as written, has a range of application which exceeds that scope. It is important, however, that in all cases an appropriate test of substantial severability should be applied. When textual severance is possible, the test of substantial severability will be satisfied when the valid text is unaffected by, and independent of, the invalid. The law which the court may then uphold and enforce is the very law which the legislator has enacted, not a different law. But when the court must modify the text in order to achieve severance, this can only be done when the court is satisfied that it is effecting no change in the substantial purpose and effect of the impugned provision. Thus, in *Dunkley v. Evans*, the legislative purpose and effect of the prohibition of fishing in the large area of the sea in relation to which the Minister was authorised to legislate was unaffected by the obviously inadvertent inclusion of the small area of sea to which his power did not extend. In *Daymond v. Plymouth City Council* the draftsman of the Order had evidently construed the enabling provision as authorising the imposition of charges for sewerage services upon occupiers of property irrespective of whether or not they were connected to sewers. In this error he was in the good company of two members of your Lordships' House. But this extension of the scope of the charging power, which, as the majority held, exceeded its proper limit, in no way affected the legislative purpose and effect of the charging power as applied to occupiers of properties which were connected to sewers.

To appreciate the full extent of the problem presented by the Greenham byelaws it is necessary to set out the full text of the prohibitions imposed by byelaw (2) which provides:

"No person shall: (a) enter or leave or attempt to enter or leave the protected area except by way of an authorised entrance or exit. (b) enter, pass through or over or remain in or over the protected area without authority or permission given by or on behalf of one of the persons mentioned in byelaw 5(1). (c) cause or permit any vehicle, animal, aircraft or thing to enter into or upon or to pass through or over or to be or remain in or upon or over the protected area without authority or permission given by or on behalf of one of the persons mentioned in byelaw 5(1). (d) remain in the protected area after having been directed to leave by any of the persons mentioned in byelaw 4. (e) make any false statement, either orally or in writing, or employ any other form of misrepresentation in order to obtain entry to any part of the protected area or to any building or premises within the protected area. (f) obstruct any constable (including a constable under the control of the Defence Council) or any other person acting in the proper exercise or execution of his duty within the protected area. (g) enter any part of the protected area which is shown by a notice as being prohibited or restricted. (h) board, attempt to board, or interfere with, or interfere with the movement or passage, of any vehicle, aircraft or other installation in the protected area. (i) distribute or display any handbill, leaflet, sign, advertisement, circular, poster, bill, notice or object within the protected area or affix the same to either side of the perimeter fences without authority of permission given by or on behalf of one of the persons mentioned in byelaw 5(1). (j) interfere or remove from the protected area any property under the control of the Crown or the service authorities of a visiting force or, in either case, their agents or contractors. (k) wilfully damage, destroy, deface or remove any notice board or sign within the protected area. (l) wilfully damage, soil, deface or mark any wall, fence, structure, floor, pavement, or other surface within the protected area."

It is at once apparent that paragraphs (a), (b), (c), (d), (g), (j) and (l) are *ultra vires* as they stand. Paragraphs (e), (f), (i) and (k) appear to be valid and paragraph (h) is probably good in part and bad in part, since the exercise by a commoner of his rights may well interfere with the movement or passage of vehicles. Textual severance can achieve nothing since it is apparent that the valid provisions are merely ancillary to the invalid provisions.

There is exhibited to the case stated by the Crown Court a letter written by an official of the Ministry of Defence to an objector at the time the byelaws were made which concludes with the sentence:

"Finally I can confirm that in accordance with the enabling Act, the Military Lands Act 1892, the byelaws will not affect rights of common."

Mr Laws has invited us to infer from this that the Secretary of State for Defence made the byelaws in the belief that the law would imply the necessary exceptions to prevent the byelaws from prejudicially affecting rights of common. I do not think we are entitled to take account of the letter in considering whether the byelaws may be upheld as valid in part. But in any event it is a matter of pure speculation as to what the writer of the letter had in mind. The draftsman of the byelaws cannot possibly have been in ignorance of the terms and effect of the proviso to section 14(1) of the Act of 1892 and the theory of an inadvertent omission appears the less plausible since five sets of byelaws in relation to common lands used for military purposes which were made by the Secretary of State for Defence under section 14 of the Act of 1892 in the years 1976 to 1980 all contain careful express provisions to safeguard rights of common.

I think the proper test to be applied when textual severance is impossible, following in this respect the Australian authorities, is to abjure speculation as to what the maker of the law might have done if he had applied his mind to the relevant limitation on his powers and to ask whether the legislative instrument

"with the invalid portions omitted would be substantially a different law as to the subject-matter dealt with by what remains from what it would be with the omitted portions forming part of it": *R. v. Commonwealth Court of Conciliation and Arbitration, ex p. Whybrow & Co.*, 11 C.L.R. 1, 27.

In applying this test the purpose of the legislation can only be inferred from the text as applied to the factual situation to which its provisions relate. Considering the Greenham byelaws as a whole it is clear that the absolute prohibition which they impose upon all unauthorised access to the protected area is no less than is required to maintain the security of an establishment operated as a military airbase and wholly enclosed by a perimeter fence. Byelaws drawn in such a way as to permit free access to all parts of the base to persons exercising rights of common and their animals would be byelaws of a totally different character. They might serve some different legislative purpose in a different factual situation, as do some other byelaws to which our attention has been drawn relating to areas used as military exercise grounds or as military firing ranges. But they would be quite incapable of serving the legislative purpose which the Greenham byelaws, as drawn, are intended to serve.

For these reasons I conclude that the invalidity of byelaw 2(b) cannot be cured by severance. It follows that the appellants were wrongly convicted and I would allow their appeals, set aside the order of the Divisional Court and restore the order of the Crown Court at Reading.

LORDS GRIFFITH, OLIVER and GOFF agreed with LORD BRIDGE.

LORD LOWRY [agreed with Lord Bridge's conclusion that the byelaw could not survive the test of substantial severability, but also made a reservation in favour of the traditional test of textual severability].

My Lords, the accepted view in the common law jurisdictions has been that, when construing legislation the validity of which is under challenge, the first duty of the court, in obedience to the principle that a law should, whenever possible, be interpreted *ut res magis valeat quam pereat*, is to see whether the impugned provision can reasonably bear a construction which renders it valid. Failing that, the court's duty, subject always to any relevant statutory provision . . . is to decide whether the whole of the challenged legislation or only part of it must be held invalid and ineffective. That problem has traditionally been resolved by applying first the textual, and then the substantial, severability test. If the legislation failed the first test, it was condemned in its entirety. If it passed that test, it had to face the next hurdle. This approach, in my opinion, has a great deal in its favour.

The basic principle is that an *ultra vires* enactment, such as a byelaw, is void *ab initio* and of no effect. The so-called blue pencil test is a concession to practicality and ought not to be extended or weakened. In its traditional form it is acceptable because, once the offending words are ignored, no word or phrase needs to be given a meaning different from, or more restrictive than, its original meaning. Therefore the court has not legislated; it merely continues to apply that part of the existing legislation which is good.

It may be argued that a policy split has developed and that it is time to show common sense and bring our thinking up to date by a further application of the *ut res magis valeat quam pereat* principle. I am, however, chary of yielding to this temptation for a number of reasons. 1. The blue pencil test already represents a concession to the erring law-maker, the justification for which I have tried to explain. 2. When applying the blue pencil test (which actually means ignoring the offending words), the court cannot cause the text of the instrument to be altered. It will remain as the ostensible law of the land unless and until it is replaced by something else. It is too late now to think of abandoning the blue pencil method, which has much to commend it, but the disadvantage inherent in the method ought not to be enlarged. 3. It is up to the law-maker to keep within his powers and it is in the public interest that he should take care, in order that the public may be able to rely on the written word as representing the law. Further enlargement of the court's power to validate what is partially invalid will encourage the law-maker to enact what he pleases, or at least to enact what may or may not be valid, without having to fear any worse result than merely being brought back within bounds. 4. *Dunkley v. Evans* [1981] 1 W.L.R. 1522 and *Thames Water Authority v. Elmbridge Borough Council* [1983] Q.B. 570 are very special cases. I recall in that regard what McNeill J. said in *R. v. Secretary of State for Transport, ex p. Greater London Council* [1986] Q.B. 556, 582D. 5. To liberalise the test would, in my view, be anarchic, not progressive. It would tend in the wrong direction, unlike some developments in the law of negligence, which have promoted justice for physically or economically injured persons, or the sounder aspects of judicial review, which have promoted freedom and have afforded protection from power. 6. The current of decisions and relevant authority has flowed in favour of the traditional doctrine.

[His Lordship concluded by noting that the sole question considered in *Daymond v. Plymouth City Council* [1976] A.C. 609 was whether section 30 of the Water Act 1973 empowered the water authority to charge occupiers of property who did not receive the benefit of the authority's services directly.]

I am therefore very reluctant to treat the case as an authority which by implication contradicts the established doctrine of textual severability for the purposes of the present appeal. Accordingly, I would allow this appeal on two grounds, (1) that there is no valid part of byelaw 2(b) which can be severed from the invalid part and stand by itself and (2) that the byelaw would not in any event survive the test of substantial severability.

Appeals allowed.

Notes

1. See comments by A.W. Bradley [1989] P.L.1. (on the decision of the Divisional Court), and [1990] P.L. 293 (on the decision of the House of Lords). Bradley is critical of the fact that it appeared:

"that the Ministry of Defence knew of the limitation upon the Secretary of State's powers and knowingly departed from the previous practice of taking care to comply with the intent of the legislation" (at 295).

He also noted that Lord Lowry's view had "the edge in terms of the previous authorities" (at 300). Lord Bridge's approach, while more generous to the lawmaker, still gave "salutary substance to the spectre of the judge over Whitehall's shoulder" (at 300).

"What previously may have seemed in danger of being entirely at the discretion of the court is now subject to a more structured review" (at 299).

2. In *R. v. Secretary of State for Transport, ex p. Greater London Council* [1986] Q.B. 556, McNeill J. quashed a direction by the Secretary of State requiring the GLC to pay a specified sum to London Regional Transport by way of grant. Through a miscalculation, this figure was too high by some £10.2 million. McNeill J. held that the direction was "single and indivisible"; that the deduction of £10.2 million would involve rewriting and changing the character of the direction; and that this could not be justified by reference to the authorities on severance. The direction "stands or falls as one".

3. *D.P.P. v. Hutchinson* was applied by the House in *R. v. Inland Revenue Commissioners, ex p. Woolwich Equitable Building Society* [1990] 1 W.L.R. 1400. The Revenue conceded that part of a regulation was *ultra vires* in that it purported to prescribe a rate of income tax for which building societies were accountable different from that of the year of assessment; the House held (reversing the Court of Appeal on this point) that this could not be severed from the rest of the regulation and that this and a linked regulation were wholly *ultra vires*. The fact that the offending part could be deleted without altering the grammatical sense of what was left was insufficient for severance:

"One has to ask also the question whether the deletion of that which is in excess of the power so alters the substance of what is left that the provision in question is in reality a substantially different provision from that which it was before deletion" (*per* Lord Oliver at 1413).

Here it was "beyond argument" that the regulation without the offending part:

"is in substance quite different from the regulation which the draftsman actually produced and intended.... What form the regulation might have taken if the invalidity of paragraph (4) had been appreciated is a matter of pure speculation" (*per* Lord Oliver at 1415–1416).

(*cf.* Lord Goff at 1417–1419.)

CHAPTER 13

EXCLUSION OF JUDICIAL REVIEW

PARLIAMENT may attempt to make a particular act or decision "judge-proof". One general method is to entrust powers in subjective form (see above, pp. 369 *et seq.*). Another general method is to use explicit exclusion clauses, purporting for example, to exclude a particular remedy, or to prevent any recourse to the courts at all. Historically these clauses have been controversial both politically and legally. Section 11 of the Tribunals and Inquiries Act 1958 (see now s.12 of the 1992 Act, above, p. 54) reduced the effects of such clauses in statutes passed before July 1958. One of the exclusion clauses expressly preserved by the 1958 Act was considered in the *Anisminic* case (above, p. 210). Another variety frequently found in legislation is the "finality" clause, which seems to have little effect beyond taking away a right of appeal which would otherwise exist. (See *R. v. Medical Appeal Tribunal, ex p. Gilmore*, below.) The other significant modern exclusionary formula is that built into the typical "statutory *ultra vires*" clause (see above, pp. 552–564). These protect compulsory purchase orders, etc., from any judicial review apart from on an application to the High Court within six weeks on the stated grounds. The effect of these clauses is discussed in *Smith v. East Elloe R.D.C.*, below, p. 799, and *ex p. Ostler*, below, p. 804. In the latter case, the Court of Appeal held that the authority of the House of Lords in *Smith v. East Elloe* has not been affected by the *Anisminic* case, and that an order cannot be challenged other than in accordance with the statutory procedure.

Another technique is that of empowering a public authority to "define" expressions used in the enabling Act which sets it up. See, for example, the Counter-inflation Act 1973, s.23 and Sched. 3, para. 1, discussed by V. Korah at (1976) 92 L.Q.R. 42.

One variety of clause to which effect has been given is a "conclusive evidence" clause (see below, p. 798). Then the courts may hold that Parliament has entrusted a matter exclusively to another tribunal (above, p. 700). Finally, the courts may refuse a particular remedy in the exercise of their discretion where an alternative remedy is available (see above, pp. 687–689).

One limiting factor is that statutory ouster clauses of whatever kind cannot be relied on to defeat actions against the state relying on community law: P. Oliver, (1987) 50 M.L.R. 881, 897–898, citing Case 224/84 *Johnston v. Chief Constable of the Royal Ulster Constabulary* [1986] I-E.C.R. 1651; [1986] 3 C.M.L.R. 240; [1987] Q.B. 129, which concerned a "conclusive evidence" certificate under Art. 53(2) of the Sex Discrimination (Northern Ireland) Order 1976.

R. v. MEDICAL APPEAL TRIBUNAL, ex p. GILMORE

[1957] 1 Q.B. 574; [1957] 2 W.L.R. 498; 101 S.J. 248; *sub nom. Re Gilmore's Application* [1957] 1 All E.R. 796 (Court of Appeal)

In 1936 the applicant, a colliery pick sharpener, sustained an injury to both eyes while at work, his right eye being rendered almost blind. In March 1955, he suffered a further injury at work, by which the condition of his left eye was so severely aggravated that in the result he was almost totally blind. On his claim for disablement benefit under the National Insurance (Industrial Injuries) Act 1946, two medical boards provisionally assessed the degree of disablement at 100 per cent; but a third board made no award. The claimant appealed to a medical appeal tribunal which had before it and incorporated in its award an extract from a specialist's report setting out the facts as to the state of both eyes; but in making its award the tribunal assessed the aggravation at only 20 per cent, showing thereby that they had failed to assess in accordance with regulation 2(5) of the National Insurance (Industrial Injuries) (Benefit) Regulations 1948 (relating to industrial injuries to paired organs). If a one-eyed man should lose the sight of his remaining good eye in an industrial accident, this regulation required his disablement to be assessed as if the blindness in the bad eye were itself the result of losing the good eye (*i.e.* as 100 per cent disablement).

Section 36(3) of the National Insurance (Industrial Injuries) Act 1946, provided that "... any decision of a claim or question ... shall be final". The applicant applied for an order of certiorari to quash the decision of the tribunal on the ground that there was a manifest error of law on the face of the record.

The Divisional Court refused leave to apply for certiorari, and so the applicant moved the Court of Appeal *ex parte*, which granted his request. The court was of opinion that they ought to extend the usual time limit of six months because he had not been guilty of any delay in seeking redress, and that there was some ground for thinking that there was an error on the face of the record.

On February 12, 1957, the application came on for hearing in the Court of Appeal. After the case had been opened, counsel for the Ministry of Pensions and National Insurance and for the tribunal informed the court that he had carefully considered the matter with the responsible officers of the Ministry and, as a result, he conceded that the decision of the medical appeal tribunal of June 13, 1956, was erroneous in point of law; he added that the Ministry were in some difficulty because the chairman of the tribunal had died.

Despite that concession, the court of its own motion considered that as the application raised points of considerable importance, judgment should be reserved.

DENNING L.J.: [held, first, that the tribunal's decision was vitiated by an error of law on the face of the record.]

The second point is the effect of section 36(3) of the Act of 1946 which provides that "any decision of a claim or question ... shall be final". Do those words preclude the Court of Queen's Bench from issuing a certiorari to bring up the decision?

This is a question which we did not discuss in *R. v. Northumberland Compensation Appeal Tribunal, ex p. Shaw* [1952] 1 K.B. 338, because it did not there arise. It does arise here, and on looking again into the old books I find it very well settled that the remedy by certiorari is never to be taken away by any statute except by the most clear and explicit words. The word "final" is not enough. That only means "without appeal". It does not mean "without recourse to certiorari". It makes the decision final on the facts, but not final on the law. Notwithstanding that the decision is by a statute made "final", certiorari can still issue for excess of jurisdiction or for error of law on the face of the record. ...

[His Lordship reviewed the authorities.]

In my opinion, therefore, notwithstanding the fact that the statute says that the decision of the medical appeal tribunal is to be final, it is open to this court to issue a certiorari to quash it for error of law on the face of the record. It would seem to follow that a decision of the national insurance and industrial insurance commissioners is also subject to supervision by certiorari (a point left open by the Divisional Court in *R. v. National Insurance Commissioner, ex p. Timmis* [1955] 1 Q.B. 139); but they are so well versed in the law and deservedly held in such high regard that it will be rare that they fall into error such as to need correction.

In contrast to the word "final" I would like to say a word about the old statutes which used in express words to take away the remedy by certiorari by saying that the decision of the tribunal "shall not be removed by certiorari". Those statutes were passed chiefly between 1680 and 1848, in the days when the courts used certiorari too freely and quashed decisions for technical defects of form. In stopping this abuse the statutes proved very beneficial, but the court never allowed those statutes to be used as a cover for wrongdoing by tribunals. If tribunals were to be at liberty to exceed their jurisdiction without any check by the courts, the rule of law would be at an end. Despite express words taking away certiorari, therefore, it was held that certiorari would still lie if some of the members of the tribunal were disqualified from acting: see *R. v. Cheltenham Commissioners* (1841) 1 Q.B. 467, where Lord Denman C.J. said (*ibid.* at 474): "The statute cannot affect our right and duty to see justice executed." So, also, if the tribunal exceeded its jurisdiction: see *ex p. Bradlaugh* (1878) 3 Q.B.D. 509; or if its decision was obtained by fraud: see *R. v. Gillyard* (1848) 12 Q.B. 527, the courts would still grant certiorari. I do not pause to consider those cases further; for I am glad to notice that modern statutes never take away in express words the right to certiorari without substituting an analogous remedy. This is probably because the courts no longer use it to quash for technical defects but only in case of a substantial miscarriage of justice. Parliament nowadays more often uses the words "final" or "final and conclusive," or some such words which leave intact the control of the Queen's courts by certiorari. . . .

ROMER and PARKER L.JJ. delivered concurring judgments.

Notes

1. *Ex p. Gilmore* considers both "finality" and "no certiorari" clauses. As to the former, it has been held that it would not even prevent an appeal by case stated on a question that might otherwise be resolved by certiorari or a declaration (*Tehrani v. Rostron* [1972] 1 Q.B. 182). In *Pearlman v. Keepers and Governors of Harrow School* [1979] Q.B. 56, Lord Denning M.R. at 71 stated *obiter* that a finality clause would only exclude an appeal on the facts and not on a point of law. Eveleigh L.J. was inclined to agree on this point (at 79). Geoffrey Lane L.J. disagreed (at 74) and his view was subsequently endorsed by Lord Diplock and Lord Keith in *Re Racal Communications Ltd.* [1981] A.C. 374, 382. The House of Lords held in that case that a provision that a decision of a High Court judge shall not be appealable meant exactly that. On "no certiorari" clauses see further the *Pearlman* case, above, p. 229. Lord Denning M.R. held at 69 that the "no certiorari" clause (County Courts Act 1959, s.107) only applied to proceedings under the 1959 Act, *Pearlman* arising under the Housing Act 1974. Both Geoffrey Lane L.J. and Eveleigh L.J. treated the clause as applicable.

2. A "finality" clause may help a court decide that no duty of care in negligence is owed: see *Jones v. Department of Employment* [1989] Q.B. 1.

3. "Conclusive evidence" clauses were considered by the Court of Appeal in *R. v. Registrar of Companies, ex p. Central Bank of India* [1986] Q.B. 1114. The Registrar of Companies registered a charge under section 95(1) of the Companies Act 1948. The Court of Appeal held, on an application for judicial review, that the registrar, in deciding to register the charge in default of delivery of the original documents by which the

charge was created or evidenced, had erred in law. However, section 98(2) of the 1948 Act provided that the registrar's certificate:

"shall be conclusive evidence that the requirements of this Part of this Act as to registration have been complied with".

The court held that this precluded it from considering evidence adduced to show non-compliance with the requirements for registration and, accordingly, from quashing the registration. This form of clause, although in a pre-1958 statute, was not negatived by section 14 of the Tribunals and Inquiries Act 1971 (now section 12 of the 1992 Act, above, p. 54). Lawton L.J. was of the view that the Registrar had acted in excess of jurisdiction; Slade and Dillon L.JJ. that he had made an error of law within jurisdiction. Slade L.J. at 1175–1176 followed Lord Diplock's approach in *Re Racal Communications Ltd* (above p. 224), concluding that the presumption that administrative authorities, in accordance with *Anisminic*, cannot determine questions of law conclusively was here rebutted in view of s.98(2). His Lordship also noted that counsel for the Registrar accepted that s.98(2) did not bind the Crown, so there was nothing to prevent intervention by the Attorney-General. Moreover, the provisions might not apply where a purported certificate disclosed an error on its face (*per* Slade L.J. at 1177), or was procured by fraud (*per* Lawton L.J. at 1169, Dillon L.J. at 1183).

Ex p. Central Bank of India was followed in *R. v. Secretary of State for Foreign Affairs, ex p. Trawnik, The Times*, February 21, 1986. Section 40(3) of the Crown Proceedings Act 1947 provides that:

"A certificate of a Secretary of State: (*a*) to the effect that any alleged liability of the Crown arises otherwise than in respect of His Majesty's Government in the United Kingdom ... shall, for the purposes of this Act, be conclusive as to the matter so certified."

The applicant sought a judicial review of two certificates under s.40(3)(a) relating to the possible liability of the Crown in nuisance in respect of the establishment of a machine-gun range in West Berlin. The Court of Appeal held on a preliminary issue that evidence in contradiction of the terms of the certificates was inadmissible. May L.J. said that:

"As a matter of construction, the words 'shall ... be conclusive as to the matter so certified' in section 40(3)(a) are equivalent to a provision that the certificate shall be conclusive evidence of the matters certified, whether these be questions of fact or law or of mixed fact and law.

Such words do not preclude an application for judicial review of the certificate but such an application if based on the proposition that that which has been certified is so clearly wrong that the certificate must be a nullity, would be bound to fail because the evidence which counsel would wish to call to prove this very thing could not be adduced."

Emery and Smythe, p. 54, argue that this reasoning cannot be reconciled with *Anisminic*.

SMITH v. EAST ELLOE RURAL DISTRICT COUNCIL AND OTHERS

[1956] A.C. 736; [1956] 2 W.L.R. 888; 120 J.P. 263; 100 S.J. 282; [1956] 1 All E.R. 855; 54 L.G.R. 233; 6 P. & C.R. 102 (House of Lords)

[For earlier litigation concerning the dispute between S and the authorities, see p. 711.]

By paragraph 15(1) of Part IV of Schedule 1 to the Acquisition of Land (Authorisation Procedure) Act 1946: "If any person aggrieved by a compulsory purchase order desires to question the validity thereof ... on the ground that the authorisation of a compulsory purchase thereby granted is not empowered to be granted under this Act ... he may, within six weeks from the date on which notice of the confirmation or making of the order ... is first published ... make an application to the High Court...."

By paragraph 16: "Subject to the provisions of the last foregoing paragraph, a compulsory purchase order ... shall not ... be questioned in any legal proceedings whatsoever...."

On November 29, 1948, the Minister of Health confirmed a compulsory purchase order in respect of 8½ acres of land owned by Kathleen Rose Smith, following a public local inquiry. A notice to treat and a notice of entry were duly served on the appellant, and in due course the compulsory purchase price for the said house and land was fixed by the Lands Tribunal at £3,000. The respondent council caused a firm of builders to demolish the house and to erect on its site and on the said land a number of houses.

On July 6, 1954, the appellant issued a writ, claiming:

1. Against the East Elloe Rural District Council: (a) Damages for trespass to the plaintiff's land; (b) An injunction restraining them by their officers, servants and agents and each and every one of them from trespassing upon the aforesaid land and premises; (c) A declaration that the compulsory purchase order was wrongfully made and in bad faith.

2. Against the Ministry of Health: A declaration that the compulsory purchase order was wrongfully confirmed and in bad faith.

3. Against the respondent, J.C. Pywell: A declaration that he knowingly acted wrongfully and in bad faith in procuring the said order and confirmation of the same.

4. Against the Ministry of Housing and Local Government: As having taken over the functions of the [Ministry of Health] a declaration that the said compulsory purchase order and confirmation of the same are in bad faith.

5. Further and other relief.

6. Damages.

7. Costs.

The writ was set aside by Master Clayton on the ground that the court had no jurisdiction to grant the relief sought as the result of paragraph 16 of Part IV of Schedule 1 to the 1946 Act. S appealed unsuccessfully to Havers J., the Court of Appeal. The House of Lords allowed an appeal as regards the claim under paragraph 3 and related matters only.

LORD MORTON OF HENRYTON: My Lords, I think there can be no doubt that the respondents were never entitled to have the writ set aside so far as it claims relief against the respondent Pywell. The relief claimed by paragraph 3 of the writ and the further relief claimed by paragraphs 5, 6 and 7, in so far as that relief affects the respondent Pywell, in no way call in question the validity of the compulsory purchase order of August 26, 1948, or of its confirmation. It is simply alleged, as against Mr Pywell personally, that he knowingly acted wrongfully and in bad faith in procuring the order and the confirmation thereof. It is equally clear that claims 1, 2 and 4 do put in issue the validity of the order....

Mr Roy Wilson, for the appellant, puts forward propositions which I summarize as follows: (1) Paragraph 15 gives no opportunity to a person aggrieved to question the validity of a compulsory purchase order on the ground that it was made or confirmed in bad faith. (2) Although, *prima facie*, paragraph 16 excludes the jurisdiction of the court in all cases, subject only to the provision of paragraph 15, it is inconceivable that the legislature can have intended wholly to exclude all courts from hearing and determining an allegation that such an order was made in bad faith. (3) Therefore, paragraph 16 should be read as applying only to an order or a certificate made in good faith.... The Attorney-General, on behalf of the respondents, contends that the opportunity of objection given by paragraph 15 extends to cases where bad faith is alleged, but, whether or not this is so, if the person aggrieved fails to apply to the court within the six weeks' period there mentioned, the jurisdiction of the court is completely ousted by paragraph 16, the terms whereof are unambiguous.

My Lords, I accept Mr Wilson's first proposition. I cannot construe paragraph 15 as covering a case in which all the requirements expressly laid down by statute have been observed, but the person aggrieved has discovered that in carrying out the steps laid down by statute the authority has been actuated by improper motives. It is to be observed that both in the earlier and in the later part of paragraph 15 there is only one ground upon which the validity of the order can be questioned.... These words seem to me to restrict the complainant to alleging non-compliance with some requirement to be found in the relevant statutes or regulations. If paragraph 15 had been intended to apply to cases of bad faith, surely the restrictive words "on the ground that", etc., would have been left out in both parts....

My Lords, having accepted Mr Wilson's first proposition, ... I reject his second and third propositions, on the short and simple ground that the words of paragraph 16 are clear, and deprive all courts of any jurisdiction to try the issues raised by paragraphs 1, 2 and 4 of the writ, whereby the appellant undoubtedly seeks to question the validity of the order of August 26, 1948.

Turning first to counsel's second proposition, it does not seem to me inconceivable, though it does seem surprising, that the legislature should have intended to make it impossible for anyone to question in any court the validity of a compulsory purchase order on the ground that it was made in bad faith. It may have been thought that the procedure which has to be followed before such an order is made and confirmed affords sufficient opportunity for allegations of bad faith to be ventilated, and it may have been thought essential, if building schemes were to be carried out, that persons alleging bad faith in the making of an order after the order has been made, should be limited to claims sounding in damages against the persons who, in bad faith, caused or procured the order to be made. The present action started nearly six years after the order now in question was made and confirmed, and illustrates the difficulty which might arise if no such limit were imposed, since houses have already been erected on the land which was the subject of the order....

LORD REID: [held, first, that allegations of misuse of power under the *Wednesbury* principles, whether in good faith or bad faith, fell outside paragraph 15, which only applied to (1) informality of procedure where, for example, some essential step in procedure had been omitted and (2) *ultra vires* in the sense that what was authorised by the order went beyond what was authorised by the enabling Act. ...]

I turn to paragraph 16. Not only does it prevent recourse to the court after six weeks in cases to which paragraph 15 does apply, but, on the face of it, it prevents any recourse to the court at all in cases to which paragraph 15 does not apply. It uses words which are general and emphatic, and, to my mind, the question is whether this use of general words necessarily leads to the conclusion that the jurisdiction of the court is entirely excluded in all cases of misuse of powers in *mala fide* where those acting in *mala fide* have been careful to see that the procedure was in order and the authority granted by the order was within the scope of the Act under which it was made. A person deliberately acting in bad faith would naturally be careful to do this. In my judgment, paragraph 16 is clearly intended to exclude, and does exclude entirely, all cases of misuse of power in *bona fide*. But does it also exclude the small minority of cases where deliberate dishonesty, corruption or malice is involved? In every class of case that I can think of the courts have always held that general words are not to be read as enabling a deliberate wrongdoer to take advantage of his own dishonesty. Are the principles of statutory construction so rigid that these general words must be so read here? Of course, if there were any other indications in the statute of such an intention beyond the mere generality of the words that would be conclusive: but I can find none.

There are many cases where general words in a statute are given a limited meaning. That is done, not only when there is something in the statute itself which requires it, but also where to give general words their apparent meaning would lead to conflict with some fundamental principle. Where there is ample scope for the words to operate without any such conflict it may very well be that the draftsman did not have in mind and Parliament did not realize that the words were so wide that in some few cases they could operate to subvert a fundamental principle.... So, general words by themselves do not bind the Crown, they are limited so as not to conflict with international law, they are commonly read so as to avoid retrospective infringement of rights, and it appears to me that they can equally well be read so as not to deprive the court of jurisdiction where bad faith is involved.... I think that there is still room for reason to point out that the general words in this case must be limited so as to accord with the principle, of which Parliament cannot have been ignorant, that a wrongdoer cannot rely on general words to avoid the consequences of his own dishonesty. As I have said, we must take this case on the footing that the appellant might allege deliberate dishonesty of the grossest kind.

It is said that Parliament may have intended that even cases of gross dishonesty should be excluded from redress because otherwise it would be embarrassing to deal with allegations of this kind after a long interval, and, if the case were proved, a local authority and ultimately the ratepayers might be involved in grievous loss. I am not entirely satisfied that the law is powerless to deal justly with such a situation. But, even if that were a possible consequence, I would hesitate to attribute to Parliament the view that considerations of that kind justify hushing up a scandal.

In my judgment this appeal should be allowed.

LORD RADCLIFFE: ... I should myself read the words of paragraph 15(1), "on the ground that the authorization of a compulsory purchase thereby granted is not empowered to be granted under this Act", as covering any case in which the complainant sought to say that the order in question did not carry the statutory authority which it purported to. In other words, I should regard a challenge to the order on the ground that it had not been made in good faith as within the purview of paragraph 15. After all, the point which concerns the aggrieved person is the same in all cases: an order has been made constituting an ostensible exercise of statutory power and his purpose in resorting to the courts is to show that there is no statutory authority behind the order. I do not see any need to pick and choose among the different reasons which may support the plea that the authorization ostensibly granted does not carry the powers of the Act. But, even if I did not think that an order could be questioned under paragraph 15 on the ground that it had been exercised in bad faith, and I thought, therefore, that the statutory code did not allow for an order being questioned on this ground at all, I should still think that paragraph 16 concluded the matter, and that it did not leave to the courts any surviving jurisdiction.

The appellant's argument for an exception rests on certain general reflections which do not seem to me to make up into any legal principle of construction as applied to an Act of Parliament. It is said that the six weeks which are all the grace that, on any view, paragraph 15 allows an aggrieved person for his taking action, are pitifully inadequate as an allowance of time when bad faith, which may involve concealment or deception, is thought to be present. And indeed they are. Further, it is said that it would be an outrageous thing if a person who by ordinary legal principles would have a right to upset an order affecting him were to be precluded from coming to the courts for his right, either absolutely or after six weeks, when the order is claimed by him to have been tainted by bad faith. And perhaps it is. But these reflections seem to me to be such as must or should have occurred to Parliament when it enacted paragraph 16. They are not reflections which are capable of determining the construction of the Act once it has been passed, unless there is something that one can lay hold of in the context of the Act which justifies the introduction of the exception sought for. Merely to say that Parliament cannot be presumed to have intended to bring about a consequence which many people might think to be unjust is not, in my opinion a principle of construction for this purpose. In point of fact, whatever innocence of view may have been allowable to the lawyers of the eighteenth and nineteenth centuries, the twentieth-century lawyer is entitled to few assumptions in this field. It is not open to him to ignore the fact that the legislature has often shown indifference to the assertion of rights which courts of law have been accustomed to recognize and enforce, and that it has often excluded the authority of courts of law in favour of other preferred tribunals.

At one time the argument as shaped into the form of saying that an order made in bad faith was in law a nullity and that, consequently, all references to compulsory purchase orders in paragraphs 15 and 16 must be treated as references to such orders only as had been made in good faith. But this argument is in reality a play on the meaning of the word nullity. An order, even if not made in good faith, is still an act capable of legal consequences. It bears no brand of invalidity upon its forehead. Unless the necessary proceedings are taken at law to establish the cause of invalidity and to get it quashed or otherwise upset, it will remain as effective for its ostensible purpose as the most impeccable of orders. And that brings us back to the question that determines this case: Has Parliament allowed the necessary proceedings to be taken?

I am afraid that I have searched in vain for a principle of construction as applied to Acts of Parliament which would enable the appellant to succeed.

On the other hand, it is difficult not to recall in the respondents' favour the dictum of Bacon: "*Non est interpretatio, sed divinatio, quae recedit a litera.*"

VISCOUNT SIMONDS and LORD RADCLIFFE were in favour of allowing the appeal to the extent proposed by LORD MORTON. LORD SOMERWELL was in favour of allowing the appeal.

Appeal allowed in part.

Notes

1. Over the two issues as to the scope of paragraphs 15 and 16 respectively, the House divided three ways. Lord Morton preferred the narrow interpretation of para. 15 and held that para. 16 barred all proceedings even in cases of bad faith. Lord Radcliffe held and Viscount Simonds "inclined to the opinion" that para. 15 extended to cover cases of misuse of power, but agreed with Lord Morton on the effect of para. 16. Lords Reid and Somerwell agreed with Lord Morton as to the effect of para. 15 but were prepared to recognise an exception to the effect of para. 16 in cases of deliberate dishonesty or fraud. Lord Morton's position that questions of bad faith could be raised *neither* under para. 15 *nor* in any other proceedings is difficult to defend. In any event, the courts have subsequently preferred Lord Radcliffe's approach to the interpretation of the grounds of challenge available under a statutory *ultra vires* clause (see above, pp. 557–558).

2. See J.S. Hall (1957) 21 Conv. (N.S.) 455; *Smith v. Pywell, The Times,* April 28, 1959.

R. v. SECRETARY OF STATE FOR THE ENVIRONMENT, ex p. OSTLER

[1976] 3 W.L.R. 288; [1977] Q.B. 122; [1976] 3 All E.R. 90; (1976) 75 L.G.R. 45; 120 S.J. 332 (Court of Appeal)

The applicant, a corn merchant with business premises in the market square of Boston, Lincolnshire, applied in December 1975 to the Queen's Bench Divisional Court for leave to apply for an order of certiorari to quash a stopping-up order made under the Highways Act 1959 and a compulsory purchase order made under the Acquisition of Land (Authorisation Procedure) Act 1946. Those orders were made to carry out a road scheme to relieve traffic congestion in the town centre. Both orders had been confirmed by the Secretary of State for the Environment on May 8, 1974. In support of his application he claimed that he had not objected to the original proposals when they were published in 1972 because they appeared not to touch his premises and for that reason had not attended the first public inquiry in September 1973, but that after the orders had been confirmed a supplementary proposed order had been published which would, if carried out, affect his premises; and that he had objected to the supplementary proposals at a further public inquiry in December 1974 but had not been allowed to question the original orders confirmed in May on the ground that they had become final. He alleged that after the supplementary order had been confirmed, it had come to his knowledge that before the 1973 inquiry there had been a secret agreement between an officer of the Department and local wine merchants who were intending to object to the original proposals, guaranteeing that if they were confirmed, the supplementary proposal would be made; that the wine merchants' objections had thereupon been withdrawn; that if he had known of the secret agreement he would have objected before the first proposals were confirmed; and that by reason of his having been deprived of the opportunity to object, the confirmed orders were invalidated by want of natural justice and bad faith verging on fraud.

A preliminary objection was taken on behalf of the Secretary of State that, whatever the facts, any attack on the validity of the confirmed orders was barred in any legal proceedings whatever because the prescribed six-week period under paragraph 2 of Schedule 2 to the Act of 1959 and paragraph 15 of Schedule 1 to the Act of 1946 had expired; that there was binding House of Lords authority (*Smith v. East Elloe R.D.C.*, above, p. 799) to that effect on the provisions of the Act of 1946 (which were in terms identical with those of the Act of 1959) and that the application for certiorari should not be permitted to proceed. The Divisional Court, after considering whether speeches in the House of Lords in the *Anisminic* case (above, p. 210) had undermined the earlier authority, adjourned the application to go into the merits but later granted the Secretary of State leave to appeal on the preliminary point of law.

LORD DENNING M.R.: ... Now it is quite clear that if Mr Ostler had come within six weeks, his complaint could and would have been considered by the court....

[His Lordship read paragraph 2 of Schedule 2 to the 1959 Act.]

That is a familiar clause which appears in many statutes or schedules to them. Although the words appear to restrict the clause to cases of *ultra vires* or non-compliance with regulations, nevertheless the courts have interpreted them so as to cover cases of bad faith. On this point the view of Lord Radcliffe has been accepted (which he expressed in *Smith v. East Elloe Rural District Council* [1956] A.C. 736, 769). In addition this court has held that under this clause a person aggrieved—who comes within six weeks—can upset a scheme or order if the Minister has taken into account considerations which he ought not to have done, or has failed to take into account considerations which he ought to have done, or has come to his decision without any evidence to support it, or has made a decision which no reasonable person could make. It was so held in *Ashbridge Investments Ltd v. Minister of Housing and Local Government* [1965] 1 W.L.R. 1320, and the Minister did not dispute it. It has been repeatedly followed in this court ever since and never disputed by any Minister. So it is the accepted interpretation. But the person aggrieved must come within six weeks. That time limit has always been applied....

[His Lordship then read paragraph 4.]

So those are the strong words, "shall not ... be questioned in any legal proceedings whatever ...".

[His Lordship summarised *Smith v. East Elloe R.D.C.*, and the *Anisminic* case.]

Some of their Lordships seem to have thrown doubt on *Smith v. East Elloe Rural District Council* [1956] A.C. 736: see what Lord Reid said at [1969] 2 A.C. 147, 170–171. But others thought it could be explained on the ground on which Browne J. explained it. Lord Pearce said, at 201: "I agree with Browne J. that it is not a compelling authority in the present case"; and Lord Wilberforce said, at 208: "After the admirable analysis of the authorities made by Browne J. ... no elaborate discussion of authority is needed."

I turn therefore to the judgment of Browne J. His judgment is appended as a note to the case at 223 *et seq.* He put *Smith v. East Elloe Rural District Council*, at 224, as one of the "cases in which the inferior tribunal has been guilty of bias, or has acted in bad faith, or has disregarded the principles of natural justice". He said of those cases:

"It is not necessary to decide it for the purposes of this case, but I am inclined to think that such decisions are not nullities but are good until quashed (*cf.* the decision of the majority of the House of Lords in *Smith v. East Elloe Rural District Council* [1956] A.C. 736, that a decision made in bad faith cannot be challenged on the ground that it was made beyond powers and Lord Radcliffe's dissenting speech ...)."

In these circumstances, I think that *Smith v. East Elloe Rural District Council* must still be regarded as good and binding on this court. It is readily to be distinguished from the *Anisminic* case [1969] 2 A.C. 147. The points of difference are these:

First, in the *Anisminic* case the Act ousted the jurisdiction of the court altogether. It precluded the court from entertaining any complaint at any time about the determination. Whereas in the *East Elloe* case the statutory provision has given the court jurisdiction to inquire into complaints so long as the applicant comes within six weeks. The provision is more in the nature of a limitation period than of a complete ouster. That distinction is drawn by Professor Wade, *Administrative Law* (2nd ed., 1967), pp. 152–153, and by the late Professor S.A. de Smith in the latest edition of *Halsbury's Laws of England* (4th ed., 1973), vol. 1, para. 22, note 14.

Second, in the *Anisminic* case, the House was considering a determination by a truly judicial body, the Foreign Compensation Tribunal, whereas in the *East Elloe* case the House was considering an order which was very much in the nature of an administrative decision. That is a distinction which Lord Reid himself drew in *Ridge v. Baldwin* [1964] A.C. 40, 72. There is a great difference between the two. In making a judicial decision, the tribunal considers the rights of the parties without regard to the public interest. But in an administrative decision (such as a compulsory purchase order) the public interest plays an important part. The question is, to what extent are private interests to be subordinated to the public interest.

Third, in the *Anisminic* case, the House had to consider the actual determination of the tribunal, whereas in the *Smith v. East Elloe* case the House had to consider the validity of the process by which the decision was reached.

So *Smith v. East Elloe Rural District Council* [1956] A.C. 736 must still be regarded as the law in regard to this provision we have to consider here. I would add this: if this order were to be upset for want of good faith or for lack of natural justice, it would not to my mind be a nullity or void from the beginning. It would only be voidable. And as such, if it should be challenged promptly before much has been done under it, as Lord Radcliffe put it forcibly in *Smith v. East Elloe Rural District Council* [1956] A.C. 736, 769–770.

[His Lordship read the passage: "But this argument is in reality a play on the meaning of the word nullity.... Has Parliament allowed the necessary proceedings to be taken?"]

The answer which he gave was "No". That answer binds us in this court today.

Since the *Anisminic* case the court has considered the position in *Routh v. Reading Corporation*, December 2, 1970, Bar Library Transcript No. 472 of 1970. Salmon L.J., supported by Karminski and Cairns L.JJ., held that *Smith v. East Elloe Rural District Council* was of good authority, even after the *Anisminic* case. In Scotland, too, it has been applied, in *Hamilton v. Secretary of State for Scotland*, 1972 S.L.T. 233.

Looking at it broadly, it séems to me that the policy underlying the statute is that when a compulsory purchase order has been made, then if it has been wrongly obtained or made, a person aggrieved should have a remedy. But he must come promptly. He must come within six weeks. If he does so, the court can and will entertain his complaint. But if the six weeks expire without any application being made, the court cannot entertain it afterwards. The reason is because, as soon as that time has elapsed, the authority will take steps to acquire property, demolish it and so forth. The public interest demands that they should be safe in doing so. Take this very case. The inquiry was held in 1973. The orders made early in 1974. Much work has already been done under them. It would be contrary to the public interest that the demolition should be held up or delayed by further evidence or inquiries. I think we are bound by *Smith v. East Elloe Rural District Council* [1956] A.C. 736 to hold that Mr Ostler is barred by the statute from now questioning these orders. He ought to be stopped àt this moment. I would allow the appeal accordingly.

GOFF L.J.: ... In my judgment, in *Smith v. East Elloe Rural District Council* the majority did definitely decide that those statutory provisions preclude the order from being challenged after the statutory period allowed, then by paragraph 15, and now by paragraph 2, and we are bound by that unless *Anisminic Ltd v. Foreign Compensation Commission* [1969] 2 A.C. 147 has to cut across it that we are relieved from the duty of following *Smith v. East Elloe Rural District Council* and, indeed, bound not to follow it.

That raises a number of problems. With all respect to Lord Denning M.R. and Professor Wade, I do myself find difficulty in distinguishing *Anisminic* on the ground that in that case there was an absolute prohibition against recourse to the court, whereas in the present case there is a qualified power for a limited period, because the majority in the *Smith* case said either that fraud did not come within paragraph 15, so that, in effect, it was an absolute ouster, or that it made no difference to the construction if it did.

Nevertheless, it seems to me that the *Anisminic* case is distinguishable on two grounds. First, the suggestion made by Lord Pearce [1969] 2 A.C. 147, 201, that *Anisminic* dealt with a judicial decision, and an administrative or executive decision might be different. I think it is. It is true that the Minister has been said to be acting in a quasi judicial capacity, but he is nevertheless conducting an administrative or executive matter, where questions of policy enter into and must influence his decision.

I would refer in support of that to a passage from the speech of Lord Reid in the well-known case of *Ridge v. Baldwin* [1964] A.C. 40, 72. I need not read it. It sets out what I have been saying.

Where one is dealing with a matter of that character and where, as Lord Denning M.R. has pointed out, the order is one which must be acted upon promptly, it is, I think, easier for the courts to construe Parliament as meaning exactly what it said—that the matter cannot be questioned in any court, subject to the right given by paragraph 2, where applicable, and where application is made in due time—than where, as in *Anisminic*, one is dealing with a statute setting up a judicial tribunal and defining its powers and the question is whether it has acted within them. I think that is supported by the passage in the speech of Lord Reid in the *Anisminic* case [1969] 2 A.C. 147, 170, where he said:

"But I do not think that it is necessary or even reasonable to construe the word 'determination' as including everything which purports to be a determination but which is in fact no determination at all."

The second ground of distinction is that the ratio in the *Anisminic* case was that the House was dealing simply with a question of jurisdiction, and not a case where the order is made within jurisdiction, but it is attacked on the ground of fraud or *mala fides*. There are, I am fully conscious, difficulties in the way of that distinction, because Lord Somervell of Harrow in *Smith v. East Elloe Rural District Council* [1956] A.C. 736, 771, in his dissenting speech, said that fraud does not make the order voidable but a nullity. Lord Reid said the same in the *Anisminic* case [1969] 2 A.C. 147, 170; and at 199 Lord Pearce equated want of natural justice with lack of jurisdiction.

Nevertheless, despite those difficulties, I think there is a real distinction between the case with which the House was dealing in *Anisminic* and the case of *Smith v. East Elloe Rural District Council* on that ground, that in the one case the determination was a purported determination only, because the tribunal, however eminent, having misconceived the effect of the statute, acted outside its jurisdiction, and indeed without any jurisdiction at all, whereas here one is dealing with an actual decision made within jurisdiction though sought to be challenged.

It cannot be gainsaid that some of the speeches in *Anisminic* do appear to cast doubts upon the correctness of the decision in *Smith v. East Elloe Rural District Council*, but it certainly was not expressly overruled, nor did any of their lordships, as I see it, say that it was wrong. There are substantial differences, such as Lord Denning M.R. and I have indicated, between the two cases, and it seems to me that *Smith v. East Elloe Rural District Council* stands, is binding on this court, and is a decision directly in point. . . .

SHAW L.J. agreed with the reasons given by Lord Denning M.R.

Appeal allowed.

Notes

1. The House of Lords refused leave to appeal: [1977] 1 W.L.R. 258.

2. For discussions of the relationship between *Smith v. East Elloe R.D.C.* and the *Anisminic* case written before *Ostler* was decided, see K. Davies (1971) 35 Conv. (N.S.) 316; J.E. Trice [1973] J.P.L. 227; E. Young [1973] J.P.L. 221; J. Alder (1975) 38 M.L.R. 274.

3. For case notes on *Ostler*, see H.W.R. W[ade] (1977) 93 L.Q.R. 8; C.A. Whomersley [1977] C.L.J. 4; J. Alder [1976] J.P.L. 270; C. Harlow [1976] P.L. 304. For a more extended discussion see the debate between Alder and Gravells: J.E. Alder (1975) 38 M.L.R. 274 and (1980) 43 M.L.R. 670; N.P. Gravells (1978) 41 M.L.R. 383 and (1980) 43 M.L.R. 173. Alder argues that *Anisminic* and *Smith v. East Elloe R.D.C.* can be reconciled by a process of conceptual reasoning; Gravells that the *Anisminic* principle, "formulated in an entirely different factual context," could have no relevance to the treatment of time-limit clauses. See also L.H. Leigh, "Time Limit Clauses and Jurisdictional Error" [1980] P.L. 34.

4. *Anisminic* is the leading example of a case where a "shall not be questioned clause" has been held not to prevent judicial review of an *ultra vires* decision. Others include *Att.-Gen. v. Ryan* [1980] A.C. 718, where the Privy Council held that a Minister's refusal of an application for citizenship without a fair hearing could be challenged

notwithstanding a provision that such a decision "shall not be subject to appeal or review in any court" (followed in *R. v. Secretary of State for the Home Department, ex p. Mohammed Al Fayed* [1997] 1 All E.R. 228). *cf. South East Asia Fire Bricks Sdn Bhd v. Non-Metallic Mineral Products Manufacturing Employees Union* [1981] A.C. 363, where the company sought certiorari to quash a decision of the Malaysian Industrial Court that favoured the union for an error of law on the face of the record. The Privy Council held that this remedy was barred by a provision that read:

"Subject to this Act, an award of the Court shall be final and conclusive, and no award shall be challenged, appealed against, reviewed, quashed or called in question in any court of law."

Lord Fraser of Tullybelton stated that this result was achieved not by the finality clause (following *ex p. Gilmore*, above, p. 796), but by the provision that the award should not be "quashed" either alone or in conjunction with the words "shall not be questioned in any court of law". The error alleged here was an error of law within jurisdiction, the Privy Council rejecting the view that all errors of law went to jurisdiction (see further above, pp. 224 *et seq.*). (If that view were to be accepted, little if any effect is left to a "shall not be questioned clause":

"... [I]f every error is now to be jurisdictional, ouster clauses will have no sphere of operation at all, and the judicial attitude will be exposed as one of naked disobedience to Parliament" (H.W.R. W[ade] (1979) 95 L.Q.R. 163, 166).)

5. *Ex p. Ostler* was applied by Pill J. in *R. v. Secretary of State for the Environment, ex p. Kent* (1988) 57 P. & C.R. 431, where the applicant applied on February 11, 1988, for judicial review of the decision of a planning inspector dated November 12, 1987, allowing an appeal against a refusal of planning permission. His Lordship rejected an argument to the effect that the six-week time limit did not apply as the Secretary of State had not had jurisdiction to entertain the appeal under section 245 of the Town and Country Planning Act 1971 as the local authority's procedure of consultation had been flawed. An appeal to the Court of Appeal was dismissed: [1990] J.P.L. 124. Here, the applicant did not find out until after the six-week period that an application for planning permission had been made in respect of land near his home or had subsequently gone on appeal to the Secretary of State.

Ex p. Ostler was also applied in *Khan v. Newport Borough Council* [1991] C.O.D. 157, in respect of a tree preservation order. Staughton L.J. commented that it was not at first sight obvious why any short time limits should be necessary in the case of such an order, as opposed to a compulsory purchase order as in *ex p. Ostler*. Then, in *R. v. Cornwall County Council, ex p. Huntingdon* [1992] 3 All E.R. 566, the Divisional Court applied *ex p. Ostler* in rejecting an application for judicial review of an order under the Wildlife and Countryside Act 1981, s.53(2)(b). The court rejected an argument that the order here was "fundamentally invalid" whereas the orders in *Smith v. East Elloe R.D.C.* and *ex p. Ostler* were not; Mann L.J. expressed the view that there were no "degrees of invalidity". *Ex p. Ostler* was also applied by Pill J. in *R. v. Secretary of State for the Environment, ex p. Upton Brickworks Ltd.* [1992] C.O.D. 31 (order under the Wildlife and Countryside Act 1981, s.29); by McCullough J. in *R. v. Devon County Council, ex p. Isaac* [1992] C.O.D. 371 (modification order relating to a by-way under the 1981 Act, ss.53, 54); by Roch J. in *R. v. London Borough of Camden, ex p. Woolf* [1992] C.O.D. 456 (traffic management order under the Road Traffic Regulation Act 1984, ss.43, 45). The respective decisions of the Divisional Court and McCullough J. were upheld by the Court of Appeal in *R. v. Cornwall County Council, ex p. Huntingdon; R. v. Devon County Council, ex p. Isaac* [1994] 1 All E.R. 694.

6. Lord Denning writing extra-judicially recanted most of his arguments in *ex p. Ostler*, accepting that a breach of natural justice or bad faith renders a decision a

nullity, and expressing the view that the decisions should rest simply on the last paragraph of his judgment (*The Discipline of Law* (1979), pp. 108–109).

7. The Interception of Communications Act 1985, s.7(8), provides that the decisions of the tribunal set up under that Act to investigate complaints concerning interception of mail or telephone-tapping, "(including any decisions as to their jurisdiction) shall not be subject to appeal or liable to be questioned in any court." A similar provision appears in the Security Service Act 1989, s.5(4), and the Intelligence Services Act 1994, s.9(4) in respect of decisions of the Commissioner and Tribunal established by each Act.

Questions

1. Has *Smith v. East Elloe R.D.C.* been overruled by *Anisminic* or can it be distinguished as suggested by *Ostler*?

2. Is the distinction made in *Ostler* between "administrative" decisions (*East Elloe*) and "judicial ones" (*Anisminic*) supportable?

3. Why should a decision made on the basis of irrelevant considerations of personal animosity be protected because it may also have been influenced by policy considerations and can be called an "administrative" decision?

4. Is it possible to draft an exclusion clause that effectively excludes the jurisdiction of the courts to review a decision of an administrative agency in *all* circumstances? Consider the provisions summarised in note 7, above.

CHAPTER 14

DELEGATED LEGISLATION[1]

"PARLIAMENT and government would grind to a halt if there were not built into our constitution an adequate system of Executive legislation" (First Special Report from the Joint Committee on Statutory Instruments, 1977–1978 (1977–1978 H.C. 169), para. 37). In the early part of this century there was considerable debate about the constitutional propriety of the delegation by Parliament, particularly to the government, of powers to legislate. The Committee on Ministers' Powers (Cmd. 4060 (1932)) concluded (p. 58) that the delegation of legislative powers:

"is legitimate for certain purposes, within certain limits, and under certain safeguards. It is plain that it is in fact inevitable."

Various reasons were put forward for this conclusion (below, p. 805). The committee noted a number of criticisms of delegated legislation that had been voiced, but did not think that the evidence justified "an alarmist view of the constitutional situation" (p. 54). What was lacking was coherence and uniformity in operation. There were "real dangers incidental to delegated legislation" and "safeguards" were necessary. The Committee recommended that the existing Rules Publication Act 1893, which required certain categories of delegated legislation to be published, should be replaced by a more comprehensive measure. The many different forms in which an enabling statute might require delegated legislation to be laid before Parliament should be replaced by a standardised procedure. These two matters were addressed by the Statutory Instruments Act 1946 (below, p. 810). It was also recommended that each House of Parliament should set up a Standing Committee for the purpose of considering and reporting (a) on every Bill containing a proposal to confer law-making power on a Minister; and (b) on delegated legislation that was subject to a laying requirement. The House of Commons acted on recommendation (b) in 1944. The House of Lords continued to scrutinise delegated legislation that required the approval of the House under arrangements that had commenced in 1925. Following the recommendations of the Joint Committee on Delegated Legislation (The Brooke Committee Report, 1971–1972 H.L. 184, H.C. 475), these separate arrangements were replaced by a Joint Committee on Statutory Instruments (below, pp. 823–824). Continuing concern as to the adequacy of arrangements for scrutiny of delegated legislation have led to further institutional developments, with the establishment by the House of Lords of the Select Committee on the Scrutiny of Delegated Powers and by the House of Commons of the

---

[1] The making of delegated legislation is considered as part of the wider legislative process, including the making of statutes and European legislation, by D.R. Miers and A.C. Page, *Legislation* (2nd ed., 1990); S.H. Bailey and M.J. Gunn, *Smith and Bailey on the Modern English Legal System* (3rd ed., 1996), Chap. 5. For an unofficial but authoritative review, see *Making the Law: The Report of the Hansard Society Commission on the Legislative Process* (1993). Delegated legislation is also considered in the standard works on administrative law: *Craig*, Chap. 7; *Wade and Forsyth*, Chap. 22; and has been the subject of a recent review by the House of Commons Select Committee on Procedure: Fourth Report, 1995–1996 H.C. 152, *Delegated Legislation* (see below, p. 821).

Deregulation Committee. Indeed, a special procedure has been developed, including scrutiny by these committees, for deregulation orders made under Part I of the Deregulation and Contracting Out Act 1994, which may have the effect of modifying substantive provisions of Acts of Parliament. See below, pp. 832–833.

(A) THE NECESSITY FOR DELEGATION

REPORT OF THE COMMITTEE ON MINISTERS' POWERS

Cmd. 4060, pp. 51–52

Necessity for Delegation

11. We have already expressed the view that the system of delegated legislation is both legitimate and constitutionally desirable for certain purposes, within certain limits, and under certain safeguards. We proceed to set out briefly—mostly by way of recapitulation—the reasons which have led us to this conclusion:—

Pressure on Parliamentary time

(1) Pressure upon Parliamentary time is great. The more procedure and subordinate matters can be withdrawn from detailed Parliamentary discussion, the greater will be the time which Parliament can devote to the consideration of essential principles in legislation.

Technicality of subject matter

(2) The subject matter of modern legislation is very often of a technical nature. Apart from the broad principles involved, technical matters are difficult to include in a Bill, since they cannot be effectively discussed in Parliament....

Unforeseen contingencies

(3) If large and complex schemes of reform are to be given technical shape, it is difficult to work out the administrative machinery in time to insert in the Bill all the provisions required; it is impossible to foresee all the contingencies and local conditions for which provision must eventually be made....

Flexibility

(4) The practice, further, is valuable because it provides for a power of constant adaptation to unknown future conditions without the necessity of amending legislation. Flexibility is essential. The method of delegated

legislation permits of the rapid utilisation of experience, and enables the results of consultation with interests affected by the operation of new Acts to be translated into practice. In matters, for example, like mechanical road transport, where technical development is rapid, and often unforeseen, delegation is essential to meet the new positions which arise.

Opportunity for experiment

(5) The practice, again, permits of experiment being made and thus affords an opportunity, otherwise difficult to ensure, of utilising the lessons of experience. The advantage of this in matters, for instance, like town planning, is too obvious to require detailed emphasis.

Emergency powers

(6) In a modern State there are many occasions when there is a sudden need of legislative action. For many such needs delegated legislation is the only convenient or even possible remedy. No doubt, where there is time, on legislative issues of great magnitude, it is right that Parliament itself should either decide what the broad outlines of the legislation shall be, or at least indicate the general scope of the delegated powers which it considers are called for by the occasion.

Note
One of the members of the Committee, Miss Ellen Wilkinson, added a note (pp. 137–138) which commenced:

> "While agreeing generally with this report I would like to add a note regarding the tone of certain passages which rather give the impression that the delegating of legislation is a necessary evil, inevitable in the present state of pressure on parliamentary time, but nevertheless a tendency to be watched with misgiving and carefully safeguarded.
> I feel that in the conditions of the modern state, which not only has to undertake immense new social services, but which before long may be responsible for the greater part of the industrial and commercial activities of the country, the practice of Parliament delegating legislation and the power to make regulations, instead of being grudgingly conceded, ought to be widely extended, and new ways devised to facilitate the process."

She went on to argue that Parliament could only deal really effectively with the principle and general plan of proposed legislation. "The details should be left to the experts." In practice, the distinction between "principle" (for primary legislation) and "detail" (for delegated legislation) can be difficult to draw. (See, *e.g.* J.A.G. Griffith, "The Place of Parliament in the Legislative Process" (1951) 14 M.L.R. 279, 425). In more recent years the Joint Committee on Statutory Instruments (see below, pp. 830–831, 832) has expressed concern:

FIRST SPECIAL REPORT FROM THE JOINT COMMITTEE ON STATUTORY INSTRUMENTS 1995–1996

Report on Proceedings 1986–1996 (1995–1996 H.L. Paper 103, H.C. 582), pp. 3–4

General aspects of secondary legislation

Number of statutory instruments

4. In 1973, when the Committee was first established, 2,227 instruments came into force. In 1992 the annual total exceeded 3,000 for the first time and it has remained above 3,000 ever since. In 1995 it reached 3,345. The overall volume of statutory instruments has increased markedly over this period. In 1988 the total length of all instruments was 6,342 pages; by 1993, the last year for which figures are available, it had grown to 7,944 pages. Instruments registered in 1995 have yet to appear in bound volumes but take up approximately two feet, six inches of bookshelf.

5. The Committee does not consider all of these, local instruments not subject to any kind of parliamentary proceeding being outside its order of reference. It is difficult to compare figures for instruments considered by the Committee as parliamentary sessions vary so much in length. Nevertheless, table 2 below[2] demonstrates clearly that the number of instruments considered by the Committee has grown over the same period....

Scope of instruments

6. It is generally accepted that the nature of statutory instruments has also changed. Instruments have become both more complex and more far-reaching in scope. As the Committee argued in its submission to the Procedure Committee in 1985, "secondary legislation has increasingly been used, not just to implement the 'nuts and bolts' of policies laid down in primary legislation, but actually to *change* policies in ways that were sometimes not envisaged when the enabling primary legislation was passed".

7. Recognition of this concern was one of the factors which led to the establishment of the House of Lords Delegated Powers Scrutiny Committee in Session 1992–1993. That Committee has the responsibility of examining the powers in proposed new primary legislation which will allow the making of statutory instruments in the future. The Committee's work is intended to reduce the risk that instruments change policies in a way that Parliament had not envisaged and to ensure that Parliament has appropriate control over the more wide-ranging powers. We accept that the trend towards the pursuance of measures through secondary rather than primary legislation is probably irreversible but hope that the Delegated Powers Scrutiny Committee will continue to contribute towards more effective scrutiny under these changing circumstances.

---

[2] Omitted (ed.). In 1994–1995 the Joint Committee considered 1,666 instruments and reported 174; the Select Committee considered 174 and reported 2.

(B) The Forms of Delegated Legislation

REPORT FROM THE JOINT COMMITTEE ON DELEGATED LEGISLATION 1971–1972

(1971–1972 H.L. 184, H.C. 475) pp. x–xii

Delegated legislation:

6. In his memorandum of evidence to Your Committee, Counsel to Mr Speaker (Sir Robert Speed) has defined delegated legislation thus:—

(1) Delegated legislation covers every exercise of a power to legislate conferred by or under an Act of Parliament or which is given the force of law by virtue of an Act of Parliament. It can be expressed in a variety of forms:—
   (a) Measures passed by the General Synod of the Church of England.
   (b) Provisional orders confirmed by a Provisional Order Confirmation Act, including those made under the Private Legislation Procedure (Scotland) Act, 1936.
   (c) Orders in Council and regulations, orders, rules, schemes or other instruments made by a Minister or Government Department or Rule Committee or similar authority.
   (d) Orders, bye-laws or other instruments, made by public or local authorities (in some cases confirmed by the Privy Council, a Minister or a Government Department).

(2) In some cases the power to legislate may be conferred by legislation which is itself a piece of delegated legislation, *e.g.* an Order in Council.

(3) The documents by which a power of delegated legislation is exercised are, in the main, statutory instruments.

(4) The definition of statutory instruments varies according to whether the Act under which the instrument is made was passed before or after January 1, 1948, the date on which the Statutory Instruments Act 1946 [below, pp. 817–821] was brought into operation.

(5) In regard to post-1947 Acts, under section 1(1) of the Statutory Instruments Act 1946 every Order in Council made in exercise of a statutory power is a statutory instrument, and every instrument made by a Minister of the Crown in exercise of a statutory power is a statutory instrument if the Act conferring the power expressly so provides.

(6) As regards pre-1948 Acts, broadly speaking, every instrument made under an Act of Parliament—
   (i) by Her Majesty in Council, or
   (ii) by a Minister of the Crown, or
   (iii) relating to any court in the United Kingdom,
is a statutory instrument if it is of a legislative and not an executive character.

(7) Measures are not statutory instruments, although in some cases the Measure does apply the Statutory Instruments Act 1946 to the subordinate legislation made thereunder. Also, as a general rule, the instruments referred to in category 1(d) above are not statutory instruments.

(8) Statutory instruments are classified as local or general according to

their subject matter. Unless there are special reasons to the contrary, a statutory instrument which is in the nature of a local and personal or private Act is classified as local, and a statutory instrument which is in the nature of a public general Act is classified as general.

(9) The classification is done in the first place by the Minister responsible for the preparation of the Order in Council or the Minister by whom the instrument is made. He, when sending the instrument to the Queen's Printer, certifies it as local or general.

(10) There is a procedure under which a Committee composed of Officers of both Houses, called the Statutory Instruments Reference Committee, may determine any question referred to them regarding the classification of instruments as general or local....

Notes

1. A number of significant categories of subordinate legislation are not "statutory instruments". These include (1) the byelaws of local authorities, made under powers conferred by the Local Government Act 1972 and other statutes (see *Cross*, Chap. 6) and below, pp. 834–838; (2) special procedure orders (see S.H. Bailey and M.J. Gunn, *Smith and Bailey on the Modern English Legal System* (3rd ed., 1996), p. 267); Orders in Council made under the royal prerogative (*ibid.*, pp. 290–291).

2. Unlike primary legislation, which is almost invariably drafted by parliamentary counsel, statutory instruments made by Ministers are normally drafted by departmental lawyers (see Report of the Joint Committee on Delegated Legislation 1971–1972 (1971–1972 H.L. 184, H.C. 475), pp. 194 *et seq.*, Memorandum by the Civil Service Department on Departmental Procedures in Producing Delegated Legislation). The Joint Committee on Statutory Instruments (First Special Report on Proceedings 1986–1996, 1995–1996 H.L. Paper 103, H.C. 582), pp. 5–6, has drawn attention to complaints that regularly arise, including common drafting errors, and observed that "many of these problems could be avoided by closer attention to the guidelines set out in Statutory Instrument Practice" (and internal guidance document used by departments). The Hansard Society Commission rejected a proposal that responsibility for drafting be transferred to Parliamentary Counsel: departmental administrators and lawyers will be much more familiar with practicalities and details regarding the application of legislation; the timing of drafting of S.I.s is closely related to decisions as to commencement of the statutory provisions, which are departmental responsibilities; the present arrangements would more easily facilitate the increased direct consultation with interested bodies recommended by the Commission (*Making the Law*, p. 49).

3. Consultation with other public bodies and outside interest groups is an established feature of the process of making delegated legislation. An example of a statutory advisory body is the Council on Tribunals, which must be consulted before procedural rules are made for a large number of statutory tribunals (Tribunals and Inquiries Act 1992, s.8 and Schedule 1) (above, pp. 103–117). Another is the Social Security Advisory Committee set up by the Social Security Act 1980 to replace the National Insurance Advisory Committee and the Supplementary Benefits Commission (see N.J. Wikeley, *Ogus, Barendt and Wikeley's, The Law of Social Security* (4th ed., 1995) pp. 625–626). One of its functions is to comment on regulations concerning social security benefits other than industrial injuries benefits, war pensions and occupational pensions (for which there are separate bodies). Draft regulations must be sent for it to comment on unless it appears to the Secretary of State "that by reason of the urgency of the matter it is inexpedient so to refer them" or the Committee agrees (Social Security Administration Act 1992, s.173(1)); other exceptions are set out in Schedule 7, Part I, and temporary exceptions are set out in section 173(5). If the Secretary of State subsequently lays the regulations before Parliament, he must lay, in addition, the Committee's report and a statement indicating the extent to which any recommendations

have been implemented, and in so far as effect has not been given to them, his reasons why not (1992 Act, s.174). Where draft regulations have not been submitted to the Committee because of urgency, the final regulations must be submitted as soon as practicable, unless the Committee agrees. Moreover, the Secretary of State may, in urgent cases where he has referred drafts to the Committee make the regulations before receiving the Committee's advice (1992 Act, s.173(3)). In these cases, the Secretary of State must lay the Committee's report before Parliament, with a statement of the extent (if any) to which he proposes to give effect to any recommendations (1992 Act, s.173(4)). See *R. v. Secretary of State for Social Services, ex p. Cotton, The Times,* December 14, 1985 (sufficient compliance with duty to consult where proposed amendments to regulations were summarised).

4. Where a statute requires consultation with particular interests, that is likely to be regarded by the courts as a mandatory procedural requirement, failure to comply with which will render the regulations *ultra vires*, at least as regards the interests not consulted (see above, pp. 407–413). In many areas of government decision-making, the courts have been prepared to imply into a statute a requirement of prior consultation with affected interests. This is one aspect of the requirements of "natural justice" and apply to those with a "legitimate expectation" of being consulted (see Chap. 8). However, the courts have been unwilling to imply such requirements prior to the making of delegated legislation. See *Bates v. Lord Hailsham of St Marylebone* [1972] 1 W.L.R. 1373 (above, p. 484).

(C) PRINTING, PUBLICATION AND LAYING BEFORE PARLIAMENT

These matters are regulated by the Statutory Instruments Act 1946 and the Statutory Instruments Regulations 1947.

STATUTORY INSTRUMENTS ACT 1946

Definition of "Statutory Instrument"

1.—(1) Where by this Act or any Act passed after the commencement of this Act to make, confirm or approve orders, rules, regulations or other subordinate legislation, is conferred on His Majesty in Council or on any Minister of the Crown then, if the power is expressed—

(a) in the case of a power conferred on His Majesty, to be exercisable by Order in Council;
(b) in the case of a power conferred on a Minister of the Crown, to be exercisable by statutory instrument,

any document by which that power is exercised shall be known as a "statutory instrument" and the provisions of this Act shall apply thereto accordingly.

(2) Where by any Act passed before the commencement of this Act power to make statutory rules within the meaning of the Rules Publication Act 1893, was conferred on any rule-making authority within the meaning of that Act, any document by which that power is exercised after the commencement of

this Act shall, save as is otherwise provided by regulations made under this Act, be known as a "statutory instrument" and the provisions of this Act shall apply thereto accordingly.

Numbering, printing, publication and citation

2.—(1) Immediately after the making of any statutory instrument, it shall be sent to the King's printer of Acts of Parliament and numbered in accordance with regulations made under this Act, and except in such cases as may be provided by any Act passed after the commencement of this Act or prescribed by regulations made under this Act, copies thereof shall as soon as possible be printed and sold by [or under the authority of] the King's printer of Acts of Parliament.

(2) Any statutory instrument may, without prejudice to any other mode of citation, be cited by the number given to it in accordance with the provisions of this section, and the calendar year.

Supplementary provisions as to publication

3.—(1) Regulations made for the purposes of this Act shall make provision for the publication by His Majesty's Stationery Office of lists showing the date upon which every statutory instrument printed and sold by [or under the authority of] the King's printer of Acts of Parliament was first issued by [or under the authority of] that office: and in any legal proceedings a copy of any list so published [. . .] shall be received in evidence as a true copy, and an entry therein shall be conclusive evidence of the date on which any statutory instrument was first issued by [or under the authority of] His Majesty's Stationery Office.

(2) In any proceedings against any person for an offence consisting of a contravention of any such statutory instrument, it shall be a defence to prove that the instrument had not been issued by [or under the authority of] His Majesty's Stationery Office at the date of the alleged contravention unless it is proved that at that date reasonable steps had been taken for the purpose of bringing the purport of the instrument to the notice of the public, or of persons likely to be affected by it, or of the person charged.

(3) Save as therein otherwise expressly provided, nothing in this section shall affect any enactment or rules of law relating to the time at which any statutory instrument comes into operation.

Statutory Instruments which are required to be laid before Parliament

4.—(1) Where by this Act or any Act passed after the commencement of this Act any statutory instrument is required to be laid before Parliament after being made, a copy of the instrument shall be laid before each House of Parliament and, subject as hereinafter provided, shall be so laid before the instrument comes into operation:

Provided that if it is essential that any such instrument should come into operation before copies thereof can be so laid as aforesaid, the instrument may be made so as to come into operation before it has been so laid; and where any statutory instrument comes into operation before it is laid before Parliament, notification shall forthwith be sent to the Lord Chancellor and to the Speaker of the House of Commons drawing attention to the fact that copies of the instrument have yet to be laid before Parliament and explaining why such copies were not so laid before the instrument came into operation.

(2) Every copy of any such statutory instrument sold by the King's printer of Acts of Parliament shall bear on the face thereof:

(a) a statement showing the date on which the statutory instrument came or will come into operation; and

(b) either a statement showing the date on which copies thereof were laid before Parliament or a statement that such copies are to be laid before Parliament.

(3) Where any Act passed before the date of the commencement of this Act contains provisions requiring that any Order in Council or other document made in exercise of any power conferred by that or any other Act be laid before Parliament after being made, any statutory instrument made in exercise of that power shall by virtue of this Act be laid before Parliament and the foregoing provisions of this section shall apply thereto accordingly in substitution for any such provisions as aforesaid contained in the Act passed before the said date.

Statutory Instruments which are subject to annulment by resolution of either House of Parliament

5.—(1) Where by this Act or any Act passed after the commencement of this Act, it is provided that any statutory instrument shall be subject to annulment in pursuance of resolution of either House of Parliament, the instrument shall be laid before Parliament after being made and the provisions of the last foregoing section shall apply thereto accordingly, and if either House within the period of forty days beginning with the day on which a copy thereof is laid before it, resolves that an Address be presented to His Majesty praying that the instrument be annulled, no further proceedings shall be taken thereunder after the date of the resolution, and His Majesty may by Order in Council revoke the instrument, so, however, that any such resolution and revocation shall be without prejudice to the validity of anything previously done under the instrument or to the making of a new statutory instrument.

(2) Where any Act passed before the date of the commencement of this Act contains provisions requiring that any Order in Council or other document made in exercise of any power conferred by that or any other Act shall be laid before Parliament after being made and shall cease to be in force or may be annulled, as the case may be, if within a specified period either House presents an address to His Majesty or passes a resolution to that effect, then, subject to the provisions of any Order in Council made under this Act, any statutory instrument made in exercise of the said power shall by virtue of this Act be subject to annulment in pursuance of a resolution of either House of Parliament and the provisions of the last foregoing subsection shall apply thereto

accordingly in substitution for any such provisions as aforesaid contained in the Act passed before the said date.

Statutory Instruments of which drafts are to be laid before Parliament

6.—(1) Where by this Act or any Act passed after the commencement of this Act it is provided that a draft of any statutory instrument shall be laid before Parliament, but the Act does not prohibit the making of the instrument without the approval of Parliament, then, in the case of an Order in Council the draft shall not be submitted to His Majesty in Council, and in any other case the statutory instrument shall not be made, until after the expiration of a period of forty days beginning with the day on which a copy of the draft is laid before each House of Parliament, or, if such copies are laid on different days, with the later of the two days, and if within that period either House resolves that the draft be not submitted to His Majesty or that the statutory instrument be not made, as the case may be, no further proceedings shall be taken thereon, but without prejudice to the laying before Parliament of a new draft.

(2) Where any Act passed before the date of the commencement of this Act contains provisions requiring that a draft of any Order in Council or other document to be made in exercise of any power conferred by that or any other Act shall be laid before Parliament before being submitted to His Majesty, or before being made, as the case may be, and that it shall not be so submitted or made if within a specified period either House presents an address to His Majesty or passes a resolution to that effect, then, subject to the provisions of any Order in Council made under this Act, a draft of any statutory instrument made in exercise of the said power shall by virtue of this Act be laid before Parliament and the provisions of the last foregoing subsection shall apply thereto accordingly in substitution for any such provisions as aforesaid contained in the Act passed before the said date.

Supplementary provisions as to ss.4, 5 and 6

7.—(1) In reckoning for the purposes of either of the last two foregoing sections any period of forty days, no account shall be taken of any time during which Parliament is dissolved or prorogued or during which both Houses are adjourned for more than four days.

(2) In relation to any instrument required by any Act, whether passed before or after the commencement of this Act, to be laid before the House of Commons only, the provisions of the last three foregoing sections shall have effect as if references to that House were therein substituted for references to Parliament and for references to either House and each House thereof.

(3) The provisions of sections four and five of this Act shall not apply to any statutory instrument being an order which is subject to special Parliamentary procedure, or to any other instrument which is required to be laid before Parliament, or before the House of Commons, for any period before it comes into operation....

Interpretation

11.—(1) For the purposes of this Act, any power to make, confirm or approve orders, rules, regulations or other subordinate legislation conferred on the Treasury, . . ., the Board of Trade or any other government department shall be deemed to be conferred on the Minister of the Crown in charge of that department.

(2) If any question arises whether any board, commissioners or other body on whom any such power as aforesaid is conferred are a government department within the meaning of this section, or what Minister of the Crown is in charge of them, that question shall be referred to and determined by [the Minister for the Civil Service].

Notes

1. The words "or under the authority of" were added to ss.2 and 3, and the words "purporting to bear the imprint of the King's printer" deleted from s.3 by the Statutory Instruments (Production and Sale) Act 1996. Indeed, s.1(1) of the 1996 Act provided that the 1946 Act "shall have effect and be taken always to have had effect" with these amendments. However, this "does not affect the operation of section 3(2) of that Act in relation to proceedings commenced before June 21, 1996" (1996 Act, s.1(2)). The changes were made to regularise the fact that the Queen's Printer had in practice contracted out the printing of S.I.s since at least 1965, failing to note that this did not comply with the statute. (Curiously, there was in fact provision for *statutes* to be printed under the authority of the Queen's Printer.) See H.C. Deb., Vol. 280, cols. 984–1009, July 3, 1996; H.L. Deb., Vol. 574, cols. 813–822, 1381–1393, July 16, 24, 1996.

2. The 1946 Act was of considerable importance in that it brought a measure of order into what had previously been a highly convoluted area, by providing one basic procedure (albeit with some variants) for the making of delegated legislation by central government. On the history of delegation, see C.K. Allen, *Law and Orders* (3rd ed., 1965), Chap. 2.

3. The Statutory Instruments Regulations 1947 (S.I. 1948 No. 1) were made under section 8 of the 1946 Act, which enables the Minister for the Civil Service, with the concurrence of the Lord Chancellor and the Speaker, to make regulations for the purposes of the Act. They were amended by S.I.s 1977 No. 641 and 1982 No. 1728. Regulation 2(3) provides that section 1(2) of the 1946 Act shall not apply to:

"(a) any document which, although of a legislative character, applies only to a named person or premises and is not required to be laid before or subject to confirmation or approval by Parliament or the House of Commons; or

(b) any Order in Council which, being an Order for which the Lord President of the Council is the responsible authority, confirms or approves subordinate legislation in the nature of a local and personal or private Act; or

(c) any such document as is mentioned in the Schedule to these Regulations."

Regulation 3 requires instruments received by the Queen's Printer to be allocated to the series of the calendar year in which they are made and numbered in that year consecutively as nearly as may be in the order in which they are received. However, instruments subject to the affirmative procedure or special parliamentary procedure are allocated as if made and received on the day they become operative. Regulation 4 provides that instruments are to be classified as local or general. Unless there are special reasons to the contrary, an instrument in the nature of a local or personal or private Act is to be classified as local, and one in the nature of a Public General Act as general. Instruments are to be certified as local or general by the responsible Minister, although the Reference Committee may direct a different classification. Regulations 5 to 8 provide for exemptions from requirements as to printing and sale for (1) local instruments, and general instruments certified by the responsible Minister "to be of a class of document which is or will be otherwise regularly printed as a series and made available to persons affected thereby" (reg. 5); (2) temporary instruments (reg. 6); (3) a schedule or other document identified by or referred to in an instrument which would otherwise be required to be included in the instrument as printed and sold, where this is "unnecessary or undesirable having regard to the nature of bulk of the document and to any other steps taken or to be taken for bringing its substance to the ntoice of the public" (reg. 7); (4) confidential instruments, where printing and sale of copies before the instrument comes into operation would be "contrary to the public interest" (reg. 8). In each case (except that of local instruments) the responsible Minister certifies that the exemption applies; in all cases the Reference Committee may direct otherwise. The responsible Minister may require the Queen's printer to comply with s.1(2) in respect of local instruments. Regulation 9 requires HMSO to publish a "Statutory Instruments Issue List" showing the serial number, short title and date of issue of each instrument issued by the office. Regulation 10 requires the publication of an "Annual Edition" comprising copies of all instruments issued (except spent and local instruments), an Annual Numerical and Issue List of Statutory Instruments, a classified list of local instruments, a table showing the effects on existing statutes and statutory instruments, and an index. Regulation 11 establishes a Statutory Instruments Reference Committee, consisting of two or more persons nominated by the Lord Chancellor and the Speaker. Its functions include that of determining any question arising as to numbering, printing or publication of instruments, their classification as general in the nature of a Public General Act or of a local and personal or private Act, and whether a document constitutes a "statutory rule" within the meaning of s.1(2) of the 1946 Act.

4. Section 9(1) of the 1946 Act enables the Queen in Council to apply the provisions of the 1946 Act to powers in pre-1948 statutes to confirm or approve subordinate legislation conferred on a Minister of the Crown, where the exercise of such a power would not constitute the making of a statutory rule within the 1893 Act and so would fall outside section 1(2). See the Statutory Instruments (Confirmatory Powers) Order 1947 (S.I. 1948 No. 2), which applied the Act to certain classes of subordinate legislation authorised by pre-1948 statutes. Most of the classes are no longer important, the legislation in question having since been repealed. One general class that is still provided for is where (1) a minister has power under a pre-1948 statute to confirm or approve subordinate legislation made by an authority which is not a "rule-making authority" under the 1893 Act, (2) the legislation is "of a legislative and not an executive character" and (3) the legislation is required to be laid before Parliament or the House of Commons.

5. Section 1 of the Laying of Documents Before Parliament (Interpretation) Act 1948 provides:

Meaning of references to laying before Parliament

"**1.**—(1) For the removal of doubt it is hereby declared that a reference in any Act of Parliament or subordinate legislation, whether passed or made before or after the passing of this Act, to the laying of any instrument, report, account or other document before either House of Parliament is, unless the contrary intention appears, to be construed as a reference to the taking, during the existence of a Parliament, of such action as is directed by virtue of any Standing Order, Sessional Order or other direction of that House for the time being in force to constitute the laying of that document before that House, or as is accepted by virtue of the practice of that House for the time being as constituting such laying, notwithstanding that the action so directed or accepted consists in part or wholly in action capable of being taken otherwise than at or during the time of a sitting of that House; and that a reference in any such Act or subordinate legislation to the laying of any instrument, report, account or other document before Parliament is, unless the contrary intention appears, to be construed accordingly as a reference (construed in accordance with the preceding declaration) to the laying of the document before each House of Parliament.

(2) It is hereby further declared that nothing in section four of the Statutory Instruments Act 1946, is to be taken as indicating an intention that any reference in that section to the laying of copies of certain statutory instruments as therein mentioned is to be construed otherwise than in accordance with the preceding declaration."

By Standing Order No. 141, the House of Commons has directed that the delivery of a copy of a statutory instrument to the Votes and Proceedings Office on any day during the existence of a Parliament shall be deemed to be laying before the House. In practice, it is normally then placed in the House of Commons Library. S.O. No. 141 does not, however, apply to instruments required to be laid for any period before it comes into operation. These can only be laid on sitting days. (See *Erskine May's Parliamentary Practice* (21st ed., 1989), pp. 543–545).

6. It is unclear whether a requirement that an instrument be laid before Parliament is "mandatory" or "directory" (*i.e.* whether laying is or is not a pre-condition to the validity of the instrument: see pp. 407 *et seq.*). The position appears to be that the matter depends on the exact wording and context of the particular case. There are authorities that suggest that laying requirements are directory: see *Bailey v. Williamson* (1873) L.R. 8 Q.B. 118; *Starey v. Graham* [1899] 1 Q.B. 406, 412; *Springer v. Doorly* (1950) L.R.B.G. 10 (West Indian Court of Appeal); A.I.L. Campbell [1983] P.L. 43; but see *de Smith, Woolf and Jowell*, p. 275, for the argument that they should be mandatory. In *R. v. Secretary of State for Social Services, ex p. Camden London Borough Council* (unreported, February 26, 1986), Macpherson J. held that the requirement in section 33(3)(c) of the Supplementary Benefits Act 1976 that certain social security regulations "shall not be made unless a draft of the regulations has been laid before Parliament and approved by a resolution of each House ..." was mandatory. Indeed, the words were "clear, strong and mandatory". On appeal, the Court of Appeal assumed this to be so without deciding the point: [1987] 1 W.L.R. 819. The other point that arose for consideration in this case was whether the laying requirement was applicable to a document referred to in the regulations. The regulations in question concerned allowances for board and lodgings and were designed to limit the maximum benefits payable according to areas, and to limit the time for which in any area those benefits would be payable to individual claimants. The regulations provided that in any particular case, the relevant amount was the amount shown as applicable for that area in a booklet entitled *Supplementary Benefit Maximum Amounts, Initial Periods and Board and Lodging Areas*, published by HMSO. The booklet was not laid before Parliament. Macpherson J. held that the booklet did not fall within the laying requirement, as it was not "part of" the statutory instrument, and was not a "document by which the Secretary of State exercises his actual powers" for the purposes of the 1946 Act. See A.I.L. Campbell [1987] P.L. 328.

R. v. SHEER METALCRAFT LTD

[1954] 1 Q.B. 586; [1954] 2 W.L.R. 777; [1954] 1 All E.R. 542
Streatfeild J.

Trial on indictment at Kingston-upon-Thames Assizes. The company, and its managing director were prosecuted for infringement of the Iron and Steel Prices Order 1951 (S.I. 1951 No. 252). The defendants argued that it was not a valid statutory instrument as its schedules, which set out maximum prices for different commodities of steel, had not been printed with the instrument by the Queen's Printer, as required by section 2(1) of the Statutory Instruments Act 1946 (above, p. 818), and the Minister had not certified under regulation 7 of the 1947 regulations (above, p. 822) that this was unnecessary. Streatfeild J. ruled on this submission.

STREATFEILD J.: ... [read sections 1, 2 and 3 of the 1946 Act (above pp. 817–818), and regulation 7 of the 1947 Regulations.]

There does not appear to be any definition of what is meant by "issue" [in section 3(1)] but presumably it does mean some act by the Queen's Printer of Acts of Parliament which follows the printing of the instrument. That section, therefore requires that the Queen's Printer shall keep lists showing the date upon which statutory instruments are printed and issued.

It seems to follow from the wording of this subsection that the making of an instrument is one thing and the issue of it is another. If it is made it can be contravened; if it has not been issued then that provides a defence to a person charged with its contravention. It is then upon the Crown to prove that, although it has not been issued, reasonable steps have been taken for the purpose of bringing the instrument to the notice of the public or persons likely to be affected by it.

I do not think that it can be said that to make a valid statutory instrument it is required that all of these stages should be gone through; namely, the making, the laying before Parliament, the printing and the certification of that part of it which it might be unnecessary to have printed. In my judgment the making of an instrument is complete when it is first of all made by the Minister concerned and after it has been laid before Parliament. When that has been done it then becomes a valid statutory instrument, totally made under the provisions of the Act.

The remaining provisions to which my attention has been drawn, in my view, are purely procedure for the issue of an instrument validly made— namely, that in the first instance it must be printed by the Queen's Printer unless it is certified to be unnecessary to print it; it must then be included in a list published by Her Majesty's Stationery Office showing the dates when it is issued and it may be issued by the Queen's Printer of Acts of Parliament. Those matters, in my judgment, are matters of procedure. If they were not and if they were stages in the perfection of a valid statutory instrument, I cannot see that section 3(2) would be necessary, because if each one of those stages were necessary to make a statutory instrument valid, it would follow that there could be no infringement of an unissued instrument and therefore it would be quite unnecessary to provide a defence to a contravention of any such instrument. In my view the very fact that subsection (2) of section 3 refers to a defence that the instrument has not been issued postulates that the instrument must have been validly made in the first place otherwise it could never have been contravened.

In those circumstances I hold that this instrument was validly made and approved and that it was made by or signed on behalf of the Minister on its being laid before Parliament; that so appears on the face of the instrument itself. In my view, the fact that the Minister failed to certify under regulation 7 does not invalidate the instrument as an instrument but lays the burden upon the Crown to prove that at the date of the alleged contraventions reasonable steps had been taken for bringing the instrument to the notice of the public or persons likely to be affected by it. I, therefore, rule that this is admissible.

[When evidence of the steps taken to bring the instrument to the notice of the public and of the contravention of it by the accused had been given. His Lordship summed up and the jury, after a retirement of two minutes, found both the accused guilty on all counts.]

Verdict: Guilty on all counts.

Notes

1. The report at [1954] 1 All E.R. 542, 545–546, states that evidence was given that the Minister of Supply issued information regarding the deposited schedules to trade journals; that the maximum permitted prices during the relevant months appeared in the *Board of Trade Journal*, the *Metal Bulletin* and the *Ironmonger*; and that the British Iron and Steel Federation sent copies of the schedules to the defendant company when the order of 1951 came into existence.

2. Some support for *Sheer Metalcraft* is provided by *Jones v. Robson* [1901] 1 K.B. 673. By section 6 of the Coal Mines Regulation Act 1896:

> "a Secretary of State on being satisfied that any explosive is or is likely to become dangerous, may, by order, of which notice shall be given in such manner as he may direct, prohibit the use thereof in any mine ... either absolutely or subject to conditions."

The Secretary of State made an Order imposing conditions as to the handling of detonators on and after October 1, 1899. The defendant, the manager of a mine, was prosecuted for breach of the Order. He was aware of the Order, but no notice of it had been published as required by section 6. The Divisional Court held that the defendant could properly be convicted. The Order came into force when it was made by the Secretary of State, and the provisions as to notice were "directory" only.

However, the ruling in *Sheer Metalcraft* that an instrument can come into effect before it is issued is inconsistent with the decision of Bailhache J. in *Johnson v. Sargant & Sons* [1918] 1 K.B. 101. The Food Controller made an Order under the Defence of the Realm regulations requisitioning, *inter alia*, imported beans. The Order was dated May 16, 1917, but only became known to the public on May 17. It stated that it did not apply to beans "which have been sold by the original consignees and paid for by the purchasers". On May 16, the plaintiff paid for and took delivery of a cargo of beans from the defendants. They subsequently claimed that the contract had been cancelled by the Order. They referred to the rule that a statute takes effect from the first moment of the day on which it is passed, unless another day is expressly named, in which case it comes into operation immediately on the expiration of the previous day. They argued that, by analogy with the position with statutes, the Order came into operation immediately after midnight on May 15. As the beans were only paid for on May 16, the transaction was caught by the Order. However, Bailhache J. did not regard the analogy as appropriate:

> "there is about statutes a publicity even before they come into operation which is absent in the case of many Orders such as that with which we are now dealing; indeed, if certain Orders are to be effective at all, it is essential that they should not be known until they are actually published. In the absence of authority upon the point I am unable to hold that this Order came into operation before it was known, and, as I have said, it was not known until the morning of May 17."

Accordingly, the transaction fell within the exemption in the Order.

Jones v. Robson was not cited in *Johnson v. Sargant*, and neither case was cited in *R. v. Sheer Metalcraft*.

3. In *Simmonds v. Newell* [1953] 1 W.L.R. 826, the Defiant Cycle Co. and two of its directors were prosecuted before justices for selling steel at a price in excess of the maximum permitted by the Iron and Steel Prices Order 1951, as amended. The Order had been made by the Minister of Supply. The maximum prices were set out in schedules. An Assistant Secretary in the Ministry of Supply decided, having regard to regulation 7 of the 1947 Regulations (above, p. 822), that the printing and sale of the schedules was not necessary. She so decided in view of the bulk of the schedules, because they would be available for inspection at Steel House in London, and because trade associations would be distributing copies of the schedules that were most in demand. The Assistant Secretary wrote to the editor of Statutory Instruments that the schedules had been certified under reg. 7 to be exempted from printing and sale, but there was not in fact a certificate to that effect. The Divisional Court held that the letter did not constitute a certificate. The Solicitor General had accepted that while this did not render the Order invalid, it threw upon the Crown the burden of proving that reasonable steps had been taken to bring the purport of the instrument to the notice of the public, or of persons likely to be affected by it or the person charged (section 3(2) of the 1946 Act). Lord Goddard C.J. commented (at 830):

"That is certainly a very reasonable attitude for the Solicitor-General to take up, because it is not desirable, in criminal matters, that people should be prosecuted for breaches of orders unless the orders can fairly be said to be known to the public."

As no evidence had been given that steps had been taken to publicise the Order, the defendants should have been acquitted.

The court left open arguments—

(1) that a contravention of section 2 of the 1946 Act in not causing to be printed an instrument required to be printed would have the effect that the instrument was invalid; and

(2) that the defence in section 3(2) was available even where the instrument was exempt from the printing requirements.

4. In *Lim Chin Aik v. The Queen* [1963] A.C. 160, the question before the Privy Council was whether a person could properly be convicted of the offence of remaining in Singapore while the subject of an order prohibiting his entry if he was unaware of the existence of the order. Most of the advice of their Lordships was directed to the issue whether the offence required the proof of *mens rea* (their Lordships held that it did). In addition, they rejected the Crown's argument that once made the Order became part of the law of Singapore and that ignorance of the law is no excuse. *Per* Lord Evershed (at 171):

"In their Lordships' opinion, even if the making of the order by the Minister be regarded as an exercise of the legislative as distinct from the executive or administrative function (as they do not concede), the maxim cannot apply to such a case as the present where it appears that there is in the State of Singapore no provision, corresponding, for example, to that contained in section 3(2) of the English Statutory Instruments Act of 1946, for the publication in any form of an order of the kind made in the present case or any other provision designed to enable a man by appropriate inquiry to find out what 'the law' is."

This appears to suggest that in the context "ignorance of the law" can be an excuse even though (and, indeed, because) there is no express statutory defence.

Lord Evershed noted that the case concerned an order directed at an individual, and that the relevant Ordinance drew a distinction between such orders and an order directed to a class of persons. It expressly provided in the latter case for "publication in the *Gazette* and presentation to the Legislative Assembly" (at 172).

5. These cases raise two questions: (1) can delegated legislation come into effect before it is published?; (2) can a person be properly convicted of an offence created by delegated legislation unless either reasonable steps have been taken to make it public or the defendant is actually aware of it? Justice requires the answer to (2) to be no (*cf.* Lord Goddard's remark in *Simmonds v. Newell*). That could be achieved by a broad general rule that delegated legislation does not come into force until published. Alternatively, and more narrowly, it could be achieved by a special defence in the criminal law. Such a defence would operate as an exception to the maxim that ignorance of the law is no excuse: the justification is that the maxim would operate harshly if even the best of endeavours would not enable the "law" to be ascertained. Section 3(2) of the 1946 Act provides a defence of that kind. *Lim Chin Aik v. The Queen* suggests such a defence might be available even in the absence of a statutory provision. This would make it more acceptable for the answer to question (1) to be yes. Note that question (2) did not arise in *Jones v. Robson*, and that the section 3(2) defence was potentially available in *Simmonds v. Newell* and *R. v. Sheer Metalcraft*, although not made out on the facts in the second case. *Johnson v. Sargant* did not concern a criminal prosecution. Thus in none of these reported cases in this country has a person been convicted of an offence under delegated legislation the details of which had not been published at the time of contravention.

6. Some commentators reconcile *Johnson v. Sargant* with the other cases by treating it as authority for the proposition that a piece of delegated legislation *which does not itself state a commencement date* comes into effect on the date of publication and not that on which it was made (see 44 *Halsbury's Laws of England*, 4th ed., para. 1003). *Jones v. Robson, Simmonds v. Newell* and *R. v. Sheer Metalcraft* all concerned instruments with specified commencement dates. Nothing was, however, made of this point in the cases themselves. Since 1947, all statutory instruments required to be laid before Parliament will show the dates they came into operation (see the 1946 Act, s.4(2)(a) (3), above p. 819).

7. D.J. Lanham, ("Delegated Legislation and Publication" (1974) 37 M.L.R. 510) argues strongly that the principle of *Johnson v. Sargant* is to be preferred, as a matter of justice, and that the general common law rule is that delegated legislation does not come into force until it is published. The contrary view is expressed by A.I.L. Campbell [1982] P.L. 569, reply by Professor Lanham [1983] P.L. 395.

8. Consider section 3(2) of the 1946 Act (above, p. 818). To what kinds of statutory instrument does it apply? (see Lanham, *op. cit.*, at 521–523). This question turns on the meaning of the words "any such statutory instrument". The possibilities are that:

(i) These words refer back to the kinds of statutory instruments specified in section 3(1), *i.e.* "every statutory instrument printed and sold by the King's printer". This would have the result that the defence would only be available where an instrument *is issued at some time*, but the contravention precedes the date of issue. It would not be available if the instrument is never issued, even where that was in breach of publication requirements. *Simmonds v. Newell* and *R. v. Sheer Metalcraft* are against this narrow interpretation.

(ii) The words are to be read as referring to "any statutory instrument", no weight being attached to the word "such". The defence would then be available wherever the instrument has not been issued at the date of contravention. This interpretation gives the broadest scope to the s.3(2) defence. Would this be an appropriate occasion for the exercise of the limited power of judges to ignore statutory words to prevent statutory provisions having an absurd result?

(iii) The defence would only be available where the instrument has not been issued at the date òf contravention, *and this is in breach of a duty to publish*. This was the situation that arose in *Simmonds v. Newell* and *Sheer Metalcraft*. Does the wording of section 3 justify this reading?

9. The defence in section 3(2) appears, with the language but not the substance modified, as clause 50 in the proposed Criminal Code Bill (see *Codification of the Criminal Law: A Report to the Law Commission* (1984–1985 H.C. 270), pp. 129–130, 198).

(D) Parliamentary Scrutiny

FOURTH REPORT FROM THE SELECT COMMITTEE ON PROCEDURE, 1995–1996, DELEGATED LEGISLATION

(1995–1996 H.C. 152)

I: Introduction

3. The House of Commons has a particular responsibility in the matter of scrutiny of delegated legislation, since the House of Lords has for a number of years operated a self-denying ordinance in this field. It neither rejects affirmative instruments nor annuls negative instruments, although it has passed technically ineffective motions calling for the amendment or withdrawal of instruments, and in July 1995 it divided on an approval Motion. In October 1994 the House of Lords formally affirmed its unfettered freedom to vote on any subordinate legislation submitted for its approval. The practice of the House of Lords may be changing. It plays a valuable role through its Delegated Powers Scrutiny Committee (see para. 14 below) and in the Joint Committee on Statutory Instruments. But for the present the onus of scrutiny and control is on the Commons.

4. Parliamentary control of delegated legislation has long been an area of concern. This is reflected in a number of select committee and other Reports over the past half century....

II: Current

Affirmative and negative

6. The current procedures for scrutinising delegated legislation differentiate between those instruments requiring a positive Resolution of the House in order to be brought into effect—"affirmative instruments"—and those which can be annulled by a Resolution of the House if passed within 40 days of their laying—"negative instruments".

Affirmative instruments

As a result of the recent implementation of the Jopling proposals, an affirmative instrument stands automatically referred for debate in a Standing Committee, unless the Government agree that it be debated on the Floor of the House. Debate in Committee is on a formal and unamendable Motion, "That the Committee has considered the draft XYZ Order 1996". Whatever the outcome of any vote, and indeed whether or not any motion is agreed, the

Chairman reports the instrument to the House. A formal approval Motion is then put forthwith on the Floor, usually after a few days interval. Those instruments taken on the Floor are debated on the approval Motion, which is also unamendable. In this session to May 1, 36 affirmative instruments have been taken on the Floor in 16 debates (several instruments being taken together on many occasions), compared to 47 debates in Committee on 63 instruments.

Negative instruments

Unless a Motion is tabled seeking to annul a negative instrument, it is not debated. When such a Motion has been tabled, the Government may agree either to refer the instrument to a Standing Committee upstairs, or, exceptionally, to allow the Motion to be brought forward on the Floor of the House; or it may freely disregard it. Instruments referred to a Committee are debated in the same way as are affirmative instruments, save that there are no subsequent proceedings on the Floor. Those taken on the Floor are debated on an annulment or revocation Motion. In the session to May 1, 22 negative instruments have been debated in Committee in 17 debates, and 4 prayers have been debated on the Floor.

7. As the evidence from the Clerk of the House emphasised, the distinction between affirmative and negative instruments, which determines the form of parliamentary control, is very much a matter of chance, "grounded as often as not on the fortuitous outcome of past debate on the parent legislation". Ministers may concede affirmative procedure in the course of debate on a bill in committee. On other occasions Parliament may let delegation of legislative powers slip through without insisting on any parliamentary procedure. The House of Lords Delegated Powers Scrutiny Committee, whose terms of reference include examination of a bill to see whether it subjects the exercise of legislative power "to an inappropriate degree of parliamentary scrutiny", has not tried to devise any precise ground rules for determining the proper level. We question whether there is any objective means of predetermining the proper degree of scrutiny to be given to an instrument.... We have arrived at a situation where the nature of parliamentary control allowed for in legislation is being dictated by the notoriously inadequate system of scrutiny and control itself, rather than by nature of the powers to be delegated. In other words, the affirmative procedure may be insisted on as a means of attracting at least *some* form of parliamentary scrutiny, rather than as a reflection of the inherent importance of the subject matter. Were there to be a respectable means of control of negative instruments, the application of that procedure in primary legislation would be more widely acceptable, and the number of relatively insignificant affirmatives reduced accordingly.

8. It is difficult to avoid the existing dichotomy of affirmative and negative instruments, rooted as it is in past statute. There would in theory be something to be said for abolishing the distinction, and creating a uniform category of instruments, with a parliamentary mechanism for determining which required positive approval, based on their inherent significance rather than their statutory basis.... The fact that it would require primary legislation, possibly wholesale amendment of much of statute law, must initially drawback. The proposals we make are less radical. Should they prove

ineffective, however, we consider that serious consideration must be given to the radical proposal of a uniform category and procedure for all delegated legislation.

Super-affirmatives

9. We consider that the House would be assisted by a procedure for instruments of particular significance which went beyond the standard affirmative procedure: a "super-affirmative" procedure, on the lines of the procedure recently established for the consideration of draft Deregulation Orders. Under such a procedure, a Minister proposing to make an order would first have to lay a proposal for a draft order. That could be examined in detail by the relevant departmental select committee, who could propose amendments to be made within the 60-day timescale used in the deregulation procedure. We doubt if the rest of the deregulation procedure is so readily transferable, since such an order is likely to be more politically controversial than deregulation orders. A Select Committee is unlikely to resolve unanimously that the subsequent draft Order be approved; nor do we consider that such orders should be exempt from debate. Such a procedure would nevertheless provide an opportunity for some detailed parliamentary examination of proposed delegated legislation of particular significance and an opportunity for effective parliamentary input. **We recommend that the Government contemplate the adoption of such a procedure in appropriate forthcoming legislation.**

Delegation of powers

14. There is in our view too great a readiness in Parliament to delegate wide legislative powers to Ministers, and no lack of enthusiasm on their part to take such powers. The result is an excessive volume of delegated legislation. It was partly in response to this that the House of Lords established in 1992–1993 a Delegated Powers Scrutiny Committee "to report whether the provisions of any bill inappropriately delegate legislative power; or whether they subject the exercise of legislative power to an inappropriate degree of parliamentary scrutiny". In response to our request, we received a very helpful memorandum on its work from the Chairman of the Committee, Lord Alexander of Weedon. It has drawn the attention of the House of Lords on several occasions to instances of inappropriate delegation of legislative power, and has also on occasions suggested the use of affirmative rather than negative procedures. The Committee is only advisory. We see no benefit in seeking to duplicate its function in the Commons. The scrutiny of powers to be delegated in primary legislation, and the procedure to be applied, are in any event already commonly part of debate on primary legislation. No procedural changes could readily influence the outcome of such debate. We have therefore concentrated on the scrutiny of the delegated legislation produced under powers granted by primary legislation, rather than on finding means of limiting the grant of such powers. . . .

Joint Committee on Statutory Instruments

19. The Joint Committee on Statutory Instruments, and the Select Committee comprised of its Commons Members, continues to provide an expert

technical legal scrutiny of all instruments laid before the House, and some not so laid. In its weekly reports, it draws attention to points arising on a number of instruments: in 1994–1995, it did so on about 1 in 10 of all the instruments it considered. Its work is painstaking, unglamorous and goes largely unregarded within the House. It nonetheless plays a vital role in policing the statutory instruments system, and it has an admirable effect on departments. Nothing should be done by way of reform which undermined its authority or diminished its standing.

20. The Chairman of the Joint Committee, Mr Andrew F. Bennett M.P., raised the question of the consideration of instruments by the House before completion of their consideration by the Joint Committee. Despite an informal agreement that this should not happen, there have been several instances in recent years of consideration by the House before completion of Joint Committee consideration. Mr Bennett revived a proposal made in earlier years that there should be a Standing Order preventing such consideration, as already exists as S.O. No. 70 in the House of Lords. He accepted that it would still be possible for such business to be proceeded with, by passage of a business motion setting aside Standing Orders: but he felt that the existence of a Standing Order in place of an informal understanding would "push departments into being a bit fairer to all of us" in terms of the timing of debates. We have much sympathy with the principle that the House—or its Committees— should not be expected to debate instruments before the Joint Committee Report is available. There is sufficient evidence of the disregard of this principle on some occasions as to merit the full force of a Standing Order. **We therefore recommend the passage of a Standing Order to provide that no decision on a statutory instrument should be made by the House until completion of its consideration by the Joint Committee on Statutory Instruments.**

Deregulation Committee

22. We received a very detailed and informative memorandum from the Chairman of the Deregulation Committee, reporting on the first year of its work. It should be recalled from the outset that Deregulation Orders are peculiar in that they all involve amendment of primary legislation, which would require further primary legislation to amend it, were it not for the terms of the Deregulation and Contracting Out Act 1994 and the parallel establishment of the Deregulation Committee with its special powers. The degree of scrutiny given by the Committee has demanded commitment of substantial resources, which could not conceivably be extended even to all affirmative orders. It is however in our view significant that the Committee has operated smoothly and effectively; that it has used its powers to persuade government to accept nearly all the amendments it has sought; that it and its House of Lords counterpart have effectively killed off one proposal; and that the end result to date is that 17 draft Orders have been agreed to by the House without any debate, but in the full confidence that they are generally acceptable. The European Legislation Committee and the Deregulation Committee have demonstrated that scrutiny by committees can work, and can engage Members' attention and commitment.

Notes
1. Among the other proposals made by the Procedure Committee were (1) that the

40-day "praying time" be extended to 60 days (as is the case for deregulation orders); (2) that debates on negative instruments be arranged before the expiry of praying time; (3) that a Sifting Committee be established to determine which negative instruments merit debate and to identify affirmative instruments which it considers do not require debate; and (4) that debates in Standing Committee be on substantive motions open to specified classes of amendment. The package of proposals if implemented would constitute a significant improvement to the formal structure for scrutiny. At the time of writing (January 1997), the report had not received a full debate.

2. The Joint Committee on Statutory Instruments considers whether the special attention of the House should be drawn to an instrument on any of the following grounds:

"(i) that it imposes a charge on the public revenues or contains provisions requiring payments to be made to the Exchequer or any government department or to any local or public authority in consideration of any licence or consent or of any services to be rendered, or prescribes the amount of any such charge of payment;

(ii) that it is made in pursuance of any enactment containing specific provisions excluding it from challenge in the courts, either at all times or after the expiration of a specific period;

(iii) that it purports to have retrospective effect where the parent statute confers no express authority so to provide;

(iv) that there appears to have been unjustifiable delay in the publication or in the laying of it before Parliament;

(v) that there appears to have been unjustifiable delay in sending a notification under the proviso to subsection (1) of section four of the Statutory Instruments Act 1946, where an instrument has come into operation before it has been laid before Parliament;

(vi) that there appears to be a doubt whether it is *intra vires* or that it appears to make some unusual or unexpected use of the powers conferred by the statute under which it is made;

(vii) that for any special reason its form or purport call for elucidation;

(viii) that its drafting appears to be defective;

or on any other ground which does not impinge on its merits or on the policy behind it and to report its decision with the reasons thereof in any particular case."
See the Committee's First Special Report on Proceedings 1986–1996, 1995–1996 H.L. Paper 103, H.C. 582.

3. On the work of the House of Lords Select Committee on the Scrutiny of Delegated Powers, see C.M.G. Himsworth [1995] P.L. 34, and the Committee's reviews of its own work in First Report, 1992–1993 (1992–1993 H.L. Paper 57); Twelfth Report, 1993–1994 (1993–1994 H.L. Paper 90); Special Report, 1995–1996 (1995–1996 H.L. Paper 120); Memorandum of Evidence of Lord Alexander of Weedon to the Select Committee on Procedure, Fourth Report, 1995–1996 H.C. Paper 152, pp. 58–64.

4. Deregulation orders are made under Part I of the Deregulation and Contracting Out Act 1994. They amend or repeal statutory provisions passed before the end of the 1993–1994 session in order to remove or reduce burdens on business. After a consultation stage, proposals are examined by a special Deregulation Committee of the House of Commons and by the House of Lords Select Committee on the Scrutiny of Delegated Powers. The committees both provide substantive scrutiny and perform the functions of the Joint Committee on Statutory Instruments. See the First Special Report of the Deregulation Committee, 1994–1995 H.C. Paper 311, and Government Response (see First Report of the Committee, 1994–1995 H.C. Paper 409); Memorandum of Barry Field M.P. to the Select Committee on Procedure Fourth Report, 1995–1996 H.C. Paper 152, pp. 72–82. The Committees cannot veto draft orders but

the Government has undertaken that where there is an adverse report it would expect in normal circumstances ot submit a revised proposal or withdraw the proposal altogether (Government Response (1993–1994 H.C. Paper 404) to the Fourth Report of the Select Committee on Procedure (1993–1994 H.C. Paper 238), p. viii).

5. For earlier surveys of arrangements for parliamentary scrutiny, see J.D. Hayhurst and P. Wallington [1988] P.L. 547 and Hansard Society Commission, *Making the Law* (1993), pp. 89–94.

(E) VIRES

Apart from the procedural matters already considered in this chapter, the validity of a statutory instrument may be challenged on the ground that it is *ultra vires* as a matter of substance.

Notes

1. Examples of challenge on this ground include the following: In *Hotel and Catering Industry Training Board v. Automobile Proprietary Ltd.* [1969] 1 W.L.R. 697, the House of Lords held that a power to make an order establishing a Training Board for persons employed "in any activities of industry or commerce" did not enable an order to be made in respect of members' clubs. In *R. v. Customs and Excise Commissioners, ex p. Hedges and Butler* [1986] 2 All E.R. 164, a power to demand production of the whole of the records of a business, including records concerning non-dutiable goods, was held not to be "incidental" or "supplementary" to powers concerning the regulation of excise warehouses and dealings in dutiable goods. In *R. v. Secretary of State for Social Security, ex p. Joint Council for the Welfare of Immigrants* [1996] 4 All E.R. 385, the Court of Appeal (Simon Brown and Waite L.JJ., Neill L.J. dissenting) held that regulations, which excluded from social security benefits persons who sought asylum otherwise than immediately on arrival in the United Kingdom and persons whose asylum claims had been rejected and were awaiting appeal, were *ultra vires*. They had the effect of rendering the rights of asylum seekers under the Asylum and Immigration Appeals Act 1993 valueless; the latter would either be deterred from pursuing their claims or be forced to live a life of utter destitution. "Parliamentary legislation alone could ... achieve that sorry state of affairs" (*per* Simon Brown L.J. at 402). The effect of this decision was subsequently reversed by the Asylum and Immigration Act 1996, although applicants for asylum may seek assistance from local authorities under section 21(1) of the National Assistance Act 1948 (*R. v. Hammersmith and Fulham London Borough Council, ex p. M, The Times,* February 19, 1997). Finally, in *R. v. Lord Chancellor, ex p. Witham* [1997] 2 All E.R. 79, the Diversional Court held an order significantly increasing fees for the issue of a writ was *ultra vires* on the ground that a citizen's common law right off access to the courts could only be abrogated by specific statutory provision or specific enabling legislation.

2. On the question whether the invalid part of an instrument can be severed, see *R. v. Inland Revenue Commissioners, ex p. Woolwich Equitable Building Society,* above, p. 795.

3. It is not clear whether a statutory instrument, as distinct from a byelaw (see below, pp. 834–838) can be challenged for unreasonableness. In *Maynard v. Osmond* [1977] Q.B. 240, regulations which did not allow police officers (other than Chief Constables and Assistant and Deputy Chief Constables) to be legally represented in disciplinary proceedings were challenged on this ground; the Court of Appeal did not express any doubt as to its jurisdiction to entertain such a challenge, but dismissed the argument on its merits. A provision in the Immigration Rules (which are not published as statutory instruments) was held to be unreasonable in *R. v. Immigration Appeal Tribunal, ex p. Manshoora Begum* [1986] Imm.A.R. 385 (below, p. 838).

The scope of review may be narrower where an instrument is approved by Parliament (*cf.* above, pp. 354–357).

4. See generally, K. Puttick, *Challenging Delegated Legislation* (1988).

(F) BYELAWS

Powers for local authorities to make byelaws are found in a large number of Acts of Parliament (see *Cross*, Appendix E). Such powers may also be conferred on other public bodies. District and London borough councils in England and county and county borough councils in Wales have a general power to

"made byelaws for the good rule and government of the whole or any part of the district [principal area] or borough, as the case may be, and for the prevention and suppression of nuisances therein" (Local Government Act 1972, s.235(1), as amended).

However, this power may not be exercised

"for any purpose as respects any area if provision for that purpose or respects that area is made by, or is or may be made under, any other enactment" (1972 Act, s.235(3)).

The procedure for making any byelaw (unless special provision is otherwise made) is found in section 236 of the 1972 Act. Byelaws have to be conferred by a Minister (usually the Secretary of State). At least one month before application for confirmation, notice of intention to apply must be given in "one or more local newspapers circulating in the area to which the byelaws are to apply" and a copy must be deposited at the authority's offices and open to public inspection without payment. The authority must provide a copy of the byelaws (or a part of them) to any person on application, on payment of such sum not exceeding 10p per 100 words as the authority may determine. The confirming authority may confirm or refuse to confirm any byelaw, and may fix the commencement date. If not date is so fixed, the byelaw comes into operation one month after confirmation. After confirmation, byelaws must be printed, deposited at the authority's offices and open to public inspection, and copies must be supplied on application or payment of such sum not exceeding 20p per copy as the authority may determine.

Byelaws are not normally confirmed unless they follow models issued by the relevant Government Department (most commonly the Home Office or the Department of the Environment).

KRUSE v. JOHNSON

[1898] 2 Q.B. 91; 67 L.J.K.B. 782; 78 L.T. 647; 14 T.L.R. 416; 62 J.P. 469; 42 S.J. 509; [1895–1899] All E.R. Rep. 105; 46 W.R. 630; 19 Cox C.C. 103
(Divisional Court (Q.B.D.))

Kent County Council made a byelaw prohibiting any person from playing music or singing in a public place within 50 yards of any dwelling-house after being required by any constable, or by an inmate of such house to desist. The byelaw was made under section 16 of the Local Government Act 1888 and section 23(1) of the Municipal Corporations Act 1882, which gave power to "make such byelaws as to them [the council], seem meet for the good rule and government of the . . . [county], and for the prevention and suppression of nuisances not already punishable in a summary manner by virtue of any Act...". K was convicted by justices of an offence against this byelaw, in that he had conducted an open-air religious service within 50 yards of a house, after being required to desist by a constable. K appealed by way of case stated to the Divisional Court, contending that the byelaw was *ultra vires* for unreasonableness.

LORD RUSSELL OF KILLOWEN C.J.: ... [stated the facts, outlined the relevant legislation, and continued:] We thus find that Parliament has thought fit to delegate to representative public bodies in town and cities, and also in counties, the power of exercising their own judgment as to what are the bye-laws which to them seem proper to be made for good rule and government in their own localities. But that power is accompanied by certain safeguards. There must be antecedent publication of the bye-law with a view, I presume, of eliciting the public opinion of the locality upon it, and such bye-laws shall have no force until after they have been forwarded to the Secretary of State. Further, the Queen, with the advice of her Privy Council, may disallow the bye-law wholly or in part, and may enlarge the suspensory period before it comes into operation. I agree that the presence of these safeguards in no way relieves the Court of the responsibility of inquiring into the validity of bye-laws where they are brought in question, or in any way affects the authority of the Court in the determination of their validity or invalidity. It is to be observed, moreover, that the bye-laws having come into force, they are not like the laws, or what were said to be the laws, of the Medes and Persians—they are not unchangeable. The power is to make bye-laws from time to time as to the authority shall seem meet, and if experience shews that in any respect existing bye-laws work hardly or inconveniently, the local authority, acted upon by the public opinion, as it must necessarily be, of those concerned, has full power to repeal or alter them. It need hardly be added that, should experience warrant that course, the Legislature which has given may modify or take away the powers they have delegated. I have thought it well to deal with these points in some detail, and for this reason—that the great majority of the cases in which the question of bye-laws has been discussed are not cases of bye-laws of bodies of a public representative character entrusted by Parliament with delegated authority, but are for the most part cases of railway companies, dock companies, or other like companies, which carry on their business for their own profit, although incidentally for the advantage of the public. In this class of case it is right that the Courts should jealously watch the exercise of these powers, and guard against their unnecessary or unreasonable exercise to the public disadvantage. But, when the Court is called upon to consider the bye-laws of public representative bodies clothed with the ample authority which I have described, and exercising that authority accompanied by the checks and safeguards which have been mentioned, I think the consideration of such bye-laws ought to be approached from a different stand-point. They ought to be supported if possible. They ought to be, as has been said, "benevolently" interpreted, and credit ought to be given to those who have to administer them that they will be reasonably administered. This involves the introduction of no new canon of construction. But, further, looking to the character of the body legislating under the delegated authority of Parliament, to the subject-matter of such legislation, and to the nature and extent of the authority given to deal with matters which concern them, and in the manner which to them shall seem meet, I think courts of justice ought to be slow to condemn as

invalid any bye-law, so made under such conditions, on the ground of supposed unreasonableness. Notwithstanding what Cockburn C.J. said in *Bailey
v. Williamson* (1873) L.R. 8 Q.B. 118, 124, an analogous case, I do not mean
to say that there may not be cases in which it would be the duty of the Court to
condemn bye-laws, made under such authority as these were made, as invalid
because unreasonable. But unreasonable in what sense? If, for instance, they
were found to be partial and unequal in their operation as between different
classes; if they were manifestly unjust; if they disclosed bad faith; if they
involved such oppressive or gratuitous interference with the rights of those
subject to them as could find no justification in the minds of reasonable men,
the Court might well say, "Parliament never intended to give authority to
make such rules; they are unreasonable and *ultra vires.*" But it is in this sense,
and in this sense only, as I conceive, that the question of unreasonableness can
properly be regarded. A bye-law is not unreasonable merely because particular judges may think that it goes further than is prudent or necessary or convenient, or because it is not accompanied by a qualification or an exception
which some judges may think ought to be there. Surely it is not too much to say
that in matters which directly and mainly concern the people of the county,
who have the right to choose those whom they think best fitted to represent
them in their local government bodies, such representatives may be trusted to
understand their own requirements better than judges. Indeed, if the question
of the validity of bye-laws were to be determined by the opinion of judges as to
what was reasonable in the narrow sense of that word, the cases in the books
on this subject are no guide; for they reveal, as indeed one would expect, a
wide diversity of judicial opinion, and they lay down no principle or definite
standard by which reasonableness or unreasonableness may be tested.

So much for the general considerations which, it seems to me, ought to be
borne in mind in considering bye-laws of this class. I now come to the bye-law
in question.

It is admitted that the county council of Kent were within their authority in
making a bye-law in relation to the subject-matter which is dealt with by the
impeached bye-law. In other words, it is conceded, and properly so, that the
local authority might make a bye-law imposing conditions under which musi-
cal instruments and singing might be permitted or prevented in public places;
but it is objected that they had no authority to make a bye-law on that subject
in the terms of this bye-law. Further, it is not contended that the bye-law
should, in order to be valid, be confined to cases where the playing or singing
amounted to a nuisance; but the objections are, as I understand them, that the
bye-law is bad—first, because it is not confined to cases where the playing or
singing is in fact causing annoyance, and next, because it enables a police
constable to bring it into operation by a request on *his* part to the player or
singer to desist. As to the first of these objections, if the general principles upon
which these bye-laws ought to be dealt with are those which I have already
stated, it is clear that the absence of this qualification cannot make the bye-law
invalid. But, further, such a qualification in my judgment would render the
bye-law ineffective. What is to be the standard of annoyance? What may be a
cause of annoyance to one person may be no annoyance, and may even be
pleasurable, to another person. Again, who is to be the judge in such case of
whether there is or is not an annoyance? Is it to be the resident of the house
within 50 yards of the playing or singing; or is it to be the magistrate who

hears the charge? It is enough to say that, in my judgment, the absence of the suggested qualification cannot make the bye-law invalid, even if it be admitted that its presence would be an improvement.

As to the second objection—namely, that the policeman has the power of putting the bye-law into operation by requiring the player or singer to desist—I again say that, even if the absence of this power would be an improvement, and would make the bye-law in the apprehension of some more reasonable, it is not, on the principles I have already stated, any ground for declaring the bye-law to be invalid. In support of this objection pictures have in argument, been drawn—more or less highly coloured—of policemen who without rhyme or reason would or might gratuitously interfere with what might be a source of enjoyment to many. In answer, I say a policeman is not an irresponsible person without check or control. If he acts capriciously or vexatiously, he can be checked by his immediate superiors, or he can be taught a lesson by the magistrates should he prefer vexatious charges. If the policeman persisted in saying that the musician should desist when the people in the neighbourhood desired his music, his gratuitous interference would promptly come to an end. Nor is it correct to say, as has been erroneously stated in some of the cases cited, that the magistrate would be bound in every case to convict where the musician did not desist when called upon. It is clear that under s.16 of the Summary Jurisdiction Act 1879, the magistrate, if he thinks the case of so trifling a nature that it is inexpedient to inflict any punishment, may, without proceeding to conviction, dismiss the information. The facts of this case are certainly no illustration of the bye-law having been gratuitously or vexatiously put in force. The case states that, although it was not proved that the occupier of the house within 50 yards had, on the day in question, requested the constable to require the appellant to desist, yet it was proved that the singing was an annoyance to the occupier, and that he had on previous occasions complained to the police of such singing. Indeed, it was stated during the argument that the conviction here appealed from was the second conviction of the appellant for an offence against this bye-law....

In my opinion, judged by the test of reasonableness, even in its narrower sense, this is a reasonable bye-law; but, whether I am right or wrong in this view, I am clearly of opinion that no Court of law can properly say that it is invalid.

Sir F.H. Jeune P. delivered a concurring judgment. Mathew J. dissented.

Chitty L.J., Wright, Darling and Channell JJ. concurred with Lord Russell of Killowen C.J.

Conviction affirmed.

Notes

1. This case has been considered and applied on many occasions. See notes in [1895–1899] All E.R. Rep. 105–106; D.G.T. Williams, *Welsh Studies in Public Law* (ed. by J.A. Andrews, 1970), "The Control of Local Authorities", pp. 128 *et seq.*

2. On the validity of byelaws in general, see Alan Wharam (1973) 36 M.L.R. 611; *Cross*, Chap. 6.

3. A byelaw may be *ultra vires* for uncertainty. See *Percy v. Hall* [1996] 4 All E.R. 523, where the Court of Appeal held that the correct test was whether "it can be given

no meaning or no sensible and ascertainable meaning, and not merely because it is ambiguous or leads to absurd results" (Lord Denning in *Fawcett Properties Ltd v. Buckingham County Council* [1961] A.C. 636, 677–678) and not whether it contains "adequate information as to the duties of those who are to obey" (Mathew J. in *Kruse v. Johnson* [1898] 2 Q.B. 91, 108). While the former test had been established in relation to the validity of planning conditions, Lord Denning expressly equated the position of such conditions and byelaws. This approach had frequently been adopted by the Court of Appeal and House of Lords in relation to planning conditions. The latter test had frequently been applied in byelaw cases, but not above the level of the Divisional Court. Furthermore, it was in itself a test of "great uncertainty" providing "no criteria or principles by which to judge the adequacy of the information, or the degree of certainty, afforded by the byelaws". (See Simon Brown L.J. at 531–537.) On the facts, however, the byelaws challenged were not invalid under either test. They prohibited entry on "lands belonging to the Secretary of State" in named parishes, the land being in the vicinity of a military communications installation. The fact that members of the public might have to enquire which lands did belong to the Secretary of State did not render the byelaws uncertain.

4. The tests set out by Lord Russell of Killowen have been applied to test the validity of immigration rules: see *R. v. Immigration Appeal Tribunal, ex p. Manshoora Begum* [1986] Imm.A.R. 385, 393–395, Simon Brown J. (requirement in para. 52 of the Immigration Rules that an applicant dependent relative must establish that he has a standard of living substantially below that of his own country held to be "partial and unequal" and "manifestly unjust" in operating adversely against applicants from poorer countries). However, arguments based on *Kruse v. Johnson* have failed in subsequent cases (see, *e.g. R. v. Immigration Appeal Tribunal, ex p. Fuller* [1993] Imm.A.R. 177; *R. v. Secretary of State for the Home Department, ex p. Kwapong* [1994] Imm.A.R. 207 (distinction between husbands and wives in immigration rules not unreasonable under *Kruse v. Johnson* given that Parliament had not applied the Sex Discrimination Act 1975 to the rules).

5. The reference to byelaws being unreasonable if "partial and unequal" in their operation has been regarded as illustrating a broader principle of English law requiring equal treatment without unfair discrimination. Acts and decisions that offend this principle may be regarded as irrational or *Wednesbury* unreasonable (see above, p. 394; *de Smith, Woolf and Jowell*, pp. 576–582, noting that the principle of equality is recognised as a fundamental principle of European Community Law and by Article 14 of the European Convention on Human rights); Sedley J. in *R. v. Minister of Agriculture, Fisheries and Food, ex p. Hamble (Offshore) Fisheries Ltd* [1995] 2 All E.R. 714, 722.

6. On the scope of collateral challenge to a byelaw, see *Bugg v. D.P.P.*, doubted in *R. v. Wicks* (above, p. 778).

INDEX